WITHDRAWN

English Riddles
from
Oral Tradition

ARCHER TAYLOR

English Riddles from Oral Tradition

OCTAGON BOOKS

A division of Farrar, Straus and Giroux

New York   1977

Copyright 1951 by The Regents of The University of California

Reprinted 1977
by special arrangement with The University of California Press

OCTAGON BOOKS
A DIVISION OF FARRAR, STRAUS & GIROUX, INC.
19 Union Square West
New York, N.Y. 10003

Library of Congress Cataloging in Publication Data

Taylor, Archer, 1890-
   English riddles from oral tradition.

   Reprint of the ed. published by the University of California Press, Berkeley.
   Bibliography: p.
   Includes index.
   1. Riddles. I. Title.
[PN6371.T3   1977]   398.6   76-55778
ISBN 0-374-97793-3

Manufactured by Braun-Brumfield, Inc.
Ann Arbor, Michigan
Printed in the United States of America

To the memory of

George Lyman Kittredge

Preface

THIS COLLECTION includes, as far as I have been able to find them, the riddles taken down from oral tradition in the British Isles and in the English-speaking parts of the Western Hemisphere. It does not include Welsh, Scotch Gaelic, or Irish riddles, except as parallels. I have added those English riddles in Renaissance collections and later jestbooks which seemed to preserve traditional materials or to have influenced later oral versions. The literary riddles of the Renaissance and later times constitute, however, a genre of their own and deserve separate study. A few texts have come to me directly from oral sources, but I have made no serious effort to gather new texts or to consult manuscript collections. The unpublished texts which have fallen into my hands are indicated as "Oral," accompanied by the name of the state in which my informant resided. Duplicates or variants of texts already in print are serviceable indications of the currency of the riddles concerned. I have given the usual bibliographical references for the texts quoted or cited.

The arrangement of a collection of riddles offers many difficulties. For this collection I have adopted a system based upon that used in Robert Lehmann-Nitsche's Argentinian collection. This system is briefly described in the Introduction. The annotation is of two kinds. The headnote, which may refer to a single riddle or a group of riddles, identifies the fundamental comparison, surveys its various uses, examines its several forms, adaptations, and elaborations, and cites what has been said about its meaning and associations. The note at the back, which ordinarily refers to a single text, more rarely to two or three very closely related texts, contains parallels and explanatory comment on difficulties in the meaning of particular words or the interpretation. I have not commented on all the difficulties that the dialect or the peculiarities in spelling might present. If, for example, the collector prints both "of" and "o'" for "of," I have let his spellings stand without change or comment. Emendation or correction of such details would offer the reader little assistance. I have italicized words which are strictly onomatopoetic and have inserted some interpretative words in square brackets into the texts of the riddles. In a few, for example, "can" signifies "can't," and I have inserted the latter to make the meaning clear.[1]

Unless I have indicated otherwise, the parallels and the English texts to which they are attached in headnote or note have the same answer, and this answer is not repeated; it is to be inferred from the English text. I have

---

[1] There is a distinct difference in intonation between "He' can go" and "He can' go." The first has a positive meaning. The second, which has a characteristic emphasis on "can" and perhaps a long *n*, has a negative meaning. See examples in Riddles Nos. 1028*a* and 1709.

usually refrained from explanatory comment on the parallels. If the similarity in the manner of describing the object is obvious, I have ordinarily been content to leave the citation at that point. The illustration of this similarity is the purpose of citing the parallel. Explanatory comment on other aspects of the foreign riddle would often lead us far afield.

I have arranged the parallels in an order according to the linguistic groups from West to East: Celtic, Germanic, Romance (Basque is, however, included with Spanish), Balto-Slavic, Finno-Ugric, Arabic, Turkish, and so on. French texts from Breton-speaking regions are cited under "Breton." When I have cited several parallels in a single language, I have usually placed first either an old version or a version from a standard collection and last the colonial versions. For example, the French parallels usually begin with a Renaissance text from *Les Adeuineaux amoureux* or one from Rolland's annotated collection and conclude with parallels from Baissac's collection of the folklore of Mauritius or Parsons' collection from the Antilles. Except for a few unpublished texts, which have chiefly come to me through the kindness of Hans Ellekilde of the Dansk Folkemindesamling,[2] a few medieval and Renaissance Latin versions, and a very few texts that I have left in the original for reasons pertinent to the discussion, I have given the parallels in translation. A translation accompanies the Danish texts. The Latin texts, which are usually in verse, are ordinarily the oldest versions to be preserved. Their age and metrical form seemed to justify printing them in the original form. The parallels are cited by number, whenever possible. A number following a proper name is always to be understood as referring to the number of the riddle. References to page, section, or chapter are always specially indicated. In a few places—notably in references to Novaković's Serbian collection—I have supplied the numbers of the riddles, starting each page anew with "No. 1." The titles of the collections either are given in a short form chosen to identify the collection among several works by the same author, or, when such an identification is not needed, are omitted.[3] When a riddle has been reprinted in a later collection or is the same as another parallel, I have often indicated the fact by the use of an equals sign (=).

The Analytical Table that follows this preface has proved extremely useful in finding riddles in this collection. I have ordinarily found it more convenient to use than the Index of Solutions. It enables one to find a riddle having the answers "stick" or "wasp" that would otherwise be concealed under such synonyms as "cane" or "dirtdauber."

The kindnesses of many friends and helpers have made possible this collection. The University of Chicago and the Committee on Research of the Uni-

---

[2] Here cited as DFS.
[3] Short titles are given in the individual entries in the Collection of Riddles Cited.

versity of California gave me generous assistance in obtaining original materials in manuscript and photostat and in translating difficult texts. The Dansk Folkemindesamling permitted me to copy its manuscript collections and the notes of H. F. Feilberg; the notes proved to be almost completely incorporated in Feilberg's *Bidrag til en ordbog over jyske almuesmål*.[4] Dorothy Vargis of the Harvard College Library aided me in identifying and obtaining rare and unusual books. Donald F. Bond of the University of Chicago verified many references and copied useful texts that would otherwise have been out of my reach. John W. Spargo gave me photostats of some rare collections in the British Museum. Gordon W. Thayer discovered some Russian collections in the John G. White Collection of the Cleveland Public Library and put them at my disposal.

Many collectors have generously allowed me to use their publications. I return thanks once more to Martha Warren Beckwith, whose interest in riddles appears in Hawaiian and Jamaican collections; Ralph S. Boggs, who also surveyed the manuscript and added a number of Cuban parallels; Paul G. Brewster, L. W. Chappell, John H. Cox, T. J. Farr, Arthur H. Fauset, Emelyn G. Gardner, H. M. Hyatt, Mrs. W. E. Greenleaf, Elsie Clews Parsons, and Vance Randolph.

The linguistic difficulties that I have encountered in assembling a satisfactory mass of comparative materials have been considerable. Only a very intelligent person with an extensive and accurate knowledge of a language can translate its riddles. I have had the good fortune to have such helpers. Alice Rakstis translated the whole of Jurgelionis' Lithuanian collection for me. Vernam Hull gave me English versions of nearly four hundred Welsh texts which we have printed as a preliminary to this collection and also a considerable number of translated Irish texts. Rajko H. Ružić supplied English versions of some two thousand Bulgarian and Serbian riddles. George R. Noyes, whose active interest has been a constant stimulus and encouragement, interpreted many difficult dialectal Polish and Russian texts. Oleg Maslenikov gave me translations of Russian versions of Georgian and Yakut riddles. Arpad Steiner translated for me Sigismund Szendrey's important additions to Antti Aarne's studies in the dissemination of riddles and often gave me counsel about obscure Hungarian idioms. Arthur Weiss also helped me with Hungarian problems. In Modern Greek, I have relied upon the able help of Anthulla Eliades. Henning Larsen has counseled me about obscurities in Danish, Norwegian, and Swedish. Yakov Malkiel translated Crimean Tatar riddles from a Russian source. Harriet Pawlowska most generously provided me with a great number of Polish texts, some in difficult dialects and others translated from Yakut or other languages. Erminie Voegelin, Karl Menges,

---

[4] Cited as Feilberg, *Ordbog*.

and especially W. D. Preston, who generously translated Hamizade's very important collection for me, supplied Turkish texts. Francis J. Carmody translated some hundreds of Irish riddles. I am warmly appreciative of the fact that so many had time and strength to turn from their own duties to help me.

The publication of this volume has been aided by a grant of the American Council of Learned Societies.

A. T.

Contents

	PAGE
Introduction	1
I. Comparisons to a Living Creature, Nos. 1–335	9
II. Comparisons to an Animal, Nos. 336–458	103
III. Comparisons to Several Animals, Nos. 459–512	155
IV. Comparisons to a Person, Nos. 513–826	183
V. Comparisons to Several Persons, Nos. 827–1035	305
VI. Comparisons to Plants, Nos. 1036–1099	411
VII. Comparisons to Things, Nos. 1100–1259	453
VIII. Enumerations of Comparisons, Nos. 1260–1408	533
IX. Enumerations in Terms of Form or of Form and Function, Nos. 1409–1495	571
X. Enumerations in Terms of Color, Nos. 1496–1572	623
XI. Enumerations in Terms of Acts, Nos. 1573–1749	639
Notes to Chapter I	691
Notes to Chapter II	718
Notes to Chapter III	735
Notes to Chapter IV	744
Notes to Chapter V	770
Notes to Chapter VI	795
Notes to Chapter VII	808
Notes to Chapter VIII	831
Notes to Chapter IX	841
Notes to Chapter X	853
Notes to Chapter XI	857
Collections of Riddles Cited	871
Collections Arranged According to Languages	899
Index of Solutions	905

Analytical Table

	PAGE
CHAPTER I. Comparisons to a Living Creature, Nos. 1–335	9
Form, Nos. 1–87	10
A Member Present, Another Member Lacking, Nos. 1–28	10
Head, Nos. 1–21	10
Head, No Body, Nos. 1–2	10
Head, No Hair, Nos. 3–4	10
Head, No Eyes, No. 5	12
Neck, No Head, No. 6	12
Head Present, Another Member Lacking, Nos. 7–9	12
Many Eyes, No Mouth (Nose), Nos. 10–16	12
Tongue, No Mouth, No. 17	14
Teeth, No Mouth (Tongue), Nos. 18–21	14
Teeth, No Mouth: A Saw, No. 18	15
Hands, No Fingers, No. 22	16
Fingers, No Toes (Flesh), Nos. 23–24	16
Other Members, Nos. 25–28	16
Several Members Occasionally Lacking, No. 29	16
Abnormality in Form, Nos. 30–87	16
Head, Nos. 30–42	17
Two Heads, No. 30	17
Heart in Its Head, Nos. 31–33	18
Parts of the Head, Nos. 34–42	18
Hair, No. 34	18
Eyes, Nos. 35–39	18
Peacock, No. 39	18
Nose, Nos. 40–41	19
Mouth, No. 42	19
Back, Belly, Nos. 43–45	19
Legs, Feet, Nos. 46–87	19
The Riddle of the Sphinx, Nos. 46–47	20
First Four, Then Two, Finally Three Feet, No. 46	22
Four Legs in the Morning, Two Legs at Noon, Three Legs at Night, No. 47	23
The Odin Riddle, Nos. 48–55	24
Members of a Pregnant Creature, Nos. 56–57	28
Pregnant Animal, No. 56	30
Pregnant Woman, No. 57	31
Feet, Tails, and Nails, Nos. 58–60	31
Goes Up with Four Legs, Comes Down with Eight Legs, No. 61	32
Seven Legs and a Tail, No. 62	32
Mouth to Mouth, Seven Legs, and a Tail, No. 63	33
Three (Four) Legs Up and Six (Four) Legs Down, Nos. 64–70	33
Black upon Black, Three Legs Up, Six Legs Down, Nos. 64–66	33
Head of the Living, Mouth of the Dead, Three Legs Up, No. 67	34
Three Legs, No. 68	35
Four Legs Up, Four Legs Down, Nos. 69–70	35

Form—*Continued*

	PAGE
Legs and Other Members, Nos. 71–82	36
Long Legs, Short Thighs, Bald (Little) Head, No (Bullet) Eyes, Nos. 79–82	37
Feet, Nos. 83–87	37

Function, Nos. 88–258 38
  Birth, Growth, Manner of Life, Nos. 88–111 38
    Birth, Growth, Nos. 88–95 38
      Buried and Begets Children, No. 95 39
    Manner of Life, Nos. 96–106 [Nos. 107–111 are vacant] 39
      I Never Was and Am Always To Be, No. 97 39
  Moving, Nos. 112–222 41
    Leaves a Locked House, No. 112 42
    Follows Everywhere, No. 113 42
    Goes; Never Stops, Nos. 114–118 43
    Goes; Never Moves, Nos. 119–132 45
      Goes Up and Down; Never Moves (Never Touches the Ground), Nos. 119–124 46
      Comes and Goes; Stands Still (Does Not Leave the Spot), Nos. 125–130 47
        Always Goes; Never Moves, Nos. 125–127 48
        Goes to a Named Spot without Moving, Nos. 128–130 48
      Turns; Does Not Move, Nos. 131–132 49
    Goes Out and In, Nos. 133–135 49
    Goes; Never Comes Back, No. 136 50
    Goes; Never Wearies, Nos. 137–140 50
      Sun, Moon, and Wind or River (Waterfall) Never Grow Weary, Nos. 138–140 50
    Goes Up, Never Down, Nos. 141–142 54
    Runs; Does Not Run Up, No. 143 54
    Goes; Touches, Nos. 144–173 55
      Goes to the Water (through the Wood), Touches Water (Every Twig), Nos. 144–146 55
      Goes; Does Not Touch, Nos. 147–173 55
        Goes; Does Not Touch the Woods (House), No. 164 57
        Goes through (over, under) the Water; Does Not Touch the Water, Nos. 165–173 59
          Goes through the Water; Is Not Wet: Egg in a Duck, Nos. 169–171 62
        Miscellaneous, Nos. 172–173 63
    Goes About; Makes a Track, Nos. 174–185 63
      Moves; Leaves No Track, Nos. 181–185 64
    Goes without a Shadow, No. 186 65
    Goes on Its Head, Nos. 187–189 66
    Carries His Way on His Neck (Shoulders), No. 190 67
    Goes; Sees, Nos. 191–197 67
      Goes to the Wood; Looks Homeward, No. 191 67
      Goes about the House; Goes (Peeps) In, Nos. 192–197 70
        Goes through the Keyhole, Nos. 194–197 71
    Comes to the House (Wood); Does Not Enter, Nos. 198–202 71
    Goes About; Leaves Something, Nos. 203–213 73
      Goes About; Leaves Its Tail Behind, No. 203 73

Analytical Table

	PAGE
Function—*Continued*	
Walks; Drops a Piece, No. 204	74
Goes About; Leaves Its Entrails Behind, Nos. 205–207	74
Goes About; Leaves Cap (Rags), Nos. 208–209	75
Goes around House; Leaves a Glove, Nos. 210–213	76
Goes around House; Drags a Harrow, No. 214	77
Swims; Does Not Sink, No. 215	77
Minor Varieties of Moving, Nos. 216–222	77
Seeing, Nos. 223–228	77
Is Not Seen, No. 226	78
Cannot See, No. 227	78
Must Be Blinded, No. 228	80
Making Sounds, Nos. 229–232	80
Eating or Drinking, Nos. 233–253	81
Can Eat; Cannot Drink, No. 235	81
Insatiability, Nos. 236–239	81
Eats with Belly; Voids through Back, No. 240	82
Chews (Eats); Does Not Swallow, Nos. 241–243	84
Smokes; Does Not Chew, No. 244	84
Does Not Eat (Drink), Nos. 245–253	84
Goes About; Does Not Drink (Eat), Nos. 246–253	84
Jingles to the Water; Does Not Drink, Nos. 251–253	85
Resting, Nos. 254–258	86
Sleeps All Day; Walks at Night, Nos. 254–255	86
Does Not Rest, Nos. 256–258	86
Can Rest in a Box; Cannot Rest in a Field, No. 257	86
Cannot Rest in a Chest, No. 258	87
Form and Function, Nos. 259–335	87
Abnormal in Form, Normal in Function; Member and Function Related, Nos. 259–265	87
Moves without Legs, Nos. 260–265	87
Runs without Legs: A Clock, No. 262	90
Without Bone (Blood), Yet Walks, Nos. 264–265	90
The Snail Riddle, No. 264	92
Abnormal in Form, Normal in Function; Member and Function Not Closely Related, Nos. 266–271	93
Normal in Form, Abnormal in Function, Nos. 272–326	94
A Member Normal in Form, Abnormal in Function, Nos. 272–310	94
Head, Nos. 272–273	94
Eyes, Nos. 274–284	94
Ears, No. 285	95
Nose, No. 286	95
Mouth, Nos. 287–291	95
Tongue, Nos. 292–296	96
Teeth, Nos. 297–300	96
Has Teeth; Cannot Eat, Nos. 297–300	96
Has Teeth and Does Not Eat: A Saw, No. 298	97
Has Teeth and Does Not Eat: A Comb, No. 299	97
Has Teeth and Does Not Eat: A Rake, No. 300	98
Hands, Nos. 301–304	98

	PAGE
Form and Function—*Continued*	
Legs, Nos. 305–310	98
Has Legs; Cannot Walk, Nos. 305–310	98
Several Members Normal in Form, Abnormal in Function Nos. 311–326	99
Abnormal in Form and Function, Nos. 327–335	100
CHAPTER II. Comparisons to an Animal, Nos. 336–458	103
Animal Not Identified, No. 336	104
Insect, Nos. 337–344	104
Biting, Stinging, Nos. 338–343	105
Hip, Hop, Jump Wide, No. 344	106
Fish, Nos. 345–346	107
Amphibian, Nos. 347–349	107
Snake, No. 350	108
Bird, Nos. 351–380	108
Form, Nos. 351–353	109
Bird and Frog, No. 352	109
Function, Nos. 354–371	110
Manner of Life, Nos. 354–355	110
Flying, Nos. 356–369	111
Has Wings; Cannot Fly, No. 356	111
Flies; Never Rests, No. 357	111
Flies High and Low, Nos. 358–366	111
Flies High and Low; Catches Chickens, No. 360	112
Flies High and Low; Eats Grass, No. 361	112
Flies High and Low; Often (Never) Changes, Nos. 362–364	112
Flies High and Does Not Leave the Place, No. 364	113
Flies High and Low without Wings (Feet), Nos. 365–366	113
White Bird Featherless Flies without Wings, Nos. 367–369	115
Sitting, Nos. 370–371	123
A Specific Bird, Nos. 372–380	123
Goose Has Legs But Walks without Them, No. 372	123
Cock or Hen, Nos. 373–380	124
Form, No. 373	124
Function, Nos. 374–380	124
Crowing, Nos. 377–380	125
Cock Crows Fire, Nos. 379–380	125
Mammal, Nos. 381–458	126
Pig, Nos. 381–387	126
Gives Birth, Nos. 381–382	127
Manner of Life, Nos. 383–384	128
Motion, Nos. 385–386	128
Leaves a Trail, No. 386	128
Squeals, No. 387	129
Rabbit, No. 388	130
Lamb, No. 389	130
Deer, Nos. 390–392	130
Form, No. 390	131
Function, Nos. 391–392	131
Shoot at a Deer, No. 391	131
Walks Alone, No. 392	131

Analytical Table

	PAGE
Mammal—*Continued*	
Cow or Bull, Nos. 393–404	132
Form, No. 393	132
Function, Nos. 394–404	132
Dashes Head on Stone; Becomes White Milk, No. 397	133
Cow's Groans Heard over the World, No. 398	134
Insatiable Red Cow (Bull, Heifer), Nos. 399–400	135
Offspring of a Bull, Nos. 401–404	136
Horse, Nos. 405–435	137
Form, Nos. 405–413	138
Abnormal Form, Nos. 409–413	138
Horse in Stable, Mane (Reins, Tail) Outside, Nos. 412–413	138
Mule in Stable, Tail Outside, No. 413	141
Function, Nos. 414–435	141
Eating, Drinking, Biting, Nos. 414–417	141
Drops Silver, No. 418	141
Is Ridden, Jumps, or Walks, Nos. 419–435	142
Goes over a Bridge, No. 420	142
Abnormal Riding, Nos. 421–435	143
Does Not Wet Feet, Nos. 431–432	144
Is Not Ridden Unless . . . , Nos. 433–435	144
Donkey, No. 436	144
Dog, Nos. 437–458	146
Form, No. 437	146
Iron (Flaxen) Tail, No. 437	146
Function, Nos. 438–458	146
Barking, Nos. 438–444	146
Cannot Bark, No. 444	147
Running About, Nos. 445–458	148
Runs About All Day; Rests under the Bed (Stove) at Night, Nos. 445–446	149
Runs About; Sits by Fire (in the Cupboard, on the Table), Nos. 447–452	149
Runs About All Day; Gapes for Bones at Night, No. 453	150
Runs About; Sits with Its Tongue Out, Nos. 454–455	151
Runs About; Sits in the Corner (on Its Head), Nos. 456–457	152
Goes over Hills and Plains; Breaks Its Neck at a River, No. 458	152
CHAPTER III. Comparisons to Several Animals, Nos. 459–512	155
Animals Not Named, Nos. 459–470	155
Animals Hunted, Nos. 459–460	155
What I Caught (Killed), I Threw Away, No. 460	159
Two-Legs Sat on Three-Legs, Nos. 461–462	160
Man, Stool, Leg of Mutton (Ham), No. 461	163
Milkmaid (Man), Stool, Cow, No. 462	164
Four-Legs Sat on Four-Legs, No. 463	164
Two-Legs (Four-Legs) Goes About, Nos. 464–465	165
No-Foot, Nos. 466–468	165
Miscellaneous, Nos. 469–470	166
Animals Named, Nos. 471–512	166
Frogs, No. 471	166
Birds, Nos. 472–475	166

xviii   *English Riddles*

	PAGE
Animals Named—*Continued*	
Chickens, No. 475	166
Hares, No. 476	166
Pigs, Guinea Pigs, Nos. 477–483	167
Form, No. 477	167
Function, Nos. 478–483	167
Eating, Nos. 481–483	168
Boars Do Not Disgorge Food, No. 483	168
Sheep, Nos. 484–490	168
Form, Nos. 484–486	169
Function, Nos. 487–490	170
Graze on the Hillside, No. 488	170
Drink Up Water, Nos. 489–490	171
Goats, No. 491	173
Cows, No. 492	173
Horses, Nos. 493–496	173
Changing Color, No. 493	173
Moving, Nos. 494–496	174
Mare and Colt, No. 496	174
Comparisons of Sheep, Cattle, Horses, etc., to Teeth, Nos. 497–510	175
Comparison of Sheep to Teeth, Nos. 497–498	177
Comparison of Cattle to Teeth, Nos. 499–501	178
Comparison of Horses to Teeth, Nos. 502–510	179
Several Different Animals, Nos. 511–512	180
CHAPTER IV. Comparisons to a Person, Nos. 513–826	183
Form, Nos. 513–660	183
Head, Eyes, Mouth, Nose, Beard, Nos. 513–549	183
Head, Nos. 513–520	184
Eyes, Nos. 521–536	185
Three Eyes, Nos. 523–524	185
One Eye, Nos. 525–534	186
One Eye: A Needle, Nos. 528–534	187
One Eye and a Tail, Nos. 531–534	187
Person with a Tail,[1] Nos. 535–536	190
Nose, Nos. 537–538	191
Mouth of Horn, Beard of Flesh, Nos. 539–543	191
Beard of Flesh, Mouth of Horn, Feet of a Griffon, No. 543	194
Beard, Nos. 544–548	194
Man in Room, Beard Outside, No. 544	194
Beard and Mouth (Lips), Nos. 545–548	198
No Tooth or Tongue, No. 549	199
Hands, Nos. 550–552	199
Belly, Nos. 553–556	200
Belly of Wood, Sides of Leather, etc., Nos. 553–554	200
Without a Belly, Nos. 555–556	201
Legs, Nos. 557–563	202
Three Feet (Legs) and a Cap, No. 558	202
Hundred Legs, No. 559	203
All Legs and No Body, No. 560	203

---

[1] A degenerate version of the preceding riddle.

Analytical Table

	PAGE
Form—*Continued*	
Long Man Legless, Nos. 561–562	203
Bandy Legs, No. 563	204
Several Abnormalities, Nos. 564–572	204
Enumeration of Qualities, Nos. 573–660	205
Temperament, Nos. 573–574	205
Form,[2] Nos. 575–578	206
A Long Person, No. 575	206
Prickly or Bumpy, Nos. 576–577	210
Bearer of Pins and Needles, No. 576	210
Several Qualities, No. 578	211
Color,[3] Nos. 579–584	212
A White Person: Tooth, Nos. 581–582	212
White Man and Red Rag, No. 582	212
Red (Black) Head (Hair, Face), Nos. 583–584	212
Dress, Nos. 585–660	213
Form, Nos. 585–600	213
The Cock Dressed as a Prophet, No. 585	213
Wears One Kind of Robe, No. 586	213
Summer and Winter Clothing, No. 587	214
Dress in the Wrong Place, No. 588	216
Torn Dress, Nos. 589–593	218
Various Kinds of Dress, Nos. 594–600	219
Colors, Nos. 601–660	219
Green, Nos. 601–606	219
Itum Paraditum, Nos. 601–603	219
Green Coat, No. 604	220
Green Cap, Yellow Shoes, Nos. 605–606	220
White, Nos. 607–631	221
Little Nancy Etticoat, Nos. 607–631	221
Versions Referring Primarily to Petticoat or Coat, Nos. 611–619	222
Nancy Etticoat and Variations, No. 611	222
Miss Netticoat, Nannicoat, and Variations, No. 612	222
Nan, Nancy, and Variations, Nos. 613–615	223
Other Names, Nos. 616–617	223
A Coat, Nos. 618–619	223
Versions Referring Primarily to Nose, Nos. 620–624	223
Fragmentary and Corrupt Versions, Nos. 625–631	224
Red, Nos. 632–644	224
Dick Red-Cap, Nos. 632–644	224
Yellow, Nos. 645–649	232
A Lady (Man) with Yellow (Red) Coat (Petticoat), Nos. 645–648	232
Yellow Breeches, No. 649	233
Several Colors, Nos. 650–656	233
Gowns of Several Colors: A Plant, Nos. 650–652	233
Colors and an Act, Nos. 657–660	234
Function, Nos. 661–822	235
Birth, Nos. 661–667	235
Speaks at Birth, Nos. 665–667	235

[2] Referring to the whole body, not to a single member.
[3] Referring to the body, not to the clothes.

Function—*Continued*

    PAGE

Born without Sin; Speaks Only Once, No. 666 236
Born without Father or Mother; Speaks at Birth, No. 667 236
A Biography, Nos. 668–680 236
  A Sequence of Colors, Nos. 668–669 238
  A Sequence of Acts, Nos. 670–680 240
    A Series of Tortures, Nos. 674–680 240
      Born of Flesh and Blood; Later Decapitated, Nos. 674–677 245
      Series of Tortures or Punishments Describing a Manufactured Object, No. 678 247
      The Tortures of Flax, No. 679 249
      The Tortures of Wheat, No. 680 251
Manner of Life, Nos. 681–822 253
  Growing, No. 681 253
  Living, Nos. 682–685 253
    Lives High in the Air, No. 685 253
  Sleeping, Nos. 686–688 254
    Sleeps Out at Night, No. 688 254
  Dirties Herself, No. 689 254
  Several Activities, Nos. 690–692 255
  Moving, Nos. 693–724 255
    Dances, Nos. 693–694 255
    Goes about the House; Stands in the Corner, Nos. 695–699 255
    Minor Varieties of Motion, Nos. 700–707 259
    Motion and an Unrelated Act, Nos. 708–713 260
      Goes and Touches, No. 712 260
      Walks and Opens Kerchief, No. 713 261
    Motion Asserted and Contradicted, No. 714–715 261
    Abnormal Motion, Nos. 716–724 261
      Makes No Track, No. 716 261
      Rides While Sitting (Walking), Nos. 717–718 261
      Walks on Head, No. 719 261
      Goes Downstairs, Not Upstairs, No. 720 262
      Goes Out in Spite of Locks, No. 721 262
      Faces Backward While Moving, Nos. 722–724 262
  Bearing, Carrying, Picking Up, Nos. 725–731 263
    Bears Burdens, Nos. 725–728 263
      Carries House on Its Back, No. 727 263
      Bears a Heavy But Not a Light Burden, No. 728 264
    Drop It; Can't Pick It Up, Nos. 729–731 264
  Sitting, Standing, Nos. 732–749 265
    Sits at (Comes to) the (King's) Table, No. 737 266
    Humpty Dumpty, Nos. 738–747 267
      Cannot Put Humpty Dumpty Together Again, No. 738 268
      Cannot Put Humpty Dumpty Back Again (As He Was Before), No. 739 268
      Cannot Stand, Nos. 740–741 269
      Cannot Be Cured, No. 742 269
      Cannot Mend, Fix, Put to Rights, Nos. 743–744 270
      Cannot Pick Up Humpy Dumpy, No. 745 270
      Miscellaneous and Corrupt Versions, Nos. 746–747 271
    Hickamore, Hackamore, Nos. 748–749 271
  Talking, Nos. 750–767 272

Analytical Table

	PAGE
Function—*Continued*	
Talks (Sings) Constantly, Nos. 751–754	272
Long Black Fellow Bellows, No. 755	273
Greets, Nos. 756–759	274
Not a Man and Yet Speaks, No. 760	275
Varieties of Talking or Roaring, Nos. 761–764	278
Can't Talk, Nos. 765–767	278
Weeping and Laughing, Nos. 768–769	278
Eating, Spitting, Nos. 770–781	280
Eats Own (Mother's) Flesh, Nos. 773–775	280
Insatiability, Nos. 776–777	281
Cries When Fed, No. 778	281
Does Not Eat, Nos. 779–780	281
Spitting, No. 781	282
Deafness, No. 782	282
Working, Practicing a Trade or Profession, Nos. 783–798	282
Works without Perspiring, No. 784	283
Works All Day; Lies in Dirt at Night, Nos. 785–786	283
Worker Keeps Head Outside, No. 787	283
Carpenter, Nos. 788–792	284
Cutting (Sawing) Wood, Nos. 788–789	284
Builds a House, Nos. 790–792	284
Smith, Nos. 793–794	285
Locking a Gate without Using Iron or Steel, No. 794	285
Weaver, No. 795	286
Shoemaker, No. 796	286
Professions, Nos. 797–798	286
Man Rules the World, No. 798	286
Shooting, Wounding, Killing, Dying, Nos. 799–822	287
Killing, Nos. 801–819	287
Small; It Kills a Man, No. 801	287
Kills Many People, Nos. 802–804	289
Kills Thieves, No. 804	290
Killing (Wounding), Eating, and Throwing Away Refuse, Nos. 805–818	290
Take Off His Head; Drink His Blood: A Bottle, No. 805	290
Pull Off His Head; Drink His Blood; Throw Away His Bones: A Fruit, Nos. 806–815	293
Corrupt and Confused Versions, Nos. 814–815	298
Shake His Hand; Suck His Blood, No. 816	298
Touch a Man; He Bleeds, No. 817	298
Strike a Man; He Bleeds, No. 818	299
Can Kill; Cannot Be Killed, No. 819	300
Dying, Nos. 820–822	300
Drowning, Nos. 821–822	300
A Man and Not a Man, Nos. 823–826	301
The Eunuch Riddle, Nos. 823–824	301
Nobody and Somebody, Nos. 825–826	303
CHAPTER V. Comparisons to Several Persons, Nos. 827–1035	305
Unrelated Persons, Nos. 827–982	306
The Dead and the Living, Nos. 828–836	306
The Dead Bears the Living, Nos. 828–829	308

English Riddles

	PAGE
Unrelated Persons—*Continued*	
The Dead Bears the Living: A Ship, No. 828	309
The Dead (Old) Speak; the Living (Young) Are Silent, Nos. 830–834	311
The Dead Bury the Living, No. 835	313
The Dead Covers the Living, No. 836	314
A Company Who Are Not Men, Women, or Children, Nos. 837–839	315
Color, Nos. 840–904	316
White, Nos. 840–861	316
White Children, Nos. 840–841	316
White Children: Teeth, No. 841	316
Whitey Drives Whitey, Nos. 842–856	320
Whitey Drives Whitey out of Whitey (Cotton Field), Nos. 842–844	321
Whitey Drives Whitey out of Whitey (Cornfield, Grainfield, Garden, Cabbage Patch, Buckwheat), Nos. 845–850	323
Whitey Drives Whitey from Whitey (Clothes), Nos. 851–853	323
Whitey Drives Whitey out of Whitey (Stable, House), Nos. 854–856	324
Whitey Goes About, Nos. 857–859	324
Whitey Goes Upstairs, Nos. 860–861	324
Black, Nos. 862–864	324
Two or More Colors, Nos. 865–904	325
Whitey and Blackie (Brownie), Nos. 865–870	325
Red Man and Black (White) Man, Nos. 871–877	325
Black Man Sits on Red Man, Nos. 875–877	328
Black Man Sits (Dances) on White Man, Nos. 878–884	329
Several Colors, Nos. 885–904	330
Nicky, Nacky, Brown Tobaccy, Nos. 887–904	330
Function, Nos. 905–982	332
Residence, Nos. 905–936	332
Residents in the Bush (Underbrush), No. 905	332
Normal People in an Abnormal House, Nos. 906–916	332
The House Leaps out of the Window, No. 906	332
Flat-top House, No. 907	334
People in a House (Chapel), Nos. 908–916	334
A Brown House for Five People, No. 908	336
A Chapel (Church, Convent) and Occupants, No. 909	337
People in a House of Unusual Colors, Nos. 910–915	339
A House within a House and Filled with People, No. 916	341
Abnormal People, Normal House, Nos. 917–928	342
Abnormal in Form, Nos. 917–918	342
Abnormal in Color, Nos. 919–924	342
Abnormal in Function, Nos. 925–928	343
A Shipload of People, Nos. 929–936	343
Abnormal in Form, Nos. 929–933	344
Abnormal in Color, Nos. 934–936	344
Waiting, No. 937	344
Moving, Nos. 938–963	344
Three Men Start for Heaven, Nos. 941–942	345
Jack and Jill Went up the Hill, No. 943	346
If They Come, They Don't Come, Nos. 944–945	346
A Company of Dancers (Workmen), Nos. 946–950	347

Analytical Table

	PAGE
Unrelated Persons—*Continued*	
Men Travel at Unequal Speeds, No. 951	349
Pursuing, Nos. 952–957	350
Men Running Cannot Overtake Each Other: Wheels, Nos. 954–957	351
One Goes In; Two Stand By, Nos. 958–960	353
Go through Rain; Are Not Wet, Nos. 961–963	354
Talking, Nos. 964–965	355
Fighting, Nos. 966–968	355
Fight; God Parts Them, No. 967	357
Fight and Embrace, No. 968	358
Killing, No. 969	358
Court Proceedings, Imprisonment, Execution, Nos. 970–975	358
Imprisonment, Nos. 974–975	363
Actors Described in Terms of Their Numbers, Nos. 976–982	363
Ten Draw Four, Nos. 976–979	364
Ten against Four, No. 977	366
Ten upon (above, about, onto) Four, No. 978	366
Ten upon Four, Hauling and Scrambling, No. 979	366
Two See It; Five (Ten) Pick It, Nos. 980–982	367
Related Persons, Nos. 983–1035	368
Sons, Nos. 983–988	368
Sons and Shirts, No. 983	368
Twelve Sons, No. 984	370
Son Appears before Father's Birth, No. 985	373
Pursuing, No. 986	375
Cannot See, No. 987	376
Cannot Talk to Each Other, No. 988	376
Brothers, Nos. 989–1006	376
Form, Nos. 989–991	376
Dressing Awry, No. 989	376
Five Brothers of Abnormal Form, No. 990	378
Full All Day, Empty at Night, No. 991	379
Function, Nos. 992–1006	380
Stand (Sit) Together, Nos. 992–993	380
Brothers under One Hat, No. 993	381
Help Each Other, Nos. 994–995	382
Pursuing One Another, Nos. 996–1001	382
Brother Pursues Brother (Sister), No. 1001	385
Brother Does Not Leave Brother, No. 1002	386
Seeing, Nos. 1003–1005	386
Brothers Are Close, But Cannot See Each Other, Nos. 1003–1004	386
Live Together; Do Not See (Touch, Speak to) Each Other, No. 1005	390
Speaking, No. 1006	392
Daughter (Daughters), Nos. 1007–1011	392
Mother Begets Daughter; Daughter Begets Mother, No. 1007	392
Mother Begets and Kills Daughter, No. 1008	394
Daughter of Wicked Father Begets Good Children, No. 1009	394
Cannot Identify Oldest Daughter, No. 1010	395
Older Daughter Speaks; Younger Cannot, No. 1011	395
Sisters, Nos. 1012–1016	395
Sister Vainly Pursues Sister, Nos. 1014–1015	395

xxiv *English Riddles*

	PAGE
Related Persons—*Continued*	
Seeing, No. 1016	396
Family, Nos. 1017–1035	397
Form, No. 1017	400
Hollow Mother, Humpbacked Father, Three Children, No. 1017	402
Colors, Nos. 1018–1020	403
Function, Nos. 1021–1035	404
Manner of Life, Nos. 1021–1035	404
Parent and Children, Nos. 1021–1024	404
Mother Lives; Children Die, No. 1022	405
Mother and Countless Children, Nos. 1023–1024	406
Children, Nos. 1025–1035	406
Children Glitter, No. 1025	406
Children Cling, No. 1026	407
Cannot Touch One Another, Nos. 1027–1028	407
Pursuing, Nos. 1029–1030	409
Bathing, Nos. 1031–1032	409
Bathe and Dry the Water, No. 1032	409
Go to School, No. 1033	409
Help Each Other, No. 1034	410
Don't Want to See Each Other, No. 1035	410
CHAPTER VI. Comparisons to Plants, Nos. 1036–1099	411
A Tree, Nos. 1036–1050	411
A Tree with Root But No Leaves, No. 1036	411
A Tree with Twelve Branches, Nos. 1037–1038	412
Twelve Branches, Fifty-two Nests, No. 1037	420
Twelve Limbs, Seven Branches, No. 1038	421
Oak, Nest, Egg, and Yolk, No. 1039	421
Trees of Unequal Height, Nos. 1040–1041	422
Trees or Grass: Hair, Nos. 1042–1044	423
Trees around a Well, No. 1044	425
Trees Representing Persons, Nos. 1045–1046	425
Miscellaneous Comparisons to Trees, Nos. 1047–1050	426
Other Plants, Nos. 1051–1065	426
Growth, Nos. 1051–1062	426
Grows with Its Root Upward, Nos. 1055–1057	427
Grew in the Wood, Nos. 1058–1062	428
Land Is White; Seed Is Black, No. 1063	435
Does Not Bear (Fruit), Nos. 1064–1065	439
Flowers, Nos. 1066–1071	439
Cannot Be Plucked, No. 1070	440
Disappear, No. 1071	441
Fruits, Seeds, Nos. 1072–1099	443
Form, Nos. 1072–1073	443
Color, Nos. 1074–1089	443
Function, Nos. 1090–1095	445
Fruits on a Tree or in a Dish (Pail), Nos. 1093–1095	445
Vanish in the Daytime, No. 1094	447
Apples Cannot Be Counted, No. 1095	449
Flour (Fruit) of England (Virginia), Fruit (Flour) of Spain, Nos. 1096–1099	449
Fruit of England, etc., Nos. 1096–1099	449

Analytical Table

	PAGE
CHAPTER VII. Comparisons to Things, Nos. 1100–1259	453
Objects in Nature, Nos. 1100–1117	453
Landscape, Nos. 1100–1108	453
Mountain, Grassy Field, No. 1100	458
Holes in a Hill, No. 1101	459
Water, Nos. 1102–1106	461
Crossing Water, No. 1103	461
Water to Wash In, Towel to Dry With, No. 1104	462
Water Stands Up, Lies Down, Does Not Stir, Nos. 1105–1106	463
Gully, No. 1107	464
Road, No. 1108	464
Stick, Stump, Wand, Wood, Nos. 1109–1117	465
Bunch of Wands, No. 1116	466
Load of Wood, No. 1117	467
A House, Nos. 1118–1164	467
Form, Nos. 1118–1119	468
Position, Nos. 1120–1126	468
House Resting on Posts, Nos. 1121–1126	468
House with Doors (Windows), Nos. 1127–1142	472
House with Many Windows, Nos. 1128–1131	472
House without Doors (Windows), Nos. 1132–1138	473
Little White House without Doors, No. 1133	475
(White) House without Doors Has an Occupant, No. 1134	475
House without Doors Contains Food, Nos. 1135–1136	476
House without Doors Contains Gold, No. 1137	476
Marble Walls, Crystal Fountain, Golden Apple, No. 1138	477
Marble Stone, Golden Ball, No. 1139	478
Castle on the Seaside, No. 1140	479
Entering (Leaving, Closing) House, Nos. 1141–1142	481
House (Cave, Garden): Human Head, Nos. 1143–1151	481
Windows: Eyes, No. 1144	483
Red House (Theater), Nos. 1145–1148	483
(Red) House and a Fence, No. 1149	484
Red Cave That Is Always Wet, No. 1150	485
Red Garden within a Fence, No. 1151	488
House of Various Colors (Materials), Nos. 1152–1155	490
House and Its Contents, Nos. 1156–1164	490
House and Furniture, Nos. 1156–1160	491
House within a House within a House, Nos. 1161–1164	494
Ship, Nos. 1165–1168	495
Mill, No. 1169	496
Household Objects, Nos. 1170–1249	496
Barrel, Tub, Pot, Tank, Well, Nos. 1170–1178	497
Barrel without Staves, No. 1171	497
Bottomless Tub, Nos. 1172–1173	497
Well (Tank) Holds Water, Nos. 1174–1176	500
Pot Boils without Fire, Nos. 1177–1178	500
Furniture, Nos. 1179–1199	501
Chair (Bed) Cannot Be Sat (Lain) In, Nos. 1183–1186	501
Box (Trunk), Nos. 1187–1188	502

English Riddles

	PAGE
Household Objects—*Continued*	
Box Cannot Be Opened, No. 1187	502
Trunk Contains Two Kinds of Clothes, No. 1188	504
Lamp, Candle, Light, Nos. 1189–1191	504
Broken Plate (Egg), Nos. 1192–1196	505
Plate Repaired When Broken, No. 1193	507
Object Is Not Broken (Smashed, Cut), Nos. 1194–1196	508
Glasses, Nos. 1197–1198	509
Bottles, No. 1199	509
Bag, Rope, Nos. 1200–1205	509
Bag, Nos. 1200–1201	509
Rope, String, Nos. 1202–1205	510
Rope Moves, Nos. 1203–1205	510
Articles of Dress, Nos. 1206–1211	511
Shoes, No. 1206	511
Clothing, Nos. 1207–1211	511
Cloth, Nos. 1212–1226	512
Neither Spun Nor Woven, No. 1212	512
Without a Seam, No. 1213	512
Can Be Washed But Not Dried, No. 1214	513
Sheet, Nos. 1215–1226	513
Sheet Cannot Be Folded; Money Cannot Be Counted; Apple Cannot Be Plucked (Cut, Eaten), Nos. 1215–1216	513
Sheet Cannot Be Folded, Nos. 1217–1218	515
Sheet Covers the World, Nos. 1219–1220	516
Sheet Cannot Be Spread, Nos. 1221–1223	517
Cloth Cannot Be Folded; Money Cannot Be Counted, Nos. 1224–1225	518
Sheet Full of Small Change, No. 1226	518
Money Cannot Be Counted, No. 1227	519
Plates Washed in Evening Vanish by Morning, No. 1228	521
Articles of Food, Nos. 1229–1249	522
Biscuits and Cloth, No. 1229	522
Articles of Food: Sun or Moon, Nos. 1230–1234	522
Food Serves the Whole World, Nos. 1232–1234	526
A Piece of Meat Fills a Crack, No. 1235	526
Salt Does Not Penetrate Food, No. 1236	526
Something to Eat, Not Fish, Flesh, or Bone, Nos. 1237–1238	527
Buying Food, Water, and Wood Simultaneously, Nos. 1239–1241	528
Miscellaneous, Nos. 1242–1249	529
Cannot Eat (Pick) It, Nos. 1247–1249	529
Members of a Person or of an Animal, Nos. 1250–1251	530
Two "Packey," No. 1252	530
Letter, Message, Gift, Nos. 1253–1258	531
Wagon, No. 1259	532
Chapter VIII. Enumerations of Comparisons, Nos. 1260–1408	533
Form, Nos. 1260–1359	533
Big or Little, Nos. 1260–1265	533
Little As a Nit: Salt, No. 1262	534
Smaller Than a Mouse, Nos. 1263–1265	534
Long or Broad, Nos. 1266–1267	535

Analytical Table

Form—*Continued*

	PAGE
High, Nos. 1268–1285	536
High As a House; Bitter As Gall and Sweet As Sugar (Bitter As Gall and Green As Grass), Nos. 1269–1275	536
High, Low; Bitter, Sweet, Nos. 1269–1272	537
High, Low; Bitter, Green, Nos. 1273–1274	538
High, Low; Many Rooms, No. 1275	538
High and Sharp, Nos. 1276–1277	539
Higher Than a House, Higher Than a Tree, Nos. 1278–1280	539
Higher Than a House, Smaller Than a Mouse, No. 1281	540
Miscellaneous Comparisons to Height, Nos. 1283–1285	541
Deep, Nos. 1286–1289	541
Straight (Crooked), Nos. 1290–1299	542
Crooked As a Rainbow, Nos. 1292–1297	542
Crooked As a Rainbow; Teeth Like a Cat, Nos. 1295–1296	543
Crooked As a Ram's Horn, Nos. 1298–1299	543
Flat, No. 1300	544
Round, Nos. 1301–1357	544
Round and Black, Nos. 1302–1308	544
Round and Busy, Nos. 1309–1313	545
Round and Clear, No. 1314	546
Round and Deep, Nos. 1315–1336	547
Round As a Hoop; Sings When Caught by the Tail, No. 1326	548
Round, Deep, and Has a Thousand Holes, No. 1333	550
Round and Flat, Nos. 1337–1338	551
Round and Green, No. 1339	551
Round and Keen, No. 1340	551
Round and Long, Nos. 1341–1342	551
Round As a Ball, Longer Than Paul's Steeple, No. 1341	552
Round As a Hoop, Long As a Snake, No. 1342	553
Round As a Mill Wheel; Luggit [Having Ears] Like A Cat, No. 1343	554
Round and Plump, Nos. 1344–1345	554
Round and Rough, No. 1346	554
Round and Shallow, No. 1347	554
Round and Sharp, No. 1348	555
Round and Slick, No. 1349	555
Round and Sweet, No. 1350	555
Round and Thick, No. 1351	555
Round and Thin, No. 1352	555
Round and Toothed, No. 1353	555
Round and White, No. 1354	556
Round and Yellow, Nos. 1355–1357	556
Round, Yellow; Holds Many Things, No. 1355	556
Hard, No. 1358	557
Soft, No. 1359	557
Colors (arranged alphabetically), Nos. 1360–1393	558
Black, Nos. 1360–1365	558
Green, Nos. 1366–1374	558
Red, Nos. 1375–1378	559
White, Nos. 1379–1393	560

xxviii *English Riddles*

	PAGE
Colors—*Continued*	
White and Black: A Magpie, Nos. 1379–1382	560
White As Milk; Beard Like a Buck, No. 1383	561
White, Green, Red, and Black, Nos. 1384–1393	561
Miscellaneous Comparisons, Nos. 1394–1408	563
Better (Higher) Than God, No. 1394	564
Comparisons to Animals or Objects, Nos. 1395–1408	565
Mouth Like a Barn Door, Nos. 1395–1402	565
Like a Cat and Isn't a Cat, Nos. 1403–1404	566
The Grasshopper Riddle, Nos. 1405–1408	567
CHAPTER IX. Enumerations in Terms of Form or of Form and Function, Nos. 1409–1495	571
Form, Nos. 1409–1458	572
Shape, Nos. 1409–1415	572
Holes, Nos. 1412–1413	573
Parts of an Animal, Nos. 1414–1415	573
Position, Nos. 1416–1447	573
In (Within), Out (Without), Nos. 1416–1423	574
Hairy Without, Hairy Within, Nos. 1416–1419	575
Rough (Red) Without, Smooth (Rough) Within, Nos. 1420–1421	576
When Out, It Wriggles, No. 1422	576
Neither In Nor Out, No. 1423	576
Around, Middle, Nos. 1424–1429	577
Hair Around, Hole in the Middle, Nos. 1425–1428	578
Soft in the Middle, Hard All Around, No. 1429	578
Front, Middle, Back, Nos. 1430–1435	579
Ends Alike, Middle Contrasting, Nos. 1430–1431	579
Alive at Both Ends, Dead in the Middle, Nos. 1432–1434	580
Tail Like a Sickle, No. 1435	581
Above, Below, Nos. 1436–1447	584
Over the Head, Under the Hat, No. 1436	588
Patch on Patch, Nos. 1437–1439	588
Patch on Patch: An Animal or a Thing, No. 1437	588
Patch on Patch: A Plant, Nos. 1438–1439	592
Patch on Patch: A Cabbage, No. 1438	593
Patch on Patch: An Onion, No. 1439	594
Water (Hell) Above, Fire (Hell) Below, Nos. 1440–1441	595
Devil Above, Devil Below, McKintosh Between, No. 1442	598
Hair Above, Hair Below, Nos. 1443–1444	598
Small Above, Big Below, Nos. 1445–1447	599
Changing According to Circumstances, Nos. 1448–1458	600
Stiff (Dry), Slack (Wet), Nos. 1448–1452	600
Straight, Cross, No. 1453	602
Higher, Lower, No. 1454	602
Full, Empty, Nos. 1455–1457	602
Full by Day, Empty at Night, No. 1455	603
Empty by Day, Full at Night, No. 1456	604
Full, Yet Holds More, No. 1457	604
Ready, Unready, No. 1458	605

	PAGE
Form and Function, Nos. 1459–1475	605
Holes Hold Water, Nos. 1459–1463	605
Long, Nos. 1464–1466	606
Long and Tickles (Scares), Nos. 1464–1466	606
Wider, No. 1467	607
Round, Nos. 1468–1471	607
Round; It Reaches the Sky, No. 1471	607
Small, Nos. 1472–1473	610
Small and Fills the House, No. 1473	610
Miscellaneous, Nos. 1474–1475	610
Several Members Described in Terms of Form and (or) Function, Nos. 1476–1495	610
Four Hang; Two Point the Way, Nos. 1476–1494	610
Two Hookers, Two Lookers, and a Switchabout, No. 1476	617
Four Stand, One Switchabout, No. 1477	618
Dillydanders, No. 1478	619
Two Lookers and a Wig-Wag, No. 1479	619
Downstanders, Upstanders, No. 1480	620
Miscellaneous, Nos. 1481–1489	620
Other Answers Than a Cow, Nos. 1490–1494	621
Half Dead, Half Living, No. 1495	621
CHAPTER X. Enumerations in Terms of Color, Nos. 1496–1572	623
Black and White, Nos. 1496–1497	623
Position, Nos. 1498–1541	624
All Over, Nos. 1498–1499	624
Inside and Outside, Nos. 1500–1538	624
Green and White (Yellow), Nos. 1500–1503	624
Yellow (Red) and White, Nos. 1504–1507	624
Various Colors, Nos. 1508–1518	625
Colored Outside, Contents Inside, Nos. 1519–1527	626
Colored Outside; Has Brown Eyes, No. 1528	627
Black at Ends, Red in Middle, No. 1529	627
Red, Black, Four Corners Round About, Nos. 1530–1535	627
Miscellaneous, No. 1536	628
Colored Inside and Outside, and an Act, Nos. 1537–1538	628
Front, Middle, No. 1539	628
Above, Below, Nos. 1540–1541	629
Changing According to Position, Nos. 1542–1558	629
In and Out, Nos. 1542–1546	629
In Red, Out Black, Nos. 1542–1543	630
In Green, Out Red, No. 1544	631
In and Out, Various Colors, Nos. 1545–1546	631
Up and Down, Nos. 1547–1558	632
Up Green, Down Red, Nos. 1547–1549	632
Up White, Down Yellow (Red), Nos. 1550–1554	632
Up and Down, Various Colors, Nos. 1555–1558	634
Colors in a Chronological Sequence, Nos. 1559–1561	634
First Green, Then White, Then Red: A Blackberry, No. 1561	635
Colors and an Act, Nos. 1562–1572	636
Red and White and Stands Up, No. 1572	637

	PAGE
CHAPTER XI. Enumerations in Terms of Acts, Nos. 1573–1749	639
Possession, Nos. 1573–1596	640
Everyone Has It, Nos. 1573–1575	640
Have It without Knowing, No. 1576	642
Have It; Are without It, No. 1577	642
Have It Here; See It There, No. 1578	643
Have It; Never See It, Nos. 1579–1581	643
Have It; Others Use It, Nos. 1582–1585	644
Have It; Give It Away, Nos. 1586–1588	645
Don't Have It; Give It Away, Nos. 1589–1590	645
Lose What Is Taken; Keep What Is Not Taken, Nos. 1591–1592	647
Haven't It; Wouldn't Want to Lose It, Nos. 1593–1595	648
Wouldn't Give It Away; Wouldn't Keep It, No. 1596	650
Motion, Nos. 1597–1627	651
"Through a Rock [Distaff], Through a Reel," Nos. 1597–1603	651
Up and Down, No. 1604	652
Goes from Hand to Hand, No. 1605	653
Miscellaneous, Nos. 1606–1607	654
Motion Denied, Nos. 1608–1627	654
You Go to It Because It Won't Come to You, No. 1608	654
Does Not (Should Not) Move (Gallop), Nos. 1609–1610	655
Cannot Overtake It, Nos. 1611–1613	655
Cannot Go without It, Nos. 1614–1615	655
Cannot Climb It, Nos. 1616–1627	656
Seeing, Nos. 1628–1631	658
It Is; You Do Not See It, No. 1628	658
It Is Not; You See It, No. 1629	658
Cannot See It, No. 1630	659
See You Where You Are Not, No. 1631	659
Finding, Seizing, Catching, Lifting, Nos. 1632–1663	659
Seek It; Cannot Find It, Nos. 1632–1642	659
A Houseful, But Cannot Seize It, Nos. 1643–1654	661
Cannot (Do Not) Touch It, Nos. 1655–1657	666
Cannot Pick It Up, No. 1658	666
Cannot Take It Off, No. 1659	666
Cannot Lift, Carry, Hold It, Nos. 1660–1662	667
One Man (a Thousand Men) Cannot Lift It, Nos. 1661–1662	667
Cannot Rear It, No. 1663	668
Tearing, Cutting, Breaking, Hitting, Nos. 1664–1673	668
Cannot Tear It, No. 1664	668
Cut It; Cannot See the Cut, Nos. 1665–1666	668
Cut It; Cannot Taste It, No. 1667	669
Break It by Naming It, Nos. 1668–1669	669
Cannot Mend It, Nos. 1670–1671	669
Knocking and Hitting, Nos. 1672–1673	670
Valued As Something Essential, Nos. 1674–1680	670
Use, But Do Not Esteem It, No. 1674	670
Use It; Find It Essential, Nos. 1675–1679	670
Without It Nothing Can Be Done, No. 1680	671

Analytical Table

	PAGE
Contradictory Acts or Contradiction between Act and Result, Nos. 1681–1703	672
An Act Producing a Result Contrary to Its Nature, Nos. 1689–1703	673
When Held, It Moves; When Released, It Stops, No. 1689	673
The More One Takes Away, the Larger It Becomes, Nos. 1690–1697	673
Miscellaneous, Nos. 1698–1703	676
Miscellaneous Acts Involving an Assertion or a Denial, Nos. 1704–1712	676
Acts Involving an Assertion, Nos. 1704–1707	677
Acts Involving a Denial, Nos. 1708–1712	677
Two or More Acts, Nos. 1713–1749	678
God and Man, Nos. 1713–1721	678
God Puts It On; Man Can't Take It Off, No. 1713	678
God Didn't Do It; Man Does It, No. 1714	678
God Never Sees It; a King Seldom; a Man Every Day, Nos. 1715–1720	679
Christ Had It Not; Napoleon Had It, No. 1721	681
Nature Requires Five, No. 1722	681
Lord and Lady, No. 1723	681
Rich Man and Poor Man, Nos. 1724–1727	682
Rich Man Keeps It; Poor Man Throws It Away, No. 1724	682
Rich Man Wants More of It; Poor Man Can't Get It, No. 1725	682
Rich (Don't) Want It; Poor Want It, Nos. 1726–1727	682
Maker Doesn't Use It; Buyer Doesn't Want It; User Is Not Aware of It, Nos. 1728–1737	683
Too Much for One, Enough for Two, Nothing for Three, No. 1738	686
Erotic Scenes, Nos. 1739–1749	687

Introduction

THIS COLLECTION of riddles serves two purposes. It is, in the first place, a corpus of English traditional riddling and is intended to stand beside similar German, French, Italian, Polish, Russian, Serbian, and Bulgarian collections.[1] The many widely scattered small collections of English popular riddles are here assembled and arranged systematically. An extensive view of the parallels and of related riddles provides a foundation for comparative studies. During the last century, scholars have made adequate collections of every category of folklore except the riddle. Although there are many standard national collections of riddles, none of them surveys the international relations of the texts at all satisfactorily. There are admirable collections of tales, ballads, proverbs, charms, and superstitions, to which one can turn for information about the national and international aspects of the respective subjects. This collection is intended to supply that information for the riddles which occur in English tradition or are related to them.

Many varieties of enigmatic and puzzling questions exist. The more important of these are the true riddle (or, in brief, the riddle), the neck-riddle, the arithmetical puzzle, the clever question with its several types, notably the Biblical question or riddle, and the conundrum. This collection includes only true riddles. These are descriptions of objects in terms intended to suggest something entirely different. The Humpty Dumpty riddle, for example, describes an egg as a man sitting on a wall. Only the queer fact, which is contradictory to the usual nature of a man, that he cannot be cured or put together again after falling gives notice that we are not listening to an incident from life; in other words, that we are being asked to guess a riddle.

The types of enigmatical questions which are not included in this collection can be briefly indicated. The neck-riddle narrates an event known only to the poser of the riddle. By thus setting an insoluble puzzle the poser, who is condemned to death, hopes to save his neck. I have invented the name "neck-riddle" for this well-established enigmatic genre. An example of it is the gruesome Ilo riddle, which is known all over Europe and is closely related to the English riddles or tales of Mr. Fox and of Mr. Horn. Clever questions of several sorts demand the possession of special knowledge on the hearer's part, the performance of an arithmetical calculation, or acquaintance with a detail of Biblical history. The conundrum or witty question owes its point to an ingenious combination of conflicting or heterogeneous ideas; it often plays with puns. I have reserved the collection and study of these and some other minor genres for a future occasion.

---

[1] The order of languages is that followed in the arrangement of the parallels. See Preface, p. viii. I have named here only the languages in which comprehensive standard collections exist.

Although the study of riddles cannot be called active, comparatively few contributions to the subject have been wholly superficial and inadequate. There is little underbrush and trash in the scholar's path. Even J. B. Friedreich's *Geschichte des Räthsels*,[2] which many have condemned, contains much that is worth noting and remembering and much that modern scholars might take to heart. Although every folklore journal has printed riddles in its early volumes, the editors print fewer and fewer riddles as time passes. The loss of the hope of finding myths in riddles, the lack of any standard system of arrangement, the lack of any generally accepted standard collection against which one can measure one's own collection, and the failure to perceive the problems of historical and comparative study as applied to riddles account for this decline in interest. In the last generation, however, a new endeavor to use riddles in mythological studies has stimulated a slight rise in interest and to it we owe some of the most important and valuable collections within our reach. With the growth, furthermore, of a broader and more systematic attention to folklore, scholars have, although in small numbers, turned to riddles again.

The collecting of riddles has been casual and unsystematic. Although many texts are in print, they are, if I may speak in general terms, difficult of access. Collections have appeared in small editions in remote places or in periodicals of limited circulation serving regional or other specialized needs. The citing of parallels has usually been haphazard and insufficient. It should perhaps be said that riddles can offer serious difficulties even to persons familiar with the language in which they are written. Inasmuch as riddles have ordinarily been collected along with other folkloristic materials, they have been more or less a side line which has not received particular attention.

Notwithstanding all of these limitations, probably enough European riddles are available to satisfy scholarly demands. There seems to be no reason for thinking that our resources are deficient in any important regard. To be sure, scarcely any Irish, Modern Greek, or Slavic riddles have been translated into a major western European language. An excellent collection of a hundred Irish riddles in a Swedish folklore journal of limited circulation does not greatly improve our situation. Inasmuch as most of us cannot easily lay hands on Bielenstein's Lettish collection or translate Jurgelionis' thousand-odd Lithuanian riddles—I cite only two out of many examples—I have given many parallels in full translation.

As for regions outside of Europe, texts are easily accessible in great numbers in standard ethnographical works. Russian journals contain an abundance of materials, and Finnish scholars have diligently collected the traditions of Finno-Ugric tribes. At the suggestion and urging of Wolfgang Schultz, who hoped to use the texts to support a curious mythological interpretation of his

---

[2] Dresden, 1860.

own, Indian scholars brought together a generous quantity of very useful texts. From countries lying between India and Europe—particularly from Arabia and Persia—we have much less than we should like to have. Although ethnologists tell us that African natives sit for hours telling riddles, they have not collected a correspondingly large amount of texts.

In the comparative notes I have made an effort to survey the distribution of the riddles but have not aimed at completeness. I have used most of the scattered Breton and French collections because these riddles are often closely related to the English parallels. I have quoted freely riddles from the Near and the Far East as well as from Africa because these are little known and may throw light on problems of origin and dissemination. I have limited my citations of the thousands of available German riddles to annotated collections for Northern Germany (Wossidlo), Southern Germany (Haffner), Czechoslovakia (Hanika-Otto), and Switzerland (Rochholz). I have used other German collections only incidentally. For other languages than those I have named I have chosen what seemed to be the standard collection and have usually looked no further.

Riddles are said to be unknown to certain peoples, notably the Jews, the Chinese, and the American Indians. Although these assertions are confidently made and often repeated, they need critical examination. Early examples of typical true riddles occur in Hebrew literature, in which the comparison of Moses entering the Red Sea to a man opening a lock of water with a wooden key is both old and well-established. Chinese riddles have never awakened much interest among sinologues, but Richard C. Rudolph turned up ample evidence of their existence. Anthropologists have maintained that American Indians know nothing of riddles, but the subject cannot be called closed.[3] E. W. Gifford has directed my attention to aboriginal Australian riddles. In sum, we can probably say that riddling is a universal art.

The arrangement of a collection of riddles offers many difficulties. The older alphabetical classifications according to answers or initial words wrench apart closely related texts and are wholly unsatisfactory. In such classifications, riddles describing an apple, an orange, and a watermelon as a house with its occupants (seeds) are widely separated. A satisfactory system should bring together riddles describing an object in the same way, however varied the answers may be. I have adapted such a system from Robert Lehmann-Nitsche's Argentinian collection. In it the answers are disregarded except for subsidiary purposes. The fundamental conception underlying the enigmatical comparison determines the place of the riddle. The main subdivisions or chapters in this collection are descriptions of (1) something living, (2) an animal, (3) several animals, (4) a person, (5) several persons, (6) a plant, (7)

---

[3] See my article, "American Indian Riddles," *Journal of American Folklore*, LVII (1944), 1-15.

a thing. In these varieties of the true riddle an object is equated to something entirely different from itself, and this latter thing forms the basis of the classification. The subsequent chapters include descriptions which accumulate mystifying and conflicting details without achieving the unity of suggesting a particular object. They include riddles enumerating (8) comparisons, (9) details of form, (10) details of color, and (11) characteristic acts. Such vague and often inchoate enumerations usually have no readily recognized unifying idea and consequently disintegrate easily or absorb incongruous elements. Many of them are nevertheless inventions with a long history and are not corruptions of more clearly conceived forms.

In the earlier chapters, which present comparisons to clearly conceived objects—something living, an animal or animals, a person or persons, or a thing (these are *not* the answers to the riddle),—the arrangement passes from form to function. For example, Humpty Dumpty in the egg riddle is abnormal in function, since he cannot be cured after suffering a fall. I have therefore placed this riddle after a description of a barrel as a man having two heads. In these chapters and in the chapter presenting enumerations of details of form, references to shape stand before references to color. As far as possible, references to shape are arranged from the top downward: references to the head of the supposed object precede references to its feet. References to the lack of the member or function stand last in the respective sections.

Any arrangement is difficult to devise and even more difficult to maintain consistently. Riddlers in England and other English-speaking countries show a declining familiarity with the genre and consequently do not always understand its technique. When they have failed to see the true nature of their comparisons and rhetorical devices, they have confused and corrupted the types. I have usually placed defective and corrupt versions with the better examples of the pattern, even when the degeneration is so far advanced as to obscure essential characteristics. Where riddling flourishes, as in Russia, Mongolia, or Africa, the types are usually less disorganized and the arrangement of them offers less difficulty.

The arranging of a collection of riddles is much the same as the arranging of the objects in the physical universe, for a riddle is a comparison or equating of the answer to some other object, be it an animal, a person, a plant, or a thing. The point lies in the fact that the answer and the object suggested are totally foreign and unrelated to each other. A man is compared to a tree or a house; and a road, a ladder, a pumpkin vine, the seasons, or a hundred other objects are called a man. Although some objects in the physical universe are not the themes or riddles or the means of comparison, the selection or restriction that might perhaps be discovered in the choice affords no basis for an arrangement. In European riddling, for example, the themes of riddles are found almost exclusively in the vicinity of the farmer's house. Earthworms, chickens, milk, and eggs, as well as household tools, are characteristic and popular themes. Yet even here the choice is extremely limited: dogs and horses are not often the answers to riddles, although often used as the means of comparison. Cats or mice are virtually never used in either sense. European riddlers rarely allude to wild animals. It would be hard to find riddles for a stork, a bear, a fox, or a wolf, frequent as these creatures are in folk story. Only a few fruits or vegetables occur as the themes of riddles: the carrot, the onion, the walnut, the blackberry, and the cherry comprise the list. Apples and pears are almost completely unknown to riddlers. The thistle, but not the rose, is the subject of riddles. There is, to be sure, a riddle for a rose in this collection, but it is a queer enigma with obscure and puzzling literary connections. Flax occurs in only one riddle, and then in a riddle of peculiar type. Sewing, candles, and domestic activities are frequently described. Provisionally at least, we can say that modern European traditional riddles deal with the objects in a woman's world or a world as seen from the windows of a house.

Outside of the immediate influence of a highly sophisticated European civilization, riddlers have ranged somewhat farther afield in the search for themes, but even here wild animals are rarely the subjects of riddles or the means of comparison. Such activities as plowing and harvesting perhaps play a somewhat larger part in unsophisticated riddling, and the comparisons employ a greater variety of ideas. This greater variety includes, for example, observations drawn from slaughtered animals. Men have obviously had a hand in such inventions.

European riddling, as well as the richer and more imaginative enigmatic traditions of peoples at lower cultural levels, employ surprisingly few means of comparisons—fewer, indeed, than the objects described. For example, pumpkin vines are the theme of riddles but are not, so far as I can recall, the means of comparison. An egg is a favorite subject for riddlers, who rarely if ever compare anything to an egg.

The many comparisons of an object to an animal refer to its most obvious characteristics. The grunting of a pig suggests a mill; the barking of a dog or the crowing of a cock, a gun; the hovering flight of a bird, a snowflake; and so on. In elaborating the supposed similarity of an object to a man, riddlers display a remarkable ingenuity in choosing and adapting the details of human form and activity. Comparisons to plants or fruits are rather rare in European riddling, but are somewhat more favored elsewhere. Comparisons of a thing to another and entirely different thing are numerous but are often vaguely and carelessly conceived.

In the notes at the back of the book I have cited parallels to both the themes and the manner of description. Since the time of Karl Müllenhoff (1855) and Gaston Paris (1877) the citing of parallels has dealt almost exclusively with the themes of riddles. It has created a secure but narrow basis for comparative and historical studies. Although a few investigations—notably those dealing with the year riddle (see the headnote to Nos. 1037–1038 below) and with writing ("Boves se pareba," which is one of the first Italian riddles to have been written down; see the headnote to No. 1063 below)—appeared in the three generations after Müllenhoff had directed attention to the international currency of many themes and had thus laid a foundation for comparative and historical investigations, little was accomplished until Antti Aarne wrote *Vergleichende Rätselforschungen* (Helsinki, 1918–1920). The excellent prefaces of Gaston Paris to Rolland's French collection (1877) and of Pitrè to his Italian collection (1897) had reiterated Müllenhoff's observations regarding the international currency of riddles and had reinforced them by abundant and well-chosen examples, but no one had undertaken a serious study of the problem. Aarne adopted the classification according to form rather than theme that Lehmann-Nitsche had devised and was therefore able to perceive more clearly than anyone before him the transfer of a pattern from one to another theme. He discussed briefly the typical variations arising in the course of oral transmission of riddles and applied the principles to be inferred from them to eight widely known riddles, or rather patterns of riddles. Among the riddles that he discussed are the two previously mentioned riddles for the year and for writing, and the riddle of the Sphinx (Nos. 46a through 47b below), the description of a cow in terms of such confusing descriptions of its members as "two hookers, two lookers, and a switchabout" (No. 1476a below), the description of a man on horseback according to the number of legs to be seen (Nos. 48 through 55 below), and the riddle of the snowflake or the bird without wings (Nos. 367 through 369 below). He published some supplementary studies in Finnish that have not been translated in the *Journal de la société finno-ougrienne*, XXXIV (1917). Although a few similar studies by later hands might be noted, Aarne has had virtually no imitators.

In the course of oral transmission many variations arise in the texts of riddles. Riddlers may misunderstand the words that they hear or may fail to grasp the import of the comparison on which the riddle rests. They may replace one conventional introductory or concluding formula by another. They may allow a comparison to degenerate into vagueness and obscurity by adding unessential or incongruous details or by omitting significant features. They may substitute one comparison for another. In the pertinent headnotes I have discussed comparisons that show some similarity to the English conceptions. The comparisons of teeth to various animals, and especially to birds, will, for example, be found in the third chapter in conjunction with the English comparisons of teeth to sheep, cattle, or horses. Riddles employing a means of comparison unknown to English riddlers are introduced in what has seemed to be the most appropriate place. The comparison of teeth to chips appears, for example, in the headnote relating to the comparisons of teeth to objects.[4]

---

[4] See the headnote to No. 1150, § 5, below.

Introduction

The stylistic peculiarities of riddles have been the object of some scholarly attention. Robert Petsch's doctoral dissertation, which was later printed as *Neue Beiträge zur Kenntnis des Volksrätsels*,[5] is the first extensive investigation of the subject. Although perhaps unnecessarily detailed in some regards, it has not been superseded or materially improved upon. We have not yet recognized every type of riddle, or traced the variations in style from country to country or from age to age, or written the history of any stylistic device.

The larger relations of riddles and riddling have not yielded much, on the whole, to scholarly study. As I have already intimated, the endeavor to find myths or mythological details proved unsuccessful. The failure is explained, at least in part, by ignorance of the nature of riddling and its themes. The place of riddles in folk thought is an unexplored field in the topography, if one may call it that, of popular literature.

[5] Berlin, 1899.

Chapter I

COMPARISONS TO A LIVING CREATURE

Nos. 1–335

RIDDLERS occasionally describe an object as something living and at the same time give so few details that we cannot know whether they intend to suggest an animal or a human being. Such inventions enumerate the members of a vaguely conceived creature,[1] or tell its functions,[2] or name both its members and their functions.[3] The members named are necessarily very few and are described in such general terms as heads or legs. Any more definite descriptive detail would probably suggest either a specific animal or a man to the hearer. The functions named are also very few, and for the same reason. Any action more characteristic than moving or eating will ordinarily identify the creature. In the riddles in this chapter the riddler conceives the functions as belonging to a creature and descriptive of it. In the final chapter[4] the riddler refers to acts and functions as performed on an object. A riddle like "What goes to a spring and never drinks?"[5] will be found in this chapter, and one like "The more you take from it, the larger it becomes,"[6] in the last chapter.

The riddles in this chapter, and particularly those involving the idea of a moving creature, are colorless and, in general, uninteresting. The folk has found them so, and parallels are consequently rather scanty. It is not improbable—and a detailed study might show it to be true—that many of these insipid products are degenerations of formerly vivid and picturesque conceptions. The English snow riddle[7] draws no effective picture of an animal touching every twig or a man leaving a cap on a stump, and even its oldest form, "When it through the wood doth goe, it toucheth everything below,"[8] is pallid and neutral. Contrast it with the Vogul "Back of the village sit those who have donned white kerchiefs,"[9] that is to say, the fence posts, each with a cap of snow. The English conception of the sun as going into and out of the woods and never touching the woods is vague, but a strong and confident hand sketched the African scene of shrubs crackling in tropical heat: "Tell me a man who is in the habit of coming and breaking to pieces trees and bushes."[10]

The number of riddles conceived in these vague terms is rather small, but the number of versions circulating in English traditional use is rather large.

---

[1] Nos. 1 through 87.
[2] Nos. 88 through 258.
[3] Nos. 259 through 335b.
[4] Nos. 1573 through 1749.
[5] No. 250.
[6] Nos. 1690 through 1697.
[7] See Nos. 145, 208.
[8] No. 145.
[9] See note to No. 208 (in separate section on notes to the riddles, p. 709).
[10] See Nos. 164a, 164b, and the notes to Nos. 164a and 164b.

English riddlers show a much greater liking for them than riddlers in other countries.

1–87. Form

Riddles enumerating the members of a creature without at the same time giving enough details to identify it as a man or an animal are, obviously, vaguely conceived. Many of them, as appears from the parallels cited in the notes, are the detritus of more adequate conceptions. English riddlers have often failed to maintain a clear notion of the fundamental comparison and have permitted it to disintegrate. Some of these riddles have, however, probably existed from the beginning in versions creating no distinct or recognizable picture. Of this latter sort are the describing a sifter or sieve[1] as a creature with many eyes and no nose, or a saw[2] as one having teeth but no mouth. The most important and interesting riddles in this section describe a creature with an unusual number of legs.[3] The riddle of the Sphinx[4] still persists in oral tradition. The many descriptions of a rider or riders on horseback[5] and some very popular riddles for a pot, for a man or an animal with a pot, or for a bed[6] also belong to this type.

1–28. A Member Present, Another Member Lacking

Riddles of this sort do not ordinarily achieve an effective personification. A single defect in form is scarcely sufficient to identify an object or a person. When a normal member of the supposed creature lacks an essential part, as in "What has a head but no hair?" the contradiction may be both striking enough to arouse curiosity and exact enough to enable the hearer to guess the answer. Many riddles of this sort involve an equivocation akin to a pun. When the speaker suggests a pin by asking "What has a head but no body?" he uses the word "head" in two senses.

1–21. Head

1–2. Head, No Body

1. Something have a head, but no body.—Pin.
Parsons, *Bermuda*, p. 258, No. 96.

2. Riddlum, riddlum, raddy, / All head and no body.—Tadpole.
Oral, West Virginia.

3–4. Head, No Hair

The following riddle for a pin[1] is perhaps a modification of the first text in this collection. The Scotch bell riddle[2] differs from most of the riddles in this sec-

---

[1] Nos. 10a, 10b, 12a, 12b, 15a, 15b. [2] No. 18.
[3] Nos. 46a through 70. [4] Nos. 46a through 47b.
[5] Nos. 49 through 54b and the headnote to Nos. 48–55. [6] Nos. 62 through 70.
[1] No. 3. [2] Nos. 4a, 4b.

tion,³ for it mentions a function of the supposed creature. One might think of placing it later in this chapter, perhaps in the section "Abnormal in Form, Normal in Function; Members and Function Not Closely Related,"⁴ but there are no close parallels to its structure there. The riddler's interest probably lies in the contrast "has a head but no hair," which he may have borrowed from the pin riddle. His reference to a supposed "head" of a bell is confusing and obscure. This poor example of the enigmatic spirit has had no wide use.

The riddles for a bell diverge widely in their choice of comparisons. The Welsh "I saw some object near to a town, in a very finely made palace between earth and heaven. It has a fine tail which almost reaches to the ground, and its tongue hangs in a very large skull. It spends most of its time in silence, but sometimes it calls its friends together"⁵ makes no clear comparison and shifts from the notion of an animal to that of a person. The Swedish "Hung high, scorched and swung, it calls to Our Lord"⁶ is a scene of tortures, and something of the same theme appears in the French "The more one pulls it, the more it cries out."⁷ Lithuanian comparisons to a horse, as in "A horse with a silver tail neighs on a high hill";⁸ "*Ting-a-ling* on a high hill, a tail of hemp and a head of silver";⁹ and "An iron stallion with a flaxen tail neighs through the heavens,"¹⁰ which contains the theme of a metal animal with a flaxen tail,¹¹ show a properly enigmatic conception. The rocking of the bell as it rings suggests the galloping of a horse. Some riddlers compare a bell to a bird,¹² and others, to an old woman with one tooth.¹³

3. What has a head, / But no hair?—Pin.
   Bacon and Parsons, *Virginia*, p. 315, No. 27.

4a. It sits high, / An cries sair, / Hiz [has] the head, / Bit wints the hair.—The townclock.
   Gregor, *Northeast Scotland*, p. 81.

4b. What is that hings heich, and cries sair, / Has a heid, and nae hair?—A bell.
   Findlay, *Edinburgh*, p. 58.

---

³ Nos. 1 through 9.
⁴ Nos. 266 through 271.
⁵ Hull and Taylor, 56.
[Throughout *English Riddles*, the arabic numeral standing alone, i.e., not preceded by a volume number in roman numerals, indicates a riddle number, unless otherwise designated, but in cross references the number of a riddle within the work itself is preceded by the abbreviation "No."]
⁶ Ström, p. 185, "Kyrkklockan," 2.
⁷ Rolland, 276.
⁸ Jurgelionis, 49.
⁹ Jurgelionis, 50. His Nos. 51 through 53 differ very slightly.
¹⁰ Jurgelionis, 59.
¹¹ See the headnote to No. 437 below. This usually refers to a needle and thread; see the examples cited in the note to No. 437 and the German riddle cited in the note to No. 421.
¹² See No. 472.
¹³ See the headnote to No. 1326.

5. Head, No Eyes

5. Them has [as] got eyes ain't got no head, / An' what got head ain't got eyes.—Needle and pin.
Fauset, *Southern Negro*, p. 287, No. 119.

6. Neck, No Head

Riddlers vary this pattern, here used for a bottle, by additions or elaborations which fit it to such themes as:

§ 1. A pitcher. Italian: Pitrè, 83.

§ 2. A shirt, a coat. French: Dardy, *L'Albret*, p. 331 (Arms without legs, back without head. He who guesses it will be the biggest fool); Mensignac, *Gironde*, p. 303, No. 41. Basque: Cerquand, 39 = Vinson, 13 (A man with a neck, without a head, with two arms, without legs). Turkish: Hamizade, 87 (It has hands, but no legs, its belly is torn, it has no blood.—Jacket). Indian, Baiga: Elwin, p. 479, No. 147 (It has a neck, but no head. It has an arm, but no hands). Malayalam: Frohnmeyer, p. 229 (It has arms but no legs; it has a neck but no head.—Coat). Indonesian: Holle, *Soenda*, p. 371, No. 8 (A body, no legs; a neck, no head; arms or hands, but no fingers.—Jacket).

6. Something has neck that has no head.—Bottle.
Parsons, *Bermuda*, p. 258, No. 93.

7–9. Head Present, Another Member Lacking

7a. Wiggle, wiggle, through the grass, / Big head, no ———.—Snake.
Fauset, *Nova Scotia*, p. 169, No. 145.

7b. Chink, chink in the grass, / Bald head, no ———.—Snake.
Fauset, *Nova Scotia*, p. 169, No. 145 var.

8. Wiggle, wiggle, through the grass, / Big head, no ———.—Grasshopper.
Fauset, *Nova Scotia*, p. 169, No. 145 var.

9. What has a face, / But no mouth?—Clock.
Bacon and Parsons, *Virginia*, p. 315, No. 31.

10–16. Many Eyes, No Mouth (Nose)

The "eyes" signify the openings in a sieve or net. In a similar way riddlers also refer to the eyes of a potato.[1] An Irish pot riddle uses eyes for the bubbles of fat floating on the surface of the contents, as in "The one in the corner has a hundred eyes"[2] and "There it is in the harbor with a hundred eyes."[3] The

---

[1] Nos. 11, 16.
[2] Christiansen, 94. The "corner" is probably the fireplace. See also Delargy, *Inis Cé*, 21 (There is an old woman in the corner, and she has a hundred eyes); De Bhaldraithe, 29 (two hundred eyes); O Dalaigh, 185.
[3] Delargy, 8. The "harbor" is the fireplace.

Vogul call the branches (which look like holes) in the wall eyes: "The room sees with a hundred eyes."[4]

The English sieve riddles usually contain the contradictory element "and no nose," which rarely occurs in the continental European parallels. Aided by rhyme, this element clings tenaciously to the introductory formula "A riddle, a riddle, as I suppose" and resists the disintegrating influence of oral transmission.

Riddlers may add new ideas[5] and may suggest a clumsy personification, as in the Lappish colander riddle, "It has many eyes, and mornings and evenings it weeps white tears,"[6] which is related to riddles about milking a cow, or the Lettish sieve riddle, "A hundred-eyed [person] makes a heap."[7] Still other details appear in the Turkish "Its face is as big as a hand, it has forty or fifty eyes. I have a few words to say to this mountebank."[8] The theme is curiously used in the Samoan "A man has one body and many eyes,"[9] signifying that he is covetous, lascivious, or stingy.

Riddlers rarely suggest a thing rather than a person, as in the Finnish sieve riddle, "A room, a thousand windows."[10]

The description of an object as a creature possessing many eyes is applicable to various themes:

§ 1. A sifter, a sieve. See below, Nos. 10a, 10b, 12a, 12b, 15a, 15b.

§ 2. A thimble. See Nos. 13a, 13b.

§ 3. A potato. See Nos. 11, 16. This differs somewhat from the other riddles because it involves the double meaning of "eyes."

§ 4. A net. Finnish: Lönnrot, 1591 = Henssen, 26 (Hundred-Eyes, the maid of death, sits in a corner of the hut); Qvigstad, note to No. 8 (A man goes to the forest and has a hundred eyes on his back). Lappish: Qvigstad, 8. Yakut: Piekarski, 321 (They say there is something which has eyes without number). African, Sukuma: Augustiny, 16 (A thing has a hundred eyes). Indonesian, Lampong: Helfrich, *Lampong*, 22.

§ 5. A reed mat. Korean: Bernheisel, p. 85 (Four ears, several hundred eyes). As in English, the word for "ears" in Korean signifies also the corners of a sack or rug.

§ 6. A basket. African, Wamajame: Ovir, 5 (A thousand tiny eyes).

§ 7. A honeycomb. African, Kamba: Lindblom, 92 (Something has a hundred eyes).

§ 8. A shoe. See No. 14 below.

10a. A riddle, a riddle, as I suppose; / A hundred eyes and never a nose.—Sifter.

---

[4] Ahlqvist, *Vogul*, p. 128, No. 20. This riddle is very widely known in Russia. See also Mordvin: Paasonen, 337.
[5] See § 4 below.
[6] Qvigstad, 40.
[7] Bielenstein, 556.
[8] Kúnos, 106.
[9] Brown, p. 345.
[10] Aarne and Krohn, 262 = Henssen, 65.

Perkins, *New Orleans*, p. 107, No. 13; Redfield, *Tennessee*, p. 39, No. 42; Bacon and Parsons, *Virginia*, p. 319, No. 58; Puckett, *Southern Negro*, p. 53; Hyatt, *Adams Co., Ill.*, p. 659, No. 10849.

Coal-sifter: Waugh, *Canada*, p. 68, No. 785; Parsons, *Bermuda*, p. 248, No. 18 (a thousand eyes). Flour-sifter: Fauset, *Nova Scotia*, p. 173, No. 187 (a thousand eyes).

10b. What got ten t'ousan' eyes an' no nose?—Sifter.
Parsons, *Sea Islands, S.C.*, p. 166, No. 86, var. 2.

11. A riddle, a riddle, as I suppose; / A hundred eyes and never a nose.—Potato.
Hyatt, *Adams Co., Ill.*, p. 659, No. 10849. A thousand eyes: Parsons, *Bermuda*, p. 248, No. 18. All eyes: Brewster, *Indiana*, 56.

12a. A riddle, a riddle, as I suppose, / Forty eyes and never a nose.—A wire sieve.
Gutch and Peacock, *Lincolnshire*, p. 399, No. 15; Burne, *Shropshire*, p. 574, No. 3. A hundred eyes: Knortz, p. 219, No. 34; Parsons, *Sea Islands, S.C.*, p. 166, No. 86. A thousand eyes: Farr, *Tennessee*, p. 325, No. 99; oral, New Hampshire.

12b. A riddle, a riddle, / Full of eyes, / But never a nose.—Sieve.
Harland and Wilkinson, *Lancashire Legends*, p. 187.

13a. A riddle, a riddle, as I suppose; / A thousand eyes and never a nose.—Thimble.
Parsons, *Bermuda*, p. 248, No. 18.

13b. Riddle me, riddle me, I suppose, / Forty eyes but never a nose.—A thimble.
Sayce, *Montgomeryshire*, p. 18.

14. Many eyes and never a nose, one tongue, and about it goes.—Shoe.
Oral, North Carolina.

15a. Thousand eyes and no mouth.—Sifter.
Fauset, *Southern Negro*, p. 280, No. 46.

15b. What has many eyes and no mouth?—A sieve.
Redfield, *Tennessee*, p. 38, No. 33.

16. What has many, many eyes and no mouth?—An Irish potato.
Redfield, *Tennessee*, p. 42, No. 87.

17. Tongue, No Mouth

17. Something has a tongue and no mouth.—Shoes.
Parsons, *Bermuda*, p. 257, No. 91.

18–21. Teeth, No Mouth (Tongue)

This notion is applicable to several quite unrelated things. When Spanish riddlers use it in describing pepper, they add such details as "has a head but not feet"[1] or "has a beard and isn't a man."[2] Its most frequent use is found

---
[1] Demófilo, 46 through 48; Rodríguez Marín, 504, 505.
[2] Rodríguez Marín, p. 347, No. 90. Chilean: Flores, 36, 40, 41.

in the description of a tool with teeth. In the fifth century Symphosius versified a description of a saw as follows: "With countless teeth my whole body is filled. A leaf-tressed race I feed upon with sharp bite, yet I chew in vain because the booty of my teeth I spew out again."[3] Other tools described in similar terms are cotton cards,[4] a flax comb,[5] and a rake or harrow.[6] The Cherekessians say of a loom, "It has a hundred teeth and only two ribs,"[7] and the Creoles of Mauritius say of a scythe, "She has teeth, she has no mouth, she can eat day and night without stopping."[8]

18. Teeth, No Mouth: A Saw

The very old comparison of a saw to a creature with many teeth is elaborated in many ways. Symphosius[1] referred to the creature's insatiability, but modern riddlers have more often connected this idea with a mill[2] than with a saw. In continental Europe, we often find vivid and picturesque scenes, but these have not commended themselves to speakers of English. The French and Germans say, "It hangs on the wall and bares its teeth,"[3] and suggest a snapping dog while at the same time denying the suggestion by the incongruous remark that "it" hangs on the wall. Inasmuch as such ideas involve the activities rather than the form of the supposed creature, I shall discuss the texts more fully elsewhere.[4]

18. Some goes north, east, south, and west, / One hundred teeth and no mouth.—Saw.
Parsons, *Bermuda*, p. 256, No. 74 (It refers perhaps to a very long saw for stone).

19a. East and west and north and south, / Ten thousand teeth and never a mouth.—Flax-comb.
Redfield, *Tennessee*, p. 39, No. 41.

19b. East and west and north and south, / Ten thousand feet and never a mouth.—Flax-comb.
Knortz, p. 219, No. 31.

20. East an' West, North an' South, / Ten thousand teeth but no mouth.—Cotton-cards.
Randolph and Spradley, *Ozark*, p. 88. Five hundred teeth and nary a mouth: Boggs, *North Carolina*, p. 322, No. 9 (a hand card for carding wool); Hudson, p. 87, No. 33.

[3] Riddle 60. For further discussion of the saw riddle see the headnote to No. 18 below.
[4] No. 20.
[5] Nos. 19a, 19b.
[6] See the note to No. 18.
[7] Tambiev, p. 59, No. 69.
[8] Baissac, *Mauritius*, p. 412.
[1] Quoted in the preceding headnote.
[2] See also the headnote to Nos. 236–239 below.
[3] German: Haase, *Thüringen*, 27; Hanika-Otto, 194. For additional examples see the headnote to Nos. 297–300 below.
[4] See the headnotes to Nos. 236–239 and 297–300.

21a. ten teeth & neer a tongue, it is sport for old & yong: j pulled it out of my yellow fleece & tickled it well on the belly piece.—it is one playing on a violin.
  Tupper, *Holme Riddles*, 116.

21b. Ten teeth without a tongue, / It is gueede sport t'aul an' young; / Take it oot o'ts yallow fleece / an' kittle't on the belly piece.—A fiddle.
  Gregor, *Northeast Scotland*, p. 78.

22. Hands, No Fingers

22. What has hands / An' no fingers?—Clock.
  Bacon and Parsons, *Virginia*, p. 313, No. 29.

23–24. Fingers, No Toes (Flesh)

23. Something has fingers but has no toes.—Glove.
  Parsons, *Bermuda*, p. 257, No. 92.

24a. Four fingers and a thumb, / Yet flesh and bone have I none.—A glove.
  Bleakney, *Canada*, p. 169, No. 23; oral, Pennsylvania.

24b. What is it has five fingers but has no flesh or bones?—Glove.
  Oral, Chicago, Illinois.

24c. What is that which is neither flesh nor bone, and yet has four fingers?—A glove.
  Waugh, *Canada*, p. 70, No. 806.

24d. As I was going over —— Bridge, I saw something in the hedge. It has four fingers and one thumb, and was neither fish, flesh, fowl, nor bone.—Glove.
  Udal, *Dorset*, p. 395.

25–28. Other Members

25. Riddlum-riddlum ranty-pole, / Half arse and no hole.—Ham of a hog.
  Fauset, *Southern Negro*, p. 285, No. 102.

26. Something has legs but no body.—Chair.
  Parsons, *Bermuda*, p. 257, No. 83.

27. What has feet and legs and nothing else?—Stockings.
  Farr, *Tennessee*, p. 319, No. 21.

28. Somet'in' have hoof, no head, no tail.—Table.
  Parsons, *Sea Islands, S.C.*, p. 171, No. 124.

29. Several Members Occasionally Lacking

29. Sometimes with a head, / Sometimes with no head at all, / Sometimes with a tail, / Sometimes with no tail at all. What am I?—Wig.
  Randolph and Taylor, *Ozarks*, 2.

30–87. Abnormality in Form

Descriptions based on an abnormality in the form of a member permit great freedom in the choice of accessory details. Notwithstanding this superficial instability, they ordinarily preserve the essential idea without serious impairment. A thoughtless riddler can, however, introduce details having no pertinence to the theme and thus confuse the hearer. It is, furthermore, easy to adapt these descriptions to new answers by a slight change.

In this section the particularly important and interesting riddles are the riddle of the Sphinx,[1] the description of a rider or riders on horseback,[2] various enumerations of the members of a pregnant creature,[3] several ways of describing a man or animal with a pot on his head,[4] and the tongs riddle, which is capable of a slight alteration to adapt it to the answer "a frog" or "a pair of scissors."[5]

The riddles in this section mention only an abnormality in form. Those mentioning both a detail of form and a detail of function stand in a later section.[6] There are two varieties of them: riddles in which the function and the abnormality in form are associated with the same bodily member and the riddles in which they are not.[7] Riddles mentioning several members, normal or abnormal, usually name the functions of these members.[8]

In this section, and generally throughout this collection, the arrangement is downward from the head of the creature or top of the thing described. A riddle based on a comparison for the head, eyes, or mouth stands before one referring to the legs or feet.

30–42. Head

30. Two Heads

A Hindu riddler combines the notion of a creature with two heads with the idea of moving without feet and gives the answer "ship" to his puzzle: "What is that which has two heads but no foot and yet can go to Calcutta?"[1] The Bengali parallel is somewhat more clearly conceived: "A śhail-fish has two heads. The śhail-fish has gone to Calcutta."[2] The two heads are the two ends of the ship. A French riddler conceives a furrow as having two heads: "What has a head at both ends?"[3]

30a. What has two heads and one body?—Barrel.
Fauset, *Nova Scotia*, p. 173, No. 189; Farr, *Tennessee*, p. 318, No. 25. Gi' me a t'ing what . . .: Johnson, *Antigua*, p. 86, No. 31. What object has . . .: Perkins, *New Orleans*, p. 111, No. 55.

30b. Something short and stout with two heads. What is that?—A barrel.
Parsons, *Sea Islands, S.C.*, p. 167, No. 94.

---

[1] Nos. 46a through 47b.
[2] Nos. 49 through 54b.
[3] Nos. 56a through 57.
[4] Nos. 62 through 64f, 66a through 67e.
[5] Nos. 79a through 82c.
[6] Nos. 259 through 335b.
[7] For further discussion see the headnotes to Nos. 259–265 and 266–271.
[8] Nos. 311 through 335b.

[1] Lakshīnātha Upasāni, XI, 3.
[2] Mitra, *Chittagong*, p. 358, No. 26.
[3] Carmeau, p. 34. Breton: Sébillot, *Devinettes*, 46a, 46b.

31–33. Heart in Its Head

31. What's this that's got a heart in his head?—Lettuce.
Parsons, *Bermuda*, p. 265, No. 161.

32a. What's this that's got a heart in his head?—Cabbage.
Parsons, *Bermuda*, p. 265, No. 161 var.

32b. It stands on its one leg with its heart in its head.—Cabbage.
Farr, *Tennessee*, p. 319, No. 20; Greenleaf, *Newfoundland*, p. 11, No. 22.

33. There is something with a heart in its head.—Peach.
Knortz, p. 231, No. 87.

34–42. Parts of the Head

34. Hair

34. All hair except the head. / Guess me right, and go to bed.—A cow-tie.
Harland and Wilkinson, *Lancashire Legends*, p. 186.

35–39. Eyes

35. Head and eye I am onely; / What I may bee tell me.—A button of copper or metall.
Prettie Riddles (1631), No. 73 = Brandl, p. 62.

36. What is that with one leg and one eye?—A needle.
Knortz, p. 211, No. 4.

37. Something has one eye and one foot.—Needle.
Parsons, *Sea Islands, S.C.*, p. 157, No. 36.

38. Eight eyes, / Sure am I. / All in white, / All know I am bright. / Can't do without me only at night.—Winder-pane.
Parsons, *Aiken, S.C.*, p. 36, No. 83.

39. Peacock

Riddles for a peacock are rather unusual. The Renaissance Latin

> Penna quidem variis me picta coloribus ornat,
> Sed doleo turpes laude carere pedes.
> Sincerum nihil est, & ab omni parte beatum:
> Et vitiis virtus, & mala mista bonis[1]

involves conceptions entirely different from those in this contemporary English riddle.

39. What is it [that] more eyes doth weare / than forty men within the land, / which glister as the christall cleare / against the sunne, when they doe stand? —A peacock's taile.
Prettie Riddles (1631), No. 70 = Brandl, p. 61.

---

[1] Buchler, *Gnomologia*, 3d ed. (1614), p. 409.

40–41. Nose

40. What is it that more noses hath within the house made of plate?—The hangers where the pot-hookes hang upon.
Prettie Riddles (1631), No. 20 = Brandl, p. 54.

41. Riddy, riddy, I suppose, / Many a nose.—Briar.
Fauset, *Southern Negro*, p. 287, No. 116.

42. Mouth

42. What is this? / *Pitty pat, pitty pat*, / With his mouth in his tail.—Duck playing in water.
Fauset, *Southern Negro*, p. 288, No. 135.

43–45. Back, Belly

43. What is this? / Only two backbones, / A thousand ribs.—Track.
Fauset, *Southern Negro*, p. 287, No. 122. Two sides . . .—Railroad. Farr, *Tennessee*, p. 323, No. 74.

44. Back as round as the belly. If you don't know it, I won't tell you.—Self-heater.
Parsons, *Bermuda*, p. 244, No. 1 var.

45a. Hump back, smoove [smooth] belly.—Self-heater.
Parsons, *Bermuda*, p. 244, No. 1. Rough back: Parsons, *Bermuda*, p. 244, No. 1, var. 1. Flat belly: Parsons, *Bermuda*, p. 244, No. 1, var. 2. Smoove stomach: Parsons, *Bermuda*, p. 244, No. 1, var. 3.

45b. Hump back, smoove [smooth] belly.—Iron. This is a four-inch-deep chamber for charcoal and a spoutlike chimney, so to speak, the handle of wood.
Parsons, *Bermuda*, p. 244, No. 1, n. 4.

46–87. Legs, Feet

Several quite different and probably unrelated riddles describe an object by enumerating its legs. In the riddles for a man on horseback[1] or a man (or a cat or a dog) with his head in a pot[2] the enigmatic contradiction is the possession of an unusual and apparently inexplicable number of legs, and complicating details are occasionally introduced. In the riddle of the Sphinx[3] the number of legs varies according to the time of day.

In a few texts, of which there seem to be no English examples, the answer is a single creature with a peculiar number of legs. Since we are not clearly aware of the number of legs possessed by a fly or an ant, a reference to them may be confusing. See, as examples, the Modern Greek riddle for a fly, "A flying bird with six legs";[4] the Turkish riddle for an insect, "It has six legs, it walks with four, two are not useless, it has horns but isn't a ram, it has

---
[1] Nos. 49 through 54b.
[2] Nos. 62 through 64f, 66a through 67e.
[3] Nos. 47a, 47b.
[4] Polites, *Neohellenika Analekta*, I, 243, No. 284.

wings but isn't a bird";[5] the Bengali riddles for an ant, "Red colored, six legs, and moves about even when its stomach is cut,"[6] which refers to the animal's constricted stomach, and for a man, "Belly, back and head, two hands, twenty fingers [digits], and one nose, eyes, and ears, one navel. Where shall I get such an animal?,"[7] which makes a puzzle of the obvious. The Mordvin louse riddle, "With six feet, with two hairs in its beard, without eyes, without bones,"[8] is a somewhat more confusing enumeration. Like the Modern Greek fly riddle, the Shor description of a cockroach involves a comparison to another animal: "A six-legged, varicolored ox."[9] The Indonesian "It has four eyes and three legs" and "It walks on three legs and sees with four eyes"[10] describe an old man with spectacles and stick. The Ghilgiti "My brother has three feet. Explain now"[11] is equally naive in its simplicity. Compare finally the Filipino riddle for a horse: "There is one creature of Our Lord God which has four legs and a tail and one head, but it has no arms."[12]

46–47. The Riddle of the Sphinx

Although the riddle of the Sphinx is very old and very widely disseminated, English versions are not numerous. Since it contains virtually no details likely to vary in the process of oral transmission, the many problems involved in its study are difficult and perhaps insoluble. Its simplicity suggests the possibility of independent origins for the Indonesian, Fijian, Samoan, and Hawaiian parallels, but any decision on this point is almost out of the question. From the very beginning of the record the riddle of the Sphinx has had literary associations, and most modern versions are perhaps derived from recollections of literature rather than from tradition. A difficult problem, which no one has examined, is the possible relation of the essential idea to Egyptian metaphors for the sun.[1] The allusions to "morning, noon, and night" in these Egyptian texts raises doubts concerning Aarne's suggestion that they were added to the riddle in the course of its history. I have divided the English versions according to Aarne's theory: Nos. 46a, 46b make no mention of "morning, noon, and night," and Nos. 47a, 47b contain these indications of time.

C. Hüsing, a member of a group of scholars defending the interpretation of myths in terms of the moon and its phases, finds a "true" solution underlying the "false" or "traditional" solution of the Sphinx-riddle. The "true" solution

---

[5] Hamizade, 74.
[6] Mitra, *Sylhet*, 14.
[7] Mitra, *Sylhet*, 10.
[8] Paasonen, 117.
[9] Dyrenkova, 24. The Shor are a Turkic tribe.
[10] Indonesian, Javanese: Ranneft, *Proza*, p. 1, No. 2. Malay: Tauern, *Patasiwa*, p. 70. See also the note to No. 48 of the present collection.
[11] Leitner, *Indian Antiquary*, I (1872), 91, No. 2.
[12] Starr, *Philippines*, 7.
[1] H. Grapow, *Die bildlichen Ausdrücke des Aegyptischen* (Leipzig, 1924), p. 130.

is the moon in its changing quarters: the waxing moon with its sickle upward is a bull, the full moon is a youth ("none other than Mithra, the ancient Aryan god of light"), the waning moon is a white horse. The white horse has legs, represented by the sickle of the moon when it is turned downward. The white horse emerges victorious from a fight with a black horse or a three-legged black ass. This explanation, which I take from J. Kreemer's summary (in an article cited in n. 7 below) of Hüsing's interpretation, is characteristic theorizing of this school. Kreemer finds it difficult to understand why a "false" solution should have maintained itself for two millennia and should have disseminated itself from Greece to Indonesia. This differentiation of "true" and "false" solutions is constantly employed by G. Hüsing and his co-workers in interpreting riddles.

In classical Greek literature Athenaeus' reference to an allusion by Aesclepiades[2] seems to be the oldest mention of the Sphinx riddle, but Hesiod's comparison[3] of a man in a snowstorm to a three-legged creature with a broken back may imply an earlier knowledge of it. Aeschylus refers to it in *Agamemnon*,[4] and the text in the *Anthologia Palatina*[5] must have been widely known in the Renaissance, when this collection enjoyed great popularity. A faint echo of the Sphinx riddle in a Silesian epithalamion curiously combines learned and popular elements.[6] The riddle of the Sphinx is one of the rather few true riddles found in folk tales.[7]

---

[2] *Deipnosophistae*, X, 465b.
[3] *Works and Days*, v. 533.
[4] V. 79.
[5] XIV, 64. It is not in the *Planudean Anthology*. For references see James Hutton, *The Greek Anthology in Italy to the Year 1800*, Cornell Studies in English, XXIII (Ithaca, 1935), 622.
[6] See Max Hippe, "Hochzeitsrätsel des 17. Jahrhunderts," *Festschrift Theodor Siebs*, Germanistische Abhandlungen, LXVII (Breslau, 1933), p. 434, No. 5. For three contemporary Latin versions see Buchler, *Gnomologia*, 3d ed. (1614), pp. 448–449.
[7] See an interpolation in the medieval French *Roman de Thèbes* cited in L. A. Paton, *Studies in the Fairy Mythology of Arthurian Romance* (Boston, 1903), p. 132; Paul Sébillot, *Contes des provinces de la France* (Paris, 1884), pp. 135–142, and J.-F. Bladé, *Contes populaires de la Gascogne* (Les Littératures populaires de toutes les nations, XIX [Paris, 1886]), I, 10, No. 1 = Ernst Tegethoff, *Französische Volksmärchen* (Märchen der Weltliteratur [Jena, 1923]), II, 293, No. 55; Bernhard Schmidt, *Griechische Märchen, Sagen und Volkslieder* (Leipzig, 1877), pp. 143–144 and his note (pp. 248–249).

For discussion of the riddle of the Sphinx see Lillio Gregorio Giraldi, as reprinted in Reusner, ed. 1599, pp. 12–16 = ed. 1602, pp. 10–14; Friedreich, pp. 85–88; Auld, *Notes and Queries*, 9th ser., XII (1903), 225; L. Laistner, *Das Rätsel der Sphinx* (Berlin, 1889), I, 18–19; Ohlert, 1st ed., pp. 31–35, and 2d ed., pp. 24–27; R. Köhler, *Kleinere Schriften*, I, 115; Tupper, *Holme Riddles*, note to No. 1; Schultz, *Rätsel*, cols. 83, 85, and 92–93, No. 17; Schultz, *Rätsel aus dem hellenischen Kulturkreise*, I, 34, No. 12, and II, 65–66; G. Hüsing, *Die iranische Ueberlieferung und das arische System* (Mythologische Bibliothek, II, ii; Leipzig, 1909), pp. 42 ff.; W. H. Roscher, *Ausführliches Lexikon der griechischen und römischen Mythologie*, IV (Leipzig, 1909–1915), cols. 1366–1368; Feilberg, *Ordbog*, II, 578, s.v. "menneske"; Mitra, *Notes on Ho Riddles*, pp. 118–119; Aarne, *Rätselforschungen*, II, 3–23; J. G. Frazer (ed.), Apollodorus, I (London, 1921), 347, n. 1 (note on III, 5, 8); Stith Thompson, *Motif-Index*, H 761; J. Kreemer, "Het

46. First Four, Then Two, Finally Three Feet

Following Aarne's procedure, I have divided the versions of the riddle of the Sphinx into two classifications: those which do not indicate the specific time of the respective scenes and those which mention "morning, noon, and night."[1] The first variety is rather rare. Buchler[2] quotes two curious Renaissance Latin versions:

> Quod pedibus binis animal meat absque ruinis,
> Claudicat hinc ternis, prorepsit & ante quaternis?

and

> Sphinx dedit ænigma hoc, quadrupes quæ bestia quondam,
> Deinde bipes fieret, tandem eademque tripes.

Some riddles, which are perhaps related to the riddle of the Sphinx, have a curious resemblance to the Biblical description of old age.[3] Typical examples are the Portuguese "Two are now many, many are now few, snows are now falling"[4] and the Modern Greek "The mountains are covered with snow, what was long is now short, the mills grind no more, and two have become three."[5] These belong to a rather poorly preserved enigmatic tradition that is almost exclusively limited to eastern Europe.[6] The Hungarian parallels are both numerous and rich in details; see "Snow on the mountain, a lake in the valley, among thirty-two there isn't a single good one";[7] "Snow on the mountain, snow in the valley, there is not a single good stone in the mill, there are more toward the back than toward the front, a confrater [pal] goes down";[8] and "On the top snow, in the valley water, roses do not bloom, and thirty-two brothers are not together."[9] The Polish "A forest in the palm of his hand, the hilltops are graying, all are not his brothers";[10] the Hungarian "On the mountain it is snow; in the hole it is a lake; among thirty-two not a single one

---

Sfinx-raadsel in Indischen archipel," *Koloniaal tijdschrift*, XVI (1927), 170–172. See also some useful notes on classical allusions in F. Jacobs, *Animadversiones in epigrammata Anthologiae Graecae*, III, ii (Leipzig, 1903), 350–351.

[In citations in the present collection the small roman numeral, unless otherwise specifically indicated, represents the number of the "Part," or of an equivalent subdivision of a volume.]

[1] Nos. 46a and 46b (no reference to time of day), and Nos. 47a and 47b (morning, noon, and night).
[2] *Gnomologia*, 3d ed. (1614), pp. 448–449.
[3] Eccles. 12:3 ff. See Schultz, *Bemerkungen*, p. 360; H. Torczyner, "The Riddles in the Bible," *Hebrew Union College Annual*, I (1924), 136–137; Denis Buzy, C.S.J., "Le Portrait de la vieillesse," *Revue biblique*, XLI (1932), 329–340; Edith Henrich, "Poetry as Communication," *The Pacific Spectator*, III (1949), 139–140.
[4] Parsons, *Cape Verde*, 240.
[5] Polites, *Neohellenika Analekta*, I, 222, No. 165, and p. 242, No. 279 (the second clause is lacking); Sakellarios, p. 291, No. 15 (the arrangement differs); Dieterich, *Rätseldichtung*, p. 100.
[6] See also the headnote to Nos. 1100–1108, nn. 11–12, below.
[7] Arany and Gyulai, II, 366, No. 84. The answer is "A white-haired old man whose eyes are bleary and teeth are bad."
[8] Arany and Gyulai, III, 298, No. 34. The "confrater" is either the tongue or a morsel of food.
[9] Kálmány, III, 175, No. 59.
[10] Kopernicki, 92.

is good";[11] and the Turkish "On the top of the ridge of Khangay snow has fallen.—Gray hairs"[12] are defective or fragmentary versions which are readily enough understood by comparison with other texts.

The Modern Greek description of carrying unfermented wine in a hide, "He comes four-legged, he descends three-legged, he holds rabbit skins and carries red milk,"[13] contains some details which may have been suggested by the riddle of the Sphinx.

46a. w^t cratur is that in the world that first goes on [MS: one] 4 foot then 2 foot then 3 foot then wth 4 foot againe.—a man for being a child creeps on [MS: one] his hands & knees in his strength on [MS: one] his 2 foot & old wth a stafe & in his second childhood creeps on [MS: one] all fore againe.
Tupper, *Holme Riddles*, 1.

46b. It first walks on four legs, then on two, then on three legs.—A man.
Redfield, *Tennessee*, p. 37, No. 16; Bacon and Parsons, *Virginia*, p. 314, No. 21.

47. Four Legs in the Morning, Two Legs at Noon, Three Legs at Night

The riddle of the Sphinx in which the various times are specified as "morning, noon, and night" is, according to Antti Aarne,[1] a later development. It originally contained no such adverbial indications. Its wide distribution and its stability in tradition suggest, however, that Aarne erred and that this is after all the original form. A Scotch Gaelic version is an interesting example of the elaboration of these ideas:

> Four feet it has in the morning,
> Yet fast movement is a-lacking.
> With two about mid-day
> He can manage much better.
> Though he gets at nightfall three,
> He moves but soft and slow.[2]

Aarne calls attention to another kind of elaboration.[3] It consists in the use of special verbs to characterize the several kinds of motion. This appears also in the Hungarian "In the morning, it crawls on four legs; at noon, it walks on two legs; in the evening, it totters about on three."[4]

In the seventeenth century Johannes Pincier versified the riddle as follows:

> Sum primum gradiendi impos, quadrupesque deinde,
> Tum bipes, inde tripes, gressus videt ultima meta
> Expertem, primus qualem quoque viderat ortus.[5]

---
[11] Kriza, p. 347, No. 76.
[12] Katanov in Radlov, IX, 104, No. 895.
[13] Stathes, p. 347, No. 92.
[1] *Rätselforschungen*, II, 14–21.
[2] Nicolson, p. 21.
[3] *Rätselforschungen*, II, 12.
[4] Oral, from Szalonta, cited by Szendrey, *Ethnographia*, XXXII (1921), 73.
[5] *Ænigmatum libri tres* (The Hague, 1655), pp. 112–113 (Book II. No. 9). He adds an interesting collection of contemporary comments on the riddle.

47a. What is that in the morning upon foure legges doth goe, / and about noone it standeth fast upon two and no moe. / In the evening againe it hath no lesser than three in store. / Which tell me, Ser, art thou not he, whom I doe take thee for?—It is a man; for when he is a childe, then doth hee creep upon hands and feet; but when he is a man, then he standeth straight upon two leggs; but when he is old and decrepit, besides his legs then he useth a staffe to support his body.
Prettie Riddles (1631), No. 65 = Brandl, p. 61.

47b. What kind of animal is that that stands on four legs in the morning, three in the day, and two in the evening?—Child creeping (two legs and two hands), man with two feet, and old woman with a stick.
Parsons, *Antilles*, III, 429, Nevis, 24; Waugh, *Canada*, p. 70, No. 811; Fauset, *Southern Negro*, p. 291, No. 174.

48–55. The Odin Riddle

Some have suggested that riddles employing the device of listing an unusual number of feet and having the answer "man on horseback" are derived from the Old Norse description of Odin riding the eight-legged Sleipnir to the annual *thing*. Inasmuch as the parallels rarely exhibit any connections with religious themes and occur, furthermore, in countries where the influence of early Germanic religious ideas is entirely out of the question, I doubt this origin of the modern riddles. The diligent searcher after parallels might cite an Estonian riddle of a one-eyed woman riding on horseback[1] and see in it a survival of the description of the one-eyed Odin riding his horse, but he would probably not convince the modern student. Probably the development has been in the reverse direction: the Old Norse riddle is a special application and exemplifies the device of introducing unusual complications in order to make riddles more difficult. Abundant illustrations of this device appear in the notes in this section. I have retained the name of Odin because it suggests this context and supplies a characteristic title.

Some Bihari versions of this theme have the answer "Śukrācarya," who is a preceptor of demons. They are of special interest on account of this mythological association. They consist in an enumeration of the various members of the god and of the creature on which he is riding. The two versions, "Three eyes, six legs, two mouths, and one tongue, before him women never walk. O learned men, find him out!"[2] and "Six feet, yet not a bee; three eyes, yet not the god Śiva; one tongue, yet two heads,"[3] need the additional explanatory comment that the god is blind in one eye and rides a frog, which is popularly believed to have no tongue. It is also pertinent to mention here the oxen of the Old Norse goddess Gefjon with their four heads and eight eyes,[4] but they

---
[1] Wiedemann, p. 267.   [2] Mitra, *Bihar*, 58.
[3] Mitra, *Bihar*, 59.
[4] H. M. Chadwick, *The Growth of Literature*, I (Cambridge, England, 1932), 515.

are not the theme of riddles. Texts of this sort, like the Old Norse version of Odin and Sleipnir, are probably adaptations of the original theme to mythological uses. The abnormalities of the mythological creatures make the riddles more difficult.

This manner of description occurs in some circumstances which do not suggest a European origin. In "A man goes in a boat that has four outriggers.—A rider on horseback"[5] or "What sort of a boat with four oars is steered from the foredeck?—A horse, four legs, but one guides it at the head with the bridle,"[6] Samoan riddlers have based their comparisons on a boat. A curious Persian riddle puns on the numerical values of the letters in *fīl* (elephant): "A man from Africa came to me; a strange weird creature he had with him; the animal by God's creating had eighty heads and ten bellies and thirty legs."[7]

Some interesting contaminations or specializations of the theme call for mention. The Turkish "Stone below, a kiosk above, eight feet, two heads.—Coach on a paved road"[8] contains elements belonging to an enumeration of the parts of an object or creature in the order "below, middle, above."[9] A continental European variation consists in specifying the number of souls as well as the number of legs or other members present.[10] A version like the Swedish "Three heads, two souls, eight feet, four tails, two standing, four going, one hanging behind"[11] includes elements belonging to a description of a cow.[12] Somewhat different from any that have been mentioned is the French "Marvel on marvel, six legs and four ears.—Man and horse."[13]

The important discussions of the many riddles describing a man on horseback by enumerating the members of both man and horse are Karl Müllenhoff, *Zeitschrift für deutsche Mythologie*, III (1855), 2–5; E. B. Tylor, *Primitive Culture* (3d ed.; London, 1891), p. 94; Schultz, *Rätsel aus dem hellenischen Kulturkreise*, II, 132–133; Antti Aarne, *Rätselforschungen*, II, 173–206; Hanika-Otto, note to No. 10. In the present headnote I have incorporated the few additions to Aarne made by Sigismund Szendrey.[14] Aarne seeks to derive the riddle of the Sphinx[15] from this riddle.[16] Wolfgang Schultz also connects them.[17] Probably the resemblances can be better explained as contaminations, although No. 49 below might support such conjectures.

[5] Heider, 124.   [6] Heider, 125.
[7] Phillott, 16.
[8] Kúnos, 20 = Kúnos, *Am Urquell*, IV (1893), 22, No. 8. See also Modern Greek: Carnoy and Nicolaides, 7.
[9] See the headnote to Nos. 1436–1447 below.
[10] Swedish: Dybeck, *Runa*, 1865–1873, p. 31, No. 31; Ericsson, *Södermanland*, I (1879), 92, No. 61; Olsson, *Västergötland*, p. 126, No. 18. See also the headnote to Nos. 56–57 below.
[11] Dybeck, *Runa*, 1865–1873, p. 65, No. 84.
[12] Nos. 1476a through 1489 below.   [13] Rolland, *Rimes*, p. 198, No. 12.
[14] *Ethnographia*, XXXII (1921), 73.
[15] Nos. 46a through 47b above.
[16] *Rätselforschungen*, II, 94.
[17] See his *Rätsel*, cols. 83–86, and also his *Rätsel aus dem hellenischen Kulturkreise*, II, 62, n. 1.

Riddlers often introduce additional complications, which serve to subdivide the versions below. The arrangement is as follows: No. 48 describes a man walking with a stick; No. 49 describes an animal that does not use all its legs in moving; Nos. 50 and 51 mention a bird on the man's wrist; No. 52 refers to sexual members; No. 53 has a reference to legs in unequal numbers on the sides of the putative animal; No. 55 has the answer "a woman milking." In the note to No. 53, since there was no more convenient place, I have cited parallels in which no unusual complicating elements are present.

The fundamental conception of a creature having an abnormal number of members, usually heads and feet, is applicable to many uses in riddling. Some of these are interesting for their picturesqueness, and others for the ingenuity displayed in choosing the object to be described. The Bihari say, "It has four feet and two heads; on it rides a heavy rider; though without life, it has life—send me that thing," and mean a pair of sandals.[18] The four feet are the sandals and the wearer's feet; the two heads are the knobs passing between the big toe and the smaller toes. A Baiga description of a dead bullock carried by four men, "Eight legs on the ground, four legs point to the sky, only one tail to the twelve legs,"[19] shows some similarity to riddles for a pot,[20] a bed,[21] and a cow.[22] I do not fully understand the Uraon "Three heads with ten legs in a mixed village.—Man and bullock cart."[23] It is probably related to the Bhil description of a well bucket drawn by a man and two oxen: "A black dog has ten feet and three heads."[24] Johannes Pincier's seventeenth-century description of a soldier on horseback and a wounded man on a crutch depicts a scene that was no doubt often seen in that warlike time:

> Martia castra adii pedibus sex sultus, & inde
> Subnixus repeto patria rura tribus.
> Quam mallem binos! valeat ternarius iste:
> Non moror, hunc Samius quod putat esse sacrum.[25]

Riddlers have often adapted this manner of description to special uses:

§ 1. A man plowing. Russian: Sadovnikov, 1150 (There are three bodies, three heads, eight legs, an iron tail, a forged nose). Turkish: Kowalski, *Zagadki*, 57 (The spirit of God has pierced it and fixed me by the neck. There are six eyes and ten feet). Indian, Ho: Sarkar, p. 354, No. 20 (Have you seen [a creature with] three heads and ten feet?). Parsee: E. W. West and M. Haug (eds.), *The Book of Arda Viraf* (Bombay, 1872), cited in E. Rolland, *Faune populaire*, V (Paris, 1882), 114 (It has ten feet, three heads, six ears, six eyes, two tails, three pairs of testicles, two hands, three noses, four horns, three backs, and the life and preservation of the world come from it). Kashmiri: Knowles, 52 ([It makes the sound of] *ha ku hukan*, walks with ten feet, [has] three fundaments

---
[18] Mitra, *Bihar*, 50.
[19] Elwin, p. 466, No. 15.
[20] Nos. 64a through 64f and 66a through 68 below.
[21] Nos. 69a through 70.
[22] Nos. 1476a through 1489.
[23] Archer, p. 194, No. 228.
[24] Hedberg, p. 876, No. 71.
[25] *Ænigmatum libri tres* (The Hague, 1655), pp. 259-260 (Book III, No. 21).

and six ears). Indonesian, Javanese: Ranneft, *Proza*, p. 3, No. 12 (A warrior rambles, he has the power to turn the earth upside down, he has ten legs and three heads. His left hand holds fast the bow and the right the sharp arrow). The "bow" is the plow (a bent stick), and the "arrow" is a whip.

§ 2. A woman milking a cow. Swedish: Hyltén-Cavallius, *Värend*, 3; Ericsson, *Södermanland*, II (1881), 95, No. 86 (Six legs in its back, two horns backwards, and a cat sits and waits). Indian, Hindi: Kavyopadhyaya, 19 (Six ears, two tails, ten legs. In one mouth, no tongue. O pandit, consider!—Milkman, cow, calf, and pail).

§ 3. A shoemaker sitting on a bench. German: Hanika-Otto, 10 (Six feet, two heads, and one mind).[26] For another example describing a man seated see the Korean riddle for a man in a palanquin: "What is it that has three heads, three mouths, three noses, six eyes, six arms, six ears, and four legs?"[27]

§ 4. A crucifix (two heads, four arms, three feet). Spanish: Demófilo, 337; Rodríguez Marín, 814.

§ 5. Scales. Modern Greek: Sakellarios, p. 291, No. 19 (Two soles [of the feet], six legs, and one tooth in the back). The "soles" are the pans of the scales and the "tooth" is the marker. Malagasy: Sibree, p. 38, No. 3 (Six legs and two feet.—Money scales). Turcoman: Samojlvich, 84 (By the abetting of the Devil there is a six-legged thing in a man's hand, and its tail is at its waist). He cites as parallels Sart: Ostrumov, 17. Kirghese: Vasiliev, 78. See further Persian: Phillott, 12 (A strange creature I saw that had six legs and two heads; stranger still, listen to me, was this: its tail was in its back); Kuka, 6. Indian: Chaina Mall, *Panjab Notes and Queries*, III (1886), 220, No. 899, § 1 (I saw a wondrous horse that had six feet and two hoofs. And more wonderful still, I tell you, it had its tail in the middle of its back). The "legs" or "feet" are the strings holding the pans of the scales; the pans are called "heads" or, more appropriately, "hoofs." The curious Armenian comparison to a house differs entirely from these ideas: "Six columns, two rooms, and a crossbeam."[28] For discussion see Schultz, *Bemerkungen*, pp. 358–359.

§ 6. A cradle, Icelandic: Árnason, 19 (This girl, who has six legs and two eyes, often prepares to go on a journey. She starts out with a bang, but still she is ever pitching [like a ship] in the same place).

§ 7. A crab. Latin: Buchler, *Gnomologia*, 3d ed. (1614), p. 477 (two arms, eight legs). Mongolian: Kotvich, 264 (A year-old, six-legged sheep).

48. Something walking down the street, / Three legs, two arms, a head, two eyes, a nose, and a mouth.—Ol' man with a stick.
Fauset, *Southern Negro*, p. 291, No. 173.

---

[26] For riddles in which the soul or mind is mentioned, see the earlier part of this head-note.
[27] Bernheisel, p. 83, and the note to No. 49 below. Compare also Nos. 56a through 57 below.
[28] Seidlitz, p. 71, No. 26.

49. Six legs, two heads, two hands and a nose, / But uses only four legs as it goes.—Man on horseback.
Parsons, *Bermuda*, p. 255, No. 64.

50. Downe in a dale there sits and stands / eight legs and two hands, / livers and lights and lives three: / I count him wise that tels this to me.—It is a man riding on horsebacke, and having a hawke sitting on his hand.
Meery Riddles (1629), No. 71 = Brandl, p. 20; Tupper, *Holme Riddles*, 28.

51. What has eight legs, two arms, three heads, and wings?—A man on horseback with a canary on his hand.
Oral, California.

52. What is that hath five legs on the one side, and three on the other, heads three, and eares sixe, and two things like my mother, and yet such another thing as hath my brother?—It is a man and a woman upon a mare's backe.
Meery Riddles (1629), No. 69 = Brandl, p. 20. See also Brandl, p. 3, No. 99.

53. Mention a thing has two heads, / Two feet, one each side, four the other, / And one tail.—Lady on horseback.
Bacon and Parsons, *Virginia*, p. 319, No. 57.

54a. What creatures are those which appear closely connected, yet upon examination are found to be three distinct bodies, with eight legs, five on one side, and three on the other; three mouths, two straight forwards, and the third on one side; six eyes, four on one side, two on the other; six ears, four on one side, and two on the other?—A Man and a Woman on Horseback.
A New Collection of Enigmas (London, 1810), pp. 199–200.

54b. Come read me this riddle without any pother, / Five legs on one side and three on the other, / Two eyes in my forehead, and four on my back, / One tongue that is silent and two that can clack.—A horse carrying a woman riding behind a man.
Wit and Humor of the Age (Chicago, n.d. [1901]), p. 731, No. 9.

55. Down in the meadow it sits and stands, / Ten feet and pair of hands, / Lugs four and livers three. / Whattan a creature can it be?—Cow, calf, and a woman milking it.
Praeger, *Béaloideas*, IV (1933–1934), 146, No. 22.

56–57. Members of a Pregnant Creature

This rather unusual riddle has been the subject of considerable discussion.[1] Wilhelm Schulze, who comments on the small number of available texts, seeks to derive the theme from pre-Christian ritual. Strabo's reference[2] to Calchas'

---

[1] See Ohlert, 1st ed., pp. 38–39, and 2d ed., pp. 29–30; Heusler, *Zeitschrift des Vereins für Volkskunde*, XI (1901), 141–142; Loewenthal, p. 12; Aarne, *Rätselforschungen*, II, 204–206; Wilhelm Schulze, "Das Rätsel vom trächtigen Tiere," *Ungarische Jahrbücher*, IV (1924), 20–26.

[2] XIV, 1, 27 (p. 642).

question about the number of young a pregnant sow was carrying is, according to Schulze, an example of interest in this theme.

A similar enumeration of the members of two or more persons serves also to describe a corpse and its bearers. Riddlers in the Near East show a particular liking for this theme. They often accompany it with mention of digits or nails (fingernails and toenails). There is probably another variety to be seen in texts specifying the number of souls (minds) present. See such parallels as the Rumanian "Five men pass by with four souls and a hundred digits.—Four living men with a corpse,"³ which combines both varieties. See further the Serbian "There are five hero heads that are going together, but there are only four minds";⁴ "There are five heads, four souls, and a hundred nails";⁵ "Five heads, a hundred nails, and four minds";⁶ "Three bodies, two souls";⁷ the Bulgarian "Five heads, four souls, a hundred digits, a hundred nails";⁸ and the Modern Greek "Five heads, ten hands, ten feet, a hundred nails";⁹ "My crazy mother sent me to get water. I met a beast, awful and frightening. It had five heads, four breaths,¹⁰ twenty hands and feet, and one hundred nails."¹¹ A slightly different variety of the theme appears in the Hungarian "There goes *tipa topa*,¹² it carries four on its back, it has four eyes, four ears, and twenty-four nails."¹³ The theme has become merely an arithmetical puzzle in the Hungarian "Your father-in-law, your mother-in-law, three priests, six turkeys. How many nails do they have?—148,"¹⁴ which may not be related to this theme but is interesting for its reference to nails. The Turkish "Eight feet, four souls, five heads.— A funeral procession"¹⁵ is the usual form of the riddle. A reference to nails occurs in one Persian version, "A strange thing I saw in this world that has a hundred nails in its feet and hands, five bodies, five heads, and four lives,"¹⁶ but not in another, "What is that animal that has [a] hundred fingers and has ten legs, but moves only with eight? It has five heads, but four souls. This wonder can be seen in this world."¹⁷

In western Europe the riddles on these themes are few and show little or no

---

³ Weigand, 15.
⁴ Novaković, p. 139, No. 3.
⁵ Novaković, p. 139, Nos. 4, 5.
⁶ Novaković, p. 139, No. 6.
⁷ Novaković, p. 139, No. 7.
⁸ Gubov, 394.
⁹ Abbott, p. 307, No. 17.
¹⁰ I.e., souls?
¹¹ Stathes, p. 350, No. 114. For additional examples see Georgeakis, pp. 294–295; Polites, *Neohellenika Analekta*, I, 241, Nos. 272 through 274, and p. 249, No. 320; Dieterich, *Rätseldichtung*, p. 100; Sakellarios, p. 290, No. 16; Schultz, *Bemerkungen*, pp. 375–376.
¹² An onomatopoetic word suggesting the sound of the hoofs.
¹³ Arany and Gyulai, II, 350, No. 5. This riddle is very popular in Hungary; see *Magyar Nyelvör*, II (1873), 178, 468; III (1874), 329; VIII (1879), 522; XII (1883), 474; XIII (1884), 574, No. 3; XVI (1887), 87; XVIII (1889), 428; and XXV (1896), 239.
¹⁴ Arany and Gyulai, II, 358, No. 47.
¹⁵ Kowalski, *North Bulgaria*, 56. He cites four parallels. See also Hamizade, 93 (Ten-handed, hundred-fingered, hundred-fingernailed, ten-legged.—Coffin carried by four persons), 94 (I saw an astonishing thing: eight legs on it, four souls, five heads, and a hundred fingers [digits]).
¹⁶ Phillott, 13.
¹⁷ Kuka, 8.

resemblance to the varieties cited thus far. The Swedish funeral riddle, "Five heads and fourteen feet, [it] is dead within and living at both ends,"[18] has borrowed elements from a description of a man plowing.[19] I can cite no parallel to the peculiar Hungarian "There are four carrying him and one guarding him.— A dead man, the one guarding him is God."[20] A long English literary riddle about a corpse contains the characteristic enumeration of the feet of the supposed creature, but shows no other significant similarity to the riddles here discussed. It is as follows:

> A man I was, a man I am,
> but yet as tame as any lambe.
> Though I am blind, the way I show
> which all men that see mee must goe.
> And to put your mind out of doubt,
> eight legs I have that beare about;
> my burthen more than any hath,
> unlese he be in my estate.
> In time therefore doe learn of me,
> as I before have done of thee.
> If he had knowne that brought our woe,
> ventred had upon his foe;
> but for his fault we subject be
> to this estate [in] which you see me;
> I am that which you lest desire,
> but that you should most require.
> Gesse what I am (good sir) therefore,
> before you do knocke at my doore.—

It is a dead man, and those foure that doo carry him to his grave, with Adam our first parent, who brought death into the world.[21]

A description of a man carried in a palanquin[22] has some similarity to these riddles about a corpse and bearers. Antti Aarne touches briefly on riddles of this sort.[23]

56. Pregnant Animal

Schulze calls attention[1] to the mention of nails in these enumerations of members of an animal as a characteristic of southeastern European riddles for a pregnant animal. As he remarks, Aldhelm's knowledge of this trait offers a

---

[18] Hyltén-Cavallius, *Värend*, 6; Ström, p. 374, "Sysselsättningar," 12.
[19] See Nos. 1432a through 1433b below, and the headnote to Nos. 1430–1431, § 3.
[20] *Magyar Nyelvör*, VII (1878), 89.
[21] *Prettie Riddles* (1631), No. 25 = Brandl, p. 56. I have inserted "in" as indicated; Brandl's "which" for "with" in the last line is not correct.
[22] See the note to No. 49 above and the headnote to Nos. 48–55, § 3.
[23] *Rätselforschungen*, II, 11.

[1] "Das Rätsel vom trächtigen Tiere," *Ungarische Jahrbücher*, IV (1924), 23, n. 6. He cites Aarne, *Rätselforschungen*, II, 195, 211; Szendrey, *Ethnographia*, XXXII (1921), 78–79; *Magazin für die Literatur des Auslandes*, 1856, p. 365; Gorovei, 270; Géza Kuun, *Codex Cumanicus* (Budapest, 1880), p. 237; and Aldhelm, 84.

difficult problem in the transmission of ideas. The versions below—one of them a half-literary Renaissance text and the other a folk riddle from Hereford—are additional western European instances. They suggest the existence of an English traditional use of this theme.²

56a. as j went on my way j heard [MS: hard] a great wonder of a monster that had 10 heads [MS: hads] 10 tayls 40 feet & fore score nayls.—a sowe wth 9 piges.
Tupper, *Holme Riddles*, 53.

56b. As I was going to church one day, I saw an ill-formed beast: ten heads, ten tails, forty feet, eight-score nails.—A sow and pigs.
Leather, *Hereford*, p. 231.

57. Pregnant Woman

Descriptions of a pregnant woman as the possessor of four legs and forty digits are abundant in southern and southeastern Europe.¹ A few versions exhibit variations or corruptions of the idea. The oldest instance, the eleventh-century Latin "Vidi hominem contra solem sedentem habentem in se VI oculos, VI manus, VI pedes, LX digitos, tres animas et unam vocem,"² complicates the scene by referring to a woman and twins. The Rumanian "Four hands or eyes, four feet, forty nails"³ and the Serbian "Four eyes, four thighs, and forty nails"⁴ contain the reference to the creature's nails which Schulze considers to be a southeastern European characteristic.⁵ The Serbian "Two heads, two arms, six legs, and only ten fingers"⁶ seems to err in the last number.

57. unto the exchange j went some knacks for to buy, within a cloister there was panting a monster certainly: foot & hands it had full eight, & four eyes clear of sight: 4 ears whereby to hear, & 2 bodies exceeding clear.—it was an exchange [MS: exchang] woman big with child.
Tupper, *Holme Riddles*, 134.

58–60. Feet, Tails, and Nails

The three following riddles for a ship, a plow with ten oxen, and a thistle clearly belong together and resemble the riddles which we have just discussed. Here, however, the tails, nails, and feet have metaphorical rather than literal meanings: in No. 58, the foot is the keel of the ship; in No. 59, the nails are some-

---

² See also the long corpse riddle cited in the headnote to Nos. 56–57 above and another riddle in the note to No. 57.

¹ See Italian: Pitrè, 246; Bernoni, *Venice*, 14; Gianandrea, *Archivio*, I (1882), 401, No. 7; Rua, *ibid.*, VII (1888), 455, No. 47; Rondini, *ibid.*, VIII (1889), 186, No. 71; Corsi, *ibid.*, X (1891), 401, No. 38.
² Malein, 1.
³ Gorovei, 146.
⁴ Novaković, p. 42, No. 1 = *ibid.*, p. 51, No. 6.
⁵ See the headnote to Nos. 56–57.
⁶ Novaković, p. 97, No. 3.

what difficult to interpret, but may be the nails or pins which attach the ropes or harness to the plow; in No. 60, the nails are the spines of the thistle and the tails are probably its shoots or tassels. The hundred nails in the ship riddle are an obvious understatement.

58. As I gaed to Falkland to a feast, / I met wi' an ugly beast; / Ten tails, a hunder nailes, / An no a fit [foot] but ane.—A ship.
Chambers, *Scotland*, p. 110; Simpkins, *Fife,* p. 306.

59. As I gaed t'ma father's fehst, / I saw a great notorious behst / Wi' ten nails and forty feet, / An aye the behst crape cot an eat.—A ten-ousen plough.
Gregor, *Northeast Scotland*, p. 80.

60. As I was a-going to a neighbor's house, / I saw an awful beast; / He had nine heads and nine tails / And ninety-nine scores of nails.—Bull's eye thistle.
Gardner, *Schoharie Hills, N.Y.*, p. 255, No. 15.

61. Goes Up with Four Legs, Comes Down with Eight Legs

This riddle is probably a vaguely remembered version of a description of a bird and a frog.[1] It is an interesting example of a conception which has survived in a very small number of widely scattered texts.

61. Goes up with four legs, / Comes down with eight.—Cat with mouse.
Knortz, p. 237, No. 128.

62. Seven Legs and a Tail

Several riddles[1] describe a man or an animal and a pot by enumerating the number of feet and adding some further details. They usually mention the head of the man or animal. The variations in the details permit us to identify several types. Since each of these types seems to be restricted to a particular region, it is something more than a purely logical construction for the purposes of classification. The historical relations of these types are obscure.[2] One type unknown to English riddlers describes a cat or dog with its head in a pot and mentions the animal's tongue.[3]

62. What strange beast is that which has no head, seven legs, and one tail?— A cat with his head jammed in a three-legged pot.
Fitzgerald, p. 186.

---

[1] See No. 352.

[1] Nos. 62 through 64f, 66a through 67e. I can cite no parallel to the French "Who has seven legs?—The dog when it licks a pot" (Queyrat, *La Creuse*, I, 363), which resembles the riddles discussed in the headnote to Nos. 46–87, above, or to the Irish "Three legs that don't walk, a big mouth that won't close, a sow without a tail.—Pot" (De Bhaldraithe, 48).

[2] For further comment see Aarne, *Rätselforschungen*, II, 206–208, and the headnote to Nos. 64–70 below.

[3] See Breton: Charlec, *Dol-de-Bretagne*, 1904, p. 378, No. 40; Kerbeuzec, *Ille-et-Vilaine*, p. 504, No. 31.

63. Mouth to Mouth, Seven Legs, and a Tail

The characteristic introductory scene, "Mouth to mouth," identifies this variety of the pot riddle. Inasmuch as the parallels to this variety occur only in the Romance languages, I conjecture that the single English example that has been recorded is ultimately of French origin.

63. Mout' to mout', / Seven legs, one tail.—Dog eatin' from pot.
Parsons, *Antilles*, III, 426, Antigua, 24.

64–70. Three (Four) Legs Up and Six (Four) Legs Down

Two chief varieties of this theme, which involves the contrast of legs pointing upward and downward, can be easily perceived: those in which the hearer meets the further difficulty of unusual numbers of legs and those in which two sets of four legs point in opposite directions. The first variety has the answer, "an animal with its head in a pot." It occurs in several subvarieties, which are identified by the introductions, "Black upon black,"[1] "Patch upon patch,"[2] which has been borrowed from another riddle; "Mouth to mouth";[3] or by mention of the contrast of the dead and the living.[4] One version[5] merely enumerates the legs and their positions. As the existence of these subvarieties shows, this idea has enjoyed a remarkable success among English riddlers. This success is explicable, at least in part, by the striking quality of an unusual scene, the sharpness of the contrasts involved, and the rhymes, which have made the texts easy to remember.

A second variety of this idea involves the contrast of four legs pointing up and four legs pointing down. In English folklore, it refers to a four-poster bed.[6] The Modern Greeks use the same idea in describing curved tiles lying on a roof: "A thousand legs up, a thousand noses down."[7]

64–66. Black upon Black, Three Legs Up, Six Legs Down

Since there are no parallels to this version in the abundant West Indian and in the less abundant British stock and since it is very widely known in North America, I conjecture that it is American in origin. Such parallels as the Danish "Black outside, hairy inside, seven legs and a tail"[1] and the Swedish "Black outside, hairy inside, four ears and seven legs"[2] show how the reference to "black" arose.[3]

---

[1] Nos. 64a through 64f.
[2] No. 65.
[3] No. 63.
[4] Nos. 67a through 67e.
[5] No. 66a.
[6] Nos. 69a through 70. No. 69d refers only to the headboard.
[7] Abbott, p. 317, No. 47.
[1] Kristensen, p. 36, § 87, No. 115.
[2] Ström, p. 371, "Djur och redskap."
[3] See also Nos. 558b, 558e, 930 below.

64a. Black upon black come through th' town, / Three legs up an' six legs down.—A Negro on horseback, carrying a three-legged kettle on his head.
Randolph and Spradley, *Ozark*, p. 88.

64b. Black upon black, / Brown upon brown, / Three feet up, / Six feet down.—Black man on brown horse, with three-legged pot on his head.
Fauset, *Nova Scotia*, p. 160, No. 83 var.; Bacon and Parsons, *Virginia*, p. 327, No. 111; Brewster, *Indiana*, 39; Hyatt, *Adams Co., Ill.*, p. 864, No. 10889 var. Negro on a brown horse and with a black pot on his head: Knortz, p. 232, No. 91; Boggs, *North Carolina*, p. 324, No. 19 (A Negro in brown breeches on a brown horse, carrying a black pot on his head).

64c. What is black upon black and black upon black, three legs up and six legs down?—A Negro upon a black mule with a black kettle upon his head.
Redfield, *Tennessee*, p. 38, No. 22.

64d. Black on top of black with six legs down and three legs up.—A Negro on a mule with a kettle on his head.
Farr, *Tennessee*, p. 325, No. 95.

64e. Black upon black, / Brown upon brown, / Three legs up, / Two legs down.—A Negro riding on a horse with a three-legged kettle on his head.
Hyatt, *Adams Co., Ill.*, p. 663, No. 10889.

64f. Blacky on blacky / And blacky on brown, / Three legs up / And six legs down.—Washpot upside down on head of Negro mounted on brown mule.
Hudson, p. 88, No. 38.

65. Patch upon patch, / Patch upon brown, / Two legs up, four legs down.—The man's name was Patch. His horse's name was Patch. The man was dressed in a suit of brown clothes.
Fauset, *Nova Scotia*, p. 159, No. 82. The man wore patch clothes and he had a brown horse: Fauset, *Nova Scotia*, p. 159, No. 82 var.

66a. Three legs up and six legs down.—Man a-ridin' a horse, with a pot on his head.
Parsons, *Robeson Co., N.C.*, p. 389, No. 18.

66b. There was a man and he was ridin' along, and he had six legs down and three legs up.—The horse had four legs—they was down—and his was down, that made six, and he had a pot on his head and it had three legs.
Halpert, *New Jersey*, p. 201, No. 8.

67. Head of the Living, Mouth of the Dead, Three Legs Up

This employs two characteristic enigmatic devices, that of the contrast of the living and the dead[1] and that of reference to closely associated ideas, in this case, of the head and the mouth. The lack of continental European parallels suggests that this is an English invention.[2]

---

[1] See the headnote to Nos. 828–836.
[2] See the headnote to No. 63, a related version.

67a. Three feet up cauld and dead, / Twa feet flesh and bluid; / The head o' the livin' i' the mouth o' the deid.—An auld man wi' a pat on his heid.
Chambers, *Scotland*, p. 113.

67b. Three feet eemist, cauld an deed, / Twa feet nethmest, flesh an bleed; / The head o' the livin' / And the mou' o' the deed.—A man with a metal pot on his head.
Gregor, *Northeast Scotland*, p. 79.

67c. Three legs up, / Cold as a stone. / Six legs down, / Blood an' bone.—A man riding a horse with a pot on his head.
Parsons, *Guilford Co., N.C.*, p. 205, No. 36.

67d. Three legs up, as hard as stone, / Two legs down, all meat and bone, / Two ears livin' an' two ears dead. / Riddle me this an' take th' head!—A man with an old-fashioned pot on his head.
Randolph and Spradley, *Ozark*, p. 88; Chappell, p. 229, No. 3.

67e. A countrie loon cam down the toon / Wi' three feet up and two feet doon, / With the moo [mouth] of the livin' and the head o' the dead. Come tell me my riddle an' I'll gee ye ma head.—A boy with a pot on his head.
Gregor, *Northeast Scotland*, p. 79.

68. Three Legs

Although the usual answer to the description of an animal which has three legs up is a pot, the specialized answer "washbasin" occurs now and again.[1] Some riddlers have elaborated the riddle by adding such details as appear in the Breton "Body without intestines, feet without nails, ears without head. —Pot."[2] In adding or omitting such details riddlers let their imaginations and powers of association range freely. Some versions[3] employ a rather complete personification. The Portuguese say, "My man with three feet and one mouth," and "A man mounted on three horses."[4] Some riddlers describe a pot and the stones on which it rests as a person sitting on three stools.[5]

68. Somet'in' sittin' on three legs got ter have a mouth an' two ear.—Pot.
Parsons, *Aiken, S.C.*, p. 31, No. 43.

69–70. Four Legs Up, Four Legs Down

The enigmatic quality of this pattern does not lie in suggesting any object or creature. It lies in the implication that these heterogeneous and apparently contradictory elements belong to the same thing. The same theme appears in the Breton cow riddle, "I have four points up and four down and bring profit

---

[1] French: A. Ferrand, *Dauphiné*, p. 227. Swedish: Ström, p. 372, "Sysselsättningar," 5. Zyrian: Wichmann, *Zyrian*, 107.
[2] Sauvé, 68b.
[3] See also Nos. 558a through 558e and No. 930 below.
[4] Parsons, *Cape Verde*, 130a, 130c.
[5] See No. 1182 below.

to the house."[1] The cow's ears and horns point upward and the teats hang downward. This Breton riddle may be a shortened form of a riddle enumerating the members of a cow.[2]

69a. Four legs up and four legs down, / Soft in the middle and hard all 'round. —Bed.

Perkins, *New Orleans*, p. 107, No. 15; Parsons, *Aiken, S.C.*, p. 31, No. 45; Redfield, *Tennessee*, p. 37, No. 21; Farr, *Tennessee*, p. 322, No. 61; Brewster, *Indiana*, 7; Hyatt, *Adams Co., Ill.*, p. 657, No. 10833; Halpert, *Riddles*, p. 38, No. 5; Waugh, *Canada*, p. 67, No. 772; Greenleaf, *Newfoundland*, p. 8, No. 1.

69b. Four foot up, / Four foot down, / Sof' in de middle, / An' hard all 'roun'. —Bedstead.

Parsons, *Barbados*, p. 284, No. 47; Parsons, *Eleuthera and Watling's Islands, Bahamas*, p. 439, No. 3.

69c. Four pos' up and four pos' down, / In the middle soft and hard all aroun'. —Bed.

Parsons, *Bermuda*, p. 258, No. 104. Four leg up and four leg down: Parsons, *Bermuda*, p. 258, No. 104 var.

69d. Two legs up and four legs down, / Soft in the middle and hard all around. —Bed.

Knortz, p. 232, No. 88.

70. Four laig up an' one broad top.—Bed.

Parsons, *Bahamas*, p. 473, No. 23.

71–82. Legs and Other Members

71. 'Tis a t'ing has one leg an' plenty of hands.—A tree.

Parsons, *Antilles*, III, 440, Anguilla, 19.

72. Four laigs, / Two ear, / Long nose, / No eyes.—Mole.

Parsons, *Aiken, S.C.*, p. 28, No. 25.

73. There is something eats chicken, it have four legs, a mouth, two years [ears], and two eyes, and a nose, and a tail.—A mongoose.

Parsons, *Antilles*, III, 445, St. Thomas, 6.

74. Two heads, no neck, no arms, no legs, no face.—Barrel.

Perkins, *New Orleans*, p. 111, No. 55.

75a. What is it have four legs, one head, and a foot?—Bed.

Fauset, *Nova Scotia*, p. 161, No. 90 var.; Parsons, *Aiken, S.C.*, p. 30, No. 35.

75b. Got one head, / One foot, / One body, / Four legs.—Bed.

Fauset, *Southern Negro*, p. 277, No. 18.

75c. One head, / One foot, / Two sides, / No stomach.—Bed.

Fauset, *Southern Negro*, p. 277, No. 16.

75d. What has four legs and only one foot?—Bed.

Fauset, *Nova Scotia*, p. 161, No. 90.

---

[1] Sauvé, 28.
[2] See Nos. 1476a through 1489 below.

76. What is it has a head, foot, and feathers, / Yet is not a fowl?—Bed.
Randolph and Taylor, *Ozarks*, 4.

77. Four eyes, / Four legs, / Four sides, / Long stem.—Stove.
Fauset, *Southern Negro*, p. 277, No. 19.

78. One top, / Two ends, / Four legs, / No bottom.—Table.
Fauset, *Southern Negro*, p. 277, No. 17.

79–82. Long Legs, Short Thighs, Bald (Little) Head, No (Bullet) Eyes

This description of a pair of tongs is popular in English-speaking lands, but seems to have no parallels elsewhere. I can offer no explanation of this very peculiar state of affairs. Inasmuch as riddles about household objects are both numerous and old and riddles about frogs are both rare and apparently recent in origin (at least in most European riddling), I am inclined to believe that the frog riddle (Nos. 82a through 82c) has been modeled on the tongs riddle.

79a. Long legs, / Short thighs, / Little head, / No eyes.—Tongs.
Fauset, *Nova Scotia*, p. 164, No. 115 var.; Burne, *Shropshire*, p. 574, No. 4; Gregor, *Northeast Scotland*, p. 80; Parker, *Oxfordshire*, p. 331; Gutch and Peacock, *Lincolnshire*, p. 399, No. 21.

79b. Long legs, crooked thighs, / Little head, and no eyes.—Tongs.
Udal, *Dorset*, p. 395 = *Folk-Lore Journal*, VII (1889), 260, No. 3; Halliwell-Phillipps, *Nursery Rhymes*, p. 128; Harland and Wilkinson, *Lancashire Legends*, p. 187; Greenleaf, *Newfoundland*, p. 9, No. 7; Fauset, *Nova Scotia*, p. 164, No. 115 var.; Parsons, *Bermuda*, p. 257, No. 81; Whitney and Bullock, *Maryland*, p. 175, No. 2685.

79c. Long legs, crooked thighs, a wee head, and no eyes.—Tongs.
Green, *South Antrim*, 8.

80a. Long legs, crooked thighs, / Bald head, and no eyes.—Pair of tongs.
Greenleaf, *Newfoundland*, p. 9, No. 7; Hyatt, *Adams Co., Ill.*, p. 669, No. 10926.

80b. Little feet, long legs, short thighs, / Bald head, no eyes.—Tongs.
Fauset, *Nova Scotia*, p. 164, No. 115.

80c. Long legs, short thighs, / Bald head, and no eyes.—Tongs.
Hudson, p. 87, No. 30.

81. Long legs, crooked thighs, / Little head, and no eyes.—Scissors.
Knortz, p. 220, No. 39.

82a. Long legs, / Short thigh, / Bald head, / An' bully eyes.—Frawg.
Parsons, *Aiken, S.C.*, p. 28, No. 24.

82b. Long legs an' short thighs, / Rusty back an' bullet eyes.—Frog.
Parsons, *Guilford Co., N.C.*, p. 201, No. 5.

82c. Long legs, crooked toes, / Glassy eyes, snotty nose.—Frog.
Hyatt, *Adams Co., Ill.*, p. 662, No. 10871.

83–87. Feet

83. A little t'in' have fo' feet, an' run night an' day, an' don' stop, so small kyan' shum [can't see him].—Ants.
Parsons, *Sea Islands, S.C.*, p. 154, No. 14.

76. What is it has a head, foot, and feathers, / Yet is not a fowl?—Bed.
Randolph and Taylor, *Ozarks*, 4.

77. Four eyes, / Four legs, / Four sides, / Long stem.—Stove.
Fauset, *Southern Negro*, p. 277, No. 19.

78. One top, / Two ends, / Four legs, / No bottom.—Table.
Fauset, *Southern Negro*, p. 277, No. 17.

79–82. Long Legs, Short Thighs, Bald (Little) Head, No (Bullet) Eyes

This description of a pair of tongs is popular in English-speaking lands, but seems to have no parallels elsewhere. I can offer no explanation of this very peculiar state of affairs. Inasmuch as riddles about household objects are both numerous and old and riddles about frogs are both rare and apparently recent in origin (at least in most European riddling), I am inclined to believe that the frog riddle (Nos. 82a through 82c) has been modeled on the tongs riddle.

79a. Long legs, / Short thighs, / Little head, / No eyes.—Tongs.
Fauset, *Nova Scotia*, p. 164, No. 115 var.; Burne, *Shropshire*, p. 574, No. 4; Gregor, *Northeast Scotland*, p. 80; Parker, *Oxfordshire*, p. 331; Gutch and Peacock, *Lincolnshire*, p. 399, No. 21.

79b. Long legs, crooked thighs, / Little head, and no eyes.—Tongs.
Udal, *Dorset*, p. 395 = *Folk-Lore Journal*, VII (1889), 260, No. 3; Halliwell-Phillipps, *Nursery Rhymes*, p. 128; Harland and Wilkinson, *Lancashire Legends*, p. 187; Greenleaf, *Newfoundland*, p. 9, No. 7; Fauset, *Nova Scotia*, p. 164, No. 115 var.; Parsons, *Bermuda*, p. 257, No. 81; Whitney and Bullock, *Maryland*, p. 175, No. 2685.

79c. Long legs, crooked thighs, a wee head, and no eyes.—Tongs.
Green, *South Antrim*, 8.

80a. Long legs, crooked thighs, / Bald head, and no eyes.—Pair of tongs.
Greenleaf, *Newfoundland*, p. 9, No. 7; Hyatt, *Adams Co., Ill.*, p. 669, No. 10926.

80b. Little feet, long legs, short thighs, / Bald head, no eyes.—Tongs.
Fauset, *Nova Scotia*, p. 164, No. 115.

80c. Long legs, short thighs, / Bald head, and no eyes.—Tongs.
Hudson, p. 87, No. 30.

81. Long legs, crooked thighs, / Little head, and no eyes.—Scissors.
Knortz, p. 220, No. 39.

82a. Long legs, / Short thigh, / Bald head, / An' bully eyes.—Frawg.
Parsons, *Aiken, S.C.*, p. 28, No. 24.

82b. Long legs an' short thighs, / Rusty back an' bullet eyes.—Frog.
Parsons, *Guilford Co., N.C.*, p. 201, No. 5.

82c. Long legs, crooked toes, / Glassy eyes, snotty nose.—Frog.
Hyatt, *Adams Co., Ill.*, p. 662, No. 10871.

83–87. Feet

83. A little t'in' have fo' feet, an' run night an' day, an' don' stop, so small kyan' shum [can't see him].—Ants.
Parsons, *Sea Islands, S.C.*, p. 154, No. 14.

84. Dere was a very busy fellow who had twenty feet on one side an' on de oder side had twenty an' in all dat were forty an' he can make you feel quite uncomfortable and change the color of your skin.—Centapede.
Parsons, *Antilles*, III, 443, St. Croix, 8.

85. My father had a thing, it had three feet.—Pot.
Parsons, *Bahamas*, p. 478, No. 62.

86. *Trip trap* in a gap, / as many feete as a hundred sheepe.—It is hayle, when it falls.
Prettie Riddles (1631), No. 60 = Brandl, p. 60.

87. Somet'in' had fo' feet an' one back.—Cheer [chair].
Parsons, *Sea Islands, S.C.*, p. 171, No. 123.

88–258. Function

88–111. Birth, Growth, Manner of Life

88–95. Birth, Growth

The notion of rejuvenescence is usually applied to the moon, but it also occurs in the Icelandic riddle for the year, "It becomes only twelve months old, but yet it shows time and is indeed young, mature, and aged."[1]

88. Something under the hill, / If it's not born, / It's there still.—Person.
Parsons, *Bermuda*, p. 255, No. 69.

89. in the last minute of my age j do wax young againe & have so still continued since the world first begane.—the moone.
Tupper, *Holme Riddles*, 102; *Prettie Riddles* (1631), No. 54 = Brandl, p. 59.

90a. There was a thing just four weeks old, / When Adam was no more; / Before that thing was five weeks old, / Old Adam was fourscore.—Moon.
Udal, *Dorset*, p. 395; Waugh, *Canada*, p. 70, No. 810.

90b. There was a thing three days old / When Adam was four score.—Moon.
Leather, *Hereford*, p. 229.

91. What is it, when Adam was four days old it was four days old, and when Adam was four-score years and four days old it remained four days old?—Moon.
Beckwith, *Jamaica*, p. 216, No. 257.

92. I was four weeks old / When Cain was born / Nor five weeks old yet.—Moon.
Parsons, *Guilford Co., N.C.*, p. 206, No. 55.

93a. Something was here since the world first made, and just a month old. What's that?—Moon.
Parsons, *Sea Islands, S.C.*, p. 174, No. 168.

---
[1] Árnason, 222.

93b. Somet'in' was yere since de wo'l' was firs' made.—Moon.
Parsons, *Sea Islands, S.C.*, p. 174, No. 168.

94. Born from de worl' mek an' nebber a month ole yet.—Moon.
Beckwith, *Jamaica*, p. 195, No. 106.

95. Buried and Begets Children

A very early instance of this theme occurs in a riddle for a grain of wheat written by Judah Halevi (born *ca.* 1080), a Neo-Hebrew poet of Castile. It is: "What is it that one lays naked into the grave, and yet it does not suffer death, it begets children there, cares for them attentively until they come forth well dressed?"[1] A simple version of the same theme is to be found in a fourteenth-century riddle recorded by Claret, "Dum moritur, generat semper: granum tibi solvat."[2]

95. Cut me up in pieces and bury me alive, / The young ones will live and the old ones die.—Potatoes.
Greenleaf, *Newfoundland*, p. 14, No. 9.

96–106. Manner of Life

The riddles in this section seem to be fragments of concepts better preserved elsewhere. A few are literary inventions that have enjoyed no wide currency. In most of them the manner of personification does not have the flavor of traditional riddling.

96. My head is round, my body small, / and I hold that that savors all.—A saltseller [saltcellar] and salt.
Prettie Riddles (1631), No. 72 = Brandl, p. 62.

97. I Never Was and Am Always To Be

A similar conception serves to describe "today." It occurs in Welsh,[1] in the Flemish "I shall be named yesterday and have been tomorrow";[2] and in the Walloon "What is not yesterday and was yesterday?"[3] It is turned into a pun in Chile: "Era i no era i siempre era.—Era."[4] Somewhat to the same purpose is the Flemish personification of leap year: "I stay away patiently for four years, then see me appear, [only] to disappear again for four years. Tell me what that signifies."[5]

Although most of the parallels are said to be from oral sources, they have the flavor of literary riddles. The English text here printed may also be found in the omnium-gatherum, *Wit and Humor of the Age*.[6] Nicolaus Reusner's distich

---

[1] Friedreich, p. 158, No. 1, quoting Jolowicz, *Der poetische Orient* (Leipzig, 1858), p. 324.
[2] P. 71, No. 62.

[1] Hull and Taylor, 1.
[2] Joos, 127.
[3] Colson, *Wallonia*, IV, 42, No. 3.
[4] Flores, 253.
[5] Joos, 129.
[6] Chicago, n.d. [1901], p. 735, No. 52.

> Quod nusquam est; simul hoc & ubique, & idem est apud omnes,
> Omne quod est (mirum!) non capit ipse locus,[7]

is to the same effect, and the very curious version in Al-Ḥarîrî's *Assemblies*, "That which was yesterday and has been today and will be tomorrow, and note! it has one of these three names,"[8] gives away the answer by including it in the riddle. See also the French "How much time is there?—Only one, for the past no longer exists, the future does not yet exist, there is consequently only the present,"[9] and the Icelandic parallel, which I quote as an example of the many literary elaborations of the theme. It is as follows: "I am without beginning, yet I am born. I am also without end, and yet I die. I have neither eyes nor ears, yet I see and hear. I am never seen, and yet my works are visible. I am long conquered, I am never conquered, and yet I am vanquished. I labor ever, but am never tired. I am wise but dwell among the foolish. I am a lover of Providence, and yet it may appear to me that it hates me. Often I die before I am born, and yet I am immortal. Without being aware of it, I often take by surprise. I live with Christians, I dwell among the heathen, among the cursed in Hell I am cursed, and I reign in the Kingdom of Glory."[10]

97. I never was by [*sic*], am always to be, / None ever saw me, nor ever will, / And yet I am the confidence of all / Who live and breathe on this terrestrial ball.—Tomorrow.
Greenleaf, *Newfoundland*, p. 8, No. 5.

98. Wha' live in de river?—Fish.
Parsons, *Sea Islands, S.C.*, p. 171, No. 127.

99. What live in de river an' crawl on fo' [*sic*] feet?—Crab.
Parsons, *Sea Islands, S.C.*, p. 171, No. 128.

100. When first I appear I seem mysterious, / But when I am explained I am nothing serious.—Riddle.
Beckwith, *Jamaica*, p. 214, No. 243.

101. I am taken from a mine, and shut up in a wooden case, from which I am never released, and yet I am used by almost everybody.—Pencil.
Knortz, p. 239, No. 141.

102. I came from beyond the ocean, / I drink water out of the sea, / I lighten many a nation, / And give myself to thee.—Sun.
Beckwith, *Jamaica*, p. 214, No. 245.

103. What is it leaves its tongue out, cold or hot?—Dog.
Parsons, *Guilford Co., N.C.*, p. 204, No. 35.

---

[7] *Ænigmata* (Frankfurt a. M., 1601), p. 83.
[8] Trans. H. Rückert, 4th ed. (Stuttgart, 1864), p. 138. I have not found it in the English translation by Chenery and Steingass. See also Friedreich, p. 169, No. 1.
[9] Rolland, *Rimes*, p. 195, No. 1.
[10] Árnason, 105. The reference to conquering involves a pun which a translator cannot render into English.

104. I tell you this riddle, / Perhaps you may tell it back to me. / There's something 'tis always yawning. What's that?—Oven.
Parsons, *Antilles*, III, 441, Anguilla, 26.

105. I bear much, devour much, and reach from pole to pole.—Sea.
Wit and Humor of the Age (Chicago, n.d. [1901]), p. 737, No. 66.

106. On my belly I am fixt, / Two holes and a bridge betwixt.—Fiddle.
Fauset, *Nova Scotia*, p. 172, No. 184.

107 through 111 vacant.

112–222. Moving

Many of the riddles which describe an object as moving and qualify this description with some unusual or contradictory detail are related among themselves or exhibit contamination or confusion of patterns. In setting up the following classification, I have not been able to identify definitely every contamination that I suspected to exist or to clarify all the confusions that I found. The number of possible patterns is rather small, and the differences in them are usually slight. The following classification may accord the dignity of a separate number to a variety scarcely meriting recognition, but in such matters consistency is difficult to achieve and even if achieved, does not necessarily give a true picture of the materials. A minor variety may have an importance in traditional use which stands in no relation to its apparent value. For example, "Mout' to mout', seven legs, one tail,"[1] which has the answer, "dog eating from pot," might seem to represent a wholly insignificant variation from the usual English type, but as a matter of fact, it is the only English example of the French and Spanish type.

The enigmatic quality of the riddles in this section arises from a contradiction between the motion and another act or from the unusual aspects of the motion. These may be of several kinds. Such a simple contradiction as "going and not moving"[2] is rather freely used. An act normally associated with motion may be varied or omitted, as in "going and touching,"[3] "going and not touching,"[4] "going and leaving a track,"[5] and "going and leaving no track."[6] Numerous as these categories are, they do not include all in which moving is the characteristic element. Some conceptions of this sort do not occur in English riddling: "going without making a sound"[7] is a theme rather widely used on the Continent but not in England. "Going around the house"[8] is perhaps more freely used in German than in English riddles and has acquired the status of a convention. So, too, "going over a bridge"[9] is a German rather

---

[1] See No. 63.
[2] Nos. 119a through 132a.
[3] Nos. 144 through 146.
[4] Nos. 147 through 173.
[5] Nos. 174 through 180.
[6] Nos. 171 and 181 through 185.
[7] See the headnote to No. 164.
[8] Hanika-Otto, 121 through 137.
[9] Hanika-Otto, 139 through 142.

than an English formula, although "As I went over London Bridge" is a familiar English introduction. "Going up and down the village"[10] is a minor but securely established German pattern. Turkish riddlers use the scene "something comes from the mountain" in descriptions of a tree, a bee, a goat, a rabbit, wind, water, and a railroad train.[11] It also occurs in a Samoan riddle for a river;[12] in the Samoan riddle, however, it does not seem to have the same conventional use as in Turkish. Such variations in forms and their uses suggest that these and similar conventional details have often developed independently and have only slowly acquired their conventional quality.

It is interesting to contrast with the idea of motion such ideas as hanging or lying, which have found a wider use in foreign lands than in England. Germans often use the idea of something or somebody hanging.[13] The idea of lying is virtually universal: something or somebody lies under the steps, on the threshing floor, under the bench, under the table. English riddlers use it perhaps most often in riddles for shoes or milk.[14]

112. Leaves a Locked House

This English riddler is so vague that we cannot perceive whether he has in mind an animal or a person. A similar comparison with the answer "sun" or "sunlight" is widely known in eastern Europe. It usually makes a rather definite suggestion of a person. See a Rumanian version[1] and such Modern Greek parallels as "I go to church, I lock my door, I return to my house and find a thief inside";[2] "I have something that manages to get inside though I shut all my windows";[3] and "I shut my house and always find a thief inside."[4] The Chileans use this comparison for a dream.[5]

112. What is it even though it's locked in can get out?—Fire.
Parsons, *Bermuda*, p. 264, No. 153.

113. Follows Everywhere

The parallels usually contain a more adequate personification than we find in this English riddle. The Indian "A lady of dark color accompanies her husband; she can be seen in the light, but disappears in the dark"[1] is remarkable

---

[10] Hanika-Otto, 143 through 146.
[11] Kowalski, *Asia Minor*, note to No. 32.
[12] Heider, 38.
[13] Hanika-Otto, 180 through 197.
[14] See below, Nos. 445a, 445b, 447, 449a through 453c, 453e through 454c, 456a, and 456b. See also Hanika-Otto, 198 through 201.
[1] Papahagi, 79.
[2] Polites, *Neohellenika Analekta*, I, 227, No. 192.
[3] Polites, *Neohellenika Analekta*, I, 227, No. 193.
[4] Stathes, p. 341, No. 56. See also Sanders, 8; Sakellarios, p. 291, No. 1.
[5] Laval, p. 93, No. 9.
[1] Lakshīnātha Upasānī, V, 3.

for its reference to the object that throws the shadow as well as to the shadow. It shows some similarity to riddles for the sun and moon or for day and night.² An African (South Sotho) riddler conceives a shadow in terms of a person in "I tried to come here and he turned hither with me";³ a Tonga-Shangaan parallel is stated in terms of an animal, "I have driven my ox to the Bileni [Lower Limpopo], and I have come back with it";⁴ and a Kxatla version is expressed in terms of a thing, "Tell me: I go south, I take care of the black thing, I come back and still take care of it."⁵ European riddlers often describe a man and his shadow as chasing one another. The Rumanians say, "You run away and I chase you."⁶ Riddlers occasionally refer to the fact that a shadow cannot be caught,⁷ a theme that is characteristic of the smoke riddle. The reference to catching a shadow in the Arabic "He goes with you to the door and then you put it in your pocket"⁸ is unusual. The ordinary theme appears with an interesting personification in the Togo "A man walks with you and you cannot catch him."⁹ The Portuguese parallel contains this theme and introduces into it the theme used in describing a thorn in the foot:¹⁰ "I run, I do not catch it; I sit down, I catch it."¹¹ The Lettish description of a shadow as something that "one cannot walk across"¹² appears to be unique.

The fundamental idea of something that follows one everywhere occurs in such other uses as the Norwegian name riddle, "What is that which follows with everything?"¹³ This is allied to a widely known riddle for a name.¹⁴ See also the Nandi belly riddle, "I have a friend, and if I send him anywhere, he runs with me. What am I?"¹⁵ and the Arabic road riddle, "He accompanies you constantly, and you pay him nothing."¹⁶

113. Somet'in' follow you ev'whey you go.—Dat's yer shadow.
Parsons, *Sea Islands, S.C.*, p. 170, No. 118.

114–118. Goes; Never Stops

The notion of the river or sea as something in constant motion is probably universal. It is often a synonym for "forever" in such phrases as "while rivers flow." It occurs in this use in Plato's epitaph for Midas:

> I am a maiden of brass,
> And I lie on the tomb of Midas.
> While water shall flow
> And the tall trees grow

---

² See No. 1001 below.
³ Cited in the note to Schapera, 84.
⁵ Schapera, 84.
⁷ See the headnote to Nos. 1643–1654, § 6, below.
⁹ Schönhärl, 108.
¹¹ Parsons, *Cape Verde*, 236b.
¹³ Christie, 93.
¹⁴ See the headnote to Nos. 1573–1575, nn. 8–13, below.
¹⁵ Hollis, *Nandi*, 8.

⁴ Junod and Jaques, p. 234, No. 32.
⁶ Gorovei, *Devinettes*, p. 505.
⁸ Stumme, *Tázerwalt*, 20.
¹⁰ Nos. 1632 through 1639 below.
¹² Bielenstein, 156, 157.

¹⁶ Stumme, *Tázerwalt*, 23.

> I shall stay here
> On his woeful bier
> And tell all who pass
> That this is the tomb of Midas.[1]

In the *Aeneid* Virgil writes "In freta dum fluvii currunt."[2] William Penn's treaty with the Pennsylvania Indians is said to have included the clause, "while grass grows and water runs." The notion is ever ready to hand and has doubtless been invented a thousand times. The following passage from a Chinese classic may serve as a final illustration: "As he stood by a tree, Confucius said of a river, 'Ah! that which is passing is just like this—never ceasing, day or night!' "[3] Ovid adapts the idea to the meaning "never,"[4] but this is an unusual variation to which I note only the parallel, "would not be more at liberty than water which descends not to the sea."[5] The notion of the perpetual motion of water has been discussed as a rhetorical figure.[6]

Riddlers describe the ceaseless motion of water in rivers, in the sea, or against the shore as "never wearying"[7] or "always talking."[8] English folklore offers no example of the vivid and picturesque comparisons of a river to a horse that runs without stopping. Such comparisons may contain mythical implications. See, for example, Lettish: Bielenstein, 738. Russian: Sadovnikov, 1472, 1479. Estonian: Dido, 5 = Widemann, p. 282 (The horse runs day and night without a bridle); Gutsleff, *Anweisung zur ehstnischen Sprache* (Halle, 1732), 116 (The horse runs, the bridle stands), as cited by Russwurm, 2. Lappish: Qvigstad, 122, citing Fellman, III, 156, No. 21. Cheremiss: Wichmann, *Cheremiss*, 203; Genetz, 30 (The horse trots, the wagon-shafts are motionless). Mordvin: Paasonen, 3. Zyrian: Wichmann, *Zyrian*, 113 (A black horse gallops between two hills), 292. Votyak: Buch, p. 98, No. 6. Arabic: Giacobetti, 10 (It gallops during the day. It gallops during the night. It never wearies). Turkish: Katanov in Radlov, IX, 94, No. 808 (A black pacer does not lie quiet by either day or night), and p. 100, No. 870 (I have a black pacer that does not lie down and does not stand up). Indian, Malayalam: Frohnmeyer, p. 229 (A horse which can run, a horse which can jump, a horse which can stand if it sees water.—Shore). Korean: Bernheisel, p. 86 (What travels day and night?). In these texts the "bridle" or "wagon-shafts" that remain motionless are the banks of the river. Possibly related to these ideas is the Irish kenning "sea horses" for waves.[9]

---

[1] *Phaedrus*, 264D. The translation is Paul Shorey's.   [2] I, 607.
[3] Lun Yu, IX, 16. Quoted in Hu Shih, *The Development of the Logical Method in Ancient China* (Shanghai, 1928), p. 28.
[4] *Metamorphoses*, XIII, 24.   [5] Dante, *Paradiso*, X, 90.
[6] Kirby Flower Smith (ed.), Tibullus, p. 283, R. H. Coon, *The Reversal of Nature as a Rhetorical Figure* (Indiana University Studies, LXXX; Bloomington, Indiana, 1928), p. 12.
[7] No. 138 below.   [8] Nos. 751a, 751b.
[9] Vernam Hull, "Old and Middle Irish do·sná," *Language*, XVII (1941), 152–155.

114. There is something that run all time and never stop.—That's the river.
Parsons, *Sea Islands, S.C.*, p. 160, No. 51, var. 2.

115. Somet'in' go night an' day an' never stop.—Tide.
Parsons, *Sea Islands, S.C.*, p. 160, No. 51, var. 1.

116a. Me riddle me racket, / S'pose I tell you dis riddle, / An' perhaps not. / Dere is somet'in' goes all night an' all day an' never stops.—Sea.
Parsons, *Antilles*, III, 432, St. Eustatius, 4.

116b. It has [read: is] some t'ing dat goes all day an' all night an' never stops.—Sea.
Parsons, *Antilles*, III, 432, Saba, 2 var.

117. Somet'in' run all day an' all night.—Clock.
Parsons, *Sea Islands, S.C.*, p. 160, No. 51.

118. There is something on yonder hill, / Rocks and rocks and never stands still.—Tree.
Hyatt, *Adams Co., Ill.*, p. 669, No. 10928.

119–132. Goes; Never Moves

The various minor varieties of this rather popular theme illustrate well the art of riddling and the effect of oral transmission. These are: (*a*) "it goes up and down";[1] (*b*) "it comes and goes and stands still [or: never leaves the spot]";[2] (*c*) "it always goes but never moves";[3] (*d*) "it goes from —— to —— and does not leave the spot";[4] (*e*) "it turns and does not move."[5] An effort to vary a familiar conception by introducing novel details or borrowing elements from allied conceptions is obvious.

The contrast of going and yet not moving is applicable to:

§ 1. A pump-handle. See Nos. 119*a*, 119*b*.

§ 2. A part of a machine about which other parts move.

§ 2*a*. A marker on a scale. See the headnote to Nos. 125–130, § 4.

§ 2*b*. An axle of a carriage wheel. Danish: Kristensen, p. 13, § 3, No. 4. Swedish: Ström, p. 145, "Vagnen," 3. The Bihari riddle for a potter's wheel is "With continual moving he became exhausted; yet he did not move a single *kōs*. His children became such that they moved away hundreds and hundreds of *kōses*."[6]

§ 3. A weaver's reed. Mordvin: Paasonen, 320. Compare the Filipino description of a weaver: "She appears to be always walking, but after all is still in her place as before" (Starr, *Philippines*, 251).

§ 4. A railroad, a railroad track. See Nos. 128, 129 below.

§ 5. A fence. See Nos. 121, 133.

§ 6. A door. See No. 127.

---

[1] Nos. 119*a* through 124*b*.
[2] Nos. 125 through 130*b*.
[3] Nos. 125 through 127.
[4] Nos. 128 through 130*b*.
[5] Nos. 131, 132*a*.
[6] Mitra, *Bihar*, 35.

§ 7. A watch, a clock. See Nos. 125, 126, 130a, 130b.

§ 8. The moon. See No. 120.

§ 9. The wind. Danish: Kristensen, p. 143, § 422, No. 669. African, Kamba: Lindblom, 16 (Tell me a person who remains in one spot although traveling and does not rest).

§ 10. A river. Icelandic: Árnason, 427 (What stands still while running?—Stream), 970 (I saw some sedate maidens who hinder the travels of some people. They run on with great speed and yet each stays in her place). African, Duala: Ebding, 83. The collector should have noted the importance of his No. 74 in interpreting this version.

§ 11. A man in a hammock. Filipino: Starr, *Philippines*, 147 (Running and running, but it cannot go away), 246 (Who was running fast but did not move from where he started?).

§ 12. A key, a lock. This usually contains the additional element, "it remains in the room." See Spanish: Demófilo, 275; Rodríguez Marín, 626. Argentinian: Lehmann-Nitsche, 126. Chilean: Flores, 192.

§ 13. A whetstone. Danish: DFS, 1906/38: H. Sørenson, 1935, No. 11 (What runs around itself and never gets any farther?).

§ 14. The heart. Gypsy: Wlislocki, 22 (It runs and runs and yet does not run away, it longs for sunlight and yet never sees it).

119–124. Goes Up and Down; Never Moves
(Never Touches the Ground)

119a. Something goes up and down / And never touches the groun'.—Pump-handle.
Parsons, *Bermuda*, p. 256, No. 73.

119b. Up and down, / Never touches sky nor ground.—Pump-handle.
Waugh, *Canada*, p. 71, No. 812; Whitney and Bullock, *Maryland*, p. 174, No. 2682; Fauset, *Philadelphia*, p. 554, No. 12; Bacon and Parsons, *Virginia*, p. 312, No. 8; Chappell, p. 234, No. 29; Farr, *Tennessee*, p. 325, No. 97; Hyatt, *Adams Co., Ill.*, p. 665, No. 10898.

120. What goes up and down, / But never goes to town?—Moon.
Hyatt, *Adams Co., Ill.*, p. 663, No. 10885.

121. Something runs up the hill and down the hill, but never moves.—Rail [fence].
Parsons, *Bermuda*, p. 255, No. 66.

122a. What is that which goes up the hill, / And down the hill, / And spite of all yet standeth still?—Road.
Waugh, *Canada*, p. 69, No. 787; Knortz, p. 233, No. 100.

122b. What goes up hill and down hill, and remains still?—The road.
Greenleaf, *Newfoundland*, p. 11, No. 24; Fauset, *Nova Scotia*, p. 168, No. 132.

122c. Up the hill, down the hill; / Stand up still.—Road.
Beckwith, *Jamaica*, p. 200, No. 156a.

122d. What goes up hill and down dale and never moves an inch?—A road.
Redfield, *Tennessee*, p. 42, No. 89.

122e. What goes up and down and never moves?—The road.
Parsons, *Antilles*, III, 447, St. Thomas, 27.

123. Up the hill and down the hill, / And yet never stand still.—Road.
Fauset, *Southern Negro*, p. 283, No. 74.

124a. What is it that stands uphill, stands downhill, stands still, and goes to mill?—Road.
Brewster, *Indiana*, 45.

124b. Up hill, down hill, / Stands still, but goes to mill every day.—Road.
Randolph and Taylor, *Ozarks*, 1.

125–130. Comes and Goes; Stands Still (Does Not Leave the Spot)

This pattern is very old. Petronius asks, "Qui de nobis currit et de loco non movetur,"[1] but does not stay for an answer. Buecheler conjectures that the answer is "eye," and supports his belief by finding two other members of the human body as answers to accompanying riddles.[2] Loewenthal adds[3] a similar late medieval riddle, but again the answer "eye" is a conjecture. Traditional parallels would support better such answers as "door" or "road."

The fundamental idea naturally suggests an animal or a person. It cannot be easily fitted to a thing except in a passive sense, as in the Indonesian riddle for a nut, "One seizes it, one opens it, but one doesn't carry it away."[4] The notion that thought ranges far but does not leave the spot[5] is a conception in animal terms.

The scene of something that goes and yet remains is applicable to:

§ 1. A clock. See Nos. 125, 126 below.

§ 2. A door. See No. 127.

§ 3. A road. See Nos. 122a through 124b above.

§ 4. A marker on a scale. French: E. H. Carnoy, *La Tradition*, VI (1892), 353, No. 5.

§ 5. A mill. German: Wossidlo, 377; August Brunk, *Blätter für pommersche Volkskunde*, III, 113. Danish: Kristensen, pp. 141–142, § 420, No. 661a (It goes and goes and gets no farther.—Windmill) and No. 661b. Portuguese: Parsons, *Cape Verde*, 153. Spanish: Demófilo, 663, and pp. 344–345, No. 22.

§ 6. A ridgepole. Perhaps the Low German riddle from Denmark, "What is that which rides and rides and does not get farther?—The ridgepole" (Wat is dat, wat dor ritt un ritt, un kømt nich widder?—De Dakridder. DFS, 1906/38: Andr. Lorenzen, Damholm, 1932, No. 1), contains a pun. Such

---

[1] *Cena Trimalchionis* (ed. L. Friedländer; Leipzig, 1906), 156, 1.
[2] See Ohlert, 2d ed., p. 50. [3] P. 117, note to line 25.
[4] Holle, *Soenda*, p. 374, No. 29. This is akin to the riddle of the wormy nut discussed in the headnote to Nos. 823–824 below.
[5] See No. 364 and the headnote to No. 1578.

strictly Danish parallels as "What is that which rides night and day and does not reach any place?—A ridgepole" (Hvad er det, der rider Nat og Dag, og ingen Steder kommer?—Kragetræ. DFS, 1906/38: O. P. Olsen, Alsted, 1912, No. 6; see also Kristensen, p. 95, § 245, Nos. 376a through 376e) make less of it. Compare the striking personification in the Filipino "I have a horseman who has been riding for a year but has not gone a bit" (Starr, *Philippines*, 172).

§ 7. The tongue. Cuban: Sánchez, 22.

§ 8. A cow's tail. Norwegian: Stafset, 187.

125–127. Always Goes; Never Moves

The description of a clock or pendulum as always going but never moving or leaving the spot involves something akin to a pun on the word "going." Such a pun is possible in many languages, and the description is correspondingly widely known. Riddlers have not often individualized the actor. For example, the Czech "An old man goes along the road[1] and the road does not get shorter,"[2] which is not completely intelligible, appears to have borrowed the contrast of longer and shorter, which is here implied, from a riddle for a candle.[3] Scandinavian riddlers[4] often include the element "goes and goes and never reaches the door." A somewhat similar idea occurs in the Russian sun riddle, "What keeps moving and never stands still?" or "What keeps going, yet does not leave its place?"[5]

A few clock riddles with a clearly conceived person as the actor introduce some very special details. See, for example, the Breton "He works all year without a salary"[6] or "I am a little body without a soul. I am always walking in my prison. I notify mortals of their greatest needs."[7]

125. Always moving while standing still.—Clock.
Fauset, *Southern Negro*, p. 283, No. 75.

126. It runs all day, / But never does run away.—Clock.
Parsons, *Sea Islands, S.C.*, p. 164, No. 66.

127. What comes and goes and yet never leaves the spot?—A door.
Dempster, *Sutherlandshire*, p. 236.

128–130. Goes to a Named Spot without Moving

This variety of the preceding riddle exhibits a kind of specialization which arises readily in traditional materials. The speaker substitutes a specific reference for a general statement. In the following texts he gains an added realism by this device.

---

[1] The translation of this word is uncertain.
[2] Hanika-Otto, note to her No. 174.
[3] See the headnote to Nos. 607–631 below.
[4] See the note to No. 125.
[5] Sadovnikov, 1810, 1810a.
[6] Sauvé, 97.
Charlec, *Dol-de-Bretagne*, 1904, p. 168, No. 26.

128. What goes the whole way to Yarmouth without moving?—The railroad.
Fauset, *Nova Scotia*, p. 168, No. 132 var.

129. What runs all the way from San Francisco to New York without moving?—Railroad-track.
Bacon and Parsons, *Virginia*, p. 319, No. 61.

130a. What went to the North Pole and stopped there, / And came back because it couldn't go there?—A watch.
Greenleaf, *Newfoundland*, p. 16, No. 7.

130b. I went to London but because I didn't go I came back.—Watch.
Oral, California.

131–132. Turns; Does Not Move

131. What turns around and never moves?—A road.
Redfield, *Tennessee*, p. 38, No. 31.

132a. What turns without moving?—Milk.
Parsons, *Bermuda*, p. 264, No. 151. But never moves: Fauset, *Nova Scotia*, p. 169, No. 144. And don't move: Fauset, *Southern Negro*, p. 283, No. 73. And never moves: Redfield, *Tennessee*, p. 38, No. 30.

132b. Something turn and you can't see when it turn. What is that?—Milk (or milk turns to clabber).
Parsons, *Sea Islands, S.C.*, p. 174, No. 166.

133–135. Goes Out and In

This conception is closely related to that of the riddles[1] for a window or door, "What is both in and out of the house?" which, however, lack the slight degree of personification here implied and involve rather a confusion in logic. Also closely related is the door riddle, "What comes and goes and never leaves the spot?"[2] A Danish door riddle "What goes into the room every day and never goes out, and what goes out of the room but never goes in?"[3] is confusing because it does not describe a single object but doors in general, which swing either out or in and do not usually swing in both directions. The gambler riddle uses the phrase "out and in" in a punning sense.[4]

133. What goes in and out, and in and out, and still never moves?—A rail-fence.
Waugh, *Canada*, p. 67, No. 767.

134. What is out and in, / But never can win?—Gambler.
Hyatt, *Adams Co., Ill.*, p. 662, No. 10872.

135. Up and down, in and out; / No one knows what it's all about.—A quivering leaf on a tree when the wind is not blowing.
Farr, *Tennessee*, p. 325, No. 93.

---

[1] See the headnote to No. 1423.
[2] No. 127.
[3] Kristensen, p. 129, § 361, No. 573.
[4] No. 134 below.

136. Goes; Never Comes Back

The Kamba describe a river in similar terms but with a more definite suggestion of a scene: "A caravan that does not return."[1] The notion of going and not returning is also applied to a bullet or an arrow.[2] It is allied to the contradictions of being able to go up but not down, or down but not up,[3] and of having it and yet giving it away.[4]

136. What goes an' never comes back?—It's yer breat'.
Parsons, *Sea Islands, S.C.*, p. 172, No. 147.

137–140. Goes; Never Wearies

Riddles having the answer "stream" or "sun" are widely known and probably represent the original forms. The lack of parallels to the answer "wind" is somewhat surprising. The answer "road" appears to be of recent origin.

137. Up the hill, down the hill; yet never tired.—Road.
Beckwith, *Jamaica*, p. 200, No. 156.

138–140. Sun, Moon, and Wind or River (Waterfall) Never Grow Weary

The three English riddles from Negro tradition that describe three objects in nature as constantly going and never wearying have been taken down quite independently. They may, however, be fragments of a single very curious and interesting riddle contrasting them in this manner. Although they are reported separately, they are nevertheless current in one place only and may therefore be fragments of an original tripartite version. I shall not insist upon this explanation, since the available texts are too few to prove or disprove it.

The tripartite riddle just mentioned is very widely known, is found in strange variations, and has a long history which has not been fully explored. Its themes are characteristically cosmological. The Kashmiri describe the water, the earth, and the firmament as "One goes on and is never tired, another sits and never rises, another stands and never sits."[1] Although very different from this, the ancient Sanskrit "Three hairy ones appear, each at his own time. One mows during the year, one contemplates the universe, the course but not the form of one is visible"[2] is perhaps related. This has been interpreted as referring to the three forms of the god Agni, but the cosmological implications are obvious. A Portuguese version from the Cape Verde Islands tells of somewhat different activities but has a similar answer: "Three things there are in the world, things which we must have, one eats, another

---

[1] Lindblom, 30. See also French: J. Roux, *Limousin*, 23.
[2] See the headnote to No. 801, § 6, below.
[3] See Nos. 141 through 143 and 1604a through 1604f.
[4] See Nos. 1586, 1588.

[1] Knowles, 62.   [2] *Rigveda*, I, 164, strophe 44.

drinks, another goes without eating.—Earth, sun, moon."[3] Perhaps related to these conceptions is the Kundu riddle for the earth, "I carry and do not grow weary."[4]

A widely known version of this tripartite riddle refers to the actors as working or not working and the like and has the answer, "sun, moon, waterfall [river]," or "sun, moon, wind." Compare the riddle, "One works in the day, another at night, and the third all the time," which is current in Germany, Sweden, and Czechoslovakia.[5] Analogous to it but somewhat different is a German riddle for water, fire, and wind.[6]

Obviously related to these cosmological themes are such answers as "water, surf, sand," and the like. Compare the Portuguese "There are three things: one says that we are going, another says that we are staying, another says that we are dancing.—Water, sand, surf."[7] This has many parallels, especially in the Slavic languages. A typical one is "One says, 'Let's go!' One says, 'Let's stand!' One says, 'Let's whisper!' "[8] with the answer, "water, bank, and reeds." A stone, water, and grass[9] as well as a road, a milestone, and the wind[10] are described similarly. These texts are probably related to the dramatic Basque conversation of water, stones, and a fish: " 'Let's go, let's go!'—'Let's stay, let's stay!'—'Let's play, let's play!' "[11] See also the Turkish "One says, 'Let's go!' but the other merely bows.—Water and trees beside the water"[12] or "One says, 'Let's go!' but the other says, 'Let's live for a while!' "[13] The Shor (a Turkic tribe) have a riddle for water, foam, and a rock: "One said, 'Let's go!' One said, 'Let's stand up!' And one said, 'Let's lie down!' "[14] A queer Abyssinian riddle introduces a new answer but is clearly a branch of the same tradition: "One says, 'Let us run, let us run!' One says, 'Let us spread out, let us spread out!' One says, 'Let us stay in the shade, let us stay in the shade!' "[15] This has the answer, "river, creeping grass, clarified butter." A Lur riddle from southwestern Persia for a river, a boulder, and a tree on the bank, "One goes, one stays, one shakes its head,"[16] is related to the previously mentioned Polish and Russian texts.

These tripartite riddles are associated with versions that replace the cos-

---

[3] Parsons, *Cape Verde*, 265.   [4] Ittmann, *Kundu*, p. 178, No. 224.
[5] The version quoted is Swedish: Sandén, *Norra Vadsbo*, 115. See also German: Wossidlo, 153 (many parallels). Swedish: Ericsson, *Södermanland*, V (1884), 70, No. 235; Ström, p. 208, "Sol, måne, fors." Czech: *Pohádky kratochvilné*, 58, cited by Flajšhans, p. 31, § 28e (sun, moon, wind).
[6] Wossidlo, 154 (many parallels).   [7] Braga, 27.
[8] Polish: Gustawicz, 452, 453: Saloni, *Łańcut*, 33; Kopernicki, 51. Russian: Sadovnikov, 1477. These riddles are analogous to a Turkish riddle for water, sand, and the trembling of the poplar: "One says, 'Let's go!' One says, 'Let's remain!' The other says, 'Praise God, praise God!' " (Hamizade, 634).
[9] Polish: Siarkowski, 90. Russian: Sadovnikov, 1507.
[10] Russian: Sadovnikov, 1136.   [11] Vinson, 43; Cerquand, 50.
[12] Katanov in Radlov, IX, 285, No. 205.   [13] Katanov in Radlov, IX, 285, No. 206.
[14] Dyrenkova, 40.   [15] Littmann, *Tigriña*, p. 618, No. 7.
[16] Mann, II, 169, No. 6. Schultz, *Bemerkungen*, p. 361, suggests the answer, "funeral."

mological themes by homelier objects. Parallels are found in the homeland and colonies of almost every European country except England, Ireland, and lands where the Romance languages are spoken. A typical example is the Surinam riddle for a bed, a chair, and a clock: "You have three things in your house. One longs for daybreak, one longs for night to come, one longs for the world to end."[17] With minor adjustments in the descriptive details, this riddle has such answers as "door, stove, and broom";[18] "candle, door, clock";[19] and "bed, gate, crevice above the gate."[20] Perhaps the best-known answer is "bed, door, window,"[21] which has such interesting variations as the Lithuanian "For whom is it easy during the day, for whom during the night, and for whom never?"[22] and "One waits for day, one waits for night, and the third says, 'It is always the same for me' ";[23] the Polish "One says, 'God give light!' The second, 'God forbid!' The third, 'As it is by day, so it is by night. My eyes are always looking' ";[24] and the perhaps fragmentary Bulgarian "One shouts, 'Let it be dark'; a second, 'Let it be light.' "[25]

Some of the parallels show more or less important modifications in detail. The Cheremiss say, "One stands, another lies, the third goes,"[26] and the Votyak express a similar conception in the riddle, "One says, 'I am going.' The second says, 'I am lying.' The third says, 'I am standing.' "[27] These have the answer, "road, block, and stump [tree trunk]." In these the riddler has altered the conception from the scene of a river to that of a road. The references to darkness and light are particularly apposite to household objects, and the riddler shows some freedom in making a choice. The Russians refer to the door, the window, and the ceiling;[28] the Serbians say, "One says, 'Make light, God!' The second says, 'Do not make light, God!' And the third says, 'Be it as it may!'—Bed, door, beams."[29] This same theme occurs in the Bulgarian "One shouts, 'Light, grow dark; Light, grow dark!' and the other, 'Dark or light, I hang and hang.'—Kettle and chain."[30] This Bulgarian riddle has only two actors, and the riddler gives an answer entirely different from any that we have met thus far. Other variations appear in the Polish "One says, 'Let me sleep!' The other says, 'It is still early.'—Bed, door"[31] and the Mordvin "They bear by day and night; they do not weary.—Legs of a

---

[17] Herskovits, 50.
[18] German: Frischbier, *Menschenwelt*, p. 246, No. 49.
[19] Czech: Erben, 19, as cited by Hanika-Otto, 3.
[20] Serbian: Karadzić, 48, as cited by Flajšhans, p. 31, § 28a.
[21] Flemish: *Ons Volksleven*, I (1889), 80, No. 51; *Volkskunde*, I (1888), 19. German: Hanika-Otto, 3. Lithuanian: Jurgelionis, 395, 396. Lettish: Ulanowska, 121. Polish: Kopernicki, 9 var.; Siarkowski, 16; Gustawicz, 62 (citing nine parallels); Saloni, *Łańcut*, 34; Saloni, *Rzeshów*,.96. Ruthenian: Kaindl, p. 320.
[22] Jurgelionis, 393.
[23] Jurgelionis, 394.
[24] Saloni, *Rzeshów*, 95. The "eyes" are the windowpanes.
[25] Palashev, 8. The answer is "door, bed."
[26] Genetz, 93.
[27] Wichmann, *Votyak*, 411.
[28] Sadovnikov, 54.
[29] Novaković, p. 104, No. 6.
[30] Gubov, 167.
[31] Gustawicz, 200.

bench,"[32] in which last the conception involves but a single group of actors with contrasting functions. The Ossete riddle for post and beam is "The one says, 'My head, my head!' The other [says], 'My back, my back!'"[33]

The typical version in which there is but a single actor may be a fragment of the original conception, as in the example last cited, or a condensation in which the three contradictory acts are ascribed to a single figure, or, finally, an entirely independent invention. A Russian description of a stove door is, for example, probably a reduction of the idea to a single actor. It is, "He works during the day, he works at night, but he sleeps in the morning."[34] Independent inventions are probably to be seen in the Korean riddle for a sheaf, "What is it that carries a load day and night?"[35] or the Zulu riddle for the closing poles of a cattle yard, "Guess ye a man who does not lie down at night; he lies down in the morning until the sun sets; he then awakes and works all night; he does not work by day; he is not seen when he works."[36]

There are, furthermore, versions with answers quite different from any that have been cited. The Russian "One says, 'Let us run!' The second says, 'Let us lie down!' The third says, 'Let us swing!'—Water, grindstone, wheel"[37] and the Polish "One begs for winter, the second begs for summer, the third says, 'Winter or summer, it is all the same to me.'—Wagon, sleigh, ax"[38] may be merely modifications of ideas already discussed. The Russian "One says, 'How to winter a winter?' The second says, 'How to summer a summer?' The third says, 'Both winter and summer bring me no change.'—Sleigh, cart, peasant"[39] exhibits a more extensive change, in the invention of the neologisms "to winter a winter" and "to summer a summer." These conceptions may be related to the Mongolian "The white one says, 'Let's go!' The black one says, 'Stay!'"[40] This employs a much-favored contrast of black and white. Finally, we can probably say that the tripartite riddle describing a spark, smoke, and ashes in terms of three contrasted persons[41] is an invention quite independent of any mentioned here.

Occasionally the three speakers prove to be animals rather than things. The Russian riddle for a horse, a cow, and a rowboat is "One says, 'Winter is good for me.' The second, 'Summer is all right.' The third, 'I am all right all the time.'"[42] An obscure Russian description of a he-goat, a ram, and a calf employs a somewhat similar device: "Three acquaintances met in the evening and I overheard their conversation. One says, 'There will be a frost.' The second, 'Perhaps, perhaps not.' And the third, 'Will it!'"[43]

---

[32] Ahlqvist, p. 41, No. 7.
[33] Schiefner, 38.
[34] Preobrazhenskii, p. 170; Arkhangel'skii, p. 77.
[35] Bernheisel, p. 62.
[36] Callaway, 8.
[37] Sadovnikov, 1107.
[38] Gustawicz, 454.
[39] Sadovnikov, 957 (with thirteen parallels, some in terms of animals). Mongolian: Zhamtsanarov, 13.
[40] Zhamtsanarov, 7.
[41] See No. 941 below.
[42] Sadovnikov, 854.
[43] Sadovnikov, 900.

In another variety of the tripartite riddle the actors appear in pairs. The themes are cosmological.[44] The Hungarians say, "Two things move, two things stand still, two things move like enemies against each other.—Heaven and earth, sun and moon, water and fire";[45] the Letts, "Two stand firm, two move constantly, two approach us, two are necessary to us.—Heaven and earth, sun and moon, darkness and light, fire and water,"[46] in which a fourth member has been introduced; and the Germans, "Two go, two stand, two always come again.—Sun and moon,"[47] which reduces the answers to the single pair characterized by the acts elsewhere applied to various objects.

The tripartite riddle has not been previously recognized as a stylistic form, and comment on it is consequently very scanty.[48]

138. Run all the time an' never get tired.—Stream.
Fauset, *Southern Negro*, p. 283, No. 77; Farr, *Tennessee*, p. 321, No. 38.

139. Go day an' night an' never get tired.—Wind.
Parsons, *Sea Islands, S.C.*, p. 160, No. 51, var. 3.

140. Is somet'in' going all day an' never get tired.—Sun.
Parsons, *Sea Islands, S.C.*, p. 160, No. 51, var. 4.

141–142. Goes Up, Never Down

141. What goes up an' never goes down?—Smoke.
Fauset, *Southern Negro*, p. 281, No. 55.

142. I know something that goes up a hill and never comes down again.—Railing [rail fence].
Parsons, *Bermuda*, p. 255, No. 66 var.

143. Runs; Does Not Run Up

"Water running uphill" is occasionally a periphrasis for "never"; see Christain Weise, *Der grünenden Jugend überflüssige Gedanken* (Neudrucke deutscher Literaturwerke des XVI. und XVII. Jahrhunderts, CCXLII–CCXLV [Halle, 1914]), p. 123 (Das Wasser wird Berg-anspatzieren, ... Wann ich mein Liebgen werde kennen); L. von Hörmann, *Schnaderhüpfeln aus den Alpen* (3d ed.; Innsbruck, 1894), p. 69, No. 187 (I werd' di' schon lieb'n, ... Wånn die Drau [a tributary of the Danube] aufwärts rinnt); W. R. S. Ralston, *Tibetan Tales* (London, 1894), p. 234; H. N. Allen, *Korean Tales* (New York, 1889), p. 132. In medieval times, it was said to be analogous to the force which saves a man from hell; see W. Grimm, *Freidanks Bescheidenheit* (Göttingen, 1834), pp. ciii–civ; Gustav Roethe (ed.), *Die Gedichte Reinmars von Zweter* (Leipzig, 1887), p. 626, note on strophe 233.

---

[44] For additional examples see Schultz, *Bemerkungen*, pp. 361–364. Rumanian: Gorovei, 1728. Russian: Sichler, p. 755. See also the headnote to Nos. 1476–1494, § 14, below.
[45] Kálmány, II, 171, No. 31.   [46] Bielenstein, 133.
[47] Frischbier, *Menschenwelt*, p. 258, No. 174.
[48] See Schultz, *Rätsel aus dem hellenischen Kulturkreise*, II, 25; Flajšhans, pp. 31–32, § 28e.

143. Dere is somet'in' runs day an' night an' never runs up.—River.
Parsons, *Antilles*, III, 432, St. Eustatius, 5.

144–173. Goes; Touches

144–146. Goes to the Water (through the Wood); Touches Water (Every Twig)

Old examples of this comparatively unimportant manner of description, which involves only a slight degree of personification, are very rare. The Renaissance riddle of the bucket which touches its bottom to the water illustrates the older, more vivid personifications and offers a contrast to the later, vaguer scenes. The theme of going about and touching is applicable to:

§ 1. A bucket and a well. See No. 144.
§ 2. Snow. See No. 145. Also see a more picturesque scene in No. 210.
§ 3. Mist. See No. 146.
§ 4. A shadow. See the headnote to No. 164, § 3.
§ 5. The sun. See the headnote to No. 164 and the notes to Nos. 164*a* and 164*b*.

144. What is it that goes to the water, and the first that touched the water is the arse?—It is a bucket or paile in a well.
Meery Riddles (1629), No. 31 = Brandl, p. 13.

145. When it through the wood doth goe, / it toucheth every twig below.— It is the snow.
Prettie Riddles (1631), No. 18 = Brandl, p. 54.

146. wᵗ is that as goes threw the wood & touches ev'y twig in the wood?— a mist in a frosty morning.
Tupper, *Holme Riddles*, 58.

147–173. Goes; Does Not Touch

In English riddling, this pattern is freely used; elsewhere, it is little favored. The rather slight degree of personification and the poor pictorial quality of th scene explain its lack of success. The idea of some person or creature going about or through a wood, which signifies a forest,[1] is found in a punning sense in the description of bark.[2] It occurs in a third sense in the Breton thread riddle, "Who goes about the wood a hundred times without touching a leaf in ts tread?"[3]—for the wood is here a spindle.

Wolfgang Schultz, who discusses the riddles using the theme of going and not touching,[4] associates them with such other themes as moving and leaving no track,[5] going about the house and entering or peeping into it,[6] and going

---
[1] No. 149.   [2] Nos. 198*a*, 198*b*.   [3] Sauvé, 92.
[4] *Rätsel aus dem hellenischen Kulturkreise*, II, 20–22.
[5] Nos. 181 through 185 below.
[6] Nos. 192*a* through 196.

without legs.[7] His cosmological interpretations lead him to give the answer "moon" to these riddles.

The theme of going about and not touching is applicable to:

§ 1. A shadow.[8] See No. 147.

§ 2. The sun.[9] See Nos. 164a, 164b, and the headnote to No. 164.

§ 3. An echo, a voice, a sound. See Nos. 149 through 159 and 161 through 163.

§ 4. The wind. See the headnote to Nos. 165–173, § 5.

§ 5. A calf in a cow's belly. See No. 160 and compare the headnote to Nos. 169–171 below.

§ 6. A penny in a purse. See No. 148.

147. Faht is't gangs our an our [o'er and o'er] the water an never touches it?—Your shadow.
Gregor, *Northeast Scotland*, p. 82.

148. w^t is that as goes throwe the woode & touches not the wood?—a penny in a mans purse.
Tupper, *Holme Riddles*, 62; *Prettie Riddles* (1631), No. 19 = Brandl, p. 54.

149. Something goes through the wood without touching it.—Echoes.
Parsons, *Bermuda*, p. 257, No. 90.

150. What goes through the woods and never touches anything?—Your echo.
Puckett, *Southern Negro*, p. 53.

151. What go through the woods an' don't touch nothing?—A voice.
Parsons, *Sea Islands, S.C.*, p. 156, No. 27, var. 3.

152a. Dere's somet'in' goin' t'rough de wood an' don' touch a limb.—Dat's yer voice.
Parsons, *Sea Islands, S.C.*, p. 156, No. 27.

152b. What goes through the wood / An' never touches a limb?—Voice.
Bacon and Parsons, *Virginia*, p. 316, No. 34.

153. Somet'in' go t'rough de branches an' never touch a limb.—Echo of your voice.
Parsons, *Sea Islands, S.C.*, p. 156, No. 27, var. 1.

154. What is that that goeth thorow the wood, and toucheth never a twig?—It is the blast of a horne or any other noyse.
Meery Riddles (1629), No. 68 = Brandl, p. 19.

155. Something goin' through the wood all day long, still can't touch a leaf.—Song of a drum.
Parsons, *Barbados*, p. 282, No. 32.

---

[7] Nos. 260 through 265.
[8] This is closely related to the description of a shadow as something that goes through water and is not wet; see the headnote to Nos. 165–173, § 3.
[9] Compare No. 1657.

156. What goes through the bush and through the bush and never touches the bush?—The tick of a watch; a watch in a man's pocket.
Waugh, *Canada*, p. 67, No. 762 and var.; Wintemberg, *Toronto*, p. 133, No. 72.

157. What goes through the bush and through the bush and never touches the bush?—The sound of a cow-bell.
Waugh, *Canada*, p. 67, No. 762.

158. Somet'in' go t'rough de bush widout touch.—Woice [voice].
Parsons, *Sea Islands, S.C.*, p. 156, No. 27, var. 2.

159. Something goes through the bushes and never touches.—Music.
Parsons, *Bermuda*, p. 257, No. 90 var.

160. Some t'ing goes through the bush an' never touches.—A calf in a cow belly.
Parsons, *Antilles*, III, 433, Saba, 5.

161. What is that which goes round the rick, and through the rick, and never touches the rick?—The sound of a bell.
Parker, *Oxfordshire*, p. 331.

162. There is something that goes through the house and never touches a thing.—Voice.
Parsons, *Bermuda*, p. 257, No. 90 var.

163. Something goes through air and never touches the earth.—Voice.
Parsons, *Bermuda*, p. 257, No. 90 var.

164. Goes; Does Not Touch the Woods (House)

These two Nova Scotian descriptions of the sun as something that does not touch the house or the woods is a somewhat inaccurate comparison of little interest or importance. They may be adaptations of riddles for a sound.[1] The usual English riddle for sunlight is of an entirely different pattern: "Hickamore Hackamore cannot be dragged off the king's kitchen door."[2]

Related descriptions of the sun, the moon, or a feather occur in continental European riddling. Such descriptions are:

§ 1. The sun goes and makes no sound.[3] See Breton: Sébillot, *Devinettes*, 3b. German: Butsch, 183; Wossidlo, 372a; Böckel, *Hesse*, 30. Swedish: Geijer and Campbell, 81; Ström, p. 206, "Solen," 10. Norwegian: Brox, *Ytre Senja*, 151, citing Riksheim, 62. French: Pineau, *Poitou*, 30. Serbian: Novaković, p. 219, Nos. 5 (The noiseless one walks through the stall), and 6 (It walks through the house and you do not hear it). Hungarian: *Magyar Nyelvör*, III (1874), 329 (It goes on the road, it doesn't make any dust; it goes on the water, it doesn't stir it up.—Sun, moon, stars); IV (1875), 282 (It crosses the bridge and doesn't make a sound; it goes on water and doesn't babble; it goes on mud and doesn't splash.—Shadow, moon); VII (1878), 476 (It goes on the

---
[1] See Nos. 149 through 159.　　[2] See Nos. 748a through 748g.
[3] The answer is "sun," unless otherwise indicated.

road, it doesn't make any dust; it goes on water, it doesn't have any foam); XVI (1887), 87 = *ibid.*, XVIII (1889), 376 (It goes on reeds and doesn't rustle; it goes on water and doesn't splash). Arabic: Stumme, *Tázerwalt*, 19, 21 (moon); Socin and Stumme, 10 (She went through the hedge without making a sound). Turkish: Kúnos, 249; Kowalski, *Asia Minor*, 19, citing parallels with the answers "mist" and "eye"; Kowalski, *Zagadki*, 113 (Without saying ćit it enters the thicket); Zavarin, *Brusa*, 9 (A man walks noiselessly into the shrubbery). Compare also the Turkish "It enters the forest and does not rustle" (Kowalski, *Zagadki*, 42) with the answers "smoke," "mist." The Arabic "He goes through the world and talks with no one.—Moon" (Stumme, *Tázerwalt*, 22) contains a better personification.

§ 2. The sun (What falls in the water and doesn't splash?). In this variety specific details suggest a specific scene. See German: Frischbier, *Menschenwelt*, p. 258, No. 175; Hanika-Otto, 84. Swiss: Rochholz, 421. Czech: Feifalik, p. 374, No. 38, and the parallels cited by Hanika-Otto in the note to her No. 84, viz., "It goes through the water and does not splash; it goes through the forest and does not rustle" (*Slavia*, I, iv [Prague, 1879], 35), and Hrnčíř, 25. Russian: Sadovnikov, 1846 (Going to the woods, it does not crackle; going by the river, it does not splash), 1846a.

The same comparison is applicable to a feather, leaf, or bit of cotton falling into water. For examples see German: Hanika-Otto, 84. Russian: Preobrazhenskii, p. 171 (The lord lorded it, he fell into the water, he did not disturb the water.—Leaf). African, Evhe: F. Müller, p. 156, No. 7 (It falls into the river, it does [not] make the sound, *Plumps!*).

§ 3. A shadow. Closely related to the preceding riddle in which water is mentioned is the shadow riddle, "It goes into the straw and does not rustle." As we have seen, the first Czech riddle quoted in § 2 combines the two themes. In general, the reference to passing through straw without rustling refers to a shadow. For examples see German: Wossidlo, 372*b*; Frischbier, *Menschenwelt*, p. 258, No. 175; Haase, *Ruppin*, 154; Renk, *Tyrol*, 120; Hanika-Otto, 148. Norwegian: Aasen, 4. Lithuanian: Schleicher, p. 208. Lettish: Bielenstein, 402, 543. Serbian: Novaković, p. xviii, No. 6 (It walks through straw, yet it doesn't rustle), and p. 206, Nos. 2 (It goes over water and doesn't make a noise; it walks over grass and does not rustle), which exemplifies once more the mingling of patterns discussed above, and 3 (It walks over straw and doesn't rustle). Hungarian: *Magyar Nyelvör*, VI (1877), 423 (It goes on sedge, it doesn't rustle; it goes on water, it doesn't splash). Arabic: Ruoff, p. 13, No. 11 (Something crosses the valley without noise); Bauer, p. 223, No. 13. Crimean Tatar: Filonenko, 79 (It passes across a fence without rustling a bit). See also the somewhat more individualized Serbian riddles for fog, "The silent one passed through the forest and yet never made a noise" (Novaković, p.

125, No. 2), and darkness, "It made neither a noise nor a clatter and entered the house" (his p. 138, No. 11).[4]

164a. What goes round the house and in the house and never touches the house?—Sun.
Fauset, *Nova Scotia*, p. 162, No. 98 var.

164b. In the woods, / Out of the woods, / And never touches the woods.—Sun.
Fauset, *Nova Scotia*, p. 162, No. 98.

165–173. Goes through (over, under) the Water;
Does Not Touch the Water

In the parallels generally, as well as in Nos. 165e, 170a, and 170b below, the formulation of the paradox may differ slightly: the object is said not to get wet. This variation does not seem to be important.

§ 1. The sun, the sun's rays, light (elaborations and additional details frequently occur). See Welsh: Hull and Taylor, 223. Welsh Gypsy: Sampson, 10. Irish: O Dalaigh, 119 (He is in a meadow but can't be cut, he is in a shop but can't be sold, he is in the river but isn't wet). Breton: Sauvé, 1 (Tell me what is on the king's plate and is not eaten, goes into the sea and is not wet, goes into the fire and is not burned.—Sun's ray). Flemish: Joos, 3, 642. German: Gilhoff, 701; Hanika-Otto, 159a; Huss, *Siebenbürgen*, 121. Norwegian: Christie, 5. Swedish: Ström, p. 205, "Solen," 7. French: Rolland, 5. Spanish: Demófilo, 847; Rodríguez Marín, p. 314, n. 5. Mallorcan: Demófilo, p. 370, No. 25. Italian: Pasquarelli, *Archivio*, XV (1896), 78, No. 29. Rumanian: Gorovei, 1872. Arabic: Löhr, p. 107, No. 17. Turkish: Kúnos, 230 (It falls into the water, it doesn't get wet). African, Galla: Cerulli, 4 (It went into everything and it caught, it went into water and it did not catch.—Fire).

For discussion see Archer Taylor, "What goes through water and is not wet?" (*Modern Language Notes*, LI [1937], 86–90). See also the description of the sun or moon as an animal that passes over water without wetting its feet (No. 431 below).

§ 2. The moon. Spanish, Argentinian: Lehmann-Nitsche, 320a through 320d. Modern Greek: Carnoy and Nicolaides, 2.

§ 3. A shadow. Irish: O Dalaigh, 113 (quoted in the headnote to Nos. 1614–1615 below), 153. Swiss: Rochholz, 565. Spanish: Demófilo, 935; Rodríguez Marín, 899. Argentinian: Lehmann-Nitsche, 107a through 107f, 320e through 320k. Chilean: Flores, 706. Dominican Rep.: Andrade, 278. New Mexican: Espinosa, 120; Campa, 89. Porto Rican: Mason, 514. Rumanian: Papahagi, 11; Gorovei, *Devinettes*, p. 505 (What stays on the water without getting wet?). Lithuanian: Jurgelionis, 1092 (It goes through fire and does not burn; it goes through water and does not drown; it goes through straw

---
[4] See also African, Bantu: Tardy, 26.

and does not rustle), 1093 (It goes through water and does not get wet; it goes through straw and does not rustle). Lettish: Bielenstein, 158, 889. Estonian: Dido, 38 (Something that cannot be wet or beaten). Gypsy: Wlislocki, 4. Arabic: Ruoff, p. 12, No. 10 (It cannot be wet or beaten). Zyrian: Wichmann, *Zyrian*, 226. Yakut: Piekarski, 59 = Priklonskii, 25 (It is black and it does not get wet in water). Indonesian, Javanese: Luinenburg, p. 27, No. 1. Malay: Harmsen, p. 277, No. 42.

§ 4. A sound. French: Rolland, 21*d*; Constantin, *Savoie*, p. 21.

§ 5. The wind. Breton: Sauvé, 2*b*. Icelandic: Árnason, 679 (Who runs over the ocean waves and crosses the sea without getting wet?). French: Fesquet, p. 176. Spanish, Cuban: Massip, 176. Lettish: Bielenstein, 771, 772. Serbian: Novaković, p. 18, No. 9 (I passed through water and did not get soaked; I passed through fire and did not burn up).

§ 6. Smoke, steam. German: Hanika-Otto, 159*d* (It goes over the brook and doesn't get wet). African, Lamba: Doke, 19 (A little thing that dresses in white calico; when it enters the water, it does not even get wet.—Steam).

§ 7. An egg in a duck's belly, an unborn calf. See Nos. 169*a* through 169*e*, 169*g* through 170*a* below.

§ 8. An eye. Spanish, Argentinian: Lehmann-Nitsche, 108 (Black, white, or blue, it goes through the river and is not wet. What is it?).

§ 9. Ice. Russian: Sadovnikov, 1496 (He neither burns in fire nor drowns in water). For the theme of not drowning see Nos. 821, 822 below.

§ 10. A name. Mordvin: Paasonen, 397 (Smaller than the smallest, a little golden firkin, it does not drown in the water nor does it burn up in the fire). The appropriateness of the comparison is somewhat obscure. The same elements appear in a Russian parallel cited in the headnote to Nos. 821–822, n. 10, below.

§ 11. A letter. Irish: Delargy, *Inis Cé*, 20. Spanish, Argentinian: Lehmann-Nitsche, 105 (It goes through water without being wet; it talks without a mouth).

165a. Under de water, / Ower de water, / Yet not touch de water.—A lady passin' ower de water wid a pail o' water on her head.
Parsons, *Bahamas*, p. 481, No. 96.

165b. Over the water and under the water and never touches the water.— a woman crossing a bridge with a pail of water on her head.
Udal, *Dorset*, p. 395; Waugh, *Canada*, p. 68, No. 786; Parsons, *Bermuda*, p. 249, No. 25 var.; Fauset, *Philadelphia*, p. 554, No. 17; Hyatt, *Adams Co.*, Ill., p. 662, No 10873.
And not touch the water: Knortz, p. 238, No. 137. An' never touch a drop: Parsons, *Aiken, S.C.*, p. 31, No. 47.

165c. A woman goes under water, / Over water, / And still not touching water.—A woman going over a bridge with a bucket of water on her head.
Burne, *Shropshire*, p. 574, No. 14. Tub of water: Parsons, *Bermuda*, p. 249, No. 25 var.

165d. Walkin' over the water, / And never touching the water.—A lady walking on the bridge, with a tub of water on her head.
Bacon and Parsons, *Virginia*, p. 313, No. 13.

165e. Under the water, / And over the water, / And still don't get vet [wet]. —A woman going over a bridge with a bucket of water on her head.
Parsons, *Bermuda*, p. 249, No. 25. A woman crossing a bridge with a tub of water on her head: Redfield, *Tennessee*, p. 40, No. 56.

165f. Over the water she walked, / Under the water she walked, / Nary a drop touched her.—Woman crossing a bridge with a bucket of water on her head.
Randolph and Taylor, *Ozarks*, 22.

165g. Above water, 'low water.—Woman with a pail of water on her head walkin' over a bridge.
Bacon and Parsons, *Virginia*, p. 313, No. 13 var.

165h. w^t is that as goes under wood to the water & under water home [MS: whome]?—a woman faching [fetching] a cruck [crock] of water.
Tupper, *Holme Riddles*, 84.

165i. A lady was walkin'. / She was under water; water was on each side of her, an' water was overhead.—A lady was walkin' across a bridge. She had a bucket of water on her head and one on each side.
Fauset, *Southern Negro*, p. 284, No. 91.

165j. Over the water and carrying water.—Girl carrying a bucket of water over a bridge.
Fauset, *Nova Scotia*, p. 162, No. 97.

166a. Oot atween two woods, and in atween two waters.—A woman going to fetch water in two wooden pails.
Gregor, *Northeast Scotland*, p. 82.

166b. I went between two woods and came home between two waters.— Going to the well with two buckets.
Green, *South Antrim*, 38.

166c. What goes away between two woods / And comes home between two waters?—Man fetching water in two pails.
Praeger, *Béaloideas*, IV (1933–1934), 144, No. 7.

167. Over water, / Under water, / Don't touch water.—A man in a boat carrying a clothes basket on his head.
Fauset, *Southern Negro*, p. 284, No. 90.

168. What goes away above the ground / And returns under it?—Man with sods on his head.
Praeger, *Béaloideas*, IV (1933–1934), 144, No. 8.

169–171. Goes through the Water; Is Not Wet: Egg in a Duck

This theme resembles that of the child that goes to town and does not see the town.[1] It is also related to the similes for the Virgin Mary, through whose body Jesus passed without harming it just as the sun's rays pass through water without being wet.[2]

169a. Water over water, / Under water, / Yet not touching the water.—Eggs inside of a duck.
Parsons, *Aiken, S.C.*, p. 31, No. 46.

169b. What goes over the water and under the water, / And never touches the water?—Egg in a duck's belly.
Greenleaf, *Newfoundland*, p. 13, No. 2; Fauset, *Nova Scotia*, p. 162, No. 96; Wintemberg, *Toronto*, p. 133, No. 74.

169c. w^t is that as goes under water & ou^r water & touches not the water.—an egge in a ducks belly.
Tupper, *Holme Riddles*, 61.

169d. Over the water and under the water and through the water, but don't touch the water.—Chicken in an egg.
Gardner, *Schoharie Hills, N.Y.*, p. 255, No. 19.

169e. Something in the water, / Something on top the water, / Something under the water, / And yet doesn't touch the water.—Egg in a duck's belly.
Parsons, *Bermuda*, p. 249, No. 24.

169f. In the water, / Out of the water, / Never touch the water.—Egg in the shell.
Bacon and Parsons, *Virginia*, p. 313, No. 14.

169g. In the water, / On top the water, / Out the water, / But does not touch the water.—Egg inside of a duck.
Bacon and Parsons, *Virginia*, p. 313, No. 15.

169h. What goes through the water and through the water and never touches the water?—An egg inside of a duck.
Green, *South Antrim*, 28; Waugh, *Canada*, p. 67, No. 763.

170a. In the water, under the water, / An' never gits wet.—Duck-egg.
Parsons, *Guilford Co., N.C.*, p. 206, No. 49.

170b. What jumps into the water and out again and don't get wet?—Egg in a duck's belly.
Fauset, *Nova Scotia*, p. 162, No. 96 var.

171. What goes over the water and under the water, / And leaves no track?—Eggs in a duck's belly.
Fauset, *Nova Scotia*, p. 162, No. 96.

---

[1] No. 711.
[2] See Wilhelm Schulze, "Das Rätsel vom trächtigen Tiere," *Ungarische Jahrbücher*, IV (1924), 20–26; Archer Taylor, "What goes through water and is not wet?" *Modern Language Notes*, LI (1937), 86–90.

172-173. Miscellaneous

A few confused riddles contain the theme of going through water without touching it. The riddler who gives the answer "nail in a ship" is clearly in error, and the answer "ship sail" is apparently a mishearing. The riddle for a watermelon (No. 173) seems to be fragmentary.

172a. In the water, / Out of the water, / Never touch the water.—Nail in the bottom of a ship.
Bacon and Parsons, *Virginia*, p. 313, No. 14.

172b. Over the water, / And under the water, / And always with its head down.—A nail in the bottom of a ship.
Halliwell-Phillipps, *Popular Rhymes*, p. 148; Knortz, p. 230, No. 78.

172c. Over the water and under the water and always with its head down.—A ship sail [a ship's nail?].
Redfield, *Tennessee*, p. 39, No. 47.

173. You go over de bridge, / Water below, / Water up top.—Watermelon on yer head.
Parsons, *Sea Islands, S.C.*, p. 166, No. 85.

174-185. Goes About; Makes a Track

The European descriptions of rain[1] going about the house and making holes do not seem to be known to English riddlers. They are allied to the theme[2] of going about the house and leaving something in the window as it is applied to snow or rain. In "What leaves tracks on the side of the road?—A cane,"[3] the Ainu have noted a physical fact not utilized by other riddlers.

174. What goes all around the house and makes just one track?—Wheelbarrow.
Fauset, *Southern Negro*, p. 282, No. 62; Parsons, *Sea Islands, S.C.*, p. 156, No. 26 and var.; Parsons, *Robeson Co., N.C.*, p. 390, No. 24; Parsons, *Guilford Co., N.C.*, p. 202, No. 9; Parsons, *Aiken, S.C.*, p. 29, No. 30; Perkins, *New Orleans*, p. 110, No. 44; Redfield, *Tennessee*, p. 38, No. 34; Bacon and Parsons, *Virginia*, p. 313, No. 12; Brewster, *Indiana*, 50; Fauset, *Philadelphia*, p. 556, No. 33; Knortz, p. 234, No. 113; Halpert, *New Jersey*, p. 202, No. 12; Parsons, *Bermuda*, p. 251, No. 38; Parsons, *Bahamas*, p. 484, No. 127; Wintemberg and Wintemberg, *Canada*, p. 123, No. 420; Fauset, *Nova Scotia*, p. 173, No. 195; Greenleaf, *Newfoundland*, p. 13, No. 39.

175. What runs all round the house and makes but one track?—Snake.
Fauset, *Nova Scotia*, p. 173, No. 195.

176. My moder had somet'in', every way it go, it leave a trackin'.—Trackin' of needle.
Parsons, *Bahamas*, p. 472, No. 14.

177. Somet'in' go all 'round the house an' don't make but two tracks.—Wagon.
Parsons, *Aiken, S.C.*, p. 29, No. 31.

---
[1] German: Hanika-Otto, 121. The answer is also "a gutter."
[2] Nos. 210a through 211 below.   [3] Starr, *Ainu*, 8.

178. What goes all round the house and makes a thousand tracks?—Green grass growing.
Fauset, *Nova Scotia*, p. 174, No. 196.

179. What goes round / An' makes a thousand tracks?—A broom.
Bacon and Parsons, *Virginia*, p. 316, No. 37.

180. Here's a thing, goes round a rick, / Makes more tracks than three-score sheep.—Hedgehog.
Cornish Notes and Queries, I (1906), 273.

181–185. Moves; Leaves No Track

The resemblance of this theme to the Biblical "There be three things which are too wonderful for me, yea four things which I know not: the way of an eagle in the air; the way of a serpent on a rock; the way of a ship in the midst of the sea; and the way of a man with a maid"[1] is obvious. A medieval Irish cleric paraphrased the passage in a riddle,[2] but except for the theme of the ship the folk has not often used these ideas. Much the same conception underlies the riddle for water, "Cut it and no mark is left,"[3] but here the comparison is to a thing and not to a living creature. In adapting the conception of a living creature that moves without leaving a trace riddlers have added details appropriate to the new answers.[4]

The description of an object as a creature moving without leaving a trace is applicable to:

§ 1. A road, a path. See Nos. 181, 182 below.

§ 2. A ship. See No. 227 and the corresponding note and headnote.

§ 3. The sun, the moon.[5] Riddlers often add such appropriate details as "it makes no hole." For example, see Danish: Kristensen, p. 123, § 343, No. 549 (What goes through a fence and makes no hole?); Feilberg, *Ordbog*, III, 458, s.v. "sol." Swedish: Johannes Sundblad, *Gammeldags Seder och Bruk* (new ed.; Stockholm, 1888), p. 131 (What pushes through the bush without making a hole?). Serbian: Novaković, p. 130, No. 5 (Our horse crossed the field and there is no trace). Votyak: Wichmann, *Votyak*, 133. Arabic: Bauer, p. 223, No. 8 (It slips into the hole but does not crumble off any dirt).

§ 4. Smoke. See No. 183 below.

§ 5. The wind. See Nos. 184a through 184c.

§ 6. Mist. Scotch Gaelic: Nicolson, p. 29 (One without virtue, strength or wile, it will traverse the ben [mountain] and its footprints can't be seen).

---

[1] Ps. 30: 18–19.
[2] Stokes, p. 134, No. 12.
[3] See one version given as No. 1665 below.
[4] For discussion see Schultz, *Rätsel aus dem hellenischen Kulturkreise*, II, 20–22.
[5] See Nos. 164a, 164b above. For a fuller personification see No. 716 below. A quite adequate personification occurs in the French "Who goes through the wood without tearing his silken robe?—Sun" (Rolland, *Rimes*, p. 197, No. 3).

Yakut: Piekarski, 26 (They say that there is one who walks without leaving a trace behind him.—Fog).

§ 7. Snow. Armenian: Seidlitz, p. 71, No. 23 (It goes and goes, but one sees no track. It runs and one sees no dust) = Blechsteiner, p. xlix, No. 12, citing a parallel in *Sbornik . . . Kavkaza*, II, No. 24, which I have been unable to find.

§ 8. Money. German: Gilhoff, 641; Wossidlo, 287 (What runs about the whole world and yet makes no track?). Compare the description of money as chips flying about.[6]

§ 9. A distaff. Faeroic: Hammershaimb, *Antiquarisk tidsskrift*, III (1849–1851), 318, No. 26 (It runs all day, no trace is seen after it).

§ 10. An arrow. African, Chinyanja: Rattray, p. 153 (Something without a spoor; what is that?).

§ 11. A flea on a dog's tail. See No. 185 below.

§ 12. Ants. Turkish: Hamizade, 336 (It has a soul, it has no blood, it goes on the road, it leaves no trace). African, Nyika: Hollis, *Nyika*, p. 137, No. 1 (Father's footprints are not visible).

181. What goes to the mill every morning and don't make no tracks?—The road.
Fauset, *Southern Negro*, p. 282, No. 64.

182. Somet'in' come to de home an' don' make no track.—Pa' [path].
Parsons, *Sea Islands, S.C.*, p. 156, No. 25.

183. Go all the way round the house, / Don't make any tracks.—Smoke.
Fauset, *Southern Negro*, p. 282, No. 63.

184a. What goes all the way around the house and doesn't make any track?—The wind.
Farr, *Tennessee*, p. 320, No. 26.

184b. Around the house, / And leaves no trail behind it.—The wind.
Chappell, p. 236, No. 37.

184c. What goes over hill and vale, / Makes a noise, but never leaves a trail?—Wind.
Hyatt, *Adams Co., Ill.*, p. 671, No. 10946.

185. What loves a dog and rides on his back; / He can travel for miles and not leave a track?—Flea on a dog's tail.
Hyatt, *Adams Co., Ill.*, p. 660, No. 10857.

186. Goes without a Shadow

The English riddler applies this idea to the description of the wind, but the usual answer is "sound" or "voice."[1]

---

[6] See the headnote to No. 1605, n. 2, below.

[1] An early instance is Claret's fourteenth-century versification of this idea: "Quid volitans umbra careat: vocem bene signa" (p. 68, No. 12). For modern examples see

186. What can pass before the sun without making a shadow?—The wind.
Knortz, p. 234, No. 104.

187–189. Goes on Its Head

This old and widely known description of a nail in a man's shoe or in a horseshoe occurs in the early medieval collection of Symphosius: "Upon my head I walk, because I hang from a single foot. With my top I touch the ground and leave behind me headprints, but many comrades suffer the same lot."[1] The degree of personification varies, but rarely attains to such picturesqueness as in the Scandinavian "Four and twenty young women gallop on their heads down the road"[2] or the Russian "I walk on my head, even though I am on foot; I walk barefoot even though shod with boots."[3] I have noted no parallel to the theme of the Swedish "Everyone walks on my head, yet I hold myself erect"[4] or the Breton "Who walks on his head and is not tired at night?"[5] The notion of walking on one's head occurs in a few contaminated versions of the nail riddle[6] and is also entangled with riddles for milk,[7] a shoe,[8] and a cowbell.[9] A somewhat similar notion occurs in the French description of a wheelbarrow: "What is a thing that walks on its head to save its feet?"[10]

187a. It goes all over the mountains on its head, / And it sleeps on its head.—A horseshoe nail.
Farr, *Tennessee*, p. 323, No. 78.

187b. What is it that goes to the water on the head?—It is a horse-shoe naile.
Meery Riddles (1629), No. 30 = Brandl, p. 13.

187c. Whut is it gallops down th' road on its head?—A horse-shoe nail.
Randolph and Spradley, *Ozark*, p. 81.

Breton: Sauvé, 15; Le Chef, *Ille-et-Vilaine*, p. 668; Kerbeuzec, *Ille-et-Vilaine*, 69. Flemish: Joos, 679. Walloon: Colson, *Wallonia*, V, 130, No. 268; Colson, *Devinettes*, 1. French: Rolland, 21a through 21g; Bladé, *Armagnac*, 81; Lacuve, *Poitou*, p. 702, No. 6; Lallemant, *Argonne*, p. 234; Carmeau, p. 33; V. S., *Mélusine*, I (1878), col. 254, No. 1 = Marchessou, *Velay et Auvergne*, p. 172, No. 1; Westphalen, *Metz*, col. 201; Constantin, *Savoie*, p. 33, De la Suie, *Savoie*, p. 472. Spanish, Argentinian: Lehmann-Nitsche, 109. Dominican Rep.: Andrade, 308. Italian: Pitrè, 911 (voice). Turkish: Hamizade, 605 (From the valley to over yonder a shadowless fellow passes.—Voice).

[1] Ohl, 57.
[2] Swedish: Dybeck, *Runa*, 1849, p. 48, No. 18; Geijer and Campbell, 19; Ström, p. 144, "Hästskosömmen." Danish: Feilberg, *Ordbog*, IV, 881, s.v. "träskosöm." Norwegian: Bugge, *Telemarken*, 14, 15.
[3] Sadovnikov, 654.
[4] Ström, p. 151, "Spiken," 2.
[5] Sébillot, *Devinettes*, 57.
[6] See Nos. 172a, 172b above.
[7] Compare No. 187a with Nos. 447, 449a through 451b, 452.
[8] Compare No. 189 with Nos. 445a, 455b, 453a through 453c, 453e, 453f, 454a through 454c, 456a, 456b.
[9] Compare No. 187b with Nos. 246 and 247a through 253.
[10] V. S., *Mélusine*, I (1878), col. 254, No. 6.

187d. What is it that gangs w'its hehd down.—A nail in a horse's shoe.
Gregor, *Northeast Scotland*, p. 82; Waugh, *Canada*, p. 68, No. 784. Walks with its head on the ground: Fauset, *Nova Scotia*, p. 173, No. 193 var. Your shoe: Gardner, *Schoharie Hills, N.Y.*, p. 258, No. 54.

188a. What goes to church with you upside down an' anywhere else?—Tacks in your shoes.
Fauset, *Southern Negro*, p. 283, No. 72.

188b. Goes upstairs and downstairs and always on its head.—Nail in a shoe.
Fauset, *Nova Scotia*, p. 173, No. 193.

188c. What goes upstairs on its head?—A shoe-tack.
Farr, *Tennessee*, p. 323, No. 71.

188d. What is it always walks with its head down?—Nail in your boot.
Praeger, *Béaloideas*, IV (1933–1934), 144, No. 4.

189. What walks on its head all day and sits in the house at night?—A shoe-tack.
Redfield, *Tennessee*, p. 39, No. 39.

190. Carries His Way on His Neck (Shoulders)

The snail riddle, on the theme of carrying a house on one's back (No. 727 below) may have suggested this conception.

190a. What is that goeth to the wood, and carieth his way on his necke?—It is a man that goeth to the wood to fell boughes, and carrieth a ladder to get up.
Meery Riddles (1629), No. 44 = Brandl, p. 15.

190b. When we by the way do goe, / upon our shoulders we beare our way; / if we were not, then many should be / wet to the skin in a rayny day.—Masons, tilers, and men of such like occupation carrying ladders upon their shoulders to build and tile houses.
Prettie Riddles (1631), No. 50 = Brandl, p. 59.

191–197. Goes; Sees

191. Goes to the Wood; Looks Homeward

Although this simple paradox is scarcely known in English riddling, it has enjoyed a noteworthy popularity in continental Europe, where an instance is found as early as the fourteenth century. At that time Claret wrote in Bohemia, "Sic ex urbe means retro spectat: acuta securis."[1] The scenes of this sort are often vividly and picturesquely portrayed. In Danzig, for example, the Germans describe a dog as "A wagon goes to the field, its tongue [i.e., the dog's tail] is toward the village."[2] Similarly, the Czechs see a jackdaw as

---
[1] P. 71, No. 68.
[2] Schmidt, *Danzig*, 51.

"A peasant goes to the wood; the tongue [of the wagon] peeps out of the wood, and when the peasant goes out of the wood, it peeps into the wood."[3] The converse of such comparisons of an animal to a wagon and its tongue appears in the Czech comparison of a plow to a cow: "We have a cow. Whenever it goes to the field, it points its horns to the barnyard, and whenever it comes from the barnyard, it points its horns to the field."[4]

Descriptions in terms of an animal, a person, or a thing who or which goes in one direction and looks or points in another are applicable to many objects. Those in which the personification is rather fully developed are exemplified by a riddle for climbing a coconut palm.[5] Typical themes are:

§ 1. Tools which are carried on the shoulder and hang over the back or have projections. Ax. See Nos. 191a, 191b below. PITCHFORK. Danish: Kristensen, p. 32, § 71, Nos. 91a through 91c. Serbian: Novaković, p. 183, No. 4. SCYTHE. Lithuanian: Jurgelionis, 606, 607. Polish: Saloni, Rzeshów, 79. HORN. Serbian: Novaković, p. 194, No. 3. PLOW. German: Hanika-Otto, 155. Danish: Kristensen, p. 102, § 273, Nos. 426a through 426d; DFS, 1906/38: T. Gravlund, 1917, No. 3. Czech: Hanika-Otto, note to Nos. 82, 83. Polish: Gustawicz, 328. Serbian: Novaković, p. 170, Nos. 6, 7, and p. 183, No. 4. POLE OF A CART. Turkish: Moshkov in Radlov, X, 270, No. 70, quoted in § 10 below.

§ 2. A knapsack. Russian: Sadovnikov, 688. Votyak: Wichmann, *Votyak*, 286.

§ 3. A gun. Serbian: Novaković, p. 182, No. 11 (When going into the forest, it looks homeward), and p. 183, Nos. 1 through 3. Baluchi: M. L. Dames, *Panjab Notes and Queries*, II (1885), 70, No. 423, § 5 (The camp is marching, but his face is backward).

§ 4. A goat. Basque: Cerquand, 17, 35, 46; Vinson, 2. Spanish: Demófilo, 182, and also p. 340, No. 3, and p. 382, No. 5. Argentinian: Lehmann-Nitsche, 125. Abchaz: Guliia, 17 (When they are going into the wood, they look backwards. When they go home, they look to the wood). Abyssinian: Littmann, *Tigriña*, 14 (When they go to the field, they say, "Homewards, homewards," and when they come home, they say, "To the field, to the field").

§ 5. A dog. See the German version quoted above.

§ 6. A horse. Danish: DFS, 1906/38: T. Gravlund, 1917, p. 1, No. 4, and S. Steffensen, 1919, No. 1 (What goes to the field and turns its apron homewards?). Catalan: Pelay y Briz, 88.

Eastern riddlers have a similar conception for the fetlocks of a horse. See the White Russian "Four old men with their beards on backwards" (Jurke-

---
[3] Hanika-Otto, note to Nos. 82, 83.
[4] Hrnčíř, 144, as cited in Hanika-Otto, note to her Nos. 82, 83.
[5] See Nos. 724a through 724c.

vich, p. 293). Russian: Sadovnikov, 853. Mordvin: Paasonen, 194 (Four old men with their beards on their backs). Cheremiss: Wichmann, *Cheremiss*, 17. Turcoman: Samojlvich, 104 (Four Sarts have beards behind).

§ 7. A magpie. Czech: Erben, p. 15, cited by Hanika-Otto in the note to her Nos. 82, 83.

§ 8. The calf of the leg. This usually occurs in the form "His back is in front, his stomach behind" and is therefore rather a description of a man's figure than of his manner of looking. The shinbone suggests the back or spinal column. See Breton: Le Pennec, 27 (Who has his belly in his back?). Swedish: Russwurm, *Eibo*, p. 135, § 316, No. 40. French: Lespy, *Béarn*, 16; Bladé, *Armagnac*, 96. Basque: Cerquand, 49; Vinson, 77. Portuguese: Parsons, *Cape Verde*, 222, 223. Lettish: Bielenstein, 328, 329. Serbian: Novaković, p. 116, No. 2 (It goes from the farm and turns its belly to the house). Finnish: Lönnrot, 883 = Henssen, 129. Estonian: Gutsleff, *Anweisung zur ehstnischen Sprache* (Halle, 1732), 65, cited by Russwurm, 93; Lönnrot, p. 186; Wiedemann, p. 277. Svanian: J. Nizheradze, pp. 66–67, No. 3 (It has its back in front and its stomach behind). Abchaz: Guliia, 19 (In front, you have a back; behind, you have a stomach). Arabic: Giacobetti, 299; Ruoff, p. 19, No. 22. Crimean Tatar: Filonenko, 101 (Seen from the front, it's a back; seen from behind, it's a belly). Yakut: Piekarski, 38 (A calf with its belly backward), 165 (They say that there is a child with its stomach in its rear); Popov, p. 286 (Children are running but their stomachs are behind). Tungus: Poppe, 4 (A little Oročon's belly [is turned] backward). The Oročon, or reindeer men, are a Tungus tribe. African, Kxatla: Schapera, 81. Bakongo: Denis, 9. Kundu: Ittmann, *Kundu*, p. 180, No. 269. Indian, Baiga: Elwin, p. 477, No. 128 (Why do you look backwards as you go?—A man has struck his foot against a stone). Indonesian, Javanese: Luinenburg, p. 29, No. 10; Malay: Tauern, *Patasiwa*, p. 70. Filipino: Starr, *Philippines*, 65. Korean: Bernheisel, p. 61.

§ 9. The heel. This is probably a variety of the preceding riddle. See German: Feifalik, *Zeitschrift für deutsche Mythologie*, IV (1859), 375, No. 77; Renk, *Tyrol*, 145; Hanika-Otto, 83. Danish: Kristensen, p. 136, § 395, No. 628 (shoe). The Basque answer "one's back" (Cerquand, 49) seems to arise from a confusion which has transferred part of the riddle to the answer. Czech: Hrnčiŕ, 106, cited by Hanika-Otto in the note to her Nos. 82, 83. African, Kundu: Ittmann, *Kundu*, p. 178, No. 206 (I keep going, but I am never in front).

§ 10. A wagon, a railroad train. Turkish: Kowalski, *North Bulgaria*, 17; Moshkov in Radlov, X, 270, No. 70 (I have an ox. When he goes to the field, he looks toward the village; when he goes to the village, he looks toward the field.—Pole laid lengthwise in a cart). In Béarn, the French ingeniously adapt this idea to describe a two-wheeled cart: "When it goes to the wood, it looks at the house from the side" (Lespy, *Béarn*, 19). In the somewhat more fully developed personification of No. 722 below, the idea of going in one direction and looking in another applies to a railroad train.

§ 11. Climbing a tree. See Nos. 724a through 724c.

§ 12. A horseshoe. Welsh: Hull and Taylor, Nos. 28 through 30. Modern Greek: Polites, *Neohellenika Analekta*, I, 225, No. 181 (There is something that goes along and turns to look behind).

§ 13. A watch. Welsh: Hull and Taylor, 31. Welsh Gypsy: Sampson, 40.

Some related riddles for an ax are conceived with admirable ingenuity, as in the Lithuanian and Russian comparisons to a dog, "It bends and bends; it comes home and stretches out,"[6] the clever French "It enters the wood before its master,"[7] and the much elaborated Cheremiss and Zyrian "It goes into the wood. It looks homeward. In the wood it barks. It goes home. While going, it looks into the wood. When arrived home, it lies down under the bench."[8]

Russian riddlers make excellent comparisons of a girl and an ax, as in "With her face to the wall, with her back to the household"[9] and "A beauty reposes with her face under the bench."[10]

191a. what is that as goes to the wood & yet looks home [MS: whome]?—hachet on [MS: one] a mans shoulder.
Tupper, *Holme Riddles*, 63.

191b. What is it goeth to the wood and his head home ward?—It is an axe hanging upon a man's backe, when he goth to the wood.
Meery Riddles (1629), No. 43 = Brandl, p. 15.

191c. When I to the wood do goe, / then my head homewards I doe show.—It is an axe.
Prettie Riddles (1631), No. 52 = Brandl, p. 59.

192–197. Goes about the House; Goes (Peeps) In

Riddlers have adapted this pattern, which seems to be especially favored in English tradition, to describe such natural phenomena as sunlight, wind, and smoke. Wolfgang Schultz, who discusses it at some length,[1] thinks that the "true" answer is "moon." "False" answers have, he maintains, disguised the original cosmological import. A description of a wheelbarrow[2] partakes of this pattern but is not completely intelligible. The Ainu "What is it that runs around the house?—A log"[3] probably refers to a log in the wall of a log cabin.

---

[6] Lithuanian: Jurgelionis, 431. Russian: Sadovnikov, 4.
[7] Rolland, 213.
[8] Cheremiss: Genetz, 23. Zyrian: Wichmann, *Zyrian*, 290. For comparisons of an ax to a barking dog, see the headnote to Nos. 438–444, § 7, below.
[9] Sadovnikov, 1.
[10] Sadovnikov, 2. Zyrian: Wichmann, *Zyrian*, 3, 142.
[1] *Rätsel aus dem hellenischen Kulturkreise*, II, 20–22.
[2] No. 225 below.   [3] Starr, *Ainu*, 54.

192a. In at a window when I doe looke (beat not your braine long about this), / then in the house about I goe. / Now tell me quickly what it is.—The shining of the sunne.
Prettie Riddles (1631), No. 16 = Brandl, p. 54.

192b. Round and round the house / And in my lady's chamber.—The sun.
Gutch and Peacock, *Lincolnshire*, p. 398, No. 9.

192c. It goes round and round the house, and peeks in every window.—A sunbeam.
Wintemberg and Wintemberg, *Canada*, p. 123, No. 421.

192d. What goes roun' the house an' roun' the house an' peeps in every wee hole?—Sun.
Green, *South Antrim*, 37.

192e. Round the house and round the house / And peeps in every corner.—The sun.
Greenleaf, *Newfoundland*, p. 9, No. 12 var.

193a. Something goes round and round the house, peeps in every crack, yet no one sees it. What is it?—The wind.
Knortz, p. 213, No. 7.

193b. Round the house, and round the house, / And peeps in every crack.—Wind.
Gardner, *Schoharie Hills, N.Y.*, p. 256, No. 29.

194–197. Goes through the Keyhole

194. It goes round and round the house, and in at the keyhole.—A sunbeam.
Burne, *Shropshire*, p. 574, No. 11.

195. Goes all around the house / And peeps in at the keyhole.—Wind.
Brewster, *Indiana*, 53.

196. It goes round and round the house, and out through the keyhole.—Smoke,—made when there were no chimneys.
Burne, *Shropshire*, p. 574, No. 12.

197. Something goes through a keyhole / Where nothing else can go through.—Key.
Knortz, p. 218, No. 26.

198–202. Comes to the House (Wood); Does Not Enter

This characteristically English description of a road may be compared to the more adequately personified descriptions in which a road or path is a messenger who sleeps out at night.[1] The conception of a road as something that does not enter the house, although it comes to the very door, is not often found outside the sphere of English riddling.

---

[1] See No. 688.

Typical themes to which this riddle pattern have been applied are as follows:

§ 1. The bark on a tree. See Nos. 198a, 198b.
§ 2. A road, a path. See Nos. 199a through 200d.
§ 3. A fence. See No. 201.
§ 4. A broom handle. See No. 202.
§ 5. A gutter. Flemish: Joos, 40 (It constantly runs around the house and says *Trip! Trap!* and never comes into the house). Walloon: Colson, *Wallonia*, IV, 146, No. 146.
§ 6. A door. Mordvin: Paasonen, 132 (It looks into the room, but does not step in). This conception is closely allied to the description of the door or window as being neither inside nor outside the house.[2]

198a. What is that goeth about the wood and cannot get in?—It is the barke of a tree; for never is the barke within the tree but alwayes without.
Meery Riddles (1629), No. 58 = Brandl, p. 18.

198b. What goes round the wood and round the wood and never gets into the wood?—Bark of the tree.
Praeger, *Béaloideas*, IV (1933–1934), 146, No. 28.

199a. Somet'in' goin' up to de step an' never come in.—Path.
Parsons, *Sea Islands, S.C.*, p. 155, No. 23; Parsons, *Aiken, S.C.*, p. 26, No. 9, var. 1.

199b. What come up to de do' but don' come in?—De pat' (i.e., path).
Johnson, *St. Helena Island, S.C.*, p. 158, No. 12.

200a. What is it from house to house and never come in?—Road (path).
Fauset, *Southern Negro*, p. 283, No. 76; Parsons, *Aiken, S.C.*, p. 26, No. 9 and varr.; Bacon and Parsons, *Virginia*, p. 322, No. 88.

200b. Goin' to everybody's house, / An' didn' go in.—Path.
Parsons, *Guilford Co., N.C.*, p. 202, No. 12.

200c. Something goes round and round the house and never comes in the room.—Road.
Parsons, *Bermuda*, p. 264, No. 155.

200d. What goes all the way 'round the house an' never come in?—Path.
Parsons, *Robeson Co., N.C.*, p. 390, No. 25; Parsons, *Aiken, S.C.*, p. 26, No. 9.

201. Something goes all around your house and never comes in. Guess what it is.—A fence.
Parsons, *Sea Islands, S.C.*, p. 156, No. 24.

202. All round the house, and never come in.—Broom-handle.
Bacon and Parsons, *Virginia*, p. 312, No. 3, var. 1.

---

[2] See below, Nos. 1423a through 1423c and the headnote to No. 1423.

203–213. Goes About; Leaves Something

203. Goes About; Leaves Its Tail Behind

Riddlers often describe a needle and thread as an animal or a person dragging a tail which may be caught in a crack. In this section I have included only those versions in which the creature is not identified. Note such elaborations or variations of the fundamental idea as the Hungarian "The shining one goes ahead, the little white one follows it, and its tail has been tied up";[1] the Modern Greek "They call her 'Little Silent' and tie her up by her tail";[2] and the French "The more it walks, the shorter its tail,"[3] which suggests somewhat the riddles involving a contradiction between the act and its result.[4]

Comparisons of a needle and thread to an animal and its tail are abundant. Typical animals in this use are a bird,[5] a pig,[6] and a horse,[7] but the obvious comparison to a snake is rather rare, although examples are very widely distributed. See the Lappish "A snake going through the grass, and its tail moves behind it";[8] the Turkish "The snake glides; the thong goes on";[9] the Kxatla "Tell me: a snake which when its tail is removed cannot walk";[10] and the Filipino "He pulled out a stick and it was followed by a snake,"[11] which is perhaps conceived as a reversal of nature.

Some miscellaneous comparisons to animals may be briefly noted. The Irish compare a needle and thread to a cow coming out of a crack and leaving a bit of its tail behind,[12] and the Uraon in Chota Nagpur, to an elephant, "The body of the elephant is inside, but its tail is outside."[13] A related Modern Greek version, "I bore holes that do not show. I leave my tail behind and it shows,"[14] is a very unusual conception. Some riddlers call a needle and thread a person,[15] or invent still other comparisons.[16]

203a. Through the hedge and through the hedge and takes a long tail behind it.—A needle.
Leather, *Hereford*, p. 230.

203b. What jumps over a fence / and leaves his tail behind him?—Needle and thread.
Parsons, *Aiken, S.C.*, p. 37, No. 88.

---

[1] *Magyar Nyelvör*, III (1874), 328.
[2] Polites, *Neohellenika Analekta*, I, 232, No. 227.
[3] Parsons, *Antilles*, III, 389, Martinique, 130.
[4] See the headnote to chapter xi and the headnote to Nos. 1681–1703 below.
[5] No. 351.
[6] No. 386.
[7] Nos. 421 through 424 and No. 426.
[8] Qvigstad, 37.
[9] Menges, p. 86, No. 16.
[10] Schapera, 112.
[11] Starr, *Philippines*, 186.
[12] Christiansen, 85.
[13] Archer, p. 189, No. 186. For a similar theme see the headnote to Nos. 412–413 below.
[14] Stathes, p. 348, No. 103.
[15] Nos. 531 through 536b below.
[16] For a survey of the various types of comparisons, see the headnotes to Nos. 205–207, 419–435, and 531–534.

203c. Somet'in' goin' t'rough a crack an' always leavin' a tail behin'.—Dat's a needle.
Parsons, *Sea Islands, S.C.*, p. 157, No. 35, var. 2.

204. Walks; Drops a Piece

204. There is a long thing walkin' / With a long tail, / An' as long as it walk / It drop piece.—Needle with the cotton.
Parsons, *Barbados*, p. 277, No. 3 var.

205–207. Goes About; Leaves Its Entrails Behind

Riddlers often elaborate this concept by naming a particular animal as the actor. Examples are found almost exclusively in regions where European influences have been dominant, but the fundamental idea is readily hit upon. Compare, as examples, the Russian description of a clock, "The heath hen sits upon a tree. Its bowels hang down until they reach the ground,"[1] which compares the dangling pendulum to bowels, and an English riddle for a gun.[2]

This manner of description is most frequently used for:

§ 1. A needle and thread. See No. 205a through 205e.

§ 2. A hen and chickens. See No. 206a, 206b.

§ 3. A pillowcase. See Nos. 207a, 207b. An early example of this is seen in Claret's fourteenth-century "Quid sine ventre venit ad aquam: plumen bene solvit" (p. 73, No. 100).

§ 4. A hook and line. Hawaiian: Judd, 92 (My little hunchback with long intestines).

§ 5. A key. Breton: Charlec, *Dol-de-Bretagne*, 1904, p. 378, No. 43 (Who goes to the fair and leaves his mouth at home?). French: Rolland, 143. This involves a pun on *trou*, signifying both "mouth" and "keyhole."

§ 6. A jar. Breton: Sébillot, *Devinettes*, 44 (pot). Danish: Kristensen, p. 21, § 45, No. 56 (What goes to Kros and forgets its entrails at home?).

§ 7. A horse and reins. Norwegian: Berge, 12 (What goes to the brook to drink and drags its guts after it?). This is also closely allied to the riddles for a bridle[3] and a bell.[4]

More vividly conceived versions of the riddle for needle and thread, of which these modern English texts may be weakened forms, name a particular animal.[5] The New Mexican Spanish "Entering and leaving and entrails hanging"[6] is also a vaguely conceived scene. Riddlers occasionally make a comparison to a person with dangling intestines, as in the Modern Greek "My Aunt Nicole with intestines at the back";[7] the Indonesian "A little child whose entrails hang out";[8] and a Batak description of an old woman.[9] The

---

[1] Sadovnikov, 283.
[2] Nos. 1266a, 1266b, below.
[3] No. 248.
[4] Nos. 247a through 247c, 252a, 252b.
[5] See the English comparison to a horse in No. 423.
[6] Campa, 119.
[7] Stathes, p. 340, No. 52.
[8] Holle, *Soenda*, p. 372, No. 15.
[9] Ophuijsen, p. 213, No. 37. See also Spanish, New Mexican: Campa, 104.

French "At every step it leaves a little"[10] is probably related to the same theme.[11] Perhaps these ideas, and particularly the last one, have proved too coarse for common use in English folklore, in which the usual metaphorical concept for a needle is an animal or a person with a dragging tail.[12]

205a. What goes t'rough de water an' leave he guts behin' 'em?—Needle.
Parsons, *Sea Islands, S.C.*, p. 157, No. 35, var. 1.

205b. Go t'rough a tree an' leave 'e guts behin'.—Needle an' t'read t'rough de cloth.
Johnson, *St. Helena Island, S.C.*, p. 157, No. 7.

205c. w^t is that as goes throw the heye [hedge?] & leves his gutes after it?— a neele and thride.
Tupper, *Holme Riddles*, 59.

205d. What is that goes through thicke and thin, and drawes his guts after him?—It is an needle that goeth through thicke and thin cloth, drawing the thred after it, which is taken for the guts.
Meery Riddles (1629), No. 61 = Brandl, p. 18.

205e. There is something dragging white guts all day.—Needle wid a t'read.
Parsons, *Antilles*, III, 441, Anguilla, 29.

206. What goes around the house all day / And drags her guts after?—A hen and little chickens.
Chappell, p. 230, No. 8.

207a. What is it that goeth to the water and leaveth his guts at home?— It is a pillow-beere; for when it goeth to washing, the pillow and the feathers bee left at home.
Meery Riddles (1629), No. 29 = Brandl, p. 13.

207b. When I doe goe to the water's side, / at home I'le leave my heart behind. / Tell me what I am without pride, / if it by any meanes you finde.— It is pillow-beare.
Prettie Riddles (1631), No. 71 = Brandl, p. 62.

208-209. Goes About; Leaves Cap (Rags)

A similar conception occurs in the Votyak riddle for a bald head, "On a post [lies] wheat dough,"[1] and is adapted to a table in the Vogul "In the room there sits a man with a silken kerchief."[2]

208. Goes all over the fields and leaves a white cap on every stump.—Snow.
Brewster, *Indiana*, 31.

---

[10] Dardy, *L'Albret*, p. 331.
[11] No. 204 above and the headnote to No. 418 below.
[12] See Nos. 203a through 203c.
[1] Buch, p. 101, No. 44.
[2] Ahlqvist, *Vogul*, p. 127, No. 7.

209. Throo the woods, and throo the woods, / And throo the woods I ran; / And every bus' that I cam' till, / I left my rags and ran.—A sheep leaving wool on every thorn.
Findlay, *Edinburgh*, p. 59.

210–213. Goes around House; Leaves a Glove

English riddlers of the seventeenth century know the description of snow as a person who goes around the house and leaves a white glove. Both in this form and with changes in the color of the glove to adapt the comparison to frost, rain, and sunlight the riddle has maintained itself to the present time. It is curious to note that a riddle which has been relatively popular in English tradition lacks parallels in continental Europe. Compare the descriptions of snow conceived as a cap or a rag.[1]

210a. ther is a thing that goes rou[n]d about the house and laves his gloves in the window.—snow.
Tupper, *Holme Riddles*, 43.

210b. Round the house and round the house, / And leaves a white glove i' th' window.—Snow.
Gutch and Peacock, *Lincolnshire*, p. 398, No. 7; Burne, *Shropshire*, p. 574, No. 10; Waugh, *Canada*, p. 70, No. 802; Fauset, *Nova Scotia*, p. 161, No. 93 var.; Randolph and Spradley, *Ozark*, p. 82. An' throw white gloves in the winder: Parsons, *Guilford Co., N.C.*, p. 206, No. 54; Gardner, *Schoharie Hills, N.Y.*, p. 256, No. 28. Drop a white glove in the window: Newell, p. 158.

210c. Round the house and over the house / And sticks a white glove in the window.—Snow.
Hudson, p. 90, No. 47.

210d. Go all around the house and put a white sheet in the window.—Snow.
Bacon and Parsons, *Virginia*, p. 322, No. 90.

211. Round the house and the round the house, / And leaves a black glove i' th' window.—Rain.
Gutch and Peacock, *Lincolnshire*, p. 398, No. 8 = E. Peacock, *A Glossary of Words Used in the Wapentakes of Manley and Cunningham* (2d ed.; English Dialect Society, LVIII; London, 1890), p. 51; Fauset, *Nova Scotia*, p. 161, No. 93; Gardner, *Schoharie Hills, N.Y.*, p. 256, No. 27; Parsons, *Bermuda*, p. 252, No. 46 and var.

212. Round the house and round the house, / There lies a white glove in the window.—Sunshine.
Parsons, *Bermuda*, p. 252, No. 46 var.

213. Around the house, around the house, / And a white glove in the window.—Frost.
Fauset, *Nova Scotia*, p. 161, No. 93.

---

[1] See especially No. 210d and the riddles cited in the note to No. 208.

214. Goes around House; Drags a Harrow

214a. What goes around the house with a harrow after it?—A hen with a flock of chickens.
Green, *South Antrim*, 10.

214b. What goes round the house and round the house and a harrow after it?—Hen with chickens.
Praeger, *Béaloideas*, IV (1933–1934), 144, No. 5.

215. Swims; Does Not Sink

The riddler has not clearly conceived the creature that he is describing. Somewhat more clearly conceived versions of related riddles may be found in Nos. 821 and 822 below.

215. Something swim on the water and never go bottom. When I get my full, I go bottom.—Answer lacking.
Parsons, *Sea Islands, S.C.*, p. 160, No. 47.

216–222. Minor Varieties of Moving

216. Goes to the door and doesn't knock, / Goes to the window and doesn't rap, / Goes to the fire and doesn't warm, / Goes upstairs and does no harm.—The sun.
Parker, *Oxfordshire*, p. 330.

217. Can run, but can't walk.—A train.
Bacon and Parsons, *Virginia*, p. 312, No. 4.

218. Runs smoother than any rhyme, / Loves to fall but cannot climb.—Water.
Hyatt, *Adams Co., Ill.*, p. 670, No. 10940.

219. What's goin' 'roun' cleanin' up de earth?—Buzzards.
Parsons, *Sea Islands, S.C.*, p. 171, No. 139.

220. Runs and jumps, stops and humps.—A rabbit.
Farr, *Tennessee*, p. 321, No. 44.

221. If deh a hun'ed room, 'e go t'rough 'em all.—Broom.
Johnson, *St. Helena Island, S.C.*, p. 57, No. 9.

222. My father have a thing in his yard and he run from yard to yard.—Dog.
Beckwith, *Jamaica*, p. 184, No. 8.

223–228. Seeing

223. Something looks at you and you can't look at that.—Death.
Parsons, *Bermuda*, p. 264, No. 150.

224. What is it that standeth on this side of the woode, and looketh over the wood?—It is a sow, that hath a yoke about her necke; for [her] feete be on this side the wood, and her head is over the wood.
Meery Riddles (1629), No. 42 = Brandl, p. 15.

225. Round the house, and round the house, / In every window seen around.
—Wheelbarrow.
Gardner, *Schoharie Hills, N.Y.*, p. 256, No. 30.

226. Is Not Seen

The conception does not clearly suggest personification and perhaps on that account has not found very wide use. Some related ideas are discussed in the following headnote. A possibly related theme is the Indonesian smoke riddle, "What is seen but not felt?"[1]

The notion of coming and going unseen is applicable to:

§ 1. The wind. See Nos. 226a, 226b.

§ 2. The breath. Lappish: Qvigstad, 120. Compare Nos. 1578a through 1578c below.

§ 3. A sound. Breton: Orain, *Ille-et-Vilaine*, p. 151 (sound of bells). Russian: Sichler, p. 119 (echo). Mordvin: Paasonen, 5, 6 (thunder). Arabic: Ruoff, p. 11, No. 1 (thunder).

§ 4. A road. Spanish, Argentinian: Lehmann-Nitsche, 122.

§ 5. Heat, cold. Zyrian: Wichmann, *Zyrian*, 5 (In every room an invisible thing.—Warmth), 52 (You can see everything but two sorts of things you do not see.—Heat, cold), 252. Mordvin: Paasonen, 131. See a Finnish riddle cited in the note to No. 183 of the present collection.

226a. Something comes and goes you never see.—Wind.
Parsons, *Bermuda*, p. 256, No. 75.

226b. The house is full of it and you can't see it.—Wind.
Fauset, *Southern Negro*, p. 281, No. 52.

227. Cannot See

Although the following riddle seems to say that a vessel cannot see where it goes, the parallels do not support the obvious interpretation of the text. We should probably emend it by inserting "you" before "can't." The parallels employ the theme that a ship leaves no track or that one cannot see where it has passed over. This theme is at least as old as the proverbs of Solomon.[1] Symphosius has a similar idea in "Long, swift daughter of the forest am I borne along, with an innumerable throng of companions equally encompassed; I speed over many paths, leaving not a trace behind."[2]

The ocean or sea is called a path in many contexts, from the Old English kennings *seglrād* (sail road),[3] *swanrād* (swan road),[4] and *hronrād* (whale road)[5]

---

[1] Malay: Harmsen, p. 277, No. 43.
[1] 30:19. See Denis Buzy, C.S.J., "Les machals numériques de la sangsue et de l'almah," *Revue biblique*, XLII (1935), 5–13.
[2] No. 13. See Ohl's explanatory comment.
[3] *Beowulf*, v. 1429.   [4] *Beowulf*, v. 200.   [5] *Beowulf*, v. 10.

to the Votyak "track of the good horse"[6] and the Louyi "One does not see its track.—A boat? No! The insect *muondu*."[7] The Yakut conceive the scene very picturesquely: "They say that a dappled mare does not leave any hoofprints behind her";[8] "They say that you cannot see the hoofprints of a dappled stallion, which is without legs, yet walks, so they say";[9] "They say that there is a gray horse[10] whose hoofprints are not visible."[11]

Some riddlers, especially members of tribes living in Russia, add the remark that the path (i.e., the creature) does not bleed when cut. They are comparing the strokes of the oars to chopping flesh. See the following examples: "I ride, I ride, there's no trace. I cut, I cut, there is no blood."[12] Also see "If it goes, there is no path. If one cuts off its neck, there is no blood."[13] This is virtually the same as "There is no road by which they come and go! There is no road if they cut the throat!"[14] and "He goes on and on without leaving a trace; he cuts and cuts, yet you see no blood.—Man in a canoe."[15] There are also parallels in Mordvin,[16] Shor,[17] and Buryat.[18] Still another theme occurs in the Crimean Tatar "Here it goes, leaving no trace; blood drips from its nose; it has no eyes.—Steamer."[19]

Some riddles based on the theme of invisible tracks are picturesque enough to merit quotation. They show how widely the fundamental conception can vary. In Iceland they say, "This fair lady is born near the forest and out in the country. She travels fast with long strides, but if you look you find no footprints."[20] The Danes make a comparison to plowing: "What plows and plows, but no furrow remains?"[21] The Serbians see a similarity of a ship to a cat: "A black cat walks along the road; there is neither mark nor trace of it."[22] The Yakut "The gray mare's tracks are not to be seen"[23] is interesting when

---

[6] Wichmann, *Votyak*, 355.
[7] Jacottet, 11.
[8] Piekarski, 323. For parallels to the comparison to a horse that leaves no track, see the headnote to Nos. 1665–1666, n. 3, below. See also the riddles on the theme, "cuts, but the cut cannot be seen," in No. 1666, the headnote to Nos. 1665–1666, and the note to Nos. 1665, 1666.
[9] Piekarski, 324.
[10] Var.: "mare."
[11] Piekarski, 325.
[12] White Russian: Wasilewski, 58. For parallels making a comparison to chopping wood see the headnote to Nos. 1665–1666, n. 2, and the note to Nos. 1665, 1666.
[13] Turkish: Menges, p. 76, No. 32.
[14] Turkish: Katanov in Radlov, IX, 272, No. 169, and p. 241, No. 79.
[15] Zyrian: Wichmann, *Zyrian*, 151. Votyak: Wichmann, *Votyak*, 133 (It goes unceasingly without leaving a trace.—Boat, sun), 287.
[16] Ahlqvist, p. 40, No. 25.
[17] Dyrenkova, 7.
[18] Gombojew, 48.
[19] Filonenko, 87.
[20] Árnason, 293. The riddler shows some familiarity with the ship riddle discussed in the headnote to Nos. 1058–1062, § 1, below.
[21] Kristensen, p. 116, § 314, No. 502. See also his Nos. 499 through 501.
[22] Novaković, p. xvii, No. 1.
[23] Popov, p. 287.

set beside their riddle for a birch-bark canoe, "The tracks of a piebald mare cannot be seen."[24] These two texts show how a slight change makes a riddle fit another idea. Quite different from anything cited thus far is the Icelandic "That I exist all can see, but no one can find me, not even those who know how to use me.—The road of birds in the air."[25]

227. My father had a thing, it walk all night and all day and [you?] can't see where it walk.—Vessel.
Parsons, *Bahamas*, p. 479, No. 75.

228. Must Be Blinded

Riddlers do not often refer to a person who can see or to one who cannot see as the means of describing an object. Such a description of scissors—that is to say, the fingers must be thrust through the holes or eyes of the scissors in order to use them—has some similarity to the Filipino spectacles riddle, "I cannot see although my eyes are wide open; if I cover, I can see,"[1] but the acts are quite different in the two riddles.

The ways of personifying a pair of scissors for enigmatic purposes vary greatly. The Argentinian "That which it meets is shortened; the handle has eyes"[2] is vaguely conceived. Some riddlers speak of a pair of scissors as a creature "with eyes in its back."[3] This conception may have been suggested by the riddles describing a comb as a creature having teeth in its back.[4]

228. My father have a thing in his yard, have to blind it to use it.—Scissors.
Beckwith, *Jamaica*, p. 184, No. 12.

229–232. Making Sounds

229. What makes a lot of noise / In a house with one door, / And if it sits in a draft, / You can't hear it no more?—Bird in a cage.
Hyatt, *Adams Co., Ill.*, p. 658, No. 10838.

230. Can holler, but can't talk.—A train.
Bacon and Parsons, *Virginia*, p. 312, No. 5.

231. Never sings a melody, never has a song, / But it goes humming all day long.—Sawmill.
Hudson, p. 85, No. 17.

232. *Bum bum* in the house, / *Bum bum* outdoors, / *Bum bum* everywhere it goes.—Bumble bee.
Parsons, *Guilford Co., N.C.*, p. 204, No. 30.

---

[24] Priklonskii, 24. [25] Árnason, 122.
[1] Starr, *Philippines*, 196. [2] Lehmann-Nitsche, 634.
[3] Spanish: Demófilo, 967, 968. Argentinian: Lehmann-Nitsche, 174, 467. Chilean: Flores, 725, 727, 729, 731.
[4] See the headnote to No. 299 below.

233–253. Eating or Drinking

Riddlers use the theme of eating or drinking in various ways and often associate it with some abnormality. The notion of eating but once a year appears only in a riddle for a coffee-pulper.[1] The widely known notion of a creature that can eat anything and yet dies from a drink of water is applied to fire.[2] Insatiability is appropriate to a stove, mill, or other domestic device that grinds or consumes materials.[3] For a plane or a saw riddlers often add to the notion of eating that of voiding in an abnormal manner.[4] Some minor abnormalities of eating[5] and the scenes in which a creature is described as not drinking or eating conclude this section.[6]

233. What is that that hath his belly full of man's meat, and his mouth full of dirt?—It is an oven, when it is full of bread or pies, for that is man's meat, and the oven's mouth is then closed with dirt.
Meery Riddles (1629), No. 8 = Brandl, p. 9.

234. My father have a thing in his yard, cry for the crop once a year.—Coffee-pulper.
Beckwith, *Jamaica*, p. 184, No. 10.

235. Can Eat; Cannot Drink

235a. As long as I live I eate, but when I drinke I dye.—It is the fire, which continueth while it hath matter to burne, but is put out with water.
Meery Riddles (1629), No. 76 = Brandl, p. 21.

235b. If you feed it, it will live, / If you give it water, it will die.—Fire.
Bacon and Parsons, *Virginia*, p. 316, No. 36.

235c. What is that you can feed, but can't give water?—Fire.
Perkins, *New Orleans*, p. 113, No. 71.

235d. The mo' you feed it, / The mo' it grow. / Ef you give it water, / It will die.—Fiah [fire].
Parsons, *Aiken, S.C.*, p. 36, No. 79.

235e. Down in the meadow is a red light, / All saddled, all bridled, all fixed for a fight. / Give it water and it'll die. / Give it salt and it'll fly.—Fire.
Hudson, p. 90, No. 45.

236–239. Insatiability

The objects usually described by reference to their insatiability are a fire, a mill, or a tool that cuts or bites. The English use[1] of the theme for the sea and a rock is unusual. Inasmuch as riddlers ordinarily employ a more indi-

---

[1] No. 234.
[3] Nos. 236, 237, 239.
[5] Nos. 241 through 244.
[1] No. 238.

[2] Nos. 235a through 235e.
[4] See the headnote to No. 240.
[6] Nos. 245 through 253.

vidualized form—often an insatiable hen,[2] a hog,[3] hogs,[4] or a cow,[5] and less often a person[6]—the following examples in which the actor is not clearly seen are perhaps degenerate versions.

Some riddlers have used this theme to describe various other objects. The Sicilians say of the grave, "It always eats meat and never gets full,"[7] which resembles somewhat the Welsh description of a cemetery, "What is yonder, yonder in the enclosure of the hollow, it kills none, it swallows a hundred?"[8] The Samoans call the earth insatiable in eating and drinking.[9] The Kundu say the same of the human eye.[10] The Palestinian Arabs describe a plow as "Something goes through the world and yet it is not satiated."[11]

236. My father has a thing in his yard; the more him feed, the more him hungry.—Stove.
Beckwith, *Jamaica*, p. 184, No. 11.

237. What eats and eats and never get full?—A sausage-grinder.
Redfield, *Tennessee*, p. 39, No. 38.

238. Me riddle me riddle, / Me randy oh. / Perhaps you can clear me dis riddle, / Perhaps you cyan't. / My father had a t'ing go all night an' all day and he cyan't get his bellie full.—Sea an' de rock.
Parsons, *Bahamas*, p. 480, No. 86.

239. Chaw fine and never tired.—Saw.
Beckwith, *Jamaica*, p. 200, No. 157.

240. Eats with Belly; Voids through Back

Riddlers vary this pattern in details which do not concern the essential idea: eating may be accomplished with eyes, belly, or some other part of the body, and the materials eaten may be passed out in any one of several places. Although many riddlers have adapted the pattern to many uses, it is scantily represented in English tradition. It is particularly well suited to household implements, a saw, an adze, a mill, a chaffcutter, or the like. In the late fourth or early fifth century, Symphosius described a saw in this way (see § 1 below). In contemporary riddling, the usual answers are "mill," "plane," or "chaffcutter" (§§ 2, 4–5 below). A good example is the Icelandic plane riddle, "Although beaten all the while, he eats running; but he spits it all out quickly through his back."[1]

Typical objects described in this manner are:

---

[2] No. 376.
[3] No. 385.
[4] Nos. 481a through 481d.
[5] Nos. 400a through 400c.
[6] No. 777 and the headnote to Nos. 776–777.
[7] Pitrè, 90, 289.
[8] Hull and Taylor, 6. See also No. 483 below.
[9] Heider, 157.
[10] Ittmann, *Kundu*, 2.
[11] Ruoff, p. 33, No. 71.
[1] Árnason, 291.

§ 1. A saw. Latin: Ohl, Symphosius; 60. French: Queyrat, *La Creuse*, I, 365.
§ 2. A plane. See No. 240 below.
§ 3. An adze, an ax, a file. Lappish: Qvigstad, 29 (When it eats, it spits out all its food.—Ax). Turkish: Kúnos, 209 (What eats with its belly and voids at its sides?—File). Hawaiian: Judd, 243 (My man, that eats at the back and voids at the front.—Adze).
§ 4. A mill. (Often expressed as "eats with its eye, voids from its side".) Danish: Kristensen, p. 77, § 193, Nos. 297a through 297c. Faeroic: Hammershaimb, *Antiquarisk tidsskrift*, III (1849–1851), 321, No. 71. Norwegian: Stafset, 184; Qvigstad, note to No. 61. Swedish: Sandén, *Norra Vadsbo*, 85; Waltman, *Lidmål*, 199; Russwurm, *Eibo*, p. 134, § 316, No. 29; Ström, p. 176, "Vaderkvärn," and p. 384, "Sysselsättningar," 52. Serbian: Novaković, p. xx, No. 2 (It eats with its throat and voids with its ribs). Bulgarian: Gubov, 41. Finnish: Qvigstad, note to No. 61. Lappish: Qvigstad, 61. Estonian: Wiedemann, pp. 262–263, 284, 286. Yakut: Piekarski, 372 (They say that he eats with his mouth but pours things all around him). Indian, Khāṛiā: Roy and Roy, II, 451, No. 24. Filipino: Starr, *Philippines*, 376 (A big woman who excretes at the back). Korean: Bernheisel, p. 84.
§ 5. A chaffcutter. German: Wossidlo, 243; Frischbier, *Menschenwelt*, p. 254, No. 138; Haase, *Ruppin*, 231; Gilhoff, 615; Hanika-Otto, 85a through 85c. Danish: Kristensen, p. 37, § 92, Nos. 120a, 120b. Swedish: Ström, p. 145, "Hackelsekistan."
§ 6. A cotton-jenny. Indian, Ho: Sarkar, 16 (There is one who eats and disgorges his food at the same time). Korean: Bernheisel, p. 84 (What is that which eats from the side and vents from the side?).
§ 7. A sieve. Filipino: Starr, *Philippines*, 386 (What animal is it which takes its food through its mouth and excretes it through its eyes?).
§ 8. A weir. Indonesian, Tounsea: De C., 20.
§ 9. A pot, a pitcher, a barrel. Portuguese: Parsons, *Cape Verde*, 133. Spanish: Rodríguez Marín, 704. Lappish: Qvigstad, 98. Indian, Bengali: Mitra, *Pābnā*, pp. 335–336; Mitra, *Chittagong*, 344, No. 5. Indonesian, Engganee: Helfrich, *Engganee*, p. 518, No. 8. In a riddle for a beer barrel, a Swedish riddler enlarges upon the theme: "What is that which drinks with its side, makes water with its skull, and has ribs outside of its skin?"[2]
§ 10. A pump, a well. Breton: Sébillot, *Haute-Bretagne*, 71. Walloon: Colson, *Devinettes*, 32. Spanish, Chilean: Flores, 622.
§ 11. A chimney. Icelandic; Árnason, 203 (A fellow with a bad habit sits outside the window. He eats with his hind end and lets it out of his mouth). Breton: Sauvé, 143.
§ 12. A bag. Korean: Bernheisel, p. 59 (What is that [which] both eats and voids with the mouth?).

---

[2] Ström, p. 149, "Öltunnan."

§ 13. A lamp. Estonian: Wiedemann, p. 270 (eats out of its stomach, voids through its side).

§ 14. A gun. Surinam: Herskovits, 58.

240. Eat through me belly, / Come through me back.—Jack-plane.
Parsons, *Barbados*, p. 284, No. 49.

241–243. Chews (Eats); Does Not Swallow

241. What chew all the time and don't swallow?—It is a cane-mill.
Parsons, *Sea Islands, S.C.*, p. 167, No. 92. Machine in corn-mill: Parsons, *Bermuda*, p. 258, No. 98.

242. Over the hills and hollows, / Bites but never swallows.—Shotgun.
Redfield, *Tennessee*, p. 39, No. 45.

243. Over hills, over hollows; / Eats but never swallows.—Rust.
Hudson, p. 90, No. 49.

244. Smokes; Does Not Chew

244. What smokes, but cannot chew?—Smoke.
Redfield, *Tennessee*, p. 38, No. 25.

245–253. Does Not Eat (Drink)

245. Somet'in' in de wood fat all de time, an' don' eat not'in'.—Fatwood.
Parsons, *Sea Islands, S.C.*, p. 171, No. 141.

246–253. Goes About; Does Not Drink (Eat)

The texts exhibit the minor variations characteristic of oral tradition: Nos. 246 through 250 mention drinking and eating or only drinking; Nos. 251a through 253 mention drinking and an onomatopoetic sound. References to eating are rather rare. A few versions pun ingeniously in one way or another. A Danish halter riddle[1] plays with å (water), which might be used as an interjection or exclamation. A French riddle, "Qui dit: je berin! je berin! et qui ne boit jamais?"[2] echoes the ringing of a bell.

The notion of a creature that goes to water and does not drink is applicable to:

§ 1. A horseshoe (properly, horseshoe nail). See Nos. 246, 251b.

§ 2. A bell. See Nos. 247a through 247c and Nos. 252a, 252b. See also No. 764.

§ 3. A bridle, a chain. See Nos. 248, 251a, 253.

§ 4. A wagon. See No. 249.

§ 5. A nail in a shoe, a horseshoe, or a wagon wheel. See No. 246.

§ 6. A mill. Spanish, Argentinian: Lehmann-Nitsche, 257 (A white heron

---
[1] Cited in the note to No. 252a.
[2] A. Ferrand, *Dauphiné*, p. 228. The verb *berin* is a future form peculiar to this dialect, according to the collector.

picks at the water, dies of thirst without drinking the water). The scoops of the mill wheel are conceived as "picking" at the water.

§ 7. A ball. Arabic: Giacobetti, 440 (It seeks the water, and the water does not quench its thirst).

§ 8. A path. See No. 250.

§ 9. A shadow.[3] Rumanian: Gorovei, *Devinettes*, p. 505 (What stays on top of the water and never drinks?). This is perhaps intended to suggest a sea gull. An Argentinian Spanish version makes a reference to both drinking and eating.[4]

§ 10. The sun. Swedish: Ström, p. 205, "Solen," 5.

246. What is it that goes down to the branch [stream] with its head down but doesn't drink?—Horseshoe [nail?].
Oral, North Carolina.

247a. It goes all over the hills, but doesn't eat. / It goes to the creek, but doesn't drink.—A cowbell.
Farr, *Tennessee*, p. 319, No. 1.

247b. What goes to the branch and drinks and don't drink?—Cow and bell.
Fauset, *Southern Negro*, p. 283, No. 80. And never drinks: Hudson, p. 86, No. 20.

247c. What is it goes to the water often and never drink?—Bell on a cow.
Fauset, *Southern Negro*, p. 283, No. 79.

248. Goes to the well three times a day, and never drinks.—Bridle.
Bacon and Parsons, *Virginia*, p. 322, No. 87.

249. Goes to the water an' never drinks.—Wagon.
Parsons, *Robeson Co., N.C.*, p. 389, No. 7; Redfield, *Tennessee*, p. 39, No. 36.

250. What goes to a spring and never drinks?—Path.
Bacon and Parsons, *Virginia*, p. 319, No. 56; Parsons, *Aiken, S.C.*, p. 26, No. 9, var. 3.

251–253. Jingles to the Water; Does Not Drink

This minor variety of the foregoing riddle occurs in an old English collection and in Nova Scotian and New York collections. There are Danish parallels. It can be contrasted with the former variety of the riddle, in which there is no mention of the sound of the bell or chain and no onomatopoetic word.

251a. w^t is that as goes to the water *gink gink* & w^n it comes ther cañot drink?—a bridle in a horse mouth.
Tupper, *Holme Riddles*, 60.

251b. Who says *clink, clink* under the water and never takes a drink?—Nail in a horse's shoe.
MacGréine, *Béaloideas*, III (1931–1932), 414, No. 11.

---

[3] See also the headnote to Nos. 165–173, § 3, above.
[4] Lehmann-Nitsche. 104*n* through 104*p*.

252a. *Chinkely, chinkely* through the water and never stop to drink.—Bell.
Fauset, *Nova Scotia*, p. 166, No. 123 var.

252b. Jingles to the brook and never takes a drink.—Bell.
Fauset, *Nova Scotia*, p. 166, No. 123 var.

253. *Chink, chink* through the brook and never drink.—A chain.
Fauset, *Nova Scotia*, p. 166, No. 123; Gardner, *Schoharie Hills, N.Y.*, p. 257, No. 31.

254–258. Resting

254–255. Sleeps All Day; Walks at Night

The following English accounts of the habits of an owl or spider lack enigmatic quality. The theme of sleeping by day and waking at night is turned to better use in a Flemish riddle for the moon, "It sleeps by day, it is awake at night, it dies in the morning, and it comes to life again in the evening,"[1] and in a Parsee description of a lighted lamp, "There is a substance which keeps awake during the night and sleeps during the daytime."[2] Riddlers often use the contrast of activities in the day and those in the night.[3]

254. I know something that sleeps all day and walks at night.—Owl.
Parsons, *Bermuda*, p. 263, No. 139.

255. I know something that sleeps all day and walks at night.—Spider.
Parsons, *Bermuda*, p. 263, No. 139.

256–258. Does Not Rest

256a. Go to work an' don't work, / Go to eat an' don't eat, / Go to rest an' don't rest.—Tongue on a wagon.
Fauset, *Southern Negro*, p. 278, No. 23.

256b. Goes to the well, can't drink, / Goes to the creek, can't drink, / Goes to the barn, can't sleep, / Goes to the house, can't lay down, / Goes up and down the street, can't walk.—Wagon-tongue.
Fauset, *Southern Negro*, p. 278, No. 22.

257. Can Rest in a Box; Cannot Rest in a Field

The comparison of an object to something that can be easily held in the hand or contained in a small space but cannot rest quietly or lie in a much larger space is applicable to various themes. A fan will lie quietly in a box, but not in an open field where the wind blows. This comparison, which is of folk origin, is also used for a goose quill, as in:

> In campis ægre jaceo, atque patentibus arvis,
> Me bene conclusum scrinia parva tenent.[1]

---

[1] Joos, 5.
[2] Munshi, p. 419.
[3] See the headnote to Nos. 445–458 below.

[1] Buchler, *Gnomologia*, 3d ed. (1614), p. 427.

It is akin to the comparison of a cane to a person who goes about freely and yet stands in a small space.[2]

257a. In open field I cannot lye, / and yet may rest quietly / within a boxe of ivory.—It is a feather in a windy day.
Prettie Riddles (1631), No. 26 = Brandl, p. 56.

257b. In open feild j canot ly within a box of ivory my lady rest me quietly.— a fan of feathers in a La: [read: lady's] cabanet.
Tupper, *Holme Riddles*, 97.

258. Cannot Rest in a Chest

258. What is that I can hold in my hand, and will not lye in a great chest?— It is a long speare.
Meery Riddles (1629), No. 65 = Brandl, p. 19.

259–335. Form and Function

259–265. Abnormal in Form, Normal in Function; Member and Function Related

English riddles of this type are limited almost exclusively to the theme of a creature that moves about without feet or flesh. There are no English parallels to the Flemish bell riddle, "I speak without a tongue and cry out without lungs. Lacking sense or understanding, I announce joy and sorrow throughout the land"[1] or the Lithuanian description of an echo as talking without a tongue.[2] A similar mating of opposites occurs in riddles based on the contradiction "normal in form, abnormal in function."[3] This is much more often used than the conception found here. In both of these conceptions the contrast should refer to the same part of the body. At times, however, riddlers have neglected this obvious unifying principle and have introduced such inharmonious elements as the mention of the mouth in the text below.

259. Something in a house has no eyes, no mouth, no hands, but it can draw as good as I can.—Mirror.
Parsons, *Bermuda*, p. 258, No. 94.

260–265. Moves without Legs

This simple enigmatic paradox is applicable to various objects. In these uses it can easily have arisen independently. This suggestion of multiple origins is strengthened by the fact that individualizing details of various kinds are often introduced in order to adapt the theme to a cloud,[1] smoke,[2] fire,[3] wind,[4] or a windmill.[5]

---

[2] No. 699 below.
[1] Joos, 279. Compare No. 268 below. [2] Jurgelionis, 1098.
[3] See Nos. 272 through 326 below.
[1] See § 5. below. [2] See § 6. [3] See § 7.
[4] See § 9. [5] See § 10.

Typical uses of the paradox are as follows:

§ 1. A snail. See No. 261.

§ 2. A snake. See 263.

§ 3. A clock. See No. 262.

§ 4. A river or water.[6] An early example of this use is the fourteenth-century versification by Claret: "Abs pede currit aqua, globus et rota, viva metalla" (p. 73, No. 97). See also the elaborate literary version in Icelandic: "There is a terrible creature with very many tails that crawls on the roadless mountains and in the valleys. It is exceedingly long and rushes on with loud bellowings full of restless energy, and it often frightens people, laughs contemptuously at accidents, and washes many away to their deaths, but it nevertheless gives gentle refreshment to the weary traveler. With its great power it is known to many. Legless, it moves on toward the sea, where ships are" (Árnason, 152). See further, Spanish, Argentinian: Lehmann-Nitsche, 193. Chilean: Flores, 657 (an elaborate comparison to a snake). Lithuanian: Jurgelionis, 1069 (What runs without feet?—River, water), 1070 (What runs without little feet?—Stream). Serbian: Novaković, p. 22, No. 1 (It has neither legs nor arms, neither soul nor body. Yet it runs over the earth as if it were alive.—Water). Armenian: Seidlitz, p. 71, No. 30 (Swaying, it moves; it has no feet and walks; it has no mouth and swallows). Persian: Phillott, 3 (What is that which travels without feet, head, or hands?—River or wind). Yakut: Piekarski, 22 (They say, that, without legs, it can run; they also say that there is that which travels without legs and runs without joints.—Cake of ice and water current); Popov, p. 283 (Even though without legs, there is one who walks, it is said.—Water current). Indonesian, Lampong: Helfrich, *Lampong*, 18 (It makes a sound, yet says nothing; it goes quickly, yet it has no feet). Filipino: Starr, *Philippines*, 407 (It runs, having no feet and it roars, having no mouth.—Waves).

§ 5. A cloud.[7] Closely allied to the answers "smoke," "fire," and "wind," the answer is also usually indicated by some individualizing details. See Welsh: Hull and Taylor, 44 (mist). Polish: Saloni, *Rzeshów*, 22 (It has no legs and it walks; it has no wings and it flies). Mandingo: Monteil, 16 (fog). Persian: Phillott, 22 (What is that fairy-shape that has no life? It laughs, yet it has no mouth; it weeps, yet it has no eyes; it travels much, yet it has no feet). Indonesian, Javanese: Ranneft, *Proza*, p. 44, No. 200 (That which has paws cannot go; that which has no paws can go.—Table and cloud).

§ 6. Smoke.[8] The riddler often adds individualizing details. See Breton: Marquer, p. 225; Sébillot, *Devinettes*, 64d, 64e. French: V. S., *Mélusine*, I (1878), col. 257, No. 34. Spanish: Rodríguez Marín, 278. Argentinian:

---

[6] For comparisons of flowing water to a creature running without cessation, see Nos. 114 through 116b and compare No. 289.

[7] See also the headnote to Nos. 365–366, § 3.

[8] See also the headnote to Nos. 365–366, § 2.

Lehmann-Nitsche, 196, 197. Dominican Rep.: Andrade, 13. New Mexican: Campa, 123. Polish: Gustawicz, 64, 66, 67; Saloni, *Rzeshów*, 29 (It has no hands, it has no feet, it will come out on top); Siarkowski, 11 (It has no arms or legs, yet it can climb up). Russian: Sadovnikov, 147 (Without hands, without legs, it climbs up the house). Bulgarian: Bozhov, 11 (The long Mara is without bones), 17 (The tall George is boneless). Finnish: Henssen, 150. Estonian: Wiedemann, p. 268. Hungarian: *Magyar Nyelvör*, II (1873), 43 (Although it has neither hands nor feet, it rises to Heaven); VII (1878), 89 (Although it hasn't any feet or hands, it can get to the attic); XXXVII (1908), 188. Modern Greek: Polites, *Neohellenika Analekta*, I, 243, Nos. 281 (A long, long old monk, he has no bones), and 282 (It has no life or soul and goes to the sky); Abbott, p. 307, No. 9.

§ 7. Fire. The addition of such details as "it eats everything" or "it eats without a tongue"[9] often differentiates riddles for fire from those for smoke. In some of the following parallels the answer "fire" has replaced other answers. See Russian: Sadovnikov, 187 (It has neither hands nor legs, yet it climbs the hill). African, Konde: Mackenzie, p. 163 (It has neither feet to walk with nor hands to seize with, yet it devours everything). Indian, Baiga: Elwin, p. 478, No. 143 (Without feet it climbs; without a tongue it eats. If it drinks water, it dies).

§ 8. The sun. German: Wossidlo, 362 (What runs through the world and yet has no legs?). Russian: Sadovnikov, 1848 (Without legs, without arms, it crawls across the fence). See also the headnote to Nos. 365–366, § 4, below.

§ 9. The wind. The versions usually include such additional details as "walks without a mouth," "runs without legs," "strikes without hands," "passes by without being seen," or the like. Compare also the headnote to Nos. 264–265, § 10, below. For examples see French: J. Roux, *Limousin*, p. 175, No. 7. Armenian: Glushakov, p. 35 (It is not visible to the eye, it does not walk with its feet, it bellows along the road like a donkey, it is as strong as a full-grown hero). Kabardin: Talpa and Sokolov, 18 (It has no arms but it opens the door). Yakut: Piekarski, 35 = Priklonskii, 14 (They say that there is something that walks about although it has no legs.—Rowboat or wind). Tungus: Poppe, 11 (Without feet, without hands, he knocks at the door). Persian: Phillott, 3 (see above, § 4).

§ 10. A windmill. Danish: Kristensen, p. 142, § 420, No. 662b (What is that: it has wings, yet cannot fly; it has no legs, but it can nevertheless walk?)

§ 11. Dough. Cheremiss: Wichmann, *Cheremiss*, 157 (Without hands, without feet, it climbs to the top of a linden). The "linden" is a wooden mixing bowl.

§ 12. A wagon, a train. Swedish: Ström, p. 144, "Vagnen," 1 (It travels all

---

[9] For examples of this theme used in describing the heat of the sun, see the headnote to Nos. 367–369.

the world about, it has no feet, no legs). Spanish, Argentinian: Lehmann-Nitsche, 194 (train).

§ 13. A flatiron. See No. 260 below.

§ 14. A ball. Lettish: Bielenstein, 265 (What leaps and goes without feet?).

§ 15. Money. Russian: Sadovnikov, 692 (They walk without feet). Indian, Uraon: Archer, p. 181, No. 39 (A pebble roves the world.—Pice [an Indian coin]).

§ 16. A bullet. Swedish: Ström, p. 173, "Kulan" (What runs over a road and has neither flesh nor blood?).

§ 17. A letter. French: Mensignac, *Gironde*, 66 (White as snow, black as jet, one who talks without a head and walks without feet). Catalan: Pelay y Briz, 194. Spanish: Demófilo, 251, 252. Californian: Espinosa, 35.

§ 18. Hops. Polish: Gustawicz, 26 (It has no legs, it has no arms, it moves around the whole pole). Cheremiss: Genetz, 15.

§ 19. A ship. See No. 372 below and the headnote to No. 227, n. 9, above.

260. Black and breet [bright], / Runs without feet.—An iron.
Baring-Gould, *Notes and Queries*, 3d ser., VIII (1865), 325.

261. Something movin' without a leg.—Snail.
Parsons, *Bermuda*, p. 258, No. 101.

262. Runs without Legs: A Clock

The observation that a clock runs or strikes has occasionally suggested the remark that it performs these feats without possessing the appropriate members. Riddlers often introduce additional elaborations in details. The concept of running without legs is also applicable to the related concept of time.[1]

262. Something runs but has no legs.—Clock.
Parsons, *Bermuda*, p. 257, No. 89.

263. What can walk on eart' an' ain't got no feet?—Snake.
Parsons, *Sea Islands, S.C.*, p. 171, No. 129.

264-265. Without Bone (Blood), Yet Walks

Riddlers describe several objects in terms of an animate creature that lacks flesh and bone. The Bretons say that a saddle is neither flesh nor bone,[1] and a Russian riddle for a spinning bench is "There is a man with neither arms nor legs; he has a head but no brains; he has a belly but no guts; he has sides but no flesh."[2] When this notion is enlarged by mention of walking or moving in these impossible circumstances, it becomes suitable to describe invertebrate

---

[1] See Swedish: Ström, p. 225, "Tiden, årstiderna, dygnet," 2. Spanish, Argentinian: Lehmann-Nitsche, 618. Lettish: Bielenstein, 321.

[1] Charlec, *Dol-de-Bretagne*, 1903, p. 396.

[2] Sadovnikov, 573.

crawling animals, wind, smoke, and some other things of less importance. Typical objects described in this manner are:

§ 1. A snail. See Nos. 264a, 264b, below.

§ 2. A louse. Spanish, Argentinian: Lehmann-Nitsche, 207. Turcoman: Samojlvich, 51 (In a young wood there roams a little boneless lamb). Malayalam: Schmolck, p. 242, No. 28 (In a jungle without thorny bushes there lives a boneless mouse), which appropriately equates the biting of the louse and that of the mouse. Filipino: Starr, *Philippines*, 206 (Dark mountain, boneless animal). The mountain is the human head.

§ 3. An earthworm. French: Roque-Ferrier, *Languedoc*, p. 332. African, Lamba: Doke, 32 (That which has no ribs.—Maggot). Indian, Ho: Sarkar, p. 255. No. 43 (There is a boneless creature; it makes holes in the earth and raises its excrements upwards); Mitra, *Notes on Ho Riddles*, p. 249. Bhil: Hedberg, p. 873, No. 50. An earthworm is also called a legless man without a staff; see Nos. 562a through 562e below.

§ 4. A leech. Breton: Sébillot, *Devinettes*, 20. French: Beauvillard, *Mélusine*, I (1878), col. 485. Spanish: Demófilo, 903 (What is the insect without bone or spine?); Rodríguez Marín, 446. Polish: Gustawicz, 316 (Without a bone, but it can swim the ocean); Saloni, *Łańcut*, 2 (It hasn't bones, but it will get across the bridge). Serbian: Novaković, p. 167, No. 11 (It is flesh without the bones. It has neither teeth nor eyes. It is living, it is ugly, and it is always hungry). Arabic: Ruoff, p. 42, No. 5. Turkish: Kowalski, *Zagadki*, 111 ([The only one] in the world [who is] without bones). Persian: Phillott, 26 (What is that which has no bones? If it fastens on you, it does no harm). Indian, Ho: Mitra, *Notes on Ho Riddles*, p. 250 (Lives in the grass, no bones, so strange to look at). Khāṛiā: Roy and Roy, II, 453, No. 40 (A man without bone). Telugu: Taylor, *Nellore*, 1. Bihari: Mitra, *Bihar*, 11 (It has no bones, no anus, no mouth, no body, no house, and no hair). Bengali: Mitra, *Chittagong*, p. 972, Nos. 19 (No bones, is strange to look at), 20 (What is that creature which is jet-black, which floats upon the water, which possesses no bones, but which possesses flesh?), 20A (The owl sat on the *arjjuna*-tree, no bones, only a strip of flesh). The last of these versions is not completely intelligible. Uraon: Archer, p. 193, No. 212 (Although it has no flesh, it lives).

§ 5. Various animals. UNIDENTIFIED INSECT. African, Kxatla: Schapera, 24 (I looked for the bone of the klipspringer [a species of antelope], but could not find it). Indian, Bengali: Mitra, *Sylhet*, 13 (The girl of the company goes about in company and lodges with the company. She has no bones). MARINE ANIMALS. Samoan: Heider, 44 (Something comes from the boundless ocean and goes up to the mountain ridge, but has no bone.—Igaga [*Electris fusca*], a small fish that ascends the river courses in the early stages of its life), 45 (Who is the man, he lives in the sea, has eight arms, is strong, but has not a single bone?—Octopus).

§ 6. Mould. Italian: Tammi, 45 (A thing without flesh and bones and it has hair on the outside).

§ 7. Plants. MUSHROOM. Modern Greek: Polites, *Neohellenika Analekta*, I, 212, No. 109 (Boneless and hairless, it bores through the earth and emerges). VINE. Turkish: Hamizade, 16 (Handless, footless, it walks on the wall).

§ 8. The tongue. Estonian: Wiedemann, p. 265 (It goes without bones).

§ 9. A shadow. See No. 265 below.

§ 10. The wind. Welsh: H. M. Chadwick, *The Growth of Literature*, I (Cambridge, England, 1932), 413–414. French: Roque-Ferrier, *Languedoc*, p. 327. Portuguese: Pires, *Archivio*, VII (1888), 246, No. 3. See also the headnote to Nos. 260–265, § 9, above.

§ 11. Fire, smoke. Rumanian: Papahagi, 23, var. 2 (A monk without bones), var. 3 (Long Kosta without bones). Estonian: Wiedemann, p. 266 (A John without feet goes up the wall) and p. 268 (A man without hand or foot runs up the corner). Turkish: Hamizade, 163 (A long boneless fellow.— Smoke). Indian, Kolarian: Wagner, 74 (A man has neither bones nor flesh nor blood; still he is wandering through the whole country.—Fire).

§ 12. A billhook. Italian: Rolland, p. 164, No. 60. See also the headnote to No. 361 below.

§ 13. A letter. Welsh Gypsy: Sampson, 37 (What travels through the land and has neither flesh nor blood?). Irish: Delargy, *Inis Cé*, 19 (A man, passing East, a man passing West, a man telling a story; without a vein, without blood).

264. The Snail Riddle

The description of a snail as fleshless and bloodless and yet walking about occurs in three classical versions. The enumeration in the *Deipnosophistae*[1] has little enigmatic quality: "It is an animal without feet, without spine, without bones, with a hard shell on its back; its eyes peer far out and also inward." The two other versions are very interesting examples of the formula "born in the forest," which is often an introduction to an enumeration of three parts of an object as having entirely different origins:[2] Athenaeus writes, "Born in the forest, without spine or blood, it walks on a damp path";[3] and Cicero, "Born in the earth, walks in the grass, bears its house, lacks blood."[4] In later times European and other riddlers have not described the snail in this way.[5]

---

[1] X, 83, p. 455ᵉ = Schultz, *Rätsel aus dem hellenischen Kulturkreise*, I, 15, 46–47.
[2] See the headnotes to Nos. 401–404, 553–554, and 1058–1062 below.
[3] *Deipnosophistae*, II, 63.
[4] *De Divinatione*, II, 64.
[5] For further discussion see Ohlert, 1st ed., p. 87, and 2d ed., p. 160; Schultz, *Rätsel*, col. 92, No. 14; and my article, "An Allusion to a Riddle in Suetonius," *American Journal of Philology*, LXVI (1945), 408–410.

264a. w^t is that as is nether fish flesh blood nor boone yet can eate meate & goe.—a snale.
Tupper, *Holme Riddles*, 89.

264b. Bloodless and boneless, / And goes to the fell footless.—A snail.
Gibson, *Notes and Queries*, 3d ser., IX (1866), 86 (East Lancashire).

265. 'Tis neither Flesh nor Bone, / Yet it passes on, / By which is fairly shewn, / The length and breadth of Man.—A Man's Shadow, whilst he is walking in the Sun.
A New Riddle Book; Or, A Whetstone for Dull Wits, p. 14.

266–271. Abnormal in Form, Normal in Function; Member and Function Not Closely Related

A few riddles describe an object in terms of a physical abnormality and a function without connecting them. Such riddles give a rather confused idea of an object that the speaker has not clearly envisaged as an animal or a person. In the turnstile riddle,[1] the bodily abnormalities—four arms and a head that is nailed on—have no close connection with the functions of being in everyone's way and stopping no one. The same defect appears in the engine riddle,[2] in which the brass toes and brass nose are scarcely the reason for the fright of the crows. Jestbooks have disseminated such puzzles. Their literary connections also appear in the use of rhyme in sophisticated ways. The three other riddles in this section probably have similar literary associations.

266. I'm in everyone's way, / Yet no one I stop; / My four arms in every way play, / And my head is nailed on at the top.—A turn-stile.
Halliwell-Phillipps, *Popular Rhymes*, p. 141; Waugh, *Canada*, p. 70, No. 801; Knortz, p. 223, No. 49; Hyatt, *Adams Co., Ill.*, p. 669, No. 10929.

267. As I was going over London Bridge, / I met a thing with brass toes and brass nose, / And upon my soul it scares the crows.—A steam engine.
Fauset, *Nova Scotia*, p. 149, No. 38.

268. ther is a body wthout a hart that hath a tongue & yet no head buried it was ere it was made & loud doth speek & yet is dead.—a bell wch wⁿ it is cast is some[time] in the ground.
Tupper, *Holme Riddles*, 18.

269. All my body belly is, / and lesser then [than] it my mouth is not. / I doe containe what makes me [read: mē, i.e., men] mad, / What I am, sir, now tell me that.—A maltsacke full of malt, wherewith strong drinke is brewed.
Prettie Riddles (1631), No. 75 = Brandl, p. 62.

270. My belly is bigger than all the rest / wherein men use to put the best. / Broad is my foote, short is my necke. / If ill you use me, then feare a checke.—A bottle of glasse.
Prettie Riddles (1631), No. 76 = Brandl, p. 62.

---

[1] No. 266.   [2] No. 267.

271. It has eighteen legs and catches flies.—A baseball team.
Farr, *Tennessee*, p. 321, No. 39.

272–326. Normal in Form, Abnormal in Function

Almost all the riddles in this section depend on a pun: the "head" of a match, nail, or cabbage, the "eye" of a needle or potato, the "face" or "hands" of a clock, the "tongue" of a wagon or shoe, the "teeth" of a rake, or the "leg" of a table is understood both as part of an object and as possessing the function of a bodily member. Only a few riddles like that for a doll, "What has a mouth but cannot eat?"[1] contain no puns. The speaker occasionally adds an unessential detail, as in the riddle for a potato, "Big and round, hard and sound, eyes and can't see,"[2] or a chair, "What is it that has four legs and one back, yet can't walk?"[3] In all these riddles introductory formulas are typically lacking. Such occasional exceptions to the rule as "All through the woods,"[4] "Down the hill and across the hollow,"[5] "Over water, under water"[6] are borrowed from other riddles on the respective themes.

272–310. A Member Normal in Form, Abnormal in Function

272–273. Head

272. It has a head, but can't think.—A match.
Farr, *Tennessee*, p. 325, No. 105.

273. What is it got a head and can't think? / It stands on the ground, sits on the ground, all at the same time. / It leaves, but yet it's there.—Cabbage.
Fauset, *Nova Scotia*, p. 171, No. 173.

274–284. Eyes

274. Somet'in' cry, / No water come out his eye.—Shoe.
Parsons, *Sea Islands, S.C.*, p. 168, No. 99.

275. White I am, and blacke withall, / I have eyes, and yet am blind, / Gaine and losse not without braule / I doe procure, as you shall find.—Dice.
Prettie Riddles (1631), No. 9 = Brandl, p. 53.

276. Many eyes, / Never cries.—Potato.
Hudson, p. 87, No. 25.

277a. Something has eyes and cannot see.—Irish potato.
Parsons, *Bermuda*, p. 258, No. 97.

277b. Got two eyes and can't see.—Potato.
Fauset, *Nova Scotia*, p. 173, No. 191.

277c. Big and round, hard and sound, / Eyes and can't see.—Irish potato.
Farr, *Tennessee*, p. 322, No. 60.

---

[1] No. 287.   [2] No. 277c.   [3] No. 306b.
[4] No. 280.   [5] No. 291.   [6] No. 295a.

277d. What's round as an egg, has eyes, and can't see?—Potato.
Halpert, *New Jersey*, p. 202, No. 14.

278. Something has eyes and cannot see.—A bough.
Parsons, *Bermuda*, p. 258, No. 97 var.

279. Some t'in' got two eyes an' only can cry out o' one.—Coconut.
Parsons, *Bahamas*, p. 475, No. 42.

280. All through the woods, / An' hasn' got but one eye.—Axe.
Parsons, *Guilford Co., N.C.*, p. 204, No. 28.

281. What's got an eye but never closes its eye?—A needle.
Fauset, *Nova Scotia*, p. 173, No. 194.

282. What has an eye, / But cannot see?—Needle.
Bacon and Parsons, *Virginia*, p. 315, No. 26; Randolph and Spradley, *Ozark*, p. 86; Parsons, *Bermuda*, p. 258, No. 97; Greenleaf, *Newfoundland*, p. 9, No. 5.

283. What has a face, / But cannot see?—Clock.
Bacon and Parsons, *Virginia*, p. 315, No. 31.

284. What is it that goes up a tree and down a tree, / Has eyes and can't see?—A button.
Farr, *Tennessee*, p. 319, No. 17.

285. Ears

The Poles have a similar pun in a bucket riddle: "What animal is it that has ears but cannot hear?"[1]

285. Something has an ear and cannot hear.—Ear of corn.
Parsons, *Bermuda*, p. 257, No. 85; Parsons, *Sea Islands, S.C.*, p. 155, No. 21; Puckett, *Southern Negro*, p. 53.

286. Nose

286. Something has a nose and can't smell.—Teapot.
Parsons, *Bermuda*, p. 257, No. 86.

287–291. Mouth

287. What has a mouth, / But cannot eat?—Doll.
Bacon and Parsons, *Virginia*, p. 315, No. 32.

288. What has a mouth but can't talk?—A river.
Farr, *Tennessee*, p. 323, No. 67.

289. What has a bed, yet never sleeps; and has a mouth, yet never eats [variant: speaks]; and always keeps a-moving?—A river.
Waugh, *Canada*, p. 69, No. 794.

290. What is it, / Got a mouth and don't speak, / Got a bed and don't sleep?—River.
Parsons, *Bermuda*, p. 261, No. 120.

---
[1] Siarkowski, 75; Gustawicz, 14. See also No. 325 below.

291. Down the hill and across the hollow, / It has a mouth and can't swallow. —A cowbell.
Farr, *Tennessee*, p. 324, No. 90.

292–296. Tongue

292. What tongue goes to the creek but never drinks?—A wagon-tongue.
Farr, *Tennessee*, p. 320, No. 70.

293. Four legs, one tongue, and one body, / Goes to the water, and never drinks.—Wagon.
Fauset, *Southern Negro*, p. 278, No. 21.

294. Wanders often over the meadow all day long, with a nice little tongue but cannot speak, goes to water but cannot drink.—Cowbell.
Oral, North Carolina.

295a. Over water, under water, / Got a tongue, / Never drunk a drop.— Wagon.
Parsons, *Guilford Co., N.C.*, p. 203, No. 20.

295b. It goes to the brook, / An' got a tongue, / But won't drink?—Wagon.
Parsons, *Guilford Co., N.C.*, p. 203, No. 20 var.

295c. What has a tongue but can't eat?—Wagon.
Redfield, *Tennessee*, p. 39, No. 37.

296a. What has a tongue and can't talk?—Shoe.
Fauset, *Nova Scotia*, p. 173, No. 192; Greenleaf, *Newfoundland*, p. 8, No. 4.

296b. What has a tongue and can't talk?—Boot.
Green, *South Antrim*, 22.

296c. What is it that has a tongue but never talks, / Has no legs but always walks?—Shoe.
Oral, West Virginia.

297–300. Teeth

297–300. Has Teeth; Cannot Eat

This conception, which is rather unimportant in English riddling, is applicable to various domestic instruments with "teeth," especially a saw,[1] a comb,[2] and a rake.[3] The related notion[4] of possessing teeth but no mouth (or tongue), which is used for much the same themes, does not mention the use of the teeth.

By naming an appropriate activity, a riddler creates a vivid picture or at least the opportunity for one, and although the parallels do not often draw a completely satisfactory scene, they are frequently picturesque. The widely known conception of a dog or other animal that bares its teeth occurs in the German "It hangs on the wall and bares its teeth"[5] and in the French "Who

---

[1] No. 298. [2] Nos. 299a, 299b.
[3] No. 300. [4] Nos. 18 through 21b.
[5] Hanika-Otto, 194 (rake); Haase, *Thüringen*, 27.

shows his teeth when you enter a house?"⁶ Those who find it hard to conceive the similarity of a saw to an animal's teeth can refresh their imaginations by calling to mind the picture of the Cheshire Cat in Lewis Carroll's *Alice in Wonderland*.

Some riddlers have conceived the creature as a person, not an animal. In Béarn, they say of a saw, "At our house there is a boy with lips drawn back,"⁷ which is a roundabout way of saying that his teeth are conspicuous.

These ideas are applicable, although only rarely, to themes of an entirely different sort. The Russian riddle for a window is "I will push and push White Martin again. Martin will look at me, will bare his teeth at me,"⁸ and the Serbian description of winter is "It has no teeth, it has no arms, it has no legs, and yet it bites."⁹

297. A thousand teeth, and can't chew.—Handcard.
Hudson, p. 87, No. 32.

298. Has Teeth and Does Not Eat: A Saw

A Breton riddler declares that a saw does eat: "Who has teeth, cries continually while eating, and often bites those who feed it?"¹

298. Have teeth, / But cannot eat.—Saw.
Parsons, *Aiken, S.C.*, p. 32, No. 52; Bacon and Parsons, *Virginia*, p. 315, No. 28.

299. Has Teeth and Does Not Eat: A Comb

Another riddle for a comb that refers to its teeth is the Walloon "What has teeth along its back?"¹ In France this query has the answer "saw."² The possibility of independent invention suggests itself on reading the Kolarian riddle for a grass mat, "A man has teeth on his back,"³ and the Munda parallel, "Someone has teeth on his back."⁴

299a. What has teeth, / But cannot eat?—Comb.
Bacon and Parsons, *Virginia*, p. 315, No. 20.

299b. What has teeth and can't bite?—Comb.
Green, *South Antrim*, 23.

---

⁶ Rolland, 150; Ledieu, *Démuin*, p. 133; Dottin, *Bas-Maine*, 16; Desaivre, *Poitou*, p. 450, No. 7; Daleau, *Gironde*, p. 105; Queyrat, *La Creuse*, I, 366; Mensignac, *Gironde*, 38; Westphalen, *Metz*, col. 201; Dardy, *L'Albret*, p. 333. Compare E. H. Carnoy, *La Tradition*, I (1887), 354, No. 20. Breton: Sauvé, 75; Sébillot, *Haute-Bretagne*, 55. See also analogous French comparisons to an animal cited in the headnote to Nos. 1295–1296 below and the discussion in the headnote to Nos. 18–21 above.
⁷ Lespy, *Béarn*, 3. See also Basque: Cerquand, 20.
⁸ Sadovnikov, 62. See also his No. 69.
⁹ Novaković, p. 61, No. 7.

¹ Le Pennec, 21. For other comparisons of sawing to eating see the headnote to No. 240, § 1, above.
¹ Colson, *Wallonia*, V, 56, No. 214.
² Sébillot, *Auvergne*, 22.
³ Wagner, 81.
⁴ Roy, *The Mundas*, p. 506, No. 47.

300. Has Teeth and Does Not Eat: A Rake

This adaptation of the preceding riddles for a comb or a saw can also be compared with the descriptions of a hoe or scythe as a creature that eats.[1] The Bermudan "A garden tool we sometimes need / When smoothing soil or sowing seed.—Rake"[2] sounds like a fragment of a children's rhyme. Since it completely lacks enigmatic quality, I have not given it a place in this collection.

300. What is it that has teeth and can't eat?—A rake.
Farr, *Tennessee*, p. 322, No. 62.

301–304. Hands

301. I know something got hand an' don't wash its face.—Clock.
Parsons, *Bermuda*, p. 257, No. 88.

302. Somet'in' have two han's, an' too dirty to wash its face.—Dat's a clock.
Parsons, *Sea Islands, S.C.*, p. 164, No. 64.

303. It has two hands, but it can't work.—Clock.
Farr, *Tennessee*, p. 325, No. 104.

304. What has a hand that cannot feel [variant: hold]?—Clock.
Parsons, *Bermuda*, p. 257, No. 87.

305–310. Legs

305–310. Has Legs; Cannot Walk

The notion of a creature that has legs and yet cannot walk is applicable to any inanimate object that has legs. The French say of a broom, "Who has so many feet (paws) and can't walk?"[1] The Koreans say that a tent has four legs and four wings and yet is unable to walk or fly,[2] and the Ainu say that a granary has four legs and does not move.[3] The Chileans use a similar idea in describing scissors: "It has eyes and can't see, legs and can't walk."[4] The eyes are the openings through which the fingers are thrust. In European riddling the notion of possessing legs that cannot walk occurs most often in riddles for a chair, a table, or a bed. A curious variation having some similarity to this notion occurs in the Icelandic chair riddle, "I stand on four legs, my arms turned toward people. High and low bow for me, but I never bow for anyone."[5]

305a. Something has leg [*sic*], but cannot walk.—Table.
Parsons, *Bermuda*, p. 257, No. 84; Bacon and Parsons, *Virginia*, p. 315, No. 20.

305b. Four legs and doesn't move around the floor.—A table.
Fauset, *Nova Scotia*, p. 174, No. 190.

---

[1] See Nos. 361a through 361c and the headnote to No. 361.
[2] Parsons, *Bermuda*, p. 263, No. 143.

[1] Lallemant, *Argonne*, p. 234.
[2] Bernheisel, p. 61.
[3] Starr, *Ainu*, 3.
[4] Flores, 726.
[5] Árnason, 25.

306a. What has legs, / But cannot walk?—Chair.
Bacon and Parsons, *Virginia*, p. 315, No. 30. Four legs: Greenleaf, *Newfoundland*, p. 11, No. 23.

306b. What is it that has four legs and one back, / Yet can't walk?—A chair.
Farr, *Tennessee*, p. 322, No. 63.

307. It has four legs, but cannot walk.—Bed.
Knortz, p. 240, No. 150.

308. What has laigs / An' cannot walk?—House.
Parsons, *Aiken, S.C.*, p. 32, No. 51.

309. Legs I have but seldom walke, / I backbite all, but never speak.—Flea.
Beckwith, *Jamaica*, p. 213, No. 241.

310. There is something on four legs and you can't ride it.—A dawg.
Parsons, *Antilles*, III, 445, St. Thomas, 3.

311–326. Several Members Normal in Form, Abnormal in Function

311. Got tongue an' can't talk, / Got eyes an' can't see.—Shoe.
Parsons, *Aiken, S.C.*, p. 32, No. 50, var. 1; Farr, *Tennessee*, p. 322, No. 58.

312a. Has a soul and tongue and can't talk, / Eyes and can't see.—Shoe.
Fauset, *Southern Negro*, p. 280, No. 43.

312b. What has got eyes but never sees? / What has got a tongue but never talks? / What has got a soul that can't be saved?—Shoe.
Randolph and Spradley, *Ozark*, p. 85; Parsons, *Aiken, S.C.*, p. 32, No. 50; Farr, *Tennessee*, p. 318, No. 27; Bacon and Parsons, *Virginia*, p. 315, No. 24; Chappell, p. 236, No. 36; Fauset, *Philadelphia*, p. 555, No. 24.

312c. What has a tongue an' can't talk, / An' a soul that can't die?—Shoe.
Parsons, *Aiken, S.C.*, p. 32, No. 50, var. 2.

313. Runs and runs, / Never walks, / Has two tongues, / Never talks.—Buggy.
Oral, West Virginia.

314. Have a tongue and kyan't talk, but kyan run all de time.—Wagon.
Parsons, *Sea Islands, S.C.*, p. 164, No. 67.

315. Runners and can't walk, / Tongue and can't talk.—Sled.
Oral, West Virginia.

316a. It can run and can't walk, / It has a tongue and can't talk.—Wagon.
Knortz, p. 219, No. 29; Brewster, *Indiana*, 22; Parsons, *Guilford Co., N.C.*, p. 203, No. 21. Great long tongue: Randolph and Spradley, *Ozark*, p. 82. Can walk: Farr, *Tennessee*, p. 319, No. 12.

316b. It can run and can't walk, / Has a tongue and can't talk. / At the river's brink, / Though it's dry, it can't drink.—Wagon.
Hudson, p. 86, No. 24.

316c. Always runs and never walks, / Has a tongue but never talks.—Wagon.
Oral, West Virginia.

317. What has eyes and can't see, legs and can't walk, cooks and wears an apron?—A cook-stove.
Redfield, *Tennessee*, p. 38, No. 26.

318a. Four legs has it, an' cannot walk, / Feather has it, an' cannot fly.—Bed.
Parsons, *Sea Islands, S.C.*, p. 155, No. 20 var.

318b. Feather it have, an' cannot fly; / Feet it have, an' cannot walk.—Bed.
Parsons, *Sea Islands, S.C.*, p. 155, No. 20.

319. Four legs and can't walk, four eyes and can't see, and smokes a pipe.—Chimney.
Perkins, *New Orleans*, p. 110, No. 51.

320. What is it that sets on four legs and smokes a pipe?—Stove.
Farr, *Tennessee*, p. 325, No. 96; Greenleaf, *Newfoundland*, p. 11, No. 29.

321. Somet'in' large, an' somet'in' small, / Has two han's, no feet at all. / It always runs, yet cannot walk, / You might [read: mought, signifying "must"] be still to hear it talk.—Clock.
Parsons, *Sea Islands, S.C.*, p. 164, No. 65.

322. Somet'in' have two eyes an' cannot see; have two hands an' cannot feel, two feet an' cannot walk, an' one face.—Clock.
Parsons, *Sea Islands, S.C.*, p. 164, No. 65 var.

323. It has two han's, / But it cannot touch me. / It has three legs, / But it cannot run from me.—Clock.
Parsons, *Aiken, S.C.*, p. 32, No. 53.

324. Legs an' don't walk, / Face an' don't talk.—Clock.
Parsons, *Guilford Co., N.C.*, p. 204, No. 24.

325. ther is a thing that hath a mouth & can not speake, 2 ears an cañot hear & 3 foot & not go.—a pote [pot].
Tupper, *Holme Riddles*, 26.

326. What has two ears an' one foot an' can't use them?—Coal pot.
Parsons, *Antilles*, III, 440, Anguilla, 21.

327–335. Abnormal in Form and Function

A few riddles describing an object as abnormal in both form and function give a relatively complete picture and yet show little of the enigmatic spirit which conjures up a deceptive and totally foreign image. The excess of contradictory and confusing material makes them poor riddles.

327. What has four eyes but cannot see?—A stove.
Redfield, *Tennessee*, p. 39, No. 40.

328a. What has four eyes and cannot see?—Mississippi.
Fauset, *Southern Negro*, p. 280, No. 45; Redfield, *Tennessee*, p. 39, No. 40 var.

328b. It has four eyes, goes out to sea, but can't see.—Mississippi River.
Redfield, *Tennessee*, p. 41, No. 62.

328c. Runs, has eyes [*i*'s], can't see.—Mississippi River.
Brewster, *Indiana*, 42.

329. What has five eyes and can't see?—Pair of shoes.
Fauset, *Southern Negro*, p. 280, No. 44.

330. What have a thousand eyes but can't see?—Thimble.
Halpert, *New Jersey*, p. 202, No. 15.

331. A thousand eyes, / But yet can't see.—A cinder-sifter.
Bacon and Parsons, *Virginia*, p. 319, No. 60; Parsons, *Aiken, S.C.*, p. 28, No. 21.

332. Four legs and four eyes, / It can't walk and can't see.—A stove.
Farr, *Tennessee*, p. 319, No. 13.

333. What has a thousand legs and can't walk?—Five hundred pairs of pants.
Halpert, *New Jersey*, p. 202, No. 16.

334. It has four legs and a foot and can't walk. / It has a head and can't talk.
—A bed.
Farr, *Tennessee*, p. 323, No. 80.

335a. Two heads, caint talk, / Four legs, caint walk, / Five ribs an' a backbone.—A flax-break [heckle].
Randolph and Spradley, *Ozark*, p. 82; Chappell, p. 230, No. 5.

335b. Two heads and cannot talk, / Four legs and cannot walk, / Five ribs and a backbone. Such a riddle has never been known.—An old-fashioned flax breaker.
Redfield, *Tennessee*, p. 38, No. 28.

Chapter II

COMPARISONS TO AN ANIMAL

Nos. 336–458

This chapter includes riddles comparing an object to an animal, either named or adequately identified by characteristic details. The riddles based on the formula "What runs about all day...?"[1] and having the answers "shoe," "cat," "milk," or "wagon," suggest a dog and therefore stand with those making a specific comparison to a dog. The arrangement follows the phylogenetic classification, except that, after the manner of popular tradition, guinea pigs are grouped with pigs. Under each heading, references to form precede those to function. Comparisons which are so vague that the creature can only be recognized as something living or moving and at the same time do not permit the hearer to know whether a man or an animal is intended will be found in chapter i.

Riddlers make comparisons to rather few animals: birds (which are occasionally called cocks or hens and more rarely gulls or doves), hogs, sheep, cows, horses, and dogs. The lack of comparisons to a cat is very striking and curious. Frogs, fish, and snakes appear very rarely as the means of comparison. The equating of a needle and thread to a snake—an idea which might seem obvious and easily hit upon[2]—is, for example, almost unknown in Europe and is completely strange to English riddlers. Except for a very curious comparison of the sun or moon to a deer,[3] riddlers do not mention the animals of the field and forest.

The introductory formulas "Here's a thing," "My father has a thing," and the like sometimes obscure the intended comparison to an animal. They do not imply that the speaker conceives the answer in terms of a thing rather than an animal, but signify merely "Here's something to guess."

These comparisons to animals refer only to their most obvious and familiar characteristics. As we have seen, riddlers rarely mention insects, fish, amphibians, or snakes as the subjects of riddles or the means of comparison. The few riddles having them as answers allude usually to the habits rather than to the shapes of the creatures and lack, almost without exception, any truly enigmatic quality. In riddles making a comparison to a bird, flight is the trait most frequently chosen as the typical characteristic, and the fundamental enigmatic contradiction is obtained by saying that the supposed bird "flies without wings." The old and very important riddle for a snowflake[4] is a

---

[1] Nos. 445a through 458.   [2] See the headnote to No. 203.
[3] Nos. 391 through 392b.
[4] Nos. 367, 368, and the headnote to Nos. 367–369.

good example of this pattern. A few riddles refer in one way or another to a cock crowing,[5] and others equate a fire to a cock[6] or a pot over a fire to a setting hen.[7] Among mammals,[8] the pig is used as a means of comparison when rooting, squealing, insatiability, or the young lying beside the sow can represent striking features of the answer.[9] The bull or cow is likely to suggest insatiability or bellowing.[10] Riddlers use the horse with especial freedom and success.[11] Its reins or mane suggest a vine lying on the ground or smoke in the wind.[12] In other uses we have references to a horse eating or drinking.[13] The most favored concept is, however, that of a horse jumping, walking, or being ridden.[14] A dog barks[15] or runs about all day and sits at home at night[16] and thus makes an apt riddle for a gun, a shoe, or a dish of milk.

Unmistakable mythological implications are rare in these riddles, as in riddles generally. The comparisons of the sun to a deer[17] and of a horse to flowing water,[18] which latter theme is unknown to English riddlers, may have a mythical background. Since the early Middle Ages the scene of the wingless bird eaten by a handless person[19] has represented a snowflake. Few riddles have attracted so much scholarly attention, and yet its history and interpretation are still obscure. Perhaps no text in this collection offers more attractive opportunities for further study.

336. Animal Not Identified

336. Although my body little is, / yet I doe please the hearer's eare; / if I were tame, it were not amisse, / then I should live in lesser feare.—The nightingale.
Prettie Riddles (1631), No. 29 = Brandl, p. 61.

337–344. Insect

Riddles describing an insect or making a comparison to an insect are rare. In English folklore the only frequent instance is the comparison of ants, wasps, or bees (or birds) to a motley company of persons.[1] Like the English descriptions of a bedbug[2] or a flea,[3] riddles for insects usually deal with the characteristic activities of the creatures and show little or nothing of an enigmatic spirit.[4]

---

[5] Nos. 377 through 380.
[6] No. 374.
[7] Nos. 375a, 375b.
[8] Nos. 381a through 458.
[9] Nos. 381a through 387.
[10] Nos. 398 through 400c.
[11] Nos. 405 through 435.
[12] Nos. 412a through 413.
[13] Nos. 414a, 415a through 416.
[14] Nos. 419 through 435.
[15] Nos. 438 through 440.
[16] Nos. 445a, 445b, 447 through 454c, 456a, 456b.
[17] Nos. 391, 392b.
[18] See the headnote to Nos. 114–118.
[19] Nos. 367 through 369 and the headnote to Nos. 367–369.
[1] See Nos. 887 through 904 below.
[2] No. 343.
[3] No. 344. See a long medieval Hebrew art-riddle in Friedreich, pp. 161–163.
[4] For other riddles of this sort see No. 83 above, Nos. 359, 360 below, the note to No. 72, and the headnote to No. 344.

337. Little titchie above ground.—Ants.
Beckwith, *Jamaica*, p. 204, No. 192.

338–343. Biting, Stinging

Although Hitty titty[1] or a similar word might mean a person, the scenes "within the wall, without the wall," "up de hill, down de hill," and the like, imply that the riddler probably conceives the actor as an animal. The parallel in the Irish nettle riddle, "*Baa, baa,* inside the fence; *baa, baa,* outside the fence; and she will not touch you unless you touch her,"[2] clearly suggests a sheep and perhaps involves a comparison of the flower and sheep's wool. In a star riddle Little Hittle might be a person, but the connotation of the name is quite obscure.[3] A smoke riddle,[4] which may have borrowed the name from the star riddle, has rendered the name even more confusing. In a Turkish rose riddle the fundamental concept of this nettle riddle is ingeniously and poetically developed; see "On a green throne there is a peri, I stretched out my arm and a rider pulled out a sword," and, in a more elaborated form, "On a green throne sat a peri, he turned his lips to the red coral. While two disturbed lovers were carrying on a conversation, look! a traitor drew his sword on the rider.—Rose, nightingale, gardener plucking a rose."[5] The Turkish "It's *hat*, it's *hut*, it's *Arnavut* [an Albanian], it grabs men, it has no jaws"[6] describes a nettle in a related but somewhat different manner.

338a. Hitty titty upstairs, / Hitty titty downstairs. / If you find Hitty titty, it'll bite you.—Wasp.
Parsons, *Robeson Co., N.C.*, p. 389, No. 11. Ippie tippie: Bacon and Parsons, *Virginia*, p. 324, No. 105. Little Tippy: Parsons, *Aiken, S.C.*, p. 27, No. 12 and var. Tip tip: Perkins, *New Orleans*, p. 111, No. 56. Hippy tippy: Knortz, p. 219, No. 20.

338b. Hitty Titty upstairs, / Hitty Titty downstairs, / You touch Hitty Titty, / Hitty Titty bite you.—Wasp.
Brewster, *Indiana*, 18.

338c. Tippy Tippy Upstairs, / Tippy Tippy Downstairs, / Don't mind [i.e., if you are not careful], Tippy Downstairs will bite you.—Wasp.
Fauset, *Southern Negro*, p. 288, No. 128.

338d. Hippety hop up stairs; hippety hop downstairs. / If you don't watch out, hippety hop will bite you.—Wasp.
Farr, *Tennessee*, p. 323, No. 75.

339. Hitty titty in the house, / Hitty titty out of doors, / Nary man can catch hitty titty.—Smoke.
Bacon and Parsons, *Virginia*, p. 327, No. 133.

---

[1] Nos. 338a through 342c.   [2] De Bhaldraithe, 7.
[3] No. 599 below. See also Little titchie in No. 337 above, Hitties Titties in No. 590 below, and a variant of No. 748a.
[4] No. 339 below.   [5] Hamizade, 217, 219.
[6] Hamizade, 294. *Hat* and *hut* are nonsense words, and *Arnavut* seems to be used for the rhyme.

340. Titty titty upstairs, / Titty titty downstairs. / Don' min' titty titty bite yer.—Rat.
Parsons, *Guilford Co., N.C.*, p. 206, No. 50.

341. Wingy-wing out de wall, / Wingy-wing in de wall, / Wingy-wing make a great man like you bawl.—A jack-spaniel [jack-spaniard] sting you, you bawl.
Parsons, *Antilles*, III, 428, Nevis, 16.

342a. hitty pitty with in the wall hitty pitty without the wall if y^u touch hitty pitty: hitty pitty will bite y^u.—a nettle.
Tupper, *Holme Riddles*, 32; *Prettie Riddles* (1631), No. 58 = Brandl, p. 60; Halliwell-Phillipps, *Popular Rhymes*, p. 49 (reprinted from the seventeenth-century *Harleian 1962*).

In the variants the differences in the places of action and the names are considerable: He Jock, my cuddy, . . . owre the dyke (Simpkins, *Fife*, p. 306); Hobbie-Stobbie on this side o' the dyke (Gregor, *Northeast Scotland*, p. 80); Hobbity-bobbity sits on this side o' the burn (Gregor, *ibid.*); Heg-beg adist the dike (Chambers, *Scotland*, p. 109); Itty-pitty on the hedge (Burne, *Shropshire*, p. 574, No. 2); Kittee up the hill (Johnson, *Antigua*, p. 87, No. 46).

342b. Hetty Bitty up de hill, / Hetty Bitty down de hill. / If you don't trouble Hetty Bitty, / Hetty Bitty won't trouble you.—Stingin' nettle.
Parsons, *Antilles*, III, 424, Antigua, 3.

342c. Hicky-picky on one side of the ditch, / Hicky-picky on the other side of the ditch / And if you touch Hicky-picky, Hicky-picky will bite you.—Nettles.
Praeger, *Béaloideas*, IV (1933-1934), 145, No. 13.

343. One thing it bites like fury, but it never stings. It crawls slow in its movements.—Bedbug.
Fauset, *Nova Scotia*, p. 170, No. 151.

344. Hip, Hop, Jump Wide

This description of a flea lacks any enigmatical contradiction.[1] The comparisons[2] of a flea to a jumping horse seem to have no connection with this text.

In Turkey, we find a very curious comparison of a flea to a bird: "I have a coffee-colored bird, it plays music in the coffeehouse, wait a little, when summer comes, my bird grows joyous";[3] "I have a coffee-colored bird. It dances in the coffeehouse like a dancer";[4] and "I have a coffee-colored bird, the female dancer makes music in the coffeehouse. Come and stay a whole summer. Take it easy, my bird, enjoy yourself."[5] The pertinence of the allusions is not obvious. For another comparison to a bird see the Arabic "A bird flies over the sea, it has no feathers. How can it live?"[6]

---

[1] For riddles of similar construction see the list in the note to No. 72 above, and, especially, the bedbug riddle, No. 343.
[2] For references see note to Nos. 344a, 344b.
[3] Kúnos, 65 = Kúnos, *Nyelvkönyv*, 13.   [4] Zavarin, *Brusa*, 24.
[5] Hamizade, 570.   [6] Ruoff, p. 43, No. 10.

Comparisons of a flea to a man are rare. The Italian "I know someone who is so annoying that even the richest man chases after him"[7] is perhaps related to the notion that a flea can make even a king move.[8] An unusual transposition of this idea to the sphere of things rather than of persons is seen in the Cheremiss "It is small and yet it sets a beam in motion."[9] Comparisons of a flea or louse to a thing are rare, but the Yakut "They say that there is a small sharp knife under the pillow"[10] is an excellent riddle. Another instance is the Cheremiss "A crumb here, a crumb there, a crumb in the space under the vestibule floor."[11]

344a. Hip hop; hip hop; jump wide.—Flea.
Beckwith, *Jamaica*, p. 203, No. 190.

344b. Dip dup, a yard wide.—Flea.
Beckwith, *Jamaica*, p. 203, No. 190a.

345–346. Fish

Riddles based on a comparison to a fish are almost unknown in English tradition and are extremely rare elsewhere. The English equating of a mill saw and a "rollin' trout"[1] is quite obscure, and the description of the mythical *gnimabraein* is Irish rather English.[2] The English have not adopted the comparison of the tongue to a fish in a stream.[3]

345. As I walked over a certain bridge, / I saw a rollin' trout, / The more she eats, the more she drinks, / The more the spits it out.—A mill saw.
Fauset, *Nova Scotia*, p. 169, No. 139.

346. What beast is that which drowns if you take him out of the sea and vivifies to throw him in?—A beast called the *gnimabraein*—probably the walrus, about which there were many strange things told in ancient Ireland.
Fitzgerald, p. 189.

347–349. Amphibian

Riddles based on a comparison to an amphibian are extremely rare. Bahamans have seen a similarity between a frog jumping across a puddle and a spider spinning its web.[1] Even more ingenious is an equating of a frog in a well to churning.[2]

---

[7] Schneller, *Wälschtirol*, p. 253, No. 6.
[8] For parallels see Polish: Kopernicki, 12; Siarkowski, 97. Bulgarian: Bozhov, 20; Chacharov, 8; Gubov, 29, 30.
[9] Genetz, 34. Compare the Polish "Very red, very tiny; it can move barrels of sauerkraut" (Siarkowski, 97); Gustawicz, 299 through 303. Mordvin: Paasonen, 288, 412. Cheremiss: Porkka, 60.
[10] Piekarski, 127.   [11] Wichmann, *Cheremiss*, 29.
[1] No. 345.   [2] No. 346.
[3] See the headnote to Nos. 497–510, § 6.

[1] No. 348. For other uses of this idea, see the headnote to Nos. 431–432.
[2] No. 349.

Riddles having the answer "frog" diverge widely and usually show little of the enigmatic spirit.[3] They ordinarily enumerate the characteristics of the creature: its croaking, its life in water, and its use for human food. Typical instances are an old text, "I gave vent to hoarse sounds in the water's midst, but my voice with praise resounds, as if it too were sounding its own praises; and though I am ever singing, no one ever praises my songs,"[4] and the Renaissance Latin

> Colla tument, albet venter, vox rauca coaxat,
> Terga caput tangunt lubrica, spina viret.[5]

347. There lives a handsome little creature the while beside the dyke; / With his eyes above his head all around he gazes; / With his feet in the swamp he dances whippertywhop. / Guesser, guesser, guesser, what creature is that? —Frog.
Gardner, *Schoharie Hills, N.Y.*, p. 256, No. 21.

348. Bull frawg jump f'om bank ter bank, an' his little feet never touch water.—Spider.
Parsons, *Bahamas*, p. 485, No. 129.

349. Splash about, dash about, / Frog in the well, can't get out.—Churning.
Randolph and Taylor, *Ozarks*, 3.

350. Snake

The only English comparison to a snake consists merely in a reference to its shedding its skin; and since the riddle should have the answer "snake," the basis of the comparison is the readily observable fact of a snake's growth and the riddle consequently lacks enigmatic spirit. Comparisons to a snake are only occasionally found in European riddling, but are somewhat more frequent in Asia. They are applicable to a needle and thread[1] or the tongue.[2] Riddles having the answer "snake" are also somewhat unusual. The best-known variety is the description of a snake as a stick lying on or beneath the surface of the ground.[3]

350. When I am old, I cast my skinne, / whereby I doe come young againe.— Snayle.
Prettie Riddles (1631), No. 8 = Brandl, p. 53.

351–380. Bird

The relatively few comparisons to a bird include only one very famous old riddle, that for a snowflake.[1] Otherwise they are casual inventions of slight

---

[3] No. 347. See also Nos. 82a through 82c.   [4] Ohl, Symphosius, 19.
[5] Buchler, *Gnomologia*, 3d ed. (1614), p. 477.
[1] See the headnote to No. 203.   [2] See the headnote to Nos. 497–510, § 5.
[3] See the note to No. 1466.
[1] Nos. 367 through 370.

interest and importance[2] or adaptations of themes ordinarily expressed in terms of other animals.[3] Riddlers have paid little attention to the special peculiarities or habits of birds and have limited themselves almost solely to flight as the *tertium quid comparationis*. The cock and the hen are, however, individualized: the cock crows[4] and the hen sits on eggs.[5] A few texts name other birds without lingering over details: a snowflake is appropriately compared to a dove[6] or a gull[7] and a pot to a crow,[8] but English riddlers have generally avoided specific details of this sort.

351–353. Form

The few comparisons mentioning the form of the supposed bird have had no great success among English riddlers, and similar ideas are also rarely used elsewhere. The theme of a bird without wings and yet able to fly is, however, very popular.[1] The comparison of a needle and thread to a bird losing its tail bit by bit has only a few parallels, and these seem to be accidental in origin rather than derived from some parent text.[2] Two riddles in this section are old and have widely disseminated parallels: the bird with an abnormal number of legs[3] is known from India to Europe as a crane bearing away a frog. It may have some connection with fable. The notion of comparing a bee to a varicolored bird[4] occurs in several forms, and these may be independent inventions.

351. A very small bird / Have a very long tail / In a large cage. / An' each time it go up and down the cage / It tail comes smaller.—Needle.
Parsons, *Barbados*, p. 277, No. 3 var.

352. Bird and Frog

This curious riddle lacks any obvious reason for its existence in the form in which it has been preserved in Europe. Nevertheless a considerable number of texts can be cited in which two or more animals—among them usually a frog, a snake, and a bird—devour one another, and a riddler makes a puzzle out of the event. This "chain of destruction," as Murray B. Emeneau calls it,[1] has more intelligible use in some very old Indian tales. In the *Hitopadeśa*, a book in which it is entangled with the Mouse-Maiden Tale,[2] it occurs in the following form: An ascetic found a young mouse that had fallen from a crow's

---

[2] Nos. 354 through 360.
[3] See the riddles for a pot (No. 371) or a mill (No. 376) and, in general, the references to specific birds (Nos. 369 through 380).
[4] Nos. 377 through 380.   [5] No. 375b.
[6] No. 369.   [7] No. 370.   [8] No. 371.
[1] See the headnotes to Nos. 365–366 and 367–369.
[2] No. 351.   [3] No. 352.   [4] No. 353.
[1] "Studies in the Folk-Tales of India. III. Jain Literature and Kota Folk-Tales," *Journal of the American Oriental Society*, LXVII (1947), 1–13, especially 3–8, 11–13.
[2] Franklin Edgerton, *The Pañcatantra Reconstructed* (New Haven, 1924), I, 340–345 (Book 3, Tale 9).

mouth and reared it. It was threatened by a cat and was transformed by the ascetic into a cat. He then transformed it into a dog and later a tiger for the same reason. The tiger's feelings were hurt because everybody knew it was really a mouse, and consequently the tiger planned to kill the ascetic. By his supernatural power the ascetic perceived this plan and reconverted the tiger into a mouse.[3] Parallels to this story tell of such "chains of destruction" as that of a frog being swallowed by a serpent, which was being swallowed by an osprey, which in turn was being swallowed by a python. The sight of these events caused a spectator to become a holy man. The versions of this theme differ greatly in details and turn the story to very varied uses. Inasmuch as the following riddle and its parallels contain the same curious series of actors, it seems probable that some connection exists between them and this ancient Indian tale.

352. A bird upon the house I saw, / sixe legges it had, yet but one taile. / Two heads besides more than a daw: / name me this bird, and win the ale.— A hearneshaw had taken a frogge, and brought it to her young ones in the nest made upon the top of an house.
Prettie Riddles (1631), No. 74 = Brandl, p. 62.

353. there is a Bird of great renown, usefull in citty & in town, none work like unto him can doe: hes [he's] yellow black & green a very pretty Bird j mean, yet he is both firce & fell, j count him [MS: "hin"] wise that this can tell.—the painfull Bee.
Tupper, *Holme Riddles*, 140; *Harleian 1962* (17th cent..), cited in Halliwell-Phillipps, *Popular Rhymes*, p. 149; Knortz, p. 231, No. 83.

354–371. Function

A few riddles having various specific birds as answers[1] recite the birds' characteristic activities and lack enigmatic quality because no puzzling contradiction is involved.[2] Among such riddles only the description of an eagle rejuvenating itself by casting its bill[3] is of any curious interest, for this preserves an old belief.

354–355. Manner of Life

354. Judge of me by perfect skill, / my youth restored by casting bill.—An eagle.
Prettie Riddles (1631), No. 7 = Brandl, p. 53.

355. Wha' makes de nes' on de ma'sh?—Ma'sh-hen.
Parsons, *Sea Islands, S.C.*, p. 171, No. 140.

---

[3] Johannes Hertel, *Das Pañcatantra* (Leipzig, 1914), p. 41 (Book 4, Tale 5).
[1] Nos. 354, 355, 359, 360.
[2] For riddles of this sort see the note to No. 72 and the headnote to Nos. 337–344, n. 4.
[3] No. 354.

356–369. Flying

356. Has Wings; Cannot Fly

The riddles in this section achieve the contradiction essential to the genre in various ways. The creature may have wings and be unable to fly[1] or may lack wings and yet be able to fly.[2] The former of these impossibilities corresponds to the theme "has legs but does not walk,"[3] but is much less often used than that theme. A rare instance is the Armenian door riddle, "I have a two-winged bird, it keeps flying but does not move from its place."[4] A literary riddle, to which I shall not assign a number in this collection, describes a spider as:

> I move without wings
> Between silken strings,
> I leave as you find,
> My substance behind.[5]

References to the quality of the flight or to the attendant circumstances are rather rare. Riddlers may mention its height, distance, or speed, or may say that it flies without resting.[6]

356. What has wings but cannot fly?—The "wings" of a cart.
Green, *South Antrim*, 42.

357. Flies; Never Rests

357. What flies and rests never?—Wind.
Gardner, *Schoharie Hills, N.Y.*, p. 258, No. 60.

358–366. Flies High and Low

358. w^t bird is that as flies 3 cubits high & yet doth nev^r rise wth more than 30 feet that mount & fall wth wings [MS: wing] that have no pens at all eating [beating] the ayre it nev^r eats nor drinks nev^r trys sing spake nor thinks aproching nere unto her cruill death she wounds [MS: wouds] & kiles us wth the stones she throwes a friend to those that spend ther derest breath in spoyles & chests in mortal wou[n]ds [MS: wouds] & blows wher in she taks her plasur & her [MS: he] fill hiding men in waues that shee doth kill.—a ship in the midst of the waues is nere to death being acustomed to rob, & kiling casteth the dead in the sea haveing 30 oares & many sailes & the stones that are cast are ment by bullets.
Tupper, *Holme Riddles*, 70.

359. Wha' fly up, an' when he see yer comin', he dive?—Duck.
Parsons, *Sea Islands, S.C.*, p. 171, No. 138.

---

[1] No. 356.
[2] Nos. 365a, 367, 368.
[3] See Nos. 305a through 308.
[4] Zelinski, p. 59, No. 33. Compare No. 127 above, in which the animal is not identified.
[5] MacGréine, *Béaloideas*, III (1931–1932), 414, No. 6.
[6] No. 357 below.

360. Flies High and Low; Catches Chickens

The description of a hawk as a flying creature that catches chickens[1] lacks enigmatic quality. Like the description of a duck as a flying creature that dives out of sight,[2] it is an unusual instance of description in terms of function. In the hoe riddle[3] this manner of description suggests something entirely foreign to the answer. Parallels to the mention of the creature eating grass—an element in the hoe riddle—are rare. They occur in a Polish goose riddle: "It supports itself with shovels. With a stick, it gathers grass"[4] and "It sits upon its hands. With its horns, it eats grass."[5]

360. Wha' flies in de sky an' come down low an' ketch people chicken?—Hawk.
Parsons, *Sea Islands, S.C.*, p. 171, No. 137.

361. Flies High and Low; Eats Grass

The conception varies somewhat. The Icelandic riddle for a scythe, "On a summer's day I am often seen in the hands of men: I am raised high in the air, but am driven at times into the ground,"[1] is a description in terms of a thing, not an animal. Contrast it with another Icelandic riddle on the same theme: "Bloodless and boneless, it bites the grass off the ground."[2]

361a. Me riddle me riddle me randy oh, / Perhaps you could clear dis clear, / An' perhaps you can't. / Some t'ing / Go up and come down / An' eat grass.—[Hoe].
Parsons, *Andros Island, Bahamas*, p. 275, No. 2 (answer lacking).

361b. Something flies high, and flies low, chops grass and eats none.—Hoe.
Parsons, *Bermuda*, p. 251, No. 36.

361c. Something goes up in the air and comes down and takes a piece out of the earth.—Hoe.
Parsons, *Bermuda*, p. 251, No. 36 var.

362–364. Flies High and Low; Often (Never) Changes

The few riddles which find a similarity between a bird and either thought or the wind have features characteristic of literary inventions: a metrical form (which is badly corrupted in some of the texts) and the failure to maintain and elaborate a single, clearly conceived idea with the necessary enigmatic contradiction. The seventeenth-century version with the answer "thought"[1]

---

[1] No. 360.   [2] No. 359.   [3] Nos. 361a through 361c.
[4] Gustawicz, 88. Compare Siarkowski, 74 (It stands on two legs and tears the grass with a peg).
[5] Gustawicz, 89.
[1] Árnason, 39.
[2] Árnason, 65. For references to the lack of blood and bone see the headnote to Nos. 264–265 above.
[1] No. 364 (Tupper, *Holme Riddles*, 67).

seems to stand closest to the original invention. The versions recovered from modern tradition exemplify the processes of oral transmission: the word "changeth" is preserved, but has shifted its meaning from "changes its place" to "alter" or "become different in nature." An Icelandic riddler develops the theme in somewhat different manner: "What bird is that, imprisoned in a house, that yet flies far, swiftest of all things? It goes through Heaven and Hell and every level between them.—Mind."[2]

362. High as the sky it flies, / Over the sea it ranges, / Still it sees no mortal rise, / Still it often changes.—Wind.
Fauset, *Nova Scotia*, p. 162, No. 95 var.

363a. Round the house, / About the house, / And oftentimes changes.—The mind.
Fauset, *Nova Scotia*, p. 161, No. 95 var.

363b. Over the water, / Under the water, / Round the world it ranges, / Never been seen by the eye of man, / But oftentimes it changes.—The mind.
Fauset, *Nova Scotia*, p. 161, No. 95.

364. Flies High and Does Not Leave the Place

364. w^t bird is that so hygt her place neu^r changeth ye[t] she flys by day & night in all the world she rangeth ouer the say [sea] at onst [once] she flys mounting above the lofty skise.—ones thought.
Tupper, *Holme Riddles*, 67.

365–366. Flies High and Low without Wings (Feet)

Riddles based on this idea exhibit many variations in details and many adaptations to particular themes. Although some of them may have originated independently, those on certain themes—notably the riddle for the wind, which has a rather limited currency—probably spring from a single invention. The idea is applicable to:

§ 1. The wind. Welsh: Hull and Taylor, 283. Danish: Kristensen, p. 143, § 422, No. 670 (What is that which flies over land and water and to the end of the world and has neither feet nor wings?). Spanish, Argentinian: Lehmann-Nitsche, 197 (Flies without wings, speaks without mouth, and you do not see it or touch it). Yakut: Piekarski, 32 (They say that there is one that flies without wings).

The wind riddle often contains the element "it takes (strikes) without hands," which occurs in a variant form in the fourteenth-century 'Absque manu pulsat: ventus circum tibi solvat" (Claret, p. 71, No. 69). See French: Rolland, 16. Spanish: Demófilo, 1043 (Flies without wings, speaks without mouth, strikes without hands, and you do not see it, do not touch it);

---
[2] Árnason, 512. See also his Nos. 883 (with the answer "time") and 923. Compare the headnote to No. 1680, § 1, below.

Rodríguez Marín, 278. Argentinian: Lehmann-Nitsche, 196. Dominican Rep.: Andrade, 13 (air). Italian: Rolland, p. 159, No. 17 (What is that thing? It is one who goes around the world and has no arm, and you do not know that he is there, and he makes those tremble whom he meets on the road?). The riddler has omitted to name a function appropriate to the arm. See also Tammi, 23 (It takes without hands, runs without legs, laughs without a mouth). Estonian: Dido, 17 (It runs without feet, tastes without a hand, cries without a throat, and sighs without sorrow). See also the description of the wind as flying without ceasing in No. 357 above.

§ 2. Smoke, a spark. Breton: Charlec, *Dol-de-Bretagne*, 1904, p. 379, No. 48. Catalan: Milá y Fontanals, 1876, p. 25, No. 16 (What is that: it strikes without a beak and flies without wings?—Spark). Italian: Tschiedel, 67 (It has no wings and yet flies, it has no beak and yet bites.—Spark). Polish: Gustawicz, 481 (What flies without wings?). Arabic: Meissner, *Iraq*, p. 167, No. 68 (A bird flew and traversed oceans, but it has no feathers and no beak.—Smoke). Compare the Yakut "They say that golden birds fly out of a deep well. They say that these birds disappear in the air" (Piekarski, 250).

This notion has some analogy to the description of smoke as "climbing without legs"[1] or "climbing without hands or feet."[2] Smoke is also called something that cannot be climbed.[3]

§ 3. A cloud. (Most of the following versions contain the additional detail, "it runs without feet.")[4] Breton: Charlec, *Dol-de-Bretagne*, 1905, p. 40 (I fly without feet). Polish: Saloni, *Rzeshów*, 22 (It has no legs and it walks; it has no wings and it flies). Russian: Sichler, p. 119. Estonian: Dido, 15. Yakut: Piekarski, 32 = Priklonskii, 26 (They say that there is one that flies without wings).

Such Spanish versions as "They fly but have no wings; they give shade but have no body; they are light or heavy, feared or desired; they kill without weapon or sword; and they revive the dead"[5] show an unusual elaboration of the antitheses.

§ 4. A sunbeam. Swedish: Ström, p. 207, "Solen," 15 (It leaps without a leg; it flies without wings in one day around nine villages).

§ 5. Dust. See Nos. 365a, 365b below.

§ 6. Snow. See Nos. 367 through 369. An old version is found in Claret's fourteenth-century "Alat alis, quamvis caret alis: nix michi solvis."[6]

§ 7. Anxiety. Persian: Phillott, 21; Chaina Mall, *Panjab Notes and Queries*,

---

[1] French: Lacuve, *Poitou*, p. 352, No. 4, and p. 703, No. 14; Fleury, *Basse-Normandie*, p. 370.
[2] Votyak: Wichmann, *Votyak*, 182. See also the headnote to Nos. 260–265, § 6, above, and compare No. 941 below.
[3] See Nos. 1616a through 1617g and No. 1626.
[4] See the headnote to Nos. 260–265, § 5.
[5] Rodríguez Marín, 270; Demófilo, 730. Argentinian: Lehmann-Nitsche, 195.
[6] P. 68, No. 14.

III (1886), 220, No. 899, § 2 (I saw a wondrous fowl. It had no feet or wings. Nor [had it sprung] from the womb of a mother or from the loins of a father. Nor from above the sky or from below the earth. It ever feeds on the flesh of man). Indian: Lakshīnātha Upasānī, I, 4 (What bird is that which has no feet, no wings, which does not dwell either on earth or in the air; but it eats away the flesh of man?). The similarity of these versions as well as their style suggests a literary origin.

§ 8. The minds of fools, lunatics, and madmen. Icelandic: Árnason, 278 (I know a bird that flies without needing a wing. It can be in Heaven, Hell, and on earth at the same time.—Mind). French: Rolland, 396 (What flies and has neither feathers nor wings, climbs on roofs and has no ladder?). Italian: Tschiedel, 19 (Who flies without feathers or wings and rises to the roofs without ladders?—Brain).

§ 9. A duck. See No. 366 below.

365a. What is it that fly high and fly low, but haven't got any wings?—Dust.
Parsons, *Sea Islands, S.C.*, p. 174, No. 172.

365b. What is that which flies high and flies low, has no feet and yet wears shoes?—Dust.
Waugh, *Canada*, p. 71, No. 813.

366. Flies high, flies low, / Got no feet, but it wears shoes.—Duck.
Fauset, *Southern Negro*, p. 287, No. 117.

367–369. White Bird Featherless Flies without Wings

This old, famous, and much-discussed riddle describes an object by a scene involving a series of interrelated contradictions. Although the supposed bird has no feathers, wings, or feet, it flies and perches like an ordinary bird and an equally strange person catches and cooks or eats it. In the anemic riddling preserved in English tradition such clearly conceived and ingeniously integrated scenes are rare.

The versions most closely allied to the English texts are of two varieties. A variety of more frequent occurrence mentions a bird, a tree, and a maiden, and a variety of less frequent occurrence mentions a bird, a tree (a dike or the sea), and a man.[1] A Russian frost riddle also belongs to the less frequent variety: "An oak stands without branches, a crow sits on it, an old man comes to it without legs, took it off without hands, killed it without a knife, cooked it without fire, ate it without teeth."[2] The relationship of these two varieties is obscure. They do not seem to reflect differences in the grammatical gender of the word for "sun."

The strange actors and events in this riddle have confused riddlers and have

---
[1] For examples, see German: Carstens, *Schleswig-Holstein*, p. 421. Danish: Kristensen, pp. 120–121, § 333, Nos. 521k, 521m, 521o, 521p.
[2] Sadovnikov, 1992.

been corrupted and garbled. See, as examples, the Icelandic "The bird flew featherless, alighted on the wall boneless. Then a handless man came and shot the bird without a bow.—The wind blew the snow away";[3] the Swedish "An unknown man without a horse sat on a fence and looked at the sun above him,"[4] which seems completely disordered; and the Tatar "A tree has fallen in our yard; it has no limbs, no branches; a bird has come and has eaten it without a tongue or bill."[5] This last text implies that the tree is the snowflake and the bird is the sun.

The earliest traces of this riddle appear in a charm written down by Marcellus Empiricus (Marcellus of Bordeaux) about A.D. 400. They have aroused scholarly interest and have been the occasion of many efforts to connect these ideas with Germanic mythology.[6]

Some clearly related riddles have not hitherto been cited as parallels and will be surveyed here briefly. The similarity of certain Slavic and Finno-Ugric descriptions of dew, rain, or frost has been overlooked. Examples are the Lithuanian "I went by night, I lost a brooch, the moon found it and gave it to the sun";[7] and "I lost a ring under a brazen bridge, the moon found it for me, the sun destroyed it";[8] the Polish "A dog crawled out to the kennel and poured out whey. The moon didn't tell; the sun rose and gathered it in,"[9] which contains some details belonging to the comparison of sunlight to sour milk spilled before the door;[10] the Polish "Saint Herelka, she grew up a little pearl, the moon saw her and said naught, the sun rose and gathered her in"[11] and "Ursula dropped her keys around, the moon knew but said nothing. Then the sun arose and gathered the keys and placed them in Ursula's palm."[12] These ideas, particularly in versions akin to the last text, seem to be widely known among Slavic peoples, for the Russians say, "A comely maiden walked along a field. She was hiding her keys; the moon saw, the sun stole them,"[13] and the Serbians, "Minda lost her keys, the moon found them, the sun snatched them from the moon,"[14] and, with the answer "summer rain," they

---

[3] Árnason, 280.
[4] Ericsson, *Södermanland*, V (1884), 65, No. 208.
[5] Kalashev and Ioakimov, p. 48, No. 5.
[6] For the text of the charm see G. Helmreich (ed.), *Marcelli de Medicamentis*, p. 295, chap. xxviii, § 16 (Leipzig, 1879); R. Heim, "Incantamenta magica graeca et latina," *Jahrbücher für klassische Philologie*, Supplementband 19 (1893), pp. 492–493, with note on p. 545. Virtually all of the many scholarly discussions of the riddle print the text of the charm. Heusler, Jacoby, and Petsch discuss the relations of the charm and the riddle at length.
[7] Jurgelionis, 107 = Schleicher, p. 210.
[8] Schleicher, p. 210. See also Jurgelionis, 104 through 106, 208 through 210.
[9] Saloni, *Rzeshów*, 153.
[10] See the headnote to No. 1659 below.
[11] Saloni, *Rzeshów*, 152.
[12] Kopernicki, 74, citing Kolberg, *Krakowskie*, IV, No. 13. See many parallels in Gustawicz, 348 through 352.
[13] Arkhangel'skii, p. 75. See also Sadovnikov, 1935a through 1935m.
[14] Novaković, p. 194, No. 7.

have the related "The pearls fell in the village, and the village gathered the pearls."[15] These themes have also been taken down by collectors of Finno-Ugric traditions. See the Finnish "The pearls fell from the girl. The moon heard it. The sun found them,"[16] which has the answer "dew and frost"; the Votyak "The keys fell behind the house, the moon saw it, the sun took it.—Frost";[17] the Mordvin "The stately daughter of the mother went to wash leg bandages. The sun saw them, took them away. The moon saw them but did not take them away.—Frost";[18] and the Zyrian "The priest goes out, his key falls, the moon notices it, the sun hides it away.—Frost."[19] In the Russian "Marya, Marïa went to fetch some water, dropped her keys"[20] the scene is applied to lightning.

Less clearly conceived versions are seen in the Hungarian riddles for dew: "The moon drops it, the sun picks it up";[21] "The moon puts it down, the sun removes it, the rake rakes it," which is not completely intelligible, and the even more confused "I went on grass, I came on grass, I lost my golden ring."[22] The Turks say for ice, "I put a silver ring into the middle. The moon came and could not take it. The sun came and took it."[23] We can probably regard the Dschagga dew riddle "I spread out malt, and the boy of the court gathered it up"[24] as an independent conception.

A very simple variety of snow riddle which is current in both Romance and Slavic lands shows a general similarity to the versions discussed thus far, but differs from them in omitting any mention of a person who eats the bird. It tells of a bird flying down and coming to rest and develops these ideas in negations of the usual sort, of which "it sits without a backside" is especially characteristic. The relation of these Romance and Slavic versions to each other and to the more elaborate forms is obscure. For examples see Walloon: Colson, *Wallonia*, IV, 44, No. 16. French: Rolland, 13 (Who flies down from above, walks and has no feet, sits down and has no backside?). Italian: Gianandrea, *Canti popolari marchigiani*, p. 298, No. 9; Pitrè, *Canti*, II, 74, No. 871; Bernoni, *Venice*, 41 (Pirolin che pirolava, / Senza gambe el caminava, / Senza cul el se sentava: / Pirolin che pirolava), which I quote in the original for its onomatopoetic effect. Lithuanian: Jurgelionis, 113 (Without feet, without wings, it flew into a tree), which may be only a defective version of the Lithuanian texts cited in the note to Nos. 367 through 369 below; see also Jurgelionis, 114 (It flew like an angel, it falls like a devil), which employs an entirely different pattern, being a misapplied version of the spark riddle, No. 941 below. Lettish: Bielenstein, 585 (A bird flew without wings, it

---

[15] Novaković, p. 88, No. 5.
[16] Lönnrot, 123 = Henssen, 247.
[17] Wichmann, *Votyak*, 109.
[18] Paasonen, 300.
[19] Wichmann, *Zyrian*, 167.
[20] Sadovnikov, 1957.
[21] Kriza, 19.
[22] *Magyar Nyelvör*, XVIII (1889), 92, No. 8, and VI (1877), 271.
[23] Hamizade, 84.
[24] Gutmann, p. 529.

have the related "The pearls fell in the village, and the village gathered the pearls."[15] These themes have also been taken down by collectors of Finno-Ugric traditions. See the Finnish "The pearls fell from the girl. The moon heard it. The sun found them,"[16] which has the answer "dew and frost"; the Votyak "The keys fell behind the house, the moon saw it, the sun took it.—Frost";[17] the Mordvin "The stately daughter of the mother went to wash leg bandages. The sun saw them, took them away. The moon saw them but did not take them away.—Frost";[18] and the Zyrian "The priest goes out, his key falls, the moon notices it, the sun hides it away.—Frost."[19] In the Russian "Marya, Marïa went to fetch some water, dropped her keys"[20] the scene is applied to lightning.

Less clearly conceived versions are seen in the Hungarian riddles for dew: "The moon drops it, the sun picks it up";[21] "The moon puts it down, the sun removes it, the rake rakes it," which is not completely intelligible, and the even more confused "I went on grass, I came on grass, I lost my golden ring."[22] The Turks say for ice, "I put a silver ring into the middle. The moon came and could not take it. The sun came and took it."[23] We can probably regard the Dschagga dew riddle "I spread out malt, and the boy of the court gathered it up"[24] as an independent conception.

A very simple variety of snow riddle which is current in both Romance and Slavic lands shows a general similarity to the versions discussed thus far, but differs from them in omitting any mention of a person who eats the bird. It tells of a bird flying down and coming to rest and develops these ideas in negations of the usual sort, of which "it sits without a backside" is especially characteristic. The relation of these Romance and Slavic versions to each other and to the more elaborate forms is obscure. For examples see Walloon: Colson, *Wallonia*, IV, 44, No. 16. French: Rolland, 13 (Who flies down from above, walks and has no feet, sits down and has no backside?). Italian: Gianandrea, *Canti popolari marchigiani*, p. 298, No. 9; Pitrè, *Canti*, II, 74, No. 871; Bernoni, *Venice*, 41 (Pirolin che pirolava, / Senza gambe el caminava, / Senza cul el se sentava: / Pirolin che pirolava), which I quote in the original for its onomatopoetic effect. Lithuanian: Jurgelionis, 113 (Without feet, without wings, it flew into a tree), which may be only a defective version of the Lithuanian texts cited in the note to Nos. 367 through 369 below; see also Jurgelionis, 114 (It flew like an angel, it falls like a devil), which employs an entirely different pattern, being a misapplied version of the spark riddle, No. 941 below. Lettish: Bielenstein, 585 (A bird flew without wings, it

---

[15] Novaković, p. 88, No. 5.
[16] Lönnrot, 123 = Henssen, 247.
[17] Wichmann, *Votyak*, 109.
[18] Paasonen, 300.
[19] Wichmann, *Zyrian*, 167.
[20] Sadovnikov, 1957.
[21] Kriza, 19.
[22] *Magyar Nyelvör*, XVIII (1889), 92, No. 8, and VI (1877), 271.
[23] Hamizade, 84.
[24] Gutmann, p. 529.

settled on a tree without branches), which, like the first Lithuanian riddle above, may be a defective version. Masurian: Frischbier, *Menschenwelt*, p. 260, No. 194. Czech: Hanika-Otto, note to No. 1, citing, among other versions, Erben, 13 (It bites, it bites, it has no teeth; it flies, it flies, it has no wings). Flajšhans, p. 11, cites Bartoš, 149 (It flies and flies, but has no wings; it sits and sits but has no backside). See further Henri Gaidoz, *Mélusine*, III (1886–1887), col. 326, No. 3. Polish: Saloni, *Rzeshów*, 179 (It flies, it has no wings; its sits, it has no backside; it bites and has no mouth). In this text the "biting" is the chill of the snowflake falling on the skin. See also Saloni, *ibid.*, 180; Gustawicz, 401, 402 (like Bartoš' Czech version), 403–405; Kopernicki, 3, citing Kolberg, *Krakowskie*, IV, No. 12 (It runs, runs; and it has no wings; it sits, sits, it has no backside); Kopernicki, 3 var. (It runs, runs, it has no wings; it bites, bites, it has no beak; it sits, sits, it has no legs). Russian: Sadovnikov, 1847 (It flies without wings, it grows without roots). The second theme has probably been borrowed from an icicle riddle. Serbian: Novaković, p. 212, No. 7 (It flies, it has no wings; it has no backside, it falls and is not hurt). The second theme occurs in the parallels discussed in the headnote to Nos. 1192–1196, § 4, below. A novel trait appears in the Turkish "It resembles sugar, but has no taste; it flies in the sky but has no wings" (Hamizade, 327).

Sigismund Szendrey's important additions[25] to Antti Aarne's exhaustive study of this riddle are difficult of access. I print them here in a translation generously made for me by the late Arpad Steiner. Szendrey comments as follows:

According to Aarne,[26] this riddle consists of four elements: (A) birds (snow) fly and (B) descend upon a tree; (C) a man (sun) goes there and (D) eats the birds. In this series, however, the element B is often missing in German, Finnish, and Hungarian versions, as it is [for example] missing in Hungarian, Nos. [1]–[4]. Aarne regards such incomplete versions as rather recent corruptions.

As for the constituent elements and their names, many agreements and also considerable divergencies may be found in the Hungarian and the foreign versions. In general, the snow is called a bird in the foreign versions, more rarely (in some Rumanian and Serbian versions) birds, according to whether only one snowflake or several are thought of.[27] The latter idea corresponds better to the Hungarian conception. Hence, the plural "birds" is more frequent[28] than the singular "bird."[29] Indeed, the more expressive "a thousand

---

[25] *Ethnographia*, XXXII (1921), 80–81. The Hungarian versions, to which Szendrey refers by the numbers 1 to 10, will be found in the note to Nos. 367 through 369 of the present collection, in which note the appropriate numbers are given in square brackets. I have adjusted Szendrey's numbering of footnotes to the present context.
[26] *Rätselforschungen*, III, 17.
[27] *Rätselforschungen*, III, 24.
[28] Hungarian, Nos. [8] through [10].
[29] Hungarian, Nos. [6], [7].

birds" occurs twice.[30] The substitute "butterfly"[31] is not found anywhere in the foreign versions, but it cannot be called appropriate in Hungarian either, since snow and butterflies do not come at the same time. The attribute of the arriving bird is generally "featherless" in the foreign versions, and it is "wingless" in only a few Finnish, Russian, Lettish, Lithuanian, Ukrainian, Serbian, and many German versions.[32] In the Hungarian versions, the attributive adjective is replaced in all four elements by an adverb, and so far as the meaning is concerned, it agrees with the rarer foreign adjective "wingless." The element "without feet" in No. [1] occurs with the verb "eats" only for the sake of the meaningless contradiction.[33] In Hungarian, the tree never has a qualifying phrase because the expression "without feet" refers not to the tree but to the descending bird, just as in some German and Finnish instances.[34] In the foreign versions, the sun is generally called a "woman," [and] less frequently but only in German, Finnish, Rumanian, and Serbian versions, "man." In one German version, "bird" stands in place of the sun.[35] In Hungarian, only the latter two occur: a man in Nos. 3 and 8, and a bird is indicated only by inference.[36] The Hungarian conception differs moreover from that of the foreign versions in four instances; once, when the sun is modified only by "one,"[37] and three times when the sun is "a king from the Orient."[38] This latter comparison, although upsetting the original form of the riddle, identifies the rising sun geographically as well as poetically.[39] The adjective with "man" is generally "mouthless" in the foreign versions and is "legless" only in German, Finnish, Russian, Lithuanian, and Serbian.[40] In Hungarian, this adjective either is missing[41] or is replaced by the adverb of place "from the Orient"[42] when "sun" is replaced by "king," but when this element is preserved, it is always "without legs," corresponding to the adjective in group II of the foreign riddles.[43] In the foreign versions, the adjective with element D is always "legless" (German, Finnish, Russian, Lithuanian, Ukrainian, Czech, Serb) or "mouthless" (German, Finnish, Lithuanian, Rumanian), so that "mouthless" appears in riddles of group I and "legless" in element C of group II;[44] the Hungarian versions agree with group II.

On the basis of the original elements Aarne[45] sets up two archetypes, as follows:

---

[30] Hungarian, Nos. [1], [2].
[31] Hungarian, Nos. [4], [5].
[32] *Rätselforschungen*, III, 26.
[33] Translator's note: This error occurs in the original.
[34] *Rätselforschungen*, III, 30.
[35] *Rätselforschungen*, III, 31.
[36] Hungarian, Nos. [1], [2].
[37] Hungarian, No. [1].
[38] Hungarian, Nos. [6], [7], [9].
[39] Compare "lord" in an English version; see Aarne, *Rätselforschungen*, III, 32.
[40] *Rätselforschungen*, III, 33.
[41] Hungarian, Nos. [1], [2].
[42] Hungarian, Nos. [6], [7], [9].
[43] Hungarian, Nos. [3] through [5], and [10].
[44] *Rätselforschungen*, III, 34.
[45] *Rätselforschungen*, III, 37.

Groups I and II

A The bird flies   without feathers
B It descends on a tree without leaves

Group I	Group II
C A man comes without a mouth	C A man comes without a leg
D He eats the bird without feathers	D He eats it all without a mouth

The Hungarian versions are consequently versions of archetype II, and since the order of their elements agrees with that of some German, Finnish, Russian, Ukrainian, Serbian, and Rumanian versions, and since two elements —"without a leg" in C, "without a mouth" in D—occur only in German versions, we must have received the riddle directly from a German source.

In any event, the riddle is of German origin. It is known in Germany as early as the tenth century[46] and it spread from Germany to other lands having snow. The southernmost place where it has been taken down is Siberia.[47] We have no versions of it from Italy or southern France. In view of the elements, their arrangement, and their geographical relations, as well as in view of the scanty Rumanian and Serbian versions and the widely scattered Hungarian versions, it must be maintained that the Serbians and the Rumanians have received this riddle from Hungarian intermediaries.

The following Hungarian riddle for snow melting at sunrise may be completely independent of the preceding: "The large beehive swarms thickly; when the sun shines on it, it gets completely soaked."[48]

For discussion of this famous riddle see Karl Müllenhoff, *Zeitschrift für deutsche Mythologie*, III (1855), 19; O. Schade, *Weimarisches Jahrbuch*, III (1855), 256–258; various authors, *Notes and Queries*, 1st ser., XI (1855), 225, 274, 313, 421; Jacob Grimm, *Kleinere Schriften*, II (Berlin, 1865), 138, No. 75, and pp. 146–148; H. Gaidoz and others, *Mélusine*, III (1886–1887), cols. 83, 129, 236, 501; Ohlert, 2d ed., pp. 98–100; Karl Müllenhoff and W. Scherer, *Denkmäler deutscher Poesie und Prosa* (3d ed.; Berlin, 1892), I, 21 (chap. vii, No. 4), and the notes (II, 59); Ohlert, *Philologus*, LIII (1894), 751; Feilberg, *Gåder*, pp. 44–46; Feilberg, *Ordbog*, III, 427, s.v. "sne"; Petsch, *Neue Beiträge*, p. 16; Schultz, *Rätsel*, col. 68; V. J. Mansikka, *Ueber russische Zauberformeln* (Univ. of Finland Diss.; Helsinki, 1909), pp. 69–74; Petsch, *Rätselstudien*, pp. 334–344; J. Bolte and G. Polívka, *Anmerkungen zu den Kinder- und Hausmärchen*, III (Leipzig, 1918), 115, n. 1; Aarne, *Rätselforschungen*, III, 31–48; Flajšhans, pp. 10–11, No. 7b; A. Heusler, "Das Rätsel vom Vogel federlos," *Schweizerisches Archiv für Volkskunde*, XXIV (1923), 109–111, A. Jacoby, "Zum Rätsel vom Vogel federlos," *ibid.*, XXV (1925), 291–298. See

---

[46] *Rätselforschungen*, III, 4.   [47] *Rätselforschungen*, III, 48.
[48] *Maygar Népköltési Gyüjtemény*, XI, 458.

many parallels collected in Carstens, *Schleswig-Holstein*, p. 421; Wossidlo, 99; Hanika-Otto, 1.

The comparison to a bird without wings which sits down without feet and eats without a mouth is also applicable to fire. See German: Aarne, *Rätselforschungen*, III, 18. Lettish: Bielenstein, 959 (A bird sits on a tree, it has no feet, no beak, no wings, and yet it devours the tree). Szendrey[49] gives the following Hungarian parallels: "The tree grew up without branches, the bird flew upon it without a wing" (*Magyar Nyelvör*, V [1876], 328); "A little tree grows up without branches, a little bird eats it without a mouth" (*ibid.*, p. 34); "A tree grew up without branches, a bird flew upon it without wings, [and] ate it all without a mouth" (*Magyar Népköltési Gyüjtemény*, II, 364, No. 73; identical with *Magyar Nyelvör*, VIII [1879], 140, which Szendrey does not cite); "A tree grew up without branches, a bird flew upon it without wings, it eats it without a mouth" (*Nyelvtudományi Füzetek*, XXVI, 50); "A tree grew up without branches, a bird flies upon it without wings, it eats it, too, without a mouth" (*Magyar Nyelvör*, II [1873], 468); "A tree grows up without its branch, the bird flies upon it without its wing, it eats it all without its mouth" (*Magyar Nyelvészet*, IV, 315); identical with the preceding except that the verbs are in the past tense (*Magyar Nyelvör*, II [1873], 90); identical with the last except that "all" is omitted (*ibid.*, XII [1883], 331); "A tree grew up without branches, a bird flew upon it without wings, it ate it all without its mouth" (oral, from Szalonta); "A tree grew up without its root, a bird flew upon it without its wing, it eats it, too, without its mouth" (*Magyar Nyelvészet*, I, 873); "The tree has grown without branches, a bird flew upon it without wings, it ate it, too, without its mouth, it digested it without smoke" (*Magyar Nyelvör*, III [1874], 38). These Hungarian texts describe lightning or the burning of a candle. Elsewhere, riddlers have developed, in quite different ways, the comparison of fire to a cock or bird on a branch.[50]

Closely related to the riddle here discussed are certain Slavic riddles for the sun. A Russian version, "There stands an oak, an aged oak, on that oak, aged oak, there sits a bird Veretenitsa. No one can catch it, neither a tsar nor a tsaritsa nor a comely maiden,"[51] is clarified by such variants as "A little spindle keeps turning, a little golden spindle. No one can reach it, neither a tsar nor a tsaritsa nor a comely maiden."[52] This has some elements belonging to our riddle and others belonging to the death riddle, "A duck sits on a raft, it boasts to a Cossack, 'No one can pass me by, neither a tsar nor a tsaritsa nor a comely maiden.' "[53] The Serbian sun riddle, "A toothless bird ate up the entire world,"[54] contains an element akin to those already discussed[55] and

---

[49] *Ethnographia*, XXXII, (1921), 81.
[51] Sadovnikov, 1817. Veretenitsa signifies "spindle."
[52] Sadovnikov, 1817d.
[54] Novaković, p. 217, No. 8.

[50] See the note to No. 374 below.
[53] Sadovnikov, 2031.
[55] See Nos. 236 through 239 above.

refers to the sun as insatiable. The contradictions and impossibilities in the Estonian "A fiery coach comes down the mountain, on it there sit a man without a foot, a blind man, a naked man; a hare meets them, the blind man sees it, the man without a foot catches it, and the naked man thrusts it into his bosom"[56] have only a slight similarity to those in the snow riddle. The answer "setting sun, night, dawn, moon" is not readily understood, and the whole has much in common with the genre of lying tales.

I do not understand how this pattern of the snowflake riddle came to be used for "sin".: "An oak stands without branches, upon it [sits] a raven without wings, a man without hands took it off without teeth, got neck-deep into the water. The water pours, he will not be satisfied"[57] or for "a month and a day": "Birds without wings continue to come, a man without feet comes, too, and they all eat without mouths."[58] Equally strange uses of this pattern are the Irish riddles for the treadle of a spinning wheel, "A white wingless goose on top of a branchless tree. A headless fox came and ate it"[59] and for footsteps, "A white goose without a shadow, its treetop without branches, there came a headless fox and ate her up."[60]

The elements which make up this riddle of the snowflake occur separately. Their relationship to the riddle is obscure. Some themes of this sort have no doubt been invented independently. Such a simple and virtually universal conception as that of fire eating without a mouth, as found in an Arabic riddle,[61] need not be derived from this riddle. Such enigmatic contradictions as "flies without wings," "walks without feet," and the like are typical material for riddlers and occur in many contexts and in many countries. The assembling of a series of such contradictions also occurs in a variety of uses. We have already noted its use in an Estonian lying tale. The Bihari describe a snake eating a frog and a crab as "A thief without feet came, and stole a cow without a tail, and stole a man without a head."[62] The Polish and White Russian riddles for eating fish, "He caught not an animal, he stripped it of not feathers, he ate not meat, he threw away not bones"[63] and "I threw not a stick, I killed not a jackdaw, I pluck not feathers, I eat not flesh,"[64] are very similar to the eunuch riddle.[65]

A comparison for snow which mentions a bird and yet has no resemblance to the texts here discussed is the Hungarian "I have a hen that lays its eggs even on the bank" and "I have a little hen that lays its eggs on top of the fence."[66]

---

[56] Wiedemann, p. 290.
[57] Russian: Sadovnikov, 2076.
[58] Hungarian: *Magyar Nyelvör*, V (1876), 422.
[59] Delargy, 1.
[60] O Dalaigh, 89.
[61] Littmann, p. 47.
[62] Mitra, *Bihar*, 10.
[63] Saloni, *Rzeshów*, 134.
[64] Wasilewski, 61.
[65] See No. 823 below.
[66] *Magyar Nyelvör*, III (1874), 38, and XL (1911), 285.

367. White fowl featherless came and lit upon the barn-door legless; out came old Rolus Bolus and shot him bloodless, cooked him fireless, ate him mouthless.—A snowflake melting on a barn-door.
Leather, *Hereford*, p. 231.

368. White bird featherless / Flew from Paradise, / Perched upon the castle wall; / Up came Lord John landless, / Took it up handless, / And rode away horseless / To the King's white hall.—Snow.
Fitzgerald, p. 180 (Westmeath, Ireland); Gregor, *Northeast Scotland*, p. 81.

369. A white dove flew down by the castle. Along came a king and picked it up handless, ate it up toothless, and carried it away wingless.—Snow melted by the sun.
Redfield, *Tennessee*, p. 36, No. 8.

370–371. Sitting

370. A milkwhite gull through the air flies down, / And never a tree but he lights thereon.—Snow.
Fitzgerald, p. 180 (Galway, Ireland).

371. One John-crow sit down on three cotton-tree.—Cooking-pot set on firestones.
Beckwith, *Jamaica*, p. 199, No. 139.

372–380. A Specific Bird

372. Goose Has Legs But Walks without Them

This rather poorly conceived riddle does not make it clear what the speaker intended by the supposed legs. He may have meant the oars. The oldest reference[1] to a ship conceived as a creature moving in this fashion seems to be an art riddle by the Turkish dervish, Mohammed ibn Osman ibn Ali Nakkash, known as Lami'î (the clever), who died in A.H. 938. The Ainu "What moves about hither and yon but has no legs?"[2] is apparently quite independent of these ideas.

A more interesting notion of a ship conceives it as a creature that "goes on its belly with its spine on top."[3] Since almost all the versions[4] diverge widely, we can suppose that riddlers have hit upon this notion independently. The Faeroic "It moves more quickly on its back than a dog can run"[5] differs greatly from the Samoan "Who is the man who lies on his back until his life comes to an end?"[6] or the three Filipino versions, "What creature made by

---

[1] See Friedreich, pp. 164–165, No. 4.
[2] Starr, *Ainu*, 4.
[3] Scotch Gaelic: Nicolson, p. 57.
[4] For texts not quoted here see Icelandic: Árnason, 151. Norwegian: Brox, *Ytre Senja*, 133. Swedish: Ericsson, *Södermanland*, V (1884), 72, No. 253. French: Ledieu, *Démuin*, p. 133. Spanish: Demófilo, 113, 114; Rodríguez Marín, 804. Chilean: Flores, 120 through 122, 770.
[5] Hammershaimb, *Antiquarisk tidsskrift*, III (1849–1851), 317, No. 21.
[6] Heider, 37.

Lord God walks on its back?" "I have a hairless dog who goes belly upward," and "He walks with his back,"[7] or the simple Korean "What goes on its back?"[8] These notions are allied to the description of a ship as a house upside down, with its floor up and its roof down.[9] Tupper[10] discusses the independent origins of some of these versions.

The theme of walking on its back is applicable to various objects. When a book is being read or when it is carried open in a procession, it lies on its back. Hence, Icelanders say, "I am often turned over on my back to be open, if you are virtuous enough to receive instruction from me."[11] The simple impossibility of going about while on its back suffices for Breton, French, and Korean book riddles.[12] Danish and French riddlers have noticed that a corpse goes when on its back,[13] and the Turks elaborate the idea in "A soldier has remained behind, the caravan has returned. What bird did you see that walks on its back?"[14] The Low Germans say of a child that is being carried into the church to be baptized: "Who comes to the church on his back?"[15]

372. I've got a goose and she is a prize. / Whoever buys her will be wise. / She's got legs and walks on none, / Seeks her fortune far from home.—A sailing ship.
Greenleaf, *Newfoundland*, p. 10, No. 18.

373–380. Cock or Hen

373. Form

The theme is very rare, but see the Mongolian "You cannot guess whether a golden anklebone lies with its convex or its concave side upwards.—You cannot guess whether the unborn child is male or female."[1]

373. My father have a hen in his yard, you kyan' tell what the chicken be till he hatch.—Wife; you can't tell whether the child will be boy or girl until it is born.
Beckwith, *Jamaica*, p. 184, No. 9.

374–380. Function

374. My father have a rooster, got no coop can keep him but one.—Fire, only water can keep fire.
Beckwith, *Jamaica*, p. 187, No. 39.

---

[7] Starr, *Philippines*, 29, 30, 34. [8] Bernheisel, p. 86.
[9] See No. 1120 below.
[10] *The Riddles of the Exeter Book*, p. xxvi.
[11] Árnason, 904.
[12] Breton: Kerbeuzec, *Ille-et-Vilaine*, p. 502, No. 4; Sébillot, *Devinettes*, 49. French: Dottin, *Bas-Maine*, p. 139, No. 17. Korean: Bernheisel, p. 86.
[13] Carmeau, p. 34. Danish: Kristensen, p. 79, § 202, No. 308.
[14] Hamizade, 543. I have interchanged the first two verbs to fit the sense.
[15] H. Meier, *Ostfriesland*, 8.
[1] Bazarov, 110.

375a. A black hen sitting on a red hen nest.—Pot sitting on fire.
Parsons, *Bahamas*, p. 478, No. 71, and p. 482, No. 107; Parsons, *Sea Islands, S.C.*, p. 155, No. 16, varr. 1, 2; Puckett, *Southern Negro*, p. 53.

375b. A black hen sitting on red aiggs.—Pot sitting on fire.
Parsons, *Bahamas*, p. 474, No. 33, and p. 475, No. 43.

376. My father had a hen, the more he eat the more he want.—Mill.
Parsons, *Bahamas*, p. 478, No. 69 var.

377–380. Crowing

Riddlers often use a comparison to a crowing cock. The West Indian answer "gun" has parallels in Spanish and Italian, but the usual means of comparison for a gun is a barking dog (see Nos. 438 through 440 below). The comparison to a dog is somewhat more appropriate, for it involves a hint of the dog's bite, which well suggests the effects of the bullet. The striking comparison of a bean pod that cracks open in the sun to a crowing cock rests on an acute observation of nature.

377. My father has a cock in his yard, doesn't crow till the sun is hot.—Castor-oil bean, which cracks open in the sun.
Beckwith, *Jamaica*, p. 184, No. 14.

378. Down in yon ha' I heard a cock craw, / A dead man seeking a drink.—Answer lacking.
Chambers, *Scotland*, p. 108.

379–380. Cock Crows Fire

This comparison for a gun is very popular in the Antilles and is occasionally found elsewhere. The more usual comparisons for a gun are a donkey braying[1] or a dog barking.[2]

The related idea of a bullet conceived as a flying bird is found almost everywhere, but the versions differ so widely among themselves that I should prefer to derive them from several sources and not from a single invention. A typical example is the Flemish "A little bird without skin flies without wings, for the pleasure of some, for the vexation of others."[3] See further, German: Wossidlo, 103; Frischbier, *Menschenwelt*, p. 264, No. 219. Lithuanian: Jurgelionis, 646 (Up flew a bird without wings, but without teeth it killed a man).[4] Russian: Sadovnikov, 1417 (The birdie is not big, it rolls along the field, it fears nobody), 1412*j* (A thin bird flies, its feathers are red and yellow, man's death is at its very end). Arabic: Ruoff, p. 24, No. 24 = Bauer, p. 223, No. 13 (A bird

---

[1] No. 436.   [2] Nos. 438 through 440.
[3] Joos, 342. For comment on the idea of a creature born without skin see the headnote to No. 667 below.
[4] For discussion of the theme of a bird without wings see the headnote to Nos 367–369.

flew with the travelers,[5] its tail of wood and its beak of fire.—Gun).[6] Turkish: Hamizade, 687 (I met a black bird; I sent it to the village across the way.— Rifle). Yakut: Piekarski, 299 (A white stork leaped away, while a crane remained standing). The "stork" and "crane" are the white puff of smoke and the prop that supports the gun when it is fired. African, Kamba: Lindblom, 26 (A vulture: its beak [is] of iron.—Arrow). Indian, Gujerati: Mehta, p. 120, No. 11 (There is a bird with feathers; it can fly, though there is no life in it. Wherever it sits, it carries death.—Bow and arrow). The unusually picturesque and well-conceived Mongolian "Fifteen ducks flew away from a lake the size of a cup, a fast black duck started after them"[7] is virtually the same as a riddle for writing.[8] The oldest version of this sort is a confused eleventh-century arrow riddle, "Vidi virginem volantem rostrum ferreum habentem et corpus ligneum, caudam pennatam, mortem portantem,"[9] which suggests both a bird and a girl.

379a. My fader had a big rooster fowl an' eve'y time he crow, he crow fire.—Gun.
Parsons, *Bahamas*, p. 481, No. 90; Parsons, *Barbados*, p. 283, No. 40 (cock); Parsons, *Eleuthera and Watling's Islands, Bahamas*, p. 440, No. 8; Beckwith, *Jamaica*, p. 183, No. 7. A cock: Parsons, *Antilles*, III, 365, Trinidad, 24; p. 379, Cariacou, 2, p. 373, Grenada, 68, p. 421, Montserrat, 4, p. 429, Nevis, 19, p. 436, St. Martin, 15, p. 442, Anguilla, 39.

379b. My father had a roost', ev'y time it crow, it crow fiah.—Gun.
Parsons, *Bahamas*, p. 481, No. 95.

379c. My fader had somet'in', ev'y time it crow, it crow fiah.—Gun.
Parsons, *Bahamas*, p. 472, No. 13, and p. 474, No. 32.

380. I have a cock on yonder hill, / I keep him for a wonder, / And every time the cock do crow, / It lightens, hails, and thunders.—A gun.
Leather, *Hereford*, p. 230.

381–458. Mammal

381–387. Pig

Riddlers in the West Indian islands and in the southern United States make comparisons to a pig, but those in other English-speaking regions rarely do. This peculiar limitation probably reflects an accident in the collecting of riddles rather than a significant variation in the choice of comparisons. Comparisons to a pig are generally known in Europe.

The few English comparisons to a pig refer to its behavior and not to its shape. For example, the squealing of a pig suggests the noise of a mill[1] to riddlers in North Carolina, Sweden, Finland, and no doubt elsewhere. The

---
[5] Bits of wadding.
[6] For riddles describing an object in terms of the members of an animal see the headnote to No. 1435 below.
[7] Kotvich, 273.   [8] Kotvich, 196.   [9] Malein, 5.
[1] No. 387.

similarity between a pig rooting in the ground and a needle passing through leather has also caught the attention of riddlers on both sides of the Atlantic Ocean;[2] it may ultimately go back to a medieval description of a cobbler's thread. A very widely known comparison for lice[3] calls up the scene of pigs feeding in a forest. It does not seem to be known to English riddlers. I have not found parallels for some minor comparisons to a pig. Of these, only the description of a pumpkin vine as a sow with a litter of young[4] is worthy of note. The parallels suggest that the West Indian versions may be ultimately of African origin.

381–382. Gives Birth

The comparison of a vine with fruits hanging from it to a sow and her young is current in the West Indies and has African parallels. The theme appears elsewhere in curious variations. Although the comparison to a snake laying its eggs might seem obvious, it is rather rare. On the shores of the Baltic riddlers describe hops as "It twists, it writhes, when it comes to the end, it lays eggs."[1] This is similar to the Kxatla pumpkin riddle: "It stretches and stretches and bears here and there."[2] The resemblance is no doubt accidental. A Kanuri gourd riddle, "A snake that stands on the neighbor's fence,"[3] turns the comparison in another direction.

Comparisons to a bird arise from the roundness of the squash or gourd, which might be conceived as an egg. Examples are current at or near the eastern end of the Mediterranean. See the Modern Greek "A rebellious partridge jumps the ditch and gives birth";[4] "My short-tailed hen, she leaps over walls and gives birth";[5] "Hippity hop, the hen jumps the wall and gives birth. She bears round-bottomed eggs, round-bottomed ones";[6] and the Swahili "My tumbwa[7] has gone thither and has laid nine eggs and then has gone away."[8]

Comparisons of a vine to four-legged animals may be illustrated by the Sukuma "Our cattle are born tied to something,"[9] which varies a little from the usual conception. There are a few comparisons to a family or persons,[10] and some others refer to a rope that moves.[11]

381a. My fader had a sow, she pig here, she pig there, she pig all about.— Pumpkin vine.

Parsons, *Antilles*, III, 426, St. Martin, 18.

---

[2] See the headnote and note to No. 386.
[3] See the headnote to Nos. 459–460.   [4] Nos. 381a through 382.
[1] Swedish: Russwurm, *Eibo*, p. 133, § 316, No. 19, citing an Estonian version in Gutsleff, *Anweisung zur ehstnischen Sprache* (Halle, 1732), No. 29.
[2] Schapera, 62.   [3] Lukas, p. 173, No. 45.
[4] Polites, *Neohellenika Analekta*, I, 204, No. 57.
[5] Sakellarios, p. 291, No. 6.   [6] Stathes, p. 344, No. 75.
[7] A bird.   [8] Büttner, p. 201.
[9] Augustiny, 13.
[10] See the headnote to Nos. 1017–1035 below.
[11] See Nos. 1203a through 1203c.

381b. Me riddle me raddle, / I might tol' you dis, I might not. / Me fader had a big sow hog, wheyever she go she always pig.—Pumpkin tree.
Parsons, *Antilles*, III, 436, St. Martin, 18 var.

381c. Some t'ing goes in the bush, where ever she goes she pigs.—Pumpkin.
Parsons, *Antilles*, III, 432, Saba, 4.

381d. Dere's somet'in', whey ewer it run it pigs (t'row de young ones).—Pumpkin wine (vine).
Parsons, *Antilles*, III, 432, St. Eustatius, 7.

382. Dere was somet'in, whey ewer it runs it kids.—Bittah gour'.
Parsons, *Antilles*, III, 432, St. Eustatius, 7 var.

383–384. Manner of Life

383. Stick a hog at its head and it bleed at its tail.—Pipe.
Beckwith, *Jamaica*, p. 199, No. 142.

384. My father have a pig; cut him at his head he don't die, cut him at his tail he die.—Tree.
Beckwith, *Jamaica*, p. 187, No. 40.

385–386. Motion

385. My fader had an ol' sow hawg, de higher you buil' de pen de more he jump.—Cookin' ochry [okra] in de pot—de more fiah, de more he will boil out.
Parsons, *Bahamas*, p. 480, No. 88.

386. Leaves a Trail

This comparison of a needle to a pig running through grass and leaving a trail behind may be a disordered recollection of a medieval riddle. The so-called St. Gall Rhetoric illustrates the figure of synecdoche with "Porcus per taurum sequitur vestigia ferri." This signifies a cobbler's thread oiled with lard and following an iron needle through a piece of leather. The St. Gall Rhetoric, which may have been composed in the ninth century, exists only in manuscripts of the eleventh century.[1] This medieval riddle survives in modern folklore; the Russian and Calmuck parallels are especially interesting examples of its preservation.[2]

The reference to the "grass" through which the pig runs may be a reminiscence of the "hedge," or cloth, found in some riddles for a needle.[3] If "grass" can be so interpreted, the American riddler has then mingled a new theme with the medieval riddle.

---

[1] See K. Müllenhoff and W. Scherer, *Denkmäler deutscher Poesie und Prosa* (3d ed.; Berlin, 1892), I, 56, and II, 130, line 18; Gustav Ehrismann, *Literaturgeschichte des deutschen Mittelalters*, I (2d ed.; Munich, 1932), 245–247. For other medieval versions see the note to No. 386 below; but I have been unable to find the allusion in John Hus's sermons as cited by Flajšhans, p. 11.

[2] See the note to No. 386 below.   [3] See No. 205c and the note to No. 205c.

386. Pig run t'rough de grass an' leave de tail behin'.—Needle.
Parsons, *Sea Islands, S.C.*, p. 157, No. 35.

387. Squeals

The scene is applicable to a mill. The choice of animal[1] varies somewhat: in some parallels it is not named,[2] in others it is a fowl,[3] several hogs,[4] or a person.[5] The comparison may refer either to the sound of the mill or to its insatiability.[6]

The noise of an animal is also applicable to other objects: a gun, as in "The tiger roars in the ant's hole";[7] a grindstone, as in "Catch hold of its tail and it growls";[8] a drum, as in "At the least touch it growls";[9] a hand loom, as in "A tiger roars as it pulls a creeper";[10] and a spinning wheel, as in "When the tail is touched, the beast snarls."[11] We may group together comparisons to a tiger's roar and add the Turcoman riddle for a mill, "In the midst of darkness a tiger roars,"[12] with its Hindi parallel "A tiger roars in a small broken hut.— The *brr brr* of a hand mill,"[13] and the Bhil riddle for a churn, "A tiger is roaring in a well,"[14] but such similarities do not necessarily imply a common origin.

The Bengali mill riddle is curiously elaborated: "The king's peevish horse runs peevishly; after having partaken of cayenne pepper worth 1,000 rupees, it wants to eat more" and "A cow with curved horns and belonging to the king's palace looks with half-closed eyes; after having taken of cayenne pepper worth a thousand rupees, it wants to eat more."[15]

When concepts of this sort are applied to an oven, there is no mention of squealing. See, for example, the Modern Greek "Our sow, the one with a snout, with the snout eaten away, it has eaten the whole world, but is not satiated."[16] A Bengali riddle for a dog describes a similar insatiability: "The earthen pitcher eats rice, [but] does not wash its mouth. Some give [it food to eat], some do not give [it food to eat, but its] hunger is not appeased."[17]

387. De hog under the hill, / The more corn you give her, / The more she squeal.—Gris' mill.
Parsons, *Guilford Co., N.C.*, p. 204, No. 27.

---

[1] See the note to No. 387.
[2] See the headnote to Nos. 236–239.
[3] No. 376.
[4] Nos. 481a through 481d.
[5] No. 777.
[6] Nos. 231, 376, 777, and the note to No. 237.
[7] Baiga: Elwin, p. 475, No. 113. Compare also Nos. 755a through 755i below.
[8] Baiga: Elwin, p. 469, No. 52.
[9] Baiga: Elwin, p. 470, No. 63.
[10] Uraon: Archer, p. 180, No. 7.
[11] Khāriā: Roy and Roy, II, 450, No. 16.
[12] Samojlvich, 143.
[13] Kavyopadhyaya, 48.
[14] Hedberg, p. 874, No. 54.
[15] Mitra, *Chittagong*, pp. 344–345, Nos. 6, 6A. The second may also be found in Mitra, *Sylhet*, 23.
[16] Dieterich, *Sporades*, 9.
[17] Mitra, *Chittagong*, p. 961, No. 1.

388. Rabbit

Comparisons to a rabbit seem to be almost unknown. Some curious Finnish descriptions of the sun, "The hare ran away over the ice, it tripped along the roads and hid under a heap of twigs,"[1] and of the moon, "A hare ran across the ice, a golden dish in its armpits,"[2] are not easily interpreted. Riddles that have a hare or a rabbit as answer are equally rare. The reference to a rabbit in the following riddle is a casual substitution for the usual figure of a man.[3]

388. I went way down the road and I saw a rabbit. I pulled its neck off and drank the blood. What was that?—A bottle of whiskey.
Puckett, *Southern Negro*, p. 53.

389. Lamb

Comparisons to a lamb or sheep are rather infrequent. They ordinarily involve a reference to a flock of sheep, as in the riddles for teeth.[1] A comparison of clouds to sheep or to stars and sheep occurs only rarely.[2]

389a. Here I have it, yonder I see it, / A black lamb with a blue fleece.—Your breath.
Fitzgerald, p. 180 (Westmeath, Ireland).

389b. Here it is under the sea. / Black lamb and blue feet.—Smoke going up the chimney.
Praeger, *Béaloideas*, IV (1933–1934), 144, No. 6.

390–392. Deer

English riddlers rarely make comparisons to a deer. A deer having teeth but no mouth[1] suggests a gorse bush, and the bush rolling before the wind may have seemed similar to a deer leaping in fright. In its international relations and possible mythical background the curious comparison of the sun or moon to a deer[2] is especially interesting. Although there are few western European parallels to this comparison, some Slavic versions and many tales based on this idea imply mythological associations which are difficult to explain fully. The classical allusions, of which the reference to the moon goddess riding on a stag is typical,[3] do not seem to be the sources of these concepts, and I shall let Keller's assertion regarding the comparison of the stag to the star-strewn sky stand on its own merits.[4]

---

[1] Lönnrot, 308 = Henssen, 234. [2] Henssen, 39.
[3] See the headnote to No. 805 below.
[1] See Nos. 497 through 498c.
[2] See Nos. 484a through 485 and No. 487.
[1] No. 390. [2] Nos. 391 through 392b.
[3] Roscher, *Ausführliches Lexikon der griechischen und römischen Mythologie*, II, ii (Leipzig, 1894–1897), cols. 3175–3176.
[4] *Tiere des classischen Altertums* (Innsbruck, 1887), pp. 76, 93; *Die antike Tierwelt* (Leipzig, 1909), p. 277.

The comparison of the sun or moon to animals moving about occurs in many forms, and it is probably impossible to trace them back to a single mythical theme. It is difficult, for example, to see a common theme in the Turcoman "Two female camels, when hiding themselves, enter a solitary place";[5] the Serbian description of the setting sun: "The ox fell into a deep ravine, nobody saw it but God alone";[6] and the Kxatla "Tell me: the bull in the East which gives birth to calves and eats them.—It is the sun [or the day,—a reference to the daily cycle of the sun]."[7]

390. Form

390. On yonder hill there is a deer, / Reaching from here to Lancashire, / East, West, North, South, / Five thousand teeth, but ne'er a mouth.— Gorsty [gorse] bush.
Leather, *Hereford*, p. 232.

391–392. Function

Riddlers rarely mention the activities of the animals to which they compare objects unless these activities contribute to the sketching of a characteristic scene.

391. Shoot at a Deer

The following description of the sun, or, more rarely, the moon, as a deer at which a hunter shoots in vain has long interested students of mythology. It occurs in many forms, both as a riddle and as an incident in a tale. The versions differ greatly, and the relations among them are often obscure. In Europe, the theme is familiar to the Czechs but is rarely found further west.[1] It is uncertain whether the riddle in which a plant sprouting toward the sun is said to "shoot"[2] is related to this idea.

391. On yonder hill there is a red deer; / The more you shoot, the more you may, / You cannot drive that deer away.—Sun.
Gardner, *Schoharie Hills, N.Y.*, p. 254, No. 12.

392. Walks Alone

392a. In Moungan's Park there is a deer, / Silver horns and golden ear; / Neither fish, flesh, feather, or bone. / In Moungan's Park he walks alone.— Moon.
Fitzgerald, p. 182 (Westmeath, Ireland).

---

[5] Samojlvich, 18.   [6] Novaković, p. 2, No. 6.   [7] Schapera, 3.

[1] For discussion see O. J. Maenchen, "Der Schuss auf die Sonne," *Wiener Zeitschrift für die Kunde des Morgenlandes*, XLIV (1936), 75–95; Adalbert Kuhn, "Der Schuss auf den Sonnenhirsch," *Zeitschrift für deutsche Philologie*, I (1872), 89–119; J. Darmstetter, "La flèche de Nimrod en Perse et en Chine," *Journal asiatique*, 8th ser., V (1885), 220–228.

[2] E.g., No. 800 below.

392b. In yonder valley there runs a deer / With golden horns and silver hair. / It's neither fish, flesh, feather, nor bone; / In yonder valley it runs alone.—The sun.
Greenleaf, *Newfoundland*, p. 14, No. 8.

393–404. Cow or Bull

Among the riddles based on comparisons to animals, those naming a cow or bull are rather numerous. They are often of great interest in comparative and historical studies. The poorly preserved description of a hare as a cow of an unusual sort[1] is the only reference to form. The references to the supposed cow's activities differ considerably among themselves. Negroes in the Bahamas conceive sewing as a wall broken down by a cow and built up again by its tail.[2] The meaning of this somewhat infelicitous comparison is obscure. A bull that feeds on three ridges is the equivalent of a pot. This riddle is especially interesting as an example of a conception occurring now with an animal actor, as here, and now with a human actor.[3] The most interesting and curious riddle in this section is the description of wheat being ground in a mill as a bull that dashes its head against stones and is brought home as milk.[4] Since there are Scandinavian and Slavic parallels to this conception and English ones are lacking, its dissemination offers a problem of some interest and difficulty.

393. Form

393a. A hopper o' ditches, / A cropper o' corn, / A wee brown cow, / And a pair of leather horns!—Hare.
Green, *South Antrim*, 4.

393b. Crop-hedge, crop-thorn, / Little cow with the leather horn.—A hare.
Wright, p. 311.

394–404. Function

A needle and thread are not often compared to a bull or a cow, but the Mongolian "A little bluish bull drags his little halter"[1] is excellently conceived. Neither the conception nor the riddler's explanation of the English version is wholly satisfactory.

394. Cow broke down a wall an' buil' it up wid his tail.—You pull a needle wid t'read, an' after it comes out you full it up again.
Parsons, *Bahamas*, p. 483, No. 117.

---

[1] Nos. 393a, 393b.
[2] No. 394.
[3] No. 395. For comparisons to human actors see No. 1182 and the corresponding note.
[4] No. 397.

[1] Zhamtsaranov, 26.

395. My father has a bull, can't feed but upon three ridges.—Cooking pot with three legs.
Beckwith, *Jamaica*, p. 187, No. 42.

396. My father kill a cow, and he went to England, and he came back and meet the blood, on the very spot where he killed the cow.—A coal-pit. Cut wood and put in hole, you can go anywhere and come back and see the same hole.
Parsons, *Antilles*, III, 372, Grenada, 57.

397. Dashes Head on Stone; Becomes White Milk

Although I have noted no precise parallel to this Scotch riddle, it is probably related to the descriptions of a mill as fighting animals between which foam falls to the ground. In such descriptions bulls, bears, boars, eagles, and even men are the actors. See the Lithuanian "Two gray wolves[1] bite each other and white blood flows";[2] the Russian "Two bulls fight, between them foam falls in abundance"[3] and "Two boars fight, foam falls between them";[4] the Modern Greek "Two young cattle fight and let milk fall,"[5] which is readily adapted to a coffee mill in "Two young cattle fight and bring forth black milk";[6] the Cherekessian "Beyond our house two eagles are quarreling";[7] the Turkish "Two swine fight until white foam shows on their mouths";[8] and the Modern Greek "Two lions fight and white smoke comes from their mouths."[9]

The Bulgarians find this scene applicable to the description of carding combs; see "Two eagles fight in the mountains; the white foam flows from them";[10] "Two rams are washing, letting white foam fall."[11] They also use it for the crests of waves: "Two eagles drub each other and leave white foam."[12] Such comparisons to fighting birds are more appropriate to a winnowing fan, as in the Ho "Two kites kick each other."[13]

We find another variation of the theme in the Swedish "Brunla and Brunla's calf went over a stone cataract. When they went to town, they were gray. When they came back, they were white."[14] The name "Brunla" suggests the

---

[1] Var.: hares.   [2] Schleicher, p. 201.   [3] Sichler, p. 219.
[4] Russian: Sadovnikov, 1088; Preobrazhenskii, p. 171. Serbian: Novaković, p. 55, Nos. 8, 9. Mordvin: Paasonen, 75.
[5] Dieterich, *Rätseldichtung*, p. 99, quoting Polites, *Neohellenika Analekta*, I, 195, No. 9.
[6] Polites, *Neohellenika Analekta*, I, 195, No. 13.
[7] Tambiev, p. 59, No. 75. See a German version with two doves in Frischbier, *Menschenwelt*, p. 257, No. 169.
[8] Katanov in Radlov, IX, 395, No. 381.
[9] Sakellarios, p. 296, No. 17.
[10] Gubov, 71.
[11] Gubov, 72.
[12] Ikonomov, 62 = Bozhov, 27.
[13] Sarkar, p. 252, No. 33.
[14] Sandén, *Norra Vadsbo*, 82. For other references to this change in color see the headnote to Nos. 1550–1554 in the present collection.

brown wheat, the stone cataract is the millstone, and the change in color recalls a similar change in a description of baking bread.[15] Riddlers sometimes refer to wheat as going up with one name and coming down with another and have in mind the change from grain to meal.[16] A Russian description of a mill, "At Pavloskoye, at Romanovskoye, a she-goat fought with a he-goat, water quarreled with sand, horses began to stamp, a bear began to roar,"[17] includes some elements characteristic of the comparison to fighting animals and shows the range of fancy possible in a flourishing tradition of riddling.

Analogous comparisons naming men rather than animals as the actors are rather unusual. See, however, the Serbian "Two old men are fighting with their bellies; between them white foam rises.—Grinders"; "The old man is pressing the old woman; from under the old woman white foam surges"; "Two brothers are cutting each other, white blood flows between them"; "Two old men are pressing each other, while white foam is surging between them";[18] the slightly different Modern Greek version, "Two in-laws are battling and put forth white earth";[19] and the Yakut "Arising early in the morning, someone spits forth a white froth, so they say."[20]

Riddles for a mill involve the notion of fighting in other ways, as in the Mongolian "The fold is narrow; the sheep are many; the ram butts continually.—The mortar for hulling millet; the millet; the pestle."[21] A mill is also said to squeal,[22] to be insatiable,[23] or to eat or drink in unusual ways.[24]

397. The brown bull o' Baverton / Gaed over the hill o' Haverton, / And dashed its head atween twa stanes, / And was brought white milk hame.— Corn sent to the mill and ground.
Chambers, *Scotland*, p. 112.

398. Cow's Groans Heard over the World

Although the examples of this theme are not numerous, they are very widely scattered. The animal named varies from case to case: a cow or a horse is perhaps most frequently mentioned.[1] The Estonian "The horse in Hiu, the reins in Russia, the voice heard here"[2] describes lightning and thunder in a single comparison. Probably the Dutch reference to lightning as a horse that cannot

---

[15] Nos. 493*a*, 493*b* below.
[16] See the headnote to Nos. 1547–1558.
[17] Sadovnikov, 1077. For the last theme see the headnote to No. 387 above.
[18] Novaković, p. 55, Nos. 5, 6, 7, and 10, respectively.
[19] Sakellarios, p. 291, No. 7.
[20] Piekarski, 374.
[21] Mostaert, 6.
[22] See No. 387 above and Nos. 481*a* through 481*d* and the headnote to Nos. 776–777 below.
[23] See Nos. 376, 777.
[24] See Nos. 241, 482, and the headnotes to Nos. 240, § 4, and 246–253, § 6.
[1] A dog occurs in No. 442 below.
[2] Dido, 22; see also his Nos. 19, 20.

be bridled[3] is a related theme. Such conceptions have analogues in the descriptions of a gun as a cock, donkey, or dog that makes a characteristic noise.[4]

Comparisons of thunder to an inanimate object making a noise are rather rare. Gypsies see a similarity between thunder and the noise of a rattling wagon that fills the whole world.[5] More widely known is the comparison exemplified by the Tatar "The sword will be struck here, its tip will flash in Dagna"[6] or the Turcoman "I strike from here with a sabre, its end clinks in Arabia."[7]

The conception of a cow's groans audible throughout the world is applicable to:

§ 1. Thunder. See No. 398 below.

§ 2. A bell. Swedish: Geijer and Campbell, 17; Ström, p. 377, "Sysselsättningar," 29. Zyrian: Wichmann, *Zyrian*, 87. Votyak: Wichmann, *Votyak*, 418. Hungarian: *Magyar Nyelvör*, VIII (1879), 140 (The bull lows, people from all over the world assemble). Turkish: Katanov in Radlov, IX, 238, No. 31 (Under the earth neighs the horse of my older sister's husband), which is not fully intelligible, and p. 242, No. 96 (As soon as it received its freedom, my light bay horse neighed). Yakut: Piekarski, 231 (They say that a stallion of this universal world neighs; oxen of this wide world roar.—Clergyman, bells), 274 (They say that oxen from the Land of the South[8] are bellowing). Tungus: Poppe, 8 (On the mountain a stallion began to neigh, from all sides his mares began to crowd together). Indian, Uraon: Archer, p. 181, No. 40 (A brown cow lows in the middle of a field).

Although the comparison of a bell to a bird[9] is readily suggested by the fact that both are in the air, only the Mordvin "A huge cuckoo raises its voice, the leaves fall"[10] refers to a noise made by the bird.

§ 3. A gun. Abyssinian: Littmann, *Tigriña*, 53 (Its bellowing is that of a lion; its being carried is that of a corpse).

398. Had a co' [cow]. When it groans it is heard all over the world.—Thunder.
Parsons, *Barbados*, p. 283, No. 39.

399–400. Insatiable Red Cow (Bull, Heifer)

This is an individualized version of a riddle which also occurs with an actor so vaguely described that it cannot be identified.[1] English riddlers give the answer "fire," which is probably original, and the answer "threshing machine," which may have been suggested by similar riddles for a mill. The Armenian

---
[3] Schrijnen, II, 102, No. 2; Sinninghe, p. 7, No. 11.
[4] See Nos. 379a through 380 above and Nos. 436 and 438 through 440 below.
[5] Wlislocki, 4.
[6] Kalashev and Ioakimov, p. 48, No. 4.
[7] Samojlvich, 23. See also the headnote to No. 436, n. 21, below.
[8] Russia.
[9] See No. 472 below.
[10] Paasonen, 42.
[1] Nos. 236 through 239.

"A red ox sits and does not rise, a black one goes and does not return,"[2] with the answer "fire and smoke," resembles the descriptions of fire and a pot as red and black animals or men.[3] Although riddlers preserve the fundamental conception rather well, they often vary the details greatly. Some riddles[4] comparing the spot where fire has burned to an animal's resting place are the last remnants of an idea current among nomadic peoples. It is first recorded in the saying that grass never grows where Attila's horse has trod.[5] The Bulgarians use the notion of an insatiable bull to describe a flood: "A red bull tears down the field."[6]

399a. Down in the meadows there was a red heifer, / Give her hay she would eat it, / Give her water she would die.—Fire.
    Knortz, p. 239, No. 142.

399b. Little cow crummy, / She sits in her stall, / Give her little or much, / She'll eat it up all. / Give her water, she'll die, / Give her butter, she'll fly.—Fire.
    Green, *South Antrim*, 18.

399c. I have a little cow, / She stands in the hall, / Give her much, give her little, / She'll eat it up all. / Give her wind and she'll fly, / Give her a white drink and she'll die.—Fire.
    MacGréine, *Béaloideas*, III (1931–1932), 414, No. 5.

400a. Upon the hill stands a red bull. / He eats and eats and never gets full.—Threshing machine.
    Brewster, *Indiana*, 34; Hyatt, *Adams Co., Ill.*, p. 689, No. 10925.

400b. Down in a green lane there stands a red cow; she eats and eats yet she never gets full.—A threshing machine.
    Wintemberg, *Ontario*, p. 150, No. 131.

400c. Over on the hill stands a big red bull, / Eats grass all day but never gets full.—Mowing machine.
    Randolph and Taylor, *Ozarks*, 5.

401–404. Offspring of a Bull

This curious and interesting pattern was once very freely used, but it has survived in English riddling in comparatively few rather poorly preserved examples. It describes an object, usually a household utensil or domestic tool, as the offspring of a bull because the object contains a bit of leather. It continues by enumerating the plants or creatures that have made other contributions, or by naming the persons who had a hand in making the object. This

---

[2] Grigorov, p. 123, No. 2.
[3] Nos. 375a, 375b above and Nos. 871 through 876 below.
[4] See No. 396 and the corresponding note.
[5] See my note in the *Journal of American Folklore*, LVI (1943), 136–137.
[6] Gubov, 278.

conception is very closely related to that discussed in the headnote to Nos. 553–554 below, which describes an object in terms of a person whose members come from many sources, and to that discussed in the headnote to Nos. 1058–1062 below, which describes an object in terms of a plant, an animal, and a person. The texts here considered often mention giving birth. Riddlers have not always held to the enigmatic types which I have here attempted to identify and they have consequently confused and disarranged the texts. They have occasionally transferred elements from one to another type.

The description of an object as begotten by several animals is applicable to:

§ 1. An arrow. See No. 403.

§ 2. A harness, a saddle, a yoke, and the like. See No. 404.

§ 3. A bellows, a forge. See Nos. 401, 402.

§ 4. A sword. Swedish: Ström, pp. 172–173, "Svärdet" (Born in the smithy, refreshed [or: cooled] in the sea, blessed in Jesus Christ, hidden in the house, that which every man bears with him, buried in an enemy, that which has a long red cap, that which dragged in the sand.—A sword, with a cross as grip, in its sheath and drawn against an enemy whose blood ran out on the earth). The text is somewhat disordered.

401. A bull bulled it, / A cow calfed it. / It growed in the woods, / And the blacksmith made it.—A forge.

Fauset, *Nova Scotia*, p. 162, No. 102.

402. A cow calved it; it grew in the wood; and a smith made it.—Pair of bellows.

Leather, *Hereford*, p. 230.

403. the Bull Bulled it, the cow calved it, the gonder [gander] gott [begat] it, the goose hatched it, the smith made it, & the stail [tail] grew in the wood.—an Arrow, the metteriall whereof proseeded from all them mentioned.

Tupper, *Holme Riddles*, 141 (I have inserted the third and fourth clauses according to the scribe's indications).

404. Bull, bull, ox, ox, / Stood in the woods, / And a carpenter made it.—Yoke.

Fauset, *Nova Scotia*, p. 174, No. 197.

405–435. Horse

The comparisons to a horse deal with its most obvious characteristics. The horse's mane,[1] which like its bridle should be in the stable when the horse is in the stable, is said to be outside the stable, and the scene makes material for a riddle. Descriptions of a horse eating or drinking[2] may be imitations of similar scenes in which other animals are the actors. The comparison of a

---

[1] No. 412c.
[2] Nos. 414a through 416.

horse to a ship³ appears to be a literary invention. The spirited and obvious comparisons to jumping, walking, or riding a horse⁴ are applicable to various objects, a needle, a pipe, and other household utensils. Riddlers equate the braying of a donkey and the firing of a gun,⁵ and in the parallels other animals appear as actors.

The mention of a horse in describing celestial bodies⁶ is very curious. The moon is, for example, called a gray horse that does not wet its feet when crossing water. This seems to be a very simple kind of mythological thinking. There are no English riddles in which the sun or moon is described as a horse that runs without stopping.⁷

405–413. Form

405. I was going over to Dingledown Hill, and I saw a grey horse.—Moon.
Beckwith, *Jamaica*, p. 192, No. 78.

406. Limber, limber, horse slippery.—Fish.
Parsons, *Bahamas*, p. 476, No. 49.

407. Way out in the field there stands a grey mare, / Hoist up her tail and sop your bread there.—Beehive with honey in it.
Hyatt, *Adams Co., Ill.*, p. 657, No. 10836.

408. Wild and wooly and full of fleas; / Never been curried above the knees.
—A horse.
Farr, *Tennessee*, p. 318, No. 8.

409–413. Abnormal Form

409. We have a horse / Without any head; / He is never alive, / And never will be dead.—A clothes-horse.
Harland and Wilkinson, *Lancashire Legends*, p. 187.

410. See, see! what shall I see? / A horse's head where his tail should be.—Answer lacking.
Halliwell-Phillipps, *Nursery Rhymes*, p. 133.

411. Many miles, many miles, or more, / Tail on a sore horse / Never seen before.—Answer lacking.
Fauset, *Nova Scotia*, p. 174, No. 198.

412–413. Horse in Stable, Mane (Reins, Tail) Outside

This conception is similar to comparisons of an object to a man in a house with his beard streaming outside.¹

---

³ Nos. 414a, 414b.
⁴ Nos. 419 through 420d, 421 through 435.
⁵ No. 436.   ⁶ Nos. 405, 431.
⁷ See No. 140 and the headnote to Nos. 138–140.

¹ See headnote to No. 544, in which this conception is discussed at length.

The comparison to an animal whose mane, reins, or tail projects in an unnatural manner is applicable to:

§ 1. Plants. See Nos. 412a through 412c. The projecting member is the root.

§ 2. A vine. Swedish: Ström, p. 131, "Linse," 8. Italian: Pitrè, 902 (vine and grape). Russian: Sadovnikov, 792 (The lady is in the house, her sleeves are in the yard). The conception is analogous to comparisons of a vine to a rope and an animal.[2]

§ 3. A spoon or a ladle. Russian: Sadovnikov, 397 (The cow is asleep in her place, but her tail is in the street), 432 (A cow in the stall, her tail is on the roof). The latter riddle is also used of an oven and an oven fork.[3] Serbian: Novaković, p. 54, Nos. 1 through 12. Finnish: Lönnrot, 142 = Henssen, 96. Mordvin: Paasonen, 280. Zyrian: Wichmann, *Zyrian*, 253. Modern Greek: Polites, *Neohellenika Analekta*, I, 239, No. 263 (There is something that submerges itself entirely except for its tail).

Some versions of this spoon riddle are unusually picturesque. See the Rumanian "The wolf is in the cabbage soup, its tail is outside";[4] the Modern Greek "A loaded mule goes to the cave and enters";[5] the Russian and Mordvin "The fish is in the water, its tail is outside";[6] the Russian, Mordvin, and Cheremiss "The duck is in the sea, her tail is on the beach";[7] the Serbian "I loaded the pack mule and drove it to the mill; the pack entered but the tail could not," with a dozen and more minor variations;[8] the Turkish "The magpie is in the nest, her tail is in the air."[9] The Armenian "Not until you hold it by the tail will it go into the stall"[10] is closely paralleled by the Tatar "I have an ox. It will not enter the stall until you take it by the tail."[11] Another variation is the Cherekessian "It eats with the guests, then jumps into the manger."[12] The Turkish macaroni riddle, "He mounts a horse and dangles his feet,"[13] is a related conception.

Analogous comparisons of a spoon to a thing are somewhat less numerous than comparisons to an animal, but see the Modern Greek "A loaded ship goes to the cave" and "A little loaded cart goes to the cave and enters."[14]

---

[2] See Nos. 1203a through 1203c and the headnote to Nos. 1203–1205 below and the note to Nos. 381a through 382.
[3] Russian: Sadovnikov, 476.
[4] Weigand, p. 271, No. 9.
[5] Stathes, p. 337, No. 32.
[6] Russian: Sadovnikov, 353, 386, 386a. Mordvin: Paasonen, 66.
[7] Russian: Sadovnikov, 386b through 386f; Preobrazhenskii, p. 172. Mordvin: Paasonen, 350. Cheremiss: Porkka, 25.
[8] Serbian: Novaković, pp. 53–54, Nos. 1 through 12. The version cited is No. 10.
[9] Kowalski, *North Bulgaria*, 24.
[10] Grigorov, p. 124, No. 17.
[11] Kalashev and Ioakimov, p. 48, No. 6. Crimean Tatar: Filonenko, 35.
[12] Tambiev, p. 58, No. 53.
[13] Kúnos, 30; Kúnos, *Nyelvkönyv*, 6. See also the Russian "It sits on a spoon, its feet hanging down" (Sadovnikov, 507).
[14] Polites, *Neohellenika Analekta*, I, 204, No. 59, and p. 250, No. 326. See also the note to Nos. 1165a through 1165c below.

§ 4. Weapons, usually a dagger, a sword, or a knife in its sheath. Lithuanian: Jurgelionis, 653 (A goat in the barn, the goat's horns outside), 654, 655 (A steed in the barn, the steed's tail outside); Schleicher, p. 195. Lettish: Bielenstein, 682 through 684 (sword). Estonian: Wiedemann, p. 264.

§ 5. Beams projecting from a house. Lithuanian: Jurgelionis, 281 (Goats in the pen, horns outside), 282 (Towels in the house, the ends outside); Schleicher, p. 193. Lettish: Bielenstein, 404 (ox and horns), 775 (Eels lie in the sea, all their heads project). Polish: Saloni, Łańcut, 13 (The ox stands in the room, he has horns outdoors); Saloni, Rzeshów, 188 (Pitchy stands in the rooms, he has horns in the yard), 189; Siarkowski, 37. Russian: Sadovnikov, 45 (A pike in the sea, its ends on the shores), 46 (A she-goat lies in the house, but her horns are in the yard), 47 (A cow in the house, her horns in the wall). Bulgarian: Gubov, 220 (All the cows are in the shed, and their tails are in the cowstable), 221 (The cowshed is full of cattle, and their tails are over the cowshed.—The spoon in the basket for the knife and fork). Finnish: Henssen, 81. Estonian: Wiedemann, p. 264 (A magpie in the city, its tail outside.—Beam ends). Mordvin: Paasonen, 24. See also the headnote to No. 544, § 6, below.

§ 6. A doorknob, a key, a latch. Lettish: Bielenstein, 973 (key). Russian: Sadovnikov, 83 (The ram is in the stall, his horns are in the wall.—Doorknob), 95 (door fastener). Estonian: Wiedemann, p. 263 (A magpie in the storehouse, its tail on the roof.—Key). The door, which incloses and holds all together, is conceived as a roof. See also the headnote to No. 544, § 7, below.

§ 7. A knot. Russian: Sadovnikov, 37 (A bull in the stall, his horns in the wall).

§ 8. A road leading from a courtyard. Russian: Sadovnikov, 724 (The bull is in the yard, but his horns are on the river).

§ 9. The sun, the moon. Russian: Sadovnikov, 1837 (A ram is in the stall, its horns are on the wall.—Moon). Yakut: Piekarski, 531 (They say that a white mare forced its tail through the window.—Sunbeam); Priklonskii, 37. Mongolian: Zhamtsaranov, 9 (A mettlesome horse in the courtyard, the end of a lasso in the felt tent). African, SeSuto: Norton and Velaphe, 45 (The brown locust comes from the Pedi country holding a bundle of spears). See also the headnote to No. 544 below, and especially § 10.

§ 10. Smoke. See No. 413.

412a. The horse in the stable and the bridle outside.—A potato in the bank and the vines outside.
Puckett, *Southern Negro*, p. 53.

412b. Horse in de stable an' range [reins] outside.—'Tatuh [potato] in de bed an' de wine [vine] outside.
Johnson, *St. Helena Island, S.C.*, p. 157, No. 1.

412c. Horse in the stable, mange [mane] outside.—Pertater in de bed, wine [vine] outside.
Parsons, *Sea Islands, S.C.*, p. 152, No. 1.

413. Mule in Stable, Tail Outside

This scene, which is here used for fire and smoke, is similar to such Oriental riddles for a lamp as the Malayalam "When the crane sits in the water, it dries up"[1] and especially to the Bhil "It is drinking water by the tail,"[2] with its Uraon parallel, "A bird drinks with its tail."[3]

413. John, the mule, in the stable, his tail outside.—Fire in the kitchen, smoke outside.
Beckwith, *Jamaica*, p. 199, No. 141.

414–435. Function

414–417. Eating, Drinking, Biting

414a. show me a horse of such a kind that in the strangest fashion neu^r eats but of the wind doth tak[e] his sustentation winged before behind strang[e] & wonddrous [wondrous] deeds he doth & w^n he runds [runs] his race upon his brest [breast] wth hast he speeds his rains wth marvelous grace comes from his sid[e]s that now bleeds & in his course he doth not faile if rightly he doth wag his taile.—a shipe.
Tupper, *Holme Riddles*, 69.

414b. Galingay-galingay, wing, / And in her big belly she carries many a thing. / Many a voyage she goes for her master in vain, / and carries her bridle quite close to her rein.—Ship.
Praeger, *Béaloideas*, IV (1933–1934), 145, No. 14.

415a. My fader has a horse, all the grass he eats it comes out at his back.—Jack plane.
Parsons, *Antilles*, III, 374, Cariacou, 4.

415b. My moder have a cattle eating food at navel, coming out at his back.—Jack-plane.
Parsons, *Antilles*, III, 372, Grenada, 56.

416. My father have a horse; carry him down to the river to drink and without he pull out the tongue, can't drink.—Bottle and cork.
Beckwith, *Jamaica*, p. 187, No. 37.

417. My father have a horse; hol' a' [at] him two ears, him bite a' him tail.—Scissors.
Beckwith, *Jamaica*, p. 187, No. 38.

418. Drops Silver

A similar riddle describing a cow does not seem to be known in English. See German: Wossidlo, 293; Renk, *Tyrol*, 66; Hanika-Otto, 124a through 124f. Czech: Feifalik, p. 369, No. 12.

---

[1] Schmolck, p. 242, No. 17.   [2] Hedberg, p. 877, No. 73.
[3] Archer, p. 180, No. 16a. See also Tabaru: Fortgens, 11. For related examples see the headnote to Nos. 1440–1441 below.

418. My father have a horse and every walk he walks he drop silver.—Snail.
    Beckwith, *Jamaica*, p. 187, No. 36.

419–435. Is Ridden, Jumps, or Walks

A horse that jumps, walks, or is ridden often describes sewing and less often other activities or things: a pumpkin vine, a pipe, spectacles, matches, a steelyard, a grasshopper, or repairing a roof. Only the riddle for sewing need be discussed. In its several versions the accessory details vary greatly. The tail or reins grow shorter with each jump.[1] Continental European riddlers often call the thread and needle a silver or iron horse with a linen tail[2] and more rarely refer to the thimble as a silver mountain.[3] English riddlers speak of a horse ridden at its tail and have in mind either the finger pushing the needle through the cloth or a sewing machine controlled at one end.[4] This idea is also applicable to a pipe.[5] It is given a new turn in the Polish needle riddle, "A peasant woman went to town and bought a horse without a tail. She brought it home and gave it a tail."[6] The Poles describe a fiddle bow in the same way: "Maček went to market, he bought a horse without a tail, and he came home and put on the tail."[7] The Xhosa use these ideas in still another way in the needle riddle, "Guess the horse that cannot gallop, if it lacks a tail."[8] Still another variation is the Turkish "When moving it makes the sound *kee-gee*, but it sits on a short white horse."[9] A few riddles describe a larger scene and introduce into it a bridge, symbolizing the finger.[10]

419. My fader have a horse, / Go anywhere he like.—Pumpkin vine.
    Parsons, *Antilles*, III, 364, Trinidad, 15.

420. Goes over a Bridge

420a. A fleety horse get up over a broken bridge.—Needle and thread.
    Beckwith, *Jamaica*, p. 199, No. 140.

420b. A steel horse going over a bony bridge with a silver whip to drive him.—The horse is the thimble, the bridge is the finger, the whip is the needle.
    Parsons, *Bermuda*, p. 255, No. 67.

420c. A steel horse going over a bone bridge and a brass whip driving him.—Woman sewing.
    MacGréine, *Béaloideas*, III (1931–1932), 414, No. 9.

420d. My father have a little pony in him yard and there's only one man, little Johnny, can ride it. Johnny ride with a pair of white reins and he go

---

[1] Nos. 421, 422.
[2] See the headnote to No. 437.
[3] See the note to Nos. 420a through 420c, 420e.
[4] Nos. 425, 426.
[5] Nos. 427a, 427b.
[6] Saloni, *Rzeshów*, 48.
[7] Saloni, *Rzeshów*, 178.
[8] Godfrey, as cited in Schapera, 112.
[9] Katanov in Radlov, IX, 91, No. 763.
[10] Nos. 420a through 420c below.

over a bridge.—Needle is the pony, thread the reins, the crooked finger is the bridge, and the thimble is Johnny.
   Beckwith, *Jamaica*, p. 183, No. 3.

420e. A steel pig going over a bone bridge and a brass man driving it.—Needle and finger with a thimble.
   Praeger, *Béaloideas*, VIII (1938), 171, No. 1.

421–435. Abnormal Riding

421. My father has a horse in his yard; it jump an' jump, an' de rein get shorter an' shorter.—Needle an' thread.
   Beckwith, *Jamaica*, p. 183, No. 4.

422. My father have a horse, ev'y time he jump he leave a piece of his tail.—Needle an' t'read.
   Parsons, *Bahamas*, p. 485, No. 133.

423. Me fader hab a horse; eb'ry lep em lep em lef' a em gut.—Needle and thread.
   Beckwith, *Jamaica*, p. 186, No. 33.

424. My father have a pony; every jump he jump he stop a gap.—Needle and thread.
   Beckwith, *Jamaica*, p. 187, No. 34.

425. My fader had a horse, saddle him on his back an' ride him on his tail.—Machine.
   Parsons, *Bahamas*, p. 476, No. 53.

426. My father saddle his horse at his head an ride him at his tail.—Needle and thread.
   Beckwith, *Jamaica*, p. 183, No. 5a.

427a. My father have a grey horse in him yard, ride him nowhere but on him tail.—Pipe.
   Beckwith, *Jamaica*, p. 183, No. 5; Parsons, *Bahamas*, p. 481, No. 97.

427b. My fader had a ol' white horse, he ride it no way but on he tail.—Pipe.
   Parsons, *Bahamas*, p. 480, No. 85.

428. Without a Bridle, / Or a Sadle, / Across a thing, / I Ride a-straddle. / And those I Ride, / By help of me, / Tho' almost Blind, / Are made to see.—A pair of Spectacles.
   A New Riddle Book; Or, A Whetstone for Dull Wits, p. 11.

429. My father have a horse and a spur; every time he spur, blood will flow.—Matchbox and match.
   Beckwith, *Jamaica*, p. 187, No. 35.

430. My father have a horse in his yard; you can't ride him or he buck into you.—Steel-yard.
   Beckwith, *Jamaica*, p. 183, No. 6.

431–432. Does Not Wet Feet

The comparison of the sun or moon to an animal crossing water without wetting its feet is rather widely known, particularly in eastern Europe.[1] Riddlers employ it in several ways.[2] It is also applicable to animals:

§ 1. A pigeon. Serbian: Novaković, p. 32, No. 12 (My horse crossed the river and did not wet its hoofs).

§ 2. A fly. Serbian: Novaković, p. 139, No. 11 (A buffalo is walking on the sea without moistening its foot).

§ 3. A spider. See No. 348 above.

§ 4. A bee. Irish: O Dalaigh, 40, 41 (A little steed which travels the world and does not wet its feet).

431. A White Mare in the Lake, / That her foot never wets, / Though she travel as far as Roscarberry.—Moon.
Fitzgerald, p. 182 (Westmeath, Ireland).

432. Two horses were goin' across the river. Only four feet get wet. How's dat?—A pregnant horse.
Johnson, *Antigua*, p. 88, No. 57b.

433–435. Is Not Ridden Unless . . .

433. My father have a thing in his yard; nobody can ride him but little Johnny.—Grass-quit [a tropical finch] riding a grass-stalk.
Beckwith, *Jamaica*, p. 183, No. 1.

434. My father has a horse, unless you raise it, he can't walk.—Chai' [chair].
Parsons, *Antilles*, III, 374, Cariacou, 5.

435. My father have a thing in his yard and never ride him till him back break.—House-roof; a man sits astride it to mend the thatch.
Beckwith, *Jamaica*, p. 183, No. 2.

436. Donkey

When applied to firing a gun, the notion of a donkey braying fire is very similar to that of a cock crowing fire.[1] The Yakut make a vivid and apt comparison for a bullet in "They say some iron mews,"[2] but references to what is heard are less frequent than references to what is seen.

Eastern riddlers often compare a bullet to a running quadruped. There are a few instances of this in Balkan riddling. The Rumanians say, "A bear without a tail runs upwards";[3] the Serbians, "A black kitten passed through the forest. If it reached anyone, it would lift its legs,"[4] which is not entirely

---

[1] For comparisons of the sun or moon to a running deer see Nos. 391 through 392b and the note to No. 391.
[2] See the headnote to Nos. 165–173 for comparisons in very vague terms.

[1] Nos. 379a through 380.
[2] Piekarski, 302.
[3] Papahagi, 73.
[4] Novaković, p. 76, No. 1.

intelligible; and also, "A black kitten swished through the forest";[5] "Behind a thornbush a doe jumped, and it jumped over 303 pickets,"[6] which has the introduction in common with the Serbian spark riddle, "A doe jumped from behind a bush. Where it landed, there it died";[7] and finally, "A sheep jumped across a valley and jumped over 303 pickets."[8]

The Asiatic versions of the gun or bullet riddle differ considerably from the preceding texts and also differ among themselves. They may mention three creatures, as in the Mongolian "The gray ox stays motionless, the brindled ox spreads his legs, the dock-tailed ox ran out.—Gunshot [barrel, trigger, bullet],"[9] or—and this is the more frequent form—two creatures, as in the Mongolian archery riddle, "In the north a cow lowed, in the south a stirrup got loose."[10] The two creatures ordinarily represent the gun and the bullet; for examples of this type see the Yakut "They say that a young mare flees while its mother remains behind to neigh"[11] and "A mare calls her colt, but the colt left a long time ago";[12] or the Baluchi "When the cow lows, the calf will run";[13] the Hindi "The black calf of a black cow. The cow remained behind, and the calf ran away";[14] or the Uraon "The black cow scares while the brown calf runs."[15]

Some riddlers refer to the pistol or gun alone, as in the Gujerati "A cow dark in color who would not eat a thorny crop, and when the air is pushed outside, she creates a havoc,"[16] or to the bullet alone, as in the Bhil "The calf of a black cow does not, when sent out, come back to me and does not come back to you."[17] This last theme of going and not returning is often expressed in terms of persons.[18]

A few riddles for a gun or a bullet may be adaptations of older themes. The Mongolians see the flash of an arrow in "A gelded camel opens its mouth; at a distance there is a flash of light,"[19] and this parallels the gun riddle, "A gray horse jumped up, the skies thundered."[20] These conceptions are akin to such riddles for lightning as the Mongolian "A golden camel opened its mouth, and suddenly there flashes a tether."[21]

436. My fader hab a donkey, an' eb'ry bray him bray fire.—Gun.
   Beckwith, *Jamaica*, p. 183, No. 7b.

---

[5] Novaković, p. 76, No. 2. [6] Novaković, p. 76, No. 7.
[7] Novaković, p. 13, No. 4.
[8] Novaković, p. 13, No. 8. His No. 9 is similar.
[9] Kotvich, 436. [10] Bazarov, 64.
[11] Piekarski, 296. See also his No. 297 and Priklonskii, 9, 10.
[12] Popov, p. 287.
[13] M. Longworth Dames, *Panjab Notes and Queries*, II (1885), 70, No. 423, § 4.
[14] Kavyopadhyaya, 47. [15] Archer, p. 194, No. 227.
[16] Mehta, p. 118, No. 7. [17] Hedberg, p. 874, No. 57.
[18] See the headnote to No. 801, § 6, below, and Turkish: Moshkov in Radlov, X, 271, No. 86.
[19] Mostaert, 27; Rudnyev, 26. [20] Rudnyev, 29.
[21] Mostaert, 89; Kotvich, 212, 271; Bazarov, 2.

437-458. Dog

In their variety and their effective and easy use of the physical aspects of a dog, the following riddles exemplify very well the qualities of the true riddle. The equating to a gun, for example, of a barking dog that, contrary to a real dog, bites at a distance[1] or emits fire[2] illustrates admirably the enigmatic technique. The scene in a riddle should suggest nature and should also contain some puzzling contradiction intended to arouse our curiosity and to lead us to seek an interpretation. The riddles based on the theme "What runs about all day. . .?"[3] with its various enlargements show well the modifications arising in oral tradition. The enlargements and variations have retained unusually well the fundamental concept.

Although riddlers have used a dog rather freely as a means of comparison, they have much more rarely composed riddles with the answer "dog." The best-known riddle[4] with that answer is clearly an adaptation of a riddle for a cow and thus illustrates once more the lack of interest in riddles with the answer "dog."

437. Form

437. Iron (Flaxen) Tail

Continental European riddles often describe a needle and thread as an animal with a flaxen tail, but English riddlers know only the following distorted example of the theme. The animal is often called a horse, as in the German riddle cited in the note to No. 421. I point out the exceptions to this rule in the parallels cited in the note to No. 437. The conception of an animal with a tail serves also to describe a bell.[1]

437. Did you ever seen a dawg wid an iron tail?—An eye [of a needle] an' a tail.

Parsons, *Sea Islands, S.C.*, p. 172, No. 149.

438-458. Function

438-444. Barking

The notion of a barking dog is applicable to:

§ 1. A gun. See Nos. 438 through 440.
§ 2. A cock. See No. 441.
§ 3. A newspaper. See No. 443.
§ 4. Thunder. See No. 442.

---

[1] No. 438.
[2] Nos. 439a through 439c.
[3] See the headnote to Nos. 445-458.
[4] See the headnote to Nos. 1476-1494, § 10.

[1] Russian: Sadovnikov, 1018. For similar riddles see the headnotes to Nos. 3-4, nn. 9-11, above and to No. 1326 below, also the note to No. 472.

§ 5. The tongue. Swedish: Russwurm, *Eibo*, p. 135, § 316, No. 39 (A red dog barks behind a stone fence).[1]

§ 6. A drum. French: Parsons, *Antilles*, III, 450, Hayti, 52 (Big dog barks at little dog).

§ 7. An ax. Rumanian: Papahagi, 91. Russian: Sadovnikov, 4, 6. Zyrian: Wichmann, *Zyrian*, 22. Cheremiss: Genetz, 23; Wichmann, *Cheremiss*, 96. Turkish: Katanov in Radlov, IX, 94, No. 805, p. 181, No. 1408, and p. 242, No. 101. Gypsy: Wlislocki, 14. Mongolian: Klukine, 30; Bazarov, 161 (A short dog barks in the woods. He throws out everything that he finds and that is lying there). Abyssinian: Mittwoch, 8. Indian, Ho: Haldar, 6. African, Kanuri: Lukas, 7.

The conception is often in terms of a person rather than of a dog, as in the Zyrian "In the middle of the forest deaf Macarius calls out,"[2] or the Turkish "He often sounds a bell in the forest."[3]

438. Some'tin' bark yere, and bitesher [bites yer, i.e., you] yonder.—Gun.
Parsons, *Sea Islands, S.C.*, p. 168, No. 100; Johnson, *St. Helena Island, S.C.*, p. 158, No. 11.

439a. Me riddle, me riddle / Me dandy o / Perhaps you can clear dis riddle, / An' perhaps you can't. / I saw my fader had a t'ing, / Eve'y ba'k he ba'k / He ba'k fiah.—Gun.
Parsons, *Bahamas*, p. 477, No. 54.

439b. My father had a dog, / Every bark he bark fire.—Gun.
Parsons, *Eleuthera and Watling's Islands, Bahamas*, p. 440, No. 18.

439c. My father have a dog in his yard; every bark it bark it bark fire.—Gun.
Beckwith, *Jamaica*, p. 183, No. 7a.

440. Jamaica bully-dog bark, Kingston bully-dog keep silent.—Great gun.
Beckwith, *Jamaica*, p. 199, No. 146.

441. Kingston bully-dog bark, Montego bully-dog answer.—Rooster. When one crows at one end of the island, another answers at the other end.
Beckwith, *Jamaica*, p. 199, No. 143.

442. Portland dog bark, Westmoreland dog hear.—Thunder.
Beckwith, *Jamaica*, p. 199, No. 145.

443. England dog bark, Jamaica dog sound.—Newspaper.
Beckwith, *Jamaica*, p. 199, No. 144.

444. Cannot Bark

444. A dog in the woods / Can't bark.—Dogwood-tree.
Parsons, *Aiken, S.C.*, p. 36, No. 82.

---

[1] For additional examples see the headnote to No. 1151 below.
[2] Wichmann, *Zyrian*, 291.   [3] Hamizade, 52.

445–458. Running About

The comparison of an object to a dog which runs about all day greatly resembles the notion of a person who runs or dances all day.[1] Both are applicable to the same themes, and details belonging to one conception are often found in the other. Riddles based on these comparisons exhibit an unusual amount of variation in details and at the same time preserve the fundamental idea with admirable clarity: the supposed dog sits in a corner, lets its tongue hang out, goes under a bed to rest, or gapes for bones.

In a few instances the riddler carries the description further by mentioning an onomatopoetic sound. A shoe "goes *trip-trap* during the day" in a Catalan riddle,[2] and the Argentinians say of sabots, "By day *click-clack* and at night under the bed."[3] Such onomatopoetic devices are rather infrequent in European riddling. The most widely known instance is the rain riddle, "It goes around the house and says, *Blirp, blarp!*"[4] In most versions of the rain riddle the sounds are intended to imitate the noise of the dripping and do not clearly suggest a dog. More vividly conceived are such riddles as the Votyak "A young dog runs around the house and whimpers.—Water in the gutter"[5] and the Mongolian "It cries 'Oh!' and runs out.—Steam."[6]

Riddlers often compare an ax to a barking dog.[7] The African "My child cried out in the road"[8] is the same conception in human terms.

The notion of a creature that runs about all day and returns at night is applicable to any domestic tool. The creature may be either an animal[9] or a person. The picturesque Russian scythe riddles rest on the similarity to a person: "It slumps, it is hunchbacked, bent toward the front. It will go all over the field. When it comes home, it will go into chinks"[10] or "A white Whitey has walked in the field. On coming home, it stretched out in the shed."[11] The conception of a person is clearly seen in an Armenian riddle for boots, "At night an Aga,[12] by day a servant,"[13] which is turned into a riddle for a bed

---

[1] See the headnote to Nos. 695–699.
[2] Pelay y Briz, 89.
[3] Lehmann-Nitsche, 15a through 15d. See also the Modern Greek "*Tac-tac* all day and no *tac* all night" (Sakellarios, p. 294, No. 6), the Arabic "Something that goes *tick, tack* by day and opens its mouth at night" (Ruoff, p. 35, No. 78; Löhr, p. 105, No. 3).
[4] German: Renk, *Tyrol*, 149; Schmidt, *Danzig*, 87; Hanika-Otto, 122. Swiss: Rochholz, 456. Danish: Kristensen, p. 132, § 379, No. 600. Norwegian: Stafset, 66; Brox, *Ytre Senja*, 11 = Bergh, *Valdres*, 45 (Who is that who runs around the house and says, *Tipp, tipp, tipp!*). Czech: Hrnčíř, 7, cited by Hanika-Otto, 122. Polish: Gustawicz, 43 (It passes by the house and says, *Cheep, chop!*). Cheremiss: Wichmann, *Cheremiss*, 51.
[5] Wichmann, *Votyak*, 15, 259, 339.
[6] Kotvich, 88.
[7] See the headnote to Nos. 438–444, § 7, above.
[8] Werner, p. 213. A comparison to a man is also suggested in the Turkish "One who jokes in the mountains; [one] with yard-long legs; [one] with a twisted moustache.—Ax, greyhound, hare" (Hamizade, 53).
[9] See the headnote to No. 191, nn. 4, 6, 8, above.
[10] Sadovnikov, 1159.
[11] Sadovnikov, 1165a.
[12] Master.
[13] Seidlitz, p. 71, No. 24.

by exchanging the expressions for time.[14] A Maltese bed riddle, "Harnessed all night, it rests by day,"[15] converts this scene into a description of a horse. Both the Maltese "A thing that is active at night and rests by day"[16] and the Parsee "There is a substance which keeps awake during the night and sleeps during the daytime,"[17] which have the answers "lamp" and "lighted lamp," are similar inventions but are stated in less vivid terms. The Tabaru application of the scene to a door in "It goes out in the morning, it returns in the evening"[18] may be cited as a final illustration.

445–446. Runs About All Day; Rests under the Bed (Stove) at Night

The conception obviously suggests a dog, and some variant forms develop it further by references to gaping for bones. Some Arabic shoe riddles suggest a camel rather than a dog: "I ask you about a rider. He rides two camels, but the rider is only a single man. They permit no one else to ride. All riding animals grow weary, but these do not";[1] and "It is a riding animal, its rider is a pedestrian, it bears him and he bears it, it stands unesteemed at the door, and it neither eats nor drinks."[2] Comparisons of this sort to persons are rather infrequent, but see the Rumanian "Two sisters run all day and sleep behind the door at night."[3]

The notion of an animal that runs about all day and rests under the stove or bed at night is applicable to:

§ 1. A shoe, a boot. See Nos. 445a, 445b.
§ 2. A cat. See No. 446.

445a. What walk all day and when night comes she go under the bed and rest? Guess what it is.—Shoe.
Parsons, *Sea Islands, S.C.*, p. 164, No. 68 var.; Bacon and Parsons, *Virginia*, p. 326, No. 128.

445b. What is it walks up hills and down, hollers all day, an' sets under a bed at night?—A pair of boots.
Randolph and Spradley, *Ozark*, p. 81.

446. What goes around the floor all day, / And sleeps under the stove at night?—The cat.
Fauset, *Nova Scotia*, p. 161, No. 92.

447–452. Runs About; Sits by Fire (in the Cupboard, on the Table)

447. It goes all over the hills and hollows; / It comes in at night and sits by the fire.—Milk.
Farr, *Tennessee*, p. 320, No. 35.

---

[14] Seidlitz, p. 71, No. 34.   [15] Stumme, *Malta*, 8.
[16] Stumme, *Malta*, 17. See also the headnote to Nos. 254-255 above.
[17] Munshi, p. 419.
[18] Fortgens, 83.
[1] Ruoff, p. 35, No. 81.   [2] Giacobetti, 145.   [3] Papahagi, 77.

448. All round t' house, / All round t' house, / And it [i' the = in the] cupboard.—A mouse.
Baring-Gould, *Notes and Queries*, 3d ser., VIII (1865), 325.

449a. All over the pasture in the day time, / Sits in cupboard at night.—Milk.
Fauset, *Southern Negro*, p. 282, No. 69.

449b. Goes all over the hills and hollows, / And comes back home and set up in the safe [i.e., cooler].—Milk.
Fauset, *Southern Negro*, p. 282, No. 70.

449c. Goes over the fields all day, / Sits in the cupboard all night.—Milk.
Brewster, *Indiana*, 54.

450. What goes all over the hillsides during the day and sits on the shelf at night?—Milk.
Redfield, *Tennessee*, p. 38, No. 32.

451a. Round the fields all day, / Sits on the table at night.—Milk.
Fauset, *Nova Scotia*, p. 161, No. 94.

451b. Go out in the fields in the day-time, and come and set upon the table at night.—Milk.
Bacon and Parsons, *Virginia*, p. 314, No. 22; Parsons, *Aiken, S.C.*, p. 31, No. 41.

452. Whut is it goes through the pasture all day, an' sets in th' water at night?—Milk.
Randolph and Spradley, *Ozark*, p. 85.

453. Runs About All Day; Gapes for Bones at Night

While still retaining the fundamental idea, riddlers have enlarged upon it in various ways:

§ 1. It eats meat all day and gapes at night. Swedish: Ericsson, *Södermanland*, I (1879), 82, No. 13. French: Lespy, *Béarn*, 12; Roque-Ferrier, *Languedoc*, p. 337. Albanian: Hahn, p. 161, No. 36. Modern Greek: Dieterich, *Rätseldichtung*, p. 96, citing Stamatiadis, V, 185; Polites, *Neohellenika Analekta*, I, 244, No. 290; Stathes, p. 347, No. 93 (All day long, "Bite, bite!" And at night, "Gape, gape!"). Arabic: Bauer, p. 223, No. 4 (At night it opens its mouth, and during the day it says *Hopp, hopp!* or *Tag, tag!*).

§ 2. It is full of flesh and blood by day; it gapes at night. In this variation the emphasis shifts to the contrast between fullness and emptiness. See Icelandic: Árnason, 418 (What is full of flesh and blood by day but gapes like a troll at night?). German: Wossidlo, 337*b*. Danish: Kristensen, p. 129, § 363, No. 575. Faeroic: Hammershaimb, *Antiquarisk tidsskrift*, III (1849–1851), 317, No. 23. Norwegian: Berge, 64 (By day it is full of flesh and blood, by night it gapes like a shoe), in which the riddler has admitted the answer into his riddle. Swedish: Dybeck, *Runa*, 1848, p. 47, No. 66; Ericsson, *Södermanland*, I (1879), 82, No. 13; Sandén, *Norra Vadsbo*, 8; Waltman, *Lidmål*, 220;

Christofferson, p. 43, No. 3 = *Folkminnen och folktankar*, II (1915), 94, No. 3. Waltman, *Lidmål*, 221 contains the same error as the preceding Norwegian riddle. French: Constantin, *Savoie*, p. 23 (What is full of meat by day and empty at night?). Spanish, New Mexican: Campa, 251. Lithuanian: Schleicher, p. 208 (By day it bears bones, at night it opens its mouth). Estonian: Wiedemann, p. 283 (All day long full of raw meat, at night full of empty wind) and on the same page (By day full of flesh and blood, at night its mouth gapes).

Analogous comparisons to persons are rare.[1] Comparisons to things, as in the Kabardin "In the daytime a cartload of bread, at night an empty bullock cart,"[2] are equally rare. Riddles employing only the contrast between full and empty[3] may be a weakened form of these concepts. The Swedish "Two thick worms with open mouths,"[4] which has the answers "stockings," "boots," seems to have no close parallels. The Estonians describe stockings as "By day a sausage, at night a gut."[5]

453a. Goes all day, an' sets under de table at night an' gapes for bone.—Boot.
Parsons, *Robeson Co., N.C.*, p. 389, No. 9.

453b. All over the hills and back home at night, / Sits under the bed and gapes for bones.—Shoes.
Farr, *Tennessee*, p. 318, No. 10.

453c. What goes all down street and comes back home, and sits in the corner and waits for a bone?—Shoe.
Bacon and Parsons, *Virginia*, p. 320, No. 64; Parsons, *Aiken, S.C.*, p. 31, No. 40, var. 3.

453d. Go around the house all day, / Gape for your bones all night.—Shoes.
Brewster, *Indiana*, 3.

453e. Faht twa black things is't, it lies at your bedside an' gapes for you behns?—Your shoes.
Gregor, *Northeast Scotland*, p. 82.

453f. What lies at your bedside all night, / Gaping for your bones?—Your slippers.
Praeger, *Béaloideas*, IV (1933–1934), 146, No. 24.

454–455. Runs About; Sits with Its Tongue Out

This comparison to a dog sitting with its tongue hanging out involves a pun on the word "tongue," which signifies either the dog's tongue or a part of a shoe or wagon.

454a. What goes over hills and hollows, comes in at night, and sits under the bed with its tongue licked out?—A shoe.
Redfield, *Tennessee*, p. 39, No. 35.

---

[1] See Nos. 991a through 991c below.
[2] Talpa and Sokolov, 6.
[3] Nos. 1455a, 1455b below.
[4] Ström, p. 161, "Stövlen," 1.
[5] Wiedemann, p. 283.

454b. Go all day long, and set up in the corner with his tongue hanging out.—Shoe.
Fauset, *Southern Negro*, p. 282, No. 67; Parsons, *Sea Islands, S.C.*, p. 164, No. 68; Parsons, *Aiken, S.C.*, p. 30, No. 40. Work all day: Fauset, *Southern Negro*, p. 282, No. 66.

454c. Runs over fields and woods all day. / Under the bed at night sits not alone, / With long tongue hanging out, / A-waiting for a bone.—Shoe.
Hudson, p. 88, No. 37.

455. Runs all day, an' stands at night wid his tongue stickin' out.—Wagon.
Parsons, *Robeson Co., N.C.*, p. 389, No. 8; Parsons, *Guilford Co., N.C.*, p. 203, No. 22.

456–457. Runs About; Sits in the Corner (on Its Head)

A few contaminations of the preceding pattern remain to be considered. The notion of the creature standing in a corner[1] has perhaps been borrowed from a riddle for a broom,[2] and that of a creature sitting on its head[3] is a reminiscence of the shoenail riddle.[4]

456a. Up hills and hollows, / And at home with its head in the corner.—Shoe.
Fauset, *Philadelphia*, p. 555, No. 30.

456b. Go ev'ywhey you go / An' come back an' sit in the corner.—Shoe.
Parsons, *Aiken, S.C.*, p. 31, No. 40, var. 1.

456c. Goes all day, / Sits in a corner all night.—Shoe.
Parsons, *Guilford Co., N.C.*, p. 204, No. 25.

457. Goes all day, / Comes in at night, / Sits on its head.—Tacks in your shoes.
Fauset, *Southern Negro*, p. 283, No. 71.

458. Goes over Hills and Plains; Breaks Its Neck at a River

The import of this description is obscure. It may signify that a path is interrupted or broken when it reaches a river, but such a comparison does not seem especially apt.[1] Some Arabic and Indian references to laying off one's shoes before crossing a stream have a curious and perhaps important similarity to this riddle. See such riddles as the following, which employ both animal and human comparisons: "It goes and goes up to the river and then stops";[2] "Something goes all day and rests at the watering place,"[3] which contains a recollection of traveling in a desert; and "He came to the brook and would not go in."[4] The comparisons in animal terms are often more picturesque and more clearly conceived: "At the sight of the water the buffaloes get afraid [var.: fall down]"[5] or "The little horse runs, the little horse gallops, yet its

---

[1] Nos. 456a through 456c.   [2] Nos. 695a through 698.
[3] No. 457.   [4] Nos. 187a through 189.
[1] For comparisons of a road to a person see the note to No. 575.
[2] Iraqi Arabic: Meissner, *Iraq*, 76.
[3] Abyssinian: Littmann, *Tigriña*, 59.   [4] Arabic: Socin and Stumme, 5.
[5] Indian, Bhil: Hedberg, p. 882, No. 108.

ride stops at the water's edge."[6] The Mordvin "I touch, they go; I do not touch it, they do not go.—Snowshoes"[7] is fundamentally the same concept.

458. It goes all over hills and plains, / But when it comes to a river, it breaks its neck.—A path.
Farr, *Tennessee*, p. 318, No. 6.

---

[6] Malayalam: Schmolck, 20. See also Berber: Basset, *Nouveaux Contes*, p. 190, No. 2.
[7] Paasonen, 327.

Chapter III
COMPARISONS TO SEVERAL ANIMALS
Nos. 459–512

WHEN MAKING comparisons to several animals, riddlers usually refer to those found in herds, namely, pigs and horses. Curiously enough, however, they never mention chickens and cows, which are the most familiar gregarious domestic creatures. With the exception of a little-known riddle for a sugar mill,[1] comparisons to chickens and cows are found only in riddles for the teeth.[2]

In this chapter the riddles of the greatest historical interest or the widest currency are the comparison of lice to animals that are hunted and, when caught, are thrown away (a riddle that is said to have so puzzled Homer that he died of annoyance);[3] the comparison of a comb to a hunter and the lice to animals in a thicket;[4] a riddle or enigmatic narrative of the man Two-Legs who sat on a stool Three-Legs while a dog Four-Legs stole a mutton or ham One-Leg,[5] and various related or analogous inventions;[6] the comparison of loaves of bread or burning coals to horses or other animals that change color;[7] and the many riddles for the teeth conceived in terms of animals.[8]

Only two riddles refer to animals of more than one kind: the enigmatic narrative of One-Leg, Two-Legs, and Four-Legs, in which the animals are not identified, and the half-literary query about the three animals—the calf, the goose, and the bee—that rule the world.[9]

As in the preceding chapter, the arrangement follows the phylogenetic classification. An exception is made, however, for the riddles comparing the teeth to animals.

459–470. Animals Not Named

459–460. Animals Hunted

Two very old and famous riddles describing animals as the object of a chase have the answer "lice." One consists in the paradox of throwing away what is caught and keeping what is not caught.[1] Another belongs to a group of riddles describing the human body, and more particularly the head. In this collection I have distributed the riddles in this group according to the various

---

[1] No. 492.
[2] See the headnote to Nos. 497–510, §§ 2, 7.
[3] See the headnote to No. 460.
[4] See the headnote to Nos. 459–460.
[5] Nos. 461a through 461d.
[6] Nos. 462a through 465.
[7] Nos. 493a, 493b.
[8] Nos. 497 through 510.
[9] Nos. 511a, 512.
[1] Nos. 460a, 460b.

underlying conceptions. A brief survey will indicate where they may be found. The head is a field or forest in which a dog or another creature pursues prey;[2] the hunters of the game are eagles;[3] the animals are sheep grazing on a hillside;[4] the head is a building and people;[5] lice are prisoners taken to court and execution;[6] the eyes are pools surrounded by grass or trees;[7] the human body is a variety of objects set one upon another;[8] the head is a hill with holes[9] or a block with seven holes;[10] the hair is a handful of wands;[11] the head is a house or theater;[12] the eyes are pools, but grass or trees surrounding them are not mentioned.[13] Vermin are described in terms of acts in "What I take, I throw away; what I take not, I keep."[14]

A widely known riddle for lice and a comb, "The dead[15] drags the living out of the bushes [forest],"[16] appears to have no parallel in English folklore. Some curious instances of it are the Icelandic "The dead drives the living from the forest";[17] the Serbian "The dead thing is pulling the living thing," "A dead thing is pulling a living thing out of the forest," and "A single dead thing is pulling a hundred living things out of the mountain";[18] the Hungarian "A plow made of bone plows around a hill, the dead pulls the living";[19] the Georgian "A dead one catches living ones";[20] and the Svanian "A dead one carries a living one."[21] The Hungarian "The dead tears the living"[22] is unusual, for the living seem here to be the hairs and not the lice.

The animals inhabiting the forest are often called pigs. The term is appropriate because lice can be said to root in somewhat the same manner as pigs. Examples illustrative of the distribution and variety of this concept are German: Frischbier, *Menschenwelt*, p. 247, No. 58. Swedish: Russwurm, *Eibo*,

[2] No. 459. [3] No. 474.
[4] No. 488. Versions in which animals are not chased or driven are cited in the headnote to No. 488.
[5] See No. 918 and the headnote to Nos. 1145–1148.
[6] Nos. 970 through 975.
[7] No. 1044. Descriptions of a razor as an animal wandering in a forest are cited in the headnote to Nos. 1042–1044.
[8] Headnote to Nos. 1100–1108. [9] No. 1101.
[10] See the headnote to No. 1101.
[11] Nos. 1116a, 1116b. For comparisons of the hair to a field in which no animals are present see the headnote to No. 1116.
[12] Nos. 1143a through 1148 and the headnote to Nos. 1143–1151.
[13] No. 1176.
[14] Nos. 1591, 1592. Compare the headnote to No. 1593, § 7.
[15] For the contrast of the dead and the living see the headnote to Nos. 828–836.
[16] See Danish: Kristensen, p. 63, § 149, No. 219; Feilberg, *Ordbog*, II, 82, s.v. "kam." Faeroic: Hammershaimb, *Antiquarisk tidsskrift*, III (1849–1851), 321, No. 59. Norwegian: Landstad, p. 812, No. 45; Stafset, 91; Brox, *Ytre Senja*, 93; Bergh, *Valdres*, 48. Swedish: Ericsson, *Södermanland*, V (1884), 71, No. 230; Ström, p. 73. Italian: Pitrè, 614. Rumanian: Gorovei, 1895 through 1899. Lithuanian: Schleicher, p. 195. Lettish: Bielenstein, 626 through 629, 909. Kashub: Patock, *Schwarzau*, 4. Finnish: Lönnrot, 597 = Henssen, 126. Lappish: Poestion, p. 267; Donner, 10. Modern Greek: Dieterich, *Rätseldichtung*, p. 97, n. 2.
[17] Árnason, 90. [18] Novaković, p. 237, Nos. 7 through 9.
[19] Arany and Gyulai, III, 296, No. 21. [20] Glushakov, p. 38, No. 94.
[21] J. Nizheradze, pp. 66–67, No. 15. [22] *Magyar Nyelvör*, XV (1886), 44, No. 3.

p. 132, §316, No. 6 (A little gray man drives many little pigs out of the forest). Rumanian: Gorovei, 1399. Serbian: Novaković, p. 237, No. 12 (Shovichko drives pigs down a shadowy place). Zyrian: Wichmann, *Zyrian*, 56 (Polish pigs). Mordvin: Paasonen, 126 (Pigs root on the house roof). Votyak: Wichmann, *Votyak*, 204. Turkish: Hamizade, 657 (A chip as big as a hand, he makes the hogs come down from the mountain), 658 (He comes from the mountain, striking, striking, scraping the hogs). Ossete: Schiefner, 9. Yakut: Piekarski, 99 (They say that there are swine in birch shavings); this involves also a comparison of blond hair to curly birch shavings. Malayalam: Schmolck, p. 242, No. 23 (Pigs in the jungle). Indonesian, Tounsea: De C., 31 (A fence that runs after pigs). To this novel and ingenious concept I can cite no parallels.

A great variety of animals other than pigs are mentioned in riddles of this sort. See Icelandic: Árnason, 819 (A king had ten shepherds. He sent them into the forest to fetch the sheep), 820 (A certain king sent sixty able shepherds into the forest to gather his sheep.—Comb and lice in hair). Lithuanian: Schleicher, p. 195 (Something knotted, entangled, drives the sparrows through the thicket.—Brush). Polish: Siarkowski, 5 (A short, fat, begirdled gentleman chases goats from the woods); Kopernicki, 48 (A thin little gentleman, a wanderer, drives goats about the woods); Gustawicz, 95 through 99, 447 (There is a black forest and it is filled with little lambs. No one can drive them out but a black shepherd). Bulgarian: Gubov, 74 (Deyan drives goats over a little forest). Zyrian: Wichmann, *Zyrian*, 201 (bears), 202 (horses). Modern Greek: Polites, *Neohellenika Analekta*, I, 204, No. 60 (A short, short monk who brings down deer), and p. 245, No. 293; Sakellarios, p. 296, No. 2 (My short dog brings down the goats from the thickly settled place), and p. 297, No. 6 (The mechanic's horse comes down the hill with ewes on its back). Turkish: Hamizade, 69 (In a clustered grove of young trees a black chicken plays); Katanov in Radlov, IX, 285, No. 203 (Into the thick grove runs at a trot a two-year-old black colt). Yakut: Popov, p. 288 (A hundred men who had gone to look for squirrels vanished without trace, it is said). Mongolian: Mostaert, 172 (In a black tree without limbs there is a black dog.—Louse in a queue). African, Pangwe: Tessmann, 64 (An antelope with a black back sleeps above), 65 (A gorilla lies stretched out on the rock). Kxatla: Schapera, 27 (Tell me: a black cow in a black thicket). Indian, Bengali: Mitra, *Chittagong*, p. 968, No. 13A (O brother! the black deer grazes in a meadow [overgrown with the plant called] Kāla Kāsinde. The rājā's son has not the ability to catch [it and] eat [it]), and p. 969, No. 13B (The bird of Ekapura grazes in Ṭekarapura, allows itself to be caught in Hariśchandrapura, and dies in Lakshmīkāntapura). Bhil: Hedberg, p. 873, No. 46 (cow). Kolarian: Wagner, 90 (In a black forest buffaloes have been tied). Malayalam: Frohnmeyer, p. 230 (In a bamboo jungle without thorns a young bandicoot without bones).

Indonesian, Alfoer: Wilken, 1 (A forest full of monkeys). Tounsea, De C., 5 (A little copse where civet cats are caught). Javanese: Ranneft, *Poëzie*, p. 29, No. 3 (A thick copse is described with any sort of tree. There are no leaves and also no flowers and no fruits. There is only one sort of beast. When the beasts eat men, they annoy the landowner).

A Rumanian "Some little dogs are running in the forest to drive out hares"[23] compares both comb and lice to animals. The muddled Kashub "A man went to a man to borrow a sheep to drive the bugs from the meadow"[24] contains some elements belonging to the riddles describing a man (boy, or dog) driving a cow, a horse, or some other animal out of a field.[25]

A few riddles of this sort are sufficiently picturesque to call for special notice. The Chileans say, "The captain on the mountain does nothing but go about and when he eats, he gets furious.—Comb";[26] the Russians, "Little, hunchbacked, toothy, he got the habit of coming to the meadows to steal little ducks and yet receives thanks"[27] or "Verenka sat on a mountain ash, she chased little cattle"[28] or "While walking through the forest, blond Gabriel chases pigs";[29] the Serbians, "A wooden man drives the goats";[30] the Bulgarians, "Black monks are strolling down the forest, a white boar is driving them";[31] and the Tungus, "In the reeds the dogs bark without sound."[32] Like the previously cited Kashub text, the Kashub "The gentleman went to the gentleman to borrow a *caban* [a large Rumanian sheep] to drive the cockchafers from the rough meadow"[33] contains elements belonging to another riddle.[34]

Discussion of this riddle for lice is very scanty; see Friedreich, p. 168; Loewenthal, p. 78, citing *Anthologia Palatina*, XIV, 19.

The Letts and perhaps other peoples use this manner of description in riddles for weaving: "A brown mare that goes through a thick birch forest" or "A yellow horse that wades through a brook."[35]

459. My prey I seek the fields and weeds about, / and have more teeth then [than] beasts within the land, / and whensoever my game I have found out, / then safe I bring it to my master's hand. / Upon my back the deere he layes / and there doth kill one, sometimes more: / he shuts me up and goes his wayes, / better contented then [than] before.—It is a combe, and a louse killed upon the backe of it.

Prettie Riddles (1631), No. 38 = Brandl, p. 58.

---

[23] Papahagi, 18. [24] Gulgowski, 19.
[25] See below, Nos. 842a through 850 and the headnote to Nos. 842–856.
[26] Flores, 614. [27] Sadovnikov, 1689.
[28] Sadovnikov, 1690d. See also "Little Jeremiah set on a little mountain ash, he has begun to drive the cattle" (Preobrazhenskii, p. 171).
[29] Sadovnikov, 1690h. [30] Novaković, p. 237, No. 1.
[31] Chacharov, 15. [32] Poppe, 33.
[33] Gulgowski, 17.
[34] See below, Nos. 842a through 850 and the headnote to Nos. 842–856.
[35] Bielenstein, 297, 298.

460. What I Caught (Killed), I Threw Away

The enigmatic spirit manifests itself in the contradiction between throwing away game and a hunter's normal behavior. It often emphasizes the situation and makes the scene more confusing by adding the remark that the hunter kept the game that he did not catch. Very similar ideas underlie the riddles for a thorn[1] and for vermin.[2] In these the lice are, however, conceived not as game but as things to be kept or thrown away.

This riddle is very old. Heraclitus, who flourished at the beginning of the fifth century B.C., may have known it in a version associated with Homer, who is said to have died from vexation at being unable to guess the answer.[3] In late classical tradition the incident becomes the theme of a proverb and an epigram.[4] The epigram is famous for having been written on the walls of Pompeii. In more recent times the incident appears in tales, notably the medieval *Salomon et Marcolfus*, and in folk tales.[5]

Flajšhans comments[6] on the similarity of this riddle to the riddle for a wormy nut, "Video et tollo, si vidissem, non tulissem."[7]

The discussion of this riddle for lice has consisted chiefly in the collection of the many instances of its use. See Friedreich, p. 181; Julius Zupitza, [Herrig's] *Archiv für des Studium der neueren Sprachen*, XCIII (1894), 173; C. Schweitzer, *Etude sur ... Hans Sachs* (Nancy, 1887), p. 170; A. L. Stiefel (ed.), *Hans Sachs-Forschungen, Festschrift zur vierhundersten Geburtsfeier* (Nuremberg, 1894), p. 66, citing K. Goedeke, *Dichtungen von Hans Sachs*, I (2d ed.; Leipzig, 1883), 84–85, No. 29;[8] Emmanuel Cosquin, *Contes populaires de Lorraine*, II (Paris, n.d. [1886]), 124, No. 49; Feilberg, *Ordbog*, II, 467, s.v. "lus"; Reinhold Köhler, *Kleinere Schriften*, I, 87 and 152; Tupper, *Holme Riddles*, p. 247; Boekenoogen, p. 45; Loewenthal, p. 81; A. Wesselski, *Mönchs-*

---

[1] Nos. 1632 through 1641 and the headnote to Nos. 1632–1642.

[2] Nos. 1591, 1592.

[3] See Ohlert, 2d ed., pp. 30–31; Wilhelm Hertz, "Der Tod von Dichtern," *Gesammelte Abhandlungen* (Stuttgart, 1905).

[4] See Ohlert, 1st ed., p. 41, and 2d ed., p. 31, n. 2; Karl Dilthey, *Epigrammatum Pompeiis repertum tres* (Programm; Zürich, 1876), p. 12; *Palatine Anthology*, I, 30, and IX, 448.

[5] See Jan de Vries, *Die Märchen von den klugen Rätsellösern*, FF Communications, LXXIII (Helsinki, 1928), pp. 131–133, and, more briefly, *Dat Dyalogus of twisprake tusschen den wisen Coninck Salomon ende Marcolphus*, Nederlandsche Volksboeken, VII (Leiden, 1941), 55; Cénac Moncaut, *Littérature populaire de la Gascogne* (Paris, 1868), pp. 90 ff., 235 ff. (cited from Reinhold Köhler's review in *Jahrbuch für romanische und englische Litteratur*, V [1864], 8, as reprinted in his *Kleinere Schriften*, I [Weimar, 1898], 87); Antti Aarne and Stith Thompson, *The Types of the Folk Tale*, FF Communications, LXXIV (Helsinki, 1928), Nos. 875, 921.

[6] Pp. 5–6, §5.

[7] For this riddle and discussion of its form see the headnote to Nos. 823–824, n. 5, below.

[8] More recent editions of this text are A. von Keller and E. Goetze (eds.), Hans Sachs, *Werke*, XXV (Bibliothek des literarischen Vereins, CCL; Tübingen, 1908), 74, No. 675; E. Goetze and K. Drescher (eds.), Hans Sachs, *Sämtliche Fabeln und Schwänke* (Neudrucke deutscher Literaturwerke des 16. und 17. Jahrhunderts, CLXIV–CLXIX; Halle, 1900), III, 130, No. 50.

latein (Leipzig, 1909), pp. 235–236, No. 102; T. Birt, *Preussische Jahrbücher*, CLXIV (1916), 272; Ohlert, 2d ed., pp. 30–32; Schultz, *Rätsel*, col. 95, No. 26; Schultz, *Rätsel aus dem hellenischen Kulturkreise*, I, 66–67, No. 102; Aarne, *Rätselforschungen*, I, 11; Eugène Rolland, *Faune populaire*, XII (Paris, n.d. [1909]), 171; J. G. Winter, "A New Fragment on the Life of Homer," *Transactions of the American Philological Association*, LVI (1925), 162, and see especially the note on line 2, on pp. 127–128; W. von Christ and W. Schmid, *Geschichte der griechischen Literatur*, I (5th ed.; Munich, 1912), 35, n. 5, and 100, n. 4; James Hutton, *The Greek Anthology in Italy to the Year 1800*, Cornell Studies in English, XXIII (Ithaca, 1935), 83; and the previous references to Wilhelm Hertz and Jan de Vries.

460a. Oncet dere was a man goin' to hunt. An' all he kill he leave it dere, an' all he didn't kill he kyarry it back.—Dat was a man was travellin', an' he get full of lice goin' in de woods. All he kill he leave it dere. All he didn' kill he kyarry out.
Parsons, *Sea Islands, S.C.*, p. 170, No. 113.

460b. Dere was a man owe anoder man ten pound, an' dis man come fah it when de time was up. He on'y meet his daughter one [?] home, an' he ax de girl whey her fader? Say her fader gone ter bruk down one gyap to buil' up anoder. Axe' whey was de moder? Say moder gone huntin'; all she ketch she kill an' what she don't ketch she bring home live. Ax de girl what she was cookin'? Say she cookin' go an' come.—His fader gone to one man to borrow ten pound to pay anoder. His moder gone to de pond wid his little broder ter wash his head; all de lice she ketch she kill; what she don' ketch she bring home alive. De girl cookin' pease, ev'y time de pot boil up, de pease goin' up an' down . . . So de gentleman ax de girl what he charge um to interpret fah him? She say twenty pound. She take de ten pound to pay fah her fader an' she have ten pou' in rase've. De girl wa' wise.
Parsons, *Bahamas*, pp. 483–484, No. 121.

461–462. Two-Legs Sat on Three-Legs

The very widely known scene in which Two-Legs (a man) sits on Three-Legs (a stool) and throws Three-Legs after Four-Legs (a dog) when Four-Legs steals One-Leg (a ham, a leg of mutton, or a boot) differs very slightly in its many versions. Since it does not seem to be known east of Finland, Germany, and Italy except for some Hungarian versions of supposedly German origin, the invention is probably western European in origin.

This manner of description has a slight similarity to the Odin riddle,[1] in which an animal and a person (or an animal and two persons) form a vaguely conceived monster possessing an unusual number of legs, and a somewhat greater similarity to the riddle of the Sphinx,[2] in which a single creature is

---
[1] Nos. 49 through 55, and the headnote to Nos. 48–55.
[2] Nos. 46a through 47b.

said to have four, two, and three legs at various stages in its life. These similarities do not seem to imply any relationship among the three riddles or to suggest a common place of origin for such conceptions.

Since Two-Legs sat on Three-Legs has puzzled some riddlers and their hearers and since, furthermore, it describes an event rather than a single object, it has been used as a neck-riddle.[3] A neck-riddle is a puzzle set by a condemned criminal. When his hearers or judges fail to guess the answer, he is set free. The puzzle ordinarily consists in describing an event in confusing terms.

Aarne sets up several varieties of the pattern, "Two-Legs sat on Three-Legs." In a very widely known type, to which these English versions belong, a dog carries off a ham or a leg of mutton. In a type limited in its currency to Germany and Hungary,[4] the dog carries off a boot; see such Hungarian versions as "Two-Legs is sitting on Three-Legs, is making One-Leg, in goes Four-Legs, snatches One-Leg, Two-Legs gets angry, grabs Three-Legs, strikes Four-Legs so that it drops One-Leg."[5]

The oldest version of the riddle appears to be the eleventh-century "Vidi bipedem sedentem super tripedem; cecidit bipes, quia corruit tripes,"[6] which has no answer.

The striking pattern of "Two-Legs sat on Three-Legs" has suggested new inventions, but only those of the dairymaid, the cow, and the stool,[7] which is found only in Germanic territory, and of the cat, the rat, and the chair or table,[8] which is most often found in Romance versions, seem to have gained much currency. The English riddle of the dragonfly[9] appears to be a casual adapting of the pattern to a new use. The reference to a man in a chair[10] may be a confusion with the riddle of the Sphinx.[11] A Polish riddle for a dog, a pot, and a man, "Four-Legs broke Three-Legs, along came Two-Legs and beat Four-Legs for breaking Three-Legs,"[12] is a variation showing some similarity to a Haitian riddle for a dog, a table, a chicken, and a pot.[13] Another riddle, which may possibly be related, tells of a man, an animal (usually a goat or a dog), and a cabbage or a hen. There is rarely any mention of the number of legs, but the actors are often given queer names.[14] It shows some similarity to the English riddles about a white person calling another to drive a white cow or other white animal out of a white field or garden.[15] For examples see the Danish manuscript versions: " 'Two-Legs, take Three-Legs and drive Four-

---

[3] Dutch: Schrijnen, II, 110, No. 38. Afrikaans: Groenewald, p. 89.
[4] *Rätselforschungen*, II, 35.
[5] *Magyar Népköltési Gyüjtemény*, XI, 477. This is virtually identical with *Magyar Nyelvör*, VII (1878), 185.
[6] Malein, 4.
[7] Nos. 462a through 462c, below.
[8] Nos. 463a through 463c.
[9] No. 465.
[10] No. 464.
[11] Nos. 46a through 47b.
[12] Gustawicz, 169, 170. See also Siarkowski, 38; Kopernicki, 36.
[13] Parsons, *Antilles*, III, 453, Hayti, 95.
[14] For this theme see Robert Petsch, "Die Scheune brennt," *Zeitschrift des Vereins für Volkskunde*, XXVI (1916), 8-18.
[15] See below, Nos. 842c, 842d, 844a through 844d, 847a, 847b, 849a, 849b, and the headnotes to Nos. 842-856 and 842-844.

Legs from One-Leg.'—A man stands on a house with twelve pillars and calls to another, 'Take the dungfork and drive the rabbit out of the cabbage patch' ";[16] "Two-Legs sat on Twenty-Legs and called down to Malene, 'Now Svankes is coming to take all your chickens.'—A man sat on the ridgepole of his house and caught sight of a raven, whereupon he called to his wife Malene that a raven was after the chickens";[17] and "Two-Legs stood on Twelve-Legs and called down to Gjælben, [saying] he should come and drive a boar [Ronnibuk] away from One-Leg.—A man standing on his house sees the ram go into the cabbage patch and calls to the dog to drive it away."[18] These Danish versions, which partially explain one another, illustrate the variations typical of the riddle. A disordered Swedish "Two-Legs on Twenty-Four Legs called Vinspjäll, [saying] 'Set Runn-man loose, the innocent is taken with Redcap,'"[19] can be partially understood by comparison with the foregoing texts and with other Swedish versions.[20] Aarne[21] cites additional Scandinavian and North German versions and gives a brief discussion of the theme.

Aarne believed that the variations which we have just discussed were North German or Scandinavian in origin. There are, however, texts which suggest that the invention is more widely known, and consequently a reexamination of his opinion is necessary. See, as examples, the Portuguese riddle about a man killing a donkey for a cabbage, "Two-Feet kills Four-Feet for One-Foot"[22] and such Hungarian versions as "Shouts the Four-legged one, 'Come on out, you Two-legged one, because the Four-legged one will devour you' ";[23] "The One-legged one shouts, 'Come on out, Two-legged one, because the Four-legged one will devour you' ";[24] "The One-legged shouts, the Two-legged should not give in, the Four-legged will devour it";[25] and "The One-legged shouts that the Two-legged should go out because the Four-legged will devour it."[26] Further evidence is necessary to clarify the meaning and relationships of these texts.[27] They are proof of the existence of a type akin to the previously discussed North German and Scandinavian riddle.

Katherine Thomas ingeniously connects this riddle with an incident in St. Giles's Cathedral, Edinburgh, in 1637. When Archbishop Laud's Church

---

[16] DFS, 1906/38: P. Skadhauge, 1918, No. 6.
[17] DFS, 1906/38: T. Buch, 1924, No. 12.
[18] DFS, 1906/38: M. Jespersen, 1919, No. 7.
[19] Dybeck, *Runa*, 1865–1873, p. 30, No. 15.
[20] Dybeck, *Runa*, 1865–1873, p. 50, No. 18; Ericsson, *Södermanland*, I (1879), 80, No. 3
[21] *Rätselforschungen*, II, 50–51.
[22] Parsons, *Cape Verde*, 275. See also her Nos. 276, 277.
[23] *Magyar Nyelvör*, III (1874), 329.
[24] *Magyar Népköltési Gyüjtemény*, XI, 460 = Kriza, 15.
[25] Lázar, 519. See n. 27 below.
[26] Oral version from Szalonta in Szendrey's possession.
[27] The foregoing texts are quoted from Sigismund Szendrey, *Ethnographia*, XXXII (1921), 73–74. I am indebted to the late Arpad Steiner for the translation. Since they are virtually unknown and are difficult to come by, I have given them in full, although the variations are very slight.

Service Book was read according to instructions, " 'Two legs,' in the person of an irate old Scotch woman, Jenny Giles, rose in her Presbyterian wrath. Seizing 'three legs,' the little stool upon which she always sat at home and in church, she hurled it after 'four legs.' The 'three legs,' so unceremoniously thrown at the head of the dean, was in reality hurled after the 'four legs' of the Four Tables of the separate committees of nobles, gentry, burghers, and clergymen quickly formed. This decisive step of the Four Tables was taken following the general riots and wild excitement which this ardor for the reading of the Service Book created in all parts of Scotland."[28] Unfortunately, no contemporary evidence of this interpretation seems to be available.

Some of the following riddles may have been modeled on this pattern, and others may be inventions entirely independent of it. It is often difficult to know which explanation is correct. Clearly the Zyrian descriptions of harrowing, "Four-Legs runs, Twenty-five-Legs chases him";[29] plowing, "Four-Legs runs, Three-Legs chases him";[30] and drawing a sledge, "Four-Legs runs, Eight-Legs chases him,"[31] are related, but it is not clear whether the original theme is derived from the riddle of the man sitting on a stool or is an independently conceived idea. Very probably the Malay riddle for a drum, "Like a bird, a four-footed animal sits on a dead wood; Two-Legs comes and beats him constantly, but he does not die,"[32] is not related to all the previously mentioned texts. And so, too, no doubt, is the Samoan description of eating a millipede, "Two-Legs seeks Twenty-Legs. When found, Two-Legs eats Twenty-Legs, eats but spits it out [rejects the inedible portions]."[33] There are, furthermore, some riddles mentioning a No-Leg,[34] but these seem to belong to an entirely different category.

For discussion see Petsch, *Neue Beiträge*, p. 80; Schultz, *Rätsel aus dem hellenischen Kulturkreise*, II, 65–72; R. Lenz, *Revista de folklore chileno*, Vol. II, No. 8 (1912), pp. 379–380, and Vol. III, No. 8 (1914), pp. 295–296; Aarne, *Rätselforschungen*, II, 24–59; Groenewald, p. 74; Flajšhans, pp. 29–30, No. 28a.

461. Man, Stool, Leg of Mutton (Ham)

461a. Two legs sate upon three legs, and had one leg in her hand. Then in came foure legs, and bare away one leg. Then up start two legs, and threw three legs at foure legs, and brought againe one leg.—That is: A woman with two legs sate on a stoole with three legs, and had a leg of mutton in her hand. Then came a dog, that hath foure legs, and bare away the leg of mutton. The up start the woman and threw the stoole with three legs at the dog with foure legs, and brought againe the leg of mutton.

---

[28] *The Real Personages of Mother Goose* (Boston, n.d. [1930]), p. 214.
[29] Wichmann, *Zyrian*, 157.
[30] Wichmann, *Zyrian*, 158.
[31] Wichmann, *Zyrian*, 156, 247.
[32] Klinkert, p. 52, No. 70.
[33] Heider, 122. See curious Swedish parallels in Olsson, *Västergötland*, p. 188, Nos. 2 through 4.
[34] See the headnote to Nos. 466–468 below.

Meery Riddles (1629), No. 1 = Brandl, p. 8; *Prettie Riddles* (1631), No. 84 = Brandl, p. 63; Tupper, *Holme Riddles*, 50; Halliwell-Phillipps, *Nursery Rhymes*, p. 131; Parsons, *Bermuda*, p. 253, No. 55 var.; Waugh, *Canada*, p. 67, No. 769; Randolph and Taylor, *Ozarks*, 6; Perkins, *New Orleans*, p. 111, No. 57.

Ham: Parsons, *Barbados*, p. 287, No. 66; Parsons, *Bermuda*, p. 253, No. 55; Parsons, *Eleuthera and Watling's Islands, Bahamas*, p. 441, No. 22; Parsons, *Sea Islands, S.C.*, p. 163, No. 61; Parsons, *Aiken, S.C.*, p. 34, No. 62; Bacon and Parsons, *Virginia*, p. 314, No. 17; Redfield, *Tennessee*, p. 37, No. 17. A bone: Knortz, p. 211, No. 3. A stick: Fauset, *Philadelphia*, p. 556, No. 35.

461b. In cums two legs an' sets hisself down / Upo' three legs, wi' one leg in his hand. / In cums four legs, an' throws three legs after four legs, / An' gets his own leg again.—A man sits on a three-legged stool in a butcher's shop, with a leg of mutton in his hand, which a dog snatches and runs away with.

Gutch and Peacock, *Lincolnshire*, p. 401, No. 31.

461c. Two legs sat on t'ree legs, wid a leg on his lap, / An' up step four legs an' took away one leg. / Up jump two legs, took up t'ree legs, / An' flung it at four legs to git back on wan leg.—A man sat on a t'ree legged stool wid a leg o' mutton. A dog come an' grabbed de leg o' mutton; de man got up an' try to hit de dog wit' his stool.

Parsons, *Antilles*, III, 440, Anguilla, 22.

461d. Two legs sat on three legs, / Up jumped four legs, / And grabs one leg.—Man sitting on a three-legged stool; up jump a dog and grabs ham on the table.

Fauset, *Southern Negro*, p. 291, No. 175.

462. Milkmaid (Man), Stool, Cow

462a. Two legs sat upon three legs, / With four legs standing by; / Four then were drawn by ten, / Read my riddle you can't, / However much you try.—Dairy-maid on a three-legged stool.

Knortz, pp. 230–231, No. 77; Halliwell-Phillipps, *Popular Rhymes*, p. 148.

462b. Four legs sat on two legs [*sic*] with four legs standing by.—Maid milking a cow.

Perkins, *New Orleans*, p. 111, No. 58.

462c. Two-legs sat upon three-legs, / One-leg knocked two-legs off three-legs, / Two-legs hit four-legs with three-legs.—A man was sitting on a three-legged stool milking a cow. The cow kicked him, and he hit her with a stool.

Chappell, p. 229, No. 4.

463. Four-Legs Sat on Four-Legs

463a. Me riddle me riddle me yander, / Tough me father have a thing, it is a very good thing, / I hope you may clare this riddle, and I hope you may not. / Four feet sitting in four feet waiting on four feet.—The cat sitting in the chair waiting on the rat.

Finlay, *Bahamas*, p. 295, No. 9.

463b. Four foot jump on four foot looking for four foot.—Cat jump on the chair looking for rat.
Parsons, *Bahamas*, p. 479, No. 77.

463c. Four sit down on four waiting till four come.—Cat on the table waiting for rat.
Beckwith, *Jamaica*, p. 202, No. 178.

464–465. Two-Legs (Four-Legs) Goes About

464. Went out on two legs / An' come back on four legs.—A man on two legs came back sitting on a chair.
Bacon and Parsons, *Virginia*, p. 314, No. 20.

465. As I was coming down the road, / I saw two-wings chase four-wings, / Till four-legs broke up the fight.—A bird was chasing a dragon-fly, when an ox came along the road and let the dragon-fly escape.
Greenleaf, *Newfoundland*, p. 18, No. 6.

466–468. No-Foot

In English riddling, a comparison to a creature without a foot signifies either a wall[1] or a bottle.[2] These riddles, to which there are very few parallels, seem to be independent English inventions in the spirit of the scenes in which actors with varying numbers of feet appear.[3] They may have been suggested by those in which No-Foot signifies a fish. This conception is rather widely known. The Swedes describe a man walking on the ice beneath which fish are swimming as "Two-Legs walks on No-Foot";[4] the French say of a fish, a stool, and a dog: "No-Legs sat on Four-Legs, Four-Legs went to take No-Legs, No-Legs got away, No-Legs was left [survived],"[5] which awkwardly uses Four-Legs in two senses. The Swedish description of a fish, a bird, a man, and a dog mentions their various ways of moving: "Footless swam below, Two-Foot swam above, Three-Foot walked between, Four-Foot came after."[6] The French "Cent pattes était sur quatre pattes, quatre pattes est arrivé, qui a pris cent pattes qui était sur quatre pattes,"[7] which, punning on *cent* and *sans*, has the answer "cat took a herring from a grill." The grill is conceived as having four legs.

466. Four foot jump up on no foot back, / No foot tumble down an' break four foot back. What dat?—Dat's a goat on a rock's back. The wall fell down an' break the goat's back.
Johnson, *Antigua*, p. 86, No. 30; Parsons, *Antilles*, III, 373, Grenada, 71.

---

[1] No. 466.   [2] No. 467a.
[3] See the headnote to Nos. 461–462.
[4] Dybeck, *Runa*, 1865–1873, p. 49, No. 53.
[5] E. H. Carnoy, *La Tradition*, VI (1892), 345–355, No. 28. This is clearly an adaptation of the riddles discussed in the headnote to Nos. 461–462 above.
[6] Dybeck, *Runa*, 1865–1873, p. 65, note to No. 69.
[7] Rolland, 41; Westphalen, *Metz*, col. 198.

467a. A no-foot man bring down a two-foot man.—Rum.
Parsons, *Barbados*, p. 283, No. 42 var.

467b. One foot throw down two foot.—A no-foot man bring down a two-foot man.
Parsons, *Barbados*, p. 283, No. 42.

468. No sense on a table, / An' ef 'e not trouble no sense, / No sense won't trouble you.—Rum.
Parsons, *Antilles*, III, 424, Antigua, 8.

469–470. Miscellaneous

469. We are little airy creatures, / All of different voice and natures; / One of us in glass is set; / One of us you will find in yet; / The other you may see in tin; / And the fourth a box within; / If the fifth you should pursue, / It can never fly from you.—A, E, I, O, U.
Knortz, p. 253, No. 98.

470. At night they come without being fetched, and by day they are lost without being stolen.—Stars.
Perkins, *New Orleans*, p. 110, No. 39.

471–512. Animals Named

471. Frogs

471. Two frawg in a double pond, an' all speakin' t'rough his laig.—Telephone.
Parsons, *Sea Islands, S.C.*, p. 171, No. 120.

472–475. Birds

472. I saw six birds all in a cage, / Each had one single wing / That they could fly and sweetly sing; / Their age did not abate their strength, / Their tails were some thirty feet in length.—Bells in the tower.
Salmon, *Kennet Valley*, p. 421.

473. A bird flyin', an' one sittin'.—A woman married, an' one single.
Parsons, *Sea Islands, S.C.*, p. 163, No. 59, var. 3.

474. in thickest woods j hunt with eagles 10 after the chase wch when (?) j doe discry j dispossesse me of [MS: off] not usefull then and w^t j take not only that keep j.—a man scratching his head wth both his hands.
Tupper, *Holme Riddles*, 12.

475. Chickens

475. A hen have six chickens; and hold the hen, the chickens cry.—Guitar with six strings.
Beckwith, *Jamaica*, p. 199, No. 137.

476. Hares

476. Sixe haires did come within a plain, / whom hounds had started out the nest. / Hill up, hill downe they runne amaine, / till they were weary and then

did rest. / They caught him once, and scapt again, / more eager went they then before, / and tooke more paine then (as I win) / to beare away the game and more. / The hounds and hunters all were one, / each liked his game and tooke his prey. / But when their sport was past and done, / they left their haires and came away.—'Tis a match at bowles played in a bowling-alley.
Prettie Riddles (1631), No. 23 = Brandl, p. 55.

477–483. Pigs, Guinea Pigs

Although guinea pigs do not belong to the same phylum as pigs, riddlers make little or no distinction and I have consequently grouped them together. Guinea pigs are mentioned for their color (Nos. 478, 479a) and are replaced in some versions by wild swine or Highland swine (Nos. 479b, 479c). A description of castor beans also refers to the color of guinea pigs (No. 477). Riddlers allude to such other aspects of pigs as grunting (No. 480) and voracity (Nos. 482, 483). Grunting suggests the crackling of peas in the shell (No. 480) or the noise of a mill (Nos. 481a through 481d; see also the headnote to No. 387). For an old and famous comparison of a cobbler's needle to a rooting pig see No. 386.

477. Form

477. Me mudder hab a whole shipload o' guinea-pig, all born at one quality head.—Castor-oil beans.
Beckwith, *Jamaica*, p. 188, No. 48b.

478–483. Function

478. As I was going 'cross London Bridge, / I met a car of guinea pigs. / They were kicked; they were hacked; / They were all yellow-backed.—Oranges.
Farr, *Tennessee*, p. 323, No. 73.

479a. As I was going o'er London bridge, / I met a drove of guinea pigs; / They were nick'd and they were nack'd, / And they were all yellow-back'd.—A swarm of bees.
Halliwell-Phillipps, *Popular Rhymes*, p. 146.

479b. As I went up a hill, I met a swarm of wild swine. / Some a nak, some a nick, / And some the color of brown tobacco.—Bees.
Redfield, *Tennessee*, p. 36, No. 10.

479c. As I came o'er the tap o' Tripatraine, / I met a drove o' Highland swine, / Some o' em black, and some o' em brawnet, / Some o' em yellow tappit. Sic a drove o' Highland swine / Never came o'er the tap o' Tripatraine.—A swarm of bees.
Chambers, *Scotland*, p. 111. Tipple Tine, . . . green-lapp'd, green-back'd swine: Halliwell-Phillipps, *Nursery Rhymes*, p. 122.

480. I have a whole pen of guinea-pig an' if you touch one, dey all holla.—Gungo peas.
Beckwith, *Jamaica*, p. 187, No. 43b.

481–483. Eating

481a. downe in a medow j have 5 swine the more meat as j give them the louder the[y] cryde the less [MS: lase] meates i give them the stiller the[y] live [lie?].—5 mills when the[y] be grinding the[y] keep a noyse.
Tupper, *Holme Riddles*, 38.

481b. Downe in a meddow I have 2 swine; the more meat I give them the lowder they cry, the lesse meat I give them the stiller they lye.—These be two milstones, which the more they grind, the more noyse they make; and they be called swine here, because swine be fed with corne, and so be they.
Meery Riddles (1629), No. 67 = Brandl, p. 19.

481c. Downe in my yard I have three swine, / the more meat I give them the lowder they cry; / the lesser I give them the stiller they lye.—It is three milles.
Prettie Riddles (1631), No. 82 = Brandl, p. 63.

481d. Twa grey grumphies lay in ae sty, / Da maer de get, da maer dey cry, / De less dey get, da stiller dey lie.—Mill.
John Spence, *Shetland Folk-Lore* (Lerwick, 1899), p. 184.

482. There were three boar hawgs in a pen, two eatin', one refusin'.—Three mai l [mill] rollers, two takin' cane, one out the trash.
Parsons, *Barbados*, p. 277, No. 8. Collector's note: The top rollers crush the cane, the bottom roller throws it out.

483. Boars Do Not Disgorge Food

This strange and only partially intelligible Irish description of a graveyard is also suggested in the literal meaning of "sarcophagus" (devourer of flesh). Spanish parallels indicate a vague comparison of a graveyard to an animal or a person; see "It eats meat but doesn't eat bread."[1] A graveyard is also said to be insatiable[2] and to have neither father nor mother.[3]

483. Four white boars over Baile-Ui-Dalaigh: They would swallow all that ever came and never disgorge so much as a grain.—The four corners of a graveyard.
Fitzgerald, p. 185 (Irish).

484–490. Sheep

English ridd'ers do not often compare objects to sheep. The few examples of such comparisons are found only in the West Indies. The similarity of clouds

---
[1] Demófilo, 189; Rodríguez Marín, 805. Chilean: Flores, 72.
[2] See the headnote to Nos. 236–239 above.
[3] See the headnote to No. 667.

to sheep (No. 485) might seem obvious, but it has found scanty acceptance in tradition. In the reference to boiling rice or peas (Nos. 489a through 489k and No. 490) the comparison is appropriate. In their other uses the sheep have no particular significance and represent only a group of similar objects.

484–486. Form

Comparisons to the form of the sheep or their number often serve to describe the stars. Perhaps the most curious of such riddles are the Mongolian "Behind the Altä Khan[1] there is a herd of a hundred thousand; taking off a number, there are seven are said to be there; crowded together, six are said to be there;[2] distinguishing black and white, two are said to be there; being abandoned, one is said to be there.—The stars; Ursa Major [the 'Seven Buddhas']; the Pleiades; sun and moon; the morning star," and the variant, "Behind the Altä Khan there is a herd of a hundred thousand; taking away a number, there are seven; crowded together, there are three; of the size of scissors there are two.—The stars; Ursa Major; the shoulder belt of Orion; two stars which stand close together and are called the eyes of a wolf [perhaps Castor and Pollux]."[3] The Mongolian parallels cited in the note make a specific reference to sheep and suggest that the "herd" in these versions also signifies sheep.

A few comparisons of the stars to domestic animals call for special comment. The Cheremiss "Two white geese, a hundred and twenty sparrows.—Sun, moon, and stars"[4] seems to have no close analogue with these answers, and may be a confused recollection of the descriptions of the year in terms of birds.[5] The year riddle is often associated with cosmic themes. I do not see the full import of the Mongolian "A rich herd of horses has its pasture ground in the northwest.—Stars rising."[6] The moon alone is signified in the Mongolian "Behind the mountain there rises a bald uncastrated ram,"[7] but the meaning of the special reference to the ram's condition is obscure. A curious series of comparisons occurs in the Mongolian "The leading camel has a star [blaze, i.e., white spot on the forehead], the female camel is wrinkled, with a halter of red silk there are numberless little camels.—Sun, moon, stars, Milky Way."[8] We find another description suggesting a parade or procession in the Hindi "Four posts, drums all around, tens of thousands of bullocks, two drivers.— Points of the compass; thunder; stars; sun and moon."[9]

---

[1] A mountain range.
[2] Only six stars in the Pleiades are clearly visible. For riddles on the Pleiades see below, No. 988 and the corresponding note.
[3] Mostaert, 3 and 3 var.
[4] Wichmann, *Cheremiss*, 91.
[5] See the headnote to Nos. 1037–1038, § 3, below.
[6] Bazarov, 33.
[7] Bazarov, 46.
[8] Bazarov, 159.
[9] Kavyopadhyaya, 14.

484a. My fader had one crowd o' sheep, an' all de people in dat town couldn' count dem.—Stars.
Parsons, *Bahamas*, p. 480, No. 84.

484b. Me fader give me a flock o' sheep to count an' I couldn' count dem.—Stars.
Parsons, *Antilles*, III, 435, St. Martin, 5 var.

484c. My fader give me some sheep to counted [sic] and I could not count dem.—Stars.
Parsons, *Antilles*, III, 442, St. Croix, 3.

484d. My fader had so many sheeps and could not count them.—Star.
Parsons, *Antilles*, III, 445, St. Thomas, 11.

485. Have a flock of sheep. Dere's no one could tell which is broder or sister.—De cloud.
Parsons, *Antilles*, III, 422, Montserrat, 13.

486. I hab a pen o' sheep, but eb'ryone hab one eye.—Needles.
Beckwith, *Jamaica*, p. 188, No. 52b.

487–490. Function

487. White sheep, white sheep, on a blue hill, / When the wind stops, you all stand still. / When the wind blow, you run away slow, / White sheep, white sheep, where do you go?—To bed.
Parsons, *Bermuda*, p. 263, No. 141.

488. Graze on the Hillside

Lice on the head are often called animals grazing or roaming on a hillside,[1] but English riddlers have only rarely used the idea. I cite elsewhere references to the animals being driven out.[2] Some interesting instances are the Yakut "A hundred men descend a hill without leaving a trace,"[3] which may refer to the teeth of the comb rather than to the lice, and "A white horse finds pasture on a rocky hill";[4] the Mongolian "A pig in the woods"[5] and "A voiceless dog among the reeds that have no joints" or "A voiceless goose in a thick forest";[6] and the Omaha "There is a mountain covered with trees. Horses are moving there; some have black hair, some red, some white."[7] The Samoan reference to ointments in "Who lives in a dense forest and yet gets aromatic things?"[8] turns the theme in a novel way.

---

[1] French: Rolland, 191; A. Ferrand, *Dauphiné*, p. 228; Baissac, *Mauritius*, p. 407. Italian: Pitrè, 613. Lappish: Qvigstad, 47, 58. Mordvin: Paasonen, 365, 405. Cheremiss: Porkka, 26, 120. Indian, Telugu: Taylor, *Nellore*, 2. Indonesian, Atjeh: Kreemer, *Atjeh*, 62, citing N. Graafland, *De Minahassa*, I (Haarlem, 1898), 287. Hawaiian: Judd, 141.
[2] See above, No. 474 and the headnote to Nos. 459–460.
[3] Popov, p. 288.   [4] Piekarski, 80.
[5] Zhamtsaranov, 16.   [6] Kotvich, 145, 146.
[7] James O. Dorsey, "Omaha Sociology," *Report of the Bureau of American Ethnology*, III (1884), 334.
[8] Heider, 110.

488. My father have a pen of sheep an' don' feed nowhere but on the hillside.—Lice on the head.
Beckwith, *Jamaica*, p. 187, No. 41.

489–490. Drink Up Water

West Indian riddlers compare the boiling of rice to the scene of sheep entering a pond and drinking it dry. In such far-removed places as the Caucasus Mountains and India, similar concepts are found. A possibility of a common origin is suggested by the fact that Indian laborers were imported into the West Indies.

The Oriental parallels to this riddle for boiling rice are often very cleverly conceived. The Cherekessians say of flour, "Six dogs drink much water";[1] the Birhor riddle for maize fried in a piece of broken earthenware is a scene from nature: "Storks have collected on a plot of high ground";[2] the Mongolians describe tea pounded in a mortar and mixed with mutton fat and condiments as "A court [i.e., sheepfold] with a hollow in it, the rams are black"[3] and rye in a sacrificial vessel as "A herd of rams in an iron sheepfold."[4] Still another variation is seen in the Tungus description of boiling tea: "From the other side of the sea clipped sheep came swimming."[5] The Bengali compare boiling rice to a growing plant: "I planted flowering shrubs in knee-deep water. When the water was reduced to a *chhātak* [became very low], the flowers bloomed."[6]

The notion of animals drinking up a pond of water or going into it is applicable to:

§1. Frost. Czech: Hanika-Otto, p. 123, No. 157 (A white ox came to our house and drank a tank of water). Polish: Saloni, *Rzeshów*, 113 (A gray ox drank up a pool); Gustawicz, 254, 255 (six parallels), 502; Kopernicki, 5.

§2. The sun and clouds. Armenian: Glushakov, p. 26, No. 30 (My horse is gray. It will go [and] drink up the water [and] will return alive).

§3. The stars. Russian: Arkhangel'skii, p. 75 (Little rollers were rolling along a little linden bridge, they saw the dawn [and] went into the water); Sadovnikov, 1855.

§4. Dumplings. Russian: Sadovnikov, 506 (From knocking and thundering there rolled little balls along a wide board. On seeing the dawn, they jumped into the water), 508, 527, 1053. For parallels to this conception see, in the present collection, the Lettish and Polish riddles quoted in the note to Nos. 1032a, 1032b. Turkish: Katanov in Radlov, IX, 101, No. 874 (A noose [for catching horses] has fallen on the horse, but a thousand of my sheep have fallen into the water.—Pulling meat out of a bowl with a hook).

---

[1] Tambiev, p. 55, No. 20.
[2] Roy, *The Birhors*, p. 540. Compare the Hindi "In a dry marsh the herons are bursting" (Kavyopadhyaya, 37).
[3] Bazarov, 186.   [4] Bazarov, 127.   [5] Poppe, 32.
[6] Mitra, *Notes on Ho Riddles*, p. 114.

§ 5. A shoot in a coconut. Samoan: Heider, 5 (Someone drinks so much that he can drink up the whole ocean). Fijian: Fison, 12 (A lake filled with water. Presently a white cloud rises in the midst and drinks the lake dry. Then the cloud grows and has leaves).

489a. A flock of sheep went in a pond wet, an' came out dry.—Rice in a pot.
Parsons, *Barbados*, p. 278, No. 9 var.

489b. Wriggle me, wriggle me, / I tell you this striggle, / Perhaps you me [may] tell me, perhaps not. / My fader got a flock o' sheep, / An' de flock suck de pan [pond] dry.—Rice.
Parsons, *Antilles*, III, 428, Nevis, 18.

489c. My fader have a flock of sheep, he send them to the river and it dry the river.—Rice.
Parsons, *Antilles*, III, 375, St. Vincent, 9 var.

489d. Onct a man did have a flock of sheep. Send dem to de river to drink water. Dey dry de river.—Pot of rice.
Parsons, *Antilles*, III, 420, Montserrat, 1 var.

489e. My fader has a lot of sheeps an' he drive dem to de river an' dey drink de river dry. Tell me de riddle an' I give you a brooch.—Rice in de pot.
Parsons, *Antilles*, III, 420, Montserrat, 1 var.

489f. My fader have a flock of sheep, when dey go to drink water dey leave de stream dry.—Pot of rice.
Parsons, *Antilles*, III, 420, Montserrat, 1.

489g. My father has a flock of sheep they went to the Bushiwé to drink water and they dried up the Bushiwé.—Rice.
Parsons, *Antilles*, III, 370, Grenada, 28.

489h. A flock of ship [sheep] went to a pond to drink water and suck up ev'y drop.—Dat's a pot of white rice.
Parsons, *Antilles*, III, 425, Antigua, 21.

489i. My fader had a flock o' sheep, an' all drink de well dry.—Rice cooked in a pan.
Parsons, *Antilles*, III, 438, Anguilla, 5 var.

489j. Father had a flock o' sheep. Send 'em in the pond, suck the pond dry. Tell me what that riddle is.—Rice.
Parsons, *Antilles*, III, 438, Anguilla, 5.

489k. A flock of white sheep went out in a field, / And dry de pond with water.—Roice [rice] in de pot.
Parsons, *Barbados*, p. 277, No. 9.

489l. My fader had a t'ing, it suck a pon' o' water dry.—Rice.
Parsons, *Bahamas*, p. 474, No. 27.

489m. Flock of sheep in the pond full of water. / The water drain out and left a flock of sheep.—Rice in a pot.
Parsons, *Barbados*, p. 277, No. 9 var.

490. My fader have a lot of sheeps, and he took them to the river, and they dried it up.—Pease.
Parsons, *Antilles*, III, 375, No. 9 var.

491. Goats

491. My fader have a flock of goat an' my fader don't know which one is his own.—Mango tree.
Parsons, *Antilles*, III, 422, Montserrat, 14.

492. Cows

492. My father had six milching cows. Out of the six which give the best butter.—First tache.
Parsons, *Barbados*, p. 277, No. 7. There are six taches or boilers in a sugar mill. The last and smallest one, through which the sugar passes, is referred to as the first.

493–496. Horses

The comparisons of teeth to horses are collected separately in Nos. 502 through 510 below.

493. Changing Color

This conception is ingeniously adapted to fit various objects. It is rather infrequently used in Europe, but is often found in such widely separated and probably unrelated traditions as the riddles of the Zyrians, the Ho, and the Kxatla. It is applicable to such objects as:

§1. Loaves of bread. See Nos. 493a, 493b.

§2. The fire under an oven and a baker or a stick poking it.[1] This scene ordinarily includes a reference to a cow or an ox of a color different from that of the herd: the coals are red and the poker is black. See Danish: Kristensen, p. 101, §260, Nos. 241a, 241b; Feilberg, *Ordbog*, II, 774, s.v. "ovn." Norwegian: Brox, *Ytre Senja*, 150. Swedish: Dybeck, *Runa*, 1850, p. 35, No. 15; Ericsson, *Södermanland*, I (1879), 83, No. 15 (A house filled with red cattle and a green calf dances in the middle); Hyltén-Cavallius, *Värend*, 42; Sandén, *Norra Vadsbo*, 41; Ström, p. 381, "Sysselsättningar," 43; Olsson, *Västergötland*, p. 127, No. 27. French: Rolland, 412; Rolland, *Rimes*, p. 209, No. 62; Marchessou, *Velay et Auvergne*, p. 168, No. 16; Sébillot, *Auvergne*, 44; Queyrat, *La Creuse*, I, 367; J. Roux, *Limousin*, 75. Catalan: Pelay y Briz, 56. Spanish: Demófilo, p. 347, No. 34, and p. 381, No. 1. Italian: Salvioni, *Archivio*, IV

---
[1] See also the descriptions of fire as a red heifer (No. 399a) and of the teeth and the tongue (Nos. 499a through 501).

(1885), 548, No. 71. Rumanian: Gorovei, 1928. Lithuanian: Jurgelionis, 348 (A field full of little red cows, when a black one runs up and with her horns chases them all away). Lettish: Bielenstein, 809 through 815, 991 (sty of red pigs). Polish: Saloni, *Rzeshów*, 192 (The little house is full of little red cattle, but a pitchy one comes in and drives them all away), 193 (A little pen is full of little red sheep and a black ox flies in among them). Russian: Sadovnikov, 309 (The stable is full of red cows. The black one will enter, will chase them all out). Finnish: Lönnrot, 1120, 1 = Henssen, 240. Estonian: Wiedemann, p. 280. Turkish: Kowalski, *North Bulgaria*, 18; and Kowalski, *Zagadki*, 123 (I have a shed full of he-mules, they all have a white spot on the forehead.— Wood); Moshkov in Radlov, X, 270, No. 75 (In the stable I have a red mare. When a black stallion comes, he drives out everybody).

Such comparisons to persons as the Swedish "A gray man goes into the house with a very long tail and drives out many people.—Poker"[2] are rare.

§ 3. Milk in coffee. Swiss: Rochholz, 559.

§ 4. Eggs and chickens. Indian, Ho: Sarkar, p. 350, No. 1 (Cattle of the same shed, when collected, [all] are white, when dispersed [hatched], some will be black, some will be white, and some will be red); Haldar, p. 276, No. 9 (In a room there were only white kine; in the morning, they came out in different colors).

493a. Six pair of white horses / Went in a storm. / When they came out, / They were black or brown.—Bread.
Parsons, *Bermuda*, p. 256, No. 72.

493b. Six white horses in a stall, / And when they come out, / They are black or brown.—Bread.
Parsons, *Bermuda*, p. 256, No. 72 var. Twenty-four white horses put up at a stable: Parsons, *Bermuda*, p. 256, No. 72 var.

494–496. Moving

494. Two horses were galloping and neither of them could catch one another. —Two mill-rollers.
Beckwith, *Jamaica*, p. 199, No. 138.

495. A frisky horse and a frisky mare was going up to mountain hill.—Needle and thread.
Beckwith, *Jamaica*, p. 199, No. 140a.

496. Mare and Colt

Comparisons of the sun and the moon to a pair of animals are not unusual, but the use of a comparison to two animals to signify the moon and a star is very rare, being found only in the Irish text appearing below as No. 496b.

---

[2] Russwurm, 13, with an Estonian parallel. See also the headnote to Nos. 875–877, n. 6, below.

As an example of the use of the comparison to represent the sun and the moon, see the Irish "Two white cows beside the house, one in the day and one in the night."[1] Such a scene as the Berber "Two falcons on a rampart; their bed is in the sea"[2] is very strange.

496a. Behind my heel, behind my house, / There is a Gray Mare and her Coult; / The King and all his men couldn't turn / That Gray Mare's tail about.—Sun or [and?] moon.
Fitzgerald, p. 182.

496b. White mare on the hill, / With her foal at her heel.—The white mare is the moon, and the colt is explained to be a certain star always near her.
Fitzgerald, p. 182.

497–510. Comparisons of Sheep, Cattle, Horses, etc., to Teeth

Although the comparison of teeth to animals is virtually universal, riddlers have varied greatly in choosing an appropriate animal. The animals which might seem to be most appropriate—sheep for their white color or dogs for their ferocity—are not particularly favored. Horses and cattle, which are naturally thought of in herds, and birds (especially chickens), which roost on perches, have been thought to be well suited for this purpose. I have noted nothing similar to the Pangwe "Young bees sit crouching on the fallen trunk of the *Pentaclethren*"[1] or the Kundu "A mountain here, a mountain there, in the middle a squirrel."[2] Jungbauer has briefly touched upon the choice of comparisons for the teeth.[3]

The animals most often mentioned in riddles for the teeth and the tongue are:

§1. Sheep, goats. See Nos. 497 through 498c. Parallels mentioning goats are cited in the note to No. 497 and in the note to Nos. 498a through 498c.

§2. Cows (the tongue is often a red bull). See Nos. 499a through 501.

§3. Horses (the tongue is often specially mentioned). See Nos. 502 through 510.

§4. Dogs, wolves. German: Haffner, 113 (wolves and a red woman). Cherekessian: Tambiev, p. 53, No. 8 (Two white dogs quarreling).

For the many comparisons of the tongue to a red dog, often a red dog behind a white fence, see the headnote to No. 1151 below.

§5. A snake. Irish: O Dalaigh, 9 (A great red worm in the hole, and white stones below and above). Spanish: Demófilo, 584, 586, 587; Rodríguez Marín, 315, 316. Argentinian: Lehmann-Nitsche, 258, 259 (red snake guarded by ivory soldiers), 260. New Mexican: Campa, 208. Surinam: Herskovits, p. 445, No. 73 (There is one thing, which is in the midst of thirty-two snakes, but the

---
[1] De Bhaldraithe, 3.
[2] Basset, *Contes populaires berbères*, p. 125, No. 3.
[1] Tessmann, 120.   [2] Ittmann, *Kundu*, 286.   [3] See pp. 354–355.

snakes do not bite it). Although the snake would be an appropriate comparison for the tongue, its aptness to suggest the teeth is not obvious. The riddler is probably confused.

§6. A fish, a crocodile. French: Parsons, *Antilles*, III, 406, Guadaloupe, 100 (A little fish plays in a basin), and 411, Les Saintes, 48. African, Pangwe: Tessmann, 123 (The water has dried up completely. A little fish [*Clarias walkeri*, Ethr.] remains twitching). Togo: Schönhärl, 74 (There is a river in which there are many levels, and in it dwells only a single fish, which can move to every side of the river, but cannot swim away). Kundu: Ittmann, *Kundu*, 218 (I caught nothing but crabs, but only a single little fish.—Teeth and tongue). Indian, Baiga: Elwin, p. 469, No. 50 (The walls of the well are made of wood. In the water swims a crocodile).

The Samoans, who are familiar with sharks, compare the teeth and not the tongue to fish. See "A man standing between two ferocious fishes" (Brown, p. 343; Turner, p. 215, No. 3) and "Someone lives among wild fish" (Heider, 137).

§7. Chickens. German: Wossidlo, 276b (also a red rooster); Simrock, p. 102; Frischbier, *Menschenwelt*, p. 242, Nos. 6, 7; Hanika-Otto, 52a through 52d (cock is mentioned). Swedish: Ström, p. 83, "Munnan, tänderna, tungan," 11. French: Parsons, *Antilles*, III, 448, Hayti, 30. Lithuanian: Schleicher, p. 211 = Jurgelionis, 172 (The perches are full of little white chickens). Lettish: Bielenstein, 381, 687 through 692. Czech: Hanika-Otto, note to Nos. 52 through 54. White Russian: Wasilewski, 32 (Under the stove you can see two white chickens). Russian: Sadovnikov, 1734 (The little henhouse full of white hens). Serbian: Novaković, p. 66, Nos. 1 (White hens peek from under the eaves. There is neither rain nor leak, yet they are always wet), 2 (A white hen, always wet, yet it never rains), 3 (White hens peek from under the eaves), 4 (The beam is full of white hens), and 5. Estonian: Wiedemann, p. 267. Zyrian: Wichmann, *Zyrian*, 189. Votyak: Wichmann, *Votyak*, 98 (On two poles sit yellow chickens), 294 (On a pole twelve heath-cocks), 360 (On a red pole white chickens); Buch, 4 (On a pole bent like a ring, there sit yellow chicks). The singular number, as in the Turkish "Under the thatch there is a white hen" (Moshkov in Radlov, X, 266, No. 11), is unusual, but some parallels will be found above. Crimean Tatar: Filonenko, 49 (I have a shed full of white chickens).

Riddlers occasionally mention other domestic fowl, especially those which are characteristically white, like the goose or swan. GEESE. German: Frischbier, *Menschenwelt*, p. 242, No. 6. Faeroic: Hammershaimb, *Antiquarisk tidsskrift*, III (1849–1851), 316, No. 10 = *Færøsk anthologi*, I, 325, No. 45. Russian: Sadovnikov, 1740 (The basement is full of geese-swans. One little goose turns over everything).[4] Vogul: Ahlqvist, *Vogul*, 33 (geese-swans).

For the last element see the headnote to No. 841 below.

PIGEONS. French: Parsons, *Antilles*, III, 410, Les Saintes, 32. Spanish, Argentinian: Lehmann-Nitsche, 248. Porto Rican: Mason, 312a. Russian: Sadovnikov, 1734g (The dovecote is full of white pigeons), 1735 (Near the opening white doves are standing). Modern Greek: Carnoy and Nicolaides, 13 (A white pigeon seated on a red hill). Arabic: Ruoff, p. 17, note to No. 12; Bauer, p. 222, No. 12. Turkish: Kúnos, 85 (On the roof of the house spotted doves), 185 (On a red tree white pigeons are lined up). STORKS. Yakut: Piekarski, 191 (They say that white storks are lying in their winter quarters). SWANS. Russian: Arkhangel'skii, p. 77 (What is it: a cellar full of white swans?); Sadovnikov, 1734c (The basement is full of white swans). TURKEYS. Spanish, Argentinian: Lehmann-Nitsche, 247a, 247d, 249. Chilean: Flores, 391, 392. Dominican Rep.: Andrade, 188. Porto Rican: Mason, 312b, 312e. See, finally, the undifferentiated conception in the Shilluk "A long row of trees full of white birds" (Westermann, p. 241, No. 15).

Riddlers only occasionally specify the bird as one noted for its song or speech. It is a songbird in Argentinian Spanish (Lehmann-Nitsche, 400), a nightingale in Modern Greek (Dieterich, *Rätseldichtung*, p. 95). Perhaps the best and most distinctly conceived version is the Panjabi "A parrot dancing on a shelf full of kauris [cowries]" (Ghulam Hussain Khán, *Panjab Notes and Queries*, III [1886], 217, No. 892, § 1).

§ 8. Insects. Shor (a Turkish tribe): Dyrenkova, 38 (In a cavity there are thirty-two firm [fixed] crickets). See also the Pangwe riddle cited above.

497–498. Comparison of Sheep to Teeth

The *tertium quid comparationis* is either the white color[1] or, when the tongue is mentioned, the contrast of white and red.[2] Solomon noted this resemblance when he said of his beloved: "Thy teeth are like a flock of sheep that are even shorn, which came up from the washing; whereof every one bear twins and none is barren among them."[3] The Mongolian "Twenty sheep coupled together, a tethered red cow with an arched back"[4] ingeniously utilizes a variety of details. A few versions[5] name goats rather than sheep. This variation occurs among peoples who are more familiar with goats than with sheep as domestic animals. The description of a single tooth is very rare, but note the Cherekessian "A white sheep drinks water."[6]

497. A flock of white sheep / On a red hill; / Here they go, there they go, / Now they stand still!—Teeth and gums.
Halliwell-Phillipps, *Popular Rhymes*, p. 142; Knortz, p. 223.

---

[1] No. 497.
[2] Nos. 498a through 498c.
[3] Song of Songs, 4:2.
[4] Mostaert, 13.
[5] These are indicated in the note.
[6] Tambiev, p. 53, No. 9. This may be an adaptation of the riddles discussed in the headnote to Nos. 489–490 above.

498a. Sixteen white sheep standing in the stall, / Great big red sheep looks over them all.—Tongue and teeth.
Fauset, *Nova Scotia*, p. 157, No. 67.

498b. Flock of white head sheep wid one brown one in it.—Yer tongue an' teet'.
Parsons, *Antilles*, III, 426, Antigua, 23.

498c. Twelve sheep in the stall, / Up jumped red sheep and overlooked them all.—Tongue licking teeth.
Fauset, *Nova Scotia*, p. 157, No. 67 var.

499–501. Comparison of Cattle to Teeth

The comparison of cattle and teeth is rather frequent in continental European riddling, but is less favored in England and America. The tongue is often called a red bull among white cattle. The English description[1] of the tongue as a whip is unusual. In the folklore of the Finno-Ugric tribes in Russia the tongue is often compared to a wet red calf[2] or, more simply, to a wet calf under the stove.[3] The Kxatla "Tell me: the red bull which surpasses the others in bellowing,"[4] which refers to the power of speech, has a parallel, so far as I have noted, only in the Tibetan "In a cave it bellows like an ox. You see it often, it never comes out, and no one uses it to carry or to pull, but you think of it at every meal."[5]

499a. four & twenty white Bulls sate upon a stall, / forth came the red Bull & licked them all.—it is ones teeth & tongue.
Tupper, *Holme Riddles*, 125. Four-and-twenty beasts: Baring-Gould, *Notes and Queries*, 3d ser., VIII (1865), 325 (Yorkshire). Twenty-four white cows and a red cow: Fauset, *Nova Scotia*, p. 157, No. 67; Randolph and Spradley, *Ozark*, p. 86. Twenty-four white cows and a red bull: Waugh, *Canada*, p. 67, No. 770. Twenty-five white steer, big red bull: Parsons, *Aiken, S.C.*, p. 24, No. 3.

499b. Thirty-two white cows standing in a stall, / Up comes a red bull and licks over all.—Teeth and tongue.
Chappell, p. 235, No. 31.

500. My moder have a pastyure, all the cattle red, except one white.—Yer teeth, yer tongue.
Parsons, *Antilles*, III, 369, No. 20.

501. Me fader hab a long whip and a number of cows; ebery wield him wield it, it touch ebery one.—Tongue and teeth.
Beckwith, *Jamaica*, p. 186, No. 32.

---

[1] See No. 501.
[2] Zyrian: Wichmann, *Zyrian*, 188. Votyak: Wichmann, *Votyak*, 79. Cheremiss: Porkka, 93, 163.
[3] Zyrian: Wichmann, *Zyrian*, 19, 57, 66, 110, 262. Cheremiss: Porkka, 99, 219.
[4] Schapera, 74.
[5] Tafel, p. 493.

502–510. Comparison of Horses to Teeth

English riddlers often compare horses and teeth and usually add a reference to the horses being in motion. The theme seems to be less popular elsewhere. The idea of the tongue as a whip appears also in a comparison of teeth to cows (No. 501).

502. Down in yonder meadow, I have a troop of white horses; now they go, now they go, now they stand still.—The teeth.
Burne, *Shropshire*, p. 574, No. 16.

503a. Thirty white horses upon a red hill, / Now they dance, now they prance, / Now they all stand still.—Teeth and gums.
Hyatt, *Adams Co., Ill.*, p. 668, No. 10922. A team of white horses: Parker, *Oxfordshire*, p. 331. Two: Parsons, *Bermuda*, p. 244, No. 2 var. Twenty: Parsons, *Bermuda*, p. 244, No. 2 var.; Parsons, *Sea Islands, S.C.*, p. 167, No. 96; Fauset, *Nova Scotia*, p. 157, No. 69. Twenty-four: Knortz, p. 213, No. 8; Parsons, *Bermuda*, p. 244, No. 2 var.; Gutch and Peacock, *Lincolnshire*, p. 399, No. 17. Thirty: Fauset, *Nova Scotia*, p. 157, No. 69 var.; Parsons, *Bermuda*, p. 244, No. 2; Perkins, *New Orleans*, p. 106, No. 9; Parsons *Aiken, S.C.*, p. 25, No. 3, var. 1; Bacon and Parsons, *Virginia*, p. 325, No. 113; Halliwell-Phillipps, *Nursery Rhymes*, p. 128. Forty-two: Parsons, *Bermuda*, p. 244, No. 2 var.

503b. White horses sit on a red hill. An' ev'ry time dey gallup, dey gallup.—Teeth.
Parsons, *Sea Islands, S.C.*, p. 167, No. 96, var. 4.

503c. Thirty white horses upon a red hill, / Now they clamp, now they tramp, / Now they stand still.—Teeth and gums.
Hyatt, *Adams Co., Ill.*, p. 688, No. 10922 var.; Randolph and Taylor, *Ozark*, 7 (chomp, ... tromp).

503d. Thirty white horses upon a red hill, / Now they champ, now they clamp, / Now they all stand still.—Teeth and gums.
Hyatt, *Adams Co., Ill.*, p. 668, No. 10922 var.

503e. Twenty white horses upon a red hill, / Now they clamp, now they clamp, / And now they stand still.—Teeth and gums.
Farr, *Tennessee*, p. 324, No. 89.

503f. Upon this red hill, / There was twenty-four white horses. / Now we rub, now we scrub, / Now we do it with all our might. / What do you think it is?—A little girl cleaning her teeth.
Fauset, *Nova Scotia*, p. 158, No. 69 var.

503g. What is way up on a red hill with twenty-two horses?—Tongue and teeth.
Fauset, *Southern Negro*, p. 276, No. 7.

504. Thirty-two horses, / Some on red hills, / Some on blue hills.—Teeth.
Parsons, *Aiken, S.C.*, p. 25, No. 3, var. 2.

505a. Two rows of white horses on a red hill.—Teeth.
Parsons, *Bermuda*, p. 244. No. 2 var.

505b. A row of white horses upon a red hill, / Here they goes, here they goes, here they stops still.—Teeth.
Greenleaf, *Newfoundland*, p. 10, No. 15.

506a. My father have twenty-five white horses in a row; if one trot, all trot; / if one gallop, all gallop; if one stop, all stop; and one cannot go without the other.—Teeth.
Beckwith, *Jamaica*, p. 183, No. 31.

506b. Twenty white horses, in a row when one star' [start], all begin one time. —Teeth.
Parsons, *Sea Islands, S.C.*, p. 167, No. 93. Lots o' white horses: Parsons, *Sea Islands, S.C.*, p. 167, No. 96, var. 1.

507. Twenty-fo' horses set upon a bridge.—Teet' in yer gum.
Parsons, *Sea Islands, S.C.*, p. 167, No. 96, var. 2.

508. My fader had thirty white horses an' one red one.—Teeth and tongue.
Parsons, *Andros Island, Bahamas*, p. 276, No. 17.

509. Sixty white horses settin' in a hill, / Out came a red horse licked them all in.—Tongue and teeth.
Fauset, *Southern Negro*, p. 276, No. 8.

510. Twenty-four horses in stall, one red man whipping hard.—Tongue and teeth.
Parsons, *Sea Islands, S.C.*, p. 167, No. 96, var. 3.

511–512. Several Different Animals

This riddle or epigram illustrates the close relationship of some riddles to proverbial thinking. The English riddle is apparently a translation of a Latin version, which I have not been able to trace beyond the middle of the eighteenth century. It is certainly much older, for the anonymous version "Anser ovem maculat, cui potum vacca ministrat" in Nicolaus Reusner's anthology of 1602[1] seems to be a related theme, and Alexandre Sylvain's sonnet (the source of which I have not discovered) shows that these ideas were known twenty years earlier. The sonnet is worth printing, since Sylvain's collection is very rare:

>Trois, qui jamais ne furent d'un accord,
>Grands biens et maux font paroistre en ce monde,
>Dont le premier, qui de simplesse abonde
>Pour cest effect, se laisse mettre à mort.
>
>Mesme au second on faict semblable tort,
>On pour le moins rudement on le sonde,
>Pour luy oter une chose assez ronde,
>Laquelle estoit son ayde et son support.

---
[1] P. 381.

> Le tiers y perd par fois de son labeur
> Ce que moins vaut, et laisse le meilleur,
> Pour sustenter la creature humaine.
>
> Depuis long temps sont employez ainsi
> Pour mettre au monde ennuy, peine, et soucy.
> Qui sont ceux-cy qui ont, et donnent peine?[2]

Hadrian Junius versified the riddle about the same time and gave a version somewhat nearer to the English riddle. His text is as follows:

> Anser, Apis, Vitulus rerum potiuntur et orbis,
>   Tergeminum brutum frena superba regit.
> Res similis monstri, condigna interprete, qualis
>   Thebigenae nodos solvere Sphingis amet.
> Membranam Vitulus praebet, calamosque canorus
>   Anser, Apes stipant cerea dona vagae.
> Fasque, nefasque tria haec obeunt, dum tergora chartae
>   Penna arat, obstringit cera notata fidem.
> His humana, tribus, divinaque jura reguntur,
>   Omneque momentum hoc ordine terna trahunt.[3]

The notion of combining three animals in symbolic uses seems to have been popular in the late Middle Ages. The English said of a government that was little to their pleasure: "The cat, the rat, and Lovell our dog all rule England under a hog," and had in mind Sir Richard Ratcliffe, Sir William Catesbie, and Lord Lovell, ministers of Richard III, whose cognizance was a wild boar.[4] According to *The New Help to Discourse*,[5] William Collingborn was hanged, drawn, and quartered for this witticism. Boniface VIII (1294–1303) was described in similar fashion as a "magnanimous sinner, who entered like a fox, reigned like a lion, and died like a dog."[6] This epigram is evidently the source of a confusing passage in a versified life of St. Lüthilt written in the fourteenth century. The passage

> Dat röimische riche
> Gewinnet einen den voisze geliche,
> De sal des mit erin walden;
> Hei salt als ein lewe halden,
> Dat sal weren eine kurte stunt;
> De sal erdrinckin als ein hunt

bothers the editor, who seeks to emend *voisze* (fox) into a word for "owl."[7]

---

[2] *Cinquante Ænigmes françoises* (Paris, 1582), pp. 16–17, No. 17 (sheep, goose, bee).

[3] Buchler, *Gnomologia*, 3d ed. (1614), p. 411.

[4] See W. G. Smith and Janet Heseltine, *Oxford Book of English Proverbs* (Oxford, 1935), pp. 422–423.

[5] Fifteenth ed. (London, 1663), p. 104. See also Lily B. Campbell (ed.), *Mirror for Magistrates* (Cambridge, England, 1938), p. 350; Hume, *History of England*, chap. xxiii.

[6] Gibbon, *Decline and Fall of the Roman Empire*, chap. lxix, citing "contemporary chronicles."

[7] J. Franck, *Westdeutsche Zeitschrift für Geschichte und Kunst*, XXI (1902), 312–313 and vv. 203–208.

This riddle has a slight resemblance to a Lübeck riddle of 1472: "Three stones, three flowers, three heads, [all] this aids the world. Guess what they are!"[8] The explanation of the three triplets will be found in Exod. 17:6, 1 Cor. 10:6, and Matt. 16:18.

511a. The calf, the goose, the bee, / The world is ruled by these three.— Parchment, quill-pen, and wax.
    Knortz, p. 227, No. 66; Halliwell-Phillipps, *Popular Rhymes*, p. 144.

511b. The cat [sic], the goose, and the bee, / The world is ruled by these three. / Who are they? What is it?—Parchment, pen, and wax.
    Bacon and Parsons, *Virginia*, p. 318, No. 49.

512. the calfe the goose & the Bee, England is ruled by these three.—vellom, the quil & wax, by wch all deeds & charter[s] are made.
    Tupper, *Holme Riddles*, 142.

---

[8] C. Walther, *Mitteilungen des Vereins für lübeckische Geschichte*, IX (1899–1900), 127–128; Paul Feit, *Korrespondenzblatt des Vereins für niederdeutsche Sprachforschung*, XXIX (1908), 52. See my comment in "Zwei niederdeutsche Rätsel," *Archiv für Literatur und Volksdichtung*, I (1949), 269.

Chapter IV

COMPARISONS TO A PERSON
Nos. 513–826

THE PRINCIPLES here adopted in subdividing the many comparisons to a person are analogous to those previously used. There are two main subdivisions: comparisons to form[1] and comparisons to function.[2] Riddles calling an object a man and yet not a man form a small group at the end of the chapter.[3]

The comparisons dealing with physical aspects of the supposed man are not very numerous.[4] I have arranged them according to the part of the body referred to, proceeding downward from the head. A few riddles mention several abnormalities,[5] and a very few, temperament or general physical qualities.[6] The comparisons referring to dress or colors[7] constitute a very important class.

The second major subdivision[8] includes riddles describing the function of the supposed person. I have arranged the texts in a rough chronology of a man's life: birth,[9] a biography,[10] and manner of life.[11] Many riddles refer to the actor as moving,[12] bearing and picking up an object or being picked up,[13] standing or sitting,[14] talking,[15] weeping or laughing,[16] or eating and spitting.[17] Some activities are represented very sparsely, notably deafness[18] or working or practicing a trade or profession.[19] A large section includes references to shooting, wounding, killing, or dying.[20] The last riddles in the chapter describe a figure as a man and not a man[21] or call it a man in one situation and not in another.[22] References to the social status of the supposed person are rare.[23] Since they usually—perhaps always—mention other aspects and can be readily entered under one of the preceding categories, I have not found it necessary to give them separate treatment.

513–660. Form

513–549. Head, Eyes, Mouth, Nose, Beard

Descriptions mentioning abnormalities of the human head are applicable to a variety of objects. The abnormality may consist in its unusual nature, the

---

[1] Nos. 513 through 660.
[2] Nos. 661 through 822.
[3] Nos. 823 through 826.
[4] Nos. 513 through 572.
[5] Nos. 564 through 572.
[6] Nos. 573 through 578.
[7] Nos. 579a through 660. Colors are also mentioned in Nos. 668, 669.
[8] Nos. 661 through 822.
[9] Nos. 661 through 667.
[10] Nos. 668 through 680.
[11] Nos. 681 through 822.
[12] Nos. 693 through 724d.
[13] Nos. 725 through 731.
[14] Nos. 732 through 749.
[15] Nos. 750 through 767.
[16] Nos. 768a through 769d.
[17] Nos. 770 through 781.
[18] No. 782.
[19] Nos. 783 through 798.
[20] Nos. 799 through 822.
[21] Nos. 823, 824.
[22] Nos. 825a through 826.
[23] Compare No. 578 and the headnotes to Nos. 539–543 and 585.

presence of more than one, or its absence. Riddles referring to unusual colors of hair stand in the section devoted to colors.[1] A few riddles involving mention of abnormal heads will be found in the section devoted to comparisons involving several abnormalities.[2]

513-520. Head

513. My face is pale, / And full and fair; / And round it, / Beauty spots there are, / By Day indeed, / I seem less bright, / and only seen, / Sometimes at Night. / And when the Sun / Is gone to Bed, / I then begin / to shew my Head.—The Moon.
A New Riddle-Book; Or, A Whetstone for Dull Wits, p. 9.

514. He wears a hat / Stuck on his neck / Because he has no head, / And many times his hat comes off / When we are sick in bed.—A bottle of medicine.
Bacon and Parsons, *Virginia*, p. 318, No. 52.

515. Woman got baby t'ree head.—Banana.
Parsons, *Bahamas*, p. 475, No. 41.

516a. Niddy, Noddy, / Two heads, one body.—Barrel.
Parsons, *Bermuda*, p. 251, No. 39; Parsons, *Bahamas*, p. 474, No. 31. Little Natty Natty: Parsons, *Bermuda*, p. 251, No. 39 var. Knitty, knotty, Tom Toddy: Boggs, *North Carolina*, p. 320, No. 2. Wriggledy, Wriggledy: Fauset, *Nova Scotia*, p. 173, No. 189 var.

516b. Me riddle me riddle, / I know somet'in', / Two heads on one body, / Nee dee noddy.—Barrel.
Parsons, *Bahamas*, p. 472, No. 7.

516c. Nib nib noddy, / Two (y)ears and one body.—Barrel.
Bacon and Parsons, *Virginia*, p. 322, No. 93.

516d. Have one man, two head an' one body.—Barrel.
Parsons, *Antilles*, III, 432, St. Eustatius, 10.

516e. A man with two heads, no foot, no hand, / Yet he stands up but on one of his head.—Barrel.
Parsons, *Eleuthera and Watling's Islands, Bahamas*, p. 440, No. 19.

517. Noody, nawdy, / Two heads and one body.—Spool.
MacGréine, *Béaloideas*, III (1931-1932), 414, No. 7.

518. Noddy, Noddy, / Two heads and one body.—Wheelbarrow.
Waugh, *Canada*, p. 70, No. 804.

519. Niddy niddy noddy, / Two heads and one body.—Rolling pin.
Brewster, *Indiana*, 16.

520. Nidy, Nody, / All head and no body.—Pumpkin.
Parsons, *Bermuda*, p. 251, No. 40.

---

[1] See Nos. 583a, 583b, 584b.
[2] See Nos. 564 through 565b, 567 through 569, and No. 572.

521–536. Eyes

521. nowe to a shepard did a dansell sit her body al full of eyes as might be in it withred she was by scorching flame a tongue she had but culd not money gaine her wind she drue above & eke beneth a wofull shepard came to kise her breth but from one part she neu^r yet did chang[e] making complaints most strang[e] the more the shepard put his mouth unto her mouth in stoping it she cryd a maine opening her eyes & shuting them againe, so now w^t this dumbe shepardise culd do, yet wher her mouth he did but kisse he waxed dum[b]e & she spaking is.—a man playing of a peere of bagpips.
Tupper, *Holme Riddles*, 65.

522. What man is he of wit so base, / that wears both his eyes in a case; / for feare of hurting them it is, / and I doe find it not amisse.—It is he that cannot see well without spectacles, and doth carry them about him in a case for feare of breaking them.
Prettie Riddles (1631), No. 37 = Brandl, pp. 57–58.

523–524. Three Eyes

This simple West Indian description of a coconut has parallels only in the Far East. A long Indian riddle,[1] which does not make a very definite comparison to a man but enumerates a series of contradictions, differs so widely from the West Indian text that a connection is unlikely. A Gujerati version has a much greater resemblance, but a connection seems improbable unless we assume that imported Hindu laborers have carried the riddle to the West Indies. A curious Sinhalese parallel suggests a bird rather than a person: "Friend, solve this. At the corner of our garden fence there is something with three eyes on the forehead, with a greasy or oily comb like that of a peacock, and with feathers spread like a peacock's."[2] Far Eastern story makes use of the notion of the three eyes in a coconut.[3]

523. A man have three eyes. He can only cry out of one.—Coconut.
Parsons, *Barbados*, p. 285, No. 56.

524a. My father has a girl with three eye, but only one he could see out.—Coconut.
Parsons, *Bahamas*, p. 478, No. 68.

524b. My fader had anoder article, had t'ree eyes, an' only one he could see out.—Coconut—have t'ree eyes, only one de water can come out.
Parsons, *Bahamas*, p. 480, No. 81.

---

[1] For references see the note to Nos. 523 through 524b.
[2] De Silva, p. 140, No. 1.
[3] See Oskar Dähnhardt, *Natursagen*, III (Leipzig, 1910), 129, citing *China Review*, V, 49, and R. Basset, *Revue des traditions populaires*, XI (1896), 611, No. 49 (buried head becomes a coconut). See further J. J. Modi, *Journal of the Anthropological Society of Bombay*, XIV (1927–1931), 520, citing Hill, *Journal of the Ceylon Branch of the Royal Asiatic Society*, XII (1891). This last seems to be an error for W. A. De Silva, "A Contribution to Sinhalese Folklore," *Journal of the Ceylon Branch of the Royal Asiatic Society*, XII (1891–1892), 124–125 and 139–140.

525–534. One Eye

The possession of a single eye characterizes a needle and a star. The needle riddle[1] usually contains the additional remark, "and has a tail." The riddle for a star, or less frequently the riddle for the sun or the moon, ordinarily contains a reference to climbing mountains. This particular conception seems to be a western European invention, but riddlers elsewhere often call these celestial bodies "travelers"; see, for example, the Ten'a "I wander over the whole earth.—Sun, moon, darkness, a goblin, kingfisher"[2] and "I reach beyond the distant hills.—Sun."[3] The notion of traveling far occurs in some versions of the needle riddle, which has probably borrowed it from the star riddle. The star riddle is very widely known among English riddlers, but parallels in other countries are rare. Its rhymes account for its persistence in tradition, and the nature of these rhymes suggests an origin in the seventeenth century.

The Portuguese call the sun and moon a man with two eyes.[4]

525a. I have a little sister called Peep, Peep, Peep, / She wades in the water deep, deep, deep. / She climbs the mountain high, high, high, / My poor little sister has but one eye.—Star.

Halliwell-Phillipps, *Popular Rhymes*, p. 145; Halliwell-Phillipps, *Nursery Rhymes*, p. 125; Fauset, *Nova Scotia*, p. 166, No. 124; Knortz, p. 224, No. 55; oral, Pennsylvania; Hyatt, *Adams Co., Ill.*, p. 667, No. 10917; Brewster, *Indiana*, 38; Fauset, *Southern Negro*, p. 281, No. 47. Bo-peep: Fauset, *Nova Scotia*, p. 166, No. 124, var. 1. "Dear" for "poor": Fauset, *Nova Scotia*, p. 166, No. 124, var. 2.

525b. I have a little sister, / Her name is Pretty Peak, / She waves over the ocean, / Deep, deep, deep! / She climbs up the mountains, / High, high, high! / My poor little sister / Has only one eye.—Star.

Parsons, *Bermuda*, p. 253, No. 54.

525c. I know a little girl by name of Sweet Pea. / She dive in the water deep, deep, deep, / She climbs up the mountain, high, high, high, / And, po' little thing, she has one eye.—Star.

Parsons, *Antilles*, III, 364, Trinidad, 14.

526a. Ol' lady peewee / Wade in de water knee dee[p]. / She looked at me wi' a funny eye.—Sun.

Parsons, *Guilford Co., N.C.*, p. 206, No. 53.

526b. Ol' lady Reet, tweet-tweet, / She wade the water knee-deep. / An' clamb the mountain sky-high, / An' haven't got but one eye.—Sun.

Fauset, *Southern Negro*, p. 281, No. 48.

527. Had a little sister, Peep-peep, / She clamb the mountain high, high. / And when she got there, / She didn't have but one eye.—Moon.

Fauset, *Southern Negro*, p. 281, No. 49.

---

[1] For discussion of the parallels see the headnotes to Nos. 528–534 and 531–534.
[2] Jetté, 71. Compare No. 102 above.
[3] Jetté, 70.
[4] Parsons, *Cape Verde*, 268.

528–534. One Eye: a Needle

Descriptions of needles or of needles and thread in terms of persons refer usually to eyes and hair or an abnormal tail.[1] The Portuguese combine the idea of a one-eyed mother (needle) with that of a pockmarked daughter (thimble).[2]

The arrangement of the texts in this section is as follows: a man with one eye,[3] a named person with one eye,[4] an unnamed person with one eye,[5] a man with one eye and a tail,[6] a woman with one eye and a tail,[7] a named woman with one eye and a tail which is gradually lost,[8] a named woman with one eye and a tail.[9] The versions in the following section do not mention the supposed person's eye; they describe a man with a tail[10] or a named person with a tail.[11] Although the number of variations might seem to be very large and the arrangement all-inclusive, some conceivable varieties have not been reported.

The analogous Icelandic "I saw two sisters lying fastened together. Each has one eye and they sting powerfully with their beaks. The keeper of merchandise brings them across the ocean"[12] probably has an answer "scissors," but the collector gives none. The eye is the opening through which the finger is thrust.

528. My fader had a son, only got one eye.—Needle.
Parsons, *Bahamas*, p. 475, No. 35.

529a. Poor little Susy on the hill with one eye.—Needle.
Parsons, *Bahamas*, p. 478, No. 67.

529b. Poor little wee-wee, only one eye.—Needle.
Parsons, *Eleuthera and Watling's Islands, Bahamas*, p. 439, No. 1.

530a. What goes all over the world / And has not but one eye?—Needle.
Parsons, *Aiken, S.C.*, p. 37, No. 89.

530b. What is long and slim, works in the light, / Has but one eye, and an awful bite?—Needle.
Hyatt, *Adams Co., Ill.*, p. 663, No. 10888.

531–534. One Eye and a Tail

The comparison of a needle to a person occurs in many extremely divergent forms.[1] The fundamental concepts are often so different that we need not

---

[1] For other varieties see the headnote to Nos. 531–534 below.
[2] Parsons, *Cape Verde*, 172b. For the theme of the pockmarked daughter see the headnotes to Nos. 576–577, and 1263–1265, n. 6, below.
[3] No. 528.   [4] Nos. 529a, 529b.   [5] Nos. 530a, 530b.
[6] No. 531.   [7] No. 532.   [8] Nos. 533a through 533d.
[9] No. 534.   [10] No. 535.   [11] Nos. 536a, 536b.
[12] Árnason, 998. See also No. 228 above.

[1] For the arrangement of the English texts see the headnote to Nos. 528–534. For a very old and interesting needle riddle see the Seventh Assembly of Al-Ḥarîrî (quoted in Friedreich, p. 168, No. 7).

suppose them to be derived from a single original invention. Contrast, as examples, the Swedish "There comes a man from England, and he was one-eyed; he could not sit, he could not stand, but he could go a little, when someone pushed him"[2] with an Argentinian Spanish scene of a young man who is about to enter a mountain.[3] Unusual conceptions, which stand more or less alone, are the Icelandic "Who is the girl trailing a tail who ran over the home field and down to the sea, then across the plain and into a corner, and then had her bed made by me?"[4] and the Polish "A lass stands near a window; her braid is wet and limp,"[5] which ingeniously compares the hole made by the needle to a window and the moistened thread to a girl's braid. The Flemish "There is a farmer who plows his land. The longer he goes, the shorter stands his plow"[6] has some similarity to the allusions to pigs running or horses in motion,[7] which are concepts often used in needle riddles, but the contrast of longer and shorter is likely to have been taken from the candle riddle.[8] An idea quite different from any that have been mentioned appears in the Malayalam "Although thin and small, the little woman does delicate work."[9]

It is difficult, if not impossible, to determine the extent to which contaminations have affected the development of these needle riddles. I have just remarked upon the similarity of a Flemish version to a riddle for a candle. An English version beginning "I had a little sister . . ."[10] may have borrowed this detail from a riddle for a star.[11] The Swedish "There comes a maiden from foreign lands, armless, one-eyed, and without a belly, but nonetheless she has helped many ahead"[12] contains elements reminding us of the description of the sun and the snowflake.[13] Still another variation that probably contains a contamination is the Swedish "There comes a maiden from a foreign land with one eye and no tooth, but she makes good profit."[14]

Characteristic actions ascribed to the person symbolizing a needle are:

§ 1. Goes over the whole world, comes from afar. This element, particularly in its first form, may be an echo of the star riddle.[15] Some examples have already been cited in this headnote. See further White Russian: Wasilewski, 43 (Little precious one, it goes over the whole world). African, SeSuto: Norton and Velaphe, 27 (The eyelet of the little horse from the sea.—A needle, as imported from the coast by people with horses). Some allusions may involve a reference to the fact that needles are, in many countries, imported articles.

---
[2] Ericsson, *Södermanland*, II (1881), 98–99, No. 104.
[3] Lehmann-Nitsche, 242.   [4] Árnason, 647.
[5] Kopernicki, 15. See also Gustawicz, 111, 112.
[6] Joos, 603.
[7] See above, Nos. 386, 420a through 426, and 495, and the headnote to No. 386.
[8] See the headnote to Nos. 607–631.
[9] Schmolck, p. 242, No. 10.   [10] No. 532.
[11] Nos. 525a through 525c.
[12] Dybeck, *Runa*, 1847, p. 42, No. 24; Ericsson, *Södermanland*, IV (1883), 69, No. 75; Geijer and Campbell, 27.
[13] See above, Nos. 367 through 369 and the headnote to Nos. 367–369.
[14] Sandén, *Norra Vadsbo*, 97.   [15] See the headnote to Nos. 525–534.

§ 2. Beautifies (dresses) the whole world. This element is naturally typical of the needle riddle and is of course limited to it. Inasmuch as it mentions "the whole world," it has perhaps suggested the borrowing or adapting of the previously mentioned element.

This element occurs in a few riddles for objects closely related to a needle; see the Danish riddle for a thimble,[16] the Swedish riddle for flaxseed, "As small as a louse, it clothes the whole world,"[17] and an Abyssinian cotton riddle, "A bush that dresses all the world."[18] These borrowings in riddles on such closely related themes are not at all surprising.

The descriptions of a needle in which reference is made to clothing all the world are very widely known. See Breton: Charlec, *Dol-de-Bretagne*, 1903, p. 288 (Who is as big as a thread and makes all the world pretty?), which admits too definite an indication of the answer into the riddle; Sébillot, *Devinettes*, 75 (Who is no bigger than a mouse's tail and makes all the world pretty?). German: Frischbier, *Menschenwelt*, p. 249, No. 80. French: Rolland, *Rimes*, p. 207, No. 52; Parsons, *Antilles*, III, 374, Cariacou, 6. Spanish, Argentinian: Lehmann-Nitsche, 293. Rumanian: Papahagi, 1 (I am small, quite small; I dress the whole army); Weigand, 1. Lithuanian: Jurgelionis, 521 (A small, small woman dresses the whole world); Frischbier, *Menschenwelt*, p. 249, No. 80, citing a text printed in 1744. Serbian: Novaković, p. 69, Nos. 5 (It dressed and adorned everybody but left itself naked), 6 (It is little and green, it dresses up the whole world but cannot dress itself), in which the adjective "green" seems to be used merely to gain a rhyme. See further, his p. 69, Nos. 7 (It is not even the size of an elbow or a palm [of the hand], yet it adorns all gentle folk), and 8 through 11. Cheremiss: Porkka, 63. Zyrian: Wichmann, *Zyrian*, 9, 79 (A little, little daughter-in-law dresses everybody). Modern Greek: Polites, *Neohellenika Analekta*, I, 202, No. 49 (I am naked and I clothe the whole world), and p. 233, No. 228 (I have something that adorns the whole world, it also adorns the king). Arabic: Ruoff, p. 31, No. 61 (Something poor and naked, [it] dresses all the country's children). Turkish: Szapszal, p. 67, No. 8 (It dresses everybody, but itself goes naked); Hamizade, 254 (As much as a tiny thorn, it sets the world in order), 256 (I have a disturbance, it sets the world in order), 260 (How tiny a thing! It dresses the world). Armenian: Zelinski, p. 59, No. 31 (It adorns the whole world, but goes bare itself). In these variants the existence of a subtype current in eastern Europe is apparent. It contrasts dressing all the world with going naked one's self.

531. There was an old man / That had but one eye, / And a long tail that he let fly; / And every time he went a gap, / He left a bit of his tail in a trap.—Needle and thread.
Spenney, *Raleigh, N.C.*, p. 110, No. 3.

---

[16] Cited in the note to Nos. 1263a, 1263b below.
[17] Hyltén-Cavallius, *Värend*, 45.   [18] Littmann, *Tigriña*, 31.

532. I had a little sister; she had one eye and a long tail. Every time she went through the gap, her tail got shorter and shorter.—Needle and thread.
Perkins, *New Orleans*, p. 108, No. 23 var.

533a. Old Mother Twitchett had but one eye, / And a long tail which she let fly; / And every time she went over a gap, / She left a bit of her tail in a trap.—A needle and thread.
Halliwell-Phillipps, *Nursery Rhymes*, p. 125; Harland and Wilkinson, *Lancashire Legends*, p. 187; Knortz, p. 222, No. 47; Hyatt, *Adams Co., Ill.*, p. 663, No. 10887; Redfield, *Tennessee*, p. 37, No. 13; Perkins, *New Orleans*, p. 108, No. 23; Parsons, *Antilles*, III, 433, Saba, 13. Old Mother Twich: Greenleaf, *Newfoundland*, p. 12, No. 33. Old Mother Hubbard: Farr, *Tennessee*, p. 324, No. 81. Old Mother Jane: Parsons, *Bermuda*, p. 261, No. 125. Old woman: Thurston, *Massachusetts*, p. 182, No. 7. Old Grandmother Pitcher: Gardner, *Schoharie Hills, N.Y.*, p. 256, No. 25.

533b. Old Mother Twitchet has but one eye, / And every time she jumps the gap, / She leaves a bit of her tail in the trap.—A needle and thread.
Waugh, *Canada*, p. 68, No. 773.

533c. Ol' Mother Twitchet went thro' a gap, / I bite off her tail, / She lef' in the crack.—Needle.
Bacon and Parsons, *Virginia*, p. 324, No. 106.

533d. Old Mrs. Twitchet with her one eye / A tail of wondrous length lets fly. / Every time she goes through the gap / She leaves a piece of her tail in the trap.—Sewing with needle and thread.
Hudson, p. 85, No. 13.

534. Miss Betsy chue chue chue / With small eye and long tail.—Needle and thread.
Parsons, *Antilles*, III, 366, Trinidad, 38.

535–536. Person with a Tail

Although closely related to the immediately preceding riddles, this version differs from them in making no mention of the needle's single eye. In No. 535, the actor is "a man"; in Nos. 536a, 536b, it is a woman or a girl, and she has a proper name. The Serbians have this same concept, but in terms of the first rather than the third person: "I am young, thin, and handsome. When I travel, I have a tail. The further I go, the shorter is my tail. In traveling, I lose my tail and I come home without it."[1] Such variations from the first to the third person often occur in the oral transmission of riddles.

Descriptions of a needle employ related incongruities, some of which are more suitable to the conception of a person. Examples are the French "A lady who drops a bit of her petticoat at every step";[2] the Basque "A lady having but a single hair"[3] and "A thin fellow having but a single hair in his beard";[4] the Turcoman "A short young girl with a long kerchief";[5] the Kashmiri "A veil one and a half yards long for my aunt who is only half a yard

---

[1] Novaković, p. 69, No. 12. [2] Guillon, *La Bresse*, p. 20.
[3] Cerquand, 51. See also French: Lespy, *Béarn*, 28.
[4] Cerquand, 21. [5] Samojlvich, 94.

high";⁶ the Uraon "A dwarf with a long beard shakes his head";⁷ the Parsee "What a stunted little thing! And it has a plait of hair a yard long";⁸ and the Gujerati "A female sex [sic] and public property, is bright and sharp. She puts on a long dress; makes gestures and coquetry; and keeps all her limbs exposed after having drilled her nose."⁹

Comparison to an animal which loses its tail is rather unusual, but see the French "What is that rat which leaves a little of its tail everywhere it goes?"¹⁰

535. A man goes into a trap, and when he comes out, leaves half of his tail.—Needle and thread.
Parsons, *Bermuda*, p. 261, No. 125 var.

536a. Old Mother Thratchell / Had a long tail. / Every stitch she took, / She lost a bit of her tail.—Needle and thread.
Fauset, *Nova Scotia*, p. 159, No. 79.

536b. Little Mary went to town, wherever she stop she leave a bit of her tail.—Needle and thread.
Parsons, *Barbados*, p. 276, No. 3.

537–538. Nose

A few West Indian riddles compare a plant and its fruit to a person with a bent nose. In the riddle for cassia¹ the resemblance concerns the shape; in the riddle for a cherry² it may also concern the color. Some candle riddles³ also involve a reference to a nose.

537a. Miss Nancy goin' upstairs with a ben'-down nose.—The cushia-seed that grows out of an applelike fruit in such a way as to resemble a nose.
Johnson, *Antigua*, p. 87, No. 45; Parsons, *Antilles*, III, 423, Antigua, 2.

537b. Miss Kitty goin' up street / Wid a ben' down nose.—Casha seed.
Parsons, *Antilles*, III, 423, Antigua, 1 var.

538a. Miss Nancy on de hill wid a bent down nose.—Cherry.
Parsons, *Antilles*, 421, Montserrat, 9.

538b. My fader have a big tree wid a bent down nose.—Cherry.
Parsons, *Antilles*, III, 421, Montserrat, 9 var.

539–543. Mouth of Horn, Beard of Flesh

This ancient pattern, which occurs in the Persian *Book of Ardâ-Virâf*,¹ survives in many modern riddles. References to the creature's head of fire² seem

---

⁶ Knowles, 22.   ⁷ Archer, p. 183, No. 58.
⁸ Munshi, 11.   ⁹ Mehta, p. 117, No. 4.
¹⁰ Mensignac, *Gironde*, p. 303, No. 40. Compare No. 422 above.
¹ Nos. 537a, 537b.   ² Nos. 538a, 538b.
³ See Nos. 620 through 624.

¹ E. W. West and M. Haug, eds. (Bombay, 1872), as cited in E. Rolland, *Faune populaire*, VI (Paris, 1883), 114. See another version in Al-Ḥarîrî's Twenty-seventh Assembly (quoted in Friedreich, p. 178, No. 8).
² See § 2 and No. 541 below.

to be later elaborations and are perhaps suggested by the candle or lamp riddle.[3] In the Renaissance, European riddlers created versions containing rather full comparisons to a cavalier or herald. The fundamental conception is closely related to descriptions of a cock as neither priest, king, sacristan, nor other functionary, although possessing some characteristic of each of them (see § 3 below), and also to descriptions of a creature having members belonging to each of many animals.[4] The parallels exhibit many confusions and contaminations. M. Sabbe's discussion,[5] which is the only study devoted to this old and curious riddle, deals with some interesting Renaissance versions, but rests on too limited an acquaintance with the parallels old and new. An Icelandic version[6] involving a series of tortures[7] is probably an entirely different theme.

The comparison of a cock to a man appears in various forms, which can be classified as follows:

§ 1. A man with mouth of horn and beard of flesh. He is often said to blow a horn like a herald.[8] A riddler adapts this description to an owl.[9]

§ 2. A man with a head of fire.[10] This has some similarity to riddles for a lamp or a pipe.[11]

§ 3. A man sings, but it is not the mass, etc. The fundamental theme is a series of antitheses: "He sings but not the mass; he has a crown but is not a king; he wears spurs but is not a cavalier."[12] Such a series of antitheses degenerates readily. Many parallels name only one or two details, and others admit incongruous elements. For examples see Danish: Feilberg, *Ordbog*, II, 250–251, s.v. "kok." Icelandic: Árnason, 289 (Once upon a time a fine dandy with a nice crown upon his head was born. He wore golden spurs and was a prophet. When his mother bore him, he was oblong and round and without head, limbs, or a soul). French: Lespy, *Béarn*, 23 (A king without a crown). Spanish, Argentinian: Lehmann-Nitsche, 623. Italian: Pitrè, *Canti*, II, 67, No. 847 (cavalier, king, sacristan); Ive, *Canti popolari istriani*, p. 299, No. 13; Gianandrea, *Archivio*, I (1882), 407, No. 17; Coronedi-Berti, *ibid.*, II (1883), 580, No. 46; Rondini, *ibid.*, VIII (1889), 191, No. 107. Russian: Sadovnikov, 946 (Not of princely stock, yet he walks abroad wearing a crown; not a fighting horseman, yet he has a spur on his foot; not a watchman, yet he awakens all early). Modern Greek: Dieterich, *Rätseldichtung*, pp. 94–95; Abbott, p. 309, No. 18. Filipino: Starr, *Philippines*, 22.

---
[3] See No. 631 and the headnote to Nos. 1440–1441.
[4] See the headnote to Nos. 1405–1408 below.
[5] "Satirische prophetie of raadselspel," *Volkskunde*, XIX (1907–1908), 34–39.
[6] Árnason, 1028.
[7] See the headnotes to Nos. 674–680, 678, and 679 below.
[8] No. 539.   [9] No. 542.   [10] No. 541.
[11] See No. 1440 and the corresponding note.
[12] Spanish: Demófilo, 786; Rodríguez Marín, 332. Argentinian: Lehmann-Nitsche, 626.

§ 4. Turk or prophet.[13] The traits described as characteristic of the creature are not its members but are other aspects. They are: its age cannot be told, its numerous wives, it cannot be shod.

§ 5. A griffon.[14] This enumeration of parts of a cock's body as unusual in several regards does not yield the picture of a single animal.[15] Although it might be placed elsewhere in this collection, I have considered it to be closely related to the descriptions of a cock as a cavalier or herald.

539. Behind the bush, behind the thorn, / I heard a stout man blow his horn, / He was booted and spurred, and stood with pride, / With golden feathers by his side; / His beard was flesh, and his mouth was horn. / I am sure such a man never could have been born.—A cock.
Burne, *Shropshire*, p. 573, No. 1.

540a. Mouth o' horn, and beard o' leather. Ye'll no guess that though ye were hanged in a tether.—A cock.
Chambers, *Scotland*, p. 109.

540b. As I went over London Bridge, / I heard some[one] cough and call. / His leg was bone, his teeth was hone [horn]. / Unriddle that riddle, I give you all my cone [corn].—A rooster.
Parsons, *Guilford Co., N.C.*, p. 206, No. 48.

540c. As I was going across London Bridge, / I looked behind, I heard a call. / The thing was brown and fleshy, / And it was never born.—Rooster.
Fauset, *Nova Scotia*, p. 149, No. 36 var.

540d. As I was going through Bramble hall, / An old man gave me a call; / His beard was flesh, his mouth was horn, / And this old man was never born. —Rooster.
Beckwith, *Jamaica*, p. 192, No. 77a.

540e. As I was goin' to Saint Paul, / I heard a man give a call. / His beard was meat, / His mouth was horn, / Such a man was never born.—A rooster.
Parsons, *Antilles*, III, 376, St. Vincent, 20. As I was goin' to Saint Ile: Parsons, *Antilles*, III, 376, St. Vincent, 20 var.

540f. As I went over London Bridge, / I heard a man call; / His beard was flesh, / His mouth was horn; / I thought there was never such a man born.— A rooster crowing under the bridge.
Chappell, p. 237, No. 43.

540g. As I went up the lane, / I heered a man give a call, / His tongue was flesh, / And his mouth was horn, / And such a man was never born.— Rooster.
Fauset, *Nova Scotia*, p. 149, No. 36.

---

[13] See Nos. 585a, 585b below.
[14] No. 543.
[15] Compare the headnote to Nos. 1405–1408.

540h. Got to a gentleman's yard and his mouth was hard and his beard was flesh.—Rooster.
Beckwith, *Jamaica*, p. 192, No. 77b.

541. When I was going up to town, I met a man; his head is fire an' his mouth is bone.—Rooster.
Beckwith, *Jamaica*, p. 192, No. 77.

542. As I was going across London Bridge, / I heard an old man give a squall. / His head was bald, his bill was —— [the missing word is probably "horn"], / Such an old man was never born.—An owl.
Bacon and Parsons, *Virginia*, p. 327, No. 130.

543. Beard of Flesh, Mouth of Horn, Feet of a Griffon

This is closely related to the description of a cavalier having a beard of flesh and a mouth of horn.[1] In the present instance, the conception has no unifying theme and is merely an accumulation of incongruous details.[2]

543. What is that that hath a beard of flesh, a mouth of horne, and feet like a Griffon?—That is a cocke, for his beard is flesh, his bill horne, and feete like a Griffon.
Meery Riddles (1629), No. 9 = Brandl, p. 9.

544–548. Beard

544. Man in Room, Beard Outside

Riddlers often use the notion of an abnormally extended member of an animal, person, or thing. Comparisons to an animal whose horns extend beyond its stall have already been noted.[1] The notion of a tree which reaches its branches into every house is applied to the sun. This notion has been discussed in an endeavor to get at the secret of the ash of Yggdrasil.[2] Sophus Bugge, who has written most fully about the pertinent riddles, comes to the conclusion: "I shall not deny the possibility that in ancient times the heathen ancestors of the Scandinavians knew a marvelous tree, [a conception] which had its origin in a mythical interpretation of such phenomena in the air or heavens as the sun with its rays, the rain, or the clouds, and that such a marvelous tree was one of the roots from which the ash of Yggdrasil sprang. But, I lack any proof. In any case, . . . we cannot seek in this idea the most fundamental and still less the sole explanation of the myth of Yggdrasil." Bugge knew only a few examples of the riddle describing the sun as a tree. See Faeroic: Hammershaimb, *Antiquarisk tidsskrift*, III (1849–1851), 316, No. 5. Norwegian:

---

[1] For discussion see the headnote to Nos. 539–543, and see M. Sabbe, "Satirische prophetie of raadselspel," *Volkskunde*, XIX (1907–1908), 34–39.
[2] For such riddles see the headnote to Nos. 1405–1408 below.

[1] See the headnote to Nos. 412–413, § 9.
[2] Sophus Bugge, *Studier over de nordiske gude- og heltesagns oprindelse*, I (Christiania, 1881–1889), 518–522. The passage quoted is on p. 520.

Sophus Bugge, *Studier over de nordiske gude- og heltesagns oprindelse*, I (Christiania, 1881–1889), 520 (There stands a tree in Billingsberge and drips in the sea. Its branches shine like gold), and a second example; Christie, 6. Polish: Saloni, *Rzeshów*, 174, 175 (An oak stands in the middle of the village and every bough hangs toward a house); Saloni, *Łańcut*, 21; Kopernicki, 50; Siarkowski, 57; Gustawicz, 390 through 395. White Russian: Sophus Bugge, *Studier over de nordiske gude- og heltesagns oprindelse*, I (Christiania, 1881–1889), 519 (There stands a tree in the middle of a village, it is visible in every hut). Hungarian: Kálmány, II, 177, No. 5 (Its trunk is in the ocean, its foliage over the sky, its limbs branching out from here to Jerusalem.—The sun, when it rises and its rays are seen everywhere). African, Tschuana: Kuhn, *Tschuana*, 15 (Tree in the North, branches reach to here). Indian, Kolarian: Wagner, 43 (Two trees are spreading their branches over the whole world.—Sun, moon).

Konrad Ohlert[3] makes a surprising comparison to an early medieval charm and cites a few additional parallels from Wilhelm Schwartz, who is the object of Bugge's attack. Romance riddlers seem not to know the notion of a tree with unusually long branches as a symbol of the sun. The variations in Scandinavian, Slavic, and African riddling suggest the probability of the independent invention of some versions, and particularly of the African parallel. Some have discussed the cosmological background of these ideas and have related them to the year riddle.[4]

Riddlers not infrequently compare the sun to an animal.[5] They only rarely compare it to a thing.[6]

Riddlers have adapted to many uses the scene of a man sitting in a room while his beard hangs out or is otherwise abnormal. Perhaps the earliest English instance is implied in the Chaucerian

> An hoor head and a green tayl,
> As hath a leek.[7]

This has many parallels, of which the Modern Greek "My Uncle Theodore the Short with his beard hanging down"[8] will be a sufficient illustration.

The conception of a man with an abnormally long beard is applicable to:

§ 1. Maize. See No. 544 below. Some riddles contain the related idea of "flesh without, hair within."[9]

---

[3] *Philologus*, LVII (1898), 601–602.
[4] See Ohlert, 2d ed., p. 101, and the discussion of the year riddle in the headnote to Nos. 1037–1038 below. For some related ideas see Uno Holmberg, "Der Baum des Lebens," *Annales Academiae Scientiarum Fennicae*, Ser. B, XVI, No. 3 (Helsinki, 1922).
[5] Nos. 391, 392b.
[6] See Nos. 1170, 1190, and the headnote to Nos. 1189–1191.
[7] *Canterbury Tales*, Prologue to "Reeve's Tale," lines 24–25. For parallels see G. L. Apperson, *English Proverbs* (London, 1929), pp. 681–682.
[8] Polites, *Neohellenika Analekta*, I, 213, No. 117. Compare No. 1383 below.
[9] See the headnote to No. 588, § 8, below.

§ 2. Flax, rushes. Danish: Kristensen, p. 48, § 130, Nos. 183a, 183b. Cherekessian: Tambiev, p. 65, No. 141 (Grandfather stands on the shore, and his beard waves.—Rushes).

§ 3. Grapes. Serbian: Novaković, p. 116, No. 4 (Mara sits at the bottom of the fortress with her hair at the top of the fortress).

§ 4. A vegetable, usually an onion, a leek, a beet, a carrot, or a radish. Welsh Gypsy: Sampson, 20 (onion). French: Constantin, *Savoie*, p. 21 (onion). Rumanian: Weigand, 2 (An old man with his beard in the ground.—Onion). Lithuanian: Jurgelionis, 523 (A Russian in a pot, his hair sticks out.—Radish), 1016 (A maiden in the bathhouse, her braids outside.—Carrot), 1025 (A White Russian in the bathhouse, his beard outside.—Radish), 1026 (Next to the bathhouse lies a White Russian, and his beard shines outside.—Radish); Schleicher, p. 207 (radish). Lettish: Bielenstein, 120 (A Russian sits in the ground, his hair outside.—Radish). White Russian: Wasilewski, 76 (Cock in the hole and the braids outside.—Beet). Polish: Gustawicz, 211 through 222 (carrot); Saloni, *Rzeshów*, 102 (A little girl in the earth and her braids on the ground.—Carrot), 103 (A little girl in the room and her braids out of doors.— Carrot), 104 (She stands in the earth and her braids show green on the earth.— Carrot). See also Kopernicki, 27 (carrot); Siarkowski, 14 (carrot). Russian: Arkhangel'skii, p. 76 (Sister sits in a dungeon, but her braids are on top.— Carrot). Serbian: Novaković, p. 121, Nos. 1 (An old man stands above ground, his beard is in the ground.—Onion) and 2 (A Turkish priest sits above ground, and his head and beard lie on the ground.—Onion), p. 193, Nos. 5 (The girl is in the house, the hair is outside.—Beet) and 6, and p. 195, Nos. 4 (The tsaritsa sits in the fort, her hair is on the fort.—Radish), and 5 (All the lords sit in the palace, and the plumes are spread outside.—Radish). Bulgarian: Chacharov, 98 (I have a thing with its beard downward and its leg up.— Beet); Gubov, 204 (A black monk in the ground; his vestments are above the ground.—Beet). Finnish: Lönnrot, 892 = Henssen, 82 (The man in the room, his hair in the wind.—Beet). Mordvin: Ahlqvist, p. 41, No. 28 (A red maiden, she sits in prison, but her braids hang out.—Beet).[10] Turkish: Zavarin, *Brusa*, 10 (Under the ground I have a bearded old grandfather.—Leek); Kúnos, 154 (My father's beard is under the ground.—Cabbage), 155 (My father's moustache is under the ground.—Onion); Kowalski, *Zagadki*, 46. Crimean Tatar: Filonenko, 67 (A beautiful maiden sits in jail, yet her hair is in the street.— Beet). Georgian: Glushakov, pp. 134–135, No. 77 (We went from below, I am all alone, I put my head down, my feet up. I surprised myself. Why should I have done this?—Onion). Dard: Leitner, *Indian Antiquary*, I (1872), 91, No. 4 (My grandfather's body is in Hades, his beard is in the world. Now, explain.—Radish).

---

[10] Since the Russian word for "red" signifies both "beautiful" and the color "red," this and the Crimean Tatar riddle below are probably translated from Russian.

§ 5. The Georgian riddle cited in the last section contains the notion of growing with one's feet in the air. This may be an entirely different riddle from those considered here. Compare the Welsh Gypsy description of an onion, "What grows head down and feet up?"[11] and the Mordvin riddle for a radish, "Its root-end grows upwards."[12] The Letts say of an apple, "It hangs on a tree, its root upwards."[13] The Bakongo riddles for a peanut, "The mouse is below and its nest is above," which is particularly ingenious, and "Its head below, its feet above,"[14] as well as the Samoan "A strong man grows straight up, but his brothers all grow down.—A variety of banana [soa'a] or the sulasula,"[15] show the wide currency of the idea, which is further discussed in the headnote to Nos. 1055–1057 below.

§ 6. The beams of a house. Lithuanian: Jurgelionis, 280 (The daughter-in-law in the house, her breasts outside). Lettish: Bielenstein, 79 (An old woman in the house, her bundle outside), 558 (A woman guest within, her fist outside), 774 (The lady of the house is within, her feet are outside). Russian: Sadovnikov, 48 (Mother in the house, her sleeves in the yard). Finnish: Henssen, 81 (The man in the room, his hair in the wind). Arabic: Ruoff, p. 34, No. 72 (Our neighbor's beard hangs down by our house.— Gutter). African, Bakongo: Denis, 20 (Papa sleeps in the house, his nose outside), 21 (The Bombata [a tribe inhabiting the region of Ngidinga, but here used in a conventional sense] bury the corpse, its head outside).

For similar comparisons to animals see the headnote to Nos. 412–413, § 5, above.

§ 7. A key.[16] Lettish: Bielenstein, 59, 60 (Maiden in the corncrib, braids outside), 61.

§ 8. A shovel. Korean: Bernheisel, p. 83 (What is [it] that has a beard about three feet long and travels upside down in a ditch only?—A Korean shovel). The "beard" signifies the ropes, tied to the end of the shovel, by which it is made to work.

§ 9. A fire (stove) and smoke. Lithuanian: Jurgelionis, 341 (An old woman stands in a cottage, but her head is outside). Russian: Sadovnikov, 142. Mordvin: Ahlqvist, p. 41, No. 5 (An old man in the ground, his beard is outside), 22 (A red maiden sits in prison, but her braids hang out). African: Cronise and Ward, p. 193 (Old man in the house, beard outside). Togo: Schönhärl, 9. Hausa: Tremearne, p. 58, No. 3 (The master is inside the hut, but his beard is outside). Kanuri: Lukas, p. 169, No. 10 (The old man sits in the hut, his beard is outside). Samoan: Heider, 81 (Someone has hair so long

---

[11] Sampson, 20.
[12] Paasonen, 377. See also the headnote to Nos. 1055–1057 below.
[13] Bielenstein, 3.   [14] Denis, 68, 71.   [15] Heider, 11.
[16] See also the headnote to Nos. 412–413, § 6, above and (for an entirely different concept for keys) No. 958 below.

that it reaches to Heaven). For a similar comparison to an animal see No. 413 above.

The Bavenda employ a somewhat different scene: "My father's spears pierce right through the roof."[17] See also the riddles in §§ 10 and 11, below, which may have suggested these riddles for fire.

§ 10. The sun. Finnish: Lönnrot, 1884 = Henssen, 80 (The old man is outside, his beard is in the room). Estonian: Dido, 34 (A man in the courtyard, his eyes in the room). Arabic: Ruoff, p. 11, No. 4 (An old man: he thrusts his chin against the wall, and his beard lies in the courtyard). This has a remote similarity to the Hickamore Hackamore riddle.[18]

Comparisons of the sun to the hair of an animal or to reins have already been noted.[19] A curious variation occurs in the SeSuto "The brown locust comes from the Pedi country, holding a bundle of spears,"[20] which mingles human and animal concepts.

For comparisons of the sun and its rays to things, especially to a tree and its branches extending into every hut, see the introductory part of this headnote. Another theme appears in the Russian "On the street are the blouses, the sleeves are in the hut" and "The lady is outside, but her sleeves are in the house"[21] and the Kxatla "Tell me: a man carries a bundle of spears. We do not know where he comes from and goes."[22]

§ 11. Light from within a house. This is merely a reversal of the preceding themes. See French: Parsons, *Antilles*, III, 381, Martinique, 16 (My father inside, his beard appears outside).

§ 12. The eye and the eyelashes. Surinam: Herskovits, p. 445, No. 71 (Look-hard sleeps on the road beside the grass and leaves his hair outside). A similar notion is perhaps vaguely implied in the Abyssinian "The door of their house consists of pieces of wood."[23] The hair and the eyelashes composed of hair are often compared to grass, wood, or sticks.[24]

544. Old man in his room and the beard out in the hall.—Ear of corn.
Beckwith, *Jamaica*, p. 195, No. 103a.

545–548. Beard and Mouth (Lips)

The riddle[1] concerning the monkey that bit Robert Portington explains this very strange invention. Only the first of the following texts retains the original answer. In the others the riddlers have supplied new answers in efforts to fit

---

[17] Stayt, p. 359, No. 5.
[18] See below, Nos. 748a through 748g and the headnote to Nos. 748–749, § 1.
[19] See the headnote to Nos. 412–413, § 9.
[20] Norton and Velaphe, 45.　　　[21] Sadovnikov, 1819, 1819a.
[22] Schapera, 2.　　　[23] Mittwoch, p. 211, No. 9.
[24] See below, Nos. 1042 through 1044, 1116a, 1116b, and the headnotes to Nos. 1042–1044, 1044, and 1116.

[1] See No. 564. Since this version describes the dress and not the shape of the creature, I have placed it in a later section.

the description and have ended in complete confusion, with the " 'mink,' or a 'little mink called a gopher' " given as the answer of No. 547. They have kept the notion of fright, but have often transferred it from the spectator to the creature that is being described.

545. As I went over tip-fer-tar, / Saw a little thing a sittin on a briar / Great wide mouth with great long beard / Bless its little soul how hit got skeered [scared].—Monkey.
Carter, *Mountain White*, p. 79.

546. As I went down that yellow bank, / I met a thing all rough and rank, / Two great lips and a hairy beard, / Darn the thing it made me afeard.— A hog.
Chappell, p. 232, No. 17.

547. I went over Tikamatug. / There I saw a little thing sticking in the mud. / Had black hair and red beard, / And draut [drat] the little thing, how it was skeered!—"Mink," or a "little mink called a gopher."
Hudson, p. 83, No. 2.

548. As I was going to Little Mentor, / I saw a little thing sitting by the fire: / Red lips, black beard. / Cuss the thing, how I was skeered.—An old-fashioned copper teakettle sitting by the fire.
Oral, West Virginia.

549. No Tooth or Tongue

549. Old Father Greybeard, / Without tooth or tongue. / If you'll give me your finger, / I'll give you my thumb.—Greybeard, says Moor, *Suffolk Words*, p. 155, was the appropriate name for a fine, large, handsome stone bottle, holding perhaps three or four or more gallons, having its handle terminating in a venerable Druidic face.
Halliwell-Phillipps, *Popular Rhymes*, p. 143 = Halliwell-Phillipps, *Nursery Rhymes* p. 134.

550–552. Hands

550a. A black man was standin' up all day / With his hands in his kimber [akimbo].—Pot.
Parsons, *Barbados*, p. 284, No. 51.

550b. A black woman with her hand in her kimber [akimbo], with three feet.— Pot.
Parsons, *Barbados*, p. 284, No. 51 var.

550c. A woman standin' all day, / Two han' in de canber, / Three foot and a hat on. Cyant move exceptin' somebody go an' move 'em.—Pot.
Parsons, *Barbados*, p. 285, No. 51 var.

551. If me stan', me kimbo; if me lie, me kimbo.—Coffee pot.
Beckwith, *Jamaica*, p. 196, No. 116.

552a. Miss Nancy behin' the door with her hand timbo.—'Tensil [chamber pot] akimbo.
Parsons, *Antilles*, III, 371, Grenada, 49 var.

552b. Miss Nancy put her hand timbo.—'Tensil akimbo.
Parsons, *Antilles*, III, 371, Grenada, 49.

553–556. Belly

553–554. Belly of Wood, Sides of Leather, etc.

In describing various objects as creatures with members of wood and metal, the riddler often fails to hold to the fundamental concept, and disorder results. The riddles in this section are descriptions of animals which are unusual because each member is of a different material. The answers are various utensils composed of several materials. Confusions readily occur in this conception. For example, a Breton riddler portrays a perhaps intentionally confused picture of a bellows in "Three holes, a long beak, and a leather ear."[1] He does not hold to the probably original intention of identifying each part as made of an unusual material. The Iraqi Arabic scales riddle, "Six of skin and two of palms and one from the forest,"[2] is an accumulation of heterogeneous details and owes its enigmatic quality to the seeming impossibility of finding an object to which they can all belong at the same time. The Kashub hoop riddle, "Beaten in the woods, bent at home, and stretched on its mistress' stomach,"[3] is both a series of tortures[4] and an invention akin to the riddles here discussed or to the violin riddle,[5] in which the several parts are said to be vegetable, animal, and human in origin. An unusually complicated comparison to a person occurs in the Icelandic knife riddle: "I have in secret a certain abbot, skillfully made by men. Three materials go to his making. The first comes from the heads of animals. The second from the innermost veins of the marrow-dregs of old Ýmir's body. The third was splendidly smelted in a brazier by the skilled makers. This abbot's face [*egg*] is on the mountain tops, but his backside [*bakki*] is at bridgeheads."[6]

Description in terms of a person composed of heterogeneous materials—usually wood, leather, and iron—is applicable to:

§1. A bellows. See Nos. 553a through 553c below.
§2. A rifle, a gun. See No. 554.
§3. A musical instrument. Italian: Pitrè, 808a (Ribs of wood, belly of leather.—Drum). Serbian: Novaković, p. 37, Nos. 8 (My back is of wood and

---

[1] Sauvé, 74a.
[2] Meissner, *Iraq*, 70. See also the headnote to Nos. 48–55, §5, above.
[3] Patock, *Strellin*, 1.
[4] See the headnote to Nos. 674–680 below.
[5] Nos. 1059a through 1062.
[6] Árnason, 42. The materials are horn, iron, and copper. *Egg* signifies both "blade" and "sharp mountain ridge"; *bakki*, both "the back of the knife" and "a river bank."

my stomach is of leather.—Gusle), 9 (A wooden belly, a leather back, and it speaks by means of hairs).

A Breton riddler retains the fundamental elements but alters the conception considerably: "I died in a forest, an iron killed me, and yet I sing with a beautiful voice.—Musical instrument."[7]

§4. A saddle. Danish: Feilberg, *Ordbog*, III, 139, s.v. "sadel." Portuguese: Parsons, *Cape Verde*, 158 (Back of skin, guts of wood, belly of rags, leg of skin, foot of iron).

Such Serbian versions as "What is cut in the forest, shorn in the corral, harvested in the field, and all put together in one piece?"[8] and "It was cut in the forest, drilled with a drill, woven on a loom"[9] do not suggest a person; these versions belong to the pattern "grew in the wood," discussed below.[10]

§5. A clothes chest. Portuguese: Parsons, *Cape Verde*, 124 (Body of wood, guts of rags). Serbian: Novaković, p. 91, Nos. 8 (Its body is of wood, its eyes are of iron, its heart is of cloth), 9, 10 (Its skin is of wood, its heart is of cloth, its mouth is of iron), and p. 92, Nos. 1, 2. Bulgarian: Palashev, 6 (The old man is of wood, his guts are of hemp).

§6. A distaff. Danish: Feilberg, *Ordbog*, III, 75, s.v. "rok."

§7. A flag. Serbian: Novaković, p. 5, No. 10 (The heart is of wood, the head is of steel, the legs are of iron, the wings are of woven stuff). The riddler suggests an unusual bird.

553a. My back and belly is wood, / And my ribs is line [lined] wi' leather. / I've a hole in my nose, and ane in my breist, / And I'm aftenest used in cauld weather.—Bellows.
Findlay, *Edinburgh*, p. 59.

553b. My belly is wood, / My sides is leather. / My nose is cold iron / And useful in cold weather.—Bellows.
Fauset, *Southern Negro*, p. 280, No. 41.

553c. My ribs is lined wi' leather, / I've a hole i' my side, / An' I'm offense [oftenest] used.—Bellows.
Gutch and Peacock, *Lincolnshire*, p. 400, No. 25.

554. Wooden belly, iron back, / Fire in th' hole, goes off with a crack.—A rifle.
Randolph and Spradley, *Ozark*, p. 85.

555–556. Without a Belly

555a. A man stan' up widout guts.—Bamboo.
Beckwith, *Jamaica*, p. 196, No. 109a.

---

[7] Sébillot, *Devinettes*, 48.
[8] Novaković, p. xxi, No. 9.
[9] Novaković, p. 187, No. 5.
[10] See the headnote to Nos. 1058–1062 below.

555b. Tallest man in Kingston don' have any belly.—Bamboo.
Beckwith, *Jamaica*, p. 196, No. 109.

556. I know a baby born widout a belly.—Skelion [tin can].
Beckwith, *Jamaica*, p. 196, No. 108.

557–563. Legs

Perhaps the most important and certainly the most interesting riddle in this section is the description of a worm as a "long man legless."[1] Some pot riddles suggest the figure of a man with three feet.[2] Some uninteresting and unimportant references to a man's legs[3] occur in riddles mentioning several bodily abnormalities. English riddlers do not seem to know the very popular conception of a mushroom[4] or an umbrella[5] as a man standing on one leg.

557. Little Polly Pickett / Run through the thicket, / Out and in and back again / With one leg tied to the door jamb.—A shuttle.
Randolph and Taylor, *Ozarks*, 12.

558. Three Feet (Legs) and a Cap

Although closely allied to the description of a pot as a creature having three feet,[1] this riddle differs from it and names the supposed person "Hoddy-doddy." This name, which occurs elsewhere,[2] may have no significance and may have been invented merely to rhyme with "body." The introduction, "Black without and black within," occurs in other riddles for a pot.[3]

558a. Hoddy, doddy, / With a round body, / Three feet and a wooden hat. / What's that?—A three-legged iron pot.
Hyatt, *Adams Co., Ill.*, p. 665, No. 10896.

558b. Hoddy-doddy, / With a round black body; / Three feet and a wooden hat. / What's that?—An iron cooking pot.
Halliwell-Phillipps, *Popular Rhymes*, p. 142; Beckwith, *Jamaica*, p. 211, No. 229; Knortz, p. 223, No. 50.

558c. Niddy-noddy, round body, / Three feet and a wooden hat.—Pot.
Praeger, *Béaloideas*, IV (1933–1934), 145, No. 16.

558d. Pee pee pattie, / Three feet and a timmer [timber] hattie.—A pot with a wooden cover.
Gregor, *Northeast Scotland*, p. 79.

558e. Black within and black without, / Three legs an' a iron cap.—A porridge pot.
Gutch and Peacock, *Lincolnshire*, p. 398, No. 13.

---

[1] Nos. 562a, 562b.   [2] Nos. 558a through 558e.
[3] Nos. 563, 566, and 568 through 572.
[4] See the headnote to Nos. 1121–1126, § 3.
[5] See the headnote to Nos. 1121–1126, § 1.
[1] Nos. 68, 85.   [2] No. 560.
[3] See No. 1537 and compare Nos. 64a through 64f.

559. Hundred Legs

559. Long neck and no hands, / Hundred legs and can't stand, / Runs through the house of a morning, / Stands behind the door when company comes.—Broom.
Randolph and Taylor, *Ozarks*, 8.

560. All Legs and No Body

This very interesting text illustrates the decay of English riddling. The speaker has no clear intent to personify a well. Hoddy Toddy, whose name he remembers as rhyming with "body," is probably taken from a riddle for a pot (Nos. 558a, 558b above). The conception "all legs and no body," which resembles in form the description of a pumpkin as "all head and no body" (No. 520 above), is appropriate enough to a well. Since only the wellsweep appears above ground, the riddler can say that, in a sense, the well has no "body," for one cannot call a hole in the ground a "body." The connection between the pumpkin riddle and the well riddle appears also in the common use of a name rhyming with "body." Thus far, the riddler is consistent and intelligible. The remainder of his text is incompatible with what has gone before. He adds a very popular description of a well in terms of a contradiction between something which is tangible and nevertheless cannot be moved.[1] This involves no sort of personification, but, rather, conflicts with it. In brief, the riddler has combined two riddles for a well without clearly understanding the technique of the enigmatic art.

560. Hoddy Toddy, all legs and no body. / Round as a hoop, and deep as a cup. / All the King's horses canna pull it up.—Draw well.
Leather, *Hereford*, p. 231.

561–562. Long Man Legless

In describing a worm as a legless man without a staff who fears ducks and hens but not dogs, the speaker evokes the figure of a beggar retreating before a barking dog. The Serbian "An old man calls from the hill, 'Defend me from hens, I am not afraid of dogs' "[1] is an unusual and ingenious reversal of the theme in order to adapt it to the answer "a sheaf of wheat." This adaptation has a parallel in the Danish riddle for a hare, "Who is he who says to you, 'Protect me from a dog, a cat lets me go'? "[2] So far as I have noted, only the Lithuanian "A gentleman in a little red coat comes [saying]: 'Drive away the chickens, I do not fear the dogs' "[3] mentions the color of the worm. This added detail has perhaps been borrowed from the riddles describing a red fruit.[4] The riddle of Long Man Legless seems to be current only in Europe

---
[1] See Nos. 1325a, 1325b.
[1] Novaković, p. 214, No. 2.
[2] Kristensen, p. 41, § 97, No. 130.
[3] Schleicher, p. 207.
[4] See the headnote to Nos. 632–644 below.

and where European riddles are known.⁵ Compare, however, the Shor "Legless, armless, he crawls on his belly.—Snake."⁶

561. Long-legged lifeless came to the door staffless, / More afraid of a rooster and hen / Than he was of a dog and ten men.—Grasshopper.
  Gardner, *Schoharie Hills, N.Y.*, p. 255, No. 18.

562a. Long man legless / Came till my door staffless, / Haud awa' yir cocks and hens, / Yir dogs an' cats I fehr na.—A worm.
  Gregor, *Northeast Scotland*, p. 81.

562b. Lang man legless, / Gaed to the door staffless; / Good wife, take up your deuks and hens, / For dogs and cats I care na.—A worm.
  Chambers, *Scotland*, p. 111.

562c. A wee man legless / Came to the door staffless, / And said: "Good wife, / Keep in your hens and ducks, / And for your dog I care not."—Worm.
  Green, *South Antrim*, 16.

562d. There was a man legless, / Came to the door staffless. / Jane Pen, keep in your hen! I'm not afraid of your dog.—Worm.
  Praeger, *Béaloideas*, IV (1933–1934), 145, No. 21.

562e. Reddichy roddichy runs on the dyke, / Keep awa' yir clockin' hen, / I care na for yir tyke.—A worm.
  Gregor, *Northeast Scotland*, p. 81.

563. Bandy Legs

563. Riddle me, riddle me randy, / My father's legs are bandy. / Bent in two and knotted in the middle.—Pot hook.
  MacGréine, *Béaloideas*, III (1931–1932), 414, No. 8.

564–572. Several Abnormalities

564. As I was goin' over Butterweek [variant: Burringham] Ferry, / I heard a thing cry, "Chickamacherry," / Wi' dorny [downy] 'ans and dorny face, / White cockade an' silver lace.—Robert Portington, a connexion of the Portingtons then of Sawcliffe, and a Royalist of note, was bitten by a monkey when crossing a ferry on the Ouse, and died from the wound.
  J. F. T., *Notes and Queries*, 10th ser., I (1904), 204.

565a. Long waist, brazen face, no great thing of beauty, / It stands most bright by day and night, / Performing of its duty.—Grandfather clock.
  Leather, *Hereford*, p. 228.

---

⁵ For parallels see the note to Nos. 562a through 562e below, and the references collected in Feilberg, *Ordbog*, III, 35, s.v. "regnorm." For other forms see the riddles cited in the note to No. 263 and the note to Nos. 264a, 264b above and in the headnote to Nos. 264–265, especially §§ 3–4.
⁶ Dyrenkova, 36.

565b. My face is marked, / My hands a-movin'. / No time to play, / Got t'run all day!—A clock.
Randolph and Spradley, *Ozark*, p. 82.

566. Two laigs, / One face, / Two han'.—Clock.
Parsons, *Aiken, S.C.*, p. 31, No. 34.

567. Excuse my revelation, / Weak but willin', / Pour but proud, / See me keep a-comin'. / Tongue-tied, / Three-posted, / Short hair I wear, / Pay fer sittin' down.—Answer lacking.
Parsons, *Guilford Co., N.C* , p. 206, No. 46.

568. I am here alone, I have one leg, one hand, and one eye. They left me here by myself, because I cannot walk, but sometime they will come and shake my hand and out of my mouth I will spit. Some of my sisters and brothers will spit so slow that people hate to shake their hand. I am very swift. I will spit a bucket so quick that some people don't believe. The longer you shake my hand the cooler I get. Can you guess my name?—A pump.
Parsons, *St. Helena Island, S.C.*, p. 228; Johnson, *St. Helena Island, S.C.*, p. 159, No. 34.

569. My legs I can venture, / To say within bound, / Are twelve, if not more, / Tho' they ne'er touch the Ground, / If you search for my Eyes, / More than thirty you'll find, / And, strange to be told, / They are always behind; / The Food that my kind / Benefactress bestows, / I receive at my Eyes, / As every one knows, / The Provision I take, / Never hinders my Sight, / I received it at Morn, / And discharge it [at] Night.—A pair of Stays.
A New Riddle Book; Or, A Whetstone for Dull Wits, p. 18.

570. Peter Flickem had a barn [bairn], / It had neither leg nor arm, / It had neither back nor belly. / Eh, poor thing! They called it Nelly.—An umbrella.
S. O. Addy, *Folk-Lore*, XII (1901), 333.

571. There was a man of Adam's race / Who had no legs, no body but waist. —Ring.
Beckwith, *Jamaica*, p. 213, No. 242.

572. No mouth, no eyes, / Nor yet a nose, / Two arms, two feet, / And as it goes, / The feet don't touch the ground, / But all the way, / The head runs round.—It is a wheelbarrow.
A New Riddle Book; Or, A Whetstone for Dull Wits, p. 3.

573–660. Enumeration of Qualities

573–574. Temperament

Descriptions of an object by a comparison to a person characterized by a particular mood or emotion are virtually nonexistent. Riddlers ordinarily refer to the physical properties of an object, or the acts that it performs. An emotional state that could be ascribed to a person or perhaps to an animal does not lend itself to enigmatic use. The following description of a rat is scarcely more than a statement of fact and lacks the paradoxical element typical of a riddle. The description of ingratitude in terms of an evil person is a literary rather than a popular conception.

573. My fader have a brother, he can't tame at all, get ferocious.—Land a rat.
Parsons, *Antilles*, III, 369, Grenada, 2.

574. j do owe most yet nothing pay, evil j am & the worse j say.—ingratitude.
Tupper, *Holme Riddles*, 103; *Prettie Riddles* (1631), No. 55 = Brandl, p. 59.

575–578. Form

Only a few riddles based on a comparison to a person refer to physical qualities rather than definite bodily abnormalities. They will be found in this section. References to bodily abnormalities of a supposed person have already been listed above. Riddles that merely enumerate the physical aspects of an object without a clear suggestion of personification will be found in chapter vii below.

575. A Long Person

Although the comparison of a road to something long—often a person, more rarely an animal, and very often a thing—is widely known, the only English example is not clearly conceived. Contrast this English version with the Russian "I shall look out of the window: there lies long Anthony."[1] In many languages, but not in English, the word for "long" has also the meaning "tall" and consequently the comparison to a tall person has an appropriateness which it lacks in English.

Riddlers have adapted the comparison to a tall person to the description of other objects than a road. See, as examples:

§1. A corner of a hut. Russian: Sadovnikov, 19 (I look out of the window; there lies long Anthony). The object intended is the beam at the corner of the hut.

§2. Smoke. German: Frischbier, *Menschenwelt*, p. 251, No. 97 (Long man, pale man reaches to Heaven). Serbian: Novaković, p. 17, Nos. 5 (The tsar reaches as far as the sky, while the tsarina [reaches] as far as his knees), 6 (The long one reaches as far as the sky and his wife up to his knees), 7 (It is long, it is thick, and it reaches as far as the sky; its children are up to its knees; its wife is reclining). Bulgarian: Gubov, 82 (The old man is so long that he reaches God, but he is without a hair). Samoan: Turner, pp. 216–217 (A man who has a white head, stands above the fence and reaches to the heavens); Brown, p. 346 (A white-headed man stands on top of the wall and reaches to

---
[1] Sadovnikov, 1327.

the sky). See also, in the headnote to No. 1471, nn. 15–18, below, the comparisons to a pole or rope that reaches to the sky, or around a field or the earth.

§3. Rain. Russian: Sadovnikov, 1917 (I look out of the window; there walks long Anthony), 1930.

§4. The moon. Russian: Sadovnikov, 1838 (I shall glance out the window; there stands long Anthony). The reference to length suggests the rays of the moon.

§5. The Milky Way. Samoan: Heider, 146 (A human being is quite extraordinarily tall. When he sleeps, he lies east and west. When morning comes, he lies north and south). The Samoan *anva*, signifying the Milky Way, is also a name for a boat and a princess.

Enigmatic descriptions of a road ordinarily refer to its length. They are of various kinds, chiefly comparisons to persons, more rarely to animals, occasionally to plants, very frequently to such objects as a rope or thong, and occasionally in terms of a contradiction or confusion in logic. The comparisons to persons are represented by the English version below and are discussed in the note. The other varieties of comparisons will be now examined briefly.

Comparisons of a road to an animal are rather unusual. The idea is not clearly put in the Argentinian "Long, long as an eel, it has neither feet nor ribs."[2] The Mordvin "Its horns reach to Heaven, its tail touches Kazan"[3] is probably a modification of a riddle for smoke.[4]

The occasional comparison of a road to a plant is best known in Africa and the Orient. The Pangwe say, "I cut down a tree, it reaches to the coast,"[5] which is essentially the same as the Bengali "Here I have cut down a tree. The tree went to a distant place called Bhānugāucha"[6] or the Filipino "I planted a calabash, its branches can reach to Manila.—Road or telegraph line"[7] and "I planted a betel tree in Dagupan, but its roots reached to here."[8] The Pangwe "A long thing, the dead trunk of *Triploehiton Tessmanni*"[9] probably involves the same idea. The Khāṛiā "A hundred creepers have joined in one knot"[10] ingeniously represents the paths converging in a village. The Polish "An oak stands in the middle of the village. A branch points to each hut"[11] is virtually the same conception, but is, in this instance, probably an adaptation of a riddle for the sun and its rays.[12]

The objects most frequently employed as the means of comparison for a road are a turban, belt, or rope. The turban is understood as a cloth that can be unrolled and stretched out, as in the Turkish "I have a turban. If one un-

---

[2] Lehmann-Nitsche, 593. [3] Paasonen, 158.
[4] See No. 413 above, and also the note to No. 413 and the headnote to No. 544, §9.
[5] Tessmann, 77. [6] Mitra, *Sylhet*, 34.
[7] Starr, *Philippines*, 328. [8] Starr, *Philippines*, 329.
[9] Tessmann, 79.
[10] Roy and Roy, II, 452, No. 32, and a very similar version in p. 449, No. 3.
[11] Siarkowski, 6. [12] See the headnote to No. 544 above.

winds it, it has no end,"¹³ and the Baiga "A king's turban that cannot be measured."¹⁴ The Swahili "Father's girdle is stretched out a long way"¹⁵ is like the Ewe "My father bought me a big loin cloth. I was going to put it on, but could not. What is it?"¹⁶ This and the Togo "My father bought me a girdle. I can never put it all on,"¹⁷ are probably derived from the same source as the Uraon "Who can measure a raja's dhoti [loincloth]?"¹⁸ It seems probable that we have here a variety of the riddle that has been spread from western Africa (Togo) to India by Arabic tellers of riddles.

The comparison of a road to a rope, lasso, or ribbon is very widely known. The Zyrians say, "A very long rope stretches about the whole world, its end is nowhere";¹⁹ the Armenians, "A long rope [stretched] to Nachitshvan";²⁰ and the Mongolians, "A long, white, silken ribbon reaches as far as Peking."²¹ Some versions say that the rope cannot be rolled up, but we need not necessarily see a connection between a Kamba "A long bast rope, it is not rolled up"²² and an Altai Turkish "In rolling up a long rope for horses, I have grown weary,"²³ which has a Mongolian parallel, and "I began to roll up a long lasso, but I could not [accomplish the task]"²⁴ or the Mingrelian and Ossete "I rolled and rolled and could not roll it up at all."²⁵ It is tempting, however, to suggest that Mohammedans might have disseminated this conception from central Africa to eastern Asia. The theme is specialized in the Lithuanian "Day and night I rolled up father's belt, but I could not roll it up."²⁶ Those texts in which the object is said to be a sheet or cover rather than a rope are probably affected by the comparison of the sky to a sheet that cannot be folded.²⁷ For examples see the Mingrelian "I have a cover. I folded it and folded it and I could not fold it up"²⁸ and the Votyak "A long blanket, which no one can roll up."²⁹

Some comparisons to a rope are more ingenious than those mentioned thus far. The oldest of them is Claret's fourteenth-century

> Omnis adest mundus cum suberibusque ligatus:
> Est via diversa dispersa sub orbe soluta,

---

¹³ Kowalski, *Asia Minor*, 26; Kúnos, 75; Hamizade, 740 (I have a turban. I wind and wind and it doesn't end). Modern Greek: Carnoy and Nicolaides, p. 279, No. 21. See also Mongolian: Bazarov, 16.
¹⁴ Elwin, p. 472, No. 81.   ¹⁵ Velten, 20.   ¹⁶ Spieth, p. 597, No. 3.
¹⁷ Schönhärl, 1.   ¹⁸ Archer, p. 193, No. 207.   ¹⁹ Wichmann, *Zyrian*, 92.
²⁰ Seidlitz, p. 70, No. 3.   ²¹ Mostaert, 80.   ²² Lindblom, 90.
²³ Radlov (German ed.), I, 261, No. 9. Mongolian: Zhamtsaranov, 79.
²⁴ Katanov in Radlov, IX, 243, No. 110, and p. 370, No. 355.
²⁵ Mingrelian: Blechsteiner, p. 157, No. 9. Ossete: Schiefner, 6.
²⁶ Jurgelionis, 687; see also his Nos. 688, 689, and Schleicher, p. 210.
²⁷ See the discussions below, in headnotes to Nos. 1215–1216, 1217–1218, 1219–1220, and 1221–1223, and see also the notes to Nos. 1215, 1216, 1217, 1219, and 1220 and the note to Nos. 1224 through 1225b.
²⁸ Petrov, p. 257, No. 6.
²⁹ Wichmann, *Votyak*, 273. See also Buch, 27.

which resembles the previously quoted Khāṛiā comparison to a creeper and knots in it.³⁰ According to Václav Flajšhans,³¹ this Latin text explains a corrupt version of the fifteenth century. Other comparisons for a road diverge greatly from one another. Examples are the Votyak "Behind the house a dirty rope.—Path to the well or river";³² the Buryat "The gaily colored twins twisted by the mother cannot be unknotted";³³ and the Gypsy "One spreads gray, endlessly long linen throughout the land."³⁴ They show the modifications which arise in a simple theme. The Nyika "A long strip of the hypenae palm, and [yet] it does not tie up firewood"³⁵ shows a clear perceiving of the notion that the rope cannot be rolled up and applies the notion to a specific situation.

There are a few, rather unimportant comparisons to a stick. The Serbian "It is a crooked stick. If it were straightened, it would reach to the sky"³⁶ is merely an adaptation of the comparison to a man. It is quite different from the Khāṛiā "Will you be able to measure the stick of the princess?"³⁷

There are, finally, riddles for a road which depend upon a contradiction in terms or on some sort of confusion in logic. The Sukuma "You will never bring it to an end,"³⁸ like the Lamba "That which has no ending,"³⁹ is merely a suggested impossibility. The Surinam "It is long in front, it is long in back"⁴⁰ seems to suggest a contradiction. The French "Long, long as a rope, beaten by horseshoes"⁴¹ is a corruption which we cannot easily set right without more parallels. Texts like the German "Longer than a tree, longer than countries, lower than grass"⁴² are probably derived from riddles for a saddle.⁴³ Another version is the confused Svanian "It does not reach a pig's legs, otherwise it is very long.—A rope,"⁴⁴ which might have the answer "saddle" or "road."

Riddlers occasionally make three assertions regarding a road: "If I were upright, I should touch the sky. If I had ears, I should hear everything. If I had a tongue, I should tell everything."⁴⁵

575. Long Aunty Long-long, no one can [be as?] long as Aunty Long-long.—Road.

Beckwith, *Jamaica*, p. 204, No. 198.

---

[30] See Claret, vv. 165–166, No. 71; and for the Khāṛiā quotation see n. 10 above.
[31] *Český lid*, XII (1903), 492, No. 1; see also his "Naše hádanky," p. 22, No. 21a.
[32] Wichmann, *Votyak*, 265. [33] Gombojew, 57.
[34] Wlislocki, 15. [35] Hollis, *Nyika*, p. 140, No. 13.
[36] Novaković, p. 181, No. 11. [37] Roy and Roy, II, 453, No. 38.
[38] Augustiny, 277. [39] Doke, 60.
[40] Herskovits, p. 443, No. 56. Compare the Berber "He is long and has no end" (Stumme, *Zeitschrift der deutschen morgenländischen Gesellschaft*, XLVIII, 406, No. 4).
[41] Beauvillard, *Mélusine*, I (1878), col. 556, No. 1.
[42] Frischbier, *Menschenwelt*, p. 264, No. 220.
[43] See the headnote to No. 1281, nn. 7–8, below.
[44] J. Nizheradze, p. 66, No. 4.
[45] Breton: Charlec, *Dol-de-Bretagne*, 1904, p. 168, No. 30. Mongolian: Zhamtsaranov, 5.

576–577. Prickly or Bumpy

The comparison of an object to a person with a bumpy skin or wearing a prickly dress is applicable to a hedgehog[1] or to a plant with protuberances.[2] A literary riddle compares the spots on the moon to beauty spots,[3] and a clock riddle,[4] which probably has a literary origin, is somewhat similar. The Samoans describe a fire and its smoke—probably a smoldering fire—in these terms: "Who is the man—his head is covered with sores and he has a long queue?"[5] Russians and others describe a thimble as a pig, or, more usually, a man, covered with holes or pockmarks.[6] Typical examples are the Altai Turkish "A rather scurvy youth"[7] or "A pockmarked man is lying under my pillow."[8] The Yakut file riddle, "They say that a pimply child is crying,"[9] contains an allusion to the scratching noise of a file. Another version, "They say that a pimply child is lying on one end of a crossbeam,"[10] refers to the Yakut custom of laying a file in a crevice of a crossbeam at one end of the foundation. The Turcoman description of the sky, "By day a clean face, at night a scarred, scabby face,"[11] employs a similar metaphor. It is akin to the Kundu comparison of the sky to an elephant covered with pustules.[12] The Mongolians compare an animal and a file, "The thin light-bay horse has eighty thousand brands."[13]

576. Bearer of Pins and Needles

A man carrying spits, stakes, or needles might be a husbandman, a Gypsy, or a peddler. He forms a convenient enigmatic parallel to a hedgehog. The Votyak hedgehog riddle, "A little Tatar boy sells needles,"[1] which also has the answer "bedbug,"[2] is an especially neat formulation of the idea. It is readily adapted to a sea urchin, as in the Modern Greek "A round, round monk loaded with pegs."[3]

Comparisons of a hedgehog to another animal are rare, since riddlers do not usually equate objects in the same category. Animals are not often represented

---

[1] Nos. 576a through 576c.
[2] Nos. 577a, 577b.
[3] No. 513.
[4] No. 565b.
[5] Heider, 79. See also his No. 82.
[6] Russian: Sadovnikov, 615. Mordvin: Paasonen, 257. See also Spanish: Rodríguez Marín, 656, 657 (dents); Demófilo, 357 (pockmarks), 358 (dents). Hungarian: *Magyar Nyelvör*, III (1874), 37 (Outside it has many little holes, but inside it has only one big one); V (1876), 34; XII (1883), 331. Kabardin: Talpa and Sokolov, 7 (It comes from the Crimea, it is pitted). Cherekessian: Tambiev, p. 57, No. 45 (He comes from the Crimea with a pockmarked face). See also the headnotes to Nos. 528–534, n. 2, above, and to Nos. 1263–1265, n. 6, below.
[7] Menges, 36.
[8] Katanov in Radlov, IX, 287, No. 237.
[9] Piekarski, 395.
[10] Piekarski, 396.
[11] Karutz, p. 97.
[12] See the two Kundu riddles quoted in the headnote to No. 1227, §4, below.
[13] Kotvich, 252.
[1] Wichmann, *Votyak*, 171.
[2] Buch, 9.
[3] Polites, *Neohellenika Analekta*, I, 237, No. 250.

in riddles by other animals. However, the Bulgarians say, "I have a little donkey loaded with needles";[4] the Serbians, "Wherever our ewe passed, it carried three hundred and three pickets."[5] Comparisons to things are also rare, but see the Bulgarian "A blue ball stuck with pins"[6] and the Algerian Arabic "My *guerba* [waterskin] is like asparagus. Its tendrils are clinging."[7] Symphosius conceived a hedgehog as a prickly house with a harmless occupant: "A house filled with prickles, but an occupant of slight form; with an unharmed back, though pierced by sharp spears, an unarmed dweller bears an armed crop."[8] The Modern Greek parallel, "A round tower loaded with cannon,"[9] makes no reference to an occupant.

In a riddle for a sieve used to filter beer a Ho riddler turns this conception very ingeniously into "Your mother's sister, that is to say, your aunt, is suffering from [a] boil. She cannot sit down."[10] The bamboo sieve used for this purpose has a conical bottom and cannot lie flat. The notion of carrying spears or spits is appropriately used of a chestnut in the Turkish "In the coat he is wearing are a thousand lancets, the whole world was the common mother."[11]

576a. As I went over Lincoln Bridge, / I met Mister Rusticap; / Pins and needles on his back, / A-going to Thorny Fair.—A hedgehog.
Gutch and Peacock, *Lincolnshire*, p. 402; Halliwell-Phillipps, *Nursery Rhymes*, p. 131; Parsons, *Bermuda*, p. 246, No. 7. Corby Fair: Gutch and Peacock, *Lincolnshire*, p. 402.

576b. As I was goin' over our gardin gap, / I spied my Uncle Ned; / With pins and needles up'n his back, / An we kep' joggin' on a-head.—A prickyotchin [urchin; i.e., hedgehog].
Gutch and Peacock, *Lincolnshire*, p. 397, No. 5.

576c. Little Billy Breek sits by the reek [rick], / He has more horns than all the king's sheep.—A hedgehog.
Kavanagh, *Béaloideas*, II (1929–1930), 295.

577a. My mother have a pretty chil', but all she have on is prickle.—Soursop.
Parsons, *Antilles*, III, 372, Grenada, 60.

577b. My moder had a chil'; all round her skin was bump.—Sugar apple.
Parsons, *Antilles*, III, 373, Grenada, 66.

578. Several Qualities

578. I am rough, I am smooth; / I am wet, I am dry; / My station is low, my title high; / My king my lawful master is, / I am used by all, though only his.—Highway.
Knortz, p. 235, No. 114.

---

[4] Charcharov, 24.
[5] Novaković, p. 78, No. 4.
[6] Gubov, 355.
[7] Giacobetti, 173.
[8] No. 29.
[9] Polites, *Neohellenika Analekta*, I, 209, No. 89.
[10] Sarkar, p. 256, No. 46.
[11] Hamizade, 383.

579–584. Color

The few riddles in this section describe an object in terms of a person of an unusual color. A related and more usual manner of description refers to the color of the supposed person's dress.[1]

579a. My flesh and skinne is red, / but white is all my heart, / where round about a wall is set / beaten with every dart.—It is a cherry and cherry stone.
Prettie Riddles (1631), No. 29 = Brandl, p. 56; Tupper, *Holme Riddles*, 92.

579b. My Skin is black, my Blood is sweet, / My heart resembles Wood, / In which there's something may be eat, / Tho' not exceeding good.—Black Cherry.
A New Riddle Book; Or, A Whetstone for Dull Wits (18th cent.), p. 9.

580. A stone wall with a golden lady.—Egg.
Parsons, *Bermuda*, p. 251, No. 42.

581–582. A White Person: Tooth

The rather unusual comparison of a single tooth to a white man is perhaps a specialized or degenerate form of the comparison of teeth to a company of white persons (see No. 841 and the headnote to No. 841, § 2).

581a. White gyirl walkin' on a red bay.—Teet' an' yer gum.
Parsons, *Bahamas*, p. 475, No. 38.

581b. White man on a red horse back.—Teet' on de gums.
Johnson, *St. Helena Island, S.C.*, p. 157, No. 4.

582. White Man and Red Rag

The description of a gum as a red rag is perhaps unique. For the comparison of the tongue to a rag see the headnote to No. 1150 below.

582. The white man take a red cloth tie his head.—Tooth and gum.
Beckwith, *Jamaica*, p. 197, No. 126.

583–584. Red (Black) Head (Hair, Face)

This conception is closely allied to the more frequently used notion of a person with a red cap.[1] Riddlers in widely separated places have hit upon it apparently independently. The Creoles in Mauritius call a bottle of wine a black man with a red head[2] and have in mind the red wax used to seal the cork. The Samoans say of a post wound with coconut fibers on which fruit is rubbed to remove the husks: "Who is the man, who stands every day with his red headdress?"[3] In modern European folklore the comparison to a man with red or black hair is often applied to a match.

---

[1] See Nos. 601a through 660.

[1] See the headnote to Nos. 632–644, in which these comparisons are more fully discussed.

[2] Baissac, *Mauritius*, p. 419.   [3] Heider, 94.

583a. Somet'in' in de house have red hair.—Matches in de box.
Parsons, *Sea Islands, S.C.*, p. 159, No. 41, var. 4.

583b. A red-head man in a red-top house.—Match.
Parsons, *Sea Islands, S.C.*, p. 159, No. 41, var. 1.

584a. A straight white man wid a red face an' a black head.—Match.
Parsons, *Sea Islands, S.C.*, p. 159, No. 41, var. 2.

584b. A tall white man with red face and blue hair. What's that?—A match.
Parsons, *Sea Islands, S.C.*, p. 159, No. 41, var. 3.

585–660. Dress

585–600. Form

585. The Cock Dressed as a Prophet

The description of a cock as a prophet, who is of uncertain age, has many wives, and wears clothes such as no man can make, occurs in several divergent forms which can probably be traced back to a late medieval or early Renaissance invention. In origin a literary rather than a popular creation, it is closely allied to the description of a cock as a cavalier, Turk, or king (see the headnote to Nos. 539–543 above). For a brief discussion of related themes see M. Sabbe, "Satirische prophetie of raadselspel," *Volkskunde*, XIX (1907–1908), 34–39.

585a. There was a prophet on this earth. / His age no man could tell; / He was at his greatest height / Before e'er Adam fell. / His wives are very numerous, / Yet he maintaineth none; / And at the day of reckoning / He bids them all begone. / He wears his boots when he should sleep; / His spurs are ever new; / There's no shoemaker on a' the earth / Can fit him for a shoe.—A cock.
Chambers, *Scotland*, p. 112.

585b. There lives a prophet in the land, / His age no man can tell, / His coat it is of many colours, / His boots are always new, / There's no tailyeor in the land / Can shape to him or shue [sew].—A cock.
Findlay, *Edinburgh*, p. 60.

586. Wears One Kind of Robe

This riddle, which is probably a literary product rather than a bit of popular tradition, contains an unusual reference to the social status of the supposed actor. Some Russian riddles for a bee use exactly the same descriptive device: "She is neither maiden nor widow nor a married wife, yet she rears children, feeds people, brings gifts to God," which refers in the last clause to the candles made of beeswax; "There lives [one who is] neither a maiden, nor a matron, nor a soldier's wife, neither a widow, nor a husband's wife. She has no husband, she does not sin, yet her children are many"; "Not a soldier's woman, nor a widow, nor a married wife, yet she gave birth to many children and was beloved by God."[1]

586. In almost every house I'm seen, / And wonder when I'm coming, / I'm neither maiden, man, nor wife, / Nor yet a married woman, / I'm penniless and poor as Job, / Yet such my state by nature / I always wear one kind of robe, / An independent creature.—Cat.
Fauset, *Nova Scotia*, p. 160, No. 85.

587. Summer and Winter Clothing

In various countries riddlers have described a tree as a person dressed in summer and naked in winter. The conception is so obvious and the variations in many of the versions are so considerable that it seems probable that it has originated independently on several occasions. The English version of this theme seems to be a literary invention which is not fully and accurately preserved in any of the four available texts. The reversal of the theme in the Turkish "On the steppe stands a naked lad.—Tree from which the bark has been removed"[1] is unusual.

In the Far East, the bamboo is often said to be dressed in its youth and naked in its maturity. The references to summer and winter are not present. See Indian, Ho: Sarkar, p. 353, No. 15 (When young, [it is] clothed; when adult, [it is] naked; on the head, [it has] matted hair; [it is] hollow within). Bengali: Mitra, *Notes on Ho Riddles*, pp. 105–106; Mitra, *Chittagong*, pp. 320–321, No. 31; Mitra, *Murshidābād*, pp. 930–931, No. 14. Khāṛiā: Roy and Roy, II, 454, No. 47 (A girl while young puts on clothes; when grown up, she casts them off). Bhil: Hedberg, p. 869, No. 17 (In childhood, it puts on a loincloth, but when it grows up, it throws it away). Indonesian, Tounsea: De C., 14. Serawaj: Helfrich, *Serawaj*, 52. Batak: Ophuijsen, p. 463, No. 60. Tabaru: Fortgens, 2, 65. Engganee: Helfrich, *Engganee*, p. 519, No. 14. Javanese: Luinenburg, p. 385, No. 27; Tauern, *Patasiwa*, p. 72. Thai: Haas, 6 (What is it? As little children, they wear a skirt; having grown up, they are quite bare). Professor Mary R. Haas has given me this unpublished text. Fijian: Fison, 14 (A man,—when a child, he was clothed; now that he is grown up, he scorns clothing). Japanese: Starr, *Japan*, p. 45 (What has many kimonos when a child, but is naked when grown?). One Javanese version conceives the riddle in terms of two persons: "The mother is naked, the child has an undershirt" (Mayer, 15).

In Europe the riddle for a tree usually refers to its various functions in serving mankind. Compare the Russian "In the spring it gladdens us, in the summer it cools us, in the autumn it feeds us, in the winter it warms us."[2] This is rather widely known in several forms. See Swedish: Dybeck, *Runa*,

---
[1] Sadovnikov, 1451, 1451a, 1451b.
[1] Katanov in Radlov, IX, 240, No. 75.   [2] Sadovnikov, 1391.

1849, p. 46, No. 2; Ström, p. 123, "Trädet." Serbian: Novaković, p. 46, Nos. 1 (In the spring I rest you, in the summer I cool you, in the fall I feed you, in the winter I warm you), and 2 (I gladden the spring, I cool the summer, I feed the autumn, and I warm the winter). See further, Spanish, Argentinian: Lehmann-Nitsche, 279. Russian: Sadovnikov, 1351 (I blossom in the spring, I bear fruit in the summer, I do not wilt in the autumn, nor do I die in the winter).

The contrast of nakedness and being dressed is applicable to various objects other than a tree. Note the Cheremiss description of a prop for a haystack, "It puts on a fur coat in the summer, it takes off its clothing in the winter,"[3] to which there is a Votyak parallel.[4] Note also the Sukuma description of a peanut, "It goes out naked and comes back with a fur dress";[5] the Uraon riddle for maize, "Young, no one noticed me. Grown up, everyone takes off my clothes";[6] and the Basque riddle for fire, "The person whom one dresses in the evening and undresses in the morning."[7]

These conceptions have a generic similarity to the enumerations of comparisons involving several references to different colors[8] and to biographical sequences of the type "born white, grows green."[9] Compare also the Turkish "The tsar's son has put on a fur coat with edgings.—Birch" and "The commander's son has put on a striped fur coat.—Poplar,"[10] which are instructive examples of the making of riddles on the same pattern.

Another variety of these comparisons in terms of a person's form is seen in the Tabaru riddle for a plant called *sajoer pakoe-pakoe* in Malay: "If she is still young, then she bows down. If she has become old, then she straightens herself upright."[11] A curious allusion to the different colors of skin appears in the Tabaru riddle for the larva of the June bug: When still small, it is a Chinese. When it is big, it is a Papuan."[12] A Chinese has a yellow skin and a Papuan a black skin.

587a. In spring I looks gay / Dress in handsome array. / De cooler it grew, / I t'row off my clothing, / In winter quite naked appear.—Answer lacking (used as a toast).
Parsons, *Andros Island, Bahamas*, p. 277.

587b. In spring I am gay, / In handsome array; / In summer more clothing I wear; / When colder it grows, / I fling off my clothes; / And in winter quite naked appear.—A tree.
Wintemberg and Wintemberg, *Canada*, p. 123, No. 424.

---

[3] Wichmann, *Cheremiss*, 40; Porkka, 52. [4] Wichmann, *Votyak*, 365.
[5] Augustiny, 15. [6] Archer, p. 193, No. 215.
[7] Cerquand, 6. Compare below, Nos. 785, 786, and the headnote to Nos. 785-786.
[8] See the headnote Nos. 1384-1393 below.
[9] Gianandrea, *Archivio*, I (1882), 84, No. 41. See also the headnote to Nos. 668-669 below.
[10] Katanov in Radlov, IX, 367, Nos. 314, 315.
[11] Fortgens, 29. [12] Fortgens, 70.

587c. In spring I am very pretty, / And in winter I am naked.—Tree.
Parsons, *Bermuda*, p. 254, No. 59.

587d. In spring, I am gray [sic] in attire, / In summer, I wear more clothing than in spring. / In winter, I am naked.—Tree.
Knortz, p. 233, No. 97.

588. Dress in the Wrong Place

A variety of animals and objects are described as persons having their dress within and their bones or skin outside, or as animals having bones outside the skin. Typical examples of this theme are the following:

§ 1. A barrel. Breton: Sébillot, *Haute-Bretagne*, 79; Charlec, *Dol-de-Bretagne*, 1903, p. 288 (Who has bones on his skin?). French: Rolland, 207 (Who has bones on his flesh?). Spanish, Argentinian: Lehmann-Nitsche, 202. Finnish: Lönnrot, 1705 = Henssen, 169 (An open mouth is on its back, the ribs are upon the skin, a horn which is turned toward everyone is on its forehead). The horn is the tap.

§ 2. A crab. Scotch Gaelic: Nicolson, p. 15 (Its flesh inside its bones). German: Wossidlo, 174. Spanish, Dominican Rep.: Andrade, 94. Porto Rican: Mason, 101. Lettish: Bielenstein, 784. Finnish: Aarne and Krohn, 128 = Henssen, 171 (Flesh below, bones above). Estonian: Lönnrot, p. 179; Wiedemann, p. 265. Hungarian: Kálmány, II, 167, No. 7 (What animal has its bones on the outside?). Surinam: Herskovits, p. 447, No. 82.

§ 3. Other animals with shells. SNAIL. Arabic: Ruoff, p. 45, No. 28 (If you are clever, shrewd, and gifted with good taste, explain: flesh within, bones outside). African, Tonga-Shangaan: Junod and Jaques, p. 236, No. 37. MUSSEL. Arabic: Littmann, p. 50.

§ 4. An egg. French: J. Roux, *Limousin*, 84. Indian, Kashmiri: Knowles, 44 (What is that animal that can be tossed up and down; inside it is flesh and outside bones?). Khāṛiā: Roy and Roy, II, 450, No. 14 (Outside white bones, inside red flesh). Chinese: Rudolph, p. 74, No. 4.

§ 5. The fingernails. See Nos. 588a through 588c and the headnote to No. 989.

§ 6. An umbrella. Indian, Bengali: Mitra, *Chittagong*, p. 357, No. 23 (Bones outside, flesh inside).

§ 7. A candle. Breton: Bayon, *Haute-Bretagne*, p. 296; Charlec, *Dol-de-Bretagne*, 1903, p. 288 (Who has his shirt in the middle of his belly?). Flemish: Joos, 154 (Outside fat, inside wool), which is perhaps intended to suggest a sheep rather than a person. German: Frischbier, *Menschenwelt*, p. 250, No. 86. Danish: Feilberg, *Ordbog*, II, 484, s.v. "lys." Faeroic: Hammershaimb, *Antiquarisk tidsskrift*, III, 316, No. 9. Icelandic: Árnason, 388 (What is hairy inside and bald outside?). French: Rolland, 162; Bladé, *Armagnac*, 85; Carmeau, p. 33; Queyrat, *La Creuse*, I, 365; Lespy, *Béarn*, 29; Mensignac, *Gironde*, p. 301, No. 23; Roque-Ferrier, *Languedoc*, pp. 335–336. Basque: Vinson, 7;

Cerquand, 33. See also Vinson, 50 = Cerquand, 38 (Shirt under the skin). Catalan: Pelay y Briz, 215. Spanish: Demófilo, 1023, 1025, and p. 391, No. 44 (Petticoat inside, flesh outside); Rodríguez Marín, 825, 826, and pp. 378–379. Cuban: Giménez Cabrera, 22. Lithuanian: Jurgelionis, 369 (A naked man, his shirt in his bosom), 370 through 372 (A flaxen heart, a tallow wrapper, a head of silver), 373 (Naked as a jacksnipe, his shirt is in his bosom); Schleicher, p. 203. Lettish: Bielenstein, 634 through 636. White Russian: Wasilewski, 115 (Naked, its shirt is in its bosom). Russian: Sadovnikov, 209 (The body is white, the soul coarse linen, the top gold), 212 (He is naked but his shirt is in his bosom); Preobrazhenskii, p. 172. Serbian: Novaković, p. 200, Nos. 5 (A naked man carries a shirt in his bosom), 7 (The heart is of cloth, the body of flesh), 8 (The heart of cloth, the body of flesh, the head of fire).[1] Bulgarian: Gubov, 102 (Its skin is inside, its flesh outside), 103 (Inside skin, outside meat), which resembles the riddle for a chicken's gizzard (§ 9 below). Finnish: Lönnrot, 29 = Henssen, 17 (A naked man wears his clothes inside). Estonian: Wiedemann, pp. 274, 286; Lönnrot, pp. 183, 193. Mordvin: Paasonen, 286 (It is naked. It has its shirts and trousers in its bosom, but it burns from head to foot). Zyrian: Wichmann, *Zyrian*, 141. Hungarian: *Magyar Nyelvör*, XXXI (1902), 532, No. 9 (I have a girl whose insides are hemp). Albanian: Hahn, p. 158, No. 10 (Wool inside, flesh without). Modern Greek: Polites, *Neohellenika Analekta*, I, 202, No. 51 (Iron sides, cotton insides). Yakut: Piekarski, 452 (They say that it is naked on the outside, but clothed on the inside); Popov, p. 288 (Outside is the meat, inside is the shirt).

§ 8. Plants. ARTICHOKE. French: Mensignac, *Gironde*, 56. NUT. French: J. Roux, *Limousin*, 84. MAIZE. African, Lamba: Doke, 48 (An old man whose gray hair is inside his belly). PINEAPPLE. African, Bavenda: Stayt, p. 359 (Bone inside, marrow outside). MANIOC. Malagasy: Sibree, 5 (Coarse *ròfia* cloth outside and white robe inside). MEALIE. African, Kxatla: Schapera, 58 (Bone in, marrow outside). Filipino: Starr, *Philippines*, 126. MANGO. Indian: Chaina Mall, *Panjab Notes and Queries*, III (1886), 220, No. 899, § 3 (What is that thing from Hindustan that has skin on its hair, and its hair on its bones?). STRAW BUNDLE CONTAINING RICE. Indian, Khariā: Roy and Roy, II, 449, No. 5 (It has its entrails outside and its flesh inside).

§ 9. The stomach, usually a chicken's gizzard. Portuguese: Parsons, *Cape Verde*, 63. Serbian: Novaković, p. 51, Nos. 3 (Flesh outside, skin inside), 4 (All around there is flesh, and in the middle skin), 5 (The body is outside, the shirt inside), which is probably suggested by the candle riddle in § 7 above. African, Lamba: Doke, 131. Swahili: Velten, 88 (Flesh without, skin within. —Stomach). Indonesian, Menangkerbau Malay: Harmsen, p. 272, No. 28.

588a. Sack a back an' not de front.—Finger-nail.
Beckwith, *Jamaica*, p. 200, No. 163.

---

[1] For parallels to the last element see the riddle for a cock, No. 541 above, and the riddles for a pipe in the headnote to Nos. 1440–1441 below.

588b. Missy apram behin' she back.—Fingernail.
Parsons, *Antilles*, III, 437, St. Martin, 34.

588c. The governor lady apron behin' her back.—Fingernails.
Parsons, *Antilles*, III, 371, Grenada, 47.

589–593. Torn Dress

589a. Biddy-widdy upstairs, / Biddy-widdy downstairs, / All the needles in the town / Couldn't sew up Biddy-widdy's night gown.—Egg.
Fauset, *Philadelphia*, p. 554, No. 20.

589b. Miss Mary goin' upstairs / Get her frock tare.—Egg.
Parsons, *Antilles*, III, 424, Antigua, 4.

590. Hitties Titties went to town, / Hitties Titties tore her nice gown, / No tailor round the town / Could mend Hitties Titties' gown like me.—Aigg.
Parsons, *Barbados*, p. 276, No. 2 var. Riddlers introduce many minor variations: Hitty Titty or Hoity Toity or Hitee Titee; wedding-gown; not a tailor in Bridgetown (Johnson, *Antigua*, p. 85, No. 25). Titty-tat . . . All the needles in the town: Fauset, *Southern Negro*, p. 282, No. 61. Miss Tatty . . . All the tailors in the town: Parsons, *Antilles*, III, 375, St. Vincent, 5. Little Peggy . . . No doctor in the town: Parsons, *Antilles*, III, 444, St. Croix, 22. Etty Etty went to town / Keety Keety tare her gown: Parsons, *Antilles*, III, 444, St. Croix, 22 var.

591a. Humpy Dumpy went up town, / Humpy Dumpy ta' [tear] his gown, / All the king's horses, all the king men, / Could not put him together again.—Egg.
Parsons, *Sea Islands, S.C.*, p. 165, No. 74, var. 3.

591b. Humpty Dumpty sat on a wall. / Humpty Dumpty got a great fall. / All the tailors in the town / Could not mend Humpty gown.—Egg.
Parsons, *Antilles*, III, 371, Grenada, 43.

591c. Humpty Dumpty went to town, / Humpty Dumpty tore his gown. / All the womens in the town / Could not men' Humpty Dumpty's gown.—Egg.
Parsons, *Aiken, S.C.*, p. 25, No. 4, var. 3.

592. Little Tommy Tucker went up a hill but he bust his gown, / But not a tailor could not mend his gown.—Egg.
Parsons, *Antilles*, III, 441, Anguilla, 35.

593a. Every time de win' blow it blow on Ber Nancy co' tail teer.—Banana leaf.
Parsons, *Bahamas*, p. 481, No. 94 var.

593b. Every time de win' blow it blow on Ber Nancy coat tail.—Banana leaf.
Parsons, *Bahamas*, p. 481, No. 94.

593c. Mrs. Queen coat-tail tear an' never mend.—Banana leaf.
Beckwith, *Jamaica*, p. 196, No. 113a.

593d. Going up to town me coatie torn-torn and not a seamstress in a town could sew it.—Banana leaf.
Beckwith, *Jamaica*, p. 196, No. 113.

593e. Wriggle-me, wriggle-de, wriggle-de wriggle, / I'll tell you this struggle. / Perhaps you may guess it, perhaps not. / My father give me a coat to sew / An' I could not get it sew.—A banana bush.
   Parsons, *Antilles*, III, 428, Nevis, 17.

593f. My father have a t'ing in him yard, cutting like a tailor cutting cloth.— Banana-leaf, because when the tree begins to fruit, the leaf slits into ribbons.
   Beckwith, *Jamaica*, p. 185, No. 20.

594–600. Various Kinds of Dress

594a. As I was going across London Bridge, / I peeped down through a crack. / I saw Old Mother Hubbard with a blanket on her back.—A mud-turtle.
   Farr, *Tennessee*, p. 319, No. 18.

594b. On London Bridge I looked down through a crack, / Saw the devil with a whirl upon his back.—Turtle.
   Hyatt, *Adams Co., Ill.*, p. 669, No. 10930.

595. I am neither queen nor king, / I wear a crown.—Grenade.
   Parsons, *Antilles*, III, 434, St. Martin, 3.

596. Miss Mary goin' upstairs wid a white ribbon tied her waist.—Snuff.
   Parsons, *Antilles*, III, 424, Antigua, 10.

597. Little Miss Nancy, shart but she have a long frock.—Needle and thread.
   Parsons, *Antilles*, III, 376, St. Vincent, 16.

598. My mother had a child, she had a long dress, every step she made, her dress came shorter.—Needle and thread.
   Parsons, *Antilles*, III, 373, Grenada, 67.

599. Little hittle, / Wrapped in a whittle, / Nineteen times as high as St. Paul's Steeple.—A star.
   Leather, *Hereford*, p. 232.

600. A little Informer, / Cloath'd in bright Armor, / Beloved by Men of Degree; / It goes fine and neat, / Without Leg or Feet, / Now tell me what this Riddle must be.—A Watch in a Silver Case; the Hand shews the Hour, while the Silver betokens bright Armour.
   A New Riddle Book; Or, A Whetstone for Dull Wits (18th cent.), p. 8.

601–660. Colors

601–606. Green

601–603. Itum Paraditum

This curious and obscure riddle has puzzled those who have handed it on in tradition. The variations in the answers show that riddlers have endeavored to make sense out of material which had become almost unintelligible.

601a. Itum Paradisum all clothed in green, / The king could not read it, no more could the queen. / They sent for the wise men out of the East, / Who said it had horns, but was not a beast.—The cabalistic Itum Paradisum is the holly-tree which from its prickly defences would seem to suggest the idea of its resemblance to the cherubim guarding the entrance of Paradise.

M. Ozmond, *Notes and Queries*, 2d ser., VI (1858), 523 = Gutch, *East Riding, Yorkshire*, p. 216. The King could not read it, nor Madam the Queen: Gutch and Peacock, *Lincolnshire*, p. 401, No. 30.

601b. Highty, tighty, paradighty, clothed in green, / The king could not read it, no more could the queen; / They sent for a wise man out of the East, / Who said it had horns, but was not a beast.—The holly tree.

Halliwell-Phillipps, *Nursery Rhymes*, p. 133 = Lina Eckenstein, *Comparative Studies in Nursery Rhymes* (London, 1906), p. 113.

602a. Itum Paraditum all clothed in green, / The king could not read it, no more could the Queen, / They sent for the wise men out of the East, / They said it had horns, but it wasn't a beast.—A parrot.

Baring-Gould *Notes and Queries*, 3d ser., IX (1866), 86 (East Lancashire).

602b. Handsome protector dressed in green, / Handsome protector sent to the queen.—Parrot.

Beckwith, *Jamaica*, p. 212, No. 232.

603. It was neither fish, flesh, blood, nor bone, / And they said it had horns and wasn't a beast.—Snail.

Green, *South Antrim*, 21.

604. Green Coat

604. My coate is greene, and I can prate / Of divers things about my grate. / In such a prison I am set / That hath more loope holes than a net.—A parret in a cage of wyer.

Prettie Riddles (1631), No. 77 = Brandl, p. 62; Tupper, *Holme Riddles*, 96 (trap-holes).

605–606. Green Cap, Yellow Shoes

605. Old grandfather Diddle Daddle / Jumped in the mud-puddle, / Green cap and yellow shoes. / Guess all your loftiness / And you can't guess these news.—Frog.

Gardner, *Schoharie Hills, N.Y.*, p. 255, No. 20.

606a. Mr. Huddle / Sat in a puddle / With a green cap and yellow shoes. — Duck.

Carter, *Mountain White*, p. 80.

606b. Little Jessie Ruddle, settin in a puddle, green garters and yaller toes. Tell me this riddle or I'll smash your nose!—Duck in a puddle.

Boggs, *North Carolina*, p. 323, No. 13; Hudson, p. 82, No. 1.

606c. Old Miss Puddididdle played in the mud-puddle; / She had red shoes and a black cap. / Now guess the riddle, and I'll give you my hat.—Duck.
Gardner, *Schoharie Hills, N.Y.*, p. 256, No. 22.

606d. Green head, yellow toes, / If you don't tell me this riddle, I'll ring your nose.—A duck.
Farr, *Tennessee*, p. 324, No. 92.

607–631. White

607–631. Little Nancy Etticoat

The description of a candle as Little Nancy Etticoat who has a white petticoat and a red nose and grows shorter as she stands is one of the most popular English riddles. The vividness and picturesqueness of the conception and the easily remembered rhymes account for its long life and wide distribution. Although the fundamental idea is virtually universal, this particular formulation appears to be of English origin. Contrast it with the Rumanian "A lad with a flower on his head"[1] or the Mongolian "It has a coral button and a juicy rump."[2] The coral button refers to a colored button symbolizing a mandarin's rank.

In the course of oral transmission riddlers have replaced or corrupted the name Nancy Etticoat. Nanny Goat,[3] which is a bit of children's speech, is a verbal echo but is appropriate enough, if we bear in mind the white fur of a goat. It has perhaps suggested the analogous Nanny Sheep.[4] Nitticoat, natticoat, which is also found in a riddle for spectacles,[5] is quite obscure. Little red ridin' coat[6] is a vague reminiscence of the nursery tale but can also refer to the red flame. A few versions[7] omit the actor's name.

A few picturesque descriptions of a candle or lamp in terms of a person deserve special mention. See the Hungarian "A queen sits on her chair. She wears a white gown, her tears fall in her lap";[8] the Swahili lamp riddle, "The gracious lady's locks flutter";[9] and the Parsee "The priestess is white-skinned with a tall stature. She is so enamoured that she burnt her whole body."[10]

The theme of the English candle riddle cannot be turned to many uses. A Dutch riddler describes snow in this manner: "There stands a maiden at the door in a white kerchief, the longer she stands the more she disappears."[11] This has some similarity to the description of a snow-capped stump.[12]

607. Little Miss Etticoat / In a white petticoat / And a red nose; / The longer she sits / The shorter she grows.—Candle.
Green, *South Antrim*, 2.

---

[1] Weigand, p. 269, No. 4; Papahagi, 27.
[2] Mostaert, 126.   [3] Nos. 620, 621 below.   [4] No. 623.
[5] No. 1723.   [6] No. 619.   [7] Nos. 627 through 631.
[8] *Magyar Nyelvör*, XXXI (1902), 532, No. 10.
[9] Büttner, p. 201.   [10] Munshi, p. 420.
[11] Schrijnen, II, 103, No. 9.   [12] See No. 208 above.

608a. Little Nancy Etticoat / In a white petticoat / And a red nose; / The longer she stands, / The shorter she grows.—A candle.

Halliwell-Phillipps, *Nursery Rhymes* (1842), p. 114 = Lina Eckenstein, *Comparative Studies in Nursery Rhymes* (London, 1906), p. 113; Parsons, *Bermuda*, p. 252, No. 45; Parsons, *Antilles*, III, 424, Antigua, 6; Parsons, *Aiken, S.C.*, p. 24, No. 1; Hyatt, *Adams Co., Ill.*, p. 658, No. 10843; Brewster, *Indiana*, 26. Little Anne Etticoat: Perkins, *New Orleans*, p. 108, No. 24. Little Anne Netticoat: Boggs, *North Carolina*, p. 321, No. 8. Little Miss Nannycot: Waugh, *Canada*, p. 69, No. 797. Little Miss Netticoat: Knortz, p. 239, No. 139. Little Nannie Netticoat: Whitney and Bullock, *Maryland*, p. 175, No. 2866; oral, Pennsylvania; Randolph and Taylor, *Ozarks*, 10. Little Nancy Hetticote: Parsons, *Sea Islands, S.C.*, p. 169, No. 111. My Nanny Etticoat: Parsons, *Antilles*, III, 443, St. Croix, 15. Nancy Metticoat: Parsons, *Aiken, S.C.*, p. 24, No. 1. Nanny-goat, nanny-goat: Gutch and Peacock, *Lincolnshire*, p. 399, No. 20; Fauset, *Nova Scotia*, p. 156, No. 62. Ninny coat: Fauset, *Nova Scotia*, p. 156, No. 62 var.

Nitticoat, natticoat: Gardner, *Schoharie Hills, N.Y.*, p. 256, No. 26. For this name see No. 1723 below.

Little Aunt Twicet: Parsons, *Bermuda*, p. 252, No. 45. The name is borrowed from the needle riddle, Nos. 533a through 533d above.

608b. Little Miss Etticoat / In a white petticoat / And a red nose; / The longer she stands, / The shorter she grows.—A lighted candle.

Udal, *Dorset*, p. 396; Halliwell-Phillipps, *Nursery Rhymes*, p. 127; Parsons, *Bahamas*, p. 484, No. 124 (omit "and a red nose").

609. Little trotty hetty coat / In a long petticoat / And a red nose; / The longer she stands / The shorter she grows.—Candle.

Spenney, *Raleigh, N.C.*, p. 110, No. 2.

610. Jenny wi' the white petticoat and the red nose / The longer she stands, the shorter she grows.—Candle.

A. Fergusson, *Notes and Queries*, 6th ser., II (1880), 323.

611–619. Versions Referring Primarily to Petticoat or Coat

611. Nancy Etticoat and Variations

611a. Little Nancy Etticoat / Has a white petticoat; / The longer she stands, / The shorter she grows; / Now cross both your hands / And tell me who knows.—A candle.

Harland and Wilkinson, *Lancashire Legends*, p. 187.

611b. Little Nancy Etticoat, / Little red petticoat, / Longer she stands, / Shorter she grows.—Candle.

Fauset, *Southern Negro*, p. 276, No. 9.

611c. Little Nanny Ettie Coat's got a white petticoat, / The longer she goes, the shorter she goes.—A candle.

Sayce, *Montgomeryshire*, p. 18.

612. Miss Netticoat, Nannicoat, and Variations

612a. Little Miss Netticoat in her white petticoat, / She has neither feet nor hands; / The longer she grows, the shorter she stands.—Candle.

Beckwith, *Jamaica*, p. 211, No. 228.

612b. Little Miss Nannicoat / Had a long petticoat. / The longer she stands, / The shorter she grows.—Candle.
Bacon and Parsons, *Virginia*, p. 317, No. 42.

612c. Nanny goat, Nanny goat, / In a white petticoat. / The longer she lives, / The shorter she goes.—A candle.
Sayce, *Montgomeryshire*, p. 17.

613–615. Nan, Nancy, and Variations

613. Little Miss Nancy, / In her white petticoat, / The longer she stands, / The shorter she grows.—Candle.
Parsons, *Barbados*, p. 286, No. 62.

614. Me riddle, me raddle, / You may tell me this riddle, / Perhaps you may not. / Dere was old Nancy goes / Wid a long petticoat, / De longer she live, / De shorter she grows.—Candle.
Parsons, *Antilles*, III, 435, St. Martin, 13.

615. Little Nan Nan in a short petticoat, / De larger she get de shorter she be.—Candle.
Parsons, *Andros Island, Bahamas*, p. 275, No. 5.

616–617. Other Names

616. Little Dora Dimple / In a white shimmy. / The longer she sets / The shorter she gets.—Candle.
Randolph and Taylor, *Ozarks*, 9.

617. Little Miss Mary / Sat on de washstan'. / De mo' she wear her petticoat, / De shorter it get.—Lam'-wick.
Parsons, *Sea Islands, S.C.*, p. 169, No. 111 var.

618–619. A Coat

A few versions refer to a coat but do not mention the name Etticoat or one of its variations. One of these belongs to the seventeenth century and may even be the original form from which the Etticoat versions have arisen.

618. j have a little boy in a whit[e] cote the biger he is the lesser he goes [probably an error for "grows"].—a whit[e] candle.
Tupper, *Holme Riddles*, 27.

619. Little red ridin' coat, / The longer she lives, / The shorter she grows.—Candlestick.
Parsons, *Guilford Co., N.C.*, p. 202, No. 19. Ol' ooman Nancy: Parsons, *Antilles*, III, 431, St. Kitts, 15.

620–624. Versions Referring Primarily to Nose

620. Nanney, nanney, nanney goat, / With a little pettycoat / The longer she stood the shorter she grew, / And when she died she had a black nose.—Candle.
Knortz, p. 220, No. 40.

621. Little Nanny Netty Goat / Dressed in a white petticoat; / The longer she stands the shorter she grows, / And when she dies, she leaves a black nose.—Candle.
Brewster, *Indiana*, 26b.

622. Nibby come nabby ko, / With a red nose. / The longer she stands, / The shorter she grows.—Candle.
Fauset, *Nova Scotia*, p. 156, No. 62 var.

623. Nanny Sheep, nanny sheep / With a red nose / The longer she stands / The lower she grows.—Candle.
Carter, *Mountain White*, p. 79.

624. Little Miss Nancy with the blue nose, / The longer she stays, the shorter she grows.—Candle.
Parsons, *Eleuthera and Watling's Islands, Bahamas*, p. 440, No. 20.

625–631. Fragmentary and Corrupt Versions

625a. Little Miss Betty / Sittin' on a stool. / The longer she sit, / the shorter she grow.—Candle.
Parsons, *Barbados*, p. 286, No. 62 var.

625b. Miss Nancy sits around de door; / The longer him stand deh, de shorter him grow.—Candle.
Beckwith, *Jamaica*, p. 211, No. 228a.

626a. Little Miss Mary / De older she grow / De shorter she come.—Candle.
Parsons, *Antilles*, III, 433, Saba, 10.

626b. Little Miss Nancy, / Larger she goes, / Shorter she becomes.—Candle.
Parsons, *Antilles*, III, 374, Cariacou, 3.

627. Met a little girl with a red head. / The longer she stands, / the shorter she grows.—Candle.
Fauset, *Nova Scotia*, p. 156, No. 62 var.

628. A white, white lady, / With a red, red hat, / De longer she lives, / De shorter she grows.—Cyandle.
Parsons, *Antilles*, III, 364, Trinidad, 12.

629. Once there was a little girl white as snow, / The longer she stands, the shorter she grows.—Candle.
Parsons, *Sea Islands, S.C.*, p. 170, No. 111, var. 2.

630. The longer something lives the shorter it gets.—Candle.
Parsons, *Bermuda*, p. 252, No. 45 var.

631. A tall white man wid a red cap on.—Cyandle.
Parsons, *Bahamas*, p. 484, No. 125.

632–644. Red

632–644. Dick Red-Cap

The English riddle in which the actor is usually called "Dick Red-Cap" describes a cherry as a person wearing a red cap and bearing a stick in his throat or other inappropriate place. The "throat" is the depression in which the stem of the cherry is attached. Such comparisons are readily adapted to other fruits and often exhibit considerable individualization in details. See the cherry riddles, "A man mounted high, dressed in a short dress, garbed in red, and going to market";[1] "A red head, a green tail, it stops the passer-by";[2] "A traveler passes on his horse; a red head makes him dismount";[3] and "Hanged high, dressed all in red."[4] These references to persons dressed in red suggest that the riddle was invented in an age when men wore gayer colors than at present. For other variations of the theme see the White Russian strawberry riddle, "A maiden sits on a hill in a red cap. Whoever passes will bow down to her"[5] and the Lappish angelica riddle, "A maiden sits on the edge of the spring with her hat on her head."[6] Angelica is a plant akin to a lily and grows near water; the hat is the unopened flower.

Some eastern European versions introduce such a phrase as "it tastes like wine," which is inconsistent with the comparison of the cherry to a person. See "A black hat, a taste like wine, a stone heart";[7] "I sit on a tower, I am as small as a mouse, red as blood, tasty as mead,"[8] which begins with a theme often used in riddles for a nut;[9] and "Red color, winey taste, stony heart. Why so?"[10]

Independent origins of the many riddles based on so simple a theme as the comparison of an object to a man in a red cap are possible, but the scanty discussion of the texts has not concerned itself with the question. The variations are sufficiently great to suggest the probability that the theme has been hit upon independently in several places. The Armenian eggplant riddle "It has a brown jacket and a green cap. What is it?"[11] differs considerably from the Russian strawberry riddle "It stands on a little hill in a red hat. Whoever passes bows to it,"[12] which is intended to suggest a sacred figure to which the passer-by does honor. Another theme, to which I have noted no parallels, is the Cheremiss "The man with a white head put on a beautiful cap.— Raspberry."[13] Such differences as these make it probable that the riddles are of independent origin.

The notion of a man or a figure that causes the passer-by to bow or bend appears frequently in Slavic riddles employing the theme of the red cap. In the Gypsy strawberry riddle, "A crone sits in the grass, nods sleepily with her

---

[1] French: Dardy, *L'Albret*, p. 331.
[2] French: Carnoy, *Picardy*, p. 54 = Carnoy, *La Tradition*, VI (1892), 354, No. 25. Compare V. S., *Mélusine*, I (1878), col. 263, No. 79.
[3] French: Carnoy, *La Tradition*, VI (1892), 354, No. 26.
[4] Breton: Duine, *Saint-Malo*, p. 517.
[5] Wasilewski, 31.
[6] Donner, 11.
[7] Lithuanian: Schleicher, p. 211.
[8] Russian: Sadovnikov, 805.
[9] See Nos. 1269a through 1275 and the headnote to Nos. 1269–1275 below.
[10] Polish: Gustawicz, 446; Saloni, *Rzeshów*, 194.
[11] Archer Taylor, *California Folklore Quarterly*, I (1942), 97.
[12] Sadovnikov, 1382a.
[13] Wichmann, *Cheremiss*, 48. Since the Russian word for "beautiful" also signifies "red," we may conjecture that this Cheremiss riddle has been translated from Russian.

head, and wears a red cap,"[14] the conception resembles some descriptions of nodding heads of grain.[15] The Serbian and Bulgarian berry riddles, viz., "It is red and small, yet it turns everybody from his way"[16] and "It is little, it is red, it makes a tsar dismount,"[17] may possibly contain reminiscences of a flea riddle.[18] The Bretons portray the scene in still another way: "I am seated on my little green tabouret. If the king or the queen passes, I shall not lift my red cap until someone takes it off my head."[19]

As is obvious from what has been said, new elements are readily introduced into the description of the man with a red cap, but these new elements do not often conflict with the spirit of the theme. The variants of this riddle show a surprisingly clear perception of the fundamental concept. See, as examples, the Italian riddles for a carnation, "Little Karl is high up on a hill with his red cap and his green leg. A knight is he who guesses it,"[20] and for a cherry, "High, high, beautiful to see, five hundred knights with bared swords and bloody heads";[21] the Polish riddles for a thistle, "A little gentleman with a little red cap stands in the path. Whoever touches him curses him,"[22] and a bedbug, "Dressed in a red jacket, a miss sits on a bone. At night she races in all directions."[23] Note the abundance of details in the Serbian riddle for an ash tree, "An old woman sits on a knoll in a red coat, staring with her eyes, showing her teeth, and threatening to shake."[24]

The idea of mentioning a color that contrasts with the red of the fruit has occurred to many riddlers. See the Baiga "Red shirt, black cap.—Flower of the *samur* [*Bombax malabaricum*]," with an Atjeh parallel "Red coat, black hat,"[25] and some descriptions of a strawberry cited elsewhere in this headnote. The seemingly obvious use of this contrast for a redheaded woodpecker appears in the Yakut "An Ažarai lad wears a bloodstained cap."[26] It is perhaps worth saying that the red cap which is a mark of the elves in Scandinavian countries[27] seems to have no connection with these ideas.

There are many varieties of scenes and themes related to this fundamental conception of a man in a red cap. See the French haw riddle, "Little black head, little red cloak, little stones in the stomach, a baton at its back";[28] the Russian mushroom riddles, "In a pine forest on a bluff there stands a little old man. His hat is red" and "The boy is no larger than a thumb. His coat is

---

[14] Wlislocki, 35.
[15] See Nos. 946a through 946d below.
[16] Novaković, p. 73, No. 10.
[17] Ikonomov, 4.
[18] See the headnote to No. 344 above.
[19] Charlec, *Dol-de-Bretagne*, 1904, p. 168, No. 31.
[20] Schneller, *Wälschtirol*, p. 253, No. 7.
[21] Schneller, *Wälschtirol*, p. 253, No. 8.
[22] Kopernicki, 20, var. 2. See also Nos. 342a through 342c above and §7 below.
[23] Kopernicki, 25 var.
[24] Novaković, p. 156, No. 6.
[25] Elwin, p. 474, No. 102; Kreemer, *Atjeh*, 56.
[26] Piekarski, 94. *Ažarai* signifies a soul from the underworld. See also No. 921 below.
[27] See Feilberg, *Ordbog*, III, 117, s.v. "rød dreng," and his *Nissens Historie* (Danmarks Folkeminder, XVIII [Copenhagen, 1919]), pp. 35–38.
[28] Westphalen, *Metz*, col. 199.

white, his hat is red,"[29] with a Mordvin parallel, "A pleasant little thing, it came forth from the earth and got a red cap";[30] and the Hindi description of a jeweler's weighing seed (*Abrus precatorius*), which is red with a black spot: "It lives in the forest crooked and in disarray. Its cap is black and its coat is red."[31] The picturesque Polish description of a chimney, "It stands on top with a red cowl,"[32] is intended to suggest a monk and may be related to the comparison between smoke rising from a chimney and a monk in gray garb.

Comparisons to persons with red beards or hair are rare. See, however, the Tatar corn riddle, "It has a red beard, is long, tall. Whoever fails to guess will be a jackal"[33] and the comparisons of matches to men with red heads.[34]

Some riddles based on a comparison to an animal resemble these descriptions of a man wearing a red cap. See the Finnish strawberry riddle, "Reddie, the red cow, is tied in the grass."[35] The figure of "Reddie, the red cow" (*Punikki, punainen lehmä*) appears with less appropriateness in some other riddles; see "Reddie, the red cow, runs along the streams and snorts through the waves.— A boat";[36] "Reddie, the red cow, the light horn, the back of a swing, ran through the bights covered with forest, flew over the mountains.—Snowshoes";[37] and "Reddie, the red cow, will not go away, even if five men should drag her and six men tempt her.—Church or forest-fire."[38] The Poles compare a poppy to an animal: "Bridled in red, the pony stands in the furrow."[39] The Mongolian jujube riddle, "A red one-year calf with a stomach of stone"[40] is very similar to the English cherry riddle.

Analogous comparisons in terms of inanimate objects are rare. Examples are the Russian raspberry riddle, "A red mortar, a white pestle,"[41] and the Turkish riddles for a cherry, "On the end of the branch a fire burns," and a pomegranate, "On top of a tree a fire burns."[42]

For discussion of riddles based on a comparison to a man wearing a red cap or dress see John Meier, "Stetit puella tunica rufa," *Zeitschrift des Vereins für Volkskunde*, XLIII (1933), 213–214; the parallels collected in Feilberg, *Ordbog*, II, 133, s.v. "kirsebær"; and my note on an Armenian riddle for an eggplant in the *California Folklore Quarterly*, I (1942), 97–98. Red is almost the only color mentioned in these inventions, but see an exception to the rule in a Yakut riddle for a whortleberry: "They say that in the woods there is a costume of figured material."[43]

---

[29] Sadovnikov, 1383, 1384. See also his Nos. 1387, 1389.
[30] Paasonen, 413. [31] Kavyopadhyaya, 24.
[32] Saloni, *Rzeshów*, 78. See also Norwegian: Brox, *Ytre Senja*, 169.
[33] Kalashev and Ioakimov, p. 50, No. 26.
[34] Nos. 583a through 584b above.
[35] Henssen, 44. See also Estonian: Lönnrot, p. 191. Lettish: Bielenstein, 394.
[36] Henssen, 45. [37] Henssen, 46 = Lönnrot, 1429.
[38] Henssen, 47 = Lönnrot, 1424. [39] Saloni, *Rzeshów*, 71.
[40] Rudnyev, 39. See also Bazarov, 95; Mostaert, 92.
[41] Sadovnikov, 907. [42] Hamizade, 390, 521.
[43] Piekarski, 18. The variant versions tell of fur decorated with silver or embroidered with silk.

The comparison to a person wearing a cap, usually a red cap, is applicable to various plants. It ordinarily refers to the fruit rather than to the flower. An exceptional variety of the theme occurs in the Hausa plum riddle, "The young men of our house have all got caps."[44] Here the caps are the circuit of leaves or sepals at the base of the flower.

Typical plants described by means of this comparison are:

§1. A cherry. See Nos. 632a through 632d and 635b. Nos. 638, 640a through 640c, and 643 through 644b contain references to red but no mention of a cap; see also Nos. 635a and 639 (no reference to red or a cap), and Nos. 637 and 642 (for a cherry in the mouth).

§2. A strawberry. German: Wossidlo, 204 (A woman stands in the wood, she wears a red cap); Gilhoff, 551, 552. Swiss: Zahler, *Münchenbuchsee*, 77. French: Lallemant, *Argonne*, p. 234 (I know a little red lady seated in a green armchair); Constantin, *Savoie*, p. 22. Hungarian: Kriza, 107 (The stem is hairy, the top is red. It is for the belly of gourmands). Gypsy: Wlislocki, 35 (A crone sits in the grass, nods sleepily with her head, and wears a red cap). See also the previously quoted examples of bowing to a man in a red cap.

§3. A pomegranate. See No. 633 below.

§4. A hip. See No. 634 (red petticoat).

§5. A pepper. See No. 645 (red petticoat).

§6. An eggplant. Armenian: Archer Taylor, *California Folklore Quarterly*, I (1942), 97–98. Arabic: Ruoff, p. 50, No. 16 (A company of Negroes comes from afar. On his head each Negro bears a green turban). The green turban is worn by Arabs descended from Mohammed. See also Littmann, p. 54, No. 38 (The lady sits by the crib, she weeps like a hoopoe; how sweet is the grass ornament on her back). Turkish: Hamizade, 559 (Short [low] in stature, decorated with velvet), 560 (Tiny lackies decorated with velvet). Crimean Tatar: Filonenko, 15 (Of small size, it wears a dress of velvet). Indian, Parsee: Munshi, 33 (Green turban, black robe).

§7. A thistle. Norwegian: Brox, *Ytre Senja*, 57; Bergh, *Valdres*, 51; Stafset, 116. Swedish: Dybeck, *Runa*, 1850, p. 37, No. 39; Ericsson, *Södermanland*, IV (1883), 72, No. 188; Sandén, *Norra Vadsbo*, 84. Polish: Gustawicz, 283 (A gentlemen stands in the field. Everybody fears him. He wears a red cap and a green garment), 284 (A little gentleman in a red cap stands by the wayside. Whoever touches him curses him).[45]

§8. A poppy. Polish: Saloni, *Rzeshów*, 101 (It stands on a little hill in a red hat). Russian: Sadovnikov, 815 (A small one, a dextrous one, went into the ground, put on a little red hat).

§9. A salak (a palm with edible fruit). Indonesian, Engganee: Helfrich,

---

[44] Fletcher, 28.
[45] See also Nos. 342a through 342c above.

Engganee, p. 519, No. 18 (A person with red hair who when one shakes him immediately afterwards stabs).

§ 10. Millet. African, Nandi: Hollis, *Nandi*, p. 133, No. 1 (I am tall and my hair has red earth in it). Compare the Kanuri riddle for the kenaski plant: "When I went around the back of the house, [I saw] a councilor with a turban."[46]

§ 11. A beet. Polish: Gustawicz, 12 (A person is sitting beneath the ground, his hair is turning red).

The figure of a person wearing red is also applicable to a few animals. In addition to the English woodpecker riddle,[47] it is used for:

§ 12. A bedbug. Polish: Gustawicz, 320 (Dressed in a red jacket, a maiden stands on a bone), 321. See also note 23 in this headnote.

§ 13. A cock. French: Rolland, 51, 402. Spanish: Rodríguez Marín, 366 and note. These French and Spanish versions are closely related to the conception of a cock as a prophet.[48] Polish: Gustawicz, 142 (It stands on a fence in a red jacket), 143 (It stands on a hill in a red bonnet).

I have noted very few instances of this pattern when used to describe a thing:

§ 14. A brick. Kashub: Gulgowski, 2 (A maiden sits in the wall in a red coat). Polish: Gustawicz, 21 (A maiden stands in the wall wearing a red bonnet).

§ 15. A religious statue. Polish: Gustawicz, 83 (A maiden stands in the corridor. She is dressed in a red jacket. Whoever passes her kneels before her).[49]

A second element characteristic of the riddle of Dick Red-cap is the assertion that he carries a stick in an unusual place—his eye, throat, stomach, or backside. It is picturesquely enlarged upon in the Turkish cherry riddles: "A red cow afraid of the stable, her tail remained behind in my hand" and "A black ox, while entering the stable, broke off his tail."[50] This characteristic element occurs in several riddles for a fruit or, more rarely, a flower:

§ 16. A grape, a raisin. Catalan: Milá y Fontanals, 1876, p. 22, No. 2 (What is that: an old, wrinkled woman who carries a little stick?—Raisin). Modern Greek: Polites, *Neohellenika Analekta*, I, 237, No. 251 (A little thing with a thorn in its end). Arabic: Littmann, p. 53, No. 32 (The lady is wrinkled and on her backside is a stalk). Turkish: Hamizade, 695 (Look! There is a crowd of ——, they have tails on their rumps). The meaning of the word indicated by a dash is obscure.

§ 17. A lotus. Arabic: Littmann, p. 54, No. 37 (As large as a hazelnut and a stick in its eye).

---

[46] Lukas, p. 174, No. 52.
[47] See No. 921 below.
[48] See the headnotes to Nos. 539–543 and 585 above.
[49] The riddler has given the theme of the comparison as the answer to the riddle.
[50] Hamizade, 391, 392.

§ 18. A pineapple. Indian, Bengali: Mitra, *Chittagong*, p. 298, No. 3 (Thing which has come out of the jungle, a stick in its backside, a load on its head).[51]

§ 19. An apple, a pear. Welsh: Hull and Taylor, 104. Breton: Sauvé, 39 (Who goes to market, his foot [var.: paw] in his backside?). Swedish: Ström, p. 125, "Päronet."

§ 20. An olive. Albanian: Hahn, p. 158, No. 8, and p. 161, No. 48 (A monk with a stick in his backside). Berber: Basset, *Nouveaux Contes*, p. 190, No. 1 (A Negro hung up by the middle of his stomach).

§ 21. A sloe. Swedish: Ström, p. 128, "Slån," 2.

§ 22. A wild popo fruit. African, Kanuri: Lukas, pp. 173–174, No. 51 (A young Fulani, who has a spear in his heart).

§ 23. A cat. Mordvin: Paasonen, 227 (An old woman climbs on the stove, there is a stick in her rump). Cheremiss: Porkka, 138 (A Tatar woman drags a hop pole after her).

632a. When I went through the garden gap, / Whom should I meet but Dick Red-Cap, / A stick in his hand, a stone in his throat. / Guess me this riddle and I'll give you a groat.—Cherry.

Halliwell-Phillipps, *Nursery Rhymes*, p. 132; Gardner, *Schoharie Hills, N.Y.*, p. 253, No. 5; Bacon and Parsons, *Virginia*, p. 324, No. 108; Brewster, *Indiana*, 43; Farr, *Tennessee*, p. 321, No. 50. Goat: Hyatt, *Adams Co., Ill.*, pp. 658–659, No. 10845; Chappell, p. 231, No. 14. I'll give you a goat.—Boy with a cherry in his mouth: Fauset, *Nova Scotia*, p. 154, No. 54. It is unusual to see the answer affected by the scene described in the riddle; it is much more frequent to see the riddle altered by an anticipation of the answer. Dick with his red cap: Parsons, *Bermuda*, p. 246, No. 6 var. A man in a tall green hat: Parsons, *Bermuda*, p. 246, No. 6 var. Garden gate: Knortz, p. 235, No. 119; Perkins, *New Orleans*, p. 108, No. 22 var.

632b. When I went through the garden gap, / Whom should I meet but Dick Red-cap, / With a stone in his hand and a stem in his throat. / Now guess this riddle and I'll give you a groat.—A cherry.

Waugh, *Canada*, p. 69, No. 796. A stem in his cap and a stone in his throat: Parsons, *Barbados*, p. 284, No. 45. Jimmie Red-cap, / A stick in his mouth, a stone in his throat: Perkins, *New Orleans*, p. 108, No. 22.

632c. I was goin' down the garden dock, / I met little Dick Red Cock. / A stick in his hand, an' stone in his throat. / Tell me that riddle, I'll give you a goat.—Cherry.

Parsons, *Antilles*, III, 446, St. Thomas, 21.

632d. Me riddle me raddle. / One mornin' as I was goin' t'rough de garden gate, / I meet up wid Mr. Dick Red Cock / With a stick in his hand an' a stone in his throat. / Tell me the riddle an' I will give you a brooch.—Answer lacking.

Parsons, *Antilles*, III, 421, Montserrat, 8.

633. As I was going through the garden gap, / I met Dick with his red cap. /

---

[51] The collector points out that the pineapple was introduced into India in A.D. 1519 or a little later, but this fact is not decisive in establishing the age of the riddle, for we may have here an adaptation of a description of a native fruit.

A stick in his hand, stones in his throat. / If you guess this riddle, / I'll give you a groat.—Pomegranate.
  Parsons, *Bermuda*, p. 246, No. 6 var.

634. Down in the meadow there sits Pat, / With a red petticoat and a black hat, / A stick in his hand and a stone in his throat. / You tell me this riddle, / I'll give you a groat.—A hip on a hedge.
  Parker, *Oxfordshire*, p. 331.

635a. As I was going to the garden gate, / I met a man with a stick in his hand, / And a stone in his throat. Who was he?—A cherry.
  Fauset, *Philadelphia*, p. 555, No. 29.

635b. As I was going up a gravelly knap' [i.e., hill], / I saw a little boy with a little red cap, / A stick in his hand, a stone in his belly; / Riddle me this and I'll give you a penny.—Cherry.
  Greenleaf, *Newfoundland*, p. 9, No. 8.

636. As I was going up a gravelly knap, / I saw a little boy with a little red cap, / A stick in his hand, a stone in his belly; / Riddle me this and I'll give you a penny.—Gooseberry.
  Greenleaf, *Newfoundland*, p. 9, No. 8 var.

637. A stick in his tail, / A stone in his throat, / Come a riddle, come a riddle, / come a tote, tote, tote.—Boy with a cherry in his mouth.
  Fauset, *Nova Scotia*, p. 154, No. 54 var.

638. hurble purple hath a red gurdle a stone in his belly a stake throw his a—— & yet hurble purple is neu^r the worse.—a cherry.
  Tupper, *Holme Riddles*, 29.

639. As I was going in dockyard gate, / I met my uncle Jack, / He had a stone in his throat, / A stick in his hand. / If you tell me this riddle, / I'll give you a groat.—Cherry.
  Parsons, *Bermuda*, p. 246, No. 6. In Somerset: Parsons, *Bermuda*, p. 246, No. 6 var.

640a. Riddle me, riddle me, rot, tot, tot, / A wee, wee mon in a red coat, / A staff in his hand, and a stane in his throat, / Riddle me, riddle me, rot, tot, tot.—Cherry.
  A. Ferguson, *Notes and Queries*, 6th ser., II (1880), 323 (Scotland). Come a riddle, come a riddle, come a rot, tot, tot: Findlay, *Edinburgh*, p. 58.

640b. Riddle me, riddle, rot-e-tot, / I saw a man with a red long coat, / A stick in his tail, and a stone in his throat, / Riddle me, riddle me, tot-e-tot.—Cherry.
  Leather, *Hereford*, p. 232; Gutch and Peacock, *Lincolnshire*, p. 397, No. 6. Staff: Gregor, *Northeast Scotland*, p. 80; Chambers, *Scotland*, p. 109.

640c. Me riddle me riddle. / A wee wee man with a red, red coat, / A stick in his hand and a stone in his throat.—Cherry.
  Parsons, *Antilles*, III, 365, Trinidad, 23.

641. Come a riddle come a riddle / Come a rat, trat, trat. / A little red man with a bone in his throat / And a staff in his hand. / Come a riddle, come a riddle / Come a rat trat trat.—Cashot nut.
Parsons, *Antilles*, III, 434, Saba, 19.

642. Ma riddledy, riddledy, rote d'tote, / A girl running around in a red petticoat, / A stick in her hand and a stone in her throat, / Ma riddledy riddledy, rote d'tote.—A girl eating a cherry.
Chappell, p. 231, No. 15.

643. Little May Margery sat on a tree, a stone in her throat, and a cane in her hand, and a red dress.—Cherry.
Knortz, p. 212, No. 5.

644a. Riddle come riddle come rarlet, / My petticoat's lined with scarlet, / A stone in the middle and stick at the tail. / Tell me this riddle without any fail.—Cherry.
Whitney and Bullock, *Maryland*, p. 174, No. 2676.

644b. Riddle cum riddle cum rawley, / Petticoat bound in scarlet, / Stone in the middle, / Stick in the tail. / Tell me this riddle, / Without any fail.—A cherry.
Thurston, *Massachusetts*, p. 182, No. 6.

645–649. Yellow

645–648. A Lady (Man) with Yellow (Red) Coat (Petticoat)

The significance of this formula is not readily apparent. It occurs in several riddles and may originally belong to one describing a rainbow. The Trinidad text with the answer "moon" seems to be a casual adaptation of the formula. Comparisons of the moon to a person are rather infrequent in riddling.[1] I can cite no parallel to the curious Icelandic description of the moon and the twenty-eight days and twenty-eight nights of the lunar month; see "When I am fully arrayed, I begin at once to lay off my bright shining attire. In dressing and undressing me fifty-six brothers and sisters are constantly occupied in the wide space."[2]

645. A lady in a boat / With a red petticoat / And a bone down her throat.—Pepper seed.
Parsons, *Antilles*, III, 371, Grenada, 42.

646. As I was going over London Bridge, / I saw a boat, / And in this boat there was something with a red coat.—A lobster.
Fauset, *Nova Scotia*, p. 149, No. 37.

647. A lady in a boat / With a yellow petticoat.—Egg.
Parsons, *Antilles*, III, 364, Trinidad, 13 var.

---
[1] See the Index of Solutions.
[2] Árnason, 12.

648. A lady in a boat / With a yellow petticoat.—Moon.
Parsons, *Antilles*, III, 364, Trinidad, 13.

649. Yellow Breeches

Although yellow jacket is a familiar term, riddlers have usually preferred to refer to wasps, bees, and similar insects as wearing yellow breeches. Simple as this comparison is, it has enjoyed a very restricted popularity. The parallels smell of the lamp.

Riddles describing a wasp are rather rare. A Bulgarian riddler mentions a bee's hum: "A strange girl sits on a strange rock, singing a strange song."[1] Some riddlers have compared a bee or wasp to a bird.[2]

649. As I was going along the road, I met a little man with a blue coat and yellow breeches on. He said, "Um, ha! I care for no man!" Who was he?—Wasp.
Leather, *Hereford*, p. 231.

650–656. Several Colors

650–652. Gowns of Several Colors: A Plant

The comparison of a plant to a person in gay and motley dress occurs in many forms, and the variety of details suggests that many of them have been invented independently. Compare these English versions with one another and with the Panjabi description of maize, "Bright was she, studded with many a pearl was she, standing out in the open, mantled in green was she."[1] The "pearls" may be the kernels or, more probably, drops of rain or dew. The French riddle for a shoot of sugar cane, "Every year I wear a white cap,"[2] resembles the Cheremiss riddle for a raspberry, "The white head put on a beautiful cap,"[3] and the Lithuanian conception of camomile, "As long as I was small, I was as green as a plant; when I was grown up, I became a young lady."[4] The colors are often arranged in a biographical sequence.[5]

650. My husband gives two gownes to me / of sundry colours every yeare; / greene is the one which I doe weare, / so long till it be all thread-bare. / White is the other as the sunne, / of many peeces up and downe, / yet like to that few workman can / devise to make another gowne. / The wiser sort, wherein they dote, / doe call me foole upon a toy; / but yet of me they take a note / that death is past when I do joy.—It is a mulberry tree, greene in the

---

[1] Ikonomov, 74.
[2] See No. 353 above.

[1] A. F. W., *Panjab Notes and Queries*, I (1884), 118, No. 899 = W. J., *ibid.*, II (1885), 106, No. 625. Compare also Bhil: Hedberg, p. 870, No. 28. See another version, in which the actor is a prince, in the headnote to Nos. 668–680, n. 8, below
[2] Parsons, *Antilles*, III, 383, Martinique, 43.
[3] Wichmann, *Cheremiss*, 40.
[4] Schleicher, p. 202.
[5] See the headnotes to Nos. 668–680 and 668–669.

summer and white with snow in the winter; who in Latine is called morus, which signifieth in Greeke a foole. That tree is of this nature, that it will not cast any buds before all other trees have, whereby we certainly know when she begins to bud that the cold and winter is altogether past for that present season.
Prettie Riddles (1631), No. 34 = Brandl, p. 57.

651. First you see me in the grass, dressed in yellow gay; / Next I am in dainty white, then I fly away.—Dandelion.
Hyatt, *Adams Co., Ill.*, p. 660, No. 1054.

652. Daffy-down-dilly has come to town, / In a yellow petticoat and a green gown.—A dandelion.
Redfield, *Tennessee*, p. 38, No. 29.

653. So black's my 'at, so white's my cap, / Magotty pie, and what's that?— This is a kind of jibe-riddle asked of very stupid persons.
Wright, p. 311.

654. I see to me, / I see from me, / Two miles over the sea, / A little blue man, / In a green boatee: His shirt is lined with a skein of red.—The rainbow.
Dempster, *Sutherlandshire*, p. 236.

655a. There is sandy, but red, white, blue. / De king can riddle an' so can de queen. / Tell me dis riddle 'fore tomorrow noon.—Rainbow.
Parsons, *Antilles*, III, 440, Anguilla, 16.

655b. Sandy's bot' red an' green, / The king an' queen can riddle so soon, / Tell me her name before tomorrow noon.—Rainbow.
Parsons, *Antilles*, III, 440, Anguilla, 16 var.

656. Mary Mack all dressed in black, / Silver buttons down her back.— Coffin.
Oral, North Carolina.

657–660. Colors and an Act

657. I am a little seed. I live in a large overcoat. And when they are going to plant me, they take my coat off and leave me in a thin little red vest. I am not tall, but some of my sisters and brothers are tall. Boys and girls are very fond of me. Can you guess who I am?—A peanut.
Parsons, *St. Helena Island, S.C.*, p. 228.

658. I am cald [called] by the name of man, / yet am as little as the mouse: / when winter comes, I love to be / with my red gorget neere the house. —A bird called Robin-Redbrest.
Prettie Riddles (1631), No. 68 = Brandl, p. 61. Tupper, *Holme Riddles*, 100 (target).

659. Mother have a boy always in one black suit, never change.—Blackbirds.
Parsons, *Antilles*, III, 369, Grenada, 8.

660. Brass button, / Blue coat, / Can't catch a billy-goat.—Policeman.
Bacon and Parsons, *Virginia*, p. 322, No. 94.

661–822. Function

661–667. Birth

661. I heard that my father was dead in Kingston. I went there and took a piece of his bone and made increase.—Kasava root.
Beckwith, *Jamaica*, p. 193, No. 85.

662. My moder have a girl, each baby she make is tweens [twins].—That's plum.
Parsons, *Antilles*, III, 369, Grenada, 13.

663. Baby born an' vanish.—Moon.
Beckwith, *Jamaica*, p. 195, No. 107.

664. Old I am, when I was borne, / and when I am hatcht, take heed of me; / or else thou mayest soone be forlorne. / if thou doest nothing looke to thee.—The grudge of a secret enemy long conceived in mind ere it be put in execution.
Prettie Riddles (1631), No. 57 = Brandl, p. 60.

665–667. Speaks at Birth

English and American riddlers do not seem to be acquainted with the variant form beginning "Born between two mountains." This is widely known on the continent of Europe. The creature suggested by the riddler may be either an animal or a person. For parallels see Scotch Gaelic: Nicolson, p. 87. German: Frischbier, *Menschenwelt*, p. 242, Nos. 10, 11. Swedish: Ström, p. 87, No. 1 var. French: Parsons, *Antilles*, III, 413, Marie Galante, 5, 7. Catalan: Pelay y Briz, 218. Spanish: Rodríguez Marín, 330. Dominican Rep.: Andrade, 251. New Mexican: Campa, 131 (A roaring bull comes from between two ranges of mountains). Porto Rican: Mason, 439. Estonian: Wiedemann, p. 293. Mordvin: Paasonen, 32. Votyak: Wichmann, *Votyak*, 13, 94. Modern Greek: Sanders, 4; Stathes, p. 334, Nos. 11 (A hill here, a hill there, a ghost rolls), 11 var. (Between two mountains a ghost rumbles). Turkish: Katanov in Radlov, IX, 291, No. 259; Moshkov in Radlov, X, 266, No. 12 (Between two burial mounds a bull bellows). African, Wanamwezi: Dahl, 47 (A mountain here, a mountain there, a lion goes through just in the middle).

This manner of description is applicable to a cough,[1] a rifle,[2] and a bell.[3]

665. I am no fish, nor flesh, nor voise; / yet when I am borne, I make a noyse.—[Crepitus ventris], or else thunder.
Prettie Riddles (1631), No. 49 = Brandl, p. 59.

---

[1] French: Baissac, *Mauritius*, p. 399.
[2] Arabic: Stumme, *Tunis*, p. 127, No. 44 (A little Negro bellows between two mountains). See also the headnote to No. 755 below.
[3] Modern Greek: Polites, *Neohellenika Analekta*, I, 211, No. 100.

666. Born without Sin; Speaks Only Once

This theme is also applicable to various Biblical figures and to Balaam's ass.

666. There is a thing, / Born without sin, / Doie [die] without skin. / He spoke one toime in his mother's womb, / And he never spoke again.—A wind that you let go.
Parsons, *Antilles*, III, 429, Nevis, 22.

667. Born without Father or Mother; Speaks at Birth

The notion of being born without father or mother also occurs in Biblical riddles, where it is applied to Adam and Eve. It occurs in a Spanish silkworm riddle[1] and is used in a sense that is not readily intelligible in a Russian riddle for a chink in a log wall: "Who is born in a house with neither a father nor a mother?"[2] A similar idea in a Breton description of a graveyard, "Who has no father, mother, or children?"[3] is an echo of the Biblical account of Melchisedec.[4]

The notion of being born without a skin (the caul) occurs in riddles for an egg,[5] dung,[6] and a bullet.[7] Its use in this English application has a Renaissance parallel:

> Pelle carens nascor, non audio, sed tamen ipse
> Audior, haud culpo, sed male culpor ego.[8]

667. Fatherless and motherless, / Born without a skin, / Spok' when it came into th' world, / An' nivir spok' sin'.—Crepitus ventris.
Gutch and Peacock, *Lincolnshire*, p. 403.

668–680. A Biography

Some riddles describe an object in terms of a biography of a supposed person. One variety, for example, associates the several stages of life with appropriate colors: the white flower with birth, the green leaf or fruit with youth, and the red fruit with maturity. A riddler may, on occasion, represent these stages by comparisons, as in the North German riddle for flax, "First as small as anise, then as green as grass, then as blue as Heaven,"[1] and thus lead away from the biographical theme. The actor is often said to wear a series of dresses of various colors, as in the dandelion riddle.[2] The contrast of "naked" and

---

[1] Demófilo, 496. [2] Sadovnikov, 27.
[3] Sébillot, *Haute-Bretagne*, 82; Millien, *Nivernais*, p. 512.
[4] Hebr. 7:3.
[5] Lettish: Bielenstein, 418.
[6] Lettish: Bielenstein, 619. Russian: Sadovnikov, 1572.
[7] Flemish: Joos, 342.
[8] Buchler, *Gnomologia*, 3d ed. (1614), p. 415. I print the shorter of two versions.

[1] Carstens, *Schleswig-Holstein*, p. 417. See also the headnote to Nos. 668–669, § 4, below.
[2] Nos. 651, 652.

"dressed" in a sequence reversing that of nature is applicable to trees and some other plants.³ When the biographical aspect is obscured, the riddles present merely a seemingly inexplicable sequence of colors.⁴ Wolfgang Schultz thinks that these conceptions are originally descriptions of a rainbow.⁵

Riddles telling a biography associated with colors ordinarily deal with plants in various stages of growth. Some of them are ingeniously constructed. The Surinam maize riddle, "When my father was young, his beard was white, but when he became old, his beard became black,"⁶ contrasts black with white and sets them in an order contrary to nature and by doing so, illustrates admirably enigmatic technique. The previously quoted Bihari maize riddle cleverly calls up the picture of an Indian prince: "During my early age, I wear a sari⁷ of green color. When I attain to my youth, a crest grows [upon my head]; and then, my beard and moustaches also grow. When I arrive at my old age, I wear pendent ornaments studded with diamonds and pearls."⁸ Such conceptions easily lead over into riddles enumerating the several parts of the supposed body as having different origins.⁹

The Hungarian lobster riddle, to which I have found no parallel, is a rare instance of a biography in terms of colors which has an animal and not a plant as answer. It is: "When alive, I had a black dress. While moving about, my castle was *lipik*. After my death, my dress turned red. Answer, my friend, and you will be my 'pal.'"¹⁰

A special variety of biographical riddle relates a series of tortures inflicted upon an innocent victim. Typical examples are the riddles for flax¹¹ and wheat.¹² It does not seem to be associated in its origin with the previously mentioned sequences of colors. It is especially interesting and curious because medieval riddlers have reworked the materials into an allegory of the life of Christ. A simple invention which probably represents fairly well the original nature of this form of riddle is the Lamba description of bark-rope, "A youngster that one doesn't beat for nothing."¹³ This could easily be enlarged upon by adding appropriate comparisons to other incidents in the life of the supposed youngster.

A very simple variety of biographical riddle sets in contrast the form or behavior of the person in youth and old age. That of "clothed in youth; naked

---

³ See the headnote to No. 587.
⁴ See the headnotes to Nos. 1384–1393 and 1559–1561.
⁵ *Rätsel aus dem hellenischen Kulturkreise*, II, 4–5.
⁶ Herskovits, p. 437, No. 19. ⁷ Gown, robe.
⁸ Mitra, *Bihari Life*, p. 28, No. 1. See also the note to No. 544 above and the headnote to Nos. 650–652 above.
⁹ See the headnote to Nos. 553–554.
¹⁰ *Magyar Nyelvör*, XV (1886), 44, and, with minor variations, XL (1911), 285. The meaning of *lipik* is obscure. Some riddles describe a lobster as turning from black to red; see the headnote to Nos. 1542–1543, §2, below.
¹¹ No. 679. ¹² No. 680.
¹³ Doke, 18. Compare No. 671 below.

in old age"[14] has already been noted. Riddlers often mention the actor's changing functions. An example is a riddle for an Indian fruit, "It was a beautiful baby. In youth, it lived in the midst of a crowd; in age, it rattled as it shook to and fro.—Channa [*Cicer aretinum*]."[15] The Lithuanian poppy riddle, "As long as I was young, I blossomed nicely. When I grew old, I made holes and through these holes I crawled,"[16] contains a confusing reference to the act of blossoming, which does not belong to a person. Better versions, which have not made this error, are "I shot up; when I shot up, I grew; when I was grown, I became a maiden; when I had become a maiden, I became a bride and married woman; when I had become a married woman, I became a crone; when I had become a crone, I got eyes and through these eyes I crawled out,"[17] and "When I was young, I blossomed like the rose; when I grew old, I got eyes; I crawled out through these eyes."[18] The Danish calf riddle, which shows some resemblance to this sort of conception, is perhaps better considered to be a version of a riddle for a drum.[19] It is as follows: "Little; [when] grown, it danced."[20] We should expect "little" to be followed by some such assertion as "it grazed."

I have noted no parallel to the clever Breton onion riddle: "I come out of earth, I am sold by my father, he who buys me cuts my tail, takes off my suit of silk, and weeps beside me when I am dead."[21]

668–669. A Sequence of Colors

A sequence of colors, each associated with a stage of human life, is easily used in describing a plant, especially a plant bearing a fruit or seed. The fundamental idea is so simple and the variations in details from country to country are often so great that we cannot confidently trace all riddles of this type back to a single origin. The English bramble riddle,[1] which has some very ancient parallels, merely lists a sequence of colors as the characteristics of an object without suggesting the idea of a person to whom they might belong. This is perhaps a degeneration of an original biographical form, but such an explanation is quite uncertain. The notion that a single object had many colors would be sufficiently confusing to make a good riddle. An instance which shows how far the variations may extend appears in the Tabaru riddle[2] for a Spanish pepper: "When still small, it is a *tjiba*.[3] When full grown, it is a *locri*."[4] The

---

[14] See the headnote to No. 587.
[15] Baiga: Elwin, p. 468, No. 42.
[16] Jurgelionis, 1002.
[17] Schleicher, pp. 203–204.
[18] Schleicher, p. 204.
[19] See the headnote to Nos. 1058–1062, §2, below.
[20] Feilberg, *Ordbog*, II, 79, s.v. "kalv."
[21] Adolphe Orain, *Mélusine*, IV (1888–1889), col. 405, No. 7, and repeated, V (1890–1891), col. 86, No. 11.

[1] See the headnote to Nos. 1384–1393.
[2] Fortgens, 101.
[3] A small green parrot.
[4] A small red parrot.

Kundu say of the African plum, "On my going into the field I dressed myself in linen, on my return I wore a black cloth."[5]

Riddlers in almost every country have used the notion of a sequence of colors. Spanish-speaking peoples have shown a particular liking for it. They have riddles for chile,[6] corn,[7] wheat,[8] and various Chilean plants[9] in this pattern. Indeed, they are so familiar with it that they have adapted it to describe a cigar.[10] The Italians use it for a mulberry.[11]

Typical uses of the biographical sequence of colors are:

§1. Coffee. See No. 668 and compare No. 1390. This differs from analogous riddles in mentioning black, which is associated with death. The contrast of red and black, which riddlers often use,[12] rarely occurs in these sequences of colors. Compare, however, the shrimp riddle from Mauritius, "I am black in my happy days, I am red in my sad days."[13]

§2. A cherry. German: Wossidlo, 184; O. Schell, *Am Urquell*, I (1890), 132, No. 13. Turkish: Hamizade, 394 (I began with white, I worked with green, I ended with red, I arrived at many lands).

§3. A blackberry.[14] Spanish: Demófilo, 668 through 671; Rodríguez Marín, 558 through 561. Argentinian: Lehmann-Nitsche, 76.

§4. Flax. Indonesian, Javanese: Ranneft, *Proza*, p. 47, No. 219 (When it is still young, it appears green, and white when it is old. It has the shape of a boat filled with *emping*).[15]

§5. A pepper. Spanish, Chilean: Flores, 32 (green, red, wrinkled). Thai: Haas MS (What is it? A little thing, she wears a white skirt; a young lady, her skirt is green; quite old, her skirt is red)—a manuscript version communicated to me by Dr. Mary Haas of the University of California, Berkeley, California. Korean: Bernheisel, p. 61 (What is that [which] wears a green apron when young and a red one when old?).

§6. Buckwheat. Hungarian: Arany and Gyulai, III, 295, No. 15 (When I was small, I wore a green garment; when grown, I wore red mourning; after my death, I wore black).

§7. A carob. Modern Greek: Polites, *Neohellenika Analekta*, I, 252, No. 339 (I was born white, became black, and in my old age my teeth became loose).

---

[5] Ittmann, *Kundu*, 138.
[6] Cuban: Giménez Cabrera, 51. New Mexican: Campa, 30.
[7] Spanish: Demófilo, 999.
[8] New Mexican: Campa, 92. See also the headnote to Nos. 1559–1561, §8, below.
[9] The *maqui* (Flores, 430 through 433), the *membrillo* (*ibid.*, 446), and the *paume* (*ibid.*, 594 through 596).
[10] Spanish: Demófilo, 287, 819, 954; Rodríguez Marín, 491.
[11] Ferraro, *Canti popolari in dialetto logodurese*, pp. 308–309, No. 32.
[12] See the headnote to Nos. 871–877 below.
[13] Baissac, *Mauritius*, p. 401. For parallels see the headnote to Nos. 1542–1543, §2, below.
[14] For versions lacking personification see Nos. 1561a through 1561d below.
[15] *Emping* is ground or powdered rice; see Kreemer, *Atjeh*, note to No. 34.

§8. A watermelon. Arabic: Ruoff, p. 52, No. 30 (The beginning of my life is white pearls, the second part emerald green, the third red as a ruby. Guess my status, Negro!).[16]

668. Born in white, live in green, die in red, bury in black.—Coffee.
Beckwith, *Jamaica*, p. 196, No. 111.

669. First white, then red; / Two days old, then dead.—Cotton blossom.
Hudson, p. 85, No. 12.

670-680. A Sequence of Acts

670. A child was born in the month of March, / We cut his umbilic in the month of August; / He gave a fall to the Parson of Paul / the black month before the nativity.—Barley that was tilled in March and reaped in August. The Parson of Paul drank the beer made of it in the month of November, and it gave him a fall.
Cornish Notes and Queries, I (1906), 273.

671. Why is a baby like a wheatfield?—First it is cradled, then it's threshed, and then it becomes the flour of the family.
Oral, Pennsylvania.

672. j was round and small like a p[e]arle then long & slender as brave as an earle since like a hermit j lived in a cell & now like a rogue in the wide world j dwell.—first an egge the[n] a silke worme then inclosed in a huske & last of all a buter fly.
Tupper, *Holme Riddles*, 17.

673. What is that which constantly changes its habit while it lives, is buried before it is dead, and whose tomb is valued wherever it is found?—Silkworm.
Waugh, *Canada*, p. 71, No. 817.

674-680. A Series of Tortures

The notion of describing an object as a person who suffers a variety of tortures exists in many widely diverging forms. It seems altogether probable that riddlers have hit upon the idea independently. The Turks, for example, compare eating a bunch of grapes to killing a ram: "I have a ram. Go, fetch it, lead it, slaughter it, eat it, spread out its skin so that its skin will dry; then, it will rise and walk."[1] This has some similarity also to the description of fruit or a bottle of liquor in terms of a man whose head is torn off, whose blood is drunk,

---

[16] This variety of riddling seems to be unknown in English folklore. It consists in describing an object, usually a fruit, in terms of precious jewels or metals. See the Palestinian Arabic riddle for the narcissus, "My wrist [is] emerald green, the palm of my hand golden yellow, my finger pure as silver. If you are a free man, the son of a free man, guess my riddle" (Ruoff, p. 53, No. 32). This manner of riddling is especially favored on the shores of the Mediterranean. See also the headnote to No. 1355, n. 5, below.

[1] Kowalski, *Asia Minor*, 44.

and whose body is thrown away.² The Serbian wine riddle, "The sun cooks me, the hand breaks me up, the foot presses me, the mouth tastes me,"³ which contains several unconnected elements, is another variation of the theme. The Russian riddle for tea, "They twisted me, they diapered me, they threw me into Chinatown [Kitaygorod],"⁴ involves, as Professor George R. Noyes tells me, something akin to a pun. Kitaygorod signifies the central, originally fortified part of Moscow adjoining the citadel or Kremlin. Here, it signifies the parcel in which the tea is packed as well as the country where it is packed.

Some instances of this theme are extremely picturesque and ingenious. A Norwegian riddle, "The first year I lay in a dark house, the second I was beaten and bound, the third year I feared neither fire nor water,"⁵ has the answer "baby" but applies equally well to a pot. Another riddle having the answer "baby" is the Russian "Forty weeks I sat in a prison cell, six weeks in a hospital, twenty weeks they kept on binding me, a year they kept me hanging."⁶ Some Russian descriptions of sheaves standing on a field are battle scenes: "On the field of Arsk, on the Tatar boundary, everyone is down, is killed, beards are shaved, and bellies slashed open";⁷ "Here upon here, here upon a local hill, all those here are beaten, their heads are shaved, and knives are stuck into their heads";⁸ and (with the answer "rye") "I was walking past the parson's, I saw bodies of this sort, their bodies were broken and their bellies slit."⁹ The Russians, who have many riddles of this sort, adapt the series of tortures to describe the earth in "I am beaten, pounded, turned over, cut; I endure everything and repay everyone with good."¹⁰

In English riddling a series of tortures describes either the preparation of a plant for human use¹¹ or the manufacture of a pen.¹² The descriptions of wheat or flax after this fashion often exhibit very curious and cleverly devised parallels to the life of Christ.¹³ They can be traced back to medieval times.

Inasmuch as some of these riddles do not suggest the events of Christ's passion, I am inclined to believe that the adjustment to fit the tortures to Christ's sufferings represents a later development. The Flemish riddle for a nut, "First I was pounded, then beaten to bits, then flayed, and then swallowed,"¹⁴ which is developed somewhat differently in Danish,¹⁵ contains materials which could be easily reshaped to suggest Christ's sufferings. The riddles for a quill pen¹⁶ rarely, if ever, suggest an analogy to Biblical events.

---

² See the headnotes to Nos. 805–818 and 806–815 below.
³ Novaković, p. 19, No. 6.   ⁴ Sadovnikov, 563.
⁵ Bugge, *Telemarken*, 39. Compare Cheremiss: Porkka, 75.
⁶ Sadovnikov, 1709.   ⁷ Sadovnikov, 1225.
⁸ Sadovnikov, 1222.   ⁹ Arkhangel'skii, p. 78.
¹⁰ Sadovnikov, 1803.
¹¹ See below, Nos. 679, 680, and the headnotes to Nos. 679 and 680.
¹² Nos. 674 through 677b and the headnote to Nos. 674–677.
¹³ See the headnotes to Nos. 679 and 680.
¹⁴ Joos, 497. See also the headnote to No. 679, n. 12, below.
¹⁵ Kristensen, pp. 98–99, §251, No. 395.
¹⁶ See below, Nos. 674 through 677b and the headnote to Nos. 674–677.

A few riddles relating a sequence of tortures mention death by fire. The German horseshoe riddle contains various medieval varieties of execution: "First they burn me, then they have drawn me, then they drive nails into me, then in death I am borne by big and little."[17] A somewhat similar riddle for a pot is widely known along the Baltic coast and in Slavic countries. The Lithuanian "When I was young, I sat in a golden chair. When I was old, not even a dog would devour my bones"[18] is a shortened and rather imperfect version of such Russian riddles as "I was at the digging, I was at the clapping, and at a fire, and a bazar. When I was young, I fed people. When I aged, they diapered me. When I died, my useless bones were thrown into a pit, where even the dogs won't gnaw me."[19] A variation on this theme is "A stony mountain gave birth to me, a fiery stream baptized me, they took me to a market to sell me, there came a good lady to buy me, she struck me with a golden ring. My poor bones fell apart, they were not placed in a coffin, people don't look at them, dogs won't eat them."[20] See also the Modern Greek "I was made of earth, I was planted in the earth, and no man undertook to bury my bones.—Pitcher."[21] and the Mordvin "Turning about itself, it grows old and is enveloped in swaddling clothes; it dies, one throws it out on the field; the wild beasts do not eat it nor do the birds peck at it nor does it decay."[22] These texts are evidence of a well-established tradition of the pot riddle in which the events contain no suggestion of Biblical history.

Some Indian parallels lead me to infer that this form of the pot riddle is very old. See, as examples, "Who is he that is carried on the head and afterwards trampled under feet? But notwithstanding this insult he procures bread for the wrongdoer?"[23] and the Baiga "When I was a virgin, they were always beating me, and I didn't mind. But now I am married, I can't endure even a clap."[24] The Baiga description of mohlain leaves made into a cup and then, after being used, cast aside has some similarity to these themes. It is as follows: "It is round when it comes from the forest. We made a hollow of its body. It eats curds and milk. Then it goes to the rubbish heap."[25] The introductory element resembles the riddles beginning with a scene in the forest,[26] and the conclusion recalls the Russian pot riddle.

In eastern Europe, Biblical allusions have been introduced into some versions of the pot riddle. The Russians say, "Taken from the earth like Adam; put into a fiery oven, like the three youths; taken from the oven and put into a vehicle, like Elijah; taken to the market, like Joseph; taken to a place of

---

[17] Wossidlo, 488.
[18] Jurgelionis, 365. The "golden chair" is the fire in which the pot is burned.
[19] Sadovnikov, 322.
[20] Sadovnikov, 333.
[21] Polites, *Neohellenika Analekta*, I, 237, No. 252.
[22] Paasonen, 86. [23] Lakshīnātha Upasānī, XII, 5.
[24] Elwin, p. 478, No. 145. [25] Elwin, p. 476, No. 119.
[26] See the headnotes to Nos. 553–554 above and 1058–1062 below.

execution and hit over the head, like Jesus. He called in a loud voice, and to this voice there came a woman, like Mary Magdalene; having bought it for a copper coin, she took it home; but he wept for his mother, he died, and to this day his bones lie unburied."[27] The Serbians say, "God made me of the same stuff as Adam. I fed everybody and gave enough people water to drink; and when I died, neither did God receive my soul nor the earth my body"; also, "It was made from the same stuff as Adam; it suffered like Adam; and when it died, neither did its soul go to God nor its body to the earth"; and "It was made of earth like Adam; it was tested in the oven like the three youths; and when it died, people did not bury its bones."[28] The Mordvin "One shoves it into the oven, one throws it into the field"[29] is probably a degenerate version. The Modern Greek "I was made of earth as was Adam; I was placed in the flames as were the three young men; in my lifetime I gave cool relief to many; and when I died, no one came forward to bury my bones"[30] represents the usual series of Biblical allusions.

Some riddles containing a reference to fire as one of the tortures seem to be inventions quite independent of the texts thus far considered. They illustrate how readily the fundamental idea can be used for a riddle. A Danish riddle for a needle is as follows: "I was born in the mine. There I was well off, but later I received blows and slaps so that I became yellow and red. My head is upright and is flat at the back. My body is both long and round and pricks the skins of girls."[31] A Lettish riddle for brandy is "Mother dressed me in green, father gave me a yellow hue, a narrow gateway made me white, fire purified me, my exterior is adorned, destructive fire is hidden in me."[32]

This sort of description is also characteristic of alchemical writing in the Middle Ages. I quote the following examples from Lynn Thorndike's *A History of Magic and Experimental Science:*

> The world was lost through a woman and hence should be recovered through a woman. Therefore take the pure mother and put her in bed with the sons according to your intention and there let her do strictest penance until she is well cleansed from all sins. And then she will bear a son for certain who will preach to all saying, "Signs have appeared in sun and moon." Therefore let him be taken and beaten well and scourged lest by reason of pride he perish. . . . Therefore take the son after he has been beaten and put him to bed to enjoy himself for a while, and when you feel that he is enjoying himself, then take him pure and extinguish in cold water. And when you have repeated the process, hand him over to the Jews to be crucified. And while he is crucified, sun nor moon will be seen, and then the veil of the temple will be rent, and there will be a great earthquake. So then the fire is to be increased, and thereupon he will give up the ghost.[33]

---

[27] Sadovnikov, 334.
[28] Novaković, p. 118, Nos. 1, 2, and p. 217, No. 2.
[29] Paasonen, 364.   [30] Stathes, p. 364 No. 137.
[31] Kristensen, p. 72, §172, No. 272. See slightly different versions in Feilberg, *Ordbog*, II, 212, s.v. "knappenål." Swedish: Ström, p. 159, "Nålen," 3.
[32] Bielenstein, 119.
[33] *A History of Magic and Experimental Science*, III (New York, 1934), 76.

Another passage in the *Metaphors* of Arnald of Villanova is similar in character and resembles these riddles even more:

> Bind the serf twice and imprison him thrice. Put him once in whitest linen, and if he is inobedient, incarcerate him again. Make him receive himself. On the third night give him a white wife. And he will impregnate her. And thus she will give birth to thirty sons who will overcome their genitor.[34]

The point of Arnald of Villanova's *Parabolae*, or, as Thorndike prefers to call it, *Exempla*, is the drawing of an analogy between the passion and resurrection of Christ and the alchemical process, such as is found also in other writings ascribed to Arnald, notably the *De Secretis naturae*. In the treatment of mercury in the process of transmutation, it is led like a lamb to the slaughter to free humanity from pauperism and attendant misery. Its sweat turns to blood like that of Jesus. To the analogies to the scourging and crucifixion found elsewhere ascribed to Arnald are here added others to the crown of thorns and the gall and vinegar which complete the four passions. And after three days burial the mercury is found more beautiful, white, and transfigured than ever before.[35]

Somewhat similar ideas occur in the Icelandic silver riddle: "At first I am always in the ground covered with heavy layers of earth. Then men come, armed with sharp axes, and cut me up pitilessly. Then I am drenched in water but cannot swim very long. Next I am crushed and tortured in fire until I turn liquid. I am given homes of various kinds, spacious, narrow, low, or small. But I end my life in the homes of the rich, where I reach the highest old age."[36]

Still other variations of the theme of a sequence of tortures are seen in the Icelandic riddles for cooking and eating a bird, "I first quickened in a round house, where I was brought up on the furniture. I broke out from thence, and being a good traveler, I got around far and wide. Then the net of a fated death caught me, and I was stripped and my belly bared. I was put over a fire but burnt only slightly, and then boiled in flaming hot oil, all the while being pierced by a three-pronged spear. I was next pushed into the whirlpool that is everyone's concern, and finally became the abomination of all men. Such is the story of my life,"[37] and for weaving, "I saw a man wearing long clothes sitting in bondage. He was strictly fettered at his head and feet. He is always wrapped up in three chains, but the fourth one around his knees is the tightest one, and is held by two boys attending at his either side. Then there came a small slave who tore and scratched him with a raven's beak, so that he gave forth a rattling sound. Then a naked woman came and ran violently to his crotch and beat and struck him so that he shook all over. Then there came a

---

[34] Thorndike, *A History of Magic* . . . , III, 76.
[35] Thorndike, *A History of Magic* . . . , III, 77–78.
[36] Árnason, 114.
[37] Árnason, 826.

king dressed in women's garments and cut his insteps with a hard ax. Some hearts of the earth squeeze each other and cause each other to wince audibly, but they have never been seen to weep."[38]

674–677. Born of Flesh and Blood, Later Decapitated

The description of the tortures which a goose quill suffers in becoming a pen employs themes which are characteristic of the literary rather than the popular riddle. Such themes are the biographical scheme, the use of the first person, and the mention of the functions of the pen in the concluding words, "I make peace between king and king and many a true lover glad." An early example found in the *Palatine Anthology*[1] was often translated and adapted.[2] Although Andrea Alciati translated this epigram, he did not include it in his *Emblemata*.[3] Had he done so, it would have gained an even wider currency than it has enjoyed.

The Latin version in Nicolaus Reusner's *Ænigmatographia*[4] is, Loewenthal conjectures,[5] translated from German. This conjecture may be correct so far as Reusner's immediate source is concerned, but the riddle is certainly not a German invention, even though Reinmar von Zweter may have alluded to it in the thirteenth century.[6] The parallels in the *Palatine Anthology*, in Modern Greek,[7] and in Persian, suggest that we should look to the East for the origin of the riddle. The Persian parallel, which Schultz mentions but does not cite precisely, is as follows: "A stranger came from the forest to the city. His head was cut off and his face was blackened. He was then mounted on three horses and was dragged through a field with his head sweeping the ground."[8] Most of the Arabic riddles for a pen have been inaccessible to me,[9] but the version in the story[10] of Tawaddud in the *Arabian Nights* is quite different from the texts with which we are concerned. I am uncertain whether the Uraon "The head of a tired hen is cut with a knife, but it goes on walking,"[11] which refers to an animal and not to a person, can be considered a variant of this riddle. Wolfgang Schultz's note[12] and an epigram in the *Palatine Anthology*[13] explain

---

[38] Árnason, 976. The word here translated "squeeze" may also be translated "pierce," but the meaning of the statement remains obscure.

[1] IX, 162.

[2] See James Hutton, *The Greek Anthology in Italy to the Year 1800*, Cornell Studies in English, XXXII (Ithaca, 1935), Register.

[3] Hutton, *The Greek Anthology in Italy* . . ., p. 201, n. 2.

[4] Ed. 1599, p. 185 = ed. 1602, p. 376.   [5] Pp. 57–58, n. 1.

[6] Gustav Roethe, *Die Gedichte Reinmars von Zweter* (Leipzig, 1887), p. 253, and strophe 188; Loewenthal, pp. 57–58, 145; Petsch, *Rätselstudien*, pp. 345–346.

[7] Sanders, p. 235.

[8] Kuka, 10. The three horses are the fingers.

[9] René Basset cites several texts; see *Revue des traditions populaires*, XIX (1904), 56.

[10] See *Tausend und eine Nacht*, ed. Max Henning, VIII (Leipzig, n.d.), 187; Victor Chauvin, *Bibliographie des ouvrages arabes*, VII (Liège, 1903), 117–119, No. 387.

[11] Archer, p. 194, No. 226.

[12] *Rätsel aus dem hellenischen Kulturkreise*, II, 126.

[13] Appendix, VII, 37.

the implications found in some versions. The nature of the many literary riddles about a pen will perhaps be sufficiently illustrated by the old and famous version of Al-Ḥarîrî. Some themes found in these English riddles will be noted in this Arabic version. It is as follows:

> One split in his head it is through whom 'the writ'
> is known, as honored recording angels take their pride in him;
> When given to drink he craves for more, as though athirst, and
> settles to rest when thirstiness takes hold of him;
> And scatters tears about him when ye bid him run, but tears that
> sparkle with the brightness of a smile.[14]

The riddle for a pen based on a series of tortures has suggested some versions having other answers. A Danish riddler probably had the pen riddle in mind when contriving this description of cheese: "I come from flesh and blood, but never are these found in me. They cut off my head with a knife and laid me on a table before priests and lords."[15] The Finnish riddle for flax, "The head is cut off, the entrails cut to bits. Yet it serves king and beggar,"[16] has some similarity to the pen riddle, but is essentially the usual flax riddle[17] with these slight contaminations.

For further discussion see Ohlert, 2d ed., pp. 170-171, and Ohlert, *Philologus*, LVII (1898), 600–601 (citing a few remote parallels to *Anthologia Palatina*, IX, 163); also Wolfgang Schultz, *Rätsel*, cols. 100–101.

674. Once I was born in flesh and blood, / As other creatures be; / But now am neither flesh nor blood, / But it all belongs to me. / They plucked me from my native soil / Where I was born and bred; / But, for the use of man, indeed / They then cut off my head. / I took a draught, a hearty draught, / Of with all the skill I had, / Which made enmity between kings and kings / And made true lovers glad. / I, oft a sword, my brother's foe, / My friendship does not fail; / I often cause the rich to weep, / The poor lament and wail.—A goose quill pen.
Leather, *Hereford*, p. 228.

675a. When I was taken from the fair fair body, / They then cut off my head, / And thus my shape was altered. / It's I that make peace between king and king, / And many a true lover glad: / All this I do, and ten times more, / And more I could do still; / But nothing I can do / Without my guider's will.—A quill-pen.
Knortz, p. 225, No. 60; Halliwell-Phillipps, *Nursery Rhymes*, p. 120; Hyatt, *Adams Co., Ill.*, p. 665, No. 10899.

---

[14] Al-Ḥarîrî, *The Assemblies* (trans. Chenery and Steingass), II, 116 (the Forty-second Assembly). See also Friedreich, p. 158, No. 2.
[15] Kristensen, p. 100, § 257, No. 408. Here the cutting of the head refers to cutting the top of the sack containing the cheese.
[16] Aarne and Krohn, 74 = Henssen, 249.
[17] No. 679 below.

675b. They took me from my mother's side / Where I was bravely bred / And when to age I did become / They did cut off my head. / They gave to me some diet drink / That often made me mad / But it made peace between two kings / And made two lovers glad.—A goosequill pen.
Oral, California.

676. I am become of flesh and blood, / As other creatures be; / Yet there's neither flesh nor blood / Doth remain in me. / I make kings that they fall out, / I make them agree; / And yet there's neither flesh nor blood / Doth remain in me.—Goosequill pen.
Halliwell-Phillipps, *Popular Rhymes*, p. 147; Knortz, p. 229, No. 74.

677a. Taken from my native soil, given monstrous drinks, 'nough to make one mad, / But it ends debates betwixt kings and queens and makes two lovers glad.—A goosequill made into a pen.
Oral, North Carolina.

677b. As I was taken from my mother's side, my head was quite cutt [sic] off. / I made peace between kings, and true lovers glad.—Goose quill.
MacGréine, *Béaloideas*, III (1931–1932), 413, No. 2.

678. A Series of Tortures or Punishments Describing a Manufactured Object

Riddlers often describe a manufactured object by a series of tortures, as in the picturesque Spanish key riddle, "I was ill-treated when I was made, my mother loves me, and although I am an honorable woman, my lord has tied me with cords."[1] The following English cask riddle suggests the punishment of transportation, but the asker probably did not perceive the import of the idea. An exact parallel to the English riddle is lacking. The Flemish cask riddle, "I was bound and beaten. Without fault, I must bear this. What availed it that I made a noise? There must be a brand in my skin,"[2] contains some analogous ideas and also shows similarities to the riddle for flax.[3]

This English cask riddle may have developed from the old and widely known description of a barrel as a man girt with iron belts. This in turn belongs to the many descriptions of an object as person who is girdled, encircled, or tied in various ways. Such descriptions refer to anything tied in bundles. Typical themes are:

§ 1. A cask or barrel. Swiss: Rochholz, 471 and note. Icelandic: Árnason, 171 (I know a woman with many girdles. Her kisses refresh and quench men's thirst.—Drinking vessel), 257 (He travels wrapped in fetters and then comes home drunk, lies down, and vomits what everyone likes.—Brandy keg). Swedish: Noreen, *Fryksdal*, 11. Serbian: Novaković, p. 6, No. 2 (The tsar's sister girdled herself with nine girdles). Cheremiss: Porkka, 132 (A little Russian girded himself with forty-one girdles). Modern Greek: Abbott, p. 313,

---
[1] Cuban: Massip, 122.   [2] Joos, 327.   [3] No. 679 below.

No. 32 (My uncle Hadji-Theodore girt with eighteen belts); Polites, *Neohellenika Analekta*, I, 240, No. 266 (My short son Theodore wears many girdles. He binds himself and unbinds himself and cannot undo himself), and also the more usual shorter version, "My short stumpy son with many girdles" (I, 199, No. 31); Sanders, 14; Stathes, p. 347, No. 96. Turkish: Katanov in Radlov, IX, 243, No. 125 (One lad girt with eight belts), 286, No. 222 (Tyorep is girt with four belts and Arap with six belts.—Pail and tub), and p. 293, No. 263. See also the comparisons of a barrel to a man dressed in patches.[4]

§ 2. A sheaf or bundle. Irish: O Dalaigh, 174 (A long bright woman with a girdle around her). Serbian: Novaković, p. 215, No. 7 (All the princes are girt, the tsar alone is not girt.—Sheaves and cock [pile of sheaves]). Estonian: Wiedemann, p. 286, No. 290. Zyrian: Wichmann, *Zyrian*, 244 (A handsome, handsome fellow, always with two girdles). Mordvin: Paasonen, 144 (Tatars bound together are lying in the river.—Bundles of flax). Zyrian: Wichmann, *Zyrian*, 244. Indian, Kashmiri: Knowles, 97 (A pandit descended thence with three girdles about him.—A bundle of wood).

The unusual elaboration in the Cheremiss "Has a hundred bands and a head of fir.—Grain stack"[5] refers to the pole in the center of the stack.

§ 3. A broom. Icelandic: Árnason, 543 (Who is the dark-haired and valiant-looking prince that has arrived in the land? He has toes and long tongs with which he trains young pigs. Both his hands are tied and ropes are strapped around his middle), 955 (I saw someone in a black dress, tied around with a string. I think he was chasing the children at Ingjaldshóll). These riddles for a bundle of twigs used for whipping a disobedient child contain some obscurities. Polish: Gustawicz, 236 (A maiden stands behind the door, wrapped in rods and switches), 237 (A maiden stands behind the door, she is wrapped and bound with ropes). Cheremiss: Genetz, 13 (Man and wife put on green cloaks, girded themselves with a silken girdle.—Bath brushes, made of short green branches). Turcoman: Samojlvich, 75 (In a dark cart there lies a slave with his waist girt about). Tibetan: Mitra, p. 465, No. 3 (One girdle for a hundred persons). Indonesian, Tabaru: Fortgens, 49 (Some hundred persons, all of whom have one girdle in common).

§ 4. Posts, a fence. Russian: Sadovnikov, 703 (A hundred and one brothers stand all in a row, all bound together). Estonian: Wiedemann, p. 267. Cheremiss: Genetz, 3. Zyrian: Wichmann, *Zyrian*, 269 (Two siblings girt with one and the same belt.—Fence posts). Votyak: Wichmann, *Votyak*, 91 (Two men bind their hips together). Turkish: Menges, 51 (Two maidens girt with one belt.—Posts in a dam); Katanov in Radlov, IX, 243, No. 119 (A hundred brothers girt with one girdle.—Grating of a yurt). The Yakut "They say that two boys are tugging at one belt, but neither one succeeds in wresting it from

---

[4] See the headnote to No. 1437, § 7, below.
[5] Porkka, 57.

the other," "They say that two brothers are tugging at a belt of silver," and "Two men are pulling a belt"⁶ are more dramatic than most versions. The Tungus "The older and the younger brother are girt with one belt"⁷ introduces a slight elaboration. The Korean "What is it that wears a girdle but no hat?"⁸ conceives a wicker fence in terms of the local dress.

§ 5. A saddle. Yakut: Priklonskii, 37 (A good peasant with three belts).

§ 6. A gun. Turkish: Katanov in Radlov, IX, 104, No. 890 (Two twins have three belts), which describes a double-barreled gun. Ossete: Schiefner, 51 (Three girdles on a little person.—Pistol).

§ 7. A tripod. Turkish: Katanov in Radlov, IX, 241, No. 91 (Three lads are girt with one belt). Compare the description of a table as four men under one hat.⁹

§ 8. A door closed by a bar. Rumanian: Papahagi, 74. Albanian: Hahn, p. 158, No. 5 (Two sisters who are girt with one girdle), and p. 161, No. 34.

§ 9. A bridge. Ossete: Schiefner, 2 (A short girdle on a long man).

678. I sailed here from the old land, / And am bound with iron bonds; / Murder have I not done; / Stolen not; cheated not; / Yet a peg is beaten into my head.—Cask.
Gardner, *Schoharie Hills, N.Y.*, p. 253, No. 6.

679. The Tortures of Flax

Recorders of folklore have noted only one English example of the old and famous series of tortures which serves to describe the preparation of flax. This theme is probably related to the somewhat similar tortures of the grape,¹ wheat, or a capon. Of these, only the wheat riddle is known to English tradition.² The acts "I pulled off his head, ate his flesh, and threw away his bones"³ are better regarded as a comparison to killing and eating an animal. In the Middle Ages the riddles for the grape, wheat, and a capon were ingeniously adapted to suggest the life and sufferings of Christ while remaining an accurate description of the object intended. Their interrelations and their connections with other themes are obscure. Blechsteiner suggests⁴ that the flax riddle is allied to some folk-tales having a chain-structure, and, perhaps independently, Wolfgang Schultz⁵ expresses a similar idea. The early medieval *Conflictus ovi et lini*⁶ exhibits some similarities to these riddles, but a connection is improbable.

---

⁶ Piekarski, 258, 259; Priklonskii, 111.   ⁷ Poppe, 5.
⁸ Bernheisel, p. 82.   ⁹ See No. 993 below.
¹ See Reusner, ed. 1602, p. 282.
² See below, No. 680 and the headnote to No. 680.
³ See the headnote to Nos. 806–815.
⁴ P. lv.
⁵ *Mitra*, I (1914–1920), col. 47.
⁶ See M. Manitius, *Geschichte der lateinischen Literatur des Mittelalters*, II (Munich, 1923), 771.

One of the oldest versions of the flax riddle is in the insufficiently studied medieval Latin dialogue known as *Adrian et Epictetus*. Although this dialogue is a branch of a widely disseminated set of questions and answers and several manuscripts of it have been listed, we have no adequate edition of the text. Walther Suchier, who has long promised an edition,[7] divides the manuscripts into two classes. Unfortunately, the two texts, *Cod. lat. monac. 8439* and *Arundel 351*, which have been printed, belong to the same class.[8] The theme of the tortures of flax occurs only in the first of these. It is uncertain whether the riddle properly belongs to the dialogue or has been introduced by a scribe. This fifteenth-century version is as follows: "Quid est quod in terra mergitur, crescit ut bibamus, in ligno pendet, in aquam mergitur, ad solem producitur, ferro disrumpitur, inde homines et ecclesie ornantur?"[9] Some obvious improvements of this corrupt text are the substitution of *nascitur* for the first *mergitur* and the recognition of *bibamus* as a peculiar spelling of *vivamus*. Suchier quotes[10] a variant reading from *Balliol 239:* "crescit sicut herba, floret sicut garba, colorem habet sicut cera." These ideas belong to an altogether different riddle for flax, but the occurrence of a flax riddle in this manuscript, which belongs to the second and virtually unknown class of texts of *Adrian et Epictetus*, suggests that a flax riddle of some sort may belong to the original version.

The last of the nineteen riddles which the Queen of Sheba asked Solomon recites the uses to which flax is put and differs greatly from the other texts discussed in this headnote. It is as follows: "It walks ahead of all; it cries out loud and bitterly; its head is like the reed; it is the glory of the noble, the disgrace of the living, the delight of birds, the distress of fishes."[11] The allusions are interpreted as follows: "The sail of the boat is made of flax; in a storm it waves to and fro, and when beaten by the wind, it emits sounds; the rich wear byssus, the poor have rags, and shrouds are usually made of linen; the birds steal the flax-seed, and the fish are caught with nets made of flax."

The rhetorical device which we find in these enigmatic narratives of the tortures and functions of flax—the device of ascribing speech to an inanimate object—is known as *prosopopeia*. It was often used in classical and medieval literatures. In an instructive essay on the Old English *Dream of the Rood* Margaret Schlauch shows how it was used in that poem.[12] A striking similarity to our riddles is seen in the pseudo-Ovidian *De Nuce* (cited by Miss Schlauch), in which a nut tree complains of its misfortunes.

[7] *L'Enfant sage*, p. 66; Daly and Suchier, p. 109.
[8] *L'Enfant sage*, pp. 66–67, 265–276; J. M. Kemble, *The Dialogue of Salomon and Saturnus* (London, 1848), pp. 212–215.
[9] *L'Enfant sage*, p. 268, No. 64. [10] *L'Enfant sage*, p. 274.
[11] L. Ginzberg, *Legends of the Jews*, IV (Philadelphia, 1913), 149 and the notes, and VI, 290–291, nn. 46–47. A versification by Krafft varies in some details; see Friedreich, p. 102.
[12] " 'The Dream of the Rood' as Prosopopeia," *Essays and Studies in Honor of Carleton Brown* (New York, 1940), pp. 23–34. For riddles reciting the sufferings of a nut or nut tree see the headnote to Nos. 674–680, nn. 14–15 above.

For old versions or discussions of the theme see Straparola, II, 3, and VII, 3; Ohlert, 1st ed., p. 144, n. 2, and, more briefly, 2d ed., p. 179; Ludwig Laistner, *Das Rätsel der Sphinx* (Berlin, 1889), I, 8–15; J. Bächtold (ed.), Nikolaus Manuel, *Werke*, Bibliothek älterer Schriftwerke der deutschen Schweiz, II (Frauenfeld, 1878), xxxi–xxxiii, ccxvii; Johannes Bolte, "Andreas Tharäus 'Klage der Gerste und des Flachses,' " *Schriften des Vereins für die Geschichte Berlins*, XXXIII (1897), 35–68; R. Köhler, *Kleinere Schriften*, II, 675, No. 1; F. W. Drijver, *Velerlei beelden* (Amsterdam, n.d. [1910]), pp. 127–130; R. Eisler, *Weltenmantel und Himmelszelt* (Munich, 1910), p. 149, n. 2, p. 242, n. 4, and p. 272, n. 3;[13] J. Volný, "Písen o lnu a konopí a predivu," *Český lid*, XXII (1912–1913), 386–392; J. Bolte and G. Polívka *Anmerkungen zu den Kinder- und Hausmärchen*, I (Leipzig, 1913), 19, n. 2, and p. 222, n. 1; Max Hippe, "Hochzeitsrätsel des 17. Jahrhunderts," *Festschrift Theodor Siebs*, Germanistische Abhandlungen, LXVII (Breslau, 1933), pp. 431–433, No. 3; *Zeitschrift des Vereins für Volkskunde*, XXXV–XXXVI (1925–1926), 60; Stith Thompson, *Motif-Index* (FF Communications, CVIII [Helsinki, 1934]), III, 280, H. 13. 2. 6. The theme also occurs in Italian folksongs; see Ive, *Canti popolari istriani*, pp. 221–222.

679. My father was a sprightly lad but now he's dead and gone. / My mother was six hundred years old the minute I was born. / I was always brought up a suckling and never eat no bread, / And never was good for nothing till after I was dead. / They best me and banged me up and down about and up and down again, / Took my body from me and left me nothing but my skin. / Then I grew old and crazy near my constitution's end. / They took me all to pieces and blew me up again. / I went among the poor and I went among the rich. / At last they got sick of me and blew me all to bits.—Flax.
E. M. Backus, *Journal of American Folklore*, XLVIII (1935), 197.

680. The Tortures of Wheat

Riddlers often compare the growth, harvesting, and grinding of wheat to events, usually tortures, in a human life. The interrelations of the many versions of this theme and its connections with the similar riddle for flax[1] are obscure. The English riddle below differs from the usual versions, which often have some similarities to the life of Jesus and end with a reference to the Host. This Christian garb is probably a reworking of the original conception.

The comparison of the growth of wheat, the grinding of flour, and the making and eating of bread to a man's life has many widely varying forms. The Icelanders say, "A multitude of us is born into the world. An abundance of us benefits and pleases man. Our destiny carries us far from our homeland, throughout the world, over sea and land, until our predestined day of

---

[13] His promised article in *Philologus* seems not to have appeared.
[1] See the headnote to No. 679.

judgment arrives, when we become dust. Then foaming waterfalls rush upon us, flinging rocks. After the judgment we receive a renewal and manifold transformations. Escaped from a hot purgatory, we are everywhere desired by men and women. Then people joyfully offer us lodging and lead us politely into the house. But in the end we leave despised by a secret passage. Such is the story of our fate, hidden under the runes of a riddle."[2] One of the oldest versions is the Syriac "I stood like a lance, the sword struck me with its edge, the bull trampled me with its feet, the air bore away my clothes, naked I entered into the master's house, he much delighted in me."[3] The Russians say, "The fiddle squeaks, the tsarina rides, she begs to be allowed to stay over night [saying,] 'I will not stay forever, I will pass one night here. The hackers will come, they will break my little bones, they will throw my body into a cylinder, they will drag my soul to Paradise.' "[4] The Cuban "Green I was raised, and white they kneaded me, red they cut me, and black they ground me"[5] employs the sequence of colors characteristic of the bramble riddle,[6] but admits too many specific references to the procedure of grinding and baking. Similar but probably quite unrelated references to colors also occur in a Kashub parallel, "He was born red, he walked about in green, he was cut down white and taken to the grave.—Rye."[7]

Perhaps the most curious and important of all early versions is that in the Twenty-ninth Assembly[8] of Al-Ḥarîrî (died 1122 or 1123). The narrator tells of hearing a man order his son to go to the market with "the one of full-moon face and pearly hue, of pure root and tormented body, who was pinched and stretched, imprisoned and released, made to drink and weaned, and pushed into the fire after he had been slapped." As the commentators explain, these details describe a loaf, which is round and white and made of pure materials. Imprisonment and release refer to the grinding of the corn; suckling and weaning to mixing water with the dough and then withholding it until it is kneaded. Inasmuch as Al-Ḥarîrî's book was often imitated, his use of the theme is very important. A curious Korean riddle for vermicelli tells the story in its own way: "What is it that goes in a wooden door, comes out an iron door, takes a hot bath, then a cold bath, and then goes to sleep on a reed mat?"[9]

For the discussion of other parallels see R. Eisler, *Weltenmantel und Himmelszelt* (Munich, 1910), pp. 148–149. He cites Ovid, *Metamorphoses*, XI,

---

[2] Árnason, 290.
[3] Furlani, *Azraq*, 37.
[4] Sadovnikov, 1235.
[5] Massip, 192.
[6] See the headnote to Nos. 1384–1393 below. Compare Nos. 1561a through 1561d and the discussion in the headnote to Nos. 668–669 above.
[7] Gulgowski, 3.
[8] Al-Ḥarîrî, *The Assemblies* (trans. Chenery and Steingass), II, 16, and the notes, pp. 194–195; Friedreich, p. 171.
[9] Bernheisel, p. 62. The wooden and the iron doors are the openings of the mill, and the reed mat lies on the bottom of the bowl in which vermicelli is served.

1-43 (a description of the death of Orpheus), Robert Burns's poem on John Barleycorn, and Johann von Krolewitz' *Vaterunser*, which gives a full allegorical comparison of the life of Jesus to the growth, harvesting, and use of wheat. See also the collectanea of Johannes Bolte and George Polívka, *Anmerkungen zu den Kinder- und Hausmärchen*, I (Leipzig, 1913), 222–223, n. 1, and p. 331, n. 3, and also the comment on the tortures of flax in the preceding headnote.

680. When I was young and in my mother's lap, / She never gave me milk or pap: / She never sang me lullaby, / But left me there to live or die. / Then I sprang up, became all green, / I looked like some fairy queen. / Then I turned from green to yellow, / And I became a noble fellow. / A rub-a-rout came and cut me down, / And in a band my body bound. / Then they carried me to the barn, / There I thought I could take no harm. / Here comes a man with a stick cut in two, / Then he places me on the floor: / He broke my back, knocked out my brains, / And thus rewarded me for my pains!—Wheat.
Leather, *Hereford*, p. 233.

681–822. Manner of Life

681. Growing

681. Father has a man, instead of growing up, he grew down.—Candle.
Fauset, *Nova Scotia*, p. 156, No. 63.

682–685. Living

682. There is a woman livin' in the worl'. From the time the worl' is create', never more than four weeks old.—Moon.
Parsons, *Barbados*, p. 288, No. 76.

683a. My mother have a child. She so pretty it is a pity she live in the bush.—Watermelon.
Parsons, *Antilles*, III, 371, Grenada, 45.

683b. My mother has a pretty, pretty daughter, but the only thing she lives in the bush.—Watermelon.
Parsons, *Antilles*, III, 371, Grenada, 45 var.

684. My moder have a boy, lives far away from her home.—Fish.
Parsons, *Antilles*, III, 369, Grenada, 14.

685. Lives High in the Air

Although the notion of a person or animal living high in the air is scarcely definite or characteristic enough to make a satisfactory riddle, there are a few examples of its use. It is not surprising that examples are rare. Typical themes are:

§ 1. A bee. See No. 685.

§ 2. A spider. Spanish: Demófilo, 77; Rodríguez Marín, 438 (He lives high, dies high, on high weaves the weaver). New Mexican: Campa, 127.

§ 3. A bell. Spanish: Rodríguez Marín, 770. Chilean: Flores, 62.

685. Riddle me ree, / There's no man knows this riddle on to me. / There is a man livin' in de ear [air], comes back in de ear, eat his feed an' go back up. / An' no man can't hear me.—A wild bee.
Parsons, *Barbados*, p. 288, No. 75.

686–688. Sleeping

686. Me fader hab a lil bwoy sleep wid him every night; and every call him call him, de lil bwoy run.—Dog-flea.
Beckwith, *Jamaica*, p. 186, No. 30.

687. What is it sleeps all night with its finger in its eye?—Crook.
Green, *South Antrim*, p. 179, No. 9.

688. Sleeps Out at Night

Although the scene of a man sleeping out at night occurs in several riddles, it has never become very popular among riddlers. I note the English comparisons of an ax or a ladder to a man sleeping outdoors[1] and of a gallows to a man standing outdoors in windy weather.[2] The Dutch mill riddle, "Old, gray-haired, gray, it stands all night in the dew, it has neither flesh nor blood and is good for everyone,"[3] embellishes the fundamental theme with details from various sources. For other uses of the element "it is good for everyone" see the dishrag riddle.[4] A nail is compared to a man with his head outside.[5]

688. From house to house he goes, / A messenger small and slight, / And whether it rains or snows, / He sleeps out in the night.—Path.
Perkins, *New Orleans*, p. 107, No. 14.

689. Dirties Herself

Similar conceptions are found in the Irish "A tall, very fair woman dissolving in tears"[1] and the Rumanian "An old man whose nose is running.—Oil lamp."[2]

689a. Miss Nancy goin' to church, / All de way she goin' she droppin', droppin'.—Candle.
Parsons, *Antilles*, III, 369, Grenada, 3.

689b. My mother has a nice little girl. / As soon as she dressed her, she dirty all her dress.—Candle.
Parsons, *Antilles*, III, 372, Grenada, 55.

---

[1] Nos. 790a through 791.
[2] No. 804.
[3] Schrijnen, II, 106–107, No. 24.
[4] See the headnote to Nos. 1674–1680 below.
[5] No. 787.
[1] Delargy, 24.
[2] Papahagi, 50.

689c. My mother has a child, she always messin' herself.—Candle.
Parsons, *Antilles*, III, 372, Grenada, 55 var.

690–692. Several Activities

690. w^t m^r that be whose m^r is his man bound like a senclese foole is he with it nothing can be unlerned [be] yet he doth abound most proud w^n that j take him by the hand although j have him not, his maining [meaning] yet j understand though him j have for yet so wise is hee though words nor motions showing yet 1000 kings he tells ine [in] words worth the knowing.—a man reading in a booke.
Tupper, *Holme Riddles*, 68.

691. My fader sen' me fe [for] go pick out a woman fe me wife; those laugh will be the bes' fe tek; but those not, better left, fe they will kill me.—Ackee. This refers to the common warning that the fruit is safe to eat only after it has ripened and split in the sun.
Beckwith, *Jamaica*, p. 190, No. 68.

692. My father have a t'ing in him yard; when it sick it look up to heaven, when it get better it look down to the devil.—Bunch of bananas.
Beckwith, *Jamaica*, p. 184, No. 13.

693–724. Moving

693–694. Dances

693. Little Miss Nance tie up her frock and wheel round three times.—Turnstick in the pot.
Beckwith, *Jamaica*, p. 198, No. 130.

694. Little Miss Nancy like to dance and dance so rough.—Pepper.
Beckwith, *Jamaica*, p. 198, No. 131.

695–699. Goes about the House; Stands in the Corner

The scene of a person going about the house and then standing at rest in a corner is analogous to that of a dog running over the fields all day and coming home at night to lie under the table. The former scene usually has the answer "broom"; the latter scene, which I have already discussed at length,[1] has the answers "shoe" and "milk." Although the two conceptions are very similar, riddlers nevertheless keep them apart. I have noted no comparisons of milk or a shoe to a person and only rare instances of the comparison of a broom to a dog. For example, the Yakut "They say that a dog's tail lies near the doorstep"[2] belongs to this set of ideas but appears to be otherwise quite independent of the usual broom riddle. The hairs in the dog's tail represent the twigs in the broom.

---
[1] See the headnotes to Nos. 445–458 and 445–446.
[2] Piekarski, 401.

Some versions of the broom riddle are couched in dramatic terms. They often suggest a dog running about and a command given to it. See the Rumanian "*Ratsch* here, *ratsch* there, he remains behind";[3] the Mordvin "Mitya here, Mitya there, Mitya went under the bench";[4] the Modern Greek "Dash! here. Dash! there. Dash! under the bed";[5] the Turkish " 'Met!' I said. 'Met!' I said. 'Lie down behind the door!' I said";[6] and *"Pst!* here. *Pst!* behind the door";[7] and the Crimean Tatar "Here *pat,* there *pat,* go and lie down behind the door!"[8] In some of these texts the word representing the noise made by the broom is onomatopoetic; in other texts it is the name of the dog.

The comparisons to other animals than a dog are less appropriate, unless we are to think of a household in which pigs and cows run freely through the rooms. See the Lettish "A scratchy young pig runs through the room"[9] and the Yakut "They say that a shaggy, starved, two-year-old calf is found in the room as well as outside the house" or "They say that a two-year-old, short-tailed calf wanders near the house."[10] The Lettish "A little black cow licks the floor"[11] may have been suggested by riddles for the fire licking the pot.[12] Somewhat less obvious is the Yakut "They say that it has been gathered and joined and now there has arisen a two-year-old calf."[13] The age of the calf is chosen to suggest its size and to suit the length of the broom.

The comparison of a broom to a person offers some very excellent and instructive examples of riddling at its best. See the Swedish "It goes and goes and dances on the floor and stands at the door and is ashamed," which has the answer "shoebrush";[14] and the French "My mother has a little girl. Every morning she does a minuet,"[15] "My mother has a captain at the door"[16] (which suggests the figure of a soldier standing guard), and "Who runs through all the rooms without saying 'Good day' to her master?"[17] Other excellent examples are the Lettish "Grandmother in the corner with her head bound up," which could refer to the ordinary binding of a broom or to a cloth on the broom for brushing down cobwebs;[18] the Russian "Under the floor, under the middle, there stands a woman with a beard";[19] the Turkish "Uncle stands behind the door, respectfully folding his hands";[20] the Nandi "I have a

---

[3] Papahagi, 60.   [4] Paasonen, 174.
[5] Polites, *Neohellenika Analekta,* I, 226, No. 185.
[6] Kúnos, 133.
[7] Kúnos, 245; Hamizade, 646 (Whisk here, whisk there, whisk behind the door).
[8] Filonenko, 20.   [9] Bielenstein, 576.
[10] Piekarski, 399, 402.   [11] Bielenstein, 575.
[12] See below, No. 872 and the headnote to Nos. 871–877.
[13] Piekarski, 400.   [14] Sandén, *Norra Vadsbo,* 9.
[15] Parsons, *Antilles,* III, 449, Hayti, 33.   [16] Parsons, *Antilles,* III, 449, Hayti, 34.
[17] Constantin, *Savoie,* p. 20.
[18] Bielenstein, 580, 581. Compare the Crimean Tatar "Formerly I was a lady dressed in green. Having come here, I become a servant with my head bandaged" (Filonenko, 36).
[19] Arkhangel'skii, p. 77.   [20] Zavarin, *Brusa,* 37.

daughter who gets a good meal every morning, but she goes to bed hungry at night,"[21] which contrasts the abundance of dust and refuse swept up in the morning with the scanty amount found at night; the Bhil "A woman turns hither and thither when leaving the house,"[22] which describes sweeping the doorstep; and the Malayalam "The old one over there in the corner, do you know how I usually name her?"[23] The Annamese say, "There is an old woman in the house who likes to lick everywhere."[24]

Some riddles for a broom employ contrasts very ingeniously. I can cite no parallel to the Yakut "They say that in the house there is one who leaps, while in the barn there is a whirlwind,"[25] which has the answer "broom and shovel" and apparently refers to the shoveling of grain or earth as raising a whirlwind. The contrast of a busy housemaid and an idle lady appears in several Balkan texts. The Serbian "In the daytime a servant, at night a lady"[26] is virtually identical with the Modern Greek "At night an idle lady, in the daytime a housemaid."[27] The Serbian "In the daytime I am both the servant and the maid, and at night I am the grandest lady"[28] shows some elaboration of detail. With only a slight change this contrast is applicable to a stove: "In the winter a lady, in the summer a servant."[29]

Riddlers have enlarged upon the fundamental idea of comparing a broom to a person by adding elements that readily suggest themselves. A broom may be a person who cannot stand alone: "As long as you hold me, I'll stand up. But, when you let me go, I'll sleep,"[30] or a person who falls from a horse: "To this room it goes, to that room it goes, when thrown off, down it falls,"[31] which has a Bengali parallel in "From this room it goes to that room. It falls to the ground with little thuds."[32] Another variation is seen in the Birhor "A boy that begins rolling over the ground in the morning. Well, name it."[33] Many versions contain a dramatic element usually lacking in western European riddling; see, for example, "Jig a hall, jig a room; go a corner, go stan' up behin' de door"[34] and the texts quoted in the first paragraph of this headnote. The Modern Greek "It goes in and sweeps, it comes out and sleeps," with the answer "oven broom,"[35] introduces too definite a reference to the answer into the riddle.

The answer is occasionally "a stick," but this may signify a stick bearing leaves and used as a broom. Compare the Sart stick riddle, "It is always going by day, it stands in the corner at night,"[36] which, like the Mordvin

---

[21] Hollis, *Nandi*, p. 134, No. 7.   [22] Hedberg, p. 878, No. 83.
[23] Schmolck, p. 242, No. 19.   [24] Dumoutier, p. 205.
[25] Piekarski, 399.   [26] Novaković, p. 130, No. 7.
[27] Abbott, p. 313, No. 34, and p. 317, No. 42.
[28] Novaković, p. 130, No. 8.   [29] Novaković, p. 167, No. 1.
[30] Indian, Baiga: Elwin, p. 477, No. 130.   [31] Indian, Ho: Sarkar, p. 352, No. 11.
[32] Mitra, *Chittagong*, p. 346, No. 9. See also Mitra, *Notes on Ho Riddles*, pp. 108–109.
[33] Roy, *The Birhors*, p. 541.   [34] No. 696b below.
[35] Stathes, p. 343, No. 68.
[36] Ostrumov, 85, quoted by Jungbauer, p. 349. For references to a stick standing in a small space see the note to No. 258 in the present collection.

parallel, "One who goes back and forth and lies down to rest behind the door,"[37] may refer equally well to a cane or walking stick. Although the Kashmiri "I have a little girl, she wanders hither and thither, at night she sits down by my door"[38] has the answer "stick," it perhaps means a broom. These comparisons are almost the same as the Dard " 'Now listen! My sister walks in the daytime and at night stands behind the door.' "[39]

As I have already said, a few riddlers compare a broom to a dog. The German "Brown doggie goes about every day in the room and sniffs out every corner"[40] is an invention to which I can cite no parallel. The Serbian "I was looking for my Tuto, looking here, looking there; and I found my Tuto behind the door,"[41] with a close Bulgarian parallel in "Tuta here, Tuta there, and it never sits down. When it sits down, it does so behind the door,"[42] are clearly adaptations of the previously discussed comparisons to a person.

The comparison to a person who goes about and then goes to stand in a corner is applicable to:

§ 1. A broom. See Nos. 695a through 698 below.

§ 2. A gun. Lithuanian: Jurgelionis, 419 (A maiden dances around a cottage, and then again stands in a corner), and 634 (He stands in the corner as if swollen, he runs outside as fast as he can). African, Duala: Ebding, 9 (Some stand, others sit on the ground.—Gun and men). This refers to a gun fired from a rest.

§ 3. A candle. Serbian: Novaković, p. xxii, No. 2 (An old woman sits in the corner and does chores over the whole house).

§ 4. A spear. Indian, Baiga: Elwin, p. 470, No. 56 (It travels everywhere, but when it returns home, it takes no room at all).

§ 5. A staff, a cane. See No. 699 below and the remarks on the answer "stick," above in this headnote (nn. 36–38). Compare the headnote to No. 257.

§ 6. A shirt. Russian: Sadovnikov, 527 (It dances all day, it rests all night).

695a. 'Roun' the house and 'round the house / And into the corner it goes.— Broom.
Greenleaf, *Newfoundland*, p. 9, No. 1; Fauset, *Nova Scotia*, p. 161, No. 91 var.; Waugh, *Canada*, p. 68, No. 780; Tupper, *Holme Riddles*, 44 (stands behind the door); Burne, *Shropshire*, p. 574, No. 13.

695b. Goes around the house all day, / Stands in the corner all night.— Broom.
Brewster, *Indiana*, 17.

695c. Some t'ing goes round an' round the house an' stands in the corner.— Broom.
Parsons, *Antilles*, III, 433, Saba, 6.

---

[37] Paasonen, 51. [38] Knowles, 64.
[39] Leitner, *Indian Antiquary*, I (1872), 91, No. 2 = Leitner, p. 17.
[40] Frischbier, *Menschenwelt*, p. 253, No. 132.
[41] Novaković, p. xix, No. 7. [42] Gubov, 228.

695d. What goes all around the house and come back and set in a corner?—A broom.
Halpert, *New Jersey*, p. 202, No. 13.

695e. What goes roun' the house an' roun' the house an' lies in every corner?—Brush.
Green, *South Antrim*, 36.

695f. What goes round the house and round the house and lies at night in the corner?—Besom.
Praeger, *Béaloideas*, VIII (1938), 171, No. 4.

696a. Drill a hall, drill a·room; lean behind the door.—Broom.
Beckwith, *Jamaica*, p. 204, No. 191.

696b. Jig a hall, jig a room; go a corner, go stan' up behin' de door.—Broom.
Beckwith, *Jamaica*, p. 204, No. 191a.

697. Set in the corner at night, / Go all over the house in the day.—Broom.
Fauset, *Southern Negro*, p. 282, No. 65; Parsons, *See Islands, S.C.*, p. 168, No. 105; Parsons, *Aiken, S.C.*, p. 30, No. 39; Parsons, *Robeson Co., N.C.*, p. 390, No. 23; Parsons, *Bermuda*, p. 256, No. 70; Bacon and Parsons, *Virginia*, p. 312, No. 3 and varr.; Randolph and Spradley, *Ozark*, p. 88.

698. What work all day long, an' stay in the corner at night?—Broom-handle.
Bacon and Parsons, *Virginia*, p. 312, No. 3, var. 1.

699. I have a grandmother who walked all day and when she get home, took up no more space than could be covered by a penny.—Cane.
Oral, North Carolina.

700–707. Minor Varieties of Motion

700. I went to see / A great big tee / That followed me / To sea.—Sea-gull.
Parsons, *Bermuda*, p. 259, No. 109.

701. My moder have a boy, he don't want to see his moder leave him.—Sun and bay.
Parsons, *Antilles*, 370, Grenada, 24.

702. My moder have a boy, don't want to let him go at all, because if you let him go, he go away.—Answer lacking.
Parsons, *Antilles*, III, 372, Grenada, 58.

703. Lillylow, lillilow, set up on an end, / See little baby go out at town end.—Candle.
Halliwell-Phillipps, *Popular Rhymes*, p. 146; Knortz, p. 228, No. 71.

704. Jackatawad ran over the moor, / Never behind, but always before!—The *ignis fatuus*, or Will o' the Wisp. Jackatawad is a provincial term for this phenomenon.
Halliwell-Phillipps, *Popular Rhymes*, p. 146; Knortz, p. 229, No. 75.

705. What force or strength cannot get through, / I, with gentle touch, can do; / And many in the street could stand, / Were I not, as a friend, at hand. —A key.
Waugh, *Canada*, p. 71, No. 815.

706. From house to house he goes a messenger, small and straight. Who is that messenger?—Lane. Park.
Parsons, *Bermuda*, p. 260, No. 118.

707. Wee man o' leather / Gaed through the heather, / Through a rock, through a reel, / Through an auld spinning-wheel; / Through a sheep-shank bane; / Sic a man was never seen.—A beetle.
Chambers, *Scotland*, p. 112.

708–713. Motion and an Unrelated Act

708. I doe resemble many a weight [wight], / yet I keepe me out of their sight, / and do not once come where they be, / yet every day they may see me.—A bell towling to a sermon.
Prettie Riddles (1631), No. 78 = Brandl, p. 62.

709. Miss Nancy goin' to heaven / Wif a tray of bread [cake] she can't reach. —Coconut.
Parsons, *Antilles*, III, 369, Grenada, 4.

710. Every jump shiney jump, whitey hold it back.—Needle and thread.
Beckwith, *Jamaica*, p. 204, No. 193.

711. I went to town, I walk in town, I eat in town, and yet I don't know town.—A woman was breedin'. She went to town an' after she come home, the baby born, grew a big man, don' know town.
Beckwith, *Jamaica*, p. 193, No. 88.

712. Goes and Touches

Riddlers often use this notion to describe a door or a latch. The Turkish riddles for a brazier, "I have a bride, the comer embraces her, the goer embraces her,"[1] and a glass or cup, "I have a girl, the comer kisses her, the goer kisses her,"[2] are variations of the theme.

712a. Tom, Tom, Tittymouse, / Everybody comes and goes, / Plays on Tom, Tom, Tittymouse.—Latch on a door.
Fauset, *Nova Scotia*, p. 164, No. 109.

712b. Up upon Titty Mouse, / Down upon Titty Mouse, / All the folk of the house / Play upon Titty Mouse.—Latch of the door.
Kavanagh, *Béaloideas*, IV (1933–1934), 342.

712c. Tetchie in, tetchie out; all hands can play on it.—Lock and key.
Beckwith, *Jamaica*, p. 203, No. 189.

---

[1] Hamizade, 475.   [2] Hamizade, 56.

712d. Tickle me in, tickle me out; all hands can play on tickle.—Lock and key.
Beckwith, *Jamaica*, p. 203, No. 189a.

713. Walks and Opens Kerchief

713. My moder have a girl, she makes one step and then she opens her white kerchief.—That's the wave.
Parsons, *Antilles*, III, 369, Grenada, 12.

714–715. Motion Asserted and Contradicted

714. Sings and can't talk, / Runs and can't walk.—Spinning wheel.
Hudson, p. 88, No. 34.

715. I do walke, yet I do not goe; / I doe drinke, yet no thirst slacke; / I doe eate, yet do not feed; / I doe worke, yet no worke make.—It is a man who dreames; who in his dreame seemes to doe all these things, yet indeed doth none of them.
Prettie Riddles (1631), No. 47 = Brandl, p. 59.

716–724. Abnormal Motion

716. Makes No Track

The comparison of the sun to a vehicle is rare, but see the Mongolian "From behind the mountain the chariot rolls."[1] The notion of moving without making a track is often applied to a boat in water.[2]

716. Vineyard man walk through vineyard grass-piece and neither make track nor road.—Sun.
Beckwith, *Jamaica*, p. 195, No. 104.

717–718. Rides While Sitting (Walking)

717. An Indian man first time in town see a white man riding. A white man is lazy; he walks while he is sitting down.—White man was riding a bicycle.
Bacon and Parsons, *Virginia*, p. 320, No. 70.

718. A man riding and still walking.—Stick-horse [hobbyhorse].
Parsons, *Bahamas*, p. 478, No. 64.

719. Walks on Head

The second version is an interesting elaboration of a folk theme. It exhibits some similarity to the riddle for a path.[1] The hint of the answer given by the rhyme with "snail" is a device often found in literary riddles.

719a. A man going up to town; he walk on his head going up, he walk on his head going back.—Horseshoe-nail.
Beckwith, *Jamaica*, p. 194, No. 90.

---

[1] Bazarov, 7.   [2] See the headnote to No. 227 above.
[1] See No. 688 above.

719b. I walk all day through rain and snow; / I scuff through sleet and hail; / I sleep a-standing on my head, / And my name it rimes with *snail*.—Nail in a man's shoe.
Hudson, p. 88, No. 36.

720. Goes Downstairs, Not Upstairs

720. Ma Nancy come downstairs and she cyan' go back upstairs.—Leaf.
Parsons, *Antilles*, III, 373, Grenada, 64.

721. Goes Out in Spite of Locks

An even more vivid comparison of a fire to a person is employed in the Pangwe riddle, "She dances zealously by raising and lowering her shoulders, she dances slowly by swaying her body back and forth, this maiden of the Mpongwe."[1]

721. What is that which, after we have fastened, bolted, locked, barred the house, placed a watchman on guard, and taken the keys with us, yet, before morning, goes out in spite of us?—A fire in the grate.
Waugh, *Canada*, p. 71, No. 818.

722–724. Faces Backward While Moving

722. A man going to town and he face town, and when he coming back, he face down to Montego Bay.—Train running between Kingston and Montego Bay.
Beckwith, *Jamaica*, p. 193, No. 89.

723. I went to de town / And my face in town.—Moon.
Parsons, *Antilles*, III, 363, Trinidad, 3.

724a. Going up to town, my face turn to town; coming back from town, my face turn to town.—Climbing a tree.
Beckwith, *Jamaica*, p. 191, No. 74.

724b. When you go to town you face the town. / When you comin' from town you face the town.—Climbing a tree.
Parsons, *Antilles*, III, 375, St. Vincent, 2.

724c. I was goin' ter town, lookin' before; coming out of town, lookin' before.—Coconut tree.
Parsons, *Bahamas*, p. 485, No. 132.

724d. Sissy Sissy went to town, / Sissy sissy face down. / Sissy Sissy from town, / Sissy Sissy face down.—Climbing a coconut tree, face is up, climbing down, face is still up.
Parsons, *Antilles*, III, 372, Grenada, 50.

---

[1] Tessmann, 15.

725–731. Bearing, Carrying, Picking Up

725–728. Bears Burdens

725. I went in a bush, / I meet a man, / He tell me carry.—Crab.
Parsons, *Antilles*, III, 364, Trinidad, 18.

726. As I was going up Himple Dimple, / I looked down on dimples do, / I saw Jack with a pack on his back, / And so merrily did he go.—Fox with a goose.
Leather, *Hereford*, p. 231.

727. Carries House on Its Back

In the fifth century, Symphosius knew this idea as characteristic of a snail and wrote:

> Porto domum mecum, semper migrare parata,
> Mutatoque solo non sum miserabilis exul,
> Sed mihi concilium de caelo nascitur ipso.[1]

This Ohl translates: "I bear my house with me, always prepared to move, and when I have shifted ground, I am no wretched exile, but my wisdom is born of heaven itself." This hits the meaning exactly, although the last line has given the editors much trouble. Ohl rightly rejects a drastic emendation by Castalio. With two exceptions, the manuscripts read *concilium*, which is often confused with *consilium*. Whichever we choose, the line is readily understood by taking *nascitur* in the sense "owes its origin to, is derived from" and *mihi* as dative of benefit. Hence the line means, "But this wisdom [this skill of bearing my house with me] comes to me from heaven itself," because it is natural to a snail. A less frequent formulation of the idea is "What is the strongest animal?—The snail, because it bears its house."[2] A fable explains why the snail must carry its house.[3]

The notion of a man carrying his house on his back is applicable to:

§ 1. A snail. See No. 727.

§ 2. A turtle. Spanish, Chilean: Flores, 741. Indian, Uraon: Archer, p. 185, No. 96 (The man with his house on his back). Filipino: Starr, *Philippines*, 322 through 325.

§ 3. A crab. Indonesian, Sangir: Adriani, p. 395, No. 47 (A stone house that is carried about). Tabaru: Fortgens, p. 538, No. 86 (A youth bearing a house). Fijian: Fison, 11 (I enter a house and run away with it.—Hermit crab). Samoan: Heider, 113.

§ 4. A beetle. Danish: Kristensen, p. 114, § 312, Nos. 496a, 496b.

---

[1] Ohl, 18.
[2] French: Rolland, 76. Norwegian: Stafset, 258. See also Hesiod, *Works and Days*, v. 569.
[3] O. Dähnhardt, *Natursagen*, IV (Leipzig, 1912), 275, No. 7.

727. Who is hee that runneth through the hedge and his house on his backe?
—That is a Snaile, which wheresoever he goeth carryeth his house on his backe.

Meery Riddles (1629), No. 34 = Brandl, p. 14.

728. Bears a Heavy But Not a Light Burden

The formulation of this paradox varies widely. It is implied in the simplest form in "What is the strongest drink?—Water."[1] In the Argonne, it is stated as an alternative: "You who are so wise, how would you like to take a load of straw to Paris without shaking [it]?—I would as soon take a load of straw to Paris without shaking as eat a loaf of bread without chewing."[2] The riddler's answer signifies that he would find both tasks equally difficult or easy.

The idea of a person who cannot bear even a light burden is applicable to smoke in the French and Lettish "It can't bear a leaf"[3] or the French "As tall as a strawstack, she cannot carry a denier."[4] A grain of sand is described in an opposite way: "Smaller than a fly, it carries a church on its back."[5]

728. I tremble at each breath of air, / And yet can heaviest burdens bear.—Water.

Waugh, *Canada*, p. 69, No. 788.

729–731. Drop It; Can't Pick It Up

The scene of a person dropping something which he cannot pick up is applicable to various objects. His failure may inhere in himself[1] or in the object, which eludes the grasp.[2] The latter idea occurs again in riddles for snuff[3] and smoke or mist.[4] The objects described in this manner with special reference to the actor are:

§ 1. A cabbage palm or cabbage-nut tree. See No. 729.

§ 2. A bird and a feather. See Nos. 730a through 731.

§ 3. Spittle. Surinam: Herskovits, p. 449, Nos. 91 (A man is riding a horse. His pocket handkerchief falls down. When he steps down to take it, he does not see it any more.—Horse's spit), and 91a (A person was riding a bicycle. His hat fell down. That person climbed down to take his hat, but he did not find it any more). The comparison of spittle in white bubbles to a handkerchief is intelligible, but the comparison to a hat is less appropriate.

---

[1] Flemish: Joos, 653. Danish: Kristensen, p. 140, § 415, No. 656. Swedish: Ström, p. 218, "Vattnet," 9.
[2] Lallemant, *Argonne*, p. 230.
[3] French: Rolland, 154. Lettish: Bielenstein, 145.
[4] Dardy, *L'Albret*, p. 327.
[5] Swedish: Dybeck, *Runa*, 1850, p. 35, No. 19; Ericsson, *Södermanland*, III (1882), 101, No. 150; Ström, p. 229, "Sanden."

[1] See §§ 1–2 below.   [2] See §§ 3–5 below.
[3] See No. 1658.
[4] See Nos. 1643a through 1644b, 1651a through 1652c, and the headnote to Nos. 1643–1654, § 1.

§ 4. An egg. See Nos. 745a through 745c.

§ 5. Crepitus ventris. Breton: Duine, *Saint-Malo*, p. 516.

§ 6. A windmill. French: Parsons, *Antilles*, III, 415, Les Saintes, 45 (man loses cap, can't pick it up).

729. A man standin' all day with his hand in his pawket drop his cot [coat] an' he cyan't bend to pick it up.—Cabbage [palm] or cabbage-nut tree.
Parsons, *Barbados*, p. 279, No. 19.

730a. A black woman goin' along dropped her handkerchief and can't turn to pick it up.—Blackbird.
Parsons, *Barbados*, p. 279, No. 19 var.

730b. Miss Nancy was going to Kingston; she drop her pocket handkerchief never turn round to pick it up.—Bird drops a feather.
Beckwith, *Jamaica*, p. 197, No. 128.

730c. Miss Nance was going upstairs and she lose her pocket handkerchief and she would not turn round to pick it up.—Bird drops a feather.
Beckwith, *Jamaica*, p. 197, No. 128a.

730d. Queen of Sheba riding out; / Her kerchief drop and couldn't pick it up. —Bird drops a feather.
Beckwith, *Jamaica*, p. 197, No. 128b.

730e. Mr. Blackman was going to town; him drop him kerchief an' couldn't pick it up.—Crow drops a feather.
Beckwith, *Jamaica*, p. 197, No. 127.

731. My father ridin' away full speed to England. His hat fall, he never turn to pick it up.—When a bird is flying and one of the feathers drop.
Parsons, *Antilles*, III, 371, Grenada, 46.

732–749. Sitting, Standing

732. Round the house is a little red spot, there's where the lady squat.— Strawberry.
Parsons, *Antilles*, III, 446, St. Thomas, 20.

733. Wha' sit up on fo' block?—House.
Parsons, *Sea Islands, S.C.*, p. 171, No. 122.

734. Down she squat, / Out it come, / Up she jumped, / Home she run.— Girl milking a cow.
Randolph and Spradley, *Ozark*, p. 87.

735. Little Miss Nancy sit at the pass; everyone that come give him a kiss.— Fly.
Beckwith, *Jamaica*, p. 197, No. 129.

736. Half a 'tumpy sit down on 'tumpy; when a go, a don' see nothing but half a 'tumpy.—Broken bottle on stump.
Beckwith, *Jamaica*, p. 203, No. 187.

737. Sits at (Comes to) the (King's) Table

The conception of an uninvited person sitting at the king's table or coming to it is applicable to various themes. With its suggestion of freedom and even impudence, it is perhaps best suited to describe a fly. The oldest instance that I have noted is in Larivey's Renaissance translation of Straparola.[1] The conception serves as well to describe various articles of food and also sunlight. Examples are as follows:

§ 1. A fly. German: Frischbier, *Thierwelt*, p. 359, No. 108. Icelandic: Árnason, 1030 (A certain maiden jumped down upon the nose of Sir Aden. She did not know where to go; she jumped on the nose of Sir Snow. She did not know where to look; she jumped on the nose of Mr. Cook. Men tried to dust her coat; she jumped down the bishop's throat. And she's still there, I know't). Swedish: Ström, p. 114, "Flugan" (I am one of the king's most distinguished guests and eat his best dishes and sit down upon his nose and bite) French: V. S., *Mélusine*, I (1878), col. 263, No. 67 (A thing no bigger than a pea goes to drink in the king's cup). Portuguese: Braga, 58. Italian: Gianandrea, *Archivio*, I (1882), 559, No. 23; Gianandrea, *Canti popolari marchigiani*, p. 301, No. 27. Serbian: Novaković, p. 140, No. 3 (*Vrts! Trts!* and it lands on the tsar's head). Maltese: Stumme, *Malta*, 6 (It goes everywhere, even to the emperor's roof). African, Kanuri: Lukas, p. 172, No. 35 (A little thing that does not fear even the king). Gouro: Tauxier, *Côte d'Ivoire*, p. 315, No. 4 (I seated myself on my chair but someone has always taken his seat before me). Slave Coast: Trautmann, p. 102 (Who eats with the king and doesn't put his napkin in order?). Sukuma: Augustiny, 22 (He sits down on the chair before you do), 51 (Even if you hurry, you will not sit down before it on the chair). Wanamwezi: Dahl, 22. Indian, Baiga: Elwin, p. 467, No. 28 (A little brat that feeds with a king).

§ 2. Condiments. SALT. Spanish, Cuban: Sánchez, 1 (I ascend the table of the king). For a comparison of salt to something small that serves the king see No. 1262 in this collection. PEPPER. White Russian: Jurkevich, p. 293 (A small, black, little one is at the king's table). Russian: Sadovnikov, 497 (She is black, she is small, she ran around the entire field and had dinner at the tsar's).

The versions differ considerably and it is therefore probable that they are independent inventions. Compare the Catalan riddle for salt, "What is that: you are very white, madame, and you will be very white. There is neither a large nor a small festival where you are not present,"[2] with the Portuguese "I am neither fish nor fisherman. I run all around the islands and give savor to all the world"[3] or other texts cited in the Index of Solutions.

---

[1] Night V, Tale 4.
[2] Milá y Fontanals, 1876, p. 23, No. 6.
[3] Parsons, *Cape Verde*, 57b.

§ 3. Articles of food. WATERMELON. Portuguese: Parsons, *Cape Verde*, 5 (Mistress so slim gives birth to Mistress so fine, who goes to serve Sir King on his table in Portugal). LEMON. Indian, Gujerati: Mehta, p. 116, No. 2 (A yellow, yellow, ball-like thing rolled on and on to occupy the lap of the king. What's that?).

§ 4. Sunlight. Scotch Gaelic: Nicolson, p. 29 (It will enter the fire without burning, it will enter the chest without smothering, it will enter the sea without drowning, it will go to the king's table without hindrance).

737. Something sits to the table when you sit.—Swallow.
Parsons, *Bermuda*, p. 258, No. 100.

738–747. Humpty Dumpty

Riddlers often embellish with pertinent details the personification of an object as a person who falls and injures himself beyond hope of cure. Since the abundant English examples of this theme rarely admit incongruous materials, they show the nature of riddling when the fundamental concept is clearly maintained. Such riddling is almost extinct in English-speaking countries. The Humpty Dumpty riddle is one of the best instances in English of a truly vigorous and intelligent tradition.[1]

The comparison of an egg to a thing that, when broken, cannot be repaired is rather rare. Riddlers do not often compare objects in the same category: a thing is usually compared to a person or an animal and less usually to another thing. See, however, Norwegian: Bergh, *Valdres*, 13, 19; Stafset, 65 (cup). Icelandic: Árnason, 69 (The cup fell from the shelf and broke. No one came to Iceland who could repair the cup and yet it was a cup). French: Rolland, *Rimes*, p. 199, No. 14; Parsons, *Antilles*, III, 438, St. Martin, 49, and p. 448, Hayti, 13, 14. Serbian: Novaković, p. 75, No. 8 (A barrel fell from the attic. A hundred coopers came to repair it and could not). Hungarian: Kriza, 109 (I have a tub. When it falls from its shelf, there is no tinker in the world who would ever be able to put it back).[2] Quite different from this is the Hungarian "I have a lock that a blacksmith could not make. Even the black gypsies could not make it. The tinsmith could not make it either."[3] Another variation of the thing that cannot be repaired is the Ossete "A tower is broken to bits and cannot be set up again."[4]

Some ideas characteristic of the Humpty Dumpty riddle occur in other connections. The notion that the egg cannot be made or repaired appears in

---

[1] For parallels and discussion see Feilberg, *Ordbog*, IV, 1143–1144; Petsch, *Neue Beiträge*, pp. 76–77; Aarne, *Rätselforschungen*, I, 21, citing *Journal de la société finno-ougrienne*, XXXIV (1917), 64–89.
[2] This is very popular in Hungarian folklore; see *Magyar Nyelvör*, III (1874), 37 and 329; IV (1875), 320; V (1876), 127 (I have a little egg that no tinker could mend, if it fell from the attic), which carelessly includes the answer in the riddle; XII (1883), 426; XVI (1887), 87; XXVI (1897), 430; XXXI (1902), 532, No. 12.
[3] *Magyar Nyelvör*, IV (1875), 375.   [4] Schiefner, 14.

the Flemish riddle for thunder, "Holderdebolder ran over the storehouse. There is no carpenter who can make Holderdebolder."[5] The name Holderdebolder is used in Flemish versions of Humpty Dumpty. The notion of something that a carpenter cannot make occurs in the ice riddle.[6] The figure of a sitting man occurs in spoon and macaroni riddles.[7]

The conception of a man who falls and cannot be cured or put together again is applicable to:

§ 1. An egg. See Nos. 738 through 747b below. For comparisons to a torn gown that cannot be mended see Nos. 590 through 592 above.

§ 2. A bottle, a pot. Flemish: Joos, 210. Russian: Sadovnikov, 332 (The Cherekessian fell to pieces. No one would put him together, neither priests, nor deacons, nor rich men). Indian, Bengali: Mitra, *Chittagong*, p. 973, No. 22 (A receptacle made of bamboo upon another receptacle of bamboo;[8] the contents fall down. If the golden amulet gets broken, nobody can repair it).

§ 3. A splinter, a match. Russian: Sadovnikov, 179, 180 (I will take a cage apart. Even the tsar will not be able to put it together). A more picturesque version is "The drinking glass has fallen apart over all the cities. Nobody can put it together; neither the tsar nor the tsarina nor a handsome maiden, neither brother nor sister."[9] Zyrian: Wichmann, *Zyrian*, 20, 168, 169, 286. Votyak: Wichmann, *Votyak*, 156.

§ 4. Ice, an icicle. Irish: Christiansen, 8 (A bridge which no one can repair).[10] Swedish: Sandén, *Norra Vadsbo*, 71 (icicle).

738. Cannot Put Humpty Dumpty Together Again

738. Humpty Dumpty sat on a wall, / Humpty Dumpty had a great fall, / All the king's horses and all the king's men / Couldn't put Humpty Dumpty together again.—Egg.

Greenleaf, *Newfoundland*, p. 11, No. 25; Fauset, *Nova Scotia*, p. 163, No. 107 var.; Knortz, p. 214, No. 10; Hyatt, *Adams Co., Ill.*, pp. 660–661, No. 10863; Puckett, *Southern Negro*, p. 53; Parsons, *Aiken, S.C.*, p. 25, No. 4; Beckwith, *Jamaica*, p. 211, No. 230; Parsons, *Bermuda*, p. 254, No. 56. Humpy Dumpy: Parsons, *Antilles*, III, 376, St. Vincent, 15; Parsons, *Guilford Co., N.C.*, p. 206, No. 51 (fourscore men). Hamsie Dumphy: Bacon and Parsons, *Virginia*, p. 314, No. 23.

739. Cannot Put Humpty Dumpty Back Again (As He Was Before)

739a. Humpty Dumpty sat on a wall, / Humpty Dumpty had a great fall; / All the king's horses, all the king's men / Cannot put Humpty Dumpty back again.—An egg.

---

[5] Joos, 16.
[6] See below, § 4, the headnote to No. 794, and the riddles for bees cited in the headnote to Nos. 793–794.
[7] See the headnote to Nos. 412–413, § 3.
[8] For this theme see the headnotes to Nos. 1105–1106 and Nos. 1436–1447 below.
[9] Sadovnikov, 180b.
[10] Compare n. 6 above and No. 1670 below.

Wintemberg and Wintemberg, *Canada*, p. 123, No. 423; Halliwell-Phillipps, *Nursery Rhymes*, p. 113 = Lina Eckenstein, *Comparative Studies in Nursery Rhymes* (London, 1906; printing used was that of 1911), p. 105; Brewster, *Indiana*, 68; Fauset, *Southern Negro*, p. 282, No. 60; Parsons, *Aiken, S.C.*, p. 25, No. 4 var.; Parsons, *Barbados*, p. 282, No. 34. Could not put him up again: Parsons, *Sea Islands, S.C.*, p. 165, No. 74.

739b. Humpty Dumpty sat on a wall, / Humpty Dumpty had a great fall. / It took five hundred man to put / Humpty Dumpty back on de wall.—Egg.
Parsons, *Antilles*, III, 434, St. Bartholomew, 2.

739c. Humpy Dumpy sittin' on de wall, / Humpy Dumpy had a fall, / All de white king ladies / Tell what do Humpy Dumpy.—Egg.
Parsons, *Antilles*, III, 423, Antigua, 1.

739d. Roly-poly 'gin the wall, / Roly-poly had a great fall. / Ten score men and ten score more / Couldn't put the roly-poly back as it was before.—Egg.
Fauset, *Nova Scotia*, p. 163, No. 107 var.

739e. Humpty Dumpty sate on a wall, / Humpty Dumpty had a great fall; / Three score men and three score more / Cannot place Humpty Dumpty as he was before.—An egg.
Halliwell-Phillipps, *Nursery Rhymes*, p. 129; Harland and Wilkinson, *Lancashire Legends*, p. 187; *Gammer Gurton's Needle* (1810), p. 47 = Lina Eckenstein, *Comparative Studies in Nursery Rhymes* (London, 1906; printing used was that of 1911), p. 105.

739f. Hoity Doity sat on a wall, / Hoity Doity got a fall, / Not the strongest man in town / Couldn't put back Hoity Doity on the wall.—Egg.
Parsons, *Barbados*, p. 282, No. 34 var.

740–741. Cannot Stand

740. Humpty Dumpty sat on a wall, / Humpty Dumpty had a great fall, / All the doctors in the land / Couldn't make Humpty Dumpty stand.—Egg.
Fauset, *Nova Scotia*, p. 163, No. 107.

741. Humpty Dumpty sat on a wall, / Humpty Dumpty had a great fall, / All the doctors in the land / Couldn't make Humpty Dumpty stand.—Sunshine.
Fauset, *Nova Scotia*, p. 163, No. 107.

742. Cannot Be Cured

742a. Humpty Dumpty went to school, / Humpty Dumpty broke his back, / No doctor in this world / Could men [mend] poor Humpty Dumpty back.—Egg.
Parsons, *Bermuda*, p. 254, No. 56 var.

742b. Humpy Tumpy wen' to town one day, / He had a fall, / Broke his head, / An' all de doctors in de town couldn' cure it.—Egg.
Parsons, *Sea Islands, S.C.*, p. 165, No. 74, var 1.

742c. Dumpy Dumpy take a fall, / Dumpy Dump mash his face, / Not a doctor couldn' 'wange [arrange?] it.—Egg.
Parsons, *Antilles*, III, 398, Dominica, 121.

742d. Humpty Dumpty had a fall. / No man could cure Humpty Dumpty.—Egg.
  Parsons, *Sea Islands, S.C.*, p. 165, No. 74, var. 2.

742e. Humpy Dumpy on the wall, / Humpy Dumpy had a fall, / All the doctor in the world could not cure Humpy Dumpy.—Fowl egg.
  Parsons, *Eleuthera and Watling's Islands, Bahamas*, p. 440, No. 13.

742f. Me riddle me riddle me yandio, / Perhaps you can tell me this riddle. / Perhaps you can't. / Humpy Dumpy on the wall, / Humpy Dumpy had a fall, / All the doctor in the world / Couldn't cure Humpy Dumpy's fall.—Fowl eggs.
  Parsons, *Eleuthera and Watling's Islands, Bahamas*, p. 440, No. 17.

743–744. Cannot Mend, Fix, Put to Rights

743a. Humpty Dumpty lay in a beck, / With all his sinews round his neck; / Forty doctors and forty wrights / Couldn't put Humpty Dumpty to rights!—An egg.
  Halliwell-Phillipps, *Nursery Rhymes*, 122. Lina Eckenstein, *Comparative Studies in Nursery Rhymes* (London, 1906; printing used was dated 1911), p. 105, cites the same riddle from an edition of Halliwell-Phillipps, *Nursery Rhymes*, printed in 1846, p. 209. This edition I have not seen.

743b. Ma riddle ma racket, / Perhaps you might tell me dis riddle, / Perhaps not. / Humpee Dumpee wen' to town, / Humpee Dumpee sit on a wall, / Humpee Dumpee bus' he gall. / Not a doctah, not a seams'ess, / Could not men' Humpee Dumpee gall.—Egg.
  Parsons, *Antilles*, III, 431, St. Kitts, 14.

744. Humpy on a wall / Humpy Bumpy got a fall / Ten men, ten more / Can't fix Humpy Bumpy / The way she was before.—Egg.
  Carter, *Mountain White*, p. 79.

745. Cannot Pick Up Humpy Dumpy

745a. Humpy Dumpy sat on a wall / Humpy Dumpy had a great fall / All de king's horses an' all de king's men / Could not pick up Humpy Dumpy again.—Egg.
  Parsons, *Antilles*, III, 421, Montserrat, 10.

745b. Humpity Trumpity fell on de flo'. / No man can't pick / Humpity Trumpity up.—Aigg.
  Parsons, *Aiken, S.C.*, p. 25, No. 4, var. 2.

745c. Humpity Dumpity sat on a wall, / Humpity Dumpity got a great fall, / The king wi' a' his men / Cudna lift Humpity Dumpity again.—An egg.
  Gregor, *Northeast Scotland*, p. 78.

746–747. Miscellaneous and Corrupt Versions

746. Humpy dumpy dead an' he never run.—Me broke a bottle an' t'row it away an' it never run.
Parsons, *Bahamas*, p. 483, No. 115.

747a. Humpty Dumpty had a great fall, / Humpty Dumpty fell on de wall.
—Egg.
Parsons, *Aiken, S.C.*, p. 25, No. 4, var. 1.

747b. Humpy Dumpy sat on a wall, / Humpy Dumpy had a great fall.—
Answer lacking.
Parsons, *Antilles*, III, 443, St. Croix, 11.

748–749. Hickamore, Hackamore

The notion of a person or thing which cannot be driven or dragged from the spot where it is found is applicable to a few phenomena of nature. English riddlers have personified the object as Hickamore Hackamore. The name or names may be intended to suggest the flickering sunbeam. Substitute names are occasionally taken from such contexts as the nursery rhyme "Hickery Dickery Dock, the mouse ran up the clock'"[1] or the nettle and the wasp riddles,[2] which yield such names as Hitchity hitchity and Hitty Kitty.[3]

Objects described in this manner are:

§ 1. Sunshine, a sunbeam, sunlight. See Nos. 748a through 748g. One version replaces personification by comparison to a thing.[4]

§ 2. A cloud. See No. 749.

§ 3. Smoke. German: Frischbier, *Menschenwelt*, p. 251, No. 98 (There is something in our house, a hundred horses can't pull it out).[5]

§ 4. A spool of thread. Swiss: Zahler, *Münchenbuchsee*, 79 (There is something as small as a mouse, and seven horses can't pull it up a mountain).[6]

748a. Hick-a-more, Hack-a-more, / On the king's kitchen-door; / All the king's horses / And all the king's men / Couldn't drive Hick-a-more, Hack-a-more / Off the king's kitchen-door!—Sunshine.
Halliwell-Phillipps, *Nursery Rhymes*, p. 120; Parsons, *Barbados*, p. 282, No. 33; Knortz, p. 224, No. 56; Bacon and Parsons, *Virginia*, p. 316, No. 40; Parsons, *Aiken, S.C.*, p. 29, No. 26; Fauset, *Southern Negro*, p. 282, No. 59; Fauset, *Philadelphia*, p. 553, No. 7.
Sunlight. Randolph and Spradley, *Ozark*, p. 84; Hyatt, *Adams Co., Ill.*, p. 668, No. 10920; Brewster, *Indiana*, 66.
Hicky More, Hocky More: Perkins, *New Orleans*, p. 108, No. 21. Hicky mo, lacky mo: Parsons, *Sea Islands, S.C.*, p. 161, No. 52. Heckhore or Hickory-kor: Parsons, *Bermuda*,

---
[1] See a variant of No. 748a.
[2] Nos. 338a through 338d, 341 through 342c.
[3] Nos. 748b, 748f, and a variant of 748a.
[4] See Nos. 1659a through 1659c and the headnote to No. 1659.
[5] See also Nos. 1268a, 1268b below.
[6] See also No. 1341 below and the headnote.

p. 254, No. 57. Hickery Dockery: Parsons, *Barbados*, p. 282, No. 33 var. Hitchity, hitchity: Beckwith, *Jamaica*, p. 212, No. 235.

748b. Ma riddle ma riddle / I'll tell you dis riddle / I don't know whether you know it or not / Hitty Kitty on de king kitchen door / Neither de king or his soldiers / Could take Hitty Kitty aff of de king kitchen door.—Sun.
Parsons, *Antilles*, III, 444–445, St. Croix, 27.

748c. Hicky-more, hacky-more / Hangs over the kitchen door. / Nothing so bright and nothing so fair / As hicky-more, hacky-more / Hangs over the kitchen door.—The sun.
Fauset, *Nova Scotia*, p. 164, No. 110.

748d. Hick-a-more, Hack-a-more / Hung on a kitchen door; / Nothing so long, and nothing so strong, / As Hick-a-more, Hack-a-more / Hung on the kitchen door.—Sunbeam.
Halliwell-Phillipps, *Nursery Rhymes*, p. 207 = Lina Eckenstein, *Comparative Studies in Nursery Rhymes* (London, 1906; printing used was that of 1911), p. 113; Carter, *Mountain White*, p. 79.

748e. Hick more, Hack more / Hanging over the kitchen door. / There is nothing more higher / Than Hick more, Hack more.—Sun.
Parsons, *Aiken, S.C.*, p. 29, No. 26, var. 2.

748f. Hitchy-hitchy hanging high, / Over the kitchen door.—Sun.
Fauset, *Southern Negro*, p. 281, No. 50.

748g. Hickamor hackamor / Hangin' over the kitchen do'. What is hickamor hackamor?—Sun.
Parsons, *Aiken, S.C.*, p. 29, No. 26, var. Hicky, hacky, more: Redfield, *Tennessee*, p. 36, No. 12. Hicky, hangy mo: Parsons, *Sea Islands, S.C.*, p. 161, No. 52, var. 1.

749. Hickamore, 'ackamore / Sits over th' kitchen-door; / Nothing so long and nothing so strong / As Hickamore, 'ackamore / Sits over th' kitchen-door.—A cloud.
Gutch and Peacock, *Lincolnshire*, p. 398, No. 10.

750–767. Talking

This theme is very frequently used for the noise of the sea or of a waterfall. The existence of an Ainu parallel, "What is that which goes crying as the river flows by?—Foam,"[1] is noteworthy.

750. I know a man; every talk he talk his mouth-corner foam.—Sea.
Beckwith, *Jamaica*, p. 195, No. 105a.

751–754. Talks (Sings) Constantly

The Portuguese find a similarity between the beating of the surf against the shore and a washerwoman: "She beats by day, she beats by night, and she

---

[1] Starr, *Ainu*, 66, which is now translated and annotated in Archer Taylor, "Ainu Riddles," *Western Folklore*, VI (1947), 166, No. 39.

does not tire."¹ This has a curious resemblance to an Irish mythical figure which foretells disaster.² Another variety of this conception occurs in the Icelandic waterfall riddle: "A certain man runs forever without leaving his seat. He has neither mouth, voice, nor throat, but roars so loud that it is heard far and wide."³ According to other riddlers the sea is insatiable.⁴

The notion of men constantly talking also serves to describe tools or acts requiring coöperation.⁵ The Filipinos say that a clock is constantly talking: "Day and night I cry."⁶

751a. I know a man talk every second.—Sea.
Beckwith, *Jamaica*, p. 195, No. 105.

751b. Mother have a boy, quarrel all day long.—Sea water.
Parsons, *Antilles*, III, 369, Grenada, 9.

752. My moder have a boy, bawl every hour in the day and six o'clock in the night.—Donkey.
Parsons, *Antilles*, III, 370, Grenada, 23.

753. My moder have a boy, all talky talk, but you can't see him.—Wind.
Parsons, *Antilles*, III, 370, Grenada, 27.

754. What sings morning, noon, and night, / And when the fire's out, shuts up tight?—Teakettle.
Hyatt, *Adams Co., Ill.*, p. 668, No. 10921.

755. Long Black Fellow Bellows

The obvious comparison of a gun to a man speaking or bellowing occurs in various forms. Some riddlers refer only to the sound; others mention accessory details. See Icelandic: Árnason, 14 (I often separate body from soul, although I have neither. My thundering voice splits the rocks and shakes the ground.—Gunpowder). Rumanian: Papahagi, 88 (The long thin woman has no voice and thunders in crying out). Mordvin: Paasonen, 106 (A crooked-breasted woman, a slant-breasted woman. Whomever she curses, dies). Albanian: Hahn, p. 158, No. 12. Modern Greek: Polites, *Neohellenika Analekta*, I, 207, No. 82 (An empty road with an ogre playing inside); Stathes, p. 342, No. 62 (Hollow body, ogre's voice). Abyssinian: Mittwoch, 5 (When it kills, it makes a noise). Indian, Uraon: Archer, p. 180, No. 18 (A ghost speaks from a piece of dry wood). Indonesian, Tabaru: Fortgens, 67 (An ugly Papuan girl who speaks as soon as her mouth is touched). Fijian: Fison, p. 408, No. 19 (There is a chief

---

¹ Parsons, *Cape Verde*, 256.
² Gertrude Schoepperle, "The Washer of the Ford," *Journal of English and Germanic Philology*, XVIII (1919), 60–66.
³ Árnason, 993. See also his No. 548 quoted in the note to No. 131 above.
⁴ See No. 238.
⁵ See Nos. 964, 960, and compare the use of quarreling discussed in the headnote to Nos. 966–968.
⁶ Starr, *Philippines*, 87.

who only speaks, and fowls and pigs and men fall down before him). A few riddlers refer to the distance over which the voice is heard; see Modern Greek: Stathes, p. 342, No. 64 (Tall, tall monk, with a far-reaching voice). African, Evhe: F. Müller, p. 157, No. 17 (A man weeps at Mono River, they hear it in the house).

More unusual conceptions of speaking, bellowing, and related ideas appear in the Turkish "Its voice crushes a mountain, but if you take it in your hands, it is only a handful";[1] the Bakongo "The *ndoki*[2] who killed the child remained with his mouth open";[3] and the Songaï "The old woman sneezes; her bowels shake."[4]

Comparisons to the noise of an animal are numerous and varied.[5] For a survey of riddles for a gun or bullet see the headnote to No. 801 below.

755a. Long big black fellow, / Pull the trigger, make it bellow.—*Bang!*—Gun.
Perkins, *New Orleans*, p. 107, No. 16.

755b. Long slick black feller, / Pull his tail an' make him beller.—Shotgun.
Parsons, *Guilford Co., N.C.*, p. 202, No. 18.

755c. Long stick, / Black feller, / Pull his cock, / And hear him beller.—Gun.
Bacon and Parsons, *Virginia*, p. 319, No. 55.

755d. What is a / long slim black feller? / When you pull his cock, / oh how it'll beller.—It's a gun.
Halpert, *New Jersey*, p. 201, No. 6.

755e. Long, tall, / Black feller, / Pull him back / An' hear him bellow.—Gun.
Parsons, *Aiken, S.C.*, p. 36, No. 80.

755f. Long, slim, black fellow, / Pull the cock and he will bellow.—A shotgun.
Redfield, *Tennessee*, p. 39, No. 44; Hyatt, *Adams Co., Ill.*, p. 662, No. 10874.

755g. Great long slick fellow / Spring his trigger and hear him bellow.—A gun.
Farr, *Tennessee*, p. 322, No. 64.

755h. Long, slim, and black, / Touch its cock and it will crack.—A gun.
Farr, *Tennessee*, p. 325, No. 106.

755i. Long, black, slick feller, / Turn 'im loose an' make 'im beller.—Gun.
Hudson, p. 87, No. 27.

756–759. Greets

Riddles making reference to the exchange of greetings usually involve reference to more than one person, and therefore the parallels to No. 759 below will be found in the note to Nos. 830 through 832c and in the note to Nos. 834a,

---

[1] Katanov in Radlov, IX, 285, No. 198. [2] Man who throws lots.
[3] Denis, 45. [4] Hamouda, 4.
[5] See above, Nos. 436, 439a, 439b, and the headnotes to Nos. 436 and 438–444.

834b. The three other riddles in this section seem to be quite independent inventions. The notion of comparing a stalk of sugar cane to a man bowing (No. 756) is analogous to the versions discussed in the headnote to Nos. 946–950 below. The reference to the rings in a rattlesnake's tail (Nos. 757a through 757d) offers no point of interest. The import of the drum riddle (No. 758) is obscure.

756. I was walkin' in de road I met a man / I bowed to him an' he bowed to me.—Cane staff [green leaves].
Parsons, *Antilles*, III, 445, St. Croix, 28.

757a. Once I was goin' to London, / I met an ol' man. / I ask him his age. / He hol' up his walkin'-stick, / An' said, "Look in my stick, / You will see my age."—Rattlesnake.
Parsons, *Sea Islands, S.C.*, p. 164, No. 69.

757b. Ah met a man, an' ax him his age. He tell me to look at his walkin'-stick.—Dat's a rattlesnake, his age on his tail.
Parsons, *Sea Islands, S.C.*, p. 164, No. 69, var. 1.

757c. Said, one day I walk, I met an ol' man. I asked him how ol' he was. Said look at de en' of his walkin'-cane.—Rattlesnake.
Parsons, *Sea Islands, S.C.*, p. 164, No. 69, var. 2.

757d. I meet a man, ax his name. He tell me look his walkin' rod.—Rattlesnake.
Johnson, *St. Helena Island, S.C.*, p. 158, No. 26.

758. Kiss me asleep, / Kiss me awake, / Kiss me for dear Willie's sake.—A man and a woman beating a drum.
Parsons, *Bermuda*, p. 261, No. 119.

759. I was going up to town one morning, met a man; I tell him "Mawnin' " and he wouldn't speak to me, and when I was coming back early in the evening, he speak to me.—Trash, noiseless to the tread when cold, crackles when warmed by the sun.
Beckwith, *Jamaica*, p. 191, No. 75.

760. Not a Man and Yet Speaks

The personification in riddles for a book varies greatly in degree. The Breton and Spanish versions, which employ the characteristic Romance device of a series of assertions and contradictions, will illustrate the different grades of personification: "I am not a tree and yet I bear leaves. I do not speak and yet I give advice. Girls and women carry me. I pierce their hearts more deeply than their necks.—A book";[1] "I am not an animal, yet I bear the skin of an animal. I am not a man, yet I talk. I am not a tree, yet I have leaves.—A

---

[1] Milin, *Batz*, p. 55.

bound book";[2] "It has leaves, but is not a tree. It has skin, but is not an animal.—A book."[3]

The riddle comparing a letter to a mute or otherwise abnormal messenger has some similarity to this conception. See Welsh: Hull and Taylor, 22, 23. Welsh Gypsy: Sampson, 37 (What travels through the land and has neither flesh nor blood?).[4] Irish: Christiansen, 18a (Black Blackson, without veins, without blood, comes hither over the sea telling a tale), 18b, 18c, 19 (He is black and he is white and he brings news to the men of Ireland); Delargy, 31 (A veinless, bloodless, little, black manikin [coming] across a hill from the East, relating his tale); O Dalaigh, 105. Breton: Charlec, *Dol-de-Bretagne*, 1903, p. 395. Flemish: Joos, 142, 889. German: Wossidlo, 362 (can talk and yet has no mind). Icelandic: Árnason, 209. Danish: Kristensen, pp. 18–19, § 28, Nos. 33b through 33e. Norwegian: Bugge, *Telemarken*, 109 (What is that which has neither life nor soul and can both speak and answer?); Qvigstad, note to No. 4. Swedish: Dybeck, *Runa*, 1847, p. 41, No. 14 (Has neither body nor soul, but can speak and answer); Ericsson, *Södermanland*, I (1879), 93, No. 64 (a lifeless messenger), and III (1882), 98, No. 132 (an elaborate literary version); Waltman, *Lidmål*, 174 (It travels over land and strand, Norway and Sweden, and when it gets to its destination, it talks like an informed man), and, with the answer "newspaper," 170; Sandén, *Norra Vadsbo*, 58 (Goes over both water and land, talks as well as answers, says never a word.—Letter); Ström, p. 189, "Brevet." Latin: Daly and Suchier, p. 72, and p. 143, Nos. 108, 109 (Quid est tacitus nuntius? Quem manu teneo. Quid tenes manu?—Epistulam tuum, magister) and the notes, p. 45; Buchler, *Gnomologia*, 3d ed. (1614), p. 487 (Femina circumfert infantes rite loquentes, / Sint mutuae quamvis, per loca quaequae volant); Pincier, *Ænigmatum libri tres* (The Hague, 1655), pp. 135–137, Book II, No. 19 (Destituor pedibus, vox est mihi nulla: remotos / Ire tamen cogor, dictaque ferre locos). French: Rolland, 251, 252; Bladé, *Armagnac*, 19; Lespy, *Béarn*, 4 (White as the snow, black as the chimney, it talks without a tongue, it laughs and weeps without mouth or eyes). Catalan: Pelay y Briz, 194. Spanish: Demófilo, 249; Rodríguez Marín, 783. Argentinian: Lehmann-Nitsche, 153. Chilean: Flores, 167, 401. New Mexican: Campa, 54. Italian: Casetti and Imbriani, *Canti popolari delle province meridionali* (Turin, 1872), II, 74, No. 13e; Salvioni, *Archivio*, IV (1885), 550, No. 86; Cimegotto, *ibid.*, XIII (1894), 435, No. 18 (No tongue or feet, yet talks and walks). Lettish: Bielenstein, 228 (speaks without a tongue). Czech: Hanika-Otto, p. 121, No. 21 (A messenger runs without feet, a scamp with four horns, he never tells anything, yet he gives it all away). It should be noted that the word

---

[2] Orain, *Ille-et-Vilaine*, p. 152.   [3] Demófilo, 608; Rodríguez Marín, 782.
[4] For parallels see the headnote to Nos. 264–265, § 13, above.

for "horns" may also be translated "corners." Mordvin: Paasonen, 266. Votyak: Buch, 40. Arabic: Giacobetti, 422 (She has come, she has traveled and has broken her fetters. Eyes look at her, and the mouth inquires), 423 (Deaf and dumb, she tells the news). African, Wolof: Seidel, p. 309 (Who teaches without talking?—Book). Persian: Mann, II, 170, No. 7 (It has neither hands nor feet, it brings news everywhere). Yakut: Piekarski, 237 (They say that there is that which has no tongue but [yet] speaks of everything). Indonesian, Javanese: Ranneft, *Poëzie*, p. 88, No. 4 (He goes everywhere, although he is blind, deaf, and dumb. When anyone who is clever sees him, such a person needs only to look at him to understand him).

Some versions differ considerably from the general idea common to the preceding texts. The Scotch Gaelic "She is whiter than mountain cotton, whiter than shirt or linen, more marked with little spots than starling's breast, and she will drink as she gets"[5] and the Portuguese "It sucks up, it drips, it speaks from here to another land"[6] are examples of such versions. The Icelandic "I know a bright maiden, who often travels between friends and is very reserved. But when she has lost her virginity, she tells news to the one who has ravished her"[7] is an unusually elaborate personification. The French "White as the snow, black as the chimney, it talks without a tongue, it laughs and weeps with neither mouth nor eyes"[8] contains comparisons for the colors ordinarily found in other uses. The contrast of the dead and the living occasionally appears in riddles for a letter.[9]

A few versions of the letter riddle involve a comparison to an animal. The Lithuanians say, "A mottled heifer goes all over the world."[10] A comparison to a bird, of which a trace may perhaps be seen in the preceding riddle, is more widely known. See the Basque "A painted bird that enters the house and without saying anything discharges its duty";[11] the Lithuanian "A blind pigeon flies through all the world" and "A little mottled bird flew all around the world";[12] the Spanish "A little black and white dove flies without wings, talks without a tongue,"[13] which has the notion of a wingless bird in common with a riddle for a snowflake;[14] the Arabic "My gray chick arrives at the sea and returns to me,"[15] which is not entirely clear; the Turkish "A happy bird comes, it pleases by speaking";[16] and the Yakut "The voice of the raven from the Land of the South [Russia] can be heard in this land.—Telegram."[17]

---

[5] Nicolson, p. 57.
[6] Parsons, *Cape Verde*, 176.
[7] Árnason, 1111.
[8] Lespy, *Béarn*, 4.
[9] See the headnote to Nos. 830–834 below.
[10] Jurgelionis, 691, 692. Lettish: Bielenstein, 227.
[11] Cerquand, 47.
[12] Jurgelionis, 692, 694.
[13] Rodríguez Marín, 796; Demófilo, 253.
[14] See above, Nos. 367 through 369 and the headnote to Nos. 367–369.
[15] Giacobetti, 425.
[16] Hamizade, 484.
[17] Piekarski, 239.

Comparisons of a letter to a thing are rare, except for the scene of chips that are hewn in one country and fly to another.[18]

760. I'm foolish, and still not foolish. / I'm covered all over with dark spots. / No principal or teacher, / I can make every one in the world talk without saying a single word.—Book.
Fauset, *Nova Scotia*, p. 163, No. 103.

761–764. Varieties of Talking or Roaring

761. He laugh plain and talk plain, but haven't any life.—Talking-machine.
Beckwith, *Jamaica*, p. 196, No. 112.

762a. Arthur O'Bower has broken his hand, / He comes roaring up the land; / The King of Scots, with all his power, / Cannot turn Arthur of the Bower!—A storm of wind.
Halliwell-Phillipps, *Nursery Rhymes*, p. 123 = Knortz, p. 226, No. 62 = Parsons, *Bermuda*, p. 261, No. 122. Broken his band: Hyatt, *Adams Co., Ill.*, p. 671, No. 10947.

762b. Old Father Boris [Boreas], he came to my door, / He came with a dash and a rush and a roar, / He whooped and he howled and he made a great din, / And at last the old fellow popped in.—North wind.
Hudson, p. 90, No. 46.

763. My father stay here and he grumble all over the world, hear him.—Thunder.
Parsons, *Antilles*, III, 370, Grenada, 34.

764. There is somet'in' right over de water hollerin' for it an' kyan't get it.—A bell 'roun' de cow's neck.
Parsons, *Sea Islands, S.C.*, p. 171, No. 121.

765–767. Can't Talk

765. Here's a t'ing. / Knockin' up to de sea night an' day, / An' none could talk to each oder.—Sea and rock.
Parsons, *Andros Island, Bahamas*, p. 275, No. 7.

766. My moder have a boy, put him in the yard, cyan't talk.—Dog.
Parsons, *Antilles*, III, 370, Grenada, 22.

767. My moder have a boy, work him so severe, but he can't talk.—Horse.
Parsons, *Antilles*, III, 369, Grenada, 18.

768–769. Weeping and Laughing

The contrast of weeping and laughing or of speaking and keeping silent occurs in the descriptions of such objects as a bucket[1] or a strap.[2] The scenes vary so widely that many of the versions have probably been invented independently.

---

[18] See the headnote to No. 1605, § 3, below.
[1] Nos. 768a, 768b.
[2] Nos. 769a through 769d.

The Votyak bucket riddle, "Going, she clasps her hands; returning, she weeps"[3] is very different from its French equivalent, "Who goes all dancing and then returns all weeping?"[4] or the Wanamwezi "It goes with *Hui!* and comes back very quietly."[5] Similar conceptions occur in widely separated places. The Tatars in the Caucasus say for a chain, "If it enters the water, it becomes mute; when it comes out of the water, it begins talking,"[6] and the Kxatla describe a scoop for water rattling in a bucket as "Tell me: little ram bleat, but when you see the river, keep quiet," which also has the answer "sandals."[7] The Kamba conceive a calabash in similar terms, but refer to a human rather than an animal actor: "Tell me: the man who, when you walk, cries for help."[8] An Omaha riddle which Professor Robert H. Lowie has pointed out to me is interesting as a probable borrowing from the French, with whom they were in contact. The Omaha kettle riddle, "A person having gone to the water and having looked at it is coming back weeping,"[9] has close parallels in French riddling, from which the Omahas may have borrowed it.

The contrast of weeping and laughing or of speaking and keeping silent is applicable to:

§ 1. A bucket. See Nos. 768a, 768b below.

§ 2. A window. Russian: Sadovnikov, 70 (In the house, who weeps and who laughs?). This refers to water running down the warm pane.

§ 3. A drum. Indian, Uraon: Archer, p. 189, No. 152 (Put down silent, picked up noisy).

§ 4. A strap. See Nos. 769a through 769d below.

§ 5. A mill. Icelandic: Árnason, 901 (I tell you of a little lady who begins to sing when she is full). Filipino: Starr, *Philippines*, 376. See also No. 231 above.

768a. Something gone down laughin' an' comin' up cryin'.—Bucket.
Parsons, *Antilles*, III, 436, St. Martin, 16.

768b. Me riddle me racket, / Perhaps you may know dis, / Perhaps you may not. / Dey have somet'ing go down laughing, / Come up croyin' [crying].—Bucket.
Parsons, *Antilles*, III, 431, St. Eustatius 1.

769a. Something going up laughing and coming down crying.—Strap.
Parsons, *Antilles*, III, 443, St. Croix, 10.

769b. Ma riddle ma racket, / I tell you dis story / An' I goin' to tell you once more. / Something go up in de air laughin' and come down cryin'.—Strap.
Parsons, *Antilles*, III, 430, St. Kitts, 1.

---

[3] Wichmann, *Votyak*, 401. [4] Ledieu, *Démuin*, p. 136.
[5] Dahl, 40.
[6] Kalashev and Ioakimov, p. 66, No. 2.
[7] Schapera, 110. Squeaking sandals become silent when wet.
[8] Lindblom, 7.
[9] J. O. Dorsey, "Omaha Sociology," *Report of the Bureau of American Ethnology*, III, (1884), 334.

769c. Dere is something go up laughin' and come down cryin'.—De strap dat moders use.
Parsons, *Antilles*, III, 443, St. Croix, 10 var.

769d. Some t'ing goin' up laughin' an' comin' down ballin' [bawling].—Lakes [licks]—chappin' [strapping] somebody and beatin' somebody.
Parsons, *Antilles*, III, 443, St. Croix, 10 var.

770–781. Eating, Spitting

770. l[e]arning doth feed me yet j know no letter j have lived among books yet am never the better j have eaten up the muses yet j know not a verse what student that is j pray y^u rehearse.—a worme bred in a booke.
Tupper, *Holme Riddles*, 13.

771. Me fader hab a man an' he kyan' stan' up till him belly full.—Bag.
Beckwith, *Jamaica*, p. 186, No. 27.

772. I had a son. As fast as he eat, he bring it back.—Plane.
Parsons, *Antilles*, III, 438, Anguilla, 1.

773–775. Eats Own (Mother's) Flesh

English riddlers rarely employ this old and widely known pattern, but the variations in their answers and the wide distribution of the few existing texts show that it was once much better known.

773. Who is he which eates his mother in his grandam's belly?—It is the worme in a nut; for of the kernell of the nut commeth the worme. Therefore the kernell is here taken for the mother of the worme, and of the shell the kernell commeth, and therefore the shell is here taken for the mother of the kernell and the grandam of the worme.
Meery Riddles (1629), No. 33 = Brandl, p. 14.

774a. The lad that eats his own flesh and drinks his own blood.—A candle.
Dempster, *Sutherlandshire*, p. 236.

774b. Who drinks his own blood and eats his own flesh?—A burning lamp.
Greenleaf, *Newfoundland*, p. 11, No. 28.

774c. I consume my mother that bare me, / I eat my nurse that fed me, / then I dye leaving all blinde that saw me.—Meant of a flame of a candle, which having consumed both waxe and weeke [wick] goeth out leaving them in the dark that saw by it.
Meery Riddles (1629), No. 75 = Brandl, p. 21.

775. I eate my nurse that feeds mee full, / consume my mother that beares me still, / and I am such an unthankfull wight, / that when I die and loosse my sight, / I make all blind that doe delight.—The sunne.
Prettie Riddles (1631), No. 67 = Brandl, p. 61.

776–777. Insatiability

The notion of insatiability is equally applicable to a fire and a mill and may be conceived in animal or human terms.[1] Comparisons to an animal have the added advantage of permitting the riddler to suggest appropriate noises in elaborating the scene. The Icelandic "What three things may be called insatiable?—Fire of fuel, a harlot of lust, and Hell of the pains of the damned,"[2] contains no truly enigmatic element.

Comparisons of a mill to a person vary greatly in details. A Russian riddler contents himself with the simple contrast, "She feeds all the world, she herself does not eat."[3] In describing a saw driven by water, the Finns introduce several figures: "One brings [it] up with a hook, another drags [it] up with a sled, and yet the eater is never satisfied."[4] More highly individualized versions are a Swedish comparison to an old fool[5] and comparisons to a woman singing.[6]

776. Bonny Kitty Brannie, she stand at the wa', / Gie her little, gie her muckle, she licks up a'; / Gie her stanes, she'll eat them,—but water, she'll dee: / Come tell this bonny riddleum to me.—The fire.
Chambers, *Scotland*, p. 109.

777. My father had a son, the more he eat the more he want.—Mill.
Parsons, *Bahamas*, p. 478, No. 69.

778. Cries When Fed

778a. Me father have a black servant and when he feed her, she bawl.—Frying-pan.
Beckwith, *Jamaica*, p. 186, No. 28.

778b. Although I feed the child, still it cry.—Frying fish in de pan.
Parsons, *Barbados*, p. 286, No. 58.

778c. The more I feed thee, the more thee cry.—Frying-pan.
Parsons, *Barbados*, p. 286, No. 58 var.

778d. I have a little sister, the more you feed her, the more she cries.—Frying-pan.
Parsons, *Barbados*, p. 286, No. 58 var.

779–780. Does Not Eat

779. On the water I will lay, / I will neither drink nor cast away, / Water make stomach swell.—Jug.
Parsons, *Sea Islands, S.C.*, p. 160, No. 50 and var.

---

[1] See the headnote to Nos. 236–239.
[2] Árnason, 697.
[3] Sadovnikov, 1071a.
[4] Lönnrot, 534 = Henssen, 132.
[5] Ström, p. 176, "Väderkvarnen."
[6] See the headnote to Nos. 768–769, § 5, above.

780a. My fader had a son twenty years / An' never eat a meal of victuals.—Clock.
Parsons, *Andros Island, Bahamas*, p. 275, No. 8.

780b. Pippety-poppety sits in my pocket, / It neither eat corn nor hay. / Up jumps the pedlar, swore he would mettle her, / And stole my wee poppet away.—Watch.
Praeger, *Béaloideas*, IV (1933–1934), 145, No. 18.

781. Spitting

The obvious comparison of a gun to a man spitting occurs in various forms, which do not seem to be derived from a single source. See Icelandic: Árnason, 879 (The tall giantess, swelling with eloquence, has many knuckles. She causes harm, talks famously, and spits grains from her mouth). White Russian: Wasilewski, 7 (Hard Martin spits far). Votyak: Wichmann, *Votyak*, 165 (The old Russian crone spits far). Albanian: Pedersen, 9 (One who eats something black and spits out something red), which employs the much-favored contrast of red and black.[1] Arabic: Stumme, *Tázerwalt*, II (It is satiated and in the district of the Ḥáḥa it belches). Crimean Tatar: Filonenko, 52 (I spit from here; it has hit the opposite side).[2] Yakut: Piekarski, 304 (There is a daredevil who cannot spit forth of his own free will, so they say); Priklonskii, 75.

The brass cap and wooden head of this English riddle may have been suggested by a pot riddle.[3]

781. Brass cap and wooden head, / Spits fire and spews lead.—Gun.
Gutch and Peacock, *Lincolnshire*, p. 399, No. 19.

782. Deafness

Folk riddlers rarely use the notion of deafness. The few examples that I have noted are literary rather than traditional in appearance.[1]

782. Deafe I am, and cannot heare, / and when I worke I feele no paine. / Some doe curse me, some speake me faire, / though well I know it is in vaine.—Dice and dicers.
Prettie Riddles (1631), No. 41 = Brandl, p. 58.

783–798. Working, Practicing a Trade or Profession

783. My father had a plantation / Little below damnation. / An' he work de finny, / An' he work de finny.—Plantation.
Parsons, *Barbados*, p. 287, No. 65.

---

[1] See the headnote to Nos. 871–877 below.
[2] This scene is often applied to thunder and lightning; see the headnote to No. 398 above.
[3] See Nos. 558a through 558e above.

[1] See, for example, the Flemish pen riddle (Joos, 331).

784. Works without Perspiring

This notion is also applicable to a gun; see the Turkish "There is a little blue dog that never sweats."[1] It is also used of the sky, "The horse *kyokketey* never sweats, but runs across the whole,"[2] and of the earth, "Even if it travels round all the land, it will not sweat."[3] The contrary notion is applicable to a window: "They say that there is that which perspires daily.—Frosted window."[4]

784. Mother have a boy, work all day long, never perspire.—Corn meal [corn mill].
Parsons, *Antilles*, III, 369, Grenada, 10.

785–786. Works All Day; Lies in Dirt at Night

This description of a fire seems to have been more popular in former days; modern instances are not numerous. It suggests an animal or a person, probably the latter.

The conception is also applicable to a bellows, as in the Turkish "It has no soul, but it breathes; night and day it lies in the ashes."[1] Something similar is seen in the well-conceived Parsee fire riddle: "What is that thing which is burned in the ground [at night] and turned into bars of gold the next morning?"[2] Still another conception is the French "One dresses it in the evening, one undresses it in the morning,"[3] which has an enigmatic effect because the events are just the opposite of the events of ordinary life.

785. w^t is that as works al day & lies in his own [MS: one] dung al night?—egge or Ashes.
Tupper, *Holme Riddles*, 40. The second answer is a later addition.

786. What is that that shineth bright all day, and at night is raked up in it[s] owne dirt?—That is the fire; that burneth bright all the day, and at night is raked up in his ashes.
Meery Riddles (1629), No. 4 = Brandl, p. 8.

787. Worker Keeps Head Outside

This scene, which is ordinarily applied to the description of a nail, occurs also with mention of several actors.[1] Comparisons of this sort to animals are rare, but see the Turkish nail riddle, "On the roof of the house there is a chicken with a fuzzy head."[2]

787. A man work for rich and work for poor and yet have his head outside.—Nail-head.
Beckwith, *Jamaica*, p. 195, No. 101.

---

[1] Katanov in Radlov, IX, 291, No. 244.   [2] Katanov in Radlov, IX, 239, No. 54.
[3] Katanov in Radlov, IX, 286, No. 208.   [4] Yakut: Piekarski, 268; Priklonskii, 41.
[1] Kúnos, 277.   [2] Munshi, 1.
[3] Lespy, *Béarn*, 8. See another version in the headnote to No. 587, n. 7, above.
[1] See No. 917.   [2] Kúnos, 88.

788–792. Carpenter

788–789. Cutting (Sawing) Wood

Riddlers find the scene of cutting or sawing wood applicable to various objects. It is characteristically used in combination with the contradiction, "and no chips fly," in describing a clock or the act of rowing.[1] The comparison of a woodpecker to a man cutting wood is so obvious as to lack interest. Money is called chips that fly about.[2]

The important uses of the scene of cutting wood by riddlers are for:

§ 1. A clock. See Nos. 789a, 789b.

§ 2. The eyelids. Faeroic: Hammershaimb, *Antiquarisk tidsskrift*, III (1849–1851), 317–318, No. 25 = *Færøsk anthologi*, I, 323, No. 20 (He hews all day, but there are no chips afterwards). Norwegian: Bugge, *Telemarken*, 43 (What is it that chops all day and does not get out a chip?); Landstad, p. 811, No. 38; Stafset, 41; Brox, *Ytre Senja*, 64. Swedish: Dybeck, *Runa*, 1848, p. 47, No. 64. Lappish: Friis, 5. Gypsy: Wlislocki, 6 (It hews constantly, but hews no chips). See also the headnote to Nos. 1665–1666, § 3, below.

788. Miss D. June cutting wood for a year, never get a bundle.—Woodpecker.
Beckwith, *Jamaica*, p. 198, No. 132.

789a. My father was in Green Island cutting chip and the chip never fly.—Clock.
Beckwith, *Jamaica*, p. 191, No. 72.

789b. Two sawyers were sawing from morning till night and never saw a bit of dust.—Clock.
Beckwith, *Jamaica*, p. 194, No. 97.

790–792. Builds a House

790a. A man walk around four corners of the world and make a house; rain come catch him a door [out of doors], dew fall on him, sun burn him, and he have no shelter of his own.—Ladder.
Beckwith, *Jamaica*, p. 195, No. 99.

790b. A man build a fine up-stairs house, and he have to sleep outside.—Ladder.
Beckwith, *Jamaica*, p. 195, No. 99a.

791. A man mek him house an' him sleep outside.—Axe.
Beckwith, *Jamaica*, p. 195, No. 100.

792. There was an old man that live never building house till rain come.—John Crow. As soon as rain come, he begin to cut posts, say he will build him a house. When sun comes out, he come to dry himself, never build house any more.
Beckwith, *Jamaica*, p. 195, No. 102.

---

[1] See the note to No. 227.   [2] See the note to No. 1605.

793–794. Smith

The comparison of a bee at its work to an artificer of unparalleled skill is both a riddle and a proverb. Aldhelm knew the idea when he wrote "Atque carens manibus fabrorum vinco metalla,"[1] and a proverb calls the bee "The little smith of Nottingham, who doeth the work no man can."[2] A cock is said to wear clothing beyond any tailor's skill to fashion: "There came a man from England, who had beautiful clothes. They were not spun, they were not bound, they were not woven, they were not sewn."[3] These ideas are akin to the Russian description of filling a chink in a wall: "I shall patch a patch with neither needle nor thread."[4]

793. I have a smith without a hand, / he workes the worke that no man can. / He serves our God, and doth man ease / without any fire in his furnace.— It is a bee that makes hony and waxe.
Prettie Riddles (1631), No. 64 = Brandl, pp. 60–61.

794. Locking a Gate without Using Iron or Steel

A similar conception appears in the comparison of ice to a bridge that a carpenter cannot make or to a bridge that is built of materials that a carpenter cannot use. See Irish: Christiansen, 10. German: Frischbier, *Menschenwelt*, p. 259, No. 186 (It is a bridge that no man has made, it is not of stone and not of wood and yet can carry men and horses). Italian: Tammi, 24 (A bridge without stones). Lithuanian: Jurgelionis, 123 (Without an ax, without a hatchet, without a drill, without a small drill, without wood, without little wood, a bridge was built). White Russian: Wasilewski, 3 (Without an ax, without a wedge, I shall build a bridge on the river). Russian: Sadovnikov, 1490 (A bridge is being bridged with no boards, ax, or wedge), 1989 (Samson himself paved the bridge, without an ax, without a wedge, without a spike.— Frost). Serbian: Novaković, p. 113, No. 5 (There is a bridge on the water without a single piece of wood). Mordvin: Paasonen, 101. Indian, Kashmiri: Knowles, 132 (O spring of the goose, the goose made its way to you; the carpenter cut it, no potter formed it; but you of yourself became hardened).

See also the riddles making a comparison to a bridge that cannot be repaired.[1]

794. Hicky-picky locked the gate, / Hicky-picky locked it weel, / Hicky-picky locked the gate / Without iron or steel.—Frost.
Praeger, *Béaloideas*, VIII (1938), 171, No. 3.

---

[1] Riddle 20, ed. Pitman, pp. 12–13.
[2] J. M. Kemble, *The Dialogue of Salomon and Saturnus* (London, 1848), p. 243; H. G. Bohn, *Handbook of Proverbs* (London, 1855), p. 218; H. L. Apperson, *English Proverbs* (London, 1929), p. 455.
[3] Swedish: Waltman, *Lidmål*, 234.
[4] Sadovnikov, 30. See also the headnote to No. 1212, n. 5, below.

[1] See the headnote to Nos. 738–747, § 4, above.

795. Weaver

795. I was tying mat ever since an' I never lay down on one.—Pumpkin-vine.
   Beckwith, *Jamaica*, p. 196, No. 115.

796. Shoemaker

The original form of the riddle is best preserved in Nos. 796b and 796c, which have been taken down in the last twenty years. Curiously enough, the oldest version, No. 796a, which was printed more than three centuries ago, omits the fundamental idea of the four elements.

796a. There dwels a shoemaker neere the hall / That makes his shoes without a nawle; / though men of them doe not were, / yet they of them have many a paire.—It is a smith which maketh shooes for horses.
   Prettie Riddles (1631), No. 83 = Brandl, p. 63.

796b. Watchmaker [what maker] makes shoes without leather, / Fire, water, earth, and aire. / Every custom[er] has two pair.—Horse shoes.
   Parsons, *Bermuda*, p. 254, No. 58 var.

796c. What shoemaker makes shoes without leather, / With all four elements put together? / Fire and water, earth and air; / Ev'ry customer has two pair. —A horseshoer.
   Halliwell-Phillipps, *Nursery Rhymes*, p. 126; Knortz, p. 220, No. 37; Hyatt, *Adams Co., Ill.*, p. 662, No. 10878.

796d. I was walking down the street and I saw a man making shoes without leather.—Horse shoe.
   Parsons, *Bermuda*, p. 254, No. 53.

797–798. Professions

797. Woman have a chile an' just begin l'arning [i.e., teaching] him fe t'ief.— Hawk.
   Beckwith, *Jamaica*, p. 196, No. 119.

798. Man Rules the World

Parallels to this conception are very rare. I can cite only the Wamajame "A single king in the land.—Moon."[1] The Pangwe "A youth stands in a father's village square, everyone sees him.—Moon"[2] contains, according the collector Tessmann, an allusion to God in the word "father's," but the African predilection for such introductory phrases as "My father gave me . . ." makes this explanation improbable.

798. My fader had one son an' he ruled de whole worl'.—Dat's de sun.
   Parsons, *Bahamas*, p. 473, No. 17.

---

[1] Ovir, 2.   [2] Tessmann, 6.

799–822. Shooting, Wounding, Killing, Dying

799. I wound the heart and please the eie, / tell me what I am by and by.—Beauty.
Prettie Riddles (1631), No. 10 = Brandl, pp. 53–54.

800. I think I will shoot God, and God say I mus' shoot the earth.—Banana shoot.
Beckwith, *Jamaica*, p. 196, No. 114.

801–819. Killing

801. Small; It Kills a Man

Riddles describing a bullet afford very interesting and instructive examples of enigmatic inventions. Although we might expect riddles for an arrow to be adapted to a bullet, there seem to be very few instances of such a development. Since the many riddles for a bullet do not agree in the use of any single theme, we may infer that they are comparatively recent inventions made independently in various places.

Typical themes used to describe a bullet or gun are:

§ 1. Small, but (usually) powerful. See No. 801. Compare "What [thing] that is never seen goes through the bush?—A shot from a gun."[1] See further, "Small as aniseseed, all the world knows it but no one can reach it";[2] "Smaller than birds, stronger than beasts";[3] "It is as big as a hornet, it drives horses from the battlefield or bumps the horses into sleep";[4] and "Smaller than a walnut, stronger than a man."[5] The contrast of something small that proves to be surprisingly strong occurs in several widely separated cultures and may be a theme which has been disseminated from a single invention. The contrast is quite in good enigmatic style. I can cite no parallel to the Icelandic gun riddle: "Who is the slim one with many handles that draws to itself a small grain of dust and also tastes small buttons? I think she wreaks harm. Guess her name."[6] Compare also the description of a bridge as being more terrifying the smaller it is, in Nos. 1703a, 1703b below.

§ 2. A bird. See Nos. 379a through 380 and the headnote to Nos. 379–380 above.

§ 3. An animal. See Nos. 436 and 438 through 440 and the discussion in the headnotes to Nos. 436, 387, n. 7, and 398, § 3.

§ 4. A man (woman) and child. Lithuanian: Schleicher, p. 199 = Jurgelionis, 645 (A hollowed-out crone bears mad children); Schleicher, p. 199 (A rotten, hollow linden bears mad children). Yakut: Piekarski, 298 (The child

---

[1] Welsh: Hull and Taylor, 49. Compare, in the present collection, No. 1630 and the corresponding note.
[2] Spanish, Argentinian: Lehmann-Nitsche, 579.
[3] Finnish: Lönnrot, 1314 = Henssen, 116. [4] Arabic: Bauer, p. 223, No. 3.
[5] Ossete: Schiefner, 49. [6] Árnason, 617.

is running away, while the mother remained behind to neigh), 300 (A mother neighed while her squealing child became playful). African, Tschuana: Kuhn, *Tschuana*, 18 (The mother screamed, the child came out and escaped). Lesotho: Franz, p. 155 (A man who, when he speaks, his children run away). Kxatla: Schapera, 121 (Tell me: his mother coughed, the child came out and ran away.—Rifle). Hausa: Harris, 20 (The harlot has beautified herself, but the men are running away.—Bow and arrows). Kundu: Ittmann, *Kundu*, 22 (Members of the secret society crowded about the door of the clubhouse), 219 (I sent off the children, but they did not return), which is akin to the versions cited in § 6 below. Indonesian, Malay: Klinkert, 54 (Mother is quiet, the children look for food). Javanese: Ranneft, *Proza*, p. 9, No. 42 (One holds the mother in his lap, and one speaks in friendly manner to her; the children are seeking food) and p. 14, No. 65; Ranneft, *Poëzie*, p. 49, No. 9 (The jewel of ladies sleeps without interruption and lies stretched out full length in bed. She never speaks; it seems she is dead. During her whole life she has no husband, and the jewel of perfumes is pregnant now and again. When she brings a child into the world, it flies away like the wind and destroys him whom it strikes. Tabaru: Fortgens, 84 (The mother is always giving commands, the child is always running.—Bow and arrow).

The Estonian "It eats fire and drinks blood"[7] is conceived in terms of a single person.

§ 5. A messenger. Welsh: Hull and Taylor, 49. Scotch Gaelic: Nicolson, p. 59 (It will go across the river, it will come across the river, it will cut the grass and will not eat it). Serbian: Novaković, p. 65, Nos. 3 (An iron youngster swishes through the forest, nobody saw him), 4 (A young man passed through the forest, nobody saw him). Hungarian: *Magyar Nyelvör*, V (1876), 88 (It goes over the mountain; it goes fast; it carries iron but is not a smith; it crawls into a hole but is not an insect). Albanian: Pedersen, 4 (One who goes away and never looks back). Turkish: Kowalski, *North Bulgaria*, 57 (I said to the yellow one, "Smoke!" It closed up and went into the forest). Georgian: Blechsteiner, p. 15, No. 30. Surinam: Herskovits, p. 443, No. 59 (You were the first to go, and yet I overtook you when I lit one firestick). African, Kundu: Ittmann, *Kundu*, 220 (I sent a child on its travels, it brought nothing back, in spite of that it did not tell me what it had seen on its journey). The Vogul "The iron ran through the birch" (Ahlqvist, *Vogul*, 3) is probably a corrupt version of a riddle akin to the first Serbian text above.

§ 6. One who goes and does not return. White Russian: Wasilewski, 113 (I'll send a messenger for a dear guest. Whether the guest is there or not, the messenger will not return). Turkish: Katanov in Radlov, IX, 104, No. 889 (I have one son and he has remained in the mountain). Indian, Khāṛiā: Roy and Roy, II, 448, No. 21 (Has been able to go, but not to return.—Arrow).

---

[7] Wiedemann, p. 290.

Kolarian: Wagner, 83 (A man can go out, but he cannot return.—Arrow, also, word). Uraon: Archer, p. 189, No. 163 (Go it can but come it cannot.—Arrow).

The idea of going and not returning in this use is very old, for Symphosius, who wrote in the fifth or sixth century A.D., used it in describing an arrow: "Bound round with heavy iron, up with feathers light encircled, through the air's midst I speed in winged flight, and when sent I return, though no one sends me back."[8] Here a return is mentioned, but it is not normal in nature.

§ 7. Spitting. See No. 781 above. For leaving entrails behind see Nos. 1266a, 1266b.

§ 8. Speaking, bellowing. See Nos. 755a through 755i. For comparisons to the noises of animals see the headnote to No. 755, n. 5.

§ 9. Miscellaneous activities. Icelandic: Árnason, 165 (comparison to giving birth). French: Parsons, *Antilles*, III, 384, Martinique, 60 (man leads a dog). Yakut: Piekarski, 301 (They say that an old man feeds on fire and air.—Gun). Indonesian, Engganee: Helfrich, *Engganee*, p. 519, No. 19 (breaking wind).

§ 10. Comparisons to things. Mordvin: Paasonen, 343 (I have a granary, it is full of deadly plants). Turkish: Kúnos, 99 (A deep well, its water *dsumbul*, whoever drinks it, dies; whoever does not drink it, lives). The meaning of *dsumbul* is obscure. Ossete: Schiefner, 50 (Harder than a stone, livelier than a horse). Mongolian: Zhamtsaranov, 22 (A little ball, a little stone, swifter than a horse).

801. Through the woods, through the woods I ran, / And as little as I am, I killed a man. What is it?—A bullet.
Perkins, *New Orleans*, p. 108, No. 20.

802–804. Kills Many People

The rare riddles for death have no common themes. The "Mr. Debt" of the Jamaican text is probably "Mr. Det'," i.e., death. The Elizabethan riddle is not fully intelligible. A different conception of death is seen in the Irish "Yonder he is through the stream, a man without a coat, a man without a belt, a man of hard slender legs, it is my woe that I cannot run."[1]

802. And smart as little Tommie be, one man kill the whole world.—Mr. Debt.
Beckwith, *Jamaica*, p. 196, No. 118.

803. Little boy bunting / sate on the house easing [sic], / with a bow and a bolt / slayeth the king and all his folke.—This is Death which slaieth Kings, princes, dukes, earles, gentlemen, and every living creature.
Meery Riddles (1629), No. 14 = Brandl, p. 10.

---
[8] Ohl, 65.
[1] De Bhaldraithe, 21.

804. Kills Thieves

804. Here I stand in windy weather. / Chief and justice is my name, / I am the death of many a thief.—A gallows.
Fauset, *Nova Scotia*, p. 158, No. 71.

805–818. Killing (Wounding), Eating, and Throwing Away Refuse

The scene of killing, eating, and throwing away refuse is applicable to any object of which part is used and part discarded. The two very popular English riddles of this sort have as answers a bottle of liquor[1] and a fruit or coconut.[2] The comparison to an animal may be illustrated by the Mordvin hemp riddle: "One wears the hide, one throws away the flesh, one eats the bones."[3] The comparison to a man may be illustrated by the many fruit riddles below. In some texts the riddler makes a comparison to a thing, usually a bag or a pot, and cannot use the idea of killing that is appropriate to the comparisons to a man or an animal. Examples are the Xhosa riddle for the entrails of a sheep. After having been cleaned, these are eaten by the Xhosa. The text is: "I buy a bag of meal, I throw away the meal and eat the bag."[4] The Turkish riddle for marrow in a bone is well conceived: "He took out the gold and threw away the box."[5] Other riddles of this sort are the Serbian descriptions of a pomegranate, "I carried a bag full of wheat;[6] I ate up the bag, and I threw away the wheat,"[7] and a plum, "I ate up the pot and threw away a thing out of the pot."[8] An Albanian entrails riddle is similar to the Xhosa text; it is "The kettle is eaten, the food is not eaten."[9] An African turtle riddle describes an actual event as "We killed an animal, ate the inside, and threw away the skin."[10] See finally the Serbian wax riddle: "I cooked meat; I threw the meat away; and I kept the broth."[11]

805. Take Off His Head; Drink His Blood: A Bottle

English riddlers show a great liking for the personification of a bottle as a person whose head is chopped off, whose blood is drunk, and whose body is left standing.[1] Although this excellent conception is in the best enigmatic style, it has surprisingly few parallels in the tradition of western Europe or in

---

[1] See Nos. 805a through 805r, 805t through 805w, and the headnote to No. 805.
[2] Nos. 806a through 813.
[3] Paasonen, 90. Compare the headnote to Nos. 806–815, § 1, below.
[4] R. Godfrey, "Kafir Riddles," *Blythswood Review*, IV (1927), as quoted in Schapera, *Kxatla*, 68 note. See also Tschuana: Kuhn, *Tschuana*, 6.
[5] Katanov in Radlov, IX, 43, No. 1162.
[6] Compare the headnote to No. 1355 below.
[7] Novaković, p. 242, No. 5.   [8] Novaković, p. 242, No. 6.
[9] Hahn, p. 163, No. 79.   [10] Ila: Smith and Dale, II, 328, No. 30.
[11] Novaković, p. 23, No. 2.

[1] The reference to leaving the body standing recalls the exposure of bodies after an execution. See a somewhat different Spanish conception of a bottle: Demófilo, 150, 618. Argentinian: Lehmann-Nitsche, 417. Chilean: Flores, 108. Dominican Rep.: Andrade, 65. Porto Rican: Mason, 484.

the more abundant and picturesque lore further east. An Italian riddler compares wine to blood,[2] but does not elaborate on the theme. The lack of parallels to the answer "bottle" leads me to infer that the original answer was a fruit.[3] The comparison of a bottle to a rabbit[4] that is treated in this way is a casual alteration of the theme.

805a. As I leukit our ma father's castle, / I saw a bodie stanin; / I took aff's head and drank's bleed, / And left's body stanin.—A bottle.
Gregor, *Northeast Scotland*, p. 76.

805b. As I went along the river, / A met a man. / I chopped off his head, / I drank his blood.—A bottle of rum.
Parsons, *Bermuda*, p. 245, No. 3, var. 2.

805c. As I gaed our the Brig o' Dee, / I met Geordie Bychan; / I took aff his head an drank his bleed, / An left his body stan'in.—A bottle of whiskey.
Gregor, *Northeast Scotland*, p. 77.

805d. When I was goin' 'cross London Bridge, / I met an old man on de way. / I brek his neck an' drank his blood, / An' t'rew his body away.—Bottle o' liquor.
Smiley, *Virginia, etc.*, p. 375, No. 6. Bottle of pop: Fauset, *Philadelphia*, p. 556, No. 36.

805e. Oncet I was goin' a-walkin', / I met ol' Mawlie on de way. / I break his neck an' suck his blood, / An' leave his body dere.—Foun' a bottle of whiskey on de way, break his neck, drunk de whiskey, an' leave de bottle right dere.
Parsons, *Sea Islands, S.C.*, p. 160, No. 46, var. 7.

805f. Once I was goin' to London, / I met somebody standin', / Cut his throat an' suck his blood, / An' leave his body standin'.—A jug of whiskey.
Parsons, *Sea Islands, S.C.*, p. 160, No. 46, var. 5.

805g. I went down the road, I met a man. I cut off his head and dranked his blood. What's that.—A man with a bottle of whiskey.
Parsons, *Sea Islands, S.C.*, p. 160, No. 46, var. 6.

805h. As I was walkin' down th' road / I met up with my very best friend, / I pulled off his head an' drinked his blood / And left his body stand!—A bottle of whiskey.
Randolph and Spradley, *Ozark*, p. 85.

805i. Round the rick and round the rick, / And there I met my Uncle Dick, / I picked him up, and sucked his blood, / And let his body stand.—A bottle of beer left near a rick.
Parker, *Oxfordshire*, p. 331. I cut off his head, and drunk his blood. Bottle of cider: Leather, *Hereford*, p. 232.

---

[2] Pitrè, 78.
[3] See the headnote to Nos. 806–815 below.
[4] No. 388 above.

805j. As I was going up London Bridge, / I met my brother John. / I chopped off his head and drank his blood / And let his body stan'.—Bottle of wine.
Greenleaf, *Newfoundland*, p. 9, No. 10.

805k. As I went over London Bridge, / I met old dirty Jay. / I cut his throat, and sucked his blood, / And throwed his heart away.—Bottle of whiskey.
Fauset, *Southern Negro*, p. 278, No. 25.

805l. As I was goin' over London Bridge, / I met my brother Will, / I cut off his head an' sucked his blood, / And threw his body away.—Bottle of whiskey.
Fauset, *Southern Negro*, p. 278, No. 26.

805m. Once I was walking along I meet a man a standin', I cut 'e t'roat an' suck 'e blood an' leave 'im still a-standin'.—Bottle o' soda water.
Johnson, *St. Helena Island, S.C.*, p. 158, No. 16.

805n. Around the rick, around the rick, / And there I found my uncle Dick! / I screwed his neck, I sucked his blood, / And left his body lying. / What was it?—A bottle of wine.
Sayce, *Montgomeryshire*, p. 18.

805o. As I was going over London Bridge, / I saw two men a-hanging, / I ate their flesh, and drunk their blood, / And left their bones a-hanging.—Two bottles of wine.
Leather, *Hereford*, p. 232.

805p. As I was walkin' across the Basin Bridge, / I met my sister Kate, / I broke her neck, / An' drank her blood. / Could you tell me what it is?—A bottle of wine.
Fauset, *Southern Negro*, p. 278, No. 24.

805q. As I was going down London Alley, / I met my sister Sally, / I broke her neck, / And suck her blood, / Left her in the alley.—Bottle of whiskey.
Fauset, *Southern Negro*, p. 278, No. 27.

805r. As I was walking down the lane, / I met my sister Mary Ann; / I knocked off her head, sucked her blood, / And let her body stan [stand].—Bottle of soda pop or bottle of wine.
Hyatt, *Adams Co., Ill.*, p. 667, No. 10912; Brewster, *Indiana*, 12.

805s. As I was going across London Bridge, / I met sister Sally Ann, / She was drunk, and I was sober, / So I kicked her over.—A bottle of whiskey.
Parsons, *Aiken, S.C.*, p. 24, No. 2, var. 4; Bacon and Parsons, *Virginia*, p. 318, No. 53. As I was crossing a street in London: Parsons, *Bermuda*, p. 245, No. 3 var.

805t. As I went over London Bridge, / I met my sister Anne, / I broke her neck and drank her blood, / And let her body stand.—Bottle of brandy.
Fauset, *Nova Scotia*, p. 150, No. 39; Brewster, *Indiana*, 12. Sister Jane: Parsons, *Bermuda*, p. 244, No. 3. Sister Mary: Waugh, *Canada*, p. 67, No. 765. Sister Nancy: Bacon and Parsons, *Virginia*, p. 318, No. 53, var. 1. A bottle of wine: Farr, *Tennessee*, p. 324, No. 82. As I was going up the road: Greenleaf, *Newfoundland*, p. 9, No. 9. I tapped her head and sucked her blood: Chappell, p. 237, No. 42. Cut off her head.—Jug of whiskey: Gardner, *Schoharie Hills, N.Y.*, p. 253, No. 3.

805u. As I was going across London Bridge, / I met my sister Sally. / I bit off her head and sucked her blood, / And left her body standing.—Bottle of wine.
Hyatt, *Adams Co., Ill.*, p. 671, No. 10948.

805v. As I went through guttery-gap, / I met my Uncle Davey. / I cut his skull and sucked his blood, / And left his body aisy.—Bottle of stout.
Praeger, *Béaloideas*, IV (1933-1934), 145, No. 15.

805w. When I was going over London bridge, / I kissed my sister Anny. / I cut off her head and sucked her blood / And left her body standing.—A bottle of wine.
Janice Neal, *New York Folklore Quarterly*, I (1945), 216.

806–815. Pull Off His Head; Drink His Blood;
Throw Away His Bones: A Fruit

The scene of killing a person, drinking his blood, and throwing away his body is applicable to the eating of a fruit and the discarding of the refuse. It is very popular among riddlers and differs so widely in its various forms that some versions may have been invented independently. The victim may be a bird, an animal, or a person. In the Kashmiri description of eating grapes, "Walking by the way and picking a crow,"[1] the black grapes are appropriately represented by a crow. Compare it with the Modern Greek "An insignificant magpie thrown into the ditch"[2] or with the Rumanian "I went into the valley, caught partridges, ate the feathers, threw away the whole body."[3] A Finnish riddler elaborates a similar conception in terms of an animal and gives the answer, "felling a tree": "We killed an ox, threw the horns on the ground ate the skin, sold the blood, burned the flesh."[4] He is relating the cutting of the tree, the trimming of its branches, the eating of the inner bark, the selling of the tar, and the burning of the wood. In the picturesquely conceived Cuban banana riddle, "I was going down a little road. I met a little Negro. I took off his clothes and ate him whole,"[5] the "undressing" of the Negro or the peeling off the covering resembles a riddle for an onion,[6] and the reference to a Negro signifies that the skin of a ripe banana is black. A Flemish riddle for a hazelnut[7] turns the theme in still another direction. These comparisons to a bird, an animal, and a man illustrate the variety inherent in this conception. Comparisons to a thing, usually a bag or a pot, are less numerous.[8]

The variety of details in the scenes and the many answers which are proposed are, however, best suited to the description of a fruit part of which is

---
[1] Knowles, 89.
[2] Polites, *Neohellenika Analekta*, I, 245, No. 296.
[3] Papahagi, 10, var. 1.   [4] Henssen, 237.
[5] Massip, 170.   [6] See the headnote to No. 1439 below.
[7] *Ons Volksleven*, II (1890), 104, No. 62.
[8] See the headnote to Nos. 805–818 above.

eaten and part of which is thrown away. A somewhat similar series of tortures[9] also usually refers to plants. Some indications of variations having a regional currency may be noted. The comparison to a bird is very rare. Description in terms of an animal is found virtually everywhere. Description in terms of a man is most frequently found in regions where western European ideas can have exerted an influence.

Perhaps the oldest evidence of this riddle is the reference to a grape in the *Palatine Anthology:* "If you had taken me in my youth, you would have drunk the blood shed from me; but now that time has finished making me old, eat me, wrinkled as I am, with no moisture in me, crushing my bones together with my flesh."[10]

The scene of killing a creature and throwing away its bones serves to describe various objects:

§ 1. Flax. Russian: Sadovnikov, 1303 (As I walked in the autumn, I found eight. I threw away the meat, I wore out the hide, I ate up the head), 1311*d* (Autumn comes. We shall slay the elk, we shall discard the bones, and sell the hide, and eat the little head ourselves). See a Mordvin text quoted in the headnote to Nos. 805–818.

§ 2. Grain. Indian: Elwin, Baiga, p. 477, No. 131 (We throw away the flesh and eat the bones).

§ 3. Birch-sap, pine-sap. Russian: Sadovnikov, 1347 (I shall climb the little hill, I shall strip the little calf, I shall put the tallow into my mouth, I shall discard the hide), 1353.

§ 4. A strawberry. Flemish: Joos, 451 (I went into a street, I saw a little red soldier standing there, I pulled off his head and let the rest stand).

§ 5. An onion. Serbian: Novaković, p. 121, Nos. 5 (I killed an ox and sold all of it except a shoulder. When the fall came, the ox was whole), 6 (I killed an ox, ate up the meat, threw away the bones, but next year he was the same as before). This shows some similarity to the description of the growth of plants from seeds or shoots.[11] Compare also the Songaï riddle for cola: "I strangled my ox, the blood did not come out; I cut it into bits, the blood did not come out. When I wanted to eat it, blood came out."[12]

§ 6. A red cabbage. Welsh Gypsy: Sampson, 23 (I went down into the garden and saw old Rustyback. I cut off his head and left his body alone).

806a. As I went over London Bridge, / I saw a lady landing; / I pulled off her head and sucked her blood / And left her body standing.—Blackberry.
Brewster, *Indiana,* 30.

---

[9] See Nos. 679, 680.
[10] XIV, 103. The reference to wrinkles applies to a dried raisin.
[11] See No. 661 above.
[12] Hamouda, 20.

806b. One day I was going 'cross London Bridge, / An' met ol' Lady Nancy. / Sucked her blood, / An' lef' her body dancin'.—I picked a blackberry, and left de bush a-shakin'.
Parsons, *Aiken, S.C.*, p. 24, No. 2, var. 3.

806c. As I went up the hill, / I met my sister Nancy, / I pulled off her head and sucked her blood / And left her body dancing.—A blackberry.
Farr, *Tennessee*, p. 324, No. 86.

807. As I was going up London Bridge, / I met my brother John. / I chopped off his head and drank his blood / And let his body stan'.—Squashberry.
Greenleaf, *Newfoundland*, p. 9, No. 10.

808. I went up de hill / An' kill a man. / I drink his blood / An' throw away his flesh.—Cane [sugar cane].
Parsons, *Barbados*, p. 280, No. 24 var.

809a. As I was passing London town / I saw a lady hanging. / I took her down and drank her blood / And left her a-hanging.—Orange.
Parsons, *Bermuda*, p. 245, No. 3 var.

809b. As I went over Padstow bridge / Upon a cloudy day, / I met a fellow clothed in yellow, / I took him up and sucked his blood, / And threw his skin away.—An orange.
Cornish Notes and Queries, I (1906), 273. London bridge: M. A. Courtney, *Cornish Feasts and Folk-Lore* (Penzance, 1890), p. 206.

809c. As I was goin' across London Bridge, / I met a yaller man, / I cut off his head, / Drank his blood, / Ate his flesh, / Chucked his skin overboard.—An orange.
Parsons, *Bermuda*, p. 245, No. 3 var.

809d. As I was going over London Brig, / I spies a little red thing; / I picks it up, I sucks its blood, / And leaves its skin to dry.—An orange.
Gutch and Peacock, *Lincolnshire*, p. 397, No. 1.

809e. I was going up Sand-hill and saw a man and suck his blood and throw him over the wall.—Orange.
Beckwith, *Jamaica*, p. 192, No. 76.

810a. Onct I was goin' 'cross London Bridge, / Met a man, / I drunked his blood, / An' t'rowed his hide away.—Watermelon.
Parsons, *Aiken, S.C.*, p. 24, No. 2.

810b. As I was going over London Bridge, / I met old Dr. Gray, / I sucked his blood, / An' threw his skin away.—Watermelon.
Parsons, *Aiken, S.C.*, p. 24, No. 2, var. 1.

810c. As I was walking in the field, / I met old Father Gray, / I ate his meat and drank his blood, / And threw his hide away.—Watermelon.
Southern Workman, March, 1894.

810d. I went upon my father's grave. I ate his meat, suck his blood, and threw his bones away.—Watermelon.
Parsons, *St. Helena Island, S.C.*, p. 228; Johnson, *St. Helena Island, S.C.*, p. 159, No. 31.

810e. As I went through the field today, / I met my grandpap old and gray. / I ate his meat, I drank his blood, / I threw his skin down in the mud.—Watermelon.
Hudson, p. 84, No. 10.

810f. As I was goin' down the street, / I met with ol' gran'father. / I ate his meat an' drank his blood, / An' threw his hide away.—Watermelon.
Parsons, *Aiken, S.C.*, p. 24, No. 2, var. 2.

811a. As I went over London Bridge, / I met old Granny gray. / I ate her meat and sucked her blood / And threw her skin away.—Watermelon.
Hudson, p. 84, No. 9.

811b. As I was going 'cross London Bridge, / I met old Sally Gray. / I sucked her blood an' ate her meat, / An' threw her skin away.—Watermelon.
Bacon and Parsons, *Virginia*, p. 319, No. 53, var. 2.

811c. As I was going down the road one day, I met old Nellie Gray. / I ate her meat, I drank her blood, and threw her skin away.—A watermelon.
Farr, *Tennessee*, p. 323, No. 69.

812a. One day I was comin' up a hill, / I met a man. / Suck his blood, / Eat his flesh, / And throw away his bones.—Coconut.
Parsons, *Barbados*, p. 280, No. 24.

812b. One day I was comin' up a hill, / I met a man. I broke his bones and throw away his skull.—Coconut.
Parsons, *Barbados*, p. 280, No. 24 var.

812c. Mah fader had a t'ing, eat he flesh, drink his blood, an' t'row away his bone.—Coconut.
Parsons, *Bahamas*, p. 482, No. 110.

812d. Me fader had a t'ing. / You drink de blood / An' t'row away de back.—Coconut.
Parsons, *Andros Island, Bahamas*, p. 277, No. 20.

812e. They eat my flesh and drink my blood, and t'row 'way my bones.—The coconut.
Johnson, *Antigua*, p. 83, No. 2.

812f. What is this you eat its flesh and drink its blood?—Coconut.
Parsons, *Bermuda*, p. 245, No. 3 var.

812g. I kill a man, / Eat his flesh, / Drink his blood, / An' leave his bawns [bones] whole.—Coconut.
Parsons, *Barbados*, p. 280, No. 24 var.

812h. I was walkin', / I met a man, / I cut his throat, / I drink his blood, / I ate his flesh.—Coconut.
Parsons, *Antilles*, III, 443–444, St. Croix, 16.

812i. I foun' a man in de road and I kill him and take off his neck, and I drink his blood an' eat his flesh an' I did not like the color of his skin and how it is an' I throw it away.—Coconut.
Parsons, *Antilles*, III, 444, St. Croix, 16 var.

812j. I met a man and licked him down, / I ate his flesh, / I drank his blood, / I threw away his bones.—Coconut.
Parsons, *Antilles*, III, 380, St. Lucia, 44.

812k. Me riddle, me raddle, / Perhaps you may tell me this riddle, / Perhaps you may not. / I kill a man, I drank his blood, / I eat his flesh, / An' I t'row away his bones.—Coconut.
Parsons, *Antilles*, III, 435, St. Martin, 12.

812l. Me an' you wa' [were] goin' along de street, we meet a man. We broke his head, we drank his blood, we eat his flesh, we t'row away his bones.—Coconut.
Parsons, *Antilles*, III, 433, Saba, 7.

812m. I kill a man, cut his throat, drink his blood, eat his meat, throw away his bones.—Coconut.
Parsons, *Antilles*, III, 423, Montserrat, 29.

812n. I cut [caught] a man, / I drink his blood, / I eat his flesh, / And chow [throw] away his bone.—Coconut.
Parsons, *Antilles*, III, 430, St. Kitts, 3.

812o. A man, eh, cut him open, eh, / I drink he blood, eh, / I eat he flesh, eh, / I t'row away de bones, eh. / Tell me day [that] riddle.—Coconut.
Parsons, *Antilles*, III, 440, Anguilla, 24.

812p. M' fader had a man, / They cut his t'roat, / Drink his blood, / Eat his flesh, / An' t'row away his bones. / Tell me dat.—Coconut.
Parsons, *Antilles*, III, 440, Anguilla, 24 var.

812q. I went up a hill, / I meet a man, / I cut he neck. / I drink his blood. / I eat his flesh.—Coconut.
Parsons, *Antilles*, III, 364, Trinidad, 19 var.

812r. I went up a hill, / I meet a man. / I cut off his head. / I drink his blood. / I eat his flesh.—Coconut.
Parsons, *Antilles*, III, 364, Trinidad, 19.

812s. Went up a hill, I met a man. I drank his blood and ate his flesh, and threw away his skin.—Coconut.
Parsons, *Antilles*, III, 447, St. Thomas, 26.

812t. I went up Saint Paul hill. / T'rew away Saint Paul skin. / Drink Saint Paul blood. / T'rew away Saint Paul bone. / I eat Saint Paul meat.—Coconut.
Parsons, *Bahamas*, p. 476, No. 46.

812u. I drinks St. Paul blood, / I eat his meat, / I t'row away de shell.—Coconut.
Parsons, *Bahamas*, p. 473, No. 22.

812v. Up St. John, / Down St. John, / I meet a man, / Drink his blood, / And I throw away his bone.—Coconut.
Parsons, *Antilles*, III, 365, Trinidad, 19 var.

812w. I went to St. Anne. / I met a man. / I cut off his neck. / I drunk his blood. / I ate his flesh. / I threw his bone.—Coconut.
Parsons, *Antilles*, III, 370, Grenada, 35.

813. As I went through a guttery gap, / I met my uncle Davy. / I laid him down / And sucked his blood / And left his body aisy.—Plum.
Green, *South Antrim*, 19.

814–815. Corrupt and Confused Versions

814a. Go up Mount Zion, drink Zion blood, eat de flesh, dash away de bone.—Climbing a coconut tree, drinking the milk, eating the flesh.
Beckwith, *Jamaica*, p. 203, No. 188a.

814b. Climb up Zion hill, pick Zion fruit, come down Zion hill, drink Zion water.—Climbing a coconut tree, picking the nut, coming down, drinking the milk.
Beckwith, *Jamaica*, p. 203, No. 188.

815. I was walkin', / I met a man, / I cut his throat, / I drink his blood, / I ate his flesh.—Dog cut the deer's throat and he drank his blood and eat his meat.
Parsons, *Antilles*, III, 443–444, St. Croix, 16.

816. Shake His Hand; Suck His Blood

This riddle represents a confusion of the preceding pattern (Nos. 805a through 815), in which the speaker sucks the man's blood and throws away his body, with the following riddles in which the pump is said to remain standing. The riddler has not clearly conceived the situation.

816. I went to London Bridge an' meet a man a-standin'. I shake 'e han' an' suck 'e blood an' lef' um still a-standin'.—Pump.
Johnson, *St. Helena Island, S.C.*, p. 158, No. 15.

817. Touch a Man; He Bleeds

This conception appears also in the Sukuma description of a sieve, "I see an old woman, who bleeds from her nose" (Augustiny, 11).

817a. Ring a man's finger ev'y day, an' always bleeding'.—Stan' poipe [standpipe]. Open the cock [wring his head], water comes out.
   Parsons, *Barbados*, p. 280, No. 25.

817b. A man standin' up all day in the sun. / When you touch him, he bleeds. —Stand pipe.
   Parsons, *Barbados*, p. 280, No. 25 var.

817c. Back in de road I met an ol' man. De mo' I shake his han', de mo' he bleed.—Dat was a pump.
   Parsons, *Sea Islands, S.C.*, p. 159, No. 46.

817d. I wen' down de road. I met a man. Shook his han'. An' I draw blood.— Pump.
   Parsons, *Sea Islands, S.C.*, p. 159, No. 46, var. 1.

817e. I went out walking one day. I met a man, an' I shook his han'. An' he began to bleed. An' I say, "Why are you bleedin'?"—Pump.
   Parsons, *Sea Islands, S.C.*, p. 159, No. 46, var. 2.

817f. Oncet I was walkin' down a road, an' met a man who shook his head an' drank his blood.—Pump.
   Parsons, *Sea Islands, S.C.*, p. 159, No. 46, var. 3.

817g. When I was goin' to London, / I met a man, / I shuk his han', / An' leave him still a-standin'.—Pump.
   Parsons, *Sea Islands, S.C.*, p. 159, No. 46, var. 4.

818. Strike a Man; He Bleeds

A similar comparison of an object to a man who is struck or beaten occurs in the Kanuri descriptions of an anvil: "A dwarf stands there and gets blows" and "When I went down into the valley, there were two dwarfs who were dying under blows from a club."[1]

818a. j saw a sight the other day, a damsell did begin the fray: she with her dayly friend did meet, then standing in the open street she gave such hard & sturdy blowes he bled 10 gallons at the nose: yet neith[r] seem to faint nor fall, nor gave her any abuse at all.—a pumpe.
   Tupper, *Holme Riddles*, 119; *Harleian 1962* (17th cent.) = Halliwell-Phillipps, *Popular Rhymes*, p. 149; Knortz, p. 230, No. 82.

818b. I saw a sight / The other night, / All standin' in the open street, / She gave me some hard and healthy blows, / And bled ten gallons at the nose.— Pump.
   Fauset, *Nova Scotia*, p. 150, No. 40.

318c. A man standin' in the road all day. You will hit him, he will bleed, but will not move. As you squeeze a man nose, it will bleed.—Stand pipe.
   Parsons, *Barbados*, p. 280, No. 25 var.

---
[1] Lukas, p. 171, Nos. 30, 31.

818d. As I went out one moonlight night, / I saw a thing that made me fright. / I hit it hard and heavy blows / Till it bled gallons at the nose.—Pump.
Green, *South Antrim*, 32.

819. Can Kill; Cannot Be Killed

The Hindi "Without arms, without legs, carried at the shoulder. Murder is in its mouth, and it eats men as they stand"[1] is a very confused conception.

819. Something can kill you, but you can't kill that.—Gun.
Parsons, *Bermuda*, p. 257, No. 80.

820–822. Dying

Except for the biographical riddles that end with the death of the sufferer after a series of tortures (see the headnote to Nos. 674–680 above) comparisons to a dying man are rare in riddling. A few texts (Nos. 821, 822) refer to drowning.

820. Miss Witty Wit wit and wit till she wit out her last wit.—Needle and thread.
Beckwith, *Jamaica*, p. 204, No. 194.

821–822. Drowning

The following English comparisons of a cork or bottle floating in a stream to a man who swims but never drowns may have been suggested by a much more widely known comparison of a floating leaf to a man. The examples of this latter riddle are, however, best known east of Poland and consequently a connection is somewhat doubtful. The leaf riddle occurs either in terms of a man in the water, as in the White Russian "The lord flew, he fell in the water, he can't swim or drown,"[1] and in the Russian "A thoroughbred gentleman fell into a well, yet he neither dirtied the water nor drowned himself,"[2] or in terms of a thing, as in the Serbian "A board fell into the sea, the sea did not rise, nor did the board break,"[3] the Bulgarian "A board fell into the sea, it did not sink nor did the sea become stirred up,"[4] and the Mordvin "Tara, Tara fell into the water, it did not sink."[5] More remote versions of the idea are seen in the Pangwe "There is a man, he sinks in the river, no water enters his mouth"[6] and the Kashmiri "I pulled it down from above with a rope. I dashed it into the water. I said, 'It is drowned,' but, it rose thence

---

[1] Kavyopadhyaya, 34.
[1] Wasilewski, 63.
[2] Sadovnikov, 1395. The same riddle is used for a feather; see his Nos. 1599 and 1595 (down).
[3] Novaković, p. 115, No. 5, and see also his No. 6.
[4] Gubov, 213. See also Gubov, 416; Chacharov, 60.
[5] Paasonen, 314.   [6] Tessmann, 35.

like a king parrot, i.e., nicely."[7] The last version is in the narrative form characteristic of many Eastern riddles.

A few excellently personified versions suggest a similar picture, but with such differences that I consider them to be independent inventions. The Surinam gin-bottle riddles, "Black woman swims a swamp" and "Every hour a black woman makes a courtesy in the swamp,"[8] call up the scene of an empty bottle bobbing on the surface of the water. A Samoan cork riddle, "A man stands on the wide ocean,"[9] is surprisingly similar to this scene.

A reference to not drowning in water, as found in a Russian riddle for ice, "It does not burn in fire, and it does not drown in water,"[10] has been suggested by the riddle for a name."[11]

821. Man goes under water never drowns.—Cork.
Parsons, *Bermuda*, p. 264, No. 156.

822. Little Johnny fell in the water and never drowned.—Bottle.
Beckwith, *Jamaica*, p. 198, No. 133.

823–826. A Man and Not a Man

823–824. The Eunuch Riddle

An old eunuch riddle that Plato knew, the scholiasts commented upon, and Athenaeus reported in the *Deipnosophistae* has a long literary history. Petrus Crinitus, a teacher of belles lettres at Florence in the first quarter of the sixteenth century, versified it as follows:

> Homo non homo, videns non videns, alitem non alitem,
> Lapide non lapide, perculit non perculit,
> Cum super arbore, non super arbore degeret.
> —Semivir quidam cæcutiens leviter attingit pumice vespertilionem in sambuco sedentem.[1]

Another version of the same period with the answer "A boy throws a piece of ice or pumice at a Junebug or a butterfly on a flaxfield" shows the changes that have occurred in the course of transmission. It is as follows:

> Un homme, qui d'estre homme a seulement semblant,
> Donne un grand coup de pierre à un oyseau volant
> Sur un arbre, qui arbre au vray ne se peut dire,
> Ny l'oiseau n'est oyseau, ny la pierre n'est pierre.[2]

The first of the following texts is a direct descendant of the classical tradition, and the second contains elements of the French version. For discussion of this

---
[7] Knowles, 101. [8] Herskovits, p. 443, Nos. 61, 62.
[9] Brown, p. 345. [10] Bardin, p. 243, No. 4.
[11] See the headnote to Nos. 165–173, § 10, above.

[1] Quoted by Buchler, *Gnomologia*, 3d ed. (1614), pp. 444–445.
[2] Alexandre Sylvain (A. van den Bussche), *Cinquante Ænigmes françoises* (1582), pp. 45–46, No. 43.

riddle see Hagen, p. 17; Pitrè, p. xlix; Ohlert, 1st ed., pp. 28–30, and 2d ed., pp. 21, n. 3, and pp. 52–53; Boekenoogen, pp. 49–50; Tupper, *Holme Riddles*, note to No. 22 and p. 223; Schultz, *Rätsel*, cols. 66–67, 77, and 96–97, No. 32; Schultz, *Rätsel aus dem hellenischen Kulturkreise*, II, 46–56; Johannes Bolte and G. Polívka, *Anmerkungen zu den Kinder- und Hausmärchen*, II (Leipzig, 1915), 365, n. 1; W. Schultz, *Mitra*, I (1914–1920), cols. 46–50, 161–176.

A similar series of assertions and denials appears in various contexts. An epigram in the *Palatine Anthology* is "No one sees me when he sees, but he sees me when he sees not; he who speaks does not speak, and he who runs does not run, and I am untruthful though I tell all truth."[3] The old riddle of finding a wormy nut is told in the same fashion. A Swedish traditional version is as follows: "It was a man. It was no man. He was walking in a meadow. It was no meadow. He found a thing. It was no thing. If he had seen it, he would not have picked it up, but since he did not see it, he picked it up."[4] The beginning of this text seems to have been suggested by the eunuch riddle, but the concluding sentence is the typical form of the riddle of the wormy nut. A medieval version of the same riddle is "Vidi et tuli. Si vidissem, non tulissem."[5] The same sort of contradictions describe counterfeit money[6] and smoke.[7] The Norwegians say for a rainbow, "There was a man, there was no man. He went on a way, there was no way. He bore water without a pail";[8] and the Russians for fishing, "I rode not along a road, I urged not with a whip, I hit not with a stick. I caught not a magpie. I plucked not feathers. I ate not meat";[9] and the Bretons for an unborn rabbit, "My father has killed what he did not see and eaten what was not born after cooking it with words.— A rabbit taken from the mother's body and cooked over a fire of burning books."[10] The Turks use similar concepts in a very strange way to describe the heart or love: "A tree in my garden is branchless and knotless, on top of it there is a featherless, wingless bird. You must shoot it without bullets or rifle. Afterwards you must cook it without grass or hearth. Then you must

---

[3] XIV, 110. No answer is given.
[4] Dybeck, *Runa*, 1847, p. 40, No. 4 = Russwurm, 63; Hyltén-Cavallius, *Värend*, 82.
[5] Karl Müllenhoff and Wilhelm Scherer, *Denkmäler*, 3d ed. (Berlin, 1892), I, 20 (VII, No. 1), and notes, II, 48 (VII, No. 1). See further Müllenhoff, *Zeitschrift für deutsche Mythologie*, III (1855), 20; Boekenoogen, p. 49; Petsch, *Rätselstudien*, pp. 332–333. Afrikaans: Groenewald, p. 81. German: Butsch, 172; Wossidlo, 391. Luxemburg: De la Fontaine, 3. Danish: Kristensen, p. 96, § 246, No. 377, and p. 99, § 252, No. 396. Flemish: M[one], *Anzeiger*, VII (1838), col. 266, No. 252. Latin: Reusner, ed. 1602, pp. 287, 382; Buchler, *Gnomologia*, 3d ed. (1614), p. 446. French: Rolland, 110; Westphalen, *Metz*, col. 199. Serbian: Novaković, p. 155, No. 5. Mordvin: Paasonen, 101 (He who bends down errs). Hungarian: Arany and Gyulai, II, 349, No. 2. Gypsy: Wlislocki, 34. See also a riddle cited in the headnote to No. 460 above.
[6] Danish: Kristensen, p. 96, § 246, No. 377. Compare the headnote to Nos. 1728–1737, § 1, below.
[7] Flemish: Joos, 45. [8] Brox, *Ytre Senja*, 123.
[9] Sadovnikov, 1622. See Polish and White Russian parallels cited in the headnote to Nos. 367–369, nn. 63–65, above.
[10] Sauvé, 36 = E. Rolland, *Faune populaire*, VII (Paris, 1906), 217.

eat it without salt or pepper."[11] Some traits in this list of par_
the comparison of a snowflake to a wingless bird eaten by the

823. A man & no man going & not going in the light & no light
no stone stroke [struck] a bird & no bird sitting in a tree & no tre_.—androgius
the eunuch being spur-blind in the twylight stroke a bat wth a pumice stone
sitting upon a mustard tree.
Tupper, *Holme Riddles*, 22.

824. A man who was not a man, / Killed a bird that was not a bird. / On a tree that was not a tree, / With a gun that was not a gun.—It means that a little boy killed a butterfly with a power gun on a cane tree.
Parsons, *Antilles*, III, 365, Trinidad, 28.

825-826. Nobody and Somebody

825a. Turn me back, I'm nobody; / Turn me face, I'm somebody.—Looking-glass.
Johnson, *Antigua*, p. 86, No. 38.

825b. Look in my face, I am somebody; / Look in my back, I am nobody.—Mirror.
Parsons, *Bermuda*, p. 258, No. 95.

826. Use me well, and I am everybody; / Scratch my back, and I am nobody. —A looking glass.
Waugh, *Canada*, p. 69, No. 798; Gardner, *Schoharie Hills, N.Y.*, p. 257, No. 41; Brewster, *Indiana*, 14.

---

[11] Hamizade, 208.
[12] See the headnote to Nos. 367-369 above.

Chapter V

COMPARISONS TO SEVERAL PERSONS

Nos. 827–1035

RIDDLES making a comparison to several persons show little similarity in choice of themes or manner of treatment to those making a comparison to a single person. In this chapter, I have placed first the riddles in which the actors have no family relationship to one another.[1] The second half of the chapter contains riddles in which the actors are said to be related to one another.[2] I have adopted this classification in imitation of Lehmann-Nitsche's procedure. It does not prove to be entirely satisfactory, in several regards. The defects are not numerous or important enough to justify a rearrangement and may therefore serve to illustrate some weaknesses in his classification.

In various ways, riddlers have established a connection among the actors who are not members of a family. They have contrasted the living and the dead,[3] and they have enlarged upon this contrast by assigning apparently impossible activities to the supposed persons: the dead bear the living,[4] the dead speak while the living keep silence,[5] and the dead even bury[6] or cover[7] the living. The notion of a company is used for a man, a woman, and a child, and also for ants.[8] Riddlers have often described objects in terms of people identified by characteristic colors.[9]

References to the functions[10] of the actors who are not members of a family are somewhat less important than references to their forms. Riddlers describe objects as people who are resident in a bush or house[11] and often assert that the house or the people are unusual in some regard.[12] Closely related to such conceptions are the descriptions of a shipload of people.[13] This variation, which is characteristically West Indian in its currency, may contain a reminiscence of the slave trade. Other descriptions in terms of functions deal with such activities as waiting, moving, talking, fighting, and carrying on a trial that culminates in the execution of a criminal.[14] Some of these scenes are ingeniously elaborated. A chase after a louse is, for example, conceived as either a court trial or a hunt.[15] The section devoted to the functions of people who are not related concludes with riddles referring to the actors according to their number.[16]

---

[1] Nos. 827 through 982.
[2] Nos. 983a through 1035.
[3] Nos. 828a through 836.
[4] Nos. 828a through 829b.
[5] Nos. 833 through 834b and the headnote to Nos. 830–834.
[6] Nos. 835a, 835b, and the headnote to No. 835.
[7] See the headnote to No. 836.
[8] Nos. 837a through 839.
[9] Nos. 840 through 904.
[10] Nos. 905 through 982.
[11] Nos. 905 through 927.
[12] Nos. 906 through 927.
[13] Nos. 929 through 936.
[14] Nos. 937 through 982.
[15] Nos. 970 through 975.
[16] Nos. 976a through 982.

The riddles in which the actors have a family relationship to one another[17] describe the interconnected and interdependent parts of an object: the wheels of a wagon, the vanes of a windmill, the segments of a nut, the stones of a fireplace and the pot standing on them, the grains of rice in a pot, the fingers, and the like. I have arranged them according to the nature of the family relationship. Those in which the actors are father and son[18] stand first. They are followed by riddles in which the actors are brothers,[19] daughters,[20] sisters,[21] and a family.[22] Riddlers often conceive the same object in several of these ways.[23]

827–982. Unrelated Persons

827. Dere is two men, not de livin', not de dead, but dey is de onniest ["onliest"] two men obey de Lawd's command.—De Bible an' de prayerbook.
Parsons, *Bahamas*, p. 484, No. 123.

828–836. The Dead and the Living

Loewenthal[1] discusses the frequently used contrast of the dead and the living as a bit of enigmatic technique. Riddlers may heighten this contrast by assigning apparently impossible activities to the dead and the living. Ingenuity and keen observation often appear in its use. For example, the Yakut description of a man blind in one eye, "A dead man and a living man lie with their legs interlocked, so they say,"[2] compares the eyeballs to men and the fibers running to them to the interlocked legs. Such a conception requires great familiarity with anatomy from both askers and hearers.

The notion of ascribing apparent impossibilities to the dead and the living is used in riddling as follows:

§ 1. The dead gives birth to the living. The answer is an egg and a chick. Although English riddlers do not seem to know this riddle, instances in other languages are abundant. See Norwegian: Bergh, *Valdres*, 21. Rumanian: Papahagi, 29. Serbian: Novaković, p. 76, No. 3 (A dead thing bears a living thing). Albanian: Pedersen, 2 (The living brings forth dead, and the dead the living). Turkish: Hamizade, 754 (From one having a soul a soulless one is born). Crimean Tatar: Filonenko, 62 (From an inanimate object a live thing is born). Svanian: J. Nizheradze, pp. 66–67, No. 7 (Out of a dead one a living one comes). Georgian: Blechsteiner, p. 15, No. 23 (I saw the lifeless pregnant, the living give birth; the mother bears the child and dies. Who guesses that?). Sart: Ostrumov, 147, as cited by Jungbauer, p. 351 (From one without life there comes one with life. If you are intelligent, guess it). Afghan: Thorburn,

---

[17] Nos. 983a through 1035.
[19] Nos. 989 through 1006.
[21] Nos. 1012 through 1016.
[18] Nos. 983a through 988.
[20] Nos. 1007a through 1011.
[22] Nos. 1017a through 1035.
[23] As an example, see the riddles for wagon wheels cited in the headnote to Nos. 954–957, n. 4.

[1] Pp. 44, 46.
[2] Piekarski, 235.

Bannu, 10 (From the living a corpse is born, the living leaves its corpse, and its corpse is broken in two). For discussion of this theme see Schultz, *Rätsel*, col. 86, and Schultz, *Bemerkungen*, pp. 368–369.

§ 2. The dead begets the living. This unusual conception has the answer "fire"; see the eleventh-century Latin "Vidi mortuos generare vivos et in ira vivorum consumpti sunt mortui."[3]

§ 3. The dead drives the living out of the bushes. The answer is a comb that drives lice from hair.[4]

§ 4. The dead entraps the living. The various answers—bait and fish, weir and fish, ant caught in resin—involve the same fundamental theme. Minor alterations adapt it to the various answers, of which bait or a rod and fish is perhaps the most frequently found.[5] The variations in the Portuguese "Dead kills living.—Fish hook,"[6] the Bengali "One rod, the rod bears a dead one, the dead one catches a living one;"[7] and the Filipino "He carries the flesh of the dead but seeks the flesh of the living.—Fish line"[8] are typical of good riddling. The theme may have been independently invented in various countries.

Answers of similar import are (*a*) a bamboo trap in which to catch fish, as in the Ho "The dead devours the living";[9] (*b*) a weir, as in the Cheremiss "The dead catches the living";[10] (*c*) a snare for birds, as in the Palestinian Arabic "One died, [and] spent the night in the open air. A living one came, snapped at the dead one, then the dead one rose and caught the living one."[11] This is slightly varied in the Iraqi parallel, "When we had buried a dead man, who had died, in a chapel, the living one came and scratched him out. Then the dead man sprang up and seized him";[12] (*d*) an ant caught in resin, as in the Cheremiss "The dead catches the living"[13] or the Votyak "The dead kills the living";[14] (*e*) a gun, as in the Votyak "One without life kills one with life";[15] and (*f*) a noose, as in the Kanuri "Something dead seized something living."[16]

§ 5. The dead bears the living. The usual answers are a ship or a shoe.[17]

§ 6. The dead serves the living. Arabic: Giacobetti, 379 (leather bottle). The reference is to a bottle made of the hide of an animal.

§ 7. The dead holds or holds back the living. French: Baissac, *Mauritius*,

---

[3] Malein, p. 233, No. 3. For a similar concept applied to plants see No. 95 above; and to salmon, see Hull and Taylor, 133, 134.
[4] See the headnote to Nos. 459–460 above.
[5] In addition to the versions cited see Spanish, Dominican Rep.: Andrade, 33. Porto Rican: Mason, 53. Hawaiian: Judd, 97; Beckwith, 30.
[6] Parsons, *Cape Verde*, 160a.
[7] Mitra, *Sylhet*, 22.
[8] Starr, *Philippines*, 182.
[9] Sarkar, p. 257, No. 50; Mitra, *Notes on Ho Riddles*, pp. 258–259.
[10] Genetz, 84.
[11] Ruoff, p. 38, No. 94.
[12] Meissner, *Iraq*, 69.
[13] Genetz, 71.
[14] Buch, 26; Wichmann, *Votyak*, 124.
[15] Wichmann, *Votyak*, 398.
[16] Lukas, p. 170, No. 22.
[17] For discussion see the headnote to Nos. 828–829 below.

p. 409 (bridle). Arabic: Giacobetti, 466 (One attaches it, one pulls it, the dead holds back the living.—Bridle). African, Bakongo: Denis, 102 (belt for climbing a palm). Indian, Kashmiri: Knowles, 104 (A dead man leading the living.—A beast held by a tether).

§ 8. The dead pursues the living. See the headnote to Nos. 1432–1434, n. 1, below.

§ 9. The dead speak; the living are silent. The usual answers are a musical instrument, trash, or dry and green peas.[18]

§ 10. The dead buries or covers the living. The answer is ashes over a fire.[19]

Some riddles contrast the relative positions of the living and the dead. For examples, see:

§ 11. Living above, dead below. Portuguese: Parsons, *Cape Verde*, 68 (Living above, dead below, the dead [in] the living.—Egg). Italian: Ferraro, *Canti popolari in dialetto logodurese*, p. 302, No. 16. The Danish allusion, "The dead stands over the living," which describes fire and ashes, reverses the order.[20]

§ 12. Living within, dead outside. The answer is usually "a house." For examples see Portuguese: Parsons, *Cape Verde*, 239. Lettish: Bielenstein, 247 (Dead round about, alive within). Albanian: Pedersen, 3 (A dead man, whose intestines move about and being alive, go in and out of his belly).[21] Indonesian, Batak: Ophuijsen, p. 210, No. 19 (The dead swallows the living). According to the collector,[22] the Batak will not accept the answer "boat."

§ 13. Alive at both ends, dead in the middle. The usual answer is a man plowing.[23]

Somewhat different in conception from any riddles cited thus far are certain descriptions of an egg. The Argentinians and Chileans say, "Not living or dead, not female or male";[24] and the Arabs in Palestine, "It has neither foot nor head, nor tail, is neither living nor dead."[25]

828–829. The Dead Bears the Living

The seeming impossibility of the dead bearing the living is applicable to descriptions of:

§ 1. A shoe. Breton: Sauvé, 89. German: Wossidlo, 442. Swiss: Rochholz, 490. French: V. S., *Mélusine*, I (1878), col. 254, No. 5 (I am born of a dead beast, I bear those who bear me, I go through the wood to the king's house).

---

[18] For discussion see the headnote to Nos. 830–834.
[19] See Nos. 835a through 836, and the discussions in the accompanying headnotes, the note to Nos. 835a, 835b, and the note to No. 836.
[20] The riddle is cited in the headnote to No. 836, n. 10, below.
[21] Compare also the riddles cited in the headnote to No. 906.
[22] Ophuijsen, p. 205.
[23] See the headnote to Nos. 1432–1434 below.
[24] Lehmann-Nitsche, 437; Flores, 355, 365.
[25] Ruoff, p. 49, No. 13.

This may have been based on the ship riddle.[1] Mention of going to the king's house is analogous to the mention of the fly that comes to the king's table.[2] Baissac, *Mauritius*, p. 406. Lettish: Bielenstein, 655 (One not alive bears the living one). Serbian: Novaković, p. 111, No. 4. Finnish: Lönnrot, 2109 = Henssen, 157. Votyak: Buch, 35 (snowshoe). Indonesian, Batak: Ophuijsen, p. 209, No. 14 (The living is borne by the dead). For discussion of this theme see Loewenthal, pp. 58–59.

§ 2. A cradle. Icelandic: Árnason, 432 (What moves, [although] dead, with life in it?). Arabic: Giacobetti, 398 (The dead bears the living. Push the dead, the living is silent).

§ 3. A ship. See Nos. 828a through 828h below.

§ 4. A train. See Nos. 829a, 829b.

§ 5. A vulture on a horse's carcass. This Argentinian riddle, "The dead bears the living,"[3] is a degenerate version of a longer riddle of an entirely different type.[4]

§ 6. A pot on a fire. Latin: Daly and Suchier, p. 141, No. 94 = Malein, p. 233, No. 2. See the notes in Daly and Suchier, p. 144, Nos. 91, 94, and compare the headnote to Nos. 871–877, n. 3, below.

828. The Dead Bears the Living: A Ship

The typical form of this riddle, which may also have the answer "oak tree" when the introductory passage describes the use of the acorns for food before the timber is used in a ship, is seen in the Lithuanian "When I was alive, I fattened the living. Dead, I carried the living."[1] The oak, which had once borne acorns for pigs, now as a ship bears living passengers. This old and famous riddle exhibits many modifications and adaptations. It was disseminated by the Apollonius romance.[2] A curious variation introduces a contrast to the essential theme of the dead bearing the living. This appears in the eighteenth-century Lithuanian "When I was alive, I fattened live ones. When I was dead, I carried living ones. The living went beneath me"[3] and is enlarged upon in the modern Swedish "I am dead but there is life in me, the living go under me, and the living hover above me, the living walk in me, and the living have regard for me."[4]

---

[1] Nos. 828a through 828g below.
[2] See the headnote to No. 737 above.   [3] Lehmann-Nitsche, 702.
[4] For the riddle see Rodolfo Lenz, "Cuentos de adivinanzas corrientes in Chile," *Revista de folklore chileno*, II, No. 8 (1912), 353–359, Nos. 2a through 2l, and "Notas comparativas," *ibid.*, III, No. 8, pp. 272–280.

[1] Jurgelionis, 898; Schleicher, p. 196.
[2] See Heinrich von Neustadt, *Apollonius von Tyrland*, ed. Samuel Singer (Berlin, 1906), vv. 16612–16632; R. W. Pettengill, *Journal of English and Germanic Philology*, XII (1913), 249; Loris, *Sbornik Bawor*, p. 428, as cited by Flajšhans, pp. 9–10, No. 7a.
[3] Jurgelionis, 663, quoting Praetorius, *Acta Borussica*, II (Königsberg, 1731), 562. See also Frischbier, *Pflanzenwelt*, pp. 65–66, No. 5. The oldest version that I have noted is Buchler, *Gnomologia*, 3d ed. (1614), p. 454.
[4] Ericsson, *Södermanland*, II (1881), 95, No. 88.

Parallels to the ship or oak-tree riddle are very numerous:[5] See the following selection intended to show its wide distribution. Norwegian: Brox, *Ytre Senja*, 114. Swedish: Dybeck, *Runa*, 1847, p. 40, No. 2; Ericsson, *Södermanland*, II (1881), 100, No. 115 (The dead bears the living on its back), and III (1882), 97, No. 127; Ström, p. 124, "Eken," 1, and p. 169, No. 3. Latin: Johannes Lauterbach, *Ænigmata* ([Frankfurt a. M.], 1601), p. 71 = Friedreich, p. 214, No. 7 (Dum vivo, vivos pasco, jam mortua, vivos / Porto: sed æquoreas denique sulco vias). French: Rolland, 89. Lithuanian: Schleicher, p. 202 (When I was alive, I fed the living. When I died, I bore the living, and the living moved beneath me). The Lettish personification, "Living, it bears a green crown. Dead, it bears the living,"[6] contains an element characteristic of the grenade riddle.[7] Slovak: Záturecky, 256 (I am the daughter of a beautiful forest, I travel to the northern land, two servants I have always with me, I leave no trace at all), which I quote from Flajšhans.[8] He believes that it is derived from the Apollonius romance. It contains elements belonging to the riddles for a violin and a ship.[9] Serbian: Novaković, p. 111, No. 4 (It was alive and fed the living, now it carries the living). Modern Greek: Polites, *Neohellenika Analekta*, I, 235, No. 243 (Lifeless itself, it takes lives and carries them away); Stathes, p. 337, No. 30. African, Kinyarwanda: Hurel, p. 153, No. 5 (The dead on the dead). Indonesian, Batak: Ophuijsen, p. 209, No. 14 (The living is borne by the dead). A French riddler in the Antilles enlarges upon the original idea: "A dead man bears a living man to take the living (pl.) to make the living (pl.) live.—Boat, fisher, fish."[10] The Turkish "A live one mounts a dead one; the dead one mounts an infidel"[11] is also an expansion, but the significance of the reference to the sea as an infidel is not obvious.

There are not many riddles for a ship. The Bihari "A populated village goes over the water"[12] represents a conception which is probably independent of those discussed here. The notions that a ship leaves no trace in the water and that rowing may be compared to chopping wood serve as bases for riddles.[13] Some have called a ship and its sails a tree with leaves.[14] The various parts of a ship are sometimes described according to their origins.[15]

828a. Look through a diamond, I see the dead carry the living.—Ship at sea.
Beckwith, *Jamaica*, p. 198, No. 136a.

---

[5] See the many parallels collected in German: Wossidlo, 78. Danish: Feilberg, *Ordbog*, III, 243, s.v. "skib."
[6] Bielenstein, 322. [7] See No. 595 above. [8] Pp. 9–10, No. 7a.
[9] The reminiscence of the violin riddle occurs in the first sentence. For parallels see the headnote to Nos. 1058–1062 below. The last sentence is found independently as a ship riddle; see the headnote to No. 227 above.
[10] Parsons, *Antilles*, III, 389, Martinique, 131.
[11] Hamizade, 1.
[12] Mitra, *Bihari Life*, p. 46, No. 30.
[13] See the headnote to No. 227 above.
[14] See Nos. 1036a through 1036d.
[15] See the headnote to Nos. 1058–1062, § 1.

828b. Dead carry the living over Napoleon's grass-piece.—Ship at sea.
Beckwith, *Jamaica*, p. 198, No. 136.

828c. It's astonish to see de dead carr' de livin'.—Boat.
Parsons, *Andros Island, Bahamas*, p. 276, No. 15.

828d. I was sitting in my chair, / I spied the dead carrying the living, / And oh, wasn't that a dreadful wonder.—A vessel.
Fauset, *Nova Scotia*, p. 170, No. 150.

828e. As I leukit out ma father's castle wa', / A saw the dead carryin the livin awa.—A ship.
Gregor, *Northeast Scotland*, p. 80.

828f. As I lookit owre my window at ten o'clock at night, / I saw the dead carrying the living.—A ship sailing.
Chambers, *Scotland*, p. 110.

828g. I stood on my father's co' [cow] pen, an' saw de dead carry in [carryin'] the livin'.—Bot [boat] carrying passengers.
Parsons, *Barbados*, p. 284, No. 50.

828h. w^n j lived j fed the liveing now j am dead j beare the live[ing] & with swift speed j walk ou^r the liveing.—a ship mad[e] of oake groweing feeds hogs with acorns now b[e]ars men & swims ou^r fishes.
Tupper, *Holme Riddles*, 15.

829a. As I looked out through my grandfather's window, / I saw the dead carryin' the livin'.—Train.
Green, *South Antrim*, 25.

829b. I stood on a high mountain, / I looked through a golden ring, / I say [saw?] the dead carrying the living. / On whattan a wonderful thing!—Seeing a train through a spyglass.
Praeger, *Béaloideas*, IV (1933-1934), 145, No. 11.

830–834. The Dead (Old) Speak; the Living (Young) Are Silent

Inasmuch as this conception is current only where African riddling is known, it is probably of African origin. Somewhat similar, however, is the Samoan description of the green and ripe coconut: "When he is grown up, he speaks; having become a gray-haired man, he does not speak,"[1] which refers to the shaking of the liquid within the shell and the gray fibers growing over the mature nut in which the liquid has dried up.

Adaptations of this fundamental idea to other objects than peas or leaves are unusual. Perhaps the most important of them is the description of a letter, which is ordinarily expressed in the singular, as in the Algerian Arabic "The dead carries the living, the living do not speak,"[2] which signifies that the

---
[1] Heider, 7.
[2] Giacobetti, 424, and see also his No. 426.

dead paper bears news of the living. The simple contrast "The dead speaks to the living" is either a letter[3] or, more rarely, a pen.[4] The Argentinian Spanish "I met a dead man, I talked to him, and he told me a secret"[5] is a more vivid personification and resembles a Spanish riddle for a book.[6] A Portuguese riddle for paper, pen, and the hand exhibits very peculiar complications: "Three men inside one house—two dead, one alive. The dead two speak, and the living one is silent."[7]

Another use of the theme of the dead speaking and the living keeping silent is seen in riddles for musical instruments. The Cuban Spanish riddle for a piano, "In a dark room are a dead and a live one, the live one touches the dead one, and the dead one screams,"[8] is probably inspired by the bell riddle, "The living pulls the dead and the dead cries out"[9] or "The living man shakes the dead man mercilessly, the dead man calls the village."[10] A Renaissance English instance of this way of thinking is:

> Oedipus, that whilome hast resolved a greater doubt,
> unfold this riddle unto me which now I shall put out:
> When I did live, then was I dumbe, and yeeld no harmony,
> But, being dead, I doe afford most pleasant melody.—
> Any musicall instrument that is made of wood.[11]

A simpler version of this idea is the medieval Latin "Verum est. Audivi mortuos multa loquentes."[12] Some widely scattered examples may be cited in further illustration.[13] The Malagasy say, "Dead before it begins to bluster."[14] The Indians describe a conch as a person: "A person who is dumb while alive but speaks fluently when he is dead. He has no skin on his body after his death, yet takes part in Hindu ceremonies."[15] The Japanese compare a triton-shell trumpet to an animal: "When alive, it does not cry; when dead, it makes a great roar. What animal is that?"[16] I do not see the import of a French mortise riddle from Mauritius: "The living do not speak, the dead speak."[17]

830. Two boys going alone, one could speak and the other could not.—Green peas and dry peas.
Parsons, *Bahamas*, p. 477, No. 60 var.

---

[3] Arabic: Ruoff, p. 21, No. 8.
[4] Arabic: Ruoff, p. 22, No. 15. Indian, Parsee: Munshi, p. 413.
[5] Lehmann-Nitsche, 356. [6] Demófilo, 605, 606.
[7] Parsons, *Cape Verde*, 177. [8] Massip, 165.
[9] Albanian: Pedersen, 1.
[10] Georgian: Blechsteiner, p. 13, No. 15.
[11] *Prettie Riddles* (1631), No. 14 = Brandl, p. 54.
[12] Daly and Suchier, p. 141, No. 92.
[13] See also a long Flemish literary riddle for a flute (Joos, 310). Swedish: Ström, p. 190, "Skinnbandet." For references to a violin as both dead and living see the note to Nos. 1059a, 1059b, below, and the headnote to Nos. 1058–1062.
[14] Sibree, p. 40, No. 19. [15] Lakshīnātha Upasānī, III, 7.
[16] Starr, *Japan*, p. 45. [17] Baissac, *Mauritius*, p. 411.

831. My moder have a tree, when she pass by an' touch dat tree, all de chil'runs cry.—Pease tree.
Parsons, *Antilles*, III, 444, St. Croix, 26.

832a. My father had two things, the old can talk, but the young cannot.—Pigeon peas.
Parsons, *Bahamas*, p. 477, No. 60. Uncle: Parsons, *Bahamas*, p. 477, No. 60 var.

832b. What kyan an ol' woman / An' young one kyan't?—Green pease and dry pease.
Parsons, *Andros Island, Bahamas*, p. 276, No. 18.

832c. I speak to de young an' dey wouldn' speak; / I speak to de ol' an' dey speak.—You shake de young pease an' dey wouldn' shake; you shake de ol' pease an' dey shake.
Parsons, *Bahamas*, p. 483, No. 116.

833. I went in the churchyard, / I spoke to the livin', / An' the livin' wouldn' speak. / I speak to the dead, / An' the dead speak.—Pease.
Parsons, *Barbados*, p. 279, No. 20.

834a. Walk on the livin', An' the livin' wont holler; / Walk on de dead, / The dead holler.—Dry leaves.
Parsons, *Barbados*, p. 279, No. 20 var.

834b. When you step on the live, the live wouldn't cry; / but when you step on the dead, the dead will cry.—Trash.
Parsons, *Sea Islands, S.C.*, p. 175, No. 182.

835. The Dead Bury the Living

This paradox usually occurs in an enigmatic message from a girl to her lover.[1] These texts may be fragments of that message, but they have an independent life, at least in Anglo-Irish folklore. The paradox, which signifies "when ashes cover the fire at night," occurs in a somewhat enlarged form in Nicolaus Reusner's distich:

> Mortua res vivam sepelit, manet illa sepulcro
> Viva suo, vivis mollit & ill cibos.[2]

Quite independent uses of the paradox appear in the Icelandic riddle for sleep, "Who is the dead one that buries the living one?"[3] and the Samoan "A living one is buried with a corpse.—The yam, which rots, and the shoot, which grows a new plant."[4] It is reversed in the Icelandic "The dead digs up the living.—Tongs pull a coal from the fire."[5]

---

[1] See No. 836.
[2] Reusner, ed. 1599, p. 264 = Reusner, *Ænigmata*, p. 70 = Buchler, *Gnomologia*, 3d ed. (1614), p. 443.
[3] Árnason, 497.
[4] Heider, 17. Compare No. 95 above. [5] Árnason, 366.

835a. I seen the dead buryin' the livin', an' that's a wonderful thing.—Shovelful of coals on the fire.
Green, *South Antrim*, 26.

835b. I sat on my hunkers, / I looked through my peepers, / I saw the dead burying the living.—Dead ashes falling on the fire.
Praeger, *Béaloideas*, IV (1933-1934), 144, No. 10.

836. The Dead Covers the Living

The use of the theme of the dead covering or burying the living is perhaps best known in an enigmatic message which is intelligible only to the recipient and remains entirely obscure to the hearers, bearers, or bystanders. I have noted three varieties of the enigmatic message: (1) a message fixing the time for an assignation;[1] (2) news of the fate of an illegitimate child which is called an apple that has fallen to the ground;[2] and (3) a vague and obscure conversation which seems to be quite independent of the preceding.[3] All of these are in dialogue or are represented as a message or the words of a speaker. Such messages or enigmatical communications are somewhat similar to paradoxical commands to come neither by day nor by night, neither riding nor walking, and the like.[4]

The message sometimes occurs in versions which have lost the form of a dialogue. This is the case in the Polish "A cloud approaches; there will be rain, but not now. When an oak and a linden fall over and a birdie sings through its horns, then it will rain.—A suitor, wishing to kidnap a daughter from her parents, told her that he would come for her toward evening when she should be ready for him at a given signal. When the time for flight came, he stood before her parents' house and said to her, 'A cloud now approaches; there will be rain.' The girl replies, 'But not now,[5] but when the linden and the oak fall over[6] and the bird sings through its horns,[7] then[8] it will rain.'"[9] A very curious Danish text, "The dead stands over the living, and the water goes over the world, now there awakens a true prophet with mouth of horn and beard of flesh.—Chick in egg,"[10] contains elements of this riddle, the

---

[1] In addition to the text below see R. Köhler, *Kleinere Schriften*, III, 508-509, No. 14; Feilberg, *Gåder*, pp. 42-43; Loewenthal, p. 106.
[2] German: Wossidlo, 976; W. Busch, *Korrespondenzblatt des Vereins für niederdeutsche Sprachforschung*, XXIII (1911), 15-16. Danish: Feilberg, *Ordbog*, III, 1136, s.v. "æble." Swedish: Dybeck, *Runa*, 1849, p. 47, No. 5; Ericsson, *Södermanland*, V (1884), 64, No. 206; Sandén, *Norra Vadsbo*, 152; Geijer and Campbell, 116.
[3] German: Wossidlo, 975.
[4] See R. Köhler, *Kleinere Schriften*, III, 513.
[5] She cannot go now.
[6] When her father and mother go to bed.
[7] The cock crows.
[8] Then she will be able to go.
[9] Siarkowski, 61.
[10] Kristensen, p. 41, § 96, No. 129; Feilberg, *Ordbog*, II, 252, s.v. "kokkeskylling." See also the headnote to Nos. 828-836, § 11, above.

comparison of dew to water which covers the world,[11] and the description of a cock as a man with an unusual face.[12]

836. tell thy Master in my name w^n trees are turned & well[s] be dry & quick be dead, then come will j.—tis midnight w^n a gentle woman correcting her maineing [meaning] promised her lord that she would com.
    Tupper, *Holme Riddles*, 99.

837–839. A Company Who Are Not Men, Women, or Children

The basis is a paradox in grammar or logic: a company made up of a man, a woman, and a child is not a company of men, women, and children. The theme may have been ultimately suggested by the description of Melchisedec's ancestry.[1] Two texts with the answer "ants"[2] are probably confused with the descriptions of ants as a company of varicolored persons.[3]

837a. As I was goin' up London Bridge, / I met three living people. / They were neither men, women or children.—Was a man, a woman, and a child.
    Bacon and Parsons, *Virginia*, p. 325, No. 111.

837b. As I went up Christ Church Steeple, / I saw three Christ Church people. / They were neither men, women, or children, / But were three Christ Church people.—Man, woman, an' chil'.
    Parsons, *Barbados*, p. 285, No. 53. Heaple Steeple: Redfield, *Tennessee*, p. 40, No. 55.

837c. As I was going up St. George's steeple, / I met some St. George's people. / They were neither men, women, or children. / Who were they?— Man, woman, and child.
    Parsons, *Antilles*, III, 375, St. Vincent, 4.

837d. As I was goin' to St. George's Steeple, / I met three of St. George's people. / Dey were neider men, chilrens, or women. What were they?—They were a man, a vooman, and a child. An' I step on a piece of lead an' my story end.
    Parsons, *Antilles*, III, 437, St. Martin, 29.

837e. I went up St. George's Street, / I met three of St. George's people, / Neither men, neither three women, / Neither three chil', yet three of St. George's people.—A man, a chil', an' a woman.
    Parsons, *Antilles*, III, 425, Antigua, 16.

837f. As I was going to St. Peter's Church / I met three Christian people, / They were not a man [men], woman [women], or child [children] / Yet they were Christian people.—Man, woman, child.
    Parsons, *Bermuda*, p. 261, No. 123. St. James' Steeple: Johnson, *Antigua*, p. 85, No. 23.

---

[11] See Nos. 1103a, 1103b, below.
[12] See the headnote to Nos. 539–543.
[1] Hebr. 7:3.
[2] Nos. 838, 839 below.   [3] Nos. 888a through 892.

837g. One mornin' I was coming down / St. John's steeple. / I met three Christian people. / They were neither man, woman or children.—A man, a woman and a chil'.
Parsons, *Antilles*, III, 371, Grenada, 41.

837h. Me riddle, me ree, / Not a man shall explain this riddle on to me. / One morning I goin' up St. John's Steeple / An' all I met was Christians people / They were neither mens, women nor children / Still they was Christians people.—Man, woman, an' chil'.
Parsons, *Barbados*, p. 285, No. 53 var.

838. Pass through St. John, / Saw eleven St. John people. / They were neither men, women or children.—They was red ants.
Parsons, *Barbados*, p. 285, No. 53 var.

839. Once I was going to London Bridge, I met a man and a crowd of ladies and gentlemen, and I couldn't tell the ladies from the gentlemen.—Ants.
Johnson, *St. Helena Island, S.C.*, p. 160, No. 47.

840–904. Color

840–861. White

840–841. White Children

The only English riddle making a comparison to white children has the alternative answers, "teeth" and "watermelon." Although the children signify the white seeds of a watermelon, the parallels, which usually mention black rather than white seeds, suggest that this version is a chance variation of the ordinary form.

840. A whole lot of little white children playin' in red.—Watermelon.
Fauset, *Southern Negro*, p. 276, No. 3.

841. White Children: Teeth

The riddles for the teeth, tongue, and (more rarely) the gums are very varied. In this headnote I review the comparisons of the teeth to persons. Comparisons to animals[1] and to things[2] are surveyed in other headnotes.

Certain ideas occur rarely in comparing teeth to persons. In Javanese riddling, for example, the front teeth are six sisters who appear and disappear and cannot be differentiated from one another.[3] Such ideas are perhaps better suited to describe the stars. The Tatars say, "We were alone, thirty-three of us girls, once we joined together in an embrasure, we took places in one line."[4]

---

[1] See the headnote to Nos. 497–510.
[2] See the headnote to No. 1150.   [3] Tounsea: De C., 6.
[4] Kalashev and Ioakimov, p. 48, No. 8. The number may refer to the thirty-two teeth and the tongue, but the latter is not specifically mentioned. The riddle is a variant of the Turkish "We were, we were, we were thirty-two girls; crunching, we drew together, we brought together two rows" (Hamizade, 155).

The Parsee "In a room there are thirty-two mendicants"[5] is not fully intelligible.

In some countries, and characteristically in Africa, the contrast of Negroes and Whites yields materials for describing the teeth. The Duala speak of "Whites in a cave,"[6] the Kundu of twenty Europeans (Whites) in a hollow stone, where they are always wet, although no rain falls.[7] The SeSuto say, "Like a red man fought by many white men."[8] The Taveta refer merely to the uniformity of the teeth in "My children are all alike."[9] The Kanuri enlarge upon the theme and make a more extensive contrast in "Thousands of blacks, thirty whites.—Hair, teeth."[10]

Typical comparisons of the teeth to men engaged in symbolic acts are:

§ 1. White (ivory) soldiers. French: Haurigot, *French Guiana*, p. 120 (White soldiers and a red corporal in barracks). Spanish: Demófilo, 583; Rodríguez Marín, 314. Argentinian: Lehmann-Nitsche, 259. Chilean: Flores, 396. Cuban: Massip, 117. Porto Rican: Mason, 319. African, Songaï: Hamouda, 33 (My warriors are thirty-three in number, a thorn pricks one, all stop.—The teeth, which in chewing strike a grain of sand). Here the riddler apparently includes the tongue in the count. Ewe: Spieth, 20 (If I were not so strong, then I should not be found among those who swing the dagger). Indonesian, Alfoer: Wilken, 56 (They are all white men; they stand in two rows beside one another and fight every day). Hawaiian: Judd, 196.

The soldiers are not always specified as white. See Spanish: Demófilo, 592, 1421; Rodríguez Marín, 318 through 320. Chilean: Flores, 91, 393. Italian: Tammi, 1. African, Bakongo: Denis, 1. Indonesian, Alfoer: Wilken, 5.

Teeth are often compared to fighting soldiers.[11]

The Bakongo employ the theme of soldiers (slaves) and a chief in describing a fire with sticks thrust into it: "The chief in the middle, the slaves round about."[12] It also serves for a pineapple: the chief is the fruit and the slaves are the pointed leaves surrounding it.[13] Similar conceptions are used for other purposes.[14]

§ 2. Nuns or monks in white. French: Rolland, 61; Westphalen, *Metz*, col. 199 (A woman dressed in red surrounded by thirty-two maidens dressed in white). Catalan: Pelay y Briz, 17, 223, Spanish: Demófilo, 136, 143, and p. 358, No. 27; Rodríguez Marín, 321. Italian: Tschiedel, 4; Ive, *Canti popolari*

---

[5] Munshi, p. 415, No. 18. [6] Ebding, 66, 67.
[7] Ittmann, *Kundu*, 121. For parallels to the theme of something being always wet see the headnote to No. 1150 below.
[8] Norton and Velaphe, 48. [9] Hollis, *Taveta*, 65.
[10] Lukas, p. 168, No. 4.
[11] See the headnote to Nos. 966–968, § 6, below.
[12] Denis, 29. See also Werner, p. 213, and a Pangwe riddle recorded by Tessmann, his No. 135.
[13] Denis, 66.
[14] See below, the headnote to No. 993, n. 6. See also the notes to Nos. 1024 and 1026.

318   *English Riddles*   [hn. 841

istriani, p. 298, No. 10; Ferraro, *Archivio*, XXI (1902), 541, No. 19; Panareo, *ibid.*, XXIII (1906–1907), 237, No. 7. Some Romance enumerations of the parts of the head contain a mention of a company of persons in white.[15]

§ 3. A company. We have already noted the rows of fighting soldiers.[16] The oldest version alluding to a company of men appears to be that in Al-Ḥarîrî's Thirty-fifth Assembly.[17] The Alfoer compare teeth to men in barracks: "The comrades keep looking through the window."[18] The Javanese "There are robbers in rows in a cave. They form in two rows. Whatever comes in surely dies, overpowered by the warriors. The bodies [of those who are killed] disappear without anyone seeing it"[19] shows an unusual degree of elaboration and some novel details. The Armenians compare the tongue to a leader of a troop: "Thirty-two warriors have one commander."[20]

§ 4. Threshing. Examples are very widely disseminated and are very curious in their details. The Portuguese say, "Press presses, broom sweeps, sends down to the cellar,"[21] which shows a surprising similarity to the Indian versions mentioned later. The Lithuanian versions differ widely among themselves and represent still other conceptions: see "A tiny, tiny house of threshers," which is merely a specialized variety of the previously mentioned notion of a company of people; "A very pretty little house full of threshers and among these threshers there lies a red dog," which is perhaps mingled with the description of the mouth as a garden in which a red dog lies;[22] "Twelve thresh and one rolls," which may be a degenerate version of conceptions cited later in this paragraph; and "Twenty-four threshed and a rack[23] turned [it] over,"[24] which is explained by the Lettish "Twenty-four threshers and only one turns [the grain]."[25] Several actors in different functions are introduced in the Russian "The cutter cuts, the wooden one carries, the bubbling son turns it in";[26] "The wooden one carries, the bony one gnaws, wet Martin constantly adds [to it]";[27] "The five-membered one carries, the city girl cuts, Martin himself turns it around";[28] "Two brothers thresh, white Andrew turns it around."[29] The Georgian "The white man threshes, the red man mixes, the poor fellow cries, 'Throw it down to me.'—Teeth, tongue, stomach,"[30] is

---
[15] See Milá y Fontanals, 1876, p. 27, No. 27, and the parallel cited in the headnote to Nos. 1100–1108, nn. 24–25, below.
[16] See § 1 above.   [17] See Friedreich, p. 176, No. 7.
[18] Wilken, 4.
[19] Ranneft, *Poëzie*, p. 87, No. 2. For other comparisons of the mouth to a cave see below, No. 1150a and the headnote to No. 1150.
[20] Zelinski, p. 57, No. 18.
[21] Parsons, *Cape Verde*, 206.
[22] Compare the headnote to No. 1151 below.
[23] The translation is uncertain.
[24] The Lithuanian texts are, in order, Jurgelionis, 175, 176, 177, 178.
[25] Bielenstein, 694.   [26] Sadovnikov, 493.
[27] Sadovnikov, 493*g*.   [28] Sadovnikov, 493*i*.
[29] Sadovnikov, 1742; Preobrazhenskii, p. 170.
[30] Blechsteiner, 24.

closely allied to the Tunisian Arabic "The white ones thresh, the red one presses it down, the camel lets it pass, the sea swallows it up."[31] The Zyrian "Thirty people threshing, one turns over the sheaves"[32] is the scene already noted in Lithuanian riddling.

The Mongolian "The white horse chops it, it pushes it back and forth, the fallow horse mixes it, it pushes it into the well"[33] and "The magpie chisels it and pushes it on, the mouse mixes it and throws it in its own well"[34] are curious adaptations of the theme to animals.

§ 5. A mill and grinding. Comparisons of this sort are rarer than one might expect. The author of the *Ancren Riwle* of the thirteenth century suggests how this concept might yield matter for a riddle: "'Wheat is holy conversation,' as St. Anselm saith. He grinds chaff who prates idly. The two cheeks [jaws?] are the grindstones; the tongue is the clapper."[35] A few modern riddles of this sort are closely related to the previously cited riddles describing threshing. See, for example, the Ho "Twenty or thirty men are grinding paddy, and only one man is stirring or moving it."[36] Comparisons which are based primarily on the notion of grinding in a mill are seen in the Kashmiri "Above is a dry mill, dry and wet will meet there; for it the world will turn, but the upper millstone will never turn";[37] the Uraon "Many grind but one collects";[38] and the Mongolian "In a bulging vessel it is chopped, with a *khuloo* it is mixed; into a well it is thrown."[39] See other examples in the note to No. 1101 below.

§ 6. Kneading bread. The conception is somewhat similar to the previously discussed scenes of threshing and grinding. I have noted only the Yakut "They say that children in little white shirts knead and knead continually and then throw below what they have kneaded."[40]

§ 7. Scenes from nature. In a few instances the riddler conceives eating as analogous to a scene in nature. Compare the Vogul "A raging stream pours in, a little shovel stirs"[41] with the Kashmiri "A great green stone—the teacher's daughter pushed it, and it descended and arrived at Khanabul."[42] The great green stone is a lump of vegetables being chewed. There is probably an allusion or a pun in the reference to Khanabul, but I have not been able to interpret it.

---

[31] Stumme, *Tunis*, 58.
[32] Wichmann, *Zyrian*, 123, 241. Mordvin: Ahlqvist, p. 41, No. 10.
[33] Mostaert, 115. [34] Zhamtsaranov, 15.
[35] Ed. J. Morton, Camden Society, LVII (London, 1853), pp. 70–71; ed. J. Påhlsson (Lund, 1918), p. 29.
[36] Sarkar, p. 251, No. 29.
[37] Knowles, 65. The mill is the palate.
[38] Archer, p. 192, No. 198.
[39] Mostaert, 116. *Khuloo* is said to mean "wax in the ear." In this context it represents an instrument for mixing the chopped materials. Probably the word also means a stick for cleaning wax from the ear.
[40] Piekarski, 168.
[41] Ahlqvist, *Vogul*, p. 128, No. 27. [42] Knowles, 83.

841. A whole lot of little white children playin' in red.—Teeth and tongue.
Fauset, *Southern Negro*, p. 276, No. 3.

842–856. Whitey Drives Whitey

In this extremely popular riddle the speaker mystifies his hearer by the use of confusing and obscure terms. He conceals his meaning in the word "Whitey," which signifies variously a white man, a white dog, a white cow, and a white field. This riddle is known only in the English-speaking areas of the Western Hemisphere. A French version collected in Dominica[1] is obviously translated from an English source. Although it has not been reported from the British Isles, its wide currency in the West Indies, Nova Scotia, and the Middle West implies an origin in England.

The conception underlying this riddle is the describing of a scene, not an object, in obscure periphrases. This is a procedure entirely different from that characteristic of the riddles in this collection. It is analogous to a conception found in many very curious and obscure European enigmas[2] and may have arisen from them. A Scotch example is as follows:

> Ho! master above a master, rise from your fortune,
> Step to your shintilews,
> The grey cat o' grapus
> Is up the step of fundus
> With montapus on her tail.
> If there come no help out of fountoclear,
> We're gane an a' that's here.[3]

If the riddler had not given us the explanation, "Master of the whole house, rise from your bed; step to your breeches; the gray cat is up the stair with fire on her tail. If there come not help out of the well, we are gone, and all that are here," we could not guess what this gibberish could mean.

Inventions of this sort are widely known and are sufficiently similar to one another to suggest making an effort to derive them from a common source. See the Icelandic "I sat on a roarer [?] and looked at a tumbler [?] and saw a rich bear running with a piece of pleasure at its mouth. Then I called my crotch-slammer, and guess what she was to do!—He saw a polar bear with a woman's breast in its mouth. Then he called his bitch to set it on the bear";[4]

---

[1] Parsons, *Antilles*, III, 389, Dominica, No. 1 var.
[2] I have included the Whitey riddle as an example of a special enigmatic type. It differs from the parallels cited in this headnote because it contains no obscure words. The parallels containing obscure names and words have been discussed in Robert Petsch, "Die Scheune brennt," *Zeitschrift des Vereins für Volkskunde*, XXVI (1916), 8–18; Walter Anderson, "Novelle popolari sammarinesi," *Acta et commentationes Tartuenses* (Dorpat), Ser. B, X, Heft 5 (1927), pp. 16–17, No. 8; Kenneth Jackson and E. Wilson, "The Burning of the Barn," *Folk-Lore*, XLVII (1936), 190–203; Martha Long, "An Old Riddle from Berkeley," *Western Folklore*, VII (1948), 64.
[3] Chambers, *Scotland*, p. 113.
[4] Árnason, 930. The meaning of the words queried is uncertain. His Nos. 929 and 931 through 937 are of similar construction.

the Lithuanian "The stealers of the bare foot run up, they catch the Meckmeck,[5] the people of Kamanten drive them away.—Wolves seize a goat, the herdsmen pursue them";[6] and the Russian "I shall go into *ukhta*.[7] I shall find *valukhta*.[8] If it were not for *kubikhta*,[9] I should not come out alive.—Forest, wild beast, gun."[10]

The only version which shows any similarity to the English Whitey riddles is the Russian "As I walked along the road, I was looking. There stands property and in another property there walks yet another property. I took that property and struck it and took property from property.—Horse and foal in a wheatfield."[11] The word *dobro*, which I have translated "property," also signifies "good." In both the scene and the manner of description this is similar to the English texts.

842–844. Whitey Drives Whitey out of Whitey (Cotton Field)

For convenience, I divide the many texts of this version into three types: Nos. 842*a* through 842*i*, in which a white creature (usually a dog but occasionally a person or an unnamed creature) drives out a white cow; Nos. 843*a*, 843*b*, in which a white dog drives out some animal not a cow; and Nos. 844*a* through 844*d*, in which a man sends a person and not a dog to drive out the animal. This system of arrangement is a rough-and-ready classification which seems to indicate what little can be guessed about the historical relations of the texts. It involves the conjecture that riddlers have replaced the dog and cow of such riddles as Nos. 842*b* and 842*f* by either another animal or a person, but in the absence of old versions and parallels from other languages any such conjectures are necessarily somewhat doubtful.

842a. Whitey run whitey outer whitey.—White man run a white cow outer white cottonfield.
 Parsons, *Aiken, S.C.*, p. 34, No. 66; Smiley, *Virginia, etc.*, p. 375, No. 3.

842b. Whitey runnin' Whitey out de cottonfield.—White dawg runn'n a cow.
 Bacon and Parsons, *Virginia*, p. 312, No. 1 var.

842c. Whitey in a whitey, whitey sent a whitey to get a whitey out of whitey. —A white cow in a white cotton patch.
 Farr, *Tennessee*, p. 320, No. 27.

842d. Whitey sen' whitey to run whitey out o' whitey.—White man sen' white boy run white cow out o' cotton fiel'.
 Johnson, *St. Helena Island, S.C.*, p. 158, No. 24.

842e. What is this? / Called white, / Called white out of white?—A white man calling a white dog to get a white cow out of white cotton.
 Fauset, *Southern Negro*, p. 283, No. 84.

---

[5] Onomatopoetic "for a goat."
[6] Schleicher, p. 211.
[7] Perhaps "shady."
[8] Perhaps "careening."
[9] Noisy one.
[10] Sadovnikov, 1405.
[11] Sadovnikov, 852; see also his Nos. 870, 879.

842f. Whitie saw Whitie in whitie; / Whitie sent Whitie to drive Whitie out of whitie, / And Whitie went and drove Whitie out of whitie.—The white man sent Whitie, the dog, to drive Whitie, the cow, out of the cotton-field.
Chappell, p. 237, No. 41.

842g. As I went by Whitey, I looked over Whitey, and I saw Whitey in Whitey. I called Whitey to drive Whitey out of Whitey.—A white dog is called to drive a cow, "Whitey," out of a field of cotton.
Brewster, *Indiana*, 35.

842h. Ber Whitey drove Whitey out o' Whitey. What's dat?—White man drove a white cow out of a cotton field.
Parsons, *Sea Islands, S.C.*, p. 152, No. 2 var.

842i. Whitey in whitey, / Whitey took whitey, / Run whitey out o' whitey. —A white man calling a white dog to get a white cow out of white cotton.
Fauset, *Southern Negro*, p. 284, No. 85.

843a. White told White to take White and run White out of Whitey.—A white man sent a white dog to drive a white rabbit out of a white cotton-patch.
Bacon and Parsons, *Virginia*, p. 326, No. 123, and p. 312, No. 1; Parsons, *Sea Islands, S.C.*, p. 152, No. 2; Puckett, *Southern Negro*, p. 53; Fauset, *Southern Negro*, p. 284, No. 87. A dog driving sheep out of a cotton-field: Bacon and Parsons, *Virginia*, p. 312, No. 1 var.

843b. Riddle m' riddle, I'll tell you this riddle, / Perhaps you may tell it to me, / Whitey send whitey to drive whitey out of whitey groun'.—White man had a white dog to chase a white chicken out of his ground.
Parsons, *Antilles*, III, 439, Anguilla, 9.

844a. Whitey sent Whitey to chase Whitey out of Whitey.—A white man sent a white lady to chase a white lamb out of a cotton field.
Parsons, *Antilles*, III, 363, Trinidad, 8.

844b. Me riddle me racket / Perhaps I may tell you / And perhaps I mightn't. / Whitey sen' Whitey to dri' Whitey out o' Whitey.—White man sent a white woman to drive a white horse out of the cotton piece.
Parsons, *Antilles*, III, 437, St. Martin, 32.

844c. White told white to go in white and get white.—A white man told a white boy to go in the white cotton-field and get the white dog.
Knortz, p. 237, No. 126; Fauset, *Southern Negro*, p. 284, No. 87.

844d. A white somepin' / Took a white somepin' / Run a white somepin' / Out a' a white somepin'.—A white man calling a white boy to get a white cow out of white cotton.
Fauset, *Southern Negro*, p. 284, No. 86.

845–850. Whitey Drives Whitey out of Whitey (Cornfield, Grainfield, Garden, Cabbage Patch, Buckwheat)

845. Whitey runnin' Whitey out de corn-field. You give up?—White dawg runnin' a cow out de corn-field.
Parsons, *Aiken, S.C.*, p. 34, No. 66, var. 2.

846. Whitey in the Whitey, / Whitey told Whitey / To drive Whitey out of the grain.—A white woman told her dog Whitey to drive a cow whose name was Whitey out of the field of grain.
Fauset, *Nova Scotia*, p. 152, No. 45 var.

847a. Whitee send whitee go an' drive out whitee out a whitee garden. What is dat?—A white man sends his white servant to drive a white horse out of a white man's garden.
Johnson, *Antigua*, p. 87, No. 52.

847b. Whitey send Whitey to go and drive out Whitey out of de Whitey gyarden.—A white man sent his white servant to drive his white horse out of his garden.
Parsons, *Antilles*, III, 430, St. Kitts, 7.

848. Whitey sent Whitey to drive Whitey out of de gyarden.—A White lady sent a white dog to drive a white fowl out of de gyarden.
Parsons, *Antilles*, III, 445, St. Croix, 30.

849a. Whitey-whitey send whitey-whitey to drive whitey-whitey from eating whitey-whitey.—White man sends his white boy to drive the white goat out of the cabbage patch.
Beckwith, *Jamaica*, p. 204, No. 199.

849b. Whitey told Whitey to drive Whitey out of Whitey.—A white man told a white boy to drive a white cow out a white cabbage head.
Parsons, *Bermuda*, p. 247, No. 10.

850. White sent white to drive white out of white.—Mr. White sent his white dog to drive the white cow out of the white buckwheat.
Gardner, *Schoharie Hills, N.Y.*, p. 257, No. 37.

851–853. Whitey Drives Whitey from Whitey (Clothes)

851. Whitey sen' Whitey to race Whitey off of Whitey.—A white woman sent a white child to race a white duck off a white clo'es.
Parsons, *Barbados*, p. 277, No. 4.

852a. Whitey sent Whitey to stop Whitey eating Whitey.—White man sent white boy to stop cow eating white clothes.
Parsons, *Eleuthera and Watling's Islands, Bahamas*, p. 439, No. 4.

852b. Ber Whitey sen' Ber Whitey to drive Ber Whitey f'om eatin' Ber Whitey.—A white lady sen' a white servan' ter drive a white cow f'om eatin' a white clo'se.
Parsons, *Bahamas*, p. 482, No. 105.

853. Whitey sent Whitey in de gyarden to dri' Whitey f'om eatin' Whitey.—De white mistress sent a white servant to drive de white horse f'om eatin' de white close [clothes].
Parsons, *Bahamas*, p. 473, No. 18.

854–856. Whitey Drives Whitey out of Whitey (Stable, House)

854. Whitey in a whitey, / Whitey told a whitey / to go drive whitey / out of whitey.—A white lady told a white dog to drive the white cow out of the white house.
Parsons, *Aiken, S.C.*, p. 34, No. 66, var. 1.

855. Whitey Whitey sent Whitey Whitey to lock up Whitey Whitey in Whitey Whitey.—A white man sent a white groom to lock up a white horse in a white stable.
Parsons, *Antilles*, III, 371, Grenada, 44.

856. Whitey sent Whitey to chase Whitey out of Whitey.—White man sent a white groom into a white stable for a white horse.
Parsons, *Antilles*, III, 363, Trinidad, 8 var.

857–859. Whitey Goes About

857. Whitie, Whitie, up and down, / Whitie, Whitie, all around town.—Teeth.
Parsons, *St. Helena Island, S.C.*, p. 227.

858. Whitey up an' down, / Whitey, whitey, all 'roun' town.—Dat's yer feet.
Parsons, *Sea Islands, S.C.*, p. 168, No. 97.

859. Whitey whitey can't climb whitey whitey.—Smoke.
Beckwith, *Jamaica*, p. 203, No. 186.

860–861. Whitey Goes Upstairs

860. Whitey went upstairs, / Whitey come downstairs.—White hen went upstairs and laid an aigg, an' she come down.
Parsons, *Aiken, S.C.*, p. 25, No. 5.

861. Whitey went upstairs / An' lef' Whitey.—White hen went upstairs and laid an aigg, an' she come down.
Parsons, *Aiken, S.C.*, p. 25, No. 5 var.; Bacon and Parsons, *Virginia*, p. 323, No. 104; Parsons, *Robeson Co., N.C.*, p. 388, No. 1; Fauset, *Southern Negro*, p. 284, No. 88.

862–864. Black

862. Two blacke leapt over the lake with their mouthes full of men's bones.—That is a payre of shoes on a man's feet, when a man leapes over a lake; for they be blacke, and they are within full of man's flesh and bones.
Meery Riddles (1629), No. 12 = Brandl, p. 10.

863. Papa take hairy-hairy, put in blackey-blackey.—Brush and blacking.
Beckwith, *Jamaica*, p. 204, No. 196.

864. Blackey cover ten.—Boots cover toes.
Beckwith, *Jamaica*, p. 203, No. 183.

865–904. Two or More Colors

865–870. Whitey and Blackie (Brownie)

865. Blacky wen' into Whitey an' drive Blackey outer Whitey.—Black boy and cottonfield.
Parsons, *Sea Islands, S.C.*, p. 152, No. 2 var.

866. Mrs. Black went in black, / And came out, left white.—Black hen went in a hollow log and left a white egg.
Fauset, *Southern Negro*, p. 284, No. 89.

867. Blackey went in blackey, blackey came out of blackey, and blackey left whitey in blackey.—A black hen went in a black stump and laid a white egg.
Farr, *Tennessee*, p. 323, No. 70.

868. Blackie upstairs, / Whitie downstairs.—Hen lays downstairs and goes up.
Parsons, *Guilford Co., N.C.*, p. 204, No. 29.

869. Blacky went up de hill, put down Whitey an' came back.—Black fowl went up and lay a white egg and came back down.
Parsons, *Antilles*, III, 445, St. Croix, 29.

870. Browney go in, / An' Whitey come out.—Rice.
Parsons, *Barbados*, p. 278, No. 10.

871–877. Red Man and Black (White) Man

Riddlers have readily hit upon the obvious symbolism of comparing a fire to a red man and a pot above it to a black man and have as readily added many minor modifications of the fundamental idea. In some instances riddlers carry personification to the extent of creating figures bearing names like Mr. Redman, John Redman, and the like or of inventing characteristic actions. These ideas are closely related to the curious proverb recorded by Cervantes and others: "Said the pot to the kettle, 'Get away, Blackface!'"[1] Themes very similar to this proverb appear in such riddles as "Black said to Red, 'Break me and you're dead!'"[2] Here the reference is to the bursting of the pot and the extinguishing of the fire. The oldest version of this theme, "Vidi mortuum

---

[1] *Don Quixote*, II, chap. lxvii. For proverbs in dialogue see Archer Taylor, *The Proverb* (Cambridge, Mass., 1931), p. 158; Samuel Singer, *Schweizerisches Archiv für Volkskunde*, XXXVIII (1940–1941), 136–137.

[2] Danish: Kristensen, p. 68, § 153, No. 250, and p. 103, § 276, No. 432. For parallels see Breton: Orain, *Ille-et-Vilaine*, p. 148; Lavenot, *Basse-Bretagne*, p. 669. French: Rolland, 77; and Rolland, *Rimes*, p. 209, No. 61; Bladé, *Armagnac*, 76; Lacuve, *Poitou*, p. 355, No. 47; Pineau, *Poitou*, 14; Carnoy, *Picardy*, p. 54; Lallemant, *Argonne*, p. 235; Sébillot, *Auvergne*, 31; Dardy, *L'Albret*, p. 329; Lespy, *Béarn*, 8; Parsons, *Antilles*, III, 409, Guadaloupe, 156, and p. 448, Hayti, 19.

sedentem super vivum, et ex risu mortui moriebatur vivus,"[3] employs the contrast of the living and the dead rather than that of red and black. It belongs to the eleventh century.

Riddlers do not usually say that the actors are related to each other, but the Italians call Red and Black mother and daughter[4] and the modern Greeks say of a fire, "Of a red mother a black child is born [who says], 'I have no wings, but fly to find the clouds.'"[5]

The activities ascribed to Red and Black range from that in the simple Hungarian description of a copper kettle, "It is a pasha, its belly is red"[6] or "There is a pasha under the bench, he has a red belly"[7] and the Abyssinian "A red boy who always stays in the house"[8] to such ingenious and complicated inventions as the Kxatla "Tell me: baboon, squat on your haunches so that the children may rejoice!"[9] In this, "baboon," who is appropriately chosen because his black fur resembles a sooty pot, might perhaps be better set off by an exclamation point.

Although the activities vary widely according to the speaker's ingenuity, three main types—sitting;[10] sitting in a chair;[11] beating, tickling, or licking Black[12]—are probably the most abundantly represented. Riddlers who mention burning, boiling, or warming[13] often admit the answer or a characteristic aspect of the answer into the riddle itself and thus exceed the limits of good enigmatic technique. As examples, consider the Mongolian "Four old women sit and warm their livers.—The stand for the cauldron and its four feet"[14] and "Four sisters warm their livers, an old woman alone burns her buttocks."[15]

Some miscellaneous comparisons of pots and men call for brief comment. The Mingrelians say, "A red man runs around a black man,"[16] and the Faeroese, "Red plays under the black bottom."[17] There are a few examples of three colors and three actors, representing fire, a pot, and milk,[18] or (more rarely) a pot, chain, and fire.[19]

Comparisons in terms of animals are cited below in the appropriate footnotes. Some themes are borrowed from other riddles. The Norwegian "Seven red cows in a ring and a black cow in the middle"[20] or the Arabic "There are

---

[3] Malein, p. 233, No. 2. See the headnote to Nos. 828–829, § 6, above.
[4] Cimegotto, *Archivio*, XIII (1894), 436, No. 30.
[5] Stathes, p. 335, No. 19.   [6] Arany and Gyulai, III, 293, No. 3.
[7] *Magyar Nyelvör*, XXXI (1902), 533, No. 35.
[8] Littmann, *Tigriña*, 8.   [9] Schapera, 103.
[10] No. 875 below.   [11] No. 876.
[12] No. 872.   [13] No. 873a.
[14] Mostaert, 37.   [15] Mostaert, 38.
[16] Blechsteiner, p. 157, No. 7.
[17] Hammershaimb, *Antiquarisk tidsskrift*, III (1849–1851), 318, No. 33 = Qvigstad, note to No. 113.
[18] Norwegian: Brox, *Ytre Senja*, 68, citing Nordeng, 11; Nergaard, p. 170, No. 43. Swedish: Ström, p. 372, "Sysselsättningar," 2, 3.
[19] Gianandrea, *Canti popolari marchigiani*, p. 299, No. 13.
[20] Brox, *Ytre Senja*, 76.

black goats, red goats come to them, and all become red,"[21] has probably been suggested by the riddles for coals or loaves of bread.[22] On the whole, the parallels mentioning animals agree rather closely with those mentioning persons. A symbolism peculiar to animals is not often found. See, however, the examples of one animal licking another. Bulgarian: Gubov, 166, 168, 171, 172, and 173 (The reddish ox licks the black one). Russian: Bardin, p. 243, No. 7 (The black cow stands still, while the red one licks it). Finnish: Lönnrot, 1414 = Henssen, 88 (A red horse licks a black mare). Turkish: Katanov in Radlov, IX, 614, No. 67 (There are a red horse and a black horse that lick each other). African, Togo: Schönhärl, 169 (A goat licks a pot), in which riddle only the fire is represented by an enigmatic equivalent. SeSuto: Norton and Velaphe, 49 (The red ox hits the black, the black the white, which leaps out of the kraal.—Fire heats the pot, the pot the milk [which boils over]). Indian, Uraon: Archer, p. 191, No. 178 (The black cow is sleeping. The red cow is licking). Indonesian, Engganee: Helfrich, *Engganee*, p. 517, No. 5. Like the Ossete "A black rider on a black horse,"[23] the Cherekessian riddles for a pot and chain, "A black dog reaches from above and raises another black dog" and "Two black dogs are quarreling,"[24] contain this theme without a contrast of colors. It is interesting that this notion of red and black animals symbolizing fire and a pot should be found in the easternmost parts of Asia. The Mongols says, "A red cow licks a black cow" and "A red cow licks a black cow and makes her weep,"[25] and the Ainu, "What is the red dog that licks a black dog?"[26] Some versions are conceived in terms of persons and animals.[27] Riddlers have also compared a pot on the fire to a hen on its nest.[28]

Comparisons of a fire to another object are rare. Riddlers ordinarily compare things of entirely different categories: a mill to an animal, a tree to a man, an egg to a man, and so on. Typical of the infrequent comparisons of a fire to a thing are the Modern Greek "Red stick strikes black bottom";[29] and "A red lash beats a black bottom";[30] the Malayalam "A thousand ripe areca nuts in a hole.—Glowing coals on the hearth."[31] The Polish flame riddle, "The red guts strike against the black sieve,"[32] becomes intelligible when we realize that the supposed sieve is a pile of crossed logs. The vague Bavenda description of a veldt fire as "Red in front, black behind"[33] outlines no clearly conceived figure and apparently involves only the seeming impossibility of combining these two colors in an actual object.

---

[21] Ruoff, p. 27, No. 39.
[22] See above, Nos. 493a, 493b, and the headnote to No. 493, § 2.
[23] Schiefner, 30.   [24] Tambiev, p. 57, Nos. 48, 49.
[25] Mostaert, 131 and var.   [26] Starr, *Ainu*, 71.
[27] See the note to No. 872 below.   [28] See No. 375a.
[29] Polites, *Neohellenika Analekta*, I, 204, No. 62.
[30] Stathes, p. 341, No. 57.
[31] Schmolck, p. 242, No. 22. Ripe areca nuts have a reddish tinge.
[32] Saloni, *Rzeshów*, 143.   [33] Stayt, 4.

Riddlers do not often use the contrast of red and black for other purposes than describing a fire, but the Modern Greek "Red rides Black.—Fez"[34] is the exception that proves the rule. It is probably adapted from the riddle for fire and a pot.

Descriptions of fire and a pot which do not mention colors are very unusual. See the Lithuanian "A tooter toots under a brazen bridge."[35]

871. As I went over London Bridge, / I saw a little house: I looked in, / Through the window, and there was / A red man making a black man sing.— A fire making the kettle boil.
Leather, *Hereford*, p. 233.

872. The red man tickles the black man all the time.—Fire under the pot.
Parsons, *Bermuda*, p. 249, No. 20.

873a. A red man tickle a black man make him belly boil up.—Fire under boiling pot.
Beckwith, *Jamaica*, p. 197, No. 124a.

873b. John Redman tickle John Blackman till him laugh *puco-puco*.—Fire under boiling pot.
Beckwith, *Jamaica*, p. 197, No. 124.

874. John Redman beat John Blackman till him gallop.—Fire under boiling pot.
Beckwith, *Jamaica*, p. 197, No. 124b.

875–877. Black Man Sits on Red Man

Riddlers usually apply this conception to a pot over a fire. Some scenes are described with unusual vividness or picturesqueness. In "I-am-black over I-am-red"[1] the Portuguese employ the first person. The Lapps say, "An old woman sitting in the corner with red berries in her lap.—Hearth and coals,"[2] and the Serbs, "A red old man looks into the pot."[3] Some riddlers make a comparison to a person sitting in a chair.[4] Some related conceptions are not easily quoted.[5] The French "There are many pretty red ladies, a black lady comes who chases them all.—Fire and oven"[6] describes the fire and the poker. It belongs with the descriptions of coals or loaves of bread in terms of animals who are driven out.[7]

Riddlers often conceive fire and a pot as a red horse on which a black man sits. Some of these inventions are unusually picturesque. The modern Greeks

---
[34] Dieterich, *Rätseldichtung*, p. 96, citing Kanellakis, p. 166, No. 19.
[35] Schleicher, p. 198.
[1] Parsons, *Cape Verde*, 132.
[2] Qvigstad, 16.   [3] Novaković, p. 16, No. 8.
[4] See below, No. 876 and note to No. 876.
[5] See French: Lespy, *Béarn*, 7. Italian: Coronedi-Berti, *Archivio*, II (1883), 433, No. 61; Ferraro, *ibid.*, XXI (1902), 542, No. 20.
[6] A. Ferrand, *Dauphiné*, p. 227. See also the headnote to No. 493, § 2, above.
[7] See the note to Nos. 493a, 493b and the headnote to No. 493, § 2.

say, "A black man rides a red horse";[8] the Uraon, "An old man washes at sunrise and jumps on a horse.—Cooking pot";[9] and the Baluchi, "The black mare is saddled, and the children's hearts are glad.—The griddle is put on the fire."[10] Slightly different is the Modern Greek "The frog spreads his legs and Blackbeard sits on him.—The kettle on the trivet."[11]

The Kolarians compare fruits composed of red and black parts to a man sitting. They say, "A Ghasi is sitting on a king.—*Sōsō* or bhelwa fruit" or, shifting the comparison to animal actors, "On a red cow a quail is sitting."[12]

875. De black man settin' on de red man head.—Pot settin' on fire.
Parsons, *Andros Island, Bahamas*, p. 276, No. 12; Parsons, *Sea Islands, S.C.*, p. 155, No. 16; Beckwith, *Jamaica*, p. 197, No. 123.

876. A black mon sitting in a red mon's chair.—Pot on a fire.
Parsons, *Antilles*, III, 422, Montserrat, 26.

877. A black sittin' on a red man head.—Fungee [corn flour].
Parsons, *Antilles*, III, 427, Antigua, 35.

878–884. Black Man Sits (Dances) on White Man

878. White man sitting on the black man's head.—Reel of thread.
Parsons, *Eleuthera and Watling's Islands, Bahamas*, p. 440, No. 5.

879. Black man sits on a white man head.—Hen sit on her nest.
Parsons, *St. Helena Island, S.C.*, p. 227; Johnson, *St. Helena Island, S.C.*, p. 159, No. 29.

880. A black man sit on a white man head.—Ackee.
Beckwith, *Jamaica*, p. 197, No. 121.

881. A white man stand upon a black man head.—Bammie on griddle.
Beckwith, *Jamaica*, p. 197, No. 122.

882a. White men sit in black men chair. What is dat?—Rice.
Parsons, *Antilles*, III, 436, St. Martin, 23.

882b. A riddle, a riddle, / Perhaps a tiggle. / A white man sittin' in a black man chair.—Rice in the pot.
Parsons, *Antilles*, III, 426, Antigua, 27.

882c. Black man sat in a white man's chair. Tell me what that riddle is.—Rice in a pot.
Parsons, *Antilles*, III, 438, Anguilla, 6.

883a. Mr. Blackman sit pon Mr. Whiteman table.—Black ink on white paper.
Beckwith, *Jamaica*, p. 197, No. 120a.

---

[8] Dieterich, *Rätseldichtung*, p. 96, citing Polites, *Neohellenika Analekta*, I, 230, No. 211.
[9] Archer, p. 182, No. 56.
[10] M. Longworth Dames, *Panjab Notes and Queries*, II (1885), 70, No. 423, § 3.
[11] Abbott, p. 313, No. 30 = Polites, *Neohellenika Analekta*, I, 212, No. 110.
[12] Wagner, 17 and 17 var.

883b. Black man dance on white man table.—Black ink on white paper.
Beckwith, *Jamaica*, p. 197, No. 120.

883c. White man dance upon a black lady's floor.—Pen and ink.
Parsons, *Bermuda*, p. 250, No. 33.

883d. Black man dance on white man sheet.—Black ink on white paper.
Beckwith, *Jamaica*, p. 197, No. 120*d*.

883e. Black man dance on white man head.—Black ink on white paper.
Beckwith, *Jamaica*, p. 197, No. 120*c*.

883f. Black man sit down on white man chair.—Black ink on white paper.
Beckwith, *Jamaica*, p. 197, No. 120*b*.

884. Black man walkin' all day on a black road, / Ev'y step he made, he stepped right.—Pencil and slate.
Parsons, *Barbados*, p. 286, No. 59.

885–904. Several Colors

885. When Ber Reddy stick Ber Blackey, make Ber Whitey laugh.—When fish stick de pot, make de water boil.
Parsons, *Bahamas*, p. 482, No. 106.

886. Mr. Redman box Mr. Blackman make Mr. Whiteman laugh.—Fire, baking pan, and bammie.
Beckwith, *Jamaica*, p. 197, No. 125.

887–904. Nicky, Nacky, Brown Tobacky

887. As I went up Heeple's Steeple, / I met a whole heap of people; / They was neither nicky nor nacky, / But they were brown as tobacky.—Wasps.
Oral, Indiana.

888a. As I went over Heepo Steeple, / I met up with a heap o' people, / Some was nicky, some was nacky, / Some was th' color o' brown tobacky.—An anthill full of ants.
Randolph and Spradley, *Ozark*, p. 75.

888b. As I went up Heeples Steeple / There I met a heap of people / Some was licker and some was lacker / And some was the color of a chaw of tobaccer.—A drove of ants going up a hill.
Carter, *Mountain White*, p. 78.

889a. I went up a heaple steeple, / Met a crowd of colored [variant: little] people; / Some was red, some was black, / Some was de color of a gingersnap.—Ants.
Parsons, *Sea Islands, S.C.*, p. 163, No. 62, var. 1.

889b. Once I was going up the hipple steeple, / I met a crowd of little people, / Some was white and some was black, / Some was the color of gingersnaps.—Ants.
Johnson, *St. Helena Island, S.C.*, p. 159, No. 30.

890. Some was Nick, / Some was Nack, / Some was de color of a gingersnap.—Ants.
Parsons, *Sea Islands, S.C.*, p. 163, No. 62, var. 2.

891. On top the church steeple a crowd o' people, / All the same kind, / Of [the color of?] my old straw kelly. Could you tell me what it is?—Ants.
Fauset, *Southern Negro*, p. 279, No. 31.

892. As I was goin' over London Bridge, / I met three kinds of men. / Some was brown, an' some was red, / An' some was black.—Ants.
Fauset, *Southern Negro*, p. 279, No. 30.

893. As I was going up Heeple Steeple, / There I saw all kind o' people, / Some was hickey, some was hackey, / Some was like old black tobaccy.—Hornet's nest in the grass.
Fauset, *Nova Scotia*, p. 155, No. 55.

894. As I went over the hill of Manoo, / I saw a flock of binny ewes. / They were naked, they were nacked, / They were white and yellow packed. / Such a flock of binny ewes / Never went over the hill of Manoo.—Skip of bees.
Praeger, *Béaloideas*, IV (1933–1934), 146, No. 27.

895. Went across of London Bridge, / Met a heap of people. / Some was nick, some was knack, / Some was colored across the back. / What was that?—A drove of partridges.
Fauset, *Southern Negro*, p. 279, No. 29.

896. As I was goin' up heeple steeple, / I met some Christian people. / Some were nickle, and some were nackle, / And some were the color of brown terbacker.—Partridge.
Bacon and Parsons, *Virginia*, p. 321, No. 78.

897. As I went across the Cumberland Mountain, / I met a gang of people. / Some were nick and some were nack, / And some had colors of their back. / What kind of people were they?—Quail.
Farr, *Tennessee*, p. 325, No. 100.

898a. As I went over London Bridge, / I saw a heap of people. / Some were nickey and some were nackey, / Some were the color of brown tobacco.—Quail.
Farr, *Tennessee*, p. 325, No. 101.

898b. As I was going through heeple steeple, / There I met a heap o' people. / Some were hicker, some were hacker, / Some were brown as chewing tobacker.—Quail.
Hudson, p. 83, No. 5.

899. I went up a heap o' steeple, / There I met a heap o' people, / Some pernickey, some pernacky, / An' some de color brown terbacky.—Bees, yellow jackets, and wasps.
Parsons, *Guilford Co., N.C.*, p. 202, No. 10.

900. I went across London Bridge, / I met a heap of people; / Some was wix, / Some was wax, / Some was the color of ol' chaw terbacker.—Swa'm o' bees.
Parsons, *Robeson Co., N.C.*, p. 390, No. 20.

901. As I was going across a London bridge, / I met a lot of little people. / Some were nicker, some were nacker, / Some were the color of a chew of tobacco.—Partridges, wasps, bees, or red ants.
Redfield, *Tennessee*, p. 36, No. 9.

902a. As I went over London Bridge, / I met a heap of people, / Some were nick, some were brown, / And some were the color of tobacco.—Bees.
Hyatt, *Adams Co., Ill.*, p. 657, No. 10834.

902b. As I was on my way to London town / To buy my wife a soda cracker, / I saw a host: some black, some brown, / The rest the color of tobacker.—Bees.
Hudson, p. 84, No. 6.

902c. I went over to London and met a heap o' people. Some was knicker; some was knacker; some was the color of brown tobaker.—Bee swarm.
Boggs, *North Carolina*, p. 321, No. 4.

903. As I was going over London Brig, / I met a load of soldiers; / Some in ickets, some in ackets, / Some in red and yellow jackets. / What were they?—A swarm of wasps.
Baring-Gould, *Notes and Queries*, 3d ser., VIII (1865), 325.

904. As I went up heeple steeple, / There I met a heap of people, / Some were black and some were blue, / Some were the color of my old shoe.—Wasps.
Hyatt, *Adams Co., Ill.*, p. 670, No. 10938.

905–982. Function

905–936. Residence

905. Residents in the Bush (Underbrush)

905. My fader have some nice children. Dey all stay in de bush.—Watermelon.
Parsons, *Antilles*, III, 371, Grenada, 45 var.

906–916. Normal People in an Abnormal House

906. The House Leaps out of the Window

Inasmuch as scholars have frequently discussed this old and famous comparison of water to a house and fish to its occupants, I have limited the citation of parallels to those not previously mentioned and to those illustrating the wide distribution of the theme. No doubt the riddle owes part of its popularity, particularly in western Europe, to its use in the Apollonius romance. Perhaps the most interesting variation is Alexandre Sylvain's versification:

> Estant bien armé dedans ma maison,
> Le larron y vient et par trahison
> Me surprend, sans sçavoir mes estres:
> Ma maison s'en fuit par quelques fenestres.
> Ie meurs tost apres, car vivre ne puis
> Hors de ma maison. Dites qu'ie suis.[1]

I have not noted any other reference to the occupant of the house being an armed man, that is to say, a fish with scales. An Icelandic parallel is executed with remarkable neatness: "A guest came to the farmer's house. The farmer hurried to the door and jumped on the guest, but the guest stood firm. Then all the servants were locked in and the house jumped out of the window."[2] Buchler gives two versions in Latin and thus adds to our knowledge of the early forms of this well-conceived riddle.[3]

For discussion of this riddle see Gaston Paris in Rolland, pp. ix–x; Rodríguez Marín, p. 337; Pitrè, pp. lxxi–lxxii; Frederick Tupper, *The Riddles of the Exeter Book*, p. 225, No. 85, and *Modern Language Notes*, XVIII (1903), 3, 5; Petsch, *Neue Beiträge*, p. 138; Petsch, "Rätselstudien," *Zeitschrift des Vereins für Volkskunde*, XXVI (1916), 1–8; Schultz, *Bemerkungen*, p. 373; Ohl, Symphosius, 12; Flajšhans, pp. 7–8, § 6c.

Some very different riddles for fish and a net call only for passing mention. For example, the Catalan "What roars and the guests are mute and both move together?"[4] is probably a degenerate version of a riddle for Jonah and the whale. A curious Finnish text, "One threw the road about, hung the thief on a tree, and carried the dead home.—The road is the water, the thief is the net, and the dead the fish,"[5] is probably connected with a lying tale made up of fantastic impossibilities.[6]

Riddlers in many parts of the world have reversed this conception and have compared a house to a fish net. The Lapps[7] have hit upon this thought, and there is a parallel in Indonesia: "An old man sets a weir. Every night he catches many fish, but when the day dawns, the fish are gone."[8] Somewhat different is the comparison of a net to a house which its occupants cannot leave.[9] The description of a house as "That which envelopes stands still, that which is enveloped moves"[10] belongs to that variety of riddle which is couched

---

[1] *Cinquante Ænigmes françoises* (1582), p. 46, No. 42.
[2] Árnason, 314.
[3] *Gnomologia*, 3rd ed. (1614), pp. 419–420.
[4] Milá y Fontanals, 1877, p. 6 = Pelay y Briz, 189.
[5] Henssen, 248.
[6] For references to this tale see Archer Taylor, "Zwischen Pfingsten und Strassburg," *Studies in Honor of John Albrecht Walz* (Lancaster, Pa., 1941), pp. 25–27.
[7] Qvigstad, 44.
[8] Tounsea: De C., p. 243, No. 23. For the comparison of stars to objects that are seen at night and vanish in daylight see Nos. 1094a through 1094e below.
[9] Indonesian, Tabaru: Fortgens, 15.
[10] Indonesian, Soenda: Holle, *Soenda*, p. 374, No. 30.

in contradictory terms and expresses the functions of the objects described.[11] More concrete conceptions in terms of a motionless container and moving contents are found in the Albanian "A big cow, worms go in and out,"[12] the Turkish "The summit has a hole, but the interior has worms.—Yurt,"[13] and the Suk "There are entrails in the stomach."[14]

I can cite no parallel to a curious equating of a house and a man in the Kamba "A rich man who is usually rich in the night; when it gets light, he becomes poor."[15]

906. The robbers came to our house, / When we were a' in. / The house lap out at the windows, / And we were a' ta'en.—Fish caught in a net.
Chambers, *Scotland*, p. 112.

907. Flat-top House

A similar conception, but in terms of things and not persons, appears in the Turkish "Tiny tub full of little rods."[1]

907. A crowd of little men livin' in a flat-top house.—Matches in a box.
Johnson, *St. Helena Island, S.C.*, p. 158, No. 18.

908–916. People in a House (Chapel)

This simple and widely used pattern admits of many elaborations and embellishments: the color of the building may be mentioned,[1] or the occupants may be nuns or soldiers.[2] Since these special varieties usually occur in rather small areas, I conjecture that many of them are local modifications of the original theme rather than original, independent inventions. The fundamental idea, which is exemplified by the Bulgarian gourd riddle, "The house is full of children,"[3] is, however, so readily hit upon and so widely known that it may have been invented separately more than once. On the other hand, some apparently simple, undifferentiated versions may reflect the degeneration and attrition of an originally complex theme.

A characteristic special development, which English riddlers do not know, consists in adding the trait, "the key is of iron." This refers to a knife for cutting the fruit. Typical examples are Serbian: Novaković, p. 118, Nos. 10, 11 (A green corral, white sheep, an iron key opens it.—Watermelon), and p. 119, Nos. 1 (A green barn, black cattle, an iron key that opens it), 4 (I take the iron key and open the green fortress and drive out the black cattle).

---

[11] For riddles of this type see below, Nos. 1689 through 1703b and the headnotes to Nos. 1689 and 1690–1697.
[12] Hahn, p. 161, No. 43. Compare the headnote to Nos. 828–836, § 12, above.
[13] Katanov in Radlov, IX, 160, No. 1328. See also his p. 238, No. 36.
[14] Beech, 10.   [15] Lindblom, 99.

[1] Kowalski, *North Bulgaria*, 22.

[1] See No. 909, the note to No. 909, and the note to Nos. 910a through 910i.
[2] See the headnote to No. 909.   [3] Ikonomov, 50.

Arabic: Ruoff, p. 52, No. 29 (A green dome full of Negroes, its lock [is] from Allah, and its key [is] of iron); Socin and Stumme, 2 (Our pot is full of black men, iron alone can open it). By some confusion on the part of either the riddler or the translator, "pot" has been substituted for "house." Turkish: Kúnos, 11 (Its house is built by Allah, its door is opened by iron); Kowalski, *North Bulgaria*, 32; Moshkov in Radlov, X, 268, No. 38 (God builds the building; iron opens a door into it). Crimean Tatar: Filonenko, 13 (God created the house, and a knife opened the door to it). A rare western European reference to the knife which cuts the melon is the French "There is neither a door nor a little door, a knife is the porter,"[4] which contains elements belonging to the riddle for an egg.[5] The Serbian "A green field, black seed; it is opened with an iron key"[6] exhibits a curious contamination with the riddle for writing.[7]

Other variations in the conception of a house as representing something entirely different involve mention of the lack of a door,[8] or the notion of a house within a house within a house,[9] or such ingenious elaborations as the Albanian "The palace of the king is green; he is dressed in red, the company in black."[10]

Some elaborations of these comparisons of an object to a house and its occupants affect the supposed residents, that is to say, the seeds, rather than the house. They are called nuns or monks or soldiers. This is analogous to comparing peas or rice boiling in a pot to sheep or dancers.[11] An ingenious conception of this sort is the Kxatla "Tell me: wizards are quarreling inside the cave.—Melon seeds crackling in a pot [over a fire.]"[12] The Georgian chestnut riddle, "A round kernel within, a velvet skin without; surrounded by people, by a numerous army,"[13] contains elements of the usual riddle for a chestnut[14] and the additional comparison of the spines on the bur to an army.

A few comparisons to a container and its contents have as answers fruit and the seeds within.[15]

A comparison to people in a house is applicable to several objects, especially fruits containing seeds. See:

§ 1. A shoe and the toes. See No. 908 below.

§ 2. Fruits. See the headnote to No. 909.

---

[4] Bladé, *Armagnac*, 73.
[5] See the headnote to Nos. 1132–1138, § 1, below.
[6] Novaković, p. 119, No. 2.
[7] See Nos. 1063a, 1063b, 1063d through 1063i below.
[8] See the headnote to No. 909 and the headnote to Nos. 1132–1138, § 2.
[9] See Nos. 1161 through 1164 and the headnote to Nos. 1161–1164.
[10] Hahn, p. 159, No. 4.
[11] See the headnote to Nos. 489–490 and the note to Nos. 489a through 489m above, and also the note to Nos. 1032a, 1032b below.
[12] Schapera, 61.
[13] Glushakov, p. 25, No. 18.
[14] See Nos. 1276, 1277 below.
[15] See the headnote to No. 1355.

§ 3. The teeth. Catalan: Pelay y Briz, 82 (A chapel full of people and it is mine.—Mouth). Spanish, New Mexican: Campa, 207. See the headnote to No. 841, § 2, above.

908. A Brown House for Five People

The description of a shoe or glove as a house with rooms for five people occurs but once in the English riddles available to me. It is, however, widely current in Romance and Slavic folklore, in such picturesque forms as "Five little squirmers in a black forest"[1] or "Five little pigs looking out of the pen.—Toes in a torn shoe."[2] The Spanish specification that there are "five brothers of unequal size"[3] is probably related to a finger riddle.[4] In some versions the toes or fingers are called prisoners.[5]

The riddler often adds the remark that each of the five brothers goes to his own room or introduces a contrast of five rooms having but one door, and says that it admits to all of them. The variations in these conceptions are often great. The Icelanders say, for example, of mittens, "I am a house with two penthouses and am occupied by five brothers. When the snowstorm rages, I shelter them from bitter cold,"[6] which is too literal a description of the function of a mitten to be considered good riddling. The Norwegian versions, "Five sisters went through a door; when they got inside, each had her own house"[7] and "Five sisters entered through one door and each came to her own room,"[8] exemplify the usual theme and resemble the Swedish "Five maidens, each has her own room."[9] The Italian "Five persons dressed in one shirt"[10] is an adaptation of the nut riddle.[11] The Russian "In five little wells there sit five young men"[12] and "All the little boys went apart to little dark storerooms, each little boy to a little storeroom,"[13] as well as the Finnish "Five boys go in one door and yet each lives in his own chamber,"[14] make minor modifications in the conception.

Allusions to animals rather than to persons are somewhat less frequent.[15] The Algerian Arabic riddle for slippers is "Our cow is yellow. She has five little ones in her stomach."[16] The Kxatla "Five hyenas go into the same hole.—Shoes"[17] is much the same as the Chilean "Twenty ducks with only one

---

[1] French: Rolland, 129.
[2] Bulgarian: Gubov, 287. See also Berber: Basset, *Contes populaires berbères*, p. 125, No. 1.
[3] Demófilo, 1055 = Rodríguez Marín, 642. Cuban: Massip, 200.
[4] See Nos. 1040, 1041 below.
[5] See the headnote to Nos. 970–975, § 7.
[6] Árnason, 115.   [7] Landstad, p. 810, No. 30.
[8] Stafset, 113. See also Bergh, *Valdres*, 11, 57.
[9] Ström, p. 85, "Fingrarne," 2.   [10] Pitrè, 355.
[11] See the note and the headnote to No. 1005 below.
[12] Sadovnikov, 684.   [13] Sadovnikov, 685.
[14] Lönnrot, 1981 = Henssen, 31.
[15] See the Bulgarian riddle quoted above.
[16] Giacobetti, 341.   [17] Schapera, 80.

foot [in common]"[18] or the Mordvin "A man goes to the forest. He drives ten ducks before him."[19] The ducks may be chosen for their white color.

Riddlers occasionally make comparisons of this sort in which neither persons nor animals are mentioned. The Swedes say for gloves: "Five rooms, one door."[20] The Italian "Five cottage cheeses in one mould"[21] is more picturesque. The Lettish "Five stalls, one door"[22] and the Russian "Five storerooms, one door"[23] show the riddler's familiarity with the farmstead. The German "Five holes in one hole"[24] and the Korean "It has six doors, but goes in and out of one. What is it?—A Korean shoe"[25] set the hearer the task of resolving a paradox. This riddle has been ingeniously connected with an incident in Thor's visit to Utgardaloki.[26] Thor spends the night in a room that proves in the morning to have been the thumb of the giant's glove. This incident may be evidence that the narrator knew the riddle.

The comparison to men entering a room or living in rooms is applicable to:

§ 1. The fingers at meals. Indian, Kolarian: Wagner, 69 (Five brothers are entering at one time a flat hollow). Compare also the headnote to Nos. 980–982 below and the note to Nos. 980a, 980b, also the Chinese "Two pieces of bamboo drive ducks through a narrow door.—Eating rice with chopsticks" (Rudolph, p. 75, No. 27).

§ 2. Buttons and buttonholes. Portuguese: Parsons, *Cape Verde*, 192 (Ten men live in a house, each has his room; if one makes a mistake, all the others make a mistake).

§ 3. Grubs. Samoan: Brown, p. 344 (A great number of brothers, each has his own little room to himself.—*Afato* [a large edible grub]).

908. Black, white, and a brown house with five people in it.—Shoe and your toes.
Parsons, *Bermuda*, p. 255, No. 65.

909. A Chapel (Church, Convent) and Occupants

English folklore has but one example of this conception. This mid-seventeenth-century example has many parallels in European, particularly Romance, riddling. These parallels occur in both generalized and particularized forms: the fruit is a house or a chapel of characteristic color.

---

[18] Flores, 564, 565. The riddler conceives the entire body as a foot. The variant "Five ducks" conceives the leg as a foot.
[19] Paasonen, 400.
[20] Russwurm, *Eibo*, p. 133, § 316, No. 15. See also Estonian: Wiedemann, p. 292.
[21] Pitrè, 354.
[22] Bielenstein, 829.
[23] Sadovnikov, 662.
[24] German: Wossidlo, 464. Luxemburg: De la Fontaine, 59. See also the note to No. 13a above.
[25] Bernheisel, p. 83.
[26] H. V., "Vad gåtor kunna lära oss," *Årsskrift utgifven af Föreningen Brage*, I (1906) 20–23.

A special variation consists in saying that the house or chapel has no door or no window. Although a similar idea occurs in riddles for an egg, English riddlers do not seem to apply it to a fruit.[1] The Spanish say of a pomegranate: "A church full of people, it has no door by which they enter."[2] This is much the same as the Russian riddle for a cucumber: "Neither doors nor windows, the church is full of people";[3] the Votyak riddle for a pumpkin, "The house is full of people, [it has] neither a door nor a window";[4] and the Armenian riddle for a pomegranate, "What sort of house is it that has neither door nor window, but in which a thousand men live?"[5]

Some versions introduce a further specialization, which is at times inappropriate to the scene.[6] There is, for example, no pertinence in references to pupils or students or, least of all, to soldiers on one leg standing in a church. A Serbian watermelon riddle is "The church is full of pupils, but it has no doors."[7] This is similar to the Bulgarian "The school is full of little students. There is no door through which they jump out.—Melon"[8] and a curious Bulgarian description of a gourd, "The church is full of soldiers, all standing on one leg. There is no door for them to get out."[9] I do not fully understand the Russian "On the ice, the ice, I shall start playing *pikul'da;* on the ice there stands a churchful of people."[10]

The comparison of an object to a chapel (house) and its occupants is applicable to:

§ 1. Fruits. See the headnote to Nos. 908–916 above and the variation already cited in this headnote.

§ 2. A beehive. Spanish: Demófilo, 308 (armed people), 309 (convent of nuns);[11] Rodríguez Marín, 410 (little castle full of nuns). Argentinian: Lehmann-Nitsche, 413 (double house with five thousand ladies). Dominican Rep.: Andrade, 6 (convent of nuns). Porto Rican: Mason, 183 (little castle full of nuns). Russian: Bardin, p. 243, No. 14 (In a crowded hut old women are weaving linen). For descriptions of the shape or color of wasps and bees see Nos. 649, 894, and 899 through 904 above.

§ 3. The teeth. See the headnotes to Nos. 841, 908–916, § 3, and 1143–1151, n. 7.

§ 4. An egg. See No. 1134.

---

[1] See Nos. 1132 through 1137e and the headnote to Nos. 1132–1138, §§ 1–3.
[2] Alcázar, p. 161.
[3] Sadovnikov, 752.
[4] Wichmann, *Votyak*, 266.
[5] *Sbornik . . . Kavkaza*, II, No. 9. I cite this riddle from Blechsteiner, p. xlviii.
[6] For additional examples see the headnote to Nos. 910–915 below.
[7] Novaković, p. 119, No. 3.
[8] Gubov, 86.
[9] Gubov, 363.
[10] Preobrazhenskii, p. 172. The meaning of *pikul'da* is obscure.
[11] For various comparisons to nuns or monks, see the headnote to No. 841, § 2, above and the headnote to Nos. 1100–1108, n. 24, below.

909. j have a chapple all in green, forty souldiers be therein & euery souldier cloathed in white, ile give y^u a groat & tell me it right.—a pumpian [pumpkin].
Tupper, *Holme Riddles*, 123.

910–915. People in a House of Unusual Colors

The description in terms of people in a house of unusual colors usually refers to a fruit and its seeds. It is easily adapted to the fruits best known in any particular locality, but is obviously especially suited to the cucumber, watermelon, and pumpkin with their many seeds. It suggests itself so readily that we cannot insist upon tracing back the theme, or even the variations in details or the adaptations to various plants, to a single invention. Riddlers often elaborate the description of the house by mentioning the lack of doors or windows[1] or by adding some other detail appropriate to a house.

Somewhat different conceptions occasionally serve to describe the fruits which are best compared to a house of unusual colors. Both the Hungarian "There is a black cow eating red hay in a green stable.—Watermelon"[2] and the Dard "In the red sheep's pen white young ones are many—attend!—Red pepper"[3] are unusual comparisons to animals. A somewhat similar Rumanian comparison for paprika, "A knife full of ants,"[4] probably refers to the seed as a knife sheath.

There are a few comparisons to the seeds as persons who are not definitely conceived as being in a house of unusual colors. The Tabaru say of a palm and its fruits, "A Papuan, who holds hundreds and thousands of people in one hand straight in front of him."[5] The Armenian pomegranate riddle, "On the outside satin, in the inside thousands," is interesting for its companion piece referring to a chestnut, "On the outside thousands, in the inside satin."[6] Here we see how one riddle can give rise to another on an entirely different theme by a slight modification.

There are a few examples of the comparison of a fruit or a pod filled with seeds to things. The similarity to a sack or box filled with coins is obvious.[7] The Parsees describe a pomegranate as "A small ball containing fifty to one hundred grains."[8] The Kháriá say that an eggplant is "A black jug which conceals paddy [rice]."[9]

Typical themes to which the description in terms of a house, church, or room filled with people is applicable are:

§ 1. A cucumber. White Russian: Wasilewski, 23 (A hut full of people,

---

[1] See the headnotes to Nos. 909 and 1132–1138, and occasional parallels in the note to Nos. 910a through 910i and in the note to No. 913.
[2] *Magyar Nyelvör*, IV (1875), 234.
[3] Leitner, *Indian Antiquary*, I (1872), 91, No. 7.
[4] Papahagi, 13.   [5] Fortgens, 37.
[6] Glushakov, p. 25, Nos. 16, 17.
[7] For examples see the headnote and the note to No. 1355 below.
[8] Munshi, p. 417, No. 23.   [9] Roy and Roy, II, 455, No. 1.

without windows or doors). Russian: Sadovnikov, 752 (With neither doors nor windows, the church is full of people). Mordvin: Paasonen, 129, 156 (A room as large as a goose egg, its interior is full of people). Cheremiss: Porkka, 33 (My little room is full of people, I don't know one of them), 62, 119. Zyrian: Wichmann, *Zyrian*, 97. Votyak: Wichmann, *Votyak*, 266 (The house is full of people, neither a door nor a window).

§ 2. A watermelon. See Nos. 910a through 910i below.

§ 3. A pumpkin. See No. 911.

§ 4. A cantaloupe. See No. 912.

§ 5. A pimiento. Spanish: Demófilo, 811; Rodríguez Marín, 530 (A little church full of people). Chilean: Flores, 23, 27, 28 (pepper).

§ 6. An apple. See No. 913.

§ 7. A papaw. See No. 914.

§ 8. A soursop. See Nos. 915a, 915b.

§ 9. A poppy. Kashub: Patock, *Strellin*, 4 (In the midst of the sea there stands a tower, of which I can assure you that it contains thousands). Mordvin: Paasonen, 370 (A regiment of soldiers in a single barracks), 411 (In a tiny city seven hundred cossacks are quarreling).

§ 10. A pea pod. Votyak: Wichmann, *Votyak*, 175 (A very small hut; the hut is full of children). Also see below, No. 1005 and the headnote to No. 1005.

§ 11. An olive. Spanish: Demófilo, 21 = Rodríguez Marín, 455 (A hundred ladies in a convent, and all of them dressed in black). Arabic: Giacobetti, 75 (Our Negress is green. She has white children who become black).

§ 12. An orange. Spanish: Demófilo, 700, 701, 703 (All dressed in yellow); Rodríguez Marín, 462. Argentinian: Lehmann-Nitsche, 423 (Many women in an enclosure). Chilean: Flores, 474. Cuban: Massip, 135 (Ladies in a castle all dressed in yellow). Dominican Rep.: Andrade, 216. Porto Rican: Mason, 63.

§ 13. Other plants. Porto Rican: Mason, 200 (sarsaparilla). Surinam: Herskovits, 16a (The church is colored green, the priest is dressed in black, and the people are in white.—Soursop).

910a. Green and red, / Got a whole lot of little fellows inside.—Watermelon.
Fauset, *Southern Negro*, p. 276, No. 2.

910b. Green, white, and red, / Whole lot of nigger babies inside.—Watermelon.
Fauset, *Philadelphia*, p. 554, No. 11.

910c. Red inside an' full of little niggers.—Watermelon.
Parsons, *Robeson Co., N.C.*, p. 388, No. 2.

910d. A lot of little black children / Live in a red house.—Watermelon.
Bacon and Parsons, *Virginia*, p. 322, No. 95, var. 2.

910e. Something has green walls outside and red inside and a lot of little black people.—Watermelon.
Parsons, *Bermuda*, p. 247, No. 13 var.

910f. A little red woman lives in a green house and has black children.—Watermelon.
Parsons, *Bermuda*, p. 248, No. 13 var. Brown children: Parsons, *Bermuda*, p. 248, No. 13 var.

910g. A green house trimmed in white and red walls, / A heap o' black children inside.—Watermelon.
Fauset, *Southern Negro*, p. 276, No. 4.

910h. House set upon the hill, / Green on the outside, / Red on the inside, / Full of people.—Watermelon.
Fauset, *Southern Negro*, p. 276, No. 5.

910i. My walls are red, / My tenants are black, / My color is green / All over my back.—Watermelon.
Perkins, *New Orleans*, p. 106, No. 3.

911. Some red chil'run live in a green and white house.—Pum'kin.
Parsons, *Barbados*, p. 278, No. 13.

912. It's white, it's green. An' inside it's full of little yaller niggers.—Muskmelon.
Parsons, *Robeson Co., N.C.*, p. 388, No. 3.

913. House painted red outside, / White inside, / And colored people [variant: black people] live in it.—Apple.
Parsons, *Bermuda*, p. 248, No. 13 var.

914. A yellow house with yellow curtains and black people living in it.—Papaw.
Parsons, *Bermuda*, p. 248, No. 13 var.

915a. White woman live in a green painted house, an' have black children.—Sore sop [soursop].
Parsons, *Barbados*, p. 278, No. 11.

915b. A woman live in a green painted house. She white, and all her children black.—Soursop.
Parsons, *Antilles*, III, 376, St. Vincent, 12.

916. A House within a House and Filled with People

The notion of a house within a house within a house resembles scenes in cumulative nursery rhymes.[1] It occurs also in a cumulative tale.[2] A similar sequence, which deals with parts of the house, appears in a riddle for blood.[3]

---

[1] See the headnote to Nos. 1156–1164 below for a discussion of this technical device.
[2] See Archer Taylor, "Formelmärchen," *Handwörterbuch des deutschen Märchens*, II (Berlin, 1935–1940), 188–189, § 21.
[3] See Nos. 1156a, 1156b below.

916a. A green and a white house, inside of that green and white house is a red house; inside of that red house are little niggers.—Watermelon.
Knortz, p. 215, No. 12.

916b. There was a green house. Inside the green house there was a white house. Inside the white house there was a red house. Inside the red house there was a lot of little black babies. What was it?—Watermelon.
Fauset, *Nova Scotia*, p. 153, No. 50.

916c. Once there was a leetle green house, / In th' leetle green house was a leetle white house, / In th' leetle white house was a leetle red house, / In th' leetle red house was a lot o' black niggers. / What was it?—Watermelon.
Randolph and Spradley, *Ozark*, p. 86.

916d. Down in the field is a little green house; / In the little green house is a little white house; / In the little white house is a little red house; / Inside the little red house are a lot of little niggers.—Watermelon.
Brewster, *Indiana*, 32.

916e. In my father's garden there was a green house; / in that green house there was a white house; / in that white house there were several black members.—Watermelon.
Parsons, *Bermuda*, p. 247, No. 13.

916f. Way down on the hill there's a little green house. / Inside that little green house is a little white house. / Inside of that little white house is a little red house. / Inside the little red house are little black babies asleep.—Watermelon.
Hudson, p. 84, No. 11.

916g. Went over there in a lady's yard, / I seen a green fence; / Inside the green fence was a red fence, / And then a whole lot o' little children.—Watermelon.
Fauset, *Southern Negro*, p. 276, No. 1.

917–928. Abnormal People, Normal House

917–918. Abnormal in Form

917. My father has a houseful of children and everyone of their heads turn out of doors.—Nails in a house.
Beckwith, *Jamaica*, p. 188, No. 47.

918. Large house, lots of people, yet you can' [can't] see them.—Head, the people are the braids [the little twists of hair].
Parsons, *Bermuda*, p. 261, No. 126.

919–924. Abnormal in Color

919. My mama have a house and white boys. She put 'em in the house and they all come out brown.—Bread.
Parsons, *Antilles*, III, 364, Trinidad, 10.

920. My father has a houseful of children; every time they come out they come out with red head.—Annata.
   Beckwith, *Jamaica*, p. 188, No. 45.

921. My father has a houseful of children and everyone of them has a red cap.—Woodpeckers.
   Beckwith, *Jamaica*, p. 187, No. 44.

922. My father has a whole house of children; everyone have a white head.—Castor-oil beans.
   Beckwith, *Jamaica*, p. 188, No. 48a.

923a. A woman has a whole lot of children and all come out with black heads and red dresses.—Ackee.
   Beckwith, *Jamaica*, p. 188, No. 46b.

923b. Me fader hab a houseful o' chil'ren an' eb'ryone a dem a black head.—Ackee.
   Beckwith, *Jamaica*, p. 188, No. 46.

924. A whole lot o' little red-head chilrun stay in a flat-top house.—Matches.
   Parsons, *Sea Islands, S.C.*, p. 158, No. 41.

925–928. Abnormal in Function

925. There was a woman in a green painted house, have plenty of brown children, an' jus' as you touch her, all the children holler out *chickadee!*—Dry pease.
   Parsons, *Barbados*, p. 278, No. 12.

926a. My father have a houseful of children; if you touch one, whole of them cry.—Gungo peas.
   Beckwith, *Jamaica*, p. 187, No. 43.

926b. My sister have a whole house o' pickney and if you touch one, everyone cry.—Gungo peas.
   Beckwith, *Jamaica*, p. 187, No. 43a.

927. There's a house full of children, / When the wind blow, they all cry.—Dry pease.
   Parsons, *Antilles*, III, 366, Trinidad, 33.

928a. My fader have a set of children / And every one turn drummer.—Dry pease.
   Parsons, *Antilles*, III, 376, St. Vincent, 19.

928b. Sets of little boys come drummers.—Dry peas.
   Parsons, *Antilles*, III, 369, Granada, 6.

929–936. A Shipload of People

West Indian riddlers, particularly those in Jamaica, describe objects in terms of a shipload of people. The themes are the same, almost without exception, as those of riddles referring to a houseful of people (Nos. 917 through 927).

929–933. Abnormal in Form

929. My father has a shipload of Guinea people, but all their heads is turned down.—Bottles packed in straw.
Beckwith, *Jamaica*, p. 188, No. 49.

930. Me fader hab a Guinea ship o' nager; eb'ryone o' dem a t'ree foot.—Cooking-pots.
Beckwith, *Jamaica*, p. 188, No. 50.

931. My father sent for a ship-load of soldiers and everyone come with one eye.—Needles.
Beckwith, *Jamaica*, p. 188, No. 52. Me fader hab a whole Guinea ship a nager: Beckwith, *Jamaica*, p. 188, No. 52a.

932. My father sent for a shipload of men and everyone come with arm akimbo.—Coffee-pots.
Beckwith, *Jamaica*, p. 188, No. 51.

933. My father sent to Africa to buy some slave; everyone came with their heart on their back.—Ring.
Parsons, *Eleuthera and Watling's Islands, Bahamas*, p. 440, No. 7.

934–936. Abnormal in Color

934. Me fader come out wid a whole shipload o' Guinea-people; everyone has red.—Woodpecker.
Beckwith, *Jamaica*, p. 187, No. 44a.

935. Me fader have a whole shipload of Bungo nager an' everyone have a white head.—Castor-oil beans.
Beckwith, *Jamaica*, p. 188, No. 48.

936. Me ma ha' one Guinea ship a pickney; eb'ryone a dem head black.—Ackee.
Beckwith, *Jamaica*, p. 186, No. 46a.

937. Waiting

937. Six and four waiting for twenty-four.—Six holes in four horseshoes waiting for twenty-four nails.
Beckwith, *Jamaica*, p. 202, No. 179.

938–963. Moving

938. Come up and let us go; go down and here we stay.—Anchor.
Perkins, *New Orleans*, p. 110, No. 4.

939. Nine run, one come, two run.—Nine man run for the doctor, one baby born, two nipples run.
Beckwith, *Jamaica*, p. 202, No. 180.

940. Three old lady was goin' along. There [read: they] was deaf, dumb, and blind, an' still they was righteous.—Hymn book, prayer book, and Bible.
Parsons, *Antilles*, III, 438, Anguilla, 4.

941–942. Three Men Start for Heaven

Three men, or less frequently in western Europe three birds, rising in the air and suffering three different fates represent sparks, smoke, and fire. The various forms of this scene diverge widely and are perhaps not related to one another. A Slavic variety describes the three persons as members of a family: "The mother is stout, the daughter is red, the son [var.: grandson] went off to the skies"[1] and "The mother is black, the daughter is red, the son is long-legged, skillful, and bending around."[2] The contrast of the black mother and the red daughter is akin to Redman and Blackman representing the fire and a pot,[3] but it is difficult to know whether the two conceptions are even remotely connected. The Russian word for "red" signifies also "beautiful," and the riddler may have intended to say, "The mother is stout, the daughter is beautiful."

Another variety of this scene calls the actors geese and not persons. The Serbians say, "Two geese flew to God for dinner. A scorched bee met them and did not let them go to God for dinner.—Sparks";[4] the Bulgarian parallel is a dialogue, "Chingur geese came from below. The roasted forehead meets them, [saying,] 'Where are you going, Chingur geese?' 'We are going, roasted forehead, to die.'—Sparks go up the chimney and are extinguished."[5] These riddles are not entirely intelligible and are not elucidated by the further Serbian parallels.[6] They are probably related to the Palestinian Arabic "Three geese flutter. One flies away, one disappears, the third devours the world insatiably.—Spark, smoke, fire."[7]

Some versions mentioning only a single actor may be defective or fragmentary, but the available evidence is so scanty and so difficult to interpret that the relationships of the texts among themselves and their relationships to the preceding varieties are obscure. Typical riddles for a spark are the Swedish "Little and red, just when it flies, it falls dead";[8] the Russian "Grandfather's reel went off to the skies";[9] and the Serbian "I started going to God and broke my leg."[10]

941. Three men fe go a heaven: one go halfway an' turn back, one go right up, an' one no go at all.—Fire: spark, smoke, and ashes.
Beckwith, *Jamaica*, p. 195, No. 98.

---

[1] Russian: Sadovnikov, 144; Preobrazhenskii, p. 172.
[2] Russian: Sadovnikov, 145. For comparisons of smoke to a long person see the headnote to No. 575, § 2.
[3] See Nos. 871 through 876, above. See also the comparisons of a fire and utensils to the members of a family, as cited in the headnote to No. 1017 *bis* below.
[4] Novaković, p. 14, No. 3.
[5] Gubov, 134. The meanings of "Chingur" and "the roasted forehead" are obscure.
[6] Novaković, p. 14, Nos. 1, 2, and 4 through 8.
[7] Ruoff, p. 23, No. 19.
[8] Dybeck, *Runa*, 1849, p. 43, No. 26; Ström, p. 223.
[9] Sadovnikov, 151.
[10] Novaković, p. 13, No. 3.

942. w^t is that mak[e]s tears without sorow, tak[e]s his iourney to heaven but dys [dies] by the way is begot wth another, yet that other is not begot wthout it.—smoake.
Tupper, *Holme Riddles*, 14.

943. Jack and Jill Went up the Hill

This curious riddle appears to be an adaptation of the nursery rhyme, to which the riddler adds the notion that Jack cannot help Jill.

943. Jack and Jill went up the hill, / and yet Jack cannot help Jill.—Legs.
Parsons, *Bermuda*, p. 250, No. 31.

944–945. If They Come, They Don't Come

Since the Latin version needs no subjects for the verbs, it lacks the inaccuracy and ambiguity of most vernacular versions.[1] A curious variation of the theme is seen in the Tatar "If I say, 'Come! Come! [*Gät! Gät!*],' they will not come. If I say, 'Do not come! Do not come! [*Gälma! Gälma!*],' they will come."[2] The answer "lips" is explained as follows: the imperative *gät* contains no labial sound. In saying *gälma* the lips approach each other to produce the labial *l*.

944a. If he comes, I no come. If he no come, I come.—A farmer planting corn. If the crows come, it will ruin his crop, then the corn will not come; but if the crows don't come, his crop will come.
Bacon and Parsons, *Virginia*, p. 312, No. 7.

944b. A man have a corn field, an' he says, "If they come, they won't come; an' if they don't come, they come." The king ask him the meaning of that. He tell him, "If your pigeons come, your corn won't come; an' if your pigeons don't come, your corn will come."—De king ask him if he will keep it a secret until he see his [the king's] face again. Now after he tell him dat, he have a coin wid de king's face on it, he relate it [i.e., he looks at the coin and feels free to reveal the secret].
Parsons, *Antilles*, III, 434, St. Bartholomew, 1. The bracketed explanations were inserted by the collector.

944c. If he come, he no come; if he us come, if he us come, he come!—If the the crow comes, the corn doesn't come; if the crow doesn't come, then the corn comes. (Thus say the S. Carolina negroes when sowing corn.)
Knortz, p. 210, No. 2.

944d. If he come, he no comes, / If he no comes, he comes.—Corn and crow. If the crow comes, the corn doesn't. If the crow doesn't come, the corn does.
Fauset, *Nova Scotia*, p. 170, No. 152; Perkins, *New Orleans*, p. 110, No. 46; Bacon and Parsons, *Virginia*, p. 327, No. 136.

---

[1] For discussion see Ohlert, 2d ed., p. 10; Albert Wesselski, *Mönchslatein* (Leipzig, 1909), p. 236, No. 102. For reference to the theme in narrative use see J. Bolte, *Zeitschrift des Vereins für Volkskunde*, VI (1896), 162.
[2] Kalashev and Ioakimov, p. 50, No. 20.

944e. A prisoner was offered his freedom if he could think of a riddle which the officers could not answer. Looking through his prison bars, he saw a farmer planting corn and crows were flying overhead. The prisoner said, "If he come, he no come; and if he no come, he come." The officers could not answer, so he was given his freedom.—If the crows come and eat the corn, the corn will not grow; but if the crows do not come, the corn will not grow.
Oral, New York.

945. When it come, it does not come; when it does not come, it come.—Rat and corn.
Beckwith, *Jamaica*, p. 202, No. 177.

946–950. A Company of Dancers (Workmen)

Riddlers have very readily and naturally hit upon the idea of comparing nodding or waving objects to dancers. It is especially suitable for flowering plants with heads swaying in the breeze. The existence of very similar riddles in such widely separated cultural traditions as Vogul, African, and Samoan indicates how easily the idea suggests itself. In European Russia, the Vogul describe an unidentified grass "with red heads" as "Women with silken kerchiefs bend up and down in the meadow."[1] In Togo, the natives call leaves "dancers."[2] The Tschuana say, "Nikete's children dance, she does not.—Twigs."[3] The Wamajame have invented a still more vivid scene in "The warriors dance a dance.—The wind shakes the leaves."[4] The Samoans see grass ripe with seed as "A countless company of brothers wearing brown hats."[5] Many more examples might be cited, but these are sufficient to suggest the probability of separate inventions.

Some riddles of this sort are interesting for the ingenuity or aptness of the comparison. The Sukuma say of castor beans, "The chief's wives dance,"[6] and have in mind the bursting of the pods. A Ho riddler describes a pipal tree in "The mother stands still. Her children are little. When the wind blows, they dance."[7] The Tabaru refer to ripe rice in "Men by the hundreds and thousands, all bow."[8] A somewhat different, but related, theme occurs in the Wamajame riddle for wheat, "Many warriors have clubs."[9] Comparisons to a single person are less numerous.[10] Comparisons to animals seem to be unknown. Comparisons to things are unusual, as we might expect,[11] but see the Ten'a "I act as a broom, sweeping the place around me.—Grass tops."[12]

---

[1] Ahlqvist, *Vogul*, 16.   [2] Schönhärl, 41.
[3] Kuhn, *Tschuana*, 7.   [4] Ovir, 28.
[5] Heider, 23.   [6] Augustiny, 18.
[7] Sarkar, p. 253. See Mitra, *Notes on Ho Riddles*, pp. 252–253, and compare below, 1022a through 1022d and the note to Nos. 1022a through 1022d.
[8] Fortgens, p. 529, No. 14, and compare Nos. 135, 756, 834a and 834b above.
[9] Ovir, 26.   [10] See No. 756 above.
[11] Comparisons in riddles ordinarily deal with objects in two entirely different categories. Things are compared to animals or persons, not to other things.
[12] Jetté, 47.

Since these riddles describing dancers usually have the answer "flax," we may conjecture that the English answers "sparks"[13] and "bees" or "bugs"[14] are casual adaptations of the pattern. The riddles for rice cooking in a pot[15] show that similar conceptions are readily associated with fire. Waves are occasionally called dancers.[16]

Analogous comparisons in terms of animals or things are rare. I have noted only the Mordvin cabbage riddle, "Along the vegetable bed swans have settled down,"[17] and the Russian flax riddle, "On the field of Arsk there stand little white pillars. Their little caps are green."[18]

The scene of a group of dancers—the color of their heads or headdresses is often mentioned—is applicable to:

§ 1. Flax. See Nos. 946a through 946d, below.

§ 2. Grass, reeds, rushes. This is virtually the same as Nos. 946a through 946d. Serbian: Novaković, p. 18, No. 6 (One is playing on a pipe, the other is dancing.—Wind and reeds), and p. 19, No. 1 (Dudulin plays on a pipe, Tankosava dances, everything is shaking in the forest). Cherekessian: Tambiev, p. 65, No. 140 (Abedezkhian girls with broad head-coverings.—Rushes). Yakut: Piekarski, 310 (They say that damsels with feather-crested caps are dancing in a clearing in the woods.—During the fishing season, small birches are placed in holes cut in the ice and moved about in order to frighten the fish from these spots to the nets).

§ 3. Bees or bugs. See Nos. 947 through 948b below.

§ 4. Sparks. See Nos. 949a, 949b.

946a. Out in the garden / I have a green spot, / And twenty-four ladies dancing on that; / Some in green gowns, / And some in blue caps. / You are a good scholar, / If you riddle me that.—Flax.

Whitney and Bullock, *Maryland*, p. 173, No. 2672.

946b. At the end of my yard there is a vat, / Four-and-twenty ladies dancing in that; / Some in green gowns, and some with blue hat. / He is a wise man who can tell me that.—A field of flax.

Halliwell-Phillipps, *Popular Rhymes*, p. 146; Knortz, p. 228, No. 73.

946c. Down in the meadow there is a tan flat; / Four-and-twenty ladies dancing on that; / Some had blue bonnets and some had black. / Guess this riddle and I'll give you my hat.—Flax.

Gardner, *Schoharie Hills, N.Y.*, p. 255, No. 14.

946d. downe by the waterside stand a house & a plat [plot] & 4 & 20 ma[i]ds [MS: mads] dancing ther at ev^r one with a bell & a blew [blue] hat & w^t is that.—a feeld of hempe or flaxe.

Tupper, *Holme Riddles*, 37.

---

[13] Nos. 949a, 949b below.
[14] Nos. 947 through 948b.
[15] See Nos. 1032a, 1032b, and the note to Nos. 1032a, 1032b.
[16] No. 713 and the note to No. 713.
[17] Paasonen, 219.
[18] Sadovnikov, 1346.

947. Behind the king's kitchen there is a great vat, / And a great many workmen working at that, / Yellow is their toes, yellow is their clothes. / Tell me this riddle and you can pull my nose.—Bees making honey.
Hyatt, *Adams Co., Ill.*, p. 657, No. 10835.

948a. Way over yonder, in yonder flat / I saw ten thousand workin' at that. / Some wore green coats, some wore black. / Come, good scholar, an' unriddle that!—Bugs of some kind.
Parsons, *Guilford Co., N.C.*, p. 205, No. 42.

948b. Jus' say for other feller what that was: / In king kitchen there was a black bat [vat?], / Ten thousand workmen a-workin' at that. / Two yaller hammers and two black bats, / Now study out your lifetime—study out that.
—'At was a dead hog and all these bugs got in him workin', and yaller hammer is a bird.
Halpert, *New Jersey*, p. 201, No. 7.

949a. As I were going over London Brig, / I pipp't into a winder, / And I saw four-and-twenty ladies, / Dancing on a cinder.—Sparks.
Baring-Gould, *Notes and Queries*, 3rd ser., VIII (1865), 325 (Yorkshire).

949b. As I was going o'er London Bridge, / And peep'd through a nick, / I saw four and twenty ladies / Riding on a stick!—A fire-brand with sparks on it.
Halliwell-Phillipps, *Nursery Rhymes*, p. 133.

950. Down in the meadow I have a piece of fat [vat?]. / Four and twenty carpenters working at that. / Some have blue bonnets, and some have straw hats. / Riddle me that, and I'll give you a grot [*sic*].—Informant says that these are the "mud-men," who dug out the mud of the bog and made it into peat bricks.
Praeger, *Béaloideas*, IV (1933–1934), 144, No. 5.

951. Men Travel at Unequal Speeds

Riddlers conceive the act of picking a coconut either in terms of two men[1] or in terms of a man and a thing[2] moving at unequal speeds. When broken loose from the stalk, the coconut falls faster than the picker can descend. By specifying the men as messenger and doctor the riddler makes the scene more vivid. A very similar conception is employed in the Kashmiri walnut riddle, "The merchant descended from above, leaving his cloak behind him."[3]

951a. I climb an' he ride, yet he still get dere before me.—Coconut. You climb and pick de coconut, yet he still get down on de ground before you.
Parsons, *Bahamas*, p. 471, No. 5.

---

[1] Nos. 951a through 951g.
[2] Nos. 1255a through 1258a and No. 1258c.
[3] Knowles, p. 53.

951b. My father sent me to call the doctor. The doctor come before me.—Coconut. When you go up to pick the coconut, coconut fall down before you come down.
Parsons, *Antilles*, III, 428, Nevis, 15.

951c. My father is sick and send for the doctor. An' the doctor came back before the bearer.—Coconut dropped from the tree.
Parsons, *Antilles*, III, 422, Montserrat, 16 var.

951d. My moder have a boy, send him to call the doctor, but the doctor reach before him.—Pickin' coconut.
Parsons, *Antilles*, III, 369, Grenada, 15.

951e. I went to call doctor, doctor reach before me.—Coconut. You climb up the tree and you pick it, thrown down, it reach before you.
Parsons, *Antilles*, III, 369, Grenada, 15 var.

951f. I went for a doctor and the doctor went before me.—Coconut. Climb tree, nut falls first.
Parsons, *Antilles*, III, 365, Trinidad, 26.

951g. Send bwoy to fetch doctor, doctor come before bwoy.—Boy climbing after a coconut; nut falls before the boy comes down.
Beckwith, *Jamaica*, p. 198, No. 135.

952–957. Pursuing

The description of an object in terms of men pursuing one another occurs in various forms, which are here separated according to the sex and family relationship of the actors. Nos. 952 through 957 include versions in which the actors are not said to be related to one another.[1] In Nos. 996 through 1001, the actors are brothers; in Nos. 1014a through 1015b, sisters; and in Nos. 1029a through 1030, a family. I have adopted a classification suggested by Lehmann-Nitsche in order to exemplify the difficulties which arise in employing a classification based on logical principles rather than on the concepts of the riddlers. Neither the sex nor the family relationship appears to be really significant to the riddler. I should prefer to call Nos. 952 through 957 vague, colorless varieties. When the actors are specified as brothers or sisters, the riddler implies the similarity or equality of the objects symbolized by these persons.

The scene of animals or unrelated persons pursuing one another is applicable to the description of:

§ 1. The hands of a clock. See the headnote to Nos. 996–1001, § 7.

§ 2. A reel. Breton: Le Chef, *Ille-et-Vilaine*, p. 667; Kerbeuzec, *Ille-et-Vilaine*, 41; Sébillot, *Devinettes*, 83. Danish: Feilberg, *Ordbog*, III, 76, s.v. "rokkehjul." Swedish: Ericsson, *Södermanland*, II (1881), 101, No. 123. Spanish: Demófilo, 367 (four little children), 368 (four little horses), p. 357, No. 23 (four students), and p. 392, No. 48 (four horses); Rodríguez Marín, 670 (four

---

[1] The note to Nos. 956a through 956d cites parallels in which the actors are not identified as persons.

little angels), 671 (four little horses), 672 (four above, four below, four never catch up). Argentinian: Lehmann-Nitsche, 265*b* (four horses), 265*f* (four horsemen), 265*j* (two horses), 266 (actors not identified). Chilean: Flores, 239. Catalan: Pelay y Briz, 20; Milá y Fontanals, 1876, pp. 26–27, No. 23 (four students). Serbian: Novaković, p. 53, No. 6 (The maiden is running around, five men are following her. When all five catch her, they turn her to dance). Modern Greek: Abbott, p. 315, No. 36 (Four boys are chasing one another). Turkish: Hamizade, 120 (Four siblings chase one another). Indonesian, Javanese: Ranneft, *Proza*, p. 5, No. 20 (Four thieves pursue one another). Karo-Batak: Joustra, p. 97 (Four people who pursue one another until evening and do not catch up).

For comparisons to brothers see the headnote to Nos. 996–1001, § 3, below; and to sisters, the headnote to Nos. 1014–1015, § 4, below.

§ 3. The wings of a windmill. See No. 952 and the list of windmill riddles in the note to No. 986.

§ 4. Mileposts. See No. 953.

§ 5. Wheels. See Nos. 954*a* through 956*d*.

§ 6. The spokes in a wheel. See No. 957. See also the headnote to Nos. 1014–1015, § 4.

§ 7. The seasons. German: Schmidt, *Danzig*, 17. For related riddles see the headnote to No. 984 below.

§ 8. A man and his shadow. French: Westphalen, *Metz*, col. 201 (I run after her and cannot catch her). Spanish, Argentinian: Lehmann-Nitsche, 100, 101. Chilean: Flores, 704. Portuguese: Parsons, *Cape Verde*, 238 (Two men run a race of twenty miles. Neither leaves the other behind, and neither tires). See also No. 113 above.

§ 9. A horse's hoofs. Spanish, Argentinian: Lehmann-Nitsche, 265 (four horses), 265*e* (four donkeys), 265*h* (four barrels), 265*i* (four sheep's pelts). The pelts refer to the hair of the fetlocks.

§ 10. The runners of a sled. Yakut: Priklonskii, 43 (Two dogs are running; one cannot outstrip the other). See also the headnote to Nos. 1014–1015, § 3, below.

952. Four men walkin' all day, an' still can't ketch one another.—Mill point [i.e., the round house or perhaps the tail tree of the mill—Collector's note].
Parsons, *Barbados*, p. 277, No. 6.

953. Some white ladies were walking to Kingston, and all the walk they walk, they couldn't catch each other.—Mile-posts.
Beckwith, *Jamaica*, p. 194, No. 94.

954–957. Men Running Cannot Overtake Each Other: Wheels

The conception of wheels as men who cannot overtake each other, run as fast as they may, is very popular. The great variety of forms in which it occurs is seen in the choice of different actors and different relations among the actors. For discussion of the theme see Wolfgang Schultz, *Rätsel aus dem hellenischen Kulturkreise*, II, 25–27; Flajšhans, pp. 20–21, §20a.

Riddlers have occasionally added elements belonging to the description of the parts of an animal, usually a cow,[1] as in the Serbian oxcart riddle, "There are four foursomes and two butterflies, they follow in each other's tracks, yet they do not catch one another."[2] The butterflies, which the collector does not interpret, may be the twitching ears of the ox. Compare with this such versions of the ox riddle as "Two run, two chase, two cut the road" or "Two run, two chase, two show the way."[3]

The actors are often persons individualized in some special way.[4] They are also occasionally animals or even devils, as appears in the following list:

§ 1. Horses. Swedish: Ström, pp. 382–383, "Sysselsättningar," 46. Spanish: Demófilo, 368, and p. 392, No. 48. Argentinian: Lehmann-Nitsche, 265a. Polish: Kopernicki, 2.

§ 2. Cattle. Modern Greek: Dieterich, *Rätseldichtung*, p. 99.

§ 3. Wolves. Russian: Sadovnikov, 963g (Two wolves run, they chase after one another, they can't catch up all their lives).

§ 4. Dogs. Polish: Saloni, *Rzeshów*, 73 (Four dogs are chasing and one wouldn't catch the other). Votyak: Buch, 50 (Two little dogs run close behind the horse's tail and yet cannot catch it). Hungarian: *Magyar Nyelvör*, XVIII (1889), 428 (four dogs). African, SeSuto: Norton and Velaphe, 68 (My four dogs roaring to one another.—Cartwheels).

§ 5. Swine. Hungarian: *Magyar Nyelvör*, V (1876), 521 (Twelve pigs are lying on a wheel, they roll in the mud, and there is not a single one of them on the side.—Spokes). This is akin to the riddles discussed in the headnote to Nos. 1027–1028, § 5, below. A closer parallel to the present theme is Hungarian: *Magyar Nyelvör*, XL (1911), 334 (I had a hog that has four young. When I drive them out, they will never reach one another).

§ 6. Devils, madmen. Hungarian: Arany and Gyulai, II, 360, No. 56 (Four devils chase one another but are never able to reach one another); *Magyar Nyelvör*, VIII (1879), 522 (devils) = *ibid.*, XII (1883), 286; *ibid.*, IX (1880), 180, No. 3 (Twelve devils keep running after one another; there is not one on the side). For parallels to the last theme see the headnote to Nos. 1027–1028, § 5, below.

954a. Four men walkin' all day, an' still can't ketch one another.—Cyart wheel.
Parsons, *Barbados*, p. 277, No. 6.

---

[1] See the headnote to Nos. 1476–1494 below.
[2] Novaković, p. 94, No. 18.
[3] Lithuanian: Jurgelionis, 666, 667.
[4] For actors as brothers, see Nos. 996 through 998e below; as sisters or women, Nos. 1014a through 1015b below; as members of a family, Nos. 1029a through 1030 below.

954b. Four boys going all day, can't ketch one anoder.—Motor cyar wheels.
Parsons, *Antilles*, III, 375, St. Vincent, 6 var.

955a. Four boys were going along the street. / Two were big and two were small, / And the two in front were walking quick, / And the two behind were walking quick. / Although the two in front stop, / The two behind could not catch him.—Carriage wheel.
Parsons, *Bermuda*, p. 250, No. 28.

955b. A little man was runnin' off all de time, an' big man was tryin' to ketch him an' couldn'.—A wagon-wheel.
Parsons, *Sea Islands, S.C.*, p. 153, No. 11.

956a. Four going, / Two big ones tryin' to ketch de little ones.—Buggy-wheel tryin' to ketch de little ones.
Parsons, *Aiken, S.C.*, p. 35, No. 71.

956b. Big thing run behind little thing, and can't ketch him.—Buggy largest wheel run behind littlest wheel, and can't ketch it.
Parsons, *Sea Islands, S.C.*, p. 153, No. 11, var. 1.

956c. Big titty run all day, an' can't ketch little titty.—Buggy-wheel.
Parsons, *Sea Islands, S.C.*, p. 154, No. 11, var. 5.

956d. Big sumpin' run after little sumpin' all day long. And when he goes to turn, he shakes hands with him.—A buggy: big wheel and little wheel.
Fauset, *Nova Scotia*, p. 169, No. 142.

957. Twenty-four man going on a road, / Dey run as fas' as dey can, / An' couldn' catch one anoder.—Spoke in de wheel.
Parsons, *Antilles*, III, 425, Antigua, 18 var.

958–960. One Goes In; Two Stand By

This rather rare comparison of a key and the bunch from which it projects to a man and his companions occurs in several widely scattered versions. The same theme is seen in a Polish riddle for bread on a baker's shovel: "Two are round, one is long. *Zips!* into a brick-walled hole they go."[1] It is closely related to the comparisons to a group of men of whom one is wet and the others are dry.[2]

958. "Hips," says I, / "Hangs by my side; / One went in; / Two hung by."
—Keys.
Hyatt, *Adams Co., Ill.*, p. 663, No. 10882.

959. Me riddle, me riddle, / You were in, / You come out, and I go in. What's that?—Sin.
Parsons, *Antilles*, III, 427, Nevis, 5.

---
[1] Kopernicki, 90. For the *tertium quid comparationis* see Italian: Ferraro, *Canti popolari in dialetto logodurese*, p. 300, No. 10. Mordvin: Paasonen, 367. Turkish: Katanov in Radlov, IX, 158, No. 1316.
[2] See below, No. 963 and the headnote to Nos. 961–963.

960. What is two things flapping and one going in and out?—A hawg with his ears flapping and his nose going in and out.

Bacon and Parsons, *Virginia*, p. 321, No. 82.

961–963. Go through Rain; Are Not Wet

Riddlers have conceived this scene in terms of both persons and things. The scene is applicable to descriptions of:

§ 1. An unborn child and a pregnant woman. See No. 961.

§ 2. A corpse in a funeral. See No. 962.

§ 3. A man under an umbrella. Spanish, Porto Rican: Mason, 382, 431. So literal an interpretation is poor enigmatic technique and suggests that the riddler has forgotten the correct answer.

§ 4. Words. Portuguese: Parsons, *Cape Verde*, 244 (I have my child. I send it into the rain; it does not get wet).

§ 5. A cow's teats. Welsh: Hull and Taylor, 227, 228. French: J. Roux, *Limousin*, 43. Polish: Gustawicz, 49 (The rain falls upon the entire woods, yet it cannot wet four fir trees). Bulgarian: Gubov, 184 (The rain came, the whole forest was soaked; only four trees remained dry), 382 through 384, 386. Hungarian: Kálmány, I, 158, No. 6 (The whole forest is soaked, but four small stakes do not get wet); *Magyar Nyelvör*, V (1876), 127 (There are four twigs in the forest that are never touched by the rain); VI (1877), 270 (A dense forest gets wet, four twigs do not get wet); XXXI (1902), 334, No. 62; XL (1911), 285. Although none of these riddles implies that the forest may signify the cow's hairs, this interpretation seems probable. Arabic: Stumme, *Tázerwalt*, 10. African, Kosi: Ittmann, *Kosi*, 56. For other riddles on this subject see Nos. 1199a through 1199d below.

§ 6. An egg in a duck (chicken). See Nos. 169a through 170b above. The conception is so vague that one cannot identify the actor.

§ 7. A shadow, the sun, the wind. See the headnote to Nos. 165–173, §§ 1, 3, 5, above.

§ 8. A distaff, spinning. Polish: Gustawicz, 292; Saloni, *Rzeshów*, 125 (Ten little boys, five under the roof, and five in the field. Those under the roof are wet, those in the field are dry), 126 (Five brothers who stand under the roof are wet, and five who chase over the field are dry), 127, 128; Siarkowski, 102 (The five brothers who were under the roof were wet, while the five who wandered over the world were dry.—The five fingers of the hand which is handling the distaff when spinning become moistened while the other hand remains dry); Kopernicki, 53. Serbian: Novaković, p. 178, Nos. 8 through 12. Hungarian: *Magyar Nyelvör*, VI (1877), 270.

961. There was two persons, goin' on, one day. One of them was in the rain. One got wet, and the other didn't get wet.—A pregnant woman.

Johnson, *Antigua*, p. 88, No. 57a.

962. Dere was four men goin' along, an' a shower o' rain an' de t'ee [three] dat run got wet, an' de one dat stan' was dry.—Four man goin' to de grave wid a fune' (funeral), an' de one inside de coffin was dry.
Parsons, *Antilles*, III, 432, St. Eustatius, 14.

963. T'ree broders, one went in, the oder two didn't go in. Went in the house of a lady. One get wet, the other two didn't get wet.—Answer lacking.
Parsons, *Antilles*, III, 445, St. Thomas, 7.

964–965. Talking

The idea of a group of people engaged in conversation has rarely caught the fancy of riddlers. Its pertinence to a riddle for the Pleiades[1] is obscure. It is used to heighten the contrast of the dead and the living.[2] In riddles mentioning a single person, talking, shouting, or singing is occasionally mentioned as a descriptive detail.[3]

964. Four men going up to town; all were talking and not one could understand the other.—Four buggy-wheels.
Beckwith, *Jamaica*, p. 194, No. 92.

965. Riding in to town, two talking to each other and none understand what the other was saying.—Two (?) new saddles creaking *ru-u-u-u*.
Beckwith, *Jamaica*, p. 194, No. 91.

966–968. Fighting

Two coöperating or interacting parts of an object are often described as fighting and the accessory details are represented by appropriate metaphors. Comparisons to fighting animals have already been discussed.[1] The notion of fighting is applicable to a great many objects: the Kamba call riverbanks "two bulls ready to fight"[2] and the Mongolians describe fingers and buttonholes as "Ökhön and Chökhön get hold of each other in the morning."[3]

The comparison to fighting men is applicable to household utensils and such tasks as sawing, grinding, and combing wool. In African and Indonesian riddling, the teeth are said to be fighting men,[4] but this aspect is not stressed in European allusions to ivory soldiers,[5] who are more probably conceived as men standing in rows. The Ossete riddle for the teeth and tongue is particularly ingenious: "Two armies destroy each other and an ambassador goes between them."[6] The Icelandic conception of carding combs is a unique variation of

---

[1] See No. 988.
[2] See Nos. 833 through 834b, the headnote to Nos. 830–834, and the note to Nos. 834a, 834b.
[3] See Nos. 750 through 755i, 757a through 757d, 759 through 764, 766, 767, and the headnotes to Nos. 751–754 and 760.

[1] See the headnote to No. 397.
[2] Lindblom, 77.
[3] Mostaert, 185.
[4] See below, § 6.
[5] See the headnote to No. 841, § 1.
[6] Schiefner, 24.

the theme: "What two brothers eat off one another?"[7] A comparison of celestial bodies to fighting men occurs now and again.[8]

Typical objects described as men fighting are:

§ 1. A pair of scissors. Turkish: Katanov in Radlov, IX, 241, No. 88 (Two ravens are beating each other on chins and cheeks). Shor (a Turkish tribe): Dyrenkova, 31 (Two crows plucked at each other with their beaks).

§ 2. Sawing. Welsh: Hull and Taylor, 125.

§ 3. Grinding. Russian: Sadovnikov, 1087 (Two brothers are quarreling, there is no end to their dispute. They fight each other, there is no end to their encounter). Albanian: Hahn, p. 159, No. 3 (Two sisters quarrel, they bite each other and cause foam to flow from their mouths). This describes the flour falling from the mill in a way similar to that used in No. 397 above.

§ 4. Pulling manioc. Portuguese: Parsons, *Cape Verde*, 26.

§ 5. Fire. Indonesian, Tabaru: Fortgens, p. 541, No. 107 (She, when she meets her husband, they fight.—Jungle weeds and fire). Mongolian: Mostaert, 48 (Old man *t'ag* from Heaven, old man *jag* from the earth, beating each other; old man gray artemisia, coming in between to separate them, gets his forehead scorched and leaves.—Steel for striking a light, flint, punk). The meanings of *t'ag* and *jag* are obscure.

§ 6. The teeth and the tongue.[9] Swedish: Ström, p. 83, "Munnen, tänderna, tungan," 8 (Red as fire, watched by white men, caught and yet free, it makes war, it makes peace). Svanian: W. Nizheradze, p. 1, No. 3 (Sixteen pairs of brothers, sometimes they are ill, sometimes they quarrel). African, Basuto: Rolland, p. 168, No. 10. Togo: Schönhärl, 73 (I am a weak man without bones,[10] yet I am very quick; and I live between two rows of strong warriors who fight together continually). Sotho: Endemann, 25. Zulu: Callaway, 7. Indonesian, Alfoer: Niemann, p. 14, No. 5 (The comrades are continually looking through the window). Compare also an Engganee riddle for the mouth (lips): "Two persons who do nothing but quarrel all day long."[11]

§ 7. Saddlebags. Bulgarian: Chacharov, 23 (Two old men pull each other's beards).

§ 8. A waterfall. Lappish: Qvigstad, 7 (A man quarrels with another man; since he cannot overcome him, he must yield.—Water dashing against the cliff). Compare the headnote to Nos. 751–754 above.

§ 9. Waves. African, Kinyarwanda: Hurel, p. 153, No. 7 (We are neighbors, we never greet one another).

---

[7] Árnason, 696.
[8] See No. 967 below.
[9] For teeth described as rows of soldiers see also the headnote to No. 841, § 1, above.
[10] See also the riddles for a leech, other animals, and various things cited in the headnote to Nos. 264–265 above.
[11] Helfrich, *Engganee*, pp. 518–519, No. 13.

§ 10. The sun and the moon. See No. 967 below.

§ 11. A comb. Indian, Bihari: Mitra, *Bihar*, 47 (There is one woman, there are many men; she meets them all at the same time; there is an interval of some four days; the men become entangled, and she separates them).

§ 12. A pair of dice. Classical Greek: Schultz, *Rätsel aus dem hellenischen Kulturkreise*, II, 25.

§ 13. Posts. Samoan: Heider, 64 (There are four brothers. If two quarrel, the two others bring about a reconciliation.—The posts opposite strain against each other and the sides hold them together); Brown, pp. 343–344. For similar riddles, in which the idea of quarreling is less prominent, see the headnotes to Nos. 992–993 and 996–1001 below.

966. Fight and scratch all day, / Set up in the corner all night.—Card for carding wool.

Fauset, *Southern Negro*, p. 282, No. 68.

967. Fight; God Parts Them

Riddlers compare the sun and moon to persons engaged in many widely differing activities. The notion is so simple and the variations are so great that we can suppose that many versions are the result of independent inventions. I find a parallel to this obscure English conception in the Wanamwezi "Two fight each other."[1] This may be related to the ultimate source of the English riddle. The Irish "Hot, hot, inside the fence; hot, hot, outside the fence; two might come toward each other and they might kill Ireland.—Sun and moon"[2] is scarcely intelligible. It may contain a reminiscence of the apocalyptic destruction of the sun and moon. R. Eisler discusses the theme of the sun and moon conceived as persons who fight.[3] The medieval Syriac "Two twin children that are born of one womb and that are not similar because they have two natures"[4] seems to represent a different tradition.

Day and night are often compared to persons,[5] but the stars are only rarely called a company of persons.[6] Two riddles for carding wool, Nos. 966 and 968, also refer to persons who fight. In a Swedish version the weaver also is mentioned: "I saw two dead men pulling each other's hair; a living man gave judgment."[7]

967. Two men fighting all day, an' no person can part them but God.—Sun an' moon.

Parsons, *Barbados*, p. 287, No. 71.

---

[1] Dahl, 64.
[2] De Bhaldraithe, 5.
[3] *Weltenmantel und Himmelszelt* (Munich, 1910), p. 225, n. 2.
[4] Furlani, *Azraq*, 2.
[5] See the headnote to No. 1001 below.
[6] Nos. 1024, 1025.
[7] Dybeck, *Runa*, 1865–1873, p. 64, No. 72.

968. Fight and Embrace

The contrast of fighting and embracing is applicable to objects with parts which separate and come together.[1] Its only use in English is for carding combs. Riddlers often describe a door and bolt in this way. The Russians say, "Two walk, two ramble, when two come together, they embrace and kiss";[2] and "Two come together and embrace";[3] and the Arabs, "They embrace at night and separate during the day."[4] Icelanders describe a hook and eye in similar fashion: "What married couple parts at night and meets again in the morning?"[5] A Rumanian riddle for scissors is "Who are the two brothers who are constantly kissing each other?"[6] For the eyelids the Sangiree say, "At night they embrace, during the day they reach for each other."[7]

968. What is: fights and scratches all day and lays in each other's arms at night?—Card for carding wool.
Carter, *Mountain White*, p. 78.

969. Killing

A few analogous riddles in which a single actor is represented as killing have been noted as applicable to a bullet and other objects.[1] The comparison of a famine to a thousand hungry men killing a thousand bullocks is not completely intelligible. Other riddles for a famine mention the fact that it afflicts men of all stations in life: "The branch by the wayside flicks great and small.— Hunger, which is no respecter of persons."[2] In two instances hunger and silence are mentioned: "I have beaten the dog. It has not cried.—It is famine. Crying is of no avail in time of famine" and "Who is the one who fights without saying a word?"[3]

969. A thousand hungry men kill a thousand bullocks.—Hunger kill men.
Beckwith, *Jamaica*, p. 196, No. 117.

970–975. Court Proceedings, Imprisonment, Execution

Riddlers have ingeniously adapted scenes of arrest, trial, and execution to describe various events in common life. They may occasionally reduce the scene to such a compact enigmatic result as "Five after one."[1] This also belongs to the category of riddles in which the actors are described in terms of their characteristic numbers.[2]

---

[1] For related patterns see Nos. 1003, 1004, and the headnote to Nos. 1003–1004.
[2] Sadovnikov, 705. This is very similar to the riddles for the sun and moon discussed in the headnote to Nos. 1476–1494, § 14, below.
[3] Sadovnikov, 706.
[4] Littmann, p. 56. [5] Árnason, 671.
[6] Papahagi, 22. [7] Adriani, 147.
[1] See Nos. 801 through 804.
[2] African, Hausa: Fletcher, p. 51, No. 6.
[3] African, Tonga-Shangaan: Junod and Jaques, p. 231, Nos. 17, 18.
[1] No. 972. [2] Nos. 976a through 982.

In a special modification of these scenes of the pursuit, trial, and execution of a criminal, the riddler assigns whimsical names to the constable, the culprit, and the place of execution. This modification is widely known everywhere but in England and in countries where English is spoken. The riddler chooses the names to suggest either the pertinent acts or the scenes of these acts. An example of the first variety of names occurs in the Low German "Two came walking, they took me prisoner, they brought me to Wribbelstadt ["Rubbing Town"?], from Wribbelstadt to Hammerschlag [Hammerblow], and there I was killed."[3] An example of the second variety occurs in the Baiga "In the thickly wooded fortress the thief is captured. He is executed in Nakanpur [City of the Nail]."[4] Both varieties of names occur also in the variant form in which an animal is slaughtered rather than a person is executed. In the western European versions the place names usually suggest acts, and in the Slavic and Oriental versions usually parts of the body,[5] but there are many exceptions to this generalization. Particularly interesting examples are the Lettish "Grandmother led a cow past Ear-inn and past Eye-inn, led it upon a wooden bridge,[6] and killed it with a bone hammer";[7] the White Russian "The lads went to the forest and found Pan Gavrilo, and Pan Gavrilo led them to Pan Patrylo, and he condemned them to death";[8] the Russian "I caught a little cow in the dark forests. I guided the little cow past Foreheadville, past Eyebrowville, past Eyeville, past Noseville, past Cheekville, past Earville, past Mouthville, past Lipville, past Moustacheville, past Beardville, past Armville, past Shoulderville. I brought the little cow to Nailville. Here I began to kill the little cow";[9] and the Bengali "The bird of Ekapura grazes in Tekarapura, allows itself to be caught in Hariśchandrapura, dies in Lakshmīkāntapura,"[10] in which the names probably have a metaphorical meaning.

Similar whimsical names occur in riddles for baking bread[11] and for roasting coffee.[12] For discussion see Petsch, *Neue Beiträge*, p. 69.

I conjecture that the original conception was a hunting scene, which later riddlers have altered into the pursuit, trial, and execution of a criminal. Other variations of the conception are a Flemish scene of a military trial and execution, "Ten men of the army went to the Noordsche Bosch. They sought out the prisoners and brought them to Peepeye,[13] from there to the scaffold Nail,

---

[3] Wossidlo, 28n.
[4] Elwin, p. 473, No. 9. See also Elwin and Hivale, p. 74, No. 72.
[5] For parallels see German: Wossidlo, 28; Gilhoff, 246 through 250; Haase, *Ruppin*, 273; Frischbier, *Thierwelt*, p. 358, Nos. 98 through 100; Schmidt, *Danzig*, 52, 52a; Böckel, *Hesse*, 85; Haffner, 83, 84; Hanika-Otto, 394. Swiss: Rochholz, 367, 368; J. Müller, *Innerschweiz*, 4.
[6] Table.
[7] Bielenstein, 630. The "bone hammer" is a comb.
[8] Wasilewski, 75.
[9] Sadovnikov, 1688.
[10] Mitra, *Chittagong*, p. 969.
[11] German: Wossidlo, 29.
[12] German: Wossidlo, 30.
[13] *Kiekoogs*.

there they were executed";[14] and a Uraon scene of a sacrifice, "Slaughtered the goat and its blood bespattered two stones.—Louse between two nails."[15]

Comparisons of a vaguer sort which mention only the numbers of the actors are rare. See as examples the Maltese "Something you pursue with five fingers and catch with two,"[16] which shows some similarity to riddles for sewing and knitting,[17] or for eating,[18] and the Tonga-Shangaan "What is the thing which you hunt with ten sticks and which you use only two sticks to kill?"[19]

The hunting scene varies greatly in details and occasionally admits elements belonging to other riddles. The horn plate[20] and the notion of catching and throwing away game[21] in the Frisian "A hunter went hunting with ten swift dogs. Each had a horn plate in front so that it could not bark. All that the hunter caught, he killed, and what he did not catch, he carried with him"[22] are borrowed matter. The Lettish "Five men hunt rabbits; past lookers, past hearers, they [the rabbits] are brought to the door of the police house, and their heads are cut off—*kranks!*"[23] confuses hunting an animal and capturing a criminal. The Russian "Little one, dextrous one, leaps like an elk, looks like a beast. Five brothers tried to catch him, could not catch him. Two brothers finally caught him and killed him"[24] begins with elements of another flea or louse riddle.[25]

The Asiatic parallels are numerous and very curious. See the Yakut "A hundred men pace the road and two arms hunt,"[26] which contains an unusual mention of the comb; the Bengali "The deer graze upon the head, the hand is stretched out, [it] walks, two knives kill," which is vaguely conceived and perhaps defective, and "Standing upon a small and tiny foundation, the small deer graze. Ten servants run, bring the deer, and two servants seize them";[27] the Bhil "A black cow comes after grazing the whole forest and coming upon a fingernail stile, dies";[28] the Baiga "In a small block of forest, a barking-deer dances. Ten went for the beat,[29] but only two did the killing,"[30] which implies the Indian manner of hunting with beaters, and the similar Javanese "There

---

[14] Joos, 596.
[15] Archer, p. 191, No. 184.
[16] Stumme, *Malta*, p. 103, No. 16.
[17] See the headnote to No. 979 below.
[18] See the headnote to Nos. 980–982, and see Nos. 980a through 981.
[19] Junod and Jaques, p. 235, No. 35.
[20] Compare Nos. 588a through 588c above, and No. 989 and the headnote to No. 989 below.
[21] See No. 460a and the headnote to No. 460.
[22] Dykstra, *Snypsnaren*, pp. 102–103.
[23] Bielenstein, 750.
[24] Sadovnikov, 1687.
[25] See the note to Nos. 344a, 344b above.
[26] Piekarski, 210.
[27] Mitra, *Chittagong*, pp. 967–968, Nos. 12, 13.
[28] Hedberg, p. 873, No. 46.
[29] Driving out animals from the jungle for the hunters.
[30] Elwin, p. 469, No. 49.

are five hunters, they are beaters in a hunt for beasts. When they have found anything, it is actually eaten up."[31]

Typical activities described by a series of events from a man's arrest to his execution are:

§ 1. Catching a louse.[32] See Nos. 970 through 973.

§ 2. Fishing. Portuguese: Parsons, *Cape Verde*, 160b (A dead policeman goes and takes a living man in his house, he carried him to the station-house), 161 (Five soldiers go to fight one man. They take two dead soldiers. One dead [soldier] falls to fighting with the living man; and the other five soldiers who are alive are filled with fear, while the other dead [soldier] does not go; and as soon as he goes, this dead man wins the fight. The living now go pack up the dead.—Five men who go in a whaler [the two dead men are the harpoon and the gun to shoot the whale]).

§ 3. Snuff-taking. Italian: Pitrè, 806. Indian, Parsee: Munshi, p. 417 (Two come to take me and they create me chief. Two come to take me and they carry me to two caves). This theme is closely related to the following:

§ 4. Picking the nose. Bulgarian: Gubov, 334 (Two pashas walk, [a group of] five [men] are waiting), 335 ("Come, get out, you scamp, [a group of] five is waiting for you"), 336 (There he walks naked, here five are waiting). Zyrian: Wichmann, *Zyrian*, 175 (Drip, drip, dripped out, [a group of] five seized it). Modern Greek: Sanders, 2; Dieterich, *Sporades*, 13 (A maiden came out of the one who is pierced, five hold her for shame); Polites, *Neohellenika Analekta*, I, 216, No. 134 (From the deep darkness comes an old woman, five servants take her and throw her against the wall), p. 222, No. 163 (A princess emerges from a palace on high, five seize her and throw her down), p. 231, Nos. 216 through 218, and p. 245, No. 297; Stathes, p. 340, No. 53 (Madame descends, she comes out of two doors, five servants seize her and throw her to the ground); Carnoy and Nicolaides, p. 278, No. 11 (A torrent flows from two holes; five brothers go to meet it). Arabic: Giacobetti, 266 (Two push and two pull.—Mucus in the nostrils). Turkish: Kowalski, *Asia Minor*, 37, 55; Kowalski, *Zagadki*, 138; Hamizade, 640 (From a black palace a prince comes, five maid servants go over to him), 641 (From a black palace a judge comes out, five maid servants go to meet him), 642 (A prince dressed in green comes from over there, five maid servants remain bowing at his side). Cherekessian: Tambiev, p. 54, No. 13 (Climbing up, five brothers force the wet part of the body to empty itself). Turcoman: Samojlvich, 12 (In the H'ur-h'ur Mountains a thief hid, they said, "Five horsemen were sent." "Chase him out," they said), citing a parallel in Radlov, VII, No. 67. Javanese: Ranneft, *Proza*, p. 6, No. 24 (There is a princess, who stands peeping from her window, she will not come down unless she is seized by five youths).

---

[31] Ranneft, *Proza*, pp. 37–38, No. 164.
[32] For discussion see Schultz, *Bemerkungen*, p. 365.

The Uraon "An old woman knocks a white hen down" (Archer, p. 180, No. 22) is quite different from these texts.

§ 5. Seeing, picking, and eating a fruit, bone, or bread. See Nos. 980a, 980b below.

§ 6. Writing. Icelandic: Árnason, 62 (I saw three brothers bent at their work, moving along, all steadying themselves on one stick. Wherever that soiled stick went, it left behind fuzzy tracks. All these brothers obey one master. Two serve as guides lest the road be lost, the third lightens the labor), 605 (Who is born fully dressed, seen by two, seized by five, stripped by ten, who cut a slit in her end? Her wine is so valuable that it is found all over the king's table), 612, 618, 637. Russian: Sadovnikov, 613 (Five hold it, five push it, two see to it that the pushing is done aright). Indonesian, Javanese: Ranneft, *Proza*, p. 39, No. 174 (Ten pallbearers carry a coffin with difficulty, five carry it with ease). This theme is often introduced into the comparisons of writing to plowing.[33]

A French scissors riddle, "Five guide, two watch,"[34] is based on a similar conception.

§ 7. The toes in a shoe. Lappish: Qvigstad, 18 (In the daytime in jail, free at night), which contains only the theme of imprisonment,[35] and 54 (Ten men taken prisoner by day and freed at night). Finnish: Koskimies, 237, as cited by Qvigstad.

§ 8. A toothpick. Indian: W. J. D'Gruyther, *Panjab Notes and Queries*, II (1885), 15, § 7 (Two bring and five use it for the adornment of thirty-two. Musalmáns preserve and Hindus destroy it.—*Dátan*, the stick used as a toothbrush). Kolarian: Wagner, 70 (They are ploughing with five men, but harrowing with ten.—Cleaning the teeth and tongue). Mongolian: Mostaert, 72 (The beloved queen fell ill, five ministers appeared, called in Dr. Toothpick, who removed some harmful stuff as big as a lizard), which admits the answer into the riddle, 73 (The little professor fell ill, five ministers galloped off to invite Dr. Incense.[36] He removed a nuisance as big as a lizard).

970. My father tek a bwoy to court; de sentence pass pon finger-nail.—[A louse].
Beckwith, *Jamaica*, p. 190, No. 67c.

971a. One man on de jail take five men to take him down.—Lice.
Parsons, *Bahamas*, p. 482, No. 10.

971b. A man standin' on a hill. / Send one man [variant: finger] to bring him, / One couldn' bring him. / Send two, and two bring him.—Lice.
Parsons, *Barbados*, p. 279, No. 22.

---

[33] See the headnote to No. 1063, n. 2, below.
[34] Fourès, p. 254.
[35] For other shoe riddles see Nos. 864, 908 above.
[36] An incense stick used as a toothpick.

971c. Some men were out in a grassy hill. / One man couldn' bring him, / Two brought him.—A louse.
Parsons, *Barbados*, p. 280, No. 22 var.

971d. One prisoner stan' pon Marley hill; ten policemen go fe tek him down; two bring him to de station do [door], an' de sentence pass pon de finger-nail. —Ten fingers to catch one louse.
Beckwith, *Jamaica*, p. 190, No. 67b.

971e. Ten men go to Bullinton fe bring down one prisoner; only two bring him down.—Ten fingers to catch one louse.
Beckwith, *Jamaica*, p. 190, No. 67a.

971f. Me father sen' ten men fe ketch one t'ief.—Ten fingers to catch one louse.
Beckwith, *Jamaica*, p. 190, No. 67.

972. Five after one!—Fingers hunting a louse in the hair.
Greenleaf, *Newfoundland*, p. 12, No. 34.

973. My moder have a boy, killing him on two tables.—Two nails, killing anything.
Parsons, *Antilles*, III, 370, Grenada, 21.

974–975. Imprisonment

974. one evening could [cold] as could might bee with frost & haile & pinching weather companions about 3 tymes 3 lay close all in a place together yet one after an other the[y] tooke a heat & dyed that night all in a sweat.—a pound of candles.
Tupper, *Holme Riddles*, 21.

975. Three prisoners, such as it was, / were shut up in a prison of a glasse. / The prison doore was made of bread, / and yet they were for hunger dead.— Those were three flyes that were shut up in a glasse, and the mouth of it stopped with a peece of bread.
Meery Riddles (1629), No. 13 = Brandl, p. 10.

976–982. Actors Described in Terms of Their Numbers

The riddle of ten drawing four or the ten fingers milking a cow is the best English illustration of this manner of describing an act in terms of the numbers of the fingers or other members used. Inventions of this sort are rather numerous and vary considerably in their fundamental ideas. Examples are the riddles for killing a louse, "Two who run and ten who chase and two who watch";[1] for setting a pot on a fire, "Three catch, ten reach over";[2] for drawing on trousers, "Five push and ten pull";[3] and for hunting, "Helter-skelter over

---

[1] French: *Les Adeuineaux amoureux*, p. lxxxviii. See, also, the headnote to Nos. 970–975 above.
[2] Malay: Klinkert, p. 48, No. 28.
[3] Breton: Ernault, *Mélusine*, I (1878), col. 511; Sébillot, *Haute-Bretagne*, 46b; Sébillot, *Devinettes*, 56. French: Bladé, *Armagnac*, 32.

the mountain and over the hill; two chase it and two wait for it.—Two dogs chase, and the hunter and gun wait";[4] and the Bhil riddle for a loaf, "Ten persons fall in quarrel. Five take leave and run away and five fall down having taken [what they quarreled about]."[5] A description of picking the nose is very widely known.[6]

Riddlers often introduce new elements into these conceptions. The Lithuanian riddles for eating from a pot suggest the flat Baltic landscape: "In Apvalain's pond a mare was drowned. Five pulled at it, ten waited" and "A mare was drowned in a marsh. Five men pulled it, two hawks waited."[7] Still another theme is introduced in the Baiga loaf riddle, "Ten brothers beat her; five brothers laid her down on the ground."[8] This substitution of numbers for persons in the Icelandic mittens riddle, "I speak of twice five and ten. I let everyone see them. I speak of twice five and ten. I show two and hide ten"[9] resembles the shopkeeper's warning to his clerk, "Two pounds ten," meaning shoplifters are about.[10]

976–979. Ten Draw Four

In its various forms this riddle is widely known in western Europe. Elsewhere, the versions deviate so widely from one another and from the European conception that a connection is often hard to make out. The Albanian "Head to the rump, rump to the stone, ten draw, two make water"[1] is clearly of this pattern, and a Bulgarian analogue,[2] which is not quotable, contains similar themes. Perhaps the first theme of the Albanian riddle has an analogue in the Bhil "Inverse buttock, reverse buttock, and buttock on the ground, too.—Calf, cow, and milking man."[3] At any rate, this theme is frequently[4] associated with the notion of ten drawing four.

Some riddles narrating the activities of men identified by their numbers seem to be quite independent of the texts here considered. The Lappish "Four give, two take"[5] is, although it is a description of milking, perhaps not connected with these riddles. The Breton "Four going, two drawing a bush behind, and a horn in front"[6] contains elements characteristic of a very popular riddle for a cow.[7]

---

[4] Serbian: Novaković, p. 61, No. 3.
[5] Hedberg, p. 881, No. 102.
[6] See the headnote to Nos. 970–975, § 4, above.
[7] Jurgelionis, 190, 191.
[8] Elwin, p. 468, No. 38.
[9] Árnason, 1074.
[10] Adolf Schirmer, *Wörterbuch der deutschen Kaufmannssprache* (Strassburg, 1911), p. xlvi, n. 1.
[1] Hahn, p. 159, No. 9.
[2] Gubov, 398.
[3] Hedberg, p. 872, No. 41. [4] See § 2, below.
[5] Qvigstad, 93. [6] Sébillot, *Devinettes*, 9b.
[7] See Nos. 1476a through 1489 below, and especially Nos. 1477a through 1477c.

The oldest version seems to be that versified by Straparola.[8]

Two varieties of the riddle can be readily recognized. The first contains mention of the milker's position and usually a reference to his rump. For examples see Irish: De Bhaldraithe, 19 (Four feet on the ground, two feet on the ground, one with a bottom,[9] and the bottom on the ground); O Dalaigh, 215. German: Wossidlo, 168. Faeroic: Hammershaimb, *Antiquarisk tidsskrift*, III (1849–1851), 320, No. 52 = *Færøsk anthologi*, I, 324, No. 34. Icelandic: Árnason, 1049 (Ten pull four, and there are two heads. Buttocks up and buttocks down and a tail behind). Danish: Kristensen, p. 75, § 176, No. 281c. Walloon: Colson, *Wallonia*, IV, 59, No. 45a (Backside on seat, ten at four); Colson, *Devinettes*, p. 147, No. 3. French: *Les Adeuineaux amoureux*, p. lxxxix = Rolland, 43b; Westphalen, *Metz*, col. 198. A second variety, "The stub stands, the mill is going, ten draw four,"[10] is found in Scandinavia and Finland with only slight variations in the numerous texts.[11]

The following minor varieties of "Ten draw four" can be recognized:

§ 1. Ten draw four. See Nos. 976a through 976e below.

§ 2. Rump on seat, ten draw four. See above in this headnote.

§ 3. Ten against four. See Nos. 977a through 977d.

§ 4. Ten upon (about, above, onto) four. See Nos. 978a through 978d.

§ 5. Ten upon four, hauling and scrambling. See No. 979.

§ 6. Four hang, ten draw. Flemish: Joos, 585, 586. Walloon: Colson, *Wallonia*, IV, 59, No. 45b. French: Rolland, 43. Compare the German "Ten bent, four drawn, . . ."[12] and the Lettish "Four stretch themselves, ten bend themselves."[13]

976a. *Ink, ank*, yon bank, / Ten drawing four.—A person milking a cow.
Waugh, *Canada*, p. 67, No. 764.

976b. *Tink, tank*, under the bank, / Ten drawing four.—An old woman milking a cow.
Fauset, *Nova Scotia*, p. 159, No. 80 var. *Scrink, scrank:* Greenleaf, *Newfoundland*, p. 11, No. 26. *Crinkety crank:* Greenleaf, *Newfoundland*, p. 11, No. 26 var. *Chink, chink*, on the bank: Fauset, *Nova Scotia*, p. 159, No. 80 var.

976c. *Ink, ank*, in the bank; / Ten a drawing four.—Men's fingers milking.
Leather, *Hereford*, p. 230.

976d. *Hink hank* under de bank, / Ten drying fo' (four).—Cyattle, milking.
Parsons, *Antilles*, III, 376, St. Vincent, 17.

---

[8] *Le piacevoli notti*, III, 5.
[9] The word also signifies "rump."
[10] Swedish: Hyltén-Cavallius, *Värend*, 10 = Wigström, p. 288, No. 5 = Ström, p. 96, "Oxen, kon, kalben," 2.
[11] Danish: Kristensen, p. 75, § 176, Nos. 281a, 281b. Norwegian: Bugge, *Telemarken*, 19; Brox, *Ytre Senja*, 122; Stafset, 183. Swedish: Ericsson, *Södermanland*, III (1882), 98, No. 134; Ström, p. 375, "Sysselsättningar," 17. Finnish: Aarne and Krohn, 267 = Henssen, 186 (The block stands, the river flows, ten draw four).
[12] Frischbier, *Thierwelt*, p. 345, No. 10.
[13] Bielenstein, 488.

976e. *Him, hum* under the bag, / Ten a-hauling four.—Man milking a cow.
Fauset, *Nova Scotia*, p. 159, No. 80.

977. Ten against Four

English riddlers compare milking a cow to ten men fighting against four. This variation seems to be an independent English development, for the few available parallels are not closely related. It has arisen from the more widely known "Ten draw four."

977a. *Clink, clank,* under the bank, / Ten against four.—Cow being milked.
Bacon and Parsons, *Virginia*, p. 327, No. 129.

977b. *Clink, clank* doon the bank, / Ten again four; / *Splish, splash* in the dish, / Till it run ower.—The milking of a cow.
Wright, p. 311.

977c. *Link, lank,* on a bank, / Ten against four.—A milkmaid.
Halliwell-Phillipps, *Popular Rhymes*, p. 148; Knortz, p. 229, No. 76.

977d. *Clink, clank,* under the bank; / Ten against four; try once more.—A girl in pattens, milking.
Harland and Wilkinson, *Lancashire Legends*, p. 186.

978. Ten upon (above, about, onto) Four

The replacement of the preposition "against" by various approximately synonymous words shows that the riddlers have failed to conceive clearly the scene of ten men fighting against four men that is implied in the preceding texts.

978a. *Pink! Pank!* Yn anëth the bank, / Ten upo' four.—Cow being milked.
J. W. Crombie, *Folk-Lore Journal*, I (1883), 267 (Buchan district, Aberdeen).

978b. *Clinke clanke* under a banke, / ten above foure and neere the stanke.—A maid milking of a cow.
Prettie Riddles (1631), No. 59 = Brandl, p. 60.

978c. *flink flank* under a bank 10 about 4.—woman milking a cowe.
Tupper, *Holme Riddles*, 36.

978d. Ten on to four.—Ten teats on a cow.
Beckwith, *Jamaica*, p. 202, No. 181.

979. Ten upon Four, Hauling and Scrambling

This description of knitting occurs but once, as far as I am aware, in English folklore. Although it is probably an adaptation of the preceding riddles for milking a cow, there are some parallels which compare knitting, sewing, or spinning to the activities of five or ten men. They seem nevertheless to be conceptions quite independent of the riddle for milking. The Danes say, "Ten red riders and five shiny soldiers march every day."[1] For sewing the Russians say, "There goes the judge to the courtroom. He is carried in by five people. He goes in boldly. He comes out like a dead man,"[2] which contains elements found in other connections.[3] The Breton "Five hold one, five turn one,"[4] the Bulgarian "Five drive it, five wait for it,"[5] and the Zyrian "Four brothers mow, five sisters rake"[6] describe spinning. The oldest example of this theme that I have noted is Claret's versification in the fourteenth century:

> Sunt deni fratres: quini stant, quinque meantes
> Sub tectoque madent, sicci currendo manebunt:
> Netricis digiti sub torno quinque locati.[7]

979. As I was going past a neighbor's house, / There I saw ten upon four; / Such hauling and scrambling and rolling about; / There's a thing for you to find out.—Person knitting.
Gardner, *Schoharie Hills, N.Y.*, p. 255, No. 16.

980–982. Two See It; Five (Ten) Pick It

Riddlers often describe eating in terms of a company of people who perform characteristic symbolic acts. I have already commented on the comparisons of eating to threshing and of teeth to white soldiers.[1] This description of eating involves the mention of groups of men in such symbolic numbers as two, five, and thirty-two, representing the eyes, fingers, and teeth.[2] The Ho adapt this conception to a series of contradictions: "There were four men under a mango tree. A mango fell from it. He who saw it did not pick it up. He who did not see it, picked it up. He who picked it up, did not eat it. He who ate it, could not satisfy his hunger. He who did not eat it, had his hunger satisfied.— The eyes, the hands, the mouth, the belly."[3] Still another variation appears in the Mongolian "Take it with the five and give it to the ten; take it with the ten and give it to the naked one; take it with the naked one and give it to the hole.—Eating: the fingers, hand, tongue, and stomach."[4] The Annamese "Five persons, holding two wands, make white egrets enter the cave"[5] shows some similarity to riddles for catching a louse.[6]

---

[1] Kristensen, p. 128, § 359, No. 571.
[2] Sadovnikov, 612.
[3] See the headnote to Nos. 970–975 above.
[4] Sauvé, 91.
[5] Gubov, 330, 331.
[6] Wichmann, *Zyrian*, 221.
[7] Claret, p. 69, No. 19. For parallels to the five wet and the five dry fingers see the headnote to Nos. 961–963, § 8, above.

[1] See the headnote to No. 841, §§ 1, 4.
[2] The Swahili use this as a children's rhyme; see Büttner, p. 201.
[3] Sarkar, p. 355, No. 22.
[4] Mostaert, 114.
[5] Dumoutier, p. 208. The "wands" are chopsticks and the "egrets," rice.
[6] See the headnote to Nos. 970–975 above.

980a. There was a white man goin' on top of a tree. / Two men saw it, / Five pick it, / Two heard it when it fell, / Ten put it up, / And one eat it.—Eye, hand, ear, finger, mouth.
Parsons, *Antilles*, III, 366, Trinidad, 32.

980b. One man go for it, five man pick it up, / And one man eat it.—[Man eating].
Parsons, *Antilles*, III, 366, Trinidad, 32 var.

981. Two men saw some mangoes. Ten men pick them. Thirty-two men eat them, and one tongue taste them.—Answer lacking.
Parsons, *Antilles*, III, 422, Montserrat, 23.

982. Eight was standin', / Two was crackin', / Two was lookin'.—Crab.
Parsons, *Antilles*, III, 366, Trinidad, 37.

983–1035. Related Persons

Comparisons to related persons are of two kinds. Brothers, sisters, sons, and daughters can easily represent the parts of an object which are identically similar, such as peas in a pod. Father and son or mother and daughter can represent objects of which one controls the other. Husband and wife can represent objects that are coördinate and complementary.

983–988. Sons

983. Sons and Shirts

Riddlers often compare day and night,[1] the days of the week, months, and seasons[2] to persons. See, as examples of comparisons for the days of the week, the Chilean comparison to seven passengers;[3] the Lettish "Six sisters bathe in a bathhouse, a seventh comes and drives them all out,"[4] which is an adaptation of riddles for loaves of bread and an oven-shovel, or for coals of fire and a poker;[5] the Arabic "Seven horsemen, each has a special name,"[6] which is paralleled by the Crimean Tatar "There are seven brothers of one age and different names";[7] the Bihari description of the four watches of the day, each of four hours, in "A man comes and goes continually, he gives birth to four sons every day. Each of these has four wives. He who understands this is a learned man,"[8] which has some similarity to a riddle for the four seasons;[9] and the Javanese "They never meet during their lives. They all die, yet they

---
[1] See the headnote to No. 1001.
[2] See the comparisons for both months and seasons cited in the headnote to No. 984.
[3] Flores, 341.
[4] Bielenstein, 391.
[5] For these riddles see the headnote to No. 493, § 2, above.
[6] Giacobetti, 58.
[7] Filonenko, 93.
[8] Mitra, *Bihar*, 73.
[9] See the headnote to No. 984 below.

revive quickly.—Days of the week."[10] These examples have been chosen to show the great variety of conceptions that have been used. I cannot cite a parallel to a curious Javanese riddle for the days of the month: "It is a ship. If one loads it with thirty persons, that is too few; with twenty, also too few; with ten, also too few; but when there are fifteen, it is full.—The moon. The men are the days of the lunar month."[11]

Riddlers have occasionally compared the days of the week to things rather than persons. These comparisons seem to be quite independent of the comparison of the year to a tree.[12] In eastern Europe the comparison of the week to a tree is well known; see Lettish: Bielenstein, 386 (A great long fir in six pieces, in the top a stork),[13] 390 (Six little golden leaves, a holy cross upon them), 391 (A long, long aspen, a golden leaf at its top). Bulgarian: Chacharov, 10 (The laurel tree blooms on Sunday.—Easter). It is uncertain whether these riddles are connected with the following obscure Flemish riddle for both the Pleiades[14] and the days of the week: "On the way to Rome there stand seven trees; these are not oaks or ash trees."[15]

The same sort of special mention of holy days occurs in the Modern Greek "A lettuce head with fifty leaves and seven hearts and in the seven hearts there sits a red rose.—Lent and Easter";[16] the White Russian "A bridge stretched for seven versts and at the end [there was] a poppy flower.—Lent, Easter";[17] and the Finnish "A swamp seven versts long, a bridge at the end of the swamp, a column at the end of the bridge, a golden apple upon the column. —Holy Week."[18] Unfortunately, neither the appropriateness of these comparisons nor their meanings are fully apparent. They show some similarity to the Turkish riddle for prayers, "Five apples fell from Heaven, three in the summer, two in the autumn."[19]

Some further comparisons have found only a limited circulation. Their meaning is often obscure. The Russians say, "In a book there are six ordinary leaves, the seventh is of gold,"[20] which is closely paralleled by the Crimean Tatar "In a copybook there are seven leaves; six aren't worth anything, the seventh is gold."[21] Other allusions to the sacredness of Sunday occur in the Lithuanian "Six parts lie outside, but the seventh lies in God's garden,"[22] the

---

[10] Ranneft, *Poëzie*, p. 24, No. 8.
[11] Ranneft, *Proza*, p. 14, No. 68.
[12] See below, Nos. 1037a through 1038b, the headnotes to Nos. 1037–1038, 1037, and 1038, the note to Nos. 1037a, 1037b, and the note to Nos. 1038a, 1038b.
[13] The stork is a holy bird.
[14] For other riddles having this answer see the note to No. 988 below.
[15] *Ons Volksleven*, I (1889), 78, No. 34.
[16] Dieterich, *Rätseldichtung*, p. 90, citing Polites, *Neohellenika Analekta*, I, 237, No. 254. For additional parallels see Aarne, *Rätselforschungen*, I, 97, and also the headnote to Nos. 1037–1038, nn. 17–20, below.
[17] Wasilewski, 121.
[18] Lönnrot, 1683 = Henssen, 101.
[19] Kúnos, 121.
[20] Sadovnikov, 2025.
[21] Filonenko, 45.
[22] Jurgelionis, 143.

curious Serbian "An old woman grew seven teeth. When she lost her teeth, she kissed everybody.—Holy Week,"[23] and the Surinam "My father has seven things. He gives six, but as for the seventh, that he does not give."[24] The Bulgarian riddle for Lent is analogous to the texts just cited: "The seven-week fast has borne a golden grain.—Easter."[25] The Serbian "A hairless, long-nosed man came and ate up seven sacks of millet"[26] is not intelligible.

There are several riddles in terms of wood. I have already noted comparisons to a tree and a bridge. The Finns say, "Six golden chips, the seventh silver."[27] The Georgian "Seven planks tied together. Neither a tsar nor his army can untie them,"[28] with the answer "week," is clearly related to the Mingrelian "Seven planks have sworn together and are firmly united, the bishop cannot dissolve them, nor the tsar's army.—The major fasts before Easter."[29] Such conceptions may be ultimately related to the Icelandic "A ladder with seven rungs stands in a house. A man and a wife who never rest are there.—Week, night, and day."[30]

983a. My fader had six sons. He gave each son a shirt. Dey wear deirs an' help him wear his own.—Six days in de week an' people still work on de seven'.

Parsons, *Bahamas*, p. 485, No. 128.

983b. My fader had six sons and seven shirts. He give each one de sons one shirt an' he take one, made de seven. De six sons wa' [wear] out deir shirts an' still help de fader to wear his.—Dere were seven days in de week. Ef you work six days in de week an' still work Sunday, you help God wid his own. (You do somet'in' you shouldn' do, you should res' on de Sabbat').

Parsons, *Bahamas*, p. 479, No. 80.

984. Twelve Sons

The personification of the various divisions of time occurs in many forms and uses, but rather few of the instances are found in riddles. The description of the twelve months as twelve men is widely known and has a long history. The one English example that I have found comes from the West Indies and may belong to Romance rather than to English folklore, for French influences seem to be strong in Saba Island. It differs from the usual personification of the twelve months in the reference to February, the shortest month, as the young-

---

[23] Novaković, p. 173, No. 9.
[24] Herskovits, p. 451, No. 104.
[25] Gubov, 33.
[26] Novaković, p. 173, No. 10.
[27] Aarne and Krohn, 336 = Henssen, 59.
[28] Glushakov, p. 38, No. 93.
[29] Blechsteiner, p. 15, No. 19.
[30] Árnason, 1025.

est son and in the lack of an allusion to the days as children. An early example of the personification of time is the riddle introduced by Jean Larivey into his translation of Straparola. It is as follows:

> Je suis un grand chasseur qui vivement pourchasse
> Infinis animaux en maintz divers quartiers;
> Je dompte à mon plaisir quatre puissans destriers,
> Qui me servent par rang quand je vas à la chasse.
>
> Par monts, par vaux, par bois, et, bref, en toute place,
> Je cours chargé de proye après deux grand levriers,
> Qui sont si diligens, si prompts et si legers,
> Qu'à peine de leurs pas on recognoist la trace.
>
> Je n'ayme qu'à chasser, et c'est pourquoy tousjours
> J'ayme un jeune chasseur, qui chasse nuicts et jours,
> Car ce seul passetemps tous les autres excelle.
>
> Je ne donrois mon heur pour l'heur du seul fœnix,
> Parce que plus souvent mes ans sont rajeunis
> Que du tortu serpent la peau ne renouvelle.[1]

Riddlers occasionally elaborate the comparison of days and nights to persons by calling them white and black respectively,[2] but this detail is perhaps more frequently found in the comparisons to leaves on a tree.

For discussion of the personification of the year and the months in riddling see H. Knust (ed.), Walter Burley, *Liber de vita . . . philosophorum* (Bibliothek des literarischen Vereins in Stuttgart, CLXXVII [Tübingen, 1886]), pp. 40–41, note *f*; Ohlert, 2d ed., p. 94; Petsch, *Rätselstudien*, p. 345; Aarne, *Rätselforschungen*, I, 160–166. The personification of the months or the representation of characteristic activities for each month in calendars does not seem to be reflected in riddling. For discussion of this pictorial tradition see J. C. Webster, *The Labors of the Months* (Evanston, 1938), and a review in *Speculum*, XVI (1941), 131–137. For a survey of riddles for the year and its divisions see the headnote to Nos. 1037–1038 below.

The conception of the seasons as four brothers occurs in various forms in eastern Europe and Asia and shows somewhat less variation in western Europe. For examples see German: Wossidlo, 156; Frischbier, *Menschenwelt*, p. 258, No. 173. Swiss: Zahler, *Münchenbuchsee*, 107, 168. Serbian: Novaković, p. 32, No. 11 (Four brothers walk all over the world and do not see one another).[3] Finnish: Aarne and Krohn, 15 = Henssen, 230 (A fellow came from the North Land, a slant-eye from Untamola, who blew fire into the room. A fellow came from the Sun Land, the son of the sun with golden brows, he drove away the

---
[1] Nuit III, Fable 1.
[2] See, for example, Buchler, *Gnomologia*, 3d ed. (1614), p. 413. Compare the curious Turkish riddle for day and night: "I have a hanging grape, one side is white, one side is black" (Hamizade, 197).
[3] For the last trait see the headnote to Nos. 1003–1004 below.

fellow of the North Land and at the same time put out the fire.—Autumn and spring), 14 = Henssen, 231 (The old lady of the North Land spread a thick sheet of linen on our floor. The old lady of the South endeavored and struggled to roll it up.—Winter and summer).[4] Turcoman: Samojlvich, 34 (In a cart I saw four young boys. For each boy I saw three maidens), to which he cites a parallel in Pantusov, *Taranchin*, 175. See also Samojlvich, 35 (A man has twelve sons: three faithless, three fierce, three simple, three noble). Armenian and Tatar: Zelinski, p. 55, No. 10, and Kalashev and Ioakimov, p. 60, No. 4 (Three are our enemies, three are gardens of paradise, three gather and bring things, three destroy). Some Turkish riddles for the three months of the hot season are constructed in similar fashion, but contain some obscurities; see "Three brothers, sons of the stars, one is of the heavens, the second from the blessed waters, the third rubs his face on his dusty feet"; "We are three brothers, we come once a year, one of us strolls in the air, one of us swims in the sea, one of us strolls in darkness"; and "Three brothers came: one fell into the water, one into the sky, one to the ground."[5] An oral Catalan parallel[6] may be a disordered recollection of these Turkish comparisons.

A few riddles for the seasons refer to animals or things instead of persons. The Yakut "A white mare has gone away, a raven one has galloped off, a black-maned and black-hoofed one remained.—Snow has thawed, spring has come and gone, summer has come"[7] seems to have lost the reference to a mare, representing autumn. I cannot satisfactorily explain the Irish "Four went yonder without ship or boat: one dead of cattle, one cut of the fields, one white rose, one fair white.—Spring, summer, autumn, winter"[8] or the Tungus "Three maidens without fathers-in-law, three mares without stallions, three deer without rumps, three mountains without an open spot in the woods.—Year."[9] The Tungus riddle is probably related to the Mongolian "Three mountain passes of the *yidam*, three *obō* of Dives [abundance], three icy cavities, three fields of flowers.—Spring, autumn, winter, summer"[10] and the variant, "The three mountain passes of the *bardo*;[11] leaves—three flowers; the three plains of riches (abundance); cold—three depressions"[12] are extremely obscure. The following explanation, which I owe to Professor F. D. Lessing, is the best

---

[4] For this theme compare the headnotes to No. 575, nn. 22-29, above, and to Nos. 1217-1218, n. 15, below.
[5] Kúnos, 271; Hamizade, 91, 92.
[6] Milá y Fontanals, 1876, pp. 25-26, No. 13.
[7] Popov, p. 283.
[8] O Dalaigh, 177.
[9] Poppe, 32. He adds the variants "three mares without bridles" and "three mountains without a pass."
[10] Mostaert, 171. The *yidam* (a Mongolian word borrowed from Tibetan) is the life-long personal *genius protector* chosen by the Lamaist after certain preparatory steps. The *obō* is a pile of stones erected by the roadside or on mountaintops; it is supposed to be the seat of a *genius loci*.
[11] *Bardo* (a Tibetan word) means the intermediate stage between death and reincarnation.
[12] Mostaert, 171 var.

available. The spring, which is a hard time for the cattle-breeding nomad, is marked by epidemics, epizoötics, and death; its three months are comparable to three mountain passes to be crossed under the protection of one's personal deity. The three *obō*, or piles of stone where sacrifices are offered, may symbolize the special activities and festivals of the three autumn months. The icy depressions, or the three winter months, are distinguished by varying degrees of cold and offer a contrast to the three blossoming fields, each with its different flowers, of the summer.

For discussion of riddles about the seasons see Gustav Roethe (ed.), *Die Gedichte Reinmars von Zweter* (Leipzig, 1887), p. 616; Loewenthal, p. 55.[13] The smaller divisions of time are occasionally personified in riddling.[14] The Flemings and the Swedes call the hours twenty-four brothers who rule the world,[15] but they are perhaps adapting a riddle for the letters of the alphabet.[16]

984. A fader had twelve sons, de second one de younges'.—Twelve months of the year, de second one February.
Parsons, *Antilles*, III, 433, Saba, 12.

985. Son Appears before Father's Birth

Riddlers use the notion of a son or daughter[1] who performs an act of some sort before the father or mother is born to describe a variety of objects, usually fire and smoke. The references to father and son usually concern fire and smoke, and those to mother and daughter usually concern ice and water.

A reference to three members of a family with characteristic actions for each of them appears in several forms. The modern Greeks say of fire, smoke, and ashes: "The first brother eats and is not satiated; the second flees and does not return; the third sleeps and does not feel."[2] Riddles for wood, fire, and a pot or stove often mention three persons.[3] Although these riddles can be grouped together as descriptions in terms of a family, they show little connection with one another.

The comparison of father and son to fire and smoke has a Western and an Eastern form. The Western form refers to the appearance of the son on the roof as in the Catalan "What is that: the father is not yet born, and the son is already running on the roof?"[4] The Kashmiri "When born, it immediately climbed to the second story"[5] is a rare Eastern instance of this form. The Eastern form refers to the son as a precocious traveler as in the Cheremiss

---

[13] See also riddles cited in the headnotes to Nos. 952–957, § 7, above, and 1037–1038, §§ 2–3, 9, below.
[14] See the headnotes to Nos. 983 and 1001.
[15] Joos, 125; Ström, "Tiden," 13.
[16] *American Notes and Queries*, III (1943), 111.
[1] For comparisons to a daughter see the headnote to No. 1007.
[2] Dieterich, *Rätseldichtung*, p. 92, citing Stamatiadis, V, 183. For other tripartite riddles on domestic objects see the headnotes to Nos. 138–140 and 941–942 above.
[3] See the headnotes to Nos. 1017–1035 and 1017 *bis*.
[4] Milá y Fontanals, 1876, p. 24, No. 10.   [5] Knowles, 102.

"While the father is putting on his boots, the son is arriving in the city."[6] The Lappish "The father is half-ready, the son is in the forest"[7] is a rare Western instance of this form. Since the versions agree rather closely, one is tempted to derive them from a common source.

Somewhat different from the scenes mentioned thus far are the Icelandic "I am tallest before my father comes to life, but not much is ever seen of me if he grows very big" and the more elaborate "What boy is born full-grown and flies from birth? At once of the same age as his father he ascends high into the air in a gray coat. As he grows old, he expands and disappears altogether from sight";[8] the Swedish "The son begins to sail, while the father is not yet born";[9] and the Lappish "The sons are workers, and the father is coming into being."[10] Few are so widely aberrant as the Italian "In the torrid zone, among blacks, I, a white, was born. I brought my father nothing but misfortune, for when I arose, he had to die. He breathed his last in my arms, may his pure spirit rise to Heaven! Unfortunate one, I was left alone in the world. It is my duty to remove spots, but guard yourself from what I conceal under a deceptive cover.—Ashes."[11]

Some versions of this riddle for fire and smoke are well conceived. See the Icelandic "He is made of steel and stone which smashes the strongest metals. The birth of the father seems slow, for the son is born before him";[12] the Serbian "The father is in the cradle, while the son walks in the house";[13] the Cheremiss "While father is putting on his boots, the son is arriving in the city";[14] the Hungarian "His father had hardly come to life, but the son is already walking on the roof";[15] the Kashmiri "The mad fellow escaped by the back-window, taking his wife on his back";[16] and the Khāṛiā "Before the birth of his father, his son goes to the dancing ground to dance."[17] The Hungarian "Although the son hasn't yet a father, he is already making shingles"[18] refers to smoke pouring out on the roof.

Some riddles for smoke employ entirely different themes. See the Nyika "If father plays in the bush, the long tail feathers of a cock are visible."[19] and the Turkish "A son larger than his father.—Fire."[20]

---

[6] Genetz, 64.
[7] Lappish: Qvigstad, 11, 62. Finnish: Koskimies, 237, as cited by Qvigstad.
[8] Árnason, 880, 566.
[9] Dybeck, *Runa*, 1865–1873, p. 64.
[10] Qvigstad, 12.
[11] Tschiedel, 18. The "duty to remove spots" refers to the use of ashes for bleaching. This literary riddle has some similarity to those discussed in the headnote to Nos. 668–680 above.
[12] Árnason, 316.   [13] Novaković, p. 16, No. 9.
[14] Genetz, 64.
[15] *Magyar Nyelvör*, XVIII (1889), 428 = XXXI (1902), 533, No. 20.
[16] Knowles, 119.
[17] Roy and Roy, II, 455, No. 50.   [18] *Magyar Nyelvör*, XVI (1887), 87.
[19] Hollis, *Nyika*, p. 137, No. 2.   [20] Hamizade, 26.

For further parallels and discussion see R. Köhler, *Kleinere Schriften*, I, 268; Ohlert, 2d ed., p. 185; Feilberg, *Ordbog*, III, 121, s.v. "røg"; Schultz, *Rätsel*, cols. 98–99; Jungbauer, pp. 350–351; Antti Aarne, *Journal de la société finno-ougrienne*, XXXIV (1917), 1–64; Flajšhans, pp. 6–7, § 6a.

The theme of a son who appears before his father's birth is applicable to:

§ 1. Smoke and fire. See No. 985 and compare the headnote to No. 1007, § 7. The fourteenth-century version noted by Claret[21] is a simple version of the theme:

Filius est captus super edem [read: aedem], quam [read: quā] pater ortus:
Ante salit fumus supra, quam fit bonus ignis.

§ 2. Steam or the heat of a stove. This can be regarded as a variation or specialization of the preceding. See Flemish: Joos, 55 (steam). Zyrian: Wichmann, *Zyrian*, 116 (the head of a stove).

§ 3. Bread and bread cake. Serbian: Novaković, p. 113, No. 10 (While the father is being born, the son walks through the house), and p. 114, Nos. 1 (I was born last night and my father this morning, and I went to fetch a priest to baptize my father), and 2 (The son is older than the father).

§ 4. Ice and water. Swedish: Ström, p. 221, "Ström, isen," 4 (The son rides a horse [river], the father is not yet born). Lappish: Qvigstad, 13. Compare Nos. 1007a, 1007b below.

§ 5. Plants. Indian, Kashmiri: Knowles, 99 (First I and my mother were born, then father. [After that] for five days nothing happened, [then] grandfather was born.—Cotton). Bihari: Mitra, *Bihari Life*, p. 47, No. 34 (While the father is still in the womb, the son went to a wedding party.—Safflower). This is explained as referring to the seed (father) in the pods and the safflower dye used for wedding clothes. Bengali: Mitra, *Chittagong*, p. 300, No. 5 (The father remained within the belly, but the son went to the market.—Plantain). The "father" is the budding stem within the trunk and the "son," the bunch of plantains taken to market.

§ 6. Hay ricks. Russian: Sadovnikov, 1271 (A stump walked out on St. Pelei's Day. The stump began to complain, "Why is it that children are born before their father?").

985. The son upon the housetop, and the father not yet born.—Smoke from a fire not yet kindled.
Fitzgerald, p. 180 (Irish).

986. Pursuing

986. My mother have four sons, she sent them to school, and not one could beat the other. What's that?—Windmill.
Parsons, *Antilles*, III, 421, Montserrat, 2 var.

---

[21] P. 74, No. 110.

987. Cannot See

987. My fadder had t'ree sons. One could not see, the other two was blind. Tell me.—Coconut.
Parsons, *Antilles*, III, 440, Anguilla, 23.

988. Cannot Talk to Each Other

The use of this scene to describe stars is rare, and its appositeness is not entirely clear.

988. My fader had seven sons, / An' all seven couldn' talk to each oders.—Seven stars.
Parsons, *Andros Island, Bahamas*, p. 275, No. 6.

989–1006. Brothers

Riddlers describe objects which occur in pairs or in larger numbers as brothers, sisters, or members of a family. They may call the eyes,[1] ears,[2] legs of a table,[3] or beans in a pod[4] "brothers." They obtain a sufficiently exact description by adding a phrase, ordinarily one suggesting an action rather than a detail of form or color. Such inventions, which are comparatively popular in lands where riddling is still vigorous, are very scantily represented in English tradition.

Only one riddle—which, moreover, has a very curious and interesting literary history and can scarcely be called a folk product—deals with the abnormal form of these so-called "brothers."[5]

989–991. Form

989. Dressing Awry

The close relationship and similarity of the fingers has suggested calling them brothers or sons. The Kundu say, "The children of my mother, nothing but twins"[1] and the Turks, "Ten boys on an island, five on each half."[2] Such comparisons are often enlarged by pointing out differences in these five supposed persons, especially a difference in height.[3]

A few riddles refer to supernumerary fingers or are otherwise curious. A Spanish riddler enumerates all five fingers individually.[4] A Zulu text mentions a supernumerary finger: "Guess ye some men who are walking, being ten in

---

[1] No. 1003.
[2] No. 1004.
[3] No. 993.
[4] No. 1005.
[5] See No. 990a and the headnote to No. 990.

[1] Ittmann, *Kundu*, 21.
[2] Katanov in Radlov, IX, 91, No. 770; Maenchen, p. 106.
[3] See the headnote to Nos. 1040–1041 below.
[4] Demófilo, 360 = Rodríguez Marín, 326 = Argentinian: Lehmann-Nitsche, 551.

number; if there is one over the ten, these ten men do not go; they say, 'We cannot go, for here is a prodigy.' These men wonder exceedingly; they are slow in settling the dispute, saying, 'How is it that one number is over ten, for formerly we did not exceed ten.' "[5]

Riddlers often add details to suggest the nails. See the Mordvin "A man is walking, he is driving ten ducks ahead of him";[6] the Duala and Aandonga comparisons to an animal: "The antelope bears a bundle of pisang"[7] and "The goats on the fence."[8] Many African comparisons of fingers to trees include a detail representing the nails. See the Basuto "Ten trees, on top of them flat rocks"[9] or the more frequent mention of green and dry wood, as in the Algerian Arabic "Tell me what is a green branch of which the flowers are dry wood"[10] and the Lamba "The Wanga-tree dry on one side."[11] The same idea also occurs in the Baiga "From the wet tree [fall] dry chips of wood."[12]

Some comparisons for the fingers or for the fingers and the nails are picturesque. See the Bulgarian "There is a plate on every point";[13] the Votyak "A piece of embroidery from Samarda with five medallions,"[14] in which the veins of the hand may be symbolized by the embroidery; the Hausa "A little bow behind an anthill";[15] and the Kashmiri "Twenty lids to twenty pots."[16]

Quite different ideas, which have no similarity to these themes, appear in the Mordvin "They can be seen from the front, they cannot be seen from the back";[17] and the Ten'a riddle from British Columbia, "Riddle me: there are backs or buttocks set in mid-air."[18] The notion of "bones over flesh" is usually reserved to describe a crab or a candle,[19] but a Portuguese riddler applies it to the nails.[20] The Annamese "Five persons wearing five horn caps climb into the forest to catch insects"[21] contains elements recalling the comparison of chasing lice to a hunt.[22] This and other references to the fingernails conceived as caps seem to have no connection with the description of a fruit or plant as a man with a red cap.[23]

---

[5] Callaway, 9.
[6] Ahlqvist, p. 39, No. 4.
[7] Bufe, 6.
[8] Pettinen, 32.
[9] Rolland, p. 169, No. 3, citing Casalis.
[10] Giacobetti, 286.
[11] Doke, 117.
[12] Elwin, p. 472, No. 78.
[13] Ikonomov, 78. See also the Turkish "Ten brothers, on the back of each one there is a stone" (Hamizade, 557).
[14] Wichmann, *Votyak*, 313. See also the comparison of the fingernails to an apron in Nos. 588b and 588c above.
[15] Harris, 3.
[16] Knowles, 108.
[17] Pasonen, 335.
[18] Jetté, 73.
[19] See the headnote to No. 588, §§ 2, 7, above.
[20] Parsons, *Cape Verde*, 226.
[21] Dumoutier, p. 209.
[22] See the headnote to Nos. 459–460 above.
[23] See the headnote to Nos. 632–644.

989. My father had ten son and every one wear their cap face turned on the back.—Fingernail.
Parsons, *Bahamas*, p. 479, No. 73.

990. Five Brothers of Abnormal Form

The history and significance of this curious comparison of five brothers to the parts of a rose are much in need of clarification. The fundamental conception appears in such Indian riddles as the Kashmiri description of a saffron flower, "Three are naked; three are coverlets; three are *parda-nishin* women";[1] the Baiga riddle for a castor bean, "Three brothers have only one nose";[2] and the Bhil riddle for the thorns of the babel tree, "Two brothers with only one buttock."[3]

In medieval Europe, this comparison for a rose was also applied the five senses as in Claret's version: "Sunt quini fratres, bini barbaque carentes et duo barbati: quintum genus probo neutri."[4] These "brothers" are respectively sight and hearing, taste and touch, and smell. This conception seems to be related to that of the five brothers representing the eyes, ears, and nose in a Ho riddle and a Munda riddle.[5] Joachim Camerarius versified the rose riddle, as follows:

> Quinque una fratres germani matre creati,
> Flavo splendentem gestant in vertice comtum:
> Glabri ex his duo, visuntur, semperque tenelli:
> Sed tres promissa cernes horrescere barba:
> Quorum gratus odor citris florentibus exit.[6]

An anonymous contemporary reduced the theme to a distich:

> Sunt quini fratres, sub eodem tempore nati:
> Barba duobus abest, & tribus illa subest.[7]

A few years later Johannes Pincier put it into other words:

> In lucem veniunt quini uno tempore fratres,
> Bini horum barbas parte ab utraque gerunt.
> Barbae aliis expers latus est utrunque duobus,
> Hinc est barbatus quintus, at inde glaber.[8]

---

[1] Knowles, 15. For "coverlets" we should probably read "covered"; *parda-nishin* refers to women in purdah.
[2] Elwin, p. 476, No. 122.
[3] Hedberg, p. 868, No. 13.
[4] P. 66, vv. 28-29.
[5] See the headnote to Nos. 1003-1004, n. 22, below.
[6] Reusner, ed. 1602, pp. 254-255 (with a translation into Greek).
[7] Reusner, ed. 1602, p. 380. See another version in Buchler, *Gnomologia*, 3d ed. (1614), p. 441.
[8] *Ænigmatum libri tres* (The Hague, 1655), pp. 147-148 (Book II, No. 24).

Much the same theme but referred to the senses and not to the parts of a rose is seen in:

> Quinque suis hominum vincunt animantia sensus,
> Horum si nosti nomina prode mihi.
> Responsio
> Nos aper auditu praecellit, aranea tactu,
> Vul[t]ur odoratu, lynx visu, simia gustu.[9]

For discussion of this curious riddle and other versions see Thomas Harrap, *Tessaradelphus or the foure Brothers; the Qualities of whom are contained in this olde Riddle* (n.p., 1616); Thomas Browne, *Works* (ed. G. Keynes; London, 1928), IV, 94, and V, 352; Flajšhans, p. 12; various authors, *Notes and Queries*, CLVIII (1930), 370, 410; Albert Wesselski, *Archiv orientální*, IX (1937), 373.

990a. Five Brethren were bred at once / without any flesh, blood, or bones; / two have beards, and two have none, / the fift have but halfe a one.—The five brethren be five greene barbs under the rose leaves which spring all at one time. Two of them have bristles like unto beards on the edges; and the other two have none, but bee plaine on the edges; and the fift is bristled, or bearded, on the one side, and plaine on the other.
Meery Riddles (1629), No. 28 = Brandl, p. 13.

990b. there is a thing wch hath five chins 2 hath beards 2 hath none, & one it hath but half an one.—a rose bud whose outward gree[n] leaves are some jaged [jagged] others plaine.
Tupper, *Holme Riddles*, 144.

991. Full All Day, Empty at Night

Riddlers often use the contrast of full and empty. It is more readily applied to things than to persons.[1] When applied to persons, it may take the form of the contrast between empty and pregnant.[2] There are a few descriptions of shoes in which other themes are used. See the Turkish "Strolling, strolling, he comes, he opens his mouth"[3] and the Georgian "There are two of them, they are brothers."[4]

991a. Two brothers we are, full all day and empty at night.—Pair of boots.
Fauset, *Nova Scotia*, p. 169, No. 147.

991b. Two brothers we are, / great burthens we bear, / By which we are bitterly prest, / In truth we may say, / we are full all day, / But empty when we go to rest.—A pair of shoes.
A New Riddle Book; Or, A Whetstone for Dull Wits (18th cent.), p. 5; Parker, *Oxfordshire*, p. 330; Hyatt, *Adams Co., Ill.*, p. 666, No. 10905.

---

[9] Buchler, *Gnomologia*, 3d ed. (1614) p., 429.
[1] See the headnote to No. 1455.
[2] See the headnote to Nos. 1455–1457.
[3] Hamizade, 437. See also No. 453 above.
[4] Glushakov, p. 25, No. 23.

991c. Two brothers we are, great burden we bear, / We're sorely oppressed, / Full all the day, an' empty at night, / When we go to rest.—Pair of shoes.
Kavanagh, *Béaloideas*, IV (1933–1934), 342.

992–1006. Function

The conception of objects as brothers possessing various normal or abnormal functions is somewhat familiar to English riddlers, but is much more popular with riddlers in other countries. The functions characteristic of these supposed brothers are: standing or sitting (Nos. 992, 993), helping one another (Nos. 994, 995), pursuing one another (Nos. 996 through 1001 and the headnote to Nos. 996–1001), seeing one another (Nos. 1003 through 1005 and the headnotes to Nos. 1003–1004 and No. 1005), and speaking (No. 1006). Of these, only the notion of brothers pursuing one another is very popular. The comparison of beams or rafters to brothers who stand or lie is widely known but has not interested English riddlers.

992–993. Stand (Sit) Together

When the parts of an object are alike in form and function and are present in numbers of two or more, they can be called "brothers" for the purposes of riddling. It is equally appropriate to call them soldiers, as in a riddle for a fence current on the Slave Coast, "Who stands motionless like a troop of warriors?"[1] They are called nuns, monks, or soldiers in some riddles for teeth and seeds.[2] This manner of description is, however, rather unfamiliar to English riddlers.

I survey here the riddles in which the actors are said to stand or sit. A similar conception is that of members of a family lying in the same bed.[3] A separation according to the sex or the relationship of the actors does not commend itself. It would lead into the inconsequential minutiae already exemplified in the classification of actors pursuing one another.[4]

Riddlers often render the scene more picturesque by elaborating its details. The persons may be conceived as hostile or quarreling.[5] The Kundu description of a gutter or, more precisely, the streams of rainwater pouring from a gutter, cleverly suggests a scene in native life: "Where do novices stand in a file?"[6] Still another variation appears in a Masai riddle for rafters, "What are my warriors like? I have many of them, and one goes out to look after the cattle."[7] This identifies the rafter which projects as a ridgepole. See finally

---

[1] Trautmann, p. 101.
[2] See the headnotes to Nos. 841, 908–916 above.
[3] See No. 1027 and the headnote to Nos. 1027–1028.
[4] See Nos. 952 through 957, 996 through 1001, 1014a through 1015b, 1029a, 1029b.
[5] See a Samoan riddle cited in the headnote to Nos. 966–968, §13.
[6] Ittmann, *Kundu*, 29.
[7] Hollis, *Masai*, p. 253, No. 2.

the Nandi "I dispatched the advisers, and they entered the earth.—Poles of a house."[8]

992. Two brothers side by side all day and at night they go to rest.—Pair of boots.
Fauset, *Nova Scotia*, p. 169, No. 148.

993. Brothers under One Hat

This scene, which ordinarily describes a table, is readily adjusted to describe a stool or the legs of a washtub. It is also applicable to:

§ 1. A hearth. Svanian: J. Nizheradze, pp. 66–67, No. 2 (Four sisters have one hat).

§ 2. Sheaves (often sheaves in a pile) or haycocks. Lithuanian: Schleicher, p. 194 (Four brothers wear one hat.—Roof resting on four posts over a haycock). Russian: Sadovnikov, 1223 (Nine brothers under one hat), 1224a (Four brothers stand under a fifth one, their heads in one pile, their backs away from one another), 1268 (Ninety-nine little brothers stand under one hat). Cheremiss: Porkka, 133. Zyrian: Wichmann, *Zyrian*, 211. This concept is closely related to the description of a sheaf as a person girt with a belt.[1]

§ 3. A chimney, a room, a building. Lithuanian: Jurgelionis, 1106 (Four brothers wear one cap.—Shed). Serbian: Novaković, p. 44, No. 3 (Four brothers wearing one cap.—Chimney). Arabic: Bauer, p. 222, No. 3 (Four robbers dressed in one nightcap.—Room and walls).

§ 4. Plants. Swedish: Dybeck, *Runa*, 1865–1873, p. 8, No. 3.

In many countries the notion of brothers standing together or joining in bearing a burden serves to describe the parts of a house. Riddlers often enlarge upon this scene with great ingenuity. See the Arabic "Four soldiers of a caisson bear a large plate.—Roof";[2] the Yakut "A hundred people, so they say, have one agreement.—Tent poles and covering" and "A hundred people under one roof.—Ceiling of a hut";[3] the Javanese "There are four gurus who are mentioned. They have no wisdom, hence they give no instruction to all their pupils. Their task is to bear something on their heads, and all their pupils do likewise; they always bear something on their heads.—Pillars of a house";[4] the Samoan "A hundred-headed company of brothers, all of whom bear their father.—Rafters"[5] and "It is a hundred brothers who surround their king,"[6] which is a variant of "A number of brothers, and it cannot be found out who is the last.—Posts which surround the round hut."[7] African

---

[8] Hollis, *Nandi*, p. 142, No. 39.
[1] See the headnote to No. 678, § 2, above.
[2] Littmann, p. 55.
[3] Piekarski, 245, and see his No. 243.
[4] Ranneft, *Poëzie*, p. 93, No. 7.
[5] Heider, 67.
[6] Heider, 68.
[7] Brown, p. 345.

riddlers use the same device; see the Nandi "I have a hundred children, and I support them all.—Center post and roof poles."[8]

993. Four brothers under one hat.—A table.
Greenleaf, *Newfoundland*, p. 12, No. 32.

994–995. Help Each Other

994. Two brothers none can help the other.—Bottle.
Parsons, *Antilles*, III, 370, Grenada, 30.

995. My father have two bottles, one can't do without the other.—Cart wheels.
Parsons, *Antilles*, III, 371, Grenada, 38 var.

996–1001. Pursuing One Another

There are similar comparisons to persons who are not related[1] and to sisters.[2] The objects described are in all of these varieties essentially the same. Perhaps the riddles in which the actors are not said to be related represent a weakened form, for the similarity or identity of the wheels is neatly symbolized by calling them brothers or sisters.[3]

The notion of brothers pursuing one another is applicable to:

§ 1. The wings of a windmill. See Nos. 999a through 999e. The Annamese description in terms of persons of opposite sexes introduces an unusual complication: "Monsieur stays in the West, Madame stays in the East; while turning, they pursue each other without ever catching each other."[4]

§ 2. The arches of a bridge. Calabrian Greek: Morosi, as cited by Rolland, 193, from Roque-Ferrier, *Languedoc*, pp. 321–322 (I have three brothers, they pursue one another and never reach one another).

§ 3. A reel. Swiss: Rochholz, 487. Italian: Pitrè, 42. Serbian: Novaković, p. 137, No. 5 (Four brothers on one steed; all are chasing at a gallop, yet one cannot catch another).

For a similar riddle in which the actors are not said to be related see the headnote to Nos. 952–957, § 2; for a version in which the actors are sisters see the headnote to Nos. 1014–1015, § 4.

§ 4. A pair of knitting needles. Lithuanian: Jurgelionis, 533 (Four brothers were taken prisoner, the fifth came to ransom them and he was captured). Serbian: Novaković, p. 69, No. 13 (There were five brothers and one pair of drawers; one brother takes them down, another puts them on), and p. 70, Nos. 1, 2, 8. Bulgarian: Gubov, 189 (Four brothers knit and the fifth helps

---

[8] Hollis, *Nandi*, p. 36, No. 13.
[1] See the headnote to Nos. 952–957.
[2] See the headnote to Nos. 1014–1015.
[3] For discussion see Flajšhans, pp. 20–21, § 20.
[4] Dumoutier, p. 205.

them), which has admitted the answer into the riddle, and 190. Albanian: Hahn, p. 161, No. 31 (Five brothers build a tower). Turkish: Hamizade, 124 through 129; Katanov in Radlov, IX, 369, No. 332 (five youths); Moshkov in Radlov, X, 272, No. 92 (Five brothers chase one another). For versions in which the actors are sisters see the headnote to Nos. 1014–1015, § 5, below.

§ 5. Sled runners. Norwegian: Christie, 73 (Two brothers go into the woods and leap and [yet] do not get away from each other). Finnish: Aarne and Krohn, 317 = Henssen, 29 (In the forest two men run on snowshoes and neither catches the other). Votyak: Buch, 46 (snowshoes). Yakut: Piekarski, 396 (They say that two brothers race each other, but neither can outrun the other), 398 (They say that two dogs are running a race, but neither can outrun the other). For parallels in which the actors are sisters see the headnote to Nos. 1014–1015, § 3, below.

§ 6. Wheels or the spokes in a wheel. See Nos. 997 through 998e. An early nstance with the answer "wheels" is Claret's fourteenth-century versification:

> Bis bini fratres currunt se non rapientes:
> Ipsa quaterna rota currus dabit ista soluta.[5]

§ 7. The hands of a clock. Flemish: Joos, 226. German: Wossidlo, 158.

§ 8. The feet. Finnish: Aarne and Krohn, 163 = Henssen, 30 (Five brothers ahead, a bald old man behind, yet he never catches them). The brothers are the toes and the old man is the heel. African, Bakongo: Denis, 8 (One says, "It is I who reigns"; the other says, "It is I who reigns"), which dramatizes the competition of the legs. The conception is akin to that underlying the fable of the Belly and its Members. Kundu: Ittmann, *Kundu*, 114 (I went on a journey with my comrade. He said he was going ahead. I said however, I am going ahead. Who are we?). Taveta: Hollis, *Taveta*, 54 (I have my two warriors who race, and neither wins). Ila: Smith and Dale, II, 326, No. 19 (The chiefs are having a dispute). Indonesian, Tounsea: De C., p. 237, No. 5 (Two brothers who follow their grandfather without stopping. Wherever their grandfather goes, they go. Neither likes to remain behind, but they contend to be first). Tabaru: Fortgens, 102. Filipino: De los Reyes y Florentino, p. 276 (Two brothers who dispute who shall go first). Tagalog: Rizal, p. 46 (Two big sticks running after one another), which is an unusual comparison to things rather than persons. Compare also No. 943 above.

This riddle for feet is very closely allied to the riddles for snowshoes and sled runners cited in § 5 above.

§ 9. The eyes and the feet. See No. 996.

§ 10. Waves. See No. 1000.

§ 11. The sun and the moon. See No. 1001.

---
[5] P. 68, No. 9.

§ 12. The seasons. See the headnote to Nos. 952–957, § 7, and the headnote to No. 984.

996. Six broders goin' along, two reach before four.—Your eyes reach before your two hands and feet.
Johnson, *Antigua*, p. 88, No. 5.

997. What's six brothers running after each other and never catching up?— A wheel with six spokes.
Greenleaf, *Newfoundland*, p. 12, No. 30.

998a. Little baba [brother] run all day, an' big baba kyan't ketch him.— Dat's a buggy-wheel.
Parsons, *Sea Islands, S.C.*, p. 154, No. 11, var. 2.

998b. Four brothers runnin' [variant: workin'] all day, an' can't catch [variant: touch] each other.—Four carriage wheels.
Parsons, *Barbados*, p. 277, No. 6 var.

998c. Four bredder walk a road and not one can touch.—Four buggy wheels.
Beckwith, *Jamaica*, p. 194, No. 93.

998d. Four brothers going to school, and not one could touch the other. What is that?—Four carriage wheels.
Parsons, *Antilles*, III, 428, Nevis, 11.

998e. Four brothers goin' to school, / Comin' from school, / Near to each other, / Could' [couldn't] catch each other.—Four carriage wheels.
Parsons, *Antilles*, III, 375, St. Vincent, 6.

999a. Four broders are runnin' a race an' not one can beat [variant: ketch] de oder.—Windmill.
Parsons, *Antilles*, III, 421, Montserrat, 2 var.

999b. Four brothers running all day to ketch one another, and could not.— A windmill with four point.
Parsons, *Antilles*, III, 428, Nevis, 12.

999c. Four broders runnin' behin' each oder an' not one could ketch de oder. —Four pint [points, vanes] of a mill.
Parsons, *Antilles*, III, 432, St. Eustatius, 6 var.

999d. Dere was onct four broder goin' by, none can ketch de oder.—De four pint of a mill.
Parsons, *Antilles*, III, 436, St. Martin, 21.

999e. Me riggle, ma riggly, / Four broders goin' alang, / All day an' night an' not one / Can't ketch each oder.—Four mill vain.
Parsons, *Antilles*, III, 425, Antigua, 18.

1000. Four broders runnin' behin' each oder an' not one could ketch de oder. —Sea swell.
Parsons, *Antilles*, III, 432, St. Eustatius, 6.

1001. Brother Pursues Brother (Sister)

Although the examples are not numerous, the comparison of the sun and moon, or, more frequently, day and night, to persons pursuing each other is both very old and very widely known. In the *Rigveda*,[1] the shining night and the dawn are two beauties who walk together, but one is going and the other is coming. In another passage,[2] the white dawn is said to be coming while a black maiden prepares a dwelling for her. The path of the two is single and eternal; they travel upon it, one behind the other, accompanied by the gods. They do not meet, and they do not stand still. Hesiod calls day and night two women, of whom one is at home while the other is abroad. They alternate in their duties so that they are never at home at the same time.[3] The Spanish say, "Two brothers, always being born one after another."[4] Such ideas suggest themselves so readily that we cannot insist upon deriving them from a single source.

There are some examples of similar ideas in traditional riddling. A French riddler in the West Indies sees day and night as "Two sisters, one black and one white";[5] an Icelander, as "Who are the man and wife who have traveled more widely than all others? They are always meeting but are never reconciled, and usurp each other's domain",[6] and also as "Although people call us brother and sister, we are quite dissimilar. My face is as white as snow and without a blemish, but my sister is very dark. Compared with me, she is also rather cold, for I am so much warmer. Each of us flees before the other. I follow her, and she chases me, but neither is oppressed by sorrow. We are never both under one roof. This is our lot of freedom that shall never end."[7] An Icelandic riddle for the day and night in midwinter deserves special notice: "I knew of a man and wife who were so different that they occupied their bed in a most unusual way. He was too short and she was too long. He looked up and she looked away and then she frowned and tore her hem. She travels around my home-district with a dark face, often frozen and never warm."[8] The interpretation of some of these details is obscure. A Polish riddler describes day and night as "A widow had two children: the daughter was black, the son glistened."[9] A Renaissance comparison of days and nights to white persons and black persons is closely related to the year riddle,[10] in which the white leaves and

---

[1] I, 123, 7.
[2] I, 113, 2-3.
[3] *Theogony*, vv. 748 ff.
[4] Demófilo, 371.
[5] Parsons, *Antilles*, III, 383, Martinique, 38.
[6] Árnason, 670.
[7] Árnason, 909. See also his No. 1039 and the Swedish riddle for the sun and moon quoted in the note to No. 967 above.
[8] Árnason, 1124.
[9] Gustawicz, 45. See also Lettish: Bielenstein, 137, 158.
[10] See below, the headnote to No. 1007, § 5, and the headnote to Nos. 1037-1038.

the black leaves of the tree represent days and nights. The text of this comparison is as follows:

> Est genitor, natos qui bis sex procreat, uni
> Cuique horum natae triginta, dispare forma;
> Quaedam sunt nigrae, quaedam sunt vultibus albae:
> Sunt immortales omnes, moriuntur et omnes.[11]

The Turks say, "I have a hanging grape, one side is white, one side is black."[12]

The comparison of the moon to a girl or princess is familiar enough in poetry but does not appear to be very popular with riddlers.[13] Comparisons of the sun and moon to things are rare. The Finns and Estonians tell of two boats that cannot overtake each other.[14]

1001. Two broders runnin' a race, not one could ketch de oder.—Sun an' moon.

Parsons, *Antilles*, III, 421, Montserrat, 3.

1002. Brother Does Not Leave Brother

1002. My moder have two boys, both of them walking together, one wouldn' go leave the other.—Two oxen.

Parsons, *Antilles*, III, 369, Grenada, 17.

1003–1005. Seeing

Riddlers often mention seeing as an act which is impossible in circumstances which seem to offer no difficulty. This enigmatic contradiction arouses the hearer's curiosity and affords matter for a riddle.

1003–1004. Brothers Are Close, But Cannot See Each Other

The old and widely known comparison of the eyes to men who are separated by a wall or mountain and are thus prevented from seeing each other may have arisen independently many times.[1] The details in its use in riddles vary considerably and lend themselves to individualization of the theme. Examples are the Polish "Two brothers look over a little mountain, but can never see each other";[2] the Modern Greek "Two brothers quarreled, and a hill separated them";[3] the Albanian "Two brothers are close to each other, and a mountain separates them";[4] the Russian "Two brothers stand across a little patch from

---

[11] Buchler, *Gnomologia*, 3d ed. (1614), p. 413.
[12] Hamizade, 197.
[13] See Spanish: Demófilo, 615, 617, 620; Rodríguez Marín, 256, 257. Indonesian, Javanese: Ranneft, *Poëzie*, p. 221, No 1. For discussion see Ohlert, 2d ed., pp. 86–92; Loewenthal, p. 53. For other comparisons of the sun and moon to persons see Rumanian: Papahagi, 20; the comment in Tupper, *The Riddles of the Exeter Book*, p. xv; No. 1001 below; and the headnote to No. 967 above.
[14] Lönnrot, 347 = Henssen, 62. Estonian: Dido, 35.

[1] Sextus Empiricus calls the eyes two lovers; see his *Adversus Mathematicos*, I, 346, ed. Immanuel Bekker (1842), p. 673.
[2] Saloni, *Rzeshów*, 116.
[3] Dieterich, *Rätseldichtung*, p. 96.   [4] Hahn, p. 158, No. 3.

each other, yet can never get together";[5] and the Sierra Leone "Two men wid ribber[6] middle dem."[7]

The obscure Pangwe "Bakon and Angbwäwodo cannot see each other,"[8] which the collector believes to be confused, may have the answer "eyes." I do not understand the Votyak "Two brothers look at each other all their lives, but cannot visit each other,"[9] for we cannot say correctly that one eye sees the other, unless in a mirror. The Bakongo use the theme of fighting brothers in a riddle for the eyelashes: "They throw objects at each other from either side."[10] Blechsteiner's derivation of the comparison of the eyes to hostile brothers from the proverb, "If the nose were not in the middle, the [one] eye would be the enemy of the [other] eye,"[11] which is current among the Georgians and Mingrelians, does not seem entirely convincing.

In riddles of this sort the actors vary greatly.[12] The following actors or things appear in riddles for the eyes:

§ 1. Birds. Slavic riddlers often compare the eyes to jackdaws. See Czech: Hanika-Otto, note to No. 214. Serbian: Novaković, p. 157, Nos. 5 (Two daws peep from the roof, but they do not see each other), 6 (Two daws lie under the hill, but one cannot see the other), and p. 158, Nos. 5 (Two daws peep from the cave), 6 (Two wingless daws peep from the cave, they fly everywhere and yet they sit in the cave).

For comparisons to other birds see Serbian: Novaković, p. 156, No. 9 (Two side by side, they saw everybody except each other), and p. 157, No. 6 (Two hens peep from under the hill, but one cannot see the other). Finnish: Aarne and Krohn, 148 = Henssen, 41 (Two golden[13] cuckoos look over the rafter). Estonian: Wiedemann, p. 288 (cocks). Tungus: Poppe, 2 (Two crows vie with each other in running, neither outruns the other).[14] Indonesian, Tabaru: Fortgens, 58 (Two doves who fight in the air.—Eyebrows). The eyes and sight are sometimes compared to birds going and returning.[15]

§ 2. Animals. RABBITS. Lithuanian: Jurgelionis, 168 (At the edge of the wood crouch two rabbits). GOATS, KIDS. Spanish, Chilean: Flores, 519. Porto Rican: Mason, 405. Albanian: Hahn, p. 160, No. 24 (Two he-goats are egged on to kill one another, and cannot reach one another.—Eyebrows). Arabic: Stumme, *Tázerwalt*, 15 (two kids). OXEN. Swedish: Russwurm, *Eibo*, p. 134,

---

[5] Sadovnikov, 1763a.
[6] River.
[7] Cronise and Ward, p. 197.
[8] Tessmann, 137.
[9] Buch, 51 = Wichmann, 375.
[10] Denis, 3. For a list of similar conceptions, see the headnote to No. 1044, n. 8, below.
[11] Blechsteiner, p. 9, No. 113 (Georgian) and p. 155, No. 97 (Mingrelian) and compare p. xxiii.
[12] For parallels in which the actors are women see No. 1016 and the corresponding note and headnote below. For general discussion see Ohlert, 2d ed., p. 207.
[13] In Finnish, the word for "golden" also signifies "beloved."
[14] For an application of this theme to the sun and moon, see No. 1001 above.
[15] See the headnote to No. 1471, nn. 30–31.

§ 316, No. 27. Estonian: Wiedemann, p. 267. DOGS. Cherekessian: Tambiev, p. 53, No. 6 (Two black dogs next to each other).

§ 3. Various objects. EGGS. Russian: Sadovnikov, 1761 (Two little eggs [or little apples] in the moss, and up above there is a carrot).[16] ROOMS. Indonesian, Sangir: Adriani, 146 (Two rooms which a tongue of land separates). BALLS. Russian: Sadovnikov, 1764 (Two balls hang across a little row from one another). CANDLES. Lithuanian: Jurgelionis, 169 (Two candles, a hill between them). POTS. Russian: Sadovnikov, 1769 (Under a little threshold there are two little pots). African, Togo: Schönhärl, 95 (Two pots never come together). STARS. Lithuanian: Jurgelionis, 165 (Two little stars which go wherever they please).

Eyes are also compared to pools or lakes[17] and to windows.[18] The Ainu "What are two things with a hill between them which never meet?"[19] lacks concreteness.

There are a few analogous comparisons for other parts of the head.[20] See also the Indian riddle for the nostrils, "There are two brothers, born in the same house, having the same name, exercising the greatest power of life, yet [they] have no power of life in themselves"[21] and for the head (ears, eyes, and nose): "On one chair sit five brethren. Although touching, they do not touch one another."[22]

The notion of persons vainly looking at each other is applicable to objects other than the parts of the head. The Bulgarian "I have four brothers. Day and night they look at one another, yet they never have enough of looking,"[23] with the answer "walls," is unusual for the mention of four brothers. The Russian "Two little brothers always look at each other, they will never meet"[24] and "Brother and sister see each other but do not come together,"[25] like the Votyak "Two brothers look at each other but never meet,"[26] have the answer "floor and ceiling." These are much the same as the Mordvin riddle for doorposts, "As they are placed, so they remain. They look across but go nowhere"[27] and the somewhat elaborated Ten'a description of the side partitions at the

---

[16] For similar riddles see the headnote to Nos. 1100–1108 below, and especially the riddle cited there in n. 22.
[17] See below, No. 1044 and the headnote and note to No. 1044.
[18] See No. 1144 and the headnote to No. 1144.
[19] Starr, *Ainu*, 28, 48.
[20] No. 1004 below.
[21] Lakshīnātha Upasānī, VIII, 1.
[22] Indian, Ho: Mitra, *Notes on Ho Riddles*, p. 117. Munda: Roy, *The Mundas*, p. 506. See also the headnote to No. 990 above.
[23] Palashev, 5. Compare also the riddle for the feet of a pot, No. 1012 below.
[24] Preobrazhenskii, p. 172.
[25] Sadovnikov, 52v.
[26] Wichmann, *Votyak*, 222.
[27] Paasonen, 107.

entrance to an underground house: "They are like relatives stretching their hands toward each other without reaching."[28]

These riddles for the walls or the floor and ceiling are rendered more vivid by individualizing the actors, as in the Zyrian, Mordvin, and Votyak "Darya and Marya look at each other"[29] or the Zyrian "Isaac and the cossack look at each other."[30] In Cheremiss, the Darya and Marya riddle has also the answer "ears of a pot."[31]

Instead of naming persons, the riddler may select animals that are traditionally hostile to each other. See the Turkish "Two bulls fixed their eyes on each other.—Two opposite corners of a yurt"[32] and the Cheremiss "The bear and the wolf look at each other.—Floor and ceiling."[33] This last riddle has the additional answers: "stove and bench,"[34] "stove and wall,"[35] "stove and window,"[36] and "floor and window."[37]

Less familiar uses of the theme of persons who are close but cannot meet or see each other are the Russian descriptions of windowpanes, "Many neighbors spend their lives side by side, yet never see one another,"[38] and of a door and the jamb, "Two godmothers bow and yet would not come together. —Doors in an entrance hall"[39] or "Two are standing, yet would not come together; two are lying, yet would not come together.—Door frames,"[40] to which the Ho "On a wooden seat, a father-in-law and his daughter-in-law are sitting together, but the one does not touch the other"[41] affords a curious parallel.

The notion of two actors who are similar in form—and are therefore represented as brothers—and do not meet is also applicable to the banks of a river or sides of a gorge, as in the Russian and Mordvin "Two little brothers look into the water, they will never meet."[42] A similar conception of riverbanks is known in Africa. Except in the Taveta "Why are there two of us and we do not quarrel?"[43] African riddlers merely say that the actors are equal in size and do not mention an act in connection with them. See, as examples, the Wamajame "Two kings are equally great"[44] and the Nuer "Guess: two big

---

[28] Jetté, 65. See the comment in my "American Indian Riddles," *Journal of American Folklore*, LVII (1944), 8–9.
[29] Zyrian: Wichmann, *Zyrian*, 138. Mordvin: Paasonen, 28. Votyak: Wichmann, *Votyak*, 235, 352; Buch, 35.
[30] Wichmann, *Zyrian*, 76. [31] Porkka, 114.
[32] Katanov in Radlov, IX, 370, No. 351.
[33] Genetz, p. 135, No. 12 = Ramstedt, p. 214, No. 11.
[34] Cheremiss: Porkka, 88.
[35] Cheremiss: Wichmann, *Cheremiss*, 49.
[36] Cheremiss: Porkka, 115. Votyak: Wichmann, *Votyak*, 11; Buch, 33.
[37] Cheremiss: Wichmann, *Cheremiss*, 109.
[38] Sadovnikov, 55. [39] Sadovnikov, 84.
[40] Sadovnikov, 85. See also the headnote to Nos. 1476–1494, § 26, below.
[41] Sarkar, p. 252, No. 32.
[42] Russian: Sadovnikov, 1475. Mordvin: Ahlqvist, p. 40, No. 16.
[43] Hollis, *Taveta*, 57. [44] Ovir, 30.

males."[45] Such riddles are very similar to African riddles for the earth and sky.[46]

A similar idea occurs in a riddle that the poet Cowper sent to a friend with a request for the answer: "What are they which stand at a distance from each other and meet without ever moving?"[47] The answer is "The trees in a colonnade." The riddle, to which I can cite no parallels, seems to be a literary rather than a popular invention. Since it has reference to seeing and perspective, I cite it here and conjecture that these riddles for the eyes may have given rise to it.

1003. Two brothers on one side of the road, / And yet they cannot see each other.—Eyes.
Parsons, *Bermuda*, p. 250, No. 29; Fauset, *Nova Scotia*, p. 174, No. 205.

1004. Jack on one side, Tom on the other; and yet Jack cannot see Tom. —Ears.
Parsons, *Bermuda*, p. 250, No. 30.

1005. Live Together; Do Not See (Touch, Speak to) Each Other

This can be considered a variety of the many descriptions in terms of persons in a house.[1] It includes an additional element referring to an act of the supposed brothers which gives them greater individuality. The number of actors is usually small. Such variations as the Spanish "More than a hundred neighbors, each in his room, not one touches or talks to another.—Nuts on a tree"[2] and the Cheremiss "Only a finger in length, yet it begets eight children.—Pea pod"[3] are rare. The notions of speaking, seeing, or touching are likely to be concerned with only a few actors. The answers are ordinarily a nut (the brothers are the segments of the kernel) or a fruit containing seeds.

For parallels having the answer "nut" see Flemish: Joos, 488, and compare his Nos. 498 through 500 and No. 502, var. 9; *Ons Volksleven*, I (1889), 79, No. 47, and II (1890), 104, No. 9. German: Hanika-Otto, 59, 258. Swiss: Rochholz, 393; Zahler, *Münchenbuchsee*, 9, 10 (apple seeds), 279. French: Rolland, 108; Bladé, *Armagnac*, 74 (pomegranate), 94; J. Roux, *Limousin*, 45; Roque-Ferrier, *Languedoc*, p. 329 and No. 72; Lacuve, *Poitou*, p. 702, No. 4; A. Ferrand, *Dauphiné*, p. 226; Dardy, *L'Albret*, p. 327; V. S., *Mélusine*, I (1878), col. 263, No. 81. Basque: Demófilo, p. 374, No. 10; Vinson, 38 (In a room [there are] four ladies who cannot go out), 39 (Room and room; in each

---

[45] Huffmann, p. 105, No. 15.
[46] See the headnote to No. 1252 below, especially nn. 8–17. For African conceptions of earth and sky as two like objects, see the note to Nos. 1252a, 1252b.
[47] Ely, *American Notes and Queries*, VIII (1891), 51. J. Stanley gives the answer on p. 78.
[1] See the headnotes to Nos. 908–916, 909, 910–915, and 1134.
[2] Rodríguez Marín, 566.
[3] Porkka, 71.

room it is a little lady); Cerquand, 32. Spanish, Mallorcan: Demófilo, p. 364, No. 20. Italian: Tammi, 14 (Four ladies in a bed), 15; Schneller, *Wälschtirol*, p. 254 (Four brothers are locked in a little room. If someone does not open it for them, they cannot come out). Rumanian: Gorovei, *Devinettes*, p. 506; Papahagi, 67, var. 1 (Four brothers in one shirt), var. 2 (A monastery with four monks). Russian: Sadovnikov, 1296 (There stands a house with neither doors nor windows, yet it is full of people.—Pod).[4] Serbian: Novaković, p. 155, Nos. 8 through 12. Bulgarian: Palashev, 9 (There are four ladies sleeping in one hole.—Walnut); Gubov, 261 (Four brothers wear one shell.—Walnut), which admits too specific a suggestion of the answer into the riddle; Chàcharov, 84 (Four brothers sleep under one cap.—Walnut), which is an adaptation of the table riddle (No. 993 above), 85 (Four brothers sleep in one shirt and cannot see one another.—Walnut); Bozhov, 21 (Four brothers are sleeping in one shirt). Hungarian: Kriza, p. 343, No. 33 (Four dear little ones live in a little round house), and p. 346, No. 70 (Four are united sweetly in an unmade house without a door or window); *Magyar Nyelvör*, XII (1883), 426 (There are four who live in it, it is a dignified house, but [also] a house that hasn't been made and hasn't any windows), 474; XVI (1887), 87 (I have a house. Four gentlemen live in it. The house has no windows at all, the inhabitants cannot see earth or heaven except when taken from the house); XIX (1890), 92 (A king sits in his house; he has four rooms in it); XX (1891), 575; XXXI (1902), 533, No. 28; Arany and Gyulai, II, 352, No. 18 (quoted in the headnote to No. 1134, n. 4, below). Modern Greek: Dieterich, *Rätseldichtung*, p. 93; Abbott, p. 307, No. 10; Stathes, p. 337, No. 37 (Closed in a little trunk, two brothers embrace each other), and p. 346, No. 90 (Locked in a little case, four brothers in an embrace). Gypsy: Wlislocki, 23 (I know four Wallachians; they sit in a fur coat, which was once green and becomes brown in winter), 39 (Four Wallachians wear a fur coat; you burn the coat, you eat the Wallachians). Arabic: Ruoff, p. 53, No. 33 (House without a door, within are four youths). Turkish: Moshkov in Radlov, X, 268, No. 54 (Four brothers in one shirt). African, Kundu: Ittmann, *Kundu*, 111 (We were born [in a house] and we have not yet seen one another). Indonesian, Tounsea: De C., 10 (Five sisters, each has a room), which resembles a riddle for gloves.[5]

This manner of describing an object is not particularly appropriate to the spokes of a wheel, as in the Serbian "There are twelve brothers in one pair of drawers."[6]

1005. Three brother in one house and never see each others' face until dead.— Three beans in one castor-oil pod.
Beckwith, *Jamaica*, p. 194, No. 95.

---

[4] For this conception of a house see the headnote to No. 1134 below.
[5] See the headnote to No. 908 above.
[6] Novaković, p. 141, No. 3.

1006. Speaking

1006. Met my two brothers. / One stopped to speak to me, / And one went on.—Two bees. One stung me, one went on.
Fauset, *Southern Negro*, p. 287, No. 127.

1007–1011. Daughter (Daughters)

1007. Mother Begets Daughter; Daughter Begets Mother

This riddle ordinarily has the answer "ice and water,"[1] but Ohlert conjectures[2] that it is ultimately derived from riddles for night and day,[3] which go back through Athenaeus to Theodectes of Phaselis (fl. 400 B.C.). Wolfgang Schultz adopted this explanation of a cosmological origin.[4]

In addition to the ordinary uses of this concept for ice and water, the river and the ocean, salt and water, and cheese and whey, riddlers have also adapted it to a mountain, smoke, and a chicken. A similar but probably independent riddle has a plant as answer.[5] The Frisian "I have it from hearing and saying that three can become one.—Ice, water, and snow"[6] contains a suggestion of the dogma of the Trinity.

Comparisons to a daughter who begets her mother are applicable to:

§ 1. Ice and water. See Nos. 1007a, 1007b below.

§ 2. Salt and water. See No. 1008.

§ 3. A river and the ocean. Icelandic: Árnason, 509 (What father eats all his children?). Rumanian: Papahagi, 3 (which mother bears sons and devours sons?). Russian: Preobrazhenskii, p. 171 (There is a mother. When her children grow big, she devours them.—River and streams). Modern Greek: Aarne, *Rätselforschungen*, II, 1. Arabic: Victor Chauvin, *Bibliographie des ouvrages arabes*, V (Liége, 1901), 192, No. 113. Yakut: Popov, p. 283 (The mother sucks her own child). Indian, Uraon: Archer, 25 (A boy goes to his father's house).

§ 4. A mountain (born when mother was born). Italian: Rolland, p. 160, No. 21.

§ 5. Day and night. Kolarian: Wagner, 60 (A black hen is sitting and hatches a white hen). For discussion see Ohlert, 2d ed., p. 96, and compare the headnote to No. 1001 above.

§ 6. The wind and a bellows. For discussion see Loewenthal, p. 42.

§ 7. Smoke and fire. Irish: Stokes, 9. Latin: Buchler, *Gnomologia*, 3d ed.

---

[1] See Reusner, ed. 1602, pp. 21–22, 82; Ohlert, 1st ed., p. 30, n. 2, and 2d ed., pp. 54–55, 96; Tupper, *Modern Language Notes*, XVIII (1903), 4, *Holme Riddles*, note to No. 5, and *Riddles of the Exeter Book*, pp. 147–158; Loewenthal, p. 42; Schultz, *Rätsel aus dem hellenischen Kulturkreise*, I, 43–48, No. 28; Flajšhans, p. 7, No. 6b.

[2] Second ed., p. 96.

[3] Athenaeus, *Deipnosophistae*, X, 451f, and *Anthologia Palatina*, XIV, 40, 41.

[4] Schultz, *Rätsel*, col. 94, Nos. 19–21; Schultz, *Rätsel aus dem hellenischen Kulturkreise*, I, 27, No. 6, and II, 23–24.

[5] See § 12 below.

[6] Dykstra, *Snypsnaren*, p. 99.

(1614), p. 475. Italian: Tschiedel, 10. Medieval Greek: Ohlert, 2d ed., p. 92. See also No. 985 above.

§ 8. A bee. Svanian: J. Nizheradze, pp. 68–69, No. 28 (At first it gives birth to young, then the young kill it).

§ 9. A viper. Latin: Ohl, Symphosius, 15 (I cannot be born, if I shall not have killed my mother. I have killed my mother, but the same end awaits me. My death undergoes what my birth has already caused). Johannes Pincier puts the same idea into other words:

> Ipsa meam matrem cum nascerer ore peremi,
> Ipsa etiam morsu prolis obibo meæ.
> Utque mecum necui crudeli morte maritum.
> Interimet pariter sic mea nata suum.[7]

§ 10. A chicken and an egg. Portuguese: Parsons, *Cape Verde*, 67 (My mother gives birth to me, I give birth to my mother). In the similarly conceived Georgian " 'I was as you now are, I shall transform you into such as I am now,' said the setting hen to the eggs, as she sat on them" has taken the words of the hen from the dialogue of the three skeletons and the three living men.[8]

§ 11. Whey and cheese. Icelandic: Árnason, 229 (The father swallows his son and is then hanged. The boy pushes out through his father and is finally whipped out of him.—Cheese in a cheesebag). Indian, Bihari: Mitra, *Bihar*, 56 (She is a lady of noble lineage; as soon as she is born, she kills her father. When she falls into the company of her grandfather, she gives birth to her father).

§ 12. Plants. The vine or stalk is often the mother or father and the fruit the daughter or son. See such instances as the Surinam riddles for sugar cane, "A child's head gives birth to its mother later," and a mango, "Always at first the father or the mother is ahead, but the child becomes bigger than the mother and later gives birth to its father and mother";[9] the Gujerati riddle for a mango, "The father gave birth to the daughter and the daughter begot the father";[10] the Surinam riddle for a cashew, "A child is born before its mother";[11] the Kashmiri riddle for a pumpkin, "The work of God; it is a spider's web; the mother gives birth to a son, and the son gives birth to a mother";[12] and the Kirghese riddle for a watermelon, "In the child lies the mother."[13]

The Bretons describe cider[14] and the Spanish and Portuguese maize[15] in

---

[7] *Ænigmatum libri tres* (The Hague, 1655), pp. 13–16 (Book I, No. 5).
[8] Glushakov, p. 29, No. 45. For the words of the hen see Henri Stegemeier, *The Dance of Death in Folksong* (Chicago, 1939), p. 26, n. 1; S. Kozáky, *Anfänge der Darstellungen des Vergänglichkeitsproblems* (Bibliotheca humanitatis historica, I [Budapest, 1936], I, 213 ff.
[9] Herskovits, p. 435, No. 47, and p. 427, No. 18.
[10] Mehta, p. 121.   [11] Herskovits, p. 429, No. 34.
[12] Knowles, 39.   [13] Karutz, p. 97.
[14] Charlec, *Dol-de-Bretagne*, 1903, p. 396.
[15] New Mexican: Campa, 111. Portuguese: Parsons, *Cape Verde*, 37.

similar fashion. A Kashmiri cotton riddle[16] describes the plant, flower, boll, and opened boll with its white hairs as child, mother, father, and grandfather, all of them appearing in an order reversing that of nature.

A curious Renaissance use of this theme in a literary riddle may have been suggested by the proverb "Familiarity breeds contempt." It is:

> Religio censum peperit, sed filia matri
> Causa suae leti pernitiosa fuit.[17]

1007a. What mother a child doth beget, / and she of it is gotten againe: / which although strange it seemed to bee, / yet it is true, I will tell you plaine. —Water turning to ice, and ice again turning to water.
Prettie Riddles (1631), No. 12 = Brandl, p. 54.

1007b. my mother brought me forth w^n shortly j her daughter brought her forth againe.—water that is made ice & then water againe.
Tupper, *Holme Riddles*, 5.

1008. Mother Begets and Kills Daughter

The ancient description of salt as begotten by water and yet killed (dissolved) by it occurs in several forms. The Levantine—Modern Greek, Arabic, and Syriac—versions exemplify best the ideas of begetting and killing and are probably derived from a common source. The connections, if any exist, among the other versions are obscure. Although the English version does not mention a mother and daughter, I have placed it here in the light of the parallels. It resembles African and Indian versions more than those current on the continent of Europe. For discussion of this theme see the second edition of Ohlert's *Rätsel und Rätselspiele der alten Greichen*, page 97.

Versions current in Russia add an allusion to fire. See as examples the Russian "Born in the ground, baptized in fire. If it falls into water, it disappears entirely";[1] and the Georgian "I threw it into water, then it was changed into water. I threw it into fire, then it was changed into a voice,"[2] which alludes to the crackling of salt when it is burned.

The notion of the daughter killing the mother appears in the Lamba match riddle, "The little thing that swallows its mother."[3]

1008. Somet'ing live in water / Still water kill it.—Salt.
Parsons, *Antilles*, III, 441, Anguilla, 33.

1009. Daughter of Wicked Father Begets Good Children

1009. A wicked father did beget / a daughter fit unto his hand, / But such

---

[16] Knowles, 99.
[17] Buchler, *Gnomologia*, 3d ed. (1614), p. 482.
[1] Sichler, p. 756.
[2] Blechsteiner, p. 13, No. 7.
[3] Doke, 7.

good children did she get, / that are the propes [props] of every land.—The divell begot sinne, and for sinne procured good lawes, which are the stayes of all governments.
Prettie Riddles (1631), No. 61 = Brandl, p. 60.

1010. Cannot Identify Oldest Daughter

1010. My father have three daughters and you can't tell me the oldest one.— Three tumblers.
Beckwith, *Jamaica*, p. 186, No. 29.

1011. Older Daughter Speaks; Younger Cannot

1011. Me riddle me riddle / Me randyo. / Perhaps yer could clear dis riddle, / Perhaps yer cyant. / My moder had two daughters, / De ol' one could a talk, / De young one cyant.—Dat's de dry pease an' de green one.
Parsons, *Bahamas*, p. 473, No. 16.

1012–1016. Sisters

1012. T'ree sisters standin' together, / None can't touch each oder.—Pot foot.
Parsons, *Andros Island, Bahamas*, p. 275, No. 4.

1013. Two sister on ribber side; no one could never wash the other.—Two bottles.
Beckwith, *Jamaica*, p. 194, No. 96.

1014–1015. Sister Vainly Pursues Sister

This pattern, which differs from related forms only in the sex and relationship of the actors, has already been discussed.[1] It is applicable to:

§ 1. Wagon wheels. See Nos. 1014a, 1014b. For similar riddles see Nos. 954a through 956d (actors not related), 998a through 998e (brothers), 1029a through 1030 (family).

§ 2. Sails or the vanes of a windmill. See Nos. 1015a, 1015b. For other riddles of this nature see Nos. 952 (actors not related), 999a through 999e (brothers). Similar riddles mentioning pursuit are collected in the note to No. 986.

§ 3. Sled runners. Finnish: Lönnrot, 365 = Henssen, 33. For similar riddles see the headnotes to Nos. 952–957, § 10, and Nos. 996–1001, § 5 (brothers).

§ 4. A reel. German: Wossidlo, 159 (six maidens). Danish: DFS, 1906/38: T. Buck, No. 7. Swedish: Ström, pp. 153–154; Waltman, *Lidmål*, 225 (Twelve Lapp women dance in a circle). French: Millien, *Nivernais*, p. 512; Fleury, *Basse-Normandie*, p. 369; J. Roux, *Limousin*, 61 (four ladies); Pineau, *Poitou*, 20; Carmeau, p. 35; Queyrat, *La Creuse*, I, 367; Roque-Ferrier, *Languedoc*, p. 322. Catalan: Milá y Fontanals, 1877, p. 7 (the missing answer is probably "reel"). Spanish, Argentinian: Lehmann-Nitsche, 265*l*. Basque: Vinson, 25;

---
[1] See the headnote to Nos. 952–957.

Cerquand, 34, 41 (four ladies); Demófilo, p. 375, No. 11. Russian: Sadovnikov, 577a, 577b (spokes of a spinning wheel), 578. Serbian: Novaković, p. 20, No. 8 (Four women ride on horseback, yet they cannot catch one another). Albanian: Hahn, p. 159, No. 14 (twelve sisters). For similar riddles see the headnote to Nos. 952–957, § 2 (animals or men who are not related), and the headnote to Nos. 996–1001, § 3 (brothers).

§ 5. Knitting needles. Rumanian: Papahagi, 44. Serbian: Novaković, p. 70, Nos. 4 through 6, 9 through 13. Bulgarian: Gubov, 191 (Five Gypsy women went through the village, only one defended herself), 192 (Four Gypsy women went on a journey, one staggered), 193 (Four Gypsy women quarrel, the fifth is pacifying them). Albanian: Hahn, p. 158, No. 6. Georgian: Blechsteiner, 17. For similar riddles see the headnote to Nos. 996–1001, § 4.

§ 6. The teeth of a harrow. Basque: Vinson, 10 (Sixteen sisters at home, staying close to one another and walking and never touching); Cerquand, 16.

§ 7. The sun and the moon. See the headnote and note to No. 1001.

§ 8. Day and night. See a Flemish riddle cited in the note to No. 1001.

1014a. Little sister ran [after?] big sister all day, an' couldn' ketch her.—Wagon-wheel.
Parsons, *Sea Islands, S.C.*, p. 154, No. 11, var 3.

1014b. Big sister always run to catch a little sister.—Buggy-wheel.
Parsons, *Sea Islands, S.C.*, p. 154, No. 11, var. 4.

1015a. There dwels foure sisters near this town, / in favour like, and like in gowne. / When they run for a prise to win, / all at once they doe begin. / One runnes as fast as doth the other, / yet cannot overtake each other.—The foure winds [sic] of a mill.
Prettie Riddles (1631), No. 17 = Brandl, p. 54.

1015b. there is 4 sister in this towne like in fauor & in gowne the hinmost [hindmost] is as forward as the first i [one] & yet the[y] can neu^r ou^{r}take one an other.—the 4 sales of a windy mile [windmill].
Tupper, *Holme Riddles*, 39.

1016. Seeing

This is merely a variant description of the eyes or ears as brothers who cannot see each other.[1] The gender of the word for eyes or ears and the sex of the actors are often not in agreement, and it seems uncertain whether such an agreement can be presupposed. In some parallels the persons are said never to kiss each other. The Chileans say "Two girls can never kiss";[2] the Rumanians express the idea in animal terms: "Two doves prepare to kiss, but they do not kiss at all."[3] The Dutch use this idea to describe the lips: "Two sisters, friendly and

---

[1] Nos. 1003, 1004, the headnote to Nos. 1003–1004, and the notes to Nos. 1003 and 1004.
[2] Flores, 520. [3] Weigand, p. 273, No. 19.

gentle, are together day and night; and more than a hundred thousand times a year they kiss each other."⁴

The notion of persons unable to see each other is occasionally applied to other things than the parts of the body. The Mongolians, for example, use it of saddlebags: "Two sisters do not look into each other's faces"⁵ or "Two brothers do not see each other's face during their whole lives."⁶

1016. Two sisters set in an upstairs window. Dey kyan't see each other.—Eyes.

Parsons, *Sea Islands, S.C.*, p. 167, No. 95; Johnson, *St. Helena Island, S.C.*, p. 159, No. 33.

1017–1035. Family

Riddlers describe closely interrelated objects as members of a family. If the objects are identical, like the rungs of a ladder or the bars of a grate, they may be called brothers, sons, sisters, daughters, or children. If the objects are connected in some way but differ among themselves—wood, fire, and smoke, for example; or the sky, the earth, and the wind—the riddler differentiates them by assigning them appropriate positions as members of a family or appropriate attributes.

Since some varieties of these conceptions do not occur in English riddling, it will be convenient to survey them all by way of introduction. The riddler may contrast the forms of the various members of the family. Typical answers to such riddles are a pot, a distaff, and other household utensils, or a plant with its leaves, flowers, and fruit.¹ The contrasting qualities may be the colors of the various objects. This is true of many riddles for plants and a few riddles for objects.²

Riddlers may contrast the functions rather than the external appearances of the members of the supposed family. English riddlers seem to be unfamiliar with such conceptions. Examples are the Ho description of a vine, "The father tethered his child behind and went off through a narrow path.—Gourd creeper,"³ and the Portuguese riddle on the same subject, "A woman gives birth. She leaves her son behind, she does not turn her face to look at him, and the son goes on growing."⁴ These riddles from widely separated places are strikingly similar, but it is difficult to trace a connection between them. Another variety of this notion of giving birth appears in the Portuguese "My

---

⁴ Sinninghe, p. 8, No. 5.   ⁵ Buryat: Gombojew, 44.
⁶ Mostaert, 98.

¹ For discussion see the headnote to No. 1017.
² For examples and discussion see Nos. 1018 through 1020, the headnote to Nos. 1018–1020, and the note to Nos. 1019a through 1020.
³ Sarkar, pp. 351–352, No. 7. Compare also the headnote to No. 1007, §12, above, and the comparisons to a rope in Nos. 1203a through 1205 below. See also the headnote to Nos. 1203–1205.
⁴ Parsons, *Cape Verde*, 33.

daughter who gives birth only at the joints."[5] Still another variety is seen in the Breton grapes riddle, "A mother without there being a father, I have many children clinging to my breast, my arms extended, I embrace the human race."[6] The ingenious Malagasy description of a lemon tree with its many leaves and thorns, "Many shields, many spears, yet cannot protect wife and children,"[7] has parallels in the comparisons of a vine to a man going to battle. The Tigriña in Abyssinia say, "Something that goes along pulling a shield in front of itself, hurling a lance, letting fall a ball of bread";[8] and the Afghans, "Like a staff in lock, it seems a flag; on its loin is a pouch, 'tis ready for battle."[9]

The examples cited thus far of members of a family having contrasted functions have had plants as answers. Objects in other categories are occasionally found. The Gypsies describe wood, fire, and smoke in "The mother stabs and strikes, the father burns, the daughter pinches,"[10] and the Mongolian "The king has iron for his father, and a mother who dances back and forth, grains are his white children, and [there is] a very black son-in-law.—Cast-iron stove, fire, ashes, poker"[11] contains one reference to an actor's function. A Polish riddle for the sky, the earth, the wind, and night is a representative of conceptions widely known in eastern Europe. It contains some elements of the kind under discussion: "A high hut, a flat mother, a mad son-in-law, a blind daughter."[12]

Riddlers have often entangled the notion of persons differentiated in their functions with that of persons differentiated in temperaments. Such entanglements are especially characteristic of riddles for the grape-vine and its products, grapes, wine, and brandy. English riddlers know nothing of such ideas, but many versions, particularly those from eastern Europe, include a preaching or bellicose son or grandson who represents the sacramental use of wine or the social effects of alcohol. Such ideas are often mingled with descriptions of the form of the vine or the grapes. Perhaps the oldest instance is in the Forty-second Assembly of Al-Ḥarîrî (died 1122 or 1123): "What is the thing, that when it corrupts, its error turns to righteousness, and when its qualities are choice, it stirs up mischief where it appears; its parent is of pure descent, but wicked that which he begets."[13] For European parallels see German: Wossidlo, 149 (Mother lives in the grass, father clings to the walls, son wanders about in

---

[5] Parsons, *Cape Verde*, 31a.
[6] Sébillot, *Devinettes*, 27a. "Embracing the human race" may refer to the use of wine in communion.
[7] Sibree, p. 40, No. 20.
[8] Littmann, *Tigriña*, 37.
[9] Thorburn, *Bannú*, 7.
[10] Wlislocki, 37. See also the comparisons of fire and smoke to father and son in the headnote and note to No. 985 above.
[11] Mostaert, 7. Compare the headnote to No. 1017 *bis* below.
[12] Gustawicz, 263. See the headnote to No. 1017, § 8, below.
[13] *The Assemblies*, trans. Chenery and Steingass, II, 118.

the world). Spanish: Demófilo, 780; Rodríguez Marín, 468 = Chilean: Flores, 553. Argentinian: Lehmann-Nitsche, 453 = Chilean: Flores, 554 (A crooked old lady, a twisting son, a beautiful daughter, a preaching grandson). New Mexican: Campa, 170. Portuguese: Parsons, *Cape Verde*, 43a, 43b (Mother coarse, son smooth, grandson bellicose). Italian: Pitrè, 909; Rondini, *Archivio*, VII (1888), 538, No. 14; Gianandrea, *Canti popolari marchigiani*, p. 289, No. 14; Tschiedel, 75 (Father is bumpy, mother is greenish, daughter so marvelously beautiful that all must fall in love with her). Serbian: Novaković, p. 20, No. 3 (The grandson is in church every day, and the son only once), which refers to the daily use of sacramental wine and the annual blessing of the vine, and p. 117, No. 1 (The father comes to church once a year, the son every holy day, the grandfather never.—Grapes, which are blessed annually at harvest time; sacramental wine; vine).[14] The Serbian "An old woman bore a handsome son and a mad grandson"[15] signifies that the vine bears wine and brandy. Bulgarian: Gubov, 214 (Ragged mother, pretty child, lively grandchild); Chacharov, 61 (A trim mother, a pretty child, a lively grandchild). Hungarian: Arany and Gyulai, II, 369, No. 99 (Crisp and curly[16] is the mother, her daughter is well grown, the son-in-law is false); *Magyar Nyelvör*, III (1874), 38 (The mother is crisp and curly, the daughter has black eyes, and the son-in-law has a thousand minds); IV (1875), 282 (The father is *itkés-botkes*,[17] the mother is crisp and curly, the daughter has pretty eyes, the son-in-law has lost his mind); VI (1877), 271, 470 (My father is long, my mother is flat, my sister is round, my brother is crazy); XXXVII (1908), 188 (The mother is curly and crisp, the father is strong like iron, the daughter has pretty eyes, the son-in-law is crazy.—Grape, leaves, hoe, vine, [and wine]). Modern Greek: Dieterich, *Rätseldichtung*, p. 92, citing Polites, *Neohellenika Analekta*, I, 203, No. 56 (A black[18] mother, a golden[19] daughter, a demonic grandchild), and p. 251, No. 332 (The father is twisted, the son good, the grandson insane); Stathes, p. 335, No. 223 (Ugly father, handsome son, and silly grandson). Carnoy and Nicolaides, p. 291 (The mother is not straight, the daughter pampered, the granddaughter mad). An obscure version for the vine, grapes, wine, and matches is "The brother is a crooked dame, the daughter cunning, the granddaughter devilish, and the great granddaughter a tantalizer."[20] Turkish: Hamizade, 17 (Its father is a bound father, its mother is a smooth, flat woman, its daughter's task is good, its son walks about in conversation.—Trunk, leaf, wine, vine). Indian, Kashmiri: Knowles, 47 (A sweet girl was born to a crooked mother).

Such Polish versions as "Without the son the church cannot be, yet the father never enters the church" and "The son goes to church every day, the

---

[14] See also Novaković, p. 228, No. 4.
[15] Novaković, p. 116, No. 7.
[16] The translation is uncertain.
[17] The meaning is obscure.
[18] Var.: wrynecked.
[19] Var.: beloved.
[20] Polites, *Neohellenika Analekta*, I, 252, No. 335.

father never"[21] are more fully developed personifications, which rest upon ideas found in versions cited above.

A few versions substitute animals for one or more members of the family, but the available examples suggest that this change is a confusion that may have been suggested by another comparison for a vine.[22] Examples are the Serbian "We have a goat, a strong goat. It gave birth to a strong son and a mad grandson" and "A pretty cow gave birth to a handsome son and a mad grandson."[23]

1017. Form

The comparison of an object to the members of a family who are contrasted in their forms is applicable to either domestic utensils, particularly those used for cooking or spinning, or a plant with its roots, stalk, fruit, or seed. Riddles of the first sort, that is, riddles having domestic utensils as answers, have enjoyed a moderate popularity with the bearers of English folklore. Versions have been taken down in Nova Scotia, South Carolina, and the West Indies. This distribution probably implies that the conception was known in Great Britain, although no examples are reported from there.

Typical objects described by a comparison to a family composed of members whose forms contrast with one another are:

§ 1. A pot. See Nos. 1017a through 1017c.

§ 2. A distaff, tow, and a spindle. Zyrian: Wichmann, *Zyrian*, 34 (The father is awry, the mother soft, the son behaves madly.—Distaff, tow, spindle), 208 (My crookbacked aunt, my godfather with a hundred eyes.—Loom and shuttle), 209 (The crookbacked aunt with her husband, Father Taras with his sons, my stepmother runs quickly back and forth.—Loom). Votyak: Wichmann, *Votyak*, 49 (The father is beardless, the son has a beard.—Distaff and spindle).

§ 3. Domestic objects. German: Wossidlo, 138 (butter-tub). Swiss: Rochholz, 498, 499 (pitchfork). Spanish, Argentinian: Lehmann-Nitsche, 452 (oven, bread, shovel, broom). Lettish: Bielenstein, 918 (A long-tailed father, a short-tailed mother, smooth, smooth children.—Bread shovel, bread trough, loaves).

A White Russian riddle for the stove, fire, and smoke includes some elements referring to the functions of the actors: "Mother is fat, daughter is pretty, and the skipping son jumped out into the yard."[1] Some Mongolian riddles on similar themes are highly elaborated: "It has something branched and tufted for its mother; it has the King of Hell[2] for its father; it has lonton[3]

---

[21] Gustawicz, 444, 445.
[22] See the headnote to Nos. 1203–1205 below.   [23] Novaković, p. 116, Nos. 6, 8.
[1] Wasilewski, 69. See other examples in the headnote to No. 1017 *bis* below.
[2] The demon Yama.
[3] The black seeds of a tree. They are also used as beads in a chaplet.

seeds for its black jacket.—Wood, fire, kettle" and "It has something branched and tufted for its mother, it has the King of Hell for its father, it has a 'thickset' coat, it has a beautiful white daughter.—Wood, fire, kettle, dishrag."[4]

§ 4. A lamp. Swiss: Zahler, *Münchenbuchsee*, 219 (An icy father, a dirty mother, a woolly child with fiery scurf on its head).

§ 5. Weapons. Indian, Ho: Sarkar, p. 252, No. 32 (The mother is hunchbacked, but the children are straight.—Bow and arrows). Lettish: Bielenstein, 458 (An iron father, a wooden mother, little tiny children, all of them bloodthirsty.—Gun), 459 through 461, 462 (A crooked father, a crooked mother, a straight son, who drinks blood.—Gun), 685 (A terrible father, a terrible mother, little tiny children, drinkers of blood.—Saber, rifle, bullets). Serbian: Novaković, p. xxi, No. 6 (The father is of wood, the mother is of iron, the two of them have a devilish child). See also the headnote to No. 801, § 4, above.

§ 6. Grapes. The versions differ widely and often introduce elements conceived in a different manner. Typical examples of the variety of conceptions are the French "A wooden mother, a straight father, a son who is somewhat humpbacked.—Vine, vine-shoot, grape"[5] and "The mother is twisted, the father is straight, the child is shaggy";[6] the Bulgarian "His father is wooden, his mother is a forest";[7] and the Turkish "The mother is an outspread aunt, the father is a two-sided uncle, the daughter is a beauty among the beautiful, the son goes around enjoying himself.—Grape arbor"[8] and "The mother is flat, the father has a crooked back, the daughter is red, the son goes through taverns."[9]

Riddles for grapes are not consistently limited to ideas of a single category. They may, on occasion, include elements referring to form, color, function, or temperament of supposed actors.[10] See, as examples, the Serbian "The grandfather is wooden, the father is green, and the child is sweet" or "The father is old, very old; the mother is young, very young; the children are sweet, very sweet."[11] I do not understand the Turcoman "A sick man goes to a sick man, the dead man goes into the grave, a son whose father is three years old goes to market.—Grapes."[12] Some elements which we have found in other riddles for grapes occur in the Crimean Tatar "His brother is a ragged man, his mother is a rank woman, his daughter is rosy sugar, and his son is mad Belsir.—Vine branches with foliage, grapes, wine."[13]

Similar themes are used in describing other plants. See the Turkish "The

---

[4] Mostaert, 117, 118.
[5] Bladé, *Armagnac*, 58.
[6] Dardy, *L'Albret*, p. 331.
[7] Gubov, 76.
[8] Kúnos, 25.
[9] Moshkov in Radlov, X, 265, No. 35. The word for "red" may also signify "beautiful."
[10] For some of these varieties see the headnote to Nos. 1017–1035 above.
[11] Novaković, p. 239, Nos. 4, 5.   [12] Samojlvich, 139.
[13] Filonenko, 33, citing a parallel in Radlov, VII, No. 135. The translations "ragged" and "rank" are somewhat uncertain. Belsir may be Abu Bekr.

body of the mother has grown hard, the father is rich in beard, and the son is fat.—Shell, cone, and kernel of a nut"[14] or the Baiga "The mother is a dwarf, and her child is red.—The ber, a small tree with red fruit."[15]

§ 7. Hops. The examples seem to be restricted to languages spoken near the Baltic Sea. See German: Wossidlo, 136. Swedish: Dybeck, *Runa*, 1848, p. 45, No. 48, and p. 46, No. 58; 1865–1873, p. 30, No. 23, and p. 49, No. 56; Russwurm, 36; Ericsson, *Södermanland*, I (1879), 90, Nos. 53, 54, and III (1882), 102, Nos. 156, 157; Hyltén-Cavallius, *Värend*, 69; Noreen, *Fryksdal*, 4; Geijer and Campbell, 72; Ström, pp. 127–128, "Humlen," 2, 3. Lettish: Bielenstein, 42 (A straight father, a twisted mother, a flat daughter, a roundish and merry son.—Hops: the pole, the flower, and the fruit or beer), 43 (A straight father, a twisted mother, a flat watchman, curly-haired children), 44 (A large, tall father, a mother in ringlets, a flat little sister, and a worthless brother). Finnish: Henssen, 36 (The father straight, the mother crooked, the daughter flat and even, the son as round as a ball.—Hop-pole, runner, leaves, flowers). Estonian: Wiedemann, pp. 265–266. Cheremiss: Porkka, 95. Votyak: Wichmann, *Votyak*, 48.

Similar ideas are found in various Indian riddles. See Baiga: Elwin, p. 469, No. 46 (The mother has a root, the daughter has a hole in her side, the grandson is a hunchback.—Mahua seed, flower, fruit). Bengali: Mitra, *Pābnā*, pp. 328–329 (The mother is tall, the children are mad, the son is round in shape.—Betel nut). Kolarian: Wagner, 9, 23 (The mother has disheveled hair, the child is smooth.—Jack fruit).

§ 8. The wind and the sky. Serbian: Novaković, p. 142, No. 5 (A tall father, a broad mother, a rambunctious son-in-law, a mad maiden.—Sky, earth, wind, fog). Bulgarian: Gubov, 70 (A mad son-in-law, a blind daughter, a short mother, a tall father.—North wind, south wind, earth, sky).

1017 *bis*. Hollow Mother, Humpbacked Father, Three Children

This description of a pot in terms of three members of a family who differ in their forms resembles a riddle for a stove or pot, fire, and smoke, in which the persons differ in their characteristic colors. The Russians, for example, say, "The mother is stout, the daughter is red, the son is brave [and] went off to the skies."[1] The reference to a red daughter recalls the riddles for a fire and pot, naming Redman and Blackman,[2] and the relations of mother and son are analogous to those in other riddles for smoke and fire.[3] To this pattern belong the Mordvin "The mother is fat, the daughter red, the son bold.—Stove, fire,

---

[14] Katanov in Radlov, IX, 287, No. 232.   [15] Elwin, p. 466, No. 16.

[1] Sadovnikov, 144. The description of the son may have been suggested by such riddles as No. 941 above and others discussed in the headnote to Nos. 941–942.

[2] See above, Nos. 871 through 876, the headnote to Nos. 871–877, and the note to No. 872.

[3] See No. 985 and the headnote to No. 985.

smoke"[4] and "The mother is fat, the daughter beautiful;[5] her son is quick; he rose to the sky";[6] the Vogul "The mother is fat, the son slim, the daughter red";[7] and the Yakut "They say that there is a fat old woman with a red daughter and a long son.—Fire, smoke, chimney"[8] with such parallels as "There is Old Mary, her long [tall] son, and her short daughter.—Chimney, smoke, spark"[9] or "A fat lady with a tall daughter, with a short, quick son."[10]

The notion of a hollow mother, humpbacked or crooked father, and children of one sort or another is applicable to a pot and occasionally to other objects. Examples are:

§ 1. A pot. See Nos. 1017a through 1017c.

§ 2. A plant. German: Wossidlo, 134 (beans), 135 (Crooked father, hollow mother, children with smooth heads.—Peas), 136 (hops).

§ 3. A fiddle. Norwegian: Bergh, *Valdres*, 40 (A humpbacked father, a hollowed-out mother, and seven singing children).

1017a. Hollow-hearted mammy, / And a pinch-backed pappy, / And three black children.—One of these pots hangs on a crane; the crane has three legs.
Fauset, *Nova Scotia*, p. 164, No. 114.

1017b. Holler belly mumma, humpback pupa, pickney wid t'ree foot.—Cooking-pot.
Beckwith, *Jamaica*, p. 196, No. 110.

1017c. Long-legged daddy, / Pot-bellied mammy, / Three black sons / And one rosy daughter.—A spit with a large pot hanging on it with three legs and a fire underneath.
Sayce, *Montgomeryshire*, p. 17.

1018–1020. Colors

The comparison of an object and its parts to the members of a family differentiated by their colors is analogous to the descriptions of a fire and a pot as Redman and Blackman (see above, Nos. 871 through 876 and the headnote to Nos. 871–877) and to the various riddles for ants, wasps, partridges, and other creatures (see Nos. 887 through 904 above). In these, however, the riddler rarely refers to a family relationship among the persons. The typical riddle mentioning the colors characteristic of several members of a family has the answer "chestnut." Although this answer does not appear to be known to English riddlers, the riddles for a chinkapin and a coconut seem to be derived from it.

---

[4] Ahlqvist, p. 40, No. 9. See also the headnote to No. 1017, § 3, above.
[5] Since the Russian word for "beautiful" means also "red," it seems probable that this text is a translation of a Russian original.
[6] Paasonen, 19.
[7] Ahlqvist, *Vogul*, p. 126, No. 11.
[8] Piekarski, 249.
[9] Piekarski, 251.
[10] Poppe, p. 288. See also a White Russian text cited in the headnote to No. 1017, § 3, above.

1018. One big black father, / Five big, black brothers, / Three red sisters, / And a big stone mother.—A stove.
Fauset, *Nova Scotia*, p. 164, No. 113.

1019a. Tall daddy, sticky mammy, black nurse, white child. What is that?—Chinkapin-tree.
Parsons, *Sea Islands, S.C.*, p. 168, No. 102.

1019b. A white chil' an' a black nurse an' a red mother.—Chinkapin. (White inside, black outside, on his en˙ reddish brown. Grows on tree in fall.)
Parsons, *Sea Islands, S.C.*, p. 168, No. 102, var. 1.

1020. Black mother, rough nurse, white baby.—A coconut.
Parsons, *Sea Islands, S.C.*, p. 168, No. 102, var. 2.

1021–1035. Function

The functions assigned to the parent and the children are very simple. The contrast of the mother living while the children die is applicable to a tree and its leaves.[1] The notion of countless children is used for stars.[2] A very freely used theme is the notion of a family whose members cannot touch one another.[3]

1021–1035. Manner of Life

1021–1024. Parent and Children

The comparison of a plant and its leaves or fruits to a mother and her children is less frequent than we might perhaps expect. It seems very obvious. A few examples of the theme are interesting for special elaborations. See the French riddle for a pomegranate, "I am the mother of more than a thousand children. Whoever wishes to know the number of them ought to pierce my side";[1] the Argentinian Spanish for an orange, "Marvel, marvel! What is it? He embraces the mother and strikes the daughter";[2] and the Arabic for grapes, "She gives birth in the hedge to children without making a sound."[3] The Ewe riddle for the fruit of the *fōyi* tree is "All of us wear hats. What is that?"[4] The Ho say of capsicum or chili, "The mother attains full development in about two months and has curly locks. She gives birth to fifty or sixty young ones, and these are green or black when immature and change color when they grow up,

---

[1] See Nos. 1022a through 1022d. See also Welsh: Hull and Taylor, 128 through 131. In riddles for potatoes, the cassava plant, and salmon, the parent is said to die, often before the birth of the offspring, but the children flourish (see the riddles listed in the note to No. 661 above).

[2] See below, No. 1024, the headnote to Nos. 1023–1024, and the note to No. 1024. The idea of countlessness is also emphasized in star riddles using as the means of comparison sheep (Nos. 484a through 484d), apples (No. 1095), biscuits (No. 1229a), and coins or other small objects (Nos. 1215, 1216, and 1224 through 1227c, the headnote to No. 1227, and the note to Nos. 1224 through 1225b).

[3] See Nos. 1027 through 1028b and the headnote to Nos. 1027–1028.

[1] Sébillot, *Auvergne*, 19.   [2] Lehmann-Nitsche, 435.

[3] Stumme, *Tázerwalt*, 22.

[4] Ewe: Spieth, p. 597, No. 6. Compare the headnote to Nos. 946–950 above.

and if you rub them with your fingers, they will quarrel with you."⁵ A Toda riddle for the wild olive is: "Every day in the year it bears children and is pregnant. What is it?"⁶ See further the Ho riddles for barley, "Children of the same mother, while young, all are calm and quiet. When grown up, all are finished,"⁷ and for cotton, "Children of the same mother are all gaping and looking white";⁸ the Malayalam for the coconut palm, "Mother is in stones and thorns, the children are in the marriage pavilion";⁹ and the Samoan for a palm leaf, "A company of two hundred brothers, all of whom lie on their faces and bear their father."¹⁰

The comparisons involving the idea of flight or running, such as the Kolarian "The children fly away, the mother remains.—An unnamed fruit,"¹¹ usually contain a reference to old age or death. See the French "I saw it living, I saw it dead, I saw it run after its death";¹² the Hungarian "When alive, it is always standing; when dead, it is always running";¹³ and the Modern Greek "When I was young, I did not run; now when I am old, I run.—Leaves."¹⁴

Comparisons of a tree and its fruit or leaves to birds are very rare. See the Arabic riddle for the olive: "A falcon which lays five thousand eggs and on the morrow these lay another five thousand."¹⁵

1021. Old Mother Old, / She lives in the cold, / And every year she brings forth young, / And every one without a tongue.—Apple tree.
Fauset, *Nova Scotia*, p. 159, No. 77.

1022. Mother Lives; Children Die

Riddlers do not often compare a plant to a living person and its leaves to the dead. In the note to Nos. 1022a through 1022d I cite parallels in which the leaves are represented as engaged in various activities, especially talking. For parallels in which a plant is represented as dancing see Nos. 946a through 946d, the headnote to Nos. 946–950, and the note to Nos. 946a through 946d.

1022a. ten thousand children beautifulle of this my body bred both sones & daughters finely deckt alive & they are dead, my sones were put to extreme greife [grief] by such as loued them well my daughters died of extrame age & why j cannot tell.—the mother is a tree the sons the fruit & the daughters the leaues.
Tupper, *Holme Riddles*, 105.

---

⁵ Haldar, p. 278, No. 24. ⁶ Rivers, p. 599, No. 5.
⁷ Sarkar, p. 353, No. 16. ⁸ Sarkar, p. 354, No. 18.
⁹ Frohnmeyer, p. 229. The marriage pavilion is covered with leaves of the coconut palm.
¹⁰ Heider, 3. ¹¹ Wagner, 1.
¹² V. S., *Mélusine*, I (1879), col. 264, No. 76; J. Roux, *Limousin*, 90. Breton: Sébillot, *Devinettes*, 24.
¹³ *Magyar Nyelvör*, III (1874), 38. The answer is: "Maize sheds leaves carried by the wind."
¹⁴ Dieterich, *Rätseldichtung*, p. 92, citing Kanellakis, 182, 106.
¹⁵ Stumme, *Tázerwalt*, 2.

1022b. Ten thousand children beautifull of this my body bred, / both sonnes and daughters finely dekt; I live; and they are dead. / My sonnes were put to extreame death by such as loved them well. / My daughters dyed with extreame age, but where I cannot tell.—The mother is a tree, the sonnes the fruit, and the daughters leaves.
Meery Riddles (1629), No. 77 = Brandl, pp. 21–22.

1022c. sisly [Cicely] sage sits in her [MS: here] kage[?] & all her children dys for age [MS: aye] yet she is a live & lusty.—the leaves of a tree.
Tupper, *Holme Riddles*, 57.

1022d. Cicily cicily sage, that sits in her cage, / A little above the well. / Her children all died of age, / And she's alive hersel'.—Thornbush.
Praeger, *Béaloideas*, VIII (1938), 171, No. 7.

1023–1024. Mother and Countless Children

Perhaps the most highly elaborated instance of this theme is the Annamese conception of the moon, sun, and stars: "During the night a mother bears hundreds of sons; at dawn they are all dead; and she bears no more. Then an immoral old man rises up, whose face is like the devil's and whom no one can look at."[1] The theme of disappearance[2] hinted at in this text is made more explicit in the Samoan "There is a numerous company of brothers; by day one does not see them, at night one can, however, see them"[3] and the Crimean Tatar "Yes, we were thirty-two maidens sitting on a board, and with the approach of dawn we disappeared."[4]

The notion of a great number of persons appears in the Tonga-Shangaan riddles for the stars, "My relatives are numerous" and "Children how numerous!"[5] References to a great number of persons or things appear in riddles for a poppyhead, like the Polish "A maiden stands on one leg in the garden. I could swear she has a thousand children."[6]

1023. Old woman had so many children, she didn't know what to do.—That was a hen. She had so many chickens, she couldn't sit on them.
Bacon and Parsons, *Virginia*, p. 316, No. 33.

1024. My moder have so many children, she can't count one ['em?].—Stars.
Parsons, *Antilles*, III, 370, Grenada, 36 var.

1025–1035. Children

1025. Children Glitter

1025. My father have so many children, they always glitterin'.—Stars.
Parsons, *Antilles*, III, 371, Grenada, 37.

---

[1] Dumoutier, p. 203.   [2] See the headnote to No. 1094 below.
[3] Heider, 148.
[4] Filonenko, 28. This seems to be an adaptation of a riddle for the teeth.
[5] Junod and Jaques, p. 235, No. 44, and p. 243, No. 91.
[6] Siarkowski, 10. For parallels to a person standing on one leg see the headnote to Nos. 1121–1126, § 5, below, and to a sack or box full of many things, the headnote to No. 1355. Compare also the Argentinian chili riddle (Lehmann-Nitsche, 445).

1026. Children Cling

1026. Somet'in' got one hundred chillun, hang all 'round um.—Net (bullet [weights] all aroun').
Parsons, *Sea Islands, S.C.*, p. 167, No. 89.

1027–1028. Cannot Touch One Another

Riddlers describe a great variety of objects as children who are close together and yet cannot touch one another. The objects so described consist of many small parts which are similar in appearance and are held fast in their respective positions. Typical objects described in this manner are:

§ 1. A nut. The children are the divisions of the nut as they appear when the nut is cut across.[1]

§ 2. A ladder. The riddler thinks of the rungs as children. For examples see German: Wossidlo, 140 (Long, long father, long, long mother, many, many children); Hanika-Otto, 47. The defective Catalan "of like form, placed between two sisters, according to equal measure and fixed number, that causes high things to be known,"[2] for which both introduction and answer are lacking, probably has the answer "ladder." See further, Lettish: Bielenstein, 725. Votyak: Buch, 39 (An innkeeper has seventy-seven guests, each has his own bed). Vogul: Ahlqvist, *Vogul*, 4 (A hundred Russians, they lie in one bed). Compare the dramatized Malagasy version, "The mother says, 'Let us stand up!' The children say, 'Let us lie across!'"[3]

§ 3. Rafters, girders, beams, shingles. Lithuanian: Jurgelionis, 278. White Russian: Shein, 9 (Some nuns went to evening parties. They lay down to sleep; and they are sleeping even now.—Framing of joists). This involves a comparison of the long, straight garb of a nun to the long, straight side of a joist. Abyssinian: Littmann, *Tigriña*, 49 (The father bears the children, the children bear the food).

There are many comparisons of rafters, joists, and girders to persons lying on a single pillow. See Russian: Sadovnikov, 50a through 50e (Brothers on one pillow). Serbian: Novaković, p. 194, No. 6 (A hundred brothers are lying on one pillow, and they cannot touch one another). Zyrian: Wichmann, *Zyrian*, 120 (Twenty boys sleeping on one pillow.—Girders and roof). Hungarian: *Magyar Nyelvör*, XIX (1890), 92. Turkish: Hamizade, 154 (He lies long lengthwise, his servants lie flat.—Beam); Katanov in Radlov, IX, 104, No. 890 (Two twins have two pillows.—Crossbeams of a yurt). Yakut: Piekarski, 244 (A hundred people have one pillow, so they say.—Covering on the tent poles); Priklonskii, 1 (A hundred men under one roof). Malagasy: Sibree, p. 39, No. 4 (Lying on the same pillow, but not on the same bed.—Rafters). Korean: Bernheisel, p. 60 (What are twelve things lying on one pillow?). See also the headnotes to Nos. 992–993 and to No. 993 above.

---

[1] See the headnote to No. 1005.   [2] Milá y Fontanals, 1877, p. 7.
[3] Sibree, p. 39, No. 13.

Riddlers occasionally add details, as in the Hungarian "Twelve boys lie in a row, not one of them is at the end of the row.—Piles under a mill"[4] or the Modern Greek "The silent, supine ones in each other's arms.—Shingles."[5]

§ 4. The floor and the ceiling, or other parts of a house taken in pairs. This theme, which is very popular in Russia, usually includes mention of the supposed persons or animals looking at each other. See the headnote to Nos. 1003–1004, nn. 23–27.

§ 5. The spokes of a wheel. Welsh: Hull and Taylor, 224. Irish: Christiansen, 78; Delargy, 22 (Twelve men in one bed and not one of them on the outer edge); O Dalaigh, 84. German: Wossidlo, 181a; Frischbier, *Menschenwelt*, p. 248, No. 71. Danish: Feilberg, *Ordbog*, II, 76, s.v. "rokkehjul" (spinning wheel). Norwegian: Stafset, 13, 96. Lithuanian: Jurgelionis, 670 (Twelve little brothers sleep in one bed). Serbian: Novaković, p. 141, No. 4 (Twelve boars are lying in one herd, none is at either end), and p. 160, Nos. 2 through 10. The Serbian version "There are twelve brothers in one pair of drawers"[6] belongs to the pattern discussed in the headnote to No. 1005 above. Hungarian: see the headnote to Nos. 954–957, §§ 5–6, above. In some versions the actors are men chasing one another[7] or brothers chasing one another.[8]

§ 6. The staves of a barrel. Scotch Gaelic: Nicolson, p. 55 (Twelve men in one bed and every one on the edge). Compare the African riddles for pegs holding a stretched-out hide: "What are many warriors like when they stand in a circle and one cannot see which is first and which is last?"[9] and "I have many children; nobody is first or last."[10] See also the riddle cited in the note to No. 1026 above.

§ 7. The corners of a pillow. German: Wossidlo, 161d (Four brothers sleep in a bed; no one sleeps in front, no one sleeps at the back, and no one sleeps in the middle). Serbian: Novaković, p. 194, No. 5 (Four brothers lie on a bed and one cannot reach the other).

§ 8. Bedposts. Swedish: Hyltén-Cavallius, *Värend*, 62.

§ 9. The Pleiades.[11] Faeroic: Hammershaimb, *Antiquarisk tidsskrift*, III (1849–1851), 321, No. 64 (Seven sisters in a bed, no one lies in front, no one lies behind). Icelandic: Árnason, 1006.

§ 10. The feet of pot. African, Wolof: Seidel, p. 309 (Three children of one mother, who are always together and yet never touch one another).

1027. Father, mother, sister, brother, / A' lies in ae bed, / An' diz [does] na touch each other.—The bars of a grate.
Gregor, *Northeast Scotland*, p. 79.

---

[4] *Magyar Nyelvör*, XIX (1890), 92.
[5] Polites, *Neohellenika Analekta*, I, 245, No. 294.
[6] Novaković, p. 141, No. 3.   [7] No. 957 above.
[8] No. 997.   [9] Masai: Hollis, *Masai*, p. 254.
[10] Taveta: Hollis, *Taveta*, 56.
[11] For other riddles on the Pleiades see the note to No. 988 above.

1028a. My moder have plenty chil'ren, / She can' touch one.—Jaspaniards [jack-spaniards, tropical wasps].
Parsons, *Antilles*, III, 363, Trinidad, 7.

1028b. The devil have a lot of children, / And he coul' [couldn't?] touch [only?] one, / He have to touch all.—Jaspaniards.
Parsons, *Antilles*, III, 363, Trinidad, 7 var.

1029–1030. Pursuing

1029a. Mother, father, sister, brother, / All runnin' after one another, / And can't catch one another.—Four wheels of a wagon.
Gutch and Peacock, *Lincolnshire*, p. 400, No. 26; Knortz, p. 238, No. 135.

1029b. My father has four children, none can' beat the other in running.—Motor car wheels.
Parsons, *Antilles*, III, 371, Grenada, 39.

1030. My moder have four children none can't go without the other.—Carriage wheel.
Parsons, *Antilles*, III, 371, Grenada, 38.

1031–1032. Bathing

1031a. My moder have four children, none can bathe the other.—Bottle.
Parsons, *Antilles*, III, 371, Grenada, 40.

1031b. My moder have three children, none can bathe the other.—Bottle.
Parsons, *Antilles*, III, 371, Grenada, 40 var.

1032. Bathe and Dry the Water

The West Indian comparison of boiling rice to people bathing in water which they dry up in the act refers to water boiling while the rice is cooking. Riddlers use many comparisons for boiling rice or parching corn.[1] A curious and perhaps unique variation appears in the Malagasy "The old man who leans against the wall,"[2] which describes the rice clinging to the side of the pot.

1032a. My mother have a lot of little children, she send them to go and bathe. They dry the water.—Rice.
Parsons, *Antilles*, III, 370, Grenada, 29.

1032b. A hundred white man went to bade [bathe] and they all come out dry.—Rice.
Parsons, *Antilles*, III, 364, Trinidad, 9.

1033. Go to School

1033a. A woman had four children. An' sen' t'ree to school first. An' the last one she send, go an' learn an' come out of school 'fore these other t'ree. How's

---

[1] See the headnote to Nos. 489–490, the note to Nos. 489a through 489m, and the note to Nos. 1032a, 1032b. See also Nos. 385 and 1537.
[2] G. Ferrand, 6.

dat?—The children are three firestones and one pot. The firestones are stationary and, so to speak, remain always in school, while the pot is put on the firestones to cook, and is then taken off again.
Johnson, *Antigua*, p. 88, No. 66.

1033b. Me riddle me raddle / Perhaps I might tell you dis riddle / An' perhaps not. / Me fader have four son, sen' dem all to school to learn, an' only one can learn.—You put you' pot on t'ree fire stone an' only you' pot can cook.
Parsons, *Antilles*, III, 421, Montserrat, 5.

1033c. My fader had four broders, send de four to school. One come out learned, an' de oder come out unlearn'.—De pot of food an' de t'ree stones.
Parsons, *Antilles*, III, 436, St. Martin, 22.

1033d. Four always goin' to school / Came from school. / One always learn his lesson, / And leaves three.—Fire stones and a pot.
Parsons, *Antilles*, III, 375, St. Vincent, 7.

1033e. Four brothers going to school. One learn and leave three. What is that?—Pot on the stove.
Parsons, *Antilles*, III, 428, Nevis, 10.

1033f. Four broders went to school one time an' one 'lone an' left t'ree.—De pot boil an' leave de t'ree stone.
Parsons, *Antilles*, III, 421, Montserrat, 5 var.

1033g. My fader have six children. He send dem to school. T'ree learn, an' t'ree remain dunces.—Pot with three rocks an' t'ree legs on the rocks. When food is ready, lift down the pot an' still t'ree stones remain.
Parsons, *Antilles*, III, 441, Anguilla, 27.

1034. Help Each Other

The Dschagga phrase the idea of coöperation very vividly: "See a law suit. An old man rises from his place and the whole case comes to a stop.—The hearthstones. If one is taken away, the lid falls into the fire."[1] The Duala "My mother bore us three, if one is not present, the other two do nothing"[2] is virtually the same as the English riddle.

1034. My mother has three children, one can't do the work without the other.—Three fire stones.
Parsons, *Antilles*, III, 372, Grenada, 54.

1035. Don't Want to See Each Other

1035. Moder have a girl, don't want to see one of her broders.—Hot water, when you put the peas to boil.
Parsons, *Antilles*, III, 369, Grenada, 11.

---

[1] Raum, p. 305, No. 14.   [2] Ebding, 45.

Chapter VI

COMPARISONS TO PLANTS

Nos. 1036–1099

RIDDLES that make a comparison to a tree stand first in this chapter. Then follow those which do not identify the plant definitely. They are arranged in a roughly chronological order, from planting and growth to the bearing of flowers and fruit.

The subjects of riddles based on comparisons to trees vary greatly. Among the most widely known are a ship,[1] the year,[2] a church,[3] and the fingers.[4] The subjects of riddles employing comparisons to plants other than trees are equally varied: the hair or eyelashes,[5] a cow's tail,[6] an icicle,[7] a violin,[8] and writing.[9] The stars are often compared to blossoms or fruits on a tree.[10] A few riddles describe a fruit and have a fruit or nut as answer.[11] Such riddles exemplify departures from the usual enigmatic technique, for the object described ordinarily belongs to a category entirely different from that of the answer. Accordingly, plants, fruits, or seeds will not, with this exception, appear as the answers of the riddles in this chapter.

There are many riddles describing plants. Descriptions in terms of an animal are rather rare, as in the Kxatla "Tell me: a green cow which bears white calves.—Mimosa tree with white thorns."[12] The most widely known instance is the comparison of a vine and a gourd to a cow and a rope.[13] The riddles in which a plant is described in terms of one or more persons are numerous.[14]

1036–1050. A Tree

1036. A Tree with Root But No Leaves

African and Indonesian riddlers ingeniously compare a ship to a tree having the peculiarity that, when it has a root (anchor), it has no leaves, and when it has no root, it bears leaves (sails). The West Indian examples of this theme seem to be derived from African sources. There is no evidence to show that European riddlers know it. A European conception of a ship with a certain

---

[1] Nos. 1036a through 1036d.
[2] Nos. 1037a through 1038b.
[3] Nos. 1039.
[4] Nos. 1040, 1041.
[5] Nos. 1043 and 1044 and the headnote to Nos. 1042–1044.
[6] No. 1056.
[7] Nos. 1055a through 1057.
[8] Nos. 1059a through 1062.
[9] Nos. 1063a through 1063i.
[10] Nos. 1071 and 1093 through 1095.
[11] Nos. 1072 through 1092.
[12] Schapera, 20.
[13] See below, Nos. 1203b, 1203c, the note to Nos. 1203a through 1203c, and the headnote to Nos. 1203–1205.
[14] See chapters iv and v.

analogy to this theme occurs in some French riddles from the West Indies[1] and in the Portuguese "My wife: whenever she reaches home, she strips."[2] Some might maintain that this, too, is of African origin and support their contention by the Swahili "There is something which covers itself, when it goes away, and when it returns, it covers itself," with a variant, "Goes with a kerchief, returns with a kerchief."[3]

1036a. There is a t'ing, when she has root, she has no leaves; and when she pull up her root, the leaves appear.—Ship at anchor has no sails; when she pulls up anchor, she has sails.
Johnson, *Antigua*, p. 87, No. 44.

1036b. 'Tis something, when they got roots, 'tain't have no branches; when it got branches, 'tain't got no roots.—Ship.
Parsons, *Antilles*, III, 440, Anguilla, 13.

1036c. My moder have a tree in her yard. When it have roots, it have no branches; when it have branches, it have no roots.—When you put down the anchor the sail sinks, when you up anchor you up sail.
Parsons, *Antilles*, III, 364, Trinidad, 16.

1036d. M'riddle, m'riddle, I'll tell you this riddle, An perhaps you may tell it to me. It is a thing has roots an' when it has no leaves, it has no roots.—Ship.
Parsons, *Antilles*, III, 440, Anguilla, 13 var.

1037–1038. A Tree with Twelve Branches

Scholars have not yet completely clarified the relations of the comparisons of the year and the world to a tree. They may be dealing with two different ideas that have influenced each other or with two ideas that have sprung from the same root. The ancient conception of the year as a tree has religious and mythical associations, as in the words of St. John: "In the midst of the street of it, and on either side of the river, was there the tree of life, which bare twelve manner of fruits, and yielded her fruit every month."[1]

Although many scholars have investigated the year riddle, no one has yet written a definitive and comprehensive account of its origin, connections, and dissemination.[2] This will involve the study of various Oriental mythical con-

---

[1] Parsons, *Antilles*, III, 375, Cariacou, 21, p. 377, St. Lucia, 7, p. 385, Martinique, 83, p. 395, Dominica, 74, and p. 452, Hayti, 82.
[2] Parsons, *Cape Verde*, 103a.
[3] Velten, 5 und 5 var.

[1] Rev. 22:2. This is very similar to a fragment of the lost Evangelium Evae; see E. Hennecke, *Neutestamentliche Apokryphen* (Tübingen, 1904), p. 42, n. 1.
[2] For a bibliography of the year riddle see my *Bibliography of Riddles*, pp. 157–158. Important references and additional ones are Friedreich, p. 89; W. Wilmanns, *Zeitschrift für deutsches Altertum*, XIII (1867), 492–493; Ohlert, 2d ed., pp. 93–95; Feilberg, *Ordbog*, III, 1195–1196, s.v. "år"; Loewenthal, pp. 52–54, 118–119; Ernst Windisch, *Zeitschrift der deutschen morgenländischen Gesellschaft*, XLVIII (1894), 353–357; August Wünsche,

cepts and the use of the tree as a symbol. It will also involve the history of some very old tales, for the year riddle occurs in the story of Aḥiḳar,[3] from which it passed into the biography of Aesop, and the story of Turandot.[4] Various Oriental mythical themes, among them the calendar plant and the tree of life, will call for examination.[5] The various types of riddles for the year have arisen in as many ways: some are modifications of an older theme and others are independent inventions.[6]

Since Sigismund Szendrey's important additions[7] to Aarne's treatise on the year riddle are difficult of access, I print them here in a translation generously made for me by the late Arpad Steiner. The seven Hungarian versions with which Szendrey begins will be found in the note to Nos. 1037a, 1037b of the present collection. Szendrey writes as follows:

This riddle may be divided, according to its components, into four parts[8] or six parts.[9] These are: (A) the tree, (B) twelve branches, (C) fifty-two flowers or four nests, (D) 365 or 366 leaves or seven eggs, (E) three or six eggs, (F) twenty-four young birds, (G) their sixty steps. These symbolize the year, the months, the weeks, the days, the first or the first two days of the three chief holy days, the hours, the minutes.

According to Aarne's findings, this riddle has spread all over the world, but he discerns several types, which are identified by the names of the parts of the year. One of these is the so-called Asiatic tree-type which designates the parts of the year solely by the parts of a tree (tree, branch, leaf, fruit). The choice of the species of tree varies locally everywhere.[10] This is shown by the Hungarian names, "God's tree, oak tree, pear tree." The adjectives "round,

---

"Das Rätsel vom Jahr und seinen Zeitabschnitten in der Weltlitteratur," *Zeitschrift für vergleichende Litteraturgeschichte*, n.s., IX (1896), 425–426; Schultz, *Rätsel aus dem hellenischen Kulturkreise*, II, 28–29; Aarne, *Rätselforschungen*, I, 74–178; J. Bolte and G. Polívka, *Anmerkungen zu den Kinder- und Hausmärchen*, II (Leipzig, 1915), 355, n. 1; Flajšhans, pp. 3–5; Schultz, *Bemerkungen*, p. 372; Jungbauer, pp. 353–354; H. Gunkel, *Das Märchen im Alten Testament* (Tübingen, 1921), pp. 24–25; Flajšhans, *Český lid*, XXIV (1924), 50–51.

[3] P. Marc, *Studien zur vergleichenden Literaturgeschichte*, II (1902), 398; Victor Chauvin, *Bibliographie des ouvrages arabes*, VI (Liége, 1902), 40.

[4] Victor Chauvin, *Bibliographie des ouvrages arabes*, V (Liége, 1901), 192, 195.

[5] Terrien de LaCouperie, "The Calendar Plant of China," *Babylonian and Oriental Record*, II (1888), 149–159; IV (1890), 21–231, 246–251; R. Eisler, *Weltenmantel und Himmelszelt* (Munich, 1910), p. 585, and *passim;* Uno Holmberg, "Der Baum des Lebens," *Annales Academiae Scientiarum Fennicae*, Ser. B, XVI, No. 3 (Helsinki, 1922), pp. 105–106, 108, and *passim*; H. Bergsma, *De Boom des Levens in Schrift en Historie* (Diss., Municipal Univ. of Amsterdam; Amsterdam, 1938).

[6] The best survey of the types is Frederick Tupper's note; see *The Riddles of the Exeter Book* (Boston, 1910), p. 117, No. 23.

[7] *Ethnographia*, XXXII (1921), 71–73.

[8] Hungarian variants, Nos. [1] through [6] in the note to Nos. 1037a, 1037b below. I have retained all of Szendrey's footnotes but have adjusted the numbering of them to this headnote.

[9] Hungarian variant, No. [7].

[10] Aarne, *Rätselforschungen*, I, 110.

old, huge" are intended to indicate the miraculous quality of the tree in the same way as the adjectives "big, tall, beautiful, golden, etc." in the parallels.[11] In the Hungarian versions the scene is indicated only by such general statements as "under the round sky, in the world," which contrast with the rather definite indications of place in the parallels.[12] The number twelve occurs generally; the number fifty-two occurs only in German, Swedish, and Russian parallels; the number 365 (366) occurs, however, only in Russian, Calmuck, West Siberian, Buryat, and Estonian folklore.[13] Parallels to the simpler form of the riddle, viz., A-B-D or tree-branch-leaf = year, month, day,[14] are very rare and occur, with numbers corresponding to those in the Hungarian riddles, only in a few West Siberian, Buryat, Calmuck, Russian, and Estonian versions. The version A-B-C-E is, on the other hand, a purely Hungarian invention that does not appear in Aarne's data because "flower" signifying "week" occurs only in a Russian version[15] and does not appear there associated with the number fifty-two. Elsewhere, the flowers signify the days.[16] Of the three or six golden apples Aladár Bán writes as follows: "This trait seems to be an original invention [of Hungarian folklore] because, so far as I know, it does not occur among other peoples."[17] Here, however, we must not lose sight of the fact that many German, Russian, Estonian, and Finnish versions[18] sharply differentiate Sunday from the other days of the week. In fact, it is called "golden apple" in a Finnish version;[19] the "golden tree" in a Russian version[20] means Easter. The idea of designating the three chief holy days by golden apples was already in existence, and consequently only the joining of the first day or the first two days of the Christmas season and Whitsunday with Easter is novel in the Hungarian versions.

Later on, a European type of riddle for the year developed alongside the Asiatic type with a tree. It indicates the week, day, hour, and minute by the nest,[21] egg,[22] and young birds. In Hungarian folklore we have only one example of this type.[23] The elements A–F are found in German, Finnish, Estonian, Danish, Russian, Ukrainian, Rumanian, and Serbian collections. The element F appears, however, in only one Finnish version, "An oak with twelve branches, on each branch twelve nests, in each nest seven eggs, in each egg twenty-four young, each one dies after he has taken some steps,"[24] as

---

[11] Aarne, *Rätselforschungen*, I, 110–111. The Hungarian word translated "huge" is very obscure and might also mean "cherry."
[12] Aarne, *Rätselforschungen*, I, 112–115.
[13] Aarne, *Rätselforschungen*, I, 130.
[14] Hungarian variants Nos. [5] and [6]. See the note to Nos. 1037a, 1037b below.
[15] Aarne, *Rätselforschungen*, I, 125.
[16] See one Finnish and three German instances in Aarne, *Rätselforschungen*, I, 93, 94, 138.
[17] *Ethnographia*, XXIX, 290.
[18] Aarne, *Rätselforschungen*, I, 93, 94, 100, 101, 130, 131.
[19] Aarne, *Rätselforschungen*, I, 132.   [20] Aarne, *Rätselforschungen*, I, 127.
[21] Aarne, *Rätselforschungen*, I, 122, 126.   [22] Aarne, *Rätselforschungen*, I, 128, 130.
[23] See Hungarian variant No. [7].   [24] Aarne, *Rätselforschungen*, I, 96.

well as in the Hungarian version. In any case, this is a noteworthy agreement in details, but lacking more ample data, we cannot easily draw any inferences.

The structure of the year riddle shows some similarity to the sequences found in nursery rhymes and folk tales. This device of uniting the elements also occurs in a few riddles.[25] This chain structure is well represented by a Votyak year riddle: "On a little fir there are twigs, on each twig a nest, in each nest birds."[26] Here the riddler neglects to mention the numbers and gives his attention solely to the structure. Perhaps some nursery rhymes are degenerate forms of the year riddle, but the question is too long and difficult for discussion here.

The year riddle also shows a striking similarity to certain Eastern riddles associating a series of objects with a series of numbers. A Georgian riddle for the sun is "Two hundred eagles flew up, opened three hundred wings, struck with four hundred talons, broke five hundred cliffs,"[27] which Blechsteiner thinks is disordered. He cites another Georgian version: "Two hundred eagles come, they spread out three hundred wings, fifteen hundred talons."[28] The interpretation of such riddles presents serious difficulties. Perhaps the numbers signify letters and these letters are then combined to make a word.

The riddles for the year are here divided according to the division proposed by Aarne, into an Asiatic type and a European type.[29] The Asiatic type mentions leaves or limbs and branches; the European type mentions branches, a nest, and birds or eggs in the nest. A curious minor variation in the Asiatic type is seen in the Turkish "On a tree twelve branches, on every branch four leaves, on every leaf seven veins."[30] The Icelandic time riddle "What tree has leaves black on one side and bright on the other?"[31] is a rare European text that might be called Asiatic in type.

A few very simple riddles making a comparison of the year or parts of the year to a tree or plant may be independent inventions. They often refer to the tree as part fresh and part dry. They are characteristically found in eastern Russia and Siberia. The Turcomans say, "Behind the cart there are two rods, one green and one dry.—Winter and summer,"[32] which is akin to the Yakut "They say that there is a tree, part of which is damp while the other part is dry.—A year with its carnival and Lenten seasons."[33] This is more suitably conceived in the Armenian "The root is damp, the middle is dry, the top is

---

[25] See Nos. 1161 through 1164 below and the headnote to Nos. 1161–1164.
[26] Buch, 15.
[27] Khakhanov, *Ocherki po istorii gruzinskoi slovesnosti*, I (Moscow, 1895), 122, cited by Blechsteiner, p. LI.
[28] Blechsteiner, p. 15, No. 26.
[29] See below, Nos. 1038a, 1038b, and Nos. 1037a, 1037b, respectively.
[30] Hamizade, 728.   [31] Árnason, 31.
[32] Samojlvich, 36.   [33] Piekarski, 11.

blossoming.—Flesh days, Lent, Easter,"[34] which is related to the Yakut "Half of the oak is dry, half is green, and it has a golden poppyhead.—Year."[35]

Riddlers rarely use the scene of a tree and its branches for other subjects than the year and the months or the sun and its rays.[36] The latter theme is not current among English riddlers. The cosmological implications of both themes are obvious, but it is not clear how closely the two riddles are related. The scenes in the two riddles are quite differently conceived.

In a few instances we can see riddlers adapting texts to special uses. For example, the obscure Hungarian riddle for the sun, "The oak tree cracks, its thousand branches crack, there are a thousand nests on the thousand branches, a thousand eggs are in the thousand nests, a thousand eggs ész-szike,"[37] has taken some elements from the year riddle. Other riddles comparing the sun to the parts of a plant may be related to the year riddle, but the nature of the relationship is quite obscure.

A strange adaptation of the year riddle applies to a girder. It is: "There lies a beam as long as Russia. In that beam are twelve nests. Each nest has twelve eggs. Each egg has twelve chickens."[38] Preobrazhenskii, who gives this parallel, "A log lies across all Russia, in that log are twelve nests, in each nest are twelve eggs, in each egg are twelve chicks,"[39] explains it in his answer, "The female roach is in the house, in the girders are roach eggs, which always, it is said, contain twelve larvae."

Riddles for the year exhibit great variety. Since we have no definitive and comprehensive investigation of them, we cannot easily perceive their connections. Typical themes are:

§ 1. Men. See No. 984 above.

§ 2. Animals other than birds. Serbian: Novaković, p. 32, Nos. 4 (There are twelve yokes, twelve oxen, all tied to one pole), 5 (There are three hundred and sixty-six oxen and twelve yokes, all tied to one pole), 6 (There are one Moor, twelve oxen, and one hundred and seventy poles).[40] Modern Greek: Dieterich, *Rätseldichtung*, pp. 89 (twelve horses), 90 (a corrupt version); Georgeakis, p. 295 (twelve asses, thirteen saddles). The saddles are the lunar months. Turkish: Maenchen, p. 106, No. 4 (My white camel mare gave birth to twelve small camels). Indian, Bihari: Mitra, *Bihar*, 72 (It has four parts

---

[34] Glushakov, p. 37, No. 88. For descriptions of objects in the order of bottom, middle, and top, see the headnote to Nos. 1436–1447 below.

[35] Khudiakov, 92, cited by Samojlvich in the note to his No. 36. For a comparison like that to the golden poppy see the headnote to No. 983, n. 17, above.

[36] See the headnote to No. 544 above.

[37] *Magyar Nyelvör*, II (1873), 177. The meaning of *ész-szike* is obscure.

[38] Sadovnikov, 43.

[39] Preobrazhenskii, p. 170.

[40] These riddles may be related to the comparison of the year to a wagon; see § 4 in this headnote.

cold, four hot, and four full of storms and high winds. It is a deer with twelve hoofs. It browse on different kinds [of fodder]).[41]

A curious Turcoman riddle for the months and days is not entirely clear: "Yesterday at noon, yesterday at noon, my horse galloped off yesterday at noon, drawing behind it a many-colored rope that is on its leg. It galloped off yesterday at noon."[42] The Turkish "My white camel has given birth to nine camel foals.—Twelve months of the year"[43] is clearly related to the previously quoted Mongolian riddle, but contains an error that I cannot explain.

For discussion of the comparison of the year to animals see the second edition of Ohlert's *Rätsel und Rätselspiele der alten Greichen*, pp. 85-86 (comment on *Odyssey*, XII, 117 ff.), 91; Loewenthal, p. 53; Schultz, *Rätsel*, col. 90, No. 3.

§ 3. Birds. The symbolism of these very curious texts is obscure. An early example is Claret's fourteenth-century version (p. 73, No. 95):

> Sunt sexaginta volucres cum quinque trecente
> Atque duodeni griffones tres quoque nidi,
> Hii simulac unum generant ovumque per annum:
> Annus habendo dies numero festivaque menses.

For modern traditional parallels, which are almost exclusively found in eastern Europe and Asia, see Lithuanian: Jurgelionis, 140 (There came an old wise man, waved his hands, and released from each hand six birds, each bird had four wings, each wing had seven feathers, and each feather was half black and half white), 142 (Twelve eagles, sixty pigeons with the strength of six hundred. —Year, months, weeks, day), 145 (Twelve eagles, fifty pigeons, three hundred and sixty-five sparrows, and four partridges); Schleicher, p. 202 (Twelve eagles, sixty doves, six hundred titmice). Polish: Saloni, Łańcut, 39 (Three hundred and sixty-five birds, fifty-two starlings, twelve eagles, they laid one egg). Serbian: Novaković, p. 32, Nos. 7 (There are twelve nests, three hundred eagles, and all of them laid only one egg), 8 (There are three hundred and sixty sparrows, and twelve pigeons, and in front of them an eagle), 9 (There are twelve birds in one bush). Mordvin: Paasonen, 92 (Twelve eagles, fifty-two jackdaws). Modern Greek: Dieterich, *Rätseldichtung*, p. 89 (twelve eagles); Polites, *Neohellenika Analekta*, I, 250, No. 327 (Three hundred and sixty cranes, thirty doves, they give birth in twelve nests, and all sit on one egg). Turkish: Kúnos, 273 = Kúnos, *Nyelvkönyv*, 47 (Three hundred and sixty-five storks, forty-eight nests, twelve eggs, two were hatched.—Two holy days [the two principal Moslem festivals]); Hamizade, 220. Kirghese or Turcoman: Karutz, p. 97 (Twelve swans bring thirty sheep, of which half are white,

---

[41] For parallels to the first part of the riddle see the headnote to No. 984 above.
[42] Samojlvich, 33.   [43] Katanov in Radlov, IX, 93, No. 784.

half are black). Siberian Turkish: Katanov in Radlov, IX, 303, No. 272 (Twelve hawks, fifty-two jackdaws, and three hundred and sixty-five starlings). Yakut: Piekarski, 10 (Three hundred and sixty-five partridges, fifty-two heath-cocks, twelve geese, and one eagle are found together; two people take turns watching them.—Days, weeks, months, year; sun, moon); Priklonskii, 83. Indian: Lakshīnātha Upasānī, VIII, 3 (A hen lays twelve eggs, four of which are hot, four are cold, four are lukewarm. What are they?). Bhil: Hedberg, p. 884, No. 121 (One eagle has twelve wings and eighteen score of feathers).

In the preceding list of comparisons to birds and eggs there seem to be at least three varieties, which are quite independent: the first Lithuanian version, which seems to stand alone; the comparisons to birds of several kinds, which probably involve symbolism of some sort; and the Indian comparison of the seasons to three kinds of eggs. This last has some similarity to the Yakut "Five sweet eggs and seven bitter ones.—Summer and winter."[44] The Turkish and the Turcoman riddles seem to be adaptations of patterns found in other forms. The discussion of these comparisons to birds is quite insufficient, but see Dieterich, *Rätseldichtung*, p. 103, for the fullest interpretation of the symbolism and additional references from folk songs; Schultz, *Rätsel aus dem hellenischen Kulturkreise*, II, 28; and Flajšhans, pp. 3–5.

These riddles seem to have no close connection with the versions which mention a tree and the birds in it.[45] Typical of them is the Serbian "There is a bush, in it are twelve poles, on every pole are four nests, in every nest there are seven chickens, each chicken has its own name."[46]

§ 4. A wagon. This is probably related to the following comparison to a wheel. For discussion see G. Roethe (ed.), *Die Gedichte Reinmars von Zweter* (Leipzig, 1887), strophe 186 and the note, p. 676; Wossidlo, 35, 36; R. Köhler, *Kleinere Schriften*, III, 359; Tupper, *The Riddles of the Exeter Book*, p. xv; R. Eisler, *Weltenmantel und Himmelszelt* (Munich, 1910), p. 497.

§ 5. A wheel. Indian, Sanskrit: Haug, p. 21, § 11, citing the wheel with twelve fiery spokes that symbolizes the year (*Rigveda*, I, 164). For discussion see W. Wilmanns, *Zeitschrift für deutsches Altertum*, XX (1876), 252; A. Wünsche, *Zeitschrift für vergleichende Litteraturgeschichte*, XI (n.s., IX; 1896), 427–429; Aarne, *Rätselforschungen*, I, 166.

§ 6. A building. Breton: Charlec, *Dol-de-Bretagne*, 1903, p. 288 (A large temple supported by twelve columns, thirty arched buttresses; two ladies walk there, one white, one black). Icelandic: Árnason, 616, 722, 731, 889, 992, 1051. French: Parsons, *Antilles*, III, 382, Martinique, 26. Italian: Pitrè, 23

---

[44] Piekarski, 12.
[45] These seem to be a development of the texts cited in the headnote and note to Nos. 1037a, 1037b below.
[46] Novaković, p. 31, No. 3.

(Palace, twelve doors, each door with thirty openings); Schneller, *Wälschtirol*, p. 256, No. 30 (There is a palace, in it are twelve rooms, each of them has thirty rafters, and in them are two, who chase each other continually and never catch each other). Czech: Hanika-Otto, note to No. 270. Modern Greek: Dieterich, *Rätseldichtung*, p. 89 (Tower of twelve stories; temple of twelve columns; ship with twelve sails); Sakellarios, p. 292, No. 12 (It is an iron mill. It puts out iron flour. It holds twelve levers, and every lever has thirty wedges), and p. 294, No. 3 (A twelve-wedged boat, each wedge with a name). Mongolian: Bazarov, 197 (One large settlement has four gates, on each gate there are thirty nails).

Two famous references to a building symbolizing the sun or the sun's course through the year may be derived from older riddles for a year and may have in turn given rise to modern riddles. Aarne's comment[47] on them is inadequate, and a new examination of these allusions is in order. They are Ovid's castle of the sun[48] and an incident in the story of Aḥiḳar.[49] The two passages do not seem to be connected closely with one another.

The concept of a building symbolizing the year appears in other and perhaps independent forms in the Icelandic "What excellent temple, most honoured and praised of all, is supported by twelve ladders raised against it? On the rungs stand a man and wife who are always busy and never rest, morning or night, and yet never weary?" and "I want to speak to you, for there is no pleasure in moping silent in the dark. It always entertains people when the ship of words leaves the landing-place of knowledge. Therefore I shall ask you, although I find it difficult to formulate what I want to say: what is the fairest and noblest of all temples? In it stands a pillar of great strength, with gold and green fields, and costlier than the noblest metal. It bears branches laden with fruits, visible to all. Although difficult expression delays me, I shall further tell you that by the pillar stand ladders, twelve in all, I think, that support the vault of the temple. There are thirty rungs in each ladder, on which people swarm, having everything according to their wills, wealth and goods in abundance. On the rungs a nobleman and his lady walk in eternal unrest, ceasing neither night nor morning, without ever wearying.

---

[47] *Rätselforschungen*, I, 154–160.
[48] *Metamorphoses*, II, 1–18. For references to the influence of this passage in medieval French literature see Achille Jubinal (ed.), *Fablel dou dieu d'amour* (Paris, 1834), which is summarized in *Histoire littéraire*, XXIII, 72 ff.; a related text in W. Foerster, *De Venus la deesse d'amor* (Bonn, 1880), especially pp. 44, 48; O. Dammann, *Die allegorische Canzone des Guiraut de Calanso "A leis cui am de cor a de saber"* (Diss., Univ. of Breslau; Breslau, 1891), pp. 11–23.
[49] For this and a related incident in the biography of Aesop see Friedreich, p. 182; Ohlert, 1st ed., pp. 15–16, 124, and 2d ed., p. 95; Meissner, *Zeitschrift der deutschen morgenländischen Gesellschaft*, XLVIII (1894), 175, 178–179, 181–183; M. Lidzbarski, *Geschichten und Lieder aus den neu-aramäischen Handschriften der Königlichen Bibliothek zu Berlin* (Beiträge zur Volks- und Völkerkunde, IV; Weimar, 1896), p. 33; Victor Chauvin, *Bibliographie des ouvrages arabes*, VI (Liége, 1902), 40; Loewenthal, p. 54; F. C. Conybeare, *The Story of Aḥiḳar* (Cambridge, England, 1912), pp. lxxxix–xc.

Now guess my riddle, good people"[50] and the Yakut "They say that the doors at the market place open first on the East, then on the West, after which the doors on the East close early, those on the West later."[51] An original variation occurs in the Icelandic hourglass riddle: "What strangely built castle has five pillars standing beside it, a very large heaven above it and an equally large heaven below it? Inside it sit two neat maidens, fair and fine and of excellent beauty. When one is satiated, the other vomits."[52]

§ 7. A cask. Modern Greek: Polites, *Neohellenika Analekta*, I, 244, No. 288 (A cask with twelve staves, and every wedge has a name).

§ 8. Flowers, fruits. See the headnote to No. 1095 and the comparisons of a week or another period of time to a plant in the headnote to No. 983, nn. 13–15.

§ 9. Household objects. Indian, Parsee: Munshi, p. 419, No. 34 (Chest with thirty drawers, thirty grains in each drawer). Baiga: Elwin, p. 479, No. 149 (In four it boils, in four it cools, in four it sinks into the water).[53]

1037. Twelve Branches, Fifty-two Nests

The Icelandic "I saw twelve trees standing in a square. They spread all over the world. They had fifty-two branches and seven apples hanging from each branch, each with its own name. Where one apple ended, another began without interruption"[1] is perhaps somewhat confused. The riddler does not clearly conceive the twelve trees. The notion of the square is perhaps related to the scene of a courtyard that occurs in some parallels. Elsewhere, the tree that spreads over the world is either the sun or the world-tree.[2]

1037a. I wot a tre, XII bowys betake / LII nestys beþ þ up ymad; / in euery nest beþ bryddys VII. I-thankyd beþ God of heuene / and euery bryd with selcouth name.—[The year].

Harleian 3362 (15th cent.), fol. 33ᵃ = M. Förster, *Anglia*, XLII (1918), 206–207.

1037b. I have a tree of great honor, / Which tree beareth both fruit and flower. / Twelve branches this tree hath nake[d], / Fifty [sic] nests therein he make[d], / And every nest hath birds seaven— / Thanked be the king of heaven; / And every bird hath a divers name. / How many all this together frame?—The tree is the yeere, the twelve branches be the twelve moneths, the fifty two nests be the fifty two weekes the seven birds be the seven days in the weeke, whereof every one hath a divers name.

Meery Riddles (1629), No. 5 = Brandl, p. 8.

---

[50] Árnason, 731, 992.
[51] Piekarski, 16. [52] Árnason, 540.
[53] For similar riddles see the headnote to No. 984 above.

[1] Árnason, 1051. For riddles referring to the months or the days of the week as having individual names see Nos. 1037a through 1038a below. Compare some curious Polish parallels cited in the note to Nos. 1063a through 1063i.
[2] See the headnote to No. 544 above.

1038. Twelve Limbs, Seven Branches

The limbs and branches ordinarily signify the months and days, and in this variety of the year riddle the division is not usually carried further. A curious variation is the Mandingo "What tree has twelve branches, each of which has thirty leaves, which protect five flowers, of which two are in the sun and three in the shade?—The year, which has twelve months of thirty days, in each day there are five prayers, two in the day and three during the night."[1] The occurrence of the year riddle in an Italian tale is perhaps worthy of mention,[2] since very few true riddles are found in tales. The variants of this tale do not usually contain the riddle.

1038a. Yonder stands a tree of honour, / Twelve limbs grow upon her; / Every limb a different name. / It would take a wise man to tell you the same. —Twelve months of the year.
Leather, *Hereford*, p. 230.

1038b. There's a tree in the valley, / Fifty-two branches round. / Each one bears seven / Which the Lord sent from Heaven.—The year.
Greenleaf, *Newfoundland*, p. 8, No. 2.

1039. Oak, Nest, Egg, and Yolk

In its style this curious riddle resembles those in which the riddler enumerates a series of objects and gives them interpretations quite at variance with their apparent natures.[1] Although the individual details in this riddle are sometimes appropriate enough—an oak might represent a church, a nest a steeple, and an egg a bell—the final comparison of the clapper to the yolk cannot be called happy. A somewhat similar and equally obscure incongruity appears in the French and Spanish parallels, but the lack of a sufficient number of texts, and especially of old texts, makes it impossible to discover the original sense underlying these obscurities.

The simple and natural comparison of a bell or crier to a bird[2] can be easily extended to suggest the congregation coming to a temple or church, as in the Altai Turkish "A goose cried out, her young assembled."[3] The European parallels to this are likely to introduce improperly definite allusions to the answer, as in the Breton "Perched high, it makes good women run to mass"[4] or "Perched high, dressed short, it makes good little women run."[5]

---

[1] Monteil, p. 189, No. 35.
[2] See the reference to Schneller in the note to Nos. 1038a, 1038b.
[1] See the headnote to Nos. 1161–1164.
[2] See below, No. 1326 and the headnote to No. 1326.
[3] Menges, p. 76, No. 29.
[4] Duine, *Saint-Malo*, p. 518.
[5] Sébillot, *Haute-Bretagne*, 80. See further, Welsh: Hull and Taylor, 56. Breton: Sauvé, 66; Sébillot, *Devinettes*, 93. French: Rolland, 274; Lespy, *Béarn*, 1; Desaivre, *Poitou*, p. 451, No. 15.

1039. beyond the seas there is an oake & in that oake ther is a nest & in that nest there is an egge & in that egge ther is a yolk wch calls together christian folke—the church is taken for the oake the steeple for the nest the bell for the egge and the clapper for the yolk wch calls the people.

Tupper, *Holme Riddles*, 104; *Meery Riddles* (1629), No. 70 = Brandl, p. 20; *The New Help to Discourse*, 9th ed., p. 129.

1040–1041. Trees of Unequal Height

The comparison of trees and fingers usually rests on the fact that both are always of varying heights. It is closely related to such queries about God's power as "What has never been, and what will never be, but every man sees it for himself?—That the fingers are not of equal height."[1] This also has the answer, "Trees in a forest."[2] Such ideas are also proverbial.[3] In speaking of peas or sola, a kind of grass growing as tall as a man, the Duala state a contrary idea: "In Bonabela one is as tall as another."[4]

In a few riddles the comparison is expressed in terms of persons rather than trees. The French say, "We are ten brothers, the fattest is not the tallest";[5] the Spanish, "A house made of the clothing of animals, and five unequal brothers inhabit it.—Shoes";[6] and the Kamba, "Tell me those born on the same day, but nevertheless of different sizes."[7]

The observation of the unequal height of trees in a forest is also used to describe the staves in a tub. The tub has two long staves on opposite sides; these are perforated and serve as handles. See the Lettish "The whole forest is of an equal height, two trees project";[8] the Russian "The whole forest is short, but two trees are higher than all [the others]";[9] and a Mordvin parallel.[10]

Comparisons of the fingers to persons are abundant,[11] but comparisons to animals are rather rare. See the Mongolian "Five geese on a rack."[12]

1040. A tree there is that boughes doth beare / in number five, as I doe know: / no equall length they never were, / and on their tops doe hornes grow. / Yet they are tied about with gold, / except the longest, without doubt, / which for use sake might be controld, / if it with gold were hoopt

---

[1] Norwegian: Christie, 111. For additional examples see below, Nos. 1629a, 1629b, the headnote to No. 1629, and the note to Nos. 1629a, 1629b.
[2] Norwegian: Bugge, *Telemarken*, 38; Landstad, p. 813, No. 48. Swedish: Ström, p. 406, No. 36.
[3] See the note to Nos. 1629a, 1629b below.
[4] Bufe, 10.
[5] V. S., *Mélusine*, I (1878), vol. 254, No. 12 = Marchessou, *Velay et Auvergne*, p. 172, No. 2. Turkish: Hamizade, 556 (We are ten brothers, the smallest one of us is the fattest one of us).
[6] Rodríguez Marín, 642. Compare Demófilo, 359. Argentinian: Lehmann-Nitsche, 462, 463.
[7] Lindblom, 54.   [8] Bielenstein, 951.
[9] Sadovnikov, 396; see also his No. 418.
[10] Paasonen, 402.
[11] See the headnote to No. 989 above.
[12] Kotvich, 25.

about.—It is one's hand and his fingers that are ful of golden rings, the middle-most excepted, because a ring doth not fit that finger.
Prettie Riddles (1631), No. 39 = Brandl, p. 58.

1041. My father have ten trees in his yard an' two taller than the rest.—Fingers.
Beckwith, *Jamaica*, p. 184, No. 16.

1042-1044. Trees or Grass: Hair

The simple and rather obvious comparison of hair to grass or trees occurs in various forms and contexts. It is occasionally elaborated by reference to the pursuit of game symbolizing the catching of lice.[1] I have arranged the pertinent texts as follows: comparisons mentioning animals;[2] comparisons mentioning trees or grass and no animals;[3] comparisons to a landscape of which a meadow or a forest forms a part;[4] and comparisons of hair to sticks or wands.[5]

In eastern Europe riddlers describe a razor as an animal that grazes in a field or roams in a forest. The conception is akin to the comparisons of lice to animals that are driven from a field by a stick or a shepherd.[6] The variations in detail are abundant and curious. See Bulgarian: Bozhov, 10 (A gray bull is grazing on the hill); Gubov, 19 (A wild hog is grazing on the hill), 20 (gray falcon), 21 (black bull), 22 (black calf); Ikonomov, 26 (A tailless pig is grazing on the hill). Turkish: Kúnos, 47 (I have a little lamb. In the morning it grazes, in the evening it bends its head and lies down); Hamizade, 690 (On a dense hill a greybound grazes). Turcoman: Samojlvich, 100 (On the hillock a lambkin frolics). African, Ewe: Spieth, p. 598, No. 10 (The antelope with a black mouth goes around a hill). Indian, Uraon: Archer, p. 181, No. 30 (A black goat grazes on a black hill). Kolarian: Wagner, 47 (A cow is grazing on the four sides of an anthill). The Serbian "An iron colt is grazing on the hill"[7] errs in admitting too definite and unequivocal a reference to the answer into the riddle; such versions as "A hairless mare grazes on the hill" and "A hairless pig grazes on the marsh"[8] exemplify a much better technique. The curious Indian "The black bird has a black nest. It feeds on the black grass. It climbs on a stone to drink water. It comes home in a litter. In a barber's house it is born as a boy"[9] is readily understood except for the last sentence.

---

[1] See No. 459, the note to No. 459, and the headnote to Nos. 459–460.
[2] In Nos. 459, 474, and the headnote to Nos. 459–560 the animals are lice. In the headnote to No. 1042–1044 the animal is a razor.
[3] See, in the note to Nos. 1042, 1043, riddles in which grass or trees signify hair; in the note to No. 1043, wood that cannot be split, signifying hair; and, in the note to No. 1044, water, signifying the eyes, and grass, trees, or shrubs, signifying eyelashes or brows. See also the classification of riddles for eyebrows in n. 26 below, and the comparisons to cutting plants in a garden, in the headnote to No. 1116, nn. 7–9.
[4] See No. 1100, the headnote to Nos. 1100–1108, and the note to No. 1100.
[5] Nos. 1116a, 1116b. Compare the headnote to No. 1116.
[6] See the headnote to Nos. 459–460.
[7] Novaković, p. 9, No. 3.
[8] Novaković, p. 9, Nos. 4, 5.
[9] Elwin and Hivale, p. 72, No. 67.

These ideas are easily adjusted to a comb in the Bulgarian "A gray pig is grazing on the hill."[10] The comparison of the black hairs to sheep in the Turkish "I chased away a thousand black sheep with an iron"[11] is unusual, but it has a parallel in a Turkish dialect.[12] The animals usually represent lice and not hairs.

The comparison of a razor to a person walking about in a field is less frequent than the comparison to an animal. For examples see the Ossete "Our little father mows hay";[13] the Sotho "A man is on a hill, he is a woodcutter who drags wood after him";[14] the Ho "A little child roams about a forest with rapid strides and came back"[15] and "There is an urchin who runs right round a little hillock";[16] or the Kashmiri "The woodcutter will go to the copse. He will cut down a thousand trees with each stroke and will destroy the jungle"; or "A sawyer went into a copse and cut and gathered some wood"; or "The mahárāj came and entered into the fight and destroyed [them]."[17]

Comparisons of a razor to a thing are rather rare, but see the Serbian "A little ax is cutting on the top of the forest,"[18] the Turkish "I have taken the stick, I have gone about the hillside,"[19] the Baiga "A little plough walks fearlessly through the jungle";[20] the Bengali "A black thorny plant[21] eats black grass. When night comes, the thorny tree goes into a refuge";[22] and the Khāṛiā "A crooked sickle cuts the jungle."[23] Ideas of this sort are easily adapted to fit a comb, as in the Hungarian "On a bone hill there moves a hand plow."[24]

Comparisons of hair to animals are rare. The Yakut riddle for eyebrows has a poetic touch: "They say that two sables lie with their feet facing each other [end to end]."[25] This resembles the Georgian "On one stone two snakes are lying"[26] and the Turkish "Adagan and Tadagan with their feet together."[27]

---

[10] Ikonomov, 16.
[11] Maenchen, 10.
[12] Katanov in Radlov, IX, 91, No. 769.
[13] Schiefner, 46.
[14] Endemann, 72.
[15] Sarkar, p. 352, No. 8.
[16] Haldar, p. 278, No. 27.
[17] Knowles, 70, 112, 129.
[18] Novaković, p. 9, No. 1.
[19] Kowalski, Zagadki, 24.
[20] Elwin, p. 465, No. 11.
[21] Argemona mexicana.
[22] Mitra, Chittagong, p. 352, No. 16.
[23] Roy and Roy, II, 451, No. 21.
[24] Kálmány, I, 160, No. 19.
[25] Piekarski, 193.
[26] Glushakov, p. 26, No. 25. References to the eyebrow or brows in riddles cited in the present collection may be classified according to the following terms of comparison:

Animals. See the text of this headnote, especially n. 25 (sables) and n. 26 (snakes), the headnote to Nos. 1100–1108, n. 20 (leeches), the headnote to No. 1116, n. 16 (cattle), and the headnote to Nos. 1003–1004, § 1 (doves).

Plants. See the note to No. 1044 (grass, etc.), the headnote to No. 1100, n. 3 (gardens), the Ho riddle cited from Sarkar in the note to No. 1100 (bush), Gubov's Bulgarian riddle No. 67 cited in the note to No. 1100 (hedges), and the headnote to Nos. 1100–1108, n. 28 (bundles of rushes).

Things. See, in the note to No. 1100, the Arabic riddle quoted from Ruoff, p. 16, No. 7 (swords), the Albanian riddle quoted from Hahn (lances), the Armenian riddle quoted from Wingate (penciled mark), and two Bulgarian riddles, Gubov's No. 66 (braids) and Ikonomov's No. 76 (plaited string).

[27] Katanov in Radlov, IX, 368, No. 328.

1042. j saw a hill on [MS: one] a day lift up above the ayre wch watered wth blood allway & tilled wth grat care herbes it brought forth of mickle worth.— that part of a horse that the[y] pule out his longest haires.
Tupper, *Holme Riddles*, 66.

1043. I had a little meadow, / And in this little meadow I had a grove of trees; / Some I could cut, but I could not cleave.—Hair on the head.
Leather, *Hereford*, p. 231; Burne, *Shropshire*, p. 574, No. 15.

1044. Trees around a Well

A somewhat similar theme occurs in the Tungus riddle for a running nose, "Between two lakes a bridge[1] gets rotten."[2] There is an apparently well-established Asiatic version of this riddle for the eyes and the eyelashes in which the lashes are compared to birds rather than to trees. Examples are the Turkish "Many geese sit on the shore of a lake"[3] and "On the shore of a lake sit many geese. What is it?"[4] The Sinhalese have a similar but more elaborate version: "On the upper shoot are five hundred songsters; on the lower shoot are five hundred songsters; between them is an infant of divine beauty. If one can solve this, he can become a Buddha."[5] The combination of a striking similarity and an equally striking difference between the more usual forms and a certain Ewe text, "There is a great river, on its banks sit many birds, but not one of them dips its beak into the water,"[6] raises interesting but probably insoluble questions regarding the origin and dissemination of the theme. Is this resemblance sufficient for us to insist upon derivation from a common source, or is the fundamental idea so obvious that it could have been independently invented? The Cheremiss "I throw twigs one year old over the lake"[7] and the Yakut "Two men bat with poles from two sides of a lake"[8] portray a similar scene in human rather than animal terms.

1044. My father had a fig-tree all hung over a well. / All the leaf dry, an' no one fall in the well.—Eye-vinker never fell in your eye.
Parsons, *Eleuthera and Watling's Islands, Bahamas*, p. 440, No. 12.

1045-1046. Trees Representing Persons

Although the notion of a family tree might suggest the comparison of trees to persons, examples of the equating of persons and trees are very rare. The comparison of daughters to fruit trees[1] is apparently a variation of the ideas found in the riddles about women one cannot marry.[2]

---

[1] The bridge is a tree laid across the stream. Compare the Malayalam "For only one bridge there are two wells" (Frohnmeyer, p. 230).
[2] Poppe, 27.
[3] Katanov in Radlov, IX, 91. No. 768.
[4] Maenchen, p. 106.
[5] Perera, p. 55.
[6] Spieth, p. 560, No. 17.
[7] Porkka, 9, and compare his No. 128.
[8] Popov, p. 285. See also Piekarski, 160, and a close parallel in his No. 159, both quoted in the note to No. 1003 of the present collection, and see also the headnote to Nos. 1003-1004, n. 10, and the note to No. 1044.

[1] No. 1045.
[2] See the headnote to No. 1070.

1045. Me riddle me riddle me yander, / Though me father have a thing, it's a very good thing, / I hope you may clare this riddle and I hope you may not. / Me father have seven fruit trees and yet he can't eat none.—A man with seven daughters and he can't marry none.
Finlay, *Bahamas*, p. 296, No. 10.

1046. A tree got a whole lot o' limbs, an' one ain't got none.—A woman got a whole crowd of chilrun.
Parsons, *Sea Islands, S.C.*, p. 168, No. 103.

1047–1050. Miscellaneous Comparisons to Trees

The import of three riddles in this section is obscure. The description of grass as a tree which only Red-mouth Johnny can climb (No. 1048) may be a disordered version of a text given in an earlier chapter (No. 433). The description of a pecan tree as something impossible to climb (No. 1049) conveys no meaning to me. Finally, the description of war as a tree (No. 1050) is perhaps a confused fragment of a riddle which is not preserved in any intelligible version.

1047. Had a tree in my garden, / The bigger it grows, the smaller it comes.—Candle.
Parsons, *Antilles*, III, 364, Trinidad, No. 11.

1048. My father has a mill tree in the yard, only red mouth Johnny can climb it.—Grass.
Parsons, *Barbados*, p. 286, No. 63.

1049. Climb all tree, / You can't climb soldier tree.—Pecan tree.
Parsons, *Antilles*, III, 366, Trinidad, No. 34 var.

1050. There stands a tree at our house-end, / It's a' clad owre wi' leather bend; / It'll fecht a bull, it'll fecht a bear, / It'll fecht a thousand men t'weir [to war].—War.
Chambers, *Scotland*, p. 108.

1051–1065. Other Plants

1051–1062. Growth

1051. My father had a field, what was the first crop he made?—His track.
Parsons, *Bahamas*, p. 478, No. 70.

1052. Somet'in' you plant one an' a whole lot get up.—Peanuts.
Johnson, *St. Helena Island, S.C.*, p. 158, No. 1.

1053. My father have one thing in his hand and throw it and it support the whole of Jamaica.—Corn-grain.
Beckwith, *Jamaica*, p. 190, No. 66.

1054. My father plant a acre a kasava; only one white belly rat a eatey off.—Grater for preparing kasava meal.
Beckwith, *Jamaica*, p. 191, No. 69.

1055–1057. Grows with Its Root Upward

Wolfgang Schultz[1] cites some cosmological parallels to this theme. With slight modifications the notion of a plant that grows upside down[2] is applicable to many objects. The Sangir description of the moon and its rays is picturesquely conceived in this manner: "Walk on its top, look up at its roots."[3] The objects most frequently described in this way are:

§ 1. An icicle. See Nos. 1055a through 1056 below, and (with the added qualification that it grows in the winter and dies in the summer) No. 1057.

§ 2. A cow's tail. See No. 1056. "To grow down like a cow's tail" is proverbial; see G. L. Apperson, *English Proverbs and Proverbial Phrases* (London, 1929), p. 119.

§ 3. A beard, braids. Bulgarian: Stoilov, 24. Indonesian: Malay: Tauern, *Patasiwa*, p. 72 (A bamboo bush grows with its root above, its top below). Menangkerbau Malay: Harmsen, p. 267, No. 11 (The tops downward, the roots upward). Simaloer: Damsté, pp. 636–637, No. 3.

The Finnish "A juniper grew on the hill with its roots up and its top down"[4] is well thought out. Two Turkish instances have the answer "braids": "Two poplars are standing on their heads" and "Two trees grow out of one place with their tops downwards."[5]

§ 4. The nose. Swedish: Olsson, *Västergötland*, p. 124, No. 4 (The root up and the branches down, in between two lakes); Ström, p. 81, "Näsan," 1. Yakut: Piekarski, 173 (They say that between two lakes there lies an uptured larch). African, Pangwe: Tessmann, 31 (I know a tree, its crown stands below and its trunk above). Tessmann's comment that this observation is peculiarly true of Negro noses is not borne out by the distribution of the riddle. Indonesian, Alfoer: Wilken, 2 (Two wood doves always look down from above;

---

[1] *Rätsel*, col. 104, No. 75. See also R. Eisler, *Weltenmantel und Himmelszelt* (Munich, 1910), p. 326, citing commentators on Dante, *Paradiso*, XXXII, 131; M. B. Emeneau, "The Strangling Figs in Sanskrit Literature," *University of California Publications in Classical Philology*, XIII (1949), 345–370. Otto Maenchen gives me the following additional references: L. von Schroeder, "Lebensbaum und Lebenstraum," *Aufsätze zur Kultur- und Sprachgeschichte vornehmlich des Orients, Ernst Kuhn . . . gewidmet . . .* (Munich, 1916), pp. 59–68; A. Jacoby, "Der Baum mit den Wurzeln nach oben und den Zweigen nach unten," *Zeitschrift für Missionskunde und Religionswissenschaft*, XLII–XLV (1928), 78–85; E. Kagarow, "Der umgekehrte Schamanenbaum," *Archiv für Religionswissenschaft*, XXVII (1929), 183–185; A. J. Wensink, "Tree and Bird as Cosmological Symbols in Western Asia," *Verhandelingen der koninklijke Akademie der Wetenschapen* (Amsterdam), Afd. Letterkunde, n.s., XXII (1921), 1–56, especially p. 33; W. W. Skeat, *Malay Magic* (London, 1900), p. 13; H. Ling Roth, *The Natives of Sarawak and British North Borneo* (London, 1896), I, 307; W. H. Furness, *Folklore in Borneo* (Wallingford, Pa., 1899), p. 20; C. Arendt, *Zeitschrift des Vereins für Volkskunde*, I (1891), 329 (Chinese).

[2] For comparisons to a person growing upside down see the headnote to No. 544, § 5, above, and compare No. 681 above.

[3] Adriani, 376; see also his No. 111. A similar idea is found in the *Rigveda*, 1, 24, 7 (see M. B. Emeneau, "The Strangling Figs in Sanskrit Literature," *University of California Publications in Classical Philology*, XIII [1949], 347, 367–368).

[4] Lönnrot, 397 = Henssen, 58.

[5] Katanov in Radlov, IX, 239, No. 46, and p. 367, No. 324.

two bamboos are turned upside down), and 9 (A gun with two barrels, the bottom is turned upwards). See also a Yakut riddle cited in the note to No. 1044 above. I have noted no parallel to the Icelandic use of this theme for an upper tooth: "What tree has its crown pointing down and its root pointing up?"[6]

§ 5. Household objects. CHIMNEY. Russian: Sadovnikov, 160. SOOT. Polish: Gustawicz, 480. Bulgarian: Gubov, 308 (The root upwards, the top downwards), 309 (The root is above, the top is below). EAVES. Hungarian: Kriza, 91 (What tree is it the roots of which grow up while its branches grow down?). Indonesian, Simaloer: Damsté, pp. 636–637, No. 4 (There is a fruit. If it falls down, one looks upwards for it.—Rain leaking out of the roof). A candle is called a man growing down.[7]

§ 6. Curtain. Indonesian, Lampong: Helfrich, *Lampong*, p. 612, No. 5. Batak: Ophuijsen, p. 202 (The leaves go upward; the roots go upward).

§ 7. Plants. See the discussion in the headnote to No. 544, § 5, above.

1055a. What doth with his roofe [root] upwards grow, / and downward with his head doth show?—It is an icesickle [icicle].
Prettie Riddles (1631), No. 45 = Brandl, p. 59.

1055b. Faht is't that grows wi' its head down?—An icicle.
Gregor, *Northeast Scotland*, p. 82.

1056. What two things grow downward?—An icicle and a cow's tail.
Fauset, *Nova Scotia*, p. 171, No. 165.

1057. Lives in winter, / Dies in summer, / And grows with its root upwards. —An icicle.
Halliwell-Phillipps, *Nursery Rhymes*, p. 134; Greenleaf, *Newfoundland*, p. 14, No. 6; Whitney and Bullock, *Maryland*, p. 174, No. 2684; Knortz, p. 224, No. 54; Thurston, *Massachusetts*, p. 182, No. 1; Hyatt, *Adams Co., Ill.*, p. 662, No. 10880; Redfield, *Tennessee*, p. 39, No. 46.

1058–1062. Grew in the Wood

The English riddles for a broom or violin belong to a very widely disseminated pattern applicable to a great variety of objects. The pattern is, I suspect, very old, for it probably suggested the popular verses about Caligula that Suetonius has preserved for us:

> In castris natus, patriis nutritus in armis,
> Iam designati principis omen erat.[1]

The characteristic feature of this pattern is the suggestion that the answer is a plant, an animal, and also a person. A very clear example of the pattern is seen in the Serbian description of a sieve, "It grew in the forest, it grazed

---

[6] Árnason, 574. [7] See No. 681 above.

[1] *Caligula*, 8. See my article, "An Allusion to a Riddle in Suetonius," *American Journal of Philology*, LXVI (1945), 408–410.

among the mares, and it danced among the women,"[2] which refers to the wooden frame, the horsehair stretched across it, and the shaking of the flour.

On the continent of Europe this pattern has been so popular that such introductory phrases as the Dutch "'T groeit in den bosch," or the Rumanian "In pădure născuiŭ (I am born in the woods)," or the Spanish "En el campo fuí criado (I was created in the field)" have virtually become mere formulas, to such an extent that the feeling for the pattern is often obscured or lost.

The Spanish candle riddle, "I was created on the mountain and I came to my end at the altar,"[3] illustrates how readily riddlers can turn this pattern to new uses. The fundamental theme of the contrast of the three origins or associations of the object has disappeared, and the riddle is a short biography of a supposed person. The reference to the mountain signifies the bees making wax out of doors. The allusion to the mountain is merely a specific scene with a general meaning. "I came to my end at the altar" signifies the burning of the candle, and at the same time aptly describes the end that any mortal might expect.

This manner of riddling resembles the descriptions of an object as being made in three ways (begotten by an ox, grown in the woods, and made by a smith or carpenter)[4] or as being a person composed of three inappropriate materials.[5] Riddlers have now and again confused these three patterns.[6] The conception may degenerate into versions which merely suggest an impossible heterogeneity of materials, as in the Turkish "Part is burning fire, part is steel, part is stone, part is wood from the field.—Flintlock gun."[7]

This description, which suggests at one and the same time a plant, an animal, and a person, is applicable to a variety of objects. An old ship riddle[8] may have been the model for later inventions. Since this pattern serves also in many very widely scattered texts for musical instruments[9] and for a sieve,[10] I cannot confidently ascribe its original use to any particular theme.

Modern riddlers use this pattern most freely for household objects. Some texts are interesting because they have admitted appropriate variations in order to adapt it to new uses. A Catalan description of sabots, "Born in the wood, made in the house, it goes to the field, it goes black and returns white,"[11] refers to the snow on the wooden shoes. The Lettish riddle for the heartwood of a tree, "Born in the wood, grown up in the wood, it has never seen the sun,"[12]

---

[2] Novaković, p. 208, No. 11.
[3] Argentinian: Lehmann-Nitsche, 53.
[4] See Nos. 401 through 404 and the headnote to Nos. 401–404.
[5] See No. 553a through 554 and the headnote to Nos. 553–554.
[6] For examples see the sword riddle cited in the headnote to Nos. 401–404, § 4, and the saddle riddle cited in the headnote to Nos. 553–554, § 4, nn. 8–10.
[7] Katanov in Radlov, IX, 547, No. 3.
[8] See § 1 below.
[9] See § 2 below and Nos. 1059a through 1062.
[10] See § 5 below.
[11] Pelay y Briz, 251. See also §13 below. [12] Bielenstein, 911.

and Rumanian riddles for a pine tree[13] and a table[14] may serve as further examples. A Rumanian description of a bridge[15] is similar to the threshold riddle[16] and illustrates the adapting of an old riddle to new uses. A Flemish coffin riddle[17] mingles elements of this pattern with the usual riddle for a coffin[18] and thus shows the familiarity of the folk with the pattern. The Polish violin riddle, "A sad tree sings gaily; a horse flicks its tail over the ram,"[19] involves some of these elements—the tree is the violin; the horse, the hairs of the bow; and the ram, the strings—but the riddler has greatly altered the conception. Such evidences of a general familiarity with this pattern are numerous.

Typical objects described in this manner are:

§ 1. A ship. Swiss: Rochholz, 602. Danish: Kristensen, pp. 115–116, § 314, Nos. 501a through 501j; DFS, 1906/38: H. Ellekilde, 1916, No. 2 (The earth is my mother, I was born in the woods. I run many a mile, and no one can find my track); DFS, 1906/38: E. Tingle, 1932, No. 32 (The wood is my mother, and I her splendid daughter; I have journeyed many a mile, and no one can see my track).[20] Norwegian: Bugge, *Telemarken*, 82. A curious Norwegian version, "It grew on the mountain, it ran in the tide, the smith forged it and the maiden span it, it went ahead in the bird's path; small as it is, it killed a man,"[21] has absorbed details from various sources. "The smith forged it" belongs to a manner of description[22] closely akin to the one here discussed. The statement "Small as it is, it killed a man" is usually found in riddles for a bullet.[23] Swedish: Ström, p. 169, "Skeppet," 1, and p. 170, "Masten," 2; Geijer and Campbell, 35. Latin: Ohl, Symphosius, 13; M[one], *Anzeiger*, VIII (1839), col. 316, No. 79. Catalan: Milá y Fontanals, 1877, p. 6. Spanish, Argentinian: Lehmann-Nitsche, 45 (I am born on the mountain, I live in the water), in which the original pattern has given place to a contrast of the mountain and the water. Polish: Gustawicz, 94 (During my lifetime, I have fed the living. I have had to die because of the wicked. Now the living are beneath me, and I carry the living. Whoever can guess this riddle, him I shall thank beautifully.—Pear tree, boat, fish, people), which has somewhat confused the

---

[13] Gorovei, 167.
[14] Gorovei, 1097.
[15] Gorovei, 1504.
[16] See § 11 below.
[17] Joos, 108.
[18] See below, Nos. 1728 through 1735, the headnote to Nos. 1728–1737, and the note to Nos. 1728 through 1735.
[19] Kopernicki, 22, citing Kolberg, *Krakowskie*, IV, No. 46. For other examples see § 2 below.
[20] Two other manuscript versions, DFS, 1906/38: N. Sørensen, 1913, No. 1, and H. Sørensen, 1935, No. 6, also contain the element "leaves no track," which is not usually found in this riddle. It belongs to another ship riddle, for which see the note and the headnote to No. 227 above.
[21] Stafset, 106.
[22] See above, Nos. 553a through 554, the headnotes to Nos. 401–404 and 553–554, and the note to No. 404.
[23] See No. 801.

answers. Finnish: Lönnrot, 846 = Henssen, 224 (It grew in the wood, came into being on the shore, lives in the water, dies in the fire). Lappish: Qvigstad, 130. Hungarian: Kálmány, I, 170, No. 21 (It grows in the forest, is born on the riverbank, lies in the water, perishes in fire).

For additional parallels and discussion see Feilberg, *Ordbog*, III, 243, s.v. "skib"; Ohlert, 2d ed., p. 190.

§ 2. A violin or other musical instrument.[24] Riddlers occasionally name an instrument without strings as an answer. See Breton: Sauvé, 114 (What sprouts in the woods and comes to the village to make an uproar?—Oboe). French: Rolland, 200 (flute). Basque: Vinson, 17 (baton). Rumanian: Gorovei, 783 (flute), and Gorovei, *Devinettes*, p. 506 (flute). Russian: Sadonikov, 272 (whistle).

The drum is a very frequently given answer. See Danish Kristensen, p. 391, Nos. 625a through 625d; DFS, 1906/38: J. Prest, p. 19, No. 7. French: Fesquet, p. 176 (tabor). Rumanian: Gorovei, 112. Arabic: Ruoff, p. 26, No. 35 (One-third from the cabinetmaker, one-third from the spice merchant, one-third from the butcher, with my eyes I saw it flying about). The cabinetmaker makes the frame, the spice merchant sells the nails, the butcher supplies the skin. The flying about is dancing. Indonesian, Batak: Ophuijsen, p. 211, No. 28 (Its mouth of flesh, its body of wood, its ribs of rattan). This seems rather more closely related to the conception of a person or animal of heterogeneous materials, as discussed in the headnote to Nos. 553–554 above. The Malagasy "Dead before it begins to bluster" (Sibree, 19) employs the contrast of the dead and the living, which I have discussed in the headnote to Nos. 828–836 above. The Tagalog "I wounded him in the wood, but he only cried at home.—Guitar" (Rizal, p. 46) is conceived ent rely in terms of a person.

Especially interesting Renaissance versions of this conception are the description of a tortoise made into a musical instrument:

In silvis cresco, per campos gramine vescor,
In domibus resono, dic modo sim quis ego?

and of a lyre:

Viva fui in silvis, sum dura occisa securi,
Dum vixi tacui, mortua dulce cano.[25]

The fundamental conception of the violin riddle has some similarity to the notion underlying the ballad of the "Twa Sisters."[26] In that ballad the body of the dead sister provides the materials for the violin: her hair is the strings, her fingers are the keys, and so on.

A special variety of this theme which is current in eastern Europe may be exemplified by the Polish "A linden tree sings gaily while a horse flicks its

---

[24] See Nos. 1059a through 1062 and the note to Nos. 1059a, 1059b.
[25] Both texts may be found in Buchler, *Gnomologia*, 3d ed. (1614), p. 446.
[26] F. J. Child, *English and Scottish Popular Ballads*, I (Boston, 1885), 118–126, No. 10.

tail over a ram."²⁷ The fiddle is the linden tree, the bow the horse, and the strings are the ram. This is intended to suggest a lying tale of impossibilities.

§ 3. A coffin. Flemish: Joos, 109. French: Rolland, 278 (I was born in the ground, I am in wood, I bear man, and I return to the earth). Portuguese: Braga, 50.

§ 4. A broom. See No. 1058 below.

§ 5. A sieve or strainer. Welsh: Hull and Taylor, 248, 249. Norwegian: Landstad, p. 806, No. 6. French: Bladé, *Armagnac*, 13. Spanish: Demófilo, 334; Rodríguez Marín, 709. Italian: Straparola, I, 3; Rondini, *Archivio*, VIII (1889), 188, No. 85. Rumanian: Gorovei, 1679. Czech: Hanika-Otto, note to Nos. 55 through 58. Kashub: Gulgowski, 10. Polish: Gustawicz, 340, 374 through 377; Saloni, *Łańcut*, 31 = Saloni, *Rzeshów*, 169 (Cut down in the forest, bent in the house, it lay under the horses and walked to the women). The motion of swinging the sieve is compared to walking. Siarkowski, 22 (It was cut down in the woods, it was fashioned at home, it rested behind the stove, it ran around the market), 40 (It idled with the horses, it hurried to the women); Kopernicki, 31. Russian: Sadovnikov, 368, 369; Arkhangel'skii, p. 77. Serbian: Novaković, p. 208, Nos. 8 (It grew among the horses, it danced among the maidens and touched their breasts), 9, 10, 11 (It grew in the forest, it grazed among the mares, and it danced among the women), and p. 209, Nos. 1 through 3. Hungarian: *Magyar Nyelvör*, II (1873), 43 = *ibid.*, III (1874), 38 = *ibid.*, XII (1883), 286 = *ibid.*, XIV (1885), 189, No. 3 (It grows in the woods, it gets fat in the meadows, it plays among women); *ibid.*, IX (1880), 37; *ibid.*, XIII (1884), 285 = *ibid.*, XXV (1896), 239 (It grows in the woods, it prospers in the meadows, they slap it in every house). Gypsy: Wlislocki, 46.

§ 6. A churn dash, a tap, or a faucet, or other implement associated with water or milk. Flemish: Joos, 115, 269. Spanish: Demófilo, 1017 through 1019, p. 373, No. 4, and p. 375, No. 12. Argentinian: Lehmann-Nitsche, 42. Lithuanian: Jurgelionis, 426 (Born in the forest, grown in the forest, it stabs everybody's throat.—Spoon), 472 (Born in a forest, raised in a barn, fastened through a hole, and it has never seen the sun.—Tap, faucet). Indian, Kashmiri: Knowles, 31 (It was born in the jungle, it gave birth in the jungle, on coming from the jungle it went out to dance.—The stick with which butter is churned).

The Lithuanian and Lettish well-sweep riddle, "Born in the wood, grown up in the wood, it comes to the house, it lifts up its tail"²⁸ illustrates the characteristic variations in the concept. In this instance the riddler suggests a horse or a dog, while the Kashmiri riddler had a person in mind.

§ 7. Implements associated with making cloth. FLAX BREAKER OR FLAIL. Flemish: Joos, 297. Lithuanian: Schleicher, p. 198 (Grown in the forest, it barks at home). Hungarian: *Magyar Nyelvör*, VI (1877), 423 = *ibid.*, XII

---

²⁷ Gustawicz, 382. For additional examples see his Nos. 381 and 383 through 387.
²⁸ Jurgelionis, 454; Bielenstein, 31.

(1883), 331 and 426 = *ibid.*, XXXI (1902), 532, No. 2 (They cut it in the woods, it resounds in the village). A more definite suggestion of a dog appears in "It grows in the woods, it barks in the village" (*ibid.*, IV [1875], 180 = *ibid.*, XIII [1884], 285 = *ibid.*, XXXVII [1908], 188). See also "They cut it in the woods, it neighs in the village" (Kriza, 43). HECKLE. German: Haffner, 203. Swedish: Ström, p. 152, "Kardan," 1; Geijer and Campbell, 25. Rumanian: Gorovei, 1132. Lettish: Bielenstein, 372 (Born in the wood, grown up in the wood, then it comes into the farmer's yard in order to bark). COMB. Spanish, Chilean: Flores, 582. DISTAFF. Danish: Kristensen, p. 106, § 292, No. 455a. Lithuanian: Jurgelionis, 505 (Grown in the forest, it waits for girls). LOOM. Rumanian: Gorovei, 1786; Papahagi, 9 (I grew in the woods, I was peeled in the woods, and at home they made *ritsch, ratsch!* with me). STICK FOR BEATING CLOTHES. Rumanian: Papahagi, 87 (I have been born in the forest, I have been cut in the forest, and now I have come to crying out in the village).

§ 8. Agricultural tools. PLOW. Rumanian: Gorovei, 476. Lithuanian: Jurgelionis, 552 (Born in a forest, grown in a forest, it goes out on a field and digs in the ground.—Wooden plow), 553. PLOW HANDLES. Polish: Gustawicz, 145 (Chopped down in the woods, fashioned at home, it squeals in the field). HARROW. Lettish: Bielenstein, 177 (Born in the forest, grown up in the forest, it comes to the people in order to scratch the dirt), 178 through 183. The riddler probably intended to suggest a hen scratching. Mordvin: Ahlqvist, p. 42, No. 16 (Born in the forest, it grew up in the forest, it doesn't creep back into the forest). SADDLE. Norwegian: Brox, *Ytre Senja*, 49. BRAKES ON A WAGON. Lithuanian: Jurgelionis, 588 (Born in the forest, grown up in the forest, it comes home to bark), 589 (Grown in the forest, it barks at home). FORK. Hungarian: Kriza, 24 (They cut it in the woods, it thrives in the meadow).

§ 9. Domestic tools. FORK FOR AN OVEN. Rumanian: Gorovei, 482. MORTAR. Georgian: Glushakov, p. 24, No. 14 (I was born in the forest, I grew up in the forest, and when I entered the house, I began to shout loudly). CLUB. Rumanian: Papahagi, 94.

§ 10. A cradle. Flemish: Joos, 201. French: Dardy, *L'Albret*, p. 331. Polish: Saloni, *Rzeshów*, 69 through 71, 72 (It grew in the forest, it had leaves, now it carries a soul and body); Siarkowski, 29 (It grew in the woods, it had many leaves, now it carries a soul and body), 29 var. (now it carries a sinful soul); Kopernicki, 30; Gustawicz, 152 through 157. This conception is very closely related to the ship riddle discussed in §1 above.

§ 11. A threshold. Lithuanian: Jurgelionis, 307 (Born in the forest, grown in the forest, it comes home to get in one's way). Bulgarian: Gubov, 279 (I grew in the forest, I came down to the field, and everybody sees me). Polish: Saloni, *Rzeshów*, 144 (It grew in the forest, it had leaves, it came home and lay down under the horse.—Stable floor). The last act might suggest a dog. The reference to the horse occurs in a different context in the sieve riddle, § 5 above. Turkish: Moshkov in Radlov, X, 270, No. 72.

§ 12. A windmill, a mill. Lithuanian: Jurgelionis, 487 (Grown in the forest, born in the forest, it goes out in the field and turns). Serbian: Novaković, p. 3, No. 2 (It was cut in the forest, it was dragged on the field, and it rattles on the water.—Wheel of water mill).

§ 13. A wooden shoe. Danish: Kristensen, p. 137, § 397, No. 633 (Grown in a forest, born in a stall, forged in a smithy). Catalan: Pelay y Briz, 251 (quoted above). Polish: Siarkowski, 100 (It had leaves in the woods; in the village it bears body and soul).[29]

§ 14. Plants. In the few instances in which a riddler gives a fruit or a plant as answer, he has probably erred by introducing the theme of his riddle into the answer, as in the Flemish nut riddles, "It grows in the wood, and it flowers in the wood, and it comes into the house to annoy girls" and "It grows in the wood, and it flowers in the wood, young people go to look for it, and the old can no longer take it in their teeth"[30] or the Argentinian description of the sacred palm, "I was born in the field, I was created on the mountain, I was made prisoner in the house, I come to be the daughter of God."[31]

1058. Grows i' the wood, an' whinnies i' the moor, / An' goes up an' down our house-floor.—A sweeping-brush (which is supposed to be of horsehair).
Gutch and Peacock, *Lincolnshire*, p. 399, No. 22.

1059a. Once it was green an' a-growin'; / Now it's dead an' a-ro'rin' [a-roaring].—Violin.
Fauset, *Southern Negro*, p. 288, No. 138.

1059b. Once 'twas green a-growin'; / Now 'tis dead a-singin'.—Fiddle.
Hudson, p. 86, No. 22.

1060. It grows in the woods; / it bellows in towns. / If you guess this riddle, / I'll give you five pounds.—A fiddle.
Farr, *Tennessee*, p. 318, No. 7.

1061a. What grows in the woods, / Winters in the town, / And earns its master many a crown?—A violin.
Fauset, *Nova Scotia*, p. 162, No. 101.

1061b. Grows i' the wood, an' yowls in the town, / An' addles it' [earns its] master many a crown.—A fiddle (the strings of which are cat-gut).
Gutch and Peacock, *Lincolnshire*, p. 400, No. 23.

1062. In the woods cryin' time, / I made my master many a dime.—Fiddle.
Fauset, *Southern Negro*, p. 283, No. 83.

---

[29] For similar themes see §§ 1, 10, above.
[30] Joos, 486, 490.
[31] Lehmann-Nitsche, 44. See the candle riddle quoted above (n. 3).

1063. Land Is White; Seed Is Black

The comparison of writing to strewing black seeds on white land is old and widely known. It often includes the idea of plowing for writing. Although riddlers have introduced many minor modifications, in the process of oral and literary transmission, they have nevertheless preserved the fundamental theme with surprising steadiness.

Some Eastern riddles contain the characteristic contrast of black and white, mention a field, and refer to animals. Since these animals are not said to be plowing, we may perhaps have an entirely different conception unrelated to the conception of black seeds and plowing in a white field. Examples are the Turkish "In the white field the black sheep grazes"[1] or the Modern Greek "A black steed runs on a white field, three hold it, two watch it."[2] Similar riddles are found in Lettish, as "A white meadow, black cattle, pleasant for a wise man to graze in,"[3] and in Mongolian, as "The enclosure is white, the sheep are black."[4] Still farther from the conception of plowing in a white field are such riddles as the Modern Greek "Three hold her when she gives birth, her birds are black, they go all over the world"[5] or "Three hold her while she gives birth. She bears black children and leaves them behind her."[6] Yet even in these we find the three men who hold the actor, just as in many comparisons of writing to plowing.

I am inclined to set apart from the conception of plowing various comparisons to birds. See the Turcoman "What sort of bird is this: how it multiplies particles of dust, there's little seed and much fruit. This bird has one mouth, two tongues. Many people are perplexed about this."[7] The Kashmiri say, "Black crows on a white bank. They are saying, 'Caw! Caw!'"[8] The Mongolian comparison to a dog is: "A black dog runs on the white snow."[9]

Scenes in which cattle, sheep, and goats appear in functions quite different from plowing can be conceived as variations and local adaptations of the original theme. See, as examples, the Icelandic "I saw three brothers bent at their work, moving along, all steadying themselves on one stick. Wherever that soiled stick went, it left behind fussy tracks. All these brothers obey one master. Two serve as guides lest the road be lost, the third lightens their

---

[1] Kowalski, *Zagadki*, 36.
[2] Polites, *Neohellenika Analekta*, I, 243, No. 285. For the themes of holding and watching see also the headnote to Nos. 970–975, § 6, above.
[3] For the reference to this riddle and other similar versions see the note to Nos. 1063a through 1063i.
[4] Kotvich, 199; Klukine, 23; Bazarov, 55.
[5] Polites, *Neohellenika Analekta*, I, 244, No. 286.
[6] Stathes, p. 348, No. 100. Compare Rumanian: Papahagi, 41.
[7] Samojlvich, 61. The two "tongues" are the nibs of the pen. The collector cites a parallel in Salikhov, *Kazan Tatar*, 58.
[8] Knowles, 109.
[9] Kotvich, 274.

labor";[10] the Modern Greek "White field and black goats"[11] and "A white meadow, black bulls. Happy is he who calls them";[12] the ingenious Lithuanian "Level fields, gray sheep, the herdsman has the whip behind his ears";[13] the Ossete "He sows black seed on a white field and what has been sowed speaks to the sower";[14] and the Mongolian "Black sheep, a white field"[15] or "He plowed the soil with five oxen and made a speech in Tibetan."[16] No colors are mentioned in the Crimean Tatar "They sow it with their hands and harvest it with their mouths."[17]

The variations in versions derived from the theme of a white field, black seed, and plowing are very great. In addition to those cited in the footnote see the Renaissance Latin versions of Johannes Lorichius:

> Seminibus variis est exornatus agellus,
> Praeteriens populus, quae sint ea semina nescit,
> Felix, qui videt, & fructus intellegit istos[18]

and Johannes Lauterbach:

> Atra seges (viden?) hic in campo cernitur albo:
> Praetereunt multi, nec patet illa seges.[19]

Adaptations of this manner of description to other themes than writing are rare. The riddler who supplies the answer "Sewing pearls on a black dress"[20] to a description of plowing in a field has probably forgotten the correct answer and has remedied his fault by a random guess. Such Finnish and Estonian descriptions of tools for making fire as "A stony field, an iron plow, and seeds of birch bark"[21] are better inventions that are clearly adapted from this riddle for writing. The Polish riddle, "A red coral plowed with some geese. He sowed black seeds over the field. He knew what was named.—Community bookkeeper,"[22] is badly confused. Quite a different conception appears in a Yakut description of a letter, "They say that there is that which has a white face, but its thoughts are speckled."[23]

Sigismund Szendrey's important commentary[24] on the Hungarian versions[25] is here added in a translation generously made for me by Arpad Steiner. Szendrey writes as follows:

---

[10] Árnason, 62.
[11] Sanders, 5.
[12] Stathes, p. 336, No. 28.
[13] Schleicher, p. 206.
[14] Schiefner, 53.
[15] Mostaert, 46. Compare n. 4 above.
[16] Bazarov, 117. The Mongols prefer to write in Tibetan.
[17] Filonenko, 18.
[18] Reusner, ed. 1602, p. 285.
[19] Ænigmata ([Frankfurt a. M.], 1601), p. 79.
[20] Cheremiss: Genetz, 68.
[21] Aarne and Krohn, 179 = Henssen, 102. Estonian: Wiedemann, p. 269.
[22] Gustawicz, 319.
[23] Piekarski, 238; Priklonskii, 90.
[24] Ethnographia, XXXII (1921), 70-71.
[25] These versions are given in the note to Nos. 1063a through 1063i below; the numbers in brackets are those used by Szendrey.

The nine components discernible in these riddles may be divided into three groups: (A) white soil, black seed; (B) the goose plows; the man drives (harrows); (C) sowing with care. These are symbols of (A) the paper and the letters; (B) the goose-quill and the man's work (sanding in place of blotting); (C) thinking.

The oldest record of this riddle may be read in the fifteenth-century French *Adeuineaux amoureux*. In the countless versions since written down, all of these nine elements—except harrowing—have been noted, but only the four elements of A are common to all versions. Consequently, Aarne[26] and before him Petsch[27] set up the archetype of this riddle in the form "White field, black seeds." Later, this was enlarged by C,[28] signifying writing or reading and its comprehension, and then by B signifying the execution of the writing. In one French, one Galician, and two Ukrainian instances C is lacking, as in "L'oie laboure, l'homme conduit, le champ blanc, la semence noir." Thus, the form of the non-Hungarian versions is, in general, A-B-C and in only four instances is it A-B.

In Hungarian folklore the form A-B, which is known only in the eastern Slavic territory of Hungary, does occur, and [also] C is joined to B alone[29] or to A-B[30] in such a manner, however, that it does not symbolize reading or writing and their understanding, but, as is more in accord with Hungarian mentality and ways of thinking, the intellectual work connected with writing, viz., thinking. Another Hungarian variation is seen in version No. [3], in which the second element of B, i.e., the man drives, was felt to be unnecessary beside the first element, but on the other hand the act of writing was felt to be incomplete without mention of sanding. Consequently, Hungarian mentality and ways of thinking produced not only a change in the form of the riddle but also a change in its meaning.

The changes did not stop here. When the steel pen had completely supplanted the goosequill, the expression "A goose plows it"[31] became unintelligible, and it was replaced by a symbol for the penholder or shaft (*lúd*), which is phonetically similar to goose (*rúd*). The riddle then assumed the following form: "White is its soil, black its seed, a shaft plows it, a man drives it, he sows with care."[32] Or, C was dropped. Or, B gained three elements, the third of which (harrowing) was added to the first two of Hungarian No. [3].

In the variants the change in the contradiction which signifies the act of writing rather than the thing written is still greater. In "Many black roads are built in a spacious white field"[33] all four elements of A and in fact the last two

---

[26] *Rätselforschungen*, I, 59.
[27] *Neue Beiträge*, pp. 135–137.
[28] Aarne, *Rätselforschungen*, I, 51–54.
[29] Hungarian, No. [4].
[30] Hungarian, Nos. [5], [6].
[31] Hungarian, No. [4], is latest occurrence of the phrase.
[32] Hungarian, No. [7]. An oral version collected by Szendrey in Szalonta.
[33] Hungarian, No. [9].

elements of B occur, but now in a completely different metaphor which accords with a peculiarly Hungarian manner of thinking.

The Hungarian version No. [10], "Black on white, in the hands of an ass; why has he it in his hands, if he knows nothing about it!" shows the widest variations. It contains only the first element of A, and the element C is striking because only this Hungarian version refers to literacy.

The curious Hungarian version No. [11], "White field, black seed, three are working, two are idling, the chick is drinking" agrees word for word with the French "Un champ blanc, la semence noire, trois qui travaillent, deux qui ne font rien et la petite poule qui boit,"[34] to which Aarne found no parallel.[35] If we consider that the Hungarian version is unique and is only fifteen years old,[36] it is clear without further investigation that a deliberately borrowed and cleverly translated French riddle has reached the folk. Consequently, this Hungarian version is only an interesting surprise and is by no means a valuable bit of evidence of the assimilative and transforming power of the Hungarian folk spirit.

Discussions of this riddle are unusually abundant; see my *Bibliography of Riddles*, pp. 156–157. Particularly important are Karl Müllenhoff, *Zeitschrift für deutsche Mythologie*, III (1855), 14, No. 16; Petsch, *Neue Beiträge*, pp. 134–137; C. Piancastelli, *Commento a un indovinello romagnolo* (Faenza, 1903); Schultz, *Rätsel aus dem hellenischen Kulturkreise*, II, 146; Karl Helm, "Zum Ackermann aus Böhmen," *Hessische Blätter für Volkskunde*, XII (1913), 217–218; Aarne, *Rätselforschungen*, I, 35–73; Flajšhans, pp. 15–16; N. Tomassia and M. Scherillo, "Un' antichissima cantilena georgica in latino volgare," *Rendiconti del Reale Istituto lombardo*, ser. 2, LVII (1924), 734–736; Pio Rajna, "Un indovinello volgare scritto alla fine del secolo VIII o al principio del IX," *Speculum*, III (1928), 291–313. A mention of this riddle would have been pertinent in Konrad Burdach's extensive commentary on *Der Ackermann aus Böhmen*, 3, 1, but he made none.

1063a. The land was white, / The seed was black. / It'll take a good scholar / To riddle me that.—Paper and writing.

Halliwell-Phillipps, *Popular Rhymes*, p. 144; Knortz, p. 226, No. 61; Hyatt, *Adams Co., Ill.*, p. 664, No. 10892.

1063b. The land was white, and the sea [seed] was black. / It will take a riddler to tell me that.—Paper and ink.

Parsons, *Bermuda*, p. 250, No. 32.

---

[34] Aarne, *Rätselforschungen*, I, 54.
[35] Neither Aarne nor Szendrey comments on the origin of this variation. It is a contamination with the virtually universal theme of finger-rhymes: the little finger gets something to eat or drink. See Sam Shiver, "Finger Rhymes," *Southern Folklore Quarterly*, V (1941), 221–234.
[36] It was written down in 1906.

1063c. Riddle me, riddle me, rine-e-go, / My father gave me some seed to sow. / The seed was black, the ground was white, / If you are a good scholar, / You can guess this by tomorrow night.—The ground was covered with snow and the boy could not plant the seed.
Hyatt, *Adams Co., Ill.*, p. 666, No. 10904.

1063d. My father gave me some seeds to sow. / The seeds were black, the ground was white. / Tell me that riddle Saturday night.—Ink on paper.
Fauset, *Nova Scotia*, p. 159, No. 81; Beckwith, *Jamaica*, p. 191, No. 71.

1063e. Me riddle, me riddle, me riddle, me row, / My fader had some seed to sow. / De lan' were white, de seed were black, / My fader gave me half of a pint.—Pen and ink.
Parsons, *Sea Islands, S.C.*, p. 161, No. 53.

1063f. Riddle me, riddle me, right-y-o, / Me mother gave me some seed to sow; / The seed was black, the ground was white. / Riddle me, riddle me, right-y-o.—Writing in ink.
Greenleaf, *Newfoundland*, p. 11, No. 27.

1063g. My father gave me seed to sow, / The seed was black / And the ground was white. / Riddle me that, an' I'll give you a pipe [variant: pint].—Writing a letter.
Green, *South Antrim*, 17.

1063h. Riddle me, riddle me, randybow, / My father gave me seed to sow, / The seed was black and the ground was white. / Riddle me that, an' I'll give you a pipe [variant: pint].—Writing a letter.
Green, *South Antrim*, 17 var.

1063i. Riddle-me, riddle-me, randy-bo! / My father gave me the seed to sow. / The seed was black and the ground was white. / Riddle-me, riddle-me, randy-bo.—Writing on white paper.
Praeger, *Béaloideas*, IV (1933–1934), 144, No. 3.

1064–1065. Does Not Bear (Fruit)

1064. My father had a thing, it hang and it never bear.—Rudder.
Parsons, *Bahamas*, p. 477, No. 59.

1065. My father has some things to hang, but they don't bear.—Windows.
Parsons, *Eleuthera and Watling's Islands, Bahamas*, p. 439, No. 2.

1066–1071. Flowers

1066. Somet'in' bloom in de mornin' an' wilt in de evenin'.—Flowers.
Parsons, *Sea Islands, S.C.*, p. 171, No. 142.

1067. Hangs and bears and never blooms.—Pot rack.
Hudson, p. 87, No. 28.

1068. If you walkin' along an' have a bunch of withered flowers, would you throw yer withered flowers to get a bunch of f'esh ones?—Ol' beau an' new beau.
Parsons, *Sea Islands, S.C.*, p. 163, No. 60.

1069. A dish full of all kinds of flowers, / You can't guess this riddle in two hours.—Honey.
Farr, *Tennessee*, p. 325, No. 103.

1070. Cannot Be Plucked

Descriptions of a person whom one cannot marry occur in various forms. They are most abundant in Africa or countries where African riddling is known, but the existence of a Scotch Gaelic parallel raises some difficult questions. Except for the English riddle here discussed, the answer is a girl rather than a man. Typical objects used as means of comparison are a tree having fruit one cannot eat,[1] bananas which one cannot eat,[2] and a chair in which one cannot sit.[3] Comparisons not represented in this collection are of very widely different kinds. The Turks say, "Come and go, come and go, come and bring. If it doesn't come, plead and bring from the untouched garden an unplanted pomegranate.—Virgin."[4] Natives in Togo and the Philippines call the person one cannot marry a tree that one cannot climb.[5] The Kxatla say, "Tell me: a quivering cane. Although you like it, you cannot cut [it]";[6] and the residents of Surinam, "My father has a barrel. The people of the house cannot take water from it, but outsiders can take.—Brother and sister cannot marry."[7] A few versions state the situation baldly; see the Dschagga "You lack women; why do you not marry the one whom you have before your eyes?—The sister, whom the brother cannot marry";[8] the Malagasy "What is good that one cannot have?—Another's wife";[9] and the rhetorical Kundu "If it were not, if it were not [my sister], then I should marry her."[10]

There are a few related riddles for mother, wife, and daughter or for unmarried persons, engaged persons, and married persons. The Turks speak in terms of animals: "I have three cows; of the first the milk is allowed and the flesh prohibited; of the second the flesh is permitted and the milk prohibited; and of the third the flesh is prohibited and the milk is prohibited.—Mother, wife, and daughter."[11] A similar theme is used of the pig in the Bulgarian "Its

---

[1] No. 1045.
[2] No. 1249.
[3] No. 1183.
[4] Hamizade, 404.
[5] Togo: Schönhärl, 52. Filipino: Starr, *Philippines*, 221, 222. For parallels to the description of an object that cannot be climbed, see the headnote to Nos. 1616–1627 below.
[6] Schapera, 92.
[7] Herskovits, p. 451, No. 100.
[8] Raum, p. 304, No. 7.
[9] G. Ferrand, 8.
[10] Ittmann, *Kundu*, 202.
[11] Kowalski, *Zagadki*, 121. For the first clause see Bulgarian: Chacharov, 31. Compare Stumme, *Tázerwalt*, 4.

flesh is eaten, but not its milk"[12] and of the bee in the Turkish "Its meat is forbidden; its milk is permitted."[13] South Carolinian riddlers compare a married person, an engaged person, and an unmarried person to a full glass, a half-full glass, and an empty one[14] or to a rigged, a half-rigged, or an unrigged ship.[15]

1070. A rose in de garden an' a rose outside. What one you take?—De rose in de garden is married man; de one outside, unmarried.
Parsons, *Sea Islands, S.C.*, p. 162, No. 58; Johnson, *St. Helena Island, S.C.*, p. 157.

1071. Disappear

A rare comparison of stars to flowers occurs in both Turkish and Indian riddling, but the two varieties of the theme do not seem to be related. The Turks draw a picture of a mosque, "Blue enameled minaret with a circular foundation. A hundred thousand flowers, one tulip.—Stars and moon,"[1] with a somewhat disordered parallel in "A thousand and one tulips, its bottom is its side, a thousand and one flowers, one tulip."[2] The abundant details in the Indian riddles are not fully intelligible: "The king's son is lying dead, and [there is nobody] to weep for him. The king's courtyard is lying [unswept], and [there is nobody to sweep it]. The flowers have bloomed, and there is no florist to pick them.—Moon, sky, stars"[3] and "The flowers of the jhingâ-creeper[4] are blooming, but there is nobody to pluck them. There lies a huge courtyard, but there is nobody to sweep it clean."[5] In a description of the Lord's angels Isaiah gives some ideas related to the comparison here discussed: "And all the host of heaven shall be dissolved, and the heavens shall be rolled together as a scroll, and all their host shall fall down, as the leaf falleth off from the vine and as a falling fig from the fig tree."[6] Even more similar to our riddle is St. John's description of the opening of the sixth seal at the Last Judgment: "And the stars of heaven fell into the earth, even as a fig tree casteth her untimely figs, when she is shaken of a mighty wind."[7]

The comparison of the sky to a field has already been noted in a riddle comparing the stars to sheep.[8] There are several instances in which the sky is a field and the stars are growing plants. The oldest of them appears to be the verses of Giovanni Francesco Straparola.[9] See also the Italian "There is a meadow quite full of carnations. Even if the Pope comes with all his

---

[12] Chacharov, 107.
[13] Hamizade, 50.
[14] See No. 1197 below.
[15] See No. 1166.
[1] Kowalski, *North Bulgaria*, 10. See also Radlov, VII, 384, No. 139.
[2] Kúnos, 52.
[3] Bengali: Mitra, *Sylhet*, p. 119, No. 23.
[4] *Luffa acutangula.*
[5] Bengali: Mitra, *Chittagong*, p. 658, No. 2 = Mitra, *Notes on Ho Riddles*, p. 102.
[6] Is. 34:4.
[7] Rev. 6:13.
[8] See Nos. 484a through 484d above.
[9] *Le piacevoli notti*, XI, 1.

popedom, even he is not able to carry away one carnation";[10] the Albanian "A plain full of red flowers";[11] the Modern Greek "A plain and melons, these two are worth everything";[12] the Mordvin "A blue field sown with silver";[13] the SeSuto "The pumpkin in the meadow.—Moon";[14] the Kashmiri "I sowed mahá[15] in a field of air; yesterday I saw it but tomorrow it is nowhere";[16] and the Tagalog "Without branches, without roots, it is loaded with flowers."[17] The conception of the sun as a flower, as in the Indian "The sky is my mother and sister. The earth is my camping ground. A flower blossoms without branch or leaves,"[18] seems to be a related theme.

The various riddles describing the stars as flowers appear to be, with the exception of the Italian and Albanian versions, more or less casual inventions which have no relations to one another. The rather restricted popularity of this idea is worthy of note. Comparisons of the stars to fruits visible at night and lost to view in the morning, as suggested in the Kashmiri text cited, are discussed at length below.[19] They may perhaps be derived from a single invention. The theme of the field of flowers representing the stars is reversed in the Suk riddle for solanum fruit: "There are stars on the plain,"[20] which refers to a field covered with yellow fruits.

A few other riddles refer to a field, but conceive it in ways not mentioned thus far. The Kamba "A very large garden and one tree-stump.—Sky and moon"[21] employs the obscure comparison of the sun or moon to a stump.[22] It is analogous to the Wanamwezi "A big field, two edible gourds."[23] The Kxatla "Tell me: a black garden with white corn.—Sky and stars"[24] seems to be an adaptation of a concept otherwise used to describe writing.[25] The Vogul "A field of peas, a hundred stones,"[26] which perhaps makes a distinction between the larger and smaller stars, conceives the scene as a plowman might. The similar Armenian "It is impossible to plow up the field, and it is impossible to count the stars"[27] has admitted the answer "stars" into the riddle in place, probably, of some such word as "peas."[28]

1071. Me fader got a rose-tree in him yard; eb'ry night he blow, an' by time de fe clean, eb'ry one gone.—Stars.
Beckwith, *Jamaica*, p. 189, No. 54b.

---

[10] Schneller, *Wälschtirol*, p. 256, No. 27.   [11] Pedersen, 14.
[12] Polites, *Neohellenika Analekta*, I, 201, No. 46.
[13] Ahlqvist, p. 41, No. 26.   [14] Norton and Velaphe, 23.
[15] *Phaseolus maximus* or *P. radiatus*.   [16] Knowles, 20.
[17] Rizal, p. 46.   [18] Elwin and Hivale, p. 74, No. 71.
[19] See the headnote to No. 1094 below.
[20] Beech, p. 45, No. 1.   [21] Lindblom, 75.
[22] See the headnote to No. 1252, nn. 4–6, below.
[23] Dahl, 89.   [24] Schapera, 6.
[25] See above, Nos. 1063a, 1063b, and 1063d through 1063i.
[26] Ahlqvist, *Vogul*, 12.   [27] Grigorov, p. 123, No. 14.
[28] See also Flajšhans, pp. 21–22.

1072–1099. Fruits, Seeds

1072–1073. Form

1072. Dere is somet'in' bear on a tree. When it's young, it have water dat you drink an' have not'in' in it but water. When it became ripe, it havin' water an' somet'in' to eat in it.—Coconut.
Parsons, *Antilles*, III, 422, Montserrat, 18.

1073. A riddle, a riddle, / Tell me this riddle, / Perhaps you know it, perhaps not. / Something having a big seed.—Mammy apple.
Parsons, *Antilles*, III, 430, St. Kitts, 9.

1074–1089. Color

1074. Once on a time something bear on a tree, when it is young, inside it is white, and outside it is green, havin' black seed. When it ripe, it still green. Havin' a load of seeds, black seeds.—Sour sop.
Parsons, *Antilles*, III, 430, St. Kitts, 4.

1075. Something bear upon a tree, when it is green, outside red; when it is ripe, outside soft.—Custard apple.
Parsons, *Antilles*, III, 430, St. Kitts, 5.

1076a. Once upon a time something bear upon a tree, when it's not ripe, it has no flesh, when it's ripe, skin black, inside white.—Skinnip.
Parsons, *Antilles*, III, 430, St. Kitts, 6 var.

1076b. Once upon a time something bear upon a tree, when it's not ripe, it has no flesh; when it's ripe, outside green and inside white.—Skinnip.
Parsons, *Antilles*, III, 430, St. Kitts, 6.

1077. A riddle ma riddle, / Come to tell you a story: / Once upon a time something bear on a tree, when it ripe, outside red, an' inside red, got a lot of seeds.—Pupaw [papaw].
Parsons, *Antilles*, III, 430, St. Kitts, 8.

1078a. A riddle ma riddle, / Come to tell you a story: / Once upon a time something bear on a tree, when it ripe, outside red, an' inside red, got a lot of seeds.—Guava.
Parsons, *Antilles*, III, 430, St. Kitts, 8 var.

1078b. Me riddle, me riddle, / Tell yer this riddle. / Something bear on a tree, inside white, outside green.—Guava.
Parsons, *Antilles*, III, 430, St. Kitts, 10.

1079. Me riddle, me riddle, / Perhaps a tiggle. / Something bear on a tree, / When it's not ripe, it's green. / Inside black. / When it ripe, inside yellow. / Havin' eight seed.—Muckle lime.
Parsons, *Antilles*, III, 426, Antigua, 26.

1080. Ma riddle ma riddle, / Perhaps I can tell you dis riddle / An' perhaps not. / It had somet'ing grow on a tree big and roun', it ripe green and it's white inside, wid plenty of white seed.—Calabash (gobee).
Parsons, *Antilles*, III, 443, St. Croix, 13.

1081. Somet'in' bears on a tree, when it is not ripe, it is white, when it full, it is white; when it ripe, it is white.—White bean.
Parsons, *Antilles*, III, 437, St. Martin, 27.

1082. Somet'ing bears on a tree, when it is not ripe, outside it is green an' havin' plenty of small seed, an' when it is ripe outside it is yellow.—Orange.
Parsons, *Antilles*, III, 429, Nevis, 28.

1083. Dere is somet'in' bear on a tree. Green outside. When it is ripe it is red inside. Tell me dat frote [fruit] name.—Watermelon.
Parsons, *Antilles*, III, 422, Montserrat, 20.

1084a. Me riddle, me riddle, / Something bear on a tree, when it is ripe it is red.—Pomegranate.
Parsons, *Antilles*, III, 427, Antigua, 36.

1084b. I went to de mountain to look fah wood. I meet a big long tree, bear a fruit red outside and seed inside.—Pomegranate.
Parsons, *Antilles*, III, 437, St. Martin, 37.

1084c. Dere's a small t'ing which grows on a tree its outside is red, and in de inside have some small seed and de t'ing of itself is painted. Can you guess what it is?—Answer lacking.
Parsons, *Antilles*, III, 442, St. Croix, 2.

1085. My fader had a tree, it bear fruit, outside green and inside white.—Coconut.
Parsons, *Bahamas*, p. 474, No. 28.

1086a. Dis is a t'ing. Dere's a tree it bear fruit once every year. It have green inside, an' green outside; and when it comes certain time, it is yellow.—Mango-fruit.
Johnson, *Antigua*, p. 88, No. 60.

1086b. A riddle, a riddle, / Perhaps a teegle, / Something bear on a tree, / When it is green it is green, / When it is ripe it is yellow. / Have one seed.—Mango.
Parsons, *Antilles*, III, 426, Antigua, 25.

1086c. Once upon a time something bear on a tree, when it is young, it is green, inside it is white; when it ripe, outside it is yellow, and inside it is yellow. It havin' one seed.—Mango.
Parsons, *Antilles*, III, 430, St. Kitts, 2.

1086d. Me riddle, me riddle, / Tell yer this riddle. / Perhaps you might get it, / And perhaps not. / Outside green and have a big seed.—Mango.
Parsons, *Antilles*, III, 422, St. Kitts, 12.

1087. Dere is somet'in' bear on a tree. When it is young it is white. When it is ripe it is either red or yellow. De outside is green. It have water —Pumpkin.
Parsons, *Antilles*, III, Montserrat, 19.

1088. Something be on a tree. Outside yellow, and inside yellow.—Clamcherry.
Parsons, *Antilles*, III, 428, Nevis, 6.

1089. Have some little long stems, outside green, inside white.—Bread fruit.
Parsons, *Antilles*, III, 431, St. Kitts, 13.

1090–1095. Function

1090. There was a tree yander have something on it. When de wind blow he shake, when de wind stop, he stop shake.—Pigeon pease.
Parsons, *Antilles*, III, 422, Montserrat, 15.

1091. Dere is somet'in' bears on a tree. De skin to t'row away, an' de flesh to eat.—Mango.
Parsons, *Antilles*, III, 432, St. Eustatius, 8 var.

1092. Dere is somet'in' bears on a tree. De skin to t'row away, an' de flesh to eat.—Banana.
Parsons, *Antilles*, III, 432, St. Eustatius, 8.

1093–1095. Fruits on a Tree or in a Dish (Pail)

Riddlers compare stars to fruits either on a tree[1] or in a dish. The distribution of these two forms indicates that we have two different riddles. It is uncertain whether the comparison of stars to fruits on a tree is connected with the mythological notion of the world-tree.[2] The comparison of stars to fruits on a tree often contains the additional detail that the fruits vanish in the daytime.[3]

The comparison of stars to fruits, grains, or seeds, which are usually said to be in a dish or scattered broadcast, is widely known and exhibits great variation in details.[4] It does not seem to be known to English riddlers. For examples see Spanish, Argentinian: Lehmann-Nitsche, 556. Arabic: Giacobetti, 24 (A flat plate covered with apples). African, Nuer: Huffman, p. 104, No. 1 (Guess what the red dates are that are in the sky but never fall). Kosi: Ittmann, *Kosi*, 172 (Beans are scattered over Mr. Pende's city). Indian, Kashmiri: Knowles, 38 (How many grains are there in one *trak*[5] of mang?[6] How many streets are there in the villages and cities? How many virgins are there?) The collector does not fully elucidate these queries. The virgins may be constellations. Bihari: Mitra, *Bihari Life*, p. 46, No. 31 (A handful of parched rice scattered over the whole yard). Ho: Haldar, 4 (A handful of fried Indian

---
[1] Nos. 1093 through 1094e.
[2] See the headnotes to Nos. 544 and 1037–1038.
[3] Riddles in which the objects are said to be countless are listed in the note to No. 1095.
[4] See the headnote to No. 1094.   [5] Dish.   [6] Beans.

corn is scattered broadcast in space). Hindi: Kavyopadhyaya, 46 (A basketful of fried paddy, which cannot be counted). Indonesian, Tabaru: Fortgens, 24 (Jasmine buds, a large dishful). Filipino: Starr, *Philippines*, 157 (A plate of roasted rice can be spread all over the town). American Indian, Quechua: Quijada Jara, 37 (On a blue field there is toasted maize).   e

In southern Europe, riddlers often compare the stars to nuts in a dish. See Serbian: Novaković, p. 128, No. 3 (The sieve is full of hazelnuts. In the middle there is a walnut). Albanian: Hahn, p. 162, No. 64 (A sieve full of nuts on the roof tiles). Modern Greek: Dieterich, *Rätseldichtung*, p. 90; Abbott, p. 317, No. 49 (Over the tiles of my roof there is a sieve full of hazelnuts). Turkish: Kowalski, *North Bulgaria*, 38 (I have a sieve full of hazelnuts, in it I have a walnut); Kowalski, *Asia Minor*, 25 = Hamizade, 731 (I have a sieve full of walnuts. I count, I count; there is no end). Crimean Tatar: Filonenko, 64 (Above the roof a sieve of nuts). Ossete: Schiefner, 4 (Grain is being dried on our house roof). In some versions the nuts are seen at night and are invisible during the day.[7]

Riddlers often compare the stars to vegetables. See Russian: Sadovnikov, 1853 (Beyond our window there is a basketful of turnips), 1854 (The trough is filled with cucumbers), 1866; Arkhangel'skii, p. 75 (Glance out the window; there stands a basket of turnips). Mordvin: Paasonen, 356 (I looked through the window. A basketful of turnips was in front of the window). Modern Greek: Stathes, p. 346, No. 87 (In your house, in mine, onions are spread out). African, Nyika: Hollis, *Nyika*, p. 137, No. 5 (Spread out the mat and let us eat some fruit). The stars in the sky are often conceived as plants growing in a field.[8]

In some versions the grains are said to lie scattered on a blanket or hide. See the Lettish "A blue blanket full of ears of wheat," "A gray woolen blanket full of white peas," and "My father had a pelt full of ears of wheat";[9] the Russian reference to a mat covered with little kernels;[10] and the Bulgarian "I spread the buffalo hide. I placed peas on it and a billy goat to guard it."[11] This idea is related to the conception of stars as lice on a blanket,[12] but apparently has no connection with the notions of the sky as a sheet that cannot be folded and the stars as coins that cannot be counted.[13] A somewhat different version of the theme occurs in the Kanuri "Two thousandfold ones on a mat. —Sun and moon."[14]

Some minor variations have obscured the full appropriateness of some com-

---

[7] See the headnote to No. 1094 below.
[8] See No. 1071 above.
[9] Bielenstein, 129, 130, 128.
[10] Sichler, p. 755. See also Sichler, p. 118; Sadovnikov, 1863, 1900.
[11] Gubov, 251. See also Estonian: Dido, 24.
[12] See the note to No. 1226 below.
[13] See Nos. 1215, 1216, 1227a, and 1227b.
[14] Lukas, 24.

parisons. In the Russian "Peas have been scattered over twelve mats,"[15] there is an allusion to the twelve months of the year. The theme is considerably altered in the Russian "Peas have spilled over a hundred roads. No one will gather them up, neither a tsar, nor a tsarina, nor a comely maiden, nor a whitefish," with the variant ". . . No one can pick them up, neither preachers nor deacons nor government officials, God alone can gather them,"[16] and also in the Kashub parallel, "Mroch scattered peas and could only pick them up at daybreak."[17]

Stars are often called fruit too numerous to count,[18] coins too numerous to count,[19] eggs or pearls or other things,[20] and (more rarely) articles of food.[21]

The riddles here discussed are closely related to the conception of the stars as figs and to that of stars as the seeds in a fig.[22] In many Eastern riddles the notion of grains or seeds scattered about represents the stars. See the Modern Greek "In your parlor and in my parlor onions are scattered about,"[23] "I was sunning little seeds atop my house," and "A long garden, a wide garden, many citrous fruits, two of them large ones";[24] the Arabic "A bushel of beans is scattered from here to Stambul";[25] the Turkish "My wheat is scattered on the ice"[26] and "In the evening I sowed and there was a great deal; in the morning I looked and there was nothing";[27] the Sukuma "Cultivating a field, I scatter seeds";[28] and the Filipino "The stars, grains of maize, disappear with the dawn."[29] Riddlers often call the stars objects that are seen only at night and disappear with the dawn.[30]

1093. Me fader hab a pepper-tree an' it nebber ripe till night come.—Stars.
Beckwith, *Jamaica*, p. 189, No. 55.

1094. Vanish in the Daytime

A special variety of the comparison of stars to fruits consists in declaring that the fruits or nuts are seen only at night and vanish in the daytime. The southeastern European comparison of stars to hazelnuts occurs with this modification in French, Catalan, and Spanish riddling. See French: Parsons, *Antilles*, III, 413, Marie Galante, 10. Catalan: Pelay y Briz, 78. Spanish: Demófilo, 433; Rodríguez Marín, 264. Argentinian: Lehmann-Nitsche, 540. Chilean:

---

[15] Sadovnikov, 1852g. [16] Sadovnikov, 1852, 1852a.
[17] Patock, *Strellin*, 6. Mroch may mean "twilight."
[18] No. 1095 below. [19] See Nos. 1227a, 1227b.
[20] See the headnote to No. 1227.
[21] See the headnote to Nos. 1230–1234, nn. 41–45.
[22] For discussion of this theme see R. Eisler, *Weltenmantel und Himmelszelt* (Munich, 1910), pp. 32, 520.
[23] Polites, *Neohellenika Analekta*, I, 211, No. 103; Sakellarios, p. 290, No. 16.
[24] Polites, *Neohellenika Analekta*, I, 213, No. 115, and p. 252, No. 336.
[25] Littmann, p. 47.
[26] Menges, p. 86, No. 17; Radlov, I, 262, No. 19.
[27] Hamizade, 730. [28] Augustiny, 47.
[29] Starr, *Philippines*, 156.
[30] See No. 1071 above and Nos. 1094a through 1094e below.

Flores, 272. Cuban: Massip, 64 (A little basket of hazelnuts, gathered up by day and scattered at night). Dominican Rep.: Andrade, 145a. New Mexican: Campa, 125. Porto Rican: Mason, 226a through 226g. These numerous Spanish parallels throw doubt on the native origin of the Aztec "What is the dish of nuts that is gathered by day and scattered at night?"[1] The Kanuri "When I had washed my calabash and had set it out to dry, and when it afterwards became morning, then it was gone.—Moon"[2] differs somewhat from the preceding conception. In Chile and in the Dominican Republic, riddlers have reversed the idea to make a riddle for chickens: "A plate of hazelnuts, which are together by night and are scattered by day."[3]

In some instances the comparison of stars to nuts seems to be independent of the previously cited texts from the shores of the Mediterranean and from Spanish America. See the Kundu "My mother bequeathed me bowls of peanuts at the door, but soon they were there no longer"[4] and "I cut an oil palm; nothing in it but worthless nuts, only one real oil nut,"[5] which has a variants in the Duala "I cut a palm nut; it had only little worthless nuts except for one large palm nut."[6] The large nut is the moon.

I can cite few analogous comparisons to persons; see the Crimean Tatar "Yes, we were, we were thirty-two maidens, sitting on a board and with the approach of dawn we disappeared"[7] and the Pangwe "The father gave birth to a daughter. She is never seen in the day, only at night.—Moon."[8] In the Tatar riddle the number of the maidens suggests that the riddler has also had in mind a riddle for the teeth, but the construction of the riddle resembles more the Russian riddle for stars and riddles for dumplings.[9]

1094a. Me fader hab a pepper-tree; eb'ry night all de pepper ripe, an eb'ry morning you wouldn't find one pepper an de tree.—Stars.
Beckwith, *Jamaica*, p. 189, No. 54.

1094b. I go to bed and leave my pepper-tree full of peppers, and wake in the morning, there isn't one there.—Stars.
Beckwith, *Jamaica*, p. 189, No. 54a.

1094c. My moder have a pepper tree, / In the night it have plenty peppers, / In the day it have none.—Stars.
Parsons, *Antilles*, III, 363, Trinidad, 6.

1094d. My fader has a pepper tree. In night it is full of yellow pepper, and in morning there are none. What's that?—Stars.
Parsons, *Antilles*, III, 422, Montserrat, 24.

---

[1] E. B. Tylor, *Primitive Culture*, 3d ed., I, 92; Abbott, p. 317, No. 49; Pauer, 49, citing Sahagún, *Historia general de Nueva España*, and Kingsborough, *Antiquities of Mexico*, p. 178.
[2] Lukas, 11. [3] Flores, 296; Andrade, 150. [4] Ittmann, *Kundu*, 98.
[5] Ittmann, *Kundu*, 146. [6] Ebding, 73. [7] Filonenko, 28.
[8] Tessmann, 7. For comparisons of the moon to a girl, see the headnote to No. 1001, n. 13, above.
[9] See the headnote to Nos. 489–490, §§ 3–4, above.

1094e. My father had a ya'd full of mangos. When he wake up in the morning, all was gone.—Stars.
Parsons, *Antilles*, III, 373, Grenada, 65.

1095. Apples Cannot Be Counted

In riddling, the apple occurs now and again[1] as a symbol for the sun or moon and (more rarely) for the stars. See the Lettish "The air is full of nuts, an apple in the middle," "A field full of nuts, an apple in the middle," "A sack full of cracked grain, an apple in the middle";[2] and the Arabic "A flat rock covered with apples."[3] It is uncertain what mythological significance can be given to such comparisons.

Since riddles for the celestial bodies and for the year are often closely related, it is pertinent to cite some Serbian comparisons of the months to apples. The texts are as follows: "The tsar sent to the tsarina twelve golden apples in a pail, in every apple there were four quarters, and in every quarter there were seven seeds"; "There is a bowl, in it are twelve apples, in every apple four quarters"; "The tsar sent twelve apples to the tsarina, in each apple there were four flowers"; "The tsar sent to the tsarina, in a golden pail, twelve golden stars, they could not arrive for a whole year"; and "The tsar sent to the tsarina, in a golden pail, twelve golden apples, they could not arrive for a whole year."[4]

1095. Me fader hab a tree full apple an' not a man can count them.—Stars.
Beckwith, *Jamaica*, p. 189, No. 56.

1096-1099. Flour (Fruit) of England (Virginia), Fruit (Flour) of Spain

The riddler puns on the word "flour," which the hearer is expected to understand as "flower" and to contrast with "fruit." Katherine Thomas finds here an allusion to the marriage of Philip II of Spain and Mary Tudor,[1] but this explanation is more than doubtful. Nor need we see in the concluding words a reference to the arrival of Count Egmont bearing the betrothal ring.

1096-1099. Fruit of England, etc.

1096a. Flour of England, fruit of Spain, / Met together in a shower of rain; / Put in a bag, tied round with a string. / If you'll tell me this riddle, / I'll give you a ring.—Plum-pudding.
Halliwell-Phillipps, *Nursery Rhymes*, p. 124; Parsons, *Bermuda*, p. 250, No. 27; Johnson, *Antigua*, p. 85, No. 24; Greenleaf, *Newfoundland*, p. 10, No. 19. Had a napkin tied

---

[1] See other references in Nos. 1215, 1216, the headnote to Nos. 1093-1095, and the notes to Nos. 1093, 1094a through 1094e, and 1215.
[2] Bielenstein, 702, 703, 704. In the last version he cites a variant "peas" for "cracked grain."
[3] Giacobetti, 24.
[4] Novaković, p. 31, Nos. 1, 2, and p. 32, Nos. 2, 3, 10.

[1] *The Real Personages of Mother Goose* (Boston, n.d. [1930]), pp. 110-111.

with string: Beckwith, *Jamaica*, p. 213, No. 236. Riddle me that and I'll give you a ring: Fitzgerald, p. 187 (Irish). Flower of England: Parsons, *Barbados*, p. 278, No. 15. Gold ring: Fauset, *Nova Scotia*, p. 149, No. 35; Redfield, *Tennessee*, p. 37, No. 14.

1096b. The fruit of England / And the flower of Spain / Met together in a shower of rain. / Put them in a bag / And tie them with a string / If you guess this riddle I'll give ye a ring.—Plum pudding.
  Carter, *Mountain White*, p. 78.

1096c. The fruit of England and the flower of Spain / Met together in a shower of rain, / Bound with a napkin, tied with a string, / Tell me this riddle, and I'll give you a ring.—Plum-pudding.
  Johnson, *Antigua*, p. 85, No. 24.

1096d. Flower of England, / Fruit of Spain, / All met together in a shower of rain. / Bound wid a napkin, / Tied wid a string, / Ef you tell me dat riddle, / I give you a ten poun' gold ring.—Plum pudding.
  Parsons, *Antilles*, III, 424, Antigua, 7.

1096e. Flower from England, / Fruit from Spain, / Put together in a shower of rain.—Steam pudding.
  Fauset, *Nova Scotia*, p. 149, No. 35 var.

1096f. Flower of Virginia, / Fruit of Spain, / Met together in a shower of rain. / Put in a bag, / Tie it up with a string. / Tell me this riddle, I'll give you a pin.—Plum pudding.
  Bacon and Parsons, *Virginia*, p. 324, No. 109. I'll give you a ring: Hyatt, *Adams Co., Ill.*, p. 665, No. 10895.

1096g. Flower of Virginia, fruit of Spain / Met together in a shower of rain. / Tell me this riddle and I'll give you a penny.—Plum pudding.
  Fauset, *Philadelphia*, p. 555, No. 25.

1096h. Flower of Virginia, fruit of Spain / Met together in a shower of rain; / Put in a bag tied round with a string. / If you tell me this riddle, I'll give you a pin.—Plum-pudding.
  Knortz, p. 219, No. 32.

1096i. Flower of England, sugar of Spain / Put together in a shower of rain. / Tell me this riddle, I'll give you a pie.—Plum pudding.
  Parsons, *Antilles*, III, 443, St. Croix, 7.

1096j. Flour of England, fruit of Spain / Met together in a shower of rain. / Homespun gown and Patenick hat. / I'll give you an hour / To tell me that.—A Christmas pudding.
  Sayce, *Montgomeryshire*, p. 17.

1097. Flour of England, fruit of Spain, / Wet an old lady in a shower of rain / With a napkin tied with a string, / Unfold this riddle, / I'll give you a gold ring.—Pudding.
  Parsons, *Bermuda*, p. 250, No. 27 var.

1098. A riddle, a riddle, aree, / Boun' with a napkin, / Tied with a string. / Tell me this riddle / And I'll give you a gol' ring.—Black pudding. You take out pig belly, clean it, grate potatoes and put in, cook in a pot with water.
Parsons, *Barbados*, p. 278, No. 14.

1099. Flower of Virginia, fruit of Spain, / Two meet together in a shower of rain. / Put in a bag and tie it wid a string. / If you guess dat riddle, / I'll give you a pin.—Dat's a man and woman, married. Dey kissin'.
Johnson, *St. Helena Island, S.C.*, p. 159, No. 37.

Chapter VII

COMPARISONS TO THINGS

Nos. 1100–1259

THE RIDDLES in this chapter involve comparisons to objects that lack life. These objects may be either found in nature or manufactured by man. The means of comparison chosen by a riddler and the answer to his riddle ordinarily belong to different categories. A lifeless shoe is compared to an animal that runs about,[1] and the head or parts of the head are compared to a house in a great variety of ways.[2] Such contrasts of animate and inanimate things are very numerous. An analogous contrast of natural and manufactured objects appears in various riddles in this chapter. The sky is compared to a sheet,[3] and the moon to a lamp.[4] In some texts the riddler has proceeded in a different fashion by describing the qualities or functions of the answer in such a way as to suggest a conflict with ordinary experience: a hole grows larger when cut[5] or an egg has no flesh and bone but after a while it walks alone.[6] Most things grow smaller when cut and do not walk without flesh and bone.

In this chapter the arrangement begins with comparisons to natural objects and goes on to comparisons to manufactured things.

1100–1117. Objects in Nature

Comparisons to natural objects that have no life are not numerous. They may have pictorial quality and suggest a scene or may concern only a stick, a road, or a gully. Comparisons to a scene are somewhat more numerous than this classification indicates. Scenes in which an animal or a plant is present will be found in earlier chapters. A riddler may compare milk to an animal that runs over hills and valleys,[1] or the eyes and eyelashes to pools surrounded by trees.[2]

1100–1108. Landscape

Riddlers often compare the human body or its members, usually the head or the hair, to a scene or to individual objects in nature.[1] The following riddles, which constitute a type very rarely found in English tradition, combine sev-

---

[1] See Nos. 445a, 445b, 453a through 454c, 456a through 456c.
[2] See Nos. 918, 1143a through 1144, 1146 through 1149a.
[3] Nos. 1215, 1217, 1219.
[4] No. 1189.
[5] Nos. 1691a, 1691b.
[6] Nos. 1237a through 1237d and 1237f through 1237h.

[1] Nos. 447 and 449a through 452.
[2] No. 1044.

[1] See the headnote to Nos. 459–460.

eral details of a landscape or a scene otherwise unified to represent either the whole human body[2] or the head.[3] In the best riddles of this sort the scene has either the unity of nature or that of a collection of objects belonging to a single sphere of activity. Examples are such very interesting and picturesque scenes as the Dutch picture of a street, "Two lanterns, two dirty allies, two files of soldiers, and a red huckster,"[4] which signifies the head and its parts; the Norwegian comparison of a man to stalks, root, and forest;[5] and the Mordvin "I have a little stove, in it are spelt grains, on the ground is a dungfork,"[6] which signifies the human body. In connection with the last riddle it is perhaps pertinent to say that a dungfork has two tines and is therefore an adequate equivalent of the legs. This Mordvin riddle is particularly interesting for its great similarity to the riddles describing a man in terms of these household objects but proceeding from below upward.[7]

Some comparisons of the human body and its members to a scene in nature are extremely ingenious and well-conceived combinations of details. The Omaha "There is a place cut up by gullies. What is it?—An old woman's face"[8] resembles the Pangwe "Crisscross network, roots of the *Bridelia stenocarpa.*—The back of the hand."[9] Obviously, however, these inventions are quite independent of one another. In "The flat mountain with the wheat on the side of it"[10] the SeSuto portray the head. The more fully described scene in the Hungarian "On the top snow, in the valley water, roses do not bloom, and thirty-two brothers are not together [i.e., no longer all together].—Hair, eyes, face, and teeth of an old man"[11] is perhaps related to the Biblical description of old age.[12] Perhaps the most clearly conceived and most picturesque of these comparisons is the Baiga "In the valley is a temple. On the temple sit two fireflies. Above the fireflies is a hill. On the hill are tigers and bears."[13]

Riddlers only rarely characterize the details by assigning specific acts to the figures as in the Hungarian "It mumbles, it sniffles, it is furtive, it resounds when knocked, a green pasture, in the green pasture short colts,"[14] which describes the mouth, nose, eyes, head, hair, and lice.

When the riddler fails to perceive and to maintain the fundamental conception, he often admits heterogeneous and inappropriate elements. Conse-

---

[2] See below, in this headnote, and see the note to No. 1100.
[3] See No. 1100, the headnote to No. 1100, and the headnote and the note to No. 1101.
[4] Sinninghe, p. 8, No. 4.   [5] Brox, *Ytre Senja*, 167.
[6] Paasonen, 185.   [7] See the note to No. 1100 below.
[8] J. O. Dorsey, "Omaha Sociology," *Report of the Bureau of American Ethnology*, III, (1884), 324. Compare this riddle with the Mongolian "The Tunke steppe without vegetation.—A woman's face" (Klukine, 12) and see my comment in "American Indian Riddles," *Journal of American Folklore*, LVII (1944), 6.
[9] Tessmann, 80.   [10] Norton and Velaphe, 38.
[11] Kálmány, III, 175, No. 59.
[12] Eccles. 12:3–4, and see the headnote to No. 46, n. 3, above.
[13] Elwin, p. 474, No. 99.   [14] Kálmány, III, 159, No. 14.

quently, these comparisons of the human body or of the head to a landscape vary greatly in their details. It is uncertain what ones can be traced to a common origin.

A very curious kind of riddling consists in accumulating many apparently unrelated objects, the implication being that they belong to one and the same object.[15] It is usually found in riddles describing a man. The description ordinarily begins at the man's feet and proceeds upward to his head. The objects seem not to be chosen entirely at random, since they are often tools and utensils found in the neighborhood of the house and barn. Typical introductory elements are "There are two poles, on the two poles is a mill," and at this point the riddler often introduces a great variety of elements. Although it is widely known on the European continent, this manner of riddling does not seem to be known to English riddlers.

A somewhat similar pattern, which usually names objects found in nature and not domestic utensils, passes from above downward. The answer is ordinarily the human head. Typical examples are the Irish "A little spring of clear water at the top of the cliff, a little window of glass in front of it, and a little double door on it,"[16] which does not get beyond describing the eye; the Icelandic "I saw a castle on a height, with five doors: a fair building. It had two splendid windows and thirty-two towers. There a rich lady dwells, but on the other hand [she is] a wretched tyrant";[17] the Hungarian "Matato in a dense forest, below Matato the blinking one, below the blinking one the sniffling one, below the sniffling one the gaping one, below the gaping one is Rottytinto."[18] This, like the Polish "A grove, a winker, a hairy breather, an eater, a little drum, and a trumpet.—Head, eyelashes, nose, mouth, stomach, and stool,"[19] which I do not fully understand, refers to the functions of the actors. The Rumanian "A wormy block, under the block a meadow, under the meadow two leeches, under the leeches two doves, under the doves a fountain with two outlets, under the fountain a mill, under the mill a hammer"[20] and the Turkish "Black mountain, black place, green meadow, cut place, bag of hair.—Head, eyebrow, eye, tooth, beard"[21] contain unusual comparisons to

[15] For examples see the note to No. 1100 below. For discussion see Schultz, *Bemerkungen*, p. 366.
[16] Christiansen, 20. See also the Albanian riddle quoted in the note to No. 1100 below, a Swedish version in Sandén, *Norra Vadsbo*, 45, and Irish parallels in the headnote to No. 1100, n. 2, below.
[17] Árnason, 70. For parallels to the castle with five doors compare the headnote to No. 1101 below, where examples of a block with seven holes are cited. For the lady in the castle compare the references to an animal and, more rarely, a person, in the headnote to No. 1151 below.
[18] Arany and Gyulai, III, 293, No. 1.
[19] Kopernicki, 36.
[20] Papahagi, 34, var. 2. For comparisons of the eyes to birds see the headnotes to Nos. 1003–1004, § 1, above, and to No. 1471 below. For descriptions of the eyebrows see the headnote to Nos. 1042–1044, nn. 25–27.
[21] Hamizade, 59.

which I have not found parallels. The leeches in the Rumanian riddle are the eyebrows of black hair, and the doves are the eyes. I have found nothing similar to a queer Russian riddle for the face: "Two apples in moss and a little carrot on top."[22] The apples are the cheeks or eyes and the carrot is the nose. A Turkish description of a sheep shows some similarity to these ideas: "Its top is a meadow, the grass is cut; its bottom is a fountain, the water is drunk."[23]

In a Romance counterpart the enumerator proceeds upward rather than downward in describing the head. The Catalan "What is that: a convent of white nuns?—The teeth. In the middle there is a bright red frater?—The tongue. Higher up, there are two trenches?—The nostrils. Higher up, two little mirrors.—The eyes. Higher up, there is a place where the gentlemen promenade.—Lice"[24] portrays a sunny town in northeastern Spain. A variation of the theme appears in the French "I enter a convent, I see the directress dressed in red, I see the sisters dressed in white, I go up to the first floor, I see two little chimneys, I go up to the second floor, I see two little windows, I go up to the third floor, I see a mountain with a meadow."[25] The Irish "A mill with a top on it, a wood above it, two hundred thieves rummaging about the wood.—A head with the itch"[26] also proceeds upward.

Góngora uses this theme in describing a lady. I quote Robert Southey's translation of the twenty-third sonnet: "Sacred temple of pure modesty, whose fair cement and elegant wall of white pearl-shell and hard alabaster was built by the divine hand. The little gate is of precious coral, and ye bright windows have forcefully usurped the pure green from the emerald. The golden covering of thy superb roof adorns the sun with light, and crowns him with beauty."[27] The Irish "Two fences of stone, two pools of water, two human graves, and two bundles of rushes.—Teeth, eyes, nostrils, and eyebrows"[28] does not adopt any discernible arrangement.

A very curious Icelandic riddle for a cat employs themes akin to those discussed here. It is, "I walked in front of the entrance to a cave. Inside I saw a leaf. Above the leaf there were two breath-houses. Above the breath-houses two pools, above the pools two peaks, and below the peaks two lava hills, and

---

[22] Arkhangel'skii, p. 77.

[23] Hamizade, 413. See also, in the same collection, such Turkish riddles for the eye, nose, and beard as "Beside that there is a shining thing, underneath it there is a faucet, then there is a bag of hair" (215) and "Beside that there is a shining thing, underneath that a murmuring thing, then a bag of hair" (214).

[24] Milá y Fontanals, 1876, p. 27, No. 27. The collector's remark that the last element is an afterthought is erroneous. It is a stable and frequently encountered element in this riddle. See also Italian: Ferraro, *Canti popolari in dialetto logodurese*, p. 323, No. 67. For the teeth described as a convent of white nuns see the headnote to No. 841, § 2, above, and compare the headnote to No. 909, n. 11, above.

[25] Rolland, *Rimes*, pp. 201–202, No. 26; Mensignac, *Gironde*, p. 297, No. 1; Westphalen, *Metz*, col. 197.

[26] De Bhaldraithe, 15.

[27] John Wood Warter (ed.), *Southey's Common-place Book* (New York, 1850), II, 148.

[28] Delargy, 36; O Dalaigh, 8.

above the lava hills a dandelion stem, and below the dandelion stem two places for soap, and below the soap places four hairy brides, and on the hairy brides twenty-four horn buckles."[29] A variation is as follows: "I walked in front of the opening of a cave. Inside I saw a flap, and around the flap twelve spikes. Above the opening were two bellows, and above the bellows two lakes, and above the lakes two peaks, and behind the peaks hills and lava, and down from the hills and lava, four pillars with twenty-four hard and curved things on them."[30] I have not made the effort to explain all these details. The Icelandic riddle for a calf's head, "Guess what I sat down on one evening. It had eight doors and three roofs,"[31] may perhaps be related to these concepts, but is probably better interpreted as a conception based on an impossible kind of house.

Only a few additional instances of the use of this pattern to describe animals rather than a man can be cited. The Votyak goose riddle, "On two poles stands a bin, on the bin stands a tube that screams, at the end of the tube is a blue spoon,"[32] is clearly related to these conceptions. The connection is somewhat less clear in the Welsh cow riddle, "Two posts on top of a mountain without touching the sky or the ground,"[33] The Serbian beehive riddle, "On top of the mountain is a clearing, on top of the clearing is a barn, and in the barn sits the mistress,"[34] is probably related to this pattern. It has a parallel in the Lithuanian poppy riddle, "There stands a little post, on that post [there stands] a manor, on that manor [there stand] a hundred million tenants."[35]

Such patterns as these, which include many incongruous elements and have only the weak unifying theme that the elements are chosen from a single sphere of human activity like the household, easily admit variations in the course of oral transmission. The variations may diverge very widely from the fundamental theme. This fundamental theme has some similarity to the conception of a grasshopper or locust as a creature composed of parts belonging to many animals.[36] The lack of old versions of these comparisons to a landscape makes it difficult, if not impossible, to discern the history and relations of the texts. I cannot, for example, readily perceive the connection of a long Icelandic description of the human body with the texts here discussed. It is as follows: "There is a big oak with twelve roots, two of them very big around. From these roots [upward] it is all hollow inside, and it contains life and death. There are two branches at its top. On each branch sit four swains and [also] the superior of the four. They always work in concord. They are

---

[29] Árnason, 304.   [30] Árnason, 305.   [31] Árnason, 326.
[32] Wichmann, *Votyak*, 89. The "blue spoon" is the beak. Compare the Cheremiss "A basket, wood chips on the basket, a large awl on the chips" (Porkka, 104). The "awl" is the beak. See also n. 40 below and the note to No. 1562.
[33] Hull and Taylor, 226.   [34] Novaković, p. 102, No. 5.
[35] Jurgelionis, 1009, and compare his No. 1012. See also the headnote to No. 1355, n. 3, below.
[᷾] See the headnote to Nos. 1405–1408.

making bark for the oak. It is smelted out of the best gold. On the top of the oak there is a little castle built by three masters. Under the castle there are piled meat and sheep, swine and goats, the fish of the sea and the seed of the earth. There are two holes, made in masterly fashion, and two windows, set with glass and stones. Furthermore, there is a gate on either side. Through these good and evil pass. A field of wool grows on top of the castle, adorned with various colors."[37] This amazing conglomeration includes elements belonging to the riddle for the year,[38] but I cannot disentangle all its complications. Only slightly less confusing is another Icelandic riddle: "I stood on two pillars, gazing at the ocean waves, and tightened the house support. I held new milk and carried the support of men. I proclaimed an ogre's work and hid flood-food under a dwarf's fair house.—Legs, threshold, spike for a walking-stick [also: bee stings], stick. The ogre's work is that a cat killed a mouse. The flood-food is bait, and the house a stone."[39] A Zyrian riddle for a cock, "On a pair of rakes a sack of feathers, on the feather sack a pot of grit, on the pot of grit two pearls,"[40] seems to have been modeled on these riddles for a man.

We have thus far considered the descriptions in terms of the features of a landscape. There are only a very few instances of the reverse procedure, in which an object in nature is described in terms of the members of a human being. Such riddles for a house or hut as the Portuguese "Side of wood, head of grass" or "Foot of stone, side of wood, coat of grass"[41] and the more detailed Finnish and Lettish parallels, "A huge hat on his head, a bunch of moss in his mouth, shoes of stone on his legs,"[42] are rather unusual inventions. A similar theme underlies a French riddle for a well, "Who has a head of iron, a belly of stone, entrails of rope, legs of water?"[43]

1100. Mountain, Grassy Field

The description of a man or a man's head in terms of a scene in nature occurs in a great variety of forms. Some have already been mentioned in the previous headnote. Since riddlers have ordinarily perceived the intent of the comparison, they have felt free to introduce changes in details. Perhaps the accumulation of heterogeneous domestic objects—a theme discussed at some length in the previous headnote—is related. The separation of it from riddles based on a more unified concept often presents considerable difficulty. The Turkish "Players, a storehouse, a fruit-store, a snore-fountain, mirrors, frowners, a meadow lawn, in it a bachelor throws the javelin.—Feet, belly, mouth, nose,

---

[37] Árnason, 145.
[38] See the headnote to Nos. 1037–1038, § 6, above.
[39] Árnason, 1027.
[40] Wichmann, *Zyrian*, 131. The "pot of grit" is the craw and the "two pearls" are the eyes.
[41] Parsons, *Cape Verde*, 113, 114.
[42] Finnish: Aarne and Krohn, 181 = Henssen, 177. Lettish: Bielenstein, 155.
[43] Rolland, *Rimes*, p. 208, No. 59a.

eyes, eyebrows, hair, louse"[1] contains some novel traits. An Irish conception of the eye in somewhat similar terms is more unified in its choice of details: "A small spring of true water in the middle of this town, little windows of glass, and little doors of clay."[2] A Turkish riddle for eyebrows is limited to a single trait: "On the face two little gardens."[3]

1100. In this world it's a mountain, and upon this mountain it's a grass piece, and in this grass piece, two glasses.—A man's head.
Parsons, *Barbados*, p. 280, No. 23.

1101. Holes in a Hill

The holes in the head, and particularly the nostrils, have aroused the interest of riddlers. They have compared the nostrils to holes in a hill[1] or the nose to a house with two doors[2] without, however, elaborating these comparisons by further details.

A notion of the seven holes in the head seems to have been disseminated from India.[3] The following examples supplement those that have already been assembled by Kozumplik, but a few characteristic or curious instances have been excerpted from his article. See Icelandic: Árnason, 70. Swedish: Russwurm, 53, citing Gutsleff, *Anweisung zur ehstnischen Sprache* (Halle, 1732), 11. French: A. Ferrand, *Dauphiné*, p. 228 (Who has seven holes in his head?). Spanish, Porto Rican: Mason, 111. Rumanian: Papahagi, 34, var. 1. White Russian: Wasilewski, 46 (In a block there are seven holes). Russian: Sadovnikov, 1724 (There stands an oak, on the oak is a ball, on the ball there are seven holes), 1728 (The ball is silken, seven holes around it). Mordvin: Paasonen, 181 (A ball with seven holes). Cheremiss: Wichmann, *Cheremiss*, 37, 138. Zyrian: Wichmann, *Zyrian*, 219, 257 (On a pitchfork a kneading trough, on the kneading trough a birchen vessel, on the birchen vessel a ball, in the ball seven holes), which is contaminated with the riddles discussed in the headnote to Nos. 1100–1108 above. Votyak: Wichmann, *Votyak*, 151 (Seven holes in a block of wood). Serbian: Novaković, p. 29, No. 6 (There is an earthen jar with seven holes. You pour water into it, and it doesn't drip). Bulgarian: Gubov, 62 (A watermelon with seven holes on the hill; water flows through five holes, two holes are dry), 63 (A jug has seven holes, pour water into it and it does not flow out), 64 (A walnut trunk with seven holes); Stoilov, § 6, Nos.

---

[1] Hamizade, 37. Compare his No. 112: "A plain (hill) with holes, a grocery store, a fountain, a dealer in mirrors, a violinist, a prominent slope, a lousy meadow.—Jaw, mouth, nose, eyes, eyebrows, forehead, head, hair."
[2] De Bhaldraithe, 18; O Dalaigh, 11. See also the headnote to Nos. 1100–1108, n. 16, above.
[3] Hamizade, 346.
[1] No. 1101.   [2] No. 1143a.
[3] W. A. Kozumplik, *Southern Folklore Quarterly*, V (1941), 1–24; Howard Meroney, "*Lecc Thollcind* and the Twelve Doors of the Soul," *Southern Folklore Quarterly*, XI (1947), 257–259.

1 (A pumpkin with seven holes), 2 (A nutwood ball with seven holes), 4 (A ball with seven holes. Whoever cannot guess it is a fool), 5 (A kettle with seven holes. You cannot pour water into it). Modern Greek: Polites, *Neohellenika Analekta*, I, 198, No. 28 (A stick with seven holes that you wear at night.— Night cap), which is obviously somewhat confused; Dieterich, *Rätseldichtung*, p. 95, citing Papazafiropoulos, 320 (A gourd with seven holes, and each has its name). This has a final element usually found in riddles for the days of the week.[4] See also Polites, *Neohellenika Analekta*, I, 232, No. 226 (A squash with five holes, and every one has a name). Berber: Basset, *Contes populaires berbères*, p. 125, No. 7. Turkish: Kúnos, 152 = Kúnos, *Nyelvkönyv*, 21; Kowalski, *Zagadki*, 71; Hamizade, 58 (A seven-holed mallet. Who doesn't know this is an idiot); Katanov in Radlov, IX, 94, No. 812 (A quadrilateral has four parts. If you add two pipes, then there will be six.—Eyes, ears, and two nostrils); Moshkov in Radlov, X, 266, No. 9 (A seven-holed block. Whoever does not know it is a fool). Crimean Tatar: Filonenko, 95 (A hammer with seven holes. He who does not know it is a fool). Astrakhan Calmuck: Kotvich, 8 (Seven holes on a hill). Mongolian: Klukine, 7; Bazarov, 185 (A beautiful stone with seven holes); Mostaert, 14 (Seven holes around a hillock). Buryat: Gombojew, 7 (Seven holes on a hill). Cherekessian: Tambiev, p. 53, No. 5 (A little stump with four openings.—Head). Armenian: Seidlitz, p. 71, No. 19 (A watermelon with seven holes). Indian, Kashmiri: Knowles, 124 (A new pot with seven holes). Ho: Mitra, *Notes on Ho Riddles*, p. 117 = Parsee: Munshi, p. 416 (A temple with seven gates). Uraon: Archer, p. 193, No. 211 (Seven holes in a single thing). Kolarian: Wagner, 46 (A clod has seven holes). Samoan: Heider, 129 (There is a marvelously beautiful and useful house with five doors.—Man with five senses). Filipino: De los Reyes y Florentino, p. 276 (What is the round fruit with seven holes?).

The Yakut riddle for a shaman and his witchcraft, "They say that there is an iron bucket with seven holes,"[5] seems to involve a misunderstanding of some sort. The Chinese philosopher Chang-tze contrasts a man and Hun-tun, a spherical chaos without members, in "Men have all seven openings for seeing, hearing, eating, and breathing, only he [Hun-tun] has none."[6]

I have noted only three instances of the nine holes in man to add to those collected by Kozumplik: "One log has nine holes";[7] "The stone *shin* with nine holes.—Eyes, nostrils, ears, and mouth";[8] and a curious old Hebrew riddle.[9]

Kozumplik recognizes two stylistic varieties of the query about the seven holes in the human head. The usual form is a declarative sentence or an in-

---

[4] See the headnotes to Nos. 983, n. 7, and 1037–1038, n. 46, above.
[5] Piekarski, 21.
[6] O. J. Maenchen, *Wiener Zeitschrift für Kunde des Morgenlandes*, XLIV (1936), 94.
[7] Turkish: Katanov in Radlov, IX, 238, No. 37.
[8] Mongolian: Rudnyev, 72.
[9] Schechter, *Folk-Lore*, I (1890), 355, No. 7; see also his p. 357.

terrogation which may involve suggesting some entirely unrelated object as "Seven holes in a block of wood"[10] or "Who has seven holes in his head?"[11] He calls a less usual form which offers the hearer the choice of two things the "tricky question." The correct answer is the one which appears less desirable. Examples are: "Which do you prefer: a shirt full of fleas or seven holes in the head?"[12] and "Which would you prefer: a golden coat or seven holes in your head?"[13] The riddler does not explain the golden coat, but it is, I conjecture, a coat of flame.

A Russian riddler uses the scene of holes in a hill to describe an oven: "The hill is steep, a hole is in the hill, in the hole are loafers, but what is in the loafers?"[14] The loafers are loaves lying in the oven.

1101. Two little holes in the side of a hill, / Just as you come to the cherry-red mill.—Nostrils and mouth.
Oral, Virginia.

1102–1106. Water

Riddlers rarely employ water as a means of comparison. In a few instances they conceive it as a pool, pond, or lake.[1] They call the eyes pools.[2] The description of the eyelashes as birds or persons standing beside a pool may have suggested the Shilluk riddle for ears, "Little children stand continually at the side of the heaps of ashes."[3] Riddlers occasionally call dew a pond too large to cross.[4] Reference to the physical qualities of water are very rarely employed as themes of comparison.[5]

1102. My fader have two ponds; when he lie down at night, he turn up one and turn down one.—Ears.
Beckwith, *Jamaica*, p. 189, No. 60.

1103. Crossing Water

The comparison of dew to a broad body of water that can, however, be crossed without danger is analogous to the comparison of ice to a broad bridge that can be crossed similarly. For this latter riddle see the Norwegian "Who builds the longest bridge?"[1] or the Swedish "Who builds the broadest bridge?"[2]

---

[10] Votyak: Wichmann, *Votyak*, 151.
[11] French: A. Ferrand, *Dauphiné*, p. 228.
[12] French: Rolland, 302.
[13] Flemish: Joos, 783.
[14] Russian: Sadovnikov, 458.
[1] See Nos. 1044, 1102, and compare the headnote to Nos. 1100–1108, nn. 28–29.
[2] See No. 1044.
[3] Westermann, p. 241.
[4] See the note to Nos. 1103a, 1103b below, and compare Nos. 1103a, 1103b.
[5] Water stands up or remains quiet; see Nos. 1105a through 1106.
[1] Brox, *Ytre Senja*, 82.
[2] Hyltén-Cavallius, *Värend*, 65. Compare Dybeck, *Runa*, 1849, p. 48, No. 17.

Other comparisons of ice to a bridge are numerous,[3] and among them the conception of ice as a bridge not made with hands is perhaps the most interesting.[4]

1103a. a water there is j must pass a broader water never was: & yet of all waters j ever did se, to pass over with less jeopardy.—a dew.

Tupper, *Holme Riddles*, 121; *Harleian 1962* (17th cent.) = Halliwell-Phillipps, *Popular Rhymes*, p. 149; *Meery Riddles* (1629), No. 47 = Brandl, p. 16; Knortz, p. 230, No. 81; Hyatt, *Adams Co., Ill.*, p. 660, No. 10855.

1103b. Which is the broadest water, and the least jeopardy to pass over?—The dew.

Demaundes Joyous (1511), No. 12 = Kemble, p. 287 = Halliwell-Phillipps, *Popular Rhymes*, p. 153.

1104. Water to Wash In, Towel to Dry With

This query or one closely related to it occurs in the curious series of impossibilities listed in the old ballad of "Captain Wedderburn's Courtship."[1] Only when scholars have clarified the origins and connections of this ballad, will it be possible see the history and associations of this riddle. A series of Lettish riddles is clearly related to the ballad and will suggest the nature of the problems to be solved: "Where did you sleep last night? On the mountain of restlessness. With what did you wash your face? Not with what fell as snow, not with what fell as rain. With what did you dry yourself? Not with what was woven, not with what was clipped."[2] The same manner of riddling is applicable to tears and hair: "Washed with something from neither rain nor snow, wrap with something neither woven nor spun";[3] and to the lining of an egg: "Hinirí Cinirí Buachail's shirt, it is a shirt which is not washed or woven or sewn."[4]

A few riddles describe drying one's self in other ways. See "You ought to do it, you will do it, but if you don't, it does itself"[5] and "What is that which the king does and everyone else does, but if one doesn't do it, it is done anyway?"[6]

1104a. I washed my hands with water, / Which was neither rain nor run, / I dried them on a towel, / Which was neither woven nor spun.—Washed in dew, dried in sun.

Fitzgerald, p. 183; Fauset, *Nova Scotia*, p. 160, No. 83; Fauset, *Southern Negro*, p. 285, No. 103.

---

[3] See Irish: Christiansen, 7b; O Dalaigh, 165. Danish: Kristensen, p. 61, §141, Nos. 201a, 201b. Norwegian: Bergh, *Valdres*, 70. For discussion of the theme see Loewenthal, p. 60; Blanche Colton Williams, *Gnomic Poetry in Anglo-Saxon* (New York, 1914), p. 137, note on line 73b.
[4] See the headnote to No. 794 above.
[1] F. J. Child, *English and Scottish Popular Ballads*, I (Boston, 1884), 414–419, No. 46.
[2] Bielenstein, 948.   [3] Lithuanian: Jurgelionis, 166.   [4] Irish: Delargy, 29.
[5] Swedish: Dybeck, *Runa*, 1849, p. 50, No. 33. See also Sandén, *Norra Vadsbo*, 24. The oldest version appears to be that in Buchler, *Gnomologia*, 3d ed. (1614), p. 427:
  Si facias fiet; si non facias quoque fiet,
  Eveniet quamvis ipse operere nihil.
[6] Swedish: Ericsson, *Södermanland*, II (1881), 99, No. 118.

1104b. She washed her hands in water / Which neither fell nor run; / She dried her hands on a towel / Which was neither woven nor spun.—Dew and sun.
    Hudson, p. 90, No. 44.

1104c. I washed my hands in water that never rained or run, / I wiped my hands on silk that was neither woven nor spun.—I washed my hands in dew and wiped them on corn silk.
    Hyatt, *Adams Co., Ill.*, p. 662, No. 10876.

1104d. I wash my han's in water / Neither rain nor run. / I dry my han's on a napkin / Neither wove nor spun.—Wash in watermelon, dry on the rind.
    Parsons, *Guilford Co., N.C.*, p. 204, No. 31.

1105–1106. Water Stands Up, Lies Down, Does Not Stir

In describing a coconut, riddlers have noted the paradox that water, that is to say, the milk in the nut, hangs in the air, or otherwise defies the laws of physics. This manner of description is known in West Indian tradition and has parallels in the folklore of Africa, Mauritius, India, Indonesia, and Hawaii. In other words, the theme does not seem to be European. It is not clear whether these widely scattered riddles derive from a single parent form or have arisen independently. A somewhat similar theme is "Sky above, sky below, water in the middle,"[1] which is used for a coconut in such widely separated lands as Chile, Indonesia, and the Philippines.

Riddlers often describe a plant and its fruit in terms of objects arranged vertically,[2] as in the coconut riddle just mentioned. A typical use of this theme is the Uraon riddle for a kesair nut lying on the ground: "Earth above and earth below and in the middle a painted pebble."[3] The analogous Bengali riddle for turmeric, "Below is the earth, above is the earth, in the middle is a beautiful girl,"[4] shows an interesting replacement of the pebble by a girl, representing the seed.

The European and Asiatic parallels to this manner of description characteristically mention domestic utensils which stand one above another, as in the Lettish riddles for horsetail (*Equisetum*): "One barrel beside another, one vat beside another";[5] "One little barrel on another, one little vat on another, and the top a cat's tail";[6] and "Little barrel on little barrel, at the top mouse dung."[7] Analogous inventions are the Albanian description of a reed, "Box over box, a fox's tail at the top,"[8] which has a Finnish and a Mongolian

---

[1] Spanish, Chilean: Flores, 198. Indonesian, Soenda: Holle, *Soenda*, p. 373, No. 20. Serawaj: Helfrich, *Serawaj*, p. 73, No. 110. Sangir: Adriani, p. 414, No. 170. Filipino: Starr, *Philippines*, 120.

[2] For further discussion of this device see the headnote to Nos. 1436–1447 below and an example cited in the headnote to Nos. 738–747, n. 8, above.

[3] Archer, p. 192, No. 193.
[4] Mitra, *Sylhet*, 2.
[5] Bielenstein, 54.
[6] Bielenstein, 392.
[7] Bielenstein, 977.
[8] Hahn, p. 160, No. 22.

parallel;[9] the Cheremiss and Votyak descriptions of an unidentified plant as "Pan over pan, pan over pan, on the top a heckle"[10] and "Barrel on barrel, brush on brush";[11] the Votyak angelica riddle, "Heckle over heckle, tub over tub";[12] and such riddles for a reed as the Turkish "A nine-bottomed keg"[13] and the Arabic "Dwelling above dwelling, and yet it holds an *okise* of oil."[14]

1105a. Water stan' up.—Sugar-cane.
Beckwith, *Jamaica*, p. 200, No. 150; Parsons, *Antilles*, III, 434, St. Martin, 2.

1105b. Ma riddle, ma riddle, / I tell you this riddle, or not, / Water stan' up.—Cane.
Parsons, *Antilles*, III, 445, St. Thomas, 1.

1105c. A riddle, a riddle, aree, / No man can explain this riddle on to me, / Water lay down, water stan' up.—Cane.
Parsons, *Barbados*, p. 277, No. 5.

1105d. Water lay down, / Water stand up.—Cane.
Parsons, *Antilles*, III, 376, St. Vincent, 11.

1105e. Water stand up, water lay down.—Cane.
Parsons, *Antilles*, III, 363, Trinidad, 1, and p. 370, Grenada, 31.

1106. My moder have a leetle pond, dig the pond, but the water in there you can never stir.—Coconut, water in them.
Parsons, *Antilles*, III, 369, Grenada, 16.

1107. Gully

The comparison of an object, usually a glove or a purse with compartments, to a road with a fork or a valley with two notches has some resemblance to the comparison of a shoe or a glove to a house with four or five rooms into which brothers retire to rest.[1]

1107. A gully with two notch in it.—Purse.
Beckwith, *Jamaica*, p. 200, No. 154.

1108. Road

A Persian riddle for a belt has some similarity to this riddle, but involves a comparison to an animal: "Snake, its head comes out of two holes."[1]

1108. A man was going to Kingston, saw two roads and took both.—Trousers.
Beckwith, *Jamaica*, p. 193, No. 84.

---

[9] Henssen, 124; Kotvich, 151.
[10] Porkka, 15; Wichmann, *Cheremiss*, 435.
[11] Genetz, 37.
[12] Wichmann, *Votyak*, 180, 213.
[13] Moshkov in Radlov, X, 268, No. 56.
[14] Bauer, p. 222, No. 7. An *okise* is a small measure.
[1] See No. 908 and the corresponding headnote.
[1] Mann, II, 169, No. 5.

1109–1117. Stick, Stump, Wand, Wood

Comparisons to a stick or to wood in some other form are rather infrequent, but the objects for which such comparisons are used are very varied: sugar cane[1] is described in an enumeration having little or no enigmatic quality. In a riddle for a hole or the grave[2] a supposed "stick" or its equivalent replaces the indeterminate "thing" usually found in this riddle. Other comparisons to a stick or to wood describe a "jigger" (probably a chigger),[3] a stick for stirring,[4] the hairs of the head,[5] and sawdust.[6] Most of these riddles show little ingenuity and have not circulated widely. English riddlers do not know the comparison of the sun and moon to stumps[7] or of a snake to a stick.[8]

1109. A long stick, juicy and sweet, and smooth back.—Sugar cane.
Parsons, *Bermuda*, p. 262, No. 128.

1110. My mother has a thing. She put it on three sticks, and she put fuel under and the fuel burn and leave three sticks.—Fire, stone, pot.
Parsons, *Antilles*, III, 423, Montserrat, 32.

1111a. Me father have a stick an' cut it an' it become longer.—Grave.
Beckwith, *Jamaica*, p. 185, No. 22b.

1111b. I had a stake, too shart [short], cut both ends to make it longer.—Dat's a grave.
Parsons, *Barbados*, p. 283, No. 43.

1111c. My father has a piece of twine. It is a bit short. He cut its two ends to get it longer.—Grave.
Parsons, *Antilles*, III, 422, Montserrat, 25.

1111d. My father make a door an' it was too short; he cut it and it become longer.—Grave.
Beckwith, *Jamaica*, p. 185, No. 22a.

1112. My father has a gig to make; the more him pare it, the bigger it get.—Hole.
Beckwith, *Jamaica*, p. 190, No. 64.

1113. Down in the meadow a tethered foal. I brought the stab [stake], and what did I leave?—A hole.
Praeger, *Béaloideas*, VIII (1938), 171, No. 10.

1114. Stump to stump; dig out stump out of dogwood heart.—Jigger [chigger].
Beckwith, *Jamaica*, p. 200, No. 160.

1115. A 'tump in a pond; all the rain can't cover the 'tump-head.—Turnstick in the pot.
Beckwith, *Jamaica*, p. 200, No. 161.

---

[1] No. 1109.
[2] Nos. 1111a through 1113.
[3] No. 1114.
[4] No. 1115.
[5] Nos. 1116a, 1116b.
[6] Nos. 1117a, 1117b.
[7] See the headnote to No. 1252, nn. 4–6.
[8] See the note to No. 1466.

1116. Bunch of Wands

The following Scotch riddle comparing hair to wands resembles somewhat the many comparisons of hair to trees or grass. It also involves the notion that the hairs are countless. The comparison of hair to trees, grass, or sticks is comparatively rare in England and on the continent of Europe. The Serbian "On the top of the stack there is a handful of reeds" and "There is a forest, and under it a meadow"[1] are probably fragments of a long description of a man's body or head.[2] There are some other instances in which hair is called grass or trees as part of a scene.[3] In India, hair is called a rattan cane, in the Bengali "From the shore I threw a knife, which cut off eighteen scores of rattan canes."[4]

This last reference to shaving as cutting off rattan canes belongs to a widely known riddle. It may be illustrated by several Serbian versions: "I went to a grove and tore out a plant, the entire world could not find its end"; "I pulled out a stick in the forest. If the entire world were to jump up, it could not find the place where I pulled it out"; "I went out into the grove and cut off a stick; the entire world jumped up and could not find its log"; "I went into the forest and cut down a beech tree. I searched for its root, but could not find it"; "I pulled an oak out of the forest. The whole world searched to find where it had been pulled from, but could not find it anywhere"; "I went into the forest and cut down seventy-seven trees and not a stump was left."[5] The Gypsy "There's a forest somewhere, one often fells it, often and often, fells it Sundays and holidays, each tree grows again quickly,—you scarcely know this forest"[6] introduces some novel ideas.

African versions usually refer to small plants and often mention that the quantity cut is insufficient to fill one's hand. The Konde say, "I hoed a large garden, and when I gathered the crop, it did not fill my hand";[7] the Ila, "I cultivated a field, and the harvest was in my hand";[8] the Kiniramba, "He cultivates a large plantation and gathers with one hand";[9] and the related Wamajame, "The magic object of your father and mother fills a fist.—Hair.[10] The Dschagga "I clear a field and yet plant nothing on it that I might eat"[11] is a somewhat different conception. The Taveta "I have slaughtered my ox, the meat does not fill the hand"[12] is a curious transposition to a metaphor concerned with an animal.

---

[1] Novaković, p. 98, No. 11, and p. 99, No. 1.
[2] See the headnote to Nos. 1100–1108 above.
[3] See the references collected in the note to No. 1100 and the riddles cited in the headnote to Nos. 1100–1108, nn. 5, 18–19, 26. See also the classification of riddles for the hair in the note to Nos. 1042, 1043.
[4] Mitra, *Chittagong*, p. 352, No. 17.
[5] Novaković, p. 44, No. 12, and p. 45, Nos. 1, 2, and 4 through 6.
[6] Wlislocki, 2. [7] Mackenzie, p. 163.
[8] Smith and Dale, II, 329, No. 45. See also Tonga-Shangaan: Junod and Jaques, p. 239, No. 177 (I hoe my field all the time and collect the harvest in my hand).
[9] F. Johnson, 8. [10] Ovir, 21.
[11] Gutmann, p. 528. [12] Hollis, *Taveta*, 42.

In many riddles for shaving the hair is mentioned. The razor is ordinarily an animal, as in the Hungarian "An iron colt neighs on a meadow of bone"[13] and the Bhil "A francoline partridge is dancing on a high hill."[14]

The statement that only God can count hairs is familiar in other contexts, but is rather rare in riddling. In African tradition I find several references to a countless number of hairs. The Kundu say, "We know the number of the Mpongwe people, that of the Kundu we do not know" and "My father gave me a book, I cannot count in it";[15] the Dschagga, "I bear things that you cannot count and yet they do not burden it," "Countless grains!—Hair of cattle," "Father has cattle that you cannot count," and "Father has a courtyard, it is full of cattle that you cannot count.—Eyebrows."[16] A somewhat similar Lamba version is "The grass on an anthill that one can't count."[17] The only parallel from outside Africa that I have noted is the Bhil "Only a bundle of hemp, still they can't be counted by me and not by you."[18] The stars are often said to be countless.[19]

More remotely similar are such comparisons as the Turkish "Beyond the roof there are little drawstrings,"[20] the Khāṛiā "Bamboo without knots,"[21] and the Bhil "One tree has no bark, no branches, and no leaves."[22]

1116a. As I look'd owre my father's castle, I saw a bunch o' wands, / And naebody could coont them, but God's own hands.—A head of hair.
Findlay, *Edinburgh*, p. 60.

1116b. As I lookit our my father's castle wa', / I saw a bunch o' waans, / An nae ane can coont them but God's ain han's.—The hair of the head.
Gregor, *Northeast Scotland*, p. 76.

1117. Load of Wood

1117a. As I went across the bridge, I met a man with a load of wood which was neither straight nor crooked. What kind of wood was it?—A load of sawdust.
Redfield, *Tennessee*, p. 40, No. 57.

1117b. I went to the wood for a load of timber, / I brought neither long sticks nor short sticks, but I brought a load of timber.—Sawdust.
MacGréine, *Béaloideas*, III (1931–1932), 413, No. 3.

1118–1164. A House

Among riddlers a house yields comparisons for a variety of objects, notably a fruit, an egg, and the mouth. They ordinarily refer to some special characteristic of a house to adapt the concept to the special purpose: covered with

---

[13] *Magyar Nyelvör*, II (1873), 559.
[14] Hedberg, p. 876, No. 70.
[15] Ittmann, *Kundu*, 119, 295.
[16] Gutmann, pp. 528 and 531.
[17] Doke, 34.
[18] Hedberg, p. 881, No. 98.
[19] See No. 1095 and the note to No. 1095 above and the headnote to No. 1227 below.
[20] Zavarin, *Brusa*, 6.
[21] Roy and Roy, II, 450, No. 15.
[22] Hedberg, p. 881, No. 100.

nails, a house is a soursop or a sea egg (sea urchin);[1] resting on a post or having many rafters, it is often an umbrella or, among non-English riddlers, a mushroom;[2] with many windows, it is a thimble, sieve, or net;[3] without a door, it is an egg;[4] with a door through which one passes with difficulties of one sort or another, it is an egg, a coconut, or the nostrils;[5] colored red, it refers to the mouth;[6] painted in colors, it is a fruit;[7] and a house with its contents or a house within a house within a house is the blood, death, a nut, a melon, or an egg.[8] This hasty survey neglects some minor themes.

Among riddlers, the comparison to a house is found virtually everywhere. Some of the most widely known forms are very scantily represented by English riddlers.[9] References to persons in a house are discussed elsewhere.[10]

1118–1119. Form

1118a. My moder have a house, right round is nail.—Soursop.
Parsons, *Antilles*, III, 370, Grenada, 25.

1118b. My father have a house, all outside of it is nail.—Sore [sour] sop.
Parsons, *Antilles*, III, 370, Grenada, 25 var.

1119. A house covered all over with pins.—Sea egg [sea urchin].
Parsons, *Barbados*, p. 285, No. 54.

1120–1126. Position

1120. My fader have a house, floor up, roof down.—Ship.
Parsons, *Antilles*, III, 435, St. Martin, 9.

1121–1126. House Resting on Posts

In England and America, where houses resting on posts are unusual, comparisons to them are rather rare, but in regions where such houses are familiar, comparisons to them are freely used. Since such a house ordinarily has four posts, the riddler obtains the characteristic enigmatic paradox by saying that the supposed house has but one post. Such comparisons are analogous to comparisons to an animal with one foot. The Turkish door riddle, "The stork goes, the stork comes, the stork stands on one foot,"[1] refers, for

---

[1] See Nos. 1118a through 1119.
[2] See Nos. 1121a through 1123b and the headnote to Nos. 1121–1126, §§ 1, 3.
[3] See Nos. 1128a through 1131.
[4] See Nos. 1132 through 1135d, 1137a through 1138b.
[5] See Nos. 1141 through 1143a.
[6] See Nos. 1146 through 1149a.   [7] See Nos. 1152, 1153.
[8] See Nos. 1156a through 1157b, 1159a through 1159d, 1161 through 1163.
[9] See especially the riddles referring to the mouth, Nos. 1146 through 1149a, and compare with the headnotes to Nos. 1145–1148, 1149, 1150, and 1151, and with the notes to Nos. 1146, 1147, 1148, 1149a.
[10] See the headnotes to Nos. 906, 908–916, 908, 909, 910–915. See also the notes to Nos. 906 and 909, and the note to Nos. 910a through 910i.

[1] Kowalski, *Asia Minor*, 11.

example, to the swinging of the door and its support at one side. A house without a supporting post is an oven.²

The comparison to a house resting on one post or to an animal standing on one leg is applicable to:

§ 1. An umbrella, a parasol. See Nos. 1121a through 1121e, 1121g through 1123a. These English versions make a comparison to a house. The colonial Spanish "An animal with several ribs and one leg,"³ the Bavenda "An old lady whose body is formed only of ribs,"⁴ and the Kolarian "The water bird in the rainy season has only one foot"⁵ make a comparison to a living creature.

§ 2. A coconut tree. See No. 1124a, 1124b.

§ 3. A mushroom. English riddlers do not know this riddle. It seems to be most popular in eastern Europe and Africa. See Rumanian: Papahagi, 30 (A pretty church built on one column). Serbian: Novaković, p. 30, No. 4 (There is a little house in a little forest on a little leg), and p. 16, Nos. 5 (There is a little house in the forest standing on one leg), 6 (The church is standing on one pillar), 7 (A white church stands on one pillar). Bulgarian: Gubov, 81 = Chacharov, 21 (The whole house stands on one pillar). Hungarian: Kriza, 22 (A white house stands on one foot); *Magyar Nyelvör*, XXXI (1902), 532, No. 116. Albanian: Hahn, p. 161, No. 39 (A house with one column); Pedersen, 7 (A bowl, a bowl like a tart, round as a buttercake, on one leg like a stork). Modern Greek: Polites, *Neohellenika Analekta*, I, 224, No. 177 (A little arched church supported by a pillar). Turkish: Kowalski, *North Bulgaria*, 27 (With a single column, with a thousand rafters), which calls the gills of the mushroom "rafters"; Kowalski, *Asia Minor*, 24 (A roof for shade on one beam). African, Taveta: Hollis, *Taveta*, p. 211, No. 59 (My house [has] one pole). Bakongo: Denis, 89 (The house that papa built [rests] on one stake). Chinyanja: Rattray, p. 154 (I built with only one post to prop up the roof. What is it?). Dschagga: Raum, p. 305, No. 12 (My father's house consists of a single pole). Nyanja: Werner, p. 213 (Such an one built his house with one post only). Swahili: Büttner, p. 201; Velten, 28 (I have built my big house, it stands on one pole).

A few versions show an interesting elaboration of details. In India, the Baiga say, "A threshing floor upside down."⁶ The Hungarian "One is a white house, the other stands on one foot.—Mushroom and a goose standing on one foot"⁷ is confused. The Armenian "What sort of thing has one foot, yet when it goes out, the wolf carries it away?"⁸ is not entirely clear, unless the picker of the mushroom is called a wolf.

Some riddlers compare a mushroom to a tree or a group of mushrooms to a forest. See Modern Greek: Polites, *Neohellenika Analekta*, I, 233, No. 229

---

² No. 1126 below.
³ Dominican Rep.: Andrade, 238.
⁴ Stayt, p. 359, No. 3.
⁵ Wagner, 94.
⁶ Elwin, p. 467, No. 34.
⁷ Kálmány, I, 162, No. 23.
⁸ Seidlitz, p. 70, No. 14.

(An orange tree supported by one column). Serbian: Novaković, p. 30, No. 5 (The entire forest stands on one pillar), in which "forest" is understood distributively, meaning each of the trees, and p. 167, No. 4 (The fir tree is waiting in the holly forest on a single leg).

The suitable and effective Uraon "A white umbrella stands in a field"[9] seems to have no parallels.

A few ambiguous versions do not make clear whether the riddler is thinking of a tree, an animal, or a man. See the Finnish "The ornament of a swamp, the favorite of the copse stands on one leg";[10] the White Russian "In the forest it is on one leg";[11] and the Turcoman "Its top is white, its bottom red. It has stuck its single foot in the ground."[12]

Although comparisons to a bird are not numerous, they are found in such widely separated versions as the Kxatla "Tell me: the guinea-fowl that stands on one leg, its thigh is very tasty"[13] and the Khāṛiā "A cock stands on one leg only."[14]

Comparisons to a man with one leg are virtually universal; they have been taken down from Brittany to eastern Asia.[15] Typical examples are the Polish "It stands by the road on one leg, it never moves at all, and it doesn't take off its cap before anything";[16] the Modern Greek "An Albanian with a hat and one foot";[17] and the Yakut "Old man Anton stands on one leg."[18]

§ 4. A cabbage.[19] German: Wossidlo, 200 (It stands on one leg, is as round as a ball, and bears its heart in its head). Danish: Kristensen, pp. 77–78, § 195, No. 300a (contaminated with Nos. 1438a, 1438b below). Lithuanian: Jurgelionis, 1043. Lettish: Bielenstein, 280 (A scamp crouches on one leg). Bulgarian: Chacharov, 32 (I have a daughter, she stands on one leg and does not tip over). Gypsy: Wlislocki, 25. Turkish: Kowalski, *North Bulgaria*, 37 (With a single foot and a molla turban). A molla turban, signifying that the wearer is a teacher, is broad and tall.

Cabbages are also conceived as animals standing on one leg, as in Serbian: Novaković, p. 108, Nos. 2 (Six hundred goats are standing on one leg), 3 (The corral is full of sheep; they all stand on one leg), 4 (A hundred eagles on a single leg), 5 (Three hundred sheep squat on a single leg). Bulgarian: Gubov, 112, 117 (A hundred goats all standing on one leg); Bozhov, 2 (A white goose stands on one leg).

---

[9] Archer, p. 179, No. 3.
[10] Lönnrot, 1689 = Henssen, 27.
[11] Wasilewski, 95.
[12] Samojlvich, 40.
[13] Schapera, 65.
[14] Roy and Roy, II, 454, No. 45.
[15] Breton: Kerbeuzec, *Ille-et-Vilaine*, 25. German: Wossidlo, 211; Haffner, 36. French: Rolland, 98; V. S., *Mélusine*, I (1878), col. 263, No. 78. Italian: Gianandrea, *Archivio*, II (1883), 426, No. 52. Estonian: Wiedemann, p. 285. Votyak: Wichmann, *Votyak*, 412.
[16] Saloni, *Łańcut*, 16.
[17] Dieterich, *Rätseldichtung*, p. 93, citing Stamatiadis, V, 179.
[18] Popov, p. 285.
[19] See also Nos. 31 through 32b and the note to No. 32b in the present collection.

§ 5. Various plants. EUPHORBIA TREE. African, Masai: Hollis, *Masai*, p. 253, No. 1 (What do my warriors resemble when they stand on one leg?). CHRISTMAS TREE. Norwegian: Brox, *Ytre Senja*, 51 (What sort of bride stands on one leg?). The splendid dress of the bride and the ornaments of the tree are equated. FLOWERS. Flemish: Joos, 510. POPPY. Polish: Saloni, *Łańcut*, 98, 99, 100 (It stands in the garden on one leg, and I could swear there's a thousand in it),[20] THISTLE. Polish: Saloni, *Łańcut*, 27 = Saloni, *Rzeshów*, 121 (It stands by the road on one leg. Whoever touches it curses).[21]

§ 6. A mill. See No. 1125 below.

§ 7. An oven. See No. 1126.

§ 8. A cresset. Russian: Sadovnikov, 193 (There stands Andy on one leg).

§ 9. A chimney. Danish: Feilberg, *Ordbog*, III, 297, s.v. "skorsten" (It stands on one leg and smokes). Zyrian: Wichmann, *Zyrian*, 240. See also, in the present collection, the note to Nos. 319, 320, and also the note to No. 320.

1121a. House with one leg.—Umbrella.
Parsons, *Bermuda*, p. 264, No. 158.

1121b. Me riddle me riddle / Me randy oh. / Perhaps you can tell me dis riddle, / Perhaps you cyan't. / My fader had a upstairs house set up on one pos'.—Umbrella.
Parsons, *Bahamas*, p. 480, No. 87.

1121c. My fader had a house standin' only on one pos'.—Umbrella.
Parsons, *Antilles*, III, 369, Grenada, 5 var., and p. 435, St. Martin, 8 (with only one post).

1121d. My moder [variant: father] have a house, stan' on one pos'.—Umbrella.
Parsons, *Antilles*, III, 369, Grenada, 5, p. 373, Cariacou, 1, and p. 363, Trinidad, 5 (with one pos').

1121e. Me fader give me a house wid one prap [prop].—Umbrella.
Parsons, *Antilles*, III, 431, St. Kitts, 16.

1121f. My father built a house with one rafter.—Umbrella.
Parsons, *Bahamas*, p. 478, No. 66 var.

1121g. My father have a house up on one post.—Umbrella.
Beckwith, *Jamaica*, p. 189, No. 59.

1122a. Perhaps you can clear these and perhaps you can't. Fifteen rafter on one post.—Umbrella.
Parsons, *Bahamas*, p. 476, No. 47, and p. 478, No. 66.

1122b. My fader had a t'ing wid one pos' an' eight rafters.—Umbrella.
Parsons, *Bahamas*, p. 482, No. 100.

---

[20] See also other Slavic parallels mentioned in the headnote to No. 1355, n. 3, below.
[21] Compare the note to Nos. 342a through 342c above.

1122c. My father have a house with so many rafters in and one pos'.—Umbrella.
Parsons, *Antilles*, III, 375, St. Vincent, 1.

1123a. Some t'in' dat stands on one post wid rafters.—Parasol.
Parsons, *Antilles*, III, 432, Saba, 3.

1123b. Had a house wid many rafters. A shower o' rain come, I wouldn' get wet.—Pawasol.
Parsons, *Antilles*, III, 432, St. Eustatius, 12.

1124a. My father had got a house on one pos', with a lot of glass window and a lot of green children.—Coconut tree.
Parsons, *Antilles*, III, 373, Grenada, 63.

1124b. My father had a house setting on one pin, with no windows, no doors.—Coconut [tree].
Parsons, *Bahamas*, p. 479, No. 78.

1125. Build the house with one post.—Mill.
Parsons, *Eleuthera and Watling's Islands, Bahamas*, p. 440, No. 10.

1126. Build the house with no post.—Oven.
Parsons, *Eleuthera and Watling's Islands, Bahamas*, p. 440, No. 11.

1127–1142. House with Doors (Windows)

1127. Man mek him house, an' him bade de a do.—Ear of corn.
Beckwith, *Jamaica*, p. 194, No. 103.

1128–1131. House with Many Windows

This comparison describes various objects having many holes. A minor elaboration, which is quite in the spirit of good enigmatic technique, consists in contrasting a thousand (many) "windows" and one "door."[1] The themes for which this comparison is used are:

§ 1. A thimble. See Nos. 1128a through 1129b.

§ 2. A net ["fishpot"]. See Nos. 1130a through 1130g.

§ 3. A sieve, a sifter. See No. 1131.

§ 4. A beehive. Indonesian, Javanese: Ranneft, *Proza*, p. 9, No. 39 (A house with a thousand doors). Filipino: Starr, *Philippines*, 212 (A palace with many rooms, each with a priest). The Cubans call a beehive a "convent without bells or tower" (Massip, 5). For elaborations of these ideas see the headnote to No. 909, § 2, above.

§ 5. A henhouse. Filipino: Starr, *Philippines*, 370 (What house is that which is full of windows?).

1128a. I have a little house, / And a mouse wouldn't fit in it, / And all the men in our town / Couldn't count the windows in it.—Thimble.
Whitney and Bullock, *Maryland*, p. 173, No. 2673.

---

[1] See Nos. 1129a, 1129b, 1130b through 1130e, 1130g, 1130i, 1131.

1128b. As I was going over London Bridge, I saw a steel house. / It had four-and-twenty windows and wouldn't hold a mouse.—A thimble.
Burne, *Shropshire*, p. 574, No. 5.

1129a. My fader had a house, have a t'ousand windows an' one door.—Thimble.
Parsons, *Bahamas*, p. 485, No. 131.

1129b. My mother has something with a thousand windows and only one door.—Thimble.
Parsons, *Eleuthera and Watling's Islands, Bahamas*, p. 440, No. 6.

1130a. My fader has a dwellin'-house. Nobody can tell how many winders in it.—Net.
Parsons, *Sea Islands, S.C.*, p. 167, No. 88; Johnson, *St. Helena Island, S.C.*, p. 158, No. 20.

1130b. There is a house with a thousand windows, and only one door.—Fish pot [a net for trapping fish].
Parsons, *Antilles*, III, 444, St. Croix, 21.

1130c. There is a house wid one door, an' many a window. Tell me dat riddle.—Fish-pot.
Parsons, *Antilles*, III, 440, Anguilla, 20.

1130d. My father have a house with so many glass windows and one door.—Fish pot.
Parsons, *Antilles*, III, 375, St. Vincent, 2.

1130e. My father has a house / All in windows, / But only one door.—Fish pot.
Parsons, *Antilles*, III, 366, Trinidad, 31.

1130f. My moder have a house, right round is glass windows.—Fish pot.
Parsons, *Antilles*, III, 370, Grenada, 26.

1130g. Something has one thousand windows and one door.—Fish-pot.
Parsons, *Bermuda*, p. 253, No. 52.

1130h. My fader had a house, had two doors an' all windows.—Fish-pot.
Parsons, *Bahamas*, p. 485, No. 130.

1130i. One hun'ed windows an' no do'.—Fish-net.
Johnson, *St. Helena Island, S.C.*, p. 157, No. 8.

1131. Somet'in' round, have one do' an' one t'ousan' winder.—Sifter.
Parsons, *Sea Islands, S.C.*, p. 167, No. 87.

1132–1138. House without Doors (Windows)

The notion of a house without doors, or without windows, or without either doors or windows, is most widely used to describe an egg, and only occasionally to describe fruits, nuts, and other objects. In English folklore it occurs in a great variety of modifications. A related theme is a fruit conceived as a house that can only be opened with an iron key.[1] The Portuguese "Little gourd of Sir King without a mouth"[2] is a curious variation of the egg riddle.

The scene of a house without doors or without windows is found in riddles for:

§ 1. An egg. See Nos. 1132 through 1135d, 1137a through 1138b below. I have subdivided the texts as follows: a house without doors or windows;[3] a white house without doors or windows;[4] a house without doors or windows but with an occupant;[5] a house without doors, but full of food;[6] a house without doors but containing gold;[7] a house containing a crystal fountain.[8] An early instance of the comparison of an egg to a house is the Renaissance Latin

> Cellula parva jacet splendens candore nivali,
> Huc aditum praebet janua nulla tibi:
> Nulla fenestra patet, teres, atque rotunda videtur,
> Marmareo cincta est aggere tota domus.
> Attamen & vivum quiddam generatur in illa,
> Cui verum corpus redditur, atque caro.
> Provenit & quaestus multis uberrimus inde,
> Hinc quoque non pauci quo satientur habent.[9]

The house is occasionally called a prison, monastery, or some other specific building. See, as examples, the Low German riddle beginning "In the cathedral at Wittenberg [To Wittenberg in'n dom]"[10] and a Swiss comparison to a monastery.[11] A Portuguese comparison to a chapel has a parallel in the Georgian "Around a little church I walked and walked, yet I found no doors."[12]

§ 2. A fruit, usually a tropical or semitropical fruit (orange, lemon, guava). Portuguese: Pires, *Archivio*, III (1884), 116, Nos. 26, 27, and p. 117, No. 29 (lemon); Braga, 11; Pires de Lima, 210. Turkish: Hamizade, 343 (A green vault has no door.—Watermelon). For comparison of a fruit to a container that holds many objects see No. 1355 and the corresponding headnote and note. For comparisons to a house and occupants see Nos. 909 through 916g and the headnotes to Nos. 908–916, 909, and 910–915.

§ 3. A nut, a seed. Swiss: Zahler, *Münchenbuchsee*, 9. Swedish: Ström, p. 135 (A three-cornered house with neither doors nor windows.—Buckwheat). African, Togo: Schönhärl, 3 (A youth built a house and he made no opening into it.—Coconut). See also No. 1136 below.

---

[1] See the headnote to Nos. 908–916.
[2] Parsons, *Cape Verde*, 69.
[3] No. 1132 below.
[4] No. 1133.
[5] No. 1134.
[6] Nos. 1135a through 1135d.
[7] Nos. 1137a through 1137e.
[8] Nos. 1138a, 1138b.
[9] Buchler, *Gnomologia*, 3d ed. (1614), p. 422.
[10] Wossidlo, 31a.
[11] Rochholz, 382.
[12] Pires de Lima, 171; Glushakov, p. 22, No. 4. For various other comparisons to a church or chapel see the headnotes to Nos. 909 and 1100–1108, nn. 24–25, above.

§ 4. A grave.¹³ African, Swahili: Velten, 3 (My house has no doors). Compare the headnote to No. 1187, n. 14, below.

1132. My father have a house without window or door.—Egg.
Beckwith, *Jamaica*, p. 185, No. 26.

1133. Little White House without Doors

Riddlers often enlarge upon this description by adding details,¹ but the adjective "white" is probably a fundamental part of the original conception. In riddles for an egg they have usually adhered to the spirit of the conception, as, for example, in the Flemish "They call it a fine, small house with a white arch and white stone. It builds its own [house] now and again, one knows where, but not how"² or the Turkish "A white vault, it has no door."³ The Breton "A little white box without key or lock"⁴ is probably adapted from a riddle for a nut.⁵

1133. A little white house, well shaped without doors or windows.—Egg.
Dempster, *Sutherlandshire*, p. 236.

1134. (White) House without Doors Has an Occupant

This scene is often applied to an egg. The oldest version appears to be a Latin versification of the seventeenth century.¹ The Uraon adapt it to a cocoon: "An old barber has a house with no doors."² Its use for a nut is rather widely known.³ The occupant is either a worm or four men representing the four quarters of the kernel; see the Hungarian "It has neither door nor window, and yet there are four living in it,"⁴ which resembles a beanpod riddle,⁵ and "I have a daughter; whenever she wants to leave her house, she has to kick out its side,"⁶ which resembles riddles for an egg.⁷ The Surinam guava riddle, "A house stands. A carpenter inside is at work, but the house has no openings,"⁸ vividly suggests the worm within. The Astrakhan Calmuck watermelon riddle, "Many thousands of merchants in a house without a door,"⁹

---

¹³ See also the headnote to No. 1134, n. 11.

¹ See Nos. 1134 through 1139.   ² Joos, 370.
³ Hamizade, 747.   ⁴ Milin, *Batz*, p. 54.
⁵ See below, Nos. 1187a, 1187b, the headnote to No. 1187, and the note to Nos. 1187a, 1187b.

¹ Buchler, *Gnomologia*, 3d ed. (1614), p. 422.
² Archer, p. 181, No. 34.
³ French: Constantin, *Savoie*, p. 22.   ⁴ Arany and Gyulai, II, 352, No. 18.
⁵ See No. 1005 above and the headnote to No. 1005, particularly the Russian riddle cited there.
⁶ *Magyar Nyelvör*, II (1873), 178.
⁷ See the headnotes to Nos. 1132–1138, §1, above, and to No. 1187, §2, below.
⁸ Herskovits, p. 435, No. 9.
⁹ Kotvich, 158. See also the Armenian "What house has neither door nor window, but a thousand people live within?—Pomegranate" (Seidlitz, p. 70, No. 9).

has many parallels.[10] The Bengali use this theme for a grave: "A house without a door and which has for its resident a man who cannot speak."[11] The Kundu description of worms in an oil palm is very ingenious: "Rich men assembled in the court of a secret club."[12] Elaborations of the theme are rather rare, but see the Togo "A man dwells in a house that has no windows. He said, 'When I die, my house will get windows.'—Egg."[13]

1134. There is a white house on the hill up yonder without a window, without a door; and yet somebody live in there.—Egg.
Beckwith, *Jamaica*, p. 185, No. 26a.

1135–1136. House without Doors Contains Food

This scene is applicable to an egg[1] and, less frequently, to a nut.[2] Although this particular use for a nut seems to be an adaptation of the egg riddle, there is a widely known description of a nut as a pot of tasty food.[3] The Icelandic grape riddle, "A house full of juice, but no door is to be found,"[4] is analogous.

1135a. I gaed by a hoosie, / An' it wiz fu o' meht, / But there wiz neither door nor window / T' let me in to eht.—An egg.
Gregor, *Northeast Scotland*, p. 79.

1135b. Little house full of meat, / No windows or doors, / To get something to eat.—Egg.
Fauset, *Nova Scotia*, p. 168, No. 131; Parsons, *Bermuda*, p. 251, No. 43 and var. White house chock full of meat: Fauset, *Nova Scotia*, p. 168, No. 131 var.

1135c. A white house full of meat / But no door to go in and eat.—An egg.
Halpert, *New Jersey*, p. 201, No. 4.

1135d. In yonder meadow there is a white store, / Full of meat and no door.—Egg.
Gardner, *Schoharie Hills, N.Y.*, p. 256, No. 23.

1136. A little house full of meat, / No door to go in and eat.—Nut.
Waugh, *Canada*, p. 68, No. 778.

1137. House without Doors Contains Gold

The notion of comparing the yolk of an egg to gold is very widespread, but occurs in English only in this and the immediately following riddles. The present riddle, which is almost certainly a fragment of the following text, Nos. 1138a and 1138b, has acquired an existence in its own right, for the

---

[10] See Nos. 910a through 910i, the headnotes to Nos. 908–916, 909, and 910–915, above, the note to No. 909, and the note to Nos. 910a through 910i. For comparisons to things in a container see the note to No. 1355 below.
[11] Mitra, *Chittagong*, p. 666, No. 16.
[12] Ittmann, *Kundu*, 15.
[13] Schönhärl, 103.
[1] Nos. 1135a through 1135d.
[2] No. 1136.
[3] See the headnote to No. 1187.
[4] Árnason, 283.

versions Nos. 1137b and 1137d have taken up characteristic introductory formulas, and No. 1137e has borrowed an idea found in No. 1133 above.

1137a. No doors there are in this stronghold, / Yet thieves break in and steal the gold.—Egg.
Knortz, p. 240, No. 147.

1137b. A riddle, a ring. / Here's a gold house, / Without winders, without doors, / And still the thieves broke in and steal the gold.—Egg.
Parsons, *Barbados*, p. 280, No. 26.

1137c. A house with no windows and no doors, and with a good strong wall, and yet thieves break in and steal the gold.—Egg.
Knortz, p. 222, No. 46.

1137d. My fader had a house / With no windows an' no doors, / Yet thieves broke in an' steal de gol'.—Egg.
Parsons, *Bahamas*, p. 477, No. 58.

1137e. A little white house with no windows or doors, but yet robbers break in and steal the gold.—Egg.
Perkins, *New Orleans*, p. 107, No. 18 var.

1138. Marble Walls, Crystal Fountain, Golden Apple

This literary comparison of an egg to a marble castle, within the walls of which are a crystal fountain (the white of the egg) and a golden apple (the yolk), circulates freely in oral tradition. Lacking older versions, I shall not speculate about the time of its invention. It has existed sufficiently long to have suffered corruption in passing from mouth to mouth.[1] The versions corrupted by oral transmission provide interesting examples of the stylistic differences between the popular and the literary riddle. Loewenthal's use of this riddle in interpreting a text in the Old English collection of riddles in the Exeter Book is a very doubtful procedure.[2] Since the fundamental ideas belong to the common stock of riddling, the ready acceptance of this rather sophisticated set of ideas by the folk is easily understood. An egg is often compared to flowers, plants, and parts of a plant.[3]

Riddlers, especially those who have been in contact with Arabic culture, tell riddles of an egg and make reference to metals and animals. See Arabic: Giacobetti, 202 (A lost beast has come from the mountain; how it mixes gold and silver!). Berber: Basset, *Contes populaires berbères*, pp. 125–126, No. 8 (I have seen a marvel: silver rising on gold). Turkish: Hamizade, 758 (Half gold, half silver, it has no soul but it is sometimes animated). Persian: Phillott, 27 (A warbler of the garden am I, and the garden is my flower ground. I'm a fire-eating bird, am I, and fire is my plumage. My bones are silver and in my

---

[1] See the corrupt versions, Nos. 1137a through 1137e.
[2] *Studien zum germanischen Rätsel*, p. 17.
[3] Examples are collected in the note to Nos. 1138a, 1138b.

belly I carry gold. He who guesses this is wiser than I). Indonesian, Alfoer: Wilken, p. 306, No. 18 (Skin and flesh of silver, heart[4] of gold). Although I have suggested a possibility of Arabic influence in these inventions, I shall not insist upon it. The Turkish "I have a well, inside it I have gold and silver water"[5] and the Yucatecan "Silver the shell, gold the center"[6] may imply that conceptions of this sort may be invented independently.

Comparisons for an egg in which yellow materials that are not gold are mentioned are rare. One example is the Turkish "I opened my box and yellow silk spilled out of it."[7]

Comparisons mentioning gold and silver are occasionally found in other uses than the description of an egg. The Portuguese say for butter, "Beat silver, gold shows up,"[8] and the Turks have a riddle for an image case, "On a gold trough is a silver trough and on the silver trough is an earthenware trough."[9]

1138a. In marble walls as white as milk, / Lined with a skin as soft as silk; / Within a fountain crystal clear, / A golden apple doth appear. / No doors there are to this stronghold— / Yet thieves break in and steal the gold.— Egg.

Waugh, *Canada*, p. 69, No. 793; Knortz, p. 219, No. 35; Hyatt, *Adams Co., Ill.*, p. 660, No. 10861; Perkins, *New Orleans*, p. 107, No. 18; Randolph and Taylor, *Ozarks*, 16; Farr, *Tennessee*, p. 319, No. 15; Halliwell-Phillipps, *Nursery Rhymes*, p. 125.

1138b. Within a noble dome confined, / Whose milk [?] / Whitewashed with silk, or lined, / A golden apple doth appear, / Steep in a bath as crystal clear, / No doors, no windows to behold, / Yet thieves break in and steal the gold.—An egg.

Fauset, *Nova Scotia*, p. 167, No. 130.

1138c. A golden apple, a marble wall, / Thieves came in and stole it all.— Aigg.

Parsons, *Bermuda*, p. 251, No. 41.

1139. Marble Stone, Golden Ball

The English comparison of an egg to a marble stone containing a golden ball is a corruption of the preceding scene of a marble castle with a crystal fountain and a golden apple. By altering the golden apple to a golden ball the riddler brings the several themes into a single category of physical objects (curtain, stone, ball), but sacrifices the concept of a house or castle. The remote parallels to the English text are of interest as examples of the use of similar materials

---

[4] Var.: liver.
[5] Hamizade, 746.
[6] M. Redfield, p. 49, No. 4.
[7] Kúnos, 215.
[8] Parsons, *Cape Verde*, 77.
[9] Katanov in Radlov, IX, 143, No. 1161.

in describing an egg, but they do not seem to be derived from the same source. Only the Danish "What sort of yellow ball is it that lies in a white cave?"[1] might conceivably have some connection with the English riddle. In the note to No. 1139 I have assembled comparisons of an egg to silver, gold, porcelain, and similar materials without, however, intending to derive them from the same original invention.

1139. A curtain drawn as fine as silk, / A marble stone as white as milk; / A thief appear and break them all, / Out start the golden ball.—Egg.
Beckwith, *Jamaica*, p. 214, No. 244.

1140. Castle on the Seaside

The defects in this inadequately conceived riddle may have arisen in the course of oral transmission. The highly elaborated conception and the traces of rhyme suggest a literary origin. The contrast of water and land probably refers to the white of the egg and the yolk.

A contrast of two liquids in a barrel occurs in a widely circulated riddle for an egg.[1] It is not found in English folklore. Typical variations of this riddle are the Danish addition that the barrel has no bung,[2] the Serbian specification of the kinds of liquids in "Wine and brandy in one barrel,"[3] and the Turkish

---

[1] Kristensen, p. 154, § 442, No. 710.
[1] Irish: O Dalaigh, 61 (A white barrel and two kinds of food in it). Dutch: Sinninghe, p. 10, No. 4; *Ons Volksleven*, VIII (1896), 190. Frisian: Carstensen, *Am Urquell*, III (1892), 327, No. 20. German: Butsch, 152; Karl Müllenhoff, *Zeitschrift für deutsche Mythologie*, III (1855), 7; Wilhelm Mannhardt, *Germanische Mythen* (Berlin, 1858), p. 415; Frischbier, *Thierwelt*, p. 352, No. 56. Swiss: Rochholz, 333; J. Müller, *Innerschweiz*, 82. Icelandic: Arnason, 1054. Norwegian: Brox, *Ytre Senja*, 181; Berge, 79. Swedish: Ericsson, *Södermanland*, I (1879), 38, No. 41, and II (1881), 98, No. 102; Wigström, p. 289, No. 18; Dybeck, *Runa*, 1847, p. 42, No. 25 = Russwurm, 19; Hyltén-Cavallius, *Värend*, 78; Sandén, *Norra Vadsbo*, 17; Geijer and Campbell, 41; Ström, p. 196, "Ägget," 2. French: Rolland, 64. Basque: Cerquand, 31; Vinson, 5. Spanish, Argentinian: Lehmann-Nitsche, 490. Chilean: Flores, 352. Italian: Gianandrea, *Archivio*, I (1882), 555, No. 19; Coronedi-Berti, *ibid.*, II (1883), 579, No. 42; Nerucci, *ibid.*, III (1884), 55; Salvioni, *ibid.*, IV (1885), 550, No. 93; Pitrè, *ibid.*, X (1891), 383; Corsi, *ibid.*, p. 401, No. 35; Cimegotto, *ibid.*, XIII (1894), 434, No. 8; Balladoro, *ibid.*, XVI (1897), 231, No. 39; Tschiedel, 74. Rumanian: Gorovei, 1286, 1291 through 1296; Wiegand, p. 269, No. 16. Lettish: Bielenstein, 416 (A little, little barrel, two kinds of beer). Polish: Gustawicz, 119 through 121; Saloni, *Łańcut*, 28 (Neither a peg nor a hole, but there are drinks in it); Saloni, *Rzeshów*, 55 (There are two kinds of wine, but there is no hole through which to get at it); Kopernicki, 24 var. Russian: Sadovnikov, 541. Bulgarian: Stoilov, p. 70, § 58, Nos. 2, 3, 5. Modern Greek: Sanders, 10; Dieterich, *Rätseldichtung*, p. 95; Polites, *Neohellenika Analekta*, I, 228, No. 201; Abbott, p. 313, No. 33; Stathes, p. 339, No. 42; Sakellarios, p. 290, No. 3. Finnish: Henssen, 69. Estonian: Wiedemann, p. 271. Lappish: Poestion, p. 269. Zyrian: Wichmann, *Zyrian*, 59, 232, 255. Votyak: Buch, 5; Wichmann, *Votyak*, 303, 406. Mordvin: Ahlqvist, p. 41, No. 30; Paasonen, 360. Cheremiss: Wichmann, *Cheremiss*, 7, 139; Ramstedt, 3. Arabic: Littmann, p. 54; Ruoff, p. 48, Nos. 8, 9. Turkish: Zavarin, *Brusa*, 26; Moshkov in Radlov, X, 267, No. 28 (A kettle full of two different drinks). Tatar: Kalashev and Ioakimov, p. 51, No. 32 (In one pitcher there are two kinds of liquids). Crimean Tatar: Filonenko, 38 (In my well I have two sorts of water). Georgian: Blechsteiner, p. xlvi, No. 4. Chinese: Rudolph, p. 74, No. 1.
[2] Feilberg, *Ordbog*, IV, 1144, s.v. "æg."
[3] Novaković, p. 74, No. 3.

in describing an egg, but they do not seem to be derived from the same source. Only the Danish "What sort of yellow ball is it that lies in a white cave?"[1] might conceivably have some connection with the English riddle. In the note to No. 1139 I have assembled comparisons of an egg to silver, gold, porcelain, and similar materials without, however, intending to derive them from the same original invention.

1139. A curtain drawn as fine as silk, / A marble stone as white as milk; / A thief appear and break them all, / Out start the golden ball.—Egg.
Beckwith, *Jamaica*, p. 214, No. 244.

1140. Castle on the Seaside

The defects in this inadequately conceived riddle may have arisen in the course of oral transmission. The highly elaborated conception and the traces of rhyme suggest a literary origin. The contrast of water and land probably refers to the white of the egg and the yolk.

A contrast of two liquids in a barrel occurs in a widely circulated riddle for an egg.[1] It is not found in English folklore. Typical variations of this riddle are the Danish addition that the barrel has no bung,[2] the Serbian specification of the kinds of liquids in "Wine and brandy in one barrel,"[3] and the Turkish

---

[1] Kristensen, p. 154, § 442, No. 710.
[1] Irish: O Dalaigh, 61 (A white barrel and two kinds of food in it). Dutch: Sinninghe, p. 10, No. 4; *Ons Volksleven*, VIII (1896), 190. Frisian: Carstensen, *Am Urquell*, III (1892), 327, No. 20. German: Butsch, 152; Karl Müllenhoff, *Zeitschrift für deutsche Mythologie*, III (1855), 7; Wilhelm Mannhardt, *Germanische Mythen* (Berlin, 1858), p. 415; Frischbier, *Thierwelt*, p. 352, No. 56. Swiss: Rochholz, 333; J. Müller, *Innerschweiz*, 82. Icelandic: Arnason, 1054. Norwegian: Brox, *Ytre Senja*, 181; Berge, 79. Swedish: Ericsson, *Södermanland*, I (1879), 38, No. 41, and II (1881), 98, No. 102; Wigström, p. 289, No. 18; Dybeck, *Runa*, 1847, p. 42, No. 25 = Russwurm, 19; Hyltén-Cavallius, *Värend*, 78; Sandén, *Norra Vadsbo*, 17; Geijer and Campbell, 41; Ström, p. 196, "Ägget," 2. French: Rolland, 61. Basque: Cerquand, 31; Vinson, 5. Spanish, Argentinian: Lehmann-Nitsche, 490. Chilean: Flores, 352. Italian: Gianandrea, *Archivio*, I (1882), 555, No. 19; Coronedi-Berti, *ibid.*, II (1883), 579, No. 42; Nerucci, *ibid.*, III (1884), 55; Salvioni, *ibid.*, IV (1885), 550, No. 93; Pitrè, *ibid.*, X (1891), 383; Corsi, *ibid.*, p. 401, No. 35; Cimegotto, *ibid.*, XIII (1894), 434, No. 8; Balladoro, *ibid.*, XVI (1897), 231, No. 39; Tschiedel, 74. Rumanian: Gorovei, 1286, 1291 through 1296; Wiegand, p. 269, No. 16. Lettish: Bielenstein, 416 (A little, little barrel, two kinds of beer). Polish: Gustawicz, 119 through 121; Saloni, *Łańcut*, 28 (Neither a peg nor a hole, but there are drinks in it); Saloni, *Rzeshów*, 55 (There are two kinds of wine, but there is no hole through which to get at it); Kopernicki, 24 var. Russian: Sadovnikov, 541. Bulgarian: Stoilov, p. 70, § 58, Nos. 2, 3, 5. Modern Greek: Sanders, 10; Dieterich, *Rätseldichtung*, p. 95; Polites, *Neohellenika Analekta*, I, 228, No. 201; Abbott, p. 313, No. 33; Stathes, p. 339, No. 42; Sakellarios, p. 290, No. 3. Finnish: Henssen, 69. Estonian: Wiedemann, p. 271. Lappish: Poestion, p. 269. Zyrian: Wichmann, *Zyrian*, 59, 232, 255. Votyak: Buch, 5; Wichmann, *Votyak*, 303, 406. Mordvin: Ahlqvist, p. 41, No. 30; Paasonen, 360. Cheremiss: Wichmann, *Cheremiss*, 7, 139; Ramstedt, 3. Arabic: Littmann, p. 54; Ruoff, p. 48, Nos. 8, 9. Turkish: Zavarin, *Brusa*, 26; Moshkov in Radlov, X, 267, No. 28 (A kettle full of two different drinks). Tatar: Kalashev and Ioakimov, p. 51, No. 32 (In one pitcher there are two kinds of liquids). Crimean Tatar: Filonenko, 38 (In my well I have two sorts of water). Georgian: Blechsteiner, p. xlvi, No. 4. Chinese: Rudolph, p. 74, No. 1.
[2] Feilberg, *Ordbog*, IV, 1144, s.v. "æg."
[3] Novaković, p. 74, No. 3.

adaptation to a household scene in "A small well with two kinds of water in it."⁴

Riddlers occasionally specify the contents in other terms. See the Turkish "I have a box with two kinds of fodder in it";⁵ the Russian "The kneading trough is small, but there are two loaves in it";⁶ the Parsee "Two kinds of ghee";⁷ and the Samoan "Two kinds of cloth, white and yellow."⁸ Perhaps the most ingenious of such inventions is the Russian "Beneath a thin little layer of ice, of ice, there stands a little cup of nice honey,"⁹ which cleverly utilizes the colors of ice and honey and suggests a paradox by naming two unrelated materials. The Swedish "Two gentlemen sit in a room without a door"¹⁰ is an unusual comparison to persons and contains an element belonging to another riddle for an egg.¹¹

An elaboration occasionally added by riddlers is that the two liquids in the barrel do not mingle.¹² It is in turn amplified in such versions as the Rumanian "The emperor's wine and the pasha's wine in one barrel, and they don't mingle";¹³ the Serbian "Wine and brandy in one barrel, and yet they do not mix";¹⁴ the Bulgarian "The wine and the butter are in one barrel, yet they do not mix."¹⁵ The Albanian "The cadi's milk and the mufti's honey are cooked in one pot and yet are not mingled"¹⁶ employs a contrast akin to the Russian use of ice and honey.

The notion of two liquids which do not mingle, though in the same container, is applicable also to the eyes.¹⁷ Interesting variations of this are the Turkish "I have a bowl of sour milk, half of it is black and half is white"¹⁸ and the Mongolian "Varicolored meat in a bowl."¹⁹

1140. I had a little castle upon the seaside. / One half was water, the other was land; / I opened my little castle door, and guess what I found; / I found a fair lady with a cup in her hand. / The cup was gold, filled with wine; / Drink, fair lady, and thou shalt be mine.—Answer lacking. [Egg.]
Halliwell-Phillipps, *Nursery Rhymes*, p. 134.

---

⁴ Kúnos, 194; Hamizade, 745, 748 (Two waters in a pitcher).
⁵ Kúnos, 66.
⁶ Sadovnikov, 548. Turcoman: Samojlvich, 120 var. (many parallels).
⁷ Munshi, p. 415. Ghee is clarified butter.
⁸ Heider, 173.
⁹ Arkhangel'skii, p. 76.
¹⁰ Russwurm, *Eibo*, p. 132, § 316, No. 1.
¹¹ See No. 1134 above.
¹² Italian: Pitrè, 869; Tammi, 10. Russian: Sadovnikov, 541. Serbian: Novaković, p. 74, Nos. 7 through 10. Bulgarian: Gubov, 425; Stoilov, p. 70, § 58, Nos. 1, 4, 6, 8. Arabic: Löhr, p. 107, No. 14.
¹³ Wiegand, p. 271, No. 16.   ¹⁴ Novaković, p. 74, No. 6.
¹⁵ Ikonomov, 15.   ¹⁶ Pedersen, 11.
¹⁷ Modern Greek: Dieterich, *Rätseldichtung*, p. 95. Mongolian: Mostaert, 143 144; Klukine, 6. Buryat: Gombojew, 8.
¹⁸ Kúnos, 163; Hamizade, 212.
¹⁹ Whymant, p. 38, No. 2.

1141-1142. Entering (Leaving, Closing) House

The closely related notions of a house that cannot be entered or cannot be departed from are often coupled together or are enlarged by the addition of accessory details. They serve to describe various objects:

§ 1. An egg. See No. 1141. Riddlers have introduced many minor modifications. The Danes, for example, say: "You must break down the wall of a pretty house in order to enter."[1] The notion that an egg is a house that can only be opened from inside appears to be found only in Hawaii.[2]

§ 2. A fishtrap. Indian, Bengali: Mitra, *Chittagong*, p. 353, No. 18 (A king's palace into which no [?] one can go, [but from which] one cannot come out). For parallels see the note to Nos. 1130a through 1130i above.

§ 3. A periwinkle. French: Baissac, *Mauritius*, p. 414 (I have a house, when I have opened it, I can never close it again).

§ 4. A nut. Spanish, Dominican Rep.: Andrade, 200 (Can open and can't close it). For parallels clearly suggesting a box rather than a house see Nos. 1187a, 1187b below. The Welsh Gypsy "High up on the tree; one can pull it down, a hundred cannot put it back; one can break it, a hundred cannot put it together again"[3] contains elements reminiscent of Humpty Dumpty.

§ 5. The earth and the sky. African, Togo: Schönhärl, 92 (There is a calabash that no one can open).

1141. My father have a white house in yard; if you go in, you kyan' come out, if you come out, you kyan' go in.—Egg.
Beckwith, *Jamaica*, p. 185, No. 25.

1142a. My father has a house with three doors and can walk only through one.—Three openings in a coconut shell; one drinks only through one.
Beckwith, *Jamaica*, p. 190, No. 63.

1142b. My fader had a house wid t'ree doors an' only one could open.—Coconut.
Parsons, *Bahamas*, p. 471, No. 1.

1143-1151. House (Cave, Garden): Human Head

I have arranged the various riddles describing the head or mouth in terms of a house, theater, or cave, as follows: Nos. 1143a, 1143b describe the nostrils as doors or rooms that cannot be entered; No. 1144 describes the eyes as windows; No. 1146 compares the mouth and teeth to a room with chairs; No. 1147 enlarges upon this last comparison by inventing the scene of a theater, in the non-English versions of which a dancer is often seen (see note to No. 1147); No. 1148 describes a house with balconies; No. 1149a, a house surrounded by a

---

[1] Feilberg, *Ordbog*, IV, 1144, s.v. "æg."
[2] Judd, 155.
[3] Sampson, 17a.

white fence; Nos. 1150a, 1150b mention a fence or a cave never rained upon but always wet; and No. 1151 mentions a fence and a garden.

The ancient comparison of the human body to a house occurs in many contexts, in tales (the fable of the Belly and the Members), proverbs, and riddles.[1] It is a commonplace in the literature of the eastern Mediterranean, where houses are made of earth and the human body is spoken of as earth.[2] St. Francis said, "Brother Body is our cell, and the soul is the hermit who dwells in it."[3]

In a few curious instances, riddlers have expanded or altered this theme. A Swiss riddler compares the head to "A door, two side-doors, two windows, two draft-holes, a forest, and in it old and young rabbits jump about."[4] This contains also elements found in the comparisons of hair to a forest and lice to the animals running about in it.[5] Much the same themes appear in Spanish parallels,[6] and in Catalonia they are enlarged by a comparison of the mouth and the teeth to a monastery filled with white monks.[7] The Tschuana "Bushman houses, they are not closed.—Nostrils"[8] refers to only one part of the face.

Riddlers occasionally call hair a thatch and may thus imply that the head is a house, but they rarely elaborate this implication. For example, the Votyak and Cheremiss description of combing the hair is unusually picturesque: "A snowshoe glides down over the houseroof."[9]

The comparisons mentioned thus far have been almost exclusively in terms of things. Comparisons in terms of men are rarely used to describe the nostrils, but see the Shilluk "Two brothers, their mouth is turned down."[10]

1143a. My fader had a house on de hill. Had two doors. An' a shower o' rain come down an' I could not get in to my fader's house.—Your nose an' two nostril holes.

Parsons, *Antilles*, III, 436, St. Martin, 25.

---

[1] See F. J. Child, *English and Scottish Popular Ballads*, II (Boston, 1885–1886), 227, headnote to his No. 77; Archer Taylor, "A Metaphor of the Human Body in Literature and Tradition," *Corona* (Durham, N.C., 1941), pp. 3–7. A very interesting instance is found in Thomas Dekker, *The Guls Hornbook* (London, 1608), chap. iii.

[2] See, as examples, Job 4:19; 2 Cor. 5:1; 2 Peter 1:13–14.

[3] Quoted in B. P. Kurtz, "Gifer the Worm," *University of California Publications in English*, II (1929), 247.

[4] Zahler, *Münchenbuchsee*, 202a. See also his Nos. 202b, 202c and the headnote to Nos. 1100–1108 above.

[5] See the headnote to Nos. 459–460 above.

[6] Demófilo, 223 through 226.

[7] Pelay y Briz, 39. For the separate use of the last theme see the headnote to No. 841, § 2, above.

[8] Kuhn, *Tschuana*, 1. Tonga-Shangaan: Junod and Jaques, p. 234, No. 31, and p. 237, No. 50.

[9] Votyak: Wichmann, *Votyak*, 258. Cheremiss: Wichmann, *Cheremiss*, 54, 115, 228.

[10] Westermann, p. 241.

1143b. A shower of rain is comin'. / Two empty rooms you cannot get shelter in.—Nose.
Parsons, *Antilles*, III, 421, Montserrat, 6.

1144. Windows: Eyes

The comparison of the eyes to windows is a riddle found in various widely separated places. The details vary considerably from text to text. This English instance is related to the comparison of the human head to a house.[1] Examples of the comparison of the eyes to windows are usually less extensive.[2] The Lithuanian "Two candles, a hill between them"[3] belongs to the comparisons to a light or lamp.[4] The Zyrian comparison to pearls in a window frame is rather unusual.[5]

The Filipino riddle, "There are seven windows; only three are shut,"[6] is an unusual variation of the riddle of the seven holes representing the openings in the human head.[7] A rare version of a cow riddle[8] and an analogous description of a horse[9] call the eyes windows.

1144. There's a house with two winder upstairs. Is red, an' downstairs is white. An' two doors.—Face.
Parsons, *Sea Islands, S.C.*, p. 167, No. 93.

1145–1148. Red House (Theater)

Riddlers occasionally compare the mouth and teeth to a house, room, or theater and its furnishings. I have here separated the minor modifications of this theme as follows: a house without mention of person,[1] a house with mention of a person,[2] and a theater, which is a specialized form of the preceding concepts, with mention, in non-English versions, of a dancer.[3] In a version[4] in which the tongue is called a chair but no house is mentioned, we may have a reminiscence of this concept. The notion of comparing the head to a house occurs in various forms, of which the Mongolian "Behind a house something dangles.—Queue"[5] is perhaps the most curious.

---

[1] See the headnote to Nos. 1100–1108.
[2] See Flemish: Joos, 72. Swiss: Zahler, *Münchenbuchsee*, 12. Swedish: Ström, p. 78, "Ögat," 1 (Two windows; one looks [can look] out of the house, but not into it), and p. 79, "Ögat," 7. Spanish: Demófilo, 143, 224, 225; Rodríguez Marín, 322, 323. Argentinian: Lehmann-Nitsche, 562. Chilean: Flores, 125. Dominican Rep.: Andrade, 63. Porto Rican: Mason, 142. Rumanian: Gorovei, 236. Zyrian: Wichmann, *Zyrian*, 64. Votyak: Wichmann, *Votyak*, 253, 156.
[3] Jurgelionis, 164.
[4] See the headnote to Nos. 1189–1191, nn. 1–2, below.
[5] Wichmann, *Zyrian*, 65.
[6] Starr, *Philippines*, 39.
[7] See the headnote to No. 1101 above.
[8] See No. 1486.
[9] Geijer and Campbell, 62.
[1] No. 1146.
[2] No. 1148.
[3] No. 1147. For references to a dancer see the note to No. 1147.
[4] No. 1180. For comparisons of the teeth to chairs, see the note to No. 1180.
[5] Mostaert, 19.

More rarely, riddlers compare a fruit or seed to a chair, as in the Kundu "Rich people sit on arm chairs,"[6] which describes pods on a pepper bush. This shows some similarity to the comparison of a thorny plant to a chair in which one cannot sit.[7]

1145. Red house, green furniture.—Melon.
Parsons, *Bermuda*, p. 248, No. 13 var.

1146. Red house, / And white sets [chairs] all around it.—Teeth and tongue.
Fauset, *Southern Negro*, p. 276, No. 6.

1147. A large theatre has two window upstairs, two window downstairs, a large door with white people, a red stage. What is that?—A person's head.
Parsons, *Sea Islands, S.C.*, p. 167, No. 93 var.

1148. Little red house surrounded by two white galleries, / And a little red man standing inside of it.—Mouth and teeth.
Fauset, *Nova Scotia*, p. 158, No. 70.

1149. (Red) House and a Fence

The comparison of teeth to a fence occurs in various forms, and we can probably reckon with the likelihood that riddlers have hit upon the idea independently. The Spanish-speaking population of the Dominican Republic refer to teeth as an "ivory wall."[1] The Turks see the teeth as "willows in a row, chewing at one another,"[2] and consequently admit too definite an indication of the answer into the question. The SeSuto say simply, "The little reed fence of Mother Knock-knock"[3] and the Louyi, "An enclosure of stakes solidly set."[4] These resemble the French "A little maiden seated on her chair surrounded by white pickets."[5] The Filipinos describe the incisors and the molars in "First the bars and then the posts,"[6] but such anatomical minutiae are rare in riddling. The Javanese "You see the other's fence, but not your own"[7] refers to a fact that other riddlers have failed to note. Some compare the tongue to a creature within a fence.[8]

1149a. Little red house / With white fence all around it, / Door keep opening and shutting.—Tongue and teeth.
Bacon and Parsons, *Virginia*, p. 314, No. 18.

1149b. Something that has a white ivory fence.—Teeth.
Bacon and Parsons, *Virginia*, p. 314, No. 19.

---

[6] Ittmann, *Kundu*, 16.
[7] See Nos. 1184a through 1185 below.
[1] Andrade, 190.
[2] Kúnos, 227.
[3] Norton and Velaphe, 36.
[4] Jacottet, 6.
[5] Mensignac, *Gironde*, p. 298, No. 2.
[6] Starr, *Philippines*, 72.
[7] Helfrich, *Bengkoela*, p. 100, No. 11.
[8] See the headnote to No. 1151 below.

1150. Red Cave That Is Always Wet

Although riddlers have often used the idea of an object that is always wet to describe the teeth or the tongue, I have noted only these two instances in English (Nos. 1150a, 1150b). The version "A well-planed little board, and it is always wet"[1] is a curious elaboration of the theme.

A weakened and perhaps degenerate version is embodied in two forms which do not clearly suggest an animal, a person, or a thing, "What is covered and yet wet?" and "What is wet all the time?"[2] This theme has a parallel in the Togo riddle for a dog's nose: "An animal has something quite naked in the sun and yet it does not dry up."[3] An Ila riddle on the same subject, "A little spring that does not dry up,"[4] is somewhat better conceived. The Arabs say for the mouth, "A well full of water, it never dries up."[5]

Comparisons of the tongue to a rag or ribbon are numerous and widely distributed. The Spanish say, "Between the wall and the wall there is a red ribbon."[6] Somewhat different conceptions are seen in the Albanian "A rag in a puddle," which is similar to the Turkish "I have a quilt; it doesn't come out of the water,"[7] and in the Ossete "Mother gave me a little cotton rag; it does not dry in the sun or by the fire."[8] Some interesting versions from eastern Europe mention various cloths used in the household. The Poles say, "Two lines of white handkerchiefs are out to dry, and they never do dry,"[9] which is not very different from the Arabic "The wash hangs in the sun. It is never dry."[10] The Georgian and Mingrelian versions differ only in a rhetorical repetition of a sort often found in Eastern riddling. The Georgian version is "I have a hand towel. I dried it, and dried it, and could not dry it."[11] The Mingrelian parallel is "I have a hand towel and it is always wet."[12] See also the Abchaz "A never drying small towel."[13] In western Europe I have noted only the German "There are wet diapers beneath a roof and they never dry out."[14]

---

[1] Redfield, *Tennessee*, p. 50, No. 18.
[2] Breton: Kerbeuzec, *Ille-et-Vilaine*, 74. Flemish: Joos, 70. Luxemburg: De la Fontaine, 49. German: Wossidlo, 42; Haffner, 109. Swiss: Rochholz, 441. Walloon: Colson, *Wallonia*, IV, 108, No. 118; Colson, *Devinettes*, p. 148, No. 11. French: Rolland, 122; Lacuve, *Poitou*, p. 354, No. 28, and p. 703, No. 19; Pineau, *Poitou*, 22; A. Ferrand, *Dauphiné*, p. 228; Mensignac, *Gironde*, p. 298, No. 3. Basque: Vinson, 59 (Always protected and always wet); Demófilo, p. 380, No. 14. Spanish: Demófilo, 593; Rodríguez Marín, 312. Svanian: J. Nizheradze, p. 69, No. 25 (It is always wet).
[3] Schönhärl, 10.
[4] Smith and Dale, II, 326, No. 20.
[5] Löhr, p. 107, No. 11.
[6] Spanish: Alcázar, 491. See also Demófilo, 595; Rodríguez Marín, 311. A version in Demófilo, 591 = Rodríguez Marín, 313 differs slightly.
[7] Albanian: Hahn, p. 160, No. 15. Turkish: Hamizade, 152.
[8] Schiefner, 25.
[9] Gustawicz, 461.
[10] Ruoff, p. 17, No. 12.
[11] Blechsteiner, p. 136, No. 6; Glushakov, p. 23, No. 6. Ossete: Schiefner, 26.
[12] Blechsteiner, p. 57, No. 8; Petrov, p. 257, No. 57.
[13] Guliia, 21.
[14] Zingerle, p. 281, No. 121.

Comparisons to a person who is always wet or to a wet house are rather infrequent,[15] but show such interesting variations as the French "A lady in a convent, she sees neither wind nor rain, but is always wet"[16] and "I am always under a roof and am always wet";[17] and the Kundu "In our homestead, even if I have an umbrella, I am wet. If I have none, I get just as wet.—Teeth."[18] Comparisons to a fish or to an animal living in water might be cited in this connection.[19]

An elaboration consists in the assertion that the board, representing the tongue, is always wet and yet never decays. Instances are numerous, especially in northern Europe.[20] Typical examples are the Faeroic "A thin board lies in the water and doesn't rot";[21] the Lithuanian "A little plank does not rot in the puddle";[22] the Russian "A log lies in a bog. It neither gets wet nor rots nor floats away from the shore";[23] and "Midst a swamp there lies a log, it does not rot, it does not emit gas."[24]

English riddlers have shown little liking for comparisons of the teeth to inanimate objects, but others have used them in great variety. The following is a survey of the themes most often used:

§ 1. Knives, axes, adzes, spears, nails, and the like. Spanish: Demófilo, 589; Rodríguez Marín, 310. Serbian: Novaković, p. xviii, No. 7 (A box full of nails). Bulgarian: Gubov, 127 (A cupboard full of chisels); Ikonomov, 48 (The house is full of hammer-axes); Bozhov, 4 (A cave full of spades), 22 (A house full of adzes); Chacharov, 35 (A house full of adzes); Stoilov, pp. 59–60, §18, Nos. 1 through 9. Modern Greek: Dieterich, *Rätseldichtung*, p. 95; Sakellarios, p. 290, No. 7. Turkish: Kowalski, *Zagadki*, 38, 61. African, Kamba: Lindblom, 38 (Tell me the man who lives in the midst of swords and spears). Duala: Ebding, 70. Evhe: F. Müller, p. 156, No. 2 (A little round house full of nails). Togo: Schönhärl, 7 (If I did not have great magical power, I could not live among those who fight with daggers). Kundu: Ittmann, *Kundu*, 296 (My father gave me a field knife. I have already worked industriously with it, but it has not become dull). Indonesian, Tabaru: Fortgens, 3 (A box with nothing but axes). Filipino: Starr, *Philippines*, 67, 68 (A deep well or box filled

---

[15] French: Lespy, *Béarn*, 6. Spanish: Demófilo, p. 390, No. 38. Argentinian: Lehmann-Nitsche, 319a through 319l. Chilean: Flores, 387; Laval, 7. Cuban: Massip, 112, 114, 116. Porto Rican: Mason, 312c, 312d, 312f. Portuguese: Pires de Lima, 53.
[16] Bladé, *Armagnac*, 39.   [17] Westphalen, *Metz*, col. 197.
[18] Ittmann, *Kundu*, 281.
[19] See the headnote to Nos. 497–510, § 6, above.
[20] Icelandic: Árnason, 597. Italian: Pitrè, 398. Rumanian: Papahagi, 51, var. 2. Polish: Saloni, *Rzeshów*, 57 (It is set in the water, but will never decay). Russian: Sadovnikov, 1743. Finnish: Henssen, 60. Estonian: Wiedemann, p. 288 (An oaken chip at the bottom of the sea never rots).
[21] Hammershaimb, *Antiquarisk tidsskrift*, III (1849–1851), 316, No. 11.
[22] Jurgelionis, 186.
[23] Sadovnikov, 1743n.
[24] Arkhangel'skii, p. 77.

with chisels). Tagalog: Rizal, p. 45 (A deep well filled with steel blades). Compare the Lithuanian "A little storehouse full of beetles used in washing clothes" (Schleicher, p. 204).

§ 2. Bones. Spanish, Argentinian: Lehmann-Nitsche, 246, 247b, 247d, 248a, 249 through 251, 471f (A corral of bones). Chilean: Flores, 242 (A box full of bones). Dominican Rep.: Andrade, 62 (A little house full of bones). Porto Rican: Mason, 205 (I have a box full of bones, and I would not give it away, not for a hundred pesos). The last theme is that of the riddle for a bald head.[25] Portuguese: Braga, 46; Pires, *Archivio*, III (1884), 114, No. 6; Parsons, *Cape Verde*, 205a through 205e (A pot or pan full of bones). Italian: Pitrè, 74.

§ 3. Stones. Italian: Pitrè, 398. Modern Greek: Dieterich, *Rätseldichtung*, p. 95; Dieterich, *Sporades*, 6 (Marble stones and a shoe). The shoe refers to the shape of the tongue. Arabic: Ruoff, p. 16, No. 9 (A hollow full of stones); Löhr, p. 106, No. 10. Turkish: Kúnos, 69 (A tiny little living thing; inside filled with tiny rocks); Zavarin, *Brusa*, 5 (Marble above, marble below, wrinkled Omar between);[26] Kowalski, *North Bulgaria*, 1. Georgian: Kapanadze, p. 144, No. 1 (My little vegetable patch is strewn with little stones). Mingrelian: Petrov, p. 257, No. 2 (Identical with the preceding, but lacks an answer). Abchaz: Guliia, 22 (There is no river about, yet there are many white stones). African, Swahili: Büttner, p. 201 (The basket of the gracious lady is quite full of little white pebbles); Velten, 40 (My sweetheart's box is full of little pebbles). Wanamwezi: Dahl, 6.

The Bulgarian "White dust lying under the bank" and "Fine dust lying under the bank"[27] are not entirely clear. The Kolarian "Bring me to the white stones, then I will go alone"[28] seems to be a fragment of a comparison of eating and threshing.[29]

§ 4. Pearls, shells. Serbian: Novaković, p. 66, No. 8 (The cave is full of fine pearls. The pearly door is worth more than a pound of fine gold. Bulgarian: Chacharov, 37 (The box is full of pearls); Stoilov, p. 59, § 18, Nos. 12 through 14. Albanian: Hahn, p. 160, No. 26 (A box of pearls). Filipino: Starr, *Philippines*, 66 (A small brook filled with shells). Compare the Aandonga "A little cave full of eggs,"[30] which appears to be an independent invention.

The comparison of teeth and pearls has some similarity to the comparison of stars and pearls,[31] but the details are appropriately varied for the two answers. The oldest example of the theme that I have noted is a Turkish art-riddle by Fani. This spice merchant, who lived about A.H. 1003, wrote: "What is the cup like a ruby which is full of pearls, is like the realm of the waves,

---

[25] See Nos. 1593a through 1593i below.
[26] For further examples of this riddle see the headnote to Nos. 1443–1444, nn. 3–4.
[27] Gubov, 123, 128.   [28] Wagner, 97.
[29] See the headnote to No. 841, § 4, above.
[30] Pettinen, 33.
[31] See the headnote to No. 1227, § 5, below.

which dissolves into naught when it is closed and which pours forth sweetness when open?"[32] Some riddlers describe a fruit as a box containing many small objects.[33]

§ 5. Miscellaneous. French: Bladé, *Armagnac*, 118 (An oven full of fagots that are neither green nor dry);[34] Dardy, *L'Albret*, p. 333 (Little laths, neither green nor dry, in a little room); Fesquet, p. 176. Italian: Schneller, *Wälschtirol*, p. 255, Nos. 17 (It is a row of linen clothes, they are always white and clean), 18 (I have a little basket full of chips, they are neither green nor dry). Bulgarian: Gubov, 126 (A vat full of small eggs), 375 (The vat is full of small eggs).[35] Turkish: Hamizade, 4 (A tiny room, inside it is full of chips); Kúnos, *Nyelvkönyv*, 38 (Willows row on row grind up one another). Altai Turkish: Radlov, I, 261, No. 3 (In the house a string of cheeses is hung up). Mongolian: Kotvich, 17 (Thirty white tents in a ditch).

Some very curious comparisons for the mouth and teeth have no parallels. The Lamba "A little hole full of grass litter"[36] is appropriate only when we think of yellowing teeth resembling grass drying into hay. The Panjabi "A parrot dancing on a shelf full of kauris"[37] is both ingeniously and correctly conceived. It has some similarity to the notion of a dog barking within a fence.[38] The teeth are often called a fence.[39] The Sukuma "A cave that is full"[40] is too scantily conceived. The strange Kundu mouth riddle, "There is a field that knows no drafts,"[41] is correctly composed, but seems to have no parallels.

1150a. In a big red cave thar's a leetle white fence. It don't never rain on th' leetle white fence, but still it's allus wet. What is it?—A feller's teeth.
Randolph and Spradley, *Ozark*, p. 83.

1150b. A little white fence that's always wet, / But never rained on yet.— Teeth.
Hudson, p. 85, No. 16.

1151. Red Garden within a Fence

The comparison of teeth to a fence leads readily to equating the mouth to a garden, but riddlers have not shown much liking for this extension of the theme. Some have compared the mouth to a garden in which a flower stands.[1]

---

[32] Friedreich, p. 163.
[33] See the headnote to No. 1355 below.
[34] The fingernails rather than the teeth are often called wood that is green and dry at the same time; see the headnote to No. 989, nn. 10–12, above.
[35] These Bulgarian riddles seem to have no connection with the Aandonga text quoted above (n. 30) in this headnote.
[36] Doke, 6.
[37] *Panjab Notes and Queries*, III (1886), 217, No. 892, §1. Kauris (cowries) are shells used as coins.
[38] See the headnote to No. 1151 below.
[39] See Nos. 1149a, 1149b, the headnote to No. 1149, and note to No. 1149a.
[40] Augustiny, 30.   [41] Ittmann, *Kundu*, 217.
[1] German: Wossidlo, 42a. Spanish, Argentinian: Lehmann-Nitsche, 471a through 471e. Chilean: Flores, 239.

A further elaboration is the comparison of the tongue to an animal, usually a dog, or, more rarely, to a person, within the fence. See the Scandinavian "A red dog behind a white fence."[2] Variations of this appear in the Serbian "A red dog barks from a hole";[3] the Bulgarian "A red bitch barks in the closet";[4] and the Gypsy "A very bad dog sits in a house of flesh."[5] The Modern Greek "A fence round about, and within a playful one"[6] is probably intended to suggest a dog. The dramatic possibilities of the theme are illustrated in the Lithuanian "A dog barks and barks. *Whish!* It's behind the door."[7]

It is not unusual in the practice of riddling to utilize a comparison of the teeth to dogs or wolves.[8]

Other animals are occasionally mentioned; see the Serbian "A red billy-goat screams in the cave";[9] the Bulgarian allusions to a fox as well as to a goat;[10] the apparently unique Arabic suggestion of a bird in "He is red and like a duck, in whose mouth will you lay him?—Tongue";[11] the Yakut "They say that the red cow tries and tries to leave the barn, but leave it she cannot," "They say that a red cow stands captive in a birch grove,"[12] and "In the midst of a forest there lies a cow";[13] the Mongolian "The red calf is tied up inside a fence of bone,"[14] "Behind the rocks there is a trained sorrel horse,"[15] and "A roan horse in a birch fence";[16] and the Pangwe "A leopard lies crouching among the [*Ficus globicarpa* Warb.]"[17]

Analogous comparisons to a person are rare, except for the Modern Greek "Round about there is a fence, and inside there is a Frank"[18] and the many comparisons of the tongue to a person in a room.[19]

1151. A little red garden, enclosed with a white fence.—Mouth.
Knortz, p. 237, No. 127.

---

[2] Danish: Kristensen, p. 137, p. 399, Nos. 636a, 636b. Swedish: Ström, p. 83, "Munnen, tänderna, tungan." Czech: Hanika-Otto, p. 125, No. 53. Estonian: Wiedemann, p. 285. Spanish, Argentinian: Lehmann-Nitsche, 247b. Bulgarian: Gubov, 91. Albanian: Hahn, p. 158, No. 9. See also the headnote to Nos. 438–444, § 5, above.
[3] Novaković, p. 79, No. 4.
[4] Bozhov, 18 = Chacharov, 25.
[5] Wlislocki, 20.
[6] Polites, *Neohellenika Analekta*, I, 206, No. 72, and p. 220, No. 153.
[7] Schleicher, p. 211.
[8] See the headnote to Nos. 497–510, § 4, above.
[9] Novaković, p. 79, No. 3.
[10] Gubov, 92 through 98.
[11] Ruoff, p. 19, No. 24. A duck and the tongue are similar in shape.
[12] Piekarski, 102, 103.
[13] Popov, p. 285. See also a Walloon riddle quoted in the note to No. 1149a in the present collection.
[14] Kotvich, 236.
[15] Mongolian, Buryat: Gombojew, 11.
[16] Klukine, 14; Bazarov, 52.
[17] Tessmann, 117.
[18] Stathes, p. 347, No. 95.
[19] See No. 1148 above. See also Spanish: Demófilo, 585 = Rodríguez Marín, 308; Demófilo, 590 = Rodríguez Marín, 309. Chilean: Flores, 394. New Mexican: Espinosa, 66.

1152-1155. House of Various Colors (Materials)

The theme is often elaborated by the mention of people of various colors who reside in a house of peculiar color. This notion is especially suited to describe a fruit and the seeds within.[1]

1152. Yellow inside, / Yellow outside, / White windows.—Orange.
Parsons, *Bermuda*, p. 248, No. 14.

1153. Painted yellow outside, / Painted yellow inside, / And a white door inside.—Mango.
Parsons, *Bermuda*, p. 248, No. 16.

1154. As I went to the school alone, / I found a little pennerie; / 'Twas painted out, 'twas painted in. / 'Twas painted our [o'er] wi' poverty; / 'T would kill a bull, 't would kill a bear, / 'T would kill a thousand men and mehr [mair; i.e., more].—Hunger.
Gregor, *Northeast Scotland*, p. 78.

1155. Iron roof, glass walls, / Burns and burns and never falls.—Lantern.
Randolph and Taylor, *Ozarks*, 15.

1156-1164. House and Its Contents

Some very curious and occasionally obscure riddles enumerate a series of objects linked with each other in a logical manner. The logical connection is not the only one, however; the repetition of a formula also links them together and reinforces the enumeration. I shall call such riddles chain-riddles. This characteristic technique of linking appears in the previously discussed riddles for a year and for a church with its bell. These riddles describe a tree with its branches, its twigs, a nest, and eggs in the nest.[1] The same device appears also in some descriptions of a man in terms of a scene in nature or in terms of a heap or collection of household utensils.[2] Some children's rhymes employ the same technique of linking.[3]

Two varieties of these chain-riddles describe an object in terms of a house and its contents. Those having the answers "blood," "death," "heart," and "ear wax"[4] name various objects in the house and proceed from larger to smaller objects. Two anomalous riddles for an egg[5] and a penny[6] proceed similarly. Riddles having the answer "walnut," "watermelon," or "canta-

---

[1] See the headnote to Nos. 910–915.

[1] See Nos. 1037a through 1039, the headnotes to Nos. 1037, 1038, and 1039, the headnote to Nos. 1037–1038, the note to Nos. 1037a, 1037b, the note to Nos. 1038a, 1038b, and the note to No. 1039.

[2] See the headnote to Nos. 1100–1108.

[3] For examples and discussion see J. Lewalter, *Deutsches Kinderlied und Kinderspiel* (Cassel, 1911), p. 384, note to No. 594; Georg Schläger, *Zeitschrift des Vereins für Volkskunde*, XXVII (1917), 201; Wolfgang Schultz, *Mitra*, I (1914–1920), col. 47; Martti Haavio, *Kettenmärchenstudien*, I (FF Communications, LXXXVIII; Helsinki, 1929), 5–92.

[4] Nos. 1156a through 1158b below.

[5] Nos. 1159a through 1159d.   [6] Nos. 1160a, 1160b.

loupe" describe a house within a house within a house and end by telling what is within the smallest house.[7] Usually, the scene portrayed is that of men dwelling within the smallest house—a conception that bears a strong resemblance to the comparison of a fruit to a house in which many persons live.[8] An obscure riddle with the answer "kite"[9] also employs this pattern. In these two varieties the differences in conception and details imply their different origins, but old texts are so few that a discussion of these matters is virtually out of the question.

A curious Porto Rican riddle for a coconut employs this device, but is based on the conception of the body of an animal and not on that of the structure of a house: "Within the skin is the hide, within the hide is the bone, within the bone is the flesh, and within the flesh is the blood."[10]

1156–1160. House and Furniture

A few curious and rather old riddles describing blood, the heart, or death in terms of a house and its furniture have maintained themselves in oral tradition with considerable success, notwithstanding the obscurity of their details. The riddler proceeds from mentioning the house to enumerating smaller and smaller parts of the house and finally tells of a shelf on which there is a cup containing something to eat or drink. This scene may preserve a recollection of the theme of a demon's life contained in the last of three objects. This theme of the so-called separable soul occurs in several *märchen*. It relates how the hero learns that the evil creature which he must defeat has its life in an egg in a wolf in a fox at the end of the world, or in the last of an equally complicated and improbable sequence of objects. By some means or other the hero must get to the end of the world and destroy the egg and with it his enemy. Both the riddle and the theme of the separable soul use the device of placing someone's life—or what implies much the same thing, his heart or blood—in an object within another object within a third object. Indeed, the fact that a variant answer to one of these riddles is "an egg"[1] seems pertinent to my effort to connect the riddle with the theme of the separable soul. The theme of the separable soul has been much discussed[2] but has not previously been connected with the riddle pattern represented by Nos. 1156a through 1159d below.

This manner of description is applied to various objects. The Russians use it in a riddle for a house, an oven, an oven-mouth, and a fire, as follows: "On the street a storehouse, in the storehouse a trunk, in the trunk a blue kerchief,

---

[7] Nos. 1161 through 1163.
[8] See the headnotes to Nos. 908–916, 909, and 910–915.
[9] No. 1164.   [10] Mason, 173.

[1] Nos. 1159a through 1159c.
[2] See J. Bolte and G. Polívka, *Anmerkungen zu den Kinder- und Hausmärchen*, III (Leipzig, 1918), 434, 439–440; J. G. Frazer, *The Golden Bough*, 3d ed., VII, ii (London, 1912), 95–152.

in the kerchief gold."³ The "blue kerchief" is the smoke of the fire, and the "gold" is the fire. In a parallel, "There stands a moist oak, in the moist oak there is a box, in the box there is a blue kerchief, in the blue kerchief there is gold,"⁴ which has the answer, "house, trunk, clothes, money," the riddler has lost the enigmatic values of his symbols and repeats their literal meanings. Riddles of this sort which have the answer "egg" are akin to the description of an egg as a wall around a precious object.⁵ The answer "penny"⁶ appears to be a recent invention, made perhaps by those who did not perceive the import of what they were saying. The answer "ear wax"⁷ is perhaps a development of the blood riddle, by the substitution of one bodily product for another.

Many instances of this manner of description seem to have no connection with the riddles here discussed.⁸ A few examples will sufficiently illustrate their variety. The Poles mingle literal and enigmatic elements in "There stands an oak, on the oak is clay, on the clay peas, and on the peas a pig.—Table, platter, peas, bacon."⁹ Perhaps a better form of this is the Cheremiss "A wooden city, in the wooden city a stone city, in the stone city an iron city, in the iron city they cook fish without bones.—Room, stove, frying pan, pancake,"¹⁰ which contains no literal elements. The Turkish "In a box there is a kind of water, in this water there is a snake, on the head of the snake there is a rose.—Lantern, oil, wick, flame"¹¹ has some similarity to a riddle for a hookah.¹² Another variation of this sort of description is seen in the Turkish "Within the large yurt is a little yurt and in the little yurt are stag's cheeks.—Boots, stockings, legs,"¹³ which has a parallel in the Mongolian "In a big house is a small house. In the small house is a fat little boy."¹⁴ The Malayalam coconut riddle, "He penetrated a jungle and saw a rock, he penetrated the rock and saw something white, he penetrated the white thing and saw water,"¹⁵ is a realistic account of a visit to a jungle (the hairy covering of the coconut).

1156a. Was a house. In de house was a table. On de table was a plate. In de plate was a saucer. In de saucer was a cup. In de cup was a spoon. In dat spoon was a drop o' somet'in' you kyan't do widout.—Drop of blood.

---

³ Sadovnikov, 167.
⁴ Sadovnikov, 689.
⁵ See the headnote to No. 1138 above.
⁶ Nos. 1160a, 1160b.
⁷ Nos. 1158a, 1158b.
⁸ See also Flemish: *Ons Volksleven*, II (1890), 104, No. 6. German: Wossidlo, 39. Danish: Kristensen, p. 154, § 445, No. 713. Italian: Coronedi-Berti, *Archivio*, II (1883), 576, No. 20. Spanish, Dominican Rep.: Andrade, 89. Zyrian: Wichmann, *Zyrian*, 173.
⁹ Saloni, *Rzeshów*, 183. See also his No. 184; Siarkowski, 2; Gustawicz, 424.
¹⁰ Porkka, 86, 134.
¹¹ Kowalski, *Zagadki*, 39.
¹² See the headnote to Nos. 1440–1441 below.
¹³ Katanov in Radlov, IX, 91, No. 771, and p. 238, No. 39.
¹⁴ Mostaert, 193.
¹⁵ Frohnmeyer, p. 229.

Parsons, *Sea Islands, S.C.*, p. 155, No. 22. House, table, saucer, cup.—Yer heart in de cup: Parsons, *Bahamas*, p. 474, No. 29.

1156b. There is a little house; and in that little house there is a little room; and in that little room there is a little shelf; and on that little shelf there is a little cup; and in that little cup there is something I would not take all the world for.—The heart's blood.

Udal, *Dorset*, p. 395; Burne, *Shropshire*, p. 574, No. 171.

1156c. As I was going over London Bridge, / I saw a house; / In that house there were a pantry, / In that pantry there were a shelf, / On that shelf there were a cup, / In that cup there / Something you can't do without.—Blood.

Greenleaf, *Newfoundland*, p. 18, No. 1.

1156d. There is a rickety hill, on this rickety hill stands a rickety house, in the rickety house is a rickety room, in the rickety room is a rickety table, on the rickety table is is a rickety cup, in the rickety cup is something everyone's got; what is it?—Blood.

Knortz, p. 215, No. 15.

1156e. Down under the hill there was a mill, / In the mill there was a chest, / And in the chest there was a till, / In the till there was a cup, / And in the cup there was a drop. / No man could drink it, / No man could eat it, / No man could do without it.—The heart's blood.

Fauset, *Nova Scotia*, p. 153, No. 49; Thurston, *Massachusetts*, p. 182, No. 4.

1156f. Upon a lone hill there was a little house, / In the little house there was a little room, / In the little room there was a little trunk, / In the little trunk there was a little cup, / In the little cup there was a little drop, / Which no man could do without.—The heart's blood.

Fauset, *Nova Scotia*, p. 153, No. 49 var.

1156g. Down yonder hill, / There stands a mill, / And in the mill, / There is a chest, / And in the chest, / Is a drop that everyone needs.—Blood.

Hyatt, *Adams Co., Ill.*, p. 658, No. 10840.

1157a. In the woods there is a pond, / In the pond there is a boat, / In that boat there is a cup, / In that cup there is / Something everyone shall taste of.—Death.

Greenleaf, *Newfoundland*, p. 18, No. 2.

1157b. There was a chist in yonders field, / And in that chist there was a till, / And in that till there was a cup, / And in that cup there was a sup / That everyone in the world must taste.—Death.

Fauset, *Nova Scotia*, p. 153, No. 49 var.

1158a. There is a ship, and in this ship is a window. In this window is a table. On this table is a cup; and in this cup is something you can neither drink it nor eat it, but you must have it.—Your ear-wax.

Parsons, *Sea Islands, S.C.*, p. 155, No. 22 var.

1158b. There was a little red house / And in the little red house / There was a little red shelf, / And on the little red shelf / Was a little red box / And in that little red box / There was something that no man eats, / No man drinks, and no man does without.—Ear wax.
Hudson, p. 86, No. 23.

1159a. On a hill there stood a house, and in that house there was a shelf, and on that shelf there was a cup; in that cup there was some suck, and you couldn't get that suck unless you broke that cup.—Egg.
Perkins, *New Orleans*, p. 110, No. 47.

1159b. Down yonder stands a little house. / In that house is a little cup. / In that cup is a little sup. / You can't get that little sup / Without breaking the little cup.—An egg.
Chappell, p. 230, No. 7.

1159c. A cup sitting in the window, / And you can't take a sup, / Without breaking the cup.—Egg.
Hyatt, *Adams Co., Ill.*, p. 660, No. 10860.

1159d. j have a little posmet & in my litt[le] posmat a litt[le] rostmeat j cannot eat my rosmeat but j must brak my posmeat.—a egg.
Tupper, *Holme Riddles*, 33.

1160a. There is a hill, / And on that hill there is a house, / And in that house there is a closet, / And in that closet there is a dress, / And in that dress there is a pocket, / And in that pocket there is an Indian head. / What is this head?—A penny.
Knortz, pp. 237–238, No. 133.

1160b. On the hill there's a house, / In that house there's a closet, / In that closet hangs a coat, / In that coat is a pocket, / In that pocket there's an Indian head.—A penny.
Bacon and Parsons, *Virginia*, p. 323, No. 97.

1161–1164. House within a House within a House

This manner of description, which is closely related to a riddle for a church, the bell, and the congregation,[1] is applicable to a fruit having a seed or seeds. English riddlers do not, however, so use it. For example, see the German "In my father's garden there stand trees, each tree has branches, on the branches hang cradles, in the cradles children are lying.—Beans."[2] This has parallels in Dutch, German, Lithuanian, and Lettish riddling; see the Lithuanian "A tiny, tiny cradle, and in that cradle there lies a small child,"[3] which seems to be a condensed version; the Lettish "In the garden there was a tree, beside the tree

---
[1] See the headnote to No. 1039.
[2] Wossidlo, 37. See also his No. 38.
[3] Jurgelionis, 1015.

one cannot marry[4] or to a thorny plant.[5] Although the comparison of a nut or fruit to a box, pot, or dish is very widely known, English riddlers have shown no great liking for it.[6] The similarity of lights and stars seems obvious, but it does not yield many riddles.[7] A variety of things are compared to bags, ropes, clothing, and cloth, but only the comparison of the sky or a cloud to cloth is generally used.[8] The section concludes with comparisons to articles of food.[9]

1170–1178. Barrel, Tub, Pot, Tank, Well

By adding appropriate details a riddler can make a description of a barrel, tub, pot, tank, or well applicable to a variety of objects. By specifying the contents as golden in color, he describes the sun. A barrel without staves or hoops that can nevertheless hold liquids is generally used on the continent of Europe as a riddle for an egg, but the English parallel[1] to this theme is not clearly expressed. Many English riddlers have compared a ring to a bottomless tub.[2] Riddles mentioning a tank or a well have as answers the eye, a joint of sugar cane, or a coco leaf.[3] The Malayalam "A pot without a bottom.—Well"[4] is a rare instance of comparing an object to something virtually identical with it. A nut is often called a pot filled with tasty food.[5]

1170. Little barrel of gold on a miry road.—Sun.
Fitzgerald, p. 181 (Irish).

1171. Barrel without Staves

Most European riddlers know this description of an egg, but this appears to be the only English instance that has been taken down. The barrel is usually said to be without hoops or bands.[1]

1171. My moder have a barrel, haven't got no staves.—Eggs.
Parsons, *Antilles*, III, 369, Grenada, 7.

1172–1173. Bottomless Tub

The concept of a bottomless tub, dish, or other vessel is applicable to a ring and to a few other objects. The ring thus described is a wide band having sides

---

[4] No. 1183. [5] Nos. 1184a through 1185.
[6] Nos. 1187a through 1188; compare with non-English riddles cited in the headnote to No. 1187, § 1, the note to Nos. 1187a, 1187b, and the note to No. 1188.
[7] See the headnote to Nos. 1189–1191.
[8] Nos. 1215, 1217 through 1222a, 1224 through 1226, 1229a, 1229b.
[9] Nos. 1229a through 1237j, and 1239a through 1249.

[1] No. 1171.
[2] Nos. 1172a through 1172c, 1172e through 1173d, 1173f through 1173j.
[3] Nos. 1174 through 1176.
[4] Frohnmeyer, p. 229.
[5] See the headnote to No. 1187 below.
[1] French: Lespy, *Béarn*, 2; Pineau, *Poitou*, 17.

bulging out slightly like the sides of a tub. This conception may be related to such apparently contradictory themes as "A hole of silver, a plug of flesh."[1] So far as I have noted, only western European riddlers know the theme of the bottomless tub. A Russian riddler turns a somewhat similar conception into a riddle having the form of a tale: "On a hill there stands a young girl. She marvels at a hole, 'Oh my bright hole, golden hole, where shall I put you?'— 'Put me on live flesh!'"[2] A somewhat simpler version is "There were two young girls walking. Each bought a little hole, put it on raw flesh."[3]

A rather inappropriate development is found in some Scandinavian parallels of the type, "Sister sends sister a bottomless tub that brews and burns and bakes and sweeps."[4] The tub should not be assigned inappropriate functions belonging to a person.

Some modifications of this pattern call for brief notice. The Lithuanians say, "A little garden of flesh, a little fence of gold"[5] and "A pot of flesh pierced at both ends."[6] In the Balkans a comparison to flesh on a spit is frequently found. The Serbians say, "The flesh is the spit, and the meat is golden"[7] and "The meat is of iron, the spit of flesh."[8] The same theme occurs in the Modern Greek and Albanian "A spit of flesh and flesh of iron"[9] and, with a reversal in the order of the elements, the Turks say, "The meat is of iron, the spit of flesh."[10] The Estonian "A kettle of flesh cooks food of iron"[11] is an analogous conception.

Somewhat different ways of describing a ring occur in the French "Round, round without a bottom, women have it, men do not, and girls want it" and "Tub without a bottom which serves for marriage."[12]

The notion of a bottomless tub or barrel filled with flesh is applicable to:

§ 1. A ring. See Nos. 1172a through 1172c, 1172e through 1173d, and 1173f through 1173j below.

§ 2. A thimble. Irish: Delargy, 17 (A bottomless barrel full of living flesh); Delargy, *Inis Cé*, 18 (A little gold keg filled with man's flesh); De Bhaldraithe, 46 (A little iron well full of human flesh); O Dalaigh, 93; Hyde, p. 172 (A bottomless barrel, it's shaped like a hive, it's filled full of flesh, and the flesh is alive); Christiansen, 80. Breton: Duine, *Saint-Malo*, p. 516 (A little bit of iron

---

[1] See the Mordvin parallel in the note to Nos. 1172a through 1173j.
[2] Sadovnikov, 679.
[3] Sadovnikov, 680.
[4] Norwegian: Christie, 115; Landstad, p. 806, No. 7; Brox, *Ytre Senja*, 67; Stafset, 147. Faeroic: Hammershaimb, *Antiquarisk tidsskrift*, III (1849-1851), 320, No. 48. Swedish: Ericsson, *Södermanland*, I (1879), 86, No. 31; Hyltén-Cavallius, *Värend*, 80; Noreen, *Fryksdal*, 20; Sandén, *Norra Vadsbo*, 101; Geijer and Campbell, 28.
[5] Schleicher, p. 198. The adjective "gold" has the variants "silver" and "brass."
[6] Schleicher, p. 198.
[7] Novaković, p. 176, No. 12.
[8] Novaković, p. 177, No. 1.
[9] Polites, *Neohellenika Analekta*, I, 231, No. 221. Albanian: Hahn, p. 161, No. 37.
[10] Kowalski, *North Bulgaria*, 44. Compare "A skewer made of meat, a roast made of silver" (Hamizade, 558).
[11] Wiedemann, p. 275.
[12] Mensignac, *Gironde*, pp. 298-299, Nos. 7, 8.

filled with flesh). Norwegian: Bugge, *Telemarken*, 49 (There stands a barrel full of flesh and blood, little and light, empty and full, many holes and none through it). Spanish, Argentinian: Lehmann-Nitsche, 578. Italian: Pitrè, 242. Lappish: Donner, 12 (Without lid or bottom, yet full of fresh meat).

A Spanish mention of "flesh in my mouth" (Demófilo, 356) suggests perhaps a dog rather than a person.

§ 3. A skirt. Danish: Kristensen, p. 131, § 373, Nos. 593a, 593b. Swedish: Ström, p. 160, "Skjortan och särkan," 2; Geijer and Campbell, 31 (What is deeper than the deepest sea?—A skirt, which is without a bottom).

§ 4. A lamp chimney. Spanish, Argentinian: Lehmann-Nitsche, 682 (Hollow, large, and round; has neither lid nor bottom).

1172a. A tub came without a bottom.—Ring.
Parsons, *Barbados*, p. 281, No. 27 var.

1172b. Me fader had a bucket wid no bottom.—Ring.
Parsons, *Bahamas*, p. 482, No. 102.

1172c. A riddle, a riddle aree, / No man can tell this riddle on to me, / A tub sailed to England from Barbados, without a bottom.—Ring.
Parsons, *Barbados*, p. 281, No. 27 var.

1172d. My father have something without top or bottom, had it with him wherever he go.—Ring.
Beckwith, *Jamaica*, p. 190, No. 62.

1172e. The Queen of Sheba / Send to the Queen of Babylon / For a bottomless dish.—Ring.
Parsons, *Barbados*, p. 281, No. 27 var.

1172f. The King of France sent to the King of Spain to get a tub without a bottom.—Ring.
Beckwith, *Jamaica*, p. 190, No. 62a.

1173a. My mama sent to your mama / To borrow a bottomless dish / To put raw flesh an' blood in.—Ring.
Parsons, *Barbados*, p. 281, No. 27 var.

1173b. The king of Manchester, / He sent to his sister, / A bottomless vessel / To put on raw flesh.—A ring.
Fauset, *Nova Scotia*, p. 164, No. 108.

1173c. The Queen of Morocco she wrote to the King / For a bottomless vessel to put flesh an' blood in.—Ring.
Kavanagh, *Béaloideas*, II (1929-1930), 295.

1173d. As I was going to Worcester, I met a man from Gloucester. I asked him where he was going, and he told me to Gloucester to buy something that had neither top nor bottom, but which would hold flesh, blood, and bones.—A wedding ring.
Eliza M. Leather, *Folk-Lore*, XXVII (1916), 415-416 (Hereford).

1173e. My moder had a pon' wid no bottom, but still yet it hol' a junk of meat.—Ring on yer finger.
Parsons, *Bahamas*, p. 472, No. 15.

1173f. My mistress send me to your mistress for a bottomless t'ing to put raw flesh in. What is dat?—A ring.
Johnson, *Antigua*, p. 88, No. 83.

1173g. A woman have a tub / Without top, without bottom, / And yet still can hold flesh and blood.—Ring.
Parsons, *Barbados*, p. 280, No. 27.

1173h. Something has neither top nor bottom and still can hold flesh and blood.—Ring.
Parsons, *Bermuda*, p. 258, No. 103.

1173i. A riddle, a ring, / Here's a gold tub, / Be 'out bottom, top, / An' still can hold in blood, bones, skin, an' nails.—Ring.
Parsons, *Barbados*, p. 281, No. 27 var.

1173j. Me riddle me riddle / Me randy oh. / Fader had a t'ing, / Perhaps you could clear dis riddle or not. / Tub hol' water wid'out no bottom.—Ring on de finger.
Parsons, *Bahamas*, p. 475, No. 40.

1174–1176. Well (Tank) Holds Water

1174. My father have a well; it have neither top nor bottom, yet it hold water.—Sugar-cane.
Beckwith, *Jamaica*, p. 190, No. 61.

1175. My father have a tank in his yard; when the rain fall, it doesn't catch and when the dew fall, it catch.—Coco leaf, because it sheds water like quicksilver.
Beckwith, *Jamaica*, p. 184, No. 18.

1176. My father got a tank in his yard, don't care how the rain come never catch water; but soon as little dirt get into it, it full.—Eye.
Beckwith, *Jamaica*, p. 184, No. 17.

1177–1178. Pot Boils without Fire

1177. As I was going over Humber, / I heard a great rumble; / Three pots a boilin', / An' no fire under.—Water under the boat.
Gutch and Peacock, *Lincolnshire*, p. 397, No. 5.

1178a. as j wend on my way j hard [heard] a grat wonder 4 & 20 pots boiling & no fire under.—many of custurds in an oven.
Tupper, *Holme Riddles*, 51.

1178b. As I went over London Bridge, / I saw a mighty wonder; / Four-and-twenty pots a-boiling, / And no fire under.—Pies in a brick oven.
Gardner, *Schoharie Hills, N.Y.*, p. 243, No. 4.

1179–1199. Furniture

1179. What is the bes' furniture for a man's house?—The daughter.
Beckwith, *Jamaica*, p. 217, No. 266.

1180. Little red rocker set on the hill, / Here he goes, here he goes, / Now he stops still.—Tongue.
Fauset, *Nova Scotia*, p. 157, No. 68.

1181. A man have a chair. When he pulled it to set down, you can hear it quite in England.—T'under.
Parsons, *Antilles*, III, 370, Grenada, 32.

1182. My mother has a daughter, if she can not get three chair, she wouldn't take a seat.—Pot and three stones.
Parsons, *Antilles*, III, 366, Trinidad, 30.

1183–1186. Chair (Bed) Cannot Be Sat (Lain) In

This conception, which does not seem particularly appropriate for the description of a man's daughter (No. 1183), is often used in the West Indies for a thorny plant (Nos. 1184a through 1186b). The Hausa "A saddle that God has made which I shall not mount" (Harris, 13) applies it to a scorpion.

1183. Me riddle me riddle burandy oh, / Perhaps I can clear dis riddle, / An' perhaps you can[:] / My fader had a cheer [chair], his own. / Couldn't come in an' set in it, / But some one else, a stranger, / Could come and set in it.—His daughter. He couldn't marry his own daughter. A stranger had to come an' marry her.
Parsons, *Andros Island, Bahamas*, p. 275, No. 1.

1184a. Me wriggle, me wriggle, / A-tell [I tell] you dis striggle, / Perhaps you may guess it, perhaps not. / My father gave me a chair to sit into, / And all that, I couldn't sit into it.—Bunch o' prickle pear.
Parsons, *Antilles*, III, 429, Nevis, 20.

1184b. My fader gave me a chair to sit in, an' still I couldn't sit in it. What's dat?—Prickle hedges.
Parsons, *Antilles*, III, 441, Anguilla, 28.

1184c. My fader gave me a large rocking chair to sit in and I couldn' sit in it.—Bunch of prickles.
Parsons, *Antilles*, III, 425, Antigua, 14.

1185. My father git me a rocking chair to rock in, and I couldn't rock in it.—A bunch of acacia.
Parsons, *Antilles*, III, 373, Grenada, 70.

1186a. My fader give me a bed to lay upon, and I could not lay upon it.—Prickly pear.
Parsons, *Antilles*, III, 442, St. Croix, 4.

1186b. My fader lay me down in a bed, an' I couldn' sleep in it.—Prickle pear.
Parsons, *Antilles*, III, 435, St. Martin, 11.

1187–1188. Box (Trunk)

1187. Box Cannot Be Opened

In the West Indies English riddlers call a nut a box which, when once opened, cannot be closed again. There are a few parallels in other languages, but the notion is usually applied to an egg.[1] The idea is analogous to the conception of an egg as a barrel without an opening,[2] a trunk without an opening,[3] or a house that cannot be easily entered or left.[4] There are a few riddles of similar construction on unusual themes: the Batak say of the kneecap, "The box of Our Lord cannot be opened"[5] and the Filipinos say of the sun, "San Juan's house—you cannot open."[6]

This idea is often applied to the stomach, as in the Bankon "My father bequeathed me a chest that no one can open. What is it?"[7] and the Mongolian "A thin rock cannot be opened."[8]

Some analogous ideas are "a chest that only God can make" and "a pot filled with tasty food." The objects described in these ways are much the same as those described by the notion of a box that cannot be opened. The notion of a chest that only God can make is applicable to:

§ 1. A nut. Spanish: Demófilo, 734; Rodríguez Marín, 564. Argentinian: Lehmann-Nitsche, 485a through 485j. Chilean: Flores, 501 through 503. Porto Rican: Mason, 399.

The closely related notion of calling a nut a pot or kettle (more rarely a box) containing tasty food does not seem to be known to English riddlers, but has circulated widely on the continent of Europe and eastward. I have not noted any African parallels. The earliest version seems to be Claret's "Dulcifluum modicum [nux], ossis que tenet ollam [sic]."[9] See further, Breton: Sébillot, *Haute-Bretagne*, 30. Flemish: Joos, 504. German: Frischbier, *Pflanzenwelt*, p. 70, No. 25. French: A. Ferrand, *Dauphiné*, p. 226 (little pot, good flavor). Lithuanian: Schleicher, p. 205. Polish: Siarkowski, 51 (Very sweet, very tiny, in a tiny cup). White Russian: Wasilewski, 96 (In a little pot tasty mush.—

---

[1] Catalan: Pelay y Briz, 27. Spanish: Demófilo, 535, 537, and p. 370, No. 4; Rodríguez Marín, 373. Argentinian: Lehmann-Nitsche, 491. Chilean: Flores, 343, 354. Dominican Rep.: Andrade, 175. New Mexican: Campa, 29. Porto Rican: Mason, 288. Rumanian: Gorovei, 1308. Filipino: Starr, *Philippines*, 102.
[2] See the note to No. 1171.
[3] French: Lallemant, *Argonne*, p. 235. Votyak: Wichmann, *Votyak*, 168.
[4] See No. 1141 above.   [5] Ophuijsen, p. 466, No. 77.
[6] Starr, *Philippines*, 159.
[7] Ittmann, *Bankon*, p. 106, No. 7. See also Kosi: Ittmann, *Kosi*, 57, 214, 215, 247. Duala: Ebding, 47.
[8] Mostaert, 170.
[9] P. 67, No. 5. The meter and the grammar require *ollā*. The scribe or the editor has erroneously taken a macron to signify *m*.

Peas). Russian: Sadovnikov, 1372. Bulgarian: Bozhov, 26 (A little pot full of sweet food.—Hazelnut); Chacharov, 66. Cheremiss: Wichmann, *Cheremiss*, 149. Mordvin: Paasonen, 395 (A little pot, a tasty soup), 421. Turkish: Kowalski, *Asia Minor*, 6 (At the end of the twig there hangs a fat morsel); Hamizade, 96 (I have a box. It holds four slices of bread.—Walnut), 97 (The food of the tiny pot is very sweet.—Walnut), 184 (I have a box; it holds a slice of bread.—Hazelnut); Katanov in Radlov, IX, 242, No. 105 (If I open the casket, it is very white. If I eat its contents, it is very sweet). Shor: Dyrenkova, 16 (Within a little colored chest there is bread.—Cedar nut). Turcoman: Samojlvich, 37 (A tiny kettle, a royal pilau in it), 38 (A little kettle, the food in it is very sweet). He cites parallels in Radlov, VII, 46; Bálint, *Kazan Tatar*, 29; and Ostrumov, *Sart*, 82. Mongolian: Kotvich, 261 (The kettle is small, the mush tastes very good); Bazarov, 123 (A little box: *crack!* Butter or fat flowed out).

The comparison to food in a dish is used almost exclusively for a nut. I have noted above a White Russian use of it for peas. The Turks say of an egg, "A tiny bit of ivory, within [there is] food for a lord,"[10] and the Taranchin in the Caucasus apply the comparison to brains in a ram's skull.[11]

The notion of a locked box is applicable to a nut, as in the Turkish "In the tree a locked chest.—Walnut" and "On top of a branch a locked chest.— Walnut, hazelnut,"[12] a beehive, as in the Turkish "On the top of a tree there is a locked box,"[13] or to the grave, as in the Turkish "On top of the road [ground] there is a locked box" and "Underneath the earth there is a locked box," or, with greater elaboration, "From behind I saw something solid; I arrived at the place and there was a locked copper box."[14]

§ 2. An egg. Indian: Lakshīnātha Upasānī, III, 1 (A powerful soldier without food dwells in a doorless house made by God. When his might sufficiently increases, he breaks through the house to the outside).

§ 3. A watermelon. Turkish: Hamizade, 349 (God makes its dwelling; a knife opens its door); Zavarin, *Brusa*, 12 (God makes, let him make. A knife opens, let it open). See also the headnote to Nos. 908–916 above.

1187a. Mah fader had a trunk. When he open it, no man can shet it.—Peanut.
Parsons, *Bahamas*, p. 482, No. 109.

1187b. Mah fader had a trunk. He open it, but he couldn't shut it.—Groun' nut [peanut].
Parsons, *Bahamas*, p. 482, No. 109 var.

---
[10] Kowalski, *Asia Minor*, 40.
[11] Pantusov, 135, as cited by Samojlvich, 37.
[12] Hamizade, 98, 101.
[13] Hamizade, 412.
[14] Hamizade, 485 through 487. His No. 654 is identical with his No. 486. Balkar: Pröhle, p. 120 (By the road there is a locked box). See also the headnote to Nos. 1132–1138, § 4, above.

1188. Trunk Contains Two Kinds of Clothes

This concept shows some similarity to the notion of an egg conceived as a barrel containing two kinds of liquid (see the headnote to No. 1140).

1188. My father had a trunk, it had only two suits of clo'es.–Groundnut [peanut].
Parsons, *Eleuthera and Watling's Islands, Bahamas,* p. 440, No. 9.

1189–1191. Lamp, Candle, Light

Comparisons to a lamp, candle, or light are surprisingly rare in riddling. The similarity of eyes to lights is noted in some of the descriptions of the head conceived as a house, ship, or street[1] and appears again in some riddles describing the various members of a cow.[2] The Lithuanian riddle "Two candles, a hill between them"[3] has as its answer "the eyes and the nose"; this scene lacks plausibility. In comparing the earth and sky to a cottage, Swedish riddlers equate the stars to sparks: "A green roof and a blue roof; sparks fly through the chimney, and water through the air."[4] Another variation of this theme is the Irish "It's a very big house, it's a candlestick of gold, it's a speckled robe. Measure it quickly, or spread it yonder.—The heavens."[5]

Perhaps the best-known use of the comparison to a lamp or candle is its application to the description of stars. The examples vary greatly among themselves and do not encourage one to seek to derive them from a common source. See the Swedish "A church full of candles";[6] the Chilean "Many lights, no one can turn them on";[7] the Gypsy "It is smaller than a tallow light and yet one sees it in the whole world";[8] the Turkish "The heavens took a golden candlestick [i.e., the moon], silver moths took the world";[9] the Uraon "A thousand candles in a dish";[10] the Kolarian "The whole country is illuminated by a small oil-filled lamp";[11] and the Korean "What is like a golden brand in an azure field?"[12]

Somewhat more remote parallels are the comparisons of the heavenly bodies to pots and pans. Such comparisons are characteristically eastern European

---

[1] See No. 1168, the headnote to Nos. 1100–1108, n. 4, and the note to No. 1144.
[2] See the Swedish, Hungarian, and Kashmiri versions in the note to Nos. 1476a through 1489 below, and compare the references to a dog's eyes in the headnote to Nos. 1476–1494, § 10.
[3] Jurgelionis, 164. For versions replacing the candles by persons see above, Nos. 1003, 1016, and the headnote to Nos. 1003–1004, particularly nn. 4–5. Comparisons of the eyes to lights are quoted in the headnote to Nos. 1003–1004, § 3, in the headnote to Nos. 1100–1108, n. 27 (bright windows), and in the note to No. 1100 (Giacobetti, 269; Ruoff, p. 16, No. 7; Jungbauer, p. 356; and Sarkar, p. 351, No. 4). For a summary of riddles for the eyes see the note to No. 1144.
[4] Ström, p. 203. [5] De Bhaldraithe, 22.
[6] Ericsson, *Södermanland,* II (1881), 99, No. 108; Ström, p. 210, "Stjärnorna," 1.
[7] Flores, 273. See also Spanish: Demófilo, 434; Rodríguez Marín, 265.
[8] Wlislocki, 27.
[9] Hamizade, 32. [10] Archer, p. 183, No. 65.
[11] Wagner, 41. [12] Bernheisel, p. 62.

and Siberian; see the Tatar "A golden bowl and a golden pan, take[13] one, put out[14] the other";[15] the Yakut "They say that a bowl of gigantic proportions sails over the deep ocean";[16] the Mongolian "On the ice a silver goblet";[17] and the Korean "What is a golden cushion under water?—Sun."[18] Other objects are mentioned less frequently: "They throw golden balls all over the woods.—Sun";[19] "A snowball is rolled all over the world.—Moon";[20] and "Chips of flaming pine are scattered over the hut.—Stars."[21] A comparison to a stick seems to belong to the folklore of the Turks and related tribes in eastern Russia: "Behind the door there is a stick of silver.—Sun";[22] "On our beam there lies a golden stick";[23] and "In our attic there lies a golden stick."[24] The idea is altered to a new theme in the Yakut candle riddle: "The sun rises from a silver stick."[25] The Irish sunlight riddle, "A little yellow thing at the king's door, and all the world won't put a withe on it,"[26] has some resemblance to the Hickamore Hackamore riddle.[27]

1189. My father has a lamp that shines over the whole world.—Moon.
Beckwith, *Jamaica*, p. 189, No. 58.

1190. A tall, tall house, / A candlestick of gold. / Riddle it right / Or let it go by you.—Sun.
Fitzgerald, p. 181 (Irish).

1191. In me are many shining lights.—It is a burning candle.
Prettie Riddles (1631), No. 53 = Brandl, p. 59.

1192–1196. Broken Plate (Egg)

The comparison of an object to a plate or other fragile thing that breaks unexpectedly and as unexpectedly remains whole when thrown down on the ground is much favored by Near Eastern riddlers. It is applicable to a variety of objects. The usual answer is paper, which falls apart in water and yet withstands a fall from a high place. The comparison is clumsily adjusted to corn in the Arabic "Something falls from the tower of prayer and does not break; if it gets between stones, it breaks,"[1] which also contains elements

---

[13] Signifying also "hide."
[14] Signifying also "show."
[15] Kalashev and Ioakimov, p. 48, No. 7.
[16] Piekarski, 7.
[17] Mostaert, 24.
[18] Bernheisel, p. 62.
[19] Hungarian: Kriza, 82.
[20] Hungarian: Kriza, 112.
[21] Yakut: Piekarski, 57.
[22] Turkish: Kowalski, *Zagadki*, 27.
[23] Cherekessian: Tambiev, p. 61, No. 90. In the Mongolian "Outside the yurt is a golden stake" (Kotvich, 100), the answer is merely "a fire."
[24] Cherekessian: Tambiev, p. 61, No. 92.
[25] Priklonskii, 30.
[26] O Dalaigh, 117.
[27] See the headnote to Nos. 748–749 above.
[1] Ruoff, p. 52, No. 27.

slightly reminiscent of a riddle for flour.² The transformation of one riddle into another is neatly exemplified by two Hungarian texts: "Bump it against a stone, [it will not break]; throw it into water, it will become snot.—Paper"³ and "Throw it into the water, it will not be spoiled; bump it against a stone, it collapses.—Egg."⁴ By slight changes the riddler obtains an entirely new riddle with a new answer.

Some versions of this conception suggest a person or an animal that is injured by the fall rather than a thing that can be broken. See, for example, the Turkish paper riddle, "You can throw it from a minaret, and it won't die. Throw it into water, and it will die."⁵ The fundamental idea is akin to the description of water as something that can be cut without leaving a mark.⁶ The modern Greeks find the comparison to an object that cannot be broken appropriate to a snake, "An earthen ring, it falls and does not break,"⁷ and the Turks modify it to suit an onion, "I threw it from a mountain, I threw a stone and it didn't break, it can't lean on my fist."⁸

Riddlers use this scene to describe:

§ 1. Paper. See No. 1192. The popularity of this conception is somewhat difficult to understand. The parallels cited in the note to No. 1192 and the following Turkish texts illustrate its variations: "It falls from the fortress and does not break, thinner than wine, whiter than snow" (Hamizade, 302); and, in the same collection, "If you throw it from a mountain, it doesn't break. It doesn't rely on spit.—Cigarette paper" (610); "I threw it from a minaret and it didn't break. I threw it into the sea and it broke" (611); "It fell to the ground and didn't break. It fell into the water and broke" (612). It also appears in a curious combination of paradoxes that are explained as references to the sun, paper, a corpse, and gold, respectively: "He falls into the water and doesn't get wet; he falls from the roof and doesn't break; on top of a horse he doesn't cry out; he falls to the ground and doesn't rust" (*ibid.*, 226).

§ 2. An anthill. See No. 1193.

§ 3. A shadow. Arabic: Littmann, p. 61.

§ 4. Snow. Dutch: Schrijnen, II, 103, No. 8. Italian: Schneller, *Wälschtirol*, p. 255, No. 21 (High, high from a palace I fell to the earth, and I do not fall to my death. I am white and become black). Hungarian: Arany and Gyulai, III, 297, No. 28 (It falls in the water and breaks. It falls on stones and does not break).

§ 5. Mucus. French: Parsons, *Antilles*, III, 406, Guadaloupe, 105, p. 410,

---

² See No. 397 above.
³ *Magyar Nyelvör*, V (1876), 268.
⁴ *Magyar Nyelvör*, V (1876), 268.
⁵ Zavarin, *Brusa*, 43. See also the note to No. 1192 below.
⁶ See No. 1665 below.
⁷ Polites, *Neohellenika Analekta*, I, 218, No. 144.
⁸ Hamizade, 629.

Les Saintes, 31, p. 417, Marie Galante, 80, and p. 438, St. Martin, 48. African, Shilluk: Westermann, p. 241 (Thrown on the ground, yet not broken).

§ 6. The sun, the moon. Icelandic: Árnason, 412 (What is it that falls down the cliff and doesn't break, falls in the water and doesn't sink, goes into the fire and doesn't burn, but finally becomes the prey of a wolf?—Sunbeam). The last allusion rests on the belief that the Fenris wolf swallows the sun at Ragnarök. Modern Greek: Dieterich, *Rätseldichtung*, p. 90, citing Polites, *Neohellenika Analekta*, I, 253, No. 342 (He wanders through the world, over land and water; he throws himself from the mountain, he falls and does not break.—Sun). The first scene is often found in a riddle for a star.[9] See also a restatement of this sun riddle in terms of a thing rather than a person: "A ring of fire, of fire, tumbles off cliffs and does not break.—Moon."[10]

1192. A woman had a plate, / She threw it down, / It wouldn't break, / She put it on water, / And it broke.—Paper.
Parsons, *Barbados*, p. 285, No. 52.

1193. Plate Repaired When Broken

This description of an anthill seems to have no parallels. The usual riddle for an anthill is a comparison to a pot boiling in the field or forest. This comparison is applicable to:

§ 1. An anthill. The statement of the riddle varies only slightly in the many printed examples. The variation ordinarily concerns the place where the pot is standing. A reference to a field, which is an unnatural place for a boiling pot, is very frequent.[1] The Lithuanians say, "A pot boils at the edge of the field";[2] the Russians, "Beyond the field there is a little pot. It boils actively. It is very hot";[3] the Serbians, "A little pot is boiling by itself in the field," or "A little pot is boiling in the middle of a field. No one puts it on, no one takes it off, no one adds to the fire," or "A red pot boils continuously in the middle of a field";[4] the Evhe, "A big pot in the jungle."[5] There are some variations in the scene. The Cheremiss say, "In an alder copse there boils a little pot";[6] the Turks, "Under the ground a kettle is boiling";[7] the Siberian Turks, "Under a fir tree there boils a cast-iron kettle";[8] and the Astrakhan Calmucks, "A black

---

[9] See the headnote to Nos. 525–534 above.
[10] Stathes, p. 337, No. 36.
[1] Serbian: Novaković, p. 138, Nos. 2, 3. Bulgarian: Gubov, 238 (A full kettle boils in the field). Finnish: Lönnrot, 408 = Henssen, 7a; Lönnrot, 1449 = Henssen, 7b. Mordvin: Paasonen, 403. Turkish: Katanov in Radlov, IX, 291, No. 751 (My pot is boiling on the desolate steppe).
[2] Jurgelionis, 859.   [3] Sadovnikov, 1662.
[4] Novaković, p. 137, No. 8, and p. 138, Nos. 1, 4.
[5] F. Müller, p. 157, No. 4.   [6] Genetz, 69.
[7] Kúnos, 158 = Kúnos, *Nyelvkönyv*, 22; Kowalski, *Zagadki*, 18. Crimean Tatar: Filonenko, 92.
[8] Katanov in Radlov, IX, 653, No. 194.

kettle boils alongside the road."[9] The scene is more concretely conceived in the Cheremiss "Porridge boils in the forest,"[10] and in the Yakut "They say that a boiler is running over in a wooded thicket."[11] A related conception is seen in the Togo "A red pot stands in the field and many soldiers live in it."[12] The answer is slightly varied in the Pangwe "In the forest a pot boils of itself.—Stump and larvae"[13] and the Evhe "A large pot in the jungle.—Termite nest."[14]

§ 2. A mole. Cherekessian: Tambiev, p. 63, No. 115 (By the well of the house a little kettle boils).

§ 3. A spring. Irish: O Dalaigh, 154 (I went to London and there I saw a marvel: three kettles boiling without a spark under them). Serbian: Novaković, p. xvii, No. 5 (A little pot is boiling in the middle of a mountain. It is neither filled nor moved), and p. 24, Nos. 4 (There is a little pot in the middle of the field, no one warms it, no one heats it, and yet it boils all the time), 5 (There is a little pot boiling in the middle of the field, no one warms it, no one heats it), and 6 (The cauldron boils, and no one fires it). Compare also the riddles for water under a boat and for custards or pies in an oven.[15]

1193. I was going to town; I mash a plate and when I was coming back, I found it new.—Ant's nest.
Beckwith, *Jamaica*, p. 193, No. 81.

1194–1196. Object Is Not Broken (Smashed, Cut)

This manner of description is applicable to water, which shows no mark of being cut,[1] and to the passage of a ship through the sea.[2] It is also applied to matter (mucus) and to a ball.[3] A few versions, which seem to be characteristically African, make a specific comparison to a tree representing a river: "I know a tree, one chops at it constantly, and yet there are no notches";[4] and "Tell me: I try to strike the *mpipi* tree,[5] but no scar appears."[6] The chopping signifies the strokes of oars or paddles. Quite different is the Filipino comparison for water in a dish: "What is the cake that cannot be cut with a knife?"[7]

1194. Something on the ground never gets smashed.—Water.
Parsons, *Bermuda*, p. 256, No. 76.

---

[9] Kotvich, 140. See also the Tatar "In the middle of the road there is a kettle; it will start to boil" (Kalashev and Ioakimov, p. 50, No. 22).
[10] Porkka, 96; Wichmann, *Cheremiss*, 97.
[11] Piekarski, 105; Priklonskii, 65.
[12] Schönhärl, 107.
[13] Tessmann, 62.
[14] F. Müller, p. 157, No. 14.
[15] Nos. 1177 through 1178b above
[1] See No. 1665.
[2] No. 1666. See also the headnote to No. 227.
[3] Nos. 1195, 1196.
[4] Pangwe: Tessmann, 32.
[5] *Boscia rehmanniana*, an evergreen.
[6] Kxatla: Schapera, 14.
[7] De los Reyes y Florentino, p. 275.

1195. Pick up an aigg, / Hit it side de wall, / He neither break, crack or fall.—Mater [mucus].
Parsons, *Barbados*, p. 282, No. 35.

1196. I had a egg an' I pitch it six mile, an' it couldn' get mash up.—Ball.
Parsons, *Antilles*, III, 432, St. Eustatius, 11.

1197–1198. Glasses

1197. Three glasses on de table, one half full, one all full, one not full.—One married, one fixin' to get married, one unmarried.
Parsons, *Sea Islands, S.C.*, p. 162, No. 59, var. 2.

1198. A riddle, a riddle aree, / No man can explain this riddle on to me, / Exceptin' he know it as well as me. / Look at a glass widout a top, / Hunt for de bottom, wont hol' a drop.—Glass [lamp chimney?].
Parsons, *Barbados*, p. 281, No. 28.

1199. Bottles

The Tschuana "The hanging nest of a bustard [*Otis tarda*], yet the eggs do not fall out" (Kuhn, *Tschuana*, 24) is an ingenious variation of this theme.

1199a. My father have four bottles of water, and he turn them down, they couldn't throw away.—Cow have four nipples, and without you milk them, you couldn't get no milk.
Parsons, *Antilles*, III, 421, Montserrat, 7 var.

1199b. Dere was four bottle milk turn' down not cark' [corked] an' yet de milk didn't t'row away.—Cattle breas'.
Parsons, *Antilles*, III, 421, Montserrat, 7.

1199c. Four bottles of milk, uncarked, turn down, and not a drap can come out.—Cow breasts.
Parsons, *Antilles*, III, 425, Antigua, 20.

1199d. My mudder give me four bottle of milk to turn down with no cork, and to t'row none away. What is dat?—A cow's four nipples.
Johnson, *Antigua*, p. 87, No. 51.

1200–1205. Bag, Rope

1200–1201. Bag

1200a. It takes ten men to haul a lilly [little] bag up a flat hill.—Man puttin' on a pair o' pants.
Fauset, *Nova Scotia*, p. 173, No. 188.

1200b. Ten drag / Wooly bag / Over Calf-hill.—Putting on a woolen stocking.
Greenleaf, *Newfoundland*, p. 12, No. 38.

1201. One little bit o' bag hold three.—Castor-oil bean-pod.
Beckwith, *Jamaica*, p. 200, No. 153.

1202–1205. Rope, String

1202. Oncet dere was a girl an' a boy. He was to Savannah. He write fo' she to come whey he was. She couldn' ride, neither walk. He had a string from Savannah to Befut [Beaufort]. An' when she get in de middle of de water, de string pop.—Fall in love.

Parsons, *Sea Islands, S.C.*, p. 170, No. 117.

1203–1205. Rope Moves

In the south of Europe a comparison of a vine to a moving rope is widely known. The following West Indian examples of the theme are the only instances in English riddling. They make an additional reference to a cow or horse and thus introduce the paradox of a motionless animal to set beside that of the moving rope. One of these West Indian riddles[1] compares the leaves to paper. This comparatively rare notion has a few parallels in Spanish folklore. Some parallels to these descriptions of a vine cite contradictions and impossibilities without achieving the unity of a scene that has been clearly thought out.[2]

Some riddles for a vine and its fruit are ingenious enough to deserve special mention. See, for example, the Modern Greek comparison to fishing, "I throw out lines and gather balls.—Squash."[3]

Comparisons of a creeping vine to an animal often refer to a pig or a goat that gives birth and runs away.[4] Variations of this theme are the Bulgarian "Long, long like a rope, yet it is not a rope; it scratches like a cat, yet it is not a cat; it covers its ears like a rabbit, yet it is not a rabbit";[5] the Kashub "Small, round, and it runs away,"[6] which may refer to a single pea slipping away under one's fingers; and the curious Engganee "A snake of no small size whose eggs one gladly eats."[7]

Comparisons of this sort to a person[8] can be illustrated by the Turkish "Tall Osman lies in the juice, his servants lie with us.—Pumpkin";[9] the Bakongo "Some continue to go on. Others sit down [crossing their legs].—Gourds";[10] and two Kolarian versions in dialogue: "'Sit down, fat fellow, I will go further to the country'"[11] and "'Go on, boys, I will curl serpent-like.'—The splitting of the lama creeper."[12] Riddlers have used this scene to describe cocoons: "In the dense forest bulls have been tied."[13]

---

[1] No. 1205.
[2] These are collected in the note to No. 1205.
[3] Polites, *Neohellenika Analekta*, I, 252, No. 337.
[4] See Nos. 381a through 382 above.   [5] Ikonomov, 13.
[6] Gulgowski, 1.   [7] Helfrich, *Engganee*, p. 519, No. 20.
[8] See also the headnote to No. 1007, § 12, above.
[9] Hamizade, 295.   [10] Denis, 85.
[11] Wagner, 4.
[12] Wagner, 13. In the month of Aghan (November–December), the fruit of the lama creeper splits asunder, by and by the fruit dries up, and the seed is curling like a serpent.—Collector's note.
[13] Indian, Kolarian: Wagner, 30.

1203a. Rope run, horse stan' up.—Pumpkin vine and pumpkin.
Beckwith, *Jamaica*, p. 199, No. 147; Parsons, *Antilles*, III, 364, Trinidad, 15, n. 1 [I suggest that the collector's note "house" is an error for "horse"].

1203b. My fader have a cow, / De cow stan' up and de rope runnin'.—Pumpkin stay one place and de vine run.
Parsons, *Antilles*, III, 364, Trinidad, 15 var.

1203c. Rope run, / Co[w] stand up.—Pumpkin stay one place and de vine run.
Parsons, *Antilles*, III, 364, Trinidad, 15 var.

1204. My father have a thing in his yard, run off cover up the whole ground.—Pumpkin vine.
Beckwith, *Jamaica*, p. 184, No. 15.

1205. There's a rope and every bump a sheet of paper.—Pumpkin vine.
Beckwith, *Jamaica*, p. 200, No. 162.

1206–1211. Articles of Dress

1206. Shoes

1206. Leather to spetch, leather to spooin, / My father brought me a pair of new shooin. / One was a thistle, the other a thorn, /—I thought in my heart they would never be worn.—Answer lacking.
Marsden, *Upper Calderdale*, p. 262.

1207–1211. Clothing

1207. It's a thing you have been wearing over two years.—Hat over two ears.
Parsons, *Eleuthera and Watling's Islands, Bahamas*, p. 441, No. 23.

1208. My father have a thing in his yard; it button from head to foot.—Pingwing [pinguin?], because the leaves are stuck with pitch.
Beckwith, *Jamaica*, p. 184, No. 19.

1209. There wiz a man bespoke a coat. / When the maker it home did bring, / The man who made it would not have it, / The man who spoke for't cudna use it, / And the man who wore cudna tell / Whether it suited him ill or well.—A coffin.
Gregor, *Northeast Scotland*, p. 79.

1210. The man that made it, never wore it, / And the man that wore it never seen it, / Formed long ago, yet made today. / Employed while others sleep, / What few would wish to give away, / Or brothers [read: others] wish to keep.—Bed.
Fauset, *Nova Scotia*, p. 154, No. 52.

1211. I have a green coat, and 'tis too short; cut a bit off it, and 'tis long enough.—The grave.
Fitzgerald, p. 186 (Irish).

1212–1226. Cloth

1212. Neither Spun Nor Woven

The old notion that a bee is an artificer who does work that no man can do is used in various ways.[1] Here he is said to make a cloth that is neither spun nor woven. The comparison to an object that no man can make is also applicable to a bridge of ice.[2] The notion of a cloth that is neither spun nor woven is occasionally used to describe the feathers of a cock. This use is akin to the description of the feathers as patches on patches, sewn without thread.[3] A riddle for a cock which combines both themes is the Swedish "There came a man from England, who had beautiful clothes. They were not spun, they were not bound, they were not woven, they were not sewn."[4] Minor uses of the notion of a cloth that is not like ordinary material are the Russian riddle for a chink in a wall, "I shall patch a patch with neither needle nor thread,"[5] and a Portuguese description of a nut.[6] The Irish say that the moonshine is a sheet that no one can weave.[7]

1212a. Mother had a piece of checkety cloth, / It was neither spun nor woven. / It had been a sheet for many years, / An' not a thread had been worn.—Beehive.
Parsons, *Aiken, S.C.*, p. 30, No. 37.

1212b. I have a sheet of checkin' comb, / Neither wove nor spun. / It's been a wearin' seven years, / And nary thread begun.—Honey comb.
Carter, *Mountain White*, p. 79.

1213. Without a Seam

Although riddlers often use this theme in describing an egg, the following example, which is not entirely clear, seems to be the only English version on record. Since this riddle suggests the comparison of an egg to a cup filled with liquid,[1] "seam" probably means "fissure, crack."

The Breton, French, and Spanish "Shirt without a seam" and the other parallels cited in the note to No. 1213 conceive the shell of the egg as a garment. This is interestingly developed in the Spanish "Dressed as a monk, I come to see the father prior; I wear white garments and [have] a red heart,"[2] in which the notion of a seamless garment is, however, not present.

---

[1] See *Demaundes Joyous* (1511), No. 40, the headnote to Nos. 793–794 above, and the note to No. 793.
[2] Irish: Christiansen, 10. See also the headnotes to Nos. 738–747, § 4, and 793–794 above, and the note to No. 1670.
[3] See the headnote to No. 1437, § 10.
[4] Waltman, *Lidmål*, 234. For another brief discussion, see the headnote to Nos. 793–794 above.
[5] Sadovnikov, 30 (cited also in the headnote to Nos. 793–794 above).
[6] Pires de Lima, 205.
[7] See the riddle quoted in the headnote to Nos. 1219–1220, n. 13, below.

[1] See the comparisons to a vessel containing liquids, cited in the headnote to No. 1140.
[2] Demófilo, 541.

The description of a chicken, a cabbage, an onion, or the clouds as "patches on patches"[3] sometimes includes the remark "and no needle passed through it," but does not further emphasize the lack of a seam.

The notion of a seamless garment is applicable to:

§ 1. An egg. See the note to No. 1213.

§ 2. A snake. Spanish: Demófilo, 350; Rodríguez Marín, 391, 392, 394. Argentinian: Lehmann-Nitsche, 335. Chilean: Flores, 219 through 221.

§ 3. A fish. German: Wossidlo, 24 (There comes a man from Seeland; he has a long coat, patch by patch, and not a single seam).

§ 4. The sky. Turkish: Kúnos, *Nyelvkönyv*, 27 (It is blue silk, the needle does not penetrate it, the scissors do not cut it, the tailor does not sew it); Hamizade, 199; Katanov in Radlov, IX, 93, No. 776 (I have some silk that has no seams). See also similar conceptions cited in the headnote to No. 1437, § 9, below.

1213. Full to the brim, / Without crack or seam.—An egg.
Waugh, *Canada*, p. 68, No. 781.

1214. Can Be Washed But Not Dried

1214. What water wash, sun can't dry.—Butter.
Beckwith, *Jamaica*, p. 200, No. 155.

1215–1226. Sheet

1215–1216. Sheet Cannot Be Folded; Money Cannot Be Counted; Apple Cannot Be Plucked (Cut, Eaten)

Riddlers have included several similes for the heavens and the celestial bodies in a single riddle. Although these similes vary somewhat in the many texts that have been recorded, we can probably safely infer that they were originally three in number. The original three may have been those named in the heading above. The wagon symbolizing Charles's Wain or the Great Bear and the bull symbolizing the sun are probably quite unrelated to this tripartite conception.

Some very curious versions connect the three objects with three actors, usually a mother, a father, and a brother or sister. It is not clear whether these actors belong to the earliest conception of the riddle. A Swedish riddler[1] interprets them as the Virgin Mary or Mother Earth, God the Father, and Jesus Christ, and a similar interpretation occurs in a New Mexican Spanish version.[2] I have discussed the possible connections of these texts elsewhere,[3] and have come to the conclusion that this association with Christian figures is a medieval embellishment of the original theme.

---

[3] See below, Nos. 1438a through 1439, the headnotes to No. 1437, §§ 9–10, and No. 1438, and the note to No. 1438b.
[1] See the note to No. 1215.   [2] See the note to Nos. 1224 through 1225b.
[3] "A Riddle for the Sun, Sky, and Stars," *California Folklore Quarterly*, III (1944), 222–231.

The various parts of this riddle appear both in combination and separately. They are here brought together, even when they appear as separate riddles. The English examples of the separate use of these themes seem to have arisen by breaking up the original tripartite riddle. Some of the examples found in other countries may represent inventions which have nothing to do with the tripartite riddle.

Riddles of a similar tripartite construction are often used for cosmological objects.[4] The Russian riddle for the sun, the earth, the stars, and a road, "Father has a stallion, the whole world cannot hold it; mother has coffers, the whole world cannot lift them; brother has a belt, the whole world cannot count it; sister has a cloth, the whole world cannot roll it up,"[5] contains a widely known riddle for a road.[6] The answers are somewhat altered but the comparisons remain the same in a Russian riddle for snow, earth, and the wind: "Father's trunk can't be raised, sister's cloth can't be gathered up, brother's horse can't be caught."[7] This has been widely disseminated, for the Yakut say, "They say that the father cannot control his horse; the mother cannot lift her trunk; the son cannot tear asunder his belt.—Wind, earth, road."[8]

Two elements appear in the Yakut "No one can catch his son's horse, and no one can clear away his daughter's linens.—Rays of the early spring sun reflected on the snow."[9] The first belongs to the conceptions discussed here, and the second is related to riddles for sunlight that cannot be removed.[10]

The previously quoted Yakut riddle containing a reference to the earth as a trunk that cannot be picked up has an analogue in a Yakut road riddle, "They say that there is that which cannot be picked up."[11] The notion is akin to Thor's vain effort to lift the Midgard serpent, representing the sea that encircles the world.[12]

The celestial bodies and the sky are often compared to animals,[13] persons,[14] fruits,[15] and miscellaneous objects.[16] Such comparisons seem to be independent of the conceptions fundamental to this tripartite riddle.

---

[4] For examples see the headnote to Nos. 138–140 above.
[5] Preobrazhenskii, p. 170. The text is obviously somewhat corrupt.
[6] See, for example, the headnote to No. 575, nn. 13–29, above, particularly n. 26.
[7] Sadovnikov, 1988; see also his Nos. 1912, 1913.
[8] Piekarski, 33.
[9] Piekarski, 40.
[10] See the headnote to Nos. 748–749 above.
[11] Piekarski, 241. This is analogous to the Yakut "They say that there is something which can never be lifted.—The earth" (his No. 39).
[12] Arthur G. Brodeur (trans.), Snorri Sturluson, *The Prose Edda* (New York, 1916), pp. 66–67.
[13] See the headnotes to No. 388 and Nos. 484–486 above and compare Nos. 391 through 392b, 405, 431, 470, 484a through 484d, 496a, 496b.
[14] See Nos. 102 and 525a through 526b and the headnote to Nos. 525–534, and compare Nos. 513, 648, 663, 682, 798, 988, 1001, 1025.
[15] See Nos. 1093 through 1094e, and 1095.
[16] See the headnote to No. 1227.

1215. I have an apple I can't cut, a blanket I can't fold, and so much money I can't count it.—Moon, stars, sky.
Perkins, *New Orleans*, p. 110, No. 38.

1216. I have a sheet I can't fold it. / I have so much money I can't count it. / I have an apple and can't eat it. / I have a diamond and can't face it.—Water, stars, moon, sun.
Fauset, *Nova Scotia*, p. 165, No. 116.

1217–1218. Sheet Cannot Be Folded

Riddlers have adjusted the comparison of the sky to a sheet or cloth to the closely related answers of a cloud[1] and sunlight.[2] It is a very old idea as riddles go, for we can probably find an example in the fourteenth-century *Codex Cumanicus*, in which a riddle reads: "One cannot fold my quilted coat."[3] This has the answer *ju*——, a defective word that Németh emends to *jumurtka* (egg). An egg is rarely, if ever, described in this way; the stars and the firmament often are. Consequently, it seems better to emend the defective word into *julduz* (stars). The reference to shaking the fat of the lynx remains obscure.

Allied comparisons are the Modern Greek scene of a tent ornamented with gold[4] and the many comparisons of earth and sky to two (usually equal) hides.[5] The Mongolian "Beautiful silk without a border, small corals without holes"[6] is well conceived.

The comparison of the stars to things often includes the assertion that the things were visible at night and vanished in the daylight. This is frequently found in connection with fruits, as in the Arabic "A tray of dates, it exists through the night without seeing the day."[7] Comparisons to objects other than fruits or nuts are rather rare, but see the Iraqi Arabic "What is it that I hung out to dry and didn't find in the morning?"[8] This is quite different from the Breton "In the forest of Cercaillette, I lost my mallet; I went at noon, I could not find it again; I went at midnight, I found it."[9] The comparison to a mallet was perhaps invented for the sake of the rhyme. An analogous riddle is told in Velay-et-Forez, "Early one morning, I went to the forest of Cercaille and found there my bell [*sonnaille*]. I lost it by day, I found it again at night."[10]

---

[1] See Nos. 1218a through 1218c, 1220, 1222a, 1224, 1225a, 1229a.
[2] Irish: Christiansen, 2a, 2b.
[3] Németh, pp. 581–582, No. 5.
[4] See the headnote to No. 1227, § 5, below.
[5] See the note to Nos. 1252a, 1252b and compare the headnote to No. 1252, n. 15.
[6] Rudnyev, 23; Bazarov, 182; Klukine, 33.
[7] Socin and Stumme, 1.
[8] Meissner, *Iraq*, p. 172, No. 78.
[9] Orain, *Ille-et-Vilaine*, p. 150.
[10] V. S., *Mélusine*, I (1878), col. 263, No. 72.

Comparisons of a cloud or the sky to a cloth are widely used. The themes differ considerably among themselves. See the Kxatla "Tell me: mat spread yourself and then remove yourself.—A cloud."[11] Allusions to color are very rare, but see the Suk "I-stretched-out-I the-skin of a-dark-colored-ox.—Dark blue sky."[12] The Turkish "I began to unroll a bare rug but could not; I began to unroll a woolen rug but could not"[13] and "What is it whose end cannot be found?"[14] as well as the Mongolian "A whole piece of silk cannot be rolled up"[15] are similar to a riddle for a road.[16] The bare rug is the cloudless sky, and the wool is fog, mist, or clouds. This contrast is explicitly stated in the Astrakhan Calmuck "A rug with wool and a rug without wool."[17]

1217. My fader had a sheet, / An' he kyouldn' fol' it.—Sky.
Parsons, *Andros Island, Bahamas*, p. 276, No. 11.

1218a. My fader gave me a large table cloth to fold up an' I couldn' fold it up.—Cloud.
Parsons, *Antilles*, III, 424, Antigua, 11.

1218b. My father git me one napkin to fold an' I couldn't fold it.—The clouds.
Parsons, *Antilles*, III, 373, Grenada, 69.

1218c. I got so many claw [clothes] until I couldn't done unfol' it.—Cloud.
Parsons, *Sea Islands, S.C.*, p. 159, No. 45.

1219–1220. Sheet Covers the World

In some widely asked riddles the sky, or, less usually, a cloud, is called a sheet that covers the world. The same description is applied, but only very rarely, to grass.[1] It is very frequently used of snow, and then usually contains the additional remark that the sheet does not cover the sea, as in the Turkish "I have a quilt that covers the world, except the sea."[2] Although this snow riddle is very widely known,[3] no English instance has been reported. On the

---

[11] Schapera, 9.   [12] Beech, p. 44, No. 7.
[13] Katanov in Radlov, IX, 243, No. 112. For the use of the idea of two similar rugs or other objects to describe the earth and the sky, see the note to Nos. 1252a, 1252b below.
[14] Hamizade, 201.   [15] Mostaert, 124.
[16] See the headnote to Nos. 575, nn. 22–29, above.
[17] Kotvich, 172.

[1] German: Wossidlo, 23.
[2] Kowalski, *Asia Minor*, 2; Kowalski, *North Bulgaria*, 37, 92; Hamizade, 324 (It covers the earth, it doesn't cover the sea), 325 (It conceals every place, it doesn't conceal one place), 330 (I have a sheet, it covers the earth, only water it does not cover). Crimean Tatar: Filonenko, 37.
[3] Breton: Sébillot, *Haute-Bretagne*, 5; Sauvé, 19. Dutch: Sinninghe, p. 5, No. 4. Flemish: *Ons Volksleven*, I (1889), 7, No. 10; *'t Daghet in den Oosten*, II, 103. German: Wossidlo, 22, 349b; Frischbier, *Menschenwelt*, p. 260, No. 192. French: Rolland, 12; Guillon, *La Bresse*, p. 20. Catalan: Milá y Fontanals, 1876, p. 22, No. 1 (What is that: a thing that puts itself on everything but does not put itself on water?); Pelay y Briz, 4. Spanish, New Mexican: Campa, 180. Rumanian: Papahagi, 65. Serbian: Novaković, p. 211, Nos. 10 through 12. Bulgarian: Chacharov, 121.

continent of Europe it has interesting variations. The Dutch "Our Lady of Laken spreads a white sheet on land and sand, but not on the strand"[4] contains a pun on Laken or Laeken, a city near Brussels, and *laken*, "a sheet." The Russian "A white blanket has covered the whole world.—First snow"[5] does not mention the sea. The Serbian "One blanket covered half the world, but it cannot cover its brother next to it"[6] is explained by "I covered the whole world, but could not cover my sister Maritsa [a river in Serbia]."[7] The confused Bulgarian "All the snow gets on Mara but cannot cover it.—River"[8] is best understood by comparison with the Serbian version. The Turkish "The snow falls, it falls everywhere, on that spot it does not fall at all" includes too much of the answer in the riddle. "I have a coverlet, it covers every country, there is one country that it does not cover"[9] is slightly different from the usual version.

Such anomalous versions as the Hungarian "My grandfather's large shirt, there are a hundred patches on it, but still there is not a single stitch in it,"[10] which contains an entirely different theme,[11] and the Turkish "I have a white house, it embraces the whole world, it does not embrace the surface of the water"[12] are rather unsuccessful inventions. Quite different from other references to a cloth is the Irish description of moonshine: "A white sheet at the side of the house, and no one was able to weave it."[13]

1219. My father has a blanket, it cover the whole world.—Sky.
Parsons, *Bahamas*, p. 477, No. 61.

1220. My father has a sheet that covers the whole world.—Cloud.
Beckwith, *Jamaica*, p. 189, No. 57.

1221-1223. Sheet Cannot Be Spread

The idea of comparing the firmament to a sheet or blanket is very old. See the Biblical "Qui extendit coelum sicut pellis,"[1] which the Middle Ages turned into a riddle, "Quid est celum?—Sicut pellis extensa."[2]

1221. My fader give me a blanket to spread over a bed, an' I could not spread it on account of de bigness of de bed.—Sky.
Parsons, *Antilles*, III, 443, St. Croix, 12.

---

[4] Schrijnen, II, 103, No. 8.
[5] Sadovnikov, 1973.
[6] Novaković, p. 211, No. 8.
[7] Novaković, p. 211, No. 9.
[8] Chacharov, 105.
[9] Kowalski, *Zagadki*, 37, 92.
[10] Arany and Gyulai, III, 295, No. 17.
[11] See the headnotes to No. 1213 above and to No. 1437, § 9, below.
[12] Kowalski, *Asia Minor*, 42.
[13] Delargy, 54.
[1] Ps. 104:2. See also Is. 40:22, 44:24. For discussion see R. Eisler, *Weltenmantel und Himmelszelt* (Munich, 1910), p. 92 (Babylonian parallels), and p. 105, n. 6, p. 224, n. 4, and p. 584, n. 3.
[2] Daly and Suchier, p. 110.

1222a. My fader gave me a sheet to spread and I couldn' spread it.—Cloud.
   Parsons, *Antilles*, III, 431, St. Eustatius, 2, p. 422, Montserrat, 12, p. 424, Antigua, 11 var., p. 435, St. Martin, 5 var. My moder: p. 435, St. Martin, 5.

1222b. Me riddle me riddle / I tell you this riddle, or not. / My moder had a sheet and she couldn't spread it.—Answer lacking.
   Parsons, *Antilles*, III, 446, St. Thomas, 12.

1223. My fader give me a sheet to spread an' I couldn' spread it.—Cistron plain [cistern floor; rain is run from the roof into a cement cistern].
   Parsons, *Antilles*, III, 436, St. Eustatius, 2 var.

1224–1225. Cloth Cannot Be Folded; Money Cannot Be Counted

These two elements are combined so often that the result may be regarded as a riddle in its own right. Although the original conception probably contained three elements,[1] this combination of two elements seems well established in the West Indies, where it has been taken down from oral tradition on three islands. It need not be connected with the Mongolian "A whole piece of silk which cannot be rolled up; ten thousand pearls which cannot be strung."[2]

In such widely separated countries as India, Sweden, and New Mexico, riddlers mention the woman who attempts to fold the cloth or sheet.[3] Since many versions name the actors, the English version gives the appearance of concealing the name by the use of the passive voice. The three English texts show corruptions which can be readily emended. Stars are sometimes called children too numerous to count.[4]

1224. A table cloth can't be folded, nor be stretched, cannot be counted.—Clouds and stars.
   Parsons, *Barbados*, p. 285, No. 55 var.

1225a. My sheet I cannot fold, / My money I cannot count.—Cloud and stars.
   Beckwith, *Jamaica*, p. 189, No. 56a.

1225b. My father have a sheet of money and he couldn't count one.—Stars.
   Parsons, *Antilles*, III, 370, Grenada, 36.

1226. Sheet Full of Small Change

English riddlers usually call the stars coins so numerous that they cannot be counted. In this instance, the riddler declares that they are numerous without referring to any effort to count them. Variations of this conception are abundant, but ordinarily refer to crumbs, stones, or lice rather than coins (see the headnote to No. 1227 for a tabulation of the themes).

---

[1] See the headnote to Nos. 1215–1216.
[2] Mostaert, 125.
[3] See my article, "A Riddle for the Sun, Sky, and Stars," *California Folklore Quarterly*, III (1944), 222–231.
[4] See No. 1024 above.

1226. My father has a large sheet, / Covers the whole world, and full of small change.—Star in the sky.
Parsons, *Eleuthera and Watling's Islands, Bahamas*, p. 440, No. 21.

1227. Money Cannot Be Counted

Riddlers have invented various comparisons for the stars in the heavens. I shall consider here only those which allude specifically to the countless number. English and western European riddlers in general call the stars money or coins that cannot be counted[1] and usually associate this comparison with descriptions of other celestial bodies. The Irish "A little white barrel full of pennies"[2] resembles a description which is more often used for a pumpkin or a poppy-head.[3] A few versions speak of biscuits so numerous that they cannot be counted[4] and may reflect a confusion with riddles describing the sun or moon as bread or cake.[5] The stars are sometimes called countless persons.[6]

The notion of countless objects is ordinarily used for stars, but there are a few instances of such references to hair.[7]

Blechsteiner calls attention to a very curious connection between some of these comparisons for stars and the words used for the human mouth.[8] He quotes a Hebrew query: " 'Count the stars of Heaven!'—*Answer.* 'Count the teeth in your mouth.' "[9] In Greek, the word *ouraniskos* signifies both "palate" and "sky," and the Latin *palatum*, as well as the corresponding Georgian word, is also used for "sky." This equating of the sky and the mouth is perhaps paralleled, thinks Blechsteiner, in such riddles for the mouth and teeth as "My little vegetable garden is strewn with stones."[10]

Riddles for the sky and stars which involve an allusion to a multitude of objects mention:

§ 1. A bag full of bones. Zyrian: Wichmann, *Zyrian*, 192 = *ibid.*, 242 (A basket full of bones, but two in it are too many), which is not entirely clear. African, SeSuto: Norton and Velaphe, 41 (Where does lanky-horse get so many bones from?). The natives in Togo compare stars to shells in water that disappear before morning (Schönhärl, 159) or to countless shells (40).

---

[1] See Nos. 1215, 1216, 1225a through 1227b, the note to No. 1215, and the note to Nos. 1224 through 1225b.
[2] Delargy, 56.
[3] See No. 1355 and the headnote to No. 1355 (especially nn. 3, 9) below, and the headnote to Nos. 1100–1108, n. 35, above.
[4] Nos. 1229a, 1229b.
[5] See Nos. 1231, 1233, 1234, the note to Nos. 1230a through 1234, and the headnote to Nos. 1230–1234.
[6] No. 1024, the headnote to Nos. 1023–1024, and the note to No. 1024.
[7] Nos. 1116a, 1116b, and the headnote to No. 1116.
[8] Blechsteiner, p. xlvi, No. 2.
[9] Sanhedrin, 39a.
[10] Mingrelian: Petrov, p. 257, No. 3. Georgian: Kapanadze, p. 144, No. 1. Blechsteiner cites parallels in German: Wossidlo, 40 through 42a.

§ 2. Lights or candles. See the headnote to Nos. 1189–1191 above.

§ 3. Household objects. Scotch Gaelic: Nicolson, p. 29 (A basin full of holes). Serbian: Novaković, p. 56, No. 6 (Tray after tray, mortar after mortar, from one end of the world to the other). Turkish: Kúnos, 98 (Its top is round, the four sides are hanging, a golden wheel, a silver broom), which is not completely intelligible. Yakut: Popov, p. 283 (In the yurt small chips are lying). Indian, Bhil: Hedberg, p. 884, No. 117 (Only a handful of jingling bells, still you can't count them). Indonesian, Sangir: Adriani, pp. 408–409, No. 134 (A pan full of gold flakes or nuggets).

§ 4. Pustules. African, Kundu: Ittmann, *Kundu*, 42 (Pustules cover an elephant.—Stars cover the firmament), 43 (Framboesia [yaws, a disease] attacked an elephant). Kosi: Ittmann, *Kosi*, 82. For riddles making a comparison to a prickly or bumpy person, see Nos. 576a through 577b above.

§ 5. Pearls, jewels, stones. Italian: Tschiedel, 71 (I have a little basket full of jewels; in the evening they are strewn and in the morning they are gathered up). Rumanian: Papahagi, 90 (A large, large blanket full of pebbles). Bulgarian: Bozhov, 80 (The sieve is full of round stones). Modern Greek: Polites, *Neohellenika Analekta*, I, 233, No. 231 (A tent, outstretched and scalloped with gold). Tatar: Kalashev and Ioakimov, p. 60, No. 5 (A tray of diamonds, it is impossible to count them). Turkish: Hamizade, 732 (I have a sieve full of imitation pearls. I throw them out in the evening, I collect them in the morning); Katanov in Radlov, IX, 93, No. 777 (I have some pearls that cannot be strung). African, Duala: Ebding, 96 (There are pearls for ornament; our ancestors could not count them and we also cannot). Indian: Lakshīnātha Upasānī, XIII, 3 (Name a person whom you may see every evening adorned with innumerable pearls).

§ 6. Clothing, buttons. Arabic: Littmann, p. 47 (A cloak with countless buttons, it cannot be folded or carried about). Astrakhan Calmuck: Kotvich, 178 (Seventy thousand buttons on the white *keshmet* [a long Caucasian coat] made of *dartsok* [cloth inscribed with conjurations and fluttering in the wind]), 179 (Among the *alchiks* that fill the skirt are two hoopnets filled with lead), 180 (In the skirt full of *alchiks* there are also two sky-blue hoopnets), 181 (Two thousand *alchiks* have two sky-blue hoopnets). The meaning of *alchiks* is obscure.

The starry sky is also compared to a blanket full of peas[11] or lice.[12]

§ 7. Eggs. Portuguese: Parsons, *Cape Verde*, 272b. Serbian: Novaković, p. 57, Nos. 1 (Hanging over the house, a sieve full of eggs), 4 (A vat full of tiny eggs). Bulgarian: Gubov, 111 (On the house a tray full of eggs), 249 (The dish is full of eggs); Bozhov, 79 (The bowl is full of eggs). Albanian:

---

[11] Compare the headnote to Nos. 1093–1095, nn. 9, 11, and 15 above.
[12] See the note to No. 1226.

Hahn, p. 162, No. 65 (A plain covered with eggs, a winged horse passes over them and does not touch them). Arabic: Stumme, *Tázerwalt*, 17 (A tray of eggs that has been overturned without the eggs falling). Turkish: Hamizade, 733 (In the evening I put a sieve full of eggs in the roof; in the morning I looked and there weren't any). Indian, Bengali: Mitra, *Chittagong*, p. 659, No. 3 (There is a boscage [thicket] upon a boscage. Upon that is a big black snake. The big black snake lays eggs that nobody can count them).

I do not fully understand the Hungarian "A *Jéger*[13] tree has two branches, there are a hundred nests on them, there are a hundred eggs in the hundred nests, but they all have only one yolk.—World, rays of the stars, the eggs are in the midst of the stars, the yolk is the moon."[14]

§ 8. Cattle, sheep. See Nos. 470 and 484a through 484d above.

§ 9. Miscellaneous. French: Parsons, *Antilles*, III, 367, Trinidad, 48. Turkish: Katanov in Radlov, IX, 238, No. 30 (I sprinkled my wheat meal on the ice). Shor: Dyrenkova, 37 (I threw wheat on blue ice). Yakut: Piekarski, 56 (Tiny fish are scattered over the hut). African, Kinyarwanda: Hurel, p. 153, No. 9 (In an incalculable manner, by themselves, by thousands, by hundreds, if you guess, I shall give you a reward). Dschagga: Gutmann, p. 526 (My patches on the father's bed pelt), and *ibid.* (I have my eyes. You cannot count them).

1227a. I got so much money I couldn't done count it.—That's a star.
Johnson, *Antigua*, p. 87, No. 49; Parsons, *Sea Islands, S.C.*, p. 159, No. 44.

1227b. My father git me some money to count and I couldn't count it.—Stars.
Parsons, *Antilles*, III, 370, Grenada, 35 var., p. 434, Antigua, 12 var., p. 432, St. Eustatius, 3, and p. 435, St. Martin, 5. A large pu'se of money: Parsons, *Antilles*, III, 414, Antigua, 12.

1227c. A riddle, a riddle, / Perhaps a tiggle. / Plenty t'ing you can't call them.—Stars.
Parsons, *Antilles*, III, 424, Antigua, 12 var.

1228. Plates Washed in Evening Vanish by Morning

This conception resembles the comparisons of the stars to household objects that I have collected in the headnote to No. 1227, § 3, but also contains the theme of their disappearance.[1]

1228. Me fader hab a heap a white plate pon a blue table; wash de plate in de evening an' turn him down, an' in de morning don' see one.—Stars.
Beckwith, *Jamaica*, p. 189, No. 54c.

---

[13] The meaning is obscure.
[14] *Magyar Nyelvör*, V (1876), 127.
[1] See the headnotes to Nos. 1094 and 1217–1218, nn. 7–10.

1229–1249. Articles of Food

Riddlers describe the stars,[1] the sun and moon,[2] an egg,[3] a pipe of tobacco,[4] and a few miscellaneous objects by comparing them to articles of food. The riddles for the sun and moon are very widely known and are of considerable interest for their special local varieties. The other riddles in this section are comparatively uninteresting. The comparison of the stars to biscuits is probably a casual variation of a more popular comparison to coins. The description of an egg as something which does not become salty even when it is cooked in salty water expresses a simple physical fact. The comparison of a burning pipe of tobacco to food boiling in a dish is rather ingenious and also interesting as a rare type of comparison. Riddlers usually compare a thing to a man or an animal, and, vice versa, a man or an animal to a thing. They do not often compare a thing to another thing.

1229. Biscuits and Cloth

1229a. I can't fold the table cloth, / I can't count my biscuits.—The clouds and stars.
Parsons, *Barbados*, p. 285, No. 55.

1229b. Biscuit can't reckon, / Our table cloth can't fall.—Sky.
Parsons, *Barbados*, p. 285, No. 55 var.

1230–1234. Articles of Food: Sun or Moon

Although the comparison of the sun or moon (more frequently the moon) to an article of food is rare in English folklore (except in the West Indian islands, where a non-English influence may be present), riddlers in continental Europe and Asia are very familiar with it. The English conundrum "What is mos' like half a cheese?—Nyew moon,"[1] which Dr. Parsons found in the West Indies, may be a defaced variety of this comparison. It is not a true riddle of the sort included in this collection. The usual answer is "The other half."[2] We naturally think also of the saying that the moon is made of green cheese, in which "green" cheese probably signifies cottage cheese.

Comparisons of the moon, and more rarely the sun, to a pancake or loaf are abundant. They are current along the Baltic coast, in Poland, and thence eastward. The earliest example that I have noted is Claret's "Aureus in

---

[1] Nos. 1229a, 1229b. See also Nos. 1094a through 1094e, 1095, the headnotes to Nos. 1093–1095, 1094, 1095, 1227, §§ 7, 9, 1230–1234, nn. 42–45, and the note to No. 1215.
[2] Nos. 1230a through 1234, the headnote to Nos. 1230–1234, and the note to Nos. 1230a through 1234.
[3] Nos. 1236a through 1236c.
[4] Nos. 1244a through 1245.

[1] Parsons, *Barbados*, p. 288, No. 77.
[2] Flemish: Joos, 941. German: Hermann Frischbier, *Am Urquell*, III (1892), 74, No. 98. French: Rolland, 384a. Spanish, Argentinian: Lehmann-Nitsche, 966. See also the headnote to Nos. 1403–1404 below.

pilatro panis stans: luna fit astro" (p. 68, No. 10) of the fourteenth century: here *panis* is glossed *Christus* and the answer is glossed *Virgo inter sanctos*. For modern examples see German: Frischbier, *Menschenwelt*, p. 258, No. 177 (A black sheet spread out, white peas sown, and in the middle is a disk).[3] Lithuanian: Jurgelionis, 76 (In the manor house there hangs a pancake). Polish: Gustawicz, 184 (A loaf of bread in the midst of beans), 185 through 187. Russian: Sadovnikov, 1842*a* through 1842*i*, 1864*a* (The oven is full of pies, in the middle is a round loaf). Cheremiss: Ramstedt, 14. Votyak: Wichmann, *Votyak*, 257 (On the house roof half a loaf), 263 (In the attic a piece of bread), 363 (The oven is full of meat-patties, but only one butter-patty is there.— Stars and moon); Buch, 34 (A plate of butter.—Moon). Turkish: Menges, p. 78, No. 48 (Above the house[4] hangs half a loaf); Kowalski, *Asia Minor*, 34, 69 (On the cupboard lies half a cake); Hamizade, 29 (Atop the roof half a round cake), 30 (Atop the house half a flat cake); Katanov in Radlov, IX, 238, No. 33 (Under the bank is lying a crust of bread). Crimean Tatar: Filonenko, 63. Shor: Dyrenkova, 3 (Above the house lies half a cake). Calmuck: Kotvich, 176 (Half a pancake on top of the yurt), 177 (Half a loaf of bread on top of the yurt). Quechua: Quijada Jara, 19. Argentinian Spanish riddlers call the moon a *tortillita*,[5] but they may know nothing of the Russian and Turkish comparison to half a loaf. When a Levantine Arabic riddler calls the moon a traveling pancake, he destroys the unity of the idea: "Equal to a flat loaf in size, it travels to the farthest kingdom" or "As small as a pancake, yet it travels."[6]

The Calmuck description of a felt cover for the opening of the yurt is an adaptation of the riddle for the moon: "There is half a pretzel on the upper jamb of the door."[7] The Yakut riddle for the moon in its first and last quarters, "Over the hut, so they say, is a crooked spoon,"[8] shows that the comparisons of the moon to a spoon refers to the waxing or waning moon.

Comparisons of the moon to cheese or to a bowl of milk or of sour milk occur generally in Baltic folklore and in the traditions of Finno-Ugric tribes in Russia.[9] They are readily understood in the light of the Cherekessian "On our roof lies half an old bowl.—Waning moon." A similar conception underlies the Cherekessian "Looking into an old vegetable garden, I see half a pumpkin."[10] The usual simile is the comparison of the moon to a bowl of milk. See Rumanian: Papahagi, 56 (A dish of sour milk standing about the house). Cheremiss: Genetz, 20 = Wichmann, *Cheremiss*, 22 (On the ridgepole

---

[3] For this comparison for the stars see the headnote to Nos. 1093–1095, nn. 9–11 and 15. The "disk" is a round loaf or roll.
[4] Var.: stable.
[5] Lehmann-Nitsche, 60*a*, 60*b*.
[6] Littmann, p. 47; Ruoff, p. 12, No. 7.
[7] Kotvich, 64.   [8] Piekarski, 51.
[9] See also French: Parsons, *Antilles*, III, 384, Martinique, 67, and p. 402, Guadaloupe, 49.
[10] Tambiev, p. 61, Nos. 91, 93.

of my room is a pot of sour milk); Porkka, 32.[11] Zyrian: Wichmann, *Zyrian*, 71 (In the corner of the sheepfold a pot of sour milk). Less well conceived are the Vogul "Behind the dark steps a mouldy half-cup"[12] and the Turkish "On the top of the house a fancy cup."[13] The Tatar "In the middle of the road is a cup of sour milk"[14] contains an unusual comparison of the Milky Way to a road.

Some of these comparisons refer only to a utensil, and not to sour milk. See the Mongolian "On the ice a silver bowl,"[15] which is analogous to "A flat pail in the steppe."[16] Mongolian pails are made of shining white birchbark. Further examples are "There is a low bucket on the wall";[17] "A sandalwood bowl on the road, a silver eating bowl on the ice.—Droppings of animals used as fuel, sun."[18] The comparison of dung to a sandalwood bowl shows how one riddle is made on the model of another.

For comparisons to cheese see the Spanish "In a dense mountain is half a cheese";[19] the Lithuanian "A cheese in the well";[20] and the Lettish "A bit of cheese in the pantry."[21] The Czech "A peasant was beating his horses, he tore open a sack of peas and lost a goat's-milk cheese"[22] is a very curious expansion of the theme.

There are a few references to other foods in versions allied to those already illustrated. The Zyrians say, "Beside the gutter a bowl of dry oatmeal" and "Beside the gutter a bowl of dry oatmeal and a bowl of malt."[23]

Comparisons of the sun to butter[24] are analogous to the comparisons of the moon to cheese. See, for example, the Modern Greek "With one tray of butter I anoint the whole world."[25] The conception varies widely and can easily have arisen independently. See the Kinyarwanda "A little pot of butter is far away, or I should dip into it"[26] and the Taveta "My house has been burned, and the fat which was hung up has been left."[27] The quite anomalous Cherekessian "Three unknown wonders. Give me three villages and I shall tell you: (1) Who climbed the sky on a ladder? (2) Who carried water in a sieve? (3) Who fried butter on a spike?—Rainbow, storm cloud, sun's rays"[28] suggests

---

[11] See also Wichmann, *Cheremiss*, 53, 116, 117, 196, 229.
[12] Ahlqvist, *Vogul*, 5.
[13] Kúnos, 87; Hamizade, 31 (Atop the roof a tinned tray).
[14] Kalashev and Ioakimov, p. 50, No. 23.
[15] Gombojew, 1; Klukine, 18.
[16] Rudnyev, 70.   [17] Bazarov, 114.
[18] Rudnyev, 52.   [19] Demófilo, 528.
[20] Jurgelionis, 80.   [21] Bielenstein, 925.
[22] Erben, 8, as cited by Flajšhans, p. 21, § 21.
[23] Wichmann, *Zyrian*, 194, 195.
[24] See the Votyak comparisons of the moon to butter, in the second paragraph of this headnote.
[25] Stathes, p. 342, No. 67; Polites, *Neohellenika Analekta*, I, 227, No. 194 = Dieterich, *Rätseldichtung*, p. 90.
[26] Hurel, p. 154, No. 18.
[27] Hollis, *Taveta*, p. 211, No. 60.
[28] Tambiev, p. 61, No. 99.

looking for an allusion to a story explanatory of the third question which would be akin to the stories of Jacob and of the Danaïds.

Riddlers mention a few other kinds of foods in descriptions of the sun and moon, but the details vary greatly from country to country. The South African Dutch mention a lemon,[29] the Antillean French a ham,[30] the modern Greeks a slice of melon.[31] The Swahili "The half of my coconut is spread over the whole city"[32] resembles comparisons for the earth and sky noted elsewhere.[33] The Tschuana "I hung up biltong,[34] it was gone in the morning"[35] contains the theme of the objects that vanish at dawn.[36] The Pangwe "Everybody gets a spoonful.—Moon"[37] seems to have no analogue. Three Filipino riddles conceive the moon in quite different ways: "Half a coconut, retreating slowly all night" and "A half coconut, scraped the whole night" and "I planted a half lemon; three priests cannot dig it up."[38] A curious Hungarian riddle for the moon, "There is a golden forest, there is a golden dish on the golden tree, there is a golden liver in the golden dish, the golden liver-meat must be cut with a golden knife,"[39] seems to stand quite alone. The Turks make a curious comparison to fish: "In a frying pan there are two fish, one is cold.—Sun, moon."[40]

Descriptions of the stars in terms of articles of food, except for the comparisons to rice, fruits, or nuts,[41] are rare. Such texts as the Lithuanian "A sieve full of scraps";[42] the Serbian "A pan full of pastry";[43] the Bulgarian "A blue pan full of pastry";[44] and the Votyak "An oven full of little cookies, in the middle a big pie.—Stars, moon,"[45] to which parallels have already been cited, are examples of riddles for stars.

The Khāṛiā and Uraon "The moon simmers in the middle of the tank,"[46] with the answer "food baking or frying in a pan," might be conceived as a reversal of these conceptions.

1230a. My father has a box of cheese. No knife can not cut it.—Moon.
Parsons, *Antilles*, III, 371, Grenada, 48.

---

[29] Groenewald, p. 85.
[30] Parsons, *Antilles*, III, 409, Les Saintes, 11.
[31] Abbott, p. 317, No. 18.
[32] Velten, 77.
[33] See the headnote to No. 1252.
[34] Dried meat.   [35] Kuhn, *Tschuana*, 22.
[36] See the headnote to No. 1094.
[37] Tessmann, 22.
[38] Starr, *Philippines*, 149, 150, 152.
[39] *Magyar Nyelvör*, XIX (1890), 92. See a perhaps imperfect version in *ibid.*, II (1873), 468.
[40] Hamizade, 225.
[41] See the headnotes to Nos. 1093–1095, 1094, and 1095.
[42] Schleicher, p. 201.
[43] Novaković, p. 57, No. 2.
[44] Gubov, 250.
[45] Buch, 41.
[46] Roy and Roy, II, 454, No. 42; Archer, p. 179, No. 1.

1230b. My fader gave me a large cheese to cut an' I could not cut it.—Moon.
Parsons, *Antilles*, III, 424, Antigua, 13.

1231. One bammie [pancake] shingle off Mt. Olivet church.—Moon.
Beckwith, *Jamaica*, p. 200, No. 152.

1232-1234. Food Serves the Whole World

1232a. My father have a piece of white yam that serve the whole world.—Moon.
Beckwith, *Jamaica*, p. 188, No. 53.

1232b. My fader had one dumpling an' he served de whole worl'.—Moon.
Parsons, *Bahamas*, p. 480, No. 83.

1233. Mah fader have a johnny cake serve de whole worl'.—Sun.
Parsons, *Bahamas*, p. 482, No. 108.

1234. I know somet'in', / My fader had two duff serve de whole worl'.—Sun an' de moon.
Parsons, *Bahamas*, p. 473, No. 19.

1235. A Piece of Meat Fills a Crack

This comparison is also applicable to drinking from a pot or tub.[1]

1235. Bellee, / Han' round de back, / Take a big piece o' meat / Ter fill de crack.—A woman nursin' a child.
Parsons, *Bahamas*, p. 473, No. 20.

1236. Salt Does Not Penetrate Food

The notion that salt does not penetrate the shell of an egg occurs very often in riddling. In its Jamaican use the notion concerns the boiling of an egg in salted water; elsewhere it seems often to refer to storing an egg in dry salt. In French and Breton riddling this notion is applied to a nut.[1]

1236a. I put one coco on the fire to boil and I put in a gallon of salt and the salt never tasted it.—Egg; the salt cannot penetrate the shell.
Beckwith, *Jamaica*, p. 191, No. 70a.

1236b. I have a t'ing and don't care how much salt I put in it, when I go to eat it, I have to put salt on it.—Egg.
Beckwith, *Jamaica*, p. 191, No. 70b.

1236c. My father gave me one root kasava an' a quart of fine salt; if I don clever, I wouldn't taste it.—Egg.
Beckwith, *Jamaica*, p. 191, No. 70.

---

[1] See Italian: Tammi, 20. Serbian: Novaković, p. 106, No. 5 (Mouth to mouth and the palm on the backside).

[1] Breton: Le Chef, *Ille-et-Vilaine*, p. 667; Kerbeuzec, *Ille-et-Vilaine*, 55. French: Lacuve, *Poitou*, No. 36.
For the comparison of a nut to a tasty dish see the headnote to No. 1187, § 1.

1237–1238. Something to Eat, Not Fish, Flesh, or Bone

1237a. As I was going through a field of wheat, / I found something good to eat. / It wasn't fish or flesh or bone. / I kept it till it ran alone.—Egg.

Waugh, *Canada*, p. 68, No. 783; Knortz, p. 221, No. 44; Johnson, *St. Helena Island, S.C.*, p. 160, No. 42; *Southern Workman*, March, 1894; Hyatt, *Adams Co., Ill.*, p. 660, No. 10862. Fish, flesh, fowl, nor bone: Gutch and Peacock, *Lincolnshire*, p. 397, No. 4; Parsons, *Sea Islands, S.C.*, p. 169, No. 110. Fish, meat, or bone: Chappell, p. 230, No. 6. It wasn't flesh, it wasn't bone: Brewster, *Indiana*, 1. I let it stay till it ran alone: Greenleaf, *Newfoundland*, p. 14, No. 10. My fields of wheat . . . picked up . . . It was neither fish, flesh, nor bone: Hudson, p. 86, No. 19.

1237b. One day I went down in the golden harvest-field, / I saw something neither fish, flesh, nor bone. In three weeks, it stood alone.—A partridge egg.

Redfield, *Tennessee*, p. 40, No. 53.

1237c. As I went across the field, I picked up something good to eat; / It was neither flesh, fish, nor bone, / But I kept it three weeks until it stood alone.—An egg.

Farr, *Tennessee*, p. 322, No. 65.

1237d. As I was going through the farm / I picked up something and put it neath my arm, / Neither fish, flesh, meat, nor bone, / I kept it till it run alone.—Egg.

Fauset, *Nova Scotia*, p. 150, No. 41 var.

1237e. As I was going through a field of wheat, / I picked up something good to eat, / It was neither fish, meat, stick, nor stone, / I kept it till it walked alone.—Egg.

Fauset, *Nova Scotia*, p. 150, No. 41. I picked up something fit to eat: Fauset, *Nova Scotia*, p. 150, No. 41 var. Feather, flesh, nor bone: Beckwith, *Jamaica*, p. 213, No. 237.

1237f. I picked up something neither flesh, fowl, feather, nor bone. I kept it three weeks, and it walked alone.—Egg.

Fauset, *Nova Scotia*, p. 150, No. 41 var.

1237g. As I was going o'er London Bridge, / I saw something under a hedge; / 'Twas neither fish, flesh, fowl, nor bone, / And yet in three weeks it runned alone.—An egg.

Halliwell-Phillipps, *Nursery Rhymes*, p. 213 = Lina Eckenstein, *Comparative Studies in Nursery Rhymes* (London, 1906), p. 110.

1237h. As I went up the hill a day, / I found a wee thing lapped in hay. / It was neither fish, flesh, blood, nor bone, / And yet I kept it till it walked its lone.—Egg.

Praeger, *Béaloideas*, IV (1933–1934), 146, No. 25.

1237i. I picked up something good to eat, / All flesh and no bone. / I kept it 'til it walked alone.—Egg.

Parsons, *Bermuda*, p. 253, No. 51.

1237j. I went out in the fiel' an' found somepin'. / It wasn't flesh an' it wasn't meat, an' still I kept it till it walked.—Egg.

Fauset, *Southern Negro*, p. 287, No. 115.

1238. Somet'in' haven' any skin or bone, but in two week time it have skin an' bone.—Chicken hatch out.
Parsons, *Sea Islands, S.C.*, p. 173, No. 158.

1239–1241. Buying Food, Water, and Wood Simultaneously

Both African and Indian riddlers have found amusing the idea of buying food and at the same time the water and the wood with which to cook it. We can probably infer that the French and Spanish instances current in the West Indies did not come from Europe, but from either African or Hindu sources. The theme is apparently very old in the Far East, for it is implied in a passage in the travels of Marco Polo.[1]

An analogous European theme is the listing of the many very different objects to be got from an acorn: "I went through the wood. I came through the wood. I picked up a small piece of wood from under my foot. In time [?] it became two spoons, in time [?] it became two cups, a tie beam for a house and a cover for bread."[2] A similar but still more involved riddle is the Russian account of getting drink, torches, splints, and bathhouse brushes from the birch: "A tree stands, at its side are four appendages; the first is an undug well, the second is light in darkness, the third joinings for a broken one, the fourth health to a tired one."[3]

1239a. I was a cook of a ship, an' the captain sent me on shore to buy three things with one cent—wood, water, an' food. Tell me that one, please.—Cook bought a coconut. It gave him shell (wood), milk (water), meat (food).
Parsons, *Antilles*, III, 439, Anguilla, 12.

1239b. I send a boy fah somet'ing to eat fah a penny, an' he brought me food an' drink fah dat penny.—Coconut.
Parsons, *Antilles*, III, 422, Montserrat, 17.

1239c. I'll give you a penny to buy food, water, and coals.—Coconut.
Parsons, *Antilles*, III, 372, Grenada, 52.

1239d. Buyin' food, water, and coals with one penny.—Coconut.
Parsons, *Antilles*, III, 380, St. Lucia, 45.

1240. I eat out St. John [i.e., the parish in which the riddler lived], / I drink out St. John, / St. John still remains.—Coconut.
Parsons, *Barbados*, p. 287, No. 68.

1241a. Going up a lane, I see a drink an' see a chaw.—Coconut.
Beckwith, *Jamaica*, p. 193, No. 83.

---

[1] For the reference see the note to Nos. 1239a through 1241b. See also some curious related folktales in W. A. Clouston, *Flowers from a Persian Garden* (London, 1890), pp. 117–118.
[2] The text quoted here is Welsh; see Hull and Taylor, 174. For parallels see German: Gilhoff, 326. Lithuanian: Schleicher, p. 196. Cheremiss: Wichmann, *Cheremiss*, 140.
[3] Preobrazhenskii, p. 173.

1241b. Dere's a cup an' in de cup dere's a chaw; no man to clear dis chaw.—Coconut.
Beckwith, *Jamaica*, p. 193, No. 83a.

1242–1249. Miscellaneous

1242. Two big biscuits, one cup of coffee, / Going to Augusta black and dirty.—Locomotive.
Bacon and Parsons, *Virginia*, p. 326, No. 124.

1243. No ca [call?] how time hard, one coco full pot.—Foot in a boot.
Beckwith, *Jamaica*, p. 200, No. 151.

1244a. Me riddle, me riddle, / Me randy-o. / I saw my fader cook a pot o' hominy, on top done an' de bottom raw.—When you light yer pipe.
Parsons, *Bahamas*, p. 476, No. 51.

1244b. I saw my fader have a t'ing, on top done an' de bottom raw.—When you light yer pipe.
Parsons, *Bahamas*, p. 476, No. 51 var.

1244c. My mother had a pot of pease and rice, done on the top and raw on the bottom.—Pipe and tobacco.
Parsons, *Bahamas*, p. 476, No. 51 var.

1245. Mother put on a pot of food to boil; the top boil before the bottom.—Pipe.
Beckwith, *Jamaica*, p. 191, No. 73.

1246a. As I was going through my grandfather's lot, / I saw something that made me squat, / It looked so sweet and tasted so sour, / Can't guess that in half an hour.—Cranberry.
Fauset, *Nova Scotia*, p. 165, No. 120.

1246b. As I was going through my grandfather's lot, / I picked up something that made me squat, / It looked so sweet and tasted so sour, / Can't guess that in half an hour.—Cranberry.
Fauset, *Nova Scotia*, p. 165, No. 120 var.

1247–1249. Cannot Eat (Pick) It

The comparing of a human hand to a bunch, or so-called "hand," of bananas rests on the obvious similarity of the bunch to the hand and fingers and on the pun.[1] The comparing of wasps to a bunch of bananas that cannot be touched[2] is probably suggested by the similarity in colors: both wasps and ripe bananas are yellow and black. The comparing of a daughter to a banana that one cannot eat is a variation of a favorite theme among African riddlers.[3]

---

[1] No. 1247.
[2] Nos. 1248a through 1248c.
[3] See the headnote to No. 1070.

1247. I gwine to town wid a hand [bunch] o' ripe plantain; I hungry an' couldn't taste it.—Fingers.
Beckwith, *Jamaica*, p. 193, No. 80.

1248a. Once was a time my fader had a bunch o' banana an' not a mahn could a gone an' pick one.—Was' [wasp].
Parsons, *Bahamas*, p. 475, No. 36.

1248b. My fader had a bunch o' bananas an' no one could touch it but his own.—Was' nest.
Parsons, *Bahamas*, p. 477, No. 57 (misnumbered 58).

1248c. My fader had a bunch o' bananas an' he could' [couldn't] touch one.—Was' nest.
Parsons, *Bahamas*, p. 482, No. 99.

1249. My fader had a bunch of banana. He couldn't eat it, his wife couldn't eat it, an' none in de house could eat it.—Dat's his daughter.
Parsons, *Bahamas*, p. 471, No. 3.

1250–1251. Members of a Person or of an Animal

1250. As I was going over London Bridge, / I met a cartful of fingers and thumbs.—Gloves.
Halliwell-Phillipps, *Nursery Rhymes*, p. 121; Knortz, p. 223, No. 53; Parsons, Bermuda, p. 260, No. 114. Brooklyn Bridge: Knortz, p. 223, No. 53 var. Fauset, *Nova Scotia*, p. 151, No. 44, adds: You tell me this riddle, I'll give you a goat.

1251. Wibbly-wobbly, / Timothy-sackitty, / Please gimme a piece of wobbly gut.—Halibut head.
Fauset, *Nova Scotia*, p. 163, No. 106.

1252. Two "Packey"

The nature of the "packey" to which the West Indian riddler compares the heaven and the earth is obscure. His conception is probably akin to the description of the sky (and often, of the earth) as a hide, blanket, sheet, or cloth,[1] but we are often told that this covering cannot be folded. It is probably not connected with the comparison of the sun and moon to articles of food.[2] It may be connected with the comparison of the heaven and the earth to pieces of wood, as in the Uraon "Two wooden planks which neither fall nor come together."[3] The usual form of this concept is seen in the Finnish "Two stumps go up and down alternately";[4] the Kamba "A very large garden with only one stump";[5] and the Bhil "In a black, well-tilled field, there are two stumps."[6] The occurrence of this theme in such widely separated places as

---

[1] See No. 1217.
[2] See the headnote to Nos. 1230–1234.
[3] Archer, p. 192, No. 194.
[4] Lönnrot, 61 = Henssen, 61. See also the headnote to No. 1071, nn. 21–22, above.
[5] Lindblom, 75.
[6] Hedberg, p. 884, No. 116.

Finland, Africa, and India raises curious and probably unanswerable questions regarding the possibility of independent origin or dissemination from a center. Inasmuch as the available texts are few and the meaning of the comparison is not obvious, any effort to answer such questions is futile. I do not know what significance to find in "Old Man Brenta sit on a stump" in one of these riddles,[7] but conjecture that some corruption has obscured the riddler's meaning.

Some curious riddles comparing the sky and earth to a pair of objects are current in Africa. See an unexplained Bakongo "The field which papa cultivated has two dungheaps."[8] Less confusing and obscure are the Togo "My father has two calabashes, they are of equal size";[9] the Ila "Bellows spouts which do not separate";[10] the Bantu "A leaf and another big leaf";[11] and the Sukuma "That in which one cooks is broad, and that with which it is covered is broad,"[12] which has a close parallel in Wanamwezi.[13] An unusual variation is seen in the Tigriña "A basket above and a basket below, what it has in the middle is a little fragment."[14] The fragment is the earth. Only a few parallels can be cited from other places. The Mongols say, "A rug with wool and a rug without wool.—Earth and sky" and "You cannot step over father's sheepskin, you cannot roll up mother's sheepskin."[15] Among related ways of describing the earth and sky[16] the notion of conceiving them as halves of an egg[17] is especially interesting.

1252a. Aunty Mary cut two packey, not one bigger than the other.—Heaven and earth.
Beckwith, *Jamaica*, p. 198, No. 134.

1252b. Ole man Brenta sit on a stump, cut two packey, not one bigger than the other.—Cloud on the earth.
Beckwith, *Jamaica*, p. 198, No. 134a.

1253–1258. Letter, Message, Gift

These represent virtually the only manufactured objects or objects not found in nature that are used as the *tertium quid comparationis*.

---

[7] No. 1252b below.
[8] Denis, 97. For comparisons of riverbanks to a pair of persons, see the headnote to Nos. 1003–1004, nn. 44–45, above.
[9] Schönhärl, 94.
[10] Smith and Dale, II, 329, No. 37.
[11] Tardy, p. 294, No. 7.
[12] Augustiny, 1.
[13] Dahl, 37.
[14] Littmann, *Tigriña*, 2. For descriptions in terms of something above and below see my headnote to Nos. 1436–1447, but they very rarely refer to the earth and sky.
[15] Kotvich, 172, 171.
[16] R. Eisler, *Weltenmantel und Himmelszelt* (Munich, 1910), p. 521, n. 2.
[17] R. Eisler, *Weltenmantel und Himmelszelt*, pp. 410–411, n. 3.

1253. j went & j went & j cannot tel whither j met & j met j cannot tell who: j had a gift given me j shall never forgo yet j came home a true Maiden altho.—a child went to be christianed.
Tupper, *Holme Riddles*, 120; *The New Help to Discourse*, 9th ed., p. 130.

1254. I sen' a letter to England, / I tell you when it reach.—Fishin' an' line.
Parsons, *Bahamas*, p. 472, No. 12.

1255a. My fader went ter England ter buy some corn, de corn reach befo' him.—If you let go a coconut f'om de coconut tree, it will reach down befo' you.
Parsons, *Bahamas*, p. 483, No. 118.

1255b. My father went to Egypt to buy some corn; the corn fell down before him.—Coconut.
Parsons, *Eleuthera and Watling's Islands, Bahamas*, p. 440, No. 15.

1255c. I went upstairs, / A bag of beans drop down an' leave me.—Coconut.
Parsons, *Bahamas*, p. 476, No. 45.

1256a. Dere's a certain fruit, if you go to pick it, it leaves you on da tree an' come down an' left you.—Dat fruit is da coconut.
Johnson, *Antigua*, p. 88, No. 81.

1256b. Sometime I went on a tree to climb an' de fruit come down before me.—Nut.
Parsons, *Antilles*, III, 422, Montserrat, 16.

1257a. I went upstairs, / I sent a message downstairs, / An' it get before me.—Coconut.
Parsons, *Bahamas*, p. 475, No. 44.

1257b. I went to de shop to buy some message, / And the message [arrives] before me.—Coconut.
Parsons, *Antilles*, III, 365, Trinidad, 26 var.

1258a. Send servant to buy bread an' bread come before servant.—Coco.
Parsons, *Antilles*, III, 435, St. Martin, 4.

1258b. Ship an' a cyargo went to race an' de ship came back befo' de cyargo.—Coconut dropped from the tree.
Parsons, *Antilles*, III, 422, Montserrat, 16 var.

1258c. I start f'om England wid mah trunk. Mah trunk reach befo' me.—Coconut.
Parsons, *Bahamas*, p. 483, No. 112.

1259. Wagon

1259. *Whimiky whamiky* / Fore board an' damiky / Stand up and lamiky / With four whirligigs. What is it?—Churn.
Randolph and Taylor, *Ozarks*, 17.

Chapter VIII

ENUMERATIONS OF COMPARISONS

Nos. 1260–1408

A FEW RIDDLES describe an object in terms of one or more comparisons that are intended to be paradoxical in some way. Those employing a single comparison usually mention some characteristic act that is in apparent contradiction to it: the eye is no bigger than a plum, but leads the king from town to town;[1] salt is as small as a nit, but nevertheless serves the king.[2] Those employing two comparisons ordinarily contrast them to gain an enigmatic effect: a walnut (or pecan) is as high as a house and as low as a mouse;[3] a ball of thread or a corsetlace is both round and long.[4]

Since the comparisons usually conflict, a unifying idea other than that of paradoxical contrast is lacking and the combination of the conflicting comparisons does not suggest an object that is not the answer to the riddle. The paradoxical contrast that holds these riddles together is occasionally strengthened by arranging the comparisons according to the positions of the members described or according to a sequence in time. The lack of a clearly perceived unifying principle causes the variants to diverge widely: elements significant to the fundamental concept are easily lost and foreign materials are readily added. Under the circumstances it is difficult to determine the original constituents of many patterns. The riddles for a walnut or pecan,[5] a chestnut,[6] a river,[7] a magpie,[8] and a bramble[9] show a remarkable stability.

1260–1359. Form

1260–1265. Big or Little

1260. Big as a barn, / Light as a feather, / And sixty horses can't pull it.—Shadow of the barn.
Faust, *Nova Scotia*, p. 174, No. 199.

1261a. ther is a thing no bigger than a plumb that l[e]ads the king from towne to towne.—his eye.
Tupper, *Holme Riddles*, 42.

1261b. It is no bigger than a plumme, / and yet it serves the king from towne to towne.—It is an eye.
Prettie Riddles (1631), No. 80 = Brandl, p. 62.

---

[1] No. 1261a.
[2] No. 1262.
[3] Nos. 1270 through 1275.
[4] No. 1341.
[5] Nos. 1269a through 1275.
[6] Nos. 1276, 1277.
[7] Nos. 1292, 1294.
[8] Nos. 1379 through 1382.
[9] Nos. 1385 through 1387 and Nos. 1389, 1391.

1262. Little As a Nit: Salt

The various enigmatic descriptions of salt differ greatly among themselves and cannot be derived from a common source. When salt is called an animal or a person, it is usually said to come to the king's table or to appear in some prominent social position.[1] The Finnish "Tidbit of lords, food of kings, pigs don't eat it, dogs don't touch it"[2] is a rather unusual series of contradictions or seeming impossibilities. It shows some similarity to the English text below.

The most favored manner of describing salt consists in comparing it to a strange, abnormal plant. The Catalan folk say, "What is that: a tree that has neither flower nor leaf, but of which the fruit is very good?—The sea"[3] and "What is that: a grumbling crone,[4] who when God wishes it is agreeable; the fruit that she carries is good to eat?—The sea."[5] Such riddles may perhaps be related to the comparisons of salt to a plant that grows without roots or is otherwise abnormal. Examples are usually found in eastern Europe; see the Polish "It grows on the ground, although it has no roots. It blossoms above ground and serves the health of the entire world";[6] "It grows in coarse grains but never blossoms";[7] "It does not grow; it does not blossom; it is useful to the entire world";[8] and "Neither foot nor blossom on it, yet the whole world has need of it."[9] Analogous texts can be cited in the Modern Greek "It is not planted in gardens or on farms; the king eats it and so does all the world,"[10] the Arabic "A grain of the grains, it is not a seed and no root grows,"[11] and the Hindi "It fruits not and flowers not, nor do its branches bend down; and as long as one lives, one eats it."[12] In a very widely known noodle tale, salt is a plant scattered as seed and then supposed to be harvested.[13]

1262. there is a thing as little as a nit that serves the king at a bit.—salt.
Tupper, *Holme Riddles*, 41; *Meery Riddles* (1629), No. 46 = Brandl, p. 16; *Prettie Riddles* (1631), No. 27 = Brandl, p. 56.

1263-1265. Smaller Than a Mouse

The comparison "smaller than a mouse" is most often found in riddles for a thimble[1] and a star.[2] It is occasionally reinforced by the contrasting compari-

---

[1] See the headnote to No. 737, § 2.
[2] Lönnrot, 152 = Henssen, 147.
[3] Milá y Fontanals, 1876, p. 23, No. 4.
[4] For comparisons of the sea to a talking or grumbling person see No. 751a, 751b, and the headnote to Nos. 751-754.
[5] Milá y Fontanals, 1876, p. 22, No. 3.
[6] Kopernicki, 21, citing a parallel in Kolberg, *Krakowskie*, IV, No. 21.
[7] Kopernicki, 21 var.
[8] Kopernicki, 21, var. 2.
[9] Siarkowski, 28. For other variations see Gustawicz, 407 through 409.
[10] Stathes, p. 345, No. 82.
[11] Löhr, p. 107, No. 22.
[12] Kavyopadhyaya, 43.
[13] M. Böhm, *Lettische Schwänke* (Reval, 1911), p. 119, No. 35.

[1] Nos. 1263a, 1263b, 1265.   [2] No. 1281.

son "bigger than a louse." The rhyme has kept the riddle alive. The comparison "higher than a house" is often combined with one or the other of these comparisons. These rhymes are characteristic of the Germanic languages. See as an example the Faeroic "Storri enn lús, minni enn mús, dýrari enn allt kongins hús.—Egynasteinurin [Larger than a louse, smaller than a mouse, more precious than all the king's house.—Pupil of the eye]"[3] and an Icelandic riddle for fire.[4] It is disguised by translation into another language and back again into English in the Welsh Gypsy plum riddle, "Smaller than a mouse and higher than a castle."[5]

Riddles for a thimble often call it an object marked with dents or a person covered with pockmarks,[6] but these texts do not usually admit the characteristic rhymes discussed here.

1263a. As I was going from barn to house, / I met a thing not as big as a mouse, / And it had more windows than all the king's house.—Thimble.
Fauset, *Nova Scotia*, p. 150, No. 42.

1263b. I have a little house, / And it wouldn't hold a mouse. / There's as many windows in it / As in the king's whole house.—Thimble.
Green, *South Antrim*, 15.

1264. Littler than a mouse, / Big as a louse. / Got more eyes than King George's house.—Thimble.
Fauset, *Nova Scotia*, p. 150, No. 42 var.

1265. What is lesser then [than] a mouse, / and hath more windows than a house?—It is a spider in the midst of his web, or else a thimble.
Prettie Riddles (1631), No. 46 = Brandl, p. 59.

1266–1267. Long or Broad

1266a. Long and slinky, like a trout, / Never sings till its guts come out.—A gun.
Greenleaf, *Newfoundland*, p. 11, No. 21.

1266b. Long and slinky, like a trout, / When it bawls, its guts come out.— A gun.
Greenleaf, *Newfoundland*, p. 11, No. 21 var.

1267. Widdicote, woddicote, over cote hang, / Nothing so broad, and nothing so lang, / As widdicote, widdicote, over cote hang.—The sky.
Raley, *Notes and Queries*, 1st ser., X (1854), 173 = G. F. Northall, *English Folk-Rhymes* (London, 1892), p. 333 = Lina Eckenstein, *Comparative Studies in Nursery Rhymes* (London, 1906), p. 114.

---

[3] Hammershaimb, *Antiquarisk tidsskrift*, III (1849–1851), 317, No. 13. For these rhymes see Nos. 1270 through 1273, 1275, 1276, 1281, and a riddle quoted in the headnote to No. 1473, n. 4, below.
[4] Árnason, 406.   [5] Sampson, 18.
[6] See the headnote to Nos. 576–577 above, and compare the headnote to Nos 528–534 n. 2. For a survey of thimble riddles see Hanika-Otto, note to No. 118.

1268–1285. High

Several well-established and clearly marked enigmatic patterns employing "as high as . . ." as an introductory formula are here separated according to the objects to which the riddler makes comparisons. "As high as a castle"[1] is ordinarily used for smoke. Contrasting comparisons to both high and low objects mark the walnut riddle,[2] which usually includes another contrasting pair of comparisons, and similarly contrasting comparisons to high and sharp objects mark the chestnut riddle,[3] which likewise usually includes another contrasting pair. Comparisons to a house and a tree and the characteristic rhyme "tree: be" occur in the star riddle,[4] and another version contains the characteristic rhyme "house: mouse."[5] A few miscellaneous and possibly fragmentary or corrupt references to something high or tall conclude the section.[6]

1268a. As high as a castle, / As weak as a wastle; / And all the king's horses / Cannot pull it down.—Smoke.

Halliwell-Phillipps, *Popular Rhymes*, p. 144; Knortz, p. 226, No. 63; Farr, *Tennessee*, p. 319, No. 19; Hyatt, *Adams Co., Ill.*, p. 667, No. 10909.

1268b. As high as a castle, / As weak [wicked?] as a wasp, / All the king's horses / Can't pull it down.—Smoke.

Parsons, *Bermuda*, p. 264, No. 154.

1269–1275. High As a House; Bitter As Gall and Sweet As Sugar (Bitter As Gall and Green As Grass)

A widely disseminated riddle describes a nut in pairs of seemingly contradictory assertions: the walnut is "as high as a house, as low as a mouse" and either "as bitter as gall and sweet after all"[1] or "as bitter as gall and as green as grass [var.: as black as ink, as white as milk]."[2] Since there are two pairs of contrasting comparisons, the number of elements is four, which is unusually large for a folk riddle. The cohesive forces holding these four elements together are not very strong. The comparisons are usually proverbial and they ordinarily rhyme. Although the contrast of these comparisons gives a certain unity, it aids little in preserving the specific form of the riddle. For this reason, the walnut riddle suffers many changes in the course of oral transmission.

In attempting to set up what might be the original types of the walnut riddle I find it difficult to go beyond what I have just said. There appear to be two fundamental types of the riddles beginning with the contrast of comparisons for the height or lowness of the object. In one the following pair of contrasting

---

[1] Nos. 1268a, 1268b.
[2] Nos. 1269a through 1275.
[3] Nos. 1276, 1277.
[4] Nos. 1278 through 1279b.
[5] No. 1281.
[6] Nos. 1283 through 1285.

[1] See Nos. 1269b through 1272.
[2] Nos. 1273, 1274.

comparisons refers to flavor and in the other to the color. Some riddles make no reference to height; see the Breton "Bitter as gall, hard as stone, good as sugar";[3] the French "What is as green as the meadow, bitter as soot, sweet as honey?"[4] See also the Albanian "Bitter, bitter as poison; sweet, sweet as honey."[5] Some, like the Albanian "Big, big as a camel; small, small as a dwarf,"[6] refer only to size.

Riddlers use this manner of description for a variety of objects:

§ 1. Fruits. APPLE. Irish: Delargy, *Inis Cé*, 8 (As high as a wall, as red as blood, as white as milk, as sweet as honey); O Dalaigh, 67. Lithuanian: Schleicher, p. 193 (As high as a roof, as small as a mouse, as sweet as honey). PEAR. Lithuanian: Schleicher, p. 194 (High as a house, hard as a lock, yellow like wax). PLUM. Welsh: Hull and Taylor, 190 (What is white and black, smaller than a mouse and higher than a horse?), 191. CHERRY. Italian: Schneller, *Wälschtirol*, p. 254, No. 9 (Sweet as honey and in the middle as bitter as gall). OLIVE. French: Roque-Ferrier, *Languedoc*, p. 330 (large, small, sweet, bitter). Spanish: Demófilo, p. 385, No. 16 (large, round, sweet, bitter). Catalan: Pelay y Briz, 156. Serbian: Novaković, p. 125, No. 9 (It is greasy, yet it is not bitter; it is green, yet it is not gall; it is sweet, yet it is not honey; it is bitter, yet it is not the bitter plant [*Sorbus domesticus*, Linn.]), and p. 156, No. 7 (bigger than a fort, smaller than an egg, more bitter than poison, sweeter than honey). Arabic: Ruoff, p. 53, No. 34. ORANGE. Portuguese: Parsons, *Cape Verde*, 16 (round, bitter, sweet). SORB APPLE. Italian: Gianandrea, *Archivio*, I (1882), 565–566, No. 35 (Larger than a house, it makes excretions like a goat, bitter, sweet).

§ 2. A nut. See Nos. 1269a through 1275.

§ 3. Honey, bees, beehive. Swiss: Rochholz, 394 (Green as clover, brown as coffee, sweet as honey, young and old like it). Swedish: Ström, p. 113, "Biet," 2 (Higher than a house, smaller than a mouse, more valuable than the farmer's oxen.—Bees and hive).

§ 4. Fire. Modern Greek: Dieterich, *Rätseldichtung*, p. 91, citing Stamatiadis, V, 185 (Small as a fly, large as a camel, sweet as honey, bitter as gall).

1269–1272. High, Low; Bitter, Sweet

1269a. What is that: as high as a hall, / as bitter as gall, / as soft as silke, / as white as milke?—That is a walnut; for it groweth as hie as a hall, and the shell is as bitter as gall, and the rinde that covereth the kernell is as silke, and the kernell is as white as milk.

Meery Riddles (1629), No. 24 = Brandl, p. 12.

---

[3] Kerbeuzec, *Ille-et-Vilaine*, p. 504, No. 26. See also French: Fourès, p. 253 (almond).
[4] Westphalen, *Metz*, col. 199.
[5] Hahn, p. 161, No. 30.
[6] Hahn, p. 159, No. 6.

1269b. As bitter as gall, / as sweet as milke, / as high as hall / and hard withall.—It is a walnut upon a tree.
Prettie Riddles (1631), No. 48 = Brandl, p. 59.

1270. High as a house, / And low as a mouse; / As bitter as gall, / But good after all.—Walnut.
Farr, *Tennessee*, p. 324, No. 83; Hyatt, *Adams Co., Ill.*, p. 669, No. 10932.

1271a. High as the house / And low as a mouse / And sweet and bitter for all.—Walnut.
Carter, *Mountain White*, p. 78.

1271b. High as a house, / Low as a mouse, / Bitter as gall, / Food for all.—Walnut.
Oral, West Virginia.

1272. Large as a house, / Small as a mouse, / Bitter as gall, / And sweet, after all.—Pecan [tree and nut].
Perkins, *New Orleans*, p. 106, No. 5.

1273–1274. High, Low; Bitter, Green

In this fourfold set of comparisons riddlers have often failed to maintain the contrast in the pairs and have introduced new elements. The nature of this development, which may occur in various ways, is readily seen in the versions of the Breton leek riddle: "Green as a meadow, white as milk, it has a beard like a goat"; "Green as a meadow that is not a meadow, white as milk that is not milk," which introduces antitheses; and "Who is as green as chives that are not chives, hairy as a goat that is not a goat, white as milk that is not milk?"[1] The last awkwardly suggests an animal or a person. Similar confusions appear in the English walnut riddle, which wavers between a suggestion of a house and a suggestion of a person.

1273. As high as a house, / As low as a mouse, / As green as grass, / As black as ink, / As bitter as gall, / Yet sweet for all.—Walnut.
Thurston, *Massachusetts*, p. 182, No. 5.

1274. as sweet as milk as greene as a leefe as bitter as galle as high as a hall & yet as little as a mouse.—a walnut.
Tupper, *Holme Riddles*, 30.

1275. High, Low; Many Rooms

1275. It's as tall as a house, / As low as a mouse, / Has as many rooms / As a gentleman's house.—Walnut.
Oral, West Virginia.

---

[1] Sébillot, *Devinettes*, 36a through 36c. See also his No. 29 and French: Mensignac, *Gironde*, 65 (White as snow, green as ivy, and bearded like a priest); Westphalen, *Metz*, col. 202 (Who has a white and a green tail?).

1276–1277. High and Sharp

The chestnut riddle combines comparisons referring to height and sharpness. Although it appears in a seventeenth-century English collection, it has not maintained itself in English folklore. Ralph Boggs reports one example from North Carolina; other collectors have failed to note it. The virtual disappearance of the chestnut from American forests as a consequence of the chestnut blight which ravaged them in the early years of the twentieth century has made it impossible for many to know the tree and the chestnut bur. Riddlers have adapted the pattern to other uses; see, for example:

§ 1. Holly. Breton: Sébillot, *Haute-Bretagne*, 33 (Pointed as a needle that is not a needle, large as an oven that is not an oven); Orain, *Ille-et-Vilaine*, p. 150; Kerbeuzec, *Ille-et-Vilaine*, p. 504, No. 34 (Large as an oven and not an oven, red as blood, green as a leek, pointed as a needle). In these a comparison referring to height is lacking.

1276. as rough as a bare as sharp as a thorne [MS: throne] as hy as a house & as litt [little] as a mouse & this thing is meet for a king.—a chestnute.
Tupper, *Holme Riddles*, 31.

1277. High as a hall, round as a ball, and sharp as a needle.—Chestnut burr
Boggs, *North Carolina*, p. 322, No. 10; Hudson, p. 88, No. 35.

1278–1280. Higher Than a House, Higher Than a Tree

The comparative adjective "higher" and the rhyme "tree: be" are earmarks of a widely used English riddle for a star.[1] The rhyme, which makes the riddle easy to remember and assures its preservation, is an English peculiarity, but the fundamental conception that a star is higher than a house occurs in many European riddles. Another star riddle employs the rhyming contrast "higher than a house and lesser [lower] than a mouse," which is possible only in the Germanic languages.[2]

1278. Higher dan a tree, / What kyan a little t'in' be?—De moon.
Parsons, *Sea Islands, S.C.*, p. 159, No. 43.

1279a. Higher than a house, higher than a tree. / Oh! Whatever can that be? —A star.
Halliwell-Phillipps, *Nursery Rhymes*, p. 129 (Yorkshire); Halliwell-Phillipps, *Popular Rhymes*, p. 146; Parsons, *Barbados*, p. 286, No. 60; Parsons, *Sea Islands, S.C.*, p. 159, No. 42 and var.; Bacon and Parsons, *Virginia*, p. 323, No. 103; Knortz, p. 230, No. 80; Redfield, *Tennessee*, p. 36, No. 6; Hyatt, *Adams Co., Ill.*, p. 667, No. 10916. Taller: Perkins, *New Orleans*, p. 106, No. 8.

1279b. Hide in de house, / Hide in de tree, / Oh ever what can dat be?— Star.
Parsons, *Sea Islands, S.C.*, p. 159, No. 42, var. 2.

---
[1] No. 1279a.
[2] No. 1281. See the headnote to Nos. 1263–1265.

1280. Higher than the house, / Higher than the tree. / Oh, what can this little thing be?—Sky.
Bacon and Parsons, *Virginia*, p. 323, No. 103.

1281. Higher Than a House, Smaller Than a Mouse

A pair of contrasting comparisons describing an object as both very high and very small or low are applicable to a star[1] and to a road. English riddlers are unfamiliar with the latter answer, which is, however, very generally reported. See Flemish: Joos, 61. Norwegian: Stafset, 206, citing Flatin, IV, 62, No. 98. Finnish: Lönnrot, 1379. Lappish: Poestion, p. 269; Donner, 1; Qvigstad, 70 (What is lower than the grass and longer [taller] than tall trees?), which contains a widely used contrast of the grass and the tree.[2] See also the Turkish and Turcoman "Higher than the mountain, lower than the grass."[3] The Mongolian "Higher than higher, lower than the grass"[4] seems to be defective. Somewhat different comparisons leading to the same answer are the Arabic "Something long but it does not reach to the udder of a goat"[5] and the Breton "Long as a strap, flat as a battledore."[6]

The contrast of high and low serves also to describe a saddle, as in the Polish, Turkish, and Turcoman "Higher than a horse, lower than a dog"[7] and the order is reversed but the answer is the same in the Crimean Tatar version.[8] The same contrast also describes the low connecting shafts of a vehicle in Turkish riddling.[9] Another version is the Polish "When down, it is as tall as a goose. When up, it stands as tall as a horse,"[10] and a similar contradiction describes a horsecollar.[11]

Various uses of similar themes are seen in the Yakut stake riddle, "Though it is lower than a fence, it is stronger than a horse";[12] the Votyak bird riddle, "Lower than weeds, higher than the tree";[13] and a similar Welsh riddle with the answer "plum."[14] The Votyak "Higher than the road, lower than the pine tree.—Grass"[15] is corrupt, for "road" (the answer) and "grass" (the means of comparison) are exchanged either in the riddler's mouth or in the collector's

---

[1] No. 1281.
[2] See the Swedish "Longer than long, and not so high as the heath" (Geijer and Campbell, 60), the Finnish "Longer than the longest [tallest] tree, lower than the grass of the earth" (Aarne and Krohn, 321 = Henssen, 114), and the Mordvin "Longer than a tree, lower than grass" (Ahlqvist, p. 42, No. 18). See also Swedish: Noreen, *Fryksdal*, 12; Ström, p. 183, "Landsvägen," 1, and, for comparisons describing a ball of thread as round and long, the headnote to No. 1341, n. 3, below.
[3] Hamizade, 739; Samojlvich, 155.   [4] Mostaert, 84.
[5] Bauer, p. 223, No. 1.   [6] Sauvé, 23.
[7] Polish: Kopernicki, 70. Turkish: Katanov in Radlov, IX, 241, No. 97. Turcoman: Samojlvich, 114. See also the analogous Hungarian "Lower than a pig and taller than a horse" (Kálmány, II, 161, No. 120); and see the headnote to No. 575, nn. 43–44, above.
[8] Filonenko, 31.   [9] Katanov in Radlov, IX, 370, No. 347.
[10] Siarkowski, 81, and see also his No. 62.   [11] Gustawicz, 28, 29.
[12] Priklonskii, 51.   [13] Wichmann, *Votyak*, 324.
[14] Hull and Taylor, 190. Welsh Gypsy: Sampson, 18.
[15] Buch, 16.

notes. The Lithuanian apple riddle, "High as a palace, wide as a fort, as yellow as beeswax,"[16] uses some of these elements, and so does the Irish description of a ball of thread, "It is higher than a castle and yet it would pass under a cup."[17]

1281. What is it that is higher then [than] a house, / And yet seemes much lesser then [than] a mouse?—It is a starre in the skie.
Meery Riddles (1629), No. 51 = Brandl, p. 17.

1282. Higher than the king's palace / And as fine as silk.—Smoke.
Fauset, *Nova Scotia*, p. 174, No. 202. A Gaelic riddle.

1283–1285. Miscellaneous Comparisons to Height

The following riddles are apparently degenerate forms of well-established patterns or casual inventions which have gained no wide currency. The cassava riddle[1] seems, for example, to be an adaptation of the walnut riddle,[2] which clarifies the significance of the word "hall" in the cassava riddle. Like some versions[3] of the walnut riddle, the riddles for sugar cane[4] and cassava refer to the flavor of the object being described. The rainbow riddle[5] contains comparisons to colors and in this regard resembles another type of riddle.[6]

1283. Hall, tall, / Bitter like gall, / But still it's a man breakfas'.—Cassava.
Parsons, *Antilles*, III, 376, St. Vincent, 13.

1284. High as the world; red as blood, but not blood; blue as indigo, but not indigo; high as granadillo temple.—Rainbow.
Beckwith, *Jamaica*, p. 202, No. 176.

1285. Some t'in' tall like a man, is very sweet.—Cane.
Parsons, *Antilles*, III, 433, Saba, 15.

1286–1289. Deep

The ordinary comparison used to suggest depth is the comparison to a cup, but its meaning and appropriateness are quite obscure. It is firmly established in a riddle for a well and is kept in place by a rhyme with "up." A single comparison[1] to the sea is a casual variation of little importance.

1286a. Riddle me riddle meree, / Perhaps you can. This riddle my be / As deep as a cup, / As round as a house, / And all the kings [sic] can't pull it up. —Well.
Parsons, *Bermuda*, p. 260, No. 112 var.

---

[16] Jurgelionis, 918.
[17] Delargy, 3; O Dalaigh, 96 (She is taller than the castle and she can get through the mouth of a cup). For other descriptions of a ball of thread see the headnote to No. 1341 below.
[1] No. 1283.
[2] Nos. 1269a through 1275.
[3] Nos. 1273, 1274.
[4] No. 1285.
[5] No. 1284.
[6] See Nos. 1360 through 1393b.
[1] No. 1288.

1286b. Riddle me, riddle me, riddle me, / Perhaps you can tell what this riddle may be: / As deep as a house, / As round as a cup, / And all the king's horses can't draw it up.—Well.
Hyatt, *Adams Co., Ill.*, pp. 670–671, No. 10943.

1286c. Somet'in' deep as a sea, / Ten t'ousan' horse cannot pull it up.—Well.
Parsons, *Sea Islands, S.C.*, p. 156, No. 28, var. 1.

1287. Black within, red without, / Deep as a cup, / All the king's horses can't pull it up.—Well.
Parsons, *Sea Islands, S.C.*, p. 156, No. 28, var. 4.

1288. Somet'in' as deep as a sea, / Ten t'ousan' horse cannot pull it up.—Well.
Parsons, *Sea Islands, S.C.*, p. 156, No. 28, var. 1.

1289. My father got a thing in his yard deep as well an' is not well, an' the whole sea does not fill it.—Sieve.
Beckwith, *Jamaica*, p. 185, No. 21.

1290–1299. Straight (Crooked)

1290. As straight as a maypole, / As little as a pin, / As bent as a bucker, / And as round as a ring.—I do not know the solution of this riddle. A bucker is a bent piece of wood by which slaughtered sheep are hung by their expanded hind legs, before being cut out. [Collector's note.]
Halliwell-Phillipps, *Popular Rhymes*, p. 148.

1291. Scrooked as an arrow, busy as a bee.—Creek.
Johnson, *St. Helena Island, S.C.*, p. 160, No. 41.

1292–1297. Crooked As a Rainbow

The significance of the comparison, which is not particularly apt in either its meaning or its application, is quite obscure. It may be a corruption of the comparison to a ram's horn.[1]

1292. Crooked as a rainbow, / Slick as a plate, / Ten thousand horses / Can't pull it straight.—River.
Parsons, *Aiken, S.C.*, p. 36, No. 76.

1293. Crooked as a rainbow, / Slim as a ja'. / Guess all de riddles, / But you can't guess dat.—Snake.
Parsons, *Sea Islands, S.C.*, p. 164, No. 70.

1294. Crooked as a rainbow, / Smooth as a slate, / Twenty-five George horse / Can't pull it straight.—River.
Parsons, *Sea Islands, S.C.*, p. 165, No. 71.

---

[1] Nos. 1298, 1299.

1295-1296. Crooked As a Rainbow; Teeth Like a Cat

A bent stalk of a raspberry hangs in a curve not unlike the arch of a rainbow and can properly be called "crookt." The rhythm of the usual form of the riddle shows that this pronounciation is correct. The speakers who begin "It's as crooked" have misunderstood the conception, for a rainbow can scarcely be called "crookéd." The parallels mention length more often than curvature and are closely related to the riddles for a saw. See the French "Long as a pole, it bares its teeth like a cat"[1] or the Walloon "Long as a string, fine as a wisp, it bares its teeth like a tomcat."[2] Such comparisons to a cat seem to be especially favored in French-speaking regions. Other descriptions of a saw suggest a dog with bared teeth.[3] A riddle from Auvergne begins with "Long as a tape" and makes a comparison to a mythical beast.[4] Still other riddles do not definitely suggest an animal but limit themselves to the contradiction "teeth without a mouth"[5] or the related theme "it has teeth but cannot eat."[6]

1295a. Crooked as a rainbow, / Teeth like a cat. / I bet a gold fiddle / You caint guess that!—A green brier.
Randolph and Spradley, *Ozark*, p. 83. Think of many things / Before you think of that: Bacon and Parsons, *Virginia*, p. 318, No. 50. Roun' as a rainbow, / Teeth like a kyat. / You can guess all de riddle, / But you kyan't guess dat: Parsons, *Sea Islands, S.C.*, p. 165, No. 72. Guess all your life time, / You can't guess that: Hudson, p. 85, No. 14; Fauset, *Southern Negro*, p. 285, No. 97; Perkins, *New Orleans*, p. 106, No. 11 var. Guess all night and you can't guess that: Brewster, *Indiana*, 52.

1295b. It's as crooked as a rainbow, and it has teeth like a cat.—A briar.
Farr, *Tennessee*, p. 321, No. 42; Knortz, p. 231, No. 86.

1296. Crooked as a rainbow, / Teeth like a cat. / Guess all your lifetime, / You never guess that.—Saw.
Parsons, *Guilford Co., N.C.*, p. 204, No. 32; Brewster, *Indiana*, 52.

1297. Crooked as a rainbow, t'iefin' [thieving] as a cat.—Snake.
Johnson, *St. Helena Island, S.C.*, p. 160, No. 45.

1298-1299. Crooked As a Ram's Horn

1298. Crooked as a ram's horn, / Flat as a plate, / All the king's horses / Couldn't pull it straight.—Sissiboo River.
Fauset, *Nova Scotia*, p. 159, No. 76. King George's men: Randolph and Spradley, *Ozark*, p. 85.

1299. As crooked as a ram's horn, / Teeth like a cat. / Guess all your lifetime, / You will never guess that.—Brier-bush.
Perkins, *New Orleans*, p. 106, No. 11.

---

[1] Sébillot, *Auvergne*, 21.
[2] Colson, *Wallonia*, IV, 95, No. 91.
[3] See the headnote to Nos. 297-300 above.
[4] Sébillot, *Auvergne*, 23.
[5] Nos. 18 through 21 above.
[6] Nos. 297 through 300.

1300. Flat

1300. Flat as a plate, / Crocked as a snake, / All the king's oxen / Can't pull it straight.—Stream.
Brewster, *Indiana*, 19.

1301–1357. Round

Riddles beginning with the comparison "Round as . . ." make up the largest group in this chapter. I have arranged them in alphabetical order according to the second adjective.[1] For example, "Round as . . ., black as . . ." precedes "Round as . . ., busy as . . ." Within the groups determined by the second adjective I have arranged the texts according to the thing that is said to be round. Thus, "Round as an apple" precedes "Round as a biscuit" in the group composed of riddles using the double theme "round and black."

Substitutions and contaminations have much disordered these riddles. As a consequence the original patterns are very difficult to identify. As both the lack of parallels and the lack of sense show, the frying-pan riddle beginning "Round as an apple"[2] is confused and contaminated. Although the comparison "round as an apple" does not belong to this conception, the original form is not readily apparent. Since the conceptions have no immediately recognizable theme like the suggesting of an animal, a person, plant, or thing, as in the chapters i–vii above, they are necessarily rather unstable.

1301a. Round like an apple, / Round like a ball. / What is that?—Moon.
Parsons, *Antilles*, III, 445, St. Thomas, 10.

1301b. Something round as an apple, plump as a ball, / Pass through Jordan City and all.—Moon.
Parsons, *Antilles*, III, 435, St. Martin, 14.

1302–1308. Round and Black

The speakers have forgotten the original import of the comparison and have introduced new and inappropriate elements. The original theme was a comparison to a magpie, that is to say, to a small, fat, black bird with a long tail. The characteristic enigmatical contradiction is the assertion that this supposed bird has a hole in its tail, that is to say, there is a hole at the end of the handle. The original theme occurs in a somewhat different formulation in the Bulgarian frying-pan riddle: "A magpie with a long tail cooks dinner quickly."[1] Interesting variations of the conception appear in the Turkish "A black bird [var.:

---

[1] The moon riddle (Nos. 1301a, 1301b), which stands first, contains two comparisons for roundness. See also No. 1303 and No. 1344.
[2] No. 1302.
[1] Chacharov, 129.

boy] is hung by his tail [leg]"; "A black raven with a long tail"; and "A turkey in the poultry yard with its tail outside."[2]

1302. Round as an apple, / Black as a coal, / Has a long tail / And a small hole.—Frying pan.
Fauset, *Nova Scotia*, p. 169, No. 140.

1303. Round as a biscuit, / Round as a cup, / Black as ink, / Can't see a wink.—Spider [frying pan].
Parsons, *Aiken, S.C.*, p. 28, No. 18.

1304. As round as a hoop, / As black as a coal, / A long tail, and / A little round hole.—Frying pan.
Leather, *Hereford*, p. 288.

1305a. As round as a moon, / As black as coal, / A long tail / And a round hole.—Frying pan.
Parsons, *Bermuda*, p. 262, No. 135.

1305b. As round as a moon, / As black as a coon, / Wid a long tail.—Frying pan.
Parsons, *Sea Islands, S.C.*, p. 173, No. 159.

1305c. What is as round as the moon, / As black as a coon, / And has a little black tail?—Skillet.
Hyatt, *Adams Co., Ill.*, p. 666, No. 10906.

1305d. Round as the moon, / Black as a coon.—Frying pan.
Fauset, *Philadelphia*, p. 554, No. 16.

1306. What is as round as the moon, black as ink, and has a tail?—A frying pan.
Oral, New Hampshire.

1307. Round as a pail and black as coal, / Little short tail and a thumping hole.—A skillet. [The collector does not explain the meaning of the last words.]
Farr, *Tennessee*, p. 323, No. 79.

1308. Round as a ring and black as coal, / Has a long thing and a toot hole.—A frying pan.
Farr, *Tennessee*, p. 323, No. 76.

1309–1313. Round and Busy

A rhyme of "biscuit [biskee]: bee" may be present, although now completely obscured. Such a rhyme was possible in the seventeenth century. The description of a watch occurs in two versions, the first ending with the assertion "the

---

[2] Hamizade, 659 through 661. For parallels to the last text see the headnote to Nos. 412–413 above.

prettiest thing you ever did see" and the second with an onomatopoetic representation of the ticking.[1]

1309a. Round as an apple, / Busy as a bee; / The prettiest thing / That ever you see.—Watch.
Thurston, *Massachusetts*, p. 182, No. 2; Bacon and Parsons, *Virginia*, p. 320, No. 67; oral, Ohio. Tell me dis riddle, / I'll give you a ring: Parsons, *Bahamas*, p. 471, No. 2 (clock). Funniest thing you ever did see: Fauset, *Nova Scotia*, p. 58, No. 73 (watch; clock).

1309b. Somet'in' roun' as an happle [apple], busy as a bee.—Watch.
Parsons, *Sea Islands, S.C.*, p. 164, No. 63, var. 2. Clock: Parsons, *Sea Islands, S.C.*, p. 164, No. 63, var. 1; Parsons, *Bahamas*, p. 482, No. 104.

1310a. Round as a biscuit, / Busy as a bee, / Purtiest leetle thing / You ever did see.—A watch.
Randolph and Spradley, *Ozark*, p. 85; Brewster, *Indiana*, 11; Parsons, *Robeson Co., N.C.*, p. 389, No. 17; Chappell, p. 235, No. 30; Hyatt, *Adams Co., Ill.*, p. 670, No. 10939; Whitney and Bullock, *Maryland*, p. 175, No. 2687; Halpert, *New Jersey*, p. 200, No. 18. Prettiest little thing I ever did see: Fauset, *Southern Negro*, p. 281, No. 56; Parsons, *Sea Islands, S.C.*, p. 163, No. 63; Parsons, *Guilford Co., N.C.*, p. 201, No. 2; Perkins, *New Orleans*, p. 106, No. 2; Halpert, *Riddles*, p. 38, No. 2. Pretties' little thing / Ever did see: Parsons, *Aiken, S.C.*, p. 28, No. 17.

1310b. Round as a biscuit, busy as a bee. / You can guess every riddle, but you can't guess me.—A watch.
Puckett, *Southern Negro*, p. 53. In the variants the summons to guess varies somewhat: If you guess that you can have poor me (Perkins, *New Orleans*, p. 105, No. 2); No man can tell that riddle on to me (Parsons, *Barbados*, p. 279, No. 18); Tell me that riddle / An' I'll give you a whole pea (Parsons, *Barbados*, p. 279, No. 18 var.); In my pocket you can see (Parsons, *Antilles*, III, 365, Trinidad, 27).

1311a. Round as a biscuit, / Go *tick, tack, tee!*—Watch.
Parsons, *Aiken, S.C.*, p. 27, No. 15, var. 2.

1311b. Round as a biscuit, / An' in de middle, / Go *tick, tick, tick!*—Watch.
Parsons, *Aiken, S.C.*, p. 27, No. 15, var. 1.

1312a. Roun' as a dollar, busy as a bee.—Watch.
Johnson, *St. Helena Island, S.C.*, p. 158, No. 22.

1312b. Round as a dollar, / Busy as a bee, / In the middle / Go *tick, tack, tee!*—Watch.
Parsons, *Aiken, S.C.*, p. 27, No. 15.

1313. Round as a ring / And busy as a bee. / Prettiest little thing / You ever did see.—A watch.
Halpert, *New Jersey*, p. 200, No. 1a.

1314. Round and Clear

1314. It's as roon's the mean / An as clear's crystal, / In [an; i.e., if] ye dinna tell me ma riddle / A'll shot ye wi' ma pistal.—A watch.
Gregor, *Northeast Scotland*, p. 76; Findlay, *Edinburgh*, p. 58.

---

[1] See No. 1312b, and compare Nos. 1311a, 1311b.

1315–1336. Round and Deep

The paradox of being both round and deep is applicable to a well. English riddlers add the contradiction that horses [oxen, mules] can't pull it up,[1] to which there are a few continental European parallels. Professor Murray Emeneau has kindly obtained a Panjabi parallel for me: "On the way a big container cannot be lifted. Help me to lift it, oh my God!" The round objects to which comparison is made vary considerably, but the deep object is almost always a cup, which is probably retained for the rhyme with "up." Some riddles for a well refer to roundness and length.[2]

When the assertion "and the Mississippi River [oceans, etc.] can't fill it up" is added to the paradox of being round and deep, the result describes a sieve or strainer.[3] Here, too, the rhyme aids in preserving the riddle with little alteration. The anomalous use of this paradox to describe a thimble[4] is a vagary of some sort.

1315a. Round as an apple, / Deep as a cup, / And all the king's horses / Can't pull it up.—Well.

Halliwell-Phillipps, *Nursery Rhymes*, p. 132; *Notes and Queries*, 3d ser., VIII (1865), 325 (Yorkshire); Harland and Wilkinson, *Lancashire Legends*, p. 167; Fauset, *Nova Scotia*, p. 158, No. 74 var.; Parsons, *Bermuda*, p. 259, No. 112. Perkins, *New Orleans*, p. 106, No. 7.
All King George's horses: Parsons, *Bahamas*, p. 483, No. 111. Little king's horses: Bacon and Parsons, *Virginia*, p. 312, No. 6.

1315b. Roun' as an apple, ship [shaped] like a cup, / All de king oxen can't pull it up.—Well.

Parsons, *Sea Islands, S.C.*, p. 156, No. 28, var. 3; Fauset, *Southern Negro*, p. 281, No. 57. King's horses: Chappell, p. 232, No. 20.

1316. As round as an apple, / As deep as a pail, / She'll never bawl out / 'Till she's caught by the tail.—Bell.

Kavanagh, *Béaloideas*, II (1929–1930), 295.

1317. As round as a ball, / As deep as a cup, / The king horse men can't pull it up.—Wheli [well].

Parsons, *Barbados*, p. 278, No. 17. All de king horses: Parsons, *Barbados*, p. 278, No. 17 var.

1318a. Round as a biscuit, / Deep as a cup, / All the king's horses / Can't pull it up.—Well.

Parsons, *Guilford Co., N.C.*, p. 201, No. 1; Randolph and Spradley, *Ozark*, p. 83; Brewster, *Indiana*, 9. Sixteen horses: Parsons, *Guilford Co., N.C.*, p. 201, No. 1 var.

1318b. Round as a biscuit, / Deep as a sea, / Ten horses kyant' pull it up.—Well.

Parsons, *Sea Islands, S.C.*, p. 157, No. 28.

---

[1] Nos. 1315a, 1315b, 1318a through 1318c, 1323, 1325a, 1325b, 1327a, 1328, 1330 through 1332. See also Nos. 1317 and 1327b.
[2] See the headnote to Nos. 1341–1342, § 1.
[3] Nos. 1319, 1321, 1322, 1324. Compare No. 1347.
[4] No. 1320.

1318c. Round as a biscuit, deep as a well, / All the king's horses can't pull it up.—Well.
Fauset, *Philadelphia*, p. 556, No. 40.

1319. Round as a biscuit, deep as a cup, / All the Mississippi River can't fill it up.—Sieve.
Brewster, *Indiana*, 10; Halpert, *Riddles*, p. 38, No. 1 (big as a cup).

1320. Round as a biscuit, / Deep as a well, / Got many winders as a hotel.—Thimbles.
Parsons, *Aiken, S.C.*, p. 27, No. 14.

1321. Round as a butter bowl, deep as a cup. / The Mississippi River cannot fill it up.—Sifter, strainer.
Perkins, *New Orleans*, p. 105, No. 1.

1322. Round as a cup and deep as a cup, / The Tennessee River can't fill it up.—Tea strainer.
Farr, *Tennessee*, p. 325, No. 94.

1323. what is that that is round as a cup yet all my lord['s] oxen canot draw it up?—A well.
Tupper, *Holme Riddles*, 82.

1324. What is round as a dishpan, deep as a tub, and still the oceans couldn't fill it up?—Sieve.
Oral, New Hampshire.

1325a. Round as a hook, / Deep as a cup, / All the king's oxen / Can't pull it up.—Well.
Knortz, p. 220, No. 38.

1325b. Round as a hoop / And as deep as a cup, / A l the king's horses / Can't pull it up.—Well.
Carter, *Mountain White*, p. 76; Parker, *Oxfordshire*, p. 330; Hyatt, *Adams Co., Ill.*, p. 670, No. 10942.

1326. Round As a Hoop; Sings When Caught by the Tail

This corrupt text seems to be the only English version of a riddle widely known in Europe. Its two parts have no close or intelligible connection with each other, for there is no obvious reason why a round object should have a tail or why it should sing. The parallels contain a much more satisfactory comparison with a bird, an animal, a person, or a thing.

Comparisons to a bird with a tail that is peculiar in some way are rather often applied to a bell. See the Swedish "A cock crows on the pine tree, and its tail hangs down to the ground";[1] the Lithuanian "A black bird sits on the fence, its tail reaching to the earth, its voice to Heaven";[2] and the Estonian

---

[1] Russwurm, *Eibo*, p. 134, § 316, No. 23.
[2] Schleicher, p. 200.

"A cock crows on the top of a haycock, its tail trails on the ground."[3] These are evidently variations of the same theme.

A special variety of the comparison of a bell to a bird consists in an elaboration in a series: "In a nest there is an egg, in the egg there is a thread, pull the thread, the egg cries out."[4] Such series constitute a special variety of enigmatic technique.[5]

Comparisons of a bell to an animal whose tail is pulled can be illustrated by the Portuguese "I have a bull; when I seize him by the tail, he bellows all over the place"[6] and the Serbian "A dead mare doesn't neigh, but when somebody pulls it by the tail, it neighs so that all men can hear it."[7] A few Serbian riddles describe a drum in a similar fashion: "A bobtailed donkey brays through the village" or "A skinned bull bellows down the valley."[8] French riddlers describe the animal representing a bell in such vague terms that it cannot be identified: "What cries out the more, the more one pulls its tail?"[9]

Comparisons of a bell to a person are not very abundant. A description in terms of an old woman with one tooth (the clapper) seems to be best known in Romance countries. See French: Queyrat, *La Creuse*, I, 365 (Who has only one tooth to call her children?); Hugues and Roux, p. 202. Catalan: Milá y Fontanals, 1876, p. 23, No. 8 (What is that: an old woman with one tooth who makes the whole world run?).[10] Other variations of the comparison of a bell to a person are the notion that this supposed person makes good women run[11] and the French "Seated high, dressed short [scantily], leg of flax, and backside open. What is that?"[12] The Chilean "Señora Carolina likes to live in a high house, and if they pull her feet, she disturbs the inhabitants"[13] is a much elaborated comparison of this sort.

1326. Round as a hoop, deep as a pail; / Never sings out 'till it's caught by the tail.—A bell.
Greenleaf, *Newfoundland*, p. 10, No. 16.

---

[3] Wiedemann, pp. 271–272.
[4] Spanish: Demófilo, p. 395, No. 62. Argentinian: Lehmann-Nitsche, 567. Dominican Rep.: Andrade, 89. Italian: Pitrè, 103. See also No. 1039 above and the note to No. 1039.
[5] See the headnote to Nos. 1156–1164 above.
[6] Parsons, *Cape Verde*, 108b. See also her Nos. 108a, 108c.
[7] Novaković, p. 59, No. 9.
[8] Novaković, p. 10, Nos. 2, 3.
[9] Louis Farges, "Proverbes, dictons et devinettes de la Haute-Auvergne," *Revue des traditions populaires*, I (1886), 378; Sébillot, *Auvergne*, 35.
[10] See further Catalan: Pelay y Briz, 37. Spanish, Californian: Espinosa, 16. Mexican: Noguera, 19; Pauer, 6. New Mexican: Espinosa, 19; Campa, 71. Porto Rican: Mason, 134. Portuguese: Braga, 30. Italian: Tschiedel, 10b; Gianandrea, *Canti popolari marchigiani*, p. 296, No. 2; Balladoro, *Archivio*, XVI (1897), 557, No. 2; Panareo, *ibid.*, XXIII (1906–1907), 240, No. 32; Schneller, *Wälschtirol*, p. 256, No. 26.
[11] See the headnote to No. 1039, nn. 4–5, above.
[12] Westphalen, *Metz*, col. 196.
[13] Flores, 144.

1327a. As round as a marble, / As deep as a cup, / And all the king's horses / Can't pull it up.—A well.
Fauset, *Nova Scotia*, p. 158, No. 74; Greenleaf, *Newfoundland*, p. 10, No. 14.

1327b. Round as a marble, deep as a cup; / Ten men from Jericho can't lift it up—Sink-hole.
Beckwith, *Jamaica*, p. 212, No. 231.

1328. Round as an orange, deep as a cup; / All the king's horses can't pull it up.—A well.
Waugh, *Canada*, p. 67, No. 768.

1329. Roun' as a riddle [sieve], / Deep as a spring, / Been de death of many a pretty thing.—Gun.
Parsons, *Robeson Co., N.C.*, p. 389, No. 6. Many a little thing: Farr, *Tennessee*, p. 320, No. 34.

1330. Round as a riddle [sieve], deep as a cup, / And all the king's horses can't pull it up.—A well.
Boggs, *North Carolina*, p. 325, No. 23.

1331a. Round as a ring / And deep as a cup, / All the king's horses can't pull it up.—Well.
Carter, *Mountain White*, p. 76.

1331b. Round as a ring, / Deep as a cup, / And all the king's mule teams / Can't pull it up.—A well dug in a hole—you can't pull that up.
Halpert, *New Jersey*, pp. 200–201, No. 2.

1332. Hits [it is] as round as a ring / And as deep as the spring / And all the king's horses / Couldn't pull it up.—Well.
Carter, *Mountain White*, p. 76.

1333. Round, Deep, and Has a Thousand Holes

A reference to an object having many holes usually suggests a thimble.[1] It is, however, not usually accompanied by comparisons to the length or depth of the thimble. See also the French riddle for a thimble, "No bigger than a chicken's wing, and it has more than a hundred holes."[2]

1333a. Round as a saucer, / Deep as a cup, / One thousand holes in the middle.—Sifter.
Parsons, *Aiken, S.C.*, p. 28, No. 30.

1333b. Round as a saucer, / Deep as a cup; / Not a Mississippi / Can fill it up.—A strainer.
Halpert, *New Jersey*, p. 201, No. 3.

1334. Round as a saucer, / Deep as a cup, / Five thousand horses / Can't pull it up.—Well.

---
[1] See No. 1413. [2] Rolland, 182.

Parsons, *Robeson Co., N.C.*, p. 389, No. 16. Ten hundred mule kyan't pull it up: Parsons, *Sea Islands, S.C.*, p. 156, No. 28, var. 2. No king horses can't pull it up: Parsons, *Aiken, S.C.*, p. 27, No. 13.

1335. Round as a saucer, / Deep as a saucer, / Three legs cannot run, / Two ears an' cannot hear.—Watch-pocket.
Parsons, *Aiken, S.C.*, p. 27, No. 16.

1336. Round as a well, deep as a bowl, / Long handle, little hole.—A frying-pan.
Waugh, *Canada*, p. 67, No. 771.

1337–1338. Round and Flat

1337. Round as an apple, / Flat as a chip, / Got two eyes, / And can't see a bit.—A button.
Fauset, *Nova Scotia*, p. 158, No. 75.

1338a. Roun' as an apple, / An' flat as a pond, / Woman on one side, man on de oder.—Das [dat's] a penny.
Parsons, *Bahamas*, p. 485, No. 134.

1338b. Round as an apple, / Flat as a pond, / Half of woman, / An' whole of a man.—Penny.
Parsons, *Antilles*, III, 424, Antigua, 8.

1338c. As round as a griddle, / As flat as a pen, / The half of a woman, / And the whole of a man.—Penny.
Green, *South Antrim*, 3.

1339. Round and Green

1339. Round as a marble, green as grass.—Green grapes.
Knortz, p. 221, No. 43.

1340. Round and Keen

1340. Round as a pin, / Keen as a pin, / Ain't got but one eye.—Needle.
Parsons, *Aiken, S.C.*, p. 32, No. 54.

1341–1342. Round and Long

This pair of comparisons, when "round" is understood as "spherical," forms a paradox suitable for use in riddles. The hearer thinks that an object cannot be both round and long. This is nevertheless true of:

§ 1. A well.[1] On the continent of Europe riddlers often term a well both round and long. See Breton: Sébillot, *Devinettes*, 43. French: Fourès, p. 253; Daleau, *Gironde*, p. 106; Mensignac, *Gironde*, p. 302, No. 27. Spanish: Demófilo, 832 (As long as a gut, round, round as an egg), which is identical with Chilean: Flores, 624; Rodríguez Marín, 598 (Long as a lasso, round as a grain

---

[1] For comparisons to the roundness and depth of a well see the headnote to Nos. 1315–1336.

sifter), which is identical with Chilean: Flores, 623. Italian: Gianandrea, *Canti popolari marchigiani*, p. 300, No. 18. Modern Greek: Polites, *Neohellenika Analekta*, I, 233, No. 233 (Long as a gut, wide as a pavilion), and p. 245, No. 295 (Long as a gut, round like a sieve).

§ 2. A ball of thread. See No. 1341.

§ 3. A corsetlace, a belt, or a girdle. See No. 1342.

§ 4. A mattress. Russian: Sadovnikov, 243a through 243h. Votyak: Wichmann, *Votyak*, 60 (In the evening a threshing floor, during the day a pile of wood), in which the riddler represents roundness and length by concrete symbols. Modern Greek: Georgeakis, p. 244; Abbott, p. 317, No. 43; Polites, *Neohellenika Analekta*, I, 236, No. 247 (All day long they are rolled up and at night they are rolled out). Turkish: Hamizade, 718 (At night it is spread out, in the daytime it is rolled up). Cherekessian: Tambiev, p. 56, No. 37 (At night it spreads out, by day it rolls up). Indonesian, Serawaj: Helfrich, *Serawaj*, p. 54, No. 38 (By day it resembles a *pĕmĕtọng* [hollowed-out tree trunk], at night it is spread out). Tabaru: Fortgens, 62.

The conception has a certain similarity to the Cheremiss shoe riddle: "Wind them up in the morning, down at night."[2]

1341. Round As a Ball, Longer Than Paul's Steeple

This description of a ball of thread as both round and long is the only English instance of a riddle widely asked on the continent of Europe. The parallels exhibit considerable variety in the choice of objects used as comparisons, particularly the object intended to suggest length. See the Irish "Round as my head, longer than a thousand feet";[1] and the Scotch Gaelic "Rounder than a ball, and longer than a ship,"[2] which errs by mentioning the answer in the riddle. The usual simile for a ball of thread mentions a road, as in "Round as an egg, longer than a road to church."[3] Another concept includes a tree or trees, as in the Irish "He's rounder than your head, he is longer than thousands of trees";[4] and the Swedish "Round as the cat's head, longer than a thousand trees."[5]

Some related manners of describing a ball of yarn occur in continental European riddling, but have not taken root in England or America. A characteristic variation consists in suggesting smallness or roundness and length by acts

---

[2] Genetz, 49.

[1] Christiansen, 83. [2] Nicolson, p. 65.

[3] Danish: Kristensen, p. 135, § 83, Nos. 108a through 108d; Feilberg, *Ordbog*, II, 723, s.v. "nøgle." Norwegian: Aasen, 17; Brox, *Ytre Senja*, 1, citing Riksheim, 66, and Nordeng, 19; Stafset, 11; Qvigstad, note to No. 85. Swedish: Dybeck, *Runa*, 1847, p. 41, No. 12; Hyltén-Cavallius, *Värend*, 44; Sandén, *Norra Vadsbo*, 20; Waltman, *Lidmål*, 231, 232. French: Roque-Feffier, *Languedoc*, p. 335; Parsons, *Antilles*, III, 368, Trinidad, 59.

[4] O Dalaigh, 76.

[5] Ström, p. 155, "Nystanet." See also *ibid.*, p. 306, "Gåtvisor," 11. Finnish: Henssen, 118. Lappish: Qvigstad, 85. Russian: Sichler, p. 120.

rather than by comparisons. See the Flemish "I have it in my hand, I throw it over the roof, and I still hold it fast."[6] The contrast involved in "What goes up round and comes down long?" does not appear to be known to English riddlers, although it is current in Wales.[7] Another variation of the fundamental theme is the Lithuanian "What do you not throw over the roof?"[8] This has also the none-too-clear alternative answer "hatred." Some parallels to this question have the answers "feather"[9] and "hops."[10] Still another version of the ball riddle is the Lithuanian "A little thing, and yet even a thousand horses do not take it over the mountain."[11] This theme is akin to that of the sunlight riddle.[12] This theme was used in the Renaissance for a ball:

> Non pugno est maius, certe mirabere cernens,
> Quatuor in montem vix traheretur equis.[13]

This English version makes the slip of mentioning the answer "ball" in the text of the riddle.

1341. What is that: round as a ball, longer than Paul's steeple, weather-cocke, and all?—It is a round bottome of thred, when it is unwound.
Meery Riddles (1629), No. 66 = Brandl, p. 19.

1342. Round As a Hoop, Long As a Snake

This riddle, which has such answers as "corsetlace," "shoelace," or "belt" or "girdle," has disappeared from modern English folklore but is still widely known on the continent of Europe. The idea is usually expressed in assertions rather than comparisons.[1] See "A snake at night, a ladder by day";[2] "A needle at night, a ladder by day";[3] "A ladder by day, a ring at night";[4] "A circle during the day, stretched out during the night."[5] The Modern Greek

---

[6] Joos, 190, and see also his No. 188. French: Queyrat, *La Creuse*, I, 364; Westphalen, *Metz*, col. 196. Hungarian: *Magyar Nyelvör*, IV (1875), 141 (On throwing it over the house, its end still remains in my hand), XIII (1884), 285.
[7] Hull and Taylor, 144. German: Wossidlo, 334. Swiss: Zahler, *Münchenbuchsee*, 115. Danish: Feilberg, *Ordbog*, II, 723, s.v. "nögle." Some versions have "comes down with a tail." For a survey of riddles employing the contrast of going up in one shape or color and coming down in another, see the headnotes to Nos. 1547–1558 and 1550–1554, below.
[8] Schleicher, p. 197.
[9] White Russian: Wasilewski, 88. Vogul: Ahlqvist, *Vogul*, 14. Mordvin: Paasonen, 355. Abyssinian: Littmann, *Tigriña*, 18 (Something which, when you throw it, does not go over the river).
[10] Mordvin: Ahlqvist, p. 40, No. 23; Paasonen, 124.
[11] Jurgelionis, 528; Schleicher, p. 202. See also German: Frischbier, *Menschenwelt*, p. 249, No. 77.
[12] Nos. 748a through 748g above.   [13] Buchler, *Gnomologia*, 3d ed. (1614), p. 417.
[1] For additional examples see German: Frischbier, *Menschenwelt*, p. 245. French: Pineau, *Poitou*, 28. Catalan: Milá y Fontanals, 1876, p. 25, No. 15.
[2] Swedish: Sandén, *Norra Vadsbo*, 57. Spanish: Demófilo, 519, and p. 355, No. 15; Rodríguez Marín, p. 362. Argentinian: Lehmann-Nitsche, 541. Rumanian: Gorovei, 684. Polish: Gustawicz, 430.
[3] French: V. S., *Mélusine*, I (1878), col. 262, No. 38; Sébillot, *Auvergne*, 43.
[4] French: V. S., *Mélusine*, I (1878), col. 262, No. 39.
[5] Modern Greek: Stathes, p. 342, No. 71 var.

"On guard all day long, and stretched out at night"[6] suggests the figure of a soldier.

1342. As round as a hoope I am, / most part when it is day; / but being night, then I am long / as any snake, I say.—It is a woman's girdle which shee weares about her middle.
Prettie Riddles (1631), No. 66 = Brandl, p. 61.

1343. Round As a Mill Wheel; Luggit [Having Ears] Like a Cat

1343. It's roon as a mill-wheel, / An luggit like a cat; / Though ye sud [should] clatter a' day, / Ye'd never clatter that.—A tub.
Gregor, *Northeast Scotland*, p. 79.

1344–1345. Round and Plump

The presence of two virtually synonymous descriptive elements in the place of contrasting adjectives is probably a sign of degeneration.[1] The riddle for the eyes[2] has some parallels that indicate clearly the *tertium quid comparationis* that is intended.[3] This theme is also applicable to a fruit; see the Filipino "Round, plump, hairy outside, red inside.—Atsuete, a red fruit used for seasoning fish."[4]

1344. As round as an apple, as plump as a ball, / Can mount the meetin' house, steeple an' all.—Sun.
Praeger, *Béaloideas*, IV, (1933–1934), 144, No. 2.

1345. Round as an apple, / Plump as a pear, / Slit in the middle, / Surrounded by hair.—Eyes.
Parsons, *Bermuda*, p. 259, No. 110.

1346. Round and Rough

1346. Round as an apple, rough as a bear. / If you guess this riddle, you may pull my hair.—Walnut.
Hyatt, *Adams Co., Ill.*, p. 670, No. 10935.

1347. Round and Shallow

1347a. Round as a sasser [saucer], / Shaller as a cup, / Mississippi / Couldn't full it up.—A sieve.
Randolph and Spradley, *Ozark*, p. 83.

---

[6] Modern Greek: Stathes, p. 342, No. 71.

[1] See another instance in the moon riddle, No. 1301b.

[2] No. 1345.

[3] See Nos. 1425 through 1428, 1443, 1444 below. Swedish: Ström, p. 79, "Ögat," 3, 4. Lettish: Bielenstein, 72 (Hair round about, in the middle "God protect us!"). Russian: Sichler, p. 119. Mordvin: Paasonen, 15 (It sits in a house, it is encircled by hair, there comes a worry, water flows).

[4] Starr, *Philippines*, 115.

1347b. Round as a saucer, / Deep as a cup, / Mississippi can't fill it up.—A sieve.
    Redfield, *Tennessee*, p. 35, No. 2.

1348. Round and Sharp

1348a. Roun' as a ball, / Sharp as an awl. / Those who can't guess / Are no account at all.—Chestnut bur.
    Parsons, *Guilford Co., N.C.*, p. 205, No. 43.

1348b. Round as a ball, sharp as a needle. Everytime you pick it up, you let it fall.—Chestnut bur.
    Oral, West Virginia.

1349. Round and Slick

1349a. Round as a biscuit, slick as a mole, / Great long tail and a thumping hole.—A skillet.
    Redfield, *Tennessee*, p. 36, No. 4.

1349b. Round as a biscuit, slight as a mole, / A great long tail with a thundering hole.—Skillet.
    Hudson, p. 85, No. 15.

1349c. Roun' as a biscuit, / Slick as a mole, / Long tail, / An' a thumb in hole.—Frying pan.
    Parsons, *Aiken, S.C.*, p. 28, No. 19.

1350. Round and Sweet

1350. Me riddle me riddle. / I know somet'in', / Round as an apple / An' sweet as not'in'.—Well.
    Parsons, *Bahamas*, p. 472, No. 9.

1351. Round and Thick

1351. Round as a biscuit, / Thick as a mole, / Whole Mississippi can't fill it up.— Sifter.
    Fauset, *Southern Negro*, p. 282, No. 38.

1352. Round and Thin

1352. Round as an apple and as thin as a knife. / Answer this riddle and I'll be your wife.—A dime.
    Farr, *Tennessee*, p. 324, No. 91.

1353. Round and Toothed

1353a. Roun' like a rainbow, / Teeth like a cat. / Guess all de riddles, / Can't guess dat.—Bamboo brier.
    Parsons, *Aiken, S.C.*, p. 35, No. 74.

1353b. Round as a rainbow, teeth like a cat, / Take your lifetime to guess that.—A brier.
Redfield, *Tennessee*, p. 36, No. 5.

1354. Round and White

1354. As roond's the mune, as white as snaw, / A holie in the middle o't, an' that's a'.—A floury "pap."
Findlay, *Edinburgh*, p. 58.

1355–1357. Round and Yellow

The riddles in this section exhibit the characteristic English degeneration of the enigmatic spirit. The description of a rabbit snare (No. 1356) has borrowed a formula from riddles for a pumpkin or an orange and uses it rather inaptly. The orange riddle (No. 1357) does not include enough details to permit one to guess the answer. The pumpkin riddle (No. 1355) is correct enough in its formulation, but portrays no clearly drawn or well-conceived picture.

1355. Round, Yellow; Holds Many Things

The concept fundamental to this riddle, that of a container holding a multitude of objects, is applicable to many fruits having an abundance of small seeds within. It often involves a comparison of a fruit to another fruit or its seeds. Riddlers do not usually compare objects in the same general category to one another. The comparisons are often ingeniously executed: a fig is a sack full of oats, a pepper a sack of money (referring to the small disklike seeds).[1] Typical variations are seen in the Bulgarian fig riddles, "The box is full of nits" and "The barn is full of millet."[2] The conception is especially well suited to the poppy, as in the Polish "In the garden there stands a tiny cane; on this tiny cane is a tiny mallet; I can swear to it that there are thousands in it."[3] This has the technique of the chain-riddle.[4] The Abyssinian pomegranate riddle, "A goblet *tarantâse*, its interior pearls, its exterior copper,"[5] illustrates the Mediterranean device of comparing a fruit to several metals or precious jewels.

Comparisons referring to animals or persons and a box or container (not a house) are rare. See, however, the Modern Greek watermelon riddles, "My well-filled basin, all marble and smooth, with black fishes and cold water"[6] and "My chilled basin, marble and smooth, you have black fishes and sweet

---

[1] For examples see the note to No. 1355.
[2] Chacharov, 119, 120. See also Gubov, 327.
[3] Siarkowski, 42. See other parallels in n. 9 below and in the headnotes to Nos. 1100–1108, n. 35, and 1121–1126, n. 20.
[4] See the headnote to Nos. 1156–1164 above.
[5] Littmann, *Tigriña*, 23. *Tarantâse* is a meaningless word. For parallels to this device see the headnote to Nos. 668–669, n. 16, above.
[6] Polites, *Neohellenika Analekta*, I, 200, No. 41.

wine";[7] the Cheremiss cucumber riddle, "Its bosom full of gold pieces, [yet] it cannot buy its freedom";[8] the White Russian poppy riddle, "The post stands and on the post a jackdaw. I can bet there are a thousand in it,"[9] which is a variation of the previously quoted Polish riddle; and the Tabaru "A lady in whose betel box there is only hail.—Papaya with its seeds."[10] The Bulgarian riddle for teeth, "The box is full of cheeseworms,"[11] is a curious variation to which there are few parallels.

The Georgian riddle for a pomegranate, "On the outside satin, on the inside thousands," is reversed for a chestnut, "On the outside a thousand, on the inside satin."[12] This is an instructive example of the process of inventing riddles.

1355. Round as an apple, / Yellow as gold, / With more things in it / Than you're years old.—Pumpkin.
Thurston, *Massachusetts*, p. 182, No. 3.

1356. Round as an apple, / Yellow as gold, / Two strings in the middle, / Hung up to a pole.—Rabbit snare tied up to a stick.
Fauset, *Nova Scotia*, p. 168, No. 137.

1357. As round's the mune, as yellow's ochre. / If ye dinna tell me that, I'll feel ye wi' the poker.—An orange.
Findlay, *Edinburgh*, p. 58.

1358. Hard

This coconut riddle may be merely a modification of the bramble riddle.[1] Since it is reported from several West Indian islands, we can infer that it is a relatively stable invention and not a casual alteration.

1358a. Hard as rock, not rock; white as milk, not milk.—Coconut.
Beckwith, *Jamaica*, p. 202, No. 175.

1358b. Hard as rock, not rock. / White as milk, not milk. / Sweet as sugar, not sugar.—Coconut.
Parsons, *Antilles*, III, 372, Grenada, 51.

1359. Soft

1359a. As soft as silk, as white as milk, / As bitter as gall, a thick wall, / And a green coat covers me all.—A walnut.
Halliwell-Phillipps, *Nursery Rhymes*, p. 122.

---

[7] Stathes, p. 337, No. 34.
[8] Wichmann, *Cheremiss*, 190.
[9] Wasilewski, 33. See also n. 3 above.
[10] Fortgens, 75.
[11] Chacharov, 38.
[12] Glushakov, p. 25, Nos. 16, 17. For riddles that more definitely suggest persons, see the headnotes to Nos. 908–916 and 910–915 above.

[1] See Nos. 1385, 1386, 1391, and the headnote to Nos. 1384–1393. See adaptations of the bramble formula to a coconut in Nos. 1393a, 1393b.

1359b. As soft as silk, as white as milk, / As bitter as gall, a strong wall, / And a green coat covers all.—A walnut.
Hyatt, *Adams Co., Ill.*, p. 669, No. 10933.

1359c. As soft as silk, / As white as milk, / As bitter as gall, / A green coat covers all.—A walnut.
Redfield, *Tennessee*, p. 36, No. 7.

1360–1393. Colors (arranged alphabetically)

1360–1365. Black

1360. What is three-fourths square / And as black as a bear? / If you don't tell me this riddle, / I will pull your hair.—Flatiron.
Hyatt, *Adams Co., Ill.*, p. 661, No. 10868.

1361a. A round, round thing as black as coal. / A long, long thing / With a little round hole.—Frying pan.
Parsons, *Barbados*, p. 287, No. 69.

1361b. As black as a mole, as slick as a coal, / With a long tail and a thundering hole.—A skillet.
Redfield, *Tennessee*, p. 36, No. 3.

1361c. Black as a coal, / Slick as a mole, / Red along tail, / And busted hole.—Frying pan.
Bacon and Parsons, *Virginia*, p. 323, No. 101.

1362. It's lang and it's roon, / An it's black's coal / Wi' a lang [——] and a plump hole.—A bottle.
Gregor, *Northeast Scotland*, p. 76. (The collector does not indicate the missing word by a dash.)

1363. As black as the De'il, / An' runs on four wheels, / An' leaves sorrow wherever it goes.—Hearse.
Green, *South Antrim*, 39.

1364. Black as ink, / An' red on de inside.—Blackberry.
Parsons, *Aiken, S.C.*, p. 32, No. 48, var. 2.

1365. Black as soot, white as milk, and sweet as sugar.—Sugar apple.
Parsons, *Bermuda*, p. 255, No. 61 var.

1366–1374. Green

1366. My fader had a thing, / Green as grass, / Ripe as an apple, / Soon get rot.—Fowl aigg.
Parsons, *Bahamas*, p. 474, No. 34.

1367. Green as grass, white as milk, black as ink, sweet as sugar.—Cherry myres.
Parsons, *Bermuda*, p. 255, No. 61 var.

1368a. Green as grass, not grass, / White as milk, not milk, / Black as jet, not jet.—Soursop.
Parsons, *Antilles*, III, 365, Trinidad, 22.

1368b. Riddle me riddle, I'll tell you this riddle, / Perhaps you may tell it to me. / Thing green as grass, grass it ain't; / White as milk, milk it ain't; / Black as ink, ink it ain't; / Sweet as sugar, sugar it ain't. / What is that?—Soursop.
Parsons, *Antilles*, III, 441, Anguilla, 30.

1369. Green as grass, white as milk, red as blood, black as ink.—Watermelon.
Parsons, *Bermuda*, p. 255, No. 61 var.

1370. Green as grass, yellow as gold, red as rose, white as milk, sweet as sugar, bitter as gall.—Pomegranate.
Parsons, *Bermuda*, p. 255, No. 61 var.

1371. Something green like grass, grass it ain't, and have a heap of little seed inside of it.—Gobee [çalabash].
Parsons, *Antilles*, III, 446, St. Thomas, 15.

1372. Something green like grass, grass it ain't, / And could speak.—Parrot.
Parsons, *Antilles*, III, 446, St. Thomas, 14.

1373a. So green as grass, / So black as coal, / Along came a silly soul / And popped it in his grinning hole.—A blackberry.
Greenleaf, *Newfoundland*, p. 14, No. 7.

1373b. Green as grass, but 'twasn't grass, / Red as blood, but 'twasn't blood, / Black as coal, but 'twasn't coal, / Long comes a pretty love / Whipped it in the grinding hole.—A blackberry.
Greenleaf, *Newfoundland*, p. 14, No. 7 var.

1374. Green as grass, not grass; stiff standing in the bed; and the best young lady is not afraid of handling it.—Onion.
Beckwith, *Jamaica*, p. 202, No. 173.

1375–1378. Red

1375. As red as an apple, as round as a ball, / Higher than the steeple, weathercock and all.—The sun.
Burne, *Shropshire*, p. 574, No. 9.

1376. Red as blood, but blood it's not; black as ink, but ink it's not; white as milk, but milk it's not; green as grass, but grass it's not.—Watermelon.
Perkins, *New Orleans*, p. 111, No. 53.

1377. It's as red as blood and not blood, / Green as grass and not grass, / White as snow and not snow.—Cedar tree.
Farr, *Tennessee*, p. 326, No. 110.

1378. Red as blood, / Black as ink.—Blackberry.
Parsons, *Aiken, S.C.*, p. 32, No. 48, var. 1.

1379–1393. White

1379–1382. White and Black: A Magpie

Riddlers describe a magpie by the contrast of black and white (which are emphasized by comparisons) and a descriptive verb. This widely circulated riddle varies from country to country in the choice of comparisons and in the action associated with them. Since the whole does not form a clearly conceived unit, riddlers often introduce foreign and inappropriate elements. The comparison "green as grass," which occurs rather frequently,[1] may perhaps refer to the green glint of the black feathers. The Mordvin "A green onion, a black earth, a white snow.—Magpie"[2] combines these colors to make a picturesque and coherent scene. It seems to be derived from a series of comparisons. Elements of the frying-pan riddle[3] occur in No. 1382. This may have come about by the association of a frying pan with the description of a bird.[4] Antithetical elements are found in a few magpie riddles.[5] In the course of oral transmission, comparisons are occasionally lost.[6]

Although it is difficult to make out the original form of the magpie riddle as far as comparisons are concerned,[7] the action associated with them varies surprisingly little. In several widely separated texts the white and black creature is said to jump like a foal or dance like a maiden. Such an act seems, therefore, to belong to the original conception. The Swedish "White as chalk, black as pitch, it dances like a maiden, it gnaws like a horse"[8] includes references to both a maiden and a horse. Some Turkish versions having a clearer personification also mention walking or jumping: "Clad in black and yellow boots, it walks by jumps";[9] "Clad in yellow camel's boots, it walks by kicks";[10] "It always walks hop, hop and on its head is a cap covered with black cloth,"[11] which is perhaps another conception; and "The gait of a maiden, a beak like a ridge."[12] which contains only a part of the riddle here discussed. Another way of describing a magpie consists in enumerating its parts from front to back.[13]

Other birds are occasionally described in the same manner as the magpie. The Turcomans say for the anka bird, "More crooked than a sickle, straighter

---

[1] See examples in the note to No. 1379 and in the note to Nos. 1381*a*, 1381*b*.
[2] Paasonen, 233.
[3] Nos. 1302 through 1308 above.
[4] See the headnote to Nos. 1435, § 4, and 1436–1447, §§ 3–4.
[5] Nos. 1381*a*, 1381*b*.   [6] No. 1496.
[7] The original form probably contained two comparisons, one each to black and white, and a description of an activity.
[8] Dybeck, *Runa*, 1847, p. 41, No. 13.   [9] Katanov in Radlov, IX, 93, No. 790.
[10] Katanov in Radlov, IX, 93, No. 791.
[11] Katanov in Radlov, IX, 240, No. 69, and p. 272, No. 172.
[12] Menges, p. 87, No. 18.
[13] See the headnote to No. 1435, § 4, below.

than a rolling pin, whiter than snow, redder than blood,"[14] which has the alternative answer "moon." This contains elements belonging to the descriptions of a magpie by enumerating its parts.

A few changes adapt this riddle for a magpie to the answer "flea," as in the Swedish "Black as coal and leaps like a foal and men cannot fetter it."[15]

1379. It's white's milk / An' as black's coal, / An' it jumps on the dyke / Like a new shod foal.—A magpie.
Gregor, *Northeast Scotland*, p. 80.

1380. What is that: / as white as milke, / as soft as silke, / as blacke as a coale, / and hops in the street like a steed foale?—It is a pye that hoppeth in the street; for part of her feathers be white and part bee blacke.
Meery Riddles (1629), No. 57 = Brandl, p. 18.

1381a. As black as ink, and is not ink; / As white as milke, and isn't milk; / As soft as silk, and isn't silk; / And hops about like a filly-foal. What's that, Miss?—A magpie.
Bingham, *Notes and Queries*, 3d ser., VIII (1865), 425 (Yorkshire).

1381b. As black as ink and is not ink; / As white as milk and is not milk; / And hops about like a filly-foal.—A magpie.
M. G. W. P., *Notes and Queries*, 7th ser., X (1890), 85.

1382. As white's the mune, as black's the coal, / A lang tail and a pumpin' hole.—A magpie.
Findlay, *Edinburgh*, p. 58.

1383. White As Milk; Beard Like a Buck

1383. It's as fite's milk, / It's saft's silk, / It hiz a beard like a buck, / An a tail cocking up.—An onion.
Gregor, *Northeast Scotland*, p. 80.

1384–1393. White, Green, Red, and Black

The perplexing relations of the several enumerations of the characteristic colors white, green, red, and black cannot be easily clarified. The riddler may tie together these colors in a biographical sequence and thus suggest a personification of the plant and its flower and fruit.[1] He may merely list the colors and lead us to guess what object could combine so many colors.[2] Although these two varieties of arrangement may be related, it is by no means certain that they are. We can suppose that the biographical sequence of the first variety survives in a weaker, less vivid form making a comparison to a thing rather than a person. Such an explanation is plausible, but must remain a hypothetical construction rather than a demonstrable reality.

---

[14] Samojlvich, 20.   [15] Waltman, *Lidmål*, 205.
[1] See No. 668 and the headnotes to Nos. 668–680 and 668–669.
[2] See the headnote to Nos. 1559–1561, n. 1.

There are some further varieties of these enumerations of colors. We may have either a series of comparisons like "Green as grass, white as milk, black as ink, sweet as sugar"[3] and "Black as soot, white as milk, and sweet as sugar,"[4] which are confusing because we cannot readily apply so many descriptive adjectives to a single object, or a series of comparisons accompanied by contradictions like "Red as blood, but blood it's not; black as ink, but ink it's not; white as milk, but milk it's not; green as grass, but grass it's not."[5] The connection between these two varieties is quite obscure.

Riddles employing these patterns vary only slightly in the choice of colors or comparisons (when comparisons are used) and are naturally best suited to describe various kinds of fruits. Since they have no clear outlines, they readily develop ideas suggested by the connotations of particular words in the texts or absorb elements belonging to other types. They should probably begin with green, then pass to white, red, and black in turn, but errors often occur. In this chapter I have arranged the versions according to the color first mentioned. As an example of the variations that occur see the Armenian blackberry riddle, "Black as a blackbird, sweet as honey in the mouth, it bites like a dog."[6]

These comparisons in the colonial Spanish "It is as white as milk and black as coal. It is as sweet as honey and bitter like the lemon" refer to a plant (*amor*) that I cannot identify.[7]

1384. Something white as cotton, green as grass, and blue as ink, and sweet as sugar. Guess what it is.—Huckleberries.
Parsons, *Sea Islands, S.C.*, p. 166, No. 61.

1385. White as a lily, it's not a lily; green as grass, it's not grass; red as fire, it's not fire; sweet as sugar, it's not sugar; black as ink, it's not ink. What is it? —Blackberry.
Perkins, *New Orleans*, p. 111, No. 52.

1386. As white as milk and not milk, / As green as grass and not grass, / As red as blood and not blood, / As black as soot and not soot.—Bramble blossom.
Parsons, *Bermuda*, pp. 255–256, No. 61; Halliwell-Phillipps, *Popular Rhymes*, p. 143, Knortz, p. 231, No. 84. Grass, snow, blood, ink: Parsons, *Guilford Co., N.C.*, p. 202, No. 11. Grass, milk, blood, ink: Fauset, *Southern Negro*, p. 276, No. 10. Milk, grass, blood, ink: Parsons, *Aiken, S.C.*, p. 32, No. 48 var.; J. S. Udal, *Notes and Queries*, 7th ser., XI (1890), 195 = Udal, *Dorset*, p. 395. Snow, grass, blood, ink: Fauset, *Southern Negro*, p. 277, No. 12; Parsons, *Aiken, S.C.*, p. 32, No. 48; Redfield, *Tennessee*, p. 35, No. 1; Hudson,

[3] No. 1367.
[4] No. 1365.
[5] No. 1376. Compare also No. 1390.
[6] Glushakov, p. 29, No. 30. For other variations see, in the present collection, the headnotes to Nos. 1269–1275 and 1273–1274, the versions cited in the note to No. 1367, and the headnote to Nos. 1559–1561.
[7] Dominican Rep.: Andrade, 28. Porto Rican: Mason, 46.

p. 87, No. 26. Snow, blood, ink: Fauset, *Nova Scotia*, p. 159, No. 78. Milk, blood, ink: Fauset, *Southern Negro*, p. 277, No. 11; Knortz, p. 221, No. 41. Grass, blood, ink: Farr, *Tennessee*, p. 320, No. 31.

1387. Something white as paper, green as grass, red as fire, large as a marble. Guess what it is.—Blackberries.
Parsons, *Sea Islands, S.C.*, p. 166, No. 82.

1388. What is that is white as snow, / and yet as blacke as any crow, / and more plyant then [than] a wand, / and is tied in a silken band. / And every day a prince's peere / looketh upon it with sad cheare?—It is a booke tyed with a silken lace, for the paper is white as snow; and the inke is as blacke as a crow and the leaves more pliant then [than] a wand.
Meery Riddles (1629), No. 53 = Brandl, p. 17. Looks on it wth a mirth that is clear: Tupper, *Holme Riddles*, 93.

1389. White as snow, green as grass, black as smut.—Blackberry.
Perkins, *New Orleans*, p. 111, No. 52 var.

1390. White as snow but not snow; green as grass but not grass; red as blood but not blood.—Coffee-blossom and berry.
Beckwith, *Jamaica*, p. 201, No. 172.

1391. White as snow and snow it isn't, / Green as grass and grass it isn't, / Red as blood and blood it isn't, / Black as tar and tar it isn't.—A blackberry. First the white blossom, then the green berry which turns red, and when ripe is black.
Hyatt, *Adams Co., Ill.*, p. 658, No. 10839. Black as ink: Brewster, *Indiana*, 2.

1392. I am within as white as snow, / without as greene as hearbs that grow; / I am higher than a house / and yet am lesser then [than] a mouse.—A walnut hanging one [on] a tree.
Prettie Riddles (1631), No. 11 = Brandl, p. 54.

1393a. White, but not as white as snow, / Green, but not as green as grass.—Coconut.
Parsons, *Sea Islands, S.C.*, p. 166, No. 63.

1393b. White as snow, not snow, / Green as grass, not grass.—Coconut.
Parsons, *Antilles*, III, 365, Trinidad, 31.

1394–1408. Miscellaneous Comparisons

A few riddles use comparisons for other aspects than shape or color. Especially interesting are the enumerations of comparisons to several aspects of an object by reference to several animals. The curious description of "nothing,"[1] which contains references to God and the Devil, probably has antecedents in medieval or Renaissance ideas and calls for historical study. The comparisons in terms of a barn door that opens, a trap that closes, or an object that has

---
[1] Nos. 1394a through 1394c.

ears like a cat[2] have suffered much disorder. The descriptions of the form "It looks like a cat and isn't a cat"[3] are very similar to conundrums. The enumeration[4] of incongruous details belonging to many animals resembles a description of a cock[5] but appears to be an independent conception with a long history.

1394. Better (Higher) Than God

This very curious riddle also occurs in a form containing no comparison.[1] I shall consider here only the versions containing the comparison "higher than God." This comparison is scarcely pertinent to the context and seems to have been borrowed from a riddle apparently not found in English folklore. It is "What is the thing that stands higher than God?—Crown"[2] or "What is above the Emperor of Russia?—Crown."[3] The answer is occasionally the Crown of Thorns.[4] The query is sometimes given a humorous turn, as in "What is higher than God [*dieu*]?—The dot over the *i*."[5] In his collection of curiosities entitled *Sphinx Theologico-philosophicus* (Herborn, 1612),[6] Johann Heidfeld makes the curious comment that this riddle and its variant "What is greater and broader than God?" must be attributed to the idolatry of the Papists and their custom of representing God the Father as an old man with a crown [higher than Him] and a cloak [broader than Him]. The Mordvin riddle for death, "Less than God, greater than the emperor,'"[7] may be related to these conceptions, but the connection is obscure. It also suggests the series of men whom Death overcomes in the Dance of Death.

1394a. Better than the Lord, / Worse than Satan, / Dead people eat it. / If you eat it, you'll die.—Nothing.
Fauset, *Philadelphia*, p. 554, No. 15.

1394b. What is greater than God, / Worse than the Devil? The dead eat [it], and if the living eat [it], they die.—Nothing.
Oral, *Ohio*.

1394c. Higher than God, lower than the devil; the dead feed on it, but not the living.—Nothing.
Beckwith, *Jamaica*, p. 216, No. 262.

[2] Nos. 1395 through 1401c.
[4] Nos. 1405 through 1408.
[3] Nos. 1403 through 1404b.
[5] See the headnotes to Nos. 539–543 and 543.
[1] See Nos. 1726, 1727 and the headnote to Nos. 1726–1727.
[2] Breton: Sauvé, 137. Portuguese: Pires, *Archivio*, III (1884), 245, No. 86.
[3] French: Ledieu, *Démuin*, p. 134.
[4] Spanish: Rodríguez Marín, 815. Argentinian: Lehmann-Nitsche, 37. Dominican Rep.: Andrade, 131. Porto Rican: Mason, 192.
[5] French: E. H. Carnoy, *La Tradition*, VI (1892), 355, No. 30; Ledieu, *Démuin*, p. 130; J. Roux, *Limousin*, 96; Parsons, *Antilles*, III, 414, Marie Galante, 34. For a tale on this theme see D. P. Rotunda, *Motif-Index of the Italian Novelle in Prose* (Indiana University Publications, Folklore Ser., II [Bloomington, Ind., 1942]), J 1262.4.
[6] P. 1312. I am indebted to R. P. McKeon for calling my attention to this passage.
[7] Paasonen, 221.

1395-1408. Comparisons to Animals or Objects
1395-1402. Mouth Like a Barn Door

1395. Opens like a barn-door, / Shuts up like a trap. / Guess all your life, / You'll never guess that.—Scissors.
Parsons, *Aiken, S.C.*, p. 35, No. 75.

1396. Mouth like a barn-door, / Ears like a kyat. / Guess all night, / And can't guess that.—Owl.
Bacon and Parsons, *Virginia*, p. 318, No. 51.

1397. Mouthed like the mill-door, luggit [lugged; i.e., having ears] like the cat; / Though ye guessed a' day, ye'd no guess that!—A large broth-pot of the old construction.
Chambers, *Scotland*, p. 109.

1398. Opens like a barn door, / Spotted like a cat. / Riddle all night, / You can't riddle that.—Newspaper.
Hudson, p. 86, No. 21.

1399a. Open like a barn-door, / Ears like a cat. / Guess all your life-time, / You can't guess that.—Waistcoat or old woman's corset.
Fauset, *Nova Scotia*, p. 155, No. 56. Overcoat: Fauset, *Southern Negro*, p. 285, No. 99.

1399b. Opens like a barndoor, / Wings like a bat, / Spread out your arms, / And jump in that.—Man's vest.
Oral, *North Carolina*.

1399c. Open like a barn-door, / Shut up like a trap. / Guess all your lifetime, / You can't guess that.—Pair of corsets.
Perkins, *New Orleans*, p. 106, No. 6.

1400. Open like a barn-door, / Eyes like a cat, / Two lookus, two hookus, / And a whiskey barrel.—Cow.
Fauset, *Nova Scotia*, p. 155, No. 57.

1401a. Open like a barn-door, / Shut like a bat. / Guess all your lifetime, / You can't guess that.—Umbrella.
Fauset, *Southern Negro*, p. 285, No. 98; Parsons, *Guilford Co., N.C.*, p. 204, No. 33; Farr, *Tennessee*, p. 321, No. 45.

1401b. Somethin' open like a barn-door an' shut up like a trap. You guess every riddle but you will never guess this.—Umbrella.
Johnson, *St. Helena Island, S.C.*, p. 160, No. 38.

1401c. Round as a bando, shut up as a trap. / Guess all the riddles, but you couldn't guess that.—Umbrella.
Parsons, *Sea Islands, S.C.*, p. 175, No. 181.

1402. Headed like a thimble, / Tailed like a rat. / You may guess to Doomsday, / But you couldn't guess that!—Pipe.
Praeger, *Béaloideas*, IV (1933-1934), 145, No. 20.

1403–1404. Like a Cat and Isn't a Cat

This kitten riddle is readily adapted to various animals, especially the ox. Its enigmatic quality consists in playing with the various names designating the old and the young or the male and female of the species. It occurs in two varieties: a description in terms of form[1] and one in terms of acts.[2] The latter variety may occasionally include some references to the animal's form. The Breton "What most resembles a cat?—A she-cat"[3] and the Hungarian "It is like a pig but is no pig. What is it?—A young pig"[4] are rare instances belonging to neither variety.

The answer to riddles of this sort is often an animal, but note the Abyssinian "Something that is like a basket but is not as big as a basket.—A little basket"[5] and the English conundrum "What most resembles half of a cheese?—The other half"[6] and the Korean "What is like the left hip?—The right hip."[7] Perhaps the most familiar instance is "What is like half the moon?—The other half."[8] This is widely current in western Europe, having been reported from Flanders, Germany, and France. An Argentinian instance shows that it was current also in Spain. The oldest example of this theme that I have noted is expressed in entirely different terms; it is:

> Quid lupi quaeso speciem rapacis
> Exprimit, formamque trucem, pilosque,
> Ut procul si tu videas, lupum ipsum
> Dixeris esse?
> Est lupa, quae similem formam sortita marito.[9]

1403. It has a head like a cat, feet like a cat, / A tail like a cat, but it isn't a cat.—A kitten.
Farr, *Tennessee*, p. 322, No. 59.

1404a. Look like a kyat an' isn' a cat. / Eat like a kyat an' isn' a cat. / Walks like a kyat an' isn' a cat.—Kitten.
Parsons, *Sea Islands, S.C.*, p. 170, No. 112.

1404b. Acts like a cat, / Looks like a cat, / Yet it isn't a cat. What is it?— A kitten.
Fauset, *Nova Scotia*, p. 170, No. 154 var.

---

[1] No. 1403.
[2] Nos. 1404a, 1404b.
[3] Le Pennec, 17.
[4] *Magyar Nyelvőr*, XVI (1887), 44, and XXXIII (1904), 529.
[5] Littmann, *Tigriña*, 61.
[6] Waugh, *Canada*, p. 72, No. 829. For parallels see Welsh: Hull and Taylor, 393, 394. Breton: Sébillot, *Haute-Bretagne*, 97. Flemish: Joos, 941. French: Rolland, 384. Catalan: Pelay y Briz, 271. Spanish, Argentinian: Lehmann-Nitsche, 967. Italian: Belladoro, *Archivio*, XVI (1897), 228, No. 2.
[7] Bernheisel, p. 84.
[8] See the headnote to Nos. 1230–1234, nn. 1–2, above.
[9] Buchler, *Gnomologia*, 3d ed. (1614), p. 421.

1405–1408. The Grasshopper Riddle

In several widely separated countries riddlers have enumerated the members of various animals and have expected their hearers to guess what single creature possesses them all.[1] The answer in one of the oldest and most characteristic versions of the theme is a grasshopper. A typical example is the modern Filipino "There is a flying thing, which stays anywhere,—even in the forest and *tayac;* its face is the face of a cow, its neck the neck of a horse, the breast the breast of a man, the wing is like the leaf of a bambu, his tail resembles a snake, and his feet look like the feet of a bird."[2] The reference in this Filipino text to part of a plant is somewhat unusual. A similar reference appears in the Yakut "There is a creature from the damp grasslands which has wings like a strip of birchbark and legs like huge pitchforks, so they say."[3] This Yakut text may be an entirely independent invention. The Bhil "Mouth like a horse, breast like a man"[4] is, on the other hand, probably a corrupt and fragmentary version of the original. Even greater alteration is to be seen in the Portuguese "Clothing of a priest, and not a priest; clothing of a bishop, and not a bishop; head of a donkey,"[5] which is still capable of being conceived as a derivative of the Oriental grasshopper riddle.

Comparisons of the members of an animal to a variety of entirely different objects occur in many connections, some of which do not appear to be related to the grasshopper riddles just discussed. See, for example, the Modern Greek description of a turtle, "Brass sky, straight earth, cat's feet, snake's head."[6] The "brass sky" is the brown dome-shaped shell above the animal, and the "straight earth" is the flat shell beneath it. Hungarian riddlers gain unity of a sort in their description of a goose by choosing objects making it up from a single category, as in "Its belly is a boat, its foot a paddle, its throat a trumpet;[7] "Its back is a heap, its foot a paddle, its neck a stick";[8] and "Its belly is a boat, its foot a paddle, its throat a bagpipe, its neck a stick."[9] In some riddles the members of a goose are arranged in the order "front, middle, back,"[10] but these texts probably belong to a quite different fundamental conception.

---

[1] For discussions, which do not deal fully with essential matters of style, see: Albert Wesselski, *Archiv orientální,* IX (1937), 365, n. 1; *L'Enfant sage,* pp. 397–398, 405, 573; Oskar Dähnhardt, *Natursagen,* I (Leipzig, 1907), 168–169, citing C. de Warloy, *La Tradition,* II (1888), 274–276. See also my article, "A Riddle for a Locust," in *University of California Publications in Semitic Philology,* XI, now in press.

A complete history of the riddle would include mention of Victor Hugo's "Puissance égale bonté" in *La Légende des siècles.* The oldest instance that I have noted is in the story of Tawaddud in the *Arabian Nights;* see Max Henning (ed.), *Tausend und eine Nacht,* VIII (Leipzig, n.d. [1924?]), 190–191.

[2] Starr, *Philippines,* 205.   [3] Piekarski, 90.
[4] Hedberg, p. 872, No. 42.   [5] Parsons, *Cape Verde,* 93.
[6] Polites, *Neohellenika Analekta,* I, 223, No. 171.
[7] *Magyar Nyelvészet,* III, 223, as cited by Szendrey, *Ethnographia,* XXXII (1921), 75.
[8] *Magyar Nyelvör,* III (1874), 37.
[9] Szendrey's manuscript collection from Szalonta; see *Ethnographia,* XXXII (1921), 75, No. 3.
[10] See the headnote to No. 1435, § 5, below.

A swallow is described in terms of its top, middle, and bottom,[11] and this also is probably a quite different theme from the one here under discussion.

A very curious Mongolian riddle for a camel, "The shape of a mouse, cloven hoofs like a cow, the breast of a tiger, the lips of a hare, the neck of a dragon, the eyes of a snake, the mane of a horse, the wool of sheep, a hump like an ape's, the comb of a rooster, the buttocks of a dog, the tail of a pig,"[12] names the animals of the Mongolian zodiac in their usual order. Various tales explain why the camel did not get a place in the zodiac and how it received compensation in the form of a member characteristic of each animal that was admitted.

This theme of combining characteristic elements belonging to various objects can be further illustrated by the Mongolian description of a cow: "Round, round little hare, how do you solve that? A cloak without seams, how do you solve that? Ten thousand white chessmen, how do you solve that? Embroidered spirals done by a skillful woman, how do you solve that? The canine teeth of a male gazelle, how do you solve that?—Rump, feet, hide, hair, eyes, horns."[13] Here the reference to the seamless coat is to the hide, but in some European riddles it is to the motley colors of the pelt.[14] There is no reason to think that these conceptions are derived from a common source.

The same theme of combining elements belonging to several quite unrelated creatures is occasionally employed in riddles which have things and not animals as answers. The Mongolians say of a gun resting on a forked support: "It has the body of a python; it has the voice of a lion; it has two feet; it has globular excrements like a camel's"[15] and "It has the voice of a dragon; it has the ear of a mule; it has bell-shaped excrements; it has fat food in an enclosure. —The cock of a gun, the bullet, the powder charge."[16] Some of these elements appear in the Mongolian riddle for a pig: "It has the four hoofs of a cow; it looks like a corpse; it has the ears of a male gazelle; it has the two eyes of a wolf that roars 'oh!' He who guesses this will have a tiger's tail for a head ornament and a multicolored lotus for a button of rank. He who does not guess this will have a kite's tail for a head ornament and the excrement of an ass for a button of rank."[17] For a curious adaptation of this theme to the description of a plant, see the Annamese "The body of the dragon, the tail of the phoenix; in winter it covers its eggs; in summer it nourishes its children,"[18] which refers to the cabbage palm.

This manner of description is used for other purposes than riddling. As the Picards say, "To be a good soldier one must have the strength of a horse, the legs of a stag, the patience of a camel, the courage of an elephant, and the

---

[11] See the headnote to Nos. 1436–1447, § 3.
[12] Mostaert, 8.   [13] Mostaert, 150.
[14] See the headnote to No. 1437, § 11, below.
[15] Mostaert, 102.   [16] Mostaert, 103.
[17] Mostaert, 168.   [18] Dumoutier, pp. 203–204.

A swallow is described in terms of its top, middle, and bottom,[11] and this also is probably a quite different theme from the one here under discussion.

A very curious Mongolian riddle for a camel, "The shape of a mouse, cloven hoofs like a cow, the breast of a tiger, the lips of a hare, the neck of a dragon, the eyes of a snake, the mane of a horse, the wool of sheep, a hump like an ape's, the comb of a rooster, the buttocks of a dog, the tail of a pig,"[12] names the animals of the Mongolian zodiac in their usual order. Various tales explain why the camel did not get a place in the zodiac and how it received compensation in the form of a member characteristic of each animal that was admitted.

This theme of combining characteristic elements belonging to various objects can be further illustrated by the Mongolian description of a cow: "Round, round little hare, how do you solve that? A cloak without seams, how do you solve that? Ten thousand white chessmen, how do you solve that? Embroidered spirals done by a skillful woman, how do you solve that? The canine teeth of a male gazelle, how do you solve that?—Rump, feet, hide, hair, eyes, horns."[13] Here the reference to the seamless coat is to the hide, but in some European riddles it is to the motley colors of the pelt.[14] There is no reason to think that these conceptions are derived from a common source.

The same theme of combining elements belonging to several quite unrelated creatures is occasionally employed in riddles which have things and not animals as answers. The Mongolians say of a gun resting on a forked support: "It has the body of a python; it has the voice of a lion; it has two feet; it has globular excrements like a camel's"[15] and "It has the voice of a dragon; it has the ear of a mule; it has bell-shaped excrements; it has fat food in an enclosure. —The cock of a gun, the bullet, the powder charge."[16] Some of these elements appear in the Mongolian riddle for a pig: "It has the four hoofs of a cow; it looks like a corpse; it has the ears of a male gazelle; it has the two eyes of a wolf that roars 'oh!' He who guesses this will have a tiger's tail for a head ornament and a multicolored lotus for a button of rank. He who does not guess this will have a kite's tail for a head ornament and the excrement of an ass for a button of rank."[17] For a curious adaptation of this theme to the description of a plant, see the Annamese "The body of the dragon, the tail of the phoenix; in winter it covers its eggs; in summer it nourishes its children,"[18] which refers to the cabbage palm.

This manner of description is used for other purposes than riddling. As the Picards say, "To be a good soldier one must have the strength of a horse, the legs of a stag, the patience of a camel, the courage of an elephant, and the

---

[11] See the headnote to Nos. 1436–1447, § 3.
[12] Mostaert, 8.   [13] Mostaert, 150.
[14] See the headnote to No. 1437, § 11, below.
[15] Mostaert, 102.   [16] Mostaert, 103.
[17] Mostaert, 168.   [18] Dumoutier, pp. 203–204.

belly of a louse."[19] This proverb has a long history behind it and is probably of Oriental origin. A similar conception which also has some aspects of a proverb appears in the comparison of the good qualities of a horse to characteristics of various other animals, as in the Renaissance Latin

> Accipe quo possis recte spectare caballum,
> Hae sunt virtutes nobilioris equi,
> Addecet hunc leporis geminas ostendere dotes,
> Convenit et vafrae vulpis habere duas.
> Tum res sint illi binae de more luporum,
> Ex asini totidem conditione petat.
> Denique femineis geminas de dotibus addat,
> Sic sonipes multum suspiciendus erit.[20]

And more briefly:

> Sint duae equo leporis dotes. vulpisque, lupique,
> Et dotes asini sint, totidemque nurus.[21]

The related comparison of the good qualities of a woman to the good qualities of a horse's members is in turn related to enumerations of feminine charms.[22]

The underlying conception of combining various members of different animals in a single creature or notion appears to be ultimately related to mythological and cosmological ideas which are especially popular in and around the eastern Mediterranean. Such a creature is similar, for example, to the classical chimera,[23] the beast of the Apocalypse,[24] and the *beste glatissant* of Arthurian romance,[25] as well as sirens, centaurs, and other Mediterranean monsters.[26]

1405. What is that like a mede, / and is not past a handfull breede, / and hath a voyce like a man[?] You will tell this, but I know not when.—It is a little hopingay; for it is greene like a mede, and is not past a handful broad, and it speaketh like a man.
Meery Riddles (1629), No. 20 = Brandl, p. 11.

---

[19] Dubois, *Proverbes picards*, as cited in Eugène Rolland, *Faune populaire*, XII (Paris, [1909]), 179. See also *L'Enfant sage*, p. 404; [Adrien Jean Victor] Le Roux de Lincy, *Proverbes* (Paris, 1859), II, 103; and the description of a greyhound in W. G. Smith and Janet Heseltine, *Oxford Book of Proverbs* (Oxford, 1935), p. 14.
[20] Buchler, *Gnomologia*, 3d ed. (1614), p. 455.
[21] Buchler, *Gnomologia*, 3d ed. (1614), p. 455.
[22] See R. Köhler, *Kleinere Schriften*, III, 22–34; Hans Sachs, *Sämtliche Fabeln und Schwänke*, IV (Neudrucke deutscher Literaturwerke der 16. und 17. Jahrhunderts, CXCIII–CXCIX; Halle, 1903), 311–312, No. 445; Pompeo Sarnelli, *La Posilecheata* (ed. V. Imbriani; Naples, 1885), pp. 120–128; and my note, "An Ordnance Map of Feminine Charms," *Modern Language Notes*, LXIII (1948), 61.
[23] W. H. Roscher (ed.), *Ausführliches Lexikon der griechischen und römischen Mythologie*, I (Leipzig, 1884–1890), cols. 893–895.
[24] Rev. 13:1 ff.
[25] William A. Nitze, "The Beste Glatissant in Arthurian Romance," *Zeitschrift für romanische Philologie*, LVI (1936), 409–418.
[26] See R. Eisler, *Weltenmantel und Himmelszelt* (Munich, 1910), p. 395 note; G. Wilke, *Kulturbeziehungen zwischen Indien, Orient und Europa* (Mannus Bibliothek, X [Würzburg, 1913]), pp. 167–183; K. Kainz, "Der cinesische Drachenwagen und die Semiramissage," *Mitra*, I (1914–1920), cols. 241–253.

1406. A head like a snake, neck like a drake; / Side like a bream, back like a beam; / Tail like a rat, foot like a cat.—Greyhound.
Leather, *Hereford*, p. 229.

1407. Ears like a barn door, / Belly like a box, / Stands on three legs, / Stinks like a fox.—Pair of snuffers.
Fauset, *Nova Scotia*, p. 168, No. 134.

1408. Ears like a mule, tail like a cotton boll, runs like a fool.—Rabbit.
Farr, *Tennessee*, p. 321, No. 51.

Chapter IX

ENUMERATIONS IN TERMS OF FORM
OR OF FORM AND FUNCTION

Nos. 1409–1495

THE RIDDLES in this chapter describe an object by enumerating the peculiarities of its form. The enumerations fall into the following types: (1) shape alone;[1] (2) form and position;[2] (3) form changing according to circumstances;[3] (4) form and function;[4] and (5) forms of several parts of the objects.[5] The importance of these types differs greatly. The first occurs only in a few insignificant and rather stupid products of the enigmatic muse. The last, although adapted to many uses, is ordinarily associated with domestic animals. The other types exist in many subtypes which are generally independent of one another.

The riddles in this chapter gain an enigmatic effect by pointing out contradictory shapes of an object. A thing is hooked, crooked, notched, and straight, and is all these at the same time.[6] It may be both full and empty.[7] This manner of riddling does not usually suggest to the hearer an object that is not the answer to the riddle. It therefore lacks the ingenuity and wit of the riddles in chapters i through vii.

Some riddles in this chapter suggest, at least in the form which probably lies behind these English versions, an object different from the answer, but the riddler is often unconscious of this implication.[8] These have been rather popular. Along with riddles for a hen (an old woman wearing a dress of many patches),[9] an onion (undressing a girl makes one weep),[10] a chimney (a man of patches),[11] a hookah (a person bearing fire on his head),[12] the eye,[13] and a cabbage,[14] they have widely known parallels. Riddles based mainly on a mere contradiction are chiefly known where European influences have predominated.

A strict adherence to the plan of arrangement adopted in this collection would call for putting all riddles based upon a comparison to an object that is not the answer to the riddle in one or another of the preceding chapters. For reasons which will be obvious to the attentive reader, some riddles involving a special class of comparisons to certain objects are included in this chapter. The

---

[1] Nos. 1409 through 1415.
[2] Nos. 1416 through 1447.
[3] Nos. 1448a through 1458.
[4] Nos. 1459 through 1475.
[5] Nos. 1476a through 1495.
[6] No. 1409.
[7] Nos. 1455a through 1457.
[8] Such riddles are Nos. 1416 through 1419a, 1425 through 1428, 1443, 1444, 1448a through 1452, 1464a through 1464c.
[9] See the headnote to No. 1437, § 10.
[10] See the headnote to No. 1439.
[11] Nos. 1437a through 1437e.
[12] See the headnote to Nos. 1440–1441 and the note to No. 1440.
[13] Nos. 1443, 1444.
[14] Nos. 1448a through 1449.

speakers have not always perceived the underlying concept, and the collectors have also failed to comprehend what they were writing down. In such circumstances I have not felt it necessary to make obvious what the speaker and the collector did not understand. In his classification, C. W. von Sydow assigns a special chapter to these riddles, but I have adopted his procedure only for those describing an object in terms of an act.[15]

A few riddles[16] are probably degenerate forms which involve, in better versions, an adequate comparison to something that is not the answer, but the English versions contain so slight evidence of this that I have disregarded it.

A second variety of riddle found in this chapter involves the suggesting of an apparent contradiction, a contradiction in terms: an object is said to be both full and empty, neither in nor out, and so on. Riddles of this sort are not degenerate forms of a personification and have no parallels suggesting a personification. Their point lies in the statement of a paradox that the hearer must solve.[17] This conception shows some similarity to riddles involving a contradiction in characteristic acts[18] rather than in characteristic details of form. Riddlers have generally considered such contradictions to be good enigmatic technique, but, even so, the examples are limited to rather sophisticated cultural levels. A Cheremiss window riddle based on the contrast of being both in and out is, for example, probably borrowed from European sources.[19] The contrast of acts seems to be readily comprehended and employed by unsophisticated peoples. The eastern European riddles for a man plowing tell the functions and not the forms of man, horse, and plow and hence represent a variation which seems independent of the European form.[20]

A third variety of riddle found in this chapter consists in the assembling of totally unrelated details of form. It is usually expressed by the arranging of objects of striking shapes in the order of the head, middle, and tail or back[21] or of the top, middle and bottom[22] or (less frequently) of the sides and the middle.[23] The members may also be described according to their forms or functions and may be at times enumerated without mention of their positions.[24] This last device shows some similarity to the descriptions of a grasshopper as composed of parts resembling several animals.[25]

1409–1458. Form

1409–1415. Shape

A few stupid riddles enumerate aspects of the form of an object without suggesting any similarity to an animal, person, plant, or thing. Since their enig-

---

[15] See Nos. 1739 and 1740 below. [16] Notably Nos. 1471, 1473.
[17] For examples see Nos. 1423a through 1423c, 1439, 1454, 1459 through 1463.
[18] See chapter xi. [19] See the note to Nos. 1423a through 1423c.
[20] See the headnote to No. 1435, nn. 1–8. [21] See the headnote to Nos. 1430–1435.
[22] See the headnote to Nos. 1436–1447.
[23] See the headnote to Nos. 1416–1447, nn. 7–18.
[24] See the headnote to Nos. 1476–1494.
[25] See the headnote to Nos. 1405–1408 and compare Nos. 1405 through 1408.

matic quality lies in the apparent impossibility of these aspects belonging to the same object, the aspects are often directly opposed.[1] In one text, which is quite unintelligible, the riddler expects us to resolve a flat contradiction.[2] Complications concerned with holes are readily connected with a strainer or a thimble.[3] One riddle referring to parts of an animal is extremely obscure.[4]

1409. Hooked, crooked, notched, and straight.—A steelyard.
Waugh, *Canada*, p. 70, No. 803.

1410. Round, oval, oblong, black, dirty, and yet clean.—Tea kettle.
Parsons, *Bermuda*, p. 258, No. 102.

1411. This corner, this corner is no corner at all.—Ring.
Beckwith, *Jamaica*, p. 200, No. 158.

1412–1413. Holes

1412. A little thing has a thousand holes.—Strainer.
Parsons, *Aiken, S.C.*, p. 28, No. 20 var.

1413. All holes, all holes, / And not a hole through.—A thimble.
Sayce, *Montgomeryshire*, p. 18.

1414–1415. Parts of an Animal

Two partially intelligible riddles naming the members of an animal constitute a category of negligible importance. In the fundamental idea they show some similarity to the grasshopper riddle,[1] which enumerates the members of several animals and tells us that they belong to one creature, and to the cow riddle,[2] which enumerates the various members according to their functions.

1414. What is narrow face Virginia?—Chicken.
Fauset, *Southern Negro*, p. 288, No. 133.

1415. Long pole, bushy tail.—Broom.
Parsons, *Bermuda*, p. 264, No. 157.

1416–1447. Position

Riddlers often describe an object by listing its parts and indicating their positions. This occurs solely, or almost solely, in European riddling, and the very rare examples found in Africa or Asia are probably borrowed from Europe.

The device of enumerating the parts of an object and naming their relative position appears in several varieties. Such confusing and contradictory formulations as "over the head and under the hat,"[1] which deals only with the position of the parts and does not mention their shape, are rare. Riddlers ordinarily refer to both the position and the shape of the parts. The texts

---

[1] Nos. 1409, 1410.
[3] Nos. 1412, 1413.
[1] See the headnote to Nos. 1405–1408.
[1] Nos. 1436a, 1436b.
[2] No. 1411.
[4] No. 1414.
[2] Nos. 1476a through 1489.

below are arranged according to the following positions: In (within), out (without);[2] Around, middle;[3] Front, middle, back;[4] Ends alike (alive), middle contrasting (dead);[5] and Above, below.[6] Within these divisions I have set up subdivisions which need not be enumerated here, but are set forth on page xxviii of the Analytical Table, above.

Riddlers do not often describe the parts of an object in horizontal order or recite the peculiarities of all its sides. The Bulgarian cradle riddle, "On both sides wooden planks, in the middle live flesh,"[7] with an Albanian parallel, "Wood on this side, wood on that side, flesh in the middle,"[8] exemplifies a description in horizontal order. The Kolarian parallel, "On the sides are the bones, the flesh [is] inside,"[9] varies the fundamental idea somewhat, since it suggests an abnormal sort of animal. Much to the same effect is an Armenian parallel in topographical terms, but it is not completely intelligible: "A mountain on one side, a mountain on the other side, in the middle it does not shake."[10] The "mountains" may be pillows, and the motionless object, the sleeping child.

The western European riddles for a horse or other animal standing between shafts[11] are very similar to the cradle riddles. See the Breton "Two sides of wood, and the middle of flesh"[12] or the Lettish "A wood on one side, a wood on the other, a hairy one comes between,"[13] which have the answer "a horse between shafts," and the closely related Breton "Wood in the middle, and flesh on both sides,"[14] the Italian "Hairy here, hairy there, the one in the middle not even the dogs eat him,"[15] or the Albanian "Flesh on this side, flesh on that side, a wood in the middle,"[16] which have the answer, "a pair of oxen and a pole between them."

For further examples of the description of the parts of an object in transverse order see the Finnish loom riddles, "On both sides a narrow board and in the middle a wobbly hole"[17] and "On both sides a balcony, in the middle a knocker."[18] The last of these suggests the façade of a house.

1416–1423. In (Within), Out (Without)

The contrast of in and out may be employed to suggest a contradiction or a *tertium quid comparationis*, which is often more specifically identified by adding

---

[2] Nos. 1416 through 1423c.
[3] Nos. 1424 through 1429c.
[4] See the headnote to Nos. 1430–1435.
[5] Nos. 1430 through 1434a.
[6] Nos. 1436a through 1447.
[7] Stoilov, § 5, No. 2.
[8] Hahn, p. 160, No. 12. See also French: Queyrat, *La Creuse*, I, 366 (The answer "trough in which bread is made" is unusual). Compare the description of the parts of a bed in horizontal order in No. 1434a below.
[9] Wagner, 71. See also Munda: Roy, *The Mundas*, pp. 506–507, No. 6.
[10] Seidlitz, 10.
[11] See also the texts cited in the headnote to Nos. 1416–1419, § 7, below.
[12] Sauvé, 49.
[13] Bielenstein, 672.
[14] Sauvé, 50.
[15] Gianandrea, *Canti popolari marchigiani*, p. 301, No. 23.
[16] Hahn, p. 160, No. 11.
[17] Henssen, 174.
[18] Henssen, 175.

details. For a discussion of this type of comparison, see Wolfgang Schultz, *Rätsel aus dem hellenischen Kulturkreise*, II, 17.

1416–1419. Hairy Without, Hairy Within

Old examples of this pattern are rare. The theme seems to be akin to that of a dialogue riddle in a fifteenth-century Weimar manuscript.[1] The widely circulated "A naked one slips into a furry one," which has answers[2] similar to those of the dialogue, need not be sharply separated from these conceptions. Typical objects described in this manner are:

§ 1. Stockings. See No. 1416.

§ 2. Shoes or boots. See No. 1417.

§ 3. Trousers. Danish: Kristensen, p. 266, § 34, No. 11. French: Lespy *Béarn*, 13; Pineau, *Poitou*, 8; Fourès, p. 254; Mensignac, *Gironde*, p. 301, No., 24; Westphalen, *Metz*, col. 199. Spanish: Demófilo, pp. 343–344, No. 18; Rodríguez Marín, 633. Californian: Espinosa, 33, 34. Dominican Rep.: Andrade, 80. Porto Rican: Mason, 361. Italian: Gianandrea, *Archivio*, I (1882), 402, No. 10. Rumanian: Gorovei, 424.

Variant descriptions of trousers are the Portuguese "Pocket inside, pocket outside, raise your feet, and put inside";[3] and the Votyak "One holds it at both sides and thrusts in the middle."[4]

§ 4. A fur cap. Hungarian: *Magyar Nyelvör*, II (1873), 177; VI (1877), 270; XXXI (1902), 533, No. 26. Gypsy: Wlislocki, 43 (Hairy within, hairy without, put hairy in it).

§ 5. Gloves, mittens. Icelandic: Árnason, 787. Walloon: Colson, *Wallonia*, IV, 110, No. 128; Colson, *Devinettes*, p. 149, No. 14. Lithuanian: Jurgelionis, 265 through 267. Russian: Sadovnikov, 659. Mordvin: Paasonen, 236, 237 (A hairy one opens, a naked one enters). Bulgarian: Gubov, 306. Cheremiss: Porkka, 66. Zyrian: Wichmann, *Zyrian*, 16, 68, 266. Hungarian: *Magyar Nyelvör*, II (1873), 467. Yakut: Piekarski, 282.

§ 6. A razor. Turkish: Kowalski, *Asia Minor*, 73 (Open your hairy one, here is my mad one).

§ 7. A man and horses plowing or drawing a cart. French: Rolland, 32; Westphalen, *Metz*, col. 198. Catalan: Pelay y Briz, 72. Spanish: Demófilo, p. 382, No. 6. New Mexican: Campa, 133. Italian: Gianandrea, *Canti popolari marchigiani*, p. 301, No. 107; Gianandrea, *Archivio*, I (1882), 406, No. 14. Lithuanian: Jurgelionis, 742 (Hair next hair, stomach next stomach, in the middle something sticks out), 743, 744. Polish: Gustawicz, 71, 72; Saloni, *Rzeshów*, 32, 33 (Bone to bone, hair against hair, and in the middle a peg shakes.—Wagon-pole and horses). See also the headnote to Nos. 1416–1447, nn. 12–16, in this collection.

---

[1] R. Köhler, *Kleinere Schriften*, III, 515–516, No. 17.
[2] Shoes, stockings, gloves.
[3] Parsons, *Cape Verde*, 190.
[4] Buch, 11.

1416. Hairy within and hairy without; lift up your foot and poke it in.—Stockings.
Beckwith, *Jamaica*, p. 201, No. 169.

1417. Got two years ["ears"; i.e., the tabs by which the boots are drawn on]. Hoist up yer foot, sho' [shove] it in, go flippity flop. What's dat?—Boots.
Parsons, *Sea Islands, S.C.*, p. 157, No. 33.

1418. Hair without, / Hair within, / All hair and no skin.—Hair-rope.
Chambers, *Scotland*, p. 109; Gregor, *Northeast Scotland*, p. 80; Findlay, *Edinburgh*, p. 59; Fauset, *Nova Scotia*, p. 174, No. 200; Carter, *Mountain White*, p. 79.

1419a. Hairy in and hairy out, / Hairy in a hairy's mout'.—Mouse in a cat's mouth.
Greenleaf, *Newfoundland*, p. 9, No. 6.

1419b. Into Hairy's mouth, / An' out o' Hairy's mouth, / An' into Hairy's mouth again.—Cat eating a mouse.
Kavanagh, *Béaloideas*, IV (1933-1934), 342.

1420-1421. Rough (Red) Without, Smooth (Rough) Within

1420a. Rough on the outside, / Smooth within, / Nothing can enter / But a big flat thing. / When it enters, / It wriggles about, / And that is the time / The goodie comes out.—Oyster.
Perkins, *New Orleans*, p. 107, No. 12.

1420b. Smood [smooth] inside, / Rough outside.—Ashter [oyster].
Parsons, *Sea Islands, S.C.*, p. 168, No. 98.

1421. What is that that is rough within, and red without, / and bristled like a bares snowt: / there is never a Lady in this Land / but will be content to take it in her hand.—It is an eglantine berry, which is rough within, and red without, and hath bristles on the top.
Meery Riddles (1629), No. 6 = Brandl, p. 9.

1422. When Out, It Wriggles

1422. Something when its out / Wriggles about, / When it's ill, it's still.—Tongue.
Parsons, *Bermuda*, pp. 258-259, No. 107.

1423. Neither In Nor Out

The contradiction involved in describing an object as neither in nor out is applicable to a window and other parts of the framework of a house. It occasionally appears in forms suggesting a personification.[1] The riddler may at times assure us of the actual existence of an object satisfying these conditions by saying "It is still about the house" or "The house cannot do without it." The Icelandic day riddle "Who is in and out at the same time, when he is not out?"[2] turns on a pun on *úti*, signifying both "out" and "over, finished." A

---

[1] See Nos. 133 through 135.   [2] Árnason, 664.

Hausa version, which is told in dialogue,³ is very curious: "'O clinging thing, why not come inside?' 'What didst thou get by going inside?'—Door and door-screen."⁴

Typical uses of the contradiction of being neither in nor out are:

§ 1. A sparrow's nest on the window frame. Votyak: Wichmann, *Votyak*, 112 (It's neither in the room nor outside). This exemplifies the introduction of a new answer by a species of specialization.

§ 2. A lintel, a threshold, a door. Irish: De Bhaldraithe, 52 (He's not inside, and he's not outside, and there is not a day that I don't see him.—Lintel). Cheremiss: Wichmann, *Cheremiss*, 212; Ramstedt, 18 (threshold). Hungarian: *Magyar Nyelvör*, XXXI (1902), 532, No. 15 (It is on the outside as well as the inside; yet it is always in the same place.—Door).

§ 3. A bolt. Irish: De Bhaldraithe, 51 (He's inside during the day, and he is outside during the night). Svanian: J. Nizheradze, pp. 68–69, No. 22 (At night it is outside, and in the daytime it is at home). Mordvin: Paasonen, 49 (Both here and there.—Door handles). Mongolian: Mostaert, 66 (One fist in the house, one fist outside.—*Ydēr*, thongs which unite and hold objects by passing through them like the thongs running through the lattice supporting a felt tent).

1423a. It isn't in / And 'tisn't out / And the house can't do without it.— A window.

Fauset, *Nova Scotia*, p. 174, No. 201. A Gaelic riddle.

1423b. What is neither in the house, nor out of the house, and still is about the house?—A window.

Gregor, *Northeast Scotland*, p. 82.

1423c. What's neither without nor within / But on the ditch drying?— Window.

Praeger, *Béaloideas*, IV (1933–1934), 146, No. 25.

1424–1429. Around, Middle

Descriptions mentioning specifically the locations "around" and "middle" are rather few. The fundamental idea of a contrast between the center and the circumference of an object occurs frequently enough; see, for example, the description of eyes as pools surrounded by grass or trees.¹ In the following riddle for a sponge the riddler's interest lies in the seeming impossibility of a hole being able to hold water.

1424. I know somet'in', / Hole all aroun', / Hole in de middle, / An' yet still hol' water.—Sponge.

Parsons, *Bahamas*, p. 472, No. 8.

---

³ For riddles of similar construction see the headnote to Nos. 138–140 above.
⁴ Fletcher, p. 55, No. 33.
¹ See No. 1044.

1425–1428. Hair Around, Hole in the Middle

The following rather poorly preserved texts exhibit various kinds of degeneration and corruption. The fundamental idea is elsewhere expressed by two comparisons[1] or a scene.[2] A well-conceived Fijian riddle for the eye affords a good contrast in enigmatic style. It is: "Breakers on this side, breakers on that side, dark-colored salt water in the middle."[3]

1425. Something round, split in the middle, / Surrounded by hair, and water comes out.—Eye.
Parsons, *Bermuda*, p. 259, No. 110 var.

1426a. A little long thing, with hair all around it, / Sorta red on the inside, an' water comes outa it.—An eye.
Boggs, *North Carolina*, p. 323, No. 14.

1426b. Something that has hair on it, and water comes out.—Eye.
Parsons, *Bermuda*, p. 259, No. 110 var.

1426c. Something you have hair around.—Eye.
Parsons, *Bermuda*, p. 259, No. 110 var.

1427. Eye ride round, air [ear] ride round, mouth in the centre.—Answer lacking.
Parsons, *Antilles*, III, 369, Grenada, 19.

1428. A dainty fine thing, / Which under her wing, / My lady does commonly wear, / With a bottomless Hole, / As black as a coal, / And cover'd all over with Hair.—It is a Muff.
A New Riddle Book; Or, A Whetstone for Dull Wits, p. 4.

1429. Soft in the Middle, Hard All Around

Although this conception is clearly related to "Four legs up and four legs down, soft in the middle and hard all around" (No. 69a above), the relationship is obscure. Inasmuch as the longer version does not contain a clear conception, it may be a later development. The small number of available versions and their restriction to a limited area make it difficult to discern the course of development.

1429a. Somet'in' sof' in the middle and hard all 'round.—Bed.
Parsons, *Sea Islands, S.C.*, p. 155, No. 19.

1429b. Hard on the edge, / And soft in the middle.—Bed.
Fauset, *Southern Negro*, p. 287, No. 123.

1429c. Hard all aroun' an' sof' in middle.—Bed.
Johnson, *St. Helena Island, S.C.*, p. 158, No. 14.

---

[1] No. 1345.
[2] Nos. 1443, 1444.
[3] Fison, 23.

1430–1435. Front, Middle, Back

The many continental European descriptions of an object in terms of its form at the front, in the middle, and at the back have very few English parallels. Inasmuch as this manner of description has found equally little favor with riddlers in Russia, Africa, the Levant and eastward, I am inclined to infer that its popularity in central Europe is of rather recent date.

We can identify two varieties of descriptions of the front, middle, and back of an object. In the first variety the front and back are said to be identical and the middle contrasts with them, either in form[1] or in function.[2] This variety is known to English riddlers. In a second variety,[3] which is virtually unknown to English riddlers, the three aspects of the object are entirely dissimilar. The enigmatic quality of the riddle arises from the difficulty of combining in a single thing three dissimilar and incongruous aspects.

1430–1431. Ends Alike, Middle Contrasting

This conception, which is best known in a riddle for a man, a plow, and a horse, may refer either to the form or the function of the members. References to form are, however, rather rare and occur only in riddles of obscure origin and limited dissemination. They may be awkward imitations of the more widely known variety in which the functions of the members are contrasted. Typical themes are:

§ 1. A clothesline. See No. 1430.

§ 2. A wasp. See Nos. 1431a through 1431d.

§ 3. A man milking or plowing. Breton: Lavenot, *Basse-Bretagne*, p. 667 (What has two heads and a middle?). Norwegian: Bugge, *Telemarken*, 17 (Heads at both ends). French: Marchessou, *Velay et Auvergne*, p. 166, No. 6 (Wood in front, wood behind); Sébillot, *Auvergne*, 11 (Wood in front, wood behind, a white fountain in the middle).

1430. Tied at both ends and raised in the middle. / If you can guess this riddle, I'll give you a fiddle.—Clothesline.
Hyatt, *Adams Co., Ill.*, p. 659, No. 10850.

1431a. Big on both ends, little in the middle, / Paws up the dirt and plays like a fiddle.—Dirt-dauber [wasp].
Farr, *Tennessee*, p. 322, No. 57.

1431b. Big at both ends, / Little in the middle; / Digs up dirt, / Sings like a fiddle.—Dirtdauber.
Halpert, *Riddles*, p. 38, No. 3.

---

[1] See the headnote to Nos. 1430–1431, "Ends Alike, Middle Contrasting."
[2] See the headnote to Nos. 1432–1434, "Alive at Both Ends, Dead in the Middle."
[3] See the headnote to No. 1435, "Tail Like a Sickle."

1431c. Big at each end, little in the middle; / Digs up the dirt and sings like a fiddle.—Dirt dauber.
Hudson, p. 84, No. 8.

1431d. Big at both ends and little in the middle; / Goes upstairs singing like a fiddle.—Mason wasp, dirt dauber, mud wasp.
Hudson, p. 84, No. 7.

1432–1434. Alive at Both Ends, Dead in the Middle

On the continent of Europe this manner of riddling has enjoyed great popularity, but in English tradition it has been reported only from the southern United States. I have recognized three subvarieties, one in which the riddlers contrast the dead and the living, as in the Votyak "The dead follows the living.—Cart";[1] another in which they contrast flesh and wood;[2] and a third in which they contrast three states of man (alive, baptized, dead).[3] Several scholars have discussed this theme.[4]

The notion of something alive at both ends and dead in the middle is applicable to:

§ 1. A man plowing. See Nos. 1432a through 1433b.
§ 2. Men carrying a slaughtered pig. Swedish: Ström, p. 372, "Sysselsättningar," 6 (What is living at both ends and dead in the middle?).
§ 3. Men carrying a watertub. Norwegian: Berge, 102.
§ 4. A person in bed. See Nos. 1434a, 1434b.

1432a. Dead in the middle, / 'Live at each end.—Horse, plough, and a man.
Bacon and Parsons, *Virginia*, p. 317, No. 44; Parsons, *Guilford Co., N.C.*, p. 201, No. 6; Parsons, *Sea Islands, S.C.*, p. 155, No. 17.

1432b. 'Live on each en', / Dead in the middle.—Horse an' man plough.
Parsons, *Aiken, S.C.*, p. 36, No. 77; Parsons, *Robeson Co., N.C.*, p. 388, No. 4; Fauset, *Southern Negro*, p. 287, No. 121; Perkins, *New Orleans*, p. 110, No. 45.

1432c. Somet'in' live on two en', dead in the middle.—Man plowing wid oxen.
Johnson, *St. Helena Island, S.C.*, p. 158, No. 19.

1433a. Flesh befo' an' flesh behin', wood an' iron in de middle.—Horse, man drivin' him, an' plough.
Parsons, *Sea Islands, S.C.*, p. 155, No. 17, var. 1.

1433b. Flesh on the two ends, an' the middle is wood.—On the one end is a man, and the other is a horse, and the middle is the plough.
Parsons, *Sea Islands, S.C.*, p. 155, No. 17, var. 2.

---

[1] Wichmann, *Votyak*, 24, 297; Buch, 2. Turkish: Hamizade, 19 (A living one fled, a dead one pursued.—Horse and cart). For the contrast of the living and the dead see also the headnote to Nos. 828–836 above.
[2] Nos. 1433a, 1433b.
[3] See the headnote to No. 1435.
[4] E. H. Meyer, *Zeitschrift des Vereins für Volkskunde*, XIV (1904), 4–5; Schultz, *Rätsel aus dem hellenischen Kulturkreise*, II, 61; Petsch, *Neue Beiträge*, p. 139.

1434a. Somet'in' live in the middle, an' dead on de two en'.—Baid [bed].
Parsons, *Sea Islands, S.C.*, p. 155, No. 18.

1434b. Live in de middle, an' dead in between.—Pussin in baid [person in bed].
Parsons, *Sea Islands, S.C.*, p. 155, No. 18 var.

1435. Tail Like a Sickle

English riddlers have preserved only this fragment of a riddle describing an object in terms of three entirely different things arranged in an order from front to back. The parallels make it clear that this description of a cockerel is to be so understood. The reasons for the neglect of this manner of description are quite obscure. It is very popular on the continent of Europe.

This manner of description occurs in two varieties: the front, middle and back of the object are identified either by their forms or by their functions. The second of these varieties is rare, and I shall comment on it before examining the first.

The description of an object in terms of three different functions which are arranged from the front backward refers usually, and perhaps always, to a man and a draft animal. The Dutch say of a man plowing, "In front it eats straw, at the back it eats bread, in the middle it is dead."[1] The Serbians conceive a man, a harrow, and oxen as "Behind a soul, in the middle a noisemaker, at the head the blower."[2] The Palestinian Arabic "Tell me of three: the first breathing, the middle is hardened, and the third is dressed,"[3] like the Filipino "There are three things: the first is walking without talking; the second is eating; the third is walking and talking,"[4] uses a formula characteristic of proverbs and ultimately derived from the Bible.[5] A few riddles of this sort contain elements which we have already met in the discussion of the formula, Alive at both ends, dead in the middle.[6] The Low German "Alive in front, dead in the middle, it eats bread and cheese behind"[7] employs that characteristic contrast of the living and the dead and at the same time partakes of this type. The Svanian "It is itself a dead thing; it has two living things; and it feeds the world,"[8] which also has the answer "men and oxen plowing," is similarly constructed.

More important than such descriptions of apparently conflicting functions are those of quite unrelated forms. The riddler may attempt to hold together these three forms by choosing them from a single sphere of human activity, as in the cat riddle, "In front like a ball, in the middle like a sack, and at the

---

[1] Sinninghe, p. 18, No. 8.
[2] Novaković, p. 239, No. 2.
[3] Ruoff, p. 28, No. 43.
[4] Starr, *Philippines*, 236.
[5] See Prov. 30:18 and 21; Archer Taylor, *The Proverb* (Cambridge, Mass., 1931), pp. 160–164.
[6] See Nos. 1432a through 1434a above.
[7] Carstens, *Schleswig-Holstein*, p. 413.
[8] W. Nizheradze, p. 1, No. 4.

back like a broomstick,"⁹ in which all the objects belong to the household. Or, he may let contrast alone serve as a unifying element. I can cite only one example which achieves more than a rhetorical unity. It is a Khāṛiā description of plowing: "Wooden horse with iron beak, in front go the storks, and after them the thief."¹⁰ Perhaps the most interesting use of this theme of three contrasting features of an object is the old and famous story¹¹ of the three blind men and the elephant. One blind man found the elephant like a water-pipe; another like a fan; and still another like a throne. They had felt the trunk, the ear, and the side of the animal and reported their sensations.

Riddlers have ingeniously modified the fundamental idea of three conflicting objects composing a single thing. The theme of the man plowing is, for example, described in terms of three elements, as in the Breton "The ends beef, the threads of iron, the body of wood, and a Christian tail,"¹² which exhibits an unusual expansion of the more ordinary "Alive in front, dead in the middle, baptized at the end"¹³ or "A beast in front, dead in the middle, baptized at the back."¹⁴ This vaguely conceived monstrosity is more clearly seen as a unit in the Argentinian Spanish "The nose [is] of animal [origin], the back-bone of wood, the third part, behind, is Christian."¹⁵ This conception is no doubt continental Spanish, for the Filipinos say, "The head is an animal, the body is wood, and its tail is man."¹⁶

The description of an object by comparisons to three altogether different things occurs ordinarily in riddles for animals. It is rarely, and more or less casually, adapted to other themes. The comparisons show considerable variation in details. They are, however, rather stable in their application to specific animals, and we are therefore justified in establishing subtypes.

This manner of description is applicable to the following:

§1. A cat. Flemish: Joos, 418, 419. German: Wossidlo, 237; Haffner, 65. Danish: Kristensen, p. 64, §155, Nos. 227a, 227b (In front like a button, at the back like a spigot, in the middle like a mealsack); Feilberg, *Ordbog*, II, 110, s.v. "kat." Faeroic: Hammershaimb, *Antiquarisk tidsskrift*, III (1849–1851), 320, No. 50. Norwegian: Aasen, 6; Berge, 12, 14; Bergh, *Valdres*, 27; Bugge, *Telemarken*, 21; Stafset, 54, 174; Brox, *Ytre Senja*, 69, citing Riksheim, 38,

---

⁹ Swedish: Ström, p. 100, "Katten," 7; Sandén, *Norra Vadsbo*, 30. For additional examples see § 1 below.
¹⁰ Roy and Roy, II, 454, No. 43.
¹¹ Jalāl al-Dīn, Rūmī, *Masnavi i ma'navi* (trans. E. H. Whinfield, Trübner's Oriental Series [2d ed.; London, 1898]), p. 122 (Book III, Story 5); R. A. Nicolson, *Tales of Mystic Meaning* (London, 1931), p. 111, No. 33, and his edition of the *Masnavi*, VIII (London, 1940), 34. Professor Stith Thompson, to whom I am indebted for the clue to these citations, reminds me of versifications by John G. Saxe and Carl Sandburg.
¹² Sauvé, 51.
¹³ Sébillot, *Haute-Bretagne*, 12.
¹⁴ Kerbeuzec, *Ille-et-Vilaine*, p. 503, No. 23. See also V. S., *Mélusine*, I (1878), 251, No. 97; Lacuve, *Poitou*, p. 355, No. 51; Pineau, *Poitou*, 25.
¹⁵ Lehmann-Nitsche, 268.
¹⁶ Starr, *Philippines*, 35.

and Nordeng, 33. Swedish: Dybeck, *Runa*, 1847, p. 41, No. 20 = Russwurm, p. 347, No. 41; Geijer and Campbell, 66; Ström, as quoted above. Lettish: Bielenstein, 260, 904 (One end like a ball of yarn, the other end like an awl). Serbian: Novaković, p. 126, Nos. 7 (In front a ball, behind a pole, in the middle a bundle), 8 (In front a ball, at the back a spit, and in the middle a roll). The Bulgarian versions, "The cat comes from below, in front there are two ears, in back the tail" and "There comes a woman from below, dragging an awl behind her" (Gubov, 175, 176), are confused and defective. Hungarian: Arany and Gyulai, II, 349, No. 4 (Its front is like an apple, the rear is like a spit, it walks around on four sticks); *Magyar Nyelvör*, IX (1880), No. 2 (The front like an apple, it is round about the waist, a sausage sticks out of the rear, it walks on four knobby sticks), and XXIX (1900), 592 (It has four little paws, two little painted buttons, it is always moving its long thingumajig). I add the following versions from Szendrey, *Ethnographia*, XXXII (1921), 75: Gönczi, 532 (Its front is like a ball of thread, its back is like a spit. What is it?); *Magyar Nyelvészet*, IV, 315 (In front a ball, in back like a spit, it walks on four little clubs); and Szendrey's manuscript text from Szalonta (In front it is like an apple, its waist is like a dumpling, in back there is a long pointed spit, it crawls about on four little clubs).

For discussion see Aarne, *Rätselforschungen*, II, 125–130. He considers this a variety of the riddles describing a cow.[17] Szendrey makes no comment on this classification, but a comparison of the two kinds of descriptions shows significant differences. Both are characteristically applied to animals, but they show great differences in their fundamental conceptions.

§ 2. A horse. German: Wossidlo, 236; Böckel, *Hesse*, 5; Hanika-Otto, 38. Norwegian: Berge, 11; Stafset, 45; Bugge, *Telemarken*, 12. Swedish: Ström, p. 91, "Hästen," 1 (In front like a tub, in the middle like a barrel, at the back like a broom), which has the unity of choosing three household objects as the means of comparison. Lappish: Donner, 24; Poestion, p. 268; Qvigstad, 110. Gypsy: Wlislocki, 26 (In front like a cucumber, in the middle like a barrel, at the back like a twig broom).

§ 3. A cow. German: Wossidlo, 234, 235; Johannes Fischart, *Geschichtklitterung* (ed. A. Alsleben; Neudrucke deutscher Literaturwerke des 16. und 17. Jahrhunderts, LXV–LXXI; Halle, 1891), chap. xxv, p. 261; Frischbier, *Thierwelt*, p. 344, No. 4; Haffner, 64; Hanika-Otto, 37. Swiss: Rochholz, 361. Danish: Feilberg, *Ordbog*, II, 241, s.v. "ko." Norwegian: Brox, *Ytre Senja*, 32. Russian: Sadovnikov, 877 (In the middle of the yard there stands a rick, in the front are pitchforks, behind a broom), which achieves a remarkable unity. Serbian: Novaković, p. 22, No. 5 (In front are pitchforks, in the middle a basket, behind the broom). Cheremiss: Wichmann, *Cheremiss*, 133; Porkka, 59. Hungarian: Kálmány, I, 161, No. 22 (In front it looks like a pitchfork, at

---

[17] See the headnote to Nos. 1476–1494 below, especially § 9.

the back it resembles a broom, its middle contains hay); *Magyar Nyelvör*, XIV (1885), 284, No. 1; *Magyar Népköltési Gyütemény*, I, 322 (Its front is a fork, its back is a broom, its middle is a bag), which I cite from Szendrey. Szendrey discusses these Hungarian variants in connection with his remarks on the cow riddle discussed in the headnote to Nos. 1476–1494 below; see *Ethnographia*, XXXII (1921), 74. Indian, Kolarian: Wagner, 49 (In front a sickle, in the middle a basket, at the end a broom).

§ 4. A magpie. German: Wossidlo, 239; Hanika-Otto, 35 (In front a pickax, in the middle a pack, in the back a handle for a frying pan. There are many such things [as this]). Swedish: Dybeck, *Runa*, 1849, p. 49, No. 26; Ström, p. 111, "Skatan," 5 (In front like a book, at the back like a sheet, in the middle like a broom); Geijer and Campbell, 70 (At the back like a flag, in front like a book, in the middle like a ball, it dances like the finest young lady); Waltman, *Lidmål*, 216. A book opens and closes like the bird's beak; the dancing young lady occurs again in the versions cited in the headnote to Nos. 1379–1382, nn. 8, 12, above, from which the trait is borrowed. Lettish: Bielenstein, 706 through 712, 974. Albanian: Pedersen, 5 (Its body is like a wine jug, its head like a needle, its tail like scissors). Although the Albanian riddler gives the answer "magpie," he is in error, for the bird's tail is not forked. He has borrowed this trait from the swallow riddle discussed in the headnote to Nos. 1436–1447, § 3, below.

For comment on this magpie riddle see Schultz, *Rätsel aus dem hellenischen Kulturkreise*, II, 61.

§ 5. A goose, a duck. German: Wossidlo, 238 = Gilhoff, 126 (In front like a broomstick, in the middle like a pillow, at the back like a hollow scoop). Hungarian: *Magyar Nyelvör*, II (1873), 90 (In front goes the dingle-dangle, behind there is a shovel).

§ 6. A distaff. Faeroic: Hammershaimb, *Antiquarisk tidsskrift*, III (1849–1851), 318, No. 27 (Behind like a spigot, in front like a button, the middle of its body like a mealsack).

1435. Round the house, round the house, / And his tail like a sickle.—Cockerel.
Sayce, *Montgomeryshire*, p. 17.

1436–1447. Above, Below

A few rather popular patterns are enumerations of the aspects of an object in a vertical order. They often introduce a contrast of some sort into the list. A description of a lamp[1] contrasts water below with fire above. This conception is the reverse of the description of a pot as Blackman sitting on Redman.[2] A churn riddle contrasts a little top and a big bottom.[3]

---
[1] No. 1440.   [2] See No. 875.
[3] Nos. 1445a through 1445e.

Riddlers have often described the aspects of an object in a horizontal[4] rather than a vertical sequence. The examples of description in a vertical sequence vary greatly among themselves. The Portuguese maize riddle, "Poor at the foot, poor at the head, rich in the middle,"[5] holds the enumeration together by the contrast of rich and poor. The picturesque Finnish fire riddle, "Dregs above, dregs below, in the middle red beer,"[6] employs the same sort of contrast and suggests a glass of beer. The Crimean Tatar riddle for *pirogue* (a Russian meat-pie) is "Bast above, bast below, and within butter stinks," and that for a sword, "At the bottom there is a board and on the top there is a board; within there is Tiran, a theological student."[7] Another variety of conception in vertical terms appears in a Pushto riddle for wheat: "Its head is in man, its middle is in the ox, its end is in the ground,"[8] and still another is used in the Turkish almond riddle: "Below, it's wood; above, it's wood; inside is a yellow theological seminarian."[9] A coconut riddle, "Sky above and sky below and water in the middle"[10] involves the apparent impossibility of water hanging in air. The Malagasy "Earth under the person, the person under dry grass, dry grass under water, and the water again surrounded by earth,"[11] which has the answer "water carrier and pot," may have included elements suggested by a curious account of the way in which the world is supported.[12] It also suggests the descriptions of a man in terms of a variety of objects heaped one upon another.[13] A Malayalam taro riddle, "The foot like a cooking pot, the body like a stick, the head like an umbrella,"[14] belongs to the class of riddles which describe an object in terms of the parts of several animals, or of animals and things.[15]

This manner of description is most widely applied to:

§ 1. A man, a saddle, and a horse. This riddle also utilizes the very popular contrast of the living and the dead discussed in the headnote to Nos. 828–836 Examples are German: Wossidlo, 242*b*; Frischbier, *Menschenwelt*, p. 254, No. 142 (Alive above, alive below, without a soul in the middle). Spanish, Dominican Rep.: Andrade, 317. Portuguese: Parsons, *Cape Verde*, 204 (Alive at the bottom, dead in the middle, alive at the top). Italian: Pitrè, 749. Lettish: Bielenstein, 541 (Something living above, something living below, something dead in the middle). Serbian: Novaković, p. 95, No. 6 (It is of iron below, of

---

[4] See the headnote to Nos. 1430–1435.
[5] Parsons, *Cape Verde*, 40.
[6] Lönnrot, 170 = Henssen, 173.
[7] Filonenko, 4, 5. Turkish: Hamizade, 398 (On the bottom a board, on the top a board, inside there is a bloody sick man).
[8] Thorburn, *Bannú*, p. 230, No. 8.
[9] Hamizade, 46. See also his No. 68.
[10] See the headnote to Nos. 1105–1106, n. 1, above.
[11] Sibree, p. 40, No. 17.
[12] R. Köhler, *Kleinere Schriften*, II, 57–60.
[13] See the headnote to Nos. 1100–1108 above.
[14] Schmolck, p. 242, No. 15.
[15] For examples and discussion see the headnotes to Nos. 1405–1408 and 1435.

wood above, and in the middle of flesh), and p. 96, Nos. 1 (On top it is wooden, below of iron, and in the middle flesh), 2 (Above wood, below iron, and in the middle flesh). The collector says that these riddles refer to a packhorse, but the answer is more correctly "a stirrup of iron, a saddle of wood, and horse of flesh." Bulgarian: Gubov, 157 (Below iron, above wood, in the middle living flesh), 158. Finnish: Lönnrot, 120 = Henssen, 172. Estonian: Lönnrot, p. 179; Wiedemann, p. 265 (Animate below, animate above, lifeless between). Hungarian: *Magyar Nyelvör*, V (1876), 422 (The living is above, and it is also below, in between is the lifeless), and XII (1883), 142 (A thing without life is between two things with life), and also p. 234. Arabic: Giacobetti, 457. Turkish: Kúnos, 18 (Iron below, wood above, flesh between).

An interesting enlargement of this idea appears in the Kxatla riddle for a man, a horse, and a saddle: "That which walks is ridden by that which is dead, that which is dead is ridden by that which is alive."[16] This rests ultimately on the contast of the living and the dead—a theme often used by riddlers.[17]

Perhaps the most ingenious description of a horse and saddle is the Arabic "The lock of blood, the bed of wood, the steps of iron."[18] The steps are imagined as leading to a bed high above the floor. The man seated in the saddle is, in a sense, a lock holding the whole together; the saddle is a resting place or bed; and the stirrups are the steps. The Turkish "I put my hands on the house and stepped on the iron gate";[19] the Zyrian "It climbs a wooden staircase, it sits on a wooden bench";[20] and the Yakut "They say there is a hill of flesh and some iron stairs"[21] are somewhat less sophisticated forms of the same conception. The Mongolian "A mountain of flesh with a pass of wood, an iron ladder, and a woolen rope.—Horse, saddle, stirrup, tether of hair"[22] contains an unusual number of details and gives the scene an Alpine air.

§ 2. Sawyers and a log. I have noted no parallels to the Breton and Filipino adaptations to this answer: "The highest one is alive, the lowest one is alive, the one between is dead and weeps and makes white meal"[23] contains the contrast of the living and the dead,[24] a rather unusual arrangement in vertical order, and the theme of the white meal which often represents a mill.[25] The Filipino "Man above, man below, wood in the middle"[26] seems to be a quite independent invention. In this riddle one man is conceived as standing in a pit under the log and another as standing above, while the saw goes up and down.

---

[16] Schapera, 115.
[17] See the headnote to Nos. 828–836 above.
[18] Meissner, *Iraq*, p. 167, No. 67.
[19] Kúnos, 108.
[20] Wichmann, *Zyrian*, 174.
[21] Piekarski, 87.
[22] Mostaert, 4. See also Gombojew, 45.
[23] Breton: Sauvé, 37.
[24] See the headnote to Nos. 828–836 above.
[25] See the headnote to No. 397.
[26] Starr, *Philippines*, 359.

§ 3. A swallow. Although this riddle has a bird as its answer and refers to what is above and below, it differs from the magpie riddle[27] in the arrangement of the parts. The order of arrangement and the comparisons of the feathers to linen, velvet, or fur and of the forked tail to scissors are features typical of this swallow riddle. For examples see Rumanian: Papahagi, 57 (Above like a frying pan, below like cotton, behind like shears). Serbian:[28] Novaković, p. 112, Nos. 2 (In front like a fork, behind there is an awl, below a lamb), which describes the beak as a fork with two tines and the whitish stomach as lamb's wool, and 5 (On top a kid, below a lamb, in front an awl, behind a fork), which contrasts the black fur of a goat with the white wool of a sheep. Hungarian: *Magyar Nyelvör*, IV (1875), 282 = *Nyelvtudomanyi Füzetek*, XXVI, 49 (Its body is of linen, its neck of velvet, there is music coming from its mouth); *Magyar Nyelvör*, VI (1877), 270 (The back is velvet, the belly is linen, the tail is a fork, the head is a stick), and XIX (1890), 92 (It came from Rome, it speaks Greek, its belly is of white linen, its back is of velvet, its head is full of curls, its tail is like a pair of scissors). In addition to these references, Szendrey[29] cites *Magyar Nyelvészet*, III, 325; a manuscript version resembling the last-quoted text; and *Magyar Nyelvészet*, I, 873 (Its belly is linen, its neck velvet, its mouth music, its tail a fork). See also Modern Greek: Stathes, p. 333, No. 21 (Above like a frying pan, below like cotton, and behind like scissors).

The reference to scissors (the forked tail) is characteristic of the swallow riddle. It appears in such simple versions as the Turkish "One would say that some scissors come through the sky"[30] and the Kashmiri "Who has a tail like a pair of scissors? Who has a necklace on her throat? Who has a rule for six months only?"[31] "Rule" is, I conjecture, better construed without an article, as signifying "domination"; the allusion is to the migratory habits of the swallow, which is absent for half the year. Still another conception occurs in the Turcoman "Beneath, it is a ram; above, it is a she-goat; its nose is long; its tail is like a pair of scissors."[32]

§ 4. A nightingale. Modern Greek: Polites, *Neohellenika Analekta*, I, 218, No. 145 (Like a frying pan above, like cotton beneath, and like a pair of scissors in the back). This is clearly a casual adaptation of the swallow riddle.

§ 5. A turtle. Italian: Ferraro, *Canti popolari in dialetto logodurese*, p. 300, No. 8. Serbian: Novaković, p. 97, No. 8 (Above a plate, below a plate, in the middle a living thing moves). Bulgarian: Gubov, 161 (Two bowls, a disgusting

---

[27] See the headnote to No. 1435, § 4, above. For another type of magpie riddle, see the headnote to Nos. 1379–1382 above.
[28] See also Novaković, p. 112, Nos. 1, 3, 4, 6, 7, and p. 113, Nos. 1, 2.
[29] *Ethnographia*, XXXII (1921), 75–76.
[30] Kowalski, *Zagadki*, 74.
[31] Knowles, 46.
[32] Samojlvich, 45.

dish), 162 (Cover above, cover below, in the middle an omelette), 163 (Cover above, cover below, an orphan in the middle); Chacharov, 28 (Skin above, skin below, flesh in the middle). Turkish: Kowalski, *Asia Minor*, 63 (Board above, board below, a strange point between); Kúnos, 23 (Wood below, wood above, a black theological student between). Turcoman: Samojlvich, 48 (Under it a stone, over it a stone, four legs, only one head). See also, in the present collection, the headnote to No. 1437, § 12, below.

§ 6. A chestnut. Modern Greek: Abbott, p. 313, No. 31 (Skin on top, skin beneath, in the middle a morsel).

1436. Over the Head, Under the Hat

1436a. Riddle me, riddle me, what is that? / Over the head and under the hat? —Hair.

Halliwell-Phillipps, *Popular Rhymes*, p. 142; Greenleaf, *Newfoundland*, p. 12, No. 35; Fauset, *Nova Scotia*, p. 160, No. 87; Knortz, p. 232, No. 90; Hyatt, *Adams Co., Ill.*, p. 662, No. 10875.

1436b. What's that over the head and under the heart?—Hair.

Parsons, *Barbados*, p. 286, No. 64.

1437–1439. Patch on Patch

Descriptions of an object as something covered with patches or, in more concrete human terms, as a person garbed in patches, are very poorly exemplified in English tradition. English riddlers scarcely hint at such distinct personifications as that of the Algerian maize riddle, "Softly, softly, she is wrapped in her cloaks."[1] I have divided the discussion of these comparisons into two sections: riddles having things or animals as answers are surveyed in the headnote to No. 1437, and those having plants as answers, in the headnote to Nos. 1438–1439.

1437. Patch on Patch: An Animal or a Thing

The English seem to be unfamiliar with the use of this notion in describing animals. They employ it only to describe a chimney[1] and a cabbage or an onion.[2] This very restricted English use of the notion gives no adequate idea of the freedom and variety with which riddlers adapt it to their purposes. I shall cite examples of its application to animals and things in this headnote and to plants in the headnote to Nos. 1438–1439. It is used to describe the following animals and things:

§ 1. A roof. Flemish: Joos, 272 (Patch on patch and seam on seam); *Ons Volksleven*, I (1889), 78, No. 37 (There were two highly learned men, and they made a cap of a hundred thousand patches). German: Hanika-Otto, 106.

---

[1] Giacobetti, 86. See also the maize riddles cited below, in the headnote to Nos. 1438–1439, especially nn. 8–9.

[1] Nos. 1437a through 1437f. [2] Nos. 1438b, 1439.

French: Rolland, 142; Marchessou, *Velay et Auvergne*, 24; Fourès, p. 253; Dardy, *L'Albret*, p. 327; Lespy, *Béarn*, 27; Daleau, *Gironde*, p. 106; Mensignac, *Gironde*, p. 303, No. 34; Desaivre, *Poitou*, p. 455, No. 34; Westphalen, *Metz*, col. 195; Roque-Ferrier, *Languedoc*, p. 333; Baissac, *Mauritius*, p. 403. Basque: Vinson, 37 (Our father's cap is all in bits); Cerquand, 30. Italian: Gianandrea, *Archivio*, II (1883), 432, note to No. 59; Schneller, *Wälschtirol*, p. 256, No. 25 (I know a cover made of nothing but patches, and there is not a stitch in it). Polish: Saloni, *Rzeshów*, 185 (Sewn and patched, the needle untouched); Saloni, *Łańcut*, 6. Russian: Sadovnikov, 112 (Forty skirts, one cover). Hungarian: *Magyar Nyelvör*, II (1873), 43 (Patches over patches, but there never was any thread in the middle).

§ 2. A window. German: Wossidlo, 365b.

§ 3. A flag. Spanish: Demófilo, 102 through 104; Rodríguez Marín, 725, 726. Chilean: Flores, 79, 80. Cuban: Massip, 27.

§ 4. A wasp nest, a honey comb. Spanish, Argentinian: Lehmann-Nitsche, 543a (Bridge on bridge, a village of bad people), 543b, 543c, 547.

§ 5. A gun. Serbian: Novaković, p. xviii, No. 9 (The tsar's maiden has nine shirts). The shirts are the rings around the gunbarrel.

§ 6. A fence. Hungarian: *Magyar Nyelvör*, XXXVII (1908), 188 (The sister-in-law's shirt is mended, but there is no stitch in it).

§ 7. A barrel and its hoops. Serbian: Novaković, p. 85, No. 11 (Our Ann has nine undergarments), p. 86, Nos. 1 (Our Ann has nine garments, and yet her ribs can be seen), 2 (My Ann has put on nine garments). For the comparison of a barrel to a person girt with many belts see above, No. 678 and the headnote to No. 678, §1.

§ 8. Turf stack. Danish: Kristensen, p. 139, § 409, Nos. 649a through 649g; Feilberg, *Ordbog*, IV, 941, s.v. "tørvestak."

§ 9. Clouds, the sky, snow on the ground. Breton: Sauvé, 5; Sébillot, *Haute-Bretagne*, 3; Duine, *Saint-Malo*, p. 515 (A coverlet that has many patches and no seam). Dutch: Schrijnen, II, 103, No. 6 (Patch, patch, a thousand patches, it is sewn without needle or thread. I give you to guess what patch that may be). Flemish: Joos, 14. French: Rolland, 11; Bladé, *Armagnac*, 83; Dardy, *L'Albret*, p. 329 (Patched and patched once again, never has the needle passed through it); V. S., *Mélusine*, I (1878), col. 263, Nos. 69 (A thing well patched, no needle has passed through it), 70 (A thing all made of patches, never has a needle passed through it); Beauvillard, *ibid.*, col. 485; Marchessou, *Velay et Auvergne*, p. 165, No. 1; Carnoy, *Picardy*, p. 53; Pineau, *Poitou*, 34; Carmeau, p. 33; Constantin, *Savoie*, p. 21; Mensignac, *Gironde*, p. 300, No. 16; Fourès, pp. 254–255; J. Roux, *Limousin*, 4; Roque-Ferrier, *Languedoc*, p. 326; Pommerel, *Auvergne*, p. 42. Catalan: Pelay y Briz, 31. Spanish: Demófilo, 285, 286. Italian: Gianandrea, *Archivio*, II (1883), 429, No. 55; Ferraro, *Canti popolari in dialetto logodurese*, p. 317, No. 56. Hungarian: Arany and Gyulai,

III, 295, No. 17 (My grandfather's large shirt, there are a hundred patches on it, but there is not a single stitch in it). Arabic: Ruoff, p. 15, No. 22 (Patch beside patch, from here to Baghdad); Bauer, p. 223, No. 10. Turkish: Kúnos, 198 (Blue satin, a needle does not pierce it, scissors will not cut it, a tailor does not sew it.—Sky). See also the headnote to No. 1213, § 4, above.

A Picard adaptation of this pattern to snow, "I have a large coat made of nothing but scraps through which a needle and thread have never passed,"[3] appears to be unique. A Polish fog riddle, "In the cellar there sits a maiden sewing without needle, without thread; she can sew the kind of flower that is found the world over,"[4] shows some remarkable features.

The pattern "Patch on patch" is applicable to feathered or mottled animals. English riddlers do not know this very popular use of the pattern. For examples see:

§ 10. A cock, a hen, (rarely) a goose. See Breton: Sébillot, *Haute-Bretagne*, 20; Kerbeuzec, *Ille-et-Vilaine*, 82; Charlec, *Dol-de-Bretagne*, 1904, p. 378, No. 41. Flemish: Joos, 356 (Mlle Hakken wears a dress of a hundred thousand pieces; without a needle, without thread), which perhaps involves some further playing with the word *hakken* (hook). Afrikaans: Groenewald, p. 75. German: Wossidlo, 365a; Frischbier, *Thierwelt*, p. 350, Nos. 38 through 41, and p. 352, No. 55; Hanika-Otto, 104. German versions often exhibit a striking personification and literary elaboration; see, for example, "There comes a man from Egypt, has a coat of a thousand patches, without thread and without seam, which no tailor makes" (Carstens, *Schleswig-Holstein*, p. 415). The "man from Egypt" recalls Joseph and his coat of many colors (Gen. 37:3). Danish: Kristensen, p. 33, § 76, No. 96, and p. 38, § 95, No. 126; Feilberg, *Ordbog*, II, 251, s.v. "kok," and p. 381, s.v. "fugl." Spanish: Demófilo, 461, and p. 347, No. 38, and p. 384, No. 13; Rodríguez Marín, 370. Argentinian: Lehmann-Nitsche, 336a through 336n. Cuban: Massip, 89 (Full of patches and stitches. —Hen). New Mexican: Campa (A very ladylike lady with many patches and not a seam). Lithuanian: Schleicher, p. 200 (A little woman has many clothes), and *ibid.* (There comes a beggar, patch on patch, no needle goes through the patches). Lettish: Bielenstein, 492. Czech: note to Hanika-Otto, 102 through 106. Kashub: Gulgowski, 12. Polish: Siarkowski, 59 (What lady is this? She wears a thousand frocks); Gustawicz, 189 (A lady dressed in a two-piece gown walks to the barn. When the wind blows, it reveals her rear end). The white Russian and Russian parallels are remarkably vivid: "Seven hundred chemises, seven hundred patches, but when the wind blows, its backside is bare" (Wasilewski, 82); "Kheriton's wife walked along the fence, found seven hundred shirts; there came the wind, all the shirts were blown away"; "Our Parasha has forty chemises. There came a wind, her back is bare"; "Seventy

---

[3] Carnoy, *Picardy*, p. 53.   [4] Siarkowski, 80.

dresses, not a single clasp"; and "An old man walks in the field, he has on a hundred fur coats, yet his body is visible" (Sadovnikov, 924, 924b, 926, and 941). Bulgarian: Chacharov, 45 (The tsar had a daughter, she dressed in a thousand shirts, as the wind blows, you can see her body). Finnish: Lönnrot, 1281 = Henssen, 125b. Mordvin: Paasonen, 190. Yakut: Piekarski, 85 (They say that there is one who has twenty-five articles of clothing, yet he cannot cover his rear). Indian, Uraon: Archer, p. 186, No. 108 (The old woman who wears a heap of clothes). Baiga: Elwin, p. 471, No. 73 (An old woman with a load of rags on her back).

Thus far, the riddles cited have been comparisons of a hen to a person wearing many garments or a garment having many patches. As we might expect, comparisons of a hen to an animal conceived in this fashion are rare. Riddlers do not often compare one animal to another, a man to a man, or a thing to a thing. An exception to this rule is the Rumanian chicken riddle, "A pack mule laden with little boards,"[5] which may have been suggested by the hedgehog riddle[6] or by the comparisons of a cabbage or an onion to an animal.[7]

A few riddlers make an analogous comparison of a hen and a thing, as in the Turkish "A mattress with several blankets. He who does not guess it is an ass"[8] or in the Indonesian "A house, whose posts [are] two pieces, whose roof is hundreds and thousands,"[9] which, like the Serawaj "Two posts and a roof of a thousand palm leaves,"[10] is analogous to the comparison of a man to a house.[11]

§ 11. A cow. Frisian: Carstensen, *Am Urquell*, III (1892), 327, No. 25 (Patch around patch and never a seam). German: Hanika-Otto, 103 (Patched and mended and nowhere a seam). Danish: Feilberg, *Ordbog*, II, 241, s.v. "ko." Spanish, Argentinian: Lehmann-Nitsche, 336c (Marvel, marvel, what is it? It bears many patches, but has no seam). Czech: Hanika-Otto, note to her Nos. 102 through 106. Polish: Gustawicz, 177 through 179: Kopernicki, 35 (Mended and patched, never touched by a needle); Siarkowski, 3 (Patched and patched, a needle can never stand in this). Mongolian: Kotvich, 106, 254 (It was cut without a measure, sewed without seams.—Spotted cattle) and another version cited in the headnote to Nos. 1405–1408, n. 13, above. Buryat: Gombojew, 19 (Although without a seam, it is striped).

Other animals are rarely described in this way. The description of a snake or a fish cited in the headnote to No. 1213, §§ 2–3, above, lays more emphasis on

---

[5] Weigand, p. 275, No. 24 = Papahagi, 28.
[6] See the headnote to Nos. 576–577 above.
[7] See the headnote to No. 1438, n. 4 (cabbage), and the headnote to No. 1439, nn. 7–10 (onion).
[8] Kowalski, *Zagadki*, 77.
[9] Tabaru: Fortgens, 61.
[10] Helfrich, *Serawaj*, p. 51, No. 27. For variations of this theme see the note to No. 1562 below.
[11] See the note to No. 1100.

the seamless coat than on the many patches. Somewhat more similar to the type here discussed is:

§ 12. A turtle. Turkish: Hamizade, 314 (He has clothes full of moles [excrescences], full of moles, he hides his head from men). This may also be related to the comparisons to bumpy or prickly men cited in the headnote to Nos. 576–577 above. African, Tschuana: Kuhn, *Tschuana*, 33 (Little grandfather with many patches on his clothing). See also Nos. 594a, 594b above.

1437a. Patch on top o' patch, wid a hole in de middle.—Chimney.
Parsons, *Sea Islands, S.C.*, p. 165, No. 73. Square hole: Knortz, p. 214, No. 9.

1437b. Patchy patchy patch, / Hole in the middle.—Chimney.
Parsons, *Aiken, S.C.*, p. 30, No. 32, var. 2.

1437c. Patched up, patched up, / Hole in de middle. / Guess dis riddle, / I'll give you a fiddle.—Fireplace.
Parsons, *Aiken, S.C.*, p. 29, No. 32, var. 1.

1437d. Patch upon patch / With a hole in the middle. / Who will tell me this riddle, / I'll give a gold fiddle.—A chimney.
Farr, *Tennessee*, p. 320, No. 33; Perkins, *New Orleans*, p. 107, No. 19; Hyatt, *Adams Co., Ill.*, p. 659, No. 10846; Brewster, *Indiana*, 8.

1437e. Patches on top o' patches.—Chimbley.
Fauset, *Southern Negro*, p. 286, No. 111.

1437f. Brick upon brick, / Hole in the middle. / Guess that riddle, / I'll give you a fiddle.—Chimney.
Parsons, *Aiken, S.C.*, p. 29, No. 32.

1438–1439. Patch on Patch: A Plant

The notion of comparing a plant composed of many layers to a person or thing having many patches upon one another suggests itself readily. Consequently we need not attempt to derive the various instances from a single source. Compare, as examples, such widely separated texts as the Mordvin riddle for a beet, "The maiden is beautiful; she is in prison; she has forty skins; she is alive in summer but in winter one eats her";[1] the Turkish description of the *martagon*, a kind of lily, "Dressed in a ninefold silk coat, she has on her head a little seven-cornered ball";[2] and the Kxatla riddles for the *lesswana* bulb, "Tell me: the mistress with a thousand dresses"[3] and for a mealie, "Tell me: the woman coming from England who has put on a thousand petticoats."[4] The usual answers are a cabbage[5] and an onion.[6]

Riddlers occasionally use this pattern to describe other plants than a cabbage or an onion. The French say for a mushroom, "What is folded, folded, and never has a needle passed through it?"[7] The Serbians say for corn (maize),

---

[1] Paasonen, 317.
[2] Katanov in Radlov, IX, 104, No. 887.
[3] Schapera, 22.
[4] Schapera, 59.
[5] See below, No. 1438b and the headnote to No. 1438.
[6] No. 1439 and the headnote to No. 1439.
[7] Desaivre, *Mélusine*, I (1878), col. 292; Desaivre, *Poitou*, p. 451, No. 9.

"One old man has nine fur coats"[8] or "Our daddy has nine drawers."[9] The Nandi riddle for a wild banana, "There lives by the river a woman who has many garments,"[10] is perhaps related to the many African descriptions of a banana as a person wearing torn or slit garments.[11] There is an interesting allusion in an Abyssinian maize riddle, "One who has a thousand garments, like the daughter of the sea."[12] A "daughter of the sea" signifies a woman of Massaua, who ordinarily wears many more garments than do the Abyssinian women of the highlands.

Comparisons of this sort in terms of animals are rather rare, but are occasionally applied to an onion.[13] See also a Cuban pineapple comparison in terms of a house, beginning "Window on window."[14]

1438. Patch on Patch: A Cabbage

The comparison of a cabbage to something wearing patches upon patches is known virtually everywhere. The variation in details is very considerable. The Lithuanians say, "A one-legged man has a hundred suits," or "Patch on patch, the end of the thread can never be found";[1] the Russians, "There stands a short priest, dressed in forty chasubles"[2] and "As a child he knew no diapers. Now that he has become an old man, he wears a hundred diapers";[3] the Bulgarians, "A sheep is dressed in twelve leather coats, yet it freezes in winter";[4] and the Arabs conceive the idea dramatically, "The lady sits in the field and has a hundred rags about her and cries out, 'Oh! the cold that pierces me!'"[5]

Comparisons suggesting a thing rather than a person are somewhat less abundant than comparisons to a person or an animal. The English example below seems to be of this sort. See also the Serbian "A rag upon a rag, it is neither stuck with a needle nor sewn with thread";[6] the Hungarian "One patch above another, but there was never a needle in them";[7] the Modern Greek "Sheet on sheet without a stitch of sewing";[8] and the Turkish "Layer on layer of mattresses; whoever does not know it is an ass."[9]

1438a. A patch upon patch without any stitches. / If you tell me this riddle, / I'll give you my breeches.—A cabbage patch.

Sayce, *Montgomeryshire*, p. 16.

---

[8] Novaković, p. 107, No. 12. See more distinct personifications cited in the headnotes to Nos. 587, n. 6; 650–652, n. 1; 1436–1447, n. 5; 1437–1439, n. 1.
[9] Novaković, p. 88, No. 11, and p. 107, No. 10.
[10] Hollis, *Nandi*, p. 138, No. 22.
[11] See Nos. 593a through 593f above.
[12] Littmann, *Tigriña*, 27. See a similar riddle cited in the headnote to Nos. 1437–1439.
[13] See the headnote to No. 1439 below.
[14] Massip, 166.

[1] Jurgelionis, 1035, 1037.
[2] Sadovnikov, 745.
[3] Bardin, p. 243, No. 13.
[4] Chacharov, 54.
[5] Littmann, 40; Ruoff, p. 52, No. 26.
[6] Novaković, p. 29, No. 7.
[7] *Magyar Nyelvör*, III (1874), 376.
[8] Polites, *Neohellenika Analekta*, I, 200, No. 36.
[9] Moshkov in Radlov, X, 268, No. 42.

1438b. Patch upon patch, without any stitches, / Riddle me that, and I'll buy you a pair of britches.—Cabbage.
Praeger, *Béaloideas*, IV (1933-1934), 146, No. 23.

1439. Patch on Patch: An Onion

The comparison of an onion to a man wearing a coat of many patches or a woman wearing many skirts is widely known. The following English instance is, however, very imperfectly conceived. It may have been suggested by the chimney riddles:[1] The onion riddles based on the comparisons to a man or woman vary greatly in details. The Spanish texts exemplify well the nature of these variations. An onion is a woman with many petticoats or one who wears dress on dress or cloth on cloth.[2] She wears cape on cape,[3] shoe on shoe,[4] hat on hat,[5] or helmet on helmet.[6] Comparisons in terms of animals are less usual. See the Serbian "Our white horse has nine blankets and yet its ribs are visible,"[7] which also has the answer "spinning wheel";[8] the Bulgarian "I have a red calf dressed in four skins";[9] and the Mongolian "A sheep has a hundred coats in a severe winter."[10]

A special modification of the theme of many garments is peculiarly appropriate to the onion. It consists in the added remark that the bystanders weep when the garments are removed. For examples see French: Carmeau, p. 35. Lettish: Bielenstein, 946. Polish: Gustawicz, 15 through 20; Saloni, *Rzeshów*, 10 (A German woman came in red garments. When they stripped her, they wept over her), 12 through 14, 15 (A toad stands in forty coats. When they stripped it, they wept over it); Kopernicki, 1 (A German girl arrived, dressed in red garments. As they were disrobing her, they wept over her) (= Kolberg, *Krakowskie*, IV, No. 73, according to Kopernicki) and 1 var. (A lady arrived with seven skirts upon her. As they were disrobing her, they wept over her) (= Kolberg, *Kujawy*, II, 203-204, according to Kopernicki); Siarkowski, 17, 30 (There is a certain lady, there are a thousand garments on her. When they disrobed her, they wept over her). Kashub: Patock, *Schwarzau*, 6. White Russian: Wasilewski, 83 (All in patches, a peasant woman sits in the garden bed. Whoever looks at her will weep). Russian: Bardin, p. 243, No. 9 (In a fur coat there sits an old man. He who undresses him sheds tears). Cheremiss: Wichmann, *Cheremiss*, 201. Mordvin: Ahlqvist, p. 41, No. 29; Paasonen, 255.

---

[1] See Nos. 1437a through 1437f and the headnote to No. 1437.
[2] Demófilo, 257, 263, and p. 349, No. 43; Rodríguez Marín, 510, 512. Argentinian: Lehmann-Nitsche, 330, 547. Californian: Espinosa, 38. Dominican Rep.: Andrade, 109. Porto Rican: Mason, 156f.
[3] Demófilo, 260, and p. 386, No. 23; Rodríguez Marín, 511.
[4] Demófilo, 266, and p. 376, No. 1.
[5] Cuban: Massip, 53, 54. New Mexican: Espinosa, 25. Porto Rican: Mason, 156a, 157.
[6] Demófilo, 264.
[7] Novaković, p. 121, No. 1.
[8] Novaković, p. 137, No. 6.
[9] Chacharov, 52.
[10] Kotvich, 260.

The Baiga "A little girl makes the king weep"[11] deserves special note. The same contrast of the small person who makes the great one weep appears in the Parsee chili riddle, "Such a stunted little peon would make the whole village weep."[12]

1439. Patches on top o' patches.—An onion.
Fauset, *Southern Negro*, p. 286, No. 111.

1440–1441. Water (Hell) Above, Fire (Hell) Below

The enigmatic quality of this conception lies in the apparent impossibility of the close conjunction of water and fire, especially when the water stands above the fire. Objects described in this manner are household utensils hanging above a fire[1] or utensils (lamp, hookah, or pipe) in which fire burns on the top. The fundamental idea of a contradiction of the laws of nature resembles somewhat that underlying the coconut riddle: "Sky above, sky below, water in the middle."[2]

Some riddlers allude to the apparent impossibility of fire standing in water. The Serbians say of a lamp, "A fire burns in the middle of the sea,"[3] which also has the variant answer "samovar,"[4] and the Turks think in still more definitely topographical terms when describing a nargileh or hookah as "The sea above, the fire below, [between them] a narrow route."[5]

Riddlers often conceive fire and the water above it in a hookah in terms of a personification. Some of these inventions are very curious and interesting. The Kashmiri say, "An adultress in an open field, with a basin of fire on her head."[6] This conception resembles that of a candle riddle,[7] but can be interpreted in a very ingenious symbolism. The allusion to the "adultress" signifies, I conjecture, the fact that many men kiss her. The scene of the "open field"— which might not seem appropriate—refers, as Professor Murray B. Emeneau tells me, to the fact that public stopping places outside a village often consist merely of a few stones for a cooking place, a platform on which to lay a bedstead, and one or more hookahs marked with colored rags to indicate the castes or groups that may properly use them. These public stopping places are often situated in an open field. Inasmuch as Indians usually punish adultery by cutting off the nose, we perhaps should not seek an allusion to a punish-

---

[11] Elwin, p. 467, No. 29.   [12] Munshi, p. 425, No. 47.

[1] See also the personifications of Red and Black discussed in the headnote to Nos. 871–877.

[2] See the headnote to Nos. 1105–1106, n. 1. See also the samovar riddle cited in n. 30 below.

[3] Novaković, p. 215, No. 4. The Bulgarians describe a lamp before an icon in a similar manner; see Ikonomov, 73.

[4] For this answer see also the Tungus "Amidst the ocean there burns a fire" (Poppe, 29).

[5] Kowalski, *Zagadki*, 131.

[6] Knowles, 98. See also the hookah riddle quoted in the note to No. 631 above.

[7] See the headnote to Nos. 607–631 above.

ment for adultery in the "basin of fire" on the woman's head, but we may have here a local variation in legal procedure.

There are many further examples of personification in Eastern riddles for a hookah. Somewhat less successful than the version just cited is the Bihari "Its waist is thin, its bowels are capacious, in its body divine water dwells, on its head is fire."[8] This shows some similarity to descriptions enumerating bodily members of a supposed creature. A clearer and better personification occurs in the excellent Bihari "She has water in her body and fire on her head. She has assumed the vermilion spot for her husband's sake. When kissed on the mouth, she speaks, but if not, the woman remains silent."[9] The "vermilion spot," or symbol of marriage, is the burning spark in the tobacco; the bubbling of the hookah when the lips are applied to the mouthpiece is the speaking of the woman. Still more ingenious is the clever comparison to suttee in "Having seated herself on Indra's head, a woman immolates herself in the fire. As she is kissed on the mouth, she burns with much lamentation."[10] Mitra explains that Indra is the god of the watery sky. The seating of the woman "on Indra's head" is therefore the placing of tobacco in the container or pipe above the water. The theme of kissing occurs also in Icelandic riddles for a pipe: "A maiden has her mouth in the middle of her head, and in it she burns flowers in a fire. No one desires her glowing lips, and therefore all kiss her rump"[11] and "Who is the slim one that has two mouths but no belly? Legless, she can go nowhere, but she kisses many."[12] Perhaps the best of all these is a Hindi comparison of a hookah to a snake charmer: "His cistern full of water and fire lighted atop. When his flute sounds, there comes forth a black snake."[13] The music of the "flute" is the bubbling of the hookah and the "black snake" the pipe leading to it. Other variations of these ideas can be seen in the Armenian "It has a cup on its head, a spear in its hand, but it is not a Turk; it rumbles but it is not a frog";[14] the Panjabi "A smallish girl, on her head a basket of ashes";[15] and the Annamese "I ask the jinni of the kitchen for fire. I light the bonze's head. The thunder groans heavily, and the dragon rises in the air,"[16] which suggests an incantation.

In countries where the samovar is an ordinary household utensil, riddles personifying it are numerous. The Turks contrasts a censer and a vase of rose water: "Two things came suddenly from the side: the stomach of one was fire, its head was smoke; the stomach of one was water, its head was a fountain.

---

[8] Mitra, *Bihar*, 43.
[9] Mitra, *Bihar*, 44.
[10] Mitra, *Bihar*, 45.
[11] Árnason, 161.
[12] Árnason, 639. For discussion of the theme of going without legs see the headnote to Nos. 260–265 above. Two other Icelandic pipe riddles employ altogether different themes; see Árnason, 491, 832.
[13] W. J. d'Gruyther, *Panjab Notes and Queries*, III (1885–1886), 15, § 64, No. 4.
[14] Zelinski, p. 59, No. 32.
[15] Emeneau and Taylor, 18.
[16] Dumoutier, p. 207.

The assembly ended, flowing out to the roads."[17] The Yakut have several variations of the samovar riddle: "They say there is a proud gentleman who breathes fire and lives in a watery home" and "They say there is a little old granny whose breath is fiery and whose food is liquid."[18] The Yakut "They say there is a tiny man with a wound in his shoulder"[19] contains a reference to the spigot at the side of the samovar, and "They say that there is a Chinese girl who feeds herself on red cloth"[20] describes the yellow of the brass and the red of the flame. The Russians say of a cresset, "Dron son of Dron, Ivan son of Ivan, walked through fire, carried fire on his head."[21]

Comparisons in terms of animals are rather unusual. I have noted the Turkish "A little well, a poisonous water, inside there is a snake, in its mouth there is some coral,"[22] which has a variant in the last clause reading "in its mouth there is a nightingale, in the nightingale's mouth a rose"; the Crimean Tatar "There is a well, in the well there is water, in the water there is a snake, the snake's head is of coral";[23] the Armenian "A certain creature, lying belly and throat down, wants to drink water, but who will give it to drink? Others will fill it up by hand, a fire will start in its head, it will make someone's glance happy. Him who will guess the answer I shall favor tomorrow with apricots"[24] and "A snake in a lake with a flashing head."[25] In Turkish riddling an extinguished lamp is described as "The well has dried up, the snake has died, the coral has been extinguished."[26] In such riddles as these the "snake" is the wick of the lamp. The Yakut "They say that the elk has a wound in its side"[27] is a variant of the previously cited personification of a samovar.

Except for the comparison of a hookah or lamp to a fire burning in the sea, the comparison to things is rather rare. There are few parallels to the Albanian "A star in the middle of the sea"[28] or the Georgian "My little vegetable patch is on fire."[29] The Russian samovar riddle, "A hole toward the sky, a hole toward the earth, in the middle fire and water,"[30] confuses the hearer by suggesting what seems to be a physical impossibility. A curious Ho riddle employs the pattern of what I have called a chain-riddle. It relates the sequence of materials in the hookah from bottom to top: "Water above fruit, wood above water, earth above wood, intoxicating drug above earth, fire above

---

[17] Hamizade, 79. [18] Piekarski, 384, 385.
[19] Piekarski, 387. Compare the English pump riddle, Nos. 817a through 817g above.
[20] Piekarski, 389. [21] Sadovnikov, 198. Compare No. 631 above.
[22] Hamizade, 466. [23] Filonenko, 82. Compare Schultz, *Bemerkungen*, p. 375.
[24] Glushakov, p. 35, No. 81.
[25] Wingate, 9. [26] Hamizade, 462.
[27] Piekarski, 386. [28] Hahn, p. 163, No. 76. See also p. 159, No. 16.
[29] Kapanadze, p. 144, No. 3.
[30] Sadovnikov, 443. See also Mordvin: Paasonen, 159, and similar riddles in the note to No. 1441 below. There is a somewhat similar impossibility of being cooked on top and raw on the bottom in Nos. 1244a through 1245 above. For other applications of the idea of water suspended in air, see the note to Nos. 1105a through 1105e, the note to No. 1424, and the note to Nos. 1461, 1462.

drug."³¹ This seems to be related to the Kolarian "In an ocean a big stump is stuck; on top of it a house is built in which heaps of treasures are stored up; the treasure burns, but the house will not burn."³²

I have noted only one comparison of a hookah to a plant. The Panjabi say, "A stalk on the way, common to all."³³ This calls for a knowledge of the custom of leaving a hookah in the public stopping place for anyone to use.

1440. Water a-bottom, fire a-top.—Lamp.
Beckwith, *Jamaica*, p. 201, No. 166; Parsons, *Antilles*, III, 363, Trinidad, 2.

1441. Hell a-top an' hell a-bottom.—Frying-pan.
Beckwith, *Jamaica*, p. 201, No. 167.

1442. Devil Above, Devil Below, McKintosh Between

The riddler is perhaps suggesting a pun on McKintosh, signifying a person and a raincoat. The notion of a raincoat resembles somewhat the comparison of the tongue to a wet rag.¹

1442. Devil on top, / Devil below, / McKintosh in the middle.—Teeth and tongue.
Parsons, *Antilles*, III, 368, Grenada, 1.

1443–1444. Hair Above, Hair Below

Although many European riddlers have used this conception, I have noted only the two following instances in English folklore. The conception is European and not African or Asiatic. The Indonesian parallels¹ are, I conjecture, borrowed from the Dutch. The fundamental theme, which English taste has found objectionable, has some similarity to that used in a riddle for the mouth, with special reference to the teeth and tongue. See the Turkish "Marble² below, marble above, the bride plays between";³ and the Modern Greek "Mortar above, mortar below, and a maiden inside is singing."⁴

1443. Hair a-top, hair a-bottom; only a dance in the middle.—Eyelashes and eye.
Beckwith, *Jamaica*, p. 201, No. 168.

1444. Hairy on top, an' hairy below, with a round thing in the middle. What is that?—An eye.
Parsons, *Antilles*, III, 446, St. Thomas, 18.

---

³¹ Sarkar, p. 353, No. 14. For comment on chain-riddles see the headnote to Nos. 1156–1164 above.
³² Wagner, 37.   ³³ Emeneau and Taylor, 20.
¹ See the headnote to No. 1150, nn. 6–14.
¹ See the note to No. 1443, and compare with European parallels in that note and in the note to Nos. 1425 through 1426c.
² Var.: iron.
³ Turkish: Kúnos, 19; Kúnos, *Nyelvkönyv*, 4; Kowalski, *Zagadki*, 29; Hamizade, 150; and a parallel quoted in the headnote to No. 1150, § 3, above. See also "On that side a wall, on this side a wall, inside he plays a game" (Hamizade, 153. The precise translation of the last words is uncertain).
⁴ Polites, *Neohellenika Analekta*, I, 206, No. 73.

1445-1447. Small Above, Big Below

Icelanders use this contrast in describing an inkstand: "Originally I am light-colored, narrow at the top and wide at the bottom. Later I become quite black but can still recover my former color."[1]

1445a. Big in the bottom, / Little at the top, / In the middle go flippity-flop.—Churn.

Bacon and Parsons, *Virginia*, p. 325, No. 112; Johnson, *St. Helena Island, S.C.*, p. 158, No. 23.

1445b. Big in the bottom, / Little at the top, / Something in the middle / Go flippety-flop.—Churn.

Fauset, *Southern Negro*, p. 277, No. 13. Little thing in the middle: Hyatt, *Adams Co., Ill.*, p. 659, No. 10848; Brewster, *Indiana*, 15. Thing in th' middle goes flippety-flop: Randolph and Spradley, *Ozark*, p. 88; Farr, *Tennessee*, p. 321, No. 43; Chappell, p. 232, No. 19. A little thing in the middle that goes pippity pop: Boggs, *North Carolina*, p. 322, No. 11. Right in the middle it goes flippety-flop: Hudson, p. 86, No. 18.

1445c. Narrow at the top, / Broad at the bottom, / Thing in the middle / Goes flippety flop.—Churn.

Parsons, *Robeson Co., N.C.*, p. 390, No. 21.

1445d. Large at the bottom, / Small at the top, / Thing in the middle / Goes flippety flop.—Churn.

Parsons, *Guilford Co., N.C.*, p. 202, No. 16.

1445e. Big at the bottom and small at the top, / And a thing in the middle goes whipperty-whop.—A churn.

Waugh, *Canada*, p. 67, No. 766.

1445f. Big to the bottom, / Little to the top, / Something goes in it / Whipperty-whop!—Horseshoe thrown into churn, to make the bewitched butter come.

W. P. Webb, *New York Folklore Quarterly*, I (1945), 11-12.

1446a. Big at the top, / Little at the bottom, / Somet'in' at the middle / Go flippity flop.—Churn.

Parsons, *Aiken, S.C.*, p. 34, No. 63. Big at the top, / Wide at each en': Parsons, *Aiken, S.C.*, p. 34, No. 63 var.

1446b. Narrow at the bottom, / Wide at the top, / A thing in the middle / Goes whipputy-whop.—Old-fashioned dash-churn.

Wintemberg and Wintemberg, *Canada*, p. 124, No. 426. All the dash-churns I have ever seen were wide at the bottom, and narrow at the top.—Collector's note.

1447. Bit [biff?] it to the bottom, / Bit it on top. / Right in the middle / Go flippity flop.—Churn.

Parsons, *Sea Islands, S.C.*, p. 157, No. 34.

1448-1458. Changing According to Circumstances

When a riddler specifies the forms an object may take in different situations, he usually chooses those which contrast. He is often content with the implication

---

[1] Árnason, 769.

that this conflict must be resolved. The Indonesian sugar-cane riddle "What goes in wet and comes out dry?"[1] arouses curiosity by the contradictory aspects of the object, but does not suggest, so far as I can see, something which is not the answer. The riddle is probably a reversing of the more usual contrast of going in dry and coming out wet. The Altai Turkish description of a horse's tail is "When it goes into water, there is much of it. When it comes out, there is little."[2] The converse (with the same answer), "If it goes into water, it is one. If it comes out, it is a hundred,"[3] with the Armenian parallel "It went into the water and scattered. It came out of the water and clung together,"[4] relies also on an apparently inexplicable contrast. Other versions are the Turcoman "From a distance I saw one black thing. When I came up near, I saw there were a thousand black things"[5] and the Shor "If it enters the water, it's a thousand; if it goes out on dry land, it is one."[6]

A better technique appears in more adequate comparisons suggesting a person or a thing. The Bhil descriptions of a water pitcher carried to the well draw a picture of a person walking: "From here she goes aslant, but from there she comes [back] straight."[7] This is much the same as the Khāṛiā "While going, it stoops; while coming, it is erect."[8]

1448–1452. Stiff (Dry), Slack (Wet)

This widely known pattern[1] is applicable to articles of food and household utensils. Characteristic themes are:

§ 1. A cabbage. See Nos. 1448a through 1449.

§ 2. A fish. See Nos. 1450a, 1450b.

§ 3. Bread and coffee. Spanish, Chilean: Flores, 771. Dominican Rep.: Andrade, 186 (I put it in dry and take it out wet). Porto Rican: Mason, 546. Italian: Tschiedel, 3. Turkish: Zavarin, *Brusa*, 38.

§ 4. Baking bread. German: Carstens, *Schleswig-Holstein*, p. 418 (At first lax, then stiff). Modern Greek: Polites, *Neohellenika Analekta*, I, 208, No. 87 (I put it in damp and remove it dry.—Pie or cake); Stathes, p. 353, No. 128 (I put it in damp and remove it dry.—Oven mop or sponge). Turkish: Kúnos, 266 (I looked at it from a distance: dark. I went near it: Last Judgment. I

---

[1] Malay: Beauregard, p. 663; Klinkert, p. 48, No. 18.
[2] Menges, p. 86, No. 8.
[3] Katanov in Radlov, IX, 239, No. 52. The riddler has reversed the conception.
[4] Zelinski, p. 58, No. 17.
[5] Samojlvich, 105, citing parallels in Pantusov, *Taranchin*, 149, and Ostrumov, *Sart*, 139.
[6] Dyrenkova, 23.
[7] Hedberg, p. 884, No. 58.   [8] Roy and Roy, II, 452, No. 27.

[1] The references to wet and dry are occasionally reversed. See a Turkish riddle for a horse's hoof: "Going into the water, it does not grow soft; coming out of the water, it does not dry up" (Katanov in Radlov, IX, 239, No. 51). The riddler has perhaps in mind only a contradiction. Versions of the theme "entering dry and coming out wet" often clearly suggest the *tertium quid comparationis*, as in No. 1452 below. Samojlvich cites parallels in Pantusov, *Taranchin*, 291, and Ostrumov, *Sart*, 138.

put it in wet, and it came out dry, the blessing of Mohammed be upon it.—Oven and bread); Kowalski, *Zagadki*, 3 (Its mouth yawns like a signal, the interior is full of tumult, the wet one enters there, the dry one comes out); Hamizade, 186 (Its jaw is a big [open] sign, inside there is a red tumult, I threw in something wet, something dry came out. Praise Mohammed!). Turcoman: Samojlvich, 88 (Its opening is a red mark; its bottom is the resurrection of the dead in purple splendor. A damp [or "invalid"] one goes in and comes out dry [or "healthy"]). The reference to the resurrection of the dead is paralleled by the allusion to the Last Judgment in the Turkish riddle collected by Kúnos and signifies in both instances the flames beneath the oven. Armenian: Zelinski, p. 58, No. 23 (It enters wet, it comes out dry).

A somewhat different idea occurs in the Serbian "It entered the city alive without bone, and it came out dead with bones."[2] The bones are the crusts. Comparisons referring to a change in colors are cited later.[3]

The comparison to an object that is at first dry and then becomes wet is also applicable to household utensils:

§ 5. A dishrag, a washboard. See Nos. 1451, 1452.

§ 6. A spoon, a bucket, a dipper. Swedish: Hyltén-Cavallius, *Värend*, 22, 23. Portuguese: Parsons, *Cape Verde*, 220 (Put in dry, take out wet.—Gourd receptacle). Modern Greek: Sakellarios, p. 292, No. 10 (I put it in limp and take it out loaded.—Bucket); Dieterich, *Sporades*, 16 (spoon in porridge). Turkish: Zavarin, *Brusa*, 36; Kowalski, *North Bulgaria*, 54 (bucket); Moshkov in Radlov, X, 271, No. 82 (*Bang*, it went in; *bang*, it came out. It went in dry, it came out wet.—Bucket in well); Hamizade, 48, 411 (I stick it in dry, I pull it out wet.—Pail). African, Swahili: Velten, 29 (I have my child. It goes dry and returns wet.—Spoon). Indian, Uraon: Archer, p. 190, No. 167 (Dry going, wet coming.—Bucket). Indonesian, Menangkerbau Malay: Harmsen, p. 280, No. 5. Filipino: Starr, *Philippines*, 369 (When I plunged it in, it was dry. When I drew it out, it was dripping.—Dipper).

§ 7. A bit in a horse's mouth. Chilean: Flores, 276, 283.

§ 8. A sleeve, a boot. Russian: Sadovnikov, 628 (I thrust it in, it stands up; I withdraw, it wilts.—Sleeve). Mordvin, Paasonen, 332 (I put it in, it swells up; I draw it out, it collapses.—Boot).

§ 9. A needle and thread. Indian, Bihari: Mitra, *Bihari Life*, p. 45, No. 26.

§ 10. A pen. Italian: Tschiedel, 63 (It has a slit head, one puts it in dry and takes it out wet). Yakut: Piekarski, 440 (They say: there is something which enters wet but comes out dry in the end. Its root is shaggy, and its point is sharp.—Goose quill used for writing).

1448a. When it goes in, / It's stiff and stout. / When it comes out, / It's limber and greasy.—Cabbage.
Spenney, *Raleigh, N.C.*, p. 110, No. 1.

[2] Novaković, p. 232, No. 3.   [3] See the headnote to Nos. 1542–1546, § 2.

1448b. Put it in stiff and stout, / Pull it out slippery and greasy.—Cabbage in a pot.
Fauset, *Philadelphia*, p. 555, No. 22.

1449. When it goes in, / It's stiff and stout. / When it goes out, / It's floppin' about.—Cabbage.
Parsons, *Guilford Co., N.C.*, p. 205, No. 38; Boggs, *North Carolina*, p. 321, No. 7.

1450a. Flip flop fleezy, / When it is in, it is easy, / But when it is out, / It flops all about. / Flip flop fleezy.—Fish.
Parsons, *Bermuda*, p. 262, No. 136.

1450b. Hibbledy hobbledy greasy, / When he's out, he's all about. / When he's in, he's easy.—Fish out o' water.
Leather, *Hereford*, p. 232.

1451. Slippery, wet, and greasy, / When it's in, it's easy; / When it's out, it slips about, / Slippery, wet, and greasy.—Dish-rag.
Hyatt, *Adams Co., Ill.*, p. 660, No. 10856.

1452. It goes in dry and comes out wet, / It tickles your stomach and makes you sweat.—A washboard.
Farr, *Tennessee*, p. 318, No. 2; Hyatt, *Adams Co., Ill.*, p. 670, No. 10937.

1453. Straight, Cross

1453. Throw it up straight and come down cross.—Scissors.
Knortz, p. 215, No. 11.

1454. Higher, Lower

1454. What is that which is lower with a head than without one?—A pillow.
Waugh, *Canada*, p. 68, No. 776.

1455–1457. Full, Empty

English riddlers show only a slight acquaintance with this contrast. It here concerns unnamed objects that are not precisely described.[1] In some Oriental riddles the same contrast is applied to buckets in a well, as in the Arabic "Down empty, up full";[2] the Bhil "From here [it] goes empty, and from there [it] returns full,"[3] which implies a more adequate characterization; and the Tabaru "Going away, [it] is hungry; returning, [it] is satiated,"[4] in which the personification is still more complete. Quite unusual is the Basque conception of a comb as climbing a mountain empty and returning full.[5]

The contrast of full and empty is also conceived in the more specific senses of pregnant and not pregnant. This conception is applicable to a variety of objects:

§ 1. A bucket. Turkish: Katanov in Radlov, IX, 243, No. 111 (When she walks forth, she is not pregnant. When she walks back, she is pregnant).

---

[1] No. 1455a, 1455b. [2] Ruoff, p. 21, No. 10.
[3] Hedberg, p. 879, No. 89. [4] Fortgens, 94.
[5] Vinson, 64.

Mongolian: Klukine, 21 (Pregnant in coming, a nonpregnant cow in going). African, Kanuri: Lukas, p. 169, No. 13 (Whenever I send out my girl, she comes back pregnant).

§ 2. A spindle. Cheremiss: Wichmann, *Cheremiss*, 79, 141 (A Russian woman became pregnant during the dance); Porkka, 70. Shor: Dyrenkova, 29 (A little girl ran and ran inside the house and became pregnant). Mongolian: Bazarov, 140 (A thin virgin played and played and became pregnant).

A spindle is also similarly conceived in terms of animals, as in the Zyrian "An ox on a halter is fattened" and "At the haystack they are fattening an ox";[6] the Turkish "[It] runs and runs and becomes pregnant,"[7] which may refer to either a person or an animal; the Turcoman "My particolored pup twirled and twirled and became pregnant";[8] the Votyak "A hitched horse grows fat";[9] the Buryat "A gray sheep becomes pregnant as it turns";[10] and the Mongolian "The yellow dog is getting fat, shaking its tail."[11] The Mongolian "A gray bobbin is spinning around and around and jumping until it becomes fat"[12] admits too definite an allusion to the answer into the riddle.

§ 3. A bed. Bulgarian: Chacharov, 100 (I have a cow. At night it is pregnant, by day it is not). Turcoman: Samojlvich, 90 (It is not pregnant by day but is with calf at night.—Quilt).[13] Some versions do not indicate the kind of animal in the riddler's mind, as in "At night it is pregnant, in the daytime it is not pregnant."[14]

A related but fundamentally different conception is seen in a Cheremiss description of a bed as a scene from nature: "In the morning a mountain, in the evening a meadow."[15]

1455. Full by Day, Empty at Night

As a Renaissance riddler says,[1] the answer may be various articles of clothing, but the usual answer is "shoes." Riddlers may make the description of shoes more vivid by personification, but this English variation says nothing about full and empty.[2] Another way to add vividness consists in comparing shoes to dogs that are full of flesh.[3]

Characteristic applications of the contrast of "full by day and empty at night" occur in riddles for:

§ 1. A dress. Spanish, Argentinian: Lehmann-Nitsche, 8.

---

[6] Wichmann, *Zyrian*, 55, 190.
[7] Katanov in Radlov, IX, 287, No. 227. See also p. 239, No. 50.
[8] Samojlvich, 150.
[9] Buch, 21.
[10] Gombojew, 47; Kotvich, 97, 98 (colt).
[11] Kotvich, 205.
[12] Mostaert, 111. See a Vogul parallel in Ahlqvist, *Vogul*, 22.
[13] He cites parallels with the answer "boots."
[14] French: J. Roux, *Limousin*, 77. Bulgarian: Gubov, 302.
[15] Wichmann, *Cheremiss*, 132; Genetz, 9.

[1] No. 1455a.
[2] No. 992. But see the comparison in Nos. 991a through 991c.
[3] See the headnote to No. 453, § 2.

§ 2. A cap, a fez. Norwegian: Stafset, 2. Faeroic: Hammershaimb, *Antiquarisk tidsskrift*, III (1849–1851), 317, No. 24. Icelandic: Árnason, 387 (What is full upside down, but empty face downwards?). Lettish: Bielenstein, 816. Lappish: Donner, 6 (Turned up, empty; turned down, full). Albanian: Hahn, p. 159 (When you see it, it is empty; when you put it on, it is full). Arabic: Bauer, p. 222, No. 10 (A kettle, if you turn it upside down, it becomes full; if you set it right, it becomes empty); Löhr, p. 107, No. 12. Turkish: Hamizade, 179 (If I turn it down, it fills. If I turn it up, it empties.—Fez).

§ 3. A peg on which blankets hang. African, SeSuto: Norton and Velaphe, 9 (What is full by day and empty at night?).

§ 4. A mousetrap. Polish: Kopernicki, 11 (During the day it is closed, at night it is open and calls out, "*Ham!*"). Compare the headnote to No. 1456, n. 1, below.

§ 5. The belly. Italian: Pitrè, 571 (Full during the day, empty at night, and the more it erupts, the more it emits groans).

Riddlers occasionally make other contrasts of the forms of an object by day and by night. A corsetlace is a "snake" at night and a "ladder" by day.[4] The Filipinos say of a window, "At night a cloud, in the day open."[5] The "cloud" is a flapping white curtain. The Batak say of a pole in the floor of a house: "Upright during the day, flat at night,"[6] and probably expect the hearer to think of a man standing during the day and sleeping prone during the night.

1455a. What be they which be full all day, and empty at night?—It is a payre of shoes; for in the day they may be full of men's feete; but at night, when he goes to bed, they be empty, and it may be assoyled by any other part of man's raiment.
Meery Riddles (1629), No. 32 = Brandl, p. 13.

1455b. What's full in the daytime and empty at night?—Pair of boots.
Fauset, *Nova Scotia*, p. 169, No. 147.

1456. Empty by Day, Full at Night

This pattern, which is the converse of the preceding, is applicable to a bed and also to a mousetrap.[1]

1456. Empty in the day, / full at night.—Bed.
Fauset, *Nova Scotia*, p. 169, No. 146.

1457. Full, Yet Holds More

1457. What's full and holds more?—Pot full of potatoes when you pour water in.
Praeger, *Béaloideas*, IV (1933–1934), 145, No. 17.

---

[4] See the headnote to No. 1342, n. 2, above.
[5] Starr, *Philippines*, 176.
[6] Ophuijsen, p. 214, No. 45.
[1] See German: Hanika-Otto, 116, and the headnote to No. 1455, § 4, above.

1458. Ready, Unready

1458. Goes up unready [with difficulty], / Comes down ready.—Wall paper.
Fauset, *Southern Negro*, p. 288, No. 140.

1459–1475. Form and Function

A few riddles describe an object insufficiently by an adjective indicating its form and then complete the description by suggesting its characteristic activity. The riddler may connect the shape and the activity of the object, but in the poorer examples of this pattern he fails to do so. A Bahaman tongue riddle, "Something roun', it rolls all day, an' it stop at night,"[1] is in good enigmatic style, for it suggests a ball and at the same time introduces the contradiction that the object described stops rolling at night. The Renaissance "Round I am, yet cannot rest, when I am spited of the best,"[2] may suggest a ball by the adjective "round," but the remainder does not sketch a picture or set up an adequate and intelligible contradiction. The scanty description of a valuable coin in "Something small, but worth a lot"[3] employs good enigmatic technique, but gives too few details for anyone to guess the answer. When the riddler does not clearly conceive his object, he goes awry. The bathtub riddle, "Round and deep and good to keep, because you use it once a week,"[4] wavers in its fundamental conception and draws no picture to interpret.

1459–1463. Holes Hold Water

Long ago Symphosius used this contradiction in describing a sponge: "I myself am not heavy, but weight of water clings to me. All my inward parts well out in caverns opened wide. The liquid lurks within, but of its own accord does not pour forth."[1] Modern Greek riddles on the same theme are conceived in a like but simpler form: "Thousand-rooted, thousand-holed, it takes water to Constantinople"[2] and "A thousand-holed ship brings water to town."[3] A riddle for a rag[4] employs the same contradiction and appears to be an adaptation of the sponge riddle. Apparently first used of sponges, the contradiction is applied, in countries where they are rare or little known, to other objects. It is once used of a spring.[5] It is used in a very confusing way in the Icelandic "This container with eighteen holes could not hold a drop, yet milk is carried in it.—A box of slats for carrying hay."[6] The hay carried in the box is converted into milk and consequently the box can be said to carry milk. Other objects described in this manner are:

§ 1. A pothook. See No. 1461.

[1] No. 1469. [2] No. 1468.
[3] No. 1472. [4] No. 1470.
[1] Ohl, 63. [2] Sakellarios, p. 290, No. 10.
[3] Sakellarios, p. 291, No. 18. [4] No. 1463.
[5] No. 1460. [6] Árnason, 40.

§ 2. A straw roof. German: Hanika-Otto, 112 (Hole beside hole, and yet it holds water). The reference is to the open ends of the straws.

1459. What is full of holes and holds water?—A sponge.
Oral, New Hampshire.

1460. What is it that holds water and yet is full of holes?—A spring.
Gardner, *Schoharie Hills, N.Y.*, p. 257, No. 32.

1461. Full of holes and holds water.—The reeken-hook, i.e., the pot-hook which hangs in the reekin', or chimney, with holes to regulate the height of the pot from the fire.
Gutch and Peacock, *Lincolnshire*, p. 398, No. 14; Alice B. Gomme, "Folk-Lore Scraps from Several Localities," *Folk-Lore*, XX (1909), 73 (Durham).

1462. Here's a thing—no bottom or top— / Holds gallons of water, never leaks a drop.—A brandis (a three-cornered rest for holding a kettle on the fire).
Cornish Notes and Queries, I (1906), 273.

1463. Somepin' hol' water an' water don't hold it.—Rag.
Fauset, *Southern Negro*, p. 283, No. 81.

1464–1466. Long

1464–1466. Long and Tickles (Scares)

Riddlers rarely describe an object as merely long. The following modifications of a single original conception which involves the suggesting of an object quite different from the answer seem not to have been fully understood by the askers of the riddles. They have introduced incongruous elements in the riddles for a comb and a snake.[1] A few riddles turn on the comparison of an object to a long or tall person.[2] Riddles which name several things as the means of comparison often refer to colors[3] but rarely to length.[4]

1464a. Long, slim, and slender, / Tickles where it's tender; / Tickles where the hair grows, / Long, slim, and slender.—A whip, applied to the back of a horse.
Hyatt, *Adams Co., Ill.*, p. 671, No. 10945.

1464b. Long, slim, and slender, / Tickles where 'tis tender.—A horsewhip.
Greenleaf, *Newfoundland*, p. 12, No. 36.

1464c. Long nose, you may suppose, / Tickles where the hair grows.—A horsewhip.
Greenleaf, *Newfoundland*, p. 12, No. 36 var.

1465. Long, slim, and slender, / Tickles where it's tender; / Two heads and nary nose, / Tickles where the hair grows.—Comb.
Brewster, *Indiana*, 26.

1466. Long, slim, and slender, / Dark as homemade thunder, / Keen eyes and peaked nose, / Scares the devil wherever he goes.—Snake.
Brewster, *Indiana*, 15.

---

[1] See Nos. 1465, 1466.
[2] See the headnote to No. 575.
[3] See, for examples, Nos. 1384 through 1391.
[4] See Nos. 1266a through 1267.

1467. Wider

1467. A very big long t'ing, de wider de hole de better to go in.—Stocking.
Parsons, *Antilles*, III, 437, St. Martin, 33.

1468–1471. Round

1468. Round I am, yet cannot rest, / when I am spited of the best.—A tennis ball, when two good players play together.
Prettie Riddles (1631), No. 36 = Brandl, p. 57. when j am mounted of the best: Tupper, *Holme Riddles*, 98.

1469. Something roun'. / It rolls all day, / An' it stop at night.—Tongue.
Parsons, *Andros Island, Bahamas*, p. 276, No. 14.

1470. Round and deep and good to keep, / Because you use it once a week.—Bathtub.
Hyatt, *Adams Co., Ill.*, p. 657, No. 10832.

1471. Round; It Reaches the Sky

The English comparison of the eye to a ball, which differs from an ordinary ball in being able to reach the sky, is rather poorly conceived. The underlying idea is widely known and is often better phrased. The object is said to be thrown, and the scene is more adequately suggested to suit a ball. The Turks say, "A tiny bit of ivory sweeps over mountain and boulder";[1] the Turcomans, "I have a particolored stone. Wherever I throw it, it reaches the mark"[2]; the Yakut, "A chamois button reaches toward the sky."[3] Similar notions are found in African riddling, in which a reference to a river often appears. See the Swahili "My two betel nuts have gone over the river";[4] the Wanamwezi "I strike the wooden ball, and it falls in Msalala";[5] the SeSuto "Two little stones far cast";[6] and the Ila "Something I threw over to the other side of the river."[7]

The idea of a projectile is expressed with unusual fullness and interesting complications in the Swahili "My arrow, which I throw in the evening, does not reach far. In the daytime, it makes the journey of a year."[8] This we might set beside the Albanian "Two arrows with black wings reach wherever they wish."[9]

Ideas of this sort are found almost everywhere. The Letts say, "One throws it far, it falls down near by";[10] the Russians, "It is round, it is small, but when you throw it, you can reach the sky";[11] the French, "A thing no longer than a nut makes a tour of the mountains";[12] and the Filipinos, "The round objects, which are projectiles, reach far."[13]

[1] Kowalski, *Asia Minor*, 3.
[2] Samojlvich, 1.
[3] Piekarski, 188.
[4] Velten, 21.
[5] Dahl, 85.
[6] Norton and Velaphe, 5.
[7] Smith and Dale, II, 330, No. 47.
[8] Velten, 23.
[9] Hahn, p. 162, No. 61.
[10] Bielenstein, 73.
[11] Sadovnikov, 1781.
[12] V. S. *Mélusine*, I (1878), col. 263, No. 66.
[13] De los Reyes y Florentino, p. 276.

A comparison to a long object that reaches far is found occasionally and may, in some instances, be an adaptation of a riddle for smoke.[14] See the Bulgarian "I have two poles reaching as far as the sky";[15] and the Votyak "A long pole that reaches to the sky."[16] Another variety of this conception is seen in the Zyrian "It reaches the city; it does not reach around the head" and "A long, long rope stretches around the field, around the water; it does not reach around the head"[17] or the Mordvin "I have reins which reach around the earth but not around me."[18]

The comparison of the eye to something small is often contrasted with the assertion that it contains, holds, or fills the whole world. Examples are the Armenian "It contains both heaven and earth,"[19] which a Georgian riddler enlarges upon in "I put it together, [it was] as large as a piece of money; I opened it, [it was] as large as the world"[20] and the Mongolian "If you take it in your hand, it fills it; if you release it, it fills the whole world."[21] The Dschagga "A little mirror that sees all the world,"[22] with the alternative answer "star," is similarly conceived, but is probably independent in origin.

The Indonesian parallels are noteworthy for their reference to the simile of a mat that is rolled up and unrolled. See the Menangkerbau Malay "Rolled up, [it is as large as a nail]; opened, [it is as large as] half the world";[23] and the Serawaj "If it is spread out, then it is as large [or broad] as the world; if it is rolled up, then it is as broad as a nail."[24] Such conceptions are probably not related to the Serbian "I stretched linen from the sea to the Danube, and I rolled it up in a walnut shell"[25] or "I stretched a golden wire across the whole world, and I rolled it up in a walnut shell."[26] These latter ideas are probably connected with the comparison of a road to a turban, rope, or belt that is rolled up.[27]

The comparison of seeing or looking to sowing a field is rare. See the Lettish "With two beans one sows all the field"[28] or "With two measures one sows the whole world."[29]

In many countries riddlers have compared the eyes to birds that have the ability to fly far afield or have other pertinent characteristics. See the Rumanian "Two doves, in whatever direction I may throw them, they go thither";[30]

---

[14] See also the comparison to a man who reaches to the skies, in the headnote to No. 575, § 2, above.
[15] Palashev, 4.
[16] Buch, 29.
[17] Wichmann, *Zyrian*, 93, 132.
[18] Ahlqvist, p. 41, No. 4.
[19] Zelinski, p. 58, No. 25.
[20] Glushakov, p. 24, No. 10 = Blechsteiner, p. 13, No. 13.
[21] Bazarov, 8; Klukine, 13; Mostaert, 2. Tungus: Poppe, 22.
[22] Raum, p. 306, No. 17.
[23] Harmsen, p. 280, No. 52.
[24] Helfrich, *Serawaj*, p. 44, No. 4.
[25] Novaković, p. 158, No. 8.
[26] Novaković, p. 158, No. 9. See also p. 159, Nos. 1, 2.
[27] See the headnote to No. 575, nn. 13-26, above.
[28] Bielenstein, 74.
[29] Bielenstein, 75.
[30] Papahagi, 69, var. 2.

the Serbian "Two wingless doves peep out from a cave, they fly everywhere and yet they sit in the cave";[31] the Bavenda "Birds fly far away, leaving tail feathers behind,"[32] in which the feathers represent the eyelashes or eyebrows; the Kxatla "Tell me: birds which graze on a place that is not near";[33] the Persian "There are a couple of black-white doves who are tied up separately. In their flights they reach the skies, but nevertheless they never come out of their nests";[34] and the Serawaj "A bird which flies to the mountain and yet remains on its perch."[35]

Comparisons to animals other than birds are rare, but see the Arabic "Two little horses which make a day's journey without stopping";[36] and the Wanamwezi "I graze father's cattle at a distance."[37] Comparisons of this sort, that is, comparisons to a thing, are very unusual.[38]

Comparisons representing the eyes as persons are very abundant. As the following examples show, they probably reflect several quite independent inventions. See the Bulgarian "As small as nuts, they are seated low but see as high as Heaven";[39] the Polish "Very tiny, very black, it runs around the world,"[40] with the parallel "Very tiny, very gray, in the name of the Father and the Son, it can circle the entire earth";[41] the Abyssinian "Without leaving its place, it reaches to a far country";[42] the Kamba "I went to Yata just now and I returned";[43] the Tschuana "I have boys; if I send them far away, they return in a short time";[44] the Kxatla "Tell me: two young men sitting on one stool, who, when the river is full, pass over it and quickly return,"[45] to which the collector cites a Xhosa parallel, "Guess my two young fellows that cross the river, however huge it may be"; the Suk "I am so swift that no one can catch me";[46] the Shilluk "It is on this side and on the other side";[47] the Persian "It travels to the sky ahead of the eye, but no one has ever seen it.—Sight";[48] the Kolarian "Now he is going away far off, now he has returned";[49] and the Tibetan "Someone walks out the door, and he is at once at the top of the heavens and he neither flew nor ran."[50]

1471. From five feet high, / Up to the Sky, / It reaches, tho' 'tis round; / Now try your Wits, / If fancy hits, / This Riddle you'll expound.—The sight of a Man's Eye.
A New Riddle Book; Or, A Whetstone for Dull Wits, p. 13.

---

[31] Novaković, p. 158, No. 6.
[32] Stayt, p. 360, No. 10.
[33] Schapera, 76.
[34] Kuka, 17.
[35] Helfrich, *Serawaj*, p. 59, No. 60.
[36] Stumme, *Tázerwalt*, 14.
[37] Dahl, 30.
[38] Indonesian, Tabaru: Fortgens, 32.
[39] Stoilov, p. 58, §12.
[40] Siarkowski, 25.
[41] Gustawicz, 276. See also his No. 277.
[42] Mittwoch, 2.
[43] Lindblom, 23.
[44] Kuhn, *Tschuana*, 29.
[45] Schapera, 75.
[46] Beech, 14.
[47] Westermann, p. 242.
[48] Phillott, 18.
[49] Wagner, 85.
[50] Tafel, p. 492.

1472–1473. Small

1472. Something small, but worth a lot.—Sovereign.
Parsons, *Bermuda*, p. 263, No. 142.

1473. Small and Fills the House

In many countries the description of a small object that nevertheless fills a house or room refers to the light of a candle or lamp. The small object is often called a grain of wheat or a flaxseed, and less often, an animal. An Indian riddler carries out the metaphor by equating the rays of light to chaff: "From a single ear the whole house is filled with chaff."[1] An example of a comparison involving mention of a person is the Breton "A child smaller than a sheep, it fills all the house."[2] I have noted no parallel to the Portuguese "Little chases out Big.—Lamp and darkness."[3]

Swiss riddlers adapt the idea to describe a snail: "There is something as small as a mouse, and it fills the whole house";[4] and a Turkish riddler gives the answer "whitewash" to the usual riddle for light: "Five kopeks' worth of sal ammoniac illuminates the interior of a house."[5]

1473. What is that which 20 will goe into a tankard, and one will fill a barne? —It is 20 candles not lighted and one lighted.
Meery Riddles (1629), No. 39 = Brandl, p. 15.

1474–1475. Miscellaneous

1474. Now thin and plain, / Now rich and sweet, / But nearly always good to eat.—Cake.
Parsons, *Bermuda*, p. 262, No. 127.

1475. Guess a riddle now you must, / Stone is fire, and fire is dust. / Black is red, and red is white; / Come and view the wondrous sight.—Coal.
Janice M. Neal, *New York Folklore Quarterly*, I (1945), 216.

1476–1495. Several Members Described in Terms of Form and (or) Function

1476–1494. Four Hang; Two Point the Way

Riddlers have almost universally applied this widely used pattern, which can be readily adapted to many animals or things, to a cow. We can probably infer that a cow was the original answer. The adaptations are occasionally awkward; see the German chaffcutter riddle, "Four hangers, ten reachers, it fetches a *Jappup* [onomatopoetic], it eats up everything."[1] In describing the male and female ass the Algerian Arabs have done better: "Four make a noise and two

---
[1] Bhil: Hedberg, p. 885, No. 126.   [2] Sébillot, *Devinettes*, 54.
[3] Parsons, *Cape Verde*, 129.
[4] Zahler, *Münchenbuchsee*, 343. For the rhyme "house: mouse" see the headnote to Nos. 1263–1265, n. 3, above.
[5] Moshkov in Radlov, X, 269, No. 64.
[1] Carstens, *Schleswig-Holstein*, p. 419.

protect it, one chases flies, and one serves for singing"[2] and "Four things make a noise [feet], two shake in the air [ears], a stick chases flies in front of the shop [udder]."[3] The Abyssinian "One that stamps, wags its tail, whose horn points at heaven, whose tail drags on the ground.—Cow"[4] shows that the riddler has failed to grasp the meaning and structure of the enumeration. It is intelligible in the light of parallels cited in the note to Nos. 1476a through 1489 below.

An essential element in the conception seems to be the contrast of pointing up and pointing down. This is turned in an apparently unique manner in the Mongolian "Turned downward, four *bandi*;[5] turned upward, one *bandi*; from the side, one *bandi* comes and sportively fills one *bandi* and carries him off. If you look at it, it is the white juice of grass.—Milking a cow; the udder, the milk bucket, the milking woman."[6] For discussion and collections of parallels see Andreas Heusler, *Zeitschrift des Vereins für Volkskunde*, XI (1901), 129–130; Petsch, *Neue Beiträge*, pp. 79, 105; Feilberg, *Ordbog*, II, 240–241, s.v. "ko"; Aarne, *Rätselforschungen*, II, 60–172.

Although Aarne[7] made a very exhaustive study of this pattern and Szendrey[8] added a considerable number of Hungarian parallels, there still remains some confusion about the fundamental conception. The characteristic features of this pattern are the naming of the members of an animal and the referring to their numbers. The members are described in terms of their functions, and the functions may be identified—and often are identified—by periphrases that are intentionally confusing. Such riddles should be separated from those describing an animal in terms of its front, middle, and back[9] or its top, middle, and bottom.[10] These three varieties are usually, but not always, carefully separated. Aarne and Szendrey failed in some instances to recognize these three varieties. The description of an animal in terms of the numbers of its members and their functions should also be kept apart from the descriptions which assemble a heterogeneous collection of elements and confuse the hearer by the obvious impossibility of uniting them in one conception.[11]

The subjects for which riddlers use this pattern are various, but are characteristically animals. In adapting it to certain creatures, some typical peculiarities arise: the riddles mentioning a man and an animal (§§ 3–4 below) usually include mention of sexual organs; those mentioning a dog (§ 10 below) often refer' to the dog making a bed for itself, and so on. By comparison of these variations, Aarne endeavors to arrive at the original form of the pattern and

---

[2] Giacobetti, 154.   [3] Giacobetti, 153.
[4] Littmann, *Tigriña*, 9.
[5] A *bandi*, who is a novice or a lama's disciple, is a conventional figure in Mongolian folklore.
[6] Mostaert, 59.   [7] *Rätselforschungen*, II, 60–172.
[8] *Ethnographia*, XXXII (1921), 74–78. See also Schultz, *Bemerkungen*, pp. 359–361.
[9] See the headnote to Nos. 1430–1435 above and also the headnote to No. 1435.
[10] See the headnote to Nos. 1436–1447.   [11] See the headnote to Nos. 1405–1408.

to identify the secondary forms invented in imitation of it. Inasmuch as he examined only a part of the available versions of the several types, I am not certain of his results.

Inasmuch as the wit of the pattern turns on the inventing of strange, yet not wholly incomprehensible, terms for the ears, horns, eyes, feet, or other members of the creature that the riddler is describing, translations are difficult to make and must be comparatively uninformative. Consequently, I shall give only a few translations of the parallels.

In a somewhat similar pattern the actors appear in pairs and usually do not have confusing and novel names. The answers are usually cosmological. Some examples are cited below.[12] The relation of such riddles to those chiefly discussed in this headnote is obscure.

Since almost any object can be described by inventions of this sort, some riddles seem to be casual and whimsical products. A Swiss riddle for snuffers, "Two little rings, two little poles, a box on the wall, a spit"[13] may serve as an example.

Characteristic themes are:

§ 1. A cow. See Nos. 1476a through 1489.

§ 2. A horse, a donkey. See No. 1490.

§ 3. A horse (an ox) and a wagon. Flemish: *Ons Volksleven*, I (1889), 78, No. 42. German: Frischbier, *Menschenwelt*, p. 256, Nos. 159, 160; Böckel, 34. Swiss: Zahler, *Münchenbuchsee*, 217; J. Müller, *Innerschweiz*, 9. Danish: Feilberg, *Ordbog*, III, 1078–1079, s.v. "vogn." Swedish: Dybeck, *Runa*, 1849, p. 47, No. 10 = Russwurm, 27; Dybeck, *Runa*, 1849, p. 47, No. 1, and p. 50, No. 34; Ericsson, *Södermanland*, II (1881), 94, No. 81; III (1882), 100, Nos. 143, 144; and V (1884), 66, No. 217; Hyltén-Cavallius, *Värend*, 72; Sandén, *Norra Vadsbo*, 126, 128; Ström, p. 144, "Vagnen," 2, and p. 381, "Sysselsättningar," 44, 45. Lithuanian: Jurgelionis, 672 (Two piercers, two pushers, six eyes, three ———.—Riding in a two-wheeled carriage), which contains elements, especially the six eyes, found also in the riddles discussed in the headnote to Nos. 48–55 above (the missing word may be one of those implied in No. 52 above). See also Jurgelionis, 749 (Eight feet, two heads, two ———, and one sways in the center), which contains a reference to the wagon tongue in the last element. Russian: Sadovnikov, 961 (Four knockers, four rattlers, also a *kokterok*, also a dangler.—Cart). The *kokterok* represents the pole of the wagon, but several helpers cannot suggest what further implications the word may contain. Hungarian: Arany and Gyulai, II, 357, No. 45, and 358, No. 48.

For discussion and additional parallels see Aarne, *Rätselforschungen*, II, 149–167.

---

[12] See § 14 below and compare some texts cited in the headnote to Nos. 138–140, nn. 44–47, above.

[13] Rochholz, 477. See another reference in § 27 below.

§ 4. A horse (an ox) and a plowman; a woman milking a cow. Irish: Delargy, 45 (Four legs on the ground, two legs on the ground, a head against a hindquarters, and a hindquarters on the ground.—Woman milking a cow). This is closely related to the riddles discussed in the headnote to Nos. 976–979 above. Swedish: Ström, p. 371, "Människan och djur," 3. Spanish, Porto Rican: Mason, 562. Italian: Ferraro, *Canti popolari in dialetto logodurese*, p. 326, No. 78. Lithuanian: Jurgelionis, 561 (Two poke, two pull, six eyes, three ———), 562 (Two stabbers, two European buffaloes, six eyes, three ———). These have some elements in common with No. 52 above. See also Schleicher, p. 205 (Two draggers drag, two hawks hook in, the snorter follows after). For discussion see Aarne, *Rätselforschungen*, II, 168.

§ 5. A man. Swedish: Ericsson, *Södermanland*, IV (1883), 72, No. 189 (Two walking, two dangling, one smiling, two sneezing, two peeping, two sheltering, and the king's beasts occasionally walk on the top). Portuguese: Pires de Lima, 51 (There are two goers, two tourists [eyes], ten pickers up, twenty-eight millers, and one mill). The last elements in both riddles are usually found in the texts discussed in the headnote to Nos. 1100–1108, above.

§ 6. A camel. Modern Greek: Sakellarios, p. 295, No. 12 (Two pliable pancakes, stuck into the ground; two pieces of glass; two cup-shaped things; and a crooked bow). The pancakes are the hoofs and should be four in number. Turkish: Hamizade, 145 (Four soft round things, one covering, and three round bony things); Katanov in Radlov, IX, 158, No. 1315 (There are four things that make *Tuk, tuk!* and there are three things that stick up). Buryat: Bazarov, 194 (Five Russians sow, two Russians stand watch, one Russian drives off flies). This conception shows some resemblances to a riddle for writing cited in the headnote to No. 1063 (n. 2), above. Mongolian: Mostaert, 5 (Four high and slow, high and slow; five younger sisters; two wobbling right and left; you poor one alone.—A camel's four legs, head and legs, humps, and tail). This is perhaps somewhat disordered. For other examples and discussion see Aarne, *Rätselforschungen*, II, 147–148.

§ 7. A ram, a sheep, a lamb. The earliest version that I have noted is Claret's

> Bis duo dant strepitum, tremet unus, agunt duo saltum:
> Agnus habendo pedes, caudem quoque cornua solves.[14]

See further, Danish: Kristensen, p. 34, § 77, No. 98 (Four runners, two lookers, and a woolen tail), and p. 147, § 435, No. 688 (Two show, they say, and two are warding off, and two [are] on each side, and one hangs behind.—Ram). Swedish: Ström, p. 97, "Fåret, lammet," 2, 4. French: V. S., *Mélusine*, I (1878), col. 262, No. 87. For discussion see Aarne, *Rätselforschungen*, II, 147.

§ 8. A goat. French: E. Rolland, *Faune populaire*, V (Paris, 1882), 213; J. Roux, *Limousin*, 41; Constantin, *Savoie*, p. 24. Finnish: Aarne, *Rätselfor-*

---

[14] P. 71, No. 61.

schungen, II, 147. Modern Greek: Stathes, p. 347, No. 91 (Four standing on the ground, two candles of the sky, head and tail together.—Goat being milked); Sakellarios, p. 292, No. 9 (There are four columns standing and two glassy [things] and two cuplike [things] and the sack in front and soft hands.—Ewe being milked), and No. 13 (Four sunk in the earth and two in heaven, the soft ones in your hands and the sack in front.—Ewe being milked). For discussion see Aarne, *Rätselforschungen*, II, 147.

§ 9. A cat. German: Frischbier, *Thierwelt*, p. 347, No. 25. Danish: Kristensen, pp. 64–65, § 155, Nos. 229a through 229p; Feilberg, *Ordbog*, II, 109, s.v. "kat." Norwegian: Brox, *Ytre Senja*, 27. Icelandic: Árnason, 517 (What is with two twinkling stars behind two flaps? Five camels hang down near by, and the entrance is hedged with spikes. Let him who cannot guess this riddle enter the hill). "Entering a hill" is entering the grave-mound and is synonymous with dying. The conception is somewhat confused. Swedish: Ericsson, *Södermanland*, I (1879), 87, No. 34: Wigström, p. 290, No. 30; Sandén, *Norra Vadsbo*, 129; Waltman, *Lidmål*, 191; Ström, p. 99, "Katten," 1a, and p. 101, No. 6. Italian: Corsi, *Archivio*, X (1891), 401, No. 40. Russian: Sadovnikov, 911 (Four fours, two spreading ones, one wagger, and two semiprecious stones), 911a through 911d. Turkish: Zavarin, *Brusa*, 23 (Two hearers, two lookers, four knockers, one twister). For additional references and discussion see Aarne, *Rätselforschungen*, II, 125–131.

§ 10. A dog. The earliest example that I have noted is Claret's

> Illucent bini lectum sternendo quarterni:
> Quatuor in pedibus canis est, duplex fit ocellus.[15]

See further, Breton: Sauvé, 33. German: Wossidlo, 426. Swedish: Ericsson, *Södermanland*, IV (1883), 71, No. 182; Ström, p. 97, "Hunden," 1, 2. Lettish: Bielenstein, 623 through 625. Russian: Sadovnikov, 901 (Four fours, two spreading ones, the seventh is a wagger, he himself is a grumbler), which is akin to the Russian riddle for a cat quoted in the previous paragraph. See also Sadovnikov, 902 (Four make the bed, two hold the light, one is lying down, won't let in anyone). The last remark may refer to the dog curled in a circle. Serbian: Novaković, p. 161, No. 12 (Two shine, four spread, and only one is thinking of lying down). Bulgarian: Gubov, 177 (Four legs, four eyes and ears, and the tail is the ninth). Yakut: Piekarski, 112 (Four people are preparing a sleeping bench, two people are listening to the bustle, two people are holding the pine torch, one person is sweeping the house, so they say), 113 (They say that one person is holding a pine torch, one prepares a sleeping bench, one sweeps the house), 114 (They say that two people held a pine torch while four people were making the bed. The master came and shaping himself into a ball, he fell down). Indonesian, Malay: Beauregard, *Proverbes*

---

[15] P. 70, No. 33.

et dictons, p. 724 (Where does one see four who act as supports and one who winnows?). American Indian, Quechua: Quijada Jara, 10. For additional references and discussion see Aarne, *Rätselforschungen*, II, 131–135; Flajšhans, pp. 30–31, § 28c. The Turkish "Two bits of rotten wood, four things set out, one thing is deaf. Two ears, four legs, and a tail of a dog" (Katanov in Radlov, IX, 467, No. 537) contains the characteristic form of description, but the details differ from those of any other version that has come to my attention.

§ 11. A pig. Breton: Lavenot, *Basse-Bretagne*, p. 666 (Two small needles, four runners, a reamer at the very bottom); Sébillot, *Devinettes*, 12. Swedish: Dybeck, *Runa*, 1848, p. 45, No. 45 = Russwurm, 61. Rumanian: Gorovei, 1483. Serbian: Novaković, p. 174, No. 8 (Four spread, two shine, and only one lies down). Hungarian: Arany and Gyulai, II, 367, No. 90 (One plows, four hold it, two look at it, two listen to it, one drives it. What is it?). This contains elements suggested by a riddle for writing; see the headnote to No. 1063, n. 2, above. See further *Magyar Nyelvör*, VI (1877), 270 (One plows, four hold, two look on, two listen, seven govern), XIV (1885), 274, No. 5. Szendrey, *Ethnographia*, XXXII (1921), 76, cites "One grubs, two lead, two listen, one drives" from a manuscript collection from Szalonta. Modern Greek: Polites, *Neohellenika Analekta*, I, 250, No. 328 (One in front sings, four behind hold him, and one comes along backward.—Hog; face, feet, tail); Stathes, p. 351, No. 117.

For discussion see Aarne, *Rätselforschungen*, II, 145–146. See also a Breton riddle for carrying a pig (Sébillot, *Devinettes*, 14).

§ 12. A rabbit. Breton: Sébillot, *Haute-Bretagne*, 42; Sébillot, *Devinettes*, 15; Sauvé, 32 (Four flic-flac and a little shred of tail); Duine, *Saint-Malo*, p. 515; Kerbeuzec, *Ille-et-Vilaine*, p. 509, No. 93; Orain, *Ille-et-Vilaine*, p. 155. French: E. Rolland, *Faune populaire*, VII (Paris, 1906), 217; Patry, *Normandie*, p. 643.

For discussion see Aarne, *Rätselforschungen*, II, 143.

§ 13. A baby in a cradle. Danish: Kristensen, p. 47, § 434, No. 786a (Two down-stumps, and four up-standers, a hush-hush, and a crier-out). For discussion see Aarne, *Rätselforschungen*, II, 170–171.

A use of pairs is conspicuous in the following:

§ 14. The sun and the moon. Other cosmological themes are often included. See also the headnote to Nos. 138–140, nn. 44–47, above. Examples are German: C. Walther, "Zwei Rätsel aus dem 15. Jahrhundert," *Mitteilungen des Vereins für lübeckische Geschichte*, IX (1899–1900), 127–128, and Archer Taylor, "Zwei niederdeutsche Rätsel," *Archiv für Literatur und Volksdichtung*, I (1949), 269. Swiss: Rochholz, 422 (Two walk, two stand, two we must have, two come anyway.—Sun and moon; heaven and earth; wood and water; day and night). Swedish: Ström, p. 208, "Sol, måne, dag och natt" (Two walk well, two stand well, two come well, two do no man any good.—Sun, moon; day, night; grass, leaves; hunger, thirst). Italian: Schneller, *Wälschtirol*, p.

256, No. 29 (Two wanderers, two who stand well, and a cardinal.—Sun and moon; heaven and earth; and the sea), in which the appositeness of the last is not clear. Russian: Sadovnikov, 1896 (Two standing, two lying, and two troublemakers, and two robbers who lay waste.—Sky, earth; sun, moon; day, night; fire, water), 1897 (Two that stand, two that walk, two that pass.— Sky, earth; sun, moon; day, night), 1897a (Two stand, two walk, two between themselves watch the hours.—Sky, earth; sun, moon; day, night). Modern Greek: Stathes, p. 346, No. 88 (Two well-fixed, two walking together, two that don't match, two that don't become empty.—Sun, moon). Although the riddler seems to conceive all these statements as applying to the sun and moon, the parallels do not support his interpretation.

§ 15. A woman kneading bread. Lithuanian: Jurgelionis, 544, 545 (Two look, two poke, two cannot reach it), 546 (Two poke, two wave, and a woman froths).

§ 16. Men threshing grain. Rumanian: Gorovei, 966 (Two stand, two give [strike], two look at each other, two bow to each other).

§ 17. Spear-grass. Lithuanian: Jurgelionis, 1076 (Two fly, two stand, two stay in place).

§ 18. An acorn. Swedish: Dybeck, *Runa*, 1847, p. 40, No. 6 (Two troughs, two contents of the trough, a spit, a bundle, and a nightcap); Ericsson, *Södermanland*, III (1882), 102, No. 154 (. . . and a priest's cap). Both the translation and the interpretation of this riddle are somewhat uncertain. The "troughs" are the two halves of the shell, the nut within is in two halves, the spit is the twig on which it hangs, and the nightcap is the crown or cup of the acorn. The "bundle," which occurs again in "en pik å en pak å en prästmossa [a spit and a bundle and a priest's cap]," is appropriate to this context (Ström, p. 124, "Eken," 2). In combining the two versions, the riddler has forgotten that the "bundle" is the same as the "two contents of the trough."

§ 19. A bed. See No. 1491.

§ 20. A mill. See No. 1492.

§ 21. A pot. See No. 1493. Also, compare § 24 below.

§ 22. A pipe. See No. 1494.

§ 23. A mangle. German: Frischbier, *Menschenwelt*, p. 250, No. 83 (Push this way, push that way, two stand in front, two lie below. What marvel is that?).

§ 24. A barrel. Swedish: Dybeck, *Runa*, 1865–1873, pp. 29–30, No. 7. Compare the Zyrian washbasin riddle, "Two ears, four feet, four girdles" (Wichmann, *Zyrian*, 15, 107). The ears are the two longer staves used as handles.

§ 25. A yoke. Russian: Sadovnikov, 988 (Two wooden ones, two crooked ones, eight turned holes, the ninth is chiseled).

§ 26. A door. Lettish: Bielenstein, 150 (Two stand; two lie; the third, a fox, dances). Russian: Arkhangel'skii, p. 77 (Two lie, two stand, a fifth walks, a sixth leads the way); Preobrazhenskii, p. 172; Sadovnikov, 74 (. . . and a seventh sings). Finnish: Lönnrot, 351 = Henssen, 201 (Two lie, two stand, one goes back and forth). Mordvin: Paasonen, 73. Compare the headnote to Nos. 1003–1004, nn. 23–28, and a Polish stove riddle (Gustawicz, 306).

§ 27. Snuffers. German: E. Meier, *Kinderreime*, p. 84, No. 340. Swiss: Rochholz, 477 (quoted above, n. 13).

§ 28. Scissors. Mordvin: Paasonen, 78 (Two rings, two ends [probably we should read "edges"], in the middle of them is a nail), 83.

§ 29. A churchyard. Swedish: Ström, p. 183, "Kyrkan och hennes omgivningar," 1 (Four fences, two stiles, a barn, a haypile and sandpit, the dead are more numerous than the living).

1476. Two Hookers, Two Lookers, and a Switchabout

The minor variations, which appear to be of little significance, make it difficult to subdivide the versions into groups of any sort. Those beginning with "two" and usually ending with a "switchabout" seem to form a somewhat coherent class of versions which are current south of the Ohio River. There is a single Nova Scotian example (No. 1476*d*).

1476a. Two hookers, two lookers, / And a switch-about.—A cow.
Knortz, p. 235, No. 123.

1476b. Two lookers, two hookers, / Four down-standers, one switch-about. —Cow.
Randolph and Spradley, *Ozark*, p. 87. Four standers: Bacon and Parsons, *Virginia*, p. 319, No. 59. Four stiff standers: Fauset, *Southern Negro*, p. 277, No. 14. One switcher: Parsons, *Sea Islands*, S.C., p. 154, No. 15. Four hang-downs: Redfield, *Tennessee*, p. 37, No. 19.

1476c. Two lookers, / Two hookers, / Four downhangers, / Four stiffstanders, / A switchabout, / And a lollout.—A cow.
Redfield, *Tennessee*, p. 36, No. 18.

1476d. Two lookers, / Two hookers, / Four hangers, / One switcher.—Milch cow.
Fauset, *Nova Scotia*, p. 155, No. 58 var.

1476e. Two lookers, two crookers, four down-hangers, and a switch about.— A horny cow.
Farr, *Tennessee*, p. 322, No. 53.

1476f. What got two look about, one lick-about, fo' run-about, two stiff-stander?—Cow.
Johnson, *St. Helena Island*, S.C., p. 158, No. 27.

1476g. Two lookers, two crookers, two fly-flappers, / Four walkers, four hang-downers, and a switchabout.—Cow.
Brewster, *Indiana*, 72*b*.

1477. Four Stand, One Switchabout

Although the riddlers do not always agree on the meaning of the four objects introducing this version, it seems probable that these texts constitute a type of the riddle. The fundamental conception is a contrast of the four legs that stand and the four teats that hang. This is enlarged by similar contrasts. Although versions are reported from North Carolina and Tennessee, most versions are found farther north, in Indiana, Illinois, New Hampshire, Nova Scotia, and Newfoundland. The English and Irish parallels are too scanty to support any conjectures regarding the relations of the types. The versions beginning with four objects represent, except for the variety discussed in the headnote to No. 1478, the usual form of the riddle in the British Isles. Some riddlers have extended the use of the number four through the entire riddle, as in the Breton "Four go, four come, four beat the backside."[1] Riddle No. 1477k below, which lacks the four down-hangers, seems to be a defective version of Nos. 1477a through 1477j.

1477a. Four standin', / Four hang downward, / One twis' about. / An' two look about.—Cow.
   Parsons, *Guilford Co., N.C.*, p. 201, No. 7.

1477b. Four long, stiff standers, four long hang downers, / Two crook, / Two look, / And one switch.—A cow.
   Redfield, *Tennessee*, p. 37, No. 20.

1477c. Four stiff stiff standers, / Four down hangers, / Two hookers, / Two lookers, / And a switch about.—Cow.
   Fauset, *Nova Scotia*, p. 155, No. 58; Hyatt, *Adams Co., Ill.*, p. 659, No. 10852. Four down standers: Fauset, *Nova Scotia*, p. 155, No. 58 var.

1477d. Four stiff standards, / Four down-hangers, / Two look-abouts, / Two hook-abouts, / One switch-about.—Cow.
   Chappell, p. 232, No. 18.

1477e. Four standers, / One lasher, / Two hunters, / Two lookers.—Cow.
   Parsons, *Barbados*, p. 284, No. 48.

1477f. Four step-standers, / Four down-hangers, / Two lookers, / Two crookers, / And one swing-em-out.—A cow.
   Greenleaf, *Newfoundland*, p. 12, No. 31.

1477g. Four upstanders, / Four downhangers, / Two lookers, / Two hookers, / And a switchabout.—Cow.
   Brewster, *Indiana*, 72.

1477h. Four stiff standers, two lookers, two crookers, and one switchbox.—Cow.
   Perkins, *New Orleans*, p. 111, No. 54.

---
[1] Sébillot, *Devinettes*, 9a.

1477i. Four stiff standers, / Four long hangers, / Two lookers, / Two crookers, / And the switchabout.—Cow.
Hudson, p. 83, No. 3.

1477j. Four down stand on, / Four down hang on, / Two hookers, / Two lookers, / And a frisk about.—Cow.
Hudson, p. 83, No. 4.

1477k. Four standers, / Two hookers, / Two lookers.—Cow.
Parsons, *Guilford Co., N.C.*, p. 201, No. 7 var.

1478. Dillydanders

A few versions refer to the cow's teats as dillydanders or danders. This word of obscure meaning occurs in texts from Lancashire, Ireland, and New Hampshire and is therefore presumably an old constituent of the text. It occurs in some folksongs, notably the "Carol of the Twelve Numbers," but is equally unintelligible in that context.

1478a. What has four stiff-standers, four dilly-danders, two hookers, two lookers, and a switchabout?—Cow.
Oral, *New Hampshire*.

1478b. Four stiff-standers, / Four diddle-dangers, / A switcher and a gatherer.—Cow.
Green, *South Antrim*, 5.

1478c. Four little danders, / Four stick standers, / A hook an' a crook, / An' a switcher.—Cow.
Green, *South Antrim*, 34.

1478d. Four stiff standers, / Two lilly landers, / A flip-flap / And a ding-dang.—Cow.
Oral, *West Virginia*.

1478e. Four steady standards, / Four diddle-diddle-danders, / Two crooks, two lookers, one licker, and a switcher.—Cow.
Praeger, *Béaloideas*, IV (1933–1934), 144, No. 1 (var.: two lookers, two hookers, and a wigwag).

1479. Two Lookers and a Wig-Wag

Although the cow's tail is usually called a "switchabout," some English riddlers have invented other terms. Parallels to "wigwag" and its varieties are such words as "flip-flap" (Nos. 1478d, 1479d) and "zum-zum" (No. 1479f).

1479a. Two lookers, two hookers, two snookers, four stiff-standers, four dilly-danders, and a wig-wag.—Cow.
Marsden, *Upper Calderdale*, p. 262.

1479b. Tweea lookers, twea crookers, fower dilly danders, four stiff standers, an' a wig-wam.—Cow.
Wright, p. 311 (Westmoreland; Lancashire).

1479c. Two crooks, / Four stiff-standers, / Four diddle-danders, / And a wigem-wagem.—Cow.
Wintemberg and Wintemberg, *Canada*, p. 123, No. 422.

1479d. Four stiff-standers, / Four dillydanders, / Two hookers, two snookers, / And a flip-flap.—Cow.
Harland and Wilkinson, *Lancashire Legends*, p. 186.

1479e. Two hookers, two lookers, / Four stiff standers, / Four down hangers, / A licker and a wagger about.—Cow.
Randolph and Taylor, *Ozarks*, 20.

1479f. Two peepers, two pokers, two waddlers, and one zum-zum.—Cow.
Beckwith, *Jamaica*, p. 203, No. 184.

1480. Downstanders, Upstanders

In an effort to gain unity, riddlers have employed such devices as the contrast of downstanders and upstanders, the repetition of "about,"[1] and rhyme.

1480a. Four downstanders, / Two upstanders, / One sweep arounder.—Cow.
Parsons, *Bahamas*, p. 481, No. 98.

1480b. Me riddle me riddle, / Four up a stander, / Four down stander, / One sweep arounder.—Cow.
Parsons, *Bahamas*, p. 475, No. 39.

1481–1489. Miscellaneous

The following nine versions illustrate the effects of associative thinking. The original conception of the cow riddle permits readily the introduction of new ideas, and the following versions show how far the consequent changes may go.

1481. Four little landers, / Four stick standers, / Two rappers, / Two lookers, / Two crookers, / And a Bownbell [variant: Wagabout].—A cow.
Leather, *Hereford*, p. 229.

1482. There were four street walkers, / Four down lookers, / Two lookers, two hookers, / And one lick about.—Co' [cow].
Parsons, *Barbados*, p. 284, No. 48.

1483. Four yellah sandals, / Two black sandals / One wheel about.—Cow (four foot, two horn, and a tail).
Parsons, *Antilles*, III, 425, Antigua, 19.

1484. My fader had a t'ing, four groun' holders, two lookers, two swingers [yeres (ears)].—Cow.
Parsons, *Bahamas*, p. 481, No. 91.

---

[1] See Nos. 1476f, 1477d.

1485. Something has: / Four ground standers, / Two uprights, / Two lamp lighters, / Two outriggers, / And one switch about, / And it goes Moo!—Cow.
Parsons, *Bermuda*, p. 247, No. 11 var.

1486. Two top timbers, / Two glass windows, / Four ground standers, / And one switch about.—Cow.
Parsons, *Bermuda*, p. 247, No. 11.

1487. Four standin' pos', / Two up timbers, / Two look about, / One wheel about, / One fly b'usher.—Cow.
Parsons, *Antilles*, III, 376, St. Vincent, 18.

1488. Two top t'under, / Four bellie bander, / And one shake about her.—Cow.
Parsons, *Antilles*, III, 425, Antigua, 19 var.

1489. His mouth was open, / And he was calling, / His fore [four] feet shaking, / And two eyes looking, / And two sticks ahead.—Cow.
Fauset, *Nova Scotia*, p. 155, No. 59 (Gaelic).

1490–1494. Other Answers Than a Cow

1490. Four ground standers, / One switch about, / Two upriggers.—Donkey.
Parsons *Bermuda*, p. 247, No. 10 (var.: two uprighters).

1491. Four ground holders, four upholders, soft in the middle, hard all around.—Bed.
Parsons, *Bahamas*, p. 479, No. 74.

1492. Two groun' holder, / Two cross stander, / Two swing around.—Cane mill.
Parsons, *Bahamas*, p. 477, No. 56.

1493. My fader had a t'ing, had two lookers an' t'ree standers.—Pot—two eye, an' t'ree foot.
Parsons, *Bahamas*, p. 481, No. 92.

1494. Two straights and one crook, / And a long handle.—Pipe.
Fauset, *Southern Negro*, p. 278, No. 20.

1495. Half Dead, Half Living

1495. One-half dead, the other half living, / And a tail waggin'.—Dog with its head in a pot.
Praeger, *Béaloideas*, IV (1933–34), 145, No. 19.

Chapter X
ENUMERATIONS IN TERMS OF COLOR
Nos. 1496–1572

RIDDLERS do not often describe an object primarily in terms of its color or colors; and when they do, they usually employ supplementary devices to round out the idea. Comparisons to persons or animals in which characteristic or unusual colors are mentioned have already been discussed. Comparisons to things, except for the comparison of an egg to a white house, do not usually mention color. This chapter contains riddles in which the reference to color is the essential element of the description. The first riddle[1] is perhaps the only example of the use of colors alone in describing an object. It is probably a defective version of a theme known elsewhere in a fuller form. The devices supplementing the mention of colors are references to the characteristic positions of the colors,[2] the changes in such varying circumstances as going in and out[3] or rising and falling,[4] the presence or absence of the color or colors at different times,[5] and the combination of colors with a characteristic act.[6]

Only a few of these riddles have enjoyed a wide circulation. The notion, for example, that an egg changes color[7] when it falls out of the air to the ground has amused many simple minds, and similarly the observation that a burning coal or stick becomes black on being put into water[8] affords matter for a riddle. It is probably merely an accident that the analogous riddles describing a change of color in grain and meal[9] and in a lobster before and after cooking[10] seem to be unknown to English riddlers. Although riddles describing a change in color are widely known, they have not appealed to riddlers outside of Europe or regions where European influences have strongly affected popular tradition.

Of the riddles mentioned in this chapter only the blackberry riddle,[11] which is mentioned in classical Greek literature, is old. Its history and connections are obscure and puzzling. Many of the riddles in this chapter are probably degenerate forms of a more clearly conceived comparison to a person of characteristic color.

1496–1497. Black and White

1496. Here's a thing, white and black, / What's that?—A magpie.
Cornish Notes and Queries, I (1906), 273.

[1] No. 1496.
[2] Nos. 1497 through 1541.
[3] Nos. 1542 through 1546.
[4] Nos. 1547a through 1558.
[5] Nos. 1559a through 1561d.
[6] Nos. 1562 through 1572c.
[7] Nos. 1550a through 1554.
[8] Nos. 1542, 1543.
[9] See the headnote to Nos. 1550–1554.
[10] See the headnote to Nos. 1542–1543, § 2.
[11] Nos. 1561a through 1561d.

1497. What is it that is all black and its bottom white?—Blackberry.
Praeger, *Béaloideas*, VIII (1938), 171, No. 8.

1498–1541. Position

1498–1499. All Over

1498a. Black and white and red all over.—Newspaper.
Fauset, *Philadelphia*, p. 554, No. 14; Bacon and Parsons, *Virginia*, p. 325, No. 119; Boggs, *North Carolina*, p. 325, No. 20; Parsons, *Guilford Co., N.C.*, p. 201, No. 8; Parsons, *Aiken, S.C.*, p. 31, No. 44; Redfield, *Tennessee*, p. 40, No. 59; Fauset, *Southern Negro*, p. 287, No. 124; Brewster, *Indiana*, 40; Randolph and Spradley, *Ozark*, p. 82; Waugh, *Canada*, p. 64, No. 705; Fauset, *Nova Scotia*, p. 156, No. 64; Parsons, *Bermuda*, p. 265, No. 162; Johnson, *Antigua*, p. 88, No. 67.

1498b. Something black and white and red all over.—Newspaper.
Parsons, *Sea Islands, S.C.*, p. 174, No. 174.

1498c. What is that is first white, then black, then red all over?—Newspaper.
Gardner, *Schoharie Hills, N. Y.*, p. 257, No. 42.

1499. Black and white and read all over, / Goes from Halifax to Dover.—Newspaper.
Fauset, *Nova Scotia*, p. 156, No. 64 var.

1500–1538. Inside and Outside

1500–1503. Green and White (Yellow)

1500a. Me riddle me riddle me randy oh. / Perhaps you can, / Perhaps you can not. / Me fader had a t'ing. / It white inside, / It green outside.—Coconut.
Parsons, *Andros Island, Bahamas*, p. 276, No. 19.

1500b. My father has a thing, it's green outside and white inside.—Coconut.
Parsons, *Antilles*, III, 423, Montserrat, 28.

1501. Some t'in' green outside an' white inside.—Sour sop.
Parsons, *Antilles*, III, 433, Saba, 14.

1502. Here's a t'ing. / Green outside / An' yaller inside.—Papaw.
Parsons, *Andros Island, Bahamas*, p. 276, No. 9.

1503a. Got somet'in' yeller inside an' green outside.—Pumpkin.
Parsons, *Antilles*, III, 437, St. Martin, 36.

1503b. Something has green walls outside and yellow inside.—Pumpkin.
Parsons, *Bermuda*, p. 248, No. 15.

1504–1507. Yellow (Red) and White

Riddlers occasionally employ picturesque or more definitely descriptive terms like comparisons to silver and gold (see Nos. 1137a through 1140 above) or define the colors as changing according to the situation (Nos. 1550a through 1561d below), or add some supplementary details.

1504. Me riddle me riddle me randy oh. / Here's a t'ing. / White outside / An' yaller inside.—Egg.
Parsons, *Andros Island, Bahamas*, p. 275, No. 3.

1505a. What is red an' white inside, an' white outside?—Aigg.
Parsons, *Sea Islands, S.C.*, p. 166, No. 76.

1505b. Me riddle me riddle / Me randy oh. / Perhaps you can tell me dis riddle / Perhaps you cyan't. / My fader had a little t'ing, white outside, red inside.—Fowl aigg.
Parsons, *Bahamas*, p. 481, No. 89.

1505c. Me riddle me riddle me randy oh. / Perhaps you could tell me, / Perhaps you can't. / It was something / White outside, / Red inside.—Foul egg.
Parsons, *Andros Island, Bahamas*, p. 276, No. 13.

1506a. White on de outside, white on de inside, an' yeller on de inside.—Aigg.
Parsons, *Aiken, S.C.*, p. 29, No. 28; Johnson, *Antigua*, p. 87, No. 43.

1506b. Got somet'ing yeller inside, white inside, white outside.—Egg.
Parsons, *Antilles*, III, 437, St. Martin, 35.

1507a. Ma riddle ma riddle / Perhaps I can tell you dis riddle / An' perhaps not. / It had somet'ing white, and round and small, white inside and it's yellow too.—Egg.
Parsons, *Antilles*, III, 442, St. Croix, 5 var.

1507b. Dere is somet'ing white outside an' yellow and white inside an' many people cyant break it in de right way up to now.—Dat is an egg.
Parsons, *Antilles*, III, 442, St. Croix, 5.

1507c. Dere is somet'in', it not bear on a tree nor on de eart'. It is white an' yellow inside. It is useable.—Egg.
Parsons, *Antilles*, III, 422, Montserrat, 11.

1508–1518. Various Colors

1508. What green outside, an' red inside?—Watermelon.
Parsons, *Aiken, S.C.*, p. 29, No. 27; Parsons, *Bahamas*, p. 478, No. 65; Parsons, *Sea Islands, S.C.*, p. 166, No. 79 var.

1509. Round an' green outside and yellow inside.—Watermelon.
Parsons, *Bahamas*, p. 473, No. 21.

1510. Me riddle, me rocket, / 'Tis a t'ing, / Green within, / Red within, / Green outside.—Prickly pear.
Parsons, *Antilles*, III, 439, Anguilla, 14.

1511. White within, black within, red without.—Ackee.
Beckwith, *Jamaica*, p. 202, No. 174.

1512. Red outside, / White inside.—Apple.
Bacon and Parsons, *Virginia*, p. 323, No. 99.

1513. Here's a t'ing. / Black outside / An' black inside.—Umbrella.
Parsons, *Andros Island, Bahamas*, p. 276, No. 16.

1514. Wha' yeller inside, an' white outside?—Cantaloupe.
Parsons, *Sea Islands, S.C.*, p. 166, No. 77.

1515. Dey had somet'ing, black inside, yellow outside, an' yellow inside.—Popa [papaw].
Parsons, *Antilles*, III, 437, St. Martin, 39.

1516. Dey had somet'ing, black inside, white inside, and green outside.—Soursop.
Parsons, *Antilles*, III, 437, St. Martin, 38.

1517. Have a thing yellow outside, yellow inside, and yellow inside again.—Mango.
Parsons, *Antilles*, III, 435, St. Martin, 10.

1518. Red inside, white inside, black inside, green outside.—Melon.
Parsons, *Bahamas*, p. 483, No. 113.

1519–1527. Colored Outside, Contents Inside

The references to seeds[1] and juice[2] within this object of mysterious color are too specific and spoil the enigmatic effect.

1519. Dere's a t'ing, it green inside, an' green outside, an' have one seed.—Dat is da white pear.
Johnson, *Antigua*, p. 88, No. 62.

1520. Something green inside, white outside with one seed.—Cennep.
Parsons, *Antilles*, III, 444, St. Croix, 19.

1521a. Something green outside, white inside with lots of little black seeds.—Soursap.
Parsons, *Antilles*, III, 444, St. Croix, 17.

1521b. There is something green outside and white inside, wid a lot of seeds.—Soursop.
Parsons, *Antilles*, III, 445, St. Thomas, 4.

1522. Ma riddle ma riddle / Perhaps I can tell you dis riddle / An' perhaps not. / It had some t'ing ripe green, lang, white inside and lats of seed.—Squash.
Parsons, *Antilles*, III, 443, St. Croix, 14.

1523. Dere is somet'ing white outside and green inside and have a painted seed inside and some time dey [they] have a green skin outside.—Sugar apple.
Parsons, *Antilles*, III, 443, St. Croix, 6.

---

[1] Nos. 1519 through 1527b.   [2] No. 1527b.

1524. Dere is some t'ing wid a reddish color outside an' in de inside is very sappy, an' have some small flat seed, it is put in pat [pot] frequently an' make de pat taste good. Can you guess what dat is?—Tomahtee.
Parsons, *Antilles*, III, 443, St. Croix, 9.

1525. Dere's a big green t'ing whi' have green in spots on de outside an' in de inside which have some small seeds and day [they] are flat. Can you guess what it is?—Pumpkin.
Parsons, *Antilles*, III, 442, St. Croix, 1.

1526. Something red outside, red inside, lots of red seed.—Maiden apple.
Parsons, *Antilles*, III, 444, St. Croix, 18.

1527a. Outside brown, have some fine little seeds.—Bell apple.
Parsons, *Antilles*, III, 430, St. Kitts, 11.

1527b. There is something yeller outside, have a lot of juice and splits inside.—Bell apple.
Parsons, *Antilles*, III, 445, St. Thomas, 5.

1528. Colored Outside; Has Brown Eyes

1528. Something green outside and red and white inside and has brown eyes.—Melon.
Parsons, *Bermuda*, p. 248, No. 13 var.

1529. Black at Ends, Red in Middle

1529. Black on both ends, red in the middle, / Hair all over it, looks like a divil.—A caterpillar.
Janice Neal, *New York Folklore Quarterly*, I (1945), 216.

1530–1535. Red, Black, Four Corners Round About

1530a. Black within and red without, / Four corners round about.—Chimney.
Perkins, *New Orleans*, p. 106, No. 4; Parsons, *Guilford Co., N.C.*, p. 206, No. 52 (fireplace); Johnson, *St. Helena Island, S.C.*, p. 160, No. 40; Gutch and Peacock, *Lincolnshire*, p. 398, No. 11; Fauset, *Philadelphia*, p. 555, No. 23; Halliwell-Phillipps, *Popular Rhymes*, p. 145; Halliwell-Phillipps, *Nursey Rhymes*, p. 130; Farr, *Tennessee*, p. 321, No. 40; Parsons, *Bermuda*, p. 252, No. 44; Hyatt, *Adams Co., Ill.*, p. 659, No. 10847; Brewster, *Indiana*, 23. All corners: Parsons, *Bermuda*, p. 252, No. 44 var. Fo' corners all about: Parsons, *Sea Islands, S.C.*, p. 166, No. 78; Waugh, *Canada*, p. 68, No. 779. Got four corners roundabout: Fauset, *Nova Scotia*, p. 164, No. 112. Four corners all round about: Bacon and Parsons, *Virginia*, p. 321, No. 9.

1530b. Black within and red without, / With four corners angling about.—Chimney.
Hyatt, *Adams Co., Ill.*, p. 659, No. 10847.

1530c. Four sides, / Black outside, / Red inside.—Chimney.
Bacon and Parsons, *Virginia*, p. 312, No. 9 var.

1530d. Red on the outside, black on the inside, four corners round about.—Chimney.
Parsons, *Aiken, S.C.*, p. 29, No. 29.

1531. Black within, white without, / Fo' corner roun' about.—Chimley.
Parsons, *Sea Islands, S.C.*, p. 166, No. 78 var.

1532. Black within, / Red without, / Four corners round about.—Fireplace.
Parsons, *Guilford Co., N.C.*, p. 206, No. 52.

1533. 'Tis black without and black within, / and hath foure corners, as I win.—A dry turfe.
Prettie Riddles (1631), No. 13 = Brandl, p. 54.

1534. Black within and black without, / Four corners round about.—The oven.
Gutch and Peacock, *Lincolnshire*, p. 398, No. 12.

1535. Red within, and red without; / Four courners round about.—A brick.
Harland and Wilkinson, *Lancashire Legends*, p. 186.

1536. Miscellaneous

1536. Feathers on the outside, / Pink on the inside. / What is it?—Turkey.
Fauset, *Philadelphia*, p. 555, No. 28.

1537–1538. Colored Inside and Outside, and an Act

1537. Black without, and black [variant: white] within, / An' a' the guts o't [of it] wallopin'.—A pot of boiling porridge.
Findlay, *Edinburgh*, p. 59.

1538a. Red inside, / Black outside, / He raises his leg an' shoves it in.—Boot.
Parsons, *Guilford Co., N.C.*, p. 205, No. 45.

1538b. Black on outside, / Red on inside, / An' hoist yer leg an' stick it in.—Boot.
Parsons, *Aiken, S.C.*, p. 35, No. 69; Hyatt, *Adams Co., Ill.*, p. 658, No. 10841.

1538c. Black without and red within, / Hop about and put your foot in.—Boot.
Hyatt, *Adams Co., Ill.*, p. 658, No. 10841 var.

1538d. Black without and red within, / Pick up your foot and stick it in.—Boot.
Hudson, p. 87, No. 29.

1538e. Outside black, inside red; cock up your foot and poke it in.—Boot.
Beckwith, *Jamaica*, p. 201, No. 170.

1538f. The old man hoists up his leg and sticks it in, / Something black on the outside and red within.—A boot.
Chappell, p. 235, No. 21.

1539. Front, Middle

1539. Here's a t'ing. / White to de en', / Black to de middle.—Walking stick.
Parsons, *Andros Island, Bahamas*, p. 276, No. 10.

1540–1541. Above, Below

Riddlers do not often describe an object with colors in a vertical order. See a Swedish riddle for a fruit, "Red at the top and black at the root."[1] In some riddles for fire and a pot, persons, who are called Red, or Red Man, and Black, or Black Man, stand or sit one above the other.[2] Mention of three colors in a vertical order is rare.

1540. White a top, black a middle, and red a bottom.—Bammie [pancake], baking-iron, and fire.
  Beckwith, *Jamaica*, p. 201, No. 171.

1541. Some t'ing red underneath, black in the middle, white on top.—Fire, baking pan, an' casava on top.
  Parsons, *Antilles*, III, 433, Saba, 8.

1542–1558. Changing According to Position

1542–1546. In and Out

The underlying idea does not lend itself easily to suggesting a personification. A Swedish description of an oven brush, "She goes in green, comes out red, nods her head, and is soon dead,"[1] is an exception to this rule, and a few other examples occur in the parallels cited below. The riddler occasionally suggests a particular object, expecially when the colors are red and white. The oldest and most widely used varieties of this pattern are In red, out black[2] and its converse. Similar contrasts of colors are applicable to:

§ 1. Soap. African, Evhe: F. Müller, p. 156, No. 6 (A black goat fell in a river and turned white).

§ 2. Bread.[3] Modern Greek: Dieterich, *Rätseldichtung*, p. 99, citing Stamatiadis, V, 179 (One puts it in white, one takes it out red). Crimean Tatar: Filonenko, 12 (God, God, these are its signs. Its interior is full of noise. You put it in white, you take it out red. May God bless Mohammed!—An oven heated in preparation for baking bread).[4]

§ 3. A china plate. See Turkish: Kúnos, 161 (I put it in green, it came out red. My goodness, what can that be?—Paint on a china dish), 234 (This fortress is all body. I put it in green, it came out red, I don't know the reason why), which is not entirely clear.

§ 4. A cork. Serbian: Novaković, p. 237, No. 2 (It goes in white and comes out red; he sticks it in white and takes it out red). Bulgarian: Bozhov, 28; Gubov, 78.

---

[1] Geijer and Campbell, 75. See also Flemish: Joos, 470.
[2] See the headnote to Nos. 875–877 above.

[1] Ström, p. 170, "Kvasten," 2 = Hyltén-Cavallius, *Värend*, 24 = Sandén, *Norra Vadsbo*, 2.
[2] See Nos. 1542, 1543 below.
[3] For comparisons in terms of animals see Nos. 493a, 493b above, and in terms of persons see No. 919 above.
[4] See similar riddles quoted in the headnote to Nos. 1448–1452, § 4, above.

§ 5. The sun and the moon. Faeroic: Hammershaimb, *Antiquarisk tidsskrift*, III (1849–1851), 316, No. 3 (Red goes under Ritufelli and comes back white). This is allied to the riddles for meal.[5] Ritufelli signifies a square field. Its import in this sun riddle is obscure.

§ 6. A log. (Goes in black, comes out white.) Votyak: Wichmann, *Votyak*, 38, 189, 381, 419. Compare the fully personified parallel: "He goes into the house in a black coat, comes out in a white winter coat."[6]

1542–1543. In Red, Out Black

The contrast of red and black is often used for a fire and a pot.[1] In this special form, in which the object suggested is a thing that changes its color, a personification similar to the one used in the riddle for a fire and a pot is unsuitable. There are, nevertheless, a few instances which approach a personification. The Letts say, "What little creature blushes when it is dead?"[2] The Italians develop the theme more fully in "All my life I am a priest, after death I am a cardinal.—Crayfish."[3] Rabelais had something of this sort in mind when he wrote of a lobster being cardinalized by boiling.[4]

In Catalan and Spanish riddling this contrast of red and black as it occurs in the coal riddle is introduced with the phrase "En el campo ...." This scene is appropriate to coal, but the phrase often occurs in contexts in which it has degenerated into a formula without meaning.[5]

The contrast of red changing to black is applicable to:

§ 1. Coal, a warming pan, an iron when heated. See Nos. 1542, 1543.

§ 2. When reversed, as in "in black, out red," the description fits boiling a lobster or a crab. See Flemish: Joos, 417, 938. German: Wossidlo, 329; Frischbier, *Thierwelt*, p. 358, Nos. 96, 97; Hanika-Otto, 92. Swedish: Ström, p. 119, Nos. 1, 2. French: Parsons, *Antilles*, III, 407, Gaudaloupe, 125. Rumanian: Papahagi, 38 (Black in the brook and red in the fire). Lithuanian: Jurgelionis, 888 through 891; Schleicher, p. 203. Czech: Hanika-Otto, note to No. 92. White Russian: Wasilewski, 15 (When he's alive, then he's black; when he's dead, then he's red). Polish: Gustawicz, 342, 491; Siarkowski, 54, 92. Russian:

---

[5] See the headnote to Nos. 1550–1554 below.
[6] Votyak: Wichmann, *Votyak*, 383.
[1] See the headnotes to Nos. 871–877 and 875–877.
[2] Bielenstein, 984. The answer is "crab."
[3] Tammi, 9.
[4] *Gargantua*, I, chap. xxxix. See also the couplet in *Hudibras*, II, ii, 31–32:

   And like a lobster boil'd the morn
   From black to red began to turn.

[5] For examples see Catalan: Pelay y Briz, 79, 197. Spanish: Demófilo, 235, and p. 351, No. 50; Rodríguez Marín, 451; *El folklore español*, IV (1884), 68. Argentinian: Lehmann-Nitsche, 690. Chilean: Flores, 160, 161. Cuban: Massip, 46, 47. Dominican Rep.: Andrade, 99. Guatemalan: Recinos, 10. Porto Rican: Mason, 143. Mexican: Noguera, 28. New Mexican: Campa, 86.

Sadovnikov, 531. Estonian: Wiedemann, p. 274. Mordvin: Paasonen, 162 (What is it that becomes red after its death?). Hungarian: *Magyar Nyelvör*, V (1876), 34 (What is it that blushes after it has died?). Gypsy: Wlislocki, 16. Hawaiian: Judd, 96 (Red skin, black skin, good to eat.—Shrimp). Samoan: Heider, 114 (*Birgus latro*, Pratt).

See also the Hungarian description of a shoulder of mutton: "It enters it [the oven] in black, it comes out in red."[6]

§ 3. A cardamon. African, Duala: Ebding, 101 (If one throws it into the water, it is red; if it comes out, it is still red).

1542. Something goes in the water red and comes out black.—Fire-stick.
Parsons, *Bermuda*, p. 250, No. 26.

1543. Something dives in the water red and comes out black.—Coal.
Parsons, *Bermuda*, p. 250, No. 26.

1544. In Green, Out Red

The change of green into red, here used by the riddler to describe a chinkapin, occurs in other connections. A Swedish riddle for a broom or oven brush, "In green, out red,"[1] and, in an elaborated form, "She goes in green, comes out red, nods her head, and soon is dead,"[2] refers to thrusting a broom of fresh green twigs into the fire or oven and withdrawing it in flames. The Turkish henna riddles, "I put on green in the evening, it came out red in the morning" and "Behind the fortress there is a body, a body. I put in green, red came forth from there" and "In the evening mud, in the morning coal"[3] as well as the Atjeh betel riddle, "In green, out red,"[4] rest on changes in the color of the materials when they are used. Although the Swedish, South Carolinian, Turkish, and Atjeh riddles employ the same enigmatic device, they probably have no connection with one another. They exemplify how riddlers have seen and used the same simple combinations and contrasts that nature offers.

1544. Somet'in' goes in green, goes out green an' stickery all ower, an' come out mahogany color.—Chinkapin.
Parsons, *Sea Island, S.C.*, p. 168, No. 101.

1545–1546. In and Out, Various Colors

1545. What is it that goes out black, and comes in white.—A black cow on a snowy day.
Gregor, *Northeast Scotland*, p. 82.

---

[6] *Magyar Nyelvör*, XXXI (1902), 532, No. 19.
[1] Ericsson, *Södermanland*, I (1879), 83–84, No. 19.
[2] Hyltén-Cavallius, *Värend*, 24 = Sandén, *Norra Vadsbo*, 2 = Ström, p. 170, "Kvasten," 2.
[3] Hamizade, 400, 401, 403.
[4] Kreemer, *Atjeh*, 32.

1546. There's a t'ing, you put one stick in the ground, at a certain time of the year it comes green, and the other time it comes yellow.—Sugar-cane.
Johnson, *Antigua*, p. 88, No. 59.

1547–1558. Up and Down

This contrast, which is readily adapted to various objects, is freely used by European riddlers and in countries where the European tradition of riddling is known. It is apparently not widely known elsewhere. The riddler usually combines references to colors with this contrast: what was green becomes red, or what was white becomes red. Some riddles describe other aspects than colors as varying. The Dutch and French say of wheat that it goes up with one name and comes down with another, and they have in mind the change of grain into flour in the mill.[1] A pair of scissors goes up straight and comes down cross.[2] A ball of yarn goes up round and comes down with a tail.[3]

1547–1549. Up Green, Down Red

This riddle, which is found in only a few West Indian versions, is perhaps an adaptation of the following much more widely disseminated egg riddle.

1547a. Go up green / An' come down red.—Watermelon.
Parsons, *Aiken, S.C.*, p. 34, No. 65.

1547b. Somet'in' throw [variant: go] up green an' come down red.—Watermelon.
Parsons, *Sea Islands, S.C.*, p. 166, No. 79.

1548. Go up green and come down ripe.—Watermelon.
Johnson, *St. Helena Island, S.C.*, p. 158, No. 12.

1549. What go up green as grass, white as cotton, and something in it black as ink, and come down red? Guess what it is.—A watermelon, because it is white on the inside before it is ripe.
Parsons, *Sea Islands, S.C.*, p. 166, No. 80.

1550–1554. Up White, Down Yellow (Red)

The bald contrast of something that rises white into the air and turns yellow when it falls to the ground is sufficient to describe an egg, and English riddlers have not chosen to enlarge upon it. Other riddlers have elaborated either the situation or the reference to the colors. The elaboration of the situation, as in "Thrown upon the roof and falling to the ground," is more frequently found

---

[1] Dutch: Sinninghe, p. 14, No. 17. French: Rolland, 272; Larivey's translation of Straparola, *Le piacevoli notti*, IX, 5; Marchessou, *Velay et Auvergne*, 15. See also Breton: Sébillot, *Devinettes*, 34. Modern Greek: Dieterich, *Rätseldichtung*, p. 99.
The French in the West Indies describe sugar cane in a similar way; see Parsons, *Antilles*, III, 385, Martinique, 85.
[2] No. 1453 above.
[3] Welsh: Hull and Taylor, 144. See the headnote to No. 1341, n. 7, above.

than the introduction of comparisons to the colors. The elaboration of the reference to colors consists in the use of comparisons: the egg is as white as snow or the yolk is as yellow as gold. Although the notion of comparing an egg to something that changes its color is widely known in continental Europe, I have noted parallels only in the southern United States and in the West Indian islands.

A similar conception, which is known to Welsh riddlers and generally elsewhere except in English-speaking territory, describes wheat or flour as something that goes up yellow or brown and comes down white. See Welsh: Hull and Taylor, 142. Icelandic: Árnason, 451 (What goes yellow under the rock [millstone] and comes out white?). Danish: Kristensen, p. 76, § 181, Nos. 226a, 226b, and p. 88, § 224, No. 247 (malt). Faeroic: Hammershaimb, *Antiquarisk tidsskrift*, III (1849–1851), 321, No. 70 (Gold goes under the square field and comes back white). Norwegian: Aasen, 12; Stafset, 90. French: Henri Carnoy, *La Tradition*, VII (1893), 353, No. 9; Parsons, *Antilles*, III, 405, Guadaloupe, 91. Italian: Pitrè, 296. Rumanian: Gorovei, 1107. Polish: Saloni, *Rzeshów*, 60 (It's given to it black, and it gives it out white.—Buckwheat). Compare also No. 870 above, and a Swedish riddle quoted in the headnote to No. 397, n. 14, above.

A Swiss riddle for snow, "On the roof it is bright and white, when it falls down it is yellow,"[1] is a confused effort to adapt the pattern to a new theme.

Riddlers also employ a similar contrast in terms of form; see the description of a ball of thread (No. 1341 above).

1550a. Goes up white and comes down yellow.—Egg.
Baring-Gould, *Notes and Queries*, 3d ser. VIII (1865), 325 (Yorkshire); Bacon and Parsons, *Virginia*, p. 312, No. 2; Perkins, *New Orleans*, p. 110, No. 48. What goes up white: Green, *South Antrim*, 33; Parsons, *Aiken, S.C.*, p. 34, No. 64; Johnson, *St. Helena Island, S.C.*, p. 160, No. 43. Somet'in' goes up white: Parsons, *Sea Islands, S.C.*, p. 165, No. 75, var. 1. I know something goes up white: Parsons, *Bermuda*, p. 251, No. 35.

1550b. Throw it up white, and comes down yellow. What is that?—Egg.
Parsons, *Sea Islands, S.C.*, p. 166, No. 75, var. 3.

1550c. Up it goes white and down it comes yellow.—Egg.
Knortz, p. 210, No. 1.

1551a. Something go up white, / Something come down red.—Aigg.
Parsons, *Sea Islands, S.C.*, p. 165, No. 75.

1551b. I heave up a t'ing white an' it come down red.—Egg.
Beckwith, *Jamaica*, p. 193, No. 86.

1552. It goes up in the air white and comes down to the ground yellow.—Egg.
Oral, Louisiana.

1553. Somet'in' go in de air w'ite, an' come down yaller an' w'ite.—Egg.
Parsons, *Sea Islands, S.C.*, p. 165, No. 75, var. 2.

---

[1] Rochholz, 425.

1554. Upon the house, white as snow; down on the ground, yellow as gold.—Egg.
Perkins, *New Orleans*, p. 110, No. 49.

1555–1558. Up and Down, Various Colors

1555. Me riddle me racket. / Somet'in' goes up white an' comes down black.—Black bottle of milk.
Parsons, *Antilles*, III, 437, St. Martin, 28.

1556. It goes upstairs red and comes downstairs black.—A warming pan.
Burne, *Shropshire*, p. 574, No. 6; Parker, *Oxfordshire*, p. 331.

1557. Something goes up brown, and comes down white.—Coconut.
Parsons, *Bermuda*, p. 251, No. 34.

1558. What goes up like a little black ball, / Comes down in a hurry and covers all?—Soot.
Hyatt, *Adams Co., Ill.*, p. 667, No. 10913.

1559–1561. Colors in a Chronological Sequence

Aeschylus and Sophocles note with interest the variety of colors to be seen in a blackberry and its fruit.[1] As in Nos. 1559a, 1559b, below, riddlers may occasionally add a characteristic act to the list of colors. The observation of a sequence of colors is true of many fruits and forms the basis of riddles describing:

§ 1. A blackberry. See Nos. 1561a through 1561d.

§ 2. A cherry. German: Wossidlo, 217. Swiss: Zahler, *Münchenbuchsee*, 195. Danish: Kristensen, p. 67, § 161, No. 243a, and p. 68, § 161, Nos. 245, 246. Swedish: Ericsson, *Södermanland*, III (1882), 103, No. 161. Latin: Reusner, ed. 1602, p. 243. See additional references in the note to Nos. 1561a through 1561d below, and compare the headnote to Nos. 668–669, § 2, above.

§ 3. A hawthorn. Danish: Kristensen, p. 46, § 121, No. 169. Swedish: Russwurm, 32.

§ 4. An olive. Spanish: Demófilo, 20, 22, 23.

§ 5. A lily. Danish: Kristensen, p. 80, § 207, No. 313.

§ 6. A grape and a raisin. Spanish, Argentinian: Lehmann-Nitsche, 83.

§ 7. A haystack. Danish: Kristensen, p. 47, § 127, No. 179.

§ 8. Wheat. Spanish: Demófilo, 999.

§ 9. A palm. African, Basa: Scheibler, p. 165, No. 7 (At first it is white, then it becomes black, and finally red).

§ 10. A pepper. Turkish: Hamizade, 67 (I sowed white, green sprouted, red leather).

---

[1] See Campbell Bonner, "Eyes That See and Ears That Hear," *Studies in the History of Culture* [dedicated to Waldo G. Leland] (Menasha, Wisc., 1942), pp. 5–6. See also Apollodorus, 3, 3, 1. For discussion of this conception see Rochholz, p. 221, No. 3; Schultz, *Rätsel aus dem hellenischen Kulturkreise*, II, 5–6; Ohlert, 2d ed., pp. 89–91.

§ 11. A candle. Spanish, Argentinian: Lehmann-Nitsche, 82.

1559a. First it is green, then white, then green again, then red, then it is picked.—Strawberry.
Gardner, *Schoharie Hills, N.Y.*, p. 257, No. 43.

1559b. First white, then red, / There isn't a lady in the land, / Who wouldn't take it in her hand.—Strawberry.
Hyatt, *Adams Co., Ill.*, p. 668, No. 10919.

1560. First green, then yaller, / All guts and no taller.—Pumpkin.
Brewster, *Indiana*, 4.

1561. First Green, Then White, Then Red: A Blackberry

An arrangement of colors in a chronological sequence often serves to describe a plant with its flower and fruit. The enigmatic quality of this arrangement lies in the surprising and seemingly impossible combination of colors belonging to a single object. It ordinarily refers to a blackberry, but is equally applicable to other fruits. The Rumanians and modern Greeks use it for a nut.[1]

This chronological sequence of colors is closely related to such enumerations of comparisons as "Green as greenness, white as curds, the color of *carapate* [a plant], but it is not [these].—*Pinha*, a plant like the pomegranate."[2] It is also closely related to the enumeration of colors according to their relative positions, usually from the outside to the inside.[3]

Riddlers may introduce some degree of personification into this chronological sequence of colors. It then becomes very similar to the descriptions of fruits in terms of a biography.[4] Typical examples are the Arabic riddles for a date, "A white pearl in my first period, in the second I wear an emerald dress, in the third I am a red hyacinth,"[5] and for a narcissus, "My arm is an emerald band, my hand is of yellow gold, my fingers are of fine silver,"[6] both of which riddles exemplify the Mediterranean device of comparing a plant to various metals or precious jewels. The Tabaru description of Spanish pepper, "While small, her sarong is green; when full-grown, her sarong is red,"[7] is a complete personification. The Basques use a curious set of comparisons to the life of a sheep in describing a blackberry, "Who is white at the age of a baby lamb, red at the age of a lamb, and black at the age of a sheep?" They describe a leek by a series of contradictions, "Green but not a lizard, white without being

---

[1] Gorovei, 1217; Dieterich, *Rätseldichtung*, p. 93.
[2] Parsons, *Cape Verde*, 22. For similar riddles see above, Nos. 1366 through 1371, 1376, 1378, and the headnote to Nos. 1384–1393.
[3] See Nos. 1497 through 1536, and especially Nos. 1500a through 1518.
[4] See the headnotes to Nos. 668–680 and 668–669.
[5] Littmann, p. 50. This is virtually identical with a Palestinian Arabic riddle for a watermelon quoted in the headnote to Nos. 668–669, § 8, above.
[6] Littmann, p. 52.
[7] Fortgens, 9.

snow, and bearded without being a man."⁸ Ohlert discusses this device of a sequence of colors.⁹

1561a. Something grow green, white, green, red, then black.—Blackberries.
Parsons, *Sea Islands, S.C.*, p. 166, No. 84.

1561b. First thing you see is white. Nex' thing you see is green. Nex' thing you see is black.—Bra'berry [blackberry].
Parsons, *Robeson Co., N.C.*, p. 388, No. 5.

1561c. First white, nex' green, nex' red, den black.—Blackberry.
Parsons, *Aiken, S.C.*, p. 38, No. 49.

1561d. What is green and yet is white? / What is white and yet is red? / What is red and then is black?—Blackberry.
Chappell, p. 232, No. 16.

1562-1572. Colors and an Act

1562. Buffy fluffy on the land, / Two pink pillars on which to stand.—A hen.
Bacon and Parsons, *Virginia*, p. 322, No. 89.

1563. Something red under the pot / Makes it hot.—Fire.
Parsons, *Bermuda*, p. 249, No. 19.

1564a. Brown I am and much admired, / Many horses have I tired, / Tire a horse and worry a man. / Tell me that riddle if you can.—Saddle.
Parsons, *Barbados*, p. 284, No. 46; Waugh, *Canada*, p. 68, No. 782; Knortz, p. 235, No. 117.

1564b. Brown I am and much admired, / Many horses have I tired, / Tire a horse and weary a man. Tell me that riddle if you can.—Saddle.
Farr, *Tennessee*, p. 322, No. 66; Greenleaf, *Newfoundland*, p. 12, No. 37.

1564c. Brown I am, though much admired, / Many horses have I tired, / Tired horses, worried men. / Guess that riddle if you can.—Saddle.
Fauset, *Nova Scotia*, p. 156, No. 60 var.

1564d. Tires a horse, worries a man. / Tell me this riddle if you can.—Saddle.
Beckwith, *Jamaica*, p. 212, No. 234.

1565a. Black we are, but much admired: / Men seek for us until they're tired; / We tire the horses, but comfort man. / Tell me this riddle if you can.—Coal.
Halliwell-Phillipps, *Nursery Rhymes*, p. 129; Parsons, *Bermuda*, p. 248, No. 17; Parsons, *Antilles*, III, 433, Saba, 9, and p. 440, Anguilla, 17; Bacon and Parsons, *Virginia*, p. 324, No. 107; Farr, *Tennessee*, p. 319, No. 14; Perkins, *New Orleans*, p. 107, No. 17; Hyatt, *Adams Co., Ill.*, p. 659, No. 10851; Knortz, p. 224, No. 57.

1565b. Black we are, but much admired; / Men seek for us until they're tired; / We tire the horses, but comfort man. Tell me this riddle if you can.—Charcoal.
Parsons, *Bermuda*, p. 248, No. 17.

---

⁸ Cerquand, 1, 45. ⁹ Second ed., pp. 89-91.

1565c. Blackee are we, much we admired, / Men look for us till this day they are tired, / Put 'to a bag, tied with a string. / If you will tell me what are we, / I will give you a ring.—Coal.
Johnson, *Antigua*, p. 85, No. 22.

1565d. Black we are, / But much admired. / Men seek for us / 'Til they are tired.—Coal.
Parsons, *Aiken, S.C.*, p. 35, No. 65.

1565e. Black I am and much admired, / Many a horse have I tired, / Tired a horse and worried a man. / Guess this riddle if you can.—Coal.
Fauset, *Nova Scotia*, p. 155, No. 60.

1565f. Black I am an' much admired, / Men may seek me while they're tired; / Weary horse an' weary man. / Tell me this riddle if you can.—Coal.
Gutch and Peacock, *Lincolnshire*, p. 400, No. 24.

1565g. Black we are but much admired, / Men to seek until we're tired, / Tired a horse, but comfort a man. / Tell me this riddle if you can.—A man with a load of coal.
Fauset, *Nova Scotia*, p. 156, No. 60 var.

1566. Black I am and much admired; / Men and horses I have tired; / Gold and silver I have made; / In the dunghill I am laid.—A coal.
Green, *South Antrim*, 7.

1567. Though black I am, / I'm much admired. / Many horses have I tired, / Tired horses and carried men. / Unfurl this riddle if you can.—Black hearse.
Parsons, *Bermuda*, p. 248, No. 17 var.

1568. Green, slender, and strong, / Ten bring it along.—Picking rhubarb.
Greenleaf, *Newfoundland*, p. 18, No. 5.

1569. Yellow and green, / Sharp and keen, / Grows in the mene. / The king can't ride it no more than the Queen; / The Duke of Northumberland brought it to shore, / And that's the best riddle that ever came o'er.—Gorse-bush.
Leather, *Hereford*, p. 232.

1570. Purple, yellow, red, and green, / The king cannot reach it nor the queen; / Nor can old Noll, whose power's so great: / Tell me this riddle while I count eight.—The allusion to Oliver Cromwell satisfactorily fixes the date of the riddle to belong to the seventeenth century. The answer is, a rainbow.
Halliwell-Phillipps, *Nursery Rhymes*, p. 129; Hyatt, *Adams Co., Ill.*, p. 665, No. 10901.

1571. Green rind, / Red meat, / Full of syrup, / Hard to beat.—Watermelon.
Bacon and Parsons, *Virginia*, p. 323, No. 96.

1572. Red and White and Stands Up

Although this riddle has been current since the Renaissance and perhaps longer and is found in Europe and America, collectors have neglected it. The parallels show that riddlers either have failed to perceive the import of the comparison or have deliberately obscured it. The changes and contaminations found in the related riddles for an onion,[1] an eglantine berry,[2] and a strawberry[3] make the meaning plain.[4]

1572a. Stiff standing in the bed, / Sometimes white and sometimes red, / Every lady in the land / Takes it in her hand, / And puts it in the hole before.—Radish.
Hyatt, *Adams Co., Ill.*, p. 665, No. 10900.

1572b. Stiff standing on the bed, / First it's white, an' then it's red. / There's not a lady in the land, / That would not take it in her hand.—Carrot.
Parsons, *Antilles*, III, 446, St. Thomas, 19.

1572c. What lies in bed, and stands in bed, / First white, and then red, / The thicker it gets the old woman likes it better?—Carrot.
Praeger, *Béaloideas*, VIII (1938), 171, No. 2.

---

[1] No. 1374.   [2] No. 1421.   [3] No. 1559b.
[4] For variations on this theme see the Scandinavian riddles for flax (Danish: Kristensen, p. 49, § 130, Nos. 184b through 184f. Swedish: Ström, p. 129, "Linet," 2) and beer (Swedish: Ström, pp. 197-198, "Ölet," 1).

Chapter XI

ENUMERATIONS IN TERMS OF ACTS

Nos. 1573–1749

THE RIDDLES in this chapter describe an object in terms of one or more acts. If, however, the riddler conceives the act as characterizing an animal or a person (running, eating, talking, etc.), I have placed the riddle in the appropriate section of chapters i–v. Examples are: "Who runs all day and never stops?" and "Who eats constantly and remains insatiable?" The riddles in chapter i give only a vague indication that the actor is a living creature. Those in chapters ii and iii clearly conceive the actor or actors as one or more animals, and those in chapters iv and v as one or more persons. We might call the riddles in chapter i less individualized forms of those in the next four chapters. Comparisons of an object to a thing (which is not the answer to the riddle) will be found in chapter vii. The subsequent chapters—chapter viii, enumerations of comparisons; chapter ix, enumerations of forms; chapter x, enumerations of colors; and chapter xi, enumerations of acts—contain riddles which do not clearly or fully equate the object to an animal, person, plant, or thing. These riddles often stand in the same relation to the riddles in chapter vii as the riddles in chapter i stand to those in chapters ii–v.

A few riddles contain both a comparison, a detail of form, or a reference to color, and also a mention of a characterizing act. I have placed them in appropriate sections of chapters ix–xi. In these riddles the characterizing act always follows the comparison, detail of form, or reference to color. Examples are the patterns, Round as a hoop; sings when caught by the tail;[1] Black and white; jumps like a foal;[2] or Hairy within, hairy without; thrust your leg in.[3] It would be difficult, if not impossible, to find riddles in which the characterizing act precedes the descriptive details. Since this arrangement separates the various types of riddles without difficulty, it is, I conjecture, in accord with their true nature.

The manner of riddling exemplified in this chapter is not very popular except in Europe and in places where European influences are strong. A few riddles—usually those involving simple contradictions like "It grows bigger the more you take away from it"[4]—have amused listeners in Africa, Mongolia, or Java, but most riddles of this sort are limited in their currency to Europe. It is therefore possible that examples found outside of Europe, in places not usually affected by European influences, have been borrowed. There is very little evidence to show the age of riddles of this sort. A few texts, notably the husband riddle[5] and its congeners, are known to have been current at the time

---

[1] See No. 1326. [2] See Nos. 1379 through 1381b. [3] See No. 1416.
[4] See Nos. 1690 through 1695. [5] See Nos. 1589a through 1589c.

of the Renaissance. The coffin riddle[6] implies a simpler mode of life than prevails generally today. We see in it a scene of the village craftsman making the coffin to order. The interest displayed in the powers of God[7] may have its origin in medieval theological discussion and disputation. The conspicuous absence of formulas in these riddles calls for remark. Few examples of "Riddle me, riddle me, me, ree..." in its several varieties occur, and the formulistic promise of a reward for guessing or of a punishment for failing to guess the riddle is virtually never present.

Merely naming an act characteristic of an object or pertinent to it ordinarily fails to provide an identification sufficient to make a good riddle. A few riddles which cite an act without further details may be fragments of longer and fuller forms. For example, the sifter riddle, "What dis yere? Pit de patte', pit de patte', t'ree times a day in anybody house,"[8] which might refer to kneading bread, is probably incomplete. When the act alone or the act with its attendant circumstances or consequences seems inherently impossible, the contradiction between the assertion and reality arouses the hearer's attention and makes a good riddle. A typical illustration is the name riddle, "What is it that everyone has at the same time?"[9] Another is the riddle for one's equal or like in "What good thing did man find on earth that God never found?"[10] Patent impossibilities in terms of acts occur now and again as riddles, and some of them enjoy a surprising popularity. They do not, however, constitute a form that is readily intelligible. I have found no clue to explain the English smoke riddle, "Up chin cherry, down chin cherry, not a man could climb chin cherry."[11] Although it is obvious that a man cannot climb up or down a bank of smoke, the maker of the riddle seems to have had more than that in mind, and the meaning of "chin cherry" remains insoluble. A few widely used riddles involve an apparent contradiction in logic like "The more you take from it, the larger it gets."[12] Others contrast the varying behavior of several persons toward the same object, as in the old and famous coffin riddle, "The man who made it had no use for it; the man who bought it didn't want it, the man who got it didn't know it."[13]

1573–1596. Possession

1573–1575. Everyone Has It

The notion that everyone owns the very same object usually serves to describe a name.[1] It also occurs in a few riddles having other answers. Such anomalous queries as the Cherekessian mouth riddle, "I have it, you have it, there is no one in the world who does not have it"[2] or the Polish death riddle, "What is

---

[6] See Nos. 1728 through 1735.
[8] No. 1707.
[10] No. 1720a.
[12] No. 1691a.
[1] See No. 1573.

[7] See Nos. 1713 through 1721.
[9] No. 1573.
[11] No. 1616d.
[13] No. 1729e.
[2] Tambiev, p. 53, No. 7.

it that man cannot do without?,"³ which is a similar idea, seem to be quite accidental inventions. The curious English riddle⁴ for the ends of a pudding is probably based on a proverb, but a similar idea appears in Claret's fifteenth-century "Omnibus appendet rebus: finis bene tendet" (p. 71, No. 70). A variation of the theme has the form, "Christ had it not; Napoleon had it."⁵ This is akin to the theme of riddles with a letter of the alphabet as answer. See, for example, the Turkish "I [ben] have it, you [sen] have it, man [insan] has it, but man [adam] does not.—The letter N."⁶

The Irish "There it is for you, and it isn't heavy for you; it isn't your soul nor your body nor any part of your life, and you have it from now on"⁷ and the Icelandic "What clings to everything?"⁸ are the only vernacular instances of this assertion that the name clings to the bearer that I have found in western Europe. It seems to underlie the Renaissance Latin distich:

> Ominbus appendet rebus, cunctisque cohaeret,
> Hoc sine quid sit res noscere nemo potest.⁹

For other instances, which are found farther east, see the Modern Greek "I have a thing that clings to everything";¹⁰ the Albanian "It clings to everyone to whom you give it";¹¹ the Russian "However I may throw it, it clings to everything";¹² the Arabic and Turkish "It is something and yet it is nothing, it penetrates into everything" and "Something is in you, clings to you, enters into you, but does not come out from you."¹³ The Turks introduce an additional theme in "It fell from heaven and floated down, it fell to the ground and stuck,"¹⁴ which has a parallel in the Tatar "It fell from the sky and has stuck."¹⁵ Novel themes appear in the Yakut "They say that there is something that is never separated from your front"; "They say that there is something one never loses"; and "There is an everlasting seal, so they say."¹⁶ The Yakut "It is an immovable black tag, it is said,"¹⁷ is somewhat obscure.

The special variation characteristic of the Turkish riddles for a name occurs also in a Turkish snow riddle: "Drifting around, it fell from heaven; it falls to the ground and sticks there."¹⁸

The notion that every creature or every object in the world has a particular thing in common is applicable to various objects. It occurs in widely known riddles for:

---

³ Gustawicz, 554.
⁴ See No. 1575 below.
⁵ See the headnote to No. 1721.
⁶ Kowalski, *Zagadki*, 132.
⁷ O Dalaigh, 206.
⁸ Árnason, 445.
⁹ Buchler, *Gnomologia*, 3d ed. (1614), p. 411.
¹⁰ Sakellarios, p. 292, No. 7.   ¹¹ Hahn, p. 161, No. 4.
¹² Sadovnikov, 2059.
¹³ Arabic: Ruoff, p. 18, Nos. 15, 16. Turkish: Hamizade, 281 (I have a thing; it enters everywhere).
¹⁴ Kúnos, 123. See also Hamizade, 280 (It fell from heaven, it sticks to the ground), 282 (It descended from the sky, it stuck to the whole world).
¹⁵ Kalashev and Ioakimov, p. 50, No. 25.   ¹⁶ Piekarski, 197 through 199.
¹⁷ Popov, p. 286.   ¹⁸ Kúnos, 122.

§ 1. A shadow. German: H. Meier, *Ostfriesland*, 36; Loewenthal, p. 89. French: Rolland, 19b (What is that which I have you have, the forests, the plants, the beasts, and everything in the world has, and even the fish that swim?), and Rolland, *Rimes*, p. 197, No. 6; Ledieu, *Démuin*, p. 327; Carmeau, p. 34; Mensignac, *Gironde*, p. 300, No. 15. Russian: Sadovnikov, 1892 (You have it, I have it, the oak in the field, the fish in the sea has [it]). Hungarian: *Magazin für die Litteratur des Auslands*, 1856, p. 364; Arany and Gyulai, II, 350, No. 8 = *Magyar Nyelvör*, IV (1875), 559, No. 74 = *ibid.*, VII (1878), 476, No. 43 (I have it, you have it, the fence in the garden has it); *Magyar Nyelvör*, III (1874), 38, No. 28 (I have one, you have one, the tree in the garden also has one); VI (1877), 270, No. 24, has "the little tree," and XII (1883), 286, No. 33, has "the oak tree," instead of "tree"; VI (1877), 423, No. 46 (I have one, you have one, each of a hundred stakes also has one). Turkish: Moshkov in Radlov, X, 265, No. 10 (You have it and I have it and the dry twig has it). Crimean Tatar: Filonenko, 51 (I have one; you have one; a tree thoroughly dried up has one).

The similarity of the French and Russian versions is striking enough to suggest tracing them back to a common medieval source, but I have not found it.

§ 2. Blood. Norwegian: Bugge, *Telemarken*, 42 (I have it, and you have it, and the white goat has it). Italian: Gianandrea, *Archivio*, I (1882), 401, No. 6 (I have it, you have it, the cat has it); Tammi, 38.

§ 3. Parents. Modern Greek: Polites, *Neohellenika Analekta*, I, 211, No. 105 (You have it, I have it, all the world has it, some have one, some have two, and some have none at all).

1573. What is it that everyone has at the same time?—A name.
Waugh, *Canada*, p. 70, No. 809.

1574. A tea-kettle is a tea-kettle, / A tea-kettle has what everything has. / Now what has a tea-kettle?—A name.
Chappell, p. 236, No. 38.

1575. Everything has it and so does the pudding.—Two ends.
Oral, New York.

1576. Have It without Knowing

1576. What is it you want but when you have it you don't know that you have it?—Sleep.
Oral, Chicago.

1577. Have It; Are without It

1577. I am without it, and yet I have it: / Tell me what it is, and pray God save it.—It is my heart, for I am without it seeing that it is within me, for ye may not understand that by the Riddle that I lacke it.
Meery Riddles (1629), No. 19 = Brandl, p. 11.

1578. Have It Here; See It There

The contradiction in having an object and yet seeing it at a distance is applicable to one's breath,[1] which is visible on a cold day. Closely related to it are such conceptions as the Portuguese riddles for thought, "Me here, me there.—Mind"[2] and "I am here and I am there";[3] the Chinyanja "However far away it be, this very day this thing reaches there";[4] the Rumanian "It was all over the world and does not change its place,"[5] which also resembles some riddles already discussed elsewhere. The Serbian riddle for a spark, "Now it's here and now it's not,"[6] and such variations as the Hungarian "When it is here, it bites; when it leaves, it dies"[7] or the Bulgarian "Here I am, there I am, and yet they cannot catch me"[8] introduce some other ideas. See also the Modern Greek descriptions of an echo, "I am here and I am found there,"[9] and of a needle, "I put it in here and I find it there."[10] Perhaps most closely related to the riddles for the mind or thought are those for the eyes and sight. Examples are found in India; see the Bhil "This came and that went.—Sight";[11] the Uraon "Quickly it comes, quickly it goes"[12] with the parallel, "Here it comes, there it goes."[13] I do not fully understand the New Mexican towel riddle, "You there and I here" (Tú allá y yo aquí),[14] but take it to be playing with the syllables making up *toalla* (towel). Such punning on syllables, somewhat in the manner of a charade, occurs frequently in Spanish riddling. Rather remote from the ideas here discussed is the notion of a thing that comes and goes, although we do not see any trace.[15]

1578a. Here I have it, and yonder I see it.—It is my breath in a misty morning; for here I have it in my mouth, and yonder I see it a yard from me.
Meery Riddles (1629), No. 50 = Brandl, p. 16.

1578b. here j sawe it & yander it is.—our breth.
Tupper, *Holme Riddles*, 54.

1578c. Yonder it is, and here I have it.—A man's breath, or other living creature's.
Prettie Riddles (1631), No. 30 = Brandl, p. 56.

1579–1581. Have It; Never See It

1579. You feel it; you never saw it, and never will.—Your heart.
Waugh, *Canada*, p. 69, No. 791.

---

[1] See No. 1578a through 1578c.
[2] Parsons, *Cape Verde*, 234.
[3] Parsons, *Cape Verde*, 235.
[4] Rattray, p. 155.
[5] Papahagi, 61. See also the headnote to Nos. 125–130 above and Straparola, *Le piacevoli notti*, IX, 3.
[6] Novaković, p. 13, No. 2.
[7] *Magyar Nyelvör*, XXXI (1902), 534, No. 61.
[8] Chacharov, 39.
[9] Polites, *Neohellenika Analekta*, I, 209, No. 92.
[10] Polites, *Neohellenika Analekta*, I, 221, No. 158.
[11] Hedberg, p. 880, No. 94.
[12] Archer, p. 190, No. 165.
[13] Archer, p. 190, No. 166. Compare also the headnote to No. 1471 above.
[14] Campa, 102.
[15] See the headnote to No. 227 above.

1580. There's a t'ing, it's no use to you, you cannot see it, but you cannot do without it, but you always have it with you. What's dat?—Your footsteps.
Johnson, *Antigua*, p. 87, No. 54.

1581. w^t is that as is now nev^r seen by eys & who doth seeke to show her hath bine [been] accounted wise yet somtymes we do knowe [of] her onely the wals by viewing well of her close house where she doth dwell.—ones thought.
Tupper, *Holme Riddles*, 72.

1582–1585. Have It; Others Use It

Alexandre Sylvain's version,[1] which is the earliest that I have seen, is interesting for the introduction of additional themes. It is as follows:

> Declairez moy quelle est la chose,
> Que vous protez mais dire i'ose,
> Que l'usage en est plus à nous,
> Que iamais il ne fut à vous.
> A vostre naissance ne l'estes:
> Mais un temps apres la receutes,
> Encore apres vostre trespas
> L'aurez, qui n'est estrange cas?

1582a. What belongs to yourself, yet is used by everybody more than yourself?—Your name.
Knortz, p. 232, No. 96; Perkins, *New Orleans*, p. 113, No. 85.

1582b. What is that which belongs to you, / But others use it more than you do?—Your name.
Greenleaf, *Newfoundland*, p. 10, No. 20.

1582c. You've got it. You know it. / Somebody else use it more than you do.—Name.
Parsons, *Guilford Co., N.C.*, p. 204, No. 26.

1583a. You've got it. / I haven't got it, / But yet I use it the mos'.—Yer name.
Parsons, *Aiken, S.C.*, p. 33, No. 56.

1583b. What's on you I use mo' dan you use yo'se'f?—Dat's a name.
Parsons, *Sea Islands, S.C.*, p. 170, No. 119.

1583c. What have you got that I use more than you do?—Your name.
Greenleaf, *Newfoundland*, p. 10, No. 20 var.

1583d. It's a thing you have that I use more than you.—Your name.
Parsons, *Eleuthera and Watling's Islands, Bahamas*, p. 441, No. 24.

1584. What is seldom used by you and generally called by others?—Your name.
Parsons, *Barbados*, p. 291, No. 118.

---

[1] *Cinquante Ænigmes françoises* (1582), p. 20, No. 21.

1585. There's a t'ing, every man has it and every woman has it as their personal property. Only once in a while they use it themselves. Other people will use it, although it is yours, whenever they want.—Dat's your name.
Johnson, *Antigua*, p. 88, No. 55.

1586–1588. Have It; Give It Away

Riddlers have shown little liking for the idea underlying the riddles in this section. Somewhat similar is the Lettish breath riddle, "What goes away so that one cannot get it again?"[1]

1586. What is it that you can keep after giving it to someone else?—Your word.
Gardner, *Schoharie Hills, N.Y.*, p. 258, No. 45.

1587. I had it and gave it to you, / You had it and can't keep it.—Money.
Fauset, *Nova Scotia*, p. 168, No. 135.

1588. I have a thing in my hand. Everybody come and take it away from me, and still I have it. What's dat.—My name.
Parsons, *Antilles*, III, 423, Montserrat, 33.

1589–1590. Don't Have It; Give It Away

The oldest example of this manner of riddling is a Czech question and answer scrawled in the Claret manuscript of the early fifteenth century: "Why do you look at me? You know that I have you. Pray to God that I may not have, that I might [give] to you again."[1] This text is supposed to be nearly as old as the manuscript and is consequently one of the oldest Czech riddles. Flajšhans believes it to be traditional and not literary in origin and cites a modern Hungarian parallel, "I gave when there was not; pray God that there may not be; I shall yet give."[2] The Czech and the Hungarian riddles have the same answer, "Old husband, young wife, lover." The interpretation of these confusing assertions is very difficult, but is greatly aided by a somewhat later version in Straparola's *Le piacevoli notti*[3] and a Modern Greek traditional text, "When I did not have it, I gave it to you. Now, when I have it, I do not give it to you. I pray that I had it not so that I might give it to you again.—A faithless woman and her lover, to whom she has given herself during the absence of her husband."[4]

The notion of giving away what one does not have occurs in several riddles. Although no longer very freely used, it has a history covering most of western Europe and extending back to the Renaissance. It may have originated in the riddle for baptism, which St. John the Baptist gave to his Master although he had it not. Typical themes described by it are as follows:

---

[1] Bielenstein, 522. See also No. 136 above.
[1] Flajšhans, p. 21.   [2] *Magyar Népköltési Gyütemény*, VI, No. 26.
[3] XII, 5.   [4] Dieterich, *Sporades*, 20.

§ 1. Baptism. Flemish: Joos, 833; Pol de Mont, *Volkskunde*, I (1888), 208, No. 45. German: Wossidlo, 414 (It was not in the world, no man had it, the servant gave it to the master, the servant did not have it, and the master gave it to the servant again); Schmidt, *Danzig*, 100; Butsch, 35. Norwegian: Stafset, 28; Brox, *Ytre Senja*, 198, citing Riksheim, 33. Latin: Claret, p. 72, No. 87 (Das hoc, quod nec habes); H. Therander (Johann Sommer), 92. French: Rolland, 266; *Les Adeuineaux amoureux*, p. lxx. Spanish: Rodríguez Marín, 893, 894. Argentinian: Lehmann-Nitsche, 656, 657. Dominican Rep.: Andrade, 57, 58 (A friend asked another for that which the world did not have. The friend gave it and yet kept it). Porto Rican: Mason, 16a through 16d, 90. Hungarian: *Magazin für die Litteratur des Auslands*, 1856, p. 364, No. 1; *Magyar Nyelvör*, V (1876), 422, No. 78 (The master didn't have it, the servant gave it to the master, the master returned it to the servant). Some of the foregoing resemble the slightly different Flemish "God had it not, the Devil didn't want it, the servant gave it to his master, and he did not have it himself" (Joos, 564).

Some of the preceding versions contain a very interesting and curious recollection of an ancient liturgy. In the antiphon for the octave of Epiphany we read "Baptizat miles regem, servus dominum, Johannes Salvatorem."[5] Neither the canticle nor the office to which it was attached are of Western origin. The words occur in a Greek versicle introduced into the Eastern ceremony of the Blessing of the Waters on the eve of Epiphany. This ritual is now obsolete in the Roman use except in the church of San Andrea della Valle at Rome.[6] Its characteristic of the less blessing the better (Quod minus est, a meliore benedicitur)[7] is reiterated in the litany chanted at the ceremony in Eastern churches and is reflected in the imperial coronation ceremonies.[8]

§ 2. A marriage, a husband, begetting a child, the name of wife. See Nos. 1589a through 1590, which ring changes on the answer. See also Breton: Duine, *Saint-Malo*, p. 518 (What is it that a young man can give a maiden that he does not have, that he cannot have, that he has never had, that he will never have, and that he cannot give to a young man?—The name of wife). Danish: Kristensen, p. 88, § 225, No. 348, and p. 154, § 443, No. 711.

---

[5] F. Procter and C. Wordsworth (eds.), *Breviarium ad usum insignis ecclesiae Sarum* (Cambridge, 1882), I, p. CCCL; André Mocquereau, *Le codex F 160 de la bibliothèque de cathédrale de Worcester* (Paléographie musicale, XII; 1922), fol. 58.
[6] See Hermann Usener, "Heilige Handlung," *Archiv für Religionswissenschaft*, VII (1904), 290 ff., reprinted in his *Kleine Schriften*, IV (1913).
[7] Heb. 7:7.
[8] F. C. Conybeare and A. J. Maclean, *Rituale Armenorum* (Oxford, 1905), pp. 426, 428, 429, 433, and compare pp. 186 ff. For the litany see A. Baumstark, "Die *Hodie*-Antiphonen des römischen Breviers und der Kreis ihrer griechischen Parallelen," *Die Kirchenmusik*, X (Paderborn, 1909), 153-160; N. Borgia, "Frammenti liturgici antichissimi inediti," *Byzantinische Zeitschrift*, XXX (1930), 347. For additional examples see E. H. Kantorowicz's forthcoming *Coronation and Epiphany*. I am indebted to his kindness and erudition for the preceding references.

Somewhat different is the Flemish description of marriage as a sacrament given by a celibate priest: "He who has it cannot give it, and he who hasn't it can give it."[9] This seems to be related to the following riddle for death.

§ 3. Death. French: Rolland, 280 (What is that, having it, you cannot give it to another, and not having it, you can give it?). Italian: Rolland, p. 16, No. 29 (a Renaissance text); Tschiedel, 47.

§ 4. A whetstone. Breton: Sébillot, *Devinettes*, 80a through 80c. French: *Les Adeuineaux amoureux*, p. lxxv = Rolland, 210. Rumanian: Gorovei, 908 (What gives that which it does not have?—A whetstone gives an edge).

1589a. Who was the man that give away what he didn't have?—There was a man who didn't have a chil', give away another man chil' at the church. Give another man daughter to her husband.
Parsons, *Barbados*, p. 290, No. 100.

1589b. What is that which a gentleman has not, and never can have, but may give to a lady?—Husband.
Knortz, p. 235, No. 116.

1589c. What is it that a man can give to a lady and can't give to another man?—A husband.
Perkins, *New Orleans*, p. 113, No. 72.

1590. S^r j would desire of y^u if y^u plase [please] it is a thing y^u neu^r had nor shall have yet give it to me y^u very esily may.—***a woman desire[s] that the man would get her wth child that she may have it by him although hee can not have it himselfe.
Tupper, *Holme Riddles*, 91.

1591–1592. Lose What Is Taken; Keep What Is Not Taken

The scene of catching game and throwing it away, or of not catching it and bringing it home,[1] here becomes a statement of vaguer acts concerned with an unnamed object. A Norwegian version, "A man went to the woods, and what he found he left and what he did not find he took with him,"[2] shows how this degeneration occurred.

Somewhat the same idea, although the inventions may very well be independent of this riddle, occur in the Batak description of a bullet, "He who gets it is sad; he who loses it is glad,"[3] and the Filipino shadow riddles, "If there is none, you are seeking it; if there is some, you do not take it" and "At noon I must depart to find [it]; if I can find [it], I will not take [it]."[4]

1591. A thing that I take, that I loose [lose], / yet nothing to my woe; / and that I take not, that I keepe, / yet would it faine foregoe.—He that is all

---

[9] Joos, 101.
[1] See No. 460a, 460b and the headnote to No. 460.
[2] Bergh, *Valdres*, 8.   [3] Ophuijsen, 203.
[4] Starr, *Philippines*, 330, 334.

lowsie: those lice that he takes [he] throwes them away, and those that he cannot take [he] keepes them still, and yet would faine be rid of them.
Prettie Riddles (1631), No. 43 = Brandl, p. 58.

1592. W^t is that that having taken wee have lost & haveing not taken we have kept.—A vermine that is taken & cast away & that al[l] they do not take the[y] keepe about them.
Tupper, Holme Riddles, 4.

1593–1595. Haven't It; Wouldn't Want to Lose It

This apparently impossible contradiction serves to describe:
§ 1. A bald head. See Nos. 1593a through 1593i.
§ 2. One eye. The oldest version seems to be the Latin

Non habeo, nec habere velim, quod si tamen adsit,
Non caream Croesi si mihi dentur opes.[1]

See also such modern versions as Danish: Kristensen, p. 155, § 450, No. 719. Hungarian: Arany and Gyulai, III, 297, No. 3 (I haven't got it, and I hope the Lord won't give it to me; however, in case He should give it to me, I wouldn't like to lose it for any treasures of the earth).

§ 3. A wooden leg. Breton: Sauvé, 123.

§ 4. Two heads. German: Butsch, 190; Hanika-Otto, 219 (No one has it, no one wants it, whoever has it doesn't want to give it up). French: Rolland, 121.

§ 5. A humpback. Danish: Kristensen, p. 104, § 282, No. 440.

§ 6. Age. The first versions that I have noted are reported in seventeenth-century Latin collections. Buchler quotes "Me cupit omnis homo, nemo non odit adeptus" and adds a variant in three lines of verse.[2] Johannes Pincier versifies it:

Me metuunt omnes, & me nihilominus omnes
Mortales optant, quotquot his orbis habet.[3]

For modern traditional versions see Breton: Kerbeuzec, Ille-et-Vilaine, 76. Flemish: Joos, 118. German: Wossidlo, 396; Gilhoff, 649. Danish: Kristensen, p. 13, § 4, No. 5, citing Skattegraveren, IV, 519 (What is that which everyone wants and yet is such that no one will pay a penny for it?). Swedish: Ström, p. 72, "Människans aldrar," 4. Serbian: Novaković, p. 215, No. 3 (Everybody desires me, but the one who has me would give all his property if he could make me vanish). Indonesian, Javanese: Ranneft, Poëzie, p. 67, No. 10 (The living desire it, and those who have it are rarely cheerful and contented in spirit).

---

[1] Buchler, Gnomologia, 3d ed. (1614), p. 446.
[2] Gnomologia, 3d ed. (1614), p. 452.
[3] Ænigmatum libri tres (The Hague, 1655), pp. 172–179 (Book II, No. 35 [wrongly numbered 30]).

§ 7. Lice or fleas. Catalan: Pelay y Briz, 116 (I don't have it, I don't want it, and I look for it). Italian: Rolland, p. 161, No. 32 (What is that thing, which when you have it, you seek it and do not wish to find it?). Modern Greek: E. Rolland, *Rapport sur une mission littéraire en Grèce* (Paris, 1877) as cited in Rolland, *Faune populaire*, III (Paris, 1881), 261 (There is a thing that you have that you don't want and that you seek.—Flea).

§ 8. A lawsuit.[5] Spanish, Dominican Rep.: Andrade, 263 (What is it that one doesn't have and doesn't want to have and if he has it, he doesn't want to lose it?). The German "Whoever has it is angry; whoever loses it is still angrier; whoever gains it has it no longer"[6] is a different theme.

1593a. What' that? / I haven't got it, / I would not have it. / If I had it, / I wouldn't take the world for it.—Bald head.
  Bacon and Parsons, *Virginia*, p. 320, No. 75; Parsons, *Guilford Co., N.C.*, p. 204, No. 34; Parsons, *Aiken, S.C.*, p. 36, No. 84.
  A million dollars: Farr, *Tennessee*, p. 318, No. 4. A thousand pounds: Greenleaf, *Newfoundland*, p. 13, No. 40.

1593b. You got it, you don't want it, / You wouldn' take the wor' for it.—Bal' head.
  Parsons, *Robeson Co., N.C.*, p. 389, No. 14.

1593c. You ain't got it, / But if you had it, / You wouldn't take nothin' for it.—Bald head.
  Fauset, *Southern Negro*, p. 288, No. 129.

1593d. What is that which if you have not you would not like to get and if you have you would not like to lose?—A bald head.
  Beckwith, *Jamaica*, p. 216, No. 256; Brewster, *Indiana*, 44; oral, New Hampshire.

1593e. I haven't got it, don't want, wouldn't have it. But if I had it, I would not take the whole world for it.—Bald head.
  Perkins, *New Orleans*, p. 110, No. 37.

1593f. I ain't got it, / You ain't got it, / Mr. State's got it, / And wouldn't give it for all the world.—Mr. State's bald head.
  Fauset, *Nova Scotia*, p. 154, No. 53.

1593g. De man who haven't got it don't want it; and de man who got it wouldn't take a thousand dollars for it.—Bald head.
  Parsons, *Sea Islands, S.C.*, p. 174, No. 165.

1593h. Didn't want it, tried not to get it, / Wouldn't give it up for a bootful of money.—A bald head.
  Randolph and Taylor, *Ozarks*, 21.

1593i. What is it that a man has and doesn't want, yet he would hate to lose it?—A bald head.
  Redfield, *Tennessee*, p. 40, No. 58.

---

[5] Compare a Danish riddle on the same subject cited in the headnote to Nos. 1632-1642 below.
[6] Gilhoff, 647.

1594. What is that no man would have, and yet, when he hath it, will not forgoe it?—It is a broken head or such like; for no man would gladly have a broken head, and yet, when he hath it, he would be loath to lose his head, though it be broken.
Meery Riddles (1629), No. 64 = Brandl, p. 19.

1595. I haven't got it and I don't want it, but if I had it, / I wouldn't sell it for a thousand pounds.—A baby.
Greenleaf, Newfoundland, p. 13, No. 40.

1596. Wouldn't Give It Away; Wouldn't Keep It

The following riddle has every appearance of having been disseminated by literary means. The interlaced rhymes and the puns also suggest its literary associations. The introductory paradox, "Formed long ago, yet made today," has not always been intelligible to those who kept it and has been distorted (No. 1596b) or lost (No. 1596c) in the process of oral transmission. It is explained by the Lettish "Ready-made many years ago and made only just now" (Bielenstein, 239), in which the contrast and obscurity of "formed [manufactured] long ago" and "made [made up, prepared for sleeping] today," as in the English riddle, confuse the hearer.

For a curious entanglement with a special variety of the coffin riddle see No. 1210 above.[1]

1596a. Formed long ago, yet made today, / Employed while others sleep; / What few would like to give away, / Nor any wish to keep.—A bed.
Halliwell-Phillipps, Nursery Rhymes, p. 131; Parsons, Bermuda, p. 261, No. 121; Beckwith, Jamaica, p. 213, No. 240; Greenleaf, Newfoundland, p. 8, No. 3; Knortz, p. 230, No. 79.

1596b. Found long ago, yet made today, / And most enjoyed when others sleep, / What few would wish to give away, / And fewer still would wish to keep.—Beds.
Leather, Hereford, p. 230; Waugh, Canada, p. 70, No. 800.

1596c. Formed long ago, made every day, / Few wish to keep it, and less to give it away.—Bed.
Kavanagh, Béaloideas, II (1929–1930), 295.

1596d. Nobody wants to keep it and nobody will give it away.—Bed.
Fauset, Nova Scotia, p. 154, No. 52 var.

1596e. Built many, many years ago, / Yet in use today, / How many would like to give it away?—Bed.
Fauset, Nova Scotia, p. 154, No. 52 var.

---

[1] Compare with No. 1209, which has the answer "coffin," and see the notes to Nos. 1209 and 1210. For a discussion of a group of coffin riddles based on a similar concept, see the headnote to Nos. 1728–1737.

1597–1627. Motion

1597–1603. "Through a Rock [Distaff], Through a Reel"

The import of this riddle, which is very widely known in England and America, is obscure. The usual answers are a worm, a spider, and lightning. In an apparent failure to understand the riddle, other answers are offered. For a curious endeavor to introduce personification into this riddle see No. 707 above. Riddlers usually add some such phrase as "Such a riddle was never known," which is a formula characteristic of neck-riddles or enigmas describing an event known only to the inventor, who hopes to save his neck by his puzzle. It is not clear whether this formula has survived in this riddle from a possibly original use as a neck-riddle or whether riddlers add it because they find the riddle unintelligible. A connection with neck-riddles appears in the fact that the poser in No. 1602 has an answer belonging to a neck-riddle.

1597a. Riddle me, riddle me, riddle meree, / Tell me what my riddle's to be? / Thruff a rock, thruff a reel, thruff an old woman's spinning wheel; / Thruff a milner's hopper, thruff a bag o' pepper, / Thruff an old mare's shink shank bone; / Such a riddle I have [never?] known.—A worm.
  Gutch and Peacock, *Lincolnshire*, p. 400, No. 28.

1597b. Riddle, riddle, ree, / Such a riddle couldn't be, / Through rocks, through reels, / Through an old spinning wheel, / Through a basin full of pepper, / Through a sheep's tetter, / Through a horse's shin bone. / If you riddle me that, / I'll let you alone.—A mat of worms.
  Whitney and Bullock, *Maryland*, p. 175, No. 2690.

1597c. Thorow a rocke, thorow a reele, / thorow an old spinning wheele, / thorow a hard shining bone: / such a riddle you have none.—It is a worme.
  Meery Riddles (1629), No. 40 = Brandl, p. 15.

1598a. Thru the rock, thru the reel, / Thru the old spinning wheel, / Thru the old sheep's shankbone, / A riddle like this was never known.—A maggot.
  Greenleaf, *Newfoundland*, p. 15 (West Virginia).

1598b. Through the rock, / Through the reel, / Through the mistress' spinning wheel, / Through the sheep shank bone, / Such a riddle was never known. —Maggot in a bone.
  Fauset, *Southern Negro*, p. 286, No. 114.

1598c. Through a rock, / Through a rill, / Through an old spinning-wheel. / Through a ladle full of pepper, / Through an old rotten heifer.—A piece of decayed meat with maggots.
  Fauset, *Nova Scotia*, p. 163, No. 104.

1599. Thru a rock, thru a reel, / Thru a hipper, thru a clipper, / Thru a basin full of pepper, / Thru an old cow's shin bone, / A riddle like this was never known.—A spider.
  Greenleaf, *Newfoundland*, p. 15.

1600. Through a rock, / Through a wheel, / Through an old spinning-wheel, / Through a basket, / Through a horse's shin bone, / Such a riddle was never known.—Frost.
Fauset, *Nova Scotia*, p. 163, No. 105.

1601a. Through a rock, / Through a reel, / Through a sheep's shank bone, / Such a riddle was never known.—Lightning.
Carter, *Mountain White*, p. 79.

1601b. Through an old maid's spinning wheel, / Through a miller's hopper, / Through a bag of pepper, / Through a horse's shinbone, / Such a riddle has never been known.—Lightning.
Redfield, *Tennessee*, p. 37, No. 15.

1601c. Through a rock, through a wheel, through a flyin' spinnin' wheel, / Through a shin bone, through a shan bone. / Such a little riddle never be known.—Lightning.
Parsons, *Antilles*, III, 376, St. Vincent, 10.

1601d. Through the rack, through the reel, / Through my grandmother's old spinning wheel, / Shelf, shank, skin, and bone. It's the best old riddle ever known.—Thunder and lightning.
Hudson, p. 90, No. 48.

1602. Through a rock, through a rill, / Through an old spinning-wheel, / Sheep, shin, shank, hair, and bone. / The awfulest riddle that ever was known.—A partridge built its nest in a dead horse's head.
Redfield, *Tennessee*, p. 44, No. 102.

1603. Through a rock, through a reel, / Through an old spinning wheel, / Through a miller's hopper, / Through a bag of pepper, / Through an old man's shin bone. / Riddle me that, or leave it alone!—Moth.
MacGréine, *Béaloideas*, III (1931-9132), 413, No. 1.

1604. Up and Down

1604a. Up the chimney down, / Down the chimney up, / Won't go up the chimney up, / Or down the chimney up.—An umbrella.
Fauset, *Nova Scotia*, p. 173, No. 186.

1604b. What goes up the chimney down, and can't go up the chimney up?—An umbrella.
Fauset, *Nova Scotia*, p. 173, No. 186 var.

1604c. What goes up the chimney down, / But can't come down the chimney up?—Umbrella.
Hyatt, *Adams Co., Ill.*, p. 669, No. 10931.

1604d. Whut won't go up th' chimney up, / But will go up th' chimney down? / Whut won't go down the chimney up, / But will go down th' chimney down?—An umbrella.
Randolph and Spradley, *Ozark*, p. 83.

1604e. What will go up a drain down, but will not go down a drain up?—An umbrella.
Farr, *Tennessee*, p. 320, No. 32.

1604f. What goes up a stovepipe down, and down a stovepipe down, but won't go up a stovepipe up, or down a stovepipe up?—Umbrella.
Oral, Ohio.

1605. Goes from Hand to Hand

Only a few riddles call money an object that passes from hand to hand. A related idea, which has some similarity to a riddle for lightning,[1] sketches a more vivid picture, comparing money to chips hewn in one country and flying about in another.[2] This latter scene is applicable to:

§ 1. Snow. Lettish: Bielenstein, 586 (Abroad wood was being hewn, here the chips are falling).

§ 2. The stars. Lettish: Bielenstein, 705 (Abroad a beam was cut, the chips flew hither).

§ 3. A letter. Afrikaans: Groenewald, p. 84. Russian: Arkhangel'skii, p. 79 (They are chopping in St. Petersburg, the chips fly here); Preobrazhenskii, p. 172. Mordvin: Ahlqvist, p. 41, No. 9; Paasonen, 35. Zyrian: Wichmann, *Zyrian*, 164 (They hew wood in St. Petersburg, but the chips fall here). Mingrelian: Blechsteiner, p. xxiv and p. 155, No. 24 (a proverb). Yakut: Piekarski, 236 (They say that the chips from the trees that are chopped in the Land of the South[3] fly to this land, while the chips of this land fly to the Land of the South).[4] Tungus: Poppe, 7 (On the other side of the sea they work wood, the chips fly to this side).

More picturesque formulations of this idea are the Zyrian "The foal whinnies, the stallion neighs, but the reins reach to here";[5] and the Turkish "I have a little bird, it flies through the world, circles about, returns, and finds me,"[6] "A little thing that walks about the world,"[7] and "At Stambul a *kete*[8] is baking, its odor reaches here,"[9] with its variant "In Instanbul he cooked some milk, its smell reached to here."[10] I can cite no parallel to the Tschuana "I stabbed an ox in Kwena land. Its blood spurted to here."[11]

§ 4. A bell ringing. Lithuanian: Schleicher, p. 200 (They chop in the wood, the chips fly about at home). Polish: Gustawicz, 79 through 81; Kopernicki, 96 (When they chop a tree in Rabka, it can be heard in Ponice), 96 var. (When they chop an oak in one village, the chips fly to another village). Hungarian: *Magyar Nyelvör*, II (1873), 43, No. 11 (Although they chop wood

---

[1] See the headnote to No. 398, nn. 6–7.   [2] Finnish: Lönnrot, 1549 = Henssen, 180.
[3] Russia.
[4] He cites the variant: "They say that the chips from the Land of the South fly here."
[5] Wichmann, *Zyrian*, 203, citing the variant "One hears the sound as far as Yaroslav."   [6] Kowalski, *Asia Minor*, 45.
[7] Kowalski, *North Bulgaria*, 141.   [8] A kind of cake.
[9] Kowalski, *Zagadki*, 122.   [10] Hamizade, 481.
[11] Kuhn, *Tschuana*, 40. Kwena land lies far distant from the Tschuana.

in Nova, the chips fly here); XIII (1884), 574, No. 4 (When they chop wood in Krasso, the chips fly here); and XVIII (1889), 376.

1605. Something goes from hand to hand, and has no owner.—Money.
Parsons, *Sea Islands, S.C.*, p. 175, No. 186.

1606–1607. Miscellaneous

The two descriptions of an object as something moving and yet as not possessing details characteristic of an animal, a person, or a thing are confused products of the folk muse. The riddle comparing a bird to a load of hay (No. 1606) refers, probably, to its feathers, but the riddler's conception wavers and leaves no clear scene. The description of candy as "going" the more it leaks (No. 1607) is a pun that is neither completely intelligible nor witty.

1606. As I was going over London Brig, / I met a load of hay, / I shot wi' my pistol, / And all flew away.—A bird.
Baring-Gould, *Notes and Queries*, 3d ser., VIII (1865), 325 (Yorkshire).

1607. What's dat de mo' it leak, de mo' it go?—Kyandy [candy].
Parsons, *Sea Islands, S.C.*, p. 172, No. 151.

1608–1627. Motion Denied

A small group of riddles describe an object in terms of a motion that it cannot or does not make. Few of them offer any points of interest. The bed riddle[1] contains an old proverbial theme;[2] the horse riddle[3] is really a proverb and not a riddle at all; the notion that a wagon or train doesn't need noise but cannot go without it[4] has a limited currency in Europe. The curious description of smoke as something (chip cherry) that cannot be climbed[5] is surprisingly popular and has suggested some analogous riddles, but its meaning remains obscure.

1608. You Go to It Because It Won't Come to You

This riddle has been suggested by the old query about Mahomet and the mountain: "Why did the prophet Mahomet go to the mountain?—Because the mountain would not come to him."[1] Many minor varieties[2] of this query occur in collections of traditional riddles. See, for example, the English "Why

---

[1] No. 1608.
[2] See the headnote to No. 1608, n. 1.
[3] No. 1610.
[4] Nos. 1614a through 1614d.
[5] Nos. 1616a through 1617g.

[1] For the origin and history of this query see G. Büchmann, *Geflügelte Worte*, 23d ed., p. 343 (In some older editions it appears in the section containing materials which were not to be kept up to date. The section was dropped in the course of time, but later editors restored the query to the canon); A. Wesselski, *Der Hodscha Nasreddin* (Weimar, 1911), II, 190–191, No. 372, and *Märchen des Mittelalters* (Berlin, 1925), pp. 263–265.
[2] French: *Les Adeuineaux amoureux*, pp. lxxxiv–lxxxv, xciii; Rolland, 320. Spanish, Mexican: Noguera, 34. Polish: Gustawicz, 551.

do lazy boys go to school?"³ or the Breton "Why does the bull go to the hedge?"⁴

1608. If you don' go dere, it never come to you.—Bed.
Parsons, *Bahamas*, p. 473, No. 24.

1609–1610. Does Not (Should Not) Move (Gallop)

1609. Something in water and can't move.—Buoy.
Parsons, *Bermuda*, p. 264, No. 147.

1610. Up the hill gallop me not, / In the level spur me not.—Horse.
Parsons, *Barbados*, p. 290, No. 102.

1611–1613. Cannot Overtake It

1611. I heard a rickety-racket, / Pulled off my shoes and stockings and couldn't o'ertak' it.—Railway-train.
Burne, *Shropshire*, p. 574, No. 8.

1612. I heard a rickety-racket, / Pulled off my shoes an run a'ter it.—Pap in a bottle, i.e., to still the child's rickety-racket.
Burne, *Shropshire*, p. 574, No. 7.

1613. One thing behind another an' never catch up.—Man shoving a wheelbarrow.
Fauset, *Southern Negro*, p. 283, No. 78.

1614–1615. Cannot Go without It

The notion which is here applied to a noise is also used of a shadow; see the Irish "I see it and don't notice it, walking on top of the coals, the dew doesn't wet it, and it doesn't travel alone"[1] and a colonial Spanish reference to the theme.[2]

1614a. What goes with a coach, / And comes with a coach, / And the coach can't go without it?—Noise.
Fauset, *Nova Scotia*, p. 174, No. 203; oral, New Hampshire.

1614b. Whut is it goes when th' wagon goes, stops when th' wagon stops, aint no good, but you caint get along without it?—The squeak.
Randolph and Spradley, *Ozark*, p. 81.

1614c. What goes along with a wagon that one doesn't need, yet cannot get along without?—A noise.
Redfield, *Tennessee*, p. 39, No. 48; Brewster, *Indiana*, 57.

---

[3] Parsons, *Sea Islands, S.C.*, p. 174, No. 177.
[4] Sébillot, *Haute-Bretagne*, 88.

[1] O Dalaigh, 113. Compare also No. 113 above, and the headnote to Nos. 165–173, § 3.
[2] Dominican Rep.: Andrade, 284.

1614d. What is that a train cannot move without and yet still it's of no use to it?—Noise.
Parsons, *Barbados*, p. 289, No. 87.

1615. Full rigged ship, / Everything to go with it, / Something that's no good to her, / But she can't go without taking it.—The weight of the ship.
Fauset, *Nova Scotia*, p. 160, No. 84.

1616–1627. Cannot Climb It

The notion that smoke cannot be climbed might seem so obvious that many riddlers would have hit upon it, but I can cite only the African parallel, "What is the unstable thing [which is strong but] which cannot be climbed?"[1] The allusion to strength refers to the power of smoke to make the eyes smart. The fact that this parallel is from Africa might suggest looking there for an explanation of the entirely obscure "chip cherry" or "chin cherry," but a similar phrase in a riddle from northeast Scotland seems to stand in the way.[2] Riddlers say that a pecan tree cannot be climbed,[3] but the import of this assertion is obscure.[4]

1616a. Chip cherry up, chip cherry down, / No man can climb chip cherry up, / No man can climb chip cherry up chip cherry down.—Smoke.
Puckett, *Southern Negro*, p. 53.

1616b. Chip chip cherry, / No man could climb chip chip cherry.—Smoke.
Parsons, *Sea Islands, S.C.*, p. 153, No. 5, var. 1; Halpert, *New Jersey*, p. 201, No. 5.

1616c. Chip cherry up, chip cherry down; no man can climb up chip cherry tree.—Smoke.
Johnson, *St. Helena Island, S.C.*, p. 157, No. 2.

1616d. Up chin cherry, / Down chin cherry, / Not a man could climb chin cherry.—Smoke.
Parsons, *Bahamas*, p. 484, No. 126; Parsons, *Antilles*, III, 435, St. Martin, 7 var. Chip-cherry: Beckwith, *Jamaica*, p. 203, No. 185.

1616e. Up chin-cherry, / Down chin-cherry, / Not a man to climb chin-cherry.—Smoke.
Parsons, *Antilles*, III, 441, Anguilla, 34.

1616f. Once upon a time, / Up chin cherry, / Down chin cherry. / Not a man could climb chin cherry.—Smoke.
Parsons, *Antilles*, III, 435, St. Martin, 7.

---
[1] Suk: Beech, p. 43, No. 1.
[2] No. 1617f below. In No. 1627 "chip-cherry" signifies something black. Can it be connected with chokecherry? See also the cry "Chickamacherry" in No. 564.
[3] No. 1709.
[4] See, however, the Togo and Filipino riddles in which a woman one cannot marry is compared to a tree that cannot be climbed, in the headnote to No. 1070, n. 5.

1617a. Chin [variant: chick] cherry up, chin [variant: chick] cherry down. / No man can climb chin cherry hill.—Smoke.
Parsons, *Sea Islands, S.C.*, p. 152, No. 5.

1617b. Chip cherry up and chip cherry down, / No one knows where it belongs. / What's that?—Smoke.
Parsons, *Sea Islands, S.C.*, p. 152, No. 5, var. 5.

1617c. No man could climb chin chee but chin chee se'f.—Smoke.
Parsons, *Sea Islands, S.C.*, p. 152, No. 5, var. 2.

1617d. Me riddle me riddle, / Perhaps you can clear dis riddle. / Up Saint Cherry, / Down Saint Cherry, / No man can climb up Sin Cherry.—Smoke.
Parsons, *Bahamas*, p. 477, No. 55. Sancharies: Parsons, *Bahamas*, p. 477, No. 55 var.

1617e. Ma shinee high, / Ma shinee low, / No man can climb ma shinee.—Smoke.
Parsons, *Sea Islands, S.C.*, p. 153, No. 5, var. 3.

1617f. Chick, chick, cherry, / A' the men in Kerry, / Cudna clum chick, chick, cherry.—Smoke.
Gregor, *Northeast Scotland*, p. 80.

1617g. Tritter, tritter, tritter tree, / No man can climb tritter tree.—Smoke.
Parsons, *Sea Islands, S.C.*, p. 153, No. 5, var. 4.

1618. Up chip cherry, down chip cherry, / Governor horse cyant climb chip cherry.—Chimney.
Parsons, *Barbados*, p. 276, No. 1.

1619a. Go up chip cherry, come down chip cherry, / No man can climb chip cherry like me.—Ants.
Parsons, *Barbados*, p. 276, No. 1 var.

1619b. Go up chip cherry, come down chip cherry, / But little Willie can climb chip cherry like me.—Ants.
Parsons, *Barbados*, p. 276, No. 1 var.

1619c. What that climb a chimney like me?—Ant.
Parsons, *Barbados*, p. 276, No. 1 var.

1620. Go up chip cherry, come down chip cherry, / No man can climb chip cherry like me.—Coconut tree.
Parsons, *Barbados*, p. 276, No. 1 var.

1621. Up chip cherry, down chip cherry, / Many man in jerry / Can climb chip cherry.—The sun.
Bacon and Parsons, *Virginia*, p. 327, No. 132.

1622. Up chip cherry, down chip cherry, / There is no rider to mount chip cherry.—Sky.
Parsons, *Barbados*, p. 276, No. 1 var.

1623. Up chip cherry, down chip cherry, / Still nobody can't climb chip cherry.—Beach.
Parsons, *Barbados*, p. 276, No. 1 var.

1624. Chick chick up, / Chick chick down.—Machine.
Parsons, *Bahamas*, p. 472, No. 11.

1625. My father have a thing go up chimbly chip chirrup.—Fire.
Beckwith, *Jamaica*, p. 190, No. 65.

1626. Me fader put me to climb a cloud an' I couldn't climb it.—Smoke.
Parsons, *Antilles*, III, 437, St. Martin, 31.

1627. Chip-cherry, beer, cedar.—White man (cedar), black wife (chip-cherry), brown child (beer).
Beckwith, *Jamaica*, p. 200, No. 159.

1628–1631. Seeing

In this section the concept "seeing" is construed in a passive sense: objects are seen or not seen and the spectator is not a significant part of the riddle. References to an animal or person that sees as themes of riddles will be found in appropriate sections of chapters i–v.

1628. It Is; You Do Not See It

This conception resembles the Renaissance conundrum, "What thynge is that neuer was no[r] neuer shall be?—Neuer mouse made her nest in a catte's ere [ear]."[1] This conundrum is still current in western European oral tradition.[2] It is also the theme of a proverb.[3] A Serbian riddle for marriage between a brother and a sister, "It never was nor will it ever be; and if it were to happen, it would be woeful,"[4] uses a similar formula.

1628. What is it we see made, / And never see after it is made?—Noise.
Hyatt, *Adams Co., Ill.*, p. 664, No. 10890.

1629. It Is Not; You See It

This awkwardly formulated paradox also appears in the form of a comparison of the fingers to the trees in a forest; both trees and fingers are of unequal heights.[1] The problem of the unequal length of the fingers puzzled Adelard of

---

[1] For references see *Demaundes Joyous* (1511), No. 14, reprinted in Kemble, p. 288, and Halliwell-Phillipps, *Popular Rhymes*, p. 153.
[2] Breton: Le Pennec, 7; Sébillot, *Levinettes*, 104. Flemish: Joos, 909. Danish: Kristensen, p. 219, XV, Nos. 1a, 1b. Swedish: Ericsson, *Södermanland*, V (1884), 72, No. 264; Ström, p. 401, "Lögngåtor," 1. French: Constantin, *Savoie*, p. 24. Basque: Vinson, 32; Cerquand, 4.
[3] See G. L. Apperson, *English Proverbs* (London, 1929), p. 431; W. G. Smith and Janet Heseltine, *Oxford Dictionary of English Proverbs* (London, 1935), p. 225.
[4] Novaković, p. 8, No. 5.

[1] See No. 1041 and the headnote to Nos. 1040–1041. In No. 1040, the unequal heights are those of the branches.

Bath,² who included it in his *Quaestiones naturales*.³ Inasmuch as this work had a considerable influence from the early twelfth century to the end of the fifteenth, it may have contributed to the dissemination of the paradox. The editors of Adelard offer no speculations about the source of the idea. In the Renaissance version,⁴ the allusion to holding up the hand has a curious and perhaps significant similarity to Adelard's explanation, which mentions the concavity of the palm of the hand.

1629a. It was not it is not nor ev^r shall be hould up your hand & y^u shall it see.—the little finger not so longe as the rest.
Tupper, *Holme Riddles*, 94; *Prettie Riddles* (1631), No. 81 = Brandl, p. 63.

1629b. Some man has never seen it done, and God have never intended for it to be so. Guess what it is.—Your little finger.
Parsons, *Sea Islands, S. C.*, p. 160, No. 48.

1630. Cannot See It

1630. What goes across the bridge and cuts the hay and you can't see it?—Bullet out of a gun.
Fauset, *Nova Scotia*, p. 172, No. 180.

1631. See You Where You Are Not

The Indonesian "Two people stand opposite each other, seek to catch each other, do not touch each another" (Fortgens, 16) is somewhat similar, but is doubtless quite independent.

1631. I've seen you where you never was, / And where you ne'er will be, / And yet you in that very same place / May still be seen by me.—In a mirror.
Halliwell-Phillipps, *Popular Rhymes*, p. 144; Knortz, p. 227, No. 67, and p. 235, No. 115; Hyatt, *Adams Co., Ill.*, pp. 665–666, No. 10902.

1632–1663. Finding, Seizing, Catching, Lifting

1632–1642. Seek It; Cannot Find It

The contradictory ideas of vainly seeking a thing that one does not want and yet at the same time having it are applicable to a thorn in the foot or hand¹ and also to fleas or lice.² The Irish "I passed and found it, I sat and searched. If I hadn't gotten it, I wouldn't have brought it, and since I didn't get it, I

---

² See Lynn Thorndike, *A History of Magic and Experimental Science* (New York, 1923), II, 19–49; George Sarton, *An Introduction to the History of Science* (Washington, 1931), II, 167–169.
³ M. Müller, *Die Quaestiones naturales des Adelardus von Bath*, Beiträge zur Geschichte der Philosophie und Theologie des Mittelalters, XXXI, ii (Münster, 1934), 40–41, Nos. 36, 37; Berachya Hanakdan, *Dodi Ve-Nechdi* (trans. H. Gollancz; Oxford, 1920), pp. 41–42 and 128–129.
⁴ No. 1629a below.
¹ Nos. 1632 through 1641.
² Nos. 1591, 1592, and the headnote to Nos. 1593–1595, § 7.

brought it"[3] is slightly elaborated, but most of the versions show no elaboration in the acts or in the accessory details. The Irish use a similar theme for crows and feathers: "Three of Clan Donald went one day to get berries, the part they picked they left behind, and the part they didn't pick they took with them."[4] Still another modification of the theme is seen in the Danish riddle for a lawsuit, "What is it that one must have; when one has it, one seeks to get rid of it; when one has found [won] it, one has it no longer?"[5] This theme is varied somewhat by Spanish riddlers.[6] Its appearance in Java[7] is rather curious, since Far Eastern riddlers do not often employ such contradictions.

1632. He went to the wood and caught it; / He sate him downe and sought it; / Because he could not finde it, / Home with him he brought it.—That is a thorne: for a man went to the wood, and caught a thorne in his foot; and then he sate him downe, and sought to have it pulled out; and because he could not finde it out, he must needs bring it home.
  Meery Riddles (1629), No. 2 = Brandl, p. 8.

1633. As I was going through the woods, / I picked up something, / I set down and looked at it, / The more I looked at it, the better I liked it, / I took it home because I couldn't help it.—Splinter in foot.
  Fauset, *Nova Scotia*, p. 150, No. 43.

1634a. I went to the wood and got it, / I sat me down and looked at it; / The more I looked at it, the less I liked it, / And I brought it home because I couldn't help it.—A thorn.
  Halliwell-Phillipps, *Nursery Rhymes*, p. 119; Knortz, p. 222, No. 48; Hyatt, *Adams Co., Ill.*, pp. 668–669, No. 10923; Greenleaf, *Newfoundland*, p. 13, No. 1, var. 2.

1634b. It goes in the woods. I set me down and look at it. The more I look, the less I like it. I took it because I couldn't help it.—Thorn.
  Parsons, *Bermuda*, p. 253, No. 50.

1635a. I went to the woods and got it / The more I looked at it, the less I liked it, / I brought it home in my hand / Because I couldn't find it.—Splinter in hand.
  Fauset, *Nova Scotia*, p. 151, No. 43 var.; Greenleaf, *Newfoundland*, p. 13, No. 1, var. 1.

1635b. I went to the woods and got it. I sit myself down and look at it. The more I look at it, the less I like it.—Thorn.
  Parsons, *Sea Islands, S.C.*, p. 175, No. 184; Fauset, *Philadelphia*, p. 553, No. 5.

1636. I went out in the woods and got it, / Came home and looked for it, / The more I looked for it, / The more I hated it.—Splinter.
  Hyatt, *Adams Co., Ill.*, p. 667, No. 10915.

---

[3] O Dalaigh, 173.
[4] Delargy, *Inis Cé*, 11; De Bhaldraithe, 38; O Dalaigh, 35 through 37.
[5] Kristensen, p. 103, § 279, No. 434.
[6] See the headnote to Nos. 1593–1595, § 8, above.
[7] Luinenburg, p. 382, No. 8.

1637. I walked an' walked / 'Til I got it. / When I got it, / I 'topped / An' looked for it. / An' when I saw it, I picked it out / An' threw it away.—Pimpler (a thorny shrub).
Parsons, *Barbados*, p. 287, No. 67.

1638. I run till I found it, / Picked it up and looked for it, / Chucked it down and runned away with it.—Splinter in foot.
Greenleaf, *Newfoundland*, p. 13, No. 1.

1639. j went to the wood & got it, j set me down & sought it: j kept it still against my will & so by force hom & j brought it.—a thorn in a man's foot, who sate down to look it out, but could not find it.
Tupper, *Holme Riddles*, 131.

1640. In the woods I done it, / I sat down and viewed it; / Against my will to keep it still / Right straight home I brought it.—A man cut his foot while working in the woods.
Greenleaf, *Newfoundland*, p. 13, No. 2.

1641. I went to the wood and I caught it; / Then I sate me down and sought it: / The longer I sought, / For what I had caught, / The less worth eating I thought it. / I would rather have sold it than bought it; / And when I had sought, / Without finding aught, / Home in my hand I brought it.—A thorn.
E. L. S., *Notes and Queries*, 3d ser., VI (1864), 288.

1642. Looked all over the house and couldn't find it, all over the barn and couldn't find it, looked out in the field and found it.—A cow-bell.
Redfield, *Tennessee*, p. 44, No. 104.

1643–1654. A Houseful, But Cannot Seize It

Riddle-makers in many countries have used this old pattern. Aldhelm says of the wind, "Cerne me nulli possunt nec prendere palmis"[1] and may have been inspired by a Biblical passage.[2] More vivid and also quite in the enigmatic style is the Norwegian "A house full of gray wool, and one cannot get a fistful."[3] The theme is closely related to the idea that horses cannot drag sunlight or a cloud away.[4] The pertinence of the comparison to a crane (No. 1647) is not obvious, and the riddler alters the idea while retaining the characteristic words to describe an old man and children (No. 1653). Inasmuch as English riddlers show a great liking for this riddle, they occasionally mingle it with other themes. The phrase "goes all the way around the house" in No. 1644a belongs to texts in which sunlight, the wind, a fence, or a road or path goes about the house peeping in or seeking entrance, or never entering.[5]

---

[1] Ed. Pitman, pp. 4–5, No. 2.
[2] See Tupper, *The Riddles of the Exeter Book*, pp. xlvi, 69–70, and 78; E. Erlemann, "Zu den altenglischen Rätseln," *Archiv für das Studium der neueren Sprachen*, CXI (1903), 49.
[3] Aasen, 2; Berge, 38; Brox, *Ytre Senja*, 2, citing Riksheim, 70; Stafset, 71.
[4] See Nos. 748a through 749 above.
[5] See Nos. 192c through 193b, 195, 199a through 201, and the headnote to Nos. 198–202.

The notion of something that is visible or very abundant and therefore ought to be tangible and yet cannot be seized is applicable to:

§ 1. Smoke. See Nos. 1643a through 1644b, and No. 1655. The idea is elaborated in a Renaissance version, "w^t is that that if [it] be seene can not be taken if it be taken can not be held & w^n it is thought to be some thing by & by it proves to be nothing?" (Tupper, *Holme Riddles*, 14b).

§ 2. The wind, the air. See Nos. 1648 through 1650 below.

§ 3. The sun, sunlight. See Nos. 1646a, 1646b.

§ 4. Dust. See No. 1645.

§ 5. Mist. See Nos. 1651a through 1652c.

§ 6. A shadow, darkness. Icelandic: Árnason, 352 (It will soon cover the roof of a high house. It flies higher than the mountains and causes the fall of many a man. Everyone can see it but no one can fetter it. It can stand both blows and the wind, and it is not harmful.—Darkness), 519 (Who is the swift one that found me on the road? Neither the sun nor any other light shines on him. I have often seen him running alongside ships at sea. He needs no clothing or food, is visible to all but tangible by none.—Shadow). French: Rolland, 19 (The living makes as much [of it] as the dead, everyone can easily see it, no one can touch it). Portuguese: Parsons, *Cape Verde*, 236 (I have a child. However I run, I do not catch him. I sit down. I catch him). Italian: Rolland, p. 158, No. 7; Tschiedel, 58 (What do you see and cannot grasp?); Balladoro, *Archivio*, XVI (1897), 552, No. 6. Lettish: Bielenstein, 164 (It's not a man, it's not a ghost, we can't catch it in our hands). Polish: Gustawicz, 475 (What cannot be embraced in the arms?—Shadow). Mordvin: Ahlqvist, p. 40, No. 13; Paasonen, 321. Turkish: Katanov in Radlov, IX, 160, No. 1326 (It is seen by the eyes but it does not yield to the hands.—A man's shadow), and p. 287, No. 234 (I cannot catch up to a certain raven; if I catch up to it, I cannot capture it.—Man's shadow). African, Bakongo: Denis, 25 (That which one can't catch). Ila: Smith and Dale, II, 331 (You have grown so clever: Can you catch hold of shadow?). Duala: Bufe, p. 59, No. 17 (Although you pursue me, you cannot catch me.—Darkness). Kundu: Ittmann, *Kundu*, 104 (My mother gave me soot, but I cannot seize it.—Darkness). Taveta: Hollis, *Taveta*, p. 202, No. 4 (You cannot catch this thing here). Chinyanja: Rattray, p. 153 (A little thing, yet that cannot be lifted). Indian, Kashmiri: Knowles, 106 (It is in your hand, catch it). Indonesian, Malay: Tauern, p. 69 (One can see it, see it, one cannot hold it tight). Tabaru: Fortgens, 55.

§ 7. Water, rain. Yakut: Priklonskii, 87; Piekarski, 23 (In your palm, you cannot hold it; in your hand, you cannot see it; thus it is, they say). African, Chinyanja: Rattray, p. 154 (Something which no number of people can lift, yet there is one person who can do so.—Rain). Pangwe: Tessmann, 108 (I know something, it is not caught in a snare). Tonga-Shangaan: Junod and Jaques, p. 234, No. 33 (What is the thing which, once poured out, cannot be gathered again?).

§ 8. A road. African, Kundu: Ittmann, *Kundu*, 134 (I follow it, but can't catch it).

Riddlers do not often use more concrete terms to express these ideas. See such riddles for the wind as the Portuguese "A race of young colts. Without running, I can't catch them; without catching, I can't hold them";[6] the Cherekessian "It gallops faster than you, gallops better than I; should you start after it, you will not catch it";[7] the Tungus "You cannot catch the tsar's horse";[8] and the Mongolian riddle for the mist, "A running, running female gazelle, a female gazelle which nobody can catch, a staying, staying female gazelle, a female gazelle which nobody can seize.—Vapors rising from the soil in the sunshine, a mirage."[9]

1643a. A house full, a yard full, / Couldn't catch a bowl full.—Smoke.
Halliwell-Phillipps, *Popular Rhymes*, p. 145; Fauset, *Nova Scotia*, p. 156, No. 65; Waugh, *Canada*, p. 71, No. 814; Knortz, p. 227, No. 69; Brewster, *Indiana*, 55; Bacon and Parsons, *Virginia*, p. 313, No. 10 var.; Fauset, *Southern Negro*, p. 281, No. 53.

1643b. A houseful, / A yardful, / Can't ketch a spoonful.—Smoke.
Bacon and Parsons, *Virginia*, p. 313, No. 10; Parsons, *Guilford Co., N.C.*, p. 201, No. 3; Redfield, *Tennessee*, p. 38, No. 23; Farr, *Tennessee*, p. 318, No. 3; Hudson, p. 90, No. 50; Hyatt, *Adams Co., Ill.*, p. 666, No. 10908.

1643c. A houseful, / A yardful, / Yet you can't a get thimbleful.—Smoke.
Bacon and Parsons, *Virginia*, p. 313, No. 10 var.

1643d. House full, room full, / And can't catch a spoonful.—Smoke.
Perkins, *New Orleans*, p. 106, No. 10. Handful: Hyatt, *Adams Co., Ill.*, p. 666, No. 10908, var. 3.

1643e. A house full, a hole full, / Yet you can't catch a bowlful.—Smoke.
Benjamin F. Taylor, "January and June," *Winter Nights* (New York, 1854), p. 253; Waugh, *Canada*, p. 71, No. 814; Fauset, *Nova Scotia*, p. 156, No. 65; Hyatt, *Adams Co., Ill.*, p. 666, No. 10908, var. 3; Randolph and Taylor, *Ozarks*, 23. You can't get....: Whitney and Bullock, *Maryland*, p. 174, No. 2678. A house full, a hoile full: Baring-Gould, *Notes and Queries*, 3d ser., VIII (1865), 325 (Yorkshire). After *hoile* he adds the explanatory "coal-hole" in brackets.

1643f. A house full, a yard full, a chimney full, / No one can get a spoonful.—Smoke.
Parsons, *Sea Islands, S.C.*, p. 153, No. 6.

1643g. A houseful, a chimneyful, / But not a bowlful.—Smoke.
Hyatt, *Adams Co., Ill.*, p. 666, No. 10908 var. 1.

1643h. House full, bowl full / Can't catch a spoonful.—Smoke.
Fauset, *Nova Scotia*, p. 157, No. 65 var.

1643i. Roomful, houseful. / Can't catch a cupful.—Smoke.
Parsons, *Bermuda*, p. 245, No. 4. Houseful, roomful: Greenleaf, *Newfoundland*, p. 9, No. 11. Kitchenful, houseful: Parsons, *Bermuda*, p. 245, No. 4 var. Can't catch a plateful: Parsons, *Bermuda*, p. 245, No. 4 var.

---

[6] Parsons, *Cape Verde*, 261.
[8] Poppe, 12.
[7] Tambiev, p. 61, No. 95.
[9] Mostaert, 157.

1643j. Roomful, hallfull; you can't get a spoonful.—Smoke.
Beckwith, *Jamica*, p. 201, No. 164.

1643k. Hands full, / House full, / Still can't ketch a spoonful.—Smoke.
Parsons, *Aiken, S.C.*, p. 26, No. 8.

1643 l. A chimneyful, houseful, / And still you can't get a thimbleful.—Smoke.
Parsons, *Bermuda*, p. 245, No. 4 var.

1643m. Houseful, everything full / And still can't catch a thing full.—Smoke.
Parsons, *Bermuda*, p. 245, No. 4 var.

1643n. A houseful, / An' can't get a spoonful.—Smoke.
Parsons, *Aiken, S.C.*, p. 26, No. 8, var. 1.

1643o. Pitcherful, cupful, / Yet you can't get you hand full.—Smoke.
Parsons, *Bermuda*, p. 245, No. 4 var.

1643p. A bowlful, / An' can't ketch any.—Smoke.
Parsons, *Aiken, S.C.*, p. 26, No. 8, var. 2.

1643q. The whole house full, / And can't catch a mouth full. / Guess what it is.—Smoke.
Parsons, *Sea Islands, S.C.*, p. 153, No. 6 var.

1643r. Kitchenful and batcherful, / Yet cannot catch a thimbleful.—Smoke.
Parsons, *Barbados*, p. 278, No. 16. Kitchenful and houseful: Parsons, *Barbados*, p. 278, No. 16 var. Kitchenful and butteryful: Parsons, *Barbados*, p. 278, No. 16 var.

1643s. A house full, a kitchen full, / Can't ketch a spoonful.—Smoke.
Parsons, *Bahamas*, p. 476, No. 50 (wrongly numbered 51).

1643t. House full, kitchen full, / Can't ketch a thimble full.—Smoke.
Parsons, *Bahamas*, p. 476, No. 50 var.; Parsons, *Eleuthera and Watling's Islands, Bahamas*, p. 440, No. 16; Parsons, *Antilles*, III, 363, Trinidad, 4, and p. 372, Grenada, 59.

1643u. Wriggle me, wriggle me, / You can't tell this wriggle, / I'll tell you a striggle. / House full, kitchen full. Can't ketch a bowl full.—Smoke.
Parsons, *Antilles*, III, 428-429, Nevis, 18.

1643v. Me riddle me riddle / Perhaps you may tell this and perhaps not. / House full / Kitchen full / I cannot ketch a spoonful. / Tell me that riddle and perhaps not.—Smoke.
Parsons, *Antilles*, III, 444, St. Croix, 20.

1644a. Goes all the way 'round the house, / An' don't ketch but a spoonful.—Smoke.
Parsons, *Aiken, S.C.*, p. 26, No. 8, var. 3.

1644b. Over the hills and out of the hole, / [Can't catch a bowlful].—Smoke.
Parsons, *Bermuda*, p. 246, No. 4 var.

1645. A house full, a yard full, / Couldn't catch a bowl full.—Dust.
Fauset, *Nova Scotia*, p. 156, No. 65 var.

1646a. House full, / Yard full, / Can't catch a bowlful.—Sun.
Fauset, *Southern Negro*, p. 281, No. 53.

1646b. The whole world full, / And can't catch a cup full.—Sun.
Fauset, *Southern Negro*, p. 281, No. 54.

1647. A house full, a yard full, / Couldn't catch a bowl full.—Crane.
Fauset, *Nova Scotia*, p. 156, No. 65 var.

1648. Goes all the way 'round the house, / An' don't ketch but a spoonful.—Wind.
Parsons, *Aiken, S.C.*, p. 26, No. 8, var. 3.

1649a. A house full, a yard full, / And yet can't get a teaspoonful.—Air.
Parsons, *Sea Islands, S.C.*, p. 153, No. 65 var.

1649b. House full, barn full, / But you caint git a spoonful.—Air.
Randolph and Spradley, *Ozark*, p. 85.

1649c. What is that which goes all through the house and yet you can't catch a thimbleful?—Air.
Parsons, *Bermuda*, p. 245, No. 4 var.

1650. Something blow day and night, / And you cannot catch a handful.—Answer lacking [wind].
Parsons, *Sea Islands, S.C.*, p. 153, No. 8.

1651a. A house full, a yard full, / Banks full, / Braes full, / Though ye gather all day, / Ye'll not gather your hands full.—Mist.
Whitney and Bullock, *Maryland*, p. 174, No. 2679.

1651b. Banks full, braes full. / Though you gather all day, / Ye'll not gather your hands full.—Mist.
Halliwell-Phillipps, *Popular Rhymes*, p. 144 (Northumberland), p. 144; Knortz, p. 266, No. 65.

1651c. Bank-fou an brae-fou, / Though ye gaither a' day, / Ye winna gaither a stoup-fou.—Mist.
Gregor, *Northeast Scotland*, p. 81.

1652a. A hill full, a hole full, / Ye cannot catch a bowl full.—Mist.
Halliwell-Phillipps, *Popular Rhymes*, p. 144.

1652b. A hillful, a hillful, / Can't catch a bowlful.—Mist.
Parsons, *Bermuda*, p. 245, No. 4 var. A holeful, a hillful: Parsons, *Bermuda*, p. 245, No. 4 var.

1652c. A hillful, / A bowlful, / An' can't ketch a bowlful.—Mist.
Bacon and Parsons, *Virginia*, p. 313, No. 11.

1653. Mout'ful, han'ful, kyan't get a spoonful.—Ol' man wid all de chillun.
Parsons, *Sea Islands, S.C.*, p. 153, No. 9.

1654. Picking juketa [?] going to town, picking juketa coming from town, and can't get my hands full.—Dew and sweat.
Beckwith, *Jamaica*, p. 192, No. 79.

1655–1657. Cannot (Do Not) Touch It

1655. Crowd o' people in de house. An' somet'in' come in de house an' don't touch one.—Smoke.
Parsons, *Sea Islands, S.C.*, p. 171, No. 136.

1656. My fader had a t'ing, no one couldn' touch it.—Was' [wasp].
Parsons, *Bahamas*, p. 475, No. 36 var.

1657. Something can touch you, but you can't touch it.—Sun.
Parsons, *Bermuda*, p. 264, No. 149.

1658. Cannot Pick It Up

1658. As I look'd out o' my chamber window, / I heard something fall, / I sent my maid to pick it up, / But she couldn't pick it up at all.—Snuff.
Halliwell-Phillipps, *Popular Rhymes*, p. 145; Halliwell-Phillipps, *Nursery Rhymes*, p. 120; Hyatt, *Adams Co., Ill.*, p. 667, No. 10910. As I was in my chamber: Bacon and Parsons, *Virginia*, p. 318, No. 48.

1659. Cannot Take It Off

In this rather poorly preserved version of the Hickamore Hackamore riddle[1] the speaker has altered the fundamental theme. The sunlight is here conceived as a thing and not as a person. This is analogous to the Irish "It is in the shop and it isn't sold; it is in the garden and it can't be taken away"[2] and the Turkish "I poured out sour milk before the door. I rubbed and rubbed, yet it did not disappear."[3] A comparison of milk to sunlight occurs in the dialogue of Salomon and Marcolf. The latter says, "Penso nullam rem esse sub celo candidiorem lacte," and receives the answer, "Numquid dies est candidior lacte."[4]

1659a. Something shines on the king's door, and twenty-four men can't take it off. What's that?—The sun.
Parsons, *Sea Islands, S.C.*, p. 161, No. 52, var. 3.

1659b. A riddle, a riddle aree, / No man can explain this riddle on to me. / Something on the king kitchen door, / Take all the soldiers in the world, and king men, / And can't get it off.—Sun.
Parsons, *Barbados*, p. 282, No. 33 var.

1659c. Somet'in' shine in de king wind'. An' all de king men an' all de king horse couldn' take it off.—Sunshine in de do'.
Parsons, *Sea Islands, S.C.*, p. 161, No. 53, var. 2.

---

[1] Nos. 748a through 748g.
[2] De Bhaldraithe, 4.
[3] Kúnos, 169 = Kowalski, *Asia Minor*, 16.
[4] Walter Benary, *Salomon et Marcolfus* (Heidelberg, 1914), pp. 26–27.

1660-1662. Cannot Lift, Carry, Hold It

1660a. What is that which you cannot hold ten minutes, although it is as light as a feather?—Your breath.
Waugh, *Canada*, p. 70, No. 805.

1660b. Light as a feather, / Nothing in it. / A stout man can't hold it / More than a minute.—Breath.
Randolph and Taylor, *Ozarks*, 19.

1661-1662. One Man (a Thousand Men) Cannot Lift It

This conception is closely related to that of a well as something round and deep that horses cannot pull up.[1] The usual answer is "egg," which can be easily picked up when it is whole but escapes the grip when it is broken. Although this answer is widely known, I have not found it in English. For examples see Scotch Gaelic: Nicolson, p. 33 (A little baby will lift it in its fist, and twelve men cannot lift it in a rope). German: Wossidlo, 347*a* through 347*c*. Danish: Kristensen, pp. 149–150, § 439, Nos. 701*a* through 701*h* (One man can hold it in his hand, ten men can't carry it on a pole); Feilberg, *Ordbog*, IV, 1144, s.v. "æg." Swedish: Ericsson, *Södermanland*, V (1884), 69, No. 229; Wigström, p. 288, No. 8; Sandén, *Norra Vadsbo*, 16; Ström, p. 196, "Ägget," 5. French: Marchessou, *Velay et Auvergne*, p. 167, No. 10.

This idea admits of various minor modifications, like those in the Breton "What is it that a dog can pick up and ten men can't?—A broken egg."[2] A variation which seems to be limited in its currency to eastern Europe and Asia alludes to the impossibility of putting an egg on a nail. Examples are the Zyrian, Cheremiss, and Votyak "One can hang up everything on the nail, except one [var.: two].—Egg [var.: egg and water]";[3] the Vogul "Something that can't be put on a nail";[4] the Russian "It is round and small, yet you cannot hang it on a match"[5] and "Small, round, one cannot stick it into the wall";[6] the Turcoman "Although there is snow on top of a stake, it won't stick there" and "What can't you put on a stake?";[7] the Yakut "They say that there is something which cannot be held in the hand or hung on a nail,"[8] "What is it, they say, that will not hold on a nail?"[9] and "You can't put it on a hook, you can't find it in the road."[10] This idea is also applied to a cough or the breath,[11] as well as to water, as in the Turkish "I could not carry it around

---

[1] See Nos. 1327*a*, 1328, 1330 through 1332, and 1334.
[2] Orain, *Ille-et-Vilaine*, p. 147; Charlec, *Dol-de-Bretagne*, 1904, p. 168, No. 29.
[3] Zyrian: Wichmann, *Zyrian*, 200, 273, 275. Cheremiss: Wichmann, *Cheremiss*, 41. Votyak: Wichmann, *Votyak*, 268, 392.   [4] Ahlqvist, *Vogul*, 13.
[5] Sadovnikov, 552.   [6] Preobrazhenskii, p. 172.
[7] Samojlvich, 119, 120.   [8] Piekarski, 151.
[9] Popov, p. 285; Priklonskii, 50.   [10] Priklonskii, 118.
[11] Swedish: Ström, p. 87, "Nysningen, rapningen, fisen."

the hut, I could not hang it on a match.—Water without a vessel to carry it in."[12]

Quite different formulations of the difficulty of placing an egg in a stable position occur in the Mordvin "What cannot be situated in a corner?"[13] and the Kolarian "You cannot put the king's and the queen's baskets one over the other."[14]

1661. What is it floats on the water as light as a feather, / And a thousand men couldn't lift it?—A bubble.
Greenleaf, *Newfoundland*, p. 13, No. 5.

1662. One man can carry it upstairs, / A thousand men can't bring it down.—Needle.
Fauset, *Philadelphia*, p. 553, No. 9. Eight men: Fauset, *Southern Negro*, p. 287, No. 120. Fifty men: Redfield, *Tennessee*, p. 40, No. 51.

1663. Cannot Rear It

1663a. ten mens strength ten mens length & ten men canot reare it.—a cable rop[e].
Tupper, *Holme Riddles*, 115.

1663b. Ten men's length, and ten men's strength, / An' ten men can't rear it.—A waggon-rope. The expected answer being a ladder.
Gutch and Peacock, *Lincolnshire*, p. 399, No. 18.

1663c. Ten men's strength, and ten men's length, and ten men cannot set it on end; yet one man may beare it.—That is a rope, or cable, of ten fathom long or more, which ten men cannot set on end, nor ten score nor ten thousand.
Meery Riddles (1629), No. 37 = Brandl, p. 14.

1664–1673. Tearing, Cutting, Breaking, Hitting

1664. Cannot Tear It

1664a. Ten men's length, ten men's strength, ten men can't tear, yet a little boy walks off with it.—A rope.
Waugh, *Canada*, p. 70, No. 808.

1664b. Ten men's length and ten men's strength, and ten men cannot teare it.—A cable rope which men cannot breake by force.
Prettie Riddles (1631), No. 24 = Brandl, p. 56.

1665–1666. Cut It; Cannot See the Cut

Here the underlying idea is similar to the notion that a ship cuts through the water and yet leaves no track.[1] With special reference to the oars rising and falling like an ax, this theme occurs in the Lithuanian riddles for a boat,

---

[12] Katanov in Radlov, IX, 286, No. 217.   [13] Paasonen, 135.
[14] Wagner, 32.

[1] See the note and the headnote to No. 227.

"I ride, I ride, no tracks are left; I chop and chop; there are no chips left" and "He rides and rides; turns around: there is no road left."[2] A somewhat longer but less clear version is: "A little rose with a snubnose goes riding. Neither tracks nor wheels nor the tracks of the horse are left."[3] The Lithuanians also employ this theme for water alone: "A silver field without paths" and "A field without paths, crossed without tracks."[4] The Tagalog "You cannot cut my brother's pudding.—Water"[5] is apparently an independent formulation of the idea.

The idea of a cut or track that becomes invisible is applicable to:

§ 1. Water. See Nos. 1665, 1666, below.

§ 2. A shadow. Malagasy: Sibree, p. 38, No. 12 (Cut and yet no wound is seen). Hawaiian: Judd, 186 (My little man which [read: who] cannot be cut).

§ 3. The eyelids. Icelandic: Árnason, 463 (What hews all day and leaves no mark?). See also the headnote to Nos. 788–789, § 2, above.

1665. What is that you would cut with a knife, and, after finish cuttin' it, you can't see where you cut it?—The water.
Johnson, *Antigua*, p. 84, No. 12.

1666. Ofttimes it has been divided, / And yet it can't be seen where it has been divided.—Vessel going through the water.
Fauset, *Nova Scotia*, p. 174, No. 204.

1667. Cut It; Cannot Taste It

1667. My father have a thing in his house, cut it every day and kyan' taste it.—Cord.
Beckwith, *Jamaica*, p. 185, No. 23.

1668–1669. Break It by Naming It

1668. What is it you will break if you even name it?—Silence.
Perkins, *New Orleans*, p. 113, No. 80.

1669. What is it you have all the time, but when you talk you break it?—Silence.
Oral, Chicago.

1670–1671. Cannot Mend It

This pattern is closely related to that of the Humpty Dumpty riddle,[1] which usually refers to a person who cannot be put together or cured after a fall. Similar also are the descriptions of objects in terms of a dress that is torn and cannot be mended.[2]

---

[2] Jurgelionis, 656, 657.　　　　　[3] Jurgelionis, 658.
[4] Jurgelionis, 1072, 1073.
[5] Rizal, pp. 45–46. See also Chinese: Rudolph, p. 74, No. 8.
[1] See Nos. 738 through 747b above.
[2] See Nos. 589a through 592 and 593c through 593e.

1670. As I was going o'er London Bridge, / I hear something crack; / Not a man in all England / Can mend that!—Ice.
Halliwell-Phillipps, *Popular Rhymes*, p. 145.

1671. As I gaed owre Bottle-brig, / Bottle-brig brak; / Though ye guess a' day, / Ye winna guess that.—The ice.
Chambers, *Scotland*, p. 110. In Lanarkshire alone would this enigma have its full effect, the word Bottle-brig being liable to be confounded with Bothwell Bridge, there popularly called Boddle Brig.—Collector's note.

1672-1673. Knocking and Hitting

1672. Knock an' stan' up.—Mat.
Beckwith, *Jamaica*, p. 201, No. 165.

1673. Riddle my riddle rocket. / You can't hit it and I can't knock it.—Smoke.
Redfield, *Tennessee*, p. 38, No. 24.

1674-1680. Valued As Something Essential

Although the description of a dishclout[1] as something much used and little esteemed is rather old as recorded riddling goes, both it and the manner of riddling that it exemplifies occur only rarely in popular tradition. An allied idea appears in the Basque description of a comb as long and thin and needed by all the world.[2] Some traditional riddles, particularly those for a key, doorknob, or latch, use the contrast "often used, little named"[3] or "small, but serves many."[4] The modern Russian riddle for a kulak, "Formerly held in esteem, but now: what the Devil!"[5] is an instructive example of propaganda made on a traditional model.

1674. Use, But Do Not Esteem It

1674a. Something is most used and least thought of.—Dish-rag.
Fauset, *Southern Negro*, p. 283, No. 82; Brewster, *Indiana*, 46.

1674b. What is the usefulest thing in the house and the least thought of?—Dish-cloth.
Perkins, *New Orleans*, p. 112, No. 66.

1675-1679. Use It; Find It Essential

This contrast, which is appropriate enough to a dishclout,[1] is not readily intelligible when applied to pen and paper or to white and black men and is not particularly appropriate when applied to a broom or a clock.

---

[1] Nos. 1674a, 1674b. [2] Vinson, 64 var.
[3] Swedish: Ericsson, *Södermanland*, I (1879) 93, No. 67; Sandén, *Norra Vadsbo*, 32.
[4] Cheremiss: Genetz, 58. [5] Bardin, p. 314, No. 1.
[1] No. 1675.

1675. though j be throwne from place to place & al unseemly as j am the nisest dame in the towne canot liue wthout me.—the dishclout.
Tupper, *Holme Riddles*, 46.

1676. I cannot do without you, / You cannot do without me.—Pen and paper.
Parsons, *Antilles*, III, 366, Trinidad, 36.

1677. I cannot do without you, / You cannot do with me.—White man and black.
Parsons, *Antilles*, III, 366, Trinidad, 36 var.

1678. Hitch it to the upstairs, / Hitch it to the downstairs. / No man can do without it.—Broom.
Parsons, *Sea Islands, S.C.*, p. 168, No. 104.

1679. Dere is a t'ing dat neither man nor woman can do without. You walk with it, you keep it in your house; if you don't have it, you don't know which way you are. What is dat?—A clock.
Johnson, *Antigua*, p. 88, No. 65.

1680. Without It Nothing Can Be Done

The following series of assertions and contradictions applied to time does not readily fall into any category in this collection. I have nevertheless included it, although it doubtless is of literary origin, because it has come to me from an oral source and has circulated as folklore. Its formulation in superlatives is characteristic of questions calling for a special bit of information rather than for the solution of an enigma.

This riddle contains various interesting themes. References to moving with great speed are frequent in riddling. Typical answers are:

§ 1. Thought, a dream. Welsh: Hull and Taylor, 38, 39, 401. Breton: Sébillot, *Devinettes*, 97. Icelandic: Árnason, 260 (I am found to be swifter than fire or wind. I travel to unknown worlds which mortal eye has never seen and change them around in the twinkling of an eye), 386 (What travels faster than light?). Latin: Sebastian Scheffer in Reusner, ed. 1602, p. 328, No. 4 = Friedreich, p. 210, No. 6 (Quid motibus cursum rotat celerrimis?—Mens, ire docta quo libet). Italian: Tschiedel, 70 (Who covers a thousand leagues in an hour?—Dream). Portuguese: Parsons, *Cape Verde*, 234, 235 (I am here, and I am there), which resembles the texts discussed in the headnote to No. 1578 above. Greek: Diogenes Laertius, *De Vitis Philosophorum*, I, i, 35-36 (What is the quickest?—Thought). Estonian: Dido, p. 35, No. 2 (What flies swifter than a bird?).

For discussion of allusions to the speed of thought see Ohlert, 2d ed., p. 108; Loewenthal, p. 62; Archer Taylor, *The Black Ox*, FF Communications, LXX (Helsinki, 1927), p. 42, n. 2. See also, above, Nos. 363a, 363b, and the headnote to Nos. 362-364.

§ 2. The sun. Russian: Sadovnikov, 1811 (What is the spryest in the world?).

§ 3. Sight. The conception in the Latin

> Dic mihi, quid ventis, rapidi quid fulminis alis,
> Quid stellis fixis ocyus orbis habet?[1]

has some parallels in the riddles previously quoted to illustrate the notion of the eye ranging far. For parallels to the speed of sight see my "American Indian Riddles," *Journal of American Folklore*, LVII (1944), 5.

§ 4. Time. See No. 1680 below.

1680. What, of all things in the world, is the longest and the shortest, the swiftest and the slowest, the most divisible and the most extended, the most neglected and the most regretted, without which nothing can be done, which devours all that is little, and enlivens all that is great?—Time.
Oral, Pennsylvania.

1681–1703. Contradictory Acts or Contradiction between Act and Result

Riddlers occasionally describe an object according to its functions in varying circumstances and often find the functions to be contradictory. This manner of description does not yield a clear picture, and it does not mislead the hearer by suggesting, as a riddle ordinarily does, something that is not the object intended. Consequently, the examples of this manner of description are few and uninteresting. One variety is, however, important. When the contrasted acts are emphasized by being set off with "more" and "less," as in the riddle for a hole, the contradiction is puzzling enough to make a good riddle, and all the more so because the acts seem to produce results contrary to their natures. We should expect an object to diminish as more is taken away from it.

1681. When pulled, it is a cane; when pushed, it is a tent.—Umbrella.
Perkins, *New Orleans*, p. 110, No. 41.

1682. It wasn't the moon, / It wasn't the stars, / But it lighted the fields.—Fireflies.
Fauset, *Nova Scotia*, p. 161, No. 89.

1683. What flares up and does a lot of good, / And when it dies, it's just a piece of wood?—Match.
Hyatt, *Adams Co., Ill.*, p. 663, No. 10884.

1684. What hangs on the wall and looks so fine, / But when it's dirty, it isn't worth a dime?—Wallpaper.
Hyatt, *Adams Co., Ill.*, p. 670, No. 10936.

---

[1] Johannes Pincier, *Ænigmatum libri tres* (The Hague, 1655), pp. 165–166 (Book II, No. 22). See also the headnote to No. 1471 above, especially nn. 40–50.

1685. Miles and miles and know your voice, / But cannot see your face.—Telephone.
Fauset, *Nova Scotia*, p. 158, No. 72.

1686. What is it hold thread / And can't hold bread?—Reel.
Parsons, *Bermuda*, p. 264, No. 148.

1687. What fastens two people yet touches only one?—Wedding ring.
Gardner, *Schoharie Hills, N.Y.*, p. 260, No. 81.

1688. Time-piece may lose, / But it cannot win.—Watch.
Parsons, *Aiken, S.C.*, p. 37, No. 91.

1689–1703. An Act Producing a Result Contrary to Its Nature

1689. When Held, It Moves; When Released, It Stops

The usual answer to this confusing statement is a shoe. See Modern Greek: Dieterich, *Rätseldichtung*, p. 96, citing Stamatiadis, V, 185, 187 (If you pull it off, it stands still. If you pull it on, it runs); Abbott, p. 319, No. 21 (sandal). Russian: Bardin, p. 243, No. 10 (If one ties them, they go; if one unties them, they stay behind). The speaker intends to suggest contradictions to the behavior of oxen. Bulgarian: Gubov, 389 (When they tie it, it walks; when they untie it, it sits). The speaker suggests a contradiction to the behavior of a dog. Turkish: Kúnos, 32 = Kúnos, *Nyelvkönyv*, 7 (If I tie it, it goes; unbound, it stops); Hamizade, 35 (I untie it and it stays still; I tie it and it walks). Crimean Tatar: Filonenko, 117. Armenian: Glushakov, p. 31, No. 60; Wingate, 1. Svanian: J. Nizheradze, pp. 68–69, No. 18 (When it is tied, it goes; when it is released, it stops). Georgian: Blechsteiner, pp. 14–15, No. 20. Tibetan: Tafel, p. 492. Korean: Bernheisel, p. 87 (What is that [which] goes when loaded, stops when empty?). The contrast suggests a bucket.

This pattern is also used in describing a cap: "If it lies flat, it is empty; if it sits up, it is full."[1] Some descriptions of objects involve the ideas of full and empty but employ more definite suggestions of an animal[2] or a person.[3]

1689. When held, it goes; when let loose, it lies down.—Pen.
Perkins, *New Orleans*, p. 110, No. 42.

1690–1697. The More One Takes Away, the Larger It Becomes

The example of this idea is a question asked at Trimalchio's dinner table: "Qui de nobis crescit et minor fit?"[1] Although this is not precisely the same as the hole riddle with which we are concerned, it involves the same kind of con-

---
[1] Modern Greek: Dieterich, *Rätseldichtung*, p. 96. See also the headnote to No. 1455, §2, above.
[2] See Nos. 453a through 453f above.
[3] See the headnote to Nos. 1455–1457.
[1] Petronius, *Satyricon*, 58.

tradiction. Petronius does not give the answer, and a modern editor suggests "hair."² Folk riddlers do not know this description of hair and would have perhaps suggested "candle."³ Somewhat similar in effect is the pun on "contract" in the English debt riddle, "What grows larger the more you contract it?"⁴ Another related idea is that of objects which become lighter as they grow. See the sieve riddle, "The more there are the less it weighs"⁵ and the hole riddle, "The larger it grows, the lighter it becomes."⁶ Still another variation appears in a Renaissance French riddle for a corpse which the soul has left: "There is less of it, and it weighs more."⁷ This involves the belief that a dead body is heavier than a living body.

The notion of an object growing larger as more and more is taken away ordinarily describes a hole or ditch.⁸

Riddlers have occasionally made the hearer's task more difficult by requiring as answer a special kind of hole or excavation: a grave,⁹ a pond,¹⁰ which has European parallels with the answers "well," or "rathole."¹¹ A Tabaru riddle for grinding sago¹² might also be cited in this category.

Versions which are interesting for their conception or formulation are not numerous. The vaguely suggested personification in the Serbian "The more I tear off you, the bigger you grow"¹³ is an unusual variation. The Bakongo "If you take it away from where it is and wish to put it back, the place is not big enough"¹⁴ is apparently a unique reference to the material taken out. Only the Mongolian "By digging it becomes longer; by taking away from its side it becomes wider"¹⁵ refers to both length and breadth. Pontanus versified the riddle for a hole as

> Dic mihi quid majus fiat quo pluria demas,

and Scriverius capped it with

> Pontano demas carmina, major erit.¹⁶

---

² See Ohlert, 2d ed., p. 50.
³ See the headnote to Nos. 607–631 above.   ⁴ No. 1698.
⁵ French: De la Suie, *Savoie*, p. 472; Westphalen, *Metz*, col. 200.
⁶ Filipino: Starr, *Philippines*, 164. See also French: Pineau, *Poitou*, 18. For French riddles having the answer "holes in a plank" see V. S., *Mélusine*, I (1878), col. 262, No. 54; Desaivre, *Poitou*, p. 450, No. 3; J. Roux, *Limousin*, 87; Daleau, *Gironde*, p. 105; Mensignac, *Gironde*, p. 303, No. 39; Queyrat, *La Creuse*, I, 367. The Catalan answer is merely "holes"; see Milá y Fontanals, 1876, p. 25, No. 17.
⁷ *Les Adeuineaux amoureux*, p. xci.
⁸ Nos. 1691a through 1695 below. See also the more definite but less successfully executed versions in Nos. 1111a through 1112 above.
⁹ No. 1695.   ¹⁰ No. 1690.
¹¹ Swedish: Christofferson, p. 36, No. 18 = *Folkminnen och folktankar*, II (1915), 88, No. 18.
¹² Fortgens, 53.   ¹³ Novaković, p. 76, No. 12.
¹⁴ Denis, 100.   ¹⁵ Mostaert, 75.
¹⁶ *Menagiana*, I (Paris, 1715), 43.

Another Renaissance Latin version is

> Fit minus adijcias si quid; si demseris illi,
> Protinus augetur, dic quid id esse putes?[17]

The notion of growing larger when part is removed, and the modifications of this notion, serve to describe:

§ 1. Darkness. Spanish: Demófilo, 750 (What is it: the greater it is, the less you see of it?), and p. 349, No. 44; Rodríguez Marín, 898. Chilean: Flores, 526. The same notion is used of light when a window shutter is removed or put back in the Icelandic "Increases with removal, decreases with addition."[18]

§ 2. A shadow. Spanish, Chilean: Flores, 702. New Mexican: Campa, 242.

§ 3. Life. Catalan: Pelay y Briz, 175 (The longer it grows, the shorter it is). Hungarian: *Magyar Nyelvör*, IV (1875), 234 (What is that: when increasing, it is decreasing?).

1690. Something the more you dig from it the larger it comes.—Pond.
Parsons, *Bermuda*, p. 256, No. 77.

1691a. The more you take from it, the larger it gets.—Hole.
Fauset, *Nova Scotia*, p. 175, No. 209 var.; Waugh, *Canada*, p. 68, No. 775; Parsons, *Bermuda*, p. 256, No. 77 var.

1691b. What is it the more you take away, the larger it becomes?—Hole.
Brewster, *Indiana*, 59; oral, New Hampshire.

1692a. What is that the more you take from it the more it grow?—Ditch.
Finlay, *Bahamas*, p. 295, No. 3.

1692b. What is it, the longer it is cut, the longer it grows?—Ditch.
Gardner, *Schoharie Hills, N.Y.*, p. 259, No. 73.

1692c. The more you cut off, the longer it grows.—Ditch.
Hudson, p. 87, No. 21.

1692d. The more you cut it, the longer it gets.—Ditch.
Parsons, *Robeson Co., N.C.*, p. 389, No. 13; Bacon and Parsons, *Virginia*, p. 316, No. 41; Chappell, p. 237, No. 44.

1693a. What is it you take from both ends and still it grows longer?—Ditch.
Fauset, *Nova Scotia*, p. 175, No. 209.

1693b. Cut either end makes it longer.—Ditch.
Parsons, *Bermuda*, p. 256, No. 78.

1694a. Me fader have a t'ing in him yard; the more you cut it, the longer it get.—Grave.
Beckwith, *Jamaica*, p. 195, No. 22.

1694b. There is one thing: the more you cut it, the longer it gets.—A grave.
Johnson, *Antigua*, p. 84, No. 13.

---

[17] Buchler, *Gnomologia*, 3d ed. (1614), p. 447. [18] Árnason, 1115.

1694c. What is that that is too short? Cut a bit off and you'll make it long!—Grave.
Kavanagh, *Béaloideas*, II (1929–1930), 295.

1695. What is short and to cut it off makes it longer?—A grave or a ditch.
Redfield, *Tennessee*, p. 40, No. 49.

1696. The more he cuts, the shorter it gets.—A tree.
Chappell, p. 237, No. 45.

1697. What snuff-box is that whose box gets fuller the more pinches he takes?—Candle-snuffers.
Perkins, *New Orleans*, p. 114, No. 91.

1698–1703. Miscellaneous

1698. What grows larger the more you contract it?—Debt.
Gardner, *Schoharie Hills, N.Y.*, p. 258, No. 51.

1699. What is it the more ye lay on, the faster it wasteth?—That is a whetstone, for the more ye whet, the lesse is the whetstone.
Meery Riddles (1629), No. 10 = Brandl, p. 9.

1700. You use it between your head and toes, / The more it works the thinner it grows.—Bar of soap.
Hyatt, *Adams Co., Ill.*, p. 667, No. 10911.

1701. What work is that: the faster ye worke, [the] longer it is ere ye have done; and the slower ye worke, the sooner ye make an end?—That is turning of a spit; for if ye turne fast, it will be long ere the meat be rosted; but if ye turn slowly, the sooner it is rosted.
Meery Riddles (1629), No. 3 = Brandl, p. 8.

1702. what is that as the more hould it hath the waker [weaker] it is & the lese [less] hould it hath the faster it houlds.—a ioyners houldfast [vise] wch will not hold any thing tell [till] it be putt at the end.
Tupper, *Holme Riddles*, 90.

1703a. What is that: the more it is, the lesse men feare it, and [the] lesse it is, the more men dread it?—It is a bridge; for if it be little, wee are affraid to goe over it, but if it be bigge, wee feare no more to go over it then [than] on the ground.
Meery Riddles (1629), No. 48 = Brandl, p. 16.

1703b. What thing is that which is more frightful the smaller it is?—A bridge.
Demaundes Joyous (1511), No. 37 = Kemble, p. 289, No. 37; Halliwell-Phillipps, *Popular Rhymes*, p. 154.

1704–1712. Miscellaneous Acts Involving an Assertion or a Denial

The riddles in this section are, for the most part, *disjecta membra* for which the classification provides no exactly suitable place. They are almost without exception confused and insignificant products. They are separated into two groups: riddles making an assertion about an act and riddles denying an act.

1704–1707. Acts Involving an Assertion

Only the earthquake riddle deserves special attention. It shows an amazing and inexplicable similarity to the story of Loki shaking his chain before Ragnarök. How it was invented, how it was brought to Jamaica, and how it is related to the Old Norse myth of the end of the world are puzzling and perhaps insoluble questions.

1704. Wha' hang on de tree like kyandle?—Pail.
Parsons, *Sea Islands, S.C.*, p. 171, No. 135.

1705. As I was going up to town, I hear the bells of heaven ring; man tremble, beast tremble, cause the Devil to break his chain.—Earthquake.
Beckwith, *Jamaica*, p. 193, No. 82.

1706. I think you live beneath a roof / That is upheld by me; / I think you seldom walk abroad, / But my fair form you see; / I'll close you in on every side, / Your very dwelling pave, / And probably I'll go with you / At last into the grave.—Wood.
Gregor, *Northeast Scotland*, p. 79.

1707. What dis yere? / Pit de patte', pit de patte', / T'ree times a day / In anybody house.—Sifter.
Parsons, *Aiken, S.C.*, p. 28, No. 22.

1708–1712. Acts Involving a Denial

1708. We have a t'ing in the yard an' no man can tell where it end.—Buggy wheel.
Beckwith, *Jamaica*, p. 185, No. 24.

1709. You beat all drum, / You can't beat soldier drum.—You climb, you can' [cannot] climb a *grugru* [pecan] tree.
Parsons, *Antilles*, III, 366, Trinidad, 34.

1710. What thing is onely upon this earth not / subject unto feare, / nor doth not weigh the threatnings of / tyrants pin or haire?—A good conscience.
Prettie Riddles (1631), No. 44 = Brandl, p. 58.

1711. What is that that freezeth never?—Hot water.
Demaundes Joyous (1511), No. 31 = Kemble, p. 289 = Halliwell-Phillipps, *Popular Rhymes*, p. 153.

1712a. There is a thing that nothing is, / And yet it has a name; / 'Tis sometimes tall and sometimes short, / It joins our walk, it joins our sport, / And plays at every game.—Shadow.
Knortz, p. 239, No. 143.

1712b. What is that which nothing is, and yet it has a name?—A shadow.
Waugh, *Canada*, p. 69, No. 799.

1713–1749. Two or More Acts

A few riddles set two or more acts against each other: God cannot do it and man can, or a rich man keeps it and a poor man throws it away. Such contrasts are widely current in Europe or where European riddling is known, but seem not to have appealed to riddlers elsewhere. For other riddles of a similar type see Nos. 1582a through 1586 and 1588 through 1590. The riddles discussed in the headnote to Nos. 138–140 have actors who are conceived to symbolize objects; they therefore differ from these riddles in their fundamental theme.

1713–1721. God and Man

The contrasted powers of God and man afford the materials for a few riddles. Some of these inventions may perhaps go back to medieval speculations about God's power and the limitations on it. The contrast usually concerns an act that God cannot perform but man can or a thing that man and not God possesses. Speculations of this sort are at least as old as Pliny's observations that God cannot commit suicide or alter past events or make twice ten anything but twenty.[1]

1713. God Puts It On; Man Can't Take It Off

1713. God kin put somepin' on you an' can't nobody take it off.—Sin.
Fauset, *Southern Negro*, p. 290, No. 160.

1714. God Didn't Do It; Man Does It

This contrast describes baptism. Riddlers introduce some minor variations into this contrast. I have noted above (headnote to Nos. 1589–1590, § 1) versions in purely human terms, describing baptism as something that the servant (St. John the Baptist) gave to his Master, although he did not have it himself. In a somewhat similar text, which is cited in the discussion of these versions, a Flemish riddler contrasts the activities of God and the Devil. I cite here riddles in which baptism is described as something that God could not or did not do and man accomplished. This notion is somewhat enlarged upon in the Flemish "God can do much, God can do everything, and I can do what God will never be able to do.—Prayer" (Joos, 137).

1714. There is a thing on earth that God could do but didn't, the devil hadn't got the power, and men do it.—Baptism.
Beckwith, *Jamaica*, p. 217, No. 264.

---

[1] See Lynn Thorndike, *A History of Magic and Experimental Science*, I (New York, 1923), 47.

1715-1720. God Never Sees It; a King Seldom; a Man Every Day

This riddle may have been ultimately inspired by a line of the Eighty-first Psalm (v. 8), "Among the gods there is none like unto thee, O Lord," which Burkhard Waldis, a Protestant dramatist of the Reformation, paraphrased as "O Father, God of Heaven, one finds in truth thy like nowhere in Heaven, Hell, nor on the earth."[1]

Several minor variations occur in the parallels. Although these do not seem worthy of special notice, I follow previous commentators in recognizing them.[2] Two varieties of the climactic order are present, a descending sequence (God, king, we)[3] and an ascending sequence (farmer, king, God; or I [we], king, God).[4] The German versions are usually of the latter variety and represent, according to Reinhold Köhler's conjecture,[5] a deviation from the original arrangement, God, king, farmer. Versions in which the order is irregular[6] are clearly corrupt. There are, furthermore, versions in which but two actors appear.[7] The Renaissance German "What does the Devil see all the time and God never?"[8] is a variety of this last form and suggests the passage quoted from the Psalms.

There are also some whimsical versions, which usually have two actors; such a version is the Lithuanian "What does a chip basket have and God himself has not?—A master."[9] When the speaker names but a single actor, as in the Lithuanian "What does God not have?—A higher or more distinguished person than himself,"[10] the question shows a resemblance to a riddle previously discussed[11] and to the Spanish "The sun tolerates no equal."[12] On the whole, the versions differ very little among themselves. Perhaps the most unusual are the Icelandic "There is one whom all see, kings as well as others, but whom the Lord of the Sun has never seen"[13] and "A man went out in the night and did what God couldn't do.—He accompanied a greater than himself."[14] The background of such questions as these seems ultimately to be medieval theological and philosophical discussions of the nature and power of God.

A variation that seems to be peculiarly Spanish consists calling the actor a shepherd, as in the Argentinian "The shepherd sees on the mountain what

---

[1] Preface to *Der verlorene Sohn*, vv. 1-3. See the edition by Gustav Milchsack (Neudrucke deutscher Literaturwerke des 16. und 17. Jahrhunderts, XXX; Halle, 1881), p. 6.
[2] See R. Köhler, *Kleinere Schriften*, III, 502-504, No. 2; Feilberg, *Ordbog*, II, 415, s.v. "ligemand"; Hanika-Otto, No. 209 note.
[3] Nos. 1715a, 1715b below. Compare the English variant, No. 1718.
[4] Nos. 1717a, 1717b.   [5] *Kleinere Schriften*, III, 504.
[6] No. 1716.   [7] Nos. 1719 through 1720b.
[8] Heinrich Adalbert von Keller, *Fastnachtspiele*, II, 559, as cited by R. Köhler, *Kleinere Schriften*, III, 504.   [9] Schleicher, p. 201.
[10] Schleicher, p. 201. Also, compare Nos. 1720a, 1720b below.
[11] Nos. 1394a through 1394c.   [12] Argentinian: Lehmann-Nitsche, 310.
[13] Árnason, 194.   [14] Árnason, 784.

the king does not see in [all] Spain."[15] A related idea, "Quid est quod homo non potest videre in mundo?—Alterius animum,"[16] occurs in medieval dialogues.
Riddlers say that God cannot see his:
§ 1. Equal or like. See Nos. 1715a through 1717a, 1718 through 1720b below.
§ 2. Brother. Spanish: Demófilo, 507; Rodríguez Marín, 923. Argentinian: Lehmann-Nitsche, 720 (I have what God does not have, and I see what God does not see). Porto Rican: Mason, 274.
§ 3. Master. Polish: Gustawicz, 477 (What is it that the Lord God has not and a hog has?). Hungarian: *Magyar Nyelvör*, IV (1875), 38, No. 3 (What doesn't the Lord have?). Also, compare Nos. 1717b, 1720a, 1720b below.

1715a. What God never sees, / What the king seldom sees, / What we see every day: / Read my riddle, I pray.—An equal.
Halliwell-Phillipps, *Popular Rhymes*, p. 43; Parsons, *Bermuda*, p. 257, No. 82; Knortz, p. 225, No. 59; Redfield, *Tennessee*, p. 44; Hyatt, *Adams Co., Ill.*, p. 661, No. 10865.

1715b. What God has never seen, the king seldom sees, and we see every day. —An equal.
Parker, *Oxfordshire*, p. 331.

1716. What the king seldom sees, / What God never sees, / We see every day. / What' that now?—Equal.
Parsons, *Barbados*, p. 286, No. 61.

1717a. What is that we see every day, King George himself sees, and God never sees?—Our equal.
Beckwith, *Jamaica*, p. 215, No. 255.

1717b. What is it that we many a time see / And the Queen seldom sees, / And God never sees?—Someone greater than ourselves.
Praeger, *Béaloideas*, VIII (1938), 171, No. 5.

1718. God never did see, / George Washington scarcely ever did, / And we see every day.—Our equals.
Parsons, *Guilford Co., N.C.*, p. 207, No. 56; oral, New Hampshire.

1719. What is that which the President has seen and the Lord has never seen?—A man equal to himself.
Bacon and Parsons, *Virginia*, p. 317, No. 47.

1720a. What good thing did man find on earth that God never found?— His equal.
Fitzgerald, p. 189.

1720b. What do we see every day that God doesn't?—Our equals.
MacGréine, *Béaloideas*, III (1931-1932), 414, No. 14.

---

[15] Lehmann-Nitsche, 721. See also Catalan: Pelay y Briz, 106. Spanish: Demófilo, 783, 915, 916, and p. 388, No. 31. New Mexican: Espinosa, 90; Campa, 3. Porto Rican: Mason, 300.
[16] Daly and Suchier, p. 86, No. 15.

1721. Christ Had It Not; Napoleon Had It

The notion that man has something that God has not occurs in various forms. The modern Greeks declare that man has a patch but God has not,[1] and express the same idea in secular terms in "There is something that all the world has; only the king does not have it."[2] Such riddles may be endeavors to put into concrete form the truth that God is without defect. The idea is stated somewhat differently in the Hungarian "Everybody has it but the Lord.—Sin."[3] I do not see the reason for applying this to a shadow, as in the Hungarian "I have it, you have it, Old Klotz has it, and God hasn't it"[4] or "Everyone has it but the Lord."[5]

1721. What is that which Christ had not, Napoleon had, Kaiser has and no woman ever has?—A wife.
Beckwith, *Jamaica*, p. 216, No. 258.

1722. Nature Requires Five

The proverbial admonition here turned into a riddle may be ultimately derived from the medieval "Sex horis dormire sat est juvenique senique, septem vix pigro, nulli concedimus octo."[1] A similar bit of advice that occurs as a riddle is "Three times a day, seven times a night, once a month.—Eating, hours of sleep, confessing."[2]

1722a. Nature requires five, / Custom gives seven, / Laziness takes nine, / And wickedness eleven.—Hours of sleep.
Perkins, *New Orleans*, p. 109, No. 31.

1722b. Nature needs but five, / Custom takes but seven, / Laziness takes nine, / And wickedness eleven.—Hours of sleep.
Parsons, *Bermuda*, p. 258, No. 105.

1723. Lord and Lady

1723. The lord and the lady walked out in the hall; / The lord picked up what the lady let fall. / 'Twas neither a handkerchief nor a gold ring, / But nitticoat, natticoat, stick your nose in.—Spectacles.
Gardner, *Schoharie Hills, N.Y.*, p. 255, No. 13.

---

[1] Dieterich, *Sporades*, Nos. 19, 21, citing several parallels.
[2] Polites, *Neohellenika Analekta*, I, 206, No. 74.
[3] *Magyar Nyelvör*, VII (1878), 134, No. 15.
[4] *Magazin für die Litteratur des Auslands*, 1856, p. 364.
[5] *Magyar Nyelvör*, XVI (1887), 429, No. 30.

[1] *Collectio Salernitana*, ed. Renzi, Book V, line 7, as cited in G. L. Apperson, *English Proverbs* (London, 1929), p. 577.
[2] Portuguese: Braga, 51. This differs only slightly from the Catalan version (Pelay y Briz, 186).

1724–1727. Rich Man and Poor Man

1724. Rich Man Keeps It; Poor Man Throws It Away

The parallels cited in the note illustrate well the minor variations characteristic of the process of oral transmission. The contrast of rich man and poor man is replaced by those of beggar and gentleman, farmer and landlord, and (in Sweden and along the eastern border of Germany) peasant and a German. Similar minor variations appear in the actions ascribed to these persons.

This contrast is used for snuff in the Danish "What is that which the young throw away but the old treasure more than the sweetish dish?"[1]

1724a. Riddle, riddle rocket; / What does a poor man throw away, a rich man puts in his pocket?—Snot.
Redfield, *Tennessee*, p. 46, No. 127; Brewster, *Indiana*, 6.

1724b. What does a rich man keep that a poor man throws away?—What he blows from his nose (the rich man using a handkerchief).
Waugh, *Canada*, p. 68, No. 774.

1724c. w^t is that as lords keep in there [their] pockets & begrs throw a way.—snot of ther noses.
Tupper, *Holme Riddles*, 45.

1724d. A rich man puts it in his pocket; / A poor man heaves it away.—Snot from the nose.
Greenleaf, *Newfoundland*, p. 10, No. 13.

1725. Rich Man Wants More of It; Poor Man Can't Get It

This riddle exemplifies the modern manner of using an equivocation in place of a truly enigmatic description. Here "pounds" signifies both "money" and "flesh," in the sense of "weight." It is possible that this riddle has been suggested by the following one.

1725. What is it a rich man has and wants more of, a fat man has and doesn't want, and a poor man wants and can't get?—Pounds.
Oral, New Hampshire.

1726–1727. Rich (Don't) Want It; Poor Want It

This is an unusual example of a theme found in two forms. In the present instance, the riddler describes the answer "nothing" in terms of the acts of the rich, the poor, and the dead. Some texts already cited[1] use such a comparison as "worse than Satan." Inasmuch as both versions contain the remark, "the dead live on it," we can probably infer a common source. The contrast of the living and the dead is a very old and popular theme among rid-

---
[1] Kristensen, p. 122, § 336, No. 534.
[1] See No. 1394a through 1394c and the note to Nos. 1394a through 1394c.

dlers.² The circumstances in which this riddle was invented are obscure, and the evidence is as yet too scanty to encourage any speculation on the subject. The cynical judgment on the course of the world is quite unusual in riddling. The Serbian "It is dead, it gives lodging to the living, the living buy it, the dead do not need it"³ with the answer "pot" may have borrowed some of these characteristic elements, but is probably more closely related to the coffin riddle.⁴

1726. The rich don't want it, the poor want it, and the dead live on it. What's that?—Nothing.
Parsons, *Sea Islands, S.C.*, p. 175, No. 183.

1727. What is it— / That we love more than life, / Fear more than death, / The rich want it, / The poor has it, / The miser spends it, / And the spend-'rift [spendthrift] saves it?—Nothing.
Johnson, *Antigua*, p. 83, No. 1.

1728–1737. Maker Doesn't Use It; Buyer Doesn't Want It; User Is Not Aware of It

Although widely disseminated in areas where European influences have predominated, this riddle has surprisingly few variations.¹ East of Germany and Italy, the folk shows little liking for it. The Finnish, Estonian, Slavic, and Modern Greek versions are probably borrowed, like those in Java and the Philippines, from western Europe.

In a very important variety, which does not seem to be known in English tradition but is characteristic of the oldest texts and the Romance versions, the riddler contrasts the joy of the coffin-maker, who has now found a task at which he will earn money, with the sorrow of the purchaser, who mourns a death in his family. In the medieval "Qui fecit est laetus, qui non desiderat emit, et qui hunc utitur nescius ille suit est,"² the joyful figure is present, but the sorrowful one is lacking. The Argentinian "He who makes it, makes it singing; he who buys it, buys it weeping; and he who uses it, does not see it"³ exhibits the contrasts effectively. Another form of the contrast appears in the Kundu corpse riddle, "They gave me my share, and I did not smile."⁴

The forces holding this riddle together are not strong enough to prevent disintegration, and substitutions and alterations often occur. The previously cited Argentinian text or the Cuban "He who makes it does not enjoy it; he who enjoys it does not see it; however pretty it may be, no one wishes to

---

² See the headnote to Nos. 828–836.   ³ Novaković, p. 118, No. 3.
⁴ See below, Nos. 1728 through 1735 and the headnote to Nos. 1728–1737.

¹ I have noted only a few exceptions to the rule. See comparisons of a coffin to a coat (No. 1209) and to a bed (No. 1210) and a version containing elements borrowed from the violin riddle (cited in the headnote to Nos. 1058–1062, n. 17).
² M[one], *Anzeiger*, VII (1838), col. 48, No. 135.
³ Lehmann-Nitsche, 687a.   ⁴ Ittmann, *Kundu*, 10.

have it"[5] or the Chilean "A strange well, he who makes it does not have the benefit of it, he who sees it does not wish it, and he who does not see it has the benefit of it.—Grave"[6] or the Yucatecan "He who weaves it, weaves it singing; he who buys it buys it weeping; and he who has to buy it, never needs it. —Shroud"[7] illustrate these variations.

The situation described in this riddle refers to a medieval or village manner of life: the coffin is made to order, and the maker is also the seller of the coffin. The distribution of the riddle suggests an origin in Europe. Such similar conceptions as the Uraon corpse riddle, "The man who orders without knowing"[8] or the Maltese coffin riddle, "A thing that you do not wish to enter but into which you must go by force"[9] can have arisen independently. There has been no adequate discussion or collection of the parallels.[10]

Some curious Javanese texts use this manner of description for entirely different themes. See a riddle for the hand, teeth, mouth, and stomach, "He who takes it does not eat it; who eats it does not test it; he who tests it is not sated; he who has no need of it gets possession of it";[11] another for the man who cuts grass, the man who buys it, and a horse, "He who gets it does not buy it; he who buys it does not eat it; he who eats it does not pay for it";[12] and still another for the maker and purchaser of coats and jackets, "He who makes it does not use it, but he who does not make it, uses it."[13]

I can quote no parallel to the excellent phrasing of the Swedish coffin riddle, "There lives a tailor in our town, he makes clothing that he does not want, the one who buys it does nothing with it, and the one who gets it knows naught of it."[14] This is one of the few instances in which the riddler compares the coffin to a specific thing.

This manner of description is limited, with the exception of a few texts which may be of European origin, to Europe and countries where European influence has been dominant. It is applicable to the following:

§ 1. Counterfeit money. Flemish: Joos, 339 (Whoever has it does not tell it; whoever takes it does not know it; whoever recognizes it does not want it). German: Wossidlo, 402; Gilhoff, 646. Polish: Gustawicz, 309 (He who makes it says nothing; he who takes it knows nothing; he who knows it does not take it). Russian: Sadovnikov, 696. Serbian: Novaković, p. 143, Nos. 4 (He who has me praises me; he who gets me does not know me; he who comes to know me does not want me), 5 (He who has it does not tell; he who gets it does not know of it; he who comes to know it does not want it).

---

[5] Massip, 25.
[6] Laval, 11.
[7] M. Redfield, p. 49, No. 11.
[8] Archer, p. 185, No. 97.
[9] Stumme, *Malta*, 15.
[10] See Petsch, *Neue Beiträge*, pp. 107-110; Feilberg, *Ordbog*, II, 422, s.v. "ligkiste."
[11] Ranneft, *Proza*, p. 5, No. 19.
[12] Ranneft, *Proza*, p. 10, No. 46. See a somewhat different version in Mayer, 47.
[13] Ranneft, *Proza*, p. 43, No. 196.
[14] Ström, p. 186, "Likkistan." See also No. 1209 above.

§ 2. Hunger. Luxemburg: De la Fontaine, 45 (When you have it, you don't want it).

§ 3. Sleep. Serbian: Novaković, p. 198, No. 3 (He who makes it doesn't need it; he who buys it doesn't want it; he who needs it knows nothing about it). This is a stupid substitution of an inappropriate answer.

§ 4. A cobweb. Polish: Gustawicz, 291 (He who cares has none; he who cares not has some).

1728. ther was a man bespoke a thing which when the owner [MS: oner] it home [MS: whon] did bring he that made [MS: mad] it did refuse it, he that bought it did not use it & he that had it did not know whether he had it, yea or noe.—A coffin bought by another for a dead man.
Tupper, *Holme Riddles*, 9.

1729a. He that made it, 'twas to sell it; he that bought it, did not want it; he that used it, never saw it.—Coffin.
Fitzgerald, p. 185.

1729b. The man who sells it don't buy it, and the man who buys it don't want it, and the man who gets it don't know it.—Coffin.
Parsons, *Bahamas*, p. 478, No. 72.

1729c. The man that makes it, he don't use it, / The man that buys it, he don't use it, / And the man that use it, he doesn't know it.—Coffin.
Fauset, *Nova Scotia*, p. 153, No. 51; Brewster, *Indiana*, 67.

1729d. Man who made it didn't use it, / The man who bought it didn't want it, / The man who used it didn't know it.—Coffin.
Bacon and Parsons, *Virginia*, p. 321, No. 86.

1729e. The man who made it had no use for it; the man who bought it didn't want it; the man who got it didn't know it.—Coffin.
Waugh, *Canada*, p. 71, No. 816.

1729f. The man that made it didn't need it, the man that sold it didn't want it, the man that used it didn't know.—A coffin.
Redfield, *Tennessee*, p. 40, No. 52.

1729g. The man who makes it does not use it, / The man who buys it does not use it, / The man who uses it does not know anything about it.—A coffin.
Farr, *Tennessee*, p. 322, No. 56.

1729h. What is it which the man that made it does not need, the man who buys it does not use for himself, and the person that uses it does not know it? —Coffin.
Gardner, *Schoharie Hills, N.Y.*, p. 257, No. 38.

1730. The man that made it, he didn't want it. The man that went after it, had no use for it. The man that got it, he didn't know that he got it.—A casket.
Fauset, *Nova Scotia*, p. 154, No. 51 var.

1731a. The man who made it did not want it; the man who used it did not want it.—Coffin.
Perkins, *New Orleans*, p. 110, No. 43.

1731b. Dere is somet'in' de man dat made it don' want. De man dat use it don' know what it is.—Coffin.
Parsons, *Sea Islands, S.C.*, p. 173, No. 160 var.

1731c. Man what made it, don't use, / Man what use it, don't know it.—Coffin.
Parsons, *Aiken, S.C.*, p. 33, No. 59.

1732a. The man that made it never used it, / The man that used it never saw it.—Coffin.
Fauset, *Southern Negro*, p. 285, No. 100.

1732b. Who made it don' use it. / Who use it don' see it.—Cawfin [coffin].
Parsons, *Sea Islands, S.C.*, p. 173, No. 160.

1733. De man who made it / Never use it. / De man who use it / Never made it.—Cawfin.
Parsons, *Bahamas*, p. 474, No. 30.

1734. There was a man made a thing, / And he that made it did it bring, / But he 'twas made for did not know, / Whether 'twas a thing or no.—Casket.
Fauset, *Nova Scotia*, p. 154, No. 51 var.

1735. There was a man made a thing, / and he that made it did it bring; / But he 'twas made for did not know / Whether 'twas a thing or no.—Coffin.
Chambers, *Scotland*, p. 108.

1736. What a man make an' don't need?—Tombstone.
Parsons, *Aiken, S.C.*, p. 33, No. 60.

1737. De man who made it / Never use it. / De man who use it / Never made it.—Rooster.
Parsons, *Bahamas*, p. 474, No. 30.

1738. Too Much for One, Enough for Two, Nothing for Three

This riddle has very close parallels in proverbs. Particularly interesting in this connection is a passage in the *Vetalapañcavinsati* or the Twenty-Five Tales of a Demon: "This is the way of the world; when an affair come to six ears, it does not remain secret; if a matter is confided to four ears, it may escape further hearing; and if to two ears, even Brahma the Creator does not know it; how then can any rumour of it come to man?"[1] This notion may also be related to the proverb, "Three may keep counsel, if two be away,"[2] which occurs in several variations.

---
[1] R. F. Burton, *Vikram and the Vampire* (London, 1870), p. 38. See also N. M. Penzer, *The Ocean of Story*, VI (London, 1926), 237.
[2] For references see W. G. Smith and Janet Heseltine, *Oxford Dictionary of English Proverbs* (Oxford, 1935), p. 490, G. L. Apperson, *English Proverbs and Proverbial Phrases* (London, 1929), p. 628.

Riddlers have found various substitutes for the answer here given. The Danes say, "For one it is too little, for two it is just right, and for three it is too strong [much].—Marriage";[3] the Swedes, "One is too few, two are neither too much nor too few, three are too many.—For kissing."[4] Such riddles have clearly been suggested by this riddle for a secret. Less variation from the original is seen in the Renaissance French "What thing is it that is too limited for one, and just right for two, and too large for three?—It is when one is angry at heart. It is too limited for him alone. And when he tells it to his companion, it is more nearly right, but when the third knows it, it is too much."[5] Virtually the same query occurs in German.[6] The Icelandic parallel with the answer "slander" conceives it in terms of a thing: "What is it that is too heavy for one and enough for two and cannot be destroyed if a third joins them?"[7]

Among the oldest versions of the secret riddle are Buchler's versions:

> Augusta [angusta] est uni, bene convenit atque duobus,
> Lata nimis res cum sit manifesta tribus

and

> Si scis, dic, homini nimis arctum quod foret uni,
> Amplum sed trinis nimium, justum bene binis.[8]

I do not see the pertinence of this theme in a Danish riddle for a stove, "What is it that is too much for one, too little for two, but suitable for three?"[9] A Swedish riddle for a glass of liquor, "One is enough, two are too many, three are too few,"[10] is readily intelligible.

1738. What is that which is too much for one, enough for two, but nothing at all for three?—A secret.

Knortz, p. 233, No. 99; Farr, *Tennessee*, p. 320, No. 29; Beckwith, *Jamaica*, p. 216, No. 259.

1739–1749. Erotic Scenes

A trick characteristic of riddling at all times has been the description of an erotic scene with the intent of confusing the hearer by an entirely innocent answer. I have deemed it sufficient to cite the answers to these riddles with the references to the places where they have been printed.

1739. Ans.: Apple.
Parsons, *Sea Islands, S.C.*, p. 157, No. 31.

---

[3] Kristensen, p. 154, § 444, No. 712. The Hungarian "If one isn't enough, there should be two of them" (Kriza, 47) is confused.
[4] Ström, p. 356, "Räknegåtor," 24.
[5] *Les Adeuineaux amoureux*, p. xcvii = Rolland, 248.
[6] Butsch, 319.   [7] Árnason, 404.
[8] *Gnomologia*, 3d ed. (1614), p. 475.
[9] Kristensen, p. 62, § 145, No. 211.
[10] Sandén, *Norra Vadsbo*, 6, 7.

1740a. Ans.: Man had apples in a measure, 'n' he shakes 'em, 'n' lady takes up her dress, an' he dump 'em in them.
Fauset, *Philadelphia*, p. 557, No. 45.

1740b. Ans.: Apple-tree.
Parsons, *Guilford Co., N.C.*, p. 202, No. 15; Boggs, *North Carolina*, p. 320, No. 1.

1740c. Ans.: The old man was shaking apples off a tree, and the old woman was catching them in her dress.
Chappell, p. 235, No. 32.

1741. Ans.: Bed.
Randolph and Spradley, *Ozark*, p. 84.

1742a. Ans.: Bed.
Parsons, *Guilford Co., N.C.*, p. 205, No. 39.

1742b. Ans.: Bed.
Parsons, *Robeson Co., N.C.*, p. 389, No. 10; Greenleaf, *Newfoundland*, p. 8, No. 2; Hyatt, *Adams Co., Ill.*, p. 661, No. 10867; Boggs, *North Carolina*, p. 321, No. 3; Chappell, p. 235, No. 33.

1743. Ans.: Mule.
Parsons, *Sea Islands, S.C.*, p. 157, No. 32.

1744a. Ans.: Door peg and door.
Parsons, *Sea Islands, S.C.*, p. 156, No. 29.

1744b. Ans.: Door bars.
Parsons, *Sea Islands, S.C.*, p. 157, No. 29 var.

1744c. Ans.: Door-peg.
Chappell, p. 235, No. 34.

1745. Ans.: Wedding ring.
Johnson, *Antigua*, p. 88, No. 64.

1746a. Ans.: Hog [being slaughtered].
Parsons, *Sea Islands, S.C.*, p. 157, No. 30.

1746b. Ans.: Hog [being slaughtered].
Fauset, *Philadelphia*, p. 557, No. 46; Halpert, *Riddles*, p. 38, No. 4.

1747. Ans.: Making a broom.
Beckwith, *Jamaica*, p. 204, No. 197.

1748. Ans.: Fish in water.
Fauset, *Philadelphia*, p. 557, No. 47.

1749. Ans.: Man selling nuts.
Parsons, *Guilford Co., N.C.*, p. 205, No. 41.

Notes

Notes

Chapter I
COMPARISONS TO A LIVING CREATURE
Nos. 1–335

1. Walloon: Colson, *Wallonia*, V, 54, No. 201 (I have a big head without foot or arm, and all the world up to the king has some of me).

3. The parallels vary greatly and follow only the general outline of the pattern. See "Twenty-five sisters, all with a piercing spirit, and their heads [are] without ears.— Twenty-five pins" (Breton: Charlec, *Dol-de-Bretagne*, 1904, p. 169, No. 36), and "I am somewhat long, I have neither feet nor arms, yet I have a head. No one can pass me, not even great kings" (French: V. S., *Mélusine*, I [1878], col. 254, No. 9), which is related to the Walloon riddle cited in the note to No. 1 of the present collection. See also the unusually elaborated Parsee version, "There is a thing which, though it is pointed, is yet not a thorn. It has the head but not the skin. Though it is shining, yet it is not silver. What, then, is its name?" (Munshi, pp. 414–415). For other varieties of the theme of a creature with a defect see, in the present collection, Nos. 5, 36, 37, and (with a definite comparison to a person) 531 through 536b.

4a, 4b. The import of the reference to the "head" is obscure.

5. Flemish: Joos, 865 (Who has one eye and no head?). Swedish: Ström, p. 160, "Nålen," 7 (What has an eye but no head? What has a head but no eyes?—Needle, pin). Indonesian, Tabaru: Fortgens, 30 (It is with a head but is without eyes; it is with eyes but without a head.—Pin, needle). Compare No. 3 in the present collection.

6. Breton: Sauvé, 71 (Guess a thing that has a body without feet, a neck without a head). Flemish: Joos, 855 (Who has a neck without a head and a belly without a body?), 856 (Who has a mouth and yet [has] no head?). French: Bladé, *Armagnac*, 9 (It has a belly, neck, and no head at all); Sébillot, *Auvergne*, 38; Marchessou, *Velay et Auvergne*, p. 175, No. 2; V. S., *Mélusine*, I (1878), col. 258, No. 47. Catalan: Pelay y Briz, 144. Russian: Sadovnikov, 438 (There lies a body; it has no head, but the throat is intact).

Other versions of the bottle riddle include more than the mention of the "head" or "neck"; see No. 270 of the present collection. At times, they may achieve a high degree of personification; see the Portuguese "My man with four hips" (Parsons, *Cape Verde*, 142), which refers to a square bottle, and the note to No. 270 in the present collection.

7a through 8. These differ from most of the riddles in this section, for the member that is present and the member that is lacking are not related.

9. Compare No. 22.

10a, 10b. Scotch Gaelic: Nicolson, p. 51. Danish: Kristensen, p. 122, § 340, Nos. 538a, 538b. French: Rolland, *Rimes*, p. 205, No. 44 (Who has so many little eyes, so many little eyes that he does not on that account see clearly?). Italian: Pitrè, 226. African, Kxatla: Schapera, 105 (Tell me: the wing of the lightning bird is full of holes.—Sieve).

11. The reference to the eyes involves a pun; compare Nos. 16 and 274 through 276 of the present collection. Such puns are not characteristic of the best enigmatic technique.

12b. The introductory formula seems incomplete, for the parallels begin with "A riddle, a riddle, as I suppose," which has been preserved in the vicissitudes of oral tradition by the rhyme with "nose."

13a. Compare the colonial French "A thousand holes in one hole" (Baissac, *Mauritius*, p. 405), in which the enigmatic paradox lies in the seeming impossibility of a hole being in a hole. For parallels to this notion see the headnote to No. 908, n. 24, of the present collection, and compare No. 1413.

15a, 15b. Batak: Ophuijsen, p. 468, No. 89 (Only one mouth, but countless eyes).

18 through 20. The import of "north, east, south, and west" and its variants is not entirely clear. It may signify "everywhere" or may refer to teeth that point in every direction. In the Swedish riddle for a fish, "It goes south, north, east, west, but is neither on the field nor in the air" (Ström, p. 118), it signifies "everywhere."

18. Flemish: Joos, 322. Luxemburg: De la Fontaine, 8 (What has many teeth and no jaw?—Harrow, saw). Danish: Kristensen, pp. 105–106, § 289, Nos. 449a through 449d; and "What is that which has teeth without a tongue and a head without lungs and a tail without a rump?—Rake" (Hvad et det som har Tænder uden Tunge og Hoved uden Lunger og Hale uden Røv?—En Rive. DFS, 1906/38: M. Jespersen, Bostrup Hedeby, 1919, p. 3, No. 12). Norwegian: Brox, *Ytre Senja*, 66 (Who has teeth and no tongue?—Saw); Stafset, 4 (Who has teeth but no tongue and no head?—Saw), 177 (What is that which has teeth and no tongue, tail and no rump?—Rake). Swedish: Ström, p. 142, "Räfsan," 2, 3 (rake), and p. 385, "Sysselsättningar," 37 (harrow). Walloon: Colson, *Wallonia*, V, 56, No. 215 (rake). French: Rolland, 209 (Who has teeth without a head and a tail without a rump?—Rake). Spanish: Demófilo, p. 434, No. 3 (comb). Cuban: Massip, 175 (steel tooth). Lettish: Bielenstein, 831 (Who has teeth and no mouth?—Ax).

19a. Flemish: Joos, 315 (I have no mouth, but I have many teeth and that which I bite grows in the country).

19b. The variant "feet" is probably a mishearing of "teeth."

20. Danish: Kristensen, pp. 63–64, §153, Nos. 225a, 225b (What is that which has as many teeth as all the men in town?). Quite different is the Algerian Arabic "It is as large as the sole of a foot, and its children are as numerous as the leaves of a forest" (Giacobetti, 525).

21a, 21b. Norwegian: Bugge, *Telemarken*, 51 (It speaks without a tongue, gives voice without lungs, one takes it in joy and sorrow, although it has no heart). In this parallel, note the allusion to the words of the marriage service, although the context is wholly different.

22. Spanish: Demófilo, 846. For the usual forms of the clock riddle, which are more detailed than this text, see Nos. 283, 322 through 324, 565a through 566 of the present collection.

23 through 24d. Welsh: Hull and Taylor, 278, 279. Breton: Kerbeuzec, *Ille-et-Vilaine*, 59. Flemish: Joos, 858 (She has neither flesh nor bone and yet [has] four fingers and a thumb)'. Walloon: Colson, *Wallonia*, IV, 110, No. 129. Portuguese: Braga, 39. Turkish: Hamizade, 172 (Bloodless, soulless, a set of five fingers.—Glove).

For comparison of a glove to a house with five rooms see the headnote to No. 908 of the present collection. For wholly different applications of the theme "has neither flesh nor blood," see the headnote to Nos. 264–265.

24d. The reference to the hedge has been suggested by the rhyme with bridge. The reference to flesh and bone is properly part of the riddle but has here been expanded by the use of elements of a proverbial phrase. For this phrase see G. L. Apperson, *English Proverbs* (London, 1929), pp. 219–220; W. G. Smith and Janet Heseltine, *Oxford Book of English Proverbs* (Oxford, 1935), p. 309; various authors, *Notes and Queries*, 9th ser., V (1900), 125, 290, 437, and VI (1901), 15. Compare also Nos. 264a, 265, 392a, 392b, 665, and 1237a through 1238 and the note to No. 665 in the present collection.

26. Italian: Pitrè, 746 (Born in the forest, it has feet and arms without having a head); this riddle has an introductory element characteristic of the texts discussed in the headnote to Nos. 1058–1062 of the present collection. For a variant form see No. 87.

28. Compare the Turkish description of an embroidery table, "I saw a wonderful thing. It had four legs but no soul, it gets many thousand thrusts but does not feel them, it has tulips and violets in full bloom, but you cannot hear the sigh of a nightingale" (Kúnos, 57).

30a, 30b. Like the potato riddle (Nos. 11, 16 of the present collection), this also involves a pun. In this instance, the head of a barrel is conceived as the head of a creature. The Breton barrel riddle, "Who has two bottoms and no head at all?" (Sébillot, *Haute-Bretagne*, 67e), is more in the folk manner. Greater detail is given in the barrel riddle numbered 74 in the present collection, and in Nos. 516a through 516e, in which the riddler conceives the barrel in terms of a person.

31 through 33. The usual answer is "cabbage." For parallels see German: Hanika-Otto, 591 (What bride has her heart in her head?). Danish: Kristensen, p. 46, § 120, Nos. 168a, 168b (What is that which has head, heart, and body, can stand but cannot walk?), and p. 78, § 195, No. 301 (What is that which has a heart but no soul?).

32b. This version combines two ways of describing a cabbage; it is both a creature with its heart in its head and, as in the versions cited in the headnote to Nos. 1121–1126, § 4, a man standing on one leg. It is the only English instance of the otherwise generally known comparison of a cabbage to a man standing on one leg. The same contamination occurs in the Flemish "It stands upon one paw and bears its heart in its head" (Joos, 522). See further German: Wossidlo, 200; Haffner, 36 var. Swiss: Rochholz, 418 (Something stands on the edge of the field, it has only one leg, a curly queue, and its heart is in its head).

34. I have not learned what a cow-tie may be. A hair rope with a metal buckle, that is to say, a halter, would satisfy the conditions of the riddler.

36, 37. Spanish, Argentinian: Lehmann-Nitsche, 37 (nail), 154 (I have a hard head, I stand on one foot, and I am of such strength that man overcame God.—Nail). The last sentence is a reference to the Crucifixion. Dominican Rep.: Andrade, 119 (nail). Porto Rican: Mason, 169 (nail). See Nos. 3, 5, in the present collection, and the more adequately personified versions also making a reference to a bodily defect in Nos. 531 through 536b and the headnotes to Nos. 531–534 and 535–536.

39. Indian, Uraon: Archer, p. 184, No. 85 (The boy with the hundred eyes behind).

40. Danish: Kristensen, p. 68, § 164, No. 251 (Eleven noses and no head.—Kettle hanger).

41. The import of the riddle is obscure.

42. The import of the riddle is obscure. For comment on the use of onomatopoeia in riddling see the note to No. 86.

43. Parallels to this invention, which is quite in the enigmatic spirit, are almost completely lacking. The enigmatic quality lies in the paradoxical number of ribs and backbones. Compare the German riddle for wagon tracks, "Two brothers lie beside each other. If they rise, they reach Heaven" (Wossidlo, 151). This is a familiar riddle for a road; see the headnote to No. 575 of the present collection. The mention of two persons is, however, unusual. The scene of brothers or members of a family lying together occurs frequently; see the headnote to Nos. 1027–1028. See, finally, the Kxatla description of a wagon track, "Tell me; two pythons which are standing by each other" (Schapera, 128).

45a, 45b. A self-heater is a flatiron in which a fire is burning.

46a, 46b. (Such indications of time as "morning," "noon," and "night" are not present.) Flemish: Joos, 693. Icelandic: Árnason, 1092. Portuguese: Parsons, *Cape Verde*, 198 (Two men country into the country. The one who has two feet tires, and the one who has one foot does not tire.—Man and cane). Although this contains something of the Sphinx riddle, it is probably a different theme. Italian: Pitrè, 865 (What animal is born with four legs, lives with two legs, and dies with three legs?). Modern Greek: B. Schmidt, *Griechische Märchen, Sagen und Volkslieder* (Leipzig, 1877), pp. 148-149, No. 12 (in a tale). Arabic: Ruoff, p. 16, No. 8. Turkish: Zavarin, *Brusa*, 1 (I saw someone with four legs, a second time with two [legs]). Indonesian, Javanese: Ranneft, *Poëzie*, p. 30, No. 7; Ranneft, *Proza*, p. 1, No. 3 (When it runs, it has two; when it stops, it has ten legs.—A *saté*-seller [when he sets down his tray with eight legs]), which seems to be an independent invention of the idea, and p. 36, No. 156 (When it is still small, it has four legs; when it is large, it has two legs; when it is old, it has three legs); Luinenburg, p. 28, No. 5. Samoan: Heider, 130 (Who is the man: at birth he can only lie down; later he goes on four feet, still later on two, is very strong, runs back and forth; then comes a time when he goes on three feet?).

47a, 47b. (Indications of time, usually as "morning," "noon," and "night," are present.) Scotch Gaelic: Nicolson, p. 21. Dutch: Sinninghe, p. 8, No. 1; Joos, p. 7, cites a version by Vondel. Afrikaans: Groenewald, p. 65. German: Wossidlo, 344; Hanika-Otto, 4a. Icelandic: Árnason, 709. Danish: Kristensen, p. 88, § 229, Nos. 352a, 352b, and p. 271, No. 57. Norwegian: Bugge, *Telemarken*, 40; Stafset, 214. Swedish: Dybeck, *Runa*, 1850, p. 37, No. 36; Ericsson, *Södermanland*, I (1879), 93, No. 66; Waltman, *Lidmål*, 208; Ström, p. 72, "Människans åldrar," 1. Latin: Reusner, ed. 1602, pp. 294-295; Buchler, *Gnomologia*, 3d ed. (1614), pp. 448-449. French: J. Roux, *Limousin*, 10; Parsons, *Antilles*, III, 405, Guadaloupe, 99, and p. 419, Marie Galante, 101. Spanish: Demófilo, 517; Rodríguez Marín, 295. Argentinian: Lehmann-Nitsche, 91. Cuban: Sánchez, 8. Dominican Rep.: Andrade, 316. Porto Rican: Mason, 654. Lithuanian: Jurgelionis, 151. Polish: Saloni, *Rzeshów*, 35; Gustawicz, 36; Pracki, p. 212. Russian: Sadovnikov, 1725; Preobrazhenskii, p. 172. Bulgarian: Stoilov, p. 68, § 47. Lappish: Qvigstad, 45. Hungarian: *Magyar Nyelvör*, XLIII, 218 (In the morning it walks on two legs; at noon on two). This defective version is cited by S. Szendrey, *Ethnographia*, XXXII (1921), 73. Mordvin: Paasonen, 354. Modern Greek: Polites, *Neohellenika Analekta*, I, 210, No. 99; Stathes, p. 355, No. 140. Armenian: Zelinski, No. 16 (cited by Blechsteiner, p. lii, No. 35); Seidlitz, *Das Ausland*, LVII (1884), 71, No. 16 = *Das Ausland*, LXII (1889), 809. Turkish: Hamizade, 290 (In the morning he crawls, at noon there are four feet, in the evening there are two feet. Time passes and there come to be three feet). Georgian: Blechsteiner, p. 17, No. 35 (In the morning I was quite small, at noon you saw me full-grown. When you met me at evening, you saw me already white). This contains little of the Sphinx riddle and more of the texts cited in the headnotes to Nos. 46 and 668-669 of the present collection. Mongolian: Whymant, 1. African, Basa: Scheibler, 1. Tonga-Shangaan: Junod and Jaques, p. 236, No. 39. Indian, Ho: Haldar, p. 276, No. 8; Sarkar, pp. 257-258, No. 52. Uraon: Archer, p. 192, No. 196 (Four legs in the morning, two legs at noon, three legs at night). Indonesian, Sangir: Adriani, p. 404, No. 105. Karo-Batak: Joustra, p. 94. Serawaj: Helfrich, *Serawaj*, p. 66, No. 86. For other Indonesian versions see A. L. van Hasselt, *De taal- en letterkunde van Midden-Sumatra* (Leiden, 1881), p. 148, as cited by Damsté, below; Jacobsen, p. 7; J. C. G. Jonker, *Rottineesche teksten* (Leiden, 1911), p. 90; H. T. Damsté, *Koloniaal tijdschrift*, VI (1917), 356 (Early in the morning it has two, at noon three [legs], and at the end it has two mouths). The last clause refers to the mouth and the implement used to grind betel. Atjeh: Kreemer, *Atjeh*, 59. Fijian: Fison, 31 = *Revue des traditions populaires*, I (1886), 87. Hawaiian: Judd, 123.

47b. The riddler has confused the order.

48. (Carrying a stick.) Lithuanian: Schleicher, p. 209 (It goes out on six feet and comes home on three.—Soldier). Indonesian, Javanese: Ranneft, *Proza*, p. 1, No. 2 (quoted in the headnote to Nos. 46-87, n. 10, of the present collection). Menangkerbau Malay: Harmsen, p. 265, No. 6 (It has three feet, and it runs; four eyes, and it sees).

The English riddle and the parallels might perhaps support Aarne's conjectural relating of this riddle to the riddle of the Sphinx; see *Rätselforschungen*, II, 184.

49. (Many legs, some of them are not used for locomotion.) German: Wossidlo, 360 (What has six legs and yet walks on only four?). Icelandic: Árnason, 1080 (There are two heads, two hands, ten toes, thrice two legs, but only four walk. How is this mystery to be understood?). Danish: Kristensen, p. 42, § 104, No. 142 (Two heads and only two arms, six feet and only ten toes, four feet in motion, how does one understand that?). Hungarian: Arany and Gyulai, II, 366, No. 85 (It has two hands, four eyes, six feet, and yet walks on four. What is it?); *Magyar Nyelvör*, III (1874), 234, No. 9 (Who is it that has six feet and yet walks on only four?). Indonesian, Javanese: Ranneft, *Poëzie*, pp. 26–27, No. 15 (Two heads are seen and also two arms. In all, it has six legs and only ten digits. Only four legs run, and the two others do not touch the ground.—Man in palanquin), and p. 90, No. 5 (It is said that it has six legs, three heads, and six arms. Only four legs are walking, the other two are outstretched. Over all this it is under a roof.—Man in palanquin). Japanese: Starr, *Japan*, p. 45 (Having six legs, it walks on four.—Man on horseback). See the discussion in Wilhelm Schulze, "Das Rätsel vom trächtigen Tiere," *Ungarische Jahrbücher*, IV (1924), 23, n. 4.

The Bihari describe Sarwen, the son of the blind sage Andhak, as follows: "Tulsī-dās thinks—two feet walk on the ground, four feet rest comfortably and happily; he has three heads and but two eyes" (Mitra, *Bihar*, 60) and "Two feet walk and four are dangling; he speaks honeyed words; he has three heads and but two eyes. This asks Surdas" (Mitra, *Bihar*, 61).

50, 51. (Carrying a bird.) These riddles have been frequently and fully discussed; see Tupper, *Modern Language Notes*, XVIII (1903), 105; his *Holme Riddles*, note to No. 28; and his *Riddles of the Exeter Book*, p. 108, No. 20, and p. 205, No. 65; and also Arthur G. Brodeur and Archer Taylor, "The Man, the Horse, and the Canary," *California Folklore Quarterly*, II (1943), 271–278.

50. "Downe in a dale" is a formula often used by Welsh riddlers; see Hull and Taylor, 6 and note.

52. (Sexual members mentioned.) Danish: Feilberg, *Ordbog*, I, 299, s.v. "fitte"; Kristensen, p. 43, § 106, No. 146b, and p. 155, § 447, Nos. 716a through 716c. Spanish: Rodríguez Marín, 347. Lithuanian: Jurgelionis, 563, 564, 740. Yakut: Piekarski, 205 (They say there is one who has four *sutki*, eight legs, two heads, two sexual organs.—Woman on mare). The meaning of *sutki* is obscure.

53. (Enumerations of heads, legs, arms, hands, and feet.) Welsh: Hull and Taylor, 76 through 79. Welsh Gypsy: Sampson, 9. Breton: Charlec, *Dol-de-Bretagne*, 1904, p. 379, No. 47. Dutch: *Volk en taal*, II, 201, No. 85. Afrikaans: Groenewald, p. 89. German: Wossidlo, 424; Gilhoff, 48; Carstens, *Schleswig-Holstein*, p. 423; Frischbier, *Menschenwelt*, p. 256, Nos. 162, 163 (many parallels cited); Böckel, *Hesse*, 38; Hanika-Otto, 9, 12 through 16. Danish: Kristensen, p. 43, § 106, No. 146a (Up hills and down dales, three noses and a tail, six ears, and three mouths. Who can get to the bottom of this?), and p. 110, § 299, Nos. 473a through 473d; Feilberg, *Ordbog*, III, 108, s.v. "rytter" (many parallels). Norwegian: Brox, *Ytre Senja*, 190. Swedish: Dybeck, *Runa*, 1848, p. 43, No. 27; and *ibid*., 1849, p. 50, No. 31 = Russwurm, p. 350, No. 70; Ericsson, *Södermanland*, I, 84, No. 20; and III, 102, No. 158; Hyltén-Cavallius, *Värend*, 2, 4, 5; Geijer and Campbell, 8, and compare their No. 121; Ström, p. 371, "Människa och djur," 1, and compare p. 371, "Gudar och djur," p. 372, "Sysselsättningar," 1, and p. 378, "Sysselsättningar," 35. Walloon: Colson, *Wallonia*, IV, 57, No. 36. French: *Les Adeuineaux amoureux*, pp. lxxxvii f.; Rolland, 35, 36; Rolland, *Rimes*, p. 198, No. 12; Westphalen, *Metz*, col. 202; J. Roux, *Limousin*, p. 177, No. 25. Catalan: Pelay y Briz, 317. Spanish: Rodríguez Marín,

p. 325. Argentinian: Lehmann-Nitsche, 204 (horse and two troopers). Italian: Pitrè, 866. Rumanian: Gorovei, 271. Lithuanian: Jurgelionis, 741 (Eight feet, three heads, and one tail). Lettish: Bielenstein, 185, 249 through 251, 678, 890 (ten feet, three stomachs), 901 (two heads, two hands, eight feet). Czech: Hanika-Otto, note to No. 10. Russian: Sadovnikov, 987a through 987c. Finnish: Aarne and Krohn, 304 = Henssen, 166. Hungarian: *Magazin für die Litteratur des Auslands*, 1856, p. 364 (cited by Rolland, note to No. 35). Cherekessian: Tambiev, p. 55, No. 21 (Six eyes, three noses, three heads, one tail, eight legs.—Two men on horseback). Kabardin: Talpa and Sokolov, 10 (Six eyes, three noses, three heads, eight legs, and only one tail. Two riders on one horse). The Bhil describe two dogs as "Eight feet in utter disorder, and two tails in the midst" (Hedberg, p. 872, No. 39).

56a, 56b. (Pregnant animal.) German: Frischbier, *Thierwelt*, p. 345, No. 5 (There comes a pair of cattle over the bridge, it has eight feet and walks on four). This employs the manner of description discussed in the note to No. 49 of the present collection. Icelandic: Árnason, 447 (What is it outside the door that chews with ten greedy tongues? It has forty feet, didn't move a step, and yet travels far and wide), 448 (What is lying outside the door? It has ten tongues, twenty eyes, forty feet, and travels far and wide.—A cat). Presumably this cat has nine unborn kittens, but they are not mentioned in the answer. Swedish: Ström, p. 98, "Svinet," 1. Latin: Pitman, Aldhelm, 84.

57. (Pregnant woman.) Welsh Gypsy: Sampson, 9. German: Frischbier, *Thierwelt*, p. 345, No. 5; Renk, *Tyrol*, 76. Icelandic: Árnason, 447, 448. According to Wilhelm Schulze (cited in the headnote to No. 56, n. 1, of the present collection), these texts are derived from the Old Norse riddles of King Heidrek (see Heusler, *Zeitschrift des Vereins für Volkskunde*, XI [1901], 141–142, No. 12). Medieval Latin: Pitman, Aldhelm, 90. See also K. Müllenhoff and W. Scherer, *Denkmäler* (3d ed.; Berlin, 1892), I, 20, § 7, No. 6. Catalan: Pelay y Briz, 317. Italian: Corsi, *Archivio*, X (1891), 401, No. 38. Bulgarian: Gubov, 100 (One soul carrying five souls [lives?].—A pregnant mare and a pregnant woman with a child on her shoulder). Finnish: Aarne, *Rätselforschungen*, II, 179–181. Estonian: Aarne, *Rätselforschungen*, II, 185, 188. Indian, Uraon: Archer, p. 187, No. 129 (The horse with the fourteen legs that quarrel as it goes.—Man, pregnant woman, pregnant mare).

58. The import of the riddle is not entirely clear. The references to nails and foot involve puns. I cannot interpret the allusion to the tails.

59. I conjecture that "ma father's fehst" may have originally been an allusion to Communion, for many riddles contain the scene of going to church. The rhyme with "behst" has preserved the formula, which was no longer understood.

60. Italian: Pitrè, 146a (Within a garden I saw an armed body. It wasn't a body and it had seven heads, it stood firmly on guard and fought against all men.—Thistle). For more satisfactory personification see Nos. 342a through 342c of the present collection.

61. German: Hanika-Otto, 21 (It goes up to the loft and has six ears, and when it comes down it has only two.—A girl with a kneading trough). Similar riddles based on the notion that an object has one form when it goes up and another when it comes down have the answers "stork catching frog" (No. 352 of the present collection), "ball of yarn" (see the headnote to No. 1341, n. 7), and "egg" (Nos. 1550a through 1554 and the headnote to Nos. 1550–1554). In Nos. 64a through 67e, the contrast of "up and down" refers to position rather than motion.

62. Breton: Sauvé, 69 (Seven feet, four ears, and a tail). Danish: Kristensen, p. 65, § 150, Nos. 250a (Four eyes and seven legs, in front like a button, behind like a spigot, in the middle like a mealsack), which contains elements belonging to the riddles discussed in the headnote to Nos. 1430–1435 of the present collection, and 230b (Seven legs and four ears, hairy within and bare without), which contains elements characteristic of the riddles discussed in the headnote to Nos. 1416–1419 of the present collection. Kristensen's Nos. 230c through 230g are like his No. 230b, which seems to be a well-established Danish version. See also Feilberg, *Ordbog*, II, 109, s.v. "kat." French: Sébillot, *Auvergne*, 9 (Seven legs, two heads, a tail). Ledieu, *Démuin*, p. 134 (Who has seven fingers, four paws, and one tail?—Gridiron).

63. Breton: Lavenot, *Basse-Bretagne*, p. 667; Charlec, *Dol-de-Bretagne*, 1903, p. 288. French: Rolland, 42; V. S., *Mélusine*, I (1878), col. 261, No. 92; Sébillot, *Auvergne*, 8; Pineau, *Poitou*, 5; A. Ferrand, *Dauphiné*, p. 226; Westphalen, *Metz*, col. 197; J. Roux, *Limousin*, 40; Baissac, *Mauritius*, p. 398. Portuguese: Parsons, *Cape Verde*, 83 (Mouth inside mouth, seven feet, one tail). Berber: Basset, *Nouveaux Contes*, p. 190, No. 5.

65. This confused riddle seems to have borrowed elements from Nos. 1437a through 1439, in which the theme "patch on patch" appears in another and more intelligible use.

66a, 66b. French: Parsons, *Antilles*, III, 394, Dominica, 57.

67a through 67e. (Legs up and four legs down, living thing in dead mouth.) Scotch Gaelic: Nicolson, p. 95. Irish: Delargy, 11; Christiansen, 96; Hyde, p. 171 (Two feet on the ground, and three feet overhead, and the head of the living in the mouth of the dead); De Bhaldraithe, 50; O Dalaigh, 187 (Three legs on high, two on the ground, the head of a live thing in the mouth of a dead thing). Manx: Cashen, p. 75.

67d. The "ears" are the ears of the man and the handles of the pot. The riddler has forgotten the proper context of the word "head," which occurs, as usual in this riddle pattern, with the meaning of a pot and also, in this particular text, as a variation of the conventional summons, "Guess this riddle and you can have my head."

68. (Three legs and other members.) Scotch Gaelic: Nicolson, p. 41. Danish: Kristensen, p. 36, § 86, Nos. 114a (I have a big mouth and cannot talk, two ears and cannot hear, three legs and cannot walk), 114b. Spanish: Demófilo, p. 348, No. 39. Argentinian: Lehmann-Nitsche, 161. Zyrian: Wichmann, *Zyrian*, 15. Mordvin: Paasonen, 109 (Three feet, two ears, the third is the belly.—Wash basin), 228 (It has ears, [but] no head.—Wash basin). Hungarian: Arany and Gyulai, II, 356, No. 38 = *Magyar Nyelvör*, V (1876), 470 = *ibid.*, XV (1886), 330 = *ibid.*, XXV (1896), 240 (It has three feet and one tail. I know it well because I held it in my hand); *Magyar Nyelvör*, IV (1875), 520 (It has three feet and one ear, it is smoky between its feet); XXIX (1900), 592 (It has three feet and one horseshoe. I know that you had it in your fist), in which the "horseshoe" probably refers to the shape of the frying pan; XXXVII (1908), 188 (What stands on three feet at the fair?). Modern Greek: Polites, *Neohellenika Analekta*, I, 207, No. 81 (Three-legged and black on top). Indian, Kashmiri: Knowles, 48 (It has four legs and does not walk; it has two ears and does not hear; we give it food and it does not eat.—A wooden dish on four legs).

69a through 69d. (Four legs up and four legs down.) Basque: Vinson, 61 (Four legs up, four legs down, in the middle *Poump!*), 61 var. (Two legs up, four legs down, in the middle some white where someone is leaping). Indian: Chaina Mall, *Panjab Notes and Queries*, III (1886), 219, No. 896, §1 (Four down, four up, with net on head, entangling the traveler at night, behold the net!). This refers to a four-post bed with a mosquito bar.

For the second contrast, "soft in the middle and hard all around," see another type of bed riddle in the present collection, Nos. 1429a through 1429c.

72. A description without enigmatic or contradictory elements. The folk believes that the mole actually has no eyes; see R. Riegler, *Handwörterbuch des deutschen Aberglaubens*, VI (Berlin, 1934–1935), vol. 8, §2; Eugène Rolland, *Faune populaire*, VII (Paris, 1906), 27. Symphosius knows a related idea (Riddle 21): "Blind is my face in dark shadows hid; the very day is night nor is any sun by me perceived; I prefer to be covered by clods; thus no one will see me either."

For examples of riddles which merely enumerate the aspects of the object without suggesting something different from it see Nos. 83, 98, 102, 254, 255, 343, 355, 359, 360 of the present collection. Many riddles for a fruit are no more than literal descriptions; see Nos. 1072 through 1089.

74. Compare Nos. 30a, 30b, and 516a through 516e.

75a through 75d. See the Abyssinian bedstead riddle, "Something that has four feet and a thousand eyes" (Littmann, *Tigriña*, p. 626, No. 50). The eyes are the interstices of the netting. See also the Batak bedmat riddle, "It has a head and a foot, but no hands" (Ophuijsen, p. 206, No. 4). For related conceptions see No. 307 of the present collection.

75d. Compare the French "What has only one foot and has nevertheless four paws?" (Carmeau, p. 34) and the Uraon cat riddle, "The boy with four legs" (Archer, p. 184, No. 84).

76. Polish: Siarkowski, 65 (What animal has four legs and feathers?).

78. Portuguese: Parsons, *Cape Verde*, 122 (Man of four feet, one level), which is not entirely clear. The level is the tabletop, but the personification is not well-executed. Mordvin: Paasonen, 198 (It has four feet, but no head).

79a through 79c. Irish: O Dalaigh, 100 (Long legs, crooked knees, a dead head without eyes), 200 (A long thigh, a crooked hip, taking care, but no eyes in its head).

82a through 82c. Compare the Italian frog riddle, "She has feet like a fan, big eyes, open mouth, big belly; poor girl, what's to become of her in the gravy?" (Pitrè, 671), and riddles cited in the headnote to No. 347.

82a. "Bully" is a mishearing or corruption of "bullet."

83. For parallels to the idea "runs night and day" see Nos. 115 through 117, 139.

84. African, SeSuto: Norton and Velaphe, 33 (The black cow with a hundred feet). Indonesian, Serawaj: Helfrich, *Serawaj*, p. 66, No. 87 (A body with a thousand feet). Lampong: Helfrich, *Lampong*, 25 (It has one body and a thousand feet). Malay: Tauern, *Patasiwa*, p. 71 (It is only a single animal and it has a thousand feet). Tabaru: Fortgens, 96.

85. Korean: Bernheisel, p. 85 (What is that which has three legs?—A *wharo*, or Korean three-legged iron vessel, in which a charcoal fire is kept). The pot riddle usually includes more descriptive elements than are found here; see, in the present collection, Nos. 68, 371, and 558a through 558e, which achieve a more or less adequate comparison to an animal or a person. The German "Black within, black without, three legs and a tail" (Wossidlo, 259), which leads into the pot riddle (Nos. 62, 63 of the present collection), has borrowed the last element from the comparison of a frying pan to a magpie (Nos. 1302 through 1308).

86. Freely used in riddling in continental Europe and elsewhere, the onomatopoetic *trip, trap* has few parallels in English folklore; see the headnote to Nos. 445–458, in which the sounds cited suggest a dog, and the note to No. 252a. The *pitty pat* of No. 42 suggests the sound of the swimming duck.

87. Norwegian: Brox, *Ytre Senja*, 3 (A reindeer with four feet and no leg stood on a stone). Spanish, Chilean: Flores, 690 (What thing has four feet in its rump?); this may represent a modification of the theme discussed in the headnote to Nos. 632–644, n. 49, of the present collection. See further, Russian: Sadovnikov, 235 (With feet but no hands, with sides but no ribs, with a rump but no belly, with a back but no head). Compare, in the present collection, Nos. 26, 306a, and 306b, which introduce other complications.

88. Italian: Ferraro, *Canti popolari in dialetto logodurese*, p. 302, No. 14. This English riddle is also a nursery rhyme:

> There was an old woman
> Liv'd under a hill,
> And if she isn't gone,
> She lives there still.

See W. H. Whitmore (ed.), *The Original Mother Goose's Melody* (Boston, 1892), p. 49.

89. Although the rejuvenescence of the moon is a familiar astronomical phenomenon, riddlers rarely refer to it. See Irish: O Dalaigh, 122 (Ever filling up and ever ebbing, that's how I am and will be forever). Spanish, Argentinian: Lehmann-Nitsche, 54a through 54c. Chilean: Flores, 412 through 414. Arabic: Ruoff, p. 11, No. 5 (An old man becomes a boy), and p. 12, No. 8. Indonesian, Serawaj: Helfrich, *Serawaj*, p. 55, No. 42 (When it is still small, it has horns; when it is large, then it loses its horns; when it is at the point of death, it gets horns again). Samoan: Heider, 144 (A thing dies and comes to life again). See also No. 663 of the present collection.

90a through 94. See also No. 682. For allusions to the fact that the moon does not grow old see Welsh: Hull and Taylor, 4. Irish: De Bhaldraithe, 9; Delargy, *Inis Cé*, 5; O Dalaigh, 121. Flemish: Joos, 646 (Do you know someone who becomes new when he is old and worn out?). Icelandic: Árnason, 498 (Who is the dancing reveler, fair to behold but hidden at times, who is full grown fifteen times and an infant thirty times, but never wearies?). Norwegian: Christie, 8; Stafset, 79; Berge, 6. Swedish: Ström, p. 210, "Månen," 8. Catalan: Pelay y Briz, 33. Spanish: Rodríguez Marín, 258. Italian: Casetti and Imbriani, *Canti popolari delle province meridionali* (Turin, 1872), II, 74; Gianandrea, *Archivio*, II (1883), 428, No. 54; Tschiedel, 45. Finnish: Lönnrot, 88 = Henssen, 155; Qvigstad, note to No. 82, citing Lönnrot, 77, 858. Estonian: Dido, 31, 32. Lappish: Qvigstad, 82. Hungarian: *Magyar Nyelvör*, IV (1875), 282 (It has always existed from the beginning of time. As long as there shall be a world, it will always exist. Yet it will never be one year old), p. 558 (As long as the earth exists, it will always exist, too. Yet it will never be five weeks old).

91. The riddler has erred; he should have said, "when Adam was two days old" (Gen. 1).

92. English and other riddlers often employ the first person; see Nos. 96, 97, 100 through 102, 105, 106, etc. This device is often found in riddles of literary origin.

94. The first element seems to mean "born at the making of the world."

95. Welsh: Hull and Taylor, 119, 132, 281 (and note, in their Nos. 133 and 134, the use of the same concept to represent the spawning of salmon). Swedish: Ström, p. 135, "Säd," 1. See also Nos. 661 and 1052 in the present collection. These ideas have some similarity to the biographies of coffee and flax; see Nos. 668, 679, and the headnote to Nos. 674–680.

See two much elaborated parallels, the Flemish "I have a father, no mother, many brothers, many sisters, but my father lay a long time in the grave before he gave me life" (Joos, 441) and the Kundu "My mother has died and they have buried her; she has risen again, but she did not bring forth her old body again" (Ittmann, *Kundu*, 102).

96. This text has a literary rather than traditional flavor. For other riddles on salt see No. 1262 and the headnote to No. 1262.

97. The first statement seems to be corrupted.

See also Icelandic: Árnason, 502 (What nothing is that to which you give a name, which was but is not, will be and never ceases to be?—Answer lacking).

98. The Swedish description of a fisherman, "Who lives on the wave and gets his livelihood from the wind?" (Ström, p. 236, "Fiskaren"), is similarly constructed. For riddles which name the characteristics of an object without achieving a paradoxical effect see the note to No. 72 of the present collection.

99. Perhaps the enigmatic quality lies in the contradiction between the suggestion that fish, which live in a river, seem to be implied and the statement that the supposed creature has feet. The riddler does not seem to have counted a crab's feet correctly. The naming of the function before naming the member is unusual in riddling.

104. For a more elaborate version see No. 233.

105. For references to water or a river bearing burdens, see No. 728 and the corresponding note and headnote.
106. Compare Swiss: Rochholz, 525. Italian: Pitrè, 904 (Three ears and the guts are on the belly).
112. Compare No. 721. Riddlers compare fire or light to a thing that cannot be locked up; see Russian: Sadovnikov, 1828 (What cannot be locked in the house?—Sun); Arkhangel'skii, p. 75. Votyak: Wichmann, *Votyak*, 399 (What is one unable to lock in a box? —Sun). Zyrian: Wichmann, *Zyrian*, 274 (What can't you shut up in a basket?—Sun). Yakut: Priklonskii, 85 = Piekarski, 54 (They say that there is a coin that you cannot shut up in a box.—Sunbeam). African, Pangwe: Tessmann, 4 (You hold things so well, then, hold here!—Fire). For descriptions of the sun or sunlight as something that cannot be seized, or gathered into a container, see, in the present collection, Nos. 1646a, 1646b, the note to Nos. 1646a, 1646b, and the headnote to Nos. 1643–1654.
113. Scotch Gaelic: Nicolson, p. 29. Flemish: Joos, 6. German: Haffner, 8. Icelandic: Árnason, 238 (He accompanies one and all, whether they rush, walk, ride, or stand still. In sunlight or moonlight we see him; in the dark he disappears. He loses his noble shape and may be compared to a giant). Danish: Kristensen, p. 118, § 326, No. 519 (I follow you faithfully, when the light rises, but when the light is swallowed up, I straightway vanish). Swedish: Geijer and Campbell, 87; Ström, p. 234, "Skuggan," 1, 2. French: Baissac, *Mauritius*, pp. 404, 415. Basque: Vinson, 49. Portuguese: Parson, *Cape Verde*, 238 (Two men run a race of twenty miles. Neither leaves the other behind and neither wins). Spanish: Demófilo, 933, 936, 937; Rodríguez Marín, 902. Chilean: Flores, 703. Cuban: Massip, 178. Rumanian: Papahagi, 11, var. 2. Polish: Gustawicz, 31 (Without flesh, without soul, it follows me wherever I go). Turkish: Kúnos, 41 (If I go, it is also going; it gets in front of me), 188 (When I run, it runs; when I stop, it stops. What a marvel that is! One gets exhausted); Kúnos, *Nyelvkönyv*, 8; Hamizade, 204 (I go, he goes, he goes before [faster than] me). Abchaz: Guliia, 8 (Wherever you go, it is everywhere with you; whatever you do, it will imitate you. Yet, it won't help you in any way). Tatar: Kalashev and Ioakimov, p. 49, No. 13 (I shall go and it will remain). Yakut: Priklonskii, 123 (You see it and it stands still; you start to catch it and it runs away). African, Kamba: Lindblom, 35. Bakongo: Denis, 26. Bavenda: Stayt, p. 360, No. 11. SeSuto: Norton and Velaphe, 61 (I tried to come here and he turned hither with me). Kxatla: Schapera, 84 (Tell me: I go south, I take care of the black thing, I come back and still take care of it). Kanuri: Lukas, p. 170, No. 25 (What does the fool wait for?). Wamajame: Ovir, 25 (I began early and I run with you, until I catch you). Dschagga: Raum, 1 (It accompanies me, but I cannot overtake it), which also has the answer "road." Hausa: Harris, 8 (I am going along with my brother, but I do not hear his movement). Indonesian, Javanese: Ranneft, *Poëzie*, p. 3, No. 4; Kreemer, *Java*, p. 5 (When one approaches it, it goes away. When one stops, it approaches). Filipino: Starr, *Philippines*, 333 (If I catch, it catches; if I run away, it chases me).
114. Basque: Cerquand, 19. Hungarian: *Magyar Nyelvör*, XXXI (1902), 533, No. 34 (It keeps on going, it never stops, it has branches but no leaves). Turkish: Kúnos, 40 (If I go, it goes also; if I stop, it does not). Armenian: Zelinski, p. 55, No. 3 (It goes for a month, it goes for a year, night and day it is on a journey). Ossete: Schiefner, 1 (It goes both night and day). African, Pangwe: Tessmann, 10 (Lady Mba [is] always on foot, have you ever seen her stop?). Tonga-Shangaan: Junod and Jaques, p. 231, No. 15. See also the headnote to Nos. 138–140 below.
116a, 116b. French: Parsons, *Antilles*, III, 384, Martinique, 54, p. 395, Dominica, 73, p. 403, Guadaloupe, 67, p. 409, Les Saintes, 7, p. 410, Les Saintes, 23.
117. Lappish: Donner, 13 (It goes days, it goes nights, it never finds the door). For

the last phrase see the note to No. 125 of the present collection. Svanian: J. Nizheradze pp. 56–57, No. 1 (It works day and night).

118. Compare Nos. 135, 946a through 946d, and the headnote to Nos. 1021–1024, in which riddlers compare a plant or its leaves to persons constantly dancing, bowing, or being otherwise in motion. A tooth is called a rocking chair; see No. 1180.

119a, 119b. Swedish: Ström, p. 177, "Gardesgården." Mordvin: Paasonen, 40 (It mounts, it descends, it does this work all day long). Indonesian, Soenda: Holle, *Soenda*, pp. 371–372, No. 18, and compare p. 374, No. 28 (When it is heavy, it goes up; when it is light, it goes down). Sangir: Adriani, p. 415, No. 70. Compare the curious Lettish pump riddle, "The god of the upper world implores the god of the lower world" (Bielenstein, 32) and the Svanian shed riddle, "It touches neither sky nor ground" (J. Nizheradze, pp. 68–69, No. 24).

120. The import of "never goes to town" is not apparent; it is perhaps a formula which the riddler has used unintelligently.

121. Compare No. 133, which suggests more definitely a zigzag rail-fence.

122a through 122e. Welsh: Hull and Taylor, 24, 25. Welsh Gypsy: Sampson, 41. German: Gilhoff, 547; Renk, *Tyrol*, 131, 132; Hanika-Otto, 603. Danish: Kristensen, p. 141, § 419, Nos. 660a through 660h. Swedish: Ström, p. 183, "Landsvägen," 2. Walloon: Colson, *Wallonia*, IV, 46, No. 33. French: Rolland, 29. Catalan: Pelay y Briz, 154. Lithuanian: Jurgelionis, 686 (We go by night and we go by day but we do not reach the end of our yard). Votyak: Buch, p. 101, No. 43 (It goes and goes, but never comes to an end). Indian, Parsee: Munshi, p. 417 (There is a substance which, though it follows us wherever we go, is stationary). Compare also the Italian "Sempre camino / E mai mi mòvo.—Il cammino" (Salvioni, *Archivio*, IV [1885], 547, No. 61) and "Io cammino e non mi muovo" (Tschiedel, 79).

The element "goes up and down" does not occur in the parallels. It is appropriately used in the Swedish steps riddle, "What goes up and down and never bestirs itself?" (Ström, p. 179, "Trappan"). The Norwegians begin a riddle for plowing in a similar manner (Bugge, *Telemarken*, 66), but here the phrase refers to the path of the plow across the field.

123. The negation appears to be an error. Compare the French "Who goes to Paris without stopping?" (Rolland, *Rimes*, p. 198, No. 9).

125, 126. Welsh: Hull and Taylor, 26, 27. Breton: Kerbeuzec, *Ille-et-Vilaine*, 54 (pendulum). Frisian: Carstensen, p. 326, No. 7. Flemish: Joos, 214 (Alas, what beats me night and day, when I cannot rest?), 220 (It stands, it goes, it does not live). German: Wossidlo, 376; Gilhoff, 402, 403; Renk, *Tyrol*, 131, 132; Hanika-Otto, 174 (It goes and goes and gets no farther). Danish: Kristensen, p. 69, § 169, Nos. 262a through 262f. Norwegian: Stafset, 48. Swedish: Ericsson, *Södermanland*, I, 93, No. 71; Ström, p. 164, "Klockan," 3. Walloon: Colson, *Wallonia*, IV, 151, No. 185. French: Carnoy, *Picardy*, p. 54; Baissac, *Mauritius*, p. 408. Spanish: Demófilo, 852, 857, 859; Rodríguez Marín, 768. Argentinian: Lehmann-Nitsche, 98 (pendulum). Chilean: Flores, 640. New Mexican: Campa, 257 (What goes day and night and is always in the [same] place?). Portuguese: Pires de Lima, 28. Italian: Pitrè, 1094. Lithuanian: Jurgelionis, 729 (I go and go and I am always in one place), 730 (It goes day and night on one foot and yet stands in one place). The "one foot" is the pendulum. Czech: Hanika-Otto, note to No. 174 (It goes all day and gets nowhere). Russian: Sadovnikov, 279. Serbian: Novaković, p. 199, Nos. 2 (It goes all day long, but moves nowhere), 3. Zyrian: Wichmann, *Zyrian*, 62.

125. The Scandinavian versions exhibit a special variation: "What is that which goes and goes, but can never reach the door?" (Hva e ded, der gaar aa gaar, men alri karj naa Staudörn? DFS, 1906/38: Louise Hansen, Svaneke, 1927, No. 9). For parallels see Danish: DFS, 1906/1: 288, B. K. Pedersen, Havrebjærg, 1910, p. 25. Norwegian: Brox, *Ytre Senja*, 6. Swedish: Waltman, *Lidmål*, 192; Sandén, *Norra Vadsbo*, 25.

126. Luxemburg: De la Fontaine, 9. Swiss: Rochholz, 493. Danish: Kristensen, p. 69, § 168, Nos. 268a through 268g. Eight manuscript Danish versions exhibit such minor variations as "goes and goes and does not leave the spot" (DFS, 1906/38, Marie Jespersen, Bostrup Hedeby, 1919, p. 3, No. 3) and "goes and goes and does not get to the end of the road" (DFS, 1906/38, K. Understrup, Ørre, 1920, p. 1, No. 1). Lettish: Bielenstein, 466.

127. Breton: Le Pennec, 24; Sébillot, *Devinettes*, 60. Danish: Kristensen, p. 22, § 48, Nos. 61a, 61b (What goes into the room every day and never goes out and what goes out of the room every day and does not go in?). Norwegian: Berge, 85. Swedish: Hyltén-Cavallius, *Värend*, 56; Ström, p. 180, "Dören," 1. Walloon: Colson, *Wallonia*, IV, 148, No. 158. French: Rolland, 149; Bladé, *Armagnac*, 16; Ledieu, *Démuin*, p. 133; J. Roux, *Limousin*, 71; Roque-Ferrier, *Languedoc*, p. 334; Constantin, *Savoie*, p. 20. Spanish, Argentinian: Lehmann-Nitsche, 128. Chilean: Flores, 626 through 628. New Mexican: Campa, 550 (Mi tía va, mi tía viene, y en un ser está). Porto Rican: Mason, 32. Portuguese: Pires de Lima, 76. Lettish: Bielenstein, 148. Russian: Sadovnikov, 71 (He does not stride, yet moves), 73 (A walker walks, but would not walk into the house). Finnish: Henssen, 188. Estonian: Wiedemann, p. 270. Turkish: Kúnos, 118 (Lejla goes, Lejla comes, Lejla stands on one foot); Szapszal, p. 67, No. 7 (It goes with a noise, it goes with a crash, but it passes over only one span). Cherekessian: Tambiev, p. 57, Nos. 42 (No matter how much it goes, it does not cover more than a foot of space), 43 (It goes day and night, yet it does not exceed the space equal to the shell of an egg), and compare the riddle for a cradle, "It goes day and night, it does not go more than a foot" (*ibid.*, p. 58, No. 57). African, Basuto: Rolland, p. 169, No. 5. Tschuana: Kuhn, *Tschuana*, 43. Indian, Baiga: Elwin, p. 467, No. 3 (All night he stands watchful, all day he sleeps).

In the present collection, see also such riddles for a door as "What is neither in nor out?" (No. 1423, § 2) and the texts quoted in the headnotes to Nos. 133–135, n. 3, and 356, n. 4.

129. A similar way of differentiating the pattern by mentioning a specific town or village appears in Flemish: Joos, 678 (What runs from Brussels to Malines without moving?). Norwegian: Stafset, 92, 263. Compare Aasen, 22 (Who goes from mountain to fjord and doesn't move?).

131. Icelandic: Árnason, 548 (Who runs forever without leaving his place? He has neither a mouth, a voice, nor a throat, but sings so loud that it is heard far and wide), 1108 (I know a woman who speedily wends her way. She goes on forever, and yet she remains in the same place).

133. "In and out" may refer to the zigzag line of a rail fence.

See also Swedish: Ericsson, *Södermanland*, III (1882), 96–97, No. 126. Compare No. 121 of the present collection.

134. "Out" is here used in the sense, "has refused to place a bet," and "in" in the sense of "has placed a bet." The riddle is a moral observation rather than a puzzle to be guessed.

135. Compare the Kxatla "Tell me: the children of someone are dancing, their mother does not dance.—It is the branches of a tree" (Schapera, 19). See also, in the present collection, No. 118 and the corresponding note.

136. Lappish: Qvigstad, 120 (It goes in and out and is never seen). Modern Greek: Dieterich, *Rätseldichtung*, p. 90 (It runs and runs and never returns.—River).

137. Compare the riddles Nos. 121 through 124b, which have practically the same introductory formula. These also have the answer "road."

138. Swedish: Ström, p. 209, "Solen, jorden, tanken." French: Lacuve, *Poitou*, p. 352, No. 2; Lallemant, *Argonne*, p. 235. Spanish: Demófilo, 428 (never sleeps). Rumanian: Gorovei, *Devinettes*, p. 506. Lappish: Qvigstad, 129 (It goes up and goes down and does not weary.—Water rising and falling). Albanian: Pedersen, 16. Svanian: J. Nizheradze, pp. 68–69, No. 23 (Everything gets tired except it.—Water). Arabic: Giacobetti, 10. Surinam: Herskovits, 38 (It works day and night). Abyssinian: Littmann, *Tigriña*, p. 618, No. 6 (Something that runs by day, runs by night, and does not grow weary). Altai Turkish: Menges, p. 78, No. 52 (At night it does not sleep, during the day it does not sleep, it does not sleep all its life). Indian, Kashmiri: Knowles, 62.
Compare also No. 750 of the present collection.

139. Danish: Kristensen, p. 143, § 422, No. 671 (goes from house to house, is killed many times, and yet exists until now). Swedish: Ström, p. 209, "Solen, jorden, tanken." French: Constantin, *Savoie*, p. 23. African, Wolof: Seidel, p. 309; Rolland, p. 168, No. 5.

140. Swedish: Ström, p. 208, "Sol, måne, fors," 2; p. 209, "Solen, jorden, tanken" (many varying answers); and p. 212, "Jorden," 3. French: Rolland, 3; Westphalen, *Metz*, col. 197 (He goes all day without resting, without eating, and goes to bed without dining).

141. The conception is allied to the patterns "Goes up and down the hill" (Nos. 121 through 124*b*) and "Goes up white and comes down yellow" (Nos. 1550*a* through 1554). Compare the Sukuma "It rises up" (Augustiny, 39).

142. Compare Nos. 121, 133.

143. See a more elaborate version in No. 218 of the present collection. Compare French: J. Roux, *Limousin*, 23 (Who never draws back?—Water).

144. Breton: Lavenot, *Basse-Bretagne*, p. 669. French: Rolland, 222.

145. Compare Swedish: Ström, p. 220, "Snö," 1, and p. 303, "Herdevisa." Zyrian: Wichmann, *Zyrian*, 287. Votyak: Wichmann, *Votyak*, 68.

The Breton and French formula, "runs from branch to branch," which perhaps suggests a squirrel, may be related to the English "goeth about the wood," which suggests a man or an animal walking about. For parallels see Breton: Sébillot, *Haute-Bretagne*, 4; Kerbeuzec, *Ille-et-Vilaine*, 47.

147. Irish: Delargy, 33 (I see it and I do not see it; I see it in a hollybush; it walks the plain and does not disturb the dew). German: Wossidlo, 372*b*. Swedish: Ström, p. 224, "Skuggan," 3. Italian: Pitrè, 525. Czech: Feifalik, p. 383, No. 81. Lithuanian: Jurgelionis, 1091 through 1093; Schleicher, p. 208. Estonian: Dido, 38.

Similar ideas appear in the riddles "What falls into the water and doesn't splash?" (see the headnote to No. 164, § 2, of the present collection), and "What goes through [over] the water and does not touch the water?" (see the headnote to Nos. 165–173, § 3).

149, 150. English riddlers do not seem to be familiar with the widely known echo riddle, "Who speaks every language?" For parallels see Breton: Sébillot, *Haute-Bretagne*, 5; Charlec, *Dol-de-Bretagne*, 1903, p. 288. German: Hermann Frischbier, *Am Urquell*, III (1892), 75, No. 100; Haffner, 324; Hanika-Otto, 272. Danish: Kristensen, p. 23, § 53, No. 66. Swedish: Ström, p. 228, "Ekot," 3. French: Fouju, *Beauce*, p. 631 (Who always speaks as you do?). Spanish, Argentinian: Lehmann-Nitsche, 273. Lettish: Bielenstein, 55, 56, 869 (talks without a mouth). Yakut: Piekarski, 2 (Who speaks all languages and yet has no education?).

153. Polish: Gustawicz, 493 (What can run through the woods without touching a thing?).

160. This answer usually belongs to the riddle "What goes through the water and never touches the water?" (see Nos. 169*a* through 170*b*).

164a. Norwegian: Stafset, 56 (moonshine). Swedish: Dybeck, *Runa*, 1849, p. 49, No. 27 (It goes into the straw and does not walk *pitapat*.—Moon).
164b. Welsh: Hull and Taylor, 21. Breton: Sauvé, 2a. French: Ledieu, *Démuin*, p. 133 (Who goes into the woods without touching the leaves?); Queyrat, *La Creuse*, I, 365; Lacuve, *Poitou*, p. 355, No. 52 (Who goes into the woods without making a sound in the leaves?). Spanish, Chilean: Flores, 691. Those who watch trees and shrubs in the African dry season describe the sun even more vividly: "Tell me a man who is in the habit of coming [and] breaking to pieces trees and bushes?" (Kamba: Lindblom, 104). See also the Sukuma "A man who parts the bushes" (Augustiny, 53).
165a through 165j. Welsh: Hull and Taylor, 262, 263. Welsh Gypsy: Sampson, 44, and p. 246. Danish: Kristensen, p. 19, § 30, Nos. 36a, 36b (A way over a way, a way under a way, and a way on a way.—Bridge). Swedish: Ericsson, *Södermanland*, I (1879), 88, No. 24.
167. Irish: O Dalaigh, 188 (I went out between two sticks and came in between two waters.—A man traveling on water with two wooden buckets). Compare the Javanese "Earth above and earth beneath.—House with a tile roof" (Ranneft, *Proza*, p. 19, No. 85).
168. Scotch Gaelic: Nicolson, p. 43. Breton: Sauvé, 25 (A girl walking between two earths.—A girl carrying a pot of milk on her head); Lavenot, *Basse-Bretagne*, p. 670. Walloon: Colson, *Wallonia*, V, 57, No. 222.
169a through 171. (Includes also the answer, "calf in its mother's belly" and other answers in terms of animals.) Welsh Gypsy: Sampson, 10. Irish: O Dalaigh, 53. Breton: Sauvé, 31; Charlec, *Dol-de-Bretagne*, 1904, p. 168, No. 28 (Who goes through the woods without touching it?). German: Hanika-Otto, 159b (What goes into the water and doesn't wet its feet?), 159c (Seven of them go through the brook and only one gets wet.—Sow and six pigs); Renk, *Tyrol*, 76. Norwegian: Brox, *Ytre Senja*, 147. French: Rolland, 46; Ledieu, *Démuin*, p. 134. Basque: Cerquand, 27; Vinson, 22. Spanish, Argentinian: Lehmann-Nitsche, 106. Rumanian: Gorovei, 1944; and Gorovei, *Devinettes*, p. 506. Arabic: Littmann, p. 49, No. 11 (It swam across the stream without getting wet). See also No. 160 of the present collection, and compare No. 961 and the notes to Nos. 711 and 961. In the note to Nos. 56a, 56b, and in the note to No. 57, are examples of the description of a pregnant creature by the enumeration of parts.
171. For parallels to the element "and leaves no track" see Nos. 181 through 185, the headnotes to Nos. 181–185 and 227, and the note to No. 227.
172a through 172c. For parallels to the element "and always with its head down" see Nos. 187a through 189, the headnote to Nos. 187–189, the notes to Nos. 187a, 187d, and 188a, and the note to Nos. 188b, 188c. Compare also No. 457.
172c. The answer seems to be the mishearing of a landlubber.
174. Frisian: Dykstra, *Snypsnaren*, p. 96. Flemish: *Ons Volksleven*, I (1889), 37, No. 33. German: Wossidlo, 286; Gilhoff, 528, 529; Hanika-Otto, 133. Icelandic: Árnason, 422. Filipino: Starr, *Philippines*, 389 (I went to Dagupan, but I left only two footprints.—Sled), 391 (What has four feet but only two footprints?—Rice sled).
176. For "every way" read "everywhe'," i.e., "everywhere." The usual formula is "My father [var.: mother] had a thing . . ."
177. The introductory "something" is often used. In West Indian and American riddling it often introduces riddles which describe an object in terms of an animal or a person.
179. Riddlers occasionally refer to a broom as having a hundred or a thousand feet; see Walloon: Colson, *Devinettes*, 26. Zyrian: Wichmann, *Zyrian*, 187. Compare the Spanish wagon riddle, ". . ., no one counts its tracks" (Demófilo, 304; Rodríguez Marín, 789).

180. The introductory formula "Here's a thing" may appear in comparisons of an object to a man or an animal. See the note to No. 177.

183. Compare the Finnish description of heat, "A man goes up and down in a room, but one sees neither the man nor his track" (Lönnrot, 910 = Henssen, 130).

184a. German: Hanika-Otto, 449 (Was geht durch die Hosen und macht kein Loch?). Mordvin: Paasonen, 278. The Kundu riddle for the air suggests a much more elaborate picture: "There is a city, people go about in it, but one sees no streets" (Ittmann, *Kundu*, 136).

184c. Flemish: Joos, 43 (It runs around the house and makes a noise in every corner). For the formula "over hill and dale," compare, in the present collection, Nos. 445b, 447, 449b, the Scotch Gaelic mist riddle cited in the headnote to Nos. 181–185, § 6, the Armenian riddle cited in the note to No. 185, and the note to No. 187a.

185. Compare German: Haffner, 83, 84. Armenian: Zelinski, p. 55, No. 4 (It goes, it goes, but leaves no traces; it knows neither dales nor hills nor plains; it bears children in both winter and summer; it has skin but no hair.—Louse).

186. Walloon: Colson, *Wallonia*, IV, 44, No. 18. French: Rolland, 15 (Who can go before the sun without making a shadow?); Westphalen, *Metz*, cols. 196, 201.

187a. (Goes over the mountain.) Like the variations, Nos. 187b, 187c, this is perhaps suggested by riddles for a shoe (Nos. 445b, 453b, 454a, 456a) or for milk (Nos. 447, 449b, 450). The notion of a nail going over a mountain is paralleled by the Norwegian "going over Dovrefjeld" (Bugge, *Telemarken*, 107) and by the Swedish "What is that which dances on its head over the fell?" (Waltman, *Lidmål*, 185) and "What is that which dances on its head between Sweden and Norway?" (*ibid.*, 186). See also, in the present collection, the note to No. 184c.

187b. (Goes to water.) There are a few European parallels. See German: Wossidlo, 280b. Danish: Kristensen, pp. 43–44, § 110, Nos. 150 through 153, and p. 137, § 394, Nos. 630b, 630c. As in descriptions of a cowbell, some riddlers add, "it does not drink"; see Nos. 246 and 251b of the present collection.

187c. (Gallops down the road.) Welsh: Hull and Taylor, 46. German: Haffner, 196.

187d. (Descriptive details lacking.) See also No. 457. German: Gilhoff, 675; Hanika-Otto, 342. Icelandic: Árnason, 423, 833 (I have learned that good luck is instable in this world. I have had to walk all over Iceland on my head). Danish: Kristensen, p. 137, § 394, No. 630a. French: Rolland, 139; Constantin, *Savoie*, p. 19; Fleury, *Basse-Normandie*, p. 370; Lacuve, *Poitou*, p. 354, No. 29; Dottin, *Bas-Maine*, p. 139, No. 8; A. Ferrand, *Dauphiné*, p. 228; Lediou, *Démuin*, p. 134; J. Roux, *Limousin*, 86; Baissac, *Mauritius*, p. 412. Lithuanian: Jurgelionis, 257 (What walks on its head?).

188a. (Goes to church.) Breton: Sébillot, *Haute-Bretagne*, 48; Le Chef, *Ille-et-Vilaine*, p. 667; Kerbeuzec, *Ille-et-Vilaine*, p. 508, No. 95. Dutch: Schrijnen, II, 114, No. 56. Flemish: *Ons Volksleven*, II (1890), 104, No. 11. German: Wossidlo, 280a; H. Meier, *Ostfriesland*, 5; Haffner, 283; Hanika-Otto, 488. Danish: Kristensen, p. 137, § 394, No. 630f; six manuscript versions in the Dansk Folkemindesamling. Norwegian: Stafset, 3. Walloon: Colson, *Wallonia*, IV, 111, No. 138. French: Rolland, *Rimes*, p. 203, No. 33; Queyrat, *La Creuse*, I, 364; Westphalen, *Metz*, col. 202. Spanish, New Mexican: Campa, 263. Serbian: Novaković, p. 88, No. 8 (It goes to church and stands on its head). Mordvin: Paasonen, 263 (They are underfoot, they walk on their heads). Hungarian: *Magazin für die Litteratur des Auslands*, 1856, p. 364 (cited by Rolland, note to No. 139); *Magyar Nyelvör*, II (1873), 178; XII (1883), 286; and XIII (1884), 245 (What enters the church upside down?).

188b, 188c. Although "goes to church" is the activity most often ascribed to the nail, riddlers may also say: "goes to market" (Breton: Lavenot, *Basse-Bretagne*, p. 666);

"goes to the village" (Welsh Gypsy: Sampson, 39); "goes to work" (Breton: Sauvé, 78; Lavenot, *Basse-Bretagne*, p. 672); "goes home" (German: Wossidlo, 454; Gilhoff, 672); "goes upstairs" (Danish: Kristensen, p. 13, § 374, No. 594); "goes up a ladder [or tree]" (Welsh: Hull and Taylor, 45, 47). See also such anomalous variations as the French "Who permits himself to walk on his head and says nothing?" (L. F. Sauvé, *Le Folk-Lore des Hautes-Vosges* [Paris, 1884], p. 310) and the Icelandic "There is one who walks all over Iceland with his head in the dirt. I would not offer his lot to anyone.—Horseshoe nail" (Árnason, 823).

189. See No. 457, which compares a shoe tack to a dog.

190a, 190b. Scotch Gaelic: Nicolson, p. 51 (I shall go over my highway. I shall come back on my highway, and I can carry my highway on my back). Irish: Christiansen, 73 (I went up the path and down the path and took the path with me on my back); Delargy, 21; Delargy, *Inis Cé*, 23; De Bhaldraithe, 61; O Dalaigh, 102.

191a through 191c. German: Butsch, 154; Wossidlo, 283; Gilhoff, 534; Hanika-Otto, 82, 224; Huss, *Siebenbürgen*, 34. Swiss: Rochholz, 501. Danish: Kristensen, p. 88, § 226, No. 349. Norwegian: Landstad, 37; Stafset, 107; Brox, *Ytre Senja*, 40; Bergh, *Valdres*, 49; Riksheim, 87 (cited by Brox). Swedish: Hyltén-Cavallius, *Värend*, 59; Sandén, *Norra Vadsbo*, 148; Waltman, *Lidmål*, 239; Geijer and Campbell, 23; Ström, p. 385, "Sysselsättningar," 56. Walloon: Colson, *Wallonia*, V, 55, No. 208. French: Lespy, *Béarn*, 16. Catalan: Pelay y Briz, 88. Basque: Vinson, 36; Demófilo, p. 373, No. 5. Portuguese: Leite de Vasconcellos, *Archivio*, I (1882), 281, No. 13. Lithuanian: Jurgelionis, 429, 430; Schleicher, p. 193. Lettish: Bielenstein, 830 (A man goes into the forest with his teeth backwards.—Saw). Czech: Feifalik, p. 378, No. 64; Hanika-Otto, note to Nos. 82, 83. Russian: Sadovnikov, 10. Finnish: Lönnrot, 476 = Henssen, 206. Estonian: Wiedemann, p. 278 (A man goes into the forest, his cheek shines homeward). Zyrian: Wichmann, *Zyrian*, 89, 90, 237, 289. Cheremiss: Genetz, 14; Wichmann, *Cheremiss*, 13. Mordvin: Ahlqvist, p. 40, No. 15. Votyak: Wichmann, *Votyak*, 25, 438.

192a. (Peeps, looks in.) Frisian: Dykstra, *Snypsnaren*, p. 96. Dutch: Schrijnen, II, 103, No. 11 (A thing goes around the house, it peeps through all the cracks). German: Wossidlo, 315*b* (Something goes around the house and looks in all the cracks), 315*c* (moon); Haffner, 2; Hanika-Otto, 131; *Blätter für pommersche Volkskunde*, III, 123. Danish: Kristensen, p. 123, § 341, No. 544*e* (What goes about the world and peeps in every man's house?), and § 343, No. 546 (What runs around the house and peeps in?—Sun's rays). Swedish: Ström, p. 205, "Solen," 3. Lappish: Qvigstad, 119 (moon). Estonian: Dido, 31. African, Togo: Schönhärl, 120 (A [piece of] wood that has been lighted looks into every city).

192b. (Enters.) The phrase "in my lady's chamber," which signifies "within the house," occurs in the nursery rhyme, "Goosey, Goosey, Gander."

For parallels to the sun's rays entering the house, see Welsh: Hull and Taylor, 48 (What comes into the house with the door shut?). Welsh Gypsy: Sampson, 5 (Who thrusts his way into the queen's chamber and asks leave of none?). Flemish: Joos, 4 (There is a thing that sticks its nose into every little house and little hole.—Moon). Swedish: Ström, p. 206, "Solen," 9, 18 (I have no hand, no leg, and no body, but travel nevertheless on all roads, creep on all roads, and play on all windows). Hungarian: *Magyar Nyelvör*, III (1874), 234, No. 5 (It rushes and runs into every house). Modern Greek: Abbott, p. 309, No. 13 (The doors are fast with locks and chains, and yet the thief admittance gains). Arabic: Ruoff, p. 13, No. 15 (Something slips into the holes, but crumbles away no earth).

192c through 192e. For parallels see the note to No. 192*a*.

193a, 193b. German: Wossidlo, 315*a* (What runs in the street and peeps into every corner?); Haffner, 3 (Something goes around the house and blows into all the cracks).

196. German: Wossidlo, 316 (It creeps around the house and looks into every hole). Danish: Kristensen, p. 111, § 300, Nos. 476a (What can fill a house and yet go out through a mousehole?), 476b.

197. Walloon: Colson, *Wallonia*, IV, 147, No. 155a. The Norwegians say that a key is the first to go through a door; see Stafset, 15. Compare also the sun riddle (No. 194 in the present collection), which describes light entering through a keyhole.

198a, 198b. Breton: Sébillot, *Haute-Bretagne*, 28; Sébillot, *Devinettes*, 26; Kerbeuzec, *Ille-et-Vilaine*, 53. German: Wossidlo, 375; Haffner, 47. Danish: Kristensen, p. 14, § 14, Nos. 13a, 13b. Swedish: Ström, p. 123, "Trädet," 3. Walloon: Colson, *Wallonia*, IV, 90, No. 78. French: Rolland, 86; Lallemant, *Argonne*, p. 235; Ledieu, *Démuin*, p. 132; E. H. Carnoy, *La Tradition*, VII (1893), 354, No. 23; Lacuve, *Poitou*, p. 355, No. 54; Pineau, *Poitou*, 12; Marchessou, *Velay et Auvergne*, p. 167, No. 13; Queyrat, *La Creuse*, I, p. 364; Westphalen, *Metz*, cols. 198 and 202.

The answer "ditch" in a Breton parallel (Sauvé, 129) probably refers to a ditch encircling a forest. See also French: Pineau, *Poitou*, 11.

199a through 200d. Welsh: Hull and Taylor, 20. Welsh Gypsy: Sampson, 42. Danish: Kristensen, p. 44, § 122, Nos. 157a, 157b (What goes in under every man's gate?—Track), and p. 141, § 419, Nos. 550a through 550h; and also "It goes from house to house but never into shelter" (Dæ gor fraa By te By u kommer aaller [aldrig] i Husly. DFS, 1906/38: J. K. Nielsen, Grindsted, 1935, No. 2, and DFS, 1906/1, 288: Bertha K. Pedersen, 1910, p. 31). French: Rolland, 29. Serbian: Novaković, p. xxi, No. 5 (It is turned and turning; turned out all over the world and turned into every house). Hungarian: *Magyar Nyelvör*, II (1873), 89 = IV (1875), 141 = XXV (1896), 240 (It runs everywhere, it runs into every house).

A related, but somewhat different, idea occurs in the Arabic riddle for a locomotive, "Our black mare runs without being alive" (Giacobetti, 567).

201. French: Rolland, *Rimes*, p. 206, No. 49 (Who goes around the house without coming in?—Walls).

202. Compare Nos. 695a through 695f, 697, 698 below, in which the riddler conceives the personification more clearly.

203a through 203c. Welsh: Hull and Taylor, 50 through 52. Welsh Gypsy: Sampson, 33. German: Hanika-Otto, 326 (It has a hole and makes a hole and drags a long tail), 327 (It has a hole, makes a hole, and goes through a hole). See further the survey of riddles for a needle in the note to Hanika-Otto, 324. Norwegian: Bergh, *Valdres*, 1. Swedish: Ström, p. 158, "Nålen," 3; pp. 235–236, "Skomakeren," 3; and compare p. 379, "Sysselsättningar," 37. Walloon: Colson, *Wallonia*, V, 54, No. 198. French: Rolland, 189; A. Ferrand, *Dauphiné*, p. 228. Catalan: Pelay y Briz, 73. Italian: Pitrè, 14 (What is the animal which goes dragging along its guts?). Czech: Hanika-Otto, note to her No. 324. Lappish: Qvigstad, 89 (It wanders through the forest and loses its tail in the forest), 121 (It slips through a hill to one side and then to the other, until it loses its tail). Gypsy: Wlislocki, 21. Arabic: Giacobetti, 528. Indian, Bihari: Mitra, *Bihar*, 49 (An exceeding small puppet, it has a long tail. When the puppet has gone to that side, the tail remains on this side).

203c. Breton: Sébillot, *Haute-Bretagne*, 68a.

204. French: V. S., *Mélusine*, I (1878), col. 262, No. 61; Sébillot, *Auvergne*, 42. The remark, "it drop piece," may be a reminiscence of a pattern which is otherwise unrecorded in English riddling, unless it be in the snail riddle (No. 418 in the present collection), which describes the animal as leaving silver behind.

205a through 205e. Scotch Gaelic: Nicolson, p. 49 (Sharp, sharp sheep, with its entrails hanging to it). Breton: Sauvé, 95; Sébillot, *Haute-Bretagne*, 68b. German: Haase, *Thüringen*, p. 182, No. 26. Danish: Kristensen, p. 99, § 254, No. 400b (What goes through small holes with a long tail dragging after it?), and p. 130, § 369, No. 583a (What drags entrails after itself?) and Nos. 583b, 583c; Feilberg, *Ordbog*, III, 711, s.v. "synål." Faeroic: Hammershaimb, *Antiquarisk tidsskrift*, III (1849–1851), 318, No. 29 = *Færøsk anthologi*, I, 323, No. 14. Icelandic: Árnason, 452. Norwegian: Stafset, 105. Swedish: Hyltén-Cavallius, *Värend*, 58. Portuguese: Braga, 74. Spanish: Demófilo, p. 344, No. 21, and p. 390, No. 41. Chilean: Flores, 19. Italian: Pitrè, 14 (seven parallels), 786 (shuttle). Rumanian: Gorovei, 23; and Gorovei, *Devinettes*, p. 505. Russian: Sadovnikov, 600. Hungarian: Meltzl, 15. Arabic: Giacobetti, 528. Tungus: Poppe, 21 (A mouse drags its gut). Indonesian, Javanese: Ranneft, *Proza*, p. 40, No. 178. Soenda: Holle, *Soenda*, p. 372, No. 15. American Indian, Aztec: E. B. Tylor, *Primitive Culture*, ed. 1891, p. 92, citing Sahagún, *Historia general de las cosas de Nueva España*. See also R. M. Campos, *Folklore litterario de México* (Mexico, 1929), p. 195.

205a. The descriptive phrase "goes through the water" may have been carelessly borrowed from the pillowcase riddle (Nos. 207a, 207b), or it may refer to wetting the thread to pass it through the eye of the needle.

205b. The import of "goes through a tree" is not fully clear. In a few parallels the phrase "goes through a hedge [or bushes]" refers to the needle passing through the cloth. See the note to No. 205c.

205c. Some parallels suggest that "heye" is "hedge"; see No. 203a in the present collection and the Welsh *drwy'r gwrych* (through the hedge) in Hull and Taylor, 51, or the Welsh Gypsy "through the hedge" (Sampson, 33).

207a, 207b. Welsh: Hull and Taylor, 34. Scotch Gaelic: Nicolson, p. 51. Breton: Sauvé, 96; Sébillot, *Haute-Bretagne*, 96; Le Chef, *Ille-et-Vilaine*, p. 667; Sébillot, *Devinnetes*, 73. German: Butsch, 184; Wossidlo, 282; Gilhoff, 431; Frischbier, *Menschenwelt*, p. 250, Nos. 91 through 93; Schmidt, *Danzig*, 80; Renk, *Tyrol*, 141; Hanika-Otto, 158a through 158f; Huss, *Siebenbürgen*, 102. Swiss: Rochholz, 564. Icelandic: Árnason, 413, 956. Danish: Kristensen, p. 21, § 46, No. 57, and pp. 103–104, § 281, Nos. 436a through 436l; Feilberg, *Ordbog*, II, 892, s.v. "pudevar"; five manuscript versions in DFS. Norwegian: Aasen, 18; Landstad, p. 811, No. 30; Christie, 67; Bugge, *Telemarken*, 13; Stafset, 105; Berge, 62; Qvigstad, note to No. 68 (many parallels). Swedish: Dybeck, *Runa*, 1848, p. 45, No. 44 = Russwurm, p. 347, No. 42; Ericsson, *Södermanland*, II (1881), 100, No. 117; and V (1884), 68, No. 224; Hyltén-Cavallius, *Värend*, 58; Sandén, *Norra Vadsbo*, 11; Geijer and Campbell, 30; Ström, p. 143; Olsson, *Västergötland*, p. 130, No. 73. Latin: Claret, p. 73, No. 100 (Quid sine ventre venit ad aquam); Huldreich Therander (Johann Sommer), 143. Walloon: Colson, *Wallonia*, IV, 151, No. 134. French: Rolland, 173; V. S., *Mélusine*, I (1878), col. 258, No. 52; Bladé, *Armagnac*, 63; Pommerel, *Auvergne*, p. 42; Lespy, *Béarn*, 20; Marchessou, *Velay et Auvergne*, p. 170, No. 31; Bon, *Auvergne*, p. 204; Carmeau, p. 34; Lacuve, *Poitou*, p. 355, No. 50; Pineau, *Poitou*, 10; Dottin, *Bas-Maine*, 15; Daleau, *Gironde*, p. 105; Mensignac, *Gironde*, p. 303, No. 36; J. Roux, *Limousin*, 81; De la Suie, *Savoie*, p. 473; Roque-Ferrier, *Languedoc*, p. 335. Spanish, Argentinian: Lehmann-Nitsche, 198. Dominican Rep.: Andrade, 121. Porto Rican: Mason, 799. Basque: Vinson, 58. Lithuanian: Schleicher, p. 194. Czech: Hrnčíř, 258, quoted by Hanika-Otto in the note to her No. 158. Serbian: Novaković, p. 77, No. 4 (A beast went for water and left its belly at home. When it returned, it put it in again). Lappish: Qvigstad, 68; Poestion, p. 268. Estonian: Wiedemann, p. 264. Hungarian: *Magyar Nyelvör*, II (1873), 42 (I have an ox the hide of which I might drive into the brook but the inside of it will be left behind).

Riddlers often conceive the scene vividly: the animal "leaves its bones at home" (Breton: Lavenot, *Basse-Bretagne*, p. 668), or "goes to bathe and leaves its belly at home" (Czech: Erben, p. 20, quoted by Hanika-Otto, note to her No. 158).

208. A more adequate personification—of which the English riddle may be a degeneration—is the Lappish "A hundred-year-old man and his head one night old.—A tree stump when it snows on it" (Donner, 28; Qvigstad, 125, citing Norwegian and Swedish parallels). In northern Europe, this pattern has many variations; see Norwegian: Bugge, *Telemarken*, 11; Stafset, 204; Berge, 70. Swedish: Dybeck, *Runa*, 1850, p. 37, No. 37; Ericsson, *Södermanland*, I (1879), 91, No. 58; Ström, p. 386, "Natur," 4; Russwurm, *Eibo*, p. 134, § 316, No. 36; Sandén, *Norra Vadsbo*, 147. Finnish: Henssen, 79 (An old man, a new cap. Each year it is sewed). Estonian: Wiedemann, p. 277; Dido, 11 (A child one day old, but older than a man of a hundred years). Votyak: Wichmann, *Votyak*, 8 (The emperor sleeps, his head slips down). Cheremiss: Genetz, 53 (The emperor's hat was set awry). Vogul: Ahlqvist, *Vogul*, 8 (Back of the village sit those who have donned white kerchiefs). Altai Turkish: Menges, p. 77, No. 43 (I am son-in-law of the sun, I wear a cap with silver ornaments). Turkish: Katanov in Radlov, IX, 93, No. 794 (Having found a convenient place, a white-headed old man is sitting), p. 615, No. 69 (A gray-haired old man sits on the ridge of a mountain). Yakut: Popov, p. 285 (There are children with snow caps, it is said), which includes too much of the answer in the riddle; Piekarski, 64 (They say that children, dressed in rabbit caps, ran in the races), 65 (They say that children dressed in leather caps are standing about); Priklonskii, 109 (In winter it wears a hat; in summer it takes it off), which is akin to the riddles discussed in the headnote to No. 587 of the present collection. Ainu: Starr, *Ainu*, 44 (What wears a white robe in the wood?). American Indian, Ten'a: Jetté, 85 (Riddle me: we have our heads in sheepskin caps).

The Cherekessian "On top of our pole lies a white egg" (Tambiev, p. 61, No. 97) is a rare comparison to a thing rather than a person.

210a through 210d. Welsh: Hull and Taylor, 17 and 18 (feather), 19 (canvas). Czech: Hanika-Otto, p. 123, No. 35 (A monster came to our house and looked into the courtyard; it left a little bit on every peg), has some resemblance to the riddles discussed in the headnotes to Nos. 205–207, nn. 9–11, and 418 of the present collection.

214a, 214b. Frisian: Dykstra, *Snypsnaren*, p. 96. German: Wossidlo, 323; Frischbier, *Thierwelt*, p. 352, No. 53; Hanika-Otto, 125a through 125c. Danish: Kristensen, p. 48, § 129, Nos. 182a (What goes around a house and drags its entrails after it?), 182b, 182c.

215. The answer may be "leaf" or "bottle." See Nos. 821, 822, which compare a cork or bottle to a man who goes under water and does not drown.

216. A composite of miscellaneous elements. For "goes to the fire" see Scotch Gaelic: Nicolson, p. 29. For "goes to the door" and similar phrases see Modern Greek: Abbott, p. 309, No. 13. For "does no harm" see Flemish: Joos, 644.

218. Compare No. 143 and the corresponding headnote.

219, 220. Riddlers do not often describe an object in terms of what it does.

221. Spanish, Argentinian: Lehmann-Nitsche, 131a through 131c. Chilean: Flores, 254 (An old woman runs into all the corners). For a more definite personification see Nos. 559, 695a through 695f, 697, 698 of the present collection.

222. The conventional introduction, "My father has a thing," has no meaning to the riddler, who continues with a descriptive detail obviously suited to an animal or a man.

Compare the picturesque Turkish "He shouted, seized his whip, and ran out" (Katanov in Radlov, IX, 93, No. 775). In this scene, which was suggested by a carter rushing out of a tavern, the whip is the dog's tail, and the shout, its barking. See also "He squealed and seizing his sword, he ran out on the street" (*ibid.*, p. 239, No. 55). See also, in the present collection, the headnote to Nos. 445–458, particularly the Mongolian riddle for steam cited there (n. 6).

223. French: Baissac, *Mauritius*, p. 405 (I look at it, it looks at me.—Death, sun). Spanish, Chilean: Flores, 698 (You can't look at it without crying.—Sun). Quite different is the Surinam "What is the country you go to from which you never come back?—Death" (Herskovits, 103), which may be a reminiscence of Hamlet's "undiscover'd country from whose bourn no traveler returns" (Act III, Scene i).

226a, 226b. Breton: Sauvé, 6. Flemish: Joos, 41 (I hear it and don't see it, I reach for it and don't have it). For the second of these ideas see the headnote to Nos. 1643–1654 of the present collection. German: Gustav Roethe (ed.), *Die Gedichte Reinmars von Zweter* (Leipzig, 1887), strophe 205 and the note. Icelandic: Árnason, 1157 (Men can find me but not see me. Fire and water always shelter me. The sails of the ship praise me, the eyeless one. Intangible myself, I touch others). The word "find" may also be translated "feel." Swedish: Ström, p. 216, "Vinden," 1. Latin: Eusebius, 8, "De Vento et Igne," v. 2: "Unus contigi patitur nec forte videtur"; Aldhelm, 2 (De Vento): "Cernere me nulli possunt nec prendere palmis" (ed. Pitman, pp. 4–5). Walloon: Colson, *Wallonia*, IV, 44, No. 19. French: Bladé, *Armagnac*, 113 (felt, not seen). Spanish: Rodríguez Marín, 277. Argentinian: Lehmann-Nitsche, 2 (air, wind). Chilean: Flores, 22. Portuguese: Parsons, *Cape Verde*, 260. Italian: Pitrè, 887 (It brings rain, it howls, and I do not see it). Rumanian: Gorovei, 1945; and Gorovei, *Devinettes*, p. 505 (Who passes the frontier without being noticed?). Lithuanian: Jurgelionis, 1097 (What can you see walking but do not hear? / What do you hear but do not see?—Shadow, wind). Serbian: Novaković, p. 18, No. 8 (You hear it, yet you don't see it). Finnish: Lönnrot, 2072 = Henssen, 152 (His voice sounds over the whole world, but no one has yet seen him), which contains an element characteristic of the thunder riddle (see, in the present collection, No. 398 and the corresponding headnote). Estonian: Dido, 18 (One does not see it, but one hears it). Hungarian: Kálmány, III, 175, No. 58 (Sometimes it whispers, sometimes it howls, but you cannot see it with your eyes). Turkish: Kúnos, 249 (Without any noise it falls out of sight), which is closely related to the riddles cited in the headnote to No. 164, §§ 2–3, of the present collection. Arabic: Giacobetti, 45; Ruoff, p. 11, No. 3. African, Kundu: Ittmann, *Kundu*, 1, 277. Duala: Ebding, 65. Lamba: Doke, 69. Indonesian, Malay: Harmsen, p. 276, No. 37 (felt, not seen). Serawaj: Helfrich, *Serawaj*, pp. 59–60, No. 61. Samoan: Heider, 151. Filipino: Starr, *Philippines*, 343 (What walks that cannot be seen?), 344 (Here it comes, yet you do not see it).

For discussion see Loewenthal, pp. 60–61, 146; Gustav Roethe (ed.), *Die Gedichte Reinmars von Zweter* (Leipzig, 1887), p. 621 (note on strophe 205). In an Eddic lay, Odin asks, "Whence comes the wind that goes over the sea; one never sees it?" (*Vafþrúþnismal*, 36, 3).

226b. For the element "The house is full of it" see Nos. 1643a through 1643i, 1643k through 1643n, 1643q, 1643s through 1643v, 1645, 1646a, 1647, 1649a through 1649c, 1651a.

227. Although the emendation proposed in the headnote seems correct in the light of the following parallels, one can support the text as it stands by such a riddle as the Turkish "It goes thus: it has no strength, its nose is black, and it has no eyes" (Kowalski, *Zagadki*, 232).

In most instances the parallels to the conception of a ship as something that moves without a trace show little elaboration. The actor and the scene are not very clearly conceived. See Icelandic: Árnason, 514 (What boar runs on eight feet over deep, roadless fens? It walks over hills and plains, but no search would reveal its footprints). Danish: Feilberg, *Ordbog*, III, 243, s.v. "skib." French: J. Roux, *Limousin*, 24. Spanish: Demófilo, 113, 114. Dominican Rep.: Andrade, 202. Lettish: Bielenstein, 112 through 117, 323. Polish: Gustawicz, 196 (It rides but not on a wagon; it shoots but not with a whip; it leaves no tracks behind it.—Rowboat). White Russian: Wasilewski, 59 (I ride, I ride, there is no trace. I cut, I cut, there are no chips). Russian: Preobrazhenskii, p. 170

(identical with Wasilewski's version, but having the fuller answer, "vessel on the water and an oar"); Sadovnikov, 1509. Serbian: Novaković, p. 111, No. 3 (It moves on water; its trace is not seen). Estonian: Wiedemann, p. 277. Zyrian: Wichmann, *Zyrian*, 151, 276. Votyak: Wichmann, *Votyak*, 133, 287. Mordvin: Paasonen, 179 (He goes, no traces; he chops, no chips.—Swimmer in water). Cheremiss: Genetz, 11 (I travel forward but leave no trace). Mingrelian: Blechsteiner, p. 157, No. 4 (It goes and comes and shows no trace); Petrov, p. 257, No. 4 (It goes and no trace is visible). Armenian: Grigorov, p. 124, No. 19 (It goes, it vanishes; you look back; there is no trace). Georgian: Blechsteiner, p. 13, No. 12 (It comes and goes and shows no trace); Glushakov, p. 23, No. 3 (It goes back and forth, it leaves no trace). Cuman: Németh, *Codex Cumanicus*, p. 601, No. 38 (This goes and yet has no track). Yakut: Piekarski, 326 (It walks and walks, they say, but its footprints are invisible, so they say). African, Duala: Ebding, 72 (On what path are no footprints left?). Kosi: Ittmann, *Kosi*, 202. Tonga-Shangaan: Junod and Jaques, p. 229, No. 9 (The track which cannot be seen?—It is lost in water). Indonesian, Tabaru: Fortgens, 71 (It follows a path over the sea and leaves no footprint). The riddler errs in admitting part of the answer into the riddle.

228. German: Wossidlo, 493. French: V. S., *Mélusine*, I (1878), col. 254, No. 8; Parsons, *Antilles*, III, 387, Martinique, 97; p. 391, Dominica, 16, 17; and p. 402, Guadaloupe, 52. Spanish: Demófilo, 969. Argentinian: Lehmann-Nitsche, 175, 176. Chilean: Flores, 733. Indonesian, Javanese: Ranneft, *Poëzie*, p. 70, No. 19.

Compare the Filipino riddle for spectacles, "I cannot see although my eyes are wide open; if I cover, I can see" (Starr, *Philippines*, 196).

231. For the suggestion of singing see the headnote to Nos. 768–769, § 5.

233. Welsh: Hull and Taylor, 7. Arabic: Ruoff, p. 19, No. 1 (Our camel, whoa! whoa! eats dung and voids bread).

234. For the suggestion of insatiability in riddles for a mill or a saw see Nos. 239 and 777 and the headnote to Nos. 776–777. See also the note to No. 237.

235a through 235e. Danish: Kristensen, p. 60, § 136, No. 196 (a long literary riddle). Swedish: Ström, p. 222, "Eldan och rokan," 3. Lettish: Bielenstein, 726 (I do not have a mouth, but I can eat; whatever I get, that do I eat; give me brandy, I devour it; give me water, and I die). Modern Greek: Dieterich, *Rätseldichtung*, p. 91; Georgeakis, pp. 293–294; Polites, *Neohellenika Analekta*, I, 221, No. 208 (It eats up everything and if it drinks water, it dies). Arabic: Giacobetti, 386 (hearth); Ruoff, p. 23, No. 20 (A devourer, it is without mouth and belly; beasts and trees are its food; if you feed it, it becomes fresh and lively; if you give it water to drink, it dies); Littmann, p. 47; Löhr, p. 107, No. 20.

Compare, in the present collection, No. 399a, which describes fire as an insatiable heifer, and No. 776, which describes fire as able to eat stones but not water.

235a. For the use of the first person in the English version see the note to No. 92 of the present collection.

235b. (Expressed in terms of a condition.) Arabic: Ruoff, p. 23, No. 18 (If you feed something, it lives; if you give it to drink, it dies).

235d. The description of fire growing as one feeds it reverses the theme found in the descriptions of a hole growing as one takes away from it; see the headnote to Nos. 1690–1697.

236. Turkish: Katanov in Radlov, IX, 256, No. 150 (Old man Toskan cannot eat his fill in nine whole years). Chinese: Rudolph, p. 75, No. 26 (What is it that sits very low and eats more grass than a buffalo?). See also a Modern Greek riddle quoted in the note to Nos. 400a through 400c.

237. German: Wossidlo, 377 (a contaminated version); H. Meier, *Ostfriesland*, 17 (Between Lage and Leer there stands a strange animal. It eats and it devours and it is never content.—Mill).

238. For other comparisons describing the restlessness of the sea, see Nos. 116a, 116b. For comparisons of the sea and the shore to persons talking incessantly see Nos. 751a, 751b, and the note to No. 751a, 751b.

239. Russian: Sadovnikov, 13a, 13b, 13c (She eats fast, she chews fine, she doesn't swallow, somebody else becomes full). Mordvin: Paasonen, 277.

For the comparison of a saw to something which has teeth but no mouth see the note and headnote to No. 18 in the present collection, and for the comparison of sawing to chewing see Nos. 241, 298, and 345 and the headnote to No. 240, § 1.

240. Breton: Sauvé, 142. German: Hermann Fischer, *Schwäbisches Wörterbuch*, V (Tübingen, 1920), 752. Swiss: Rochholz, 479. Icelandic: Árnason, 184 (On every farm in the land is a boy who eats with his rump and then excretes with his mouth), 186, 442 (Who eats running and excretes through his back?), 444. Walloon: Colson, *Wallonia*, V, 55, No. 210. French: V. S., *Mélusine*, I (1878), col. 258, No. 45; A. Ferrand, *Dauphiné*, p. 227; Millien, *Nivernais*, p. 578; Lacuve, *Poitou*, p. 355, No. 45; J. Roux, *Limousin*, 70; Baissac, *Mauritius*, p. 398; Parsons, *Antilles*, III, 407, Guadaloupe, 124. Portuguese: Parsons, *Cape Verde*, 144a, 144b. Spanish: *El folklore andaluz*, I (1882–1883), 30; Paul Sébillot, *Revue des traditions populaires*, X (1895), 159. Catalan: Pelay y Briz, 286. Lettish: Bielenstein, 632 (auger). Serbian: Novaković, p. 192, Nos. 8, 9. Bulgarian: Gubov, 99 (A strange beast voids on its hump), 319 (auger). Estonian: Wiedemann, p. 263 (auger). Lappish: Qvigstad, 90. Modern Greek: Dieterich, *Rätseldichtung*, p. 99. Arabic: Ruoff, p. 27, No. 38. Yakut: Piekarski, 343 (They say that something eats with its hips but throws off with the back of its skull). African, Kxatla: Schapera, 118 (Tell me: the animal which, when it coughs, sends out food through the hump). Indian, Bengali: Mitra, *Pābnā*, p. 336, No. 9. Indonesian, Tounsea: De C., 20. Lampong: Helfrich, *Lampong*, 19. Soenda: Holle, *Soenda*, p. 375, No. 34. Engganee: Helfrich, *Engganee*, p. 517, No. 4. Filipino: Starr, *Philippines*, 358. Samoan: Heider, 170. Hawaiian: Judd, 216.

241. French: Baissac, *Mauritius*, p. 412. Portuguese: Parsons, *Cape Verde*, 153. The contrast is usually expressed as the paradox of eating without being satiated; see riddles cited in the notes to Nos. 237 and 239 and the headnote to Nos. 236–239 in the present collection. A contrast of eating and not drinking, which occurs in the fire riddle (Nos. 235a through 235e), is less frequently found; see the Arabic "Something goes, it does not grow weary, it eats but does not drink.—Mill" (Ruoff, p. 31, No. 58, and compare his No. 59).

242. The conventional phrase "over the hills and hollows" here refers to the places where the gun is carried.

244. The answer probably should be "chimney"; see Nos. 319, 320.

245. Fatwood is any pinewood full of pitch.

246. The answer should be "horseshoe nail." For parallels see Flemish: Joos, 434 (It goes to the stable and doesn't eat, it goes to the pond and doesn't drink). German: Wossidlo, 382; Gilhoff, 54. Danish: Kristensen, p. 131, § 375, No. 596 (What goes on its head to water, but never drinks?—Nails in a wagon wheel). Swedish: Ström, p. 93, "Hästen," 9 (What is the remarkable person who goes to the brook to drink with twenty-five heads and drinks with only one?—Horse).

247a. (Does not eat or drink.) German: Wossidlo, 383; Gilhoff, 36; Hanika-Otto, 157a (It walks on the meadow and does not eat or drink, and yet when it gets home, it is merry), 157b. Spanish: Demófilo, 271; Rodríguez Marín, 745. Argentinian: Lehmann-Nitsche, 104a through 104m. Chilean: Flores, 189, 190. Basque: Demófilo, p. 375, No. 13.

247b. (Does not drink.) Breton: Sébillot, *Haute-Bretagne*, 9; Orain, *Ille-et-Vilaine*, p. 149. German: Butsch, 56; Frischbier, *Thierwelt*, pp. 345–346, Nos. 13, 14; Wackernagel,

14. Swiss: Rochholz, 363. Danish: Kristensen, p. 34, § 80, Nos. 102a (What gapes over the water and yet cannot get water?), 102b, 102c; Feilberg, *Ordbog*, I, 408, s.v. "fåreklokkar." Norwegian: Stafset, 8; Landstad, p. 812, No. 44; Aasen, 19; Christie, 71; Brox, *Ytre Senja*, 113. Swedish: Russwurm, p. 348, No. 47; Hyltén-Cavallius, *Värend*, 60; Waltman, *Lidmål*, 198; Ström, p. 141, "Bjällran," 1. Walloon: Colson, *Wallonia*, IV, 59, No. 44. French: V. S., *Mélusine*, I (1878), col. 262, No. 53 (Goes to drink singing, returns singing without having drunk). Basque: Vinson, 76. Serbian: Novaković, p. 57, Nos. 7 (Popagan shouting all day long walks through the forest, it comes to the water, it neither eats nor drinks anything), 8 (It goes to the water and does not drink; it goes to the salt and does not eat), 9, 10, and p. 58, Nos. 1 (It goes to the salt and does not eat it), 3 (The wheel spun in the forest, it came home, it did not lick salt, nor did it drink water), 4 (The wheel spun in the forest, it neither drank water nor grazed grass, yet it came home alone). The import of these two last examples is not obvious to me. Bulgarian: Gubov, 107 (It sits in water and [yet] walks about thirsty), 108 (It walks over the water, it does not drink it; it walks over grass, it does not eat it). Gypsy: Wlislocki, 29 (It goes along to the brook and drinks and yet does not drink).

248. Danish: Kristensen, p. 70, § 170, Nos. 269a and 269b (halter) and "What is that which goes to the water and gapes over the water and cannot get any?—Halter on a cow" (Hvad er som gaar til Vands og gaver over Vandet og kan ikke faa noget?—Klaptræ paa Koen. DFS, 1906/38: H. Ellekilde, 1916, No. 40); Feilberg, *Ordbog*, II, 173, s.v. "klaptræ."

249. Compare Nos. 292, 293, 295a through 295c and 316a through 316c, in which the description is in terms of bodily members.

250. Compare the riddles for shoes taken off before crossing a stream cited in the headnote to No. 458, nn. 2–6.

251a through 253. It is curious that this popular and stable English riddle has no close parallels in other languages.

252a. Danish: Kristensen, pp. 75–76, § 178, No. 283b (What goes to the water and says, "Å, å [water, water]," and can get none?).

255. This summary of the normal activities of a spider lacks enigmatic quality. Compare the Malay riddle for a cricket, "Who sleeps during the day and cries out at night?" (Beauregard, *Proverbes et dictons*, p. 724). For other riddles enumerating the members or acts of an object and lacking enigmatic quality see the note to No. 72 of the present collection.

256a, 256b. See also Nos. 292, 293, and 295a through 295c.

258. (The answer is usually a rake, a pole, or some other long object.) Swiss: Rochholz, 497 (It can stand where an egg [stands] and cannot lie where a cow lies.—Pole for a fruit tree). Norwegian: Stafset, 165, citing Bergh, *Sagn* (Christiania, 1879), p. 123, No. 61. Faeroic: Hammershaimb, *Antiquarisk tidsskrift*, III (1849–1851), 321, No. 67; Hammershaimb, *Færøsk anthologi*, I, 324, No. 41. Swedish: Ström, p. 142, "Räfsan," 4 (What is that which can stand in a rat hole, but cannot turn around in a horse-stall?—Rake). Bulgarian: Chacharov, 86 (The hand holds it, the door cannot hold it.—Goad). Finnish: Lönnrot, 535 = Henssen, 160 (It has room enough in an open hand, but not in a room.—Pole); Henssen, 161 (It has space enough in a small field, but not in a large forest). Lappish: Qvigstad, 87; Poestion, p. 268. Cheremiss: Porkka, 27 (It has room enough in the hand, but not in a *pud*-measure), 28; Genetz, 62 (It can be hung on a nail, it does not fit in a box.—Gun). This last riddle may be suggested by a riddle for an egg; see the headnote to Nos. 1661–1662 in the present collection. Albanian: Hahn, p. 162, No. 66 (The hand holds it, the chest does not). Turkish: Kowalski, *Asia Minor*, 27 (I have an ox, unless one breaks off the horns, it will not go into the stall.—Goad); Hamizade, 622

(It enters the hand, it doesn't enter the warehouse.—Pole). Svanian: J. Nizheradze, pp. 66–67, No. 5 (It can be held in the cup of the hand, but not in the arc [of the hand]). Ossete: Schiefner, 47. Compare also Nos. 1603, 1604, and the note to Nos. 1604a through 1604f in the present collection.

259. Icelandic: Árnason, 54 (I saw a youth whose office it was, without hands or tools, to paint every man or thing he saw), 99 (I found a treasure, a precious thing, which could make a man in my own likeness), 991 (Tell me what comes across the sea that shows a picture when asked and that can imitate every creature).

261. Flemish: Joos, 394. Spanish: Demófilo, 228, 231; Rodríquez Marín, 444, and p. 342, n. 76. Argentinian: Lehmann-Nitsche, 591. Chilean: Flores, 155, 156. Italian: Pitrè, 407; Ferraro, *Canti popolari in dialetto logodurese*, pp. 299–300, No. 7. Czech: Hanika-Otto, p. 131, No. 95. In Persian, the answer is variously given as "water," "wind," or "worm" (Phillott, 3). Indian, Bengali: Mitra, *Notes on Ho Riddles*, p. 249 (There is a creature which has no hands, which has no legs, and which does not possess two ears; my *nāduyā* son walks about from ditch to ditch). The meaning of *nāduyā* is obscure.

For personifications containing additional details see Nos. 264a, 264b, 603, 727 of the present collection.

262. Flemish: Joos, 219 (There is something that walks, it has no legs, it walks lying or hanging). German: Wossidlo, 97a through 97e. Icelandic: Árnason, 719. Swedish: Ström, p. 305, "Gåtvisor," 8. Walloon: Colson, *Wallonia*, IV, 151, No. 185d. Spanish, Chilean: Flores, 654 (It walks without feet, blows without a trumpet). Lettish: Bielenstein, 467 (What goes without feet and strikes without hands?). Indonesian, Javanese: Ranneft, *Proza*, p. 14, No. 67 (It is not a man and not an animal; it does not eat, it does not sleep, but it can live. It lives and cannot speak. It is lame, but it can run. When it is sick, there are few who can cure it).

Compare the Swedish "Who can strike without hands?" (Ericsson, *Södermanland*, V [1884], 70, No. 238) and Nos. 301 through 304 and 321 through 323 in the present collection.

263. Flemish: Joos, 391 (earthworm), 428. Spanish, Chilean: Flores, 685. White Russian: Wasilewski, 2 (Without hand, without leg, it crawls). Serbian: Novaković, p. 63, No. 10 (It has legs, yet it does not walk on them, but hides them day and night). Indian, Kashmiri: Knowles, 110 (Neither with hands nor with feet; by its own power it goes on). Uraon: Archer, p. 193, No. 105 (One who moves without legs).

Some versions introduce additional ideas. See the French "Who flays himself, does not die from it, and walks without feet?" (Rolland, 73). The Togo versions declare that a snake moves faster than a man, but they do not explain how this is to be understood. See "There is something, it has no feet and no arm, but it runs faster than a man" (Schönhärl, 21) and "A man has children, they have no feet, yet they go faster than those who have feet" (*ibid.*, 27). Compare also Nos. 562a through 562e and the headnotes to Nos. 350 and 561–562 of the present collection.

264a, 264b. Scotch Gaelic: Nicolson, p. 15 (Black wether in the wood, / Without joint in its back, / Without juice or fat, / Without head of bone). Flemish: Joos, 396 (Although I have no blood and feed on grass, yet I have power enough and strength enough that for whole days I can bear my house). For the last trait see No. 727 of the present collection.

For the formula "fish, flesh, blood, nor bone" see the note to No. 24d.

264b. For the trait "goes to the fell" see the note to No. 187a. For references to a "footless" (or "legless") animal see the discussion of the snowflake riddle in the headnote to Nos. 367–369, and see the note to Nos. 367 through 369.

265. Estonian: Wiedemann, p. 268 (bloodless, visible).

Compare the Welsh mist riddle, "What goes up the rock, it has neither feet nor bones nor a drop of blood?" (Hull and Taylor, 44); the Parsee shadow riddle, "What is that thing which has neither flesh nor bone, and which, though inanimate, moves freely about?" (Munshi, p. 98, No. 7); the German sun riddle, "What goes through the whole world and yet has no legs?" (Wossidlo, 362); and the Modern Greek smoke riddle, "A tall, tall monk, but he has no bones" (Stathes, p. 342, No. 63). For discussion see Schultz, *Rätsel aus dem hellenischen Kulturkreise*, II, 20–22.

266. Jestbooks have disseminated this literary version. See, for example, "I'm in every one's way, / Yet no Christians I stop. / My Four Hornes ev'ry Day / Horizontally play, / And my Head is nail'd down at the Top" (*Complete London Jester*, [12th ed.; London, 1784], p. 136, No. 6). A few eastern European riddles with the answer "road sign" show some similarity. See "An old woman with outstretched feet" (Rumanian: Papahagi, 92); "By the road it stands, waving its hands and saying nothing" (Polish: Gustawicz, 53); "A girl lies by the wayside with outspread arms and legs. Forked pole or stake" (*ibid.*, 406).

267. Riddlers usually associate the conventional introduction, "As I was going over London Bridge," with riddles for a bottle (Nos. 805d, 805j through 805l, 805o, 805s through 805u, and 805w), partridges, quail, bees, and wasps (Nos. 895, 898a, 900 through 902a, 903), the name "Andrew," and a few other themes.

268. Danish: Kristensen, p. 66, § 159, Nos. 239a through 239c, and p. 70, § 169, No. 268. See also "What is that which talks without a tongue and shrieks without a lung?— A church bell" (Hvad er det, som taler uden Tunge og skriger uden Lynge?—En Kirkeklokke. DFS, 1906/38: M. Jespersen, Bostrup Hedeby, 1919, p. 3, No. 13). Swedish: Ericsson, *Södermanland*, I (1879), 84, No. 20 (The dead shrieks); Geijer and Campbell, 106, 107; Ström, pp. 184–185, "Kyrkklockan," 1, 4, and pp. 272–273, "Gåtberättelser," 21 through 23. Spanish: Demófilo, 202, 203, 204 (citing Perez de Herrera, A.D. 1628); Rodríguez Marín, 814, 815. Argentinian: Lehmann-Nitsche, 357. Russian: Sadovnikov, 1006 (What has ears and a tongue, yet neither hears nor understands anything?), 1011 (A living one hits a dead one; the dead one manifests its voice; people come to its call), which resembles the themes discussed in the headnote to Nos. 828–836 of the present collection. Zyrian: Wichmann, *Zyrian*, 186.

269. Compare Nos. 467a through 468 below. See also Swedish: Ström, p. 176, "Mjölsacken."

270. French: Roque-Ferrier, *Languedoc*, p. 336. For the personification of a bottle see Nos. 6, 388, 514, 805a through 805w, and a Portuguese riddle in the note to No. 6 of the present collection. Compare the Turkish riddle for a pot, "My dark blue bull has no neck" (Katanov in Radlov, IX, 367, No. 320).

277a through 277d. Scotch Gaelic: Nicolson, p. 35 (It has eyes, yet cannot see, it is useful as food, a skin covers its every part, it is neither sheep nor tree). German: Wossidlo, 385a. Compare, in the present collection, Nos. 11 and 16, which are modeled on the riddle for a sieve (Nos. 10a, 10b). For the paradox of having an eye or eyes and yet not seeing, see the note to No. 330.

277c, 277d. The additional descriptive details confuse the effect of the pun and were probably added by a riddler who did not perceive the significance of the riddle.

278. The import of the riddle is not clear.

279. See Nos. 523 through 524b below, which employ personification.

280. The "eye" is the opening through which the helve is inserted.

281. Compare Arabic: Ruoff, p. 32, No. 63 (It has braids, which hang behind it in coming and going; it has one eye, which has never known sleep or shed a tear; it has never dressed itself in a garment, in compensation for that it dresses men in many fashions).

282. German: Wossidlo, 385b. Danish: DFS, 1906/38: Aage Sørenson, Mellerup, 1934, No. 1 (What is that which has only one eye and cannot see?—A darning needle. Hvad er det, der kun har ét Øje og ikke kan se?—En Stoppenaal). Swedish: Ström, p. 156, "Nystanet," 7.

For the paradox of having an eye or eyes and yet not seeing, see the note to No. 330 in the present collection.

284. This riddle represents an unusual application of the paradox of having an eye or eyes and yet not seeing, for which see the note to No. 330.

286. Compare "It has an ear and does not hear, it has a belly and does not eat, and it gives everybody something to eat" (German: Frischbier, *Menschenwelt*, p. 252, No. 113); "It has ears and does not hear, it has feet and does not walk" (*ibid.*, No. 114).

288. Swedish: Ström, p. 219, "Vattnet," 16 (Mouth but no head; arms but no hands; runs but has no feet). Lettish: Bielenstein, 737 (It runs day and night, it has also a voice, but it cannot run away). Russian: Sadovnikov, I465 (It proceeds without legs, its sleeves have no arms, its mouths have no speech). The Russian *rukav* signifies both "sleeves" and "a branch of a river."

289. Flemish: Joos, 26 (It has a mouth and no head, arms and no hands; it runs without feet). Swedish: Ström, p. 218, "Vattnet," 13. Spanish, Argentinian: Lehmann-Nitsche, 135. Arabic: Giacobetti, 12.

292. See another version in No. 256*b*.

293. The comparison to a creature with four legs usually occurs in riddles for a table, chair, or bed (see Nos. 305*b*, 306*b*, 307). The riddler may have conceived the four legs as representing the four posts of a hayrack.

295a. The formula "over water, under water" has probably been borrowed from the riddle of a girl carrying water over a bridge; see Nos. 165*a* through 165*g* and 165*i*.

296a through 296c. Compare Nos. 311 through 312*c* for texts containing the same theme in greater elaboration.

298. German: Gilhoff, 532. Swedish: Ström, p. 151, "Sägen," 2. Walloon: Colson, *Wallonia*, V, 55, No. 209. French: Rolland, 210. Hungarian: *Magyar Nyelvör*, V (1876), 422 = VII (1878), 134.

299a, 299b. Welsh: Hull and Taylor, 8. Flemish: Joos, 196 (It has teeth and doesn't bite). Swedish: Ström, p. 171, "Kammen." Spanish: Demófilo, 788, and p. 345, No. 27. Chilean: Flores, 583, 584. Russian: Sadovnikov, 571 (What teeth do not bite and do not eat?—Teeth in a weaver's comb).

305a. Flemish: Joos, 212 (There is a thing that has four paws and cannot walk). Spanish, Dominican Rep.: Andrade, 205. The wooden dish from which the Mohammedans in Kashmir eat stands on four legs and has two handles. Riddlers describe it thus: "It has four legs and does not walk; it has two ears and does not hear; we give it food and it does not eat" (Knowles, 48).

306a, 306b. Norwegian: Brox, *Ytre Senja*, 165. Swedish: Ström, p. 163, "Stolen," 1, 2. Walloon: Colson, *Wallonia*, IV, 150, No. 180. The Javanese say that a chair has four legs, not for walking but for standing (Ranneft, *Proza*, p. 27, No. 17). See also Nos. 26 and 87 of the present collection.

307. Lithuanian: Jurgelionis, 401 (Has feet, does not walk. Has straw, does not eat. Has a soul but not always). Lappish: Qvigstad, 43 (A horse stands on four feet; it bears a heavier load at night than during the day). See also Nos. 75*a* through 76, 318*a*, and 318*b* in the present collection.

308. The four legs are the posts on which the house rests. A Porto Rican Spanish version includes more details: "Has feet and doesn't walk; has wings and doesn't fly; has eyes and doesn't see; has a mouth and doesn't eat" (Mason, 152).

309. Compare the wasp riddle, Nos. 338*a* through 338*d*.

317. The "eyes" are the openings in the top of the stove. The details "cooks and wears an apron" refer to the person cooking and do not properly belong to the riddle.

318a, 318b. The parallels vary greatly in details. See Nos. 75a through 76, 307, and 334, in the present collection. See also German: Wossidlo, 514. Lithuanian: Jurgelionis, 402 (Has feet but does not walk; has feathers but does not fly; has straw, but does not eat; has a soul but not always), 403 (Has straw, does not eat; has feet, does not walk; has wings, does not fly), 404 (Has feet, does not run; has feathers, does not fly; has straw, does not eat; and no one feeds it). Another variation is "What bird has four legs and feathers?" (Lithuanian: Jurgelionis, 405. Polish: Gustawicz, 199). See also "I have four feet, but am not an animal; I have down, but am not a bird; I have a soul, but not always" (Lithuanian: Jurgelionis, 406). Lettish: Bielenstein, 900. Russian: Sadovnikov, 242. Compare the Danish windmill riddle, "What has four wings and can't fly, no legs but can go?" (Kristensen, pp. 142–143, § 420, Nos. 662a, 662b, and 667).

319, 320. The European parallels have the answer "chimney." See German: Wossidlo, 320a; Hanika-Otto, 298. Danish: Kristensen, p. 117, § 321, No. 513 (Who stands on one leg and smokes a pipe?), which is similar to the riddles cited in the headnote to Nos. 1121–1126, § 9, in the present collection. Swedish: Ström, p. 178, "Takbjälkerna." Lithuanian: Jurgelionis, 323 (A tall maiden smokes a pipe), 324 (A short stout little German boy smokes a pipe), 325 (On a tall hill an old man smokes a pipe), 326 (An old, old man sits on the roof and smokes a pipe), 327 (The young gentleman smokes a cigar on the roof). Czech: Hanika-Otto, note to No. 298. Mordvin: Paasonen, 125, 126. Cheremiss: Porkka, 1, 142.

319. Since the four "eyes" are the openings of a stove, the answer should be "stove."

320. This anomalous riddle suggests a dog or some other quadruped to the hearer and contradicts the suggestion by saying that the creature smokes a pipe. I have not noted precisely this sort of contradiction elsewhere and have therefore, as a matter of convenience, considered this riddle to be a variety of the preceding, more usual form.

321. Compare Swedish: Ström, p. 164, "Klockan," 4 var.

322. Flemish: Joos, 216, 217 (It has no mouth and it tells everyone the truth), 225 (a literary riddle). German: Frischbier, *Menschenwelt*, p. 247, Nos. 59, 60, and p. 248, Nos. 65, 66. Spanish, New Mexican: Campa, 96 (I have a face but no head; I have hands but no feet; I can communicate ideas but not talk; I can run but not walk). See also Nos. 130a, 130b in the present collection.

323. Spanish, Chilean: Flores, 641, 647 (. . . although I speak, I have no mouth, and I walk and I have no feet). Polish: Gustawicz, 459 (It has no legs or arms, yet it goes and beats), 460.

324. Spanish: Demófilo, 853 (It talks, has no mouth; it walks, has no feet); Rodríguez Marín, 772. Chilean: Flores, 647. Indonesian, Lampong: Helfrich, *Lampong*, 24 (Lives, has no soul; makes sounds, has no mouth; speaks twelve times a day).

325, 326. See No. 68 and the headnote to No. 285.

327. The "eyes" are the openings in the top of the stove. For the paradox of having eyes and not seeing, see the note to No. 330.

329. For various uses of the paradox of having eyes and yet not seeing, see the note to No. 330.

330. French: Fleury, *Basse-Normandie*, p. 369. The same idea is used in the Flemish thimble riddle quoted in the note to No. 1264 of the present collection.

In English riddling, the paradox of having an eye or eyes and yet not seeing is applied to a potato (see Nos. 277a through 277d) and also to a needle (No. 282), a button (No. 284), a stove (No. 327), and a pair of shoes (No. 329).

331. Swedish: Ström, p. 147, "Sållet" 1, 3.

334. Compare Nos. 318a, 318b.

335b. The phrase "such a riddle has never been known" is characteristic of neckriddles, which are not included in this collection.

CHAPTER II
COMPARISONS TO AN ANIMAL
Nos. 337-458

337. The import of the riddle is obscure. "Little titchie" is perhaps a reminiscence of "Hitty titty" and the like; see Nos. 338a through 342c.

338a through 338d. French: Parsons, *Antilles*, III, 368, Trinidad, 65, and p. 373, Grenada, 78. African, Bakongo: Denis, 53 (We went to the village, there where the dunghill is, someone greeted us.—*Chagre*, an insect). A riddler alters this slightly and gives the answer, "cock" (*ibid.*, 54).

338c. "Don't mind" signifies "If you don't mind," that is, "If you are not careful."

339. For the idea "no one can catch Hitty titty" see Nos. 1643a through 1644b and the headnote to Nos. 1643-1654, § 1.

340. See the note on No. 338c.

342a through 342c. The parallels usually show a higher degree of personification than these English texts. The actor is ordinarily a person. The well-conceived Georgian "I put my hand through the fence. A black dog bit me" (Glushakov, p. 26, No. 31) is an interesting instance of a comparison to an animal.

For versions naming a person as actor see Welsh Gypsy: Sampson, 19, and p. 246. Irish: Delargy, 66 (Niungenaí Neangenaí on this side of the fence and Niungenaí Neangenaí on the other side of the fence. He who would meddle with Niungenaí Neangenaí, Niungenaí Neangenaí would meddle with him); Delargy, *Inis Cé*, 9 (Viog, Viog inside the fence; Viog, Viog outside the fence; don't touch Viog and Viog won't touch you [the word for "touch" means also "cut, prick"]); O Dalaigh, 169 (Bridget on the fence, frightening my heart). Flemish: M[one], *Anzeiger*, VII (1838), col. 268, No. 285; *Ons Volksleven*, V (1893), 108, No. 99. German: Wossidlo, 51 (Behind the house stands Peter Kraus. If one attacks him, then he bites). Swedish: Ström, pp. 131-132, "Tisteln," 1, 2 (There stands a soldier in a gray coat and a red cap and presents his musket to all whom he sees); Geijer and Campbell, 73 (There stands a lad in our meadow. He can stab but cannot jump. He has a red cap). For parallels to a figure wearing a red cap see the headnote to Nos. 632-644, § 7, of the present collection. Polish: Kopernicki, 20 (A little gentleman stands in the field; everybody fears him), 20 var. (A maiden stands in the field; everybody fears her), 20, var. 2 (A little gentleman with a little red cap stands in the path. Whoever touches him curses him); Siarkowski, 20 (It stands in the path on one leg. Whoever touches it curses it); Gustawicz, 283 through 289, 331, 332. Crimean Tatar: Filonenko, 97 (Near the road, "Ai! Ai!"). The cry of pain "Ai!" dramatizes the scene. African, Dschagga: Gutmann, p. 530 (I climb up into the mountain forest and find there an old woman who threatens me with her fists.—Ferns growing [the young fronds are curled]) and *ibid.* (There is an old woman with only three fingers.—Fern). Kanuri: Lukas, p. 173, No. 48 (A dwarf stands there and throws spears.—Kanga, a thorny plant).

343. "One thing" is probably equivalent to the formula "There is a thing" and might be better set off by a semicolon, but I retain the collector's punctuation. For the formula "Here is a thing," which Nova Scotian riddlers do not often use, see the headnote to chapter ii.

The style of the riddle is literary and not popular.

344a, 344b. Swiss: Rocholz, 369 (There is something on a "Stöckli" [little stick; also: breast of a shirt, dickey], and it jumps like a goat), which depends partly on a pun. Swedish: Dybeck, *Runa*, 1850, p. 36, No. 22 (Small and nimble, it hops over the plain, no man can bridle it right); Ström, p. 115, Nos. 1, 2, and p. 117, No. 1. Basque: Vinson, 14 (A jump here, a jump there, a little black Mary). Portuguese: Parsons, *Cape Verde*, 91 (Jump here, jump there, so laborious). Lithuanian: Schleicher, p. 199 (A little black horse hops through the whole world), and *ibid.* (A black horse leaps, footprints are not to be seen). White Russian: Wasilewski, 20 (A little black horse, not to sit on, not to stroke). Russian: Arkhangel'skii, p. 76 (Little, blackish, fuzzy). Bulgarian: Ikonomov, 64 (It is as black as the tsar, but clowns like a clown). Finnish: Lönnrot, 2164 = Henssen, 112 (It is as black as a vicar and hops like a Lapp. Nine men can't tame it). For a parallel to the idea that an animal cannot be tamed see No. 573 in the present collection. Lappish: Poestion, p. 269 (What is as black as a priest, leaps like a horse, and a hundred men can't bridle it?). Hungarian: Arany and Gyulai, II, 361, No. 63 (It is black, but is no swallow, it jumps like a he-goat). Modern Greek: Polites, *Neohellenika Analekta*, I, 222, No. 164 (A black-faced mule, all blood and hide. What impudence!). Turkish: Kúnos, 173 (On a dark top a mule is kicking around). Turcoman: Samojlvich, 52 (A raven stallion jumped hippety-hop). Kirghese: Melioranskii, 11 (cited by Samojlvich). Georgian: Glushakov, p. 37, No. 91 (A certain creature that quickly picks up its legs. No youth of our land can put a bridle on it). Arabic: Ruoff, p. 43, No. 12 (A hopping horse hops, hops; five [men] hunt it, two catch it), which concludes with elements belonging to Nos. 971a through 971f of the present collection; Meissner, *Iraq*, 79 (Black, black as asphalt, and it leaps like a wild boar).

345. For the comparison of sawing to chewing see No. 239. "The more she drinks" refers to the water which turns the wheels of the mill and drives the saw. The meaning of "rollin' trout" is obscure, and the words may be a corruption rather than a reference to a fish.

346. Although a mammal, the walrus is popularly conceived of as a fish or amphibian.

347. Latin: Buchler, *Gnomologia*, 3d ed. (1614), p. 477. Russian: Sadovnikov, 1614 (Its eyes wide open, there it sits, talking in French, leaping like a flea, swimming like a human being). Serbian: Novaković, p. 50, Nos. 1 (Over the forest, *Shum, shum!* Over the field, *Kas, Kas!* And into the water, *Bump!*), 2 (Something is walking along the road in a little green coat. It is gnashing its teeth, it spreads its eyes and cries, *Baka, baka!*). Modern Greek: Dieterich, *Rätseldichtung*, p. 94, citing Stamatiadis, V, 181 (It has a voice like a bagpipe and has neither tail nor hair); Papakristodoulos, *Laographia*, II (1910), 194, No. 11 (It is hairless, but has no fleece. It has legs but no tail). Finnish: Lönnrot, 655 = Henssen, 228 (A little round fellow was on the road, a little golden [also signifying "dear, beloved"] button wandered along, it danced in the courtyard, it danced when it came across the courtyard. Its eyes are reversed in its head). Hungarian: *Magyar Nyelvőr*, IV (1875), 559 = XXXI (1902), 533, No. 36 = XL (1911), 334 (Young gentlemen are jumping all over the roads). Turkish: Kowalski, *Asia Minor*, 71 (In a dark spot it makes the sound *gum-gum*); Zavarin, *Brusa*, 21 (A chattering lady, an easygoing lady, elegant to the sight, jumping like a partridge, the youngest among the girls, a raving beauty, a pocket pistol. Then in color like Egyptian rice, a watermelon from the archipelago, brooklets of cream, the chattering lady lives in genuine paradise). This is not entirely intelligible; the reference to the pocket pistol concerns the jerky croaking of the frog. Turcoman: Samojlvich, 46 (Now, my horse, now, now, my horse! In motley caparison a stallion, my horse! I'll give you some barley. My horse doesn't eat. In a waterless spot my horse does not roam). Astrakhan Calmuck: Kotvich, 133 (Cheese dropped from the sky; it has four legs). The first clause probably means "food found unexpectedly." Cherekessian: Tambiev, p. 64, No. 129 (A winding road, a piece of fat meat.—River, frog). Mongolian: Mostaert, 50 (Jump, jump, spotty one, with your cramped toes, spotty one, with your flat mouth and tongue, spotty one!), 51 (Jump,

jump, spotty one, dappled one, with one spot, as big as a camel, spotty one!), 52. "As big as a camel" means "very large."

For other descriptions of a frog see Nos. 82a through 82c and 605 in the present collection.

348. Bulgarian: Chacharov, 92 (Dule went across the sea, the sea did not stir nor did Dule drown).

350. The answer "snail" does not agree with the information given by the riddler, for a snail does not cast its skin. This answer probably resulted from a scribal or typographical error for "snake." See a parallel in the Dschagga riddle for a snake, "I was old and became young again" (Gutmann, p. 528). For references to the snake casting its skin see J. G. Frazer, *Folklore in the Old Testament*, I (London, 1918), 66–74.

351. German: Frischbier, *Menschenwelt*, p. 249, No. 79 (What shiny bird has a flaxen tail?); Hanika-Otto, 324b (It is a leaden bird, it has a flaxen tail). Danish: Kristensen, p. 99, § 254, Nos. 399a through 399c, and compare his p. 130, § 379, Nos. 589a, 589b, 589e. Swedish: Ström, p. 160, "Nålen," 8. French: Parsons, *Antilles*, III, 451, Hayti, 68. Rumanian: Papahagi, 2 (A bird with a long, long and thin tail). Czech: Feifalik, p. 379, No. 74. Polish: Kopernicki, 33 = Gustawicz, 42 (A birdie flies about the street, dragging its entrails after it.—Weaver's shuttle), which contains the theme of Nos. 205a through 205e of the present collection; Gustawicz, 37 = 38 = 39 (A birdie flies beneath the roof, its entrails dragging behind.—Shuttle), *ibid.*, 40, 41. Russian: Bardin, p. 243, No. 1 (The duck was ducking and ducking and lost its tail). Serbian: Novaković, p. 69, Nos. 3 (It roots with its beak, and it moves the roots with its tail), 4 (A bird with fine plumage adorned the whole village but could not adorn itself). For discussion of this last theme see the headnote to Nos. 531–534, § 2, of the present collection. See also Indian: Lakshīnātha Upasānī, I, 2 (My tail is ten times longer than my body), which may refer to an animal rather than a bird.

For surveys of the riddles for a needle and thread see the headnotes to Nos. 203, 205–207, 419–435, 528–534, and 531–534 of the present collection. For comparisons of a needle to an animal with a flaxen tail see the note to No. 437.

352. Insert a comma after "besides," and interpret the riddle as "[It has] two heads besides, [these are] more than a daw [has]."

For parallels see Flemish: Joos, 594; *Volk en taal*, I, 5, No. 6; *Ons Volksleven*, I (1889), 80, No. 52 (Two-Legs bore No-Legs [a fish] in the air), which contains elements belonging to the riddles discussed in the headnotes to Nos. 461–462 and 466–468 of the present collection. See German: Wossidlo, 113 (bird with eight feet and a beak), and compare his No. 969 (two storks carrying a frog); Frischbier, *Thierwelt*, p. 348, No. 30; Gilhoff, 202 through 207 (frog and mouse); Schmidt, *Danzig*, 12; Haffner, 69; Hanika-Otto, 14 through 16; Renk, *Tyrol*, 98. Indian, Khāṛiā: Roy and Roy, II, 455, No. 4 (The carrier has no legs, the spectator has no head, the deceased has four legs.—Frog carried by snake and seen by crab). Bihari: Mitra, *Bihar*, 10 (A thief without feet came and stole a cow without a tail and stole a man without a head.—Snake eats frog and crab), which seems to be a disordered version of the preceding riddle. Kolarian: Wagner, 77 (The bearer's feet were not seen, but four of the corpse he takes away.—Snake, frog. The onlooker crab [*katkom*] has no head).

For discussion see Aarne, *Rätselforschungen*, II, 208–210. The conception has some similarity to the description of a man on horseback; see the headnote to Nos. 48–55 in the present collection.

The Irish "Food went to three on the shore of Loch Léin. The food ate the three and came away itself.—An eagle bore a cat to its fledgelings and left it in their nest. The cat ate the fledgelings and got away safe and sound" (Delargy, 47) is perhaps a different riddle.

353. Tupper notes the lack of parallels and gives a helpful note on riddles for bees. For the theme "none work like unto him can do" see the headnote to No. 793-794 of the present collection.

A few descriptions of a bee compare it to a bird. See the Bengali "The bird is yellow-colored, possesses legs of bamboo, and swooping down from a distance, stings one, which act causes the latter's body to smart with pain" (Mitra, *Chittagong*, pp. 965-966, No. 10 B). The bees in a hive are birds; see the Argentinian "A round thing occupied by many birds and full of delicious things to eat" (Lehmann-Nitsche, 664), the Chilean "A tree full of birds" (Flores, 201), and the Turkish "Little birds, they are working in Baghdad, they prepare it and give it to others" (Kúnos, 264). The identification of bee and bird in the Spanish "A bird with two beautiful daughters.—Bee, honey, wax" (Rodríguez Marín, 409) is slightly confused. Mention of form and a rare mention of function appear in "It flies through the air, without feathers or heart, gives food to the living, and consolation to the dead" (Spanish: Rodríguez Marín, 406, 408. Cuban: Massip, 4. Porto Rican: Mason, 8a through 8e).

The colors of a bee or a wasp suggest comparison to a man in yellow and black; see Nos. 649, 899 through 902, 947 in the present collection. The multitude of bees in a hive suggests the occupants of a convent or a house with many rooms or windows; see the headnotes to Nos. 909, § 2, and 1128-1131, § 4. The Kxatla have an interesting comparison for a bee's sting: "Tell me: Sekeleremeisi [a name of a cow] with the sharp hoof" (Schapera, 32).

354. The psalmist does not explain how the eagle rejuvenates himself (Ps. 103:5), but later writers speak of the eagle bathing in a spring (for references see E. W. Hopkins, *Journal of the American Oriental Society*, XXVI, i [1905], 1-87, and ii, 411-415; Archer Taylor, "OHG. Quecbrunno," *Modern Language Notes*, XXXII [1917], 48-50). Aldhelm alludes to the bathing eagle in Riddle 57 (ed. Pitman, p. 33) and may be the source of the Swedish parallel (Ström, p. 104, "Heliga fåglar," 4). For references to the rejuvenation of the eagle by casting its bill see M. Goldstaub and R. Wendriner, *Ein tosco-venezianischer Bestiarius* (Halle, 1892), p. 132, n. 2, and p. 386; J. Klapper, *Erzählungen des Mittelalters* (Wort und Brauch, XII [Breslau, 1914]), pp. 220 and 410, No. 208. For the snake casting its skin see No. 350 and the corresponding headnote in the present collection.

356. The riddler is more interested in playing with the word "wings" than in developing an adequate personification.

357. For references to the trait "never rests" see the headnotes to Nos. 114-118 and 138-140. For the usual description of the wind see the headnote to Nos. 365-366, § 1.

358. The meaning of "nev^r trys" is obscure, and other passages in this badly preserved text are not easily understood.

359, 360. These are examples of description containing no enigmatic comparison. For a list of similar descriptions, see the note to No. 72.

361a through 361c. African, Ila: Smith and Dale, II, 325, No. 6 (At your house there is a calf that grazes lying down.—Hoe). Indian, Ho: Sarkar, p. 352, No. 13 (It whirls in the sky and enters the earth.—Spade). Japanese: Starr, *Japan*, p. 8 (Shines in heaven, strikes earth, cleaves earth.—Mattock).

362. Probably we should read: "No mortal sees it rise [arise]."

For a remote, unrelated parallel see Spanish: Demófilo, 1042.

363a. This degenerate version has borrowed the formula "round the house" from such texts as Nos. 174 and 192b through 196.

363b. Somewhat less corrupt than No. 363a, this version has the introductory formula found in Nos. 165a through 165c, 165e through 165g, 167, 169a through 169e, 171, 172b through 173.

364. Tupper quotes a long Spanish literary riddle (Demófilo, pp. 435–436, No. 8) and an English literary riddle. An Argentinian parallel contains the ideas, "it cannot be seen, flies to the skies without wings, is the cause of knowledge" (Lehmann-Nitsche, 191). The notion that thought ranges far and returns quickly is very old. See, for example, Freidank, *Bescheidenheit*, § 29. For other comparisons to the speed of thought see the headnote to No. 1680, § 1, in the present collection, and also Welsh: Hull and Taylor, 38, 39, 40, 401.

This conception is allied to the descriptions of sight or the eye as something that ranges far (see No. 1471 and the headnote to No. 1471, in the present collection). Compare the Turkish "An arrow shot from here flew to Pekin.—Man's thought" (Katanov in Radlov, IX, 91, No. 760).

365b. The riddler's meaning is obscure. Although "wears" may be used here in the meaning "wears out," this interpretation seems somewhat unlikely in view of the Welsh parallel, in which the meaning "wears out" is not possible. See Hull and Taylor, 65, 66.

366. The import of the riddle is obscure. "Shoeing a goose" is a proverbial equivalent of wasting one's time in trifling or unnecessary labor; see W. G. Smith and Janet Heseltine, *Oxford Dictionary of English Proverbs* (Oxford, 1935), p. 238 (It is no more pity to see a woman weep than to see a goose go barefoot), which states the idea in another way, and p. 541. Probably an obscure allusion remains to be interpreted. See also Murray Aiken Cowie, *Proverbs and Proverbial Expressions in the German Works of Albrecht von Eyb* (Diss., Univ. of Chicago; Chicago, 1942), pp. 8–9, No. 27.

367 through 369. The usual series is a bird, a tree, and a girl. For parallels see Scotch Gaelic: Nicolson, p. 27. Frisian: Dykstra, I, 260. Dutch: Sinninghe, p. 5, No. 2. Flemish: Joos, 541. German: Butsch, 137; Wossidlo, 99; Frischbier, *Menschenwelt*, p. 260, No. 193; Haffner, 6; Hanika-Otto, 1a through 1g; Ludwig Erk and F. M. Böhme, *Deutscher Liederhort*, III (Leipzig, 1894), 6, No. 1065; and many references collected in Aarne, *Rätselforschungen*, III, 9–10. Swiss: E. H.-K., *Schweizerisches Archiv für Volkskunde*, III (1899), 162. Icelandic: Árnason, 279 (I know a featherless bird that alighted on a wall without a foundation. Then a handless lady seized the bird, fried it without fire, and ate it without a mouth). Danish: Grundtvig, *Gamle danske Minder*, I, 237, No. 36; Kristensen, p. 119, § 331, No. 528, pp. 120–121, § 333, Nos. 535a through 535j, 535l, 535n, and p. 273, No. 87. The variations in the modern Danish versions show some vitality in the riddle (translations are omitted, since the variations are not great enough to need interpretation and are more readily perceived in the original). Typical examples are "Der kom en hvid Fowl, fjærrløs, ɛa sat sæ o mi Faars Hus, farrerløs; der blöw ildløs stegt aa mundløs ædt. Hvad et det?" (DFS, 1906/38: S. Steffensen, 1919, No. 1); "Der kom en Fugl vingeløs og satte sig paa en gærdestaver, saa kom der en Fugl benløs og aad den op hudløs" (DFS, 1906/38: T. Buch, 1924, No. 10); DFS, 1906/38: P. Bjerge, 1912, No. 3; and "Fugl, fugl fjerløs / kom og sat sig paa bom, bom bladløs / saa kom jomfru mundløs / og aad fugl, fugl fjerløs" (DFS, 1906/38: J. Prest, 1933, No. 3). Faeroic: Hammershaimb, *Antiquarisk tidsskrift*, III (1849–1851), 315, No. 1 = *Zeitschrift für deutsche Mythologie*, III (1855), 129 = *Færøsk anthologi*, I, 322, No. 1. Norwegian: Christie, 1; Stafset, 85; Berge, 1; Bugge, *Telemarken*, 10; Brox, *Ytre Senja*, 65, citing Bergh, *Sagn* (Christiania, 1879), p. 130, Nos. 94, 95; many texts from manuscript sources in Aarne, *Rätselforschungen*, III, 10. Swedish: Dybeck, *Runa*, 1847, p. 40, No. 1 = Russwurm, p. 351, No. 79; Ericsson, *Södermanland*, I (1879), 82, Nos. 9, 10; III (1882), 100, No. 147; and V (1884), 65, No. 208; Hyltén-Cavallius, *Värend*, 77; Geijer and Campbell, 83; Christofferson, p. 45 = *Folkminnen och folktankar*, II (1915), 96; Dybeck, *Runa*, 1865–1873, p. 29, No. 5, and p. 65, Nos. 85, 90; Sandén, *Norra Vadsbo*, 23; Ström, p. 219, "Snö och is"; Olsson, *Västergötland*, p. 135, Nos. 132, 133. Renaissance Latin: J. Camerarius in Reusner, ed. 1599, p. 88 = *ibid.*, ed. 1602, p. 254 = Friedreich, p. 214, No.

5. Rumanian: Gorovei, *Devinettes*, p. 113 (Thousands of birds fly, there comes a man without feet who eats all of them). Lithuanian: Jurgelionis, 115 = Schleicher, p. 208 (Up flew a bird from the East, it perched on a tree without branches, there came a maiden and ate the bird without lips), Jurgelionis, 116 (Up flew a bird without wings, it perched on a tree without branches, there arose a toothless maid and ate the wingless bird), 117 (There grew a tree without roots, up flew a bird without wings, a toothless old woman ate the wingless bird). Lettish: Bielenstein, 583 (Little white birds, they settle down and the hedges are full of them, then the shining one comes and eats them all up), 584 (Birds without wings come, without wings they settle on the tree, the maiden without teeth comes, takes the birds, and eats them). Czech: *Pohádky* (1695), No. 137 (a translation of Butsch's German text). Hanika-Otto, note to No. 1, cites Erben, 11 (A featherless bird flew down into our leafless tree; a toothless fellow came upon it and ate up the featherless thing). The oldest version from Bohemia is the Latin "Alat alis, quamvis caret alis: nix michi solvis" (Claret, v. 62, No. 14). Russian: Sadovnikov, 1986 (A twigless tree is lying, a wingless bird flies down upon it, a mouthless girl comes and eats the wingless bird); Aarne, in *Rätselforschungen*, III, 11, cites *Zhivaia starina*, VIII (1898), 432, No. 298, and *ibid.*, XIII (1903), 482, No. 15. Serbian: Novaković, p. 212, No. 8 (White hens fell from the sky and covered our doors), p. 213, Nos. 1, 2 (White bees alighted on the ground. One creature alone could destroy them, but the whole world could not), 3 (Birds without feathers flew, they alighted on a tree without leaves; a young man without a mouth came and ate up the birds without feathers), 4 (A swan without wings flew up and alighted on an oak without branches, a tsar without arms killed it, and a tsarina without teeth ate it up), 5 (From the sky there fell a wingless bird, the tsar killed it without a gun, and the tsarina ate it up without teeth), 6 (A wingless pigeon fell, a toothless queen ate it up), 7 (A wingless king fell, a tsar without arrows killed it, a toothless tsarina ate it up), 8 (A white pigeon fell on an oak with many branches, it was killed by an armless prince).

Hungarian: [1] *Magyar Nyelvőr*, XXXI (1902), 539 (A thousand birds descend without feet, and one eats them without a mouth) [2] p. 532, No. 17 (identical with the preceding); [3] V (1876), 422 (Birds come without wings, one man comes without legs, eats them all without a mouth); [4] *Magyar Nyelvészet*, III, 327 (A butterfly flies without wings, a man comes without his legs, eats it all without his mouth); [5] IV, 316 (identical with the preceding); [6] *Magyar Nyelvőr*, XXXVII (1908), 188 (The bird flies without wings, descends on the tree without its legs, the king comes from the Orient, eats it all without a mouth); [7] III (1874), 376 (identical with No. [6] except for the reading "a king"); [8] *Magyar Nyelvészet*, I, 873 (Birds come without wings, descend on a tree without feet, a man comes without his legs, eats them all without his mouth); [9] oral version from Szalonta, a manuscript version in Szendrey's possession (Birds fly without wings, descend on a tree without feet, a king comes from the Orient, eats them all without his mouth); [10] *Magazin für die Litteratur des Auslandes*, 1856, p. 354, No. 6 (Birds come without wings and descend on the tree without feet; one comes without a foot and devours all without a mouth).

Tatar: Aarne, *Rätselforschungen*, III, 12.

367. "Lit upon the barn-door" is probably a reminiscence of the sunlight riddle; see Nos. 748a through 748g.

370. Snow on a stump suggests a man's hat; see No. 208.

371. Comparisons of a pot to a bird occur now and again. The riddler sees a similarity between the pot and its handle and the bird's fat body and extending tail. See the Kamba "A large black bird that feeds the growing children" (Lindblom, 40); the Sukuma "A vulture that stands on three branches" (Augustiny, 23); and Indonesian comparisons to a raven sitting on three ridges (Batak: Ophuijsen, p. 466, No. 76. Serawaj: Helfrich,

724   *English Riddles*

Serawaj, pp. 51–52, No. 29). See also, in the present collection, the comparison to a hen on its nest (Nos. 375a, 375b) and the comparison of a frying pan to a magpie (Nos. 1302 through 1308). This last riddle, which is still very popular in American tradition, is rarely recognized as a comparison to a bird. For comparisons to persons note the Portuguese riddle of a man sitting on three horses (Parsons, *Cape Verde*, 131) and, in the present collection, the equating of a pot to a three-legged person (No. 68). See, finally, the comparison to a bull (No. 395) and the description of the three stones on which the pot rests (Nos. 1110, 1182).

372. Swedish: Dybeck, *Runa*, 1850, p. 34, No. 6 (Who goes to church on his back?—Boat). Ström, p. 212, "Molner," 3. Spanish: Rodríguez Marín, 801. Argentinian: Lehmann-Nitsche, 152 (battleship). Lithuanian: Jurgelionis, 659 (It has wings but does not fly, there are feet but it cannot be caught). Russian: Sadovnikov, 1511 (There are neither arms nor legs, neither eyes nor ears, yet it bears the brave young man along the steep shore), 1512 (With neither legs nor arms, it crawls on its belly), 1524. Turkish: Kúnos, 125 (*Hi daily, daily*, the lark is the camp of the rose. I saw a bird among birds, its feet [i.e., sails or oars] are on its head). Yakut: Priklonskii, 112 (It lifts without a back, it runs without legs). See also the riddle cited in the headnote to No. 227, n. 9, in the present collection.

374. Mordvin: Paasonen, 53 = Ahlqvist, p. 40, No. 22 (A red cock runs along a stick); Paasonen, 122 (A red cock runs from house to house). Votyak: Wichmann, *Votyak*, 434 (Red chicks run back and forth along a white pole). Cheremiss: Wichmann, *Cheremiss*, 3. Modern Greek: Stathes, p. 344, No. 79 (A rooster without trousers with a red moustache runs all over woods and mountains, and when he finds water, he perishes); Polites, *Neohellenika Analekta*, I, 222, No. 167 (A little red bird, wherever it rolls, grass will never grow again), which contains the theme discussed in the note to No. 396 in the present collection. Indian, Baiga: Elwin, p. 475, No. 107 (A red crane stands in the valley. Suddenly, it climbs the hill with a great crackling noise). Hindustani: Elwin and Hivale, p. 72, No. 68 (The crane climbs up the mountain and feeds on the grass without a tongue. It dies when it drinks water).

This comparison appears in the German proverbial phrase "den roten Hahn aufs Dach setzen," which is discussed in F. Seiler, *Deutsche Sprichwörterkunde* (Munich, 1922), p. 245; W. Borchardt and G. Wüstmann, *Die sprichwörtlichen Redensarten der deutschen Sprache* (5th ed.; Leipzig, 1925), p. 173; *Deutsches Wörterbuch*, s.v. "Hahn." Richard Jente has generously given me these references and adds that the oldest instance known to him is Hans Sachs, *Werke* (ed. A. von Keller and E. Goetze), IX (Bibliothek des literarischen Vereins [Tübingen, 1895], CXXV), 55. See also, in the present collection, the comparisons of smoke or a spark to a flying bird (headnote to Nos. 365–366, § 2). For descriptions of fire as something locked in a box or house see Nos. 112, 721. For comparisons to an animal see Nos. 399a through 399c, the note to Nos. 399a through 399c, and the headnote to Nos. 399–400.

375a, 375b. German: Frischbier, *Menschenwelt*, p. 252, No. 120. Swedish: Ström, p. 146, "Grytan," 3. Russian: Sadovnikov, 347 (A black hen sits on red eggs), 354 through 354c, 359. Finnish: Henssen, 96. Zyrian: Wichmann, *Zyrian*, 10, 69, 128 (A basket full of red spoons.—Coals in the stove).

The comparison of a pot on a fire to a hen sitting on coals does not seem to be closely connected with the comparison of fire to a cock on a stick, in No. 374 of the present collection. For riddles describing fire and a pot see Nos. 871 through 876, the headnote to Nos. 871–877, the notes to Nos. 872 and 876, and the note to Nos. 873a, 873b.

A picturesque reversal of this pattern appears in a Kashmiri riddle for a hen sitting on eggs: "A pot full of rice under a nettle" (Knowles, 139).

376. Comparisons of a mill to a bird are very rare, for there are few similarities upon which even the most ingenious riddler can seize. A windmill does not seem to have been considered. For comparisons to a handmill, see the Russian "A snipe sits on the swamp. He does not reap, he does not thrash, but only pounds money for grain" (Arkhangel'skii, p. 78), which admits too many suggestions of the answer into the text; also, the Serbian "A sparrow is sitting, its tears are falling of themselves, [it says:] 'I have eaten the whole world, and yet I have not had enough'" (Novaković, p. 134, No. 8).

Typical riddles for a mill describe it as an insatiable creature (see, in the present collection, the note to No. 237, and compare No. 239), a squealing or roaring animal (No. 387 and the corresponding note and headnote), animals fighting (see the headnote to No. 397, nn. 2-9), an insatiable person (No. 777, the note to No. 777, and the headnote to Nos. 776–777), and a thing, as in the Zyrian "A small, small porridge pot never becomes full" (Wichmann, *Zyrian*, 80).

377. Armenian: Zelinski, p. 58, No. 19 (A whole drove of horses grazing in the meadow. When the time comes, their noses will break open.—Cotton bolls).

The sudden explosions occasioned by the bursting of the sheath of the bamboo resemble the sounds of an insect cracking its chrysalis. Chinese poets have likened it to the roar of thunder and the whiplike crackle of lightning; see W. C. White, *An Album of Chinese Bamboos* (Toronto, 1939), p. 6. Ou-yang Hsiu (A.D. 1007–1072) wrote of the bursting bamboo:

> As startling thunder cracks a maddening whip,
> So their misty sheaths unfold from patterned stem.
>
> —White, p. 11

See also Indonesian, Tabaru: Fortgens, 52. Quite different is the African conception of popping castor beans in the Kiniramba "You go to the back of the house and find your grandmother cutting firewood" (F. Johnson, 18), or of the bursting pods of *Pentaclethra macrophylla*, Benth., in the Pangwe "The father's women clap their hands in the swamp near the beach" (Tessmann, 67), or of cotton in the Hausa "I went into the country, and the country laughed at me" (Fletcher, 19). See also No. 691 in the present collection.

378. The Kundu call a cock an insatiable animal: "I rose early in the morning and ate until evening, yet I was not satiated" (Schönhärl, 34).

379 through 380. French: Parsons, *Antilles*, III, 368, Trinidad, 58, and p. 390, Dominica, 12. Spanish, Argentinian: Lehmann-Nitsche, 252 (I have a cock with six beaks, with a comb, and when it crows, everybody is frightened). Italian: Tammi, 33. Russian: Sadovnikov, 1412 (There flies the eagle, carrying fire in its teeth. Across its tail is man's death), 1413 (A black rooster wants to bellow). Turkish: Katanov in Radlov, IX, 97, No. 834 (There is a bird that calls out and throws itself on guarded meat.—Feathered arrow). Cherekessian: Tambiev, p. 56, No. 32 (A short rooster bellows in the wood.—Pistol).

For comparisons of a gun to a donkey see, in the present collection, No. 436, and to a dog, see Nos. 438 through 440.

381a through 382. Modern Greek: Sakellarios, p. 294, No. 10 (My reddish piggy, lying in the field, tied to a chain). African, Togo: Schönhärl, 170 (The pig on the other side of the lagoon gets seven young.—Okra [*Hibiscus esculenta*]). Tschuana: Kuhn, *Tschuana*, 19 (It crept hither and thither and gave birth behind there). Indian, Hindi: Kavyopadhyaya, 44 (The bullock grows up and the cow runs away). Indonesian, Alfoer: Wilken, 22 (A pig has young, but is not bad-tempered. However, its young, which surround it, bite sharply.—Alang-alang, a grass that pricks when young).

Compare the Khāṛiā cocoon riddle, "In a deep forest a dwarfish calf is tethered to a peg" (Roy and Roy, II, 448, No. 1). For comparisons of a vine to a rope see Nos. 1203a through 1203c and 1205 in the present collection. See also the comparisons of plants to animals in Nos. 412a through 412c and in No. 419, and the references cited in the note to Nos. 412a through 412c and in the headnote to Nos. 412–413, § 2.

384. The import of the riddle is obscure.

385. For the comparison of rice cooking in a pot to a company of bathers see Nos. 489a, 1032a, 1032b. In Nos. 489b through 490, the rice or peas, usually as a flock of sheep, go to a watering place and drink the pond or river dry.

386. This English riddle may be derived from the medieval "Porcus per taurum sequitur vestigia ferri" (M[one], *Anzeiger*, VIII [1839], 316, No. 75), which is the source of many of the following. See German: M[one], *Anzeiger*, VII (1838), col. 261, No. 179; Frischbier, *Menschenwelt*, p. 249, No. 78. Danish: Feilberg, *Ordbog*, III, 68, s.v. "risp." Norwegian: Landstad, p. 808, No. 17; Stafset, 59; Brox, *Ytre Senja*, 121. Swedish: Dybeck, *Runa*, 1849, p. 49, No. 21; Ericsson, *Södermanland*, (1879), 92, No. 62; and IV (1883), 69, No. 176; Sandén, *Norra Vadsbo*, 146; Ström, p. 235, "Skomakeren," 1; Olsson, *Västergötland*, p. 127, No. 26. Latin: M[one], *Anzeiger*, VII (1838), col. 48, No. 125; Buchler, *Gnomologia*, 3d ed. (1614), p. 445. Lithuanian: Jurgelionis, 517. Lettish: Bielenstein, 14, 15. Czech: Hanika-Otto, note to her No. 324 (An iron pig, a tail of hemp), which belongs with the riddles discussed in the note to No. 437 of this collection. Russian: Sadovnikov, 603 (A little piggie runs, its little back is of iron, its little tail is of flax), 657. Don Calmuck: Kotvich, 253 (The iron pig has a tail made of string).

Versions which show little or no resemblance to the medieval Latin text are Serbian: Novaković, p. 68, No. 8 (It roots with its snout and pulls the roots with its backside). Modern Greek: Stathes, p. 339, No. 43 (I have a little pig, I tie its rump and pull its nose). African, Bakongo: Denis, 46 (The pig which Papa has bought, if one has tied it by the neck [the point of the needle], it does not go; if one has tied it by the tail [the eye of the needle], then it goes). This last conception is similar to that of No. 426 in the present collection and also resembles a shoe riddle (see the examples cited in the headnote to No. 1689).

Comparisons to animals other than a pig are numerous; see a review of them in the headnotes to Nos. 203 and 205–207. Although the rooting of a pig might suggest sewing, the comparison, except for derivatives of the medieval Latin text, are rather rare.

387. The animals chosen as comparisons to a mill vary somewhat. Swedish: Ericsson, *Södermanland*, II (1881), 94, No. 85 (hog); Ström, p. 384, "Sysselsättningar," 50 (hog). Polish: Kopernicki, 10 (hogs). Russian: Sadovnikov, 1072 (It knocks, it rattles, there run a hundred horses, they will eat all the grain in the vicinity); 1075 (horse, dog, bear), 1091 (bull), 1092 (horses), 1093 (horse), 1094 (bear), 1111 (horse, bear). Finnish: Aarne and Krohn, 258 = Henssen, 51 (The pig squealed under the bridge, I held it by the tail, I tweaked it by the tail.—Handmill). Mordvin: Paasonen, 136 (bear), 362 (bear). Cheremiss: Porkka, 92 (cow). Hungarian: Kriza, p. 342, No. 27 (The bear walks along, his lever [?] purrs); *Magyar Nyelvör*, V (1876), 268 (bear); and XXXI (1902), 533, No. 38 (bear). Modern Greek: Polites, *Neohellenika Analekta*, I, 248, No. 315 (Our bad sow, our greedy one, ate all the world and her hunger is not yet satisfied), which has the alternative answer, "Hades" (see the note to No. 483 in the present collection). Armenian: Glushakov, p. 30, No. 46 (A boar growls and throws out dust). Persian: Phillott, 2 (A strange thing I saw in this world: it roared and wailed and circled round). Filipino: Starr, *Philippines*, 375 (howling monkey), 393 (I have a large pig. During the night he grunts.—Sugarmill).

388. The usual form of this riddle is a comparison to a man; see Nos. 805a through 805w.

389a. Portuguese: Parsons, *Cape Verde*, 235 (I am there, and I am here).
The first part of this riddle usually has the answer "breath"; see Nos. 1578a through 1578c of the present collection. The import of the second part is not clear; compare No. 487, in which clouds are said to resemble sheep. For the formula contrasting "here" and "there" see also the Serbian belt riddle, "I went here, I went there, we met at the buckle field" (Novaković, p. xviii, No. 8).

390. For comment on the theme of many teeth and no mouth, see the headnote to Nos. 18–21.

391. See Portuguese: Parsons, *Cape Verde*, 270 (My heifer from fifteen to sixteen, I tie her on the horn of praise to God.—Moon), which is not completely intelligible. Czech: Hanika-Otto, p. 118, No. 1 (A stag leaps over the sea and does not even wet its feet), which includes a trait discussed in the headnote to Nos. 431–432 of the present collection. Russian: Sadovnikov, 1816 (A brown cow looks through the crossbar.—Sun), 1816a (A white ox looks in the gate). Serbian: Novaković, p. 39, Nos. 1 (A dark ox is lying down, a white ox comes and chases it away), 2 through 6, 7 (Our white ox and our brown ox gore each other morning and evening. In the morning the white ox wins; in the evening the brown, and they lie in the same place, yet their place cannot be recognized). Crimean Tatar: Filonenko, 105 (In front of a house a white heifer boasts of her beauty). African, Shilluk: Westermann, p. 241, No. 11 (The black-white cow makes the earth white.—Moon).

The Bengali "A piebald cow with broken horns. She is neither to be had in the market nor found in the country" (Mitra, *Chittagong*, pp. 657–658, No. 1) describes the sky speckled with clouds that give down rain.

For the comparisons of celestial objects to animals see, in the present collection, Nos. 392a, 392b, 405, 431, 496a, 496b, and the headnote to Nos. 412–413, § 9.

392a, 392b. The formula "fish, flesh, feather, or bone" and its variations—and also the rhyme with "bone"—appear again in an egg riddle; see Nos. 1237a through 1237h and the note to No. 24d.

393a, 393b. The leather horns are the hare's ears.

394. The answer is not precisely correct, for building up the wall should refer to mending the fabric rather than to threading the needle; see No. 424. The notion of comparing sewing to making a fence is rather rare, but see the Tatar awl riddle, "A short man weaves a fence" (Kalashev and Ioakimov, p. 49, No. 9).

For other comparisons of a needle to a bull or cow, see the Bulgarian "A little gray bull is pulling the rope" (Gubov, 130) and the Yakut "They say that a gray ox pulls its nose strap behind it" (Piekarski, 380) and "A brown bull drags a rope" (Priklonskii, 117). For parallels describing a needle as an animal with a hempen tail see, in the present collection, the notes to No. 386 and 437 and the comment in the headnote to No. 437.

395. Compare the Argentinian "Three mules carrying one load.—Pot" (Lehmann-Nitsche, 234) and the Nandi "I moved my abode and left three goats behind; when I returned, there were still three goats.—The firestones" (Hollis, *Nandi*, p. 143, 43). The three ridges or stones on which the pot rests while over the fire appear also in No. 371 of the present collection.

396. The explanation makes it clear that the word "coal" signifies "charcoal," but the full import of the comparison remains obscure. It has a resemblance to the eastern European descriptions of the spot where a fire has burned or the yurt of a nomadic tribe has stood. See the Svanian "Where the red ox has rolled, nothing comes up" (J. Nizheradze, pp. 68–69, No. 26); the Turcoman "On the earth where a red cow has grazed, grass will not grow.—Forest fire" (Samojlvich, 28), which has shifted the answer slightly; the Estonian "An ox lies on the ground, the spot remains for seven years"

(Wiedemann, p. 265); the Georgian "Where the red ox has grazed, no grass will grow" (Blechsteiner, p. 15, No. 31), which is virtually identical with the Abchaz "Where the reddish brown ox once sits down, no grass will ever grow" (Guliia, 20); the Ossete "I have an ox, and where he lies down, there grass never grows again" (Schiefner, 3); and the Mongolian "On the ground where a three-year-old cow has lain there grows no grass for three years" (Bazarov, 84). The westernmost versions of this theme are the previously cited Estonian version and the Albanian "Where the red ox sits, there no grass comes" (Hahn, p. 161, No. 38).

Riddlers have conceived this idea in terms of other animals than an ox. See the Serbian "A log here, a log there, and in the middle lives a dragon, where the grass does not grow"; "There are two valleys, between them lies a dragon, where the dragon lies, there grows no grass"; and "Where our Red lives, there no grass ever grows" (Novaković, p. 15, Nos. 4 through 6). Turkish riddlers in Siberia say, "Where the red goat was lying, the grass does not grow for forty years" (Katanov in Radlov, IX, 241, No. 86) and "I have a red horse. Where it lies down, there grass will not grow" (Moshkov in Radlov, X, 265, No. 7, citing a Ukrainian parallel). The Bulgarians say, "The grass does not grow where the red dog lies" (Ikonomov, 10). The Calmucks say, "The footsteps of a three-year-old camel will not be erased for three years" (Kotvich, 50), which is identical with a Mongolian version (Mostaert, 181), or "The traces of a castrated camel will not be erased for ten years" (Kotvich, 51). Some animals are only rarely mentioned in this connection. The Turks say, "A yellow lion, where he lies grass doesn't grow" (Hamizade, 22). In Polites' Modern Greek parallel (quoted in the note to No. 374 of the present collection), the actor is a red bird. This conception is the basis of the saying that grass never grew again where Attila's horse had trod; see my note in the *Journal of American Folklore*, LVI (1943), 136–137. It has some similarity to the Turkish "The young crane flew away, but a hillock remained.—Place from which a yurt has been removed" (Katanov in Radlov, IX, 272, No. 171; see also his p. 258, No. 153).

Other comparisons of a fire and an ox are the Hungarian "A dark bull sticks his red tongue in and out.—Fire in the fireplace" (Kálmány, I, 162, No. 24) and the Turkish "A yellow ox lies down, a black ox gets up.—Fire and smoke" (Hamizade, 27).

397. Compare Basque: Vinson, 34 (The white mare in the brook). African, Kanuri: Lukas, p. 170, No. 17 (A white cow, as white as tin, lies on its back and chews over again its food). Polish: Siarkowski, 24 (A fat ox throws off manure from beneath him.—Grinding stone and grain).

398. Riddlers vary somewhat in their choice of the animal used as the means of comparison, and also in their selection of details. In the following list of parallels I have left undesignated those naming an ox or cow. See Norwegian: Bugge, *Telemarken*, 1 (horse); Brox, *Ytre Senja*, 186. Swedish: Geijer and Campbell, 82; Ström, p. 215, "Åskan," 3; Russwurm, *Eibo*, p. 132, § 316, No. 2 (horse). Portuguese: Parsons, *Cape Verde*, 259. Spanish, Argentinian: Lehmann-Nitsche, 245. Lithuanian: Jurgelionis, 100 (Far away a horse neighs, close by a bridle clinks); Schleicher, p. 195. Lettish: Bielenstein, 430. Kashub: Patock, *Strellin*, 5 (An ox bellows louder than a hundred mountains and a thousand lakes). The translation or the riddle itself is probably incorrect, as appears from the following Polish and Russian parallels. Polish: Gustawicz, 100 through 102; Saloni, *Łańcut*, 23 (The ox bellows. You can hear him beyond a hundred mountains and beyond a thousand); Kopernicki, 29 (An ox bellows over a hundred hills, but is heard over three hundred hills); Siarkowski, 91 (An ox bellows over a hundred hills, but can be heard over a million). Russian: Sichler, p. 756; Sadovnikov, 1945 (A colt has begun to neigh on Mount Zion; a mare has heard it in the Russian land), 1945a, 1946 (A gray colt neighs across a whole empire), 1947 (A bull has bellowed across a hundred villages, across a hundred streams), 1948 (A crow has cawed across a hundred towns, across a thousand lakes), 1949 (A duck gave a grunt that was felt the world over), 1950 (A monk has begun to roll down Mount Zion with fire-crackers on his head). Finnish: Lönnrot, 131 = Henssen, 236 (horse). Estonian: Wiedemann, p. 282 (horse); Dido, 21 (horse); Lönnrot, p. 179 (horse). Zyrian: Wichmann, *Zyrian*, 170 (A red cat runs along the fence). Turkish: Katanov in Radlov, IX, 93, No. 786 (The lion roared and sparkled). Calmuck: Kotvich, 182 (The dark gray foal began neighing; ninety-nine mares of this world began to foal.— Thunder and rain), 270 (When the roan prairie stallion neighed, the mares, about one billion head, appeared at once with their udders and began to foal), 271 (The castrated camel yawned, the end of the rope flashed.—Thunder and lightning). Turkish in Siberia: Katanov in Radlov, IX, 272, No. 167 (My blue bull is bellowing and is heard by the whole nation). Yakut: Popov, p. 283 (The stallion of the universe neighs, the bull of an important country bellows). Filipino: Starr, *Philippines*, 242.

The Nandi "A tree fell in Lumbwa and its branches reached Nandi.—A great noise" (Hollis, *Nandi*, p. 45, No. 52) is an interesting example of a comparison to a thing rather than to an animal.

The unintelligible Swahili "A lion has roared here, people heard it everywhere.— Crow" (Büttner, p. 201) is perhaps disordered, for Velten gives a Swahili thunder riddle as "When the lion roars, one hears it everywhere" (his No. 44).

399a through 399c. Except for these texts and the Welsh "A hideous red cow, running over the gorse" (Hull and Taylor, 73), the parallels are found in eastern Europe and India. See Serbian: Novaković, p. 15, No. 2 (A red cow stopped at the edge). Bulgarian: Chacharov, 83 (Here a valley, there a valley, in the middle a red ox. Whatever it finds, it licks). Zyrian and modern Greek riddlers compare smoke to a black bull and fire to a red bull; see Wichmann, *Zyrian*, 21, 180, 222, 267; Carnoy and Nicolaides, 15. Modern Greek: Polites, *Neohellenika Analekta*, I, 213, No. 143 (My little lamb eats wood and thrives, drinks water and dies), p. 230, No. 209 (At Argos in the meadow a red beast eats stones, eats wood, drinks water, and dies), p. 248, No. 313 (lamb); Sakellarios, p. 293, No. 9 (My goat, my sharp-nosed goat went far off and found grass to eat, found water and died). For parallels to the theme of drinking water and dying see the note to Nos. 235a through 235e. Indian, Bhil: Hedberg, p. 885 (The red cow is grazing, the black cow is overturning, and the black calf is going on sucking.—A forest fire); Kukka Mall, *Panjab Notes and Queries*, II (1884–1885), 34, No. 208 (The red cow that eats, drinks water, and dies). Uraon: Archer, p. 191, No. 185 (A brown bullock feeds on branches and dies when it drinks water). See also Nos. 235a through 235d and 776 in the present collection.

400a through 400c. For riddles describing a mill or saw in terms of other creatures than a cow or an ox, see Nos. 345, 376, and the headnote and note to No. 397. For comparisons turning on the idea of insatiability see the headnote to Nos. 236–239.

Riddles for a mill are readily applicable to an oven; see the Modern Greek "A black-faced cow eats oak" (Polites, *Neohellenika Analekta*, I, 212, No. 106). This refers to a sooty oven consuming oaken sticks.

401, 402. Danish: Kristensen, p. 60, §139, Nos. 199a through 199c. Hungarian: Kálmány, I, 158, No. 10 (Here it is used to help a horse bear a colt, it grows in the country, and it has iron on the nose.—Bellows). Arabic: Giacobetti, 533 (Its back [is] of wood, its belly of skin, its nose is plunged into the fire), which resembles greatly the pattern of Nos. 553a through 554 in the present collection. Indian, Kolarian: Wagner, 57 (Dead cows are sighing.—Bellows).

403. Norwegian: Landstad, p. 806, No. 5. French: *Les Adevineaux amoureux*, p. lxxx = Rolland, 204. Catalan: Milá y Fontanals, 1877, p. 8 = Pelay y Briz, 212. The

Welsh riddle for a gun, "A crooked suitable wood, the carpenter cut it, the smith completed it" (Hull and Taylor, 253) is probably to be interpreted as a modernization of this riddle.

404. (The answer is usually "saddle.") Danish: Kristensen, pp. 111–112, § 302, Nos. 478, 479; Feilberg, *Ordbog*, III, 139, s.v. "sadel." Norwegian: Brox, *Ytre Senja*, 50; Riksheim, 27 (cited by Brox). Swedish: Dybeck, *Runa*, 1848, p. 47, No. 62; and 1865–1873, p. 31, No. 38; Hyltén-Cavallius, *Värend*, 8; Waltman, *Lidmål*, 215; Geijer and Campbell, 18; Ström, p. 143, "Sadeln," and p. 144, "Selen." Arabic: Giacobetti, 458 (The forest says, "It is mine." The smith says, "It is mine." The cow, the sheep, the goat say, "It is mine"), which, as Giacobetti explains in a note, refers to the share of each in the saddle.

In the English riddle, the asker seems not to be familiar with the import of "Bull, bull, ox, ox"—words which are intelligible only by comparison with the preceding riddles.

405. Lithuanian: Jurgelionis, 82 (A horse with a white spot on its forehead looks over the gate). Russian: Sadovnikov, 1833a through 1833i, 1836 (From evening on, a gray stallion looks under the gate. At midnight the stallion runs across the roof). Mordvin: Ahlqvist, p. 40, No. 19 (A gray stallion looks over the gate). The meaning of the "gate," which one might compare to the "bar of Heaven" in Rossetti's "The Blessed Damozel," is obscure. A Yakut riddle for summer and winter, "They say that a stallion and a mare are standing, delousing each other" (Piekarski, 14), is apparently related to this riddle, but it also is not fully intelligible.

The Votyak use the same comparison to describe a cloud: "A gray stallion runs about the world" (Wichmann, *Votyak*, 211). A Czech riddle with the answer "moon" resembles a tale: "A farmer beat the horses, tore open a sack of peas, and lost a cheese made of goat's milk" (Hanika-Otto, p. 118, No. 2). This is not completely clear, but the peas must signify the stars (see the headnote to Nos. 1093–1095, nn. 9–11, 15, in the present collection) and the cheese, the moon (see the headnote to Nos. 1230–1234, nn. 9, 19–22).

For comparisons of the day and night to horses, see Aarne, *Rätselforsuchungen*, I, 146; for a comparison of stars to sheep see Nos. 484a through 484d in the present collection and G. Polívka, *Zeitschrift des Vereins für Volkskunde*, XXVI (1916), 321–322. For comparisons to animals that do not wet their feet in crossing water see the note to No. 431 of the present collection. A comparison of day and night to a ball of yarn that is both white and black is found in tales as well as riddles; see Polívka, as cited, pp. 317–318.

406. Perhaps a defective version of another fish riddle; see Nos. 1450a, 1450b.

407. The import of the riddle is obscure. The comparison of honey to offensive objects is rather frequent. See Dutch: Dykstra, I, 99. Compare the Low German "Achter min Vatters Hüschen då steit en klare Kabüschen [cottage], då schidden se in, då pissen se in, då döppen [dip] de riken se's Brod in" (DFS, 1906/38: A. Lorenzen, 1938, No. 2). The same spirit inspires the Italian bottle riddle: "Ho un cagnolino veramente bellino: gli alzo la coda, e gli bacio il dietro" (Pitrè, 257); see the punishments illustrated in *Jahrbuch für historische Volkskunde*, I (1925), Plate 13 (opposite p. 110).

408. The import of the riddle is obscure.

409. The mention of "horse" in the riddle and in the answer and the use of the word in two senses are not good enigmatic devices.

410. Although this sounds like a question belonging to the ballad "Our Goodman" (F. J. Child, *English and Scottish Popular Ballads* [Boston, 1885–1898], V, 88–95, No. 274), I have not found it in any version. The import of the riddle is entirely obscure.

411. The collector throws no light on this riddle, and I have found no parallel to elucidate it.

412a through 412c. (Root or tuber.) Russian: Sadovnikov, 770 (horse-radish), 772a through 773e (carrot). Finnish: Lönnrot, 892 = Henssen, 82 (beet). Mordvin: Paasonen, 23 (beet), 155 (carrot).

For comparisons of a root vegetable to a person with projecting hair, see the headnote to No. 544, § 4, in the present collection.

413. German: Frischbier, *Menschenwelt*, p. 251, No. 100. Norwegian: note to Qvigstad, 119. Swedish: Dybeck, *Runa*, 1848, p. 46, No. 52; and 1865-1873, p. 8, No. 5 (The ox within, the tail outside, the entrails far away in the wood); Hyltén-Cavallius, *Värend*, 46; Ström, p. 372, "Redskap" (The white horse stands in the room and sticks its tail through the roof); Sandén, *Norra Vadsbo*, 43 = Waltman, *Lidmål*, 227; Russwurm, *Eibo*, p. 134, § 316, No. 31; note to Qvigstad, 119. French: Baissac, *Mauritius*, pp. 400, 422; Parsons, *Antilles*, III, 399, Guadaloupe, 22 (lamp, light). Portuguese: Parsons, *Cape Verde*, 152 (sheep). Finnish: Henssen, 85. Estonian: Wiedemann, pp. 283, 288. Lappish: Qvigstad, 42, 119. Votyak: Buch, 45 (cow); Wichmann, *Votyak*, 369, 426. African, Sierra Leone: Cronise and Ward, p. 193. Songaï: Hamouda, p. 280, No. 26 (I have put my horse in the last of three adjoining and connected rooms. Its tail was projecting in spite of that.—Smoke).

For comparisons to a man see the headnote to No. 544, § 9, in the present collection.

414a. The scribe has copied the riddle with some inaccuracies, but these do not seem so confusing that I should endeavor to set them right. The parallels illustrate the comparison of a ship to a horse, but vary considerably in details and do not resemble closely the English riddle. See Spanish, Cuban: Massip, 136 (Air and water sustain me; I have food and do not eat). Dominican Rep.: Andrade, 54 (A little horse without entrails or stomach, goes all the way to Porto Rico and never gets tired). Porto Rican: Mason, 542. Russian: Sichler, p. 756 (In the middle of the mountains [i.e., waves] runs a black horse covered with a carpet, decorated with nails); Sadovnikov, 1525, 1526.

For comparisons of a ship to an animal that neither eats nor drinks although plenty of food is available, see Indian, Parsee: Munshi, p. 418. Gujerati: Mehta, p. 119, No. 9.

415a, 415b. See No. 240 and the note to No. 240, in which the animal is not identified.

415b. Since the meaning of "cattle" is vague, I have considered this to be a variant of riddle No. 415a and have not given it a separate number.

416. This may have been suggested by the riddle for a cowbell, Nos. 247a through 247c and 252a, 252b.

417. The openings of a pair of scissors through which the fingers are thrust are occasionally called "eyes"; see No. 228.

418. Latin: Hadrian Junius, 26 = Eugène Rolland, *Faune populaire*, XII (Paris, n.d. [1909]), 48 (quaqua incedo, tractu illino mucum). French: Rolland, 77 (There is a thing that loses its fat at every step); Lespy, *Béarn*, 18 (Who leaves a trace of mucus at every spot it passes?); Baissac, *Mauritius*, p. 409. Italian: Pitrè, 415a. Albanian: Hahn, p. 162, No. 60 (It is not an ox and has horns; it is not a donkey and bears a saddle; wherever it passes, it leaves silver), and p. 163, No. 78. Arabic: Ruoff, p. 46, No. 29 (*Ha, ha u ha*, oh you who long for it, her chain of pearls, and it runs after her), which the translator does not make completely intelligible. Modern Greek: Carnoy and Nicolaides, 27. African, Togo: Schönhärl, 154 (All the animals went over the stone, yet they left no tracks. Banidzē also went over it and did leave tracks). Taveṭa: Hollis, *Taveta*, p. 209, No. 49 (When my lamb walks, he pours fat on the road). Dschagga: Raum, 15 (My father feeds his ram. When he goes away, it leaves its fat on the way).

419. Compare Nos. 381a through 382, 1203a through 1204.

420a through 420c, 420e. (An unusual landscape.) Danish: Kristensen, p. 130,

§ 370, Nos. 589c, 589d (steel horse, brass street). The street is the thimble. Swedish: Ericsson, *Södermanland*, I (1879), 91, No. 55 (silver horse, silver mountain). Modern Greek: Carnoy and Nicolaides, 10 (I have been running on the hill, and I have attached the halter to the ancon).

420b. An alternative explanation, which I should prefer, is: the "horse" is the needle; the "bridge," the finger; and the "whip," the thread.

420d. Note the similarity to the grassquit riddle. See No. 433 and the corresponding note.

421. Breton: Sauvé, 94. Afrikaans: Groenewald, p. 79. German: Wossidlo, 265 (iron horse, flaxen tail), which is discussed more fully in the note to No. 437 of the present collection. Spanish, Argentinian: Lehmann-Nitsche, 230 (Moorish mare with reins on its tail). This allusion to reins appears also in Nos. 425, 426 of the present collection. Dominican Rep.: Andrade, 10. Porto Rican: Mason, 26. Cheremiss: Wichmann, *Cheremiss*, 77, 204. African, SeSuto: Norton and Velaphe, 50 (Like the gray horse running smartly with a white tail), 51 (My horse with one eye). Tschuana: Kuhn, *Tschuana*, 48 (I have a horse with long legs). Compare the Buryat "A goat drags its tail after it" (Gombojew, 39).

422, 423. Breton: Sauvé, 94. French: Dottin, *Bas-Maine*, 7. Swedish: Ström, p. 375, "Kombinationsgåtor," 20.

For descriptions of a needle and thread as an animal losing its tail or intestines, see the headnotes to Nos. 203, 205–207. For references to a creature with a flaxen tail see the note to No. 437.

424. (Stops a gap.) German: Hanika-Otto, 328 (It creeps through the hedge and closes all holes). Modern Greek: Polites, *Neohellenika Analekta*, I, 202, No. 48 (You are very long and have a tail and close up the secret gaps).

425. See the Arabic "It is bridled at its tail and free at its head.—Needle" (Bauer, p. 223, No. 12), and compare the Bakongo parallel in the note to No. 386 of the present collection.

426. Portuguese: Parsons, *Cape Verde*, 168a (I have my male, a fast runner. When he reaches a step, unless I push him in the backsides, he will not go up). The word "male" is a misprint for "mule." Polish: Gustawicz, 108 (A peasant rode the market and bought himself a tailless horse. When he came home, he attached a tail to the horse), 109, 110.

427a, 427b. French: Parsons, *Antilles*, III, 383, Martinique, 45, p. 393, Dominica, 47, and p. 401, Guadaloupe, 37. Portuguese: Parsons, *Cape Verde*, 185a (I saddle my horse, I keep from mounting on his back, I mount on his tail), 185b, 185c (Saddle a horse and mount on his tail).

428. Russian: Bardin, p. 243, No. 12 (Uncle Pahom sits mounted on a horse; he reads a book, and yet he is unable to read).

431. Irish: Christiansen, 4. Scotch Gaelic: Nicolson, p. 59. Czech: Hanika-Otto, p. 118, No. 1. Serbian: Novaković, p. 130, Nos. 1 (The donkey jumped across the sea and never wet its hoofs.—Moon), 2 (horse), 3, 4 (My horse tramped over the whole field and never touched the ground). Mordvin: Paasonen, 211 (A black-gray horse looks along the crossbeam of the gate.—Moon). Modern Greek: Sakellarios, p. 291, Nos. 11 (My fire-red mule crossed seven seas and did not wet her body), and 6 (My small goat dressed in red wears a stone bell; she crossed seven seas and did not get wet).

Although this might be considered to be a more vividly conceived version of the familiar riddle, "What goes through water and is not wet?" (see the headnote to Nos. 165–173, §§ 1–2, of the present collection), I do not feel sure that the two riddles are closely related. The notion of light passing through water and remaining unchanged is very old and seems to have existed independently of the scene mentioning an animal.

432. Swedish: Ström, p. 96, "Oxen, kon, kalven," 13. French: Rolland, 46 (It has eight feet, goes through water, and is not wet.—Pregnant cow). Hungarian: *Magazin für die Litteratur des Auslands*, 1856, p. 364. See also, in the present collection, Nos. 56a through 57, 711, 961, and the note to Nos. 56a, 56b.

433. African, Togo: Schönhärl, 137 (There is a tree on which no one but an ant can climb —Rushes). Compare the same theme in Nos. 420d, 1048, 1709 of the present collection.

434. The two next following and many other riddles show that the phrase "My father has . . ." is a conventional introduction in West Indian riddling. A horse and a chair have one quality in common: one sits on both of them.

436. Spanish, Argentinian: Lehmann-Nitsche, 231. Lithuanian: Jurgelionis, 645 (A bay mare neighed at the end of the field). Calmuck: Kotvich, 222 (A camel makes a noise on the other side of the Don; dust rises at a given point), 223 (The gray ox stays motionless; the brindled ox spreads his legs; the ox with the docked tail ran out.—Barrel, trigger, bullet). The brindled ox should be the rest on which the gun stands. Turkish: Katanov in Radlov, IX, 101, No. 875 (A castrated camel cried, *Khayt!* His lasso cried, *Khyzash!*—Gun and bullets), p. 285, No. 199 (It goes with a knock and calls like a stag and a *moral* [another kind of stag]). Abyssinian: Littmann, *Tigriña*, 53 (Its bellowing is the bellowing of a lion; its being carried about is the carrying about of a dead body). Sinhalese: Perera, p. 55 (What is it that cries on the bank but drops its dung on the other [bank]?). Compare, in the present collection, Nos. 379a through 380, in which the gun is a cock, and Nos. 438 through 440, in which it is a dog.

437. This badly confused riddle is intelligible in the light of the parallels cited below. For additional references to a dog representing a needle, see Serbian: Novaković, p. 68, No. 6 (A black bitch drags a white gut behind it). Hungarian: *Magyar Nyelvör*, II (1873), 467 (A clumsy thing that drives a tiny iron fork, and a white greyhound runs after it), which is an unusual comparison of the thread, and not the needle, to a dog. Cherekessian: Tambiev, p. 58, No. 52 (A little gray dog drags its tail). Astrakhan Calmuck: Kotvich, 96 (A gray wolf runs, dragging a blanket). Arabic: Giacobetti, 328 (A little dog dragging its entrails).

The notion of an animal with a flaxen tail is often applied to a needle and thread. The animal is usually a horse—exceptions are noted in the following list. Irish: O Dalaigh, 91 (An iron sheep with a woolen tail), 214; De Bhaldraithe, 47 (A little iron wether and a tail of wood in front). Dutch: Sinninghe, p. 22, No. 23. Flemish: Joos, 191; *Ons Volksleven*, I (1889), 8, No. 13. German: Wossidlo, 265, 268; Frischbier, *Menschenwelt*, p. 249, No. 78 (mule); Renk, *Tyrol*, 140 = Hanika-Otto, 324a; Hanika-Otto, 324b (bird), 324d. Danish: Kristensen, p. 130, § 370, Nos. 589c, 589d. Norwegian: Stafset, 185. Swedish: Russwurm, *Eibo*, p. 134, § 316, No. 26 (Iron mouse with woolen tail). Portuguese: Braga, 1; Parsons, *Cape Verde*, 169 (gray mule, white tail) and her Nos. 168, 173, 175. Rumanian: Gorovei, 15. Lithuanian: Jurgelionis, 515 (An iron horse with a hempen tail), 516 (An iron horse with a silver tail), which may refer to the silver thimble, and 518; Schleicher, p. 204. Lettish: Bielenstein, 13. Czech: Hanika-Otto, note to her No. 324; Feifalik, 74 (iron bird). White Russian: Jurkevich, p. 293 (The wolf is of iron, but its tail is of hemp). Russian: Sadovnikov, 601 through 606. Finnish: Henssen, 84. Mordvin: Paasonen, 193. Cheremiss: Genetz, 8 (ox); Wichmann, *Cheremiss*, 77 (stallion). Votyak: Buch, 24 (steer). Turkish: Hamizade, 252 (I am of iron, my tail is of hemp). Mongolian: Kotvich, 96 (A gray wolf runs dragging a blanket). Buryat: Gombojew, 39.

438. (Heard or bites, often at a distance.) Welsh: Hull and Taylor, 71. Lettish: Bielenstein, 893. Serbian: Novaković, p. 184, No. 2 (Lajka barks in the valley; it is heard far off in the forest). Since the Serbian word for "bark" is *lajati*, the dog's name involves a play on words. Turkish: Kowalski, *North Bulgaria*, 40 (His passageway is narrow, his dog bites). African, Evhe: F. Müller, p. 157, No. 17 (A man weeps at Mono River, they hear it at home). Indian, Baluchi: M. Longworth Dames, *Panjab Notes and Queries*, II (1885), 70, No. 483, § 4 (When the cow lows, the calf will run). The modern Greeks compare a gun to a dragon bellowing in a hollow tube or tree; see Dieterich, *Rätseldichtung*, pp. 98–99.

See also, in the present collection, Nos. 379a through 380 (comparisons to a cock) and No. 436 and the note and headnote to No. 436 (comparisons to a donkey, camel, ox, or stag).

439a through 439c. (Sparks from mouth.) Finnish: Lönnrot, 112 = Henssen, 251 (Hali barks from his barrel, sparks fly from his mouth). Russian: Sadovnikov, 1407 (It breathes fire, it puffs flame).

442. Flemish: Joos, 17 (Far above the fallow fields I heard a little horse snort; there is neither man nor woman who can bridle the little horse).

For comparisons of thunder to the bellowing of a cow or an ox, see, in the present collection, No. 398 and the note and headnote to No. 398. Thunder and lightning are occasionally compared to things. The Russians call it a bell; see Sadovnikov, 1020. For such a comparison as the Turkish "From here I stabbed with the sword, its point came out in Aleppo.—Lightning" (Kowalski, *Asia Minor*, 47), see the headnote to No. 398, nn. 6–7, of the present collection.

452. Milk is set in water to cool.

453a through 453f. Breton: Sébillot, *Devinettes*, 58. German: Wossidlo, 337a; August Brunk, "Volksrätsel aus Osnabrück und Umgegend," *Zeitschrift des Vereins für Volkskunde*, XVII (1907), 302, No. 44d; Frischbier, *Menschenwelt*, p. 245, Nos. 36, 38, and p. 250, No. 95. Danish: Kristensen, p. 136, § 393, No. 627. Norwegian: Stafset, 6. French: Rolland, 136; Bladé, *Armagnac*, 222; Lespy, *Béarn*, 12; Roque-Ferrier, *Languedoc*, p. 337; Fesquet, p. 177. Portuguese: Pires, *Archivio*, III (1884), 120, No. 53. Catalan: Pelay y Briz, 147, 248. Spanish: Demófilo, 1058, and p. 367, No. 6; Rodríguez Marín, 639. Argentinian: Lehmann-Nitsche, 9, 10. Chilean: Flores, 790. New Mexican: Espinosa, 135. Italian: Pitrè, 726b; Rondini, *Archivio*, VIII (1889), 186, No. 68. Rumanian: Gorovei, 1282. Lithuanian: Jurgelionis, 253; Schleicher, p. 208. Modern Greek: Dieterich, *Rätseldichtung*, p. 96.

457. German: Wossidlo, 280, 454. The English riddler has borrowed the last element from such texts as Nos. 187a through 189 of the present collection.

458. Compare No. 250.

CHAPTER III

COMPARISONS TO SEVERAL ANIMALS

Nos. 459–512

459. Flemish: Joos, 197, 199, 200. German: Wossidlo, 456; Hanika-Otto, 400. Swiss: Rochholz, 491, 563. Danish: Kristensen, p. 63, §149, Nos. 221a, 221b. Swedish: Ström, p. 400, "Kvicka svar," 6. Catalan: Pelay y Briz, 147. In Spanish, *ganado* (herd) is a colloquial term for lice, and consequently cattle are often mentioned in Spanish parallels (exceptions are indicated): Demófilo, 226, 789, and p. 378, No. 7 (work horses), and p. 291, No. 47 (beasts). Argentinian: Lehmann-Nitsche, 221, 222. Chilean: Flores, 125 (rabbits), 581 (I was begotten in the woods, I was dressed in green, and now I am met when herding cattle in the woods), which contains elements characteristic of the riddles discussed in the headnote to Nos. 1058–1062 of the present collection. Dominican Rep.: Andrade, 247. Porto Rican: Mason, 444. Rumanian: Gorovei, 1395 through 1399. Bulgarian: Ikonomov, 27 (A hog comes from the forest driving swine before it). African, Kxatla: Schapera, 27 (Tell me: a black bull which is in a black thicket). Arabic: Ruoff, p. 28, No. 44; Giacobetti, 344 (My grandmother in wooden shoes brings back the goats of the forest). Indonesian, Sangir: Adriani, p. 446, No. 380. Alfoer: Wilken, 1 (forest full of apes).

The version "It is no larger than a mule's hoof and drives a hundred beasts from the pasture" (German: Butsch, 155 [as big as a fist]. French: *Les Adeuineaux amoureux*, p. lxxii = Rolland, 191. Catalan: Pelay y Briz, 100) is a comparison to a thing and not to an animal. It seems to have been popular at the time of the Renaissance, but is now scarcely known.

For the contrast of the living and dead, see Gypsy: Wlislocki, 8, and the headnote to Nos. 828–836 in the present collection. For other comparisons of lice to animals, see Nos. 474, 488, and the headnote to Nos. 1042–1044. A classification of riddles comparing the hair of the head to grass or trees, subdivided according to the omission or the inclusion of animals, hunted or merely grazing, is given in the note to Nos. 1042, 1043.

460a. The phrase "in the woods" belongs in the riddle and not in the answer. For parallels see Welsh: Hull and Taylor, 271. Irish: Christiansen, 60. Breton: Sauvé, 35; F. M. Luzel, *Mélusine*, I (1878), col. 465 (in a tale). Frisian: Dykstra, *Snypsnaren*, pp. 102–103 (A hunter went hunting with ten swift dogs. Each had a horn plate in front so that it could not bark. All that the hunter caught, he killed, and what he did not catch, he carried with him). Flemish: Boekenoogen, p. 45; *Volkskunde*, I (1888), 206, No. 17; and II (1889), 36; Joos, 1st ed., No. 318, and 2d ed., No. 597. German: Wossidlo, 450, 990, and compare his 992; Eckart, 720; Gilhoff, 255; Renk, *Tyrol*, p. 147, No. 1; Schmidt, *Danzig*, 22; Hanika-Otto, 649. Swiss: Rochholz, 508; Zahler, *Münchenbuchsee*, 225. Icelandic: Árnason, 95 (Some boys went hunting. They threw away what they caught and carried home what they didn't catch). Danish: Kristensen, p. 177, §10, "Utøjet." Norwegian: Stafset, 98; Bergh, *Valdres*, 8. Latin: Ohl, Symphosius, 30; Daly and Suchier, p. 144, No. 95; Huldreich Therander (Johann Sommer), 414 (cited by Tupper, *Holme Riddles*, 12); O. Schreger, *Studiosus jovialis* (2d ed.; Munich, 1751), cited by Rochholz, p. 359 (Quod captum est, periit; sed quae non cepimus, adsunt); Tupper, *Holme Riddles*, note to No. 12, cites many texts and the manuscript version in *Sloane 955*, fol. 1. The distich "In densis silvis venor cum quinque catellis; / Quod capio, perdo, quod fugit, hoc habeo" was once widely known; see S. M. Prem, *Anzeiger für deutsches Altertum*, XV (1889), 143 (A.D. 1300–1350); Reusner, ed. 1599, pp. 10–11 = *ibid.*, ed. 1602, p. 9

= *Carmina proverb. loci communes* (1570), p. 3, as cited in Eugène Rolland, *Faune populaire*, XII (Paris, n.d. [1909]), 171. Walloon: Colson, *Wallonia*, IV, 63, No. 70; Colson, *Devinettes*, 5. French: Alexandre Sylvain (A. van den Bussche), *Cinquante Ænigmes françoises* (1582), 24 (a translation of "In densis silvis . . ."); Rolland, 80; Cénac-Moncaut, *Littérature populaire de la Gascogne* (Paris, 1868), p. 93; E. Cosquin, *Contes populaires de Lorraine* (Paris, [1887]), II, 126–127. Spanish: Demófilo, 843; Rodríguez Marín, p. 211, Nos. 439, 440, and p. 340, n. 74. Argentinian: Lehmann-Nitsche, 858. Finnish: Lönnrot, 884 = Henssen, 232. Lappish: Qvigstad, 102. Surinam: Herskovits, p. 449, Nos. 89, 89a. African, Tschuana: Kuhn, *Tschuana*, 50.

460b. The story is much the same as that of "Clever Gretel"; see Jan de Vries, *Das Märchen von den klugen Rätsellösern*, FF Communications, LXXIII (Helsinki, 1928).

461a through 461d. Welsh: Hull and Taylor, 188, 189. Frisian: Carstensen, p. 327, No. 30. Flemish and Dutch: M[one], *Anzeiger*, VII (1838), cols. 371–372, No. 292; Schrijnen, II, 112, No. 45; *Ons Volksleven*, I (1889), 80, No. 53; and II (1890), 104, No. 5; *Volkskunde*, II (1889), 26; van Vloten, p. 168, No. 40; *Driemandelijksche bladen*, II, 76; and III, 29; Joos, 632. Afrikaans: Groenewald, p. 74. Luxemburg: De la Fontaine, 56. German: Butsch, 131; Wossidlo, 15; Schmidt, *Danzig*, 24; H. Meier, *Ostfriesland*, 18; H. Volksmann, *Am Urquell*, I (1890), 171; Gilhoff, 623 through 626; Frischbier, *Thierwelt*, p. 345, No. 11; Renk, *Tyrol*, 13; Haffner, 251, 252; Hanika-Otto, 6a through 6h. Swiss: Rochholz, 464 through 467 (No. 467 is much elaborated). Faeroic: Hammershaimb, *Antiquarisk tidsskrift*, III (1849–1851), 319, No. 47 = *Zeitschrift für deutsche Mythologie*, III (1855), 129. Icelandic: Árnason, 1075. Danish: Kristensen, p. 185, § 4, Nos. 1 through 2k, and pp. 178–180, § 1, Nos. 1 through 3, and pp. 180–183, § 2, Nos. 2, 4, 7 through 12, 14, 18, 20, 22, 28 through 32, 34, 35; Feilberg, *Ordbog*, III, 815 (citing many German parallels). Norwegian: Bergh, *Valdres*, 59; Christie, 109; Berge, p. 263, No. 99; Stafset, 40; Brox, *Ytre Senja*, 53a, 53b citing H. E. Bergh, *Sagn* (Christiania, 1879), p. 129, No. 75. Swedish: Dybeck, *Runa*, 1847, p. 41, No. 11; and 1850, p. 36, No. 28 (a curious contaminated version); Ericsson, *Södermanland*, I (1879), 79–80, No. 2; and V (1884), 63, No. 201; Hyltén-Cavallius, *Värend*, 83; Sandén, *Norra Vadsbo*, 141; Geijer and Campbell, 105; Ström, p. 269, "Gåtberättelser," 13. Latin: Pseudo-Bede, *Flores*, 13 (ed. Migne, *Patrologia Latina*, XCIV, col. 539); Huldreich Therander (Johann Sommer), 2 (cited by Tupper, *Holme Riddles*, 4). Walloon: Colson, *Wallonia*, IV, 58, No. 42; French: Sébillot, *Auvergne*, p. 165, No. 3; Marchessou, *Velay et Auvergne*, p. 165, No. 3; A. Ferrand, *Dauphiné*, p. 226; Parsons, *Antilles*, III, 395, Dominica, 79. Catalan: Pelay y Briz, 158. Portuguese: Braga, 86; Pires, *Archivio*, VIII (1889), 94–95, Nos. 13, 14. Spanish: Demófilo, pp. 389–390, No. 36. Argentinian: Lehmann-Nitsche, 576. Porto Rican: Mason, 770. Italian: Pitrè, 923; Coronedi-Berti, *Archivio*, II (1883), 578–579, Nos. 36, 37; Salvioni, *ibid.*, IV (1885), 552, No. 101. Czech: Hanika-Otto, note to No. 6. Flajšhans comments as follows (pp. 29–30, § 28a):

In his treatise Aarne discusses (*Rätselforschungen*, II, 22–59) the narrative riddle "Two-Legged, Three-Legged, Four-Legged," adding (p. 25): "In den slavischen Ländern habe ich keine einzige [Variante] gefunden." Even though Erben has not recorded it, this riddle is, however, well known in Bohemia, as we shall see immediately. Bartoš (159) has taken down three versions in Moravia; and T. Šmýd records a variant from Skřipov in Silesia (in Prasek, *Vlastivěda*, No. 140), as follows: "Two-Legged sat on Three-Legged and was eating a leg. Four-Legged came by and snatched Two-Legged's leg. Two-Legged became angry, broke off Three-Legged's leg, and threw it at the legs of Four-Legged, and broke Four-Legged's leg." We have a Czech variant in the *Pohádky*,

1695, No. 132, in this form: "Four-Legged snatched one bone. Then, Two-Legged took Three-Legged, being much wroth; Four-Legged dropped that one bone, for he swiftly threw Three-Legged at him." From the slavishly literal Germanism "one bone" (*ein Bein*), which is, moreover, incorrect, we see that the Czech riddle is a translation of a German text, the earliest example of which was . . . [text omitted; it is Butsch, p. 14, No. 131 = Aarne, No. 30, as found in *Rätselforschungen*, II, 30]. The slavishly literal and meaningless errors of the Prague text of 1695 were, of course, subsequently noted and corrected. In both places the eighteenth-century Olomouc text has "One-Leg" instead of "one bone," and continues after the third verse thus: "Then Two-Legged took that One-Leg, sat down on Three-Legged, and ate that One-Leg," and substitutes "shoemaker" for the original German solution, "cook," as in the modern Moravian and Silesian versions. Here we see cinematographically, so to speak, the change from the original German to the Czech text.

Polish: Gustawicz, 429 (cabbage, stool, dog). Hungarian: Kriza, 110 (Two-Feet sit on Three-Feet; they together make One-Foot; Four-Feet enters; seizes One-Foot; Two-Feet gets angry, picks up Three-Feet, strikes Four-Feet, [who] drops One-Foot immediately.—Shoemaker, boot, dog, three-footed stool); *Magyar Nyelvör*, VII (1878), 38, No. 1 (cobbler); *Magyar Népköltési Gyüjtemény*, I, 322 (cited by Szendrey, *Ethnographia*, XXXII [1921], 73).

It is clear that Aarne's comment on the failure of the riddle to establish itself east of Germany is essentially correct. The Czech versions are, as Flajšhans shows, either borrowings from Germany or subsequent developments of such borrowings, and the same may be said of the Hungarian texts.

462a through 462c. (One-Leg is not mentioned.) Dutch: Schrijnen, II, 112, No. 44 (Two-Legs sat on Three-Legs and draws on Four-Legs). German: Carstens, *Schleswig-Holstein*, p. 420; Frischbier, *Menschenwelt*, p. 244, No. 31 (cobbler); Hanika-Otto, 7a, 7b. Danish: Kristensen, p. 184, § 3, Nos. 1 through 4; "Two-Legs sat on Three-Legs and milked Four-Legs" (Toben sad pag Treben og malkede Fireben. DFS, 1906/1: 288, B. K. Petersen, 1910, p. 25. See also DFS, 1906/38: M. Jespersen, 1919, No. 6, and T. Bush, 1924, No. 11). Serbian: Novaković, p. 103, No. 3 (The biped sits on the tripod and tugs at the quadruped).

For discussion see Aarne, *Rätselforschungen*, II, 45; Flajšhans, pp. 29–30, § 28a.

462a. For the element "four were then drawn by ten" compare Nos. 976a through 976e.

462b. The first "four" should be "two," and the "two" should be "three."

463a through 463c. Irish: Delargy, 48 (Off [goes] the *tó-tó;* in [goes] the *tó-tó*. The quadruped king came and snatched up the *tó-tó*.—A cat which caught a mouse that was playing by itself throughout the house). Breton: Sébillot, *Haute-Bretagne*, 14; Kerbeuzec, *Ille-et-Vilaine*, 62; Duine, *Saint-Malo*, p. 515 (Four-Legs on Four-Legs, Four-Legs goes away, Four-Legs are left.—Cat leaves a chair on which it had been sitting). French: Rolland, 40; Carmeau, p. 35; E. H. Carnoy, *La Tradition*, VI (1892), 353, No. 15; Pineau, *Poitou*, 6; Desaivre, *Poitou*, p. 451, No. 10; Westphalen, *Metz*, col. 198; Baissac, *Mauritius*, pp. 399, Nos. 410, 411; Parsons, *Antilles*, III, 404, Guadaloupe, 81, and p. 415, Marie Galante, 49. Italian: Corsi, *Archivio*, X (1891), 401, No. 37. Samoan: Heider, 128 (Four-Legs on Four-Legs eats Four-Legs.—Cat eats rat). For discussion see Aarne, *Rätselforschungen*, II, 48–50.

464. Compare the riddle of the Sphinx, Nos. 46a through 47b.

467a, 467b. French: Parsons, *Antilles*, III, 401, Guadaloupe, 34, p. 410, Les Saintes,

25, p. 413, Marie Galante, 18, p. 437, St. Martin, 41 (I make men shake.—Rum). Finnish: Lönnrot, 1411 = Henssen, 16a (A red man in a red fur coat overcame the wisest men and weakened even the strongest.—Beer cask). See also No. 670 of the present collection.

469. Ascribed to Mrs. Barbauld; see I. S. Olveall, *Enigmas of Every Variety* (London, 1882), pp. 4–5.

470. French: Baissac, *Mauritius*, pp. 400, 411–412. Spanish: Demófilo, 435 = Argentinian: Lehmann-Nitsche, 11 (Always still, always moving, sleeping in the daytime, awake at night). Cuban: Giménez Cabrera, 5 (stars), 6 (flies). African, Wamajame: Ovir, 15 (My father guards the cattle by night, I do not see them by day). Malagasy: Sibree, p. 38, No. 1.

The Spanish "Appears in motion, sleeps in the daytime, disappears at night" (Demófilo, 12) is a confused series of contradictions, yielding no definite picture.

The contrast in "Spread out at night, taken up by day" (Italian: Gianandrea, *Archivio*, II [1883], 427, No. 53; and Indonesian, Sangir: Adriani, p. 438, No. 318) occurs again in the comparisons of stars to fruit on a plate or on a tree, and to objects on a cloth. Riddlers have compared the celestial bodies to animals; see, in the present collection, Nos. 391 through 392b (deer), and 484a through 484d (sheep). In Nos. 1093 through 1094e, the stars are fruit or nuts. For other means of comparison and for a survey see the headnotes to Nos. 1093–1095, 1094, and 1227.

472. Welsh: Hull and Taylor, 56. Lithuanian: Jurgelionis, 54 (Pigeons are cooing in the church), 55 (A rooster on the perch, his guts on the ground), 56 (A black cock is perched on the fence, its tail hangs down to the ground, its voice rises to Heaven). Armenian: Glushakov, p. 30, No. 53 (The eagle began to cry out, put its young on their wings; they are not its children, they are its grandchildren). The phrase "put its young on their wings" signifies "set them in motion" and is a metaphorical description of the congregation moving to church. We should perhaps emend the fourth line to read "Their strength did not abate with age" and thus gain a rhyme with "cage." Compare the headnotes to Nos. 1039 and 1326 in the present collection.

473. For riddles about married and single men and women, see the headnote to No. 1070. The subject seems to be of particular interest to African riddlers. Riddle No. 473 does not seem to be a very apt comparison.

474. The "eagles" are, I conjecture, a scribal error for "beagles." See the Renaissance Latin version (Buchler, *Gnomologia*, 3d ed. [1614], p. 450):

> In densis silvis venor bis quinque catellis,
> Quod capio perdo, quod non capio mihi servo.

See also Lettish: Bielenstein, 283 (Ten dogs hunt in the forest).

For additional parallels and discussion, see, in the present collection, the headnotes to Nos. 459–460 and 460 and the notes to Nos. 459 and 460a. For references to the ideas of keeping what is useless and throwing away what has been caught, or of seeking what cannot be found, see Nos. 460a, 460b, 1591, 1592, 1632 through 1642, and the headnotes to Nos. 460, 1591–1592, and 1632–1642.

475. In Argentinian Spanish parallels (Lehmann-Nitsche, 409 through 412), the actors are imprisoned men.

478. Usually, the answers are ants, bees, and partridges and the actors are represented as persons; see Nos. 887 through 904. The meanings of some words in these texts are obscure; they may have been invented to make rhymes.

479a through 479c. See Nos. 887 through 904.

480. See the similar descriptions of peas as persons in Nos. 830 through 833, 1011, and the note to Nos. 830 through 832c. Compare also No. 377 and the riddles collected in the note to No. 377, in which the speakers refer to the sound made when a bud bursts open.

481a through 481d. Danish: Kristensen, p. 94, § 241, No. 370, and § 242, Nos. 373a, 373b. Persian: Phillott, 23 (What is that which has no bones; in its body it has neither breath nor life? When hungry, it is at rest; when full, it complains), which includes the contrast of full and empty discussed in the headnote to Nos. 1455–1457 in the present collection.

For comparisons of a mill to a single hog, see No. 387 and the corresponding note and headnote, and compare the review of parallels in the note and headnote to No. 387.

For comparisons to an insatiable animal see the headnote to Nos. 236–239. For comparisons to two animals fighting and dropping foam between them, see the headnote to No. 397; the animals are occasionally boars. A Nandi riddle for axes, which is most probably quite independent of the texts here discussed, shows how readily riddlers can hit upon these ideas: "What are the things that make a noise at one another like bulls bellowing before a fight, but which do not hurt one another?" (Hollis, *Nandi*, p. 139, No. 28).

483. I do not understand the import of the riddle, which seems to be related to the Irish "Four wild boars looking southwestward.—The four corners of the church" (Delargy, 70) and the similar versions collected by O Dalaigh (Nos. 140, 141). See a very curious Modern Greek parallel, "Our bad sow, our greedy one, ate all the world and her hunger is not satisfied.—Hades" (Polites, *Neohellenika Analekta*, I, 248, No. 315).

The rather numerous riddles for a cemetery exhibit only a general resemblance to the foregoing texts. See Welsh: Hull and Taylor, 6. Irish: De Bhaldraithe, 23 (It might eat whoever might come and whoever did come, and it won't defecate much grain). Spanish: Demófilo, 189; Rodríguez Marín, 805 (It eats meat, but doesn't eat bread). Chilean: Flores, 72. Hungarian: *Magyar Nyelvör*, VII (1878), 89 (It has four corners and one gate, many people dwell in it). Arabic: Giacobetti, 330 (Chain on chain, it contains your mother and your father as well as the king of kings). According to the collector, "chain on chain" refers to skeletons. Arabic: Stumme, *Tázerwalt*, 1 (A herd of sheep which however bear no young; there is increase among them but there are no children). Turkish: Kúnos, 179 (Once I saw a fortress. I approached it. It was a rose garden. It devoured all, and it vomits out all.—Military tent), which may perhaps have some connection with the Oriental notion of paradise and the land of the dead as a garden of roses (see E. Jacobs, *Rosengarten im deutschen Lied, Land, und Brauch* [Halle, 1897]; Archer Taylor, "A Parallel to the 'Rosengarten' Theme," *Modern Language Notes*, XXXI [1916], 248–250). Kúnos, 263 (The building is earthen, it is the door of the Last Judgment; how many people are there and their status and number are unknown). African, Dschagga: Gutmann, p. 527 (Out there I have a place of assembly that is never filled). See also a Meistersinger's comparisons for a cemetery in M[one], *Anzeiger*, VII (1838), cols. 374–375, No. 304.

484a through 484d. Welsh: Hull and Taylor, 88 through 91 (only No. 88 refers to sheep; the others refer to cows). Compare the dispute of Nynniaw and Pebiaw in the *Mabinogion* and a manuscript parallel cited in J. A. Herbert, *Catalogue of Romances in the British Museum*, III (London, 1910), 710, No. 10. Welsh Gypsy: Sampson, 4. Irish: Delargy, 57 (*Aillavaí, aillavaí*, two hundred *aillavaí*, and the old black-faced sheep [goes] out in front of them.—Sky and stars). The meaning of *aillavaí* is obscure. See also De Bhaldraithe, 6 (Two hundred little lambs going to Seana Moínín with the big sheep in front); O Dalaigh, 150 (Little bleat, little bleat, two hundred little bleats, and the strong sheep outside before them). German: Frischbier, *Menschenwelt*, p. 258, No. 176. Danish:

Kristensen, p. 127, § 354, No. 564 (pigs). Swedish: Geijer and Campbell, 77; Ström, p. 204, "Himmelen," 3; Russwurm, *Eibo*, p. 133, § 316, No. 16. French: Rolland, 3. Portuguese: Braga, 53 (answer: sky, stars, sun, wind); Pires de Lima, 1; Parsons, *Cape Verde*, 273 (goats). Lettish: Bielenstein, 131, 132, 360. Czech: Hanika-Otto, p. 127, No. 65. Polish: Siarkowski, 60 (In a huge field there are thousands of tiny sheep and in the middle of the field there is a crossroads, and there is a bald-headed shepherd who sometimes has horns). The horns refer to the horns of the moon. Russian: Sadovnikov, 1865 (The field is measureless; the sheep are countless; the shepherd has horns), 1865a through 1865k, 1868 (Great is the Romanovsk field; there are many horned cattle, the shepherd hid behind a willow bush, and was tending them). The "shepherd" behind the "willow bush" is the man in the moon. See also Sichler, p. 755 (field, cattle, herdsman, two precious stones). Serbian: Novaković, p. xix, No. 6 (Numberless sheep are grazing all over the field and their shepherd is a horned sheep.—Stars, sky, moon), p. 56, Nos. 2 (The corral is full of sheep. I know the name of all of them, but not their number), 3 (The corral is full of sheep and they are all on one leg [and] are silent), p. 128, Nos. 6 (The field is full of sheep, among them a horned shepherd), 7 (The corral is full of sheep with golden fleece; among them is the chief shepherd in golden clothes), p. 129, Nos. 1 (The corral is full of sheep; among them is the white one), 2 (There is an immeasurable field; there are uncounted sheep; among them is a horned shepherd). This ingenious reference to the horns of the moon is of a type which occurs only infrequently. Estonian: Wiedemann, p. 274 (goat and herd of sheep); Dido, 35. Mordvin: Paasonen, 390 (All are sheep, all are sheep, only one ram among them). Turkish: Katanov in Radlov, IX, 100, No. 871 (A multitude of my sheep has gone out; only one humpbacked bull has remained), p. 240, No. 65 (My hundred sheep ran away and old man Chus-Alday rose). Crimean Tatar: Filonenko, 128 (The kettle is full of white lambs). Turcoman: Samojlvich, 22 (In the evening I scatter sheep. In the morning I rise and there is nothing there). The theme of disappearance is discussed in the headnote to No. 1094 of the present collection. Mongolian: Mostaert, 77 (Among a thousand sheep a massive round ram), 103 (After ten thousand sheep have grazed and gone, a stout white ram rises from sleep and follows them); Klukine, 3 (A stable full of sheep, among the sheep a golden ram.—Stars and sun). Indian, Hindi: Kavyopadhyaya, 28 (My maternal uncle has nine hundred cows, which graze by night and are folded by day). African, Wamajame: Ovir, 15. Kiniramba: F. Johnson, 5 (It herds with the young sheep.—Moon and stars). Hausa: Tremearne, p. 59, No. 12 = Harris, 19 (The cows are lying down, but the big bull is standing up.—Stars and moon). Dschagga: Gutmann, p. 526 (The chief's cattle on a meadow are countless). Aandonga: Pettinen, 36 (The gnu among the antelopes.—Moon among stars).

For the comparison of the sun or moon to a deer see Nos. 391 through 392b of the present collection.

485. See No. 487.

486. The reference to sheep is a casual variation without particular importance. It has a certain appropriateness because sheep are usually seen in herds, as needles are found in bundles. Riddlers often describe a needle as a one-eyed person or animal; see Nos. 36, 37, 281, 282, 528 through 533b, 533d, 534, 931, and 1340. No. 931 refers to a shipload of soldiers.

487. The answer is probably "clouds." See No. 485, and compare Nos. 389a, 389b. The riddler has admitted elements from the nursery rhyme "Rockaby baby in the treetop" and, misled by the association, has given the answer "to bed."

488. Spanish, Argentinian: Lehmann-Nitsche, 115. Portuguese: Parsons, *Cape Verde*, 87a through 87d. Polish: Saloni, *Rzeshów*, 46 (There's a forest here and in that forest partridges parade along paths), in which the riddler may have specified the "partridges" in order to gain a rhyme, and 47 (A bobtailed, sawed-off lordling drives sheep from the forest). Mordvin: Paasonen, 187 (swine on the heath). Modern Greek: Carnoy and Nicolaides, 4 (hogs).

For a review of the riddles simultaneously comparing hair to grass or trees and lice to animals see, in the present collection, the classification at the end of the note to Nos. 1042, 1043, and also the headnotes to Nos. 459-460, 1100-1108, nn. 14, 24, and 1100, n. 1.

489a through 489m. White Russian: Jurkevich, p. 293 (Little birds [*čiričiki*] were running along a linden bridge, slap into a bog.—Peas). Russian: Sichler, p. 118. Turkish in Siberia: Radlov, I, 262, No. 14 (A thousand sheep fell in a well and died.—Porridge). Surinam: Herskovits, p. 443, No. 48 (Little toads jump from the pot.—When a pot of rice boils over). African, Tschuana: Kuhn, *Tschuana*, 22 (White birds that gather in the hollow tree trunk.—Milk which is being milked into a wooden pail). Indian, Ho: Haldar, p. 277, No. 12 (The white stones which slip straight in.—Rice in a pot). On the very curious "The dance of white herons in a ruined homestead" (Haldar's p. 276, No. 2), see Mitra, *Notes on Ho Riddles*, pp. 114-115. The "ruined homestead" is a potsherd. Javanese: Ranneft, *Proza*, p. 4, No. 18 (The sea is in motion and the mountains fall in). The last is a rare example of a comparison of a thing to a thing rather than to an animal. For comparisons to persons bathing, see, in the present collection, Nos. 1032a, 1032b.

489l. The riddler's use of the word "t'ing" does not necessarily imply a comparison to an object.

490. For another comparison of peas to animals, see No. 480.

493a, 493b. Flemish: Joos, 640 (brown mice). German: Wossidlo, 277; Haase, *Ruppin*, 244; Carstens, *Schleswig-Holstein*, p. 419; Böckel, *Hesse*, 7; Hanika-Otto, 53a through 53e. Swiss: Rochholz, 559 (It goes to the bath white and comes home brown). Danish: Feilberg, *Ordbog*, II, 271, s.v. "korn." Swedish: Russwurm, *Eibo*, p. 132, § 316, No. 7. French: V. S., *Mélusine*, I (1878), col. 263, No. 75. Spanish, Argentinian: Lehmann-Nitsche, 288. New Mexican: Campa, 58 (In a little black field there is a herd of white cows; when some lie extended, others rise.—Loaves). Lithuanian: Jurgelionis, 476. Lettish: Bielenstein, 992 (white sheep without tails). Czech: Hrnčíř, 96 (A little stone cellar full of red hens and no one but an old humpback drives them out), as cited by Hanika-Otto, under her No. 53. Polish: Gustawicz, 307, 308; Saloni, *Rzeshów*, 17 (A stable full of red cattle, a black cow comes and scatters them all), 18 (A stable full of fat horses, a thin one comes and drives them out), 19 (A pen full of little sheep, and one little black bull drove them all out), 20 (fat sheep and a dry one); 21 (black sheep, black one drives them out); Kopernicki, 87 (The stable is filled with thin mares, but when someone enters, all of them flee). Russian: Sadovnikov, 473 (I will plow up a clear field, I will chase black sheep there), 473a (I will plow, and I will plow the clear field; I will chase there and I will chase white cattle. With the white cattle is a golden rooster), 475 (The little stall is full of tailless sheep. One had a tail, but that one went away). Serbian: Novaković, p. 232, No. 5 (I drove in a white ox and drove out a black ox). This theme is similar to that discussed in the headnote to Nos. 1542-1543, § 2, of the present collection. Estonian: Wiedemann, p. 273 (sheep). Votyak: Wichmann, *Votyak*, 442 (in the cellar a yellow sheep.—Loaf). Zyrian: Wichmann, *Zyrian*, 235 (A stall full of sheep, but only one tail.—Bread in oven and handle to pull it out). Turkish: Zavarin, *Brusa*, 33 (A long train of camels, one drives [impels] the next.—Plank for loaves which are carried to the public bakery). African, Kxatla: Schapera, 69 (Tell me: the white horse which when it goes into the stable becomes brown).

For the comparison of loaves to boys who turn brown, see No. 919 of the present collection.

494. Scotch Gaelic: Nicolson, p. 45 (mill wheel and water).

496a. Irish: Christiansen, 5; Delargy, *Inis Cé*, 4 (There are two bulls on Bald Hill, one in the night and one by day. If the pair come together, this place would not be what it is). The meeting of the sun and moon is an event marking Judgment Day. Dutch: Schrijnen, II, 104, No. 10. Swedish: Ström, p. 207, "Solen," 12. Spanish, Argentinian: Lehmann-Nitsche, 226. Turkish: Katanov in Radlov, IX, 239, No. 49 (Behind a blue cow there walks a white cow), and p. 370, No. 350 (A dark-blue [var.: light-blue] horse and a white horse are chasing each other). See also, in the present collection, Nos. 392a, 392b, 405 and 431 and the notes to Nos. 391 and 405.

496b. The reference to a star is unusual.

497. (The tongue is not mentioned.) Scotch Gaelic: Nicolson, p. 57. Norwegian: Christie, 26. Russian: Sadovnikov, 1733 (The tiny stall is full of white sheep). Estonian: Wiedemann, p. 262 (A barn full of white sheep). Arabic: Giacobetti, 274 (Lift the curtain and the lambs appear), 276 (I have twenty-four lambs, of which four are two years younger. When one touches the head of a lamb, the shepherd spends the night without sleeping), 283 (I have young lambs and eight sheep. Let a bit of wood touch the head of a sheep, and the shepherd spends the night without sleeping). The eight sheep are the molars. Ossete: Schiefner, 23. Balkar: Pröhle, p. 120 (A sheepfold full of white lambs). Indian, Kashmiri: Knowles, 41 (White lambs in a stall). Mongolian, Buryat: Gombojew, 10 (Twenty goats in a hole).

498a through 498c. (The tongue is mentioned.) Irish: Delargy, *Inis Cé*, 24 (A herd of sheep going in company, and a little red lamb inside in the middle). Dutch: Sinninghe, p. 8, No. 6. Flemish: Joos, 547, var. 13. German: Hanika-Otto, 52e (white sheep, red cock). Swedish: Ström, p. 82, "Munnan, tänderna, tungan," 2 (White goats, red ram). Polish: Gustawicz, 438 (There is a little pen filled with little lambs and among them a little red bull); Saloni, *Rzeshów*, 41, 42 (Little pen full of white sheep and among them a red ram); Siarkowski, 8 (A tiny stable is filled with little white lambs; a shepherd guards them). White Russian: Wasilewski, 26 (A pen full of sheep and a ram bleats). Serbian: Novaković, p. 78, No. 7 (The oven is full of sheep, among them a red shepherd bleats), which is sadly disordered. Mongolian: Rudnyev, 1 (Twenty sheep are crippled, a bluish horse with a hollow back is tied up).

499a, 499b. (The tongue is mentioned.) Welsh: Hull and Taylor, 86, 87. Irish: Christiansen, 21a, 21b; Delargy, 35 (A field full of white cows and a red calf within among them); De Bhaldraithe, 17; O Dalaigh, 4. Breton: Sébillot, *Haute-Bretagne*, 45a; Sébillot, *Devinettes*, 55. Frisian: Dykstra, *Snypsnaren*, p. 105 (Two rows of white cows and the red bull). German: Frischbier, *Menschenwelt*, p. 242 (A red cow in a wet stable). Icelandic: Árnason, 961 (I saw a house full of white cows with a red calf playing in the floor-drain). Danish: Kristensen, p. 93, §233, Nos. 358a through 358c, and pp. 137–138, §399, Nos. 537a, 537b (red herdsman watching white cows). Norwegian: Bugge, *Telemarken*, 44; Berge, 20; Brox, *Ytre Senja*, 42, citing Riksheim, 82; Bergh, *Valdres*, 17. Swedish: Dybeck, *Runa*, 1850, p. 35, Nos. 14, 15; Hyltén-Cavallius, *Värend*, 43; Ericsson, *Södermanland*, I (1879), 83, No. 16; Sandén, *Norra Vadsbo*, 42; Geijer and Campbell, 2; Ström, pp. 81–82, "Munnen, tänderna, tungan," 1, 4, 5; Olsson, *Västergötland*, p. 124, Nos. 5a through 5c. French: Rolland, *Rimes*, p. 202, No. 27 (A red cow surrounded by white calves). Spanish, Argentinian: Lehmann-Nitsche, 247c, 251. Dominican Rep.: Andrade, 189. Polish: Saloni, *Rzeshów*, 43, 44 (Little stable full of little white calves and among them a red bullock); Kopernicki, 6; Gustawicz, 437 (There is a little pen filled with little calves and among them a little red bull), 439, 462 (Thirty-two little white heifers with a little bull in their midst). African, Kxatla: Schapera, 72 (Tell me: the white cows with the red bull). Suk: Beech, p. 43, No. 3 (White cows-my; all-red bull). Tonga-Shangaan: Junod and Jaques, p. 251, No. 132 (I have white cattle in my kraal and one [that] is red). Indonesian, Atjeh: Kreemer, *Atjeh*, 61 (buffalo).

500. The riddler is in error regarding the color of the cattle.

501. (In the following parallels the tongue is not mentioned.) Swiss: Rochholz, 442. Lettish: Bielenstein, 686 (A little, little stable full of little white oxen). Bulgarian: Gubov, 124 (White oxen tied in the stable). Tungus: Poppe, 28 (In the stable piebald oxen are attached). Mongolian: Kotvich, 16 (Thirty oxen in a ditch).

502 through 507. (The tongue is not mentioned.) The subdivision is as follows: No. 502, horses in a meadow; No. 502a through 503g, horses on a red hill; No. 504, horses on red or blue hills (probably a reference to the so-called blue-gum Negro); Nos. 505a, 505b, rows of horses; No. 506a, 506b, horses trot or gallop in unison; No. 507, horses on a bridge.

For parallels see Welsh Gypsy: Sampson, 15. Breton: Sauvé, 116a, 116b; Sébillot, *Haute-Bretagne*, 43b. Flemish: Joos, 547, var. 10, and 548. German: Carstens, *Schleswig-Holstein*, p. 413; Haffner, 112. French: Rolland, 123e; Lacuve, *Poitou*, p. 703, No. 13. Italian: Rondini, *Archivio*, VII (1888), 539, No. 23; Tschiedel, 27. Rumanian: Papahagi, 31 (A church with white horses). Lettish: Bielenstein, 379. Bulgarian: Gubov, 125 (When your white horses become playful, where do you put them?—Into bread). Modern Greek: Dieterich, *Rätseldichtung*, p. 95, citing Polites, *Neohellenika Analekta*, I, 245, No. 292 (A cave filled with white horses). Turkish: Katanov in Radlov, IX, 238, No. 31 (In the lowlands I have thirty light-blue horses). African, SeSuto: Norton and Velaphe, 47 (I have many white horses which feed in a cave).

508 through 510. (The tongue is mentioned.) The subdivision is as follows: No. 508, a red horse represents the tongue; No. 509, a red horse licks white horses; No. 510, a red man represents the tongue.

508. (The tongue is a red horse.) Breton: Sébillot, *Devinettes*, 55d. French: Carmeau, p. 34 (Thirty-two little white mares with a big red one in the middle). Italian: Gianandrea, *Archivio*, I (1882), 399, No. 3; Corsi, *ibid*., X (1891), 402, No. 45. Tungus: Poppe, 17 (In the stable a bay horse is attached).

509. (Red horse kicks, licks, etc.) Italian: Coronedi-Berti, *Archivio*, II (1883), 576, No. 12. Bulgarian: Gubov, 129 (All the horses are white; one is red, kicking all of them). Turkish: Katanov in Radlov, IX, 241, No. 85 (Among thirty light-blue horses there runs a red stallion).

510. (Red man.) Swedish: Ström, p. 82, "Munnen, tänderna, tungan," 6.

511a through 512. Latin: O. Schreger, *Studiosus jovialis* (2d ed.; Munich, 1751), chap. viii = Friedreich, pp. 229–230, No. 19 (Quae animalis gubernant mundum?— Oves dant membranum; apes ceram; quibus decreta principum constant et mundus regitur).

Chapter IV

COMPARISONS TO A PERSON

Nos. 513–826

513. The text is somewhat disordered; for "and" in the seventh line read "am." The use of meter and the use of the first person are characteristics of literary riddling. The date of composition may perhaps be inferred from the rhyme "fair: are." For the comparison of an object to a person with a rough skin, see the headnote to Nos. 576–577.

514. French: J. Roux, *Limousin*, 94 (Earthen body, water belly, wooden head). Rumanian: Papahagi, 14 (A Negro with a long neck). Lappish: Qvigstad, 3 (A man stands and has a four-cornered hat on his head.—Vent cover of a chimney). Hungarian: Kálmány, I, 168, No. 14 (Its four feet are made of wood, its hat is also wooden, the neck is made of skin.—Canteen). This resembles the riddles discussed in the headnote to Nos. 553–554 of the present collection. African, Wanamwezi: Dahl, 11 (A gleaming nubile girl). Pangwe: Tessmann, 38 (I know a man. When he eats, he pulls off his head.—Barx box). This is allied to the riddles discussed in the headnote to Nos. 805–818 of the present collection. Malagasy: Sibree, p. 39, No. 18 (When the little one comes, the great one takes off its hat.—Great stone, water pot, and ladle). Indonesian, Tabaru: Fortgens, 27 (She has a mouth, a neck, a body, but no head, hands, or feet).

For the comparison of medicine bottles to soldiers, see Spanish: Demófilo, 151 through 154; Rodríguez Marín, 619 through 622. For a similar comparison of a shirt to a man, see the headnote to No. 6, § 2, of the present collection.

516a through 517. Compare Nos. 30a, 30b, in which the personification is less complete.

516c. The parentheses indicate that the speaker said "years," which is to be understood as "ears." The "ears" are the projecting staves used as handles.

520. African, Nandi: Hollis, *Nandi*, p. 140, No. 32 (I met a woman carrying something which resembled a man's head.—Pumpkin).

523 through 524b. French: Parsons, *Antilles*, III, 407, Guadaloupe, 118. Surinam: Herskovits, p. 436, No. 15 (My mother has three eyes). Indian: Lakshīnātha Upasānī, IX, 8 (I am found on the trees, but a bird I am not. I have three eyes, but Śiva I am not. I have water which from clouds fell not. I have not to walk, so ride on a bullock. Tell me what is my name). Gujerati: Mehta, pp. 119–120, No. 10 (There is a thing in which flows the Ganges,—sweet Gangetic flow, and there is matted hair on its head; it has two, three eyes, and in it abide blessings).

For what seems to be a defective version, see No. 279 of the present collection. For a confused comparison to three sons, see No. 987. For a comparison to a house with three doors, see No. 1142a, 1142b.

525a through 525c. Swedish: Hyltén-Cavallius, *Värend*, 20 (Lilla Lod lies on the floor and gazes, peeps with one eye). The name Bo-peep in the Nova Scotian version is borrowed from a nursery rhyme; the choice of the name is suggested by the word "peep."

527. The Pushto compare the moon to a single eye: "From above came a red eye, a full eye steeped in blood. If I eat, I become an infidel; if I don't, I fall sick" (Thorburn, *Bannú*, p. 229, No. 2). I have omitted "it" after "eat," since the riddler alludes, not to the moon, but to the month of Ramadan, when Mohammedans must fast.

528 through 530b. Norwegian: Berge, 59 (It goes over land and shore and has but one eye); Brox, *Ytre Senja*, 29. Turkish: Hamizade, 258 (I have a girl, she has one eye), 259 (By God! There is a master's eye). Yakut: Piekarski, 120 (One-eyed Tunguses have come from the South). "The South" signifies Russia.

529a, 529b. The proper names "Susy" and "Wee-wee" suggest that the riddler has in mind the star riddle (Nos. 525a through 525c of the present collection), in which names often occur. Another trait of this star riddle is the adjective "poor."

530a. This is probably an adaptation of a riddle for a star (Nos. 525a through 525c) to which the remark "goes all over the world" is appropriate. It may be a confused echo of a reference to the foreign origin of the needle, a theme often mentioned (see the headnote to Nos. 531–534, § 1). The parallels often exhibit a higher degree of personification; see "Master One-Eye from foreign lands cannot sit or stand" (Swedish: Ericsson, *Södermanland*, I [1879], 91, No. 56) and "A maiden from foreign lands has one eye and no head" (his No. 57). See further Norwegian: Bugge, *Telemarken*, 50. Swedish: Ström, p. 158, "Nålen," 1.

530b. References to the sharpness of the needle are rare. See "keen as a pin" (No. 1340).

531 through 533d. Few parallels have the three elements characteristic of the English versions. These elements are: (1) possession of one eye; (2) possession of a tail; (3) the constant diminution of the tail as it goes through a gap. An example containing all these elements is the Welsh "Who is the little old woman, she is known throughout the shire; she has but one eye and a long slender tail? Although pushing through brambles, she comes through them instantly, but each time she leaves a bit of her tail in a trap" (Hull and Taylor, 96).

533a through 533d. The scene "went through a gap" may be a recollection of the cherry riddle beginning "When I went through the garden gap" (see Nos. 632a, 632b, 633) but here the "gap" is the opening through which the needle goes.

535. (Actor without a personal name.) Icelandic: Árnason, 150 (There is a blameless maiden who drags a long tail. With every step she takes, the tail gets shorter). Norwegian: Bergh, *Valdres*, 1. French: Rolland, 189 (Who goes back and forth, leaving each time a little tip of his tail?); Constantin, *Savoie*, p. 21; Haurigot, *French Guiana*, p. 119 (There is a woman, who, while she runs, consumes a bit of her tail). Indian: Ghulam Hussain Khán, *Panjab Notes and Queries*, III (1886), 217, No. 892, § 2 (A bit of a girl and walking off with the *paránda* [string to tie the hair]).

536a, 536b. (Actor with a personal name.) Modern Greek: Polites, *Neohellenika Analekta*, I, 225, No. 180 (My aunt Nicole with an intestine behind her).

536a. The riddler includes an unnecessary allusion to the answer.

536b. The scene "going to town" is conventional. See, for example, Nos. 541, 1705.

539 through 540h. Welsh: Hull and Taylor, 201, 202, which is confused with a magpie riddle found in German (Wossidlo, 240) and elsewhere. Scotch Gaelic: Nicolson, p. 21. Breton: Le Pennec, 25. German: Wossidlo, 21 (coat of a thousand patches, leather beard), in which the first comparison belongs to riddles discussed in the headnote to No. 1437, § 10, of the present collection; Wossidlo, 504; Frischbier, *Thierwelt*, p. 350, No. 42; Schmidt, *Danzig*, 3; Haase, *Ruppin*, 217; Renk, *Tyrol*, 81; Hanika-Otto, 68. Swiss: Rochholz, 378; Zahler, *Münchenbuchsee*, 134. Swedish: Dybeck, *Runa*, 1848, p. 44, No. 34; and 1865–1873, p. 48, No. 45; Ericsson, *Södermanland*, I (1879), 79, No. 1 (like the first German riddle above); Noreen, *Fryksdal*, 5; Sandén, *Norra Vadsbo*, 78, 79; Geijer and Campbell, 65; Ström, pp. 106–107, "Tuppen, hönan," 1, 2. French: *Les Adeuineaux amoureux*, p. ci = Rolland, 52; Rolland, 51; Mensignac, *Gironde*, p. 299, No. 11; Lallemant, *Argonne*, p. 233 (Beak of horn and beard of flesh make so loud a cry that he awakes a sleeping body, which goes to pull a baptized body without a soul, which awakens another body, which enters his mother's house to eat his father.—Cock, sacristan, bell, priest, church, the Host). Spanish: Demófilo, 460, 468; Rodríguez Marín, 367, 368. Argentinian: Lehmann-Nitsche, 170. 203. Chilean: Flores, 289, 290, 292, 293. Cuban:

Massip, 90 (crown, spur, red beard, early to bed and rises at dawn). New Mexican: Campa, 101. Portuguese: Coelho, *Zeitschrift für romanische Philologie*, III (1879), 197, No. 1. Italian: Pitrè, *Canti*, II, 647, No. 847. Lithuanian: Jurgelionis, 817, 818 = Schleicher, p. 200 (A man comes on crutches with beard of flesh and mouth of bone); Jurgelionis, 821 (A little mouth of bone, a little beard of flesh, patch on patch, and in a patched hole), 822 (A cap of feathers, a mouth of bone, and a beard of flesh). Lettish: Bielenstein, 198, 199. Russian: Sadovnikov, 945. Bulgarian: Gubov, 296 (I have spurs, yet I am not a horseman). Finnish: Aarne and Krohn, 109 = Henssen, 170. Turcoman: Samojlvich, 117 (*An can tan!* His voice is borne from the settlement, his mouth is of steel, his beard is of flesh), 118 (His beard is of flesh, his nose of bone). African, Kxatla: Schapera, 52 (Tell me: when I was in the hut, I heard someone calling me outside. When I came out, I found that the mouth was a bone, the beard was flesh, and the hair was flesh). The hair of flesh is the cock's comb.

The Swedish "An old father dances with a dish of meat on his head" (Russwurm, *Eibo*, p. 133, § 316, No. 14) and the Filipino "Which creature is with meat on its head?" (Starr, *Philippines*, 25) represent another conception of a cock.

541. The detail "his head is on fire" suggests comparison with the hookah riddle (see the headnote to Nos. 1440–1441, n. 6), but there is probably no connection.

543. French: Rolland, 53 (In this year several will be born who will have the feet of griffons, beards of feathers, and mouths of horn); V. S. *Mélusine*, I (1878), col. 256, No. 2 = Marchessou, *Velay et Auvergne*, p. 173, No. 8, a long literary riddle of which only "A beast will arise that will have the feet of a griffon" (line 1) is pertinent here.

544. Serbian: Novaković, p. 88, Nos. 9 (The master stands in the house and his beard is outside.—Maize), 10 (A fairy went out of the oven and let her hair down her back), p. 107, No. 9 (The master is in the palace and his beard outside), and p. 201, No. 1. African, Kamba: Lindblom, 44 (Me tell [i.e., tell me:] a man habitually sitting in his hut and his beard is outside). Swahili: Velten, 47 (There is an old man. He is inside, but his beard is outside). Bakongo: Denis, 90 (A village where everybody has a beard.—Maize). Indian, Bihari: Mitra, *Bihari Life*, p. 28, No. 1 (During my early age, I wear a sari [garment, robe] of green color. When I attain to my youth, a crest grows [upon my head]; and then, my beard and mustaches also grow. When I arrive at my old age, I wear pendent ornaments studded with diamonds and pearls). The last clause describes the grains of corn. Compare also the Bhil riddle for grass, "A tall lady with pearls in her nose" (Hedberg, p. 870, No. 28). The pearls are perhaps drops of dew. For parallels to the comparison of a plant to a person whose biography is recited, see the headnotes to Nos. 668–680 and 668–669 of the present collection. Indonesian, Lampong: Helfrich, *Lampong*, 13 (It has a beard from childhood, it wears a shirt from its youth). Korean: Bernheisel, p. 62 (What is it that stands with its hair disheveled in the field?).

For the comparison of plants to gaily dressed dancers or workers, see, in the present collection, Nos. 946a through 948b and the headnote to Nos. 946–950.

549. According to Halliwell-Phillipps, this riddle may be intended in *Harleian 7316*, p. 61: "I'm a dull senseless blockhead, 'tis true, when I'm young, / And like old grandsire Greybeard without tooth or tongue, / But by the kind help and assistance of arts / I sometimes attain to politeness of parts."

550a through 552b. French: Parsons, *Antilles*, III, 449, Hayti, 39. Rumanian: Papahagi, 16 (A little child who is always standing with its hands in its pockets). Russian: Sadovnikov, 444 (There stands a fop, his arms akimbo.—Samovar). Albanian: Hahn, p. 160, No. 18 (An Arabian with his hand at his side). Surinam: Herskovits, p. 441, Nos. 45 (A little girl is sitting with her hand at her hip.—That is a chamber pot), 45a (My mother has a man. But never does his hand come away from his side).

For a parallel in the plural, which is inappropriate to the subject, see No. 932 of the present collection.

550c. A contaminated version including elements found in Nos. 558a through 558e.

553a through 553c. Welsh: Hull and Taylor, 74, 75. Breton: Sauvé, 74a; Orain, *Ille-et-Vilaine*, p. 146; Charlec, *Dol-de-Bretagne*, 1903, p. 288. Arabic: Giacobetti, 533 (Its back is wooden, its belly leather, its nose is plunged in the fire). Indian, Bhil: Hedberg, p. 879, No. 87 (Strong leather, iron and wood. If you don't know, it must be a witch).

554. Portuguese: Parsons, *Cape Verde*, 156a (Body of wood and iron, guts of sand).

555a, 555b. Portuguese: Parsons, *Cape Verde*, 54a (Stalk by stalk, it has no marrow, it blossoms, it does not flower.—*Cariç*, a bamboo-like reed), 54b. Samoan: Heider, 19 (Someone is four to five *gafa* tall, but has no intestines.—Bamboo. *Gafa* is the length of the outstretched arms).

556. White Russian: Shein, 11 (A little blue cock is running without guts.—Bottle).

558a through 558e. Irish: Christiansen, 92 (A little black man with a big stomach, three legs in the air, and his mouth in the middle). German: Gilhoff, 499. Portuguese: Parsons, *Cape Verde*, 130a, 130b, 130c (A woman rides on three horses), 131. Lappish: Qvigstad, 31 (It stands on three feet and has a bundle on its back.—Spinning wheel). Crimean Tatar: Filonenko, 23 (It moves about on three legs and brags about its power.— Pot), 24 (It has three legs, its stomach is a drum.—Stove). The Bhil say of a tripod used in winnowing grain, "One man has three feet" (Hedberg, p. 875, No. 60). See also No. 1182 in the present collection.

558e. The formula "Black within, black without" occurs in various connections; see Nos. 1533, 1534, and compare Nos. 64a through 64f.

559. Swedish: Dybeck, *Runa*, 1865–1873, p. 81, No. 100. Shor: Dyrenkova, 28 (A little girl with tousled hair runs about the room.—Whisk broom). Compare No. 221 and the headnote to Nos. 695–699 in the present collection.

560. A sadly confused riddle. The name "Hoddy Toddy" has a parallel in the various forms of "Niddy Noddy" in Nos. 516a through 516c and 517 through 520. The comparisons for the roundness and depth of the well are discussed in the headnotes to Nos. 1286–1289 and 1315–1336.

562a through 562e. Irish: O Dalaigh, 52 (I got down through the slippery gap. I saw a little boy with a red cap on his head. "I'm more afraid," he said, "of a hen than of the army of any king on earth"). Dutch: Sinninghe, p. 12, No. 15. Flemish: Joos, 1st ed., 205, and 2d ed., 390. German: Wossidlo, 215; Gilhoff, 234 through 239; Schmidt, *Danzig*, 8; Frischbier, *Thierwelt*, p. 352, No. 49; Hanika-Otto, 62a through 62e. Danish: Kristensen, p. 78, § 196, No. 302, p. 88, § 223, Nos. 346a, 346b, and p. 100, § 258, Nos. 459a through 459c. French: Bladé, *Armagnac*, 109; *Mélusine*, I (1878), col. 88, and col. 265, No. 86; Dardy, *L'Albret*, p. 329; Lespy, *Béarn*, 24; Marehessou, *Velay et Auvergne*, p. 179, No. 10; Sébillot, *Auvergne*, 16; Fesquet, p. 176. Portuguese: Parsons, *Cape Verde*, 94 (*Reng, reng*, vexation in the fields, they have no fear except of hens.—Caterpillar). Italian: Gianandrea, *Archivio*, I (1882), 562, No. 30. Rumanian: Gorovei, 1551. Lithuanian: Jurgelionis, 883 (There comes a young gentleman with a red coat; "Chase away the chickens, I am not afraid of dogs"), 884, 885; Schleicher, p. 207. Czech: Hanika-Otto, note to No. 62 (A guest who grew up in the woods came to us, "Don't set the cock on me; I am not afraid of the dog."—Ant). Serbian: Novaković, p. 30, No. 1 (The bride called to the bride from behind the mountains, "Lead me, bride, past the hens; I am not afraid of dogs"), and p. 64, Nos. 3 (One godmother called to another over the hill, "Do not give me to the hens, I am not afraid of the dogs."—Snake), 4 (A slim bride sings behind the hill, "Do not give me to the hens; I am not afraid of dogs."—Snake). Bulgarian: Gubov, 68 (Vela shouts through nine parts of the world, "Do not protect me from dogs, but save me from hens"), 390 (Vida . . .), 391 (Yela shouts over nine regions, "Protect me from a goose, a hen; I am not afraid of the dog); Ikonomov, 23 (Vida shouts from a high hill, "Protect me! I am not afraid of the dogs, I am afraid of the hens"); Chacharov, 136 (A man is walking from downtown and shouting, "Do not protect me from dogs; save me from the hens").

564. See the headnote to Nos. 545–548.

565a, 565b. For objects described as prickly, pimply, or pockmarked persons, see the headnote to Nos. 576–577.

568. The significance of the "eye" is obscure. It may be an ornamental opening in the housing of the pump. The fundamental conception is akin to that of Nos. 816 through 818d.

571. For the comparison of a ring to a bottomless tub see Nos. 1172a through 1173j. The meaningless introductory formula, "There was a man of Adam's race," belongs to the Jonah riddle, for which see Leather, *Hereford*, p. 229; Chambers, *Scotland*, p. 108; Gregor, *Northeast Scotland*, p. 76; Hyatt, *Adams Co., Ill.*, pp. 662–663, No. 10881.

572. Welsh: Hull and Taylor, 92. Indian: Lakshīnātha Upasānī, III, 3 (A car rolls along in the sky, but touches not the ground. Its driver is on earth, but the vehicle remains in the sky).

573. The collector does not explain "land a rat." Compare the Turkish mouse riddle, "What is it whose name is *geme* [a large mouse]; it has constant trouble with people; its mother gave birth to a thief; one has to make a noise to make it go into the ground?" (Kúnos, 210).

575. German: Wossidlo, 216b (Long man, sway man [*Swankmann*]; if he could rise, he would go to Heaven to confess). French: V. S., *Mélusine*, I (1878), col. 263, No. 74 (Aunt Bandylegs goes under the door; if she rose straight, she would touch the sky). Portuguese: Parsons, *Cape Verde*, 251a (Long John martyred [twisted].—Path). Italian: Rondini, *Archivio*, VII (1888), 546, No. 63. Lithuanian: Schleicher, p. 210 (If it straightened itself up, it would support the sky; if it had hands, it would catch the thief). Polish: Gustawicz, 52 (Very narrow, very low, but should it rise, it would reach the skies). White Russian: Wasilewski, 107 (A prince lies stretching himself out. When he gets up, he will reach Heaven), 126 (Vasia lies down, stretching out, and when he gets up, he'll reach the sky). Russian: Sadovnikov, 1327; Arkhangel'skii, p. 79 (Were I to arise, I would reach the sky. If I had hands and feet, I would catch the thief. If I had mouth and eyes, I would tell everything), which has some curious resemblances to the Breton riddle quoted in the headnote to No. 575, n. 45, in the present collection. Serbian: Novaković p. 181, No. 11 (Long as I am, if I were straight, I would reach as high as the sky). Bulgarian: Bozhov, 16 = Chacharov, 103 (Long as I am, if I were straight, I would reach Heaven). Hungarian: *Magyar Nyelvör*, V (1876), 470 (like Arkhangel'skii's Russian version). Tatar: Kalashev and Ioakimov, p. 49, No. 11 (My uncle is long, his belt is short.—River and bridge). Cherekessian: Tambiev, p. 55, No. 22 (Longer than you, longer than I, [dressed] in a long coat of mail). Altai Turkish: Menges, 35 (I lie there and do not rise, but if I rise, then I go to Heaven); Katanov in Radlov, IX, 370, No. 359 (If I had legs, then I should reach to the sky; if I had arms, then I should catch the thief). Yakut: Piekarski, 240 (There is one, so they say, who says, "Should I rise I would reach the skies"); Popov, p. 290 (Were I to arise, I should reach the sky); Priklonskii, 77 (If it were to stand up, it would reach the sky). Mongolian, Buryat: Gombojew, 58 (A tall man, [he] does not reach to the foal's mane). African, Masai: Hollis, *Masai*, p. 255, No. 8 (What does your mother resemble? She is long, and yet she does not reach up to a sheep's udder). Nandi: Hollis, *Nandi*, p. 148, No. 64 (It is drawn out but does not break). Kamba: Lindblom, 89 (A man who is tall but nevertheless unable to pluck the fruit on a *kitó*-tree). Kanuri: Lukas, p. 169, No. 8 (It is long and without an end). Suk: Beech, p. 45, No. 15 (I am long, there is not [another longer than I]).

Similar ideas occur in riddles for men or animals moving along a path. See the Nandi riddle for a war party in single file: "What is like a thong which when stretched reaches from Nandi to Kavirondo?" (Hollis, *Nandi*, p. 139, No. 29) and the Kundu riddle for ants: "When we go to war, then we march one behind another in long files" (Ittmann, *Kundu*, 35).

576a through 576c. Irish: Delargy, 50 (An oaken waistcoat and ashen buttons, a frieze periwig, a cravat of nettles); O Dalaigh, 26 (A little pig in a bush; [the pig is] full of thorns), 27, 28. Rumanian: Papahagi, 6 (An old man with his coat inside out). Basque: Vinson, 70 (That which has its dress full of spits); Cerquand, 15 (Who is dressed in spits?). Russian: Sadovnikov, 883 (A peasant walks into the forest. His back is full of stakes.—Pig). Bulgarian: Gubov, 356 (Stoiko walks through the field with a hundred stakes on his shoulder), 358 (Chirko, Korndirko strolled through the field carrying countless stakes). Modern Greek: Polites, *Neohellenika Analekta*, I, 254, No. 347 (My son Theodore the Short holds a hundred short pegs). Finnish: Aarne and Krohn, 97 = Henssen, 11 (A man went into the forest, his back full of spits). Estonian: Wiedemann, p. 278; Lönnrot, p. 187. Votyak: Wichmann, *Votyak*, 171 (A little Tatar boy sells needles). Cheremiss: Porkka, 135 (Eram Obraska bears a basket of needles). See also Turcoman: Samojlvich, 42 (With quick legs, with eight tens of stakes), in which the translation of the first phrase is uncertain.

576a. The reference to Thorny Fair suggests a thicket.

577a, 577b. (A plant or fruit.) See an English chinkapin riddle in which the adjective "sticky" is used to signify "prickly," No. 1019a. Armenian: Glushakov, p. 25, No. 19 (In summer I am high, in winter I am in the house; on the outside I am covered with thorns; [if] I take them off, I am a nobleman; to Tiflis I was sent by a merchant. Who knows where I come from?—Chestnut). Indian, Ho: Sarkar, p. 354, No. 19 (A woman wearing earrings all over her body.—Pod of the masur). Uraon: Archer, p. 182, No. 44 (A boy with itches goes to the raja's palace.—Jack fruit); this riddle combines with the idea of a bumpy body the theme of describing an article of food as "going to the king's palace," for which see the headnote to No. 737 in the present collection. Kolarian: Wagner, 22 (A man covered with teeth over the whole body.—Jack fruit). The Bihari description of a jack fruit suggests rather a box or chest: "What has thorns and prickles on its outside, but contains fibers and tendrils? There is a club hidden in it" (Mitra, *Bihari Life*, p. 35, No. 11). Indonesian, Javanese: Mayer, p. 324, No. 2.

578. The contrast of rough and smooth occurs also in a riddle for an oyster; see Nos. 1420a, 1420b.

579a, 579b. For a similar manner of description see Spanish, Argentinian: Lehmann-Nitsche, 341 (A girl dressed in green has a red heart.—Watermelon), 783 (Red heart, red blood.—Watermelon).

580. Chinese: Rudolph, p. 74, Nos. 2 (On the outside is a stone wall, and beyond it again there are two walls. In the inside is a small golden lady), 3 (Two white plaster walls, and between them there is a red beauty).

581a, 581b. For riddles comparing teeth to horses see Nos. 502 through 510.

581a. The meaning of "red bay" is obscure.

582. For comparisons of the teeth or the tongue to something that is always wet, see Nos. 1150a, 1150b, and the headnote to No. 1150, nn. 1–5, 7–22.

583a through 584b. German: Haffner, 219 (little red hats). Norwegian: Brox, *Ytre Senja*, 24 (White body, red top), 77. Walloon: Colson, *Wallonia*, IV, 149, No. 171 (small woman with white petticoat, yellow face, and red hat). Spanish, Argentinian: Lehmann-

Nitsche, 385 (white child, colored hair), 424 (women with white dresses and red hats). Zyrian: Wichmann, *Zyrian*, 84 (A small, small boy has a red cap), 245 (A handsome, handsome fellow always has a yellow cap). Turkish: Hamizade, 361 (On that side a stone, on this side a stone, inside there are forty black heads). Samoan: Heider, 161 (There is a company of almost a hundred brothers, all with black hats, but one puts all of them in a box), 175 (A company of soldiers numbering a hundred men of small stature lives in a single house, but something violent can happen by which all are destroyed). For another use of the comparison to men wearing caps see No. 989 and the corresponding note in this collection.

585a, 585b. Breton: Sébillot, *Devinettes*, 16. Flemish: Joos, 349, 351; *Ons Volksleven*, VI (1894), 149, No. 18. German: Wossidlo, 504; Frischbier, *Thierwelt*, p. 351, Nos. 44 through 46. Icelandic: Árnason, 488 (Who is born twice, wears a crown every day, and engages in prophecies that are known to all, although no one understands a word that he says?). Danish: Kristensen, pp. 37–40, § 95, Nos. 127a through 127h. Norwegian: Stafset, 158; Swedish: Sandén, *Norra Vadsbo*, 79; Ström, pp. 106-107, "Tuppen, hönan," 2, var. 3, and Nos. 4, 5. French: Rolland, 57, 402; V. S., *Mélusine*, I (1878), col. 256, No. 27; Baissac, *Mauritius*, p. 402. Portuguese: Braga, 12; Parsons, *Cape Verde*, 58a through 58c. Italian: Pitrè, 319; Tschiedel, 36. Modern Greek: Stathes, p. 355, No. 141 (He is a prophet and not even a man, he wears a garment not made by hands, and when he dies, he is baptized); Georgeakis, p. 295. Samoan: Heider, 100 (Name for me the prophet who makes forecasts, his coat is blue, he wears a starched shirt-front and a white necktie, his hat is blue.—The kingfisher, whose cries foretell rain).

The Danish and Swedish "Who is the farmer's prophet?" (Kristensen, p. 37, § 95, No. 123; Ström, pp. 108–109, "Tuppen, hönan," 9) may be a derivative of this riddle. The Wamajame in Africa say simply "It wakens people" (Ovir, 17), which is a rare instance of description in terms of function rather than form. The Samoan "Who first tells us that morning is near?" (Heider, 123) involves, as the collector points out, a pun on *toa*, which signifies both "cock" and "hero."

585a. "He was at his greatest height before e'er Adam fell" probably refers to the creation of animals before the creation of men (Gen. 1).

585b. Joseph's coat (Gen. 37:3) may have suggested the "coat of many colors."

586. The general import of the riddle is obvious, and since the full original literary version will no doubt come to light, I have not felt it necessary to attempt emendations. I call attention to the rhymes "Job: robe" and "nature: creature."

587a through 587d. Breton: Sauvé, 63. German: Haffner, 45. Lithuanian: Schleicher, p. 197 (In the summer with an old fur coat, in the winter without a fur coat.—Peas). Serbian: Novaković, p. 45, No. 11 (During the summer it is dressed all the time; during the winter it is naked. It is stronger than an ox or a horse), and p. 53, No. 3 (In the winter it is green, and in summer it is bushy.—Wheat). Finnish: Lönnrot, 1084 = Henssen, 220. Mordvin: Ahlqvist, p. 40, No. 22 = Paasonen, 104 (In fur in the summer, naked in winter). Votyak: Wichmann, *Votyak*, 433 (In winter in a white winter coat, in summer in fur.—Birch). Yakut: Piekarski, 62 (They say that there is one who dons a fur garment in the summer and throws it off in the winter.—Frost); Priklonskii, 64. Samoan: Heider, 18 (Who is the man who comes naked from the jungle, is then clothed in the village, and wears this dress until death?—*Lafo*, a kind of bamboo. It is cut and trimmed of leaves in the jungle, then wrapped with cane-straw for thatching).

587d. "Gray" is a corruption of "gay."

588a through 588c. French: Parsons, *Antilles*, III, Grenada, 73, p. 374, Cariacou, 18, p. 379, St. Lucia, 36, p. 380, Martinique, 5, p. 392, Dominica, 27, p. 399, Guadaloupe, 11, p. 409, Les Saintes, 3, p. 415, Marie Galante, 42.

See the riddles for the fingernails cited in the headnote to No. 989.

589a through 593f. African, Togo: Schönhärl, 147 (It is rent, but one can't patch it with a thread).

591a through 591c. For the usual Humpty Dumpty riddles see Nos. 738 through 747*b*.

593a through 593f. French: Baissac, *Mauritius*, p. 408 (A crowd of little ladies in the house; all their clothes are in tatters); Parsons, *Antilles*, III, 406, Martinique, 106. Indian, Malayalam: Schmolck, p. 242, No. 21 (The leaves torn to bits, the fruit full of thorns.—Momoridia fruit). The last clause has a parallel expressed in terms of persons in the Bakongo pineapple riddle, "We went to the village where everybody has arrows" (Denis, 65). For similar riddles see the headnote to Nos. 576–577 in the present collection.

594a, 594b. I have noted no parallel to the Nyika turtle riddle, "The son of a gentleman, he wears a suit of iron" (Hollis, *Nyika*, p. 140, No. 14).

595. French: Parsons, *Antilles*, III, 410, Les Saintes, 26. Surinam: Herskovits, p. 435, No. 2 (In the deep bush a man sits with a crown on his head).

601a, 601b. In these texts, "read" signifies "interpret."

601b. The riddler has substituted a jingle for Itum Paraditum.

605. Italian: Salvioni, *Archivio*, IV (1885), 539, No. 1.

607 through 631. Welsh: Hull and Taylor, 98. Welsh Gypsy: Sampson, 30. Breton: Sauvé, 113. Frisian: Dykstra, *Snypsnaren*, pp. 102, 107; H. Meier, *Ostfriesland*, p. 228, No. 19; Schrijnen, II, 104, No. 16 (There sits a maiden in the green, with a pretty red coat. When one pinches her, *she* screams, and yet she has a heart of stone). Flemish: Joos, 1st ed., 78 through 83, and 2d ed., 153, 155, 156 (There stands a maiden at the door with a white apron. The longer she stands, the shorter she is); *Ons Volksleven*, II (1890), 104, No. 17. German: Wossidlo, 275, 416; Frischbier, *Menschenwelt*, p. 250, Nos. 84, 87; Gilhoff, 434, 435; W. Busch, *Korrespondenzblatt des Vereins für niederdeutsche Sprachforschung*, XXIV (1903), 28; L. Strackerjan, *Aberglauben und Sagen aus dem Herzogtum Oldenburg* (2d ed.; Oldenburg, 1909), II, 66, No. 333. Danish: Kristensen, p. 83, § 217, No. 328; Feilberg, *Ordbog*, II, 484, s.v. "lys," citing *Skattegraveren*, VI, 31, No. 387. Norwegian: Landstad, p. 810, No. 36. Spanish, Argentinian: Lehmann-Nitsche, 343. Dominican Rep.: Andrade, 302. Porto Rican: Mason, 552. Lithuanian: Schleicher, p. 203, Jurgelionis, 378 (There stands a man on a hill. The longer he stands, the shorter he becomes), 379 (A white maiden with a little red hood, her shirt made of all the plants [wax]). For the last theme see the honey riddle, No. 1069 of the present collection. Lettish: Bielenstein, 638 (A tall, graceful maiden, the longer she lives, the shorter she becomes), 957 (A tall, delicate maiden, a golden cap on her head). Gypsy: Wlislocki, 42 (It has a white coat, it has a little red cap and a black head). Arabic: Friedreich, p. 178, No. 15 (I saw a graceful woman, who grew shorter and shorter, so that when she died, there was nothing to bury), which is quoted from Seetzen; Ruoff, p. 28, No. 45 (Something,—the greater its age, the shorter it becomes). Surinam: Herskovits, p. 441, No. 40. Chinese: Rudolph, p. 75, No. 29 (There is a red-faced mandarin whose tongue is thrust out a third of an inch. From his mouth flows bloody water, and he dares not stand in the wind).

625a, 625b. (Woman or man sitting.) Flemish: Joos, 32 (Madame de Wit [White], the longer she sits, the shorter she becomes), 159. Danish: Kristensen, p. 83, § 217, No. 327. Walloon: Colson, *Wallonia*, IV, 150, No. 178 (A lady who is so sure in her seat, the more she sits, the more she goes away).

631. (Flames or fiery colors on head.) Icelandic: Árnason, 611 (Who is that fair lady that has a headdress standing straight up? Her top is wrapped in flames). Indonesian,

Tabaru: Fortgens, 59 (A snake with a golden head). See also the descriptions of matches in Nos. 583a through 584b of the present collection, the Dard hookah riddle, "My father's mother, on her head fire is burning" (Leitner, *Indian Antiquary*, I [1872], 91, No. 5), and the hookah riddle quoted in the headnote to Nos. 1440–1441, n. 6.

632a through 632d. The answer is "a cherry," unless otherwise noted. Irish: De Bhaldraithe, 15. Welsh: Hull and Taylor, 179 through 182 (plum). Breton: Sébillot, *Haute-Bretagne*, 36. Dutch: Joos, 452; *Ons Volksleven*, I (1889), 79, No. 46 (Saint Job with his red head, with his stone heart, and his green tail); Schrijnen, II, 104, No. 16. German: Wossidlo, 181, 182, 204; Gilhoff, 285 through 288; Haffner, 25 (A maiden sits on a tree. She wears a red hem on her skirt, her heart is a red stone), 27 (Something stands on the bank, has only one leg, wears a red cap); Hanika-Otto, 31a (A maiden sits in a green bower, wears a little red coat. If you squeeze her, she weeps, and yet she has a heart of stone). Swiss: Rochholz, 387; Zahler, *Münchenbuchsee*, 196. Danish: Kristensen, p. 46, § 122, No. 170, and p. 67, § 161, No. 244. Norwegian: Stafset, 63; Aasen, 8 (A black hat, red staff, stone in stomach, tree in foot.—*Hjupa Njupa* [a phrase signifying a cherry]); Bergh, *Valdres*, 10; Berge, 27; Landstad, p. 810, No. 31. Swedish: Dybeck, *Runa*, 1847, p. 40, No. 5 = Hyltén-Cavallius, *Värend*, 28 (Red body, black top, wooden leg to stand on); Dybeck, *Runa*, 1850, p. 35, No. 9; 1865–1873, p. 31, No. 36; Ström, p. 126, "Korsbärsträdet," 4. French: Bladé, *Armagnac*, 53; Marchessou, *Velay et Auvergne*, p. 179, No. 9; A. Ferrand, *Dauphiné*, p. 226; Sébillot, *Auvergne*, 17; Dardy, *L'Albret*, p. 331 (quoted in the headnote to Nos. 632–644, n. 1, of the present collection). Catalan: Milá y Fontanals, 1876, p. 24, No. 12 (What is that: Don Galindoy is in his field, with ten thousand men around him, all wear red caps except Don Galindoy, who is the oldest?). Spanish, Argentinian: Lehmann-Nitsche, 85, 167. Chilean: Flores, 310, 312, 313. Lithuanian: Jurgelionis, 927, 928 (A little stomach of gold, a little cup of bone.—Plum), 929 (A high helmet, it tastes like wine, it has a heart of stone.—Plum), 930 (A black helmet, the taste of wine, the heart of stone.—Cherry), 931 (Red, taste of wine, heart of stone.—Cherry). Hungarian: Kriza, 13 (The outside is red, the inside is hairy, there is headgear on its head, and a stick in its bottom.—Gooseberry).

634. Irish: Hyde, p. 171 (On the top of the tree see the little man red, a stone in his belly, a cap on his head); Christiansen, 58. German: Wossidlo, 209; Haffner, 28; Hanika-Otto, 24. Norwegian: Brox, *Ytre Senja*, 116. Swedish: Ericsson, *Södermanland*, I (1879), 89, No. 44; Ström, p. 128, "Nyponbusken," 1 through 3; Sandén, *Norra Vadsbo*, 12. Latin: Johannes Lorichius, as printed in Reusner, ed. 1599, p. 107 = ed. 1602, p. 281 (arbutus). Walloon: Colson, *Wallonia*, IV, 91, No. 85c. French: Rolland, 99; Guillon, *La Bresse*, p. 20 (dog rose). Bulgarian: Gubov, 410 (Daddy is red, on top he has a little red cap), 412 (A red thing, on its top its cap is red), 413 (A red thing, its red cap reaches down to its shoulders).

645. The boat may represent the shape of the pod, and the bone down the woman's throat may be the seed or the membranous thread through the pod. For parallels see French: Parsons, *Antilles*, III, 400, Guadaloupe, 25, p. 416, Marie Galante, 58 (soldier in a red cap). Spanish, Argentinian: Lehmann-Nitsche, 85, 167. For comparisons to a skirt that changes from green to red see the headnote to Nos. 668–669, § 5, in the present collection.

646. See the Irish lobster riddle, "He comes to you amidst the brine, the butterfly of the sun, the man of coat so blue and fine, with red thread his shirt is done" (Hyde, p. 170), which might, with a few changes, suit a rainbow. See a slightly different version in De Bhaldraithe, 31; O Dalaigh, 64. In the English riddle the introductory formula "As I was going over London Bridge" is scarcely appropriate.

647. Compare the Cuban "From Santo Domingo I come, from preaching a sermon;

I wear a white habit, and yellow is my heart" (Massip, 100), which suggests a monk in white and the cackling of the hen, and the Balkar "In a white castle there is a yellow princess" (Pröhle, p. 120).

649. English: Tupper, *Holme Riddles*, 140 note (There's a short little gentleman / That wears the yellow trews), which the editor cites from a literary source and not from tradition. Scotch Gaelic: Nicolson, pp. 17 (A little one under a rock, though little it ever hums; a cap on it, two horns on it, and a yellow French coat), 19 (A little wife comes to this township, and good she is at droning; a cowl of meadow-sweet on her, and a yellow coat of blanket cloth), and another on the same page (A little old man in my father's house is oftentimes a-droning, a cowl on him when lying down, and a long French coat). Swiss: Zahler, *Münchenbuchsee*, 34 (yellow trousers). Italian: Schneller, *Wälschtirol*, p. 253, No. 5 (I wear a golden cloak which serves to adorn me; I go through meadows and gardens for a meal, and everyone licks his fingers with my dung). Turkish: Moshkov in Radlov, X, 267, No. 32 (Into the woods it goes, a little Negro; out of the woods it goes, yellow stockings on its legs). Crimean Tatar: Filonenko, 7 (From far off a young man comes and he wears a sock on his leg). The Yakut "In a caftan [coat] of silk and satin, a short tailless shaman buzzes" (Popov, p. 284) makes no mention of color. Indian, Bengali: Mitra, *Chittagong*, p. 965, Nos. 10 (What is that animal whose body is yellow, whose legs are like toothpicks?), 10*a* (Lady Binodini is weltering turmeric, and after seizing and kissing one, flies away after causing the latter to weep with pain), 10*b* (The bird is yellow-colored, possesses legs of bamboo, and swooping down from a distance, stings one, which act causes the latter's body to smart with pain). For the comparison of a fly to a person who gives a kiss, see No. 735 of the present collection; and for the comparison of a bee to a bird, see No. 353 and the corresponding note. Gujerati: Mehta, p. 120, No. 12 (It is some animal which is yellow in color, but it is not a parrot. It is dark, but it is not a serpent. It is, forsooth, equipped with wings, but it cannot be put under the category of birds; and lastly, it bites and yet it is not a snake. —Wasp). Indonesian, Tabaru: Fortgens, p. 537, No. 78 (A man whose middle is golden).

For comparisons of a swarm of bees or wasps to a company of motley persons, see Nos. 887, 893, 894, and 899 through 904, in the present collection.

650. For comparisons to objects that few workmen can make, see No. 793 and the headnote to Nos. 793–794.

651, 652. Compare Lettish: Bielenstein, 52 (A little, little man, a green dress, a little black girdle.—Horsetail [*Equisetum*]). Malay: Klinkert, 55 (When little, it had a green dress; when large, a red dress.—Spanish pepper), 57 (When little, it had a green dress and white heart; when grown, it had a yellow dress and a black heart.—Papaya), 66 (When it is little, it has a green dress; when grown, it has a white dress. It looks like a Chinese boat filled with baked rice.—The fruit of the white *laboe*).

653. The import of the insult and also that of the riddle are obscure.

655b. A formula fixing a time within which a riddle should be guessed is unusual.

656. This curious text is a fragment of an obscure game rhyme; see Alice B. Gomme, *The Traditional Games of England, Scotland, and Ireland*, I (London, 1894), 7–8, "Alligoshee." It is not clear how it came to be applied to a coffin, but see an altogether different comparison of a coffin to a coat in No. 1209 of the present collection.

657. The riddler has admitted the answer, or at least a very definite suggestion of the answer, into the riddle. He does not explain the "sisters and brothers," who are, I conjecture, the shoots. The whole smacks of the Sunday-school magazine.

658. The comparison to a mouse and the rhyme of "house" and "mouse" are characteristic of riddles for a walnut (Nos. 1271*a*, 1271*b*, 1273, 1275) and for a star (No. 1281). The first sentence alludes to the name Robin.

659. Polish: Gustawicz, 455 (It stands on the fence in a black overcoat).
660. Not a riddle, but a rhyme mocking a policeman. For a riddle describing a policeman, see the clever Parsee "A black jar with a yellow cork" (Munshi, p. 410), which refers to the uniform of the Bombay police.
661. An exact parallel is lacking. For similar conceptions see Welsh: Hull and Taylor, 132 through 134. Serbian: Novaković, p. 120, No. 6 (I killed a buffalo ox, cut it into pieces, and each piece returned as an ox.—Garlic). African, Duala: Ebding, 4. Swahili: Velten, 57 (One begets a hundred.—Seed-corn). Bakongo: Denis, 88 (Papa ate the pig. With the hairs that were left, I made a new pig.—The head of the sweet potato). For related conceptions see, in the present collection, Nos. 95, 1052, the headnote to Nos. 828–836, §§ 1–2, and a riddle quoted in the note to Nos. 810a through 811c.
662. The "twins" are the two halves of the plum.
665 through 667. Breton: Charlec, *Dol-de-Bretagne*, 1903, p. 395. German: Carstens, *Schleswig-Holstein*, p. 423; Frischbier, *Menschenwelt*, p. 242, No. 11. Icelandic: Árnason, 420. Danish: Kristensen, p. 25, § 65, Nos. 81b, 83a, 83b. Swedish: Dybeck, *Runa*, 1865–1873, p. 30, No. 16; Ström, pp. 86–87, "Nysningen, rapningen, fisen," 1, 3, 4. French: Rolland, 132; Lallemant, *Argonne*, p. 234; Fourès, p. 253. Catalan: Pelay y Briz, 189 (Born singing, it dies without bones.—Sneeze). Spanish, Chilean: Flores, 571. Cuban: Massip, 155 through 158. Guatemalan: Recinos, 53. New Mexican: Campa, 262. Portuguese: Parsons, *Cape Verde*, 230 (Born singing, dead roosting). Italian: Pitrè, 605, 680 (born without wings); Coronedi-Berti, *Archivio*, II (1883), 578, No. 32; Pasquarelli, *ibid.*, XV (1896), 76, No. 7 (born, sings, dies).
665. (Thunder.) Catalan: Pelay y Briz, 133. The introductory phrase "I am no fish, no flesh" occurs now and again and with various modifications; see the note to Nos. 1237a through 1237j of the present collection. It limits the range of choice in guessing the answer.
656. (Born without sin.) German: Frischbier, *Menschenwelt*, p. 242, No. 9.
668. German: Wossidlo, 484 (a literary riddle); Carstens, *Schleswig-Holstein*, p. 417. Swiss: Zahler, *Münchenbuchsee*, 182. Norwegian: Stafset, 212 (So they put on it a shirt so white, so they laid it down like another corpse, so they set on it a crown of red gold, so it was living and not dead). In Norway, a corpse wears a crown something like a bridal crown. Spanish, Domican Rep.: Andrade, 74. Porto Rican: Mason, 113. Modern Greek: Stathes, p. 346, No. 86 (I was born in the Land of the Franks; I wear white clothing. When they take me, they quickly dress me; they "pound" me into black clothes), which is not completely intelligible. Turkish: Kúnos, 138 (Twins grew tall in the same locality. We were girls; our house and domicile was burned; we were beaten; they threw us into the water; in the water they beat us; we threw ourselves into the sea; this was our fate).
670. Riddlers occasionally use the idea that intoxicating liquor gives a man a fall. See Breton: Sébillot, *Devinettes*, 17b. Indian, Uraon: Archer, p. 484, No. 88 (The boy who knocks a man down). See also No. 467a of the present collection.
671. Note that this riddle is cast in the form of a conundrum. It is included here because it exemplifies a biographical sequence of acts.
672, 673. I have not noted any close parellels. See, for example, "Born without father and mother, [I am] within my tomb; while the fruit I give is good fortune to others, it is death to me" (Spanish: Demófilo, 496); "Imprisoned in the jail which I myself have made, and for food I have the richest cloth" (Spanish, Chilean: Flores, 321); "It digs its own grave" (Tatar: Kalashev and Ioakimov, p. 51, No. 31); "It eats and relieves itself day and night for two months and then for six months it buries itself in its hiding place" (Indian, Ho: Haldar, p. 277, No. 20). See also the Malay riddle for a spider,

"What is it that builds a house within a house, getting the materials out of his own body?" (W. W. Skeat, *Malay Magic* [London, 1900], p. 484, n. 1). See the many references to riddles for a silkworm in De Filippis, Index.

674 through 677. The versions differ widely and show that the riddlers have not always preserved the original import of the underlying comparison. Loewenthal's helpful discussion (pp. 57–58) only touches on the many difficult problems in the history of this riddle.

For parallels see Scotch Gaelic: Nicolson, p. 59. Irish: De Bhaldraithe, 35 (Not blood and not flesh and not bone is he, but from blood and flesh he grew. They touch his head to it and take a drop from it and spread it between two enemies). This confused text is partially intelligible in the light of the following parallels. Breton: Charlec, *Dol-de-Bretagne*, 1904, p. 168, No. 27 (I am neither flesh nor bone, yet I have come from flesh and bone. I announce peace and war. I walk on land and sea. I enter the cabinet of kings. One dips my head in a liquid, and I drink). Flemish: Joos, 327, 329, 332, 333. German: Wossidlo, 85*d*, 85*e*. The rather widely divergent themes of Wossidlo, 83, 84, and 86, are perhaps remotely connected with this riddle. See further: Frischbier, *Thierwelt*, pp. 356–357, Nos. 84 through 88; Müllenhoff, *Zeitschrift für deutsche Mythologie*, III (1855), 16, No. 21 (They flayed me, they cut me, they tore my soul from my body, then I went over the white field and wept my black tears). This contains elements characteristic of the riddle on the tortures of flax, given in the present collection (No. 679 and the headnote to No. 679), and of the riddle for writing (Nos. 1063*a* through 1063*i*). It contains very little of the present theme. See further, Butsch, 3 (It is a strange thing. In life it was weak; after death it became strong; it makes great business for many; it is ready for good and evil; it makes joy for one, sorrow for another), which is a series of generalities perhaps not related to our theme; Hanika-Otto, 76, 77; H. Meier, *Ostfriesland*, 33; Haase, *Ruppin*, 136. Swiss: Rochholz, 521. Danish: Kristensen, pp. 26–32, § 67, Nos. 85 through 87*c*; Feilberg, *Ordbog*, II, 805, s.v. "pennefjer." Norwegian: Brox, *Ytre Senja*, 182. Swedish: Dybeck, *Runa*, 1848, p. 47, No. 67 = Russwurm, 24; Ericsson, *Södermanland*, I (1879), 86, No. 29, and p. 90, No. 50; II (1881), 94, No. 89; and V (1884), 66, Nos. 215, 216; Sandén, *Norra Vadsbo*, 103; Christofferson, pp. 34–45, Nos. 11, 12 = *Folkminnen och folktankar*, II (1915), 88, Nos. 11, 12; Ström, pp. 186–187, "Svanpennan," and pp. 187–189, "Gåspennan," 1 through 4. Latin: Reusner, ed. 1599, p. 126 (by Johannes Stigelius) = *ibid.*, ed. 1602, p. 302 = Friedreich, p. 212, No. 4; Huldreich Therander (Johann Sommer), 236. See also Reusner, ed. 1602, pp. 284–285. French: Rolland, 253; V. S. *Mélusine*, I (1878) col. 254, No. 11; Lallemant, *Argonne*, p. 233; Souché as cited in Eugène Rolland, *Faune populaire*, VI (Paris, 1883), 176 (Its mother loses it; someone finds it, passes it through the flames, tears its soul from it, and makes it work in a field without soil). This last riddle shows some similarity to the riddles for a pot or other manufactured object discussed in the headnote to No. 678 of the present collection. See also Spanish: Demófilo, 826, and pp. 439–440, Nos. 19, 20; Rodríguez Marín, p. 372, nn. 172–174. Argentinian: Lehmann-Nitsche, 307. Chilean: Flores, 620. Italian: Rua, *Archivio*, VII (1888), 461, No. 116; Balladoro, *ibid.*, XVI (1897), 556, No. 46. Rumanian: Gorovei, 516. Lithuanian: Jurgelionis, 695 (Cut off my head, take out my heart, let me speak), 696 through 698; Schleicher, p. 197. Lettish: Bielenstein, 590. Polish: Gustawicz, 318 (When I used to be on my own, I flew about in the heavens. Now I am cut into pieces, dipped in black blood, and told to speak). Russian: Sadovnikov, 2140 (My mother wore me; my mother dropped me; people picked me up, took me to the fair to trade, cut off my head; I began to drink, to speak clearly), 2141 (I was born of flesh, but have no blood; I know no grammar, but write my whole life), 2142 (Twice born, not once christened, it was taken, cut up, the heart was taken out, it was given to drink, and it began to talk), which contains in the first two clauses elements belonging to a widely known riddle for a cock. See also Sadovnikov, 2143 (It will be taken out of a live and dead one, its head will be taken off, its heart will be taken out, it will be given to drink, it will begin to talk), 2143a through 2143d; Arkhangel'skii, p. 79. Serbian: Novaković, p. 163, Nos. 5 (It came out of flesh, yet is not flesh. It brought much profit and did much damage, yet it is not to blame), 6 (It fell out of a living thing, a living thing, splitting its tongue, and it spoke 77 languages), 7 (A living thing gave it. A living thing cut its head in two, and it spoke all the languages), 9 (I am dead and I was produced by a living thing, but when you cut off my head and give me water, I answer the whole world). Modern Greek: Ohlert, 2d ed., pp. 170–171. Finnish: Aarne and Krohn, 299 = Henssen, 156 (Born of flesh and blood, it is not flesh and is not blood. Great lords bear it. It brings honor to many and deprives many of honor). Votyak: Wichmann, *Votyak*, 370 (One cuts its head, tears out its heart; from the latter blood is continually flowing). Mordvin: Paasonen, 241 (I cut off its head, I draw out its heart, I give it something to drink, it begins to speak), 270 (It does not speak without much ado, but if you seize it with your hand, it begins to speak.—Pencil), which is probably an altogether different riddle. Hungarian: *Magyar Nyelvör*, VIII (1879), 521, No. 4 (I was not made of flesh, but I have grown out of flesh. I lost my flesh. They cut my body. They made me drink, they took me dancing, they use me for many purposes). Arabic: Ruoff, p. 21, No. 13 (Something: you cut off its head, you take out its heart, if you give it something to drink, it speaks). His Nos. 14 through 16 show only a remote resemblance.

The Turkish, Persian, and Indian versions probably belong to an entirely different set of ideas. See Turkish: Kowalski, *Asia Minor*, 59 (The more one rubs and stabs with it, the more tears it produces; while it goes back and forth, it does its business); Kúnos, 268 (Its shape is long, its head is split, it has a white sheet beneath it, its liquid flows in spurts, by going progressively it finishes its task). See more explicit versions in Kowalski, *Asia Minor*, 72. Persian: Phillott, 10 (A headless crane I saw; nor barley does it eat nor wheat; water it drinks from the river and it benefits all mankind). Indian: Lakshīnātha Upasānī, VIII, 2 (There is a thing that is honoured much and is allowed to take its place near the head; it has to do with the decision of the fate of each criminal, but its face is made black when it records such decision). Kashmiri: Knowles, 94 (His head is cut off, his head is cut off, I struck at his head with an axe. He drank the water at Nila Nág, and the people heard of it at Bárámúlá). In this Kashmiri riddle the last semblance resembles somewhat the riddles for thunder (see the headnote to No. 398, nn. 6–7, in the present collection) and for a letter (see the headnote to No. 1605, § 3). The series of tortures has also a vague similarity to the killing of a louse, discussed in the headnote to Nos. 970–975.

The variations in the English versions are too great to permit of reconstructing the original text from which they are derived. I have not endeavored to point out the minor defects which a careful reading discloses. A few typical examples of such defects are indicated in the notes to Nos. 674, 675b, 676, 677a.

674. The phrase "but it all belongs to me" is probably corrupt; something is lacking after "a hearty draught of . . ."; and probably "am" should be inserted in "I oft a sword."

675a. Here, as elsewhere, the identity of Knortz's and Halliwell-Phillipps' versions throws some doubt on Knortz's sources. He declares that his texts were collected from school children in Cincinnati. It is evident that the children had access to Halliwell-Phillipps. Since Hyatt has the same version, I conjecture that it was disseminated by some text of *Mother Goose* or a similar children's book.

675b. The phrase "diet drink" is evidently corrupt.

676. The repetition of the last two lines is evidently a corruption.

677a. This rewritten version substitutes the third person for the first person.

679. Although the general import of this corrupt text is clear, the explanation of the details—for example, the father or the mother—is often obscure and uncertain. The final references to visiting the poor and the rich refer to the conversion of rags into paper, that is to say, letters, and the last sentence alludes to the use of rags for wadding, which is literally blown to bits. The English text differs considerably from its parallels.

For parallels see Breton: Sébillot, *Haute-Bretagne*, 37a; Charlec, *Dol-de-Bretagne*, 1903, p. 396 (When I was young, I am green. I serve all the world. I serve at the table of the great. I have the first place there, and when I am old, they send me to school.— Flax, linen, paper); and 1904, p. 379, No. 51 (I stayed three months in my mother's stomach. They snatched me out with violence, they put me in water, they exposed me to great heat, they broke my bones, and I have accompanied the dead to the tomb); Sébillot, *Devinettes*, 37, 38; Orain, *Ille-et-Vilaine*, p. 154. Dutch: Schrijnen, II, 104, No. 13; Sinninghe, p. 13, No. 1. Flemish: Joos, 444 through 447, 455; *Ons Volksleven*, I (1889), 79, No. 45. Afrikaans: Groenewald, p. 82. German: Wossidlo, 77a through 77i; Gilhoff, 359, 360; Frischbier, *Pflanzenwelt*, p. 73, Nos. 41, 42; Woeste, 14; Schmidt, *Danzig*, 41a; O. Schell, "Vokswitz in Rätseln," *Am Urquell*, I (1890), 132, No. 12 (H. Volksmann cites parallels in a note on p. 172); R. Scharnweber and O. Jungrichter, *Sagen, Anekdoten und Schnurren aus dem Kreise Lackau, Niederlausitz* (Berlin-Adlershof, 1933), "Flachses Qual"; Böckel, *Hesse*, 21; Hanika-Otto, 250. Somewhat less closely related are Wossidlo, 96 and 222. Swiss: Zahler, *Münchenbuchsee*, 97. Danish: Kristensen, pp. 54–55, § 130, Nos. 185, 186a through 186q, and pp. 55–59, § 131, Nos. 187 through 190. Norwegian: Bugge, *Telemarken*, 34; Stafset, 226 (First they buried me deep in the earth, then I grew up and became big. Then there grew upon me a fair flower, then they wove me and I became thin. So I sit at table with great people, so I follow the dead into the ground). This introduces too many direct allusions to flax and therefore loses somewhat the air of a biography of a person. Swedish: Ström, pp. 129–131, "Linet," 3, 7. Latin: Reusner, ed. 1602, p. 190. French: Rolland, 93, 97; E. H. Carnoy, *La Tradition*, VI (1892), 353, No. 8; V. S., *Mélusine*, I (1878), col. 255, Nos. 22, 23; Marchessou, *Velay et Auvergne*, p. 172, Nos. 6, 14; Sébillot, *Auvergne*, 27; Queyrat, *La Creuse*, I, 366; Lallemant, *Argonne*, p. 234; Mensignac, *Gironde*, p. 305, No. 50; Westphalen, *Metz*, col. 199. Spanish: Demófilo, p. 419, No. 3; *El folklore andaluz*, I (1882–1883), 127. Portuguese: Pires de Lima, 191. Italian: Pitrè, 111; Gianandrea, *Archivio*, II (1883), 85, No. 42, and p. 86, No. 43. Russian: Sadovnikov, 1300 (I was beaten time and again, I was hot and hot again, I was torn in pieces, I was dragged in the field, I was locked under key, then seated at table), 1300a (I was beaten and hit, I was promoted to all the ranks, I was seated upon the throne with the tsar), 1300b, 1300c. Some elements belonging to the pot riddle, which I have discussed in the headnote to No. 679 of the present collection, appear in "The head is eaten [linseed], the skin [linen] is worn, but even the dogs will not eat the meat" (Arkhangel'skii, p. 76). Serbian: Novaković, p. 102, No. 7 (They beat me, choked me, trounced me, and yet I sit upon the throne with the tsar.—Shirt). Finnish: Aarne and Krohn, 74 = Henssen, 249 (The heat is cut off, the entrails cut to bits, yet it serves king and beggar), which is perhaps an adaptation of the pen riddle (Nos. 674 through 677b of the present collection) to flax. Mordvin: Paasonen, 31, 305. Georgian: Blechsteiner, p. lv, No. 2, comments on a rhyme that shows some similarity to the flax riddle: "In the pit I strewed millet, in order to store it; water flowed into the pit, in order to make it rotten. I threw it out of the pit to dry; a bird sat on the fence to pick it up. I raised a stick against the bird, in order to kill it. He [the bird] made complaint to the lord, that I might be punished. The latter took away everything that I had."

Although there are considerable differences, this shows some resemblance to such a cumulative tale as "The Old Woman and Her Dog." African, Lamba: Doke, 12 (A little animal of many death-places.—Bark-cloth. It is cut down in one place, stripped from the tree in another, soaked in water in another, beaten soft in another, and worn in another).

680. German: Wossidlo, 482; Böckel, *Hesse*, 22. Danish: Kristensen, p. 109, § 295, No. 469 (rye), and p. 131, § 372, No. 592 (seed grain); Feilberg, *Ordbog*, II, 271, s.v. "korn"; and III, 87, s.v. "rug." Swedish: Ström, p. 193, "Brödet," 1. French: V. S., *Mélusine*, I (1878), col. 256, Nos. 2, 4, 5; Marchessou, *Velay et Auvergne*, p. 173, No. 7 (the Host); Mensignac, *Gironde*, p. 306, No. 61. Spanish: Demófilo, 996. Argentinian: Lehmann-Nitsche, 47. Italian: Straparola, IX, 5, and XIII, 2; Guiseppe Pitrè, "Seminagione, mietitura, trebbiatura del frumento. Usanze e practiche popolari siciliane," *Archivio*, VI (1887), 216; Rondini, *ibid.*, VIII (1889), 192, No. 116; Ferraro, *ibid.*, XXI (1902), 536, No. 11. Russian: Sadovnikov, 1225 (On the field of Arsk, on the Tatar boundary, everyone is down, is beaten, beards are shaven, and bellies slashed open.—Sheaves), 1226 (I beheld a miracle miraculous. The head is hacked; the belly is slashed; the guts dangle, streaming forth; bodies are carted into the yard; the soul is carried to Paradise.—Sheaves), 1275 (They cut me, they bind me, they hit me mercilessly. I pass through fire and water, and my end is: a knife and teeth). Mordvin: Paasonen, 30 (I grow up in one year; they cut me off from my feet, they beat me, they seize me, they take me, they set me before the emperor).

681. The Letts describe wheat as a man whose beard grows upward (Bielenstein, 763). Compare the typical description of a plant as a person whose beard or hair projects (see the headnote to No. 544 in the present collection). Compare also the description of an icicle or a cow's tail as a plant with its root above and its top below (Nos. 1055a through 1057).

682. Norwegian: Bergh, *Valdres*, 67 (Who was two weeks old when Christ died and is not yet any older?). Italian: Tammi, 25 (It is a girl only one month old who goes into all countries). For the notion of traveling widely see the headnotes to Nos. 525–534 and 531–534, § 1, in the present collection. Samoan: Heider, 147 (Somebody lives only fourteen days.—Moonlight). See also the riddles for the moon in Nos. 89 through 94 of the present collection.

683a, 683b. The details are quite insufficient for one to guess the answer. The same defect appears in No. 905, which is couched in the plural. The conception is related to the Filipino squash riddle, "The mother creeps, and the son sits" (Starr, *Philippines*, 402). For conceptions involving an animal and an object, as in the White Russian "Under the fence a hen nests" (Shein, 1), see, in the present collection, Nos. 1203a through 1203c and the note to Nos. 1203a through 1203c.

687. The import of the comparison is not clear. Welsh riddlers describe a horsecollar in the same way (Hull and Taylor, 112, 113), but are representing the peg on which the collar hangs by the finger and the opening of the collar by the eye.

688. Irish: Hyde, p. 171; Christiansen, 65 (A little messenger from house to house and he is out at night); De Bhaldraithe, 70; O Dalaigh, 103. Lithuanian: Schleicher, p. 210 (I go all day, I go all night, I do not come to the end of the village). For a defective version omitting mention of sleeping outdoors see No. 706 in the present collection.

689a through 689c. Spanish, Argentinian: Lehmann-Nitsche, 314a (A large dry old woman who drips butter). Basque: Vinson, 8 (A gentleman who is always befouling himself).

691. African, Dschagga: Gutmann, p. 530 (Father's grandmother opens her mouth.—

Notes 759

Dried bananas). For a discussion of the theme and for parallels in terms of animals or things, see the note to No. 377 of the present collection.
692. The import of the riddle is obscure.
695a through 695f. (Goes; goes and stands.) Welsh: Hull and Taylor, 33. Welsh Gypsy: Sampson, 33. Breton: Sauvé, 67a (Mr. Rummage rummaging in the house, without eyes and without nose), 67b (What goes all about the house without eye and without nose?); Duine, *Saint-Malo*, p. 517. Flemish: Joos, 192. German: Wossidlo, 291a, 291c; Frischbier, *Menschenwelt*, p. 253, Nos. 133, 134; Gilhoff, 520 through 522. French: Rolland, 177; Bladé, *Armagnac*, 46 (What goes from room to room, has but one leg?); V. S., *Mélusine*, I (1878), col. 262, No. 51; Ledieu, *Démuin*, p. 135; A. Ferrand, *Dauphiné*, p. 228; Mensignac, *Gironde*, p. 302, No. 31; De la Suie, *Savoie*, p. 472 (Who rests in the corner after going about the room?); Marchessou, *Velay et Auvergne*, p. 170, No. 32; E. H. Carnoy, *La Tradition*, VI (1892), 353, No. 4; Parsons, *Antilles*, III, 407, Guadaloupe, 117, and p. 410, Les Saintes, 18. Italian: Pitrè, 344a, 344b. Lettish: Bielenstein, 580, 581 (see also the headnote to Nos. 695–699, n. 18, of the present collection). Czech: Hanika-Otto, p. 22, No. 31 (A girl came to our house, looked into every corner, and crouched in one of them). White Russian: Wasilewski, 92 (Look here, look there, sleep under the stove), which has some resemblance to the riddles for a shoe or milk (see the headnote to Nos. 445–458 in the present collection). Russian: Sadovnikov, 291 (I will grope and grope again, then will take my place in the corner), 291a, 291b, 293a through 293g, 297, and compare his Nos. 298, 301, 313. Modern Greek: Polites, *Neohellenika Analekta*, I, 194, No. 7 = Stathes, p. 337, No. 35 (He goes round and round and sits in the corner).
696a, 696b. (Dancing.) Swedish: Ström, p. 171, "Kvasten," 4. Lettish: Bielenstein, 574. Polish: Gustawicz, 246 (Dressed in a raincoat of red, she dances about the room). Zyrian: Wichmann, *Zyrian*, 263 (Little Matthias dances on the floor).
696a. "Drill" seems to be used in the old sense of "twirl," and "a hall" signifies the extent of the motion.
697. Compare Nos. 221, 559.
(The following parallels contain no mention of "going" or "dancing".) German: Wossidlo, 291b (What is that which stands in the corner and looks in all the corners, and when he has done the looking, then he goes to stand again in his corner?); Frischbier, *Menschenwelt*, p. 254, No. 135 (In the corner there stands a maiden with a torn jacket). French: Baissac, *Mauritius*, p. 414 (In all the houses the place of my good wife is upright in a corner). Italian: Pitrè, 344c (*Ntantarantà!* Where I put it, there it is). Lithuanian: Jurgelionis, 420 (A maiden stands in a corner, her skirt is green.—Broom with leaves [a broom of birchen twigs]). Polish: Saloni, *Rzeshów*, 109 (It stands at the end in a black coat), 110 (The maiden stands at the end in a black coat), 111 (It stands at the end in a red belt), 112 (It stands at the end in a black belt); Gustawicz, 236 (A maiden stands behind the door wrapped in rods and switches), 237 (A maiden stands behind the door; she is wrapped and bound with rope), 238 (A maiden stands behind the door; she is covered with dirt), 239 (A maiden stands behind the door; she is covered with millet seed), 240 (A maiden stands in the vestibule. Whoever passes her, bows to her [this refers to brushing the snow off the shoes]), 241, 245. Russian: Sadovnikov, 292.
699. Lappish: Donner, 16 (What has room in a mousehole and cannot turn in an oxstall?—Staff). Indian, Bhil: Hedberg, p. 875, No. 63 (After having run through the whole forest, he is sitting on a place not bigger than a pice). A pice is a small Indian coin. For other parallels see the note to No. 258 in the present collection and the remarks on the answer "stick" in the headnote to Nos. 695–699, nn. 36–39.
703. The import of the riddle is not wholly clear. "Lillylow" is a north country term

for a fire or blaze; see Joseph Wright, *English Dialect Dictionary*, III (London, 1902), 605. The presence of this riddle in Knortz's collection, which he says was derived from American sources (perhaps in Cincinnati, where he was a teacher), raises serious doubts regarding the reliability of his sources. Other similarities to the collections made by Halliwell-Phillipps confirm these doubts.

705. The riddle has a literary flavor, but I have not found its source. Other riddles for a key are not precisely parallel. They usually involve a comparison to an animal conceived as a guardian. See the Spanish "Small as a mouse, and it guards the house like a lion" (Demófilo, 626; Rodríguez Marín, 627. Argentinian: Lehmann-Nitsche, 608. Chilean: Flores, 147, 148, 150 through 152). Other equivalents of a key may be seen in the Mordvin "He is small, but holds fast a whole city" and "A sparrow holds fast an ox.—A chest with its lock" (Ahlqvist, pp. 40–41, Nos. 21 and 11). Somewhat farther off stands the versification of Symphosius: "Great powers from little strength I bring. I open closed houses, but again I close the open. I guard the house for the master, but in turn am guarded by him" (Ohl, 4).

706. This is probably a defective version of No. 688. I conjecture that the answers should be "lane, path" and that "park" is "pa'" misheard and misinterpreted. By "pa'" the speaker intended to signify "path."

707. For the usual form of this riddle, see Nos. 1597a through 1603. See also the headnote to Nos. 1597–1603.

710. Hungarian: Meltzl, 15.

711. Rumanian: Papahagi, 64. Arabic: Ruoff, p. 18, No. 2 (One saw the bridge and walked on it; one saw the bridge and didn't walk on it; one neither saw the bridge nor walked on it.—A pregnant woman with a child in her arms). Turkish: Kúnos, 189 (Three are involved in crossing, one can see, the other two cannot.—Bridge, pregnant woman). Does this mean that the bridge is personified as a blind creature? See also Hamizade, 11 (Three persons pass over a bridge. One looks, stops, and passes. One looks, does not stop, and passes. Whatever the one [the first] looks at, whatever the one [the second] steps on, he [the third] passes.—Woman, nursing child, child in womb); 122 (He looks, he walks, he passes; he looks, he does not walk, he passes; he does not look, he does not walk, he passes.—Child walking, child at breast, child in womb); 414 (Two sheep passed over a bridge; one looked, walked, and passed over; the other did not look, did not walk, and passed over).

For descriptions of a pregnant creature in which the members of mother and child are enumerated see Nos. 56a through 57 in the present collection, and for descriptions in which the unborn child is said to go through the rain without being wet see No. 961 and the headnote to Nos. 961–963. Also see Nos. 169a through 170b and the note to Nos. 169a through 171.

712a through 712d. Lithuanian: Jurgelionis, 295 (Grasped by the wedded, grasped by the unwedded.—Door), 296 through 298. Russian: Sadovnikov, 262 (It hangs, it shakes, everyone grasps it.—Towel). Cheremiss: Wichmann, *Cheremiss*, 167; Genetz, 41 (I hold the mother-in-law of my child a little tightly). Zyrian: Wichmann, *Zyrian*, 280 (Night and day it goes back and forth, everybody seizes it). Vogul: Ahlqvist, *Vogul*, 32 (Every day we stand and seize the same cow-tail.—Latch). Turkish: Kowalski, *Asia Minor*, 43 (I have a daughter-in-law; she kisses the hand of everyone who arrives, she kisses the hand of everyone who leaves). He cites four Turkish parallels and three more with the answer "jug." See also Kowalski, *Zagadki*, 133; Kúnos, 81 (Our little bride kisses the hand of the one who comes and of the one who goes); Hamizade, 320. African, Bakongo: Denis, 23 (When you go out, you touch it; when you come in, you touch it.—Door). Indian, Khāṛiā: Roy and Roy, II, 449, No. 6 (If you want to go, do go; but you must touch me on going). Korean: Bernheisel, p. 84 (What is that which, on going out, one takes in his arms, and on entering, one takes on one's back?).

712a, 712b. "Tom, Tom, Tittymouse" and the variation contain a reminiscence of a nursery rhyme. The ultimate origin may perhaps be found in the name "Thomas Didymus."

712c. Compare "little titchie" in No. 337.

713. Compare the *Vegtamskviþa*, 12, in the *Elder Edda*, which compares waves to maidens throwing up their kerchiefs. See also Heusler, *Zeitschrift des Vereins für Volkskunde*, XI (1901), 125; Ludwig Uhland, *Schriften*, III (Stuttgart, 1866), 291, n. 26. For parallels in riddling see Swedish: Ström, p. 217, "Vattnet," Nos. 3 through 5 (waves are also called brothers). Portuguese: Parsons, *Cape Verde*, 235 (My white *galan* [a cotton shawl with white stripes]). See also the comparison of flax to dancing maidens discussed in the headnote to Nos. 946–950.

715. Compare the medieval Latin "Quidam ignotus mecum sine lingua et voce locutus est, qui numquam ante fuit nec postea erit, et quem non audiebam nec novi.—Somnium te forte fatigavit, magister" (Daly and Suchier, p. 141, No. 90).

716. For the notion of making no tracks see the headnotes to Nos. 181–185 and 227 and the note to No. 227.

719a, 719b. Latin: Ohl, Symphosius, 57 (Upon my head I walk, because I hang from a single foot. With my top I touch the ground, and leave behind me headprints; but many comrades suffer the same lot). See also, in the present collection, Nos. 187a through 189, in which the personification is less explicit.

721. See No. 112 and the headnote to No. 112. "Goes out" is here understood in two senses. This version of the riddle for a fire or the sun's rays shows many features indicating a literary rather than a popular origin. Riddlers have compared the sun or a fire to a person who cannot be kept in a house or, being outside of it, cannot be kept out. These comparisons are widely scattered and appear to be without interrelations. See Bulgarian: Chacharov, 118 (I went out. When I came in, a bandit was in the house); Ikonomov, 40 (I closed it, I locked it, yet I found a burglar at home.—Sun). Turkish: Kúnos, 53 (I have a palace with a thousand rooms, nowhere is there an opening, and yet there is a thief inside), 168 (The door is closed, the chimney is covered, and yet there is a thief in the house). African, Kamba: Lindblom, 2 (Tell me the youth in our village who is very handsome but [whom it is] impossible to wrap a piece of cloth around.—Fire). Indian, Uraon: Archer, p. 192, No. 197 (A jack of all trades, but no one can hold him.—Fire), which is perhaps related to some smoke riddles in the present collection, cited in the headnote to Nos. 1643–1654 and in the note to Nos. 1643a through 1643v.

724a through 724d. See the ax riddle, Nos. 191a, 191b. The scene is also applicable to the calf of the leg (see the headnote to No. 191, § 8). A Portuguese version with that answer, "I go to Pico, my face toward Moste'r" (Parsons, *Cape Verde*, 223), much resembles these texts.

725. This may be related to the crab riddle cited in the headnote to No. 727, § 3. The collector suggests that "carry" may be *carré*.

726. See Nos. 576a, 576b, which compare a hedgehog to a man carrying needles on his back. See further the various comparisons to a man bearing stakes or to a peddler, in the note to Nos. 576a through 576c.

727. Welsh: Hull and Taylor, 54, 55. Irish: Christiansen, 49a, 49b; Delargy, 52 (A man walking along the strand with his little house on his back); and Delargy, *Inis Cé*, 29; O Dalaigh, 47 through 49. Breton: Duine, *Saint-Malo*, p. 516. Flemish: Joos, 396, 397, 916, 917. Luxemburg: De la Fontaine, 20. German: Wossidlo, 359, 803, 804; Frischbier, *Thierwelt*, p. 359, No. 109; Hanika-Otto, 232 (From within it never sees its house, and all its life it does not come out). See additional references in Feilberg, *Ordbog*, III, 429–430. Swiss: Rochholz, 374; Zahler, *Münchenbuchsee*, 344. Danish: Kristensen, p. 121, § 334; Nos. 532a, 532b; Kamp, p. 248, No. 30; Grundtvig, *Gamle danske Minder*, III, 133, No. 16. Norwegian: Brox, *Ytre Senja*, 145, 152. Swedish: Ström, p. 120, "Snigeln," 1. Latin: Ohl, Symphosius, 18 (quoted in the headnote to No. 727 in the present collection). Walloon: Colson, *Wallonia*, IV, 63, No. 68. French: Rolland, 75; and Rolland, *Faune populaire*, XII (Paris, n.d. [1909]), 47–48, and a proverb quoted on p. 45; Bladé, *Armagnac*, 106; Lacuve, *Poitou*, p. 353, No. 20; Lespy, *Béarn*, 31; Westphalen, *Metz*, col. 202; Daleau, *Gironde*, p. 105; Fourès, p. 253; Baissac, *Mauritius*, p. 401. Catalan: Pelay y Briz, 54. Spanish: Demófilo, 227 (a versification by Perez Herrera, A.D. 1628). Argentinian: Lehmann-Nitsche, 143. Portuguese: Pires de Lima, 154. Italian: Pitrè, 408; Tammi, 6. Rumanian: Gorovei, 619; and Gorovei, *Devinettes*, p. 505. Estonian: Wiedemann, p. 268. Russian: Sadonikov, 1702. Serbian: Novaković, p. 180, Nos. 2 (It walks all day long and yet does not get out of the house), 3 (It walks all over the world and yet never gets out of the house), 4 (I get out of the house every day and yet I always stay in the house). Bulgarian: Chacharov, 88 (When it walks, it carries its house on its back). Modern Greek: Dieterich, *Rätseldichtung*, p. 94. Albanian: Hahn, p. 163, No. 77. Gypsy: Wlislocki, 31. African, Dschagga: Gutmann, p. 536 (The people of Oru have been defeated and emigrate with their houses). Indian, Ho: Haldar, p. 278, No. 29 (As long as it lives, it carries its own body about; as soon as it dies, it casts off the body). Indonesian, Tabaru: Fortgens, 86 (an edible sea snail or slug). Korean: Bernheisel, p. 86.

Another snail riddle refers to a creature moving without feet or living without bones; see Nos. 261, 264a, and 264b of the present collection.

728. The parallels, which usually have the answer "river," do not contain the remark, "I tremble at each breath of air," but contrast the power of carrying a hundred bundles or some other heavy weight with the inability to carry a stone or a coin. For examples see Breton: Sauvé, 11a, 11b; Sébillot, *Haute-Bretagne*, 7; Sébillot, *Devinettes*, 7a through 7c; Kerbeuzec, *Ille-et-Vilaine*, p. 502, No. 14; Orain, *Mélusine*, IV (1888–1889), col. 424, No. 8; Orain, *Ille-et-Vilaine*, p. 149; Charlec, *Dol-de-Bretagne*, 1904, p. 169, No. 35 (What is as big as a mare's footprint and would easily raise a hundred pounds of grain?—Yeast). Flemish: Joos, 655. French: *Les Adeuineaux amoureux*, p. lxxiv = Rolland, 23a; Rolland, 23b; and Rolland, *Rimes*, p. 214, No. 84; Roque-Ferrier, *Languedoc*, p. 326; Bladé, *Armagnac*, 43, Ledieu, *Démuin*, p. 133 (Who bears a barrel, but not a sou?); De la Suie, *Savoie*, p. 473. Spanish, Argentinian: Lehmann-Nitsche, 855 (Who bears a hundred *arrobas* of potatoes, but not a quail?). Estonian: Wiedemann, p. 268 (Whose back cannot bear a grain of sand but can carry many large houses at the same time?).

For related conceptions see Nos. 105, 1651a through 1651c and 1661 of the present collection.

729. The word "cabbage" signifies the cabbage palm and not the vegetable. Compare the French riddle for a tree, "Who lets his handkerchief fall and cannot pick it up?" (Rolland, *Rimes*, p. 200, No. 20).

The usual European comparison for a cabbage (the vegetable) is that found in "A man shaking his rags in the wind," or the like. For examples see Danish: Kristensen, pp. 77–78, § 195, Nos. 300a through 300f. Swedish: Ström, p. 131, "Kålen," 3. See also, in the present collection, the description of a banana leaf as a torn dress (Nos. 593a through 593f) and that of a cabbage as "patches on patches" (see No. 1438b and the headnote to No. 1438).

730a through 730e. French: Parsons, *Antilles*, III, 392, Dominica, 33, 34.

732. Cherekessian: Tambiev, p. 65, No. 149 (At the edge of the wood there lies congealed blood.—Strawberry).

735. Compare French: Larivey's translation of Straparola, V, 4. For the notion of giving everyone a kiss, see the riddles for a spoon (Swedish: Ström, p. 148, "Matskedan," 1. Spanish, Chilean: Flores, 214, 215) and a pump (Spanish, Argentinian: Lehmann-Nitsche, 295).

736. This obscure riddle has some similarity to an equally obscure description of clouds and the earth; see No. 1252b.

737. The import of the riddle is obscure.

738 through 747b. Irish: Delargy, 10 (Fílimín Fálaimín is up on the wall. Fílimín Fálaimín fell down to the ground. If twelve and three and two more men were to come, they could not put Fílimín Fálaimín up on the wall); O Dalaigh, 59, 60. Frisian: Dykstra, *Snypsnaren*, p. 101. Dutch: Schrijnen, II, 105, Nos. 19, 20. Flemish: Joos, 1st ed., 11, 85, 101, 133, 134, and 2d ed., 371; *Volkskunde* (Ghent), VI (1893), 152; XV (1903), 83; *Ons Volksleven*, II (1890), 104, No. 8; P. D. K., *Oostvlaamsche Zanten*, I–II (1926–1927), 41–42; J. Cornelissen, F. V. E., and P. D. K., *ibid.*, III (1928), 24; A. H. van Dyck, *ibid.*, V (1930), 68–73, and VIII (1933), 140. Many of the Flemish texts are counting-out rhymes, not riddles. "Holderdebolder," the characteristic Flemish name for the egg, may signify "head over heels"; see Kremer, *De Navorscher*, XXXII (1882), 291. Afrikaans: Groenewald, p. 83. German: Wossidlo, 20, and, without mention of a proper name, 279; A. Hoefer, *Germania* (ed. F. H. von der Hagen), V (1843), 252–254, and VI (1844), 155–156; *Korrespondenzblatt des Vereins für niederdeutsche Sprachforschung*, VII (1882), 86, No. 3, p. 87, No. 7, and p. 88; XI (1886), 54, No. 15; XXVIII (1908), 10, 26, 33–39, 43, 61, 96; Carstens, *Schleswig-Holstein*, p. 415; Frischbier, *Thierwelt*, p. 351, Nos. 58 through 62; Bock, *Der Urquell*, II (1898), 213; Haffner, 165, 166; Hanika-Otto, 382. Swiss: Rochholz, 427; Zahler, *Münchenbuchsee*, 61. Danish: Kristensen, pp. 150–151, § 439, Nos. 704, 705a through 705y; Feilberg, *Ordbog*, III, 1144, s.v. "æg." Faeroic: Hammershaimb, *Antiquarisk tidsskrift*, III (1849–1851), 317, No. 16. Norwegian: Berge, 80; Bugge, *Telemarken*, 98; Brox, *Ytre Senja*, 13, citing H. Bergh, *Sagn* (Christiania, 1871); p. 128, No. 18, and p. 129, No. 19. Swedish: Dybeck, *Runa*, 1848, p. 43, Nos. 28, 29; and 1865-1873, p. 64, No. 78; Russwurm, 20; Ericsson, *Södermanland*, III (1882), 102, No. 155; V (1884), 65, Nos. 211, 212; and compare I (1879), 89, No. 44; Sandén, *Norra Vadsbo*, 16; Noreen, *Fryksdal*, 6; Hyltén-Cavallius, *Värend*, 18; Christofferson, p. 46, Nos. 1, 2 = *Folkminnen och folktankar*, II (1915), 96, Nos. 1, 2; Geijer and Campbell, 42, 43: Ström, p. 195, "Ägget," 1. Latin: *Notes and Queries*, 8th ser., XI (1897), 135, 252; and XII (1897), 134, 277. Walloon: Colson, *Wallonia*, IV, 61, No. 58. French: Rolland, 20; Parsons, *Antilles*, III, 404, Guadaloupe, 71, and p. 417, Marie Galante, 75. Czech: Hanika-Otto, note to No. 382. Finnish: Aarne and Krohn, 119 = Henssen, 255. Modern Greek: Abbott, p. 315, No. 37 (My little uncle Theodor rolling in the straw). Georgian: Blechsteiner, p. lv, No. 8. Surinam: Herskovits, p. 439, No. 28.

743b. The "gall" is the yolk.

745a, 745b. For parallels to the idea that a broken egg cannot be picked up, see the headnote to Nos. 1661–1662.

748a, 748b. For comparisons of sunlight to milk that cannot be scraped or swept away, see the headnote to No. 1659, nn. 2–3. For the formula "all the king's men" and its variations see the riddles listed in the note to No. 1260.

751a, 751b. Depending on the circumstances, the answer is either "a waterfall" or "the surf." For parallels see Scotch Gaelic: Nicolson, p. 31 (In time of storm and time of calm, in time of flow and time of ebb, and at every time from the beginning of the year, its roar will not be subdued by us.—Waterfall). Swedish: Sandén, *Norra Vadsbo*, 91 (They cry out and complain together, but no one goes to help them.—Waterfall). Russian: W. R. S. Ralston, *Songs of the Russian People* (London, 1872), p. 357; Sadovnikov, 1482 (He cries day and night, yet his voice does not get tired), 1487 (What is there that never gets quiet?). Finnish: Lönnrot, 1912 = Henssen, 190 (It complains by night, it complains by day, but no one ever comes to help.—Rapids). This may be a fragment of the tripartite riddle of the sun, moon, and river discussed in the headnote to Nos. 138–140 of the present collection. Gypsy: Wlislocki, 19 (It cries by day and by night and yet does not become hoarse.—Waterfall). African, Kundu: Ittmann, *Kundu*, 255 (What child comes into the world complaining?—Waterfall). Pangwe: Tessmann, 8 (My father bore a child there, the same kind of speech that it had at the beginning, that same kind it naturally still has here in the neighborhood). Samoan: Heider, 39, 40; Brown, p. 344 (A man cries out continuously both by day and by night.—Surf on reef); Turner, p. 216, No. 5. Hawaiian: Judd, 93 (My tapa log that is always sounding without rest), 220 (My little man that cries day and night, all the year round).

753. Compare two Renaissance Latin riddles cited by Buchler, *Gnomologia*, 3d ed. (1614), p. 474: "Sit vox nulla mihi, vel nulla sit ala licebit, / Persono, et immensas pervolo, sæpe plagas" and "Dic, quid nec linguam, nec vocem habet: attamen illud, / Dulci homines captos detinet harmonia?"

755a through 755i. African, Kundu: Ittmann, *Kundu*, 8 (If he has caught nothing, then he roars. If he has caught something, he also roars.—Gun). Yakut: Piekarski, 295 (The girl Abrāsy does not allow anyone to touch her pubic hair.—Hair on the bow of a spring gun or, also, a bear). Abrāsy is the daughter of darkness or evil.

756. Polish: Gustawicz, 433 (An old man stands by the water, nodding his beard). Cuman: Németh, *Codex Cumanicus*, p. 594, No. 26 (On the plain the new daughter-in-law bows.—Reed). Kabardin: Talpa and Sokolov, 24 (An old man stands on the bank; his beard flutters). Yakut: Piekarski, 63 (They say that in the midst of a dense forest a shaman performs his rituals.—Aspen); Popov, p. 285 (In the forest a shaman tells fortunes.—Aspen); Priklonskii, 20. African, Dschagga: Gutmann, p. 532 (There is a man who dances continually.—Grass stalk in flowing water). Sotho: Endemann, 35. Taveta: Hollis, *Taveta*, 24 (My warrior has slept trembling all night.—A small tree that grows in a river). Indian, Bhil: Hedberg, p. 870, No. 26 (An exorcist is nodding at the river.—Lavha-grass).

Riddlers often express this idea in the plural; see, in the present collection, Nos. 946a through 946d and the headnote to Nos. 946–950.

759. In the West Indies "trash" signifies the refuse of sugar cane left in the fields.

This scene, which usually includes two actors, is applicable to green and dry leaves (Nos. 834a, 834b, and the note to Nos. 834a, 834b) or to green and dry beans or peas (Nos. 830 through 833 and the note to Nos. 830 through 832c).

For a list of references to sounds associated with plants, see the note to Nos. 830 through 832c.

760. Flemish: Joos, 145 (I am dumb and cannot talk and yet I rebuke faults) and, with the answer "newspaper," 141 (I am deaf, blind, and dumb. I have never read or studied. I can neither walk nor stand, yet I journey to many lands and can tell many things) and 889 (Who can speak without a mouth and make you sad or glad? Who creates many good and evil things in the world?). Icelandic: Árnason, 390 (What is it in the house that keeps silent and yet speaks to all?). Norwegian: note to Qvigstad, 4. Spanish: Demófilo, 604. Argentinian: Lehmann-Nitsche, 92 (newspaper), 158 (book). Rumanian: Papahagi, 36 (It has no voice but says a great deal.—Book). Lappish: Qvigstad, 4 (A white man goes through every land and talks like a man; he has neither tongue nor teeth), 49 (Dumb and speechless, and yet it tells all that is to be had in the world). Turkish: Hamizade, 483 (It has no mouth, it has no tongue, it speaks like a man). Yakut: Priklonskii, 16 (Without a tongue, but it tells everything). African, Senegalese: Rolland,

p. 168, No. 6 (Who teaches without talking?), cited from Boilat, *Esquisses sénégalaises* (Paris, 1853).

763. Breton: Sébillot, *Devinettes*, 6. Mordvin: Paasonen, 45 (Beyond the great water a great old man calls out). The actor in riddles for thunder is often an animal; see No. 398 and the corresponding note in the present collection.

764. Riddlers usually describe a cowbell in such vague terms that the actor is not clearly perceived to be an animal or a person; see Nos. 247a through 247c, 252a, 252b, 291. For a comparison of a cowbell to a thing see No. 1642.

768a, 768b. Breton: Sauvé, 76; Sébillot, *Devinettes*, 45a, 45d; Charlec, *Dol-de-Bretagne*, 1905, p. 40, No. 566 (Who cries out when going and weeps on returning?); Duine, *Saint-Malo*, p. 516; Lavenot, *Basse-Bretagne*, p. 670. French: Rolland, 98; Bladé, *Armagnac*, 12; V. S., *Mélusine*, I (1878), col. 254, No. 7; Carmeau, p. 33; Lallemant, *Argonne*, p. 234; Queyrat, *La Creuse*, I, 367; Mensignac, *Gironde*, p. 302, No. 30; Dottin, *Bas-Maine*, p. 138, No. 10; Fouju, *Beauce*, p. 631; J. Roux, *Limousin*, 70. Basque: Vinson, 31; Cerquand, 7. Catalan: Milá y Fontanals, 1876, p. 24, No. 11; Pelay y Briz, 13. Italian: Corsi, *Archivio*, X (1891), 397, No. 4 (pitcher); Tschiedel, 24. Lithuanian: Jurgelionis, 460 (As I put it in, it murmurs. As I take it out, it drips). Serbian: Novaković, p. 26, No. 8 (It goes from the house singing and returns weeping), and p. 106, No. 3. Cheremiss: Wichmann, *Cheremiss*, 179. Hungarian: *Magyar Nyelvör*, XXXVII (1908), 188 (It goes to the well singing; it returns weeping). Modern Greek: Polites, *Neohellenika Analekta*, I, 226, No. 187 (I have something that descends laughing and rises weeping); Stathes, p. 341, No. 55 (He goes down laughing and comes up weeping). Arabic: Ruoff, p. 21, No. 11 (If it goes down, it speaks. If it comes up, it is silent). African, Nandi: Hollis, *Nandi*, p. 134, No. 6 (What are the things which as they go to the cattle-kraal sing, whilst as they return are silent.—The milk-calabashes). Kamba: Lindblom, 7 (Tell me the man who when you walk cries for help). Togo: Schönhärl, 111. Taveta: Hollis, *Taveta*, 66 (When my youths go to war, they talk; when they return, they are silent). Fijian: Fison, p. 408, No. 18 = *Revue des traditions populaires*, I (1886), 88 (It speaks as I take it to the salt water, it is silent as I return.—The *kitu*, or large coconut shell, used for carrying salt water). Mongolian: Mostaert, 34 (When going, they jangle. When coming, they weep). Korean: Bernheisel, p. 60 (What is that on going out beats a new tom-tom and on coming back bears a drum?—Water-pot).

The contrast of joy and sorrow in the African granary riddle, "I see something which, when it is full, makes the household smile, when it is empty, makes them weep" (Tauxier, p. 520, No. 1) is quite a different theme.

769a through 769d. African, Tschuana: Kuhn, *Tschuana*, 47 (Cock that crows with the tip of its tongue.—Whip).

770. Icelandic: Árnason, 761 (I pore over books but learn nothing. Yet I look so closely at the letters that my tooth destroys them. I have a multitude of namesakes in the world, who gnaw the foot-soles of every tramp.—Moth). The Icelandic *melur* (moth) also means "stony or gravelly ground." Latin: Ohl, Symphosius, 16.

772. For parallels see No. 240 and the corresponding note and headnote. This version is very definitely personified.

774a through 774c. Breton: Charlec, *Dol-de-Bretagne*, 1904, p. 379, No. 45. Flemish: Joos, 160, 164, 165; *Ons Volksleven*, I (1889), 78, No. 39. German: Wossidlo, 405d and note to No. 405. Danish: Kristensen, p. 138, § 401, No. 640. Norwegian: Christie, 52; Brox, *Ytre Senja*, 178; Stafest, 118. Swedish: Ström, p. 164, "Oljelampan." Walloon: Colson, *Wallonia*, IV, 150; Colson, *Devinettes*, p. 151, No. 25. French: Rolland, *Rimes*, p. 209, No. 60; Bladé, *Armagnac*, 23; V. S., *Mélusine*, I (1878), col. 262, No. 46; Marchessou, *Velay et Auvergne*, p. 170, No. 29; A. Ferrand, *Dauphiné*, p. 227; Pineau, *Poitou*,

24; Desaivre, *Poitou*, p. 453, No. 33; Millien, *Nivernais*, p. 512; Sébillot, *Auvergne*, 32, 40; Pommerol, *Auvergne*, p. 42; Lallemant, *Argonne*, p. 235; J. Roux, *Limousin*, 67; Constantin, *Savoie*, p. 20; Baissac, *Mauritius*, p. 398; Haurigot, *French Guiana*, p. 119; Parsons, *Antilles*, III, 387, Martinique, 102. Spanish: Rodríguez Marín, 828. New Mexican: Campa, 260. Lettish: Bielenstein, 640. Serbian: Novaković, p. 199, No. 14, and p. 215, No. 5 (The son bites off the mother's tongue), which may have been suggested by the famous story of the badly reared son who bites off his mother's nose just before he is hanged (for references see J. Bolte [ed.], Johannes Pauli, *Schimpf und Ernst* [Berlin, 1924], No. 19). See also Novaković, p. 199, No. 15 (It eats itself), and p. 200, No. 9 (The cat sits on the shelf in a yellow tray; it makes its own grief; it eats its own flesh), which is a rare example of setting the riddle in animal terms. Hungarian: *Magyar Nyelvör*, II (1873), 515 (I saw an animal held by an ox; some parts of it were rolled about by a stout man; it was eating itself but it did not harm others; it was of no use or any harm to itself). Arabic: Ruoff, p. 38, No. 91 (Something sits in its shop and sucks at its entrails). Berber: Basset, *Contes populaires berbères*, p. 125, No. 5. Turkish: Kowalski, *Asia Minor*, 28 (I saw a strange thing: it is one span tall, it comes from the fish, cow, and ox. It devours itself and destroys itself, such a despicable habit does it have), which he quotes from Konja, 28 = Hamizade, 505. See also Hamizade, 504 (In stature he is tall. His family is infidel. He himself eats his own flesh); Kúnos, 62 (Its size is the span of one hand, it comes from a species of cattle, it eats its own flesh); Moshkov in Radlov, X, 269, No. 66 (I have a servant, he eats himself). Modern Greek: Abbott, p. 309, No. 16 (A little snake swallows the lake and then the lake swallows the snake), which has parallels in the texts cited in the headnote to Nos. 1440–1441, nn. 22–23, 25–26, in the present collection. The Javanese call a lamp a "princess who dies when the sea dries up" (Ranneft, *Proza*, p. 15, No. 73). Filipino: Starr, *Philippines*, 81 (What son burns his mother's intestines?).

776. Indian, Kolarian: Wagner, 76 (A man is not satisfied, even after having eaten up all the riches of the whole country). The usual riddle for a fire is a comparison to an insatiable animal; see Nos. 399a through 399c in the present collection and compare Nos. 235d and 236.

777. Swedish: Dybeck, *Runa*, 1850, p. 35, No. 12 (It complains, when it gets something; it is silent, when it gets nothing). Russian: Sadovnikov, 1121 (On a threshing floor there stands a woman. She grumbles and moves her hands wide apart. No matter how much the country will deliver to her, she will not eat at all). Albanian: Hahn, p. 158, No. 19 (It devours all its possessions and is not satisfied). For references to insatiable creatures in riddles see the headnote to Nos. 236–239.

778a through 778d. Italian: Tschiedel, 60 (If I give her something to eat, she weeps; if I give her nothing, she is quiet); Tammi, 18. Surinam: Herskovits, p. 441, No. 46 (My mother has a child. As long as you feed it, it cries). African, Swahili: Velten, 24 (A grandmother sits on the stool and weeps there.—Cooking pot).

778d. The introductory phrase occurs in the star riddle (No. 525a) and may have been borrowed from it.

779. The swelling stomach seems to have been suggested by a waterskin rather than a jug, but the riddle is obscure.

780b. Polish: Gustawicz, 458 (It neither drinks nor eats but goes and beats).

781. Compare Icelandic: Árnason, 879 (The tall giantess, swelling with eloquence, has many knuckles. She causes harm, talks famously, and spits grains from her mouth). French: Baissac, *Mauritius*, p. 404 (When I am angry, I vomit forth fire). For a survey of riddles describing a gun or bullet see the headnote to No. 801 of the present collection.

783. The import of the riddle is obscure.

785. Breton: Sébillot, *Haute-Bretagne*, 53; Lavenot, *Basse-Bretagne*, p. 669; Duine, *Saint-Malo*, p. 517. Danish: Kristensen, p. 60, § 137, No. 198. Norwegian: Bugge, *Telemarken*, 6. Icelandic: Árnason, 567 (What boy sleeps in dirt and dies if he drinks?). Swedish: Ström, p. 222, "Elden och rökan," 2. French: Rolland, 152; Bladé, *Armagnac*, 64; V. S., *Mélusine*, I (1878), col. 262, No. 37; Mensignac, *Gironde*, p. 299, No. 12; Westphalen, *Metz*, col. 202 (Who sleeps in his dung?). Italian: Rua, *Archivio*, VII (1888), 456, No. 60; Rondini, *ibid.*, VIII (1889), 186, No. 67. Turkish: Hamizade, 23 (I cover him and he sleeps; I uncover him and he wakes up). Indonesian, Sangir: Adriani, p. 431, No. 179 (If it is buried, it will not live).

787. French: Parsons, *Antilles*, III, 381, Martinique, 7. Bulgarian: Ikonomov, 7 (Everything is inside, the head is outside). Modern Greek: Dieterich, *Rätseldichtung*, p. 98, citing Stamatiadis, 185. Turkish: Kúnos, 84 (The whole body is inside, the head is outside); Kowalski, *Zagadki*, 7. In No. 917 of the present collection the riddler describes several nails in a similar way.

788. The meaning of "Miss D. June" is obscure.

789a, 789b. German: Frischbier, *Menschenwelt*, p. 263, No. 215. Norwegian: Qvigstad, 22 note. Swedish: Ericsson, *Södermanland*, I (1879), 93, No. 70; Sandén, *Norra Vadsbo*, 26; Ström, p. 164, "Klockan"; Qvigstad, 22 note; Russwurm, *Eibo*, p. 134, § 316, No. 24. Serbian: Novaković, p. 242, No. 2 (It cuts wood all day long and yet there are no chips). Lappish: Qvigstad, 22, 117, 126; Poestion, p. 267; Donner, 5. Finnish: Lönnrot, 2082 = Henssen, 187; Qvigstad, 22 note. Estonian: Lönnrot, p. 187; Wiedemann, p. 278. Votyak: Wichmann, *Votyak*, 377, 415. A similar comparison is used occasionally to describe rowing a boat; see the examples cited in the note to No. 227 in the present collection, especially the Russian, White Russian, and Mordvin versions.

790a, 790b. African, Kamba: Lindblom, 81 (What little brother of yours did you leave outside, when you returned from the herding?—A rod). Compare the path riddle, No. 688 of the present collection.

793. Russian: Sadovnikov, 1427 through 1433, 1460, 1461 (Peasants went into the forest without axes, they built a house without corners.—Ants), 1644 (Twelve axes build a church without corners.—Wasp's nest). Mordvin: Ahlqvist, p. 40, No. 18. Georgian: Blechsteiner, p. 15, No. 29 (I built a wooden house, it is not of wooden chips, they go in and out, that is God's command.—Beehive); Glushakov, p. 29, No. 47 (I have a house of wood and not made of a chip. They come in and go out, as decreed by God). Indian, Kashmiri: Knowles, 56 (I built a house up in the seventh heaven, I spoke not to a mason, I spoke not to a carpenter, I built it myself, [and all of the] hundreds of rooms in it), 60 (I built a splendid house, I brought neither a carpenter nor a blacksmith.—Beehive).

The remark "serves God" in the English riddle refers to the use of wax for sacramental candles. For comparisons of wax to cloth that is neither spun nor woven, see Nos. 1212a, 1212b, in the present collection.

797. African, Nandi: Hollis, *Nandi*, 10 (I have a child who is known to steal. What is my child?—Rat).

798. African, Wamajame: Ovir, 2 (A single king in the country.—Moon). Taveta: Hollis, *Taveta*, 26 (There is only one king on the earth). Indian, Gujerati: Mehta, p. 136 (A hot[-tempered] preceptor coming out at every dawn, sinks down in the evening; if, however, he fails to come for a day, the world itself would be no more).

The comparison of the sun to a man is old and widely known. A sufficient illustration is Psalm 19: 4-6: "... the sun, which is as a bridegroom coming out of his chamber, and rejoiceth as a strong man to run a race. His going forth is from the end of the heaven, and his circuit unto the ends of it."

800. Indian, Uraon: Archer, p. 182, No. 43 (A cotton-tree looks to the sky and has only one joint.—Durhi-grass).

801. (Killing, biting, injuring.) Flemish: Joos, 341 (I am of lead and yet as swift as the wind. Where I come, Death comes. Tell me who I am, my friend). Spanish, Argentinian: Lehmann-Nitsche, 113 (I killed a man, I didn't know him). Serbian: Novaković, p. 64, No. 8 (A mad youngster goes through the forest; woe to him whom he reaches!). Mordvin: Paasonen, 11 (It cannot be gnawed to bits; it cannot be beaten to bits, but yet it kills many), 357 (It sees one from afar; it bites one sorely). African, Kundu: Ittmann, *Kundu*, 225 (I am small and yet I shall kill you.—Fishhook). Wamajame: Ovir, 9 (It kills people). Indian: Lakshīnātha Upasānī, IX, 3 (Though I am found in a wood, I am not a bird; if I am supplied with food, I cry out immediately! I am lifeless, still many creatures I kill. What am I?).

802. "Debt" should probably be "det'," signifying "death."

803. A personification of death is rarely the theme of riddles. The Germans ask: "What makes all men equal?" (Hanika-Otto, 522), and the Sukuma say: "Unforeseen, it strikes us" (Augustiny, 50). A Pushto riddler suggests a vague sort of personification in "It has neither mouth, nor teeth, nor bowels; / Yet it eats its food steadily. / It has neither village, nor home, nor hands, nor feet; / Yet it wanders everywhere. / It has neither country, nor means, nor office, nor pen; / Yet it is ready for fight always. / By day and night there is wailing about it. / It has no breath; yet to all it appears" (Thorburn, *Bannú*, p. 229, No. 3).

805a through 805w. Turkish: Katanov in Radlov, IX, 286, No. 216 (If good people come, then we will seize the good youth by the neck.—Bottle).

806a through 806c. (The answer is usually "a grape.") The Spanish "Round as the moon, they crush me to death, skin me, swallow my juice, throw my skin away" (Demófilo, 1010; Rodríguez Marín, 469. Argentinian: Lehmann-Nitsche, 597. Chilean: Flores, 758, begins with a somewhat inappropriate comparison. In the Bengali "[It is the] king's son [named] Madana Hânsa. [Its] rind is eaten, [but its] kernel is thrown away.— The fruit of the chhāltā tree [*Dillenia speciosa*]" (Mitra, *Murshidābād*, p. 927, No. 9), which seems confusing to the collector, we should understand "rind" to mean "skin" and "kernel" to mean "heart" in order to carry out the metaphor.

808. Filipino: Starr, *Philippines*, 280 (I chop your feet; I drink your blood).

809a through 809e. Welsh Gypsy: Sampson, 24 (I was going over the bridge. I saw a little yellow man. I lifted him up. I drank his blood and I threw him down). Arabic: Giacobetti, 64 (We have come to a marvelous *douâr*. There one eats the silver and throws away the gold). The gold is the rind. *Douâr* signifies "round," "going around," or "a circuit," and may refer to an idol, the circuit made about a sacred object, or, specifically, a temple at Mecca.

810a through 811c. African, Pangwe: Tessmann, 44 (I killed a man there, the knife was below, against the stomach; with it I shall cut him up for you.—Raphia fruits). For comparisons to animals rather than persons see "My fat pig—I eat the flesh, I throw away the fat" (Portuguese: Parsons, *Cape Verde*, 4); and "I kill my cow, I eat the flesh, I throw away the bones, it turns again into a cow.—Manioc patch" (*ibid.*, 29), which contains an element found in No. 611 of the present collection. See also "Our cow is gray. One eats the flesh and throws away the skin" (Arabic: Giacobetti, 95).

814a, 814b. The allusion to Zion is obscure. It may be connected with the proper name in "I eat out St. John, / I drink out St. John, / St. John remains," which is another manner of describing a coconut (see No. 1240 in the present collection). Inasmuch as the allusions to Zion in Jamaica and to St. John in Barbados show a similarity in sound, I am inclined to believe that there is no reference to the parish of St. John in Barbados, where the latter riddle was collected. Perhaps an allusion lies behind these proper names, but the texts are too uncertain to permit of any guess as to its nature. See another reference to St. John in No. 838.

817a through 817g. German: Frischbier, *Menschenwelt*, p. 255, No. 147. Walloon: Colson, *Wallonia*, V, 58, No. 27. Bulgarian: Ikonomov, 37 (I have a sister. Whoever passes by throws her down, and I do so, too).

818a through 818d. (The following parallels contain comparisons to an animal.) Welsh Gypsy: Sampson, 31 (As big as a man, as empty as a box; lift up his tail and his nose will run). Flemish: Joos, 273 (I walked into a farmer's yard. I saw there a fattie standing. I pulled it by the snout, and the water ran out). Compare the White Russian riddle for an oven door, *"Baju, baju,* I have a goat and raise it by the tail" (Wasilewski, 1).

820. The riddler refers to the gradual loss of thread in sewing, but the precise import of his comparison is obscure.

821, 822. Compare No. 215.

823. Welsh: Hull and Taylor, 288. Flemish: Joos, 618, 619, and compare his Nos. 577, 1290. German: H. Frischbier, "Rätsel-Geschichten," *Am Urquell*, II (1891), 167, No. 5; Hanika-Otto, 420. Icelandic: Árnason, 136 (I saw a man and not a man under an oak and not an oak. He killed a bird and not a bird with a precious stone and not a stone), 968 (I saw a man and not a man, sitting on a tree and not a tree. He held a stone and not a stone and hit a bird and not a bird.—A fairy man sat on a chunk of lignite and threw a piece of charcoal at a kitty-wren). Swedish: Dybeck, *Runa*, 1865–1873, p. 31, No. 35; Ericsson, *Södermanland*, I (1879), 86, No. 36; Sandén, *Norra Vadsbo*, 140; Geijer and Campbell, 104. French: Alexandre Sylvain (A. van den Bussche), *Cinquante Ænigmes françoises* (1582), 53. Classical and Medieval Greek: Plato, *De Repub.ica* V, 479E; Athenaeus, *Deipnosophistae* X, 452e; Suidas, s.v. "ainos"; C. F. G. Heinrici, "Griechisch-byzantinische Gesprächsbücher und Verwandtes aus Sammelhandschriften," *Abhandlungen der k. sächsischen Gesellschaft der Wissenschaften, phil.-hist. Klasse*, XXVIII, No. 8 (1911), p. 11. Hungarian: Kálmány, I, 169, No. 18 (The man, who is not a man, went into the garden, which is not a garden, [and] hit a bird, which is not a bird, with a stone, which is not a stone; the bird, which was not a bird, fell from the tree, which was not a tree.—Clergyman, secretary, bat, a piece of a tombstone, wooden cross at the grave). Turkish: Kúnos, 235 (Opposite here is a person, neither male nor female. He threw a stone and hit a bird, but it was not a stone that he threw nor a bird that he hit.—Soap, fish, guard of the seraglio); Hamizade, 582 (I threw a stone, I struck a bird. What is the stone that I threw, what is the bird that I struck?—A frog is struck with soap).

CHAPTER V

COMPARISONS TO SEVERAL PERSONS

Nos. 827–1035

828a through 828h. Welsh Gypsy: Sampson, 27. Scotch Gaelic: Nicolson, p. 57. Manx: Cashen, p. 76; *Manx Notes and Queries*, p. 7. Irish: Christiansen, 67. Breton: Sauvé, 93; Sébillot, *Haute-Bretagne*, 76; Kerbeuzec, *Ille-et-Vilaine*, 10. German: Butsch, 12; Wossidlo, 78. Danish: Kristensen, p. 116, § 314, Nos. 503a through 503c, and compare his p. 23, § 53, No. 65. Swedish: Dybeck, *Runa*, 1847, p. 40, No. 2 = Russwurm, 78; Ericsson, *Södermanland*, II (1881), 100, No. 115; and III (1882), 98, No. 135; Christofferson, 95; Geijer and Campbell, 37; Ström, p. 168, "Båten," 4, 5; p. 169, "Skeppet," 2; and pp. 169–170, "Krigsskeppet." Latin: Claret, p. 74, No. 112 (Mortua restat equa perducens corpora viva: / Trabs homines navis per aquas ducit quoque puppis). A second version, "Mortuus extat equs, sine pulvere strata" (p. 68, No. 13), shows some similarity to these ideas, but is probably quite a different riddle. French: Baissac, *Mauritius*, p. 419. Spanish: Rodríguez Marín, 803. Argentinian: Lehmann-Nitsche, 152 (battleship). Rumanian: Gorovei, 526; and Gorovei, *Devinettes*, p. 506. Lithuanian: Schleicher, pp. 192, 202. Czech: *Pohádky kratochvilne* (1695), Nos. 12 (It has neither blood nor flesh and yet it carries flesh and blood. And many a one has the strength of a lion and can travel a path no man can walk), 32 (It is huge and strong; it passes through many foreign lands; it contains body and soul [also a woman and perhaps a man of some kind]; it goes back and forth over living things and also bears living things on it). Flajšhans, from whom I take these texts, believes them to be of German origin; see Flajšhans, p. 9. Serbian: Novaković, p. 110, No. 1 (The dead bears the living over a field). Finnish: Lönnrot, 71 = Henssen, 158.

The Modern Greek "She is soulless, has no soul, and yet she takes souls and flees" (Abbott, p. 315, No. 40), which is probably quite a different riddle, is related to the medieval Latin "Portat animam et non habet animam; non ambulat super terram neque in caelo" (K. Müllenhoff and W. Scherer, *Denkmäler*, 3d ed. [Berlin, 1891], I, 20 [chap. vii, No. 2], and the notes in II, 58–59. See also Petsch, *Rätselstudien*, p. 343. This riddle sometimes has the answer "Jonah's whale").

The description of a ship partly according to its origin, as in the Hungarian "It grows in the wood, it goes on water, it carries souls inside it" (*Magyar Nyelvör*, V [1876], 422), is discussed in the headnote to Nos. 1058–1062, §1, of the present collection. This Hungarian version is a contamination of the two patterns.

828a. The "diamond" is a lozenge-shaped window.

828b. The meaning of "Napoleon's grass-piece" is obscure. Could it be a corruption of "Napoleon's glass piece" [spyglass]? A reference to looking is often present in this riddle. On the other hand, a few parallels call the sea "a field"; see, for instance, the Serbian version in the note to Nos. 828a through 828h.

829a, 829b. Indian, Parsee: Munshi, pp. 422–423 (Such a pest I have seen and never have I seen such a pest in my life. O brother, it runs quickly with thousands of men in its belly).

830 through 832c. French: Parsons, *Antilles*, III, 374, Cariacou, 7, p. 392, Dominica, 29, p. 399, Guadaloupe, 19 through 21, p. 410, Les Saintes, 29, p. 411, Les Saintes, 39, p. 416, Marie Galante, 56, p. 438, St. Martin, 46, p. 449, Hayti, 44. Spanish, Dominican Rep.: Andrade, 156 (I went past a house; I said, "Good day." The dead answered to my greeting; the living faltered in silence), 157. Porto Rican: Mason, 249. African, Swahili:

Velten, 70 (I was going my way, the old greeted me, the young did not greet me). Tonga-Shangaan: Junod and Jaques, p. 239, No. 61. In No. 1011 of the present collection the actors are daughters.

For other references to sounds associated with plants see Nos. 377, 480, 759, 833 through 834b, the note to 377, and the note to Nos. 834a, 834b.

830. "Going alone" is an error for "going along."

834a, 834b. French: Haurigot, *French Guiana*, p. 120. African riddlers occasionally call leaves the residents of a village. See the Bakongo "We went to a village. The living did not greet us. The dead gave us good-day" (Denis, 93 = Tauxier, *Côte d'Ivoire*, p. 315, No. 2). Hausa: Fletcher, 29. Duala: Ebding, 76, 79. Togo: Schönhärl, 12 (I met many men on a road in the morning and they did not offer a greeting. They offered a greeting in the afternoon), 70 (I greeted the living, they gave no answer. I greeted the dead, and they gave answer at once). Kosi: Ittmann, *Kosi*, 137. Kundu: Ittmann, *Kundu*, 195 (I travel, they make a noise.—Grass), 271 (On going away you spoke with me, on returning you also greeted me.—A kind of grass). This latter riddle is in the singular, like No. 759 of the present collection. Surinam: Herskovits, p. 439, Nos. 26 (I go to the bush. The living people do not speak to me, but the dead ones speak to me), 26a. Samoan: Heider, 26 (Who are the singing maidens living in the air?—Fruit of the *pu'a* [*Hernandia peltata*]). For comment on the contrast of the living and the dead, see the headnote to Nos. 828–836 of the present collection. For a comparison of leaves to a hand piano see African, Lamba: Doke, 5. For leaves compared to dancing persons see the headnote to Nos. 946–950 in the present collection and the note to Nos. 1022a through 1022d.

This conception of greeting is also applicable to a plant which scratches passers-by, as in "We have just gone to the village. The big ones did not greet us, the small ones greeted us" (African, Bakongo: Denis, 92).

834b. "Trash" is the West Indian term for the refuse of sugar cane left in the fields.

835a, 835b. Welsh: Hull and Taylor, 293. Scotch Gaelic: Nicolson, pp. 55, 93. German: R. Köhler, *Kleinere Schriften*, III, 508–509, No. 14 (with many parallels); Wackernagel, 3. Faeroic: Hammershaimb, *Antiquarisk tidsskrift*, III (1849–1851), 319, No. 38 (The dead dug up the living.—Tongs and fire). Norwegian: Bugge, *Telemarken*, 145. Swedish: Ström, p. 223, "Elden och rokan," 2. Italian: Straparola, XIII, 6; Pitrè, 171; Ferraro, *Canti popolari in dialetto logodurese*, p. 298, No. 3. Malagasy: Sibree, p. 39, No. 8 (Fetch the dead on which to place the living.—Ashes on which to carry a coal on the palm of the hand).

836. Welsh: Hull and Taylor, 293. Scotch Gaelic: Nicolson, p. 93. Frisian: Dykstra, *Snypsnaren*, pp. 109–110. Flemish: Joos, 637. Afrikaans: Groenewald, p. 90. German: R. Köhler, *Kleinere Schriften*, III, 508–509, No. 14; Adalbert von Keller, *Erzählungen aus altdeutschen Handschriften* (Stuttgart, 1855), p. 482, No. 2 = Friedreich, p. 242; Wackernagel, 14; Renk, *Tyrol*, 5. Danish: Kristensen, pp. 175–176, chap. v, Nos. 1a through 1h; Feilberg, *Ordbog*, II, 402, s.v. "levende." Norwegian: Bugge, *Telemarken*, 140, 141, 145; Stafset, 199. Swedish: Dybeck, *Runa*, 1848, p. 45–46, Nos. 49, 50, and p. 50, No. 56; 1849, p. 47, No. 7; 1850, p. 34, No. 1; 1865–1873, p. 30, No. 14, and p. 48, No. 41; Hyltén-Cavallius, *Värend*, 93; Geijer and Campbell, 117, 118; Christofferson, pp. 50–51, No. 1b = *Folkminnen och folktankar*, II (1915), 99–100, No. 1b; Ström, pp. 281–286, Kärleksgåtor," Nos. 1 through 6 (his Nos. 7 through 9 are more remotely related); Ericsson, *Södermandland*, I (1879), 91–92, No. 60. Latin: *Ænigmata*, p. 70. Portuguese: Parsons, *Cape Verde*, 291. Polish: Saloni, *Rzeshów*, 217; Siarkowski, 61. Hungarian: *Magyar Nyelvör*, III (1874), 233, No. 16; XI (1882), 527; XVII (1888), 379; Kálmány, I, 159, No. 16 (Wait, flower, wait until the old tree shall fall, and the broken limbs be gathered, and then we shall go, where the dry shall hold the raw.—The servant girl called her lover "Flower"; she told him to wait until all the old people retired, then she will make the bed [gather the broken limbs] where the body [the dog] will lie naked [raw]). The explanations are supplied by Kálmány. See also Arany and Gyulai, II, 349, No. 1; Kriza, 6, 7, 67, 86.

837a through 837h. German: Adalbert von Keller, *Erzählungen aus altdeutschen Handschriften* (Stuttgart, 1855), p. 483, No. 5 = Friedreich, p. 243. French: *Les Adeuineaux amoureux*, pp. xcviii–xcix (I see people going into fields who are not sons, men, or women.—Daughters).

838. The Palestinian Arabic "A company which comes in multitudes in which you do not know male from female nor old woman from maiden" (Ruoff, p. 41, No. 2) enlarges upon this theme. See also Nos. 887 through 892 and 901 of the present collection. For comment on St. John see the note to Nos. 814a, 814b in the present collection.

839. Spanish: Rodríguez Marín, 435, 436. Italian: Gianandrea, *Archivio*, I (1882), 559, No. 25 (bees). African, Kamba: Lindblom, 78 (I give greeting to the work gang who return the greeting.—Ants). This conversation resembles those in certain Spanish and African riddles quoted in the note to Nos. 830 through 832c and in the note to Nos. 834a, 834b, of the present collection; see also Nos. 830 through 830b.

840. The collector also gives the answer "teeth and tongue." Riddles for a watermelon or other fruit containing seeds often refer to persons in a building; see Nos. 909 through 916f and the corresponding notes, and the headnotes to Nos. 908–916 (nn. 3, 10) and 909.

841. The answer "watermelon" is an alternative to "teeth and tongue." The parallels do not specifically mention children. See Norwegian: Stafset, 159 (A house full of white maidens and a red minstrel in their midst). French: Rolland, 123 (A lady dressed in red, surrounded by thirty-two ladies dressed in white); Carmeau, p. 34. Bulgarian: Chacharov, 36 (The church is full of pupils), which is probably borrowed from the riddle for a fruit and its seeds. African, SeSuto: Norton and Velaphe, 10 (The white men in the red cave). Zulu: Callaway, 6 (Guess ye some men who are many and form a row; they dance the wedding dance, adorned in white hip-dresses). Indian, Parsee: Munshi, p. 413 (In a room there are thirty-two mendicants).

For the comparison of teeth to persons seated in chairs see No. 1146 of the present collection.

859. Compare Nos. 1616a through 1617g.

861. Compare a queer Swedish riddle about an egg in meal (White lay in white . . .); the egg is given to a cow and an old woman snatches it out of the cow's mouth (Dybeck, *Runa*, 1865–1873, p. 65, No. 83).

862. Welsh: Hull and Taylor, 160. Scotch Gaelic: Nicolson, p. 56. Breton: Sauvé, 88. Flemish: Joos, 252, 253, 255, 456, 457. Danish: Kristensen, p. 136, § 393, Nos. 627a through 627f. Norwegian: Christie, 78 (snowshoes); Stafset, 189 (snowshoes). Swedish: Geijer and Campbell, 32; Ström, p. 162, "Stövlen," 3. Italian: Rolland, p. 163, No. 53. Lappish: Qvigstad, 105. Compare also the headnote to No. 453 of the present collection.

863. Danish: Kristensen, p. 168, § IV, Nos. 1, 2.

864. Compare No. 908.

866. Serbian: Novaković, p. 93, 3 (The black one rose, the white one remained).

867. Flemish: Joos, 592 (Blackie and Whitie go into the woods. Whitie stays and Blackie comes out).

870. French: Baissac, *Mauritius*, p. 402 (Some white in something very black). For a contrast of colors in describing meal falling through the mill, see the headnote to Nos. 1550–1554 of the present collection.

871. (Singing.) Spanish, Mexican: Boas, p. 230, No. 20.

872. (Tickling, beating, licking.) Icelandic: Árnason, 915 (Something red flutters against a black rump). Norwegian: Nergaard, p. 170, No. 43 (The red one struck the black one). Swedish: Dybeck, *Runa*, 1865–1873, p. 8, No. 4 (Black hangs, Red thwacks), and p. 31, No. 39; Ström, p. 148, "Kitteln" (Black hanging, Red beating). Walloon: Colson, *Devinettes*, p. 150, No. 22. French: *Les Adeuineaux amoureaux*, p. xcviii; Carnoy, *Picardy*, p. 54; V. S., *Mélusine*, I (1878), col. 262, Nos. 57 through 59; J. Roux, *Limousin*, 62. Lithuanian: Jurgelionis, 356 (They are whipping a black —— [rump] with red straps), 357 (A black Gypsy on a red horse). Polish: Gustawicz, 27 (The red licks the black). Serbian: Novaković, p. 169, Nos. 4 (The blue one licks the black one), 5. Albanian: Hahn, p. 162, No. 56 (Redbottom beats Blackbottom). Surinam: Herskovits, p. 441, No. 47b. Indonesian, Malay: Tauern, *Patasiwa*, p. 70 (What little prince licks his slave's rump?).

A few versions leave the nature of the creatures obscure, as in the Lithuanian "A red one licks a black one" (Jurgelionis, 353) and in the Serbian versions above. For references to riddles making a comparison to an animal licking another, see the headnote to Nos. 871–877 of the present collection.

873a, 873b. (Burning, boiling, or warming itself.) Flemish: *Ons Volksleven*, I (1889), 37, No. 19. Icelandic: Árnason, 979 (I saw a black fellow who chose his residence above the bed of embers and had his belly all burned), 1035 (A black rump sits by the fire and burns itself). Norwegian: Berge, 42. French: Rolland, 160b; Baissac, *Mauritius*, p. 407 (Three little black ones watch their mother's belly burn). The three black ones are the stones on which the pot rests; see No. 1182 in the present collection. Italian: Ive, *Canti popolari istriani*, p. 296, No. 4. Russian: Sadovnikov, 336 (An old man stands in the fire. Laughing hard, he sits too long), 337 (A brave black one, gold up to his knees). Votyak: Wichmann, *Votyak*, 317 (A black Tatar warms his backside); Buch, 18 (A black ram warms his rump). Hungarian: *Magyar Nyelvör*, III (1874), 557 (A black devil is grilling his bottom).

876. (Sitting in a chair.) French: A. Ferrand, *Dauphiné*, p. 227 (A black lady on a chair and a red lady beneath it). Spanish, Argentinian: Lehmann-Nitsche, 349a, 349b (A black lady sitting on a golden chair). Lithuanian: Jurgelionis, 359 (On a golden chair there sits a black devil.—Pot). For other comparisons to a seated person see the headnote to Nos. 875–877 of the present collection.

879. Portuguese: Parsons, *Cape Verde*, 64 (I-am-black over I-am-white).

881. Compare an Irish riddle in animal terms: "A black sheep with white fleece on it" (Delargy, 12). For other pancake riddles in the present collection, see No. 886, in which there are three actors, and No. 1540, in which the riddler does not portray a scene.

883a through 883f. Indian, Bihari: Mitra, *Bihar*, 52 (A sheep with a black face leaps; upside down it dances on the finger. When it takes a plunge into the well, it communicates the secrets of the heart noiselessly).

891. "Kelly" signifies "hat."

901 through 904. For the comparison of a beehive to a convent or monastery see the headnote to No. 909, § 2. For the comparison of bees to soldiers see Spanish: Demófilo, 10 (quoted from Perez Herrera, A.D. 1628) = Argentinian: Lehmann-Nitsche, 291. See also Argentinian: Lehmann-Nitsche, 416. Italian: Gianandrea, *Canti popolari marchigiani*, p. 297, No. 4. The Batak describe ants as soldiers wearing red (Ophuijsen, p. 467, No. 80).

903. See No. 649, in which a wasp is compared to a man wearing yellow breeches.

905. Compare Nos. 683a, 683b.

906. I have selected parallels to illustrate the distribution of the riddle and to add unusual texts not seen by R. Petsch ("Rätselstudien," *Zeitschrift des Vereins für Volks-*

kunde, XXVI [1916], 1–8). See Breton: Sébillot, *Devinettes,* 22. German: Heinrich von Neustadt, *Apollonius von Tyrland* (ed. S. Singer, Deutsche Texte des Mittelalters, VII [Berlin, 1906]), p. 264, vv. 16571–16576). Swedish: Ericsson, *Södermanland,* III (1882), 98, No. 136; Ström, p. 274, "Gåtberättelser," and p. 386, "Natur och människoverk," 5. Latin: Daly and Suchier, p. 142, No. 98; Claret, p. 69, No. 27; and the Apollonius romance (see R. W. Pettengill, *Journal of English and Germanic Philology,* XII [1913], 251, No. 2). Walloon: Colson, *Wallonia,* IV, 63, No. 65. French: *Les Adeuineaux amoureux,* p. xcvii; Alexandre Sylvain (A. van den Bussche), *Cinquante Ænigmes françoises* (1582), 42; Rolland, 71; Desaivre, *Poitou,* 36; Baissac, *Mauritius,* p. 403. Spanish: Demófilo, 801 = Caballero, *Cuentos,* 150; Rodríguez Marín, 401, 402. Argentinian: Lehmann-Nitsche, 557. Italian: Pitrè, 600; Rondini, *Archivio,* VII (1888), 536, No. 1. Rumanian: Gorovei, 1383 through 1385; and Gorovei, *Devinettes,* p. 506. Lithuanian: Jurgelionis, 649 (The two men came; the hosts were frightened; the house crowded through the windows), 650 (A house with guests crawls through the window), 651 (A house goes out through the windows); Schleicher, p. 205. Czech: Hanika-Otto, p. 127, Nos. 62, 63. Russian: Sadovnikov, 1623. Serbian: Novaković, p. 193, No. 10 (I caught the folk, but their house ran away through the window). Mordvin: Paasonen, 122. Hungarian: Meltzl, 9; Kriza, 63 (The enemy came upon my house; my house fled through the enemy's window, and I remained in the enemy's fist); *Magyar Nyelvör,* IV (1875), 424 = VI (1877), 271 = XXIX (1900), 591 (The house departed through the window, the landlady remained inside). Modern Greek: Abbott, p. 311, No. 22; Dieterich, *Rätseldichtung,* p. 98; Polites, *Neohellenika Analekta,* I, 239, No. 261. Turkish: Katanov in Radlov, IX, 614, No. 63 (The robbers are gathering in the nets and the enemies are gathering in the army). Surinam: Herskovits, p. 449, No. 96. Indian: Lakshīnātha Upasānī, XI, 4 (A gang of robbers attack a house with tremendous noise; the house itself slips away between the legs of the gang, but the dwellers in the house are caught). Uraon: Archer, p. 194, No. 229 (The house escapes, while the inmates are caught). Kolarian: Wagner, 72 (In a house is a window, the house goes through the window, but the inmates of the house cannot pass through the window).

907. For comparisons of matches to animals see No. 429. Compare Nos. 583a through 584b and 924.

908. Finnish: Lönnrot, 1189 = Henssen, 64 (Four rooms, ten men in them.—Mittens). Turkish: Katanov in Radlov, IX, 286, No. 220 (Five brothers live in one den.—Shoe).

909. Various fruits and vegetables, especially those containing seeds, are described in this manner. A pomegranate is a convent of nuns separated by a thin veil (Spanish: Demófilo, 482 through 484; Rodríguez Marín, 546 through 548. Argentinian: Lehmann-Nitsche, 420. Chilean: Flores, 304), a convent of nuns in red habits (Spanish: Demófilo, 480), a church full of people (Spanish: Rodríguez Marín, 544. Chilean: Flores, 307), and a fortress full of soldiers (Spanish: Demófilo, 478). See also, in the present collection, Nos. 923a, 923b, 935, and 936 and the list of references in the note to No. 840.

Some versions of this comparison of a fruit containing seeds are interesting for their ingenuity or as examples showing the wide range of the idea. See the Modern Greek riddles for a pomegranate, "A thousand million monks all wrapped in one cloak" (Stathes, p. 349, No. 109); a watermelon, "A green tower, red curtains, black monks sitting inside" (Polites, *Neohellenika Analekta,* I, 201, No. 42), with the variant, "A green palace, red flowers, black monks sitting inside" (*ibid.,* p. 241, No. 271); or a cantaloupe, "A yellow tower, white curtains, and yellow monks sitting inside" (*ibid.,* p. 201, No. 43). Somewhat longer than usual are the Surinam riddle for a soursop, "The church is colored green, the priest is dressed in black, and the people are in white" (Herskovits, p. 437, No. 16a), and the Low German riddle for an apple, "White are the walls, green are the men, brown are the priests, who sleep in the monastery" (H. Meier, *Ostfriesland*, 27). A Serbian adapts the pattern to Mohammedanism: "The mosque is full of black Arabs" (Novaković, p. 205, No. 9). The Bulgarian riddle, which also has the answer "watermelon," does not hold fast to a single concept: "The box is full of black monks" (Chacharov, 67). The existence of the Samoan description of the kernel of the *pu'a* fruit (*Hernandia peltata*), "Who is the black person who lives in a beautiful round white house?" (Heider, 25) is a proof of the wide dissemination of the idea.

910a through 910i. Spanish: Demófilo, 482, 483, 902 (monks in green habits, red hearts). Argentinian: Lehmann-Nitsche, 420. Dominican Rep.: Andrade, 153, 244. Porto Rican: Mason, 259. Russian: Sadovnikov, 794 (With neither windows nor doors, the house is full of people). Albanian: Hahn, p. 159, No. 4 (The king's palace [is] green; he [is] dressed in red; the company is black). Modern Greek: Abbott, p. 319, No. 50 (red monastery, black monks); Dieterich, *Rätseldichtung*, p. 93 = Polites, *Neohellenika Analekta*, I, 201, No. 42 (Green tower, red curtains, black monks sitting inside); Stathes, p. 345, No. 81 (Green tower, red pillows, blacks sitting inside.—Watermelon). Samoan: Heider, 28 (There are five hundred brothers, who grow up as real white men; later, however, when they are grown, one sees that they are coal-black and live in a house that has no door, invisible to the world, the house hangs in the air.—Papaya), 29 (A numerous company of brothers hides in a cave that has no opening.—The kernels of the papaya).

910b. The sequence "green, white, and red" seems to have had little significance to the riddler. He may have thought of the colors of the watermelon from the rind to the core, or he may have had in mind the blackberry riddle, Nos. 1385 through 1387, 1389, and 1391 of the present collection.

910d. The "house" is usually the watermelon and is "red inside." In this version, however, the riddler conceives the red flesh of the watermelon as a house. See other instances of this conception in Nos. 916a through 916d and 916f.

910h. The "hill" is that on which the watermelon is growing. See also Nos. 916f and 1162a through 1163.

See French: Baissac, *Mauritius*, p. 408 (My house is painted with rose within, it is painted in green outside with a little company of people from Mozambique inside).

913. Flemish: Joos, 474, 477; *Ons Volksleven*, I (1889), 6, No. 7. Russian: Sadovnikov, 802 (With neither doors nor windows, there are six people).

914. French: Baissac, *Mauritius*, p. 400. Indian, Parsee: Munshi, p. 100, No. 14 (Which is that mother whose skin is white and whose babies are black?—Cardamon), and a variant on his p. 417.

915a, 915b. See Nos. 577a and 577b (comparison to a single person), and Nos. 1118a, 1118b (comparison to the rough walls of a house).

916a. Forgetting that the "white house" should signify the inner white lining within the green shell, the riddler has described a watermelon striped in green and white.

916f. The element "on the hill" is also found in Nos. 910h and 1162a through 1163.

917. Compare No. 787.

918. Riddlers do not often compare braids to people in a house. The comparison of lice to people is much more frequently found and fits better the remark, "yet you can't see them." For related or similar riddles see the notes to Nos. 459 and 460a. For the comparison of the head or the mouth to a house or theater see Nos. 1144 and 1146 through 1149a; for the comparison of the head to a mountain covered with grass see No. 1100; for the comparison of the hairs to wands that cannot be counted see Nos. 1116a and 1116b.

919. Danish: Kristensen, p. 101, § 259, No. 410 (What room is full of little brown fellows?), and § 261, No. 412. French: Parsons, *Antilles*, III, 368, Trinidad, 57. For the comparison of loaves to animals see Nos. 493a, 493b in the present collection. For references to change of color without mention of persons or animals, see the headnote to Nos. 1542–1546, § 2.

921. Yakut: Piekarski, 31 (The devil's sow in a red hat). See also the Yakut text cited in the headnote to Nos. 632–644, n. 26, of the present collection.

922. Compare No. 935.

923a, 923b. Ackee is a fruit. For further description of it, see Nos. 691 and 936.

924. French: Parsons, *Antilles*, III, 409, Les Saintes, 6. Spanish: Demófilo, 452 (brothers in prison). Chilean: Flores, 278 (brothers in a house), 279 (people in a house). Turkish: Kowalski, *Zagadki*, 2 (A house above, a house below, a hundred coifed with busbies within). African, SeSuto: Norton and Velaphe, 35 (Many men with black heads).

For comparisons in terms of animals see Welsh: Hull and Taylor, 150 (cows in a stable). Serbian: Novaković, p. 46, No. 4 (All the black-headed cattle are going home.—Cordwood). Finnish: Lönnrot, 802 = Henssen, 90 (A copper stall, iron cows). African, Kxatla: Schapera, 120 (Tell me: the white cattle with black heads.—Matches).

925 through 928b. French: Parsons, *Antilles*, III, 394, Dominica, 58, and p. 399, Guadaloupe, 18. Compare with Nos. 830 through 832a, 832c, 833, and the note to Nos. 830 through 832c, in the present collection.

930. Spanish: Demófilo, 992 = Rodríguez Marín, 885 (A Negress on a three-legged donkey). Argentinian: Lehmann-Nitsche, 377 through 379. Portuguese: Parsons, *Cape Verde*, 130b (A black man walks on three feet). Albanian: Pedersen, 15 (A Negro with three legs). Indian, Bhil: Hedberg, p. 875, No. 60 (One man has three feet). Indonesian, Tabaru: Fortgens, 66 (Three men standing opposite one another), 104 (Three men beat her, and yet she sings a national song).

932. See Nos. 550a through 552b, in which a comparison to a single person is made.

935. Portuguese: Parsons, *Cape Verde*, 41 (My black horse, his mane white.—Bean), 42 (My plain of black horses—there is no man to ride them.—Black beans). African, Kamba: Lindblom, 46 (Tell me: a village of old men exclusively), which may involve a reference to the white hair of old men (compare No. 922 of the present collection), and 47 (Tell me: a village of nothing but baldpates).

939. A version of this curious riddle is ascribed to the Queen of Sheba in the Midrash on Proverbs; see Friedreich, p. 98; Wilhelm Hertz, "Die Rätsel der Königin von Saba," *Zeitschrift für deutches Altertum*, XXVII (1883), 3–4; S. Schechter, "The Riddles of Solomon in Rabbinic Literature," *Folk-Lore*, I (1890), 355, No. 1, and his notes on p. 356, citing the Midrash on Lamentations, chapter i, and Perles, *Zur rabbinischen Sprach- und Sagenkunde*, p. 97, n. 1; Louis Ginzberg, *Legends of the Jews* (Philadelphia, 1913), IV, 145–146, and VI (1928), 290; Max Grünbaum, *Neue Beiträge zur semitischen Sagenkunde* (Leiden, 1893), p. 221. Hertz prints a translation of the text of the Midrash on Proverbs by John Lightfoot, a seventeenth-century commentator: "Dicit ea [the Queen of Sheba]: Quid hoc est? Septem exeunt, et novem intrant. Duo miscent, et unus bibit. Dicit ille [Solomon]: Septem dies separationis foeminae exeunt, et novem menses foetationis intrant. Duo ubera parant poculum, et unus sugit." A Syriac version is adapted to Jesus and the Virgin Mary; see Furlani, *Azraq*, 28. For further comment see Jan de Vries, *Die Märchen von den klugen Rätsellösern*, FF Communications, LXXIII (Helsinki, 1928), p. 306.

940. The meaning of the riddle is obscure.

941. Italian: Pitrè, 299 (We are two brothers and a sister along the beach. The brother goes out and doesn't come back, the second eats and is not satisfied, and the sister sleeps and is never awakened again.—Fire, smoke, ashes). The comparison of fire to something insatiable occurs in various forms; see the headnote to Nos. 236-239 in the present collection. The tripartite form has some similarity to the riddles discussed in the headnote to Nos. 138-140 and especially to German: Wossidlo, 154. This Italian text is closely related to the Modern Greek "One eats and is not satiated; one flies and does not return; one sleeps and does not feel" and "One works; one flies; one sits" (Dieterich, *Rätseldichtung*, p. 91, citing Stamatiadis, V, 183). Lithuanian: Jurgelionis, 113 (I flew like an angel, I fall like a devil.—Snow); Schleicher, p. 208. Serbian: Novaković, p. 211, No. 2 (I flew up like an eagle, I fell like an emperor, and I died like a dog.—Snow), and p. 151, No. 7 (Two dead brothers got into a fight and gave birth to a third, alive). Hungarian: Kálmány, I, 162, No. 29 (Out of three dead comes a living one.—Steel, flint, tinder, spark). Turkish: Hamizade, 538 (He eats and eats and is not satisfied; he lies and doesn't get up; he goes and doesn't come back.—Hearth, wood, smoke); this version has the structure of the tripartite riddles discussed in the headnote to Nos. 138-140 in the present collection. See further Katanov in Radlov, IX, 287, No. 230 (A white lad is walking to the *ulus* [yurt village], but a red lad is walking to give an invitation), and p. 291, No. 242 (A handsome lad is going in answer to a call). Yakut: Piekarski, 248 (It sleeps on a rock, it falls over a beam, over the beam it leaps, it runs to heaven.—Spark), 260 (They say that a five-year-old boy is going up in a swing.—Soot).

943. Compare the texts cited in the headnote to Nos. 996-1001, § 8.

944a through 944e. Breton: Sauvé, 120; Lavenot, *Basse-Bretagne*, pp. 667-668; Le Pennec, 33. Frisian: Dykstra, *Snypsnaren*, p. 101. Flemish: Joos, 1236. Luxemburg: De la Fontaine, 60. German: Wossidlo, 922; Carstens, *Schleswig-Holstein*, p. 415; August Stöber, *Elsässisches Volksbüchlein* (2d ed.; Mühlhausen, 1859), pp. 94-95, Nos. 404, 405; Renk, *Tyrol*, 114; Hanika-Otto, 565, 654. Swiss: Rochholz, 413; Zahler, *Münchenbuchsee*, 75; J. Müller, *Innerschweiz*, 7. Danish: Kristensen, p. 222, No. 51; Feilberg, *Ordbog*, III, 1154, s.v. "ærte." Swedish: Dybeck, *Runa*, 1850, p. 35, No. 20; Ericsson, *Södermanland*, II (1881), 99, No. 105; Geijer and Campbell, 140. Walloon: Colson, *Wallonia*, IV, 62, No. 62. French: Rolland, 69; Bladé, *Armagnac*, 92; Roque-Ferrier, *Languedoc*, p. 331; Baissac, *Mauritius*, p. 413. Italian: Tschiedel, p. 276, n. 1. Surinam: Herskovits, p. 449, No. 88.

944e. The speaker employs the riddle of crows and corn as a neck-riddle.

945. German: Huss, *Siebenbürgen*, 90 (mice).

946a through 946d. Irish: Delargy, 64 (A bed full of noble children wearing blue hats and green hoods); Hyde, p. 170 (There a garden that I ken, / Full of little gentlemen, / Little caps of blue they wear, / And green ribbons very fair); Christiansen, 62 (A soldier in an orchard with a blue cap). German: Haffner, 33, 34; Hanika-Otto, 249; Renk, *Tyrol*, 153. Swedish: Ström, "Linet," 7. Catalan: Demófilo, p. 360, No. 6. Spanish: Demófilo, p. 369, No. 19, and p. 386, No. 22. Compare the cotton riddle from the Dominican Republic and Porto Rico: "Many ladies on a bank and all are dressed in white" (Andrade, 24; Mason, 39). Lithuanian: Jurgelionis, 984 (Boy: Greenish bluish, yellowish gray, and white). Russian: Sadovnikov, 1304 (A bright little flower entered the moist earth, found a blue hat), which admits part of the answer into the riddle. Finnish: Aarne and Krohn, 241 = Henssen, 207 (A hundred times a hundred times, a thousand times a thousand, they bow to one another.—Wheatfield). Lappish: Qvigstad, 50 (A maiden sits by a spring and has a cap on her head.—Flax). Votyak: Wichmann, *Votyak*, 4 (In the field stands a man with a green cap.—Hemp); Buch, 42 (Forty maidens wink their eyes.—Aspen leaves). Vogul: Ahlqvist, *Vogul*, 16 (Women with silken kerchiefs bend up and down in the meadow.—"Grasses with red head"). Turkish: Katanov in Radlov, IX, 258, No. 146 (The tsar scolds and all the people bow down.—Swaying of the trees when the wind blows). African, Kamba: Lindblom, 36 (A dance that has not a conductor.—The leaves of the taro plants). Taveta: Hollis, *Taveta*, 53 (I have my warriors who fight all day long.—Reeds). Pangwe: Tessmann, 121. Swahili: Velten, 76 (All my children have bowed to the earth.—Rice). Indian, Ho: Sarkar, p. 253, No. 36 (The mother stands still, her children are little. When [the] wind blows, they dance). Samoan: Heider, 23 (A countless company of brothers wearing brown hats.—Grassseeds).

Compare also Nos. 135, 756, 1022a, and 1022b in the present collection.

951a through 951g. French: Parsons, *Antilles*, III, 373, Grenada, 79, p. 375, Cariacou, 20, p. 379, St. Lucia, 37, p. 380, Martinique, 4, p. 390, Dominica, 8, p. 398, Guadaloupe, 10, p. 409, Les Saintes, 4, p. 416, Marie Galante, 54, p. 447, Hayti, 4. Serbian: Novaković, p. 23, No. 3 = p. 162, No. 4 (I sent a servant on a job, the job came home, but the servant remained there.—Club and nut). African, Bakongo: Denis, 75 (Papa went to market. He bought a dog. Papa hasn't returned to the village, but the dog is already there.—Palm nut). Kundu: Ittmann, *Kundu*, 197 (I went to visit my brother, I and my dog. Yet before I entered the house, he [the dog] had already arrived). Duala: Ebding, 75 (I went to the East and bought a man. He went alone to the lowlands and left me behind). This is a curious reminiscence of the slave trade. Indonesian, KaroBatak: Joustra, p. 95 (That which one fetches is quicker than the one who goes for it).

952. See Nos. 999a through 999e (brothers) and 1015a and 1015b (sisters). French: Carnoy, *Picardy*, p. 54 (four gendarmes); Daleau, *Gironde*, p. 106 (four maidens); Mensignac, *Gironde*, p. 304, No. 43 (four ladies); Baissac, *Mauritius*, p. 416 (three blacks). Portuguese: Parsons, *Cape Verde*, 152 (Two men a-running from morning to night, and neither can catch the other.—Pole of the sugarcane-press [its two ends]). Spanish: Demófilo, 807 (millstone). Porto Rican: Mason, 533 (mother and son). Modern Greek: Dieterich, *Rätseldichtung*, p. 99, citing Polites, *Neohellenika Analekta*, I, 238, No. 258 (Twelve little monks who chase and chase and never catch one another).

954a, 954b. (Actors identified as persons, not related.) Welsh Gypsy: Sampson, 16. German: Wossidlo, 157a (four women); Hanika-Otto, 70f (girls). Swedish: Ericsson, *Södermanland*, II (1881), 98, No. 99 (four girls); Hyltén-Cavallius, *Värend*, 61, (four maidens). French: A. Ferrand, *Dauphiné*, p. 227 (Who runs constantly and never catches up?). Basque: Cerquand, 41 (four girls). Spanish, Argentinian: Lehmann-Nitsche, 265g (four boys), 265k (two girls), 265m (two boys). Chilean: Flores, 662 (four fathers), 664 (two godmothers and a godfather; the godfather is the wagon shaft). New Mexican: Espinosa, 111 (four little wheels). Mordvin: Paasonen, 4 (old people). Maltese: Stumme, *Malta*, p. 102, No. 4 (Seven girls who run after one another; not one catches another).

955a, 955b. (Actors are persons, some large and some small.) See also No. 998a (brothers). Walloon: Colson, *Wallonia*, V, 57, No. 220 (Two women running after two little girls). Turkish: Katanov in Radlov, IX, 239, No. 60 (The father is already running up to his son).

956a through 956d. (Actors are not identified as persons.) Breton: Sauvé, 105. Swedish: Dybeck, *Runa*, 1850, p. 37, No. 40 = Russwurm, 67 (Two small ones run ahead, two large ones run after, they run swiftly, they never overtake one another). Lithuanian: Schleicher, p. 207 = Jurgelionis, 666 (Two run, two pursue, two cut the road.—Wagon and horse). Polish: Kopernicki, 2 (four horses). Hungarian: Kriza, 102 (What is it? They start out at the same time, they are running at the same time, but they never reach one another).

957. Polish: Gustawicz, 412 (Twelve boys are racing one another, but not one can catch the other). See also, in the present collection, Nos. 997 (brothers) and a Russian riddle cited in the headnote to Nos. 1014–1015, § 4 (sisters), and the list given in the note to No. 997.

958. In the English version, "Hips" seems to be an interjection. The Danes compare a bunch of keys to a poverty-stricken man who enters while his brothers laugh (Kristensen, p. 99, § 253, No. 397). See also Italian: Ferraro, *Canti popolari in dialetto logodurese*, p. 299, No. 5 (key and lock). The Portuguese "Three men went to steal, one steals, two look on" (Parsons, *Cape Verde*, 221) is a conception of the same sort. See also a Portuguese description of earrings (*ibid.*, 237). Some riddles for a shirt are similar, but they should properly refer to a man and three roads, as in the examples cited in the note to No. 1108 of the present collection. For examples of shirt riddles involving a comparison to persons, see "One goes in, three come out" (Spanish, Dominican Rep.: Andrade, 88); "Two children sleep, one prances" (Bulgarian: Gubov, 246); and Baiga: Elwin, p. 420 and p. 478, No. 142.

959. Perhaps a reference to the confessional is intended. Compare also "One inside, two outside.—A corpse in the ground; outside are good and bad deeds" (Tatar: Kalashev and Ioakimov, p. 49, No. 18). Nor do I understand the Turkish "In he went, out he he came; the ingoer went in and came out, the ingoer went in and came out. Those used to going in went in and came out. Those not used to going in went in and came out.—The prophet Adam, the Devil, the unbelievers" (Kúnos, 119, and compare his No. 134).

Perhaps the speaker has been misled into thinking of the theme of the comparison as the answer while forgetting the proper answer, "keys." "Going in and out" has no connection with the similar phrase in a riddle for a gambler (No. 134 of the present collection).

960. Serbian: Novaković, p. 201, No. 5 (One pushes, two sway). Bulgarian: Gubov, 311 (One is sniffing, two are shaking), which is intended to suggest a dog's ears and nose, and 313 (One is pushing, two are shaking). The conception has a slight resemblance to the riddles discussed in the headnote to Nos. 1476–1494 of the present collection.

961. French: Parsons, *Antilles*, III, 396, Dominica, 82, p. 403, Guadaloupe, 70, 70a, p. 414, Marie Galante, 29. Spanish, Dominican Rep.: Andrade, 239. Compare Mordvin: Paasonen, 209, and the riddle of the unborn child that goes to town and doesn't know the town (No. 711 in the present collection). The idea of going through the water without becoming wet is applied to the eggs in a duck or a chicken (see Nos. 169a through 170b), as well as to an unborn animal (see the note to Nos. 169a through 171), and a very similar notion is expressed in the English riddle for a calf which goes through the bush (No. 160).

966. (Quarreling.) Icelandic: Árnason, 79 (There are two brothers who follow women and seldom come into men's company. Many a day shall they engage in a tug of war over that which they both want. In sheep fat is their bed prepared, where they shall rest), 81 (Two brothers lived long together in the cliff of rings. They tore off each other's hair. That was their whole amusement), in which the "cliff of rings" is an obscure kenning, 277 (Two cousins were fighting over food. Each one snatches furiously what is given to the other), 1060 (Two brothers snatch away from each other). Swedish: Ström, p. 375, "Sysselsättningar," 21 (two dead men). Portuguese: Parsons, *Cape Verde*, 145a through 145c. Serbian: Novaković, p. 33, Nos. 2 (Two old men quarreled; each pulled the other's beard), 3 (Two brothers are pulling at each other's beards over the fence), 4 (Two tomcats are fighting over the priest's dump). Albanian: Hahn, p. 161, No. 45. Modern Greek: Abbott, p. 311, No. 26 (Two little maidens tearing each other's hair).

For comparisons describing eyelids as men quarreling men see Yakut: Piekarski, 159, 160 (quoted in the note to No. 1003), and Popov, p. 285 (quoted in the headnote to No. 1044, n. 8).

The scene of sitting in the corner at night may be borrowed from the broom riddle, in the present collection (see Nos. 695a through 698), or the shoe riddle (Nos. 456a through 456c). For another variety of the concept underlying No. 966, see No. 968.

967. Most of the parallels describe the sun and moon as persons fleeing from each other; see the note and headnote to No. 1001. See German: Wossidlo, 499; Hanika-Otto, 288e (There are two riders, cut round, they have ridden together into France), which has variants substituting disks, chips, and boards for the riders. Swedish: Ström, p. 226, "Tiden, årstiderna, dygnet," 5 (A brother and a sister change about in ruling, but can never meet. When one comes, the other runs), 6, 7. Syriac: Furlani, *Azraq*, 2 (Two twin children, born of one womb and who are not alike, because they have two natures). Georgian: Kapanadze, pp. 144–145, No. 8 (In one country two brothers have the same color; one is always young, while old age has approached the other; one has a countless army, while the other has only a throne). Yakut: Piekarski, 4 (They say that two gentlemen are simultaneously pulling at each other's silken belts, yet neither one nor the other succeeds in seizing the belt or in tearing it asunder.—Day and night). Indian, Parsee: Munshi, p. 97, No. 5 (The brother goes out for a walk in the morning, and the sister strolls about at night). Indonesian, Javanese: Kreemer, *Java*, p. 3 (When the master comes, the pupil leaves; when the pupil comes, the master leaves). Samoan: Heider, 158 (There are two friends. One is in heaven, one on the earth. If the man on the earth does not see the man in heaven, he cries out all night long.—Sun and cricket). Hawaiian: Judd, 221 (The king goes alone, the queen with the soldiers).

Similar ideas occur in the tripartite riddles discussed in the headnote to Nos. 138–140 of the present collection. See, for example, Latin: Daly and Suchier, p. 119, No. 20, and their note on p. 122. Modern Greek: Dieterich, *Rätseldichtung*, p. 90, citing Stamatiadis, V, 181 (Two are motionless, two only run, two have an irreconcilable quarrel.—Sky and earth, sun and moon and water). For the notion that the sun and moon fight each other, see the headnote to this riddle (No. 967 of the present collection). Compare also No. 1001, in which the actors are brothers, and other riddles cited in the headnote and note to No. 1001.

968. (Quarreling and embracing.) For parallels to the final clause, see the note to No. 966. See further, Faeroic: Hammershaimb, *Færøsk anthologi*, I, 317, No. 22 (They claw and bite each other like trolls all day; they embrace at night). Icelandic: Árnason, 79 (quoted in the note to No. 966 of the present collection), 82. Serbian: Novaković, p. 33, Nos. 6 (By day they fight with their heads and pull each other's beards, at night they embrace each other), 7 (Two brothers scratched each other today, and this evening they went to bed together), 8 (Two brothers fought all day long, and in the evening they kissed each other).

969. This obscure riddle is probably connected with the equally obscure Nos. 1050 and 1154. In all these, bulls and one thousand men are mentioned. See also several other versions quoted in the notes to Nos. 1050 and 1154.

971a through 971f. Icelandic: Árnason, 921 (I see five bold knights urging on a baldheaded slave to drive the sheep from the mountain into the plain and then into a pond). French, *Les Adevineaux amoureux*, pp. lxxxviii f. = Rolland, 79 (Two who run and ten who chase them, two who look at them, and one who puts them to death), which, in the mention of the two onlookers, shows some similarity to the riddle for writing (see, in the present collection, the headnotes to Nos. 970–975, § 6, and 1063, n. 2). Italian: Pitrè, 620. Modern Greek: Stathes, p. 355, No. 139 (In the month of March there is born a black beast. It is not a lion or a bear. It upsets kings and leaders. It is hunted down by five tyrants and caught by two and is killed between two ivory boards), and the variant (In the month of March is born a blackish beast. It leaps like a deer, it is caught by five and ends its days in the ivory city.—Flea). Gypsy: Wlislocki, 30 (Two brown men come walking and bring a white one as prisoner. They lay him on a stone and say, "Now someone must die"). He cites his *Kinderlied*, No. 30, as parallel. The reference to laying the criminal on a stone before execution has historical parallels; see Paul G. Brewster,

"Traces of Ancient Germanic Law in a German Game-Song," *Southern Folklore Quarterly*, II (1938), 138–143. African, Kaguru: Busse, p. 62, No. 4 (I have killed my magic doctor with two clubs). Zulu: Callaway, 9 (Guess ye an ox which is slaughtered in two cattle-pens). Indian, Bihari: Mitra, *Bihar*, 14 (He is king of the town-like crown of the head, he is seized with the finger-tips, tried on the palm of the hand, and killed on the finger-nails). Uraon: Archer, p. 193, No. 210 (Theft in the hair, trial in the hand, death between the thumbnails). Indonesian, Javanese: Ranneft, *Poëzie*, p. 2, No. 3 (Bad robbers are named, who execute a task together. When the person who is the object of attack rests, they bend over and run slowly. The group of five usually attack together. When the attacked has been seized, five comrades come, who have been at one side, to give aid to those who have not been acting in vain), and p. 24, No. 7 (There are five hunters who hunt in a woods. Two slip in everywhere, three follow after. When they catch something, they kill it actually in the house [mouth?] and yet it is not as if it were eaten up); Ranneft, *Proza*, p. 5, No. 17 (There are five thieves; three of them stand watch and the two others abduct the princess. The princess escapes and the thieves blame one another). Atjeh: Kreemer, *Atjeh*, 20 (It is no roe; it is no stag; two kill him and eight track him). Kreemer cites three parallels with hunters, not constables. Malay: Tauern, *Patasiwa*, p. 72 (Ten people, they hunt the stag on the mountain, but only two kill him, eight do not).

For riddles in which the scenes receive symbolic names, see the headnote to Nos. 970–975, nn. 3–14, of the present collection.

971a. The riddler introduces the word "jail" somewhat too early; the capture should occur on the "hill," and the prisoner should then be taken to the "jail" for execution.

971c. For the comparisons of hair to grass, see the headnote to Nos. 1042–1044, nn. 2–4, and the note to Nos. 1042, 1043.

972. Spanish, New Mexican: Campa, 261.

976a through 976e. Welsh: Hull and Taylor, 232. Welsh Gypsy: Sampson, 14 (In a field I saw ten pulling four). Irish: Christiansen, 33. Danish: Kristensen, p. 75, § 176, No. 281d, which is contaminated by admixture with the conception of Nos. 1476a through 1489 of the present collection. Norwegian: Bugge, *Telemarken*, 18 (Ten draw four, it stands as in a stump, and runs like water), which is disordered. Swedish: Dybeck, *Runa*, 1850, p. 36, No. 21 = Russwurm, 54; Dybeck, *Runa*, 1865–1873, p. 30, No. 22; Christoffer-son, p. 42, No. 3 = *Folkminnen och folktankar*, II (1915), 93, No. 3; Geijer and Campbell, 40 (Two draw four out of flesh and blood into a tree [wooden bucket] and out of the tree into a tree [churn] and into flesh and blood again). Polish: Siarkowski, 93 (Ten crooked ones, four straight ones, one rump down, the other up). Hungarian: Kriza, 56 (Ten pull four).

976a. The introduction is confused.

976b. "In the bank" seems to be an error. "Under the bank," which is the usual form, perhaps refers to a bank or slope signifiying the side of the cow.

976d. The riddler may have misheard "drawing" as "drying."

976e. The riddler has substituted "bag" (udder) for "bank," which he found unintelligible.

977a through 977d. Welsh: Hull and Taylor, 229 through 231. Breton: Kerbeuzec, *Ille-et-Vilaine*, p. 504, No. 30 (I went into a loft, I raised a little trap door, I saw ten who were fighting against four). French: E. H. Carnoy, *Mélusine*, I (1878), col. 293 (I entered a farmhouse, I heard fighting. Ten against four, when the four were well beaten, the ten went away).

977b. Taken in conjunction with No. 977d, these versions are readily understood: *clink, clank* refers to the clatter of wooden shoes (pattens), "down the bank" or "under the bank" refers to a hillside (perhaps the side of the cow), and *splish, splash* to the milk falling in the bucket. In many versions the riddler seems to have understood *clink, clank*, if he gave the matter any thought at all, as the sound of falling milk, but in No. 977*b* it seems to refer to the cow's bell (see, for example, No. 252*a*).

977d. The command "Try once more" probably implies the hearer's failure to guess the riddle.

979. Rumanian: Weigand, 5 (Five fellows make a well.—Knitting needles and stocking). Turkish: Kowalski, *North Bulgaria*, 3 (Five brothers noisily weave a hedge); Moshkov in Radlov, X, 272, No. 91 (Four brothers are weaving a fence).

980a, 980b. See Irish: Christiansen, 56; O Dalaigh, 7 (Five took it, twenty swallowed it, and one more ate it.—Apple eaten at leisure), 68 (A little thing was growing on a tree. Two saw it, five took it, twenty chewed it, one left it behind, and it was only one person). Breton: Charlec, *Dol-de-Bretagne*, 1905, pp. 40–41, No. 57. French: Dottin, *Bas-Maine*, 13. Bulgarian: Ikonomov, 53 (Five brothers caught Tsar Kuzuman and threw him into Altuman City.—Fingers and bread). Modern Greek: Polites, *Neohellenika Analekta*, I, 206, No. 132 (Five brothers grab it, thirty-two hammers break it, a maiden embraces it and sends it down), p. 239, No. 260 (Five, ten do the carrying, white files pound it, the broom sweeps it up, the channel takes it down and stores it in the hold); Stathes, p. 344, No. 78, and p. 346, No. 89 (The hammer hammers, the five transport [it], Theodora calls them down the long passage). Arabic: Ruoff, p. 17, No. 11 (Five cut it, ten pull it, thirty-two divide it, one eats it.—Orange); Stumme, *Tázerwalt*, 7 (Five butchers take a morsel and throw it into the shambles.—Fingers put a bone in the mouth). Turkish: Kúnos, 180 (Over there I saw an illuminated dome, it shines now and then, the hands are covered with roses, five or ten bravos demolished this building, constantly striking at it. —Pilau, borsch, and spoon), 190 (Glass dome, light shining on it, five or ten warriors digging at it dug up the whole building); Zavarin, *Brusa*, 2 (Ach comes, Vach comes, and a kerchief comes in the middle, it comes to Zendeli Ahmed; the Egyptian Mehmed Ali comes and thirty-two teachers come, collecting all clean, they go off). The collector gives some explanatory comment for this last riddle. Persian: Kuka, 12 (Four persons fought with thirty-two, and being all killed, the narrow pit wherein they fought was filled with their blood.—Betel leaf, betel nut, slaked lime, catechu). Betel turns red when chewed; the pit is the mouth. Yakut: Piekarski, 169 (They say that ten people wait upon thirty people, thirty people serve a wheat cake, the wheat cake is thrown below.—Fingers of both hands, teeth, tongue, stomach). The last element in this somewhat confused text occurs also in riddles cited in the headnote to No. 841, nn. 21, 30, 33, 34, 39, 40, 42, of the present collection. Indian, Baiga: Elwin, p. 477, No. 132 (You may go to eat, but unless five of us help, you can't.—Five fingers). Gujerati: Mehta, p. 135 (I saw a female who became wedded to five males, thirty-two males embraced her so that her limbs were all shattered but while dying she put forth all coquetry and she displayed beauty in the bargain). The five materials chewed by Indians are betel nut, catechu, chunan, clove, tobacco. The "coquetry" is the aroma of the materials; the "beauty" is the brilliant red of the spittle. Toda: manuscript version given me by Murray B. Emeneau (Six men go by one path, having pushed one over a cliff, five return. What is it?). Indonesian, Javanese: Ranneft, *Proza*, p. 4, No. 13 (There are five thieves, three go in through an opening, one keeps watch to see when the alarm is, and the other keeps watch at the door), and p. 38, No. 170 (There are five thieves who want to enter to steal. Four go in and one stays out. When the four thieves come out, they shed blood.—Betel). Annamese: Emeneau and Taylor, 1 (One house has five brothers; they urge one another and take hold of a pair of bamboo sticks; they drive before them a herd of white buffaloes which run and enter a cave.—Your hand holds a pair of bamboo chopsticks and puts rice into your mouth).

983a, 983b. The significance of the "shirt" is not clear; the parallels do not include this element. See Spanish: Demófilo, pp. 408–409, No. 13 (seven brothers, the first is the smallest); Rodríguez Marín, 892. Argentinian: Lehmann-Nitsche, 464. Porto Rican: Mason, 193, 500. Portuguese: Pires de Lima, 8 (A man with seven sons, five [of them] just, one holy, one as he ought to be); Parsons, *Cape Verde*, 247 (seven sons). Polish: Saloni, *Rzeshów*, 187 (Seven brothers chase each other the whole year and no one can catch another), which is perhaps suggested by the riddles for spokes or wheels (see Nos. 997 through 998e in the present collection and the Turcoman riddle quoted below in this note). Russian: Sadovnikov, 2024 (There are seven brothers, equal in age, different in names). Serbian: Novaković, p. 173, No. 7 (Seven sisters strolled in Paradise and brought great joy to us.—Holy Week). Turcoman: Samojlvich, 144 (Seven brothers chase after one another.—Wheels or week). Samoan: Heider, 171 (Seven brothers, but the firstborn is the smartest).

984. German: Wossidlo, 36; H. Meier, *Ostfriesland*, 16 (man, twelve daughters, each with thirty children). Icelandic: Árnason, 189 (There is a great circle that set out on its travels with twelve brothers longer ago than anyone can remember), 192 (A father has twelve sons, each of whom has thirty sons, fair and bright, and thirty black daughters of no beauty. These are now here and now gone and never remain). Walloon: Colson, *Wallonia*, IV, 42, No. 2. French: Alexandre Sylvain (A. van den Bussche), *Cinquante Ænigmes françoises* (1582), 3 (twelve children, thirty bright sons, thirty dark daughters, with 144 daughters [hours] and 64 granddaughters); Rolland, 1 (twelve sons, who have thirty sons, half black and half white), which involves an allusion to the day and night; Friedrich, p. 196, No. 10, quoting a literary riddle from Theodor Hell, *Agrionen* (Leipzig, 1811). Portuguese: Braga, pp. 361–362 (a long Renaissance text). Catalan: Pelay y Briz, 107. Spanish: Demófilo, 69 (king with twelve sons), 71 (giant with twelve sons), 72 (black man with twelve sons), 655 (man has many brothers); Rodríguez Marín, 263 (giant, twelve sons, thirty grandsons, half black and half white). Argentinian: Lehmann-Nitsche, 447 (man with many brothers), 461 (young man, twelve sons, four grandsons, seven great-grandsons who are white and black). Dominican Rep.: Andrade, 26 (father with twelve sons). New Mexican: Campa, 112 (twelve sons, thirty grandchildren), 128 (hours are twelve daughters). Porto Rican: Mason, 56 (father with twelve sons), 58. Italian: Rua, *Archivio*, VII (1888), 451, No. 5. Russian: Sadovnikov, 2022 (Twelve brothers follow one another, do not pass one another).

985. Welsh: Hull and Taylor, 122. Irish: Stokes, 10 (What daughter tells of her mother's birth and without having seen the mother?). Scotch Gaelic: Nicolson, p. 53; Campbell, p. 404. Flemish: Joos, 1st ed., 294, and 2d ed., 49, 535, 536. German: Wossidlo, 148; Frischbier, *Menschenwelt*, p. 251, Nos. 102, 103; Haase, *Ruppin*, 223; Renk, *Tyrol*, 118; Hanika-Otto, 280; Huss, *Siebenbürgen*, 103. Swiss: Rochholz, 468. Danish: Kristensen, p. 111, § 301, Nos. 477a through 477c. Faeroic: Hammershaimb, *Antiquarisk tidsskrift*, III (1849–1851), 319, No. 40 = *Zeitschrift für deutsche Mythologie*, III (1855), 130 = *Færøsk anthologi*, I, 323, No. 25 (The son stood in the door, when the father was being born). Norwegian: Karl Müllenhoff, *Zeitschrift für deutsche Mythologie*, III (1855), 9, No. 42; Landstad, p. 812, No. 42; Berge, 44; Bugge, *Telemarken*, 8; Stafset, 68; Brox, *Ytre Senja*, 36. Swedish: Dybeck, *Runa*, 1848, p. 43, No. 30 = Russwurm, 68; Hyltén-Cavallius, *Värend*, 41 (The son goes to the forest, while the father is being born); Geijer and Campbell, 85; Ström, p. 232, "Elden ock rokan," 6. The version "The father makes day; the son makes night; they are always companions" (Hyltén-Cavallius, *Värend*, 40) is adapted from the conceptions discussed in the headnote to No. 1001 of the present collection. Latin: Ohl, Symphosius, 7; Claret, p. 74, No. 110. Walloon: Colson, *Wallonia*, IV, 148, No. 161. French: *Les Adevineaux amoureux*, p. xcviii = Rolland, 155;

V. S., *Mélusine*, I (1878), col. 254, No. 1; Parsons, *Antilles*, III, 367, Trinidad, 53, p. 373, Grenada, 75. Catalan: Pelay y Briz, 8; Demófilo, p. 354, No. 10. Spanish: Demófilo, 548, 550; Rodríguez Marín, 290 through 292. Argentinian: Lehmann-Nitsche, 438a through 438c (mother and son). Chilean: Flores, 368 through 371 (mother and son). Dominican Rep.: Andrade, 182 (mother and son). Porto Rican: Mason, 638 (mother and son). Portuguese: Braga, p. 378; Pires de Lima, 16. Italian: Pitrè, 297 (mother and daughter); Tschiedel, 31 (father and mother), 32 (father), 33 (mother); Gianandrea, *Archivio*, II (1883), 432, No. 60; Rondini, *ibid.*, VII (1888), 538, No. 11; Gianandrea, *Canti popolari marchigiani*, p. 301, No. 24 (father); Ive, *Canti popolari istriani*, p. 399, No. 12 (father); Bernoni, *Venice*, 56 (father). Rumanian: Gorovei, 828 (father and child); Papahagi, 23 var. (The father is not yet born; the son has gone to Stambul). Lithuanian: Jurgelionis, 130 (An unborn father, a son grown gray); Jurgelionis, 131 = Schleicher, p. 207 (The son has gone to war, the father is not yet born); Jurgelionis, 133 = Schleicher, p. 198 (The father is not yet born, the son braces himself against the heavens); Jurgelionis, 134 (Scarcely born and already gray). Lettish: Bielenstein, 727 through 731; Ulanowska, 108, 136, as cited by Flajšhans, pp. 6-7, No. 6a. Czech: Feifalik, p. 383, No. 100; Hanika-Otto, note to No. 280. Polish: Gustawicz, 68 through 70; Saloni, *Rzeshów*, 30 (The father was born and the son walked along the roof), 31 (. . . and the son was walking through the field). Russian: Sadovnikov, 146 (The father is not yet born, but the son is already going to the forest), 146a (. . ., but the son is already sitting on the roof). Serbian: Novaković, p. 17, Nos. 1 (While the father is being born, the son is already walking through the house), 2 (The son is dashing through the house, while the father has not yet been born), 3 (The father has not yet been born, but the son is already flying higher than the house). Finnish: Henssen, 127 (The father is not yet born; the sons are already racing about). Estonian: Lönnrot, p. 184; Wiedemann, p. 265. Lappish: Poestion, p. 267; Donner, p. 19, No. 3; Qvigstad, 11, and compare his Nos. 12, 13, 62. Votyak: Wichmann, *Votyak*, 28, 35, 46, 223, 224, 349. Cheremiss: Porkka, 64; Wichmann, *Cheremiss*, 100 (brothers), 125 (brothers), 215 (brothers). Mordvin: Ahlqvist, p. 40, No. 8; Paasonen, 209. Modern Greek: Dieterich, *Rätseldichtung*, p. 104, citing *Anthologia Palatina*, III, 575 and 549, and a monograph by N. G. Polites in *Syll. Konst.*, VIII, 525; Stathes, p. 333, No. 19 (A black child, I am born of a red mother. I have no wings, but I fly through the clouds). Albanian: Hahn, p. 158, No. 14, and p. 163, No. 24 (son goes to the well). Turcoman: Samojlvich, 31 (While the father is mounting the horse, the son is arriving at the bazar), with Turcoman, Kazan Tatar, and Kirghese parallels. Indian, Uraon: Archer, p. 192, No. 204 (The son who is born before his father). Bihari: Mitra, *Bihari Life*, p. 47, No. 33 (The son goes toward the back, before the birth of the father).

986. Compare Nos. 952, 999a through 999e, 1015a, 1015b. See the note to No. 997 for other uses of the theme of persons or animals running.

987. For the usual form of this riddle see Nos. 523 through 524b.

988. The rare enigmatic descriptions of the Pleiades vary widely in their fundamental conception and in details. See the headnotes to Nos. 484–486, n. 3, and Nos. 1027–1028, § 9, of the present collection, and Flemish: Joos, 9 (seven shards), 10 (seven trees). The last is identical with Dutch: Schrijnen, II, 102, No. 4. Joos, 11 (seven nests), may be a reminiscence of the year riddle (see Nos. 1037a, 1037b in the present collection). Afrikaans: Groenewald, pp. 85-86. German: Wossidlo, 40, 41; Petsch, *Neue Beiträge*, pp. 49–50. Norwegian: Brox, *Ytre Senja*, 203 (Seven stars in a ring journey around the world), in which the riddler should not have admitted the answer into the riddle. Latin: Aldhelm, 8 (ed. Pitman, pp. 8–9) = Friedreich, p. 192, No. 1. Aldhelm shows an especial interest in riddles about the stars and constellations; he has enigmas for the Great Bear, Lucifer the morning star, the evening star, the sun and the moon, the celestial spheres,

and the moon. Italian: Schneller, *Wälschtirol*, p. 256, No. 28 (Plate on plate, a well-armed man, a beautifully dressed woman, a well-equipped cavalry.—Heaven and earth, sun, moon, stars). Serbian: Novaković, p. 21, No. 6 (Everybody waits happily for St. George's Day. Only seven do not), which involves an unexplained allusion. The three following riddles in Novaković have the answer "Pleiades"; they are difficult to understand and are therefore not quoted. Turkish: Katanov in Radlov, IX, 92, Nos. 778a (Seven chestnut horses remembered their own land.—Great Bear), 778b (The bearded prince remembered his native land.—Moon); Maenchen, 9 (The bearded prince remembered his home; the seven foxes remembered their home.—Moon and Dipper). Mongolian: Mostaert, 78 (On the summit of the eastern mountain there grow six kinds of flowers. They are flowers which do not grow in summer. They grow in winter. What are they?), 78 var. (On the summit of the sandalwood mountain six *tawak* artemisia grow in winter, they do not grow in summer). The seventh star of the Pleiades, Merope, has a very feeble light. She is said to hide out of shame, because she yielded to a mortal man. The meaning of *tawak* is obscure; it may refer to a variety of artemisia (*Artemisia campestris*), or it may be merely a rhyme word with *săwak* (artemisia). Yakut: Popov, p. 263 (On the bottom lie seven coins). The Samoans refer to the stars in somewhat similar fashion, but do not apply the riddle especially to the Pleiades; see "There is a company of many brothers; by day one does not see them; at night, however, one can see them" (Heider, 148). For this last notion see also the headnote to No. 1094 of the present collection.

For stories about the Pleiades see R. Andree, "De Plejaden im Mythus," *Globus*, LXIV (1893), 362–366; K. van den Steinen, "Plejaden und Jahr bei den Indianern," *ibid.*, LXV (1894), 243–246; E. Förstemann, "Die Plejaden bei den Mayas," *ibid.*, p. 246; an article by Stilpon P. Kyriakides cited in *Zeitschrift des Vereins für Volkskunde*, XXXV–XXXVI (1925–1926), 70; F. Normann, *Mythen der Sterne* (Gotha, 1922).

989. The fundamental idea of this riddle is found rarely in Europe, but is known to Yakut and Samoan riddlers. Its distribution and the comparison to a turban, which it implies, suggest a Levantine origin and dissemination by Mohammedan agencies. Some versions—notably the Portuguese text from the Cape Verde Islands—suggest, however, the possibility of independent origins. For parallels see German: Carstens, *Schleswig-Holstein*, p. 413. French: Haurigot, *French Guiana*, p. 120; Baissac, *Mauritius*, p. 401 (I have ten little gentlemen, all of them have white heads). Portuguese: Parsons, *Cape Verde*, 225 (I have a child; he has worked since the age of ten years; he is dressed in the back of a vest; he cannot dress in front). Italian: Pitrè, 237. Rumanian: Weigand, p. 275, Nos. 25 (Five women with saucers on their heads), 30 = Papahagi, 19 (Twenty brothers with plates on their heads). Serbian: Novaković, p. 144, No. 11 (Our governor has a stone head), and p. 179, No. 1 (My mother gave birth to twenty sons, all of them under hard caps). Albanian: Hahn, p. 161, No. 33 (Five brothers with plates on their heads), and p. 158, No. 7 (Some dervishes with ivory caps). Arabic: Ruoff, p. 15, No. 4 (Five youths [stand] on a plate. Who are they?), and p. 32, No. 64 (A black slave bears a tablet). Turkish: Kowalski, *Zagadki*, 67 (On the flesh a little chip); Kúnos, 67 = Kúnos, *Nyelvkönyv*, 12 (A tiny little Arab with a table on his head); Katanov in Radlov, IX, 180, No. 1404 (Five brothers loaded ice on their shoulders); p. 238, No. 38 (Ten Russians are carrying ice on their shoulders). Mongolian: Mostaert, 104 (On their backs ten old women carry ice). Yakut: Piekarski, 177 (They say that there are five children wearing caps of ice), 178 (They say that five children carry five pieces of ice on their backs), 179 (Ten children carry a load of ice apiece, so they say), 192 (They say that all these twenty people have their faces in back.—Fingers and toes), which last riddle is related to the theme discussed in the headnote to No. 191 in the present collection. See also

Popov, p. 286 (Ten children carry ice); Priklonskii, 46 (Twenty men, all with their faces backwards). African, Kxatla: Schapera, 79 (Tell me: ten boys who have hats at the back). Swahili: Büttner, p. 201 = Velten, 46 (My children all have clothes, they also wear a cap on the side, whoever has no clothing and no cap is not my child). Louyi: Jacottet, 7 (Scamps clothed in white shirts). Konde: Mackenzie, p. 163 (All my children have red hats). Sinhalese: Perera, p. 55 (What is the tree by the door that has twenty branches and bark strips? Twenty knocks on the head of the person who fails to solve it). Coorg: Emeneau manuscript version (Little, little children, caps on the backs of their heads). Samoan: Heider, 135 (Twenty white brothers with black hats). This alludes realistically to dirt gathered under the nails. See also Brown, p. 343 (There are twenty brethren, each with his hat on). Fijian: Fison, 9 = *Revue des traditions populaires*, I (1886), 12 (Twenty men with white turbans). Filipino: Starr, *Philippines*, 53 (Five princes, their hat is one half [of them]); De los Reyes y Florentino, p. 236 (Ten sisters with white kerchiefs). For the comparison of matches to men wearing caps, see the note to Nos. 583a through 584b of the present collection.

990a, 990b. Flemish: Joos, 513. German: Wossidlo, 155; Carstens, *Schleswig-Holstein*, p. 417; Hanika-Otto, 252. Latin: Ebert, p. 12 (Tatwine, 26); M[one], *Anzeiger*, VII (1838), col. 48, No. 126, and col. 49, No. 141; Hagen, p. 46, n. 18 (*Codex Bernensis 611*, No. 26).

991a through 991c. German: Wossidlo, 333b. French: J. Roux, *Limousin*, 76. Spanish: Demófilo, 1056 = Rodríguez Marín, 644 = Chilean: Flores, 789. Italian: Pitrè, 725 (We are two sisters come to serve a gentleman; we are always with him when he is well but by [bad] chance when this master is in bed, we rest with our stomachs empty).

991b. See the parallel in the Hungarian knapsack riddle, "I have an ox that is not hungry when I drive him out. When driven back home, he however gets hungry" (*Magyar Nyelvör*, II [1873], 559).

991c. The Irish riddler has lost the significance of the word "prest" in No. 991b. It refers to the punishment of pressing, or the *peine forte et dure*.

992. Breton: Charlec, *Dol-de-Bretagne*, 1904, p. 378, No. 37. Modern Greek: Carnoy and Nicolaides, 22. Indonesian, Tounsea: De C., 21 (Two friends dressed in black never part, but accompany each other everywhere. Where one goes, they both go).

993. German: Frischbier, *Menschenwelt*, p. 252, No. 109 (Three maidens wear one garland.—Tripod); Hanika-Otto, 346 (four boys). French: Rolland, 193 (Three brothers in the same waistcoat). Portuguese: Parsons, *Cape Verde*, 121. Rumanian: Papahagi, 72. Lithuanian: Jurgelionis, 294 (Two maidens bound with one girdle.—Door), 384 (Four maidens under one umbrella), 385 (Under one hat sit four brothers), 465 (Two brothers sit under one hat.—Buckets under one covering); Schleicher, p. 195 (Three sisters wear one wreath.—Tripod). Polish: Gustawicz, 422 (Four peasants stand under one hat). White Russian: Wasilewski, 9 (Four little ladies stand under one hat), 53 (Four young gentlemen under one hat); Jurkevich, p. 293 (Four little masters sit under one cape). Russian: Sadovnikov, 228 (Four brothers belted with one belt stand under one hat), 229 (In a wide yard, on a smooth field, four priests under one hat), 230 (Under one veil stand four sisters), 402 (Three little brothers stand under one hat.—Legs of a washtub), 402a (Three maidens stand under one parasol); Arkhangel'skii, p. 76 (Four little brothers stand all under one hat); Preobrazhenskii, p. 172. Serbian: Novaković, p. 143, Nos. 11 (Four brothers are standing under one hat), 12 (Brothers are living under one hat, yet they do not know one another), and p. 215, Nos. 6 (Four brothers wear a single cap.—Table), 10 (Three brothers and one cap.—Stool), 11 (Three brothers wear one shirt.—Stool). Bulgarian: Gubov, 222 (Four brothers wear one cap). Mordvin: Ahlqvist, p. 39, No. 1, and p. 41, Nos. 1, 2; Paasonen, 195. Cheremiss: Porkka, 41 (Four girls under one hood), 103 (Four girls under a veil); Genetz, 87 (Four Tatar women have

Notes

drawn a single cloth over their heads); Wichmann, *Cheremiss*, 18, 46, 101, 222; Ramstedt, 12. Zyrian: Wichmann, *Zyrian*, 161, 278 (Four sisters under one cloth). Votyak: Wichmann, *Votyak*, 32 (Under the same coverlet four Russian women are sleeping), 290 (Four bridesmaids have only one cap.—Bench for a tub). Hungarian: *Magyar Nyelvör*, III (1874), 37 (Four devils stand under one hat); XII (1883), 473 (Four Germans are living under the same hat); XVI (1887), 87 (Four misses wear the same hat); XX (1891), 575 (four ladies); XXXVII (1908), 188 (Six brothers and sisters who have only one hat). Turkish: Kúnos, 274 (Three brothers wearing one *takké* [top]); Katanov in Radlov, IX, 291, No. 250 (Four lads have one shoulder.—Sofa, divan). Armenian: Seidlitz, p. 71, No. 16. I have not found Blechsteiner's reference to *Sbornik . . . Kavkaza*, II, No. 17. Mingrelian: Petrov, p. 257, No. 1. Tungus: Poppe, 13 (Three brothers wear one cap.—Tripod).

For riddles describing staves, rungs, or rafters as persons lying in the same bed see, in the present collection, the headnote to Nos. 1027–1028, §§ 2–3, 6. For comparisons to persons bound together see the headnote to No. 678.

994. The import of the riddle is not clear. See Nos. 1013, 1031a, 1031b.

995. "Bottles" may be a corruption of "brothers." See Nos. 954a through 957, 998a through 998e, 1014a, 1014b, 1029a, 1029b.

996. Turkish: Katanov in Radlov, IX, 95, No. 814 (As yet he has not come himself, but something round and black has already come). For other riddles for the eye and sight, see the headnote to No. 1471 in the present collection.

997. The spokes of the wheel are not usually mentioned; see, however, No. 957. A Russian riddle for the spokes of a spinning wheel is cited in the headnote to Nos. 1014–1015, § 4, and virtually the same concept is found in riddles for the vanes of a windmill (see Nos. 952, 986, 999a through 999e, 1015a, 1015b, and the corresponding notes). A number of non-English riddles about a reel, cited in the headnotes to Nos. 952–957, § 2, 996–1001, § 3, and 1014–1015, § 4, are based on the same idea. As a rule, the actors are persons, though in a few riddles they are horses or other animals; in practically every instance, however, they are represented as equals vainly pursuing one another.

998a through 998e. Flemish: Joos, 308. German: Wossidlo, 157b; Gilhoff, 550; Hanika-Otto, 70a through 70e, 70g. Swiss: Zahler, *Münchenbuchsee*, 408. Catalan: Pelay y Briz, 207. Italian: Pitrè, *Canti*, II, 72. Rumanian: Gorovei, 1578. Czech: Flajšhans, pp. 20–21, § 20. Polish: Saloni, *Rzeshów*, 74 (Four brothers are chasing and will never catch one another), 75, 76 (Four old men are chasing around the field and not one will catch the others); Kopernicki, 2 var.; Gustawicz, 147 through 151. White Russian: Wasilewski, 102 (Two brothers run, two chase after and can't catch [them]). Russian: Sadovnikov, 963a through 963f. Serbian: Novaković, p. 223, No. 9 (Four brothers run along the road and cannot reach one another). Bulgarian: Bozhov, 25 (Four brothers chase one another all the time and yet cannot reach one another). Mordvin: Ahlqvist, p. 39, No. 2. Cheremiss: Genetz, 4; Porkka, 39. Turcoman: Samojlvich, 144 (Seven brothers chase after one another.—Wheels or week). Turkish: Hamizade, 6 (Four brothers chase one another); Katanov in Radlov, IX, 287, No. 224; Moshkov in Radlov, X, 269, No. 68. Tatar: Kalashev and Ioakimov, p. 48, No. 1 (Two brothers are running and two are chasing them until doomsday, unless they catch up). For other riddles about wheels as persons in vain pursuit of one another, see, in the present collection, Nos. 954a through 956d; for riddles with the answer "spokes," see Nos. 957 and 997 and the list given in the note to No. 997.

998a. Crimean Tatar: Filonenko, 68 (There are four brothers, all children of one mother, two big ones, two small ones; the big ones, being the older ones, hunt the small ones, yet cannot catch them.—Wheels of a canopied bullock cart).

998d, 998e. The element "Four brothers going to school" occurs in various forms in Nos. 1033a through 1033g.

999a through 999e. German: Wossidlo, 156*h*; Gilhoff, 589. Danish: Kristensen, p. 95, § 244, Nos. 375*a* through 375*h*. Swedish: Christofferson, p. 27 = *Folkminnen och folktankar*, II (1915), 82. French: Rollard, 193; Bladé, *Armagnac*, 95; Fourès, p. 254; Baissac, *Mauritius*, p. 406. Italian: Panareo, *Archivio*, XXIII (1906–1907), 240, No. 28. Lettish: Bielenstein, 616 (Four brothers go through the air and not one catches up with another). Russian: Sadovnikov, 1122. Turkish: Moshkov in Radlov, X, 269, No. 59. Indonesian, Malay: Harmsen, p. 265, No. 7 (There are four brothers who are competing to be first). The actors are often called sisters; see Nos. 1015*a*, 1015*b* of the present collection and compare the list in the note to No. 997.

1000. French: Parsons, *Antilles*, III, 416, Marie Galante, 68. Serbian: Novaković, p. xviii, No. 2 (Two brothers run over the field, one cannot catch the other until both reach the shore).

1001. Scotch Gaelic: Nicolson, p. 13 (I see yonder on the horizon on the rocky heights of the red bank the son coming from the mother and the mother fleeing from it [him]). Flemish: Joos, 124 (Two sisters pursue each other, one wears a white and the other a black apron). Lettish: Bielenstein, 537 (Sister and brother go daily over a lake). Bulgarian: Gubov, 120 (Two things looking at each other, two things following each other.— Earth and sky, sun and moon), which resembles the riddles discussed in the headnote to Nos. 1476–1494, §14, in the present collection. Finnish: Henssen, 28*a* (Two Lapps from Turja glide on skis on a single track); Lönnrot, 367 = Henssen, 28*b* (Two Lapps from Turja go cautiously through a blue forest; one does not catch the other); Lönnrot, 673 = Henssen, 28*c* (A Lapp, a thin fellow, glides all his life on the trail of his holy brother). Indian, Parsee: Munshi, p. 97, No. 5 (The brother goes out for a walk in the morning, and the sister strolls about at night). Kolarian: Wagner, 40 (In the world are two men walking all night and day).

For other riddles describing the sun and moon or day and night as persons see the headnote and the note to No. 967 in the present collection.

1003. Breton: Sébillot, *Haute-Bretagne*, 44; Kerbeuzec, *Ille-et-Vilaine*, 22; Duine, *Saint-Malo*, p. 516; Orain, *Ille-et-Vilaine*, p. 154. German: Wossidlo, 150; Gilhoff, 4; Zingerle, p. 271, No. 3; Renk, *Tyrol*, 6; Hanika-Otto, 214. French: Carmeau, p. 35. Spanish, Argentinian: Lehmann-Nitsche, 523 (There are two walls; they cannot see between them). New Mexican: Campa, 215, 216. Portuguese: Parsons, *Cape Verde*, 209*h*. Italian: Tammi, 2. Rumanian: Papahagi, 69. Polish: Kopernicki, 17 (Two brothers look across a small hill, yet they are never able to see each other); Gustawicz, 268, 269. White Russian: Wasilewski, 55 (Two brothers live across the boundary and one can't see the other). Serbian: Novaković, p. 157, Nos. 2 (They see everybody but themselves), 7 (The brothers stood side by side, but one can't see the other), 9 (We are two brothers and are twins, alike in everything; day and night we are chums but we do not see each other). Bulgarian: Stoilov, p. 58, §11, Nos. 1 through 3. Zyrian: Wichmann, *Zyrian*, 114 (Two brothers stand each on one side of the road, but do not see each other). Votyak: Wichmann, *Votyak*, 333 (Two brothers look at a single spot, but they don't see each other), 375 (Two older brothers keep looking, but never meet). Cheremiss: Porkka, 54, 108. Modern Greek: Dieterich, *Rätseldichtung*, p. 96, citing Polites, *Neohellenika Analekta*, I, 231, No. 220 (Two brothers were quarreling, and a hill separated them). Yakut: Piekarski, 158 (Fishermen with their rods stand on both sides of the hill.—Eyelashes), 159 (They say that people stand on both sides of a tiny lake, simultaneously striking at one another with long thin poles.—Eyelashes), 160 (They say that two boys stand on either side of a body of water striking at each other with long thin poles). A close parallel to the last two riddles is cited in the headnote to No. 1044, n. 8, of the present collection (see also the note to No. 1044). African, Sierra Leone: Cronise and Ward, p. 197 (Two man bin close togedder, but dey nebber see each odder). Indian, Uraon: Archer, p. 185, No. 98 (The two brothers who sit together but never look at each other), which may contain a reminiscence of the riddles discussed in the headnote to Nos. 1003–1004 of the present collection. See also No. 1016 (sisters).

1004. Spanish, Porto Rican: Mason, 408. Zyrian: Wichmann, *Zyrian*, 102 (Two dolls look at each other.—Ears of a horse). Turkish: Katanov in Radlov, IX, 238, No. 42 (Two brothers do not see each other and do not exchange greetings), p. 242, No. 107 (My granddad lives over the mountain, but I have not seen him), and p. 255, No. 133 (Two sisters do not see each other until death itself). African, Hausa: Tremearne, p. 59, No. 9 (The great twins turned around, but they did not meet); Fletcher, 5; Harris, 26; Trautmann, p. 101 (Who looks to the right, looks to the left, but does not see its sister?). Indonesian, Tabaru: Fortgens, 89.

1005. (The answers in the following parallels are peas, beans, oats, barley, and similar seeds.) German: Haffner, 32. French: Mensignac, *Gironde*, 55 (Four maidens in a convent who see neither rain nor wind.—Nut); Westphalen, *Metz*, col. 199 (Four maidens who are enclosed in a room; they have the key and cannot open the house.—Nut); Parsons, *Antilles*, III, 384, Martinique, 57. Catalan: Pelay y Briz, 138. Spanish, Chilean: Flores, 527 (Five Negroes in one shirt). Lithuanian: Jurgelionis, 972 (Many sisters rock in one cradle.—Peas in a pod). Lettish: Bielenstein, 64 (Two little sisters under one kerchief.—Oats in the panicle). This resembles the riddle for a table; see No. 993 of the present collection. Serbian: Novaković, p. 163, No. 1 (Eight brothers and one pair of drawers.—Peapod). Bulgarian: Gubov, 210 (Two brothers sleeping in one shirt.—Barley). Arabic: Giacobetti, 102 (It is divided into equal parts and covered with solid skin. Praise be to God, who made it, and how do the Arabs call it?—Bean). Filipino: Starr, *Philippines*, 283 (There are three princesses; each has a separate room, and they cannot see each other.—*Tabunboa*, a shrub with a pod divided into three parts). For the notion of persons, each with a separate room, see, in the present collection, the headnote to No. 908, nn. 7–9, 13–14.

See also the Jamaican riddle, "One little bit o' bag hold three.—Castor-oil bean-pod" (No. 1201 in the present collection).

1007a, 1007b. Medieval Irish: Stokes, 10 (What father is born in his daughter's womb?). Flemish: Joos, 543. German: Wolfram von Eschenbach, *Parzival*, p. 659, line 24 (ein muoter ir fruht gebirt: diu fruht sinr muoter muoter wirt); Carstens, *Schleswig-Holstein*, p. 422. Danish: Kristensen, p. 61, §142, No. 202, and p. 141, §416, No. 657. Latin: Ohlert, 2d ed., p. 54, citing "Dic mihi, quid est hoc, est quaedam filia matris et mater filiae et filiae duae?" from Pompeius' commentary on the Latin grammar of Donatus (H. Keil, *Grammatici Latini* [Leipzig, 1868], V, 311). See other references cited by Ohlert; Ohl, Symphosius, p. 134; Pseudo-Bede, *Flores*, in Migne, *Patrologia Latina*, XCIV, col. 544b; Claret, p. 72, No. 88 (Quam genetrix genuit, genetricem nate regignit: unda fit in glaciem, glacies in aquam fit ibidem). This is said to come from Alexander, Claret's unidentified source. Alexander's version is "Quam mater genuit, generavit filia matrem." See further Buchler, *Gnomologia*, 3d ed. (1614), p. 452; Friedreich, p. 205, No. 1, and p. 214, No. 7; J. M. Kemble, *The Dialogue of Salomon and Saturnus* (London, 1848), p. 325; a Greek version composed by Camerarius, in Reusner, ed. 1602, p. 259; and many references collected by Tupper, *Holme Riddles*, 5. Spanish: Demófilo, 712, 713, 715 (snow); Rodríguez Marín, 281 (snow). Argentinian: Lehmann-Nitsche, 439 (snow), 440 (river and snow), 446a. Chilean: Flores, 489 (snow). Italian: Rua, *Archivio*, VII (1888), 455, No. 49; Balladoro, *ibid.*, XVI (1897), 553, No. 14. Lettish: Bielenstein, 327. Russian: Sadovnikov, 1493 (Had you not been born, I would not have died), 1494 (Mother gives birth to me, I to her), 1495 (Clean and clear like a diamond, he is torn from his mother; he himself gives birth to her), 1967 (It saw its mother, it died again.—Snow); Arkhangel'skii, p. 75. Serbian: Novaković, p. 113, Nos. 7 (I give birth to my mother and my mother gives birth to me), 8 (I an neither the father nor the son, yet [once] born, I give birth to my mother). Turkish: Katanov in Radlov, IX, 240, No. 74 (The son rode off and the father stayed.—Overflowing of water and the stones remaining after high water). Yakut: Popov, p. 283 (In the evening my mother bore me, in the morning I bore my mother.—Freezing and melting of snow). Surinam: Herskovits, p. 441, No. 39. Filipino: Starr, *Philippines*, 232 (The mother becomes the daughter and the daughter becomes the mother).

1008. Breton: Sauvé, 13 (My mother is the sea, and she or her sister is always my executioner). French: Rolland, 119 (What is it, then? Everybody wants it at his table, and its mother undoes it?). Spanish, Dominican Rep.: Andrade, 276. Italian: Straparola, XII, 9; Rolland, p. 159, No. 11 (What is it that every person wants at table and that its own mother undoes?); Pitrè, 704. Russian: Sadovnikov, 489 (It is born in the water, yet it fears the water), 490 (It is born from water, and it is good to be put into water, but when it sees its mother, it dies), 490a through 490d. Finnish: Aarne and Krohn, 42 = Henssen, 223 (It is born in water, it grows up in water, and it dies when it sees its mother). Zyrian: Wichmann, *Zyrian*, 212. Modern Greek: Dieterich, *Rätseldichtung*, p. 91, citing Stamatiadis, V, 90 (Water begets me and I feed in the sun, yet if I see my mother, I die); Polites, *Neohellenika Analekta*, I, 214, No. 120 (My mother bore me, I think on the air, and if my mother should strike me, I would melt and die); Stathes, p. 355, No. 138 (The mother bears the child, the sun brings it up, and when the mother turns to look upon her child, it dies). Arabic: Littmann, p. 54 (Son of water and it dies on touching water). Syriac: Furlani, *Azraq*, 32 (It lives when taken out of water, it dies when put into water). Abchaz: Guliia, 1 (Born of water, reared by the sun, it dies on seeing its mother). African, Swahili: Velten, 81 (Tongo is a child of the water. It was born in the water and grew up there. When a man comes to seek it, the child is told, "You may not drink hot or even cold water"). Indian, Bengali: Mitra, *Chittagong*, p. 664, No. 11 (Is produced in the sea and is resident in towns. If its mother touches it [the son], what becomes of the son?). Baiga: Elwin, p. 472, No. 85 (The little yogi comes whence we know not. Put him in anything and he will die. And then we eat him).

1009. Compare the Renaissance proverb "The law groweth of sin and chastiseth it" (Brandl, p. 27, No. 39).

1010. See No. 1197, which is a more intelligible comparison of persons to glasses of water.

1011. See Nos. 830 through 832c and the parallels in the note to Nos. 830 through 830c, in which the actors (peas) are not related to one another.

Some English riddles for castor beans are constructed on the idea of like persons, related (No. 1005) or unrelated (Nos. 922, 935), and the sound is represented as that made by an animal (cock crows, No. 377), but the two ideas of making a noise and of brothers or other similar persons seem not to have been combined in English riddles about castor beans.

1012. German: Wossidlo, 162. The theme of members of a family who are together but do not touch one another is also, in the present collection (No. 1027), used for bars of a grate.

1013. The import of the riddle is not entirely clear: "ribber side" is "river's side," and the reference to "no one could never wash the other" may involve ideas similar to those in the Danish eye riddle, "There are two sisters who wash themselves in the same water and dry themselves with the same cloth and still cannot come together" (Kristensen, p. 200, §11, No. 25d). The first elements in this Danish riddle occur in another context; see the note to Nos. 1104a, 1104b in the present collection. See also such descriptions of the eyes as are given in Nos. 1003 and 1016 and compare the obscure bottle riddle, No. 994.

1014a, 1014b. The sisters are usually four in number, and a difference in them is only rarely indicated. Frisian: Dykstra, *Snypsnaren*, p. 100. Flemish: *Ons Volksleven*, II (1890), 104, No. 12. German: Frischbier, *Menschenwelt*, pp. 254–255, Nos. 144, 145. Danish: Kristensen, p. 147, § 430, No. 680a; DFS, 1906/1: 288, B. K. Pedersen, 1910, p. 25. Swedish: Hyltén-Cavallius, *Värend*, 61; Sandén, *Norra Vadsbo*, 21; Russwurm, *Eibo*, p. 133, § 316, No. 18. Latin: Ohl, Symphosius, 77; J. Pontanus in Friedreich, p. 205, No. 4 (Quattuor aequales current ex arte sorores. Sex quasi certantes, cum sit labor omnibus unus, et propre sunt pariter, nec se contingere possunt). This may have been disseminated by the Apollonius romance; see Flajšhans, pp. 20–21, § 20a. French: Constantin, *Savoie*, p. 22; Lespy, *Béarn*, 21; Westphalen, *Metz*, col. 203. Italian: Ive, *Canti popolari istriani*, p. 23, No. 23. Modern Greek: Polites, *Neohellenika Analekta*, I, 227, No. 191 (I have four sisters, two small, two large; the large ones run after the small ones and never catch them).

Sisters in vain pursuit of one another represent spokes in a spinning wheel, in a Russian riddle cited in § 4 of the headnote to Nos. 1014–1015 of the present collection, and various references to spokes and to similar whirling parts are listed in the note to No. 997.

1015a, 1015b. Breton: Sébillot, *Haute-Bretagne*, 65; Sauvé, 106; Duine, *Saint-Malo*, p. 517; Lavenot, *Basse-Bretagne*, p. 669. Flemish: Joos, 304 (eight versions, one refers to men); *Ons Volksleven*, II (1890), 105, No. 24 (four old women). German: Wossidlo, 156; Carstens, *Schleswig-Holstein*, p. 419 (with parallels); Frischbier, *Menschenwelt*, p. 257, No. 168. Danish: Feilberg, *Ordbog*, II, 651, s.v. "møllevinger." Swedish: Ericsson, *Södermanland*, II (1881), 98, No. 99; Ström, p. 383, "Sysselsättningar," 48. Walloon: Colson, *Wallonia*, V, 93, Nos. 230, 231. French: *Les Adeuineaux amoureux*, p. xci; Rolland, 235, 236; Fertiault, *Bourgogne*, p. 168 (four girls); De la Suie, *Savoie*, p. 472 (four ladies). Catalan: Milá y Fontanals, 1877, p. 6 (answer lacking). Italian: Bernoni, *Venice*, 48 (four sisters); Ferraro, *Canti popolari in dialetto logodurese*, p. 300, No. 9 (four ladies); Pasquarelli, *Archivio*, XV (1896), 76, No. 12 (four girls); Schneller, *Wälschtirol*, p. 256, No. 24. Rumanian: Gorovei, 1578. Russian: Sadovnikov, 577. White Russian: Wasilewski, 10 (four little sisters). Finnish: Aarne and Krohn, 257 = Henssen, 34. Modern Greek: Stathes, p. 339, No. 41 (twelve sisters); Gorovei, note to No. 1578.

1016. Spanish, Chilean: Flores, 493, 520 (Two girls can never kiss). Dominican Rep.: Andrade, 226. Portuguese: Parsons, *Cape Verde*, 209b, 209c, 209f, 209g. Italian: Tammi, 2. Lithuanian: Schleicher, p. 193. White Russian: Wasilewski, 13 (Two sisters live across a boundary; one can't visit the other). Serbian: Novaković, p. 157, No. 1 (The tsar's two sisters sit on a fort, they see everybody but themselves). Bulgarian: Chacharov, 90 (I have two sisters. They are looking at each other, yet they cannot see each other); Stoilov, p. 58, § 11, Nos. 4 through 7, and § 15. Albanian: Hahn, p. 161, No. 47.

As in certain riddles mentioned in the headnote to Nos. 1003–1004 of the present collection (nn. 2–4), the element "and a mountain separates them" may be included; see Portuguese: Parsons, *Cape Verde*, 209a. Lithuanian: Schleicher, p. 193 (Two sisters cannot meet across a little mountain). Bulgarian: Ikonomov, 59 (There is a hill between two sisters. It projects day and night and yet it cannot be seen). Albanian: Hahn, p. 159, No. 8.

1017a through 1017c. Dutch: Van Vloten, p. 169, No. 46. Flemish: Joos, 598; *Ons Volksleven*, I (1889), 38, No. 30. Afrikaans: Groenewald, p. 79. German: Wossidlo, 137;

Weigand, "Volksräthsel," *Zeitschrift für deutsche Mythologie*, II (1854), 434, No. 3; Carstens, *Schleswig-Holstein*, p. 418; Frischbier, *Menschenwelt*, p. 252, Nos. 111, 112; Böckel, *Hesse*, 8. Swiss: Rochholz, 469; Zahler, *Münchenbuchsee*, 170. Danish: Kristensen, pp. 35–36, § 86, Nos. 113a through 113c; DFS 1906/38, J. K. Nielsen, 1935, No. 9, and A. Lorenzen, No. 4 (A humpbacked man, a hollow wife, and three singed children). Faeroic: Hammershaimb, *Antiquarisk tidsskrift*, III (1849–1851), 318, No. 31 = *Zeitschrift für deutsche Mythologie*, III (1855), 130 = *Færøsk anthologi*, I, 323, No. 16. Norwegian: Bugge, *Telemarken*, 78 (Hollow mother, humpbacked father, three headless children every day); Berge, 43; Stafset, 32; Brox, *Ytre Senja*, 34, 149; Bergh, *Valdres*, 39, 69; Qvigstad, note to No. 14. Swedish: Dybeck, *Runa*, 1865–1873, p. 81, No. 97; Ericsson, *Södermanland*, I (1879), 86, No. 33; and V (1884), 65, No. 209 (headless children); Hyltén-Cavallius, *Värend*, 68; Sandén, *Norra Vadsbo*, 56; Waltman, *Lidmål*, 179, 180; Noreen, *Fryksdal*, 3; Christofferson, p. 26, No. 1 = *Folkminnen och folktankar*, II (1915), 82, No. 1; Ström, pp. 146–147, "Grytan," 2; Russwurm, *Eibo*, p. 133, § 316, Nos. 21 (A bigbellied mother, a humpbacked father, and twisting, twisting daughters.—Sausage kettle), 22 (A hollowed-out mother, a crooked father, and a thickheaded son.—Kettle and spoon). Walloon: Colson, *Wallonia*, IV, 149, No. 167. Finnish: Aarne and Krohn, 222 = Henssen, 35. Lappish: Qvigstad, 14, 23; Poestion, p. 270. African, Togo: Schönhärl, 82 (A mother has three children who can never touch one another.—Legs of the pot), 133. SeSuto: Norton and Velaphe, 11 (The mother is hollow, the father crooked, the brethren [are] three.—A pot with a handle and three legs).

1019a through 1020. The answer is usually "chestnut," but I have included a few parallels with other answers. Breton: Sébillot, *Haute-Bretagne*, 31; Kerbeuzec, *Ille-et-Vilaine*, 27; Lavenot, *Basse-Bretagne*, p. 667. German: Wossidlo, 136; Haffner, 29. French: Rolland, 112; Bladé, *Armagnac*, 50; V. S., *Mélusine*, I (1878), col. 255, No. 18; Lacuve, *Poitou*, p. 703, No. 7; Pineau, *Poitou*, 35; Dardy, *L'Albret*, p. 331; Sébillot, *Auvergne*, 20; Dottin, *Bas-Maine*, 5; A. Ferrand, *Dauphiné*, p. 226; J. Roux, *Limousin*, 51; Constantin, *Savoie*, p. 23; De la Suie, *Savoie*, p. 473. Basque: Vinson, 33. Catalan: Milá y Fontanals, 1876, p. 25, No. 14; Pelay y Briz, 38, 253, 309. Spanish: Demófilo, 813 (tall father, short mother, black son, white grandson.—Pine-nut); Rodríguez Marín, 464, 465, 467. Portuguese: Braga, 6, 26. Italian: Gianandrea, *Archivio*, I (1882), 565, No. 34; Menghini, *ibid.*, XIV (1895), 278, No. 10; Tschiedel, 13 (tall father, bewitched mother, splendid daughter), 14 (tall father, thorny mother, black daughter), 65. Indian, Parsee: Munshi, p. 421 (The father is stalwart, the mother is rough-looking, and the babes plump and healthy.—Coconut). Bengali: Mitra, *Chittagong*, p. 311, No. 18 (Mother is tall, children are mad, sons are round in shape.—Areca nut).

1019a. The word for the adjective "sticky" signifies "prickly."

1022a through 1022d. (Members of a family.) Lithuanian: Jurgelionis, 893 (Mother is in the center, the children all around). African, SeSuto: Norton and Velaphe, 6 (The little one sings, the one stays still.—Whispering branches on steady trunks). Gouro and Gagou: Tauxier, *Côte d'Ivoire*, p. 316, No. 10 (The daughters of a certain mother are numerous and the hats which they wear are of the same color). Kxatla: Schapera, 19 (Tell me: the children of someone are dancing; their mother does not dance). Dschagga: Gutmann, p. 538 (The men dance, the chief rests.—Tree and twigs). Pangwe: Tessmann, 41, 66 (My father's wives have nothing but dancing caps.—Sugar-cane tassels). Indian, Ho: Sarkar, pp. 253–254, No. 36 (The mother stands still, her children are little. When [the] wind blows, they dance); Haldar, p. 277, Nos. 19 (The mother stands still while her children, with white turbans, go flying all over the country.—The cotton-tree) and 21 (The mother brings forth offspring to the number of ten or fifteen within five or six months; she holds all in her lap while the young ones themselves cling to each other.—The arum roots), and p. 278, Nos. 22 (It comes of age in three months and brings forth two or three children at the same time and holds them in its lap well covered with folds of cloth.—Indian corn) and 28 (The mother stands still while her children giggle.—A tree called *sekrē-dāru*, the leaves of which seem to smile). Malayalam: Schmolck, p. 242, No. 3 (The mother has many children; they all tremble day and night).

1022c. Tupper queries "her kage," which may mean merely "cage."

1023. This is a fragment of a nursery rhyme and not properly a riddle. A few riddlers have conceived a hen or a goose in similar terms; see the German "A little crone has many tiny children.—Goose and feathers" (Frischbier, *Thierwelt*, p. 356, No. 82); the Armenian "It became a woman, an army followed it.—Setting hen" (Glushakov, p. 24, No. 15).

1024. Portuguese: Braga, 65. Surinam: Herskovits, p. 445, No. 77 (A mother had a hundred thousand children. The mother sent the children to clean the square. The children did not clean the square well. But the moment the mother herself went, the place was clean). This contains the theme of cleaning the courtyard, which is discussed in the headnote to No. 1071 of the present collection. Arabic: Ruoff, p. 13, No. 17 (A large rug with many soldiers, a son of a king wears epaulettes.—Sky, stars, moon). The import of the reference to the epaulettes is obscure. Africa, Bavenda: Stayt, p. 359, No. 1 (A chief presided, and the people surrounded him). This resembles the scene in No. 1026 of the present collection. Kamba: Lindblom, 48 (A district exclusively of youths and the old man is exactly one.—Stars and moon). See also Indian, Gujerati: Mehta, p. 136 (I have many brothers, so many as cannot be counted. They are asleep during the day, but come out for playing at night), which contains the theme discussed in the headnote to No. 1094 of the present collection.

For riddles involving the idea of a brother and sister appearing alternately see the headnote to No. 1001, n. 7. The notion of stars as a countless multitude of persons occurs in many contexts; see, for example, George Meredith's sonnet, "Lucifer." For comparisons of the stars to animals or objects so numerous that they cannot be counted see the headnote to Nos. 1021–1035, n. 2.

1025. African, Kaguru: Busse, p. 62, No. 5 (What glitters?).

1026. African, Tschuana: Kuhn, *Tschuana*, 23 (Youths who stand around the king. —Pegs holding a hide stretched out to dry). For some similar conceptions see, in the present collection, the headnote to No. 841, nn. 12–13, and the headnote to No. 993, n. 6.

1028a, 1028b. African, Kundu: Ittmann, *Kindu*, 86 (The *Heisasachen* has a child.— Thorn of the wild yam). *Heisasachen* is a whimsical term used only in this riddle.

1029a, 1029b. See the headnotes to Nos. 954–957 (actors are not related), 996–1001 (actors are brothers), and 1014–1015 (actors are sisters).

1031a, 1031b. The import of the riddle is obscure, but compare Nos. 994, 1013.

1032a, 1032b. Spanish, Argentinian: Lehmann-Nitsche, 425 (In a dark, hot place many people are dancing.—Toasting corn). Lettish: Bielenstein, 680, 681 (Three hundred men dance on an iron bridge.—Peas in a pot). Polish: Gustawicz, 92 (Many guests rode over a linden bridge.—Beans). The linden bridge is a wooden spoon. See also Gustawicz, 341, and, in the present collection, the headnote to Nos. 489–490, §§ 3–4, and the note to Nos. 1165a through 1165c. Abyssinian: Littmann, *Tigriña*, pp. 625–626, No. 46 (Something that shuts its house and hops up and down.—Soup [boiling] in a closed pot). African, SeSuto: Norton and Velaphe, 25 (The madman dances in the thorns.—Mealies in the pot). The thorns are the firewood. Lesotho: Franz, p. 155 (The wizards are dancing in the cave.—Ears of corn being roasted in a pot). Kxatla: Schapera, 61 (Tell me:

the wizards are quarreling inside the cave.—Melon seeds crackling in a pot). Indian, Kolarian: Wagner, 12 (In a ruinous house are small evil spirits dancing.—Maize flour). The piece of broken pottery on which the flour is being cooked is called a "broken house." For other examples of this see Ho: Haldar, p. 276, No. 2 (The dance of white herons in a ruined homestead). Bengali: Mitra, *Chittagong*, p. 662, No. 10 (A faquir is dancing in a dilapidated hut.—Parched paddy [rice]). As is apparent, these seem to constitute a North Indian variation of the riddle. See further, Uraon: Archer, p. 180, No. 14 (The white storks dance in the pond.—Maize frying). Baiga: Elwin, p. 469, No. 51 (A boy dances and as he dances, ties a turban on his head.—Grain popping). Bengali: Mitra, *Chittagong*, p. 662, Nos. 8 (A black cat is dancing in the midst of a pond. Six scores of dancing boys are dancing to the beating of a drum by an old woman.—Parched paddy), 9 (Bitten by shrimps, she skips and frisks.—Parched paddy).

For a comparison of cooking to an animal dancing or leaping, see No. 385 of the present collection. The cooking of rice or peas is compared to animals drinking a pond or river dry in Nos. 489*b* through 490. For comparisons of plants, bees, bugs, or sparks to persons dancing or working, see Nos. 946*a* through 949*a*, the headnote to Nos. 946-950, and the note to Nos. 946*a* through 946*d*.

1033a through 1033g. The fundamental conceptions, as well as the accessory details, often vary greatly. See "Three Negro women in a pen, one cannot work without the others.—Firestones" (Spanish, Porto Rican: Mason, 453); "Three, three, even at the village chief's" (African, Swahili: Velten, 50); "There are three children. If one goes away, no work is done" (*ibid.*, 56); "Our children are similar to one another" (Sukuma: Augustiny, 5); "Nyakahindi is the fourth" (*ibid.*, 24); "I have three warriors. What is a discussion between two of them like, if the third is not present?" (Masai: Hollis, *Masai*, p. 254, No. 4); "They stood in threatening attitude" (Suk: Beech, p. 44, No. 9); "One man get t'ree slave: ef one gone, two no able fo' work" (Sierra Leone: Cronise and Ward, p. 196). See also Kosi, Ittmann, *Kosi*, 152, 226, 244. It is tempting to derive the Porto Rican Spanish version from an African source.

A few Far Eastern versions represent a slightly different conception. See "Three old folks warm themselves constantly" (Indonesian, Alfoer: Niemann, p. 14, No. 6); "Three old folks who do not desert one another; they are besmeared with ashes" (*ibid.*, No. 7), which recalls the ceremonial use of ashes in Eastern ritual; "Three ghosts endure much heat" (Filipino: Starr, *Philippines*, 346); "Three brothers suffer heat" (*ibid.*, 347).

A few African riddles conceive the stones in terms of animals. See "In one house there are three lions" (Swahili: Velten, 43); "I moved my abode and left three goats behind. When I returned, there were still three goats" (Nandi: Hollis, *Nandi*, p. 143, No. 43).

1034. Compare African, Nyika: Hollis, *Nyika*, p. 142, No. 21 (If one of my sons stands up, rice is not eaten). Kundu: Ittmann, *Kundu*, 93 (My mother has given birth to us there. If one is absent, the other two of us can do no work).

1035. The import of the riddle is not clear.

CHAPTER VI
COMPARISONS TO PLANTS
Nos. 1036–1099

1036a through 1036d. French: Baissac, *Mauritius*, p. 409 (I have a tree; when it has leaves, it has no roots; when it has roots, it has no leaves); Parsons, *Antilles*, III, 368, Trinidad, 63, p. 385, Martinique, 82, p. 390, Dominica, 4, p. 411, Les Saintes, 49, and p. 414, Marie Galante, 31. Indonesian, Tounsea: De C., p. 243, No. 36 (A piece of wood that has a form different from that of other wood; when the root puts forth shoots, it has no leaves, and when it has leaves, it lacks a root). Sangir: Adriani, p. 439, No. 329 (It has leaves but no roots). Tabaru: Fortgens, p. 541, No. 106 (When the root dies the leaf lives; when the leaf dies, the root lives).

1036d. The riddler has not understood the import of the comparison and has confused it.

1037a, 1037b. (Nests mentioned.) Welsh: Hull and Taylor, 138. Scotch Gaelic: Nicolson, p. 13. Frisian: Dykstra, *Snypsnaren*, p. 103. Dutch: Schrijnen, II, 104, No. 17. Flemish: Joos, 545. German: Wossidlo, 35; Frischbier, *Menschenwelt*, p. 257, No. 170; H. Meier, *Ostfriesland*, 15; Carstens, *Schleswig-Holstein*, p. 421; Butsch, 255; Böckel, *Hesse*, 18; Hanika-Otto, 276. Swiss: Rochholz, 419. Icelandic: Árnason, 141 (I know a tree on a high mountain. It has thirteen branches. On each branch there are four nests. In each nest there are six birds and a seventh one with golden feathers), 546 (What grove grows with twelve blossoms, with four nests in each blossom, and seven birds in each nest, each of which has its own name, although they are all called the same?), 590 (What oak has a hundred branches, with twelve twigs on each branch, four nests on each twig, and seven young on each nest, each of which has its own name?—A century), 741, 745. Danish: Kristensen, pp. 157–158, § 462, Nos. 735, 736, and p. 276, No. 116; DFS, 1906/38: M. Jespersen, 1919, No. 4 (What sort of tree is it that has twelve branches, on each branch four twigs, on each twig seven nests, in each nest are two eggs, one black and one white?). Norwegian: Christie, 96, 97 = Stafset, 131 (There stands a tree in Austerland with fifty-two branches and an apple on each branch and three golden ones in the middle); Stafset, 123 (There stands a tree on Reine with twelve golden branches, four nests on each branch, seven eggs in each nest, the seventh egg is golden). Faeroic: Hammershaimb, *Antiquarisk tidsskrift*, III (1849–1851), 316, No. 6 = *Zeitschrift für deutsche Mythologie*, III (1855), 29 = *Færøsk anthologi*, I, 325, No. 47 (I know a tree, the highest on the mountain, with thirteen branches, four nests on each branch, six birds in each nest, the seventh has golden feathers). Swedish: Ericsson, *Södermanland*, II (1881), 97, No. 96; Dybeck, *Runa*, 1848, p. 43, No. 31 = Russwurm, 31; Sandén, *Norra Vadsbo*, 117; Geijer and Campbell, 91; Ström, p. 225, "Tiden," 4. Latin: Reusner, ed. 1599, p. 98, and ed. 1602, p. 374 (by an unnamed author); Huldreich Therander (Johann Sommer), 411. Walloon: Colson, *Wallonia*, IV, 42, Nos. 1, 2. Catalan: Pelay y Briz, 203. Spanish: Demófilo, 70, 73; Rodríguez Marín, 261 through 263; Alcázar, 443. Argentinian: Lehmann-Nitsche, 569a through 569f. Chilean: Flores, 56. Cuban: Massip, 20. Dominican Rep.: Andrade, 34. Guatemalan: Recinos, 5. Porto Rican: Mason, 55. Portuguese: Pires de Lima, 9; Pires, *Archivio*, III (1884), 113, No. 2; Parsons, *Cape Verde*, 246. Italian: Gianandrea, *Archivio*, II (1883), 431, No. 58; Salvioni, *ibid.*, IV (1885), 548, No. 69; Rondini, *ibid.*, VII (1888), 540, No. 27; Bernoni, *Venice*, p. 2. Rumanian: Gorovei, 60 through 70; and Gorovei, *Devinettes*, p. 505. Lithuanian: Jurgelionis, 139 (There stands a tree with twelve branches, on each branch are four nests, in each nest are six children, and the seventh is the mother); Schleicher, p. 201. Lettish: Bielenstein, 191 (An oak has twelve branches, each branch four nests, each nest six eggs), 192 (A luxuriant oak has twelve branches, each branch four nests, each nest seven birds, each bird its particular name but always the same one), 193 (On an open field there stands a luxuriant tree, this tree has twelve branches, each branch four nests, each nest seven eggs), 194 (A great thick oak with twelve branches, on each branch four nests, in each nest seven eggs). Czech: Hanika-Otto, note to No. 276. Polish: Saloni, *Rzeszów*, 150 (The oak stands in the whole world. On that oak are twelve branches, on them four nests apiece, and in these nests are seven birds apiece), 151 (One oak, on that oak are twelve branches, on each branch, four nests, in each nest seven eggs); Gustawicz, 347 (There is a single tree, on this single tree there are twelve limbs, on each limb there are thirty branches, on each branch there are four nests, and in each nest there are seven birds). Russian: Arkhangel'skii, p. 75 (A beam lies across all Russia; in it are twelve little nests, in each nest are four eggs). Serbian: Novaković, p. 31, No. 3 (quoted in the headnote to Nos. 1037–1038, § 3, n. 46, of the present collection), and p. 32, No. 11 (There is a big oak, on it there are twelve poles, on each pole there are four chickens). Finnish: Lönnrot, 1744 = Henssen, 97 (An oak under the winter sky, twelve branches on the oak, four nests on each branch, seven eggs in each nest). Estonian: Lönnrot, p. 196; Wiedemann, pp. 291–292.

Hungarian: the seven versions here cited are taken from Szendrey's additions to Aarne's discussion of the riddle; see the headnote to Nos. 1037–1938, n. 7, of the present collection. The numbers in square brackets are those assigned by Szendrey. [1] *Magyar Nyelvészet*, III, 323 (Under the round sky, there is a round God's tree; the round God's tree has twelve beautiful branches, the twelve beautiful branches have fifty-two flowers, there are three golden apples among the fifty-two flowers); [2] *Magyar Nyelvör*, VII (1878), 234 (It is a round God's tree [*istenfa*], it has twelve beautiful branches, there are fifty-two flowers on its twelve beautiful branches, there are three golden apples among its fifty-two flowers. He who guesses it will get a pint of wine); [3] oral, from Szalonta (identical with the first Hungarian version); [4] *Magyar Nyelvör*, XLIII (1914), 218 (An old oak tree has twelve big branches, six golden apples have fifty-two flowers); [5] *ibid.*, XVI (1887), 87 (There is in this world a pear tree, which has twelve branches, three hundred and sixty-six leaves, and three big apples. What is it?); [6] *ibid.*, XX (1891), 575 (There is in the world a pear tree, it has twelve branches, three hundred and sixty-five leaves, three big apples); [7] *Ethnographia*, XI, 401 (A huge oak has twelve branches, on every branch there are four nests, in every nest there are seven eggs, in every egg there are twenty-four young birds, each of which dies after taking sixty steps).

Modern Greek: Dieterich, *Rätseldichtung*, p. 90, citing Polites, *Neohellenika Analekta*, I, 237, No. 254 (A head of lettuce with fifty leaves and seven hearts, and in the seven hearts there is a red rose), which describes the fifty fast days before Easter, the seven Sundays of this period, and the Easter festival); Polites, *Neohellenika Analekta*, I, 237, No. 253 (A forty-leaved head of lettuce, it has forty leaves, and within its heart it has another head of lettuce.—Lent); Carnoy and Nicolaides, p. 295 (I am a lettuce of fifty leaves and bear a carnation in my top). Turkish: Kowalski, *North Bulgaria*, 36 (On a walnut tree two branches, on two branches twelve nests, in the twelve nests forty-eight eggs, on the forty-eight eggs three hundred and sixty-six crows). Kowalski cites Hamizade, 38, 220. Berber: J. Rivière, *Recueil de contes populaires de la Kabylie du Djurdjura* (Paris, 1882), p. 159 (an episode in a tale). Yakut: Piekarski, 9 (They say that a huge tree stands in a field: an oak with twelve branches, on each branch there are four nests, in each nest there are seven eggs).

1038a, 1038b. (Nests, eggs, apples, and the like are not mentioned.) German: Frischbier, *Menschenwelt*, p. 257, Nos. 171, 172. Norwegian: Landstad, p. 812, No. 40 (What sort of tree has white leaves on one side and black on the other?). French: Parsons, *Antilles*, III, 368, Trinidad, 56. Spanish, Argentinian: Lehmann-Nitsche, 478a (What is the tree of which one part is white and the other black?), 478b (A tall tree with leaves white on one side and black on the other), 570 (In the square I have a pine tree, on the pine tree twelve branches, on each branch four twigs, and on each twig seven leaves, [a defective version of Nos. 1037a, 1037b of the present collection]), and 571 (I was walking on a little road, I met a little tree, each little branch [had] its name). Italian: Schneller, *Wälschtirol*, pp. 132–137, especially p. 133 (an incident in a tale). Rumanian: Weigand, p. 273, No. 23 (A tall tree with many leaves, [each is] half black and half white), and p. 275, No. 32. Lithuanian: Jurgelionis, 141 = Schleicher, p. 201 (My father has a flat field, in that field is an oak, on that oak are twelve limbs, and on each limb are four branches). Russian: Preobrazhenskii, p. 171 (A tree stands, from one side its leaves are white, from the other black). Serbian: Nováković, p. 31, Nos. 4 (There are twelve branches on one tree, from each branch there issue four twigs), 5 (I cut down a pole, dry inside; from it there grew twelve branches; from each branch there grew four twigs). Modern Greek: Dieterich, *Rätseldichtung*, p. 89; Polites, *Neohellenika Analekta*, I, 249, No. 317 (A tree: half of its leaves are white, half black). See further, Sart: Ostrumov, 19, as cited by Jungbauer, p. 353 (There are twelve branches on a tree; there are three hundred and sixty leaves). Arabic: Giacobetti, 53 (Four branches on a tree; one is sweet, one is bitter, one is green, one is dry), which has some analogies to the description of the seasons as four brothers, cited in the headnote to No. 984 of the present collection; Ruoff, p. 11, No. 2 (A tree has twelve branches, each branch bears thirty leaves, and each leaf has a white and a black side). Aramaic: M. Lidzbarski, *Geschichten und Lieder aus der neu-aramäischen Handschriften der königlichen Bibliothek zu Berlin* (Beiträge zur Volk- und Völkerkunde, IV [Weimar, 1896]), p. 273 (in a series of Biblical riddles). Abyssinian: Littmann, *Tigriña*, p. 632, No. 81 (Something that has a root, twelve branches with thirty fruits each). Turkish: Kúnos, 46 (I have a tree; my tree has twelve limbs; each limb has thirty leaves, black on one side and white on the other). Yakut: Piekarski, 8 (They say that there is a certain fir tree which has twelve branches, fifty-two knots, three hundred and sixty-five pine-cones), 15 (They say that a certain fir has twelve branches); Priklonskii, 76 (One fir with twelve branches). Turkish: Hamizade, 38 (Twelve-branched, thirty-leaved, seven-fruited tree); Maenchen, 5 (A golden poplar has twelve branches and sixty leaves) = Katanov in Radlov, IX, 180, No. 1405. Georgian: Blechsteiner, p. 12, No. 8 (Twelve branches hanging on a plantain tree. There fell and fell a leaf and yet it bore as many as ever). Persian: Friedreich, pp. 103–105, quoting various passages in the *Shah Nameh*. See also Jules Mohl (trans.), Abou'l Kasim Firdousi, *Le Livre des rois* (Paris, 1876), I, 261; A. G. Warner and E. Warner (trans.), *The Shâhnáma of Firdausi* (London, 1905), I, 308. Indian: Lakshīnātha Upasānī, X, 3 (A bushy tree bears twelve fruits. When they are ripe, they become one). Hindi: Kavyopadhyaya, 26 (A tree of dense leaves with twelve branches. Each with a bunch of thirty [fruits] and each with a different name). Khāṛiā: Roy and Roy, II, 452, No. 29 (Twelve branches have only seven leaves). Indonesian, Javanese: Ranneft, *Proza*, p. 13, No. 64 (A tree with twelve branches and each of its branches has twenty-nine or thirty leaves); Ranneft, *Poëzie*, p. 45, No. 2 (A large strange trée is named. A tree with eight names that one uses in turn. Of its branches it is said that they do not number more than twelve, some with thirty and some with twenty-nine leaves. The fruits on the branches are [in groups], each of seven. The flowers and fruits are in part white, in part black); Kreemer, *Java*, p. 134 (There was once a tree that had seven branches, five leaves, thirty flowers, and twelve fruits.—Year, week, *pasar* week, days, and months) and p. 3 (There are four branches, five directions [*richtingen*], seven leaves, thirty little buds, countless flowers, the fruits are a prince and a princess). These last two riddles offer difficulties which I cannot completely resolve. The word *pasar* (derived from "bazar"?) signifies "market," which may explain why the *pasar* week is compared to five leaves. The five *richtingen* are obscure, and "directions" seems to be the only possible translation. There is probably some connection with *Rigveda*, I, 162, §§ 11-12: "The wheel of the course of nature, the twelve-spoked one, turns in the heavens, yet without being worn out; on it stand—Oh, Agni!—children in pairs, seven hundred and twenty in number. They say, the five-footed, twelve-formed father is wet in the upper half, but others say, that he in the lower half who sees through everything is set in a wagon with seven wheels [each] having six spokes." Martin Haug, who comments on this passage (pp. 21-22), interprets the wheel as the year, the children as the days, the father in the upper half as probably Varuṇa, the lord of the waters, his twelve forms as the twelve months, his five feet as the five seasons, for the Brahmans often reckon the seasons *hemanta* and *śiśira* together and thus reduce the six seasons to five. The one in the lower half of the universe who sees through everything is the sun; the seven wheels are its seven rays; and the six spokes are the six regions of the world. Haug continues with § 13, "On that revolving five-spoked wheel all creatures [in the world] are standing; its heavily laden axle does not become hot and it does not break at its hub." Here he interprets the five spokes as the five chief divisions of time (*ahorātra, paksha, māsa, ṛitu,* and *ayana*) or, less probably, as the cycle of five years called *pañchasā vatsara*. We need not delve more deeply into the intricacies of Indian methods of reckoning time; it is evident that the Javanese riddler is using some such reference to the number five. Malay: Klinkert, p. 47, No. 1 (A tree with twelve branches and thirty leaves, of which fifteen are black and fifteen white, strewn with open flowers of yellowish white), in which the stars are "flowers." For the comparison of Lent or Holy Week to a tree, see the headnote to No. 983 of the present collection.

1039. French: V. S., *Mélusine*, I (1878), col. 264, No. 94 (In a wood there is a pine, on this pine there is a nest, in this nest there is an egg, in this egg there is a bull. When the bull bellows, all the world moves). The pine is the bell-tower, the nest the belfry, the egg the clapper, and the bull the bell. See also Dardy, *L'Albret*, p. 331. Spanish, Cuban: Massip, 40 (road, pine tree, nest, egg, hair; the riddler concludes: "I pulled on the hair and it screamed"), 41 (woods, tree, nest, egg, hair). Argentinian: Lehmann-Nitsche, 567. Chilean: Laval, p. 182, No. 55. Porto Rican: Mason, 132. See also the headnote to No. 1326, n. 4, in the present collection.

1040, 1041. Danish: Kristensen, pp. 23-24, § 58, No. 71. Norwegian: Bugge, *Telemarken*, 38. Spanish, Dominican Rep.: Andrade, 135. Porto Rican: Mason, 202. Italian: Pitrè, 443. Indonesian, Atjeh: Kreemer, *Atjeh*, 72 (A tree with five tops; the roots unite in one trunk). Filipino: Starr, *Philippines*, 52 (Five coconut palms, one is higher).

For a comparison in human terms see "Five men have one waist" (Turkish: Katanov in Radlov, IX, 368, No. 327).

1042, 1043. For riddles comparing hair to grass or trees without mentioning a body of water see Walloon: Colson, *Wallonia*, IV, 107, No. 109. French: Baissac, *Mauritius*, p. 403 (Some ebony wood on a rampart.—Moustache). Spanish: Demófilo, 178, 179, 790. Argentinian: Lehmann-Nitsche, 474. Chilean: Flores, 583 through 587. Italian: Pitrè, 72, 613. Lithuanian: Jurgelionis, 159 (A thick thicket, and yet not a thicket). Finnish: Lönnrot, 560 = Henssen, 55 (Gold is the golden object, silver is the silver object, which one bears on the edge of a black forest.—Ear-rings). Turkish: Kúnos, 223 (There are eight olive trees growing thickly and closely in Veli effendi's uncultivated grass patch.

—Beard). Ossette: Schiefner, 22 (Beam ends overgrown by grass). Abyssinian: Littmann, *Tigriña*, p. 631, No. 78 (Something that sprouts in the sun and is mowed off in water). African, Nandi: Hollis, *Nandi*, p. 45, No. 51 (A hut has been made and the thorn enclosure is in the process of construction). Nuer: Huffman, 10 (Guess what forest it is which one may cut down but it is never finished). Yatenga: Tauxier, 2 (I have a thing always dry that bears verdure and something always wet that has none.— Skull and tongue [for the second theme see the headnote to No. 1150 of the present collection]). Wanamwezi: Dahl, 2 (The sesame that one has planted does not grow; that which one left in the gourd grows). Malagasy: Sibree, p. 38, No. 2 (Cut down and yet not withering). Indian, Uraon: Archer, p. 180, No. 13 (There is only grass on the top of the mountain).

Riddles describing the hair of the head as grass or trees, and quoted or otherwise cited in the present collection, are listed in the following classification:

For comparisons to grass, without reference to animals representing lice, see No. 1100 and some examples in the corresponding note, the headnote to Nos. 1042–1044, the headnote to Nos. 1100–1108, nn. 10, 25, and (sheep's head) 23, and the headnote to No. 1116, nn. 7–9.

For comparisons of lice to creatures hunted or driven through the fields or grass, see No. 459, the note to No. 459, and the headnote to Nos. 459–460.

Sometimes, the creatures are merely said to be grazing or roaming through the fields; see No. 488 and the corresponding note, the headnote to Nos. 459–460, n. 32, the headnote to No. 488, nn. 1 and 4, the headnote to Nos. 1100–1108, nn. 14, 24, the headnote to No. 1100, n. 1, and the note to No. 1100.

For riddles containing comparisons of the hair to trees or wood, but not including any references to creatures representing lice, see No. 1043 (wood that cannot be split), Nos. 1116a and 1116b (countless wands), the headnote to Nos. 1042–1044, the headnote to Nos. 1100–1108, nn. 5, 26, the headnote to No. 1116, the examples in the present note, and the note to No. 1043.

For the frequent comparisons of lice in the hair to creatures hunted or driven through the woods, see the headnote to Nos. 459–460, the notes to Nos. 459 and 460a, the headnote to Nos. 970–975, nn. 9, 22, and 30, and the note to No. 1100.

Less frequently, birds or beasts are said to be feeding or roaming in the woods but are not said to be chased or hunted; see the headnote to Nos. 459–460, the headnote to No. 488, nn. 5–6, and the notes to Nos. 459 and 488.

1042. The import of the riddle is obscure. Compare the Chinyanja hair riddle, "A tree which you cut down today, and the next it begins to sprout" (Rattray, p. 155).

1043. The notion that hair cannot be split is very old. In the fifth century A.D. Symphosius wrote: "None can split me, though many cut me; but I am of changeable hue, at some time hence I shall be white. I prefer to stay black, the less I shall fear my fate" (Ohl, 58). Modern instances are the Argentinian Spanish "On a thickly wooded mountain I cut a stick. I could shorten it, but not split it" (Lehmann-Nitsche, 474a); the Kundu "What reed of the old man cannot be split?" and "The reed [*Arundo indica*] of the old people cannot be split" (Ittmann, *Kundu*, 223, 224); and the Kolarian "Can you split the king's or the queen's thin bamboo?" (Wagner, 88).

For the comparison of hair to wands or sticks, and the variation in which the sticks are said not to have branches or knots, see the headnote to No. 1116, and particularly nn. 21–22, in this collection.

1044. (Comparisons to pools surrounded by grass or trees.) Modern Greek: Polites, *Neohellenika Analekta*, I, 213, No. 118 (A trellis of forty hairs and a damp garden). Turkish: Kowalski, *Zagadki*, 85 (A very wet garden of which the guardian is hairy);

Katanov in Radlov, IX, 258, No. 144 (Around the lake are many trees). Surinam: Herskovits, p. 445, No. 69 (My mother has a well with weeds around it. Yet none falls inside). Abyssinian: Littmann, *Tigriña*, 77 (At the edge of an abyss a few twigs). African, SeSuto: Norton and Velaphe, 37 (The pools amid the watergrass). Ila: Smith and Dale, II, 325, No. 2 (When the brook dried up, the grass [on the bank] was left.—When the eye goes blind, the eyebrows and eyelashes remain). Indian: Lakshīnātha Upasānī, IX, 2 (What are those two gardens surrounded by hedges and watched carefully by two ladies who are of the same size and equal in every respect?). Kashmiri: Knowles, 34 (A little hedge around the lake). Bengali: Mitra, *Sylhet*, p. 112, No. 11 (On this bank a reed, and on the other bank [another] reed. There is a quarrel between the reeds); Mitra, *Chittagong*, p. 665, No. 13 ([A pond] on one bank of which there is a bush and on the other there is also another bush. The two bushes strike each other.—The two eyes). Indonesian, Serawaj: Helfrich, *Serawaj*, 3 (A little water surrounded by stakes, which one finds in the *idjock*. It is surrounded with stiff hair). An *idjock* is the part of the aren palm between the trunk and the leaf. Javanese: Ranneft, *Proza*, p. 14, No. 65 (A shallow puddle surrounded by a hedge). See also, in the present collection, the French riddle quoted in the note to No. 1176.

Riddlers occasionally enlarge upon this idea by referring to foreign matter falling into the well; see No. 1176. In the Yakut "They say that between two little lakes there lies an upturned larch" (Piekarski, 173), the tree signifies the nose and belongs to the category of plants growing upside down (see the headnote to Nos. 1055–1057, and particularly § 4, in the present collection), and this we can contrast with another Yakut riddle, "Between two lakes there stands a hill" (Priklonskii, 108), which makes no mention of vegetation. For more extensive comparisons of the head to a scene in nature see the headnote to Nos. 1100–1108 and the note to No. 1100 in the present collection.

For a collection of riddles describing the eyelashes as twigs, rods, or poles held or thrown across a body of water, or as birds beside a lake or stream, see the headnote to Nos. 1003–1004 in the present collection.

A Bulgarian riddle uses the comparisons to water and hedges to represent the eyes and eyebrows; see Gubov, 67 (A hill; above the hill a hole; above the hole, two openings; above the openings, two wells; above the two wells, two hedges; above the two hedges, a wide field; above the field, a thick forest; in the forest, a dumb cow). Similarly, in the Irish riddle quoted in the headnote to Nos. 1100–1108 in the present collection (see n. 28) the brows are compared to two bundles of rushes above two pools. For descriptions of the brows as growing plants in riddles not simultaneously describing the eyes as bodies of water, see the comparison to gardens, in the headnote to No. 1100, n. 3, and the comparison to a bush, in a Ho riddle cited from Sarkar (p. 351, No. 4) in the note to No. 1100. For comparisons of the brows to animals and such inanimate objects as swords, see the collection of references in the headnote to Nos. 1042–1044, n. 26.

Comparisons of the eyes to bodies of water, without comparisons of the eyelashes or eyebrows to vegetation, are collected in the note to No. 1176.

1045. African, Pangwe: Tessmann, 18 (A tree on the place behind the house, they eat up its fruits.—Girl gossiping with lovers). Bakongo: Denis, 17 (A good edible mushroom on a tomb.—Brothers and sisters [in the clan]. A mushroom on a grave is not eaten, and brothers and sisters do not marry), 18 (The caterpillars are back of my house, strangers take them).

1047. The comparison of a candle to a tree is rare; see the Turkish "A solitary tree stands and blazes" (Katanov in Radlov, IX, 241, No. 93).

The most common English riddle for a candle is a comparison to a human being called Little Nancy Etticoat or some similar name; see Nos. 607 through 616 and 619 through 626*b* of the present collection.

1048. This is probably a disordered version of No. 433, which compares a tall grass-stalk to a horse. An obscure Duala riddle may be related: "The oil palm from the Mpo a Murgonjo must not be cut down by anyone except itself.—No one can climb the reed except the dwarf titmouse" (Bufe, p. 59, No. 18). The collector adds the explanatory remark that the oil palm is often cut down to make palm wine.

1049. The import of the riddle is obscure. Compare the parallel in No. 1709 of the present collection and the Gouro "One can climb all the trees but one.—Reed" (Tauxier, *Côte d'Ivoire*, p. 315, No. 3). For the notion that smoke cannot be climbed, see Nos. 1616a through 1617g in the present collection. Compare the preceding riddle, No. 1048.

1050. The disordered text is only partially intelligible. Similar riddles with the answers "hunger" or "war" make comparisons to several men (No. 969 and the corresponding note) and to a building (No. 1154), but they, too, are not readily understood. I note some curious African parallels; see the Lamba "What breaks up a village?—Hunger, when it scatters people" (Doke, 76), the Sukuma "I climb a high cliff. I make Kangabu weep.—Thirst" (Augustiny, 21), and the Slave Coast "Little switch that chases mother and daughter from their field.—Hunger" (Trautmann, p. 102).

1051. The question usually refers to Adam, but this name appears to have no particular significance. For examples see Flemish: Joos, 809. Danish: Kristensen, p. 227, § 16, Nos. 9a through 9c.

1052. Welsh: Hull and Taylor, 119 (potato). Flemish: Joos, 441 (I have a father, no mother, many brothers, many sisters, but my father lay long in the grave before he gave me life.—Potato). Russian: Sadovnikov, 1308 (I shall throw but a tiny bit of it; it will grow a whole lot.—Hemp). Arabic: Bauer, p. 224, No. 16 (Black sheep, whose herdsman is a staff. As often as it is broken, it increases.—Bamboo writing pen). Yakut: Piekarski, 375 (Man came of men; then he grew old, eight of the bones fell apart, and he died; one skin was left behind. Through this skin he came to life and became man.—Kernel of grain).

In Nos. 95 and 661 of the present collection the riddler employs a somewhat inapt comparison.

1053. The enigmatic quality of the riddle is somewhat obscure. I have taken "support" to mean "maintain, nourish," but am not sure that this is correct. For descriptions of a grain of sand as small and yet able to support a church, see the headnote to No. 728, n. 5.

1055a, 1055b. Flemish: Joos, 36; *Ons Volksleven*, I (1889), 37–38, No. 28 (Bright and clear, bright and dry, and it grows with its root up). German: Wossidlo, 339b. Swiss: Rochholz, 420. Danish: Kristensen, p. 61, § 142, No. 203; DFS, 1906/38: J. K. Nielsen, Grindsted, 1935, p. 4, No. 27 (Dæ haar æ Ru'd opad, u æ Taap ni'rad. It has a root above and a top below). Old Norse: *Heidreks gátur*; see A. Heusler, "Die altnordischen Rätsel," *Zeitschrift des Vereins für Volkskunde*, XI (1901), 130–131; Faeroic: *Zeitschrift für deutsche Mythologie*, III (1855), 127. Norwegian: Stafset, 76; Christie, 2; Brox, *Ytre Senja*, 31b; Bergh, *Valdres*, 56; Qvigstad, note to No. 71. Swedish: Dybeck, *Runa*, 1848, p. 46, No. 55 = Russwurm, 23 (In one night there grew a winter tree, root above and top below); Dybeck, *Runa*, 1849, p. 48, No. 12; Ericsson, *Södermanland*, III (1882), 104, No. 168; Hyltén-Cavallius, *Värend*, 32; Waltman, *Lidmål*, 187; Christofferson, p. 36, No. 22 = *Folkminnen och folktankar*, II (1915), 89, No. 22; Geijer and Campbell, 84; Ström, p. 177, "Takåsen," and p. 221, "Isen," 3; Olsson, *Västergötland*, p. 135, No. 131. Lithuanian: Schleicher, p. 196. Finnish: Aarne and Krohn, 32 = Henssen, 142. Lappish: Qvigstad, 71. Mordvin: Paasonen, 113, 161. Gypsy: Wlislocki, 1.

1055b. The riddler may be conceiving the icicle as a man. For parallels see a candle riddle, No. 681, and the corresponding note.

1056. (The riddles cited in this note are only those which have the answer "cow's tail.") Scotch Gaelic: Nicolson, p. 39. Norwegian: Brox, *Ytre Senja*, 131. Lappish: Qvigstad, 28; Poestion, p. 267; Donner, 8. Estonian: Wiedemann, p. 290. Zyrian: Wichmann, *Zyrian*, 25. Modern Greek: Stathes, p. 344, No. 77 (Roots on top, tassels below). Yakut: Popov, p. 285 (A Verkhoyansk fir grows upside down); Priklonskii, 125; Piekarski, 78 (A fir near the Olonetz River reaches into the air, while a fir near the Tatta River has grown downward, so they say.—Horn and tail of a cow), 79 (They say there is a fir that grows downward). Abyssinian: Littmann, *Tigriña*, 11 (Its root above and its tuft below). Hawaiian: Judd, 80.

Here two utterly different and unrelated objects are said to possess the same characteristic peculiarity. Riddles constructed in this way resemble conundrums rather than the texts in this collection.

1057. The comparison of an icicle to a plant that "grows in winter" is rather well known; see German: Böckel, *Hesse*, 59. Danish: Feilberg, *Ordbog*, II, 31, s.v. "is-tap." Norwegian: Aasen, 3; Berge, 2; Christie, 2; Landstad, p. 809, No. 22; Brox, *Ytre Senja*, 31. Swedish: Dybeck, *Runa*, 1848, p. 46, No. 55; Waltman, *Lidmål*, 188). A comparison to something that "sees sun and moon, but never the summer" (Swedish: Hyltén-Cavallius, *Värend*, 32; Sandén, *Norra Vadsbo*, 5) is more rarely used.

1058. The riddler or the collector—whichever has added the explanatory note to the answer—has failed to perceive the nature of the riddle. The riddle aims to suggest a plant that grows in the wood, an animal that whinnies on the moor, and a person or an animal that goes up and down the floor. The plant represents the wood of the brush, the animal represents its hairs, and the person going up and down the floor represents the whole brush.

For parallels see Flemish: Joos, 191, 193. Latin: Reusner, ed. 1599, p. 229 = Johannes Lauterbach, *Ænigmata* ([Frankfurt a. M.], 1601), p. 36, No. 88. French: Parsons, *Antilles*, III, 387, Martinique, 101. Catalan: Pelay y Briz, 164. Spanish: Demófilo, 397, 399. Argentinian: Lehman-Nitsche, 148, 149. New Mexican: Campa, 152. Rumanian: Gorovei, 1127. Czech: Hanika-Otto, note to her Nos. 55 through 58.

1059a, 1059b. (The answer is a stringed instrument, and unless otherwise indicated, it is a violin.) Welsh Gypsy: Sampson, p. 246. Breton: Sébillot, *Haute-Bretagne*, 43. Dutch: Boekenoogen, p. 48. German: Wossidlo, 441; Frischbier, *Menschenwelt*, p. 263, Nos. 217, 218; Ehlers, 10; Gilhoff, 689; Hanika-Otto, 55, 519. See a version in seventeenth-century verse in R. Köhler, *Kleinere Schriften*, III, 529–530; Köhler cites a number of parallels. Swiss: Rochholz, 602. Danish: Kristensen, pp. 24–25, § 63, Nos. 78a through 78c. Norwegian: Bugge, *Telemarken*, 52, 53; Berge, 74. Swedish: Dybeck, *Runa*, 1847, p. 41, No. 9; and 1865–1873, p. 30, No. 19; Russwurm, 29 = Dybeck, *Runa*, 1850, p. 37, No. 32; Ericsson, *Södermanland*, I (1879), 84–85, No. 23; Geijer and Campbell, 29; Hyltén-Cavallius, *Värend*, 7; Ström, p. 280, "Sysselsättningar," 42. Latin: M[one], *Anzeiger*, VIII (1839), col. 316, No. 79; Reusner, ed. 1599, p. 182 = ed. 1602, p. 380. Walloon: Colson, *Wallonia*, IV, 152, No. 190; and V, 95, Nos. 233, 243. French: Rolland, 201; *Recueil des énigmes de ce temps* (Paris, 1661), III, 17. Catalan: Pelay y Briz, 71 (Born in the wood, grown in the wood, it sings at the house), 329. Portuguese: Pires de Lima, 64, 81. Spanish, Argentinian: Lehman-Nitsche, 43a, 43b (guitar). New Mexican: Campa, 159. Italian: Pitrè, 132a (guitar), 906. In the sixteenth century, this riddle was often inscribed on Bolognese violins; see W. W. Skeat and others, *Notes and Queries*, 6th ser., VIII (1883), 212. The Sienese version is contaminated with the contrast of the living and the dead (for which see the headnote to Nos. 828–836 in the present collection); see Corsi, *Archivio*, X (1891), 403, No. 58 (Born in the wood, fed in the meadow, resounds in the city, the living bears the dead, and the dead resounds). Rumanian: Gorovei, 783 (flute); and Gorovei, *Devi-*

nettes, p. 506. Lithuanian: Schleicher, p. 200; Jurgelionis, 713 (Hewn in a forest, bought in a store, having come home it cries dolefully), 714 (. . . store, it cries on the hands), 715 through 718; A. Schleicher, *Briefe über die Erfolge einer . . . Reise nach Litauen*, p. 7 = R. Köhler, *Kleinere Schriften*, III, 530, No. 28 (Born in the forest, made in the city, weeps on one's hand). Lettish: Bielenstein, 433 (Born in the wood, grown up in the wood, turned [on a lathe] by the cabinet-maker, rocked on the arm), 434 (. . . wood, it comes home and weeps bitterly), 435 (. . . wood, then it is dandled on the hands), 436 (. . . wood, it comes to sit behind the table), 437 (Grown in the wood, brought to the castle, rocked on the arm, then it cries in pain), 438 (Found in the wood, carried home, rocked on the arm, it weeps bitterly), 439 (Cut in the wood, bought in the city, carried home, rocked in the arm). Czech: Hanika-Otto, note to Nos. 55 through 58, and p. 129, No. 81. Kashub: Gulgowski, 8 (Grew in the wood, had leaves, came to the house, and began to sing). Polish: Gustawicz, 3 (It had been in the woods, it had leaves. When it came into the world, it wailed hoarsely.—Bass viol), citing four parallels, 4 (In the woods it grew, it had leaves. When it came to the village, it wailed hoarsely.—Violin), citing three parallels, and 388 (It is cut down in the woods and is fashioned at home. Around the village it wanders and leads girls astray), 389 (It was cut down in the woods and fashioned at home. It lay down near the horses, it sang at wakes); Saloni, *Rzeshów*, 170 (Cut in the forest, bent in the house, it will take into its hands sorrowful weeping), 171 (In the forest, bent in the house, it walks through the village and seduces people), 172 (Maple tree, it sings merrily, the horse [also: fiddle-bow; a pun is involved] brandishes its tail over the ram [i.e., gut strings]). This has a close parallel in "A little red tree which sings beautifully. The horse flourishes its tail over the ram" (Saloni, *Łańcut*, 29). See further Saloni, *Rzeshów*, 174 (It grew in the forest, it had leaves, it came home and began to whine), which resembles the sieve riddle (see the headnote to Nos. 1058–1062, § 5, of the present collection); Siarkowski, 23 (It was cut down in the woods, it was fashioned at home, take it in your hands, it weeps), 68 (When in the woods it had many leaves, it came to the village and wept). White Russian: Wasilewski, 94 (Cut in the forest, taken from the closet, it weeps in the hands). Russian: Sadovnikov, 273*a*, 273*b* (balalaika). Finnish: Lönnrot, 847, § 2 = Henssen, 222 (*kantele*, a stringed instrument). Hungarian: Meltzl, 29; Kriza, 42 (They cut it in the woods, it collects the crazy people of the village. —Music), 97 (They cut it in the woods, it became fat in the meadows, and it resounds in the village); *Magyar Nyelvör*, XXI (1892), 527 (They cut it in the woods; its sound can be heard at home). Mordvin: Ahlqvist, p. 41, No. 27 (Grown in the wood, brought out of the wood, it weeps in every man's hands, it causes people to move about on the floor); Paasonen, 407.

1063a through 1063i. Welsh: Hull and Taylor, 175 through 177. Scotch Gaelic: Nicolson, p. 57. Breton: Sébillot, *Haute-Bretagne*, 40; Kerbeuzec, *Ille-et-Vilaine*, 80; Charlec, *Dol-de-Bretagne*, 1904, p. 168, No. 34; Duine, *Saint-Malo*, p. 518. Afrikaans: Groenwald, p. 79. German: Wossidlo, 70; Butsch, 329; Hanika-Otto, 425, and 643, vv. 30-37, and No. 644, vv. 119–120; Frischbier, *Menschenwelt*, p. 262, No. 207 (Three blind men guide a lame one, the lame man bestrews the white land at every step and pace with black sand), 208 (White field plowed up, black seed sowed on it. If a fool passes by, he doesn't know what is standing on it); Schmidt, *Danzig*, 20. Swiss: Rochholz, 523. Danish: Kristensen, p. 117, § 323, No. 516; Feilberg, *Ordbog*, III, 312, s.v. "skrift." Norwegian: Landstad, p. 808, No. 14. Swedish: Ström, p. 186, "Svanpennan," and p. 189, "Griffeltavlan." Latin: Claret, p. 74, No. 122 (Albus ager, nigrum semen, nullus sciet ipsum, quid sit in hoc, laycus.—Liber excipitur bene scriptus); Johannes Lauterbach, *Ænigmata* ([Frankfurt a. M.], 1601), p. 79 = Friedreich, p. 215, No. 16. Walloon: Colson, *Wallonia*, V, 95, Nos. 249, 250; Colson, *Devinettes*, p. 153, No. 38. French: *Les Adeuineaux amoureux*, p. lxxv;

Rolland, 250; V. S., *Mélusine*, I (1878), col. 255, No. 13, and No. 14 = Marchessou, *Velay et Auvergne*, p. 173, No. 3; Bladé, *Armagnac*, 27; Lallemant, *Argonne*, p. 233; J. Roux, *Limousin*, 30; Constantin, *Savoie*, p. 25; Roque-Ferrier, *Languedoc*, p. 338; Baissac, *Mauritius*, p. 415; Parsons, *Antilles*, III, 385, Martinique, 79, and p. 417, Marie Galante, 85. Catalan: Pelay y Briz, 25; Demófilo, p. 357, No. 21. Portuguese: Braga, 1; Pires, *Archivio*, III (1884), 114, No. 7, and p. 245, No. 80; and VII (1888), 247, No. 24; Pires de Lima, 29, 30. Spanish: Demófilo, 405, 775, 777, p. 343, No. 14, p. 359, No. 1, and p. 388, No. 32; Rodríguez Marín, 790 through 794. Argentinian: Lehmann-Nitsche, 560a through 560i. Californian: Espinosa, 31. Chilean: Flores, 548, 549. Cuban: Giménez Cabrera, 37 (White field, black seed, five till and one sows). Dominican Rep.: Andrade, 290. Guatemalan: Recinos, 49. New Mexican: Campa, 44. Porto Rican: Mason, 148, 149, 151, 470. Italian: V. de Bartholomeis, *Rime giullaresche et popolari d'Italia* (Bologna, n.d.), p. 1, No. 1, and notes, p. 75; Rolland, p. 165, No. 73; Pitrè, *Canti*, II, 77-78, Nos. 881, 882; Gianandrea, *Canti popolari marchigiani*, p. 302, No. 28; Ferraro, *Canti popolari in dialetto logodurese*, p. 307, No. 29; Salvioni, *Archivio*, IV (1885), 550, No. 85; Rondini, *ibid.*, VII (1888), 542, No. 36; Balladoro, *ibid.*, XVI (1897), 554, No. 24; Panareo, *ibid.*, XXIII (1906-1907), 237, No. 9; Ive, *Canti popolari istriani*, p. 305, No. 26; Tschiedel, 62; Schneller, *Wälschtirol*, p. 255, No. 20. Rumanian: Gorovei, 244, 1614 through 1619; and Gorovei, *Devinettes*, p. 505. Lithuanian: Schleicher, p. 206 (An honorable field, marvelous seed); Jurgelionis, 699 (White field, black grain, [it is] being ploughed by a goose), 700 (White fields, black sheep), 701 (White fields, black sheep. He who understands herds them), 702, 703 (He who is born clever plows with a goose), 704 (Black seed, white sod, a little goose as harrow), 705, 706 (Flat fields, gray sheep, behind the shepherd's ear a little whip). Lettish: Bielenstein, 217 (A white field, black cows), 218 (A white field, black cattle), 219 (A white meadow, black cattle, pleasant for a wise man to graze in [var.: it needs a wise guardian]), 220 (A white field, black cattle, it is well for him who knows how to guard it), 221, 222, 223 (White earth, black seeds). Czech: Hanika-Otto, note to No. 423. Flajšhans, p. 16, cites Bartoš, 158 (A white field plowed with a goose quill), which has admitted too much of the answer into the riddle, and Erben, 111 (A white field, a black furrow, plowed by a goose). Polish: Saloni, Łańcut, 20 (On the white mountain he sowed peas. He gave a different name to each one), 20a (The red coral sowed with geese, on the white field black poppies are sown), which is not fully intelligible; Saloni, *Rzeshów*, 134 (Over the white mountain it plows with geese, it sows black millet and will never gather it in), 135 (Over the white mountain it plows with geese, and when it plows, it will not obliterate [the mountain]), 136 (A red mountaineer, he plowed with geese, and the white field he sowed with black grains, and of every grain he knew how it was called), 137 (A mountaineer was here, he plowed with geese, on the white field he sowed black grains, and of every grain he knew how it was called); Siarkowski, 64 (White soil, black grain); Kopernicki, 82 (Over a white hill he plows with geese, he sows with black millet, but he never reaps it). The reference in some of these Polish riddles to each letter being called by name has parallels in riddles for the months or the days of the week (see the headnote to No. 1037, n. 1). Russian: Sadovnikov, 2146 (The earth is white, but the birds on it are black), 2147 (A white field, black seed. He who sows it has knowledge), 2148 (The seed is flat, the field is smooth. Whoever has knowledge, that one sows. The seed does not sprout, but it does bear fruit), 2149 (The seed is gray, sown by hand, reaped by mouth), 2156 (It is neither the sky nor the earth, it is white to the sight. Three walk along it [and] lead one, two look on, one commands), 2156a (It is neither the sky nor the earth. It is white in itself. Two look on, three work, one commands), 2157 (A white cloth is spread along the court, a horse tramples upon it, one walks, another leads, black birds sit upon it), 2158. Serbian: Novaković, p. 90, Nos. 8 (White field, black seed, a wise head that sows.—Book), 9 (A white tribe, black seed, a wise head that sows it in the field), and p. 163, No. 8 (I caught a floating bird, I took off its curving fir, I sowed with it the white field, and the field saw the world), which is not completely intelligible. Bulgarian: Palashev, 1 (White soil, black furrows, the man learns, the goose screeches), the last clause of which refers to the squeaking of the quill; Chacharov, 43 (A white field, black seed, it is sown by hand and harvested by mouth).

Hungarian (the first eleven versions here cited are extracted from Szendrey's additions to Aarne's discussion of the riddle; see the headnote to No. 1063 of the present collection): [1] *Magyar Nyelvör*, II (1873), 90 (White is its soil, black its seed, a goose plows it, man drives it); [2] *ibid.*, p. 514 (What tale I tell is a very merry tale: black is its seed, white its soil, they say a goose plows it, but a man drives it; tell me what it is, stay here for luncheon); [3] *Magyar Nyelvészet*, III, 320 (A goose plows it, a man harrows it, white is its soil, black its seed); [4] *Magyar Népköltési Gyüjtemény*, I, 320 (A goose plows it, a man drives it, it is sown with care); [5] *ibid.*, XI, 470 = Kriza, 74 (A goose plows it, a man drives it, white is its soil, black its seed, it is sown with care); [6] *Magyar Nyelvör*, IV (1875), 327 (It is in a soil which was plowed by a goose, the handle of the plow was held by my friend, he put seed into its white soil, he thought a great deal about its sowing); [7] Szendrey's manuscript collection from Szalonta (White is its soil, black its seed, a shaft plows it, a man drives it, he sows with care); [8] *Magyar Nyelvör*, III (1874), 329 (In a white field a black furrow, a man drives it, plows it with a shaft, dries it with a rain of dust); [9] *Magyar Népköltési Gyüjtemény*, XI, 466 (Many black roads are built in a spacious white field); [10] communicated to Szendrey by Ernest Révész (Black on white, in the hands of an ass; why has he it in his hands, if he knows nothing about it!); [11] *Magyar Nyelvör*, XXXVII (1908), 187 (White field, black seed, three are working, two are idling, the chick is drinking).

See further Hungarian: Meltzl, 41; Kriza, 59 (They cut many black roads through a wide white meadow). Finnish: Aarne and Krohn, 302 = Henssen, 103 (White field, black seed. Who is able to sow it?). Estonian: Wiedemann, p. 293. Zyrian: Wichmann, *Zyrian*, 91. Cheremiss: Wichmann, *Cheremiss*, 184. Votyak: Buch, 12 (A white field, black seed, he who sows it knows it); Wichmann, *Votyak*, 47, 280 (They have sown seed-grain on the snow). Modern Greek: Dieterich, *Rätseldichtung*, p. 98, citing Kanellakis, p. 163, No. 1; Abbott, p. 309, No. 14; Stathes, p. 333, No. 27 (White is the field and black the seed. It meets and converses with him who planted it). Albanian: Hahn, p. 158, No. 2 (The field is white, the seed black, it is sown with the hand and harvested with the mouth). Arabic: Giacobetti, 301 (I have sowed seed in my field and water runs in every furrow. The cereal grains have not produced straw or spines, all is green.—Tattooing), 414 (The land is white, the seed is black, five oxen drag the yoke), 415 (The land is wooden, the plow is of reed, the seed is of gold.—Koran). This refers to paper as wooden (since it is made from a plant) and is couched in the characteristic Levantine and Mediterranean form of references to three different materials (usually metals or precious stones). See also Giacobetti's No. 416 (I went into a white land, I threw some black seed there, I had one workman and three husbandmen). Tunisian: Stumme, *Tunis*, 53. Turkish: Hamizade, 397 (On a white plowed field a black pip), 482 (A white plowed field, a black seed, the hand sows, the tongue reaps.—Letter), 723 (It is sown with the hand, it is reaped with the mouth.—Writing, reading). Turcoman: Samojlvich, 62 (That man walking has a little pole. In the middle of a white ravine a black bird is found). Armenian: Wingate, p. 471, No. 8 (A snow-white field I own, with my hand it is sown, with my lips it is mown). See also Grigorov, p. 123, No. 6 (A white field, black seeds. I sow with my hand, I reap with my tongue); Seidlitz, p. 71, No. 35 (Sowed with the pen, harvested with the eyes, eaten by the head, digested by the memory.—Instruction). Georgian: Blechsteiner, p.

13, No. 10; Glushakov, p. 28, No. 42 (White earth, black seeds, six men came up). The six men are the five fingers and the pen. Ossete: Schiefner, 53 (He sows black seed on a white field, and that which is sowed speaks with the one who sows). Cherekessian: Tambiev, p. 53, No. 2 (What has white furrows and black seeds?—The Koran). Surinam: Herskovits, 32 (A black savannah, a white savannah, and three men run past). African, Kxatla: Schapera, 122 (Tell me: a white field with black corn). Indian: Lakshīnātha Upasānī, IX, 6 (What seeds are sown by the hand and picked up by the mouth?). Kashmiri: Knowles, 109 (Black crows on a white bank; they are saying, *Caw, caw!*—Black paddy growing in a white field). The riddler has forgotten the correct answer. Ho: Haldar, p. 276, No. 7; Sarkar, p. 252, No. 30. Bihari: Mitra, *Bihari Life*, p. 45 (There are black seeds in white furrows. They were sown by the hands, but they are rooted out by the teeth). Munda: Roy, *The Mundas*, p. 506 (On white field grows karhāni paddy). Karhāni paddy is black rice. Khāriā: Roy and Roy, II, 455, No. 3 (With my hands I sow black kurthi [rice] on a white field), which the authors say is "borrowed from neighboring Hindu castes." Baiga: Elwin, p. 473, No. 89 (Sow black seed on a white field; cut the crop, and it awakes and sings). Bhil: Hedberg, p. 877, No. 78 (The ploughed field as well as the ploughshare is thin, the one who ploughs, he knows.—Paper and pen). Uraon: Archer, p. 180, No. 11 (In a white field are the black seeds). Kolarian: Wagner, 99 (On a white field black rice is sown). Indonesian, Javanese: Ranneft, *Poëzie*, p. 3, No. 5 (Two brothers are named who are one, when they are working. They have only one tool. In working they use it daily and run together. Those who have been instructed need only to look at the traces of the tool to know exactly what secret the brothers have).

1063b. The riddler has carelessly substituted the conventional contrast of land and sea, which is virtually meaningless, for "land and seed."

1063c. The riddler has obviously forgotten the answer.

1063f. Riddlers do not often repeat an introductory formula as a conclusion.

1064. Compare the sails riddle, Nos. 1036a through 1036d.

1065. Perhaps hanging a window as a carpenter does in building a house is meant. It is also possible that the riddler is giving only a vague answer to his riddle and really means the curtains.

1066. This may be a degenerate form of the riddle for the stars; see No. 1071.

1069. Breton: Sébillot, *Haute-Bretagne*, 32. French: Rolland, *Rimes*, p. 201, No. 25 (wax). Portuguese: Pires de Lima, 176. Compare the Lithuanian riddle for a wax candle, "A white maiden with a little red hood, her shirt made of all the plants" (Jurgelionis, 379).

1070. Scotch Gaelic: Nicolson, p. 61 (A crooked rowan tree beside the farmer's house. Though the world's folk should come, they would not be allowed to pluck it.—Farmer's wife). African, Wanamwezi: Dahl, 42 (At the boundary a fresh maize stalk cannot be plucked.—Your sister).

1071. Walloon: Colson, *Wallonia*, IV, 43, No. 12 (What is this? A flower of Bengal that blooms a dozen times a year. I wager twenty francs that you will not guess it in a dozen years.—Moon). The collector offers no explanation of "a flower of Bengal." Turkish: Kowalski, *Zagadki*, 8 (An enameled minaret, its base is black, a little flower worth a hundred thousand ducats.—Sun); Moshkov in Radlov, X, 265, No. 2 (*Min min minola, libi kanola*, three thousand flowers, one tulip.—Moon and stars). Armenian: Zelinski, p. 59, No. 29 (A thousand thousand minarets, a hundred thousand flowers on one leaf.—Moon, stars). Indian, Kashmiri: Knowles, 16 (The rose has bloomed and nobody cuts it.—Sun). Uraon: Archer, p. 184, No. 7 (A blossoming flower that cannot be plucked.—Fire). Indonesian, Javanese: Ranneft, *Proza*, p. 20, No. 93 (There is a pair of flowers; when they open, they fill the whole world.—Sun and moon).

I do not understand "by time de fe clean." It may be a reminiscence of the versions in which the sky is a courtyard to be swept (see the headnote to No. 1071, nn. 3, 5, in the present collection).

1072. African, Duala: Ebding, 95 (My father bequeathed me a cup always filled with water). Annamese: Emeneau and Taylor, 6 (It does not arrive at the river, it does not go to the quay. It is suspended in the middle of the sky. How does it happen that it has liquid?). Compare better versions of this theme in the headnote to Nos. 1105–1106, n. 1, and the note to Nos. 1105a through 1105e.

1074, 1076a, 1076b. The introductory formula belongs to tales rather than to riddles. See also No. 1086c.

1085. This probably degenerate version has admitted part of the answer into the riddle. See versions making no reference to tree and fruit, Nos. 1500a, 1500b. For a list of English riddles consisting of mere descriptions and lacking enigmatic quality, see the note to No. 72.

1091, 1092. The unusual comparison is a more nearly adequate personification and calls to mind a person or animal whose flesh, body, or skin is thrown away and whose blood is drunk; for examples see Nos. 808, 809b, 813, and other riddles classified under the headnote to Nos. 806–815. The introductory sentence gives more information than good enigmatic technique allows.

1093. (Fruit on a tree is visible by night and invisible by day.) Portuguese: Parsons, *Cape Verde*, 272a (A tree: at night with many figs, in the morning it has none). For references to the mention of figs in this connection see, in the present collection, the headnote to Nos. 1093–1095, n. 22. See also Parsons, *Cape Verde*, 272c. Modern Greek: Polites, *Neohellenika Analekta*, I, 247, No. 308 (I had an apple tree, it produced apples, in the daytime it would lose them, and at night it would regain them). Georgian: Kapanadze, p. 145, No. 11 (I have a tree that bears fruit every night). African, Pangwe: Tessmann, 72 (A tree [*Irvingia barteri*] sprouts many fruits at night; [they exist] no longer by day).

1094a through 1094e. (In this note are collected riddles making comparisons to objects seen at night and lost by day.) French: A. Ferrand, *Dauphiné*, p. 225 (I lost my nut in the wood of Cocagne. I lost it during the day. I found it at night); Parsons, *Antilles*, III, 450, Hayti, 55 and var. Armenian: Zelinski, p. 58, No. 20 (A whole cup of apples, it will not remain until morning). Tatar: Kalashev and Ioakimov, p. 66, No. 6 (A tray of apples, it will not keep until morning). African, Kxatla: Schapera, 4 (Tell me: I spread out sprouted corn in my yard; when I woke up, I could not find it). Taveta: Hollis, *Taveta*, 34 (I put out my bananas to dry. When I awake in the morning, they are not there and I miss them). Indian, Kashmiri: Knowles, 20 (I sowed mahá [*Phaseolus maximus* or *P. radiatus*] in a field of air; yesterday I saw it, but tomorrow it is nowhere).

For comparisons in terms of animals, see the list in the note to No. 470 of the present collection.

1095. (In this note are grouped riddles mentioning countless objects, usually fruits, seeds, or grains.) Dutch: Schrijnen, II, 102, No. 5 (Back in my father's yard there stands a tree with pearls; he who can count the pearls is the master of all). Indian, Kolarian: Wagner, 95 (Can you count the flour of Indian corn in a leaf-bowl?). Ho: Sarkar, p. 351, No. 5 (You will not be able to count [the grains in] a cupful of fried maize). Parsee and Ho: Munshi, 6 = Mitra, *Notes on Ho Riddles*, p. 101 (A plateful of mustard seed which could not be counted by anybody). Bhil: Hedberg, p. 884, No. 118 (The shade of a small pipri tree broken through by gleams of light, and around it birds and a number of small flowers. When the latter parts, a number of small jasmine flowers [appear].—Moon and stars). Indonesian, Javanese: Ranneft, *Proza*, p. 43, No. 199 (Beneath, one sees no roots; above, there are no leaves; there are two flowers and countless fruits). For comparisons of stars to countless persons, animals, or things see the headnote to Nos. 1021–1035, n. 2.

CHAPTER VII
COMPARISONS TO THINGS
Nos. 1100–1259

1100. (Only parallels mentioning several members of the human body are cited.) See Breton: Kerbeuzec, *Ille-et-Vilaine*, 60; Lavenot, *Basse-Bretagne*, p. 671 (A drum on forks); Sébillot, *Devinettes*, 53. Frisian: Dykstra, I, 260. Dutch: van Vloten, p. 166, No. 31. Flemish: Joos, 546; *Ons Volksleven*, I (1889) 78, No. 36. Afrikaans: Groenewald, p. 74. German: Butsch, 80; Wossidlo, 164; Frischbier, *Menschenwelt*, pp. 240–241, No. 1; Carstens, *Schleswig-Holstein*, p. 412; Haffner, 108; Renk, *Tyrol*, 2 through 4; Karl Müllenhoff, *Zeitschrift für deutsche Mythologie*, III (1855), 9, No. 26; Hanika-Otto, 208; Huss, *Siebenbürgen*, 91; Böckel, *Hesse*, 3; Haase, *Ruppin*, 151, 210, 269; H. Meier, *Ostfriesland*, 23. Swiss: Rochholz, 434 through 437, 439, 440; Zahler, *Münchenbuchsee*, 243; J. Müller, *Innerschweiz*, 3; J. Müller, *Uri*, 17. Danish: Kristensen, pp. 88–91, § 229, Nos. 353a through 353y, 353z (Two plates on two posts, a meal-sack, a button, a forest with wild animals); Feilberg, *Ordbog*, II, 578, s.v. "menneske" (many references). Norwegian: Landstad, p. 809, No. 26; Bugge, *Telemarken*, 41; Brox, *Ytre Senja*, 167; Berge, 97; Christie, 103; Stafset, 144. Swedish: Hyltén-Cavallius, *Värend*, 81; Ericsson, *Södermanland*, II (1881), 95–96, No. 90; IV (1883), 71, No. 183; and V (1884), 66, No. 214; Dybeck, *Runa*, 1850, p. 35, No. 28 = Russwurm, 53; Sandén, *Norra Vadsbo*, 124; Ström, pp. 73–76 and p. 77, No. 4; Geijer and Campbell, 1; Christofferson, p. 92; Russwurm, *Eibo*, p. 134, § 316, No. 25. French: Bladé, *Armagnac*, 116; Carnoy, *Picardy*, p. 55; Constantin, *Savoie*, p. 22; A. Ferrand, *Dauphiné*, p. 228 (The forest on the oven, the oven on the barn, and the fountain on two pegs); V. S., *Mélusine*, I (1878), cols. 264–265, Nos. 95, 96. Basque: Cerquand, 8 (A scoop on the earth, a stick on the scoop, a sack on the stick, a mill on the sack), but here the significance of "scoop" (*pelle*) is not entirely clear; Vinson, 35. Spanish: Demófilo, 223, 226; Rodríguez Marín, 324, 325. Chilean: Flores, 518; Laval, 4. Cuban: Massip, 32 (God gave me a well and a rope [*lazo*] for it. Stretched out, it does not reach, and doubled, it does.—Mouth and arm). Italian: Pitrè, 838, and compare his No. 73; Salvioni, *Archivio*, IV (1885), 540, No. 8; Rondini, *ibid.*, VII (1888), 544, No. 53. Rumanian: Gorovei, 1833 through 1836. Lithuanian: Jurgelionis, 152 (There stands a two-pronged fork, on that fork is a beehive, on that hive a ball, on that ball a forest, and in that forest are found little beasts), 153 (which substitutes "many birds" for the "little beasts" of the preceding), 154 (On the fork a beehive, on the beehive a ball, on the ball a thicket, and in those thickets [*sic*] are rabbits); Schleicher, p. 203. Lettish: Bielenstein, 820 (Two posts, on the posts a barrel, on the barrel a ball of yarn, on the ball a forest, in the forest small game), 821 (Two posts, on these a porridge-tub, on the porridge-tub two laths, on these two flutes, on the flutes a big forest), 822 (On two posts a barrel, on the barrel a cross, on the cross a forest), 823 (Two little posts, on the posts a little barrel, on the barrel two catchers, on the catchers a forest with much small game), 824 (Two posts, on the posts a drum, on the drum a piano, on the piano a forest, and in the forest much small game), 825 (Two posts, on the posts a leather sack, on the sack a block, on the block two poles, on the poles a mill of bones, over the mill two flowing brooks, on the brooks two glass windows, on the windows a high mountain, on the mountain a big forest, in the forest many sheep from foreign lands), 826 (My father has two posts; on the posts a barrel, on the barrel a funnel, on the funnel a taster, on the taster a smeller, on the smeller a peeper, on the peeper a ball [var.: mountain], on the ball [var.: mountain] a forest, in the forest roe-deer and rabbits [var.: partridges]. One man goes and drives them all out), 995 (On two posts a barrel, on the barrel a taster, on the taster two smellers, on the smellers two peepers, on the peepers a forest, in the forest delicate little beasts). Czech: Hanika-Otto, note to No. 208. Polish: Gustawicz, 34 (There stands a pitchfork, on the pitchfork there is a sack, on the sack there is a mill, on the mill there is a wood, in the wood a shepherd tends his sheep), 35 (There stands an oak, and on the oak a boiler, and on the boiler a club, and on the club a forest, and in that forest some quail are running about); Saloni, *Rzeshów*, 23 (An oak stands, on that oak there are branches, under these branches little ladybugs, under the ladybugs little poppy-seeds, under the poppy-seeds an iron door, and behind the iron door a stammerer stutters), 24 (There stand two oaks, over the oaks a drum, over the drum an iron bridge, above the iron bridge a bellows, above the bellows a bald mountain, on the bald mountain a little sheep pasture, and there little sheep are pastured by an old man with teeth). Russian: Sadovnikov, 1722 (There stands a pitchfork with two tines. On it there is a barrel. On the barrel there is a shaker. On the shaker there is a swinger. On the swinger there is a yawner. On the yawner there is a blower. On the blower there is a winker. On the winker there is a grove. In the grove there are piggies, which are golden-bristled), 1722a through 1722v, 1729 (In a clear field two trumpets sounded, two sables played.—Face, mouth, nose, eyes). Serbian: Novaković, p. 99, No. 2 (There grew a thick little forest, under the forest there was a meadow, under the meadow the lookout, under the lookout the *Gostur*-city, and in the city, the master), 3 (There is a thick forest, under the thicket there is a meadow, under the meadow there are two springs, under the two springs the cut grass, under the cut grass the hole, under the hole a whetstone), 4 (There is a black mountain, under the black mountain a wide field, under the wide field the lookers, under the lookers two little holes, under the holes a big chasm. May God break you, if you do not guess); p. 100, Nos. 1 through 6, and p. 101, Nos. 1 through 4 and No. 5 (There is a meadow, in the meadow is a mirror, next to the mirror is a pump, next to the pump is a fortress, and in the fortress the master). The foregoing Serbian riddles have the answer: the hair, forehead, eyebrows, eyes, nostrils, mouth, teeth, tongue, and beard (or chin). See also Novaković, p. 143, No. 10 (The barrel is standing on two pillars; on top of the barrel is a gourd.— Feet, trunk, head). Bulgarian: Gubov, 65 (A little mound; above the mound, the mouth; above the mouth, the nose; then, eyes; then, a clearing; then, thick woods [some add: the wolves are howling]), 66 (A thick, thick forest; under the forest, braids; under the braids, wells; under the wells, hollows; under the hollows, a little hole; above the hole, a little hill), 67 (A hill; above the hill a hole; above the hole, two openings; above the two openings, two wells; above the two wells, two hedges; above the two hedges, a wide field; above the field, a thick forest; in the forest, a dumb cow). Gubov's first riddle (his No. 65) fails to maintain a consistent enigmatic spirit and admits some parts of the answer into the text. See further Ikonomov, 76 (A thick forest, below the forest a shelf, below the shelf a plaited string, below the plaited string a mirror, below the mirror the sneezer, below the sneezer a field); Stoilov, § 25, Nos. 1 through 16. Finnish: Henssen, 176 (Below, a storehouse; above it a mill, a dense forest above the mill, in the forest little birds). Estonian: Lönnrot, p. 178; Wiedemann, p. 263 (A fork below, on the fork a knapsack, on the knapsack a cross, on the cross a button, on the button a forest, in the forest animals live). See another riddle on the same page (A fork below, on it a knapsack, on the knapsack a cross, on the cross a button, on the button a forest, in the forest [there are] pigs, a boy with a broad hat drives the pigs out of the forest.—Man and comb for the head) and also one on p. 277 (In the forest there are pigs, a little boy with an iron pelt pursues the pigs.—Lice). Hungarian: Kálmány, I, 164, No. 36 (Two arms, above them two gallons, above them mimble-mumble, above that snuffle-sniffle, round about that mash-lash, above that a thick forest filled with little pigs); *Magyar Nyelvör*, III

(1874), 233–234 (Two sticks, a barrel above them *hörcsög-börcsög, csillag-billag* [meaning obscure]. Below, a dense forest in which *siska* pigs [meaning obscure] live), 328 (Above the one that gapes is one that sniffs, above the one that sniffs is one that peeps, above the one that peeps is a flat meadow; above the flat meadow are oak trees; in the oak trees is a small colt); IV (1875), 559 (Below, there are two sticks, above these sticks there is a barrel, then it broadens, above that there is a *szortyon bortyon* [words suggestive of eating and drinking], above that there is a peeper, above the peeper is a dense forest, there are pigs in that forest); V (1876), 34 (like *ibid.*, III [1874], 328, above), 127 (There grows a tree with two branches, above the tree with two branches is a barrel that contains eight pints, above the barrel that contains eight pints is a tree with two branches, above the tree with two branches is a snail, above the snail is a mill, above the mill are two cans of oil, above the two cans of oil are two ravens, above the two ravens are two things that can see, above them is a dense forest), which is confused by the mention of two trees signifying the legs and the arms respectively; XII (1883), 234 (Above the thing with a mouth *ordics* [meaning obscure] is light, above the *ordics* is light, above the light is a clean meadow, above the meadow is a small pine forest in which blonde pigs graze); XV (1886), 44, No. 8 (A tree grows with two branches, above the two branches was a barrel of eight pints, above the barrel was a snail [the word can also mean pulley], above that were two things to see with, and above them a dense forest); XIX (1890), 92 (There is a filled-up bag on two stakes, there is a cross on the bag, there is a button on the cross, there is a dense forest on the button); XXVIII (1899), 527 (like *ibid.*, III [1874], 328, above). Albanian: Hahn, p. 159, No. 1 (A forest, after this a plain, after this there are two lances, after these there are two springs, after these there are two whistling holes, after these is a nightingale, and after this is a man). Arabic: Giacobetti, 269 (Above a cave there are two caves, above the two caves there are two fires, above the two fires, there is a terrace, above the terrace there is a forest, above the forest there are boars), 270 (On two bare feet it walks with its heels, above its feet there is the beater on a gate, above the beater on a gate a village, above the village two belts, above the two belts one belt, above the belt a cave, above the cave two caves, above the two caves a plain, above the plain a forest); Ruoff, p. 16, No. 7 (I have a large cave full of stones, above it lie two holes, above the holes two lights, above the two lights two swords [blackened eyebrows resemble Turkish swords], above the swords a plain, and above the plain a great forest, in it many sheep graze), No. 8a (It is two columns, above them a sack, above it a gourd, above the gourd grazing camels). Turkish: Kúnos, 17 = Kúnos, *Am Urquell*, IV (1893), 21, No. 5 (Below a baker's shop, above it the spring Hor-hor, still higher the seller of mirrors, still higher the bow-maker, still higher a meadow, a grassy spot, in it lambs graze). Sart: Ostrumov, 20, cited by Jungbauer, p. 356 (Above the pond two springs, above the two springs two lights, above the lights young poplars, above the poplars a hill, above the hill a forest, and young pigs in the forest). Armenian: Wingate, 19 (There is a spreading leafy tree, beneath the tree a level park, beneath the park a pencilled mark, beneath the mark a burning glass, beneath the glass a trumpet crass, beneath the horn a roomy loft, the loft is full of shining scythes). For the comparison of teeth to scythes see the similar comparisons in the headnote to No. 1150, § 1, in the present collection. Yakut: Piekarski, 82 (They say that there is a pitchfork, on the pitchfork there is a *tymtaj* [utensil made of birchbark], on the *tymtaj* are two stakes, on the stakes there is a cup, on the cup there is a thicket, in the thicket there are hogs [var.: animals]), 157 (On the pitchfork there is a flat utensil made of birchbark, on the utensil there are branches, on the leaves there are some rough cones.—Man's legs, stomach, arms, hair, lice). Indian, Kashmiri: Knowles, 50 (A fireplace on a candlestick. On this fireplace another fireplace with three holes. On this three-hole is a hedge of thorn. On this hedge

[is] Khájá Bábá). The head is usually called a block with seven holes; see, in the present collection, the headnote to No. 1101. Ho: Sarkar, p. 351, No. 4 (It twinkles under the bush. A breeze blows underneath. It chatters under the breeze. Do ye hear [what it is] or not?). Baiga: Elwin, p. 469, No. 48 (One crooked well. One hill of kachnar trees. Thirty-two pipal trees. One leaf.—Throat, mouth, teeth, tongue). I cannot discover the peculiar appropriateness of the trees here named. Indonesian, Javanese: Ranneft, *Poëzie*, p. 47, No. 6.

Some similar concepts occur as riddles for a single part of the head. The ears are called winnowing baskets behind a mountain (French: Baissac, *Mauritius*, p. 397); the forehead, a mountain the summit of which cannot be seen (Filipino: Starr, *Philippines*, 56). For other comparisons of the hair to a forest, see, in the present collection, the classification at the end of the note to Nos. 1042, 1043. For the comparison of the human head or mouth to a house, cave, or yard, see the riddles cited in the headnote to Nos. 1143–1151 and the pertinent headnotes and notes.

1101. The rhyme "hill: mill" and the adjective "cherry-red" suggest that this text is a fragment of some nursery rhyme describing the face.

In riddling the underlying comparison of the head and nostrils to a hill and holes appears in various forms; see the headnote to No. 1101. For the specific comparison of nostrils to holes in a hill or wall, see Bulgarian: Stoilov, § 16, Nos. 1 (Two holes in a wall, water comes out of them), 2 (Water flows out of two holes). Similar conceptions are found in the riddles cited in the note to No. 1143a, 1143b of this collection. See also African, Lamba: Doke, 86 (Two burrows beneath an anthill). Indonesian, Javanese: Ranneft, *Poëzie*, p. 89, No. 1 (There is a big mountain with two caves near one another. Within, they are grown over with weeds. Uninterruptedly there blows a strong wind, [which] fills [the caves], and there is a spring that overflows. When it storms, a worm appears).

Some versions are noteworthy for the mention of characteristic details. See, for example, "Two portable ovens in the midst of a plain" (French: Baissac, *Mauritius*, p. 406); "A log has two little ovens [in it]" (Russian: Sadovnikov, 1737); "Two wells side by side and separated by a partition" (Russian: Sadovnikov, 1758), which is related to the versions collected in the note to Nos. 1143a, 1143b of the present collection. A Parsee snuff riddle, "Two come to take me, and they create mischief. Two come to take me, and they carry me to two caves" (Munshi, p. 417), contains the theme of this riddle, but otherwise exhibits a marked resemblance to the riddles for picking the nose collected in the headnote to Nos. 970–975, § 4, of the present collection.

Riddlers compare the mouth to a mill; see the headnote to No. 841, § 5, and also Votyak: Wichmann, *Votyak*, 220. Arabic: Giacobetti, 267 (A mill on a hillock). Indian, Kashmiri: Knowles, 65 (Above is a dry mill, dry and wet will meet there; for it the world will turn, but the upper millstone will never turn). Indian, Karo-Batak: Joustra, p. 93 (A mill that one cannot pass). See also the description of an old man cited in the headnote to No. 46, nn. 5, 8, of the present collection.

1102. The import of the riddle is not clear. Compare the Kamba riddle for the ears: "You are rained upon by the rain, you have sleeping skins. Why?" (Lindblom, 61).

1103a, 1103b. Irish: Whitley Stokes, "The Bodleian 'Amra Choluimb chille,'" *Revue celtique*, XVII (1899), 259. German: Köhler, *Kleinere Schriften*, III, 511, No. 15; Butsch, 51. German hunters set this as an initiatory question; see *Archiv für die Geschichte deutscher Sprache und Dichtung*, I (1873), 148. Danish: Feilberg, *Ordbog*, II, 29, s.v. "is." Swedish: Ericsson, *Södermanland*, II (1881), 99, No. 109; Ström, p. 219, "Vattnet," 19. French: *Les Adeuineaux amoureux*, p. xcvii; Rolland, 14. Hungarian: Kálmány, II, 165, No. 45 (What water is widest in the world?—Dew). Indian: W. J. D'Gruyther, *Pan-*

jab Notes and Queries, II (1885), 15, § 5 (Trees can be sunk in it, elephants bathe in it, but a pot cannot sink in it and the thirsty bird goes to it.—Dew).

1104a, 1104b. Norwegian: Stafset, 95 (Two sisters, one sits south of the fjord and one sits north of the fjord; they both wash in one water and dry themselves on one towel). Swedish: Dybeck, *Runa*, 1865–1873, p. 31, No. 33 (Two kings in two kingdoms wash in one water and dry themselves at one fire.—Dew, sun). Breton: Sébillot, *Haute-Bretagne*, 6 (If your brother were on the other side of the river, how would you wash in the same basin and dry yourself on the same towel?). French: Lallemant, *Argonne*, p. 231. Spanish: Demófilo, 948; Rodríguez Marín, 329. Chilean: Flores, 711.

1105a through 1105e. French: Baissac, *Mauritius*, p. 397 (Some water upright.—Sugar cane), and another on the same page (Some water suspended.—Coconut). See also Parsons, *Antilles*, III, 377, St. Lucia, 1 through 3, p. 380, Martinique, 1, 2, p. 390, Dominica, 13 through 15, p. 398, Guadaloupe, 1 through 4, p. 409, Les Saintes, 1, 2, p. 413, Marie Galante, 14 through 17, p. 434, St. Martin, 1, and p. 447, Hayti, 1 through 3. African, Sierra Leone: Mudge-Paris, p. 320 (Water stands); Cronise and Ward, p. 197 (Water hang.—Orange), and another on the same page (Water 'tan up, water grow.—Sugar cane). Pangwe: Tessmann, 86 (I know water that doesn't flow.—Sugar cane), 136 (A little pot hangs on something swaying.—Fruit of the *Minuops djave* Lan.). Slave Coast: Trautmann, p. 102 (What is the canoe, wrecked on the beach and containing water?—Coconut that has been opened). Togo: Schönhärl, *Togo*, 134 (A calabash is in the air and is full of water). Indian, Bengali: Mitra, *Sylhet*, 4 (Below are the roots of Bhikmati's *chhāni* [water pot]. In what country have you seen water at the top of a tree?). Kolarian: Wagner, 20 (Hanging high, on the earth the mouth full of water.—Tamarind, mango). Indonesian, Sangir: Adriani, p. 414, No. 170 (Water vessels in the air). Soenda: Holle, *Soenda*, 20. Annamese: Emeneau and Taylor, 6 (It does not arrive at the river, it does not go to the quay. It is suspended in the middle of the sky. How does it happen that it has liquid?). Samoan: Heider, 2 (What sort of lake is it that hovers between heaven and earth?), 6. Hawaiian: Judd, 28 (My sweet-water spring, suspended in air). The idea of water above the earth but beneath the sky, used in the last few riddles quoted, as well as in the Sierra Leone orange riddle cited above, is also used in the coconut riddle quoted in the headnote to Nos. 1105–1106, n. 1.

Compare No. 1174, in which a joint of sugar cane is described as a well without top, or bottom.

1108. (In the following parallels the answer is usually shirt, coat, or trousers.) The parallels often employ the contrast "enter by one door, come out at two doors." See German: Wossidlo, 463. Swedish: Ström, p. 378, "Sysselsättningar," 34. Portuguese: Parsons, *Cape Verde*, 188 (Enter at one, come out at two.—Trousers), 189 (Enter at one, come out by three.—Shirt). Russian: Sadovnikov, 633 (I walked along the road. I found two roads. I walked along both), 648 (Two roads came in. I entered both.—Shoes). Serbian: Novaković, p. 2, No. 7 (I jumped into a hole and came out through the doors.—Trousers), and p. 102, No. 8 (I entered through one door and went out through three.—Shirt), and p. 237, No. 1 (One wolf walks along two creeks). Finnish: Henssen, 164 (One goes in at one door, and one comes out at three doors before one is properly inside). Lappish: Poestion, p. 268; Donner, p. 20, No. 14; Qvigstad, 81 (It creeps in at one hole and appears at three.—Coat). Arabic: Ruoff, p. 26, No. 36. Crimean Tatar: Filonenko, 103 (In the morning I got up and started running along two roads). Yakut: Popov, p. 289 (It is a whole house with three doors, they say). African, Hausa: Tremearne, p. 58, No. 2 (I have two roads open; though I follow the wrong one, I am not lost.—A pair of loose and shapeless Hausa trousers). Duala: Bufe, p. 60, No: 19 (A man has a house. Wherever he goes, he enters by one door; when he goes out, he must leave by many doors.

—Pulling on one's clothes). Indian, Bengali: Mitra, *Chittagong*, p. 354, No. 20 (The grass called Helāiyā is waved to and fro on both banks of the canal. [Who is that fellow who has] no neck but swallows a man?). The waving grass signifies the hands. Indonesian, Bengkoela: Helfrich, *Bengkoela*, p. 98, No. 2 (A house with three doors). American Indian, Aztec: Pauer, p. 343, No. 2. I do not understand the Turkish "The path for two geese is open, but for two cranes it is closed.—Putting on trousers and boots" (Katanov in Radlov, IX, 287, No. 225).

See, in the present collection, the comparison of a shirt to a man with arms but no legs (headnote to No. 6, § 2) and the shirt riddles making comparisons to persons (note to No. 958).

1110. Ainu: Starr, *Ainu*, 49 (What are three trees on top of a burnt mountain?). For other comparisons see, in the present collection, Nos. 68, 375a, 375b, and 395, which employ comparisons to animals, and Nos. 1033a through 1033e and 1182, which employ a comparison to a person.

1111a through 1111d. The riddler does not usually name the object to which he compares a hole; see Nos. 1690 through 1695 and the headnote to Nos. 1690–1697.

1112. This casual variation is probably a derivative of the somewhat better established version Nos. 1111a through 1111d. They are not especially appropriate comparisons for a hole.

1115. "Turn-stick" is a stick for stirring the contents of a pot.

1116a, 1116b. Mongolian, Buryat: Gombojew, 9 (God's children play with willow twigs.—Eyelashes). For other riddles equating the eyelashes with twigs, see also, in the present collection, the headnote to No. 1044, n. 7, and the Abyssinian riddle quoted in the note to No. 1044.

1117a, 1117b. Welsh: Hull and Taylor, 290, 291. Welsh Gypsy: Sampson, 25. Irish: De Bhaldraithe, 70 (Cars full of timber, and not one inch of it bent or straight). For discussion see J. G. Campbell, *Popular Tales of the Western Highlands* (Edinburgh, 1862), III, 336 note; J. G. G. McKay, *More West Highland Tales* (Edinburgh, 1940), I, 453.

1118a, 1118b. For a personification of a soursop, see No. 577a.

1119. This resembles the comparison of a hedgehog to a man bearing needles; see Nos. 576a, 576b.

1120. For a description of a ship as a creature going on its back, see the headnote to No. 372, nn. 5, 7–8.

1121a through 1121e, 1121g. (Only the post is mentioned.) French: Parsons, *Antilles*, III, 381, Martinique, 9, p. 394, Dominica, 68, p. 399, Guadaloupe, 15, p. 410, Les Saintes, 13, p. 417, Marie Galante, 78, and p. 448, Hayti, 21. Sierra Leone: Cronise and Ward, p. 195 (One big ho'se bin deh, he got one post, no mo'). Swahili: Velten, 28 (I have built my big house, it stands on one pole). Surinam: Herskovits, p. 445, No. 65 (I make a house with one post).

1121f. This is obviously a defective version; the riddler seems to have confused the pattern of Nos. 1121a through 1121e with that mentioning rafters as well (Nos. 1122a through 1122c).

1122a through 1122c. (Rafters and post.) Hawaiian: Judd, 135 (My house with eight rafters and one post). Compare also his nose riddle, No. 187 (My house, it has one rafter and two doors), and other similar nose riddles in the note to Nos. 1143a, 1143b.

1123b. The riddler errs in admitting the function of the answer into the riddle.

1124a. The significance of "glass window" is obscure; the words may have been thoughtlessly borrowed from such a text as No. 1130d below. The "green children" are probably the unripe coconuts.

1124b. For parallels to the idea "no windows, no doors" see Nos. 1132 through 1135b.

1125. The "post" is the arm by which the mill is turned.
1127. The import of the riddle is obscure.
1128a, 1128b. (Windows only.) Irish: Delargy, 18 (I have a house and a mouse could not sit in it and no one could count how many windows there are in it). Lithuanian: Jurgelionis, 526 (A small house, a hundred windows), 527 (A little dark house with a hundred windows). Polish: Gustawicz, 261 (A tiny wee house with a hundred windows).
1129a, 1129b. (Windows and one door.) French: Baissac, *Mauritius*, p. 401 (My house has many windows, one door).
1130a through 1130i. Breton: Sauvé, 80 (Riddle me ree: a prison with a thousand little rooms). Lettish: Bielenstein, 719 (A big dwelling, windows round about; he who enters does not come out). Cheremiss: Genetz, 1 (My little room is of aspen wood, made with windows round about). African, Sierra Leone: Cronise and Ward, p. 197 (Me daddy buil' ho'se, soso [entirely] windah). Togo: Schönhärl, 104. Ewe: Spieth, p. 560, No. 18. Indian: Kukka Mall, *Panjab Notes and Queries*, II (1885), 214, No. 112, § 2 (There are holes all over it, nor flesh nor blood at all in it; it astonishes me how it can exist). Baiga: Elwin, p. 466, No. 20 (Many windows, no door), and p. 471, No. 75 (The palace has many tiles on the roof, many windows in its walls. But there is only one big door. When the king enters, he cannot get out again). Hawaiian: Judd, 108 (Many holes, many holes, but [only] one to enter [by]).
This is related to the conception of fish as residents in a house that "leaps" out of the windows; see No. 906 of the present collection.
1130d, 1130f. The glass windows are probably water shining in the meshes of the net.
1131. Danish: Kristensen, p. 122, § 340, No. 539. Arabic: Ruoff, p. 36, No. 84 (Holes as countless as the stars). Filipino: Starr, *Philippines*, 387 (Guiring-guiring's house is full of holes). A Bhil sieve riddle makes a picturesque and ingenious comparison to looking up through leaves and branches to the sky: "The shade of a little pipri-tree broken through with gleams of light" (Hedberg, p. 874, No. 59).
1132. (Color not mentioned.) Irish: Christiansen, 82. German: Butsch, 15. French: Rolland, 65; Bladé, *Armagnac*, 120. Spanish: Demófilo, p. 350, No. 49; Rodríguez Marín, 374. Argentinian: Lehmann-Nitsche, 503. Cuban: Massip, 101, 103. Lettish: Bielenstein, 417 (A little, little houselet without doors or windows). Bulgarian: Gubov, 423 (it has no opening); Ikonomov, 14 (it has neither a hole nor a window); Stoilov, p. 70, § 58, No. 9 (Walled in, walled out, there is no hole or window). Cheremiss: Wichmann, *Cheremiss*, 126, 208, 235. Votyak: Wichmann, *Votyak*, 12. Modern Greek: Dieterich, *Rätseldichtung*, p. 95. Berber: Basset, *Contes populaires berbères*, p. 126, No. 11. Cuman: Németh, *Codex Cumanicus*, p. 582, No. 6. Turcoman: Karutz, p. 97. Ossete: Schiefner, 13. Abyssinian: Littmann, *Tigriña*, 17 (A little round hut that has no door). African: Werner, p. 213. Konde: Mackenzie, p. 163. Swahili: Velten, 3 (My house has no doors). Nyika: Hollis, *Nyika*, p. 141, No. 16 (I build my house, it has no door). Nyanja: Werner, p. 213 (I built my house without a door). Chinyanja: Rattray, p. 155 (A hut without a doorway). Pangwe: Tessmann, 50. Kaguru: Busse, p. 62, No. 1. Kanuri: Lukas, p. 170, No. 21 (The hut of a young woman without a door). Ila: Smith and Dale, II, 331 (You who are so smart, can you make out the doorway of a fowl's egg?). Songaï: Hamouda, 12. Indian, Baiga: Elwin, p. 477, No. 135 (A beautiful palace without a door). Indonesian, Simaloer: Damsté, 2.
For comparisons of an egg to a box, barrel, or trunk without an opening, see the headnote to No. 1187 in the present collection.
1133. (White house without door or window.) Breton: Sauvé, 44a (I have a little white room which has neither door nor bar), 44b (Guess: a little white box that has neither hole nor lock); Milin, *Batz*, p. 54 (A little white box which has neither key nor lock).

For other comparisons of an egg to a box see the headnote to No. 1187 in the present collection. Swiss: Rochholz, 382. Basque: Vinson, 6 (A white, decorated room locked without a key). Spanish: Demófilo, 539; Rodríguez Marín, 374. Chilean: Flores, 351. Cuban: Massip, 105. Portuguese: Coelho, *Zeitschrift für romanische Philologie*, III (1879), 198, No. 10; Braga, 10; Parsons, *Cape Verde*, 70a through 70c. Lithuanian: Jurgelionis, 804 (A bright [or: white] cottage without doors or windows). Cheremiss: Porkka, 112; Genetz, 16 (My aspenwood room has no window). Arabic: Ruoff, p. 48, No. 11 = Bauer, p. 233, No. 11 (A whitewashed well without an opening); Socin and Stumme, 4 (Our house with a dome is whitewashed but has no door). Indian, Bhil: Hedberg, p. 882, No. 107 (There is a white bungalow without a door).

1134. Scotch Gaelic: Nicolson, p. 33. Irish: Christiansen, 39. Breton: Sébillot, *Haute-Bretagne*, 21b. Flemish: Joos, 369 (I know a neat white house, but without door or room. In it dwells a golden lady, and Dortje is her name). Dutch: Schrijnen, II, 106, No. 21 (I knocked on a white door, there came forth a brown father [*pater*]). German: Wossidlo, 32; Frischbier, *Thierwelt*, p. 354, Nos. 64, 65; Hanika-Otto, 383, 386 (A white church, a yellow bishop in it). Swedish: Ericsson, *Södermanland*, I (1879), 88, No. 42; Wigström, p. 291, No. 61. Latin: Huldreich Therander (Johann Sommer), 405; Reusner, ed. 1599, p. 106 = ed. 1602, p. 280 = Friedreich, p. 207, No. 13. Walloon: Colson, *Wallonia*, IV, 62, No. 59 var. (I knock on a white door, a yellow curé comes to open the door). French: Bladé, *Armagnac*, 122; Marchessou, *Velay et Auvergne*, p. 166, No. 8. Spanish: Demófilo, 831; Rodríguez Marín, 381. Chilean: Flores, 366. Dominican Rep.: Andrade, 176. Porto Rican: Mason, 291. Italian: Salvioni, *Archivio*, IV (1885), 550, No. 92 (chapel). Hungarian: Arany and Gyulai, II, 360, No. 59 (There is a cloister without any steeple, it admits light without windows, flesh and blood live in it, they promise profit to man). Ossete: Schiefner, 12, 15. African, Swahili: Steere, 1; Velten, 4. Lamba: Doke, 20. Bakongo: Denis, 44. Sierra Leone: Cronise and Ward, p. 193 (De king he get ho'se, do'-mout' no deh, windah no deh, but pusson duh talk inside). Indian: Lakshīnātha Upasānī, III, 2, (A doorless house made by God is sat upon by a fasting devotee; the occupant breaks the house). Fijian: Fison, p. 409, No. 27 (quoted in the note to Nos. 1135a through 1135d of the present collection). Filipino: Starr, *Philippines*, 104.

1135a through 1135d. Welsh: Hull and Taylor, 147 through 149. German: Frischbier, *Thierwelt*, p. 355, No. 73; Hanika-Otto, 385. Danish: Kristensen, p. 149, § 439, Nos. 695a through 695d, 696a, 696b, 697; Feilberg, *Ordbog*, III, 1144, s.v. "æg." Faeroic: Hammershaimb, *Antiquarisk tidsskrift*, III (1849–1851), 317, No. 15 = *Færøsk anthologi*, I, 322, No. 7. Norwegian: Landstad, p. 811, No. 33 (A house full of food and no door into it); Brox, *Ytre Senja*, 63, 196; Berge, 81; Stafset, 87. Swedish: Ericsson, *Södermanland*, I (1879), 88, No. 40; Wigström, p. 288, No. 9, and p. 291, No. 60; Geijer and Campbell, 59; Ström, p. 196, "Ägget," and p. 371, "Växter och djur." French: Rolland, 65; Sébillot, *Auvergne*, 14. Serbian: Novaković, p. 76, Nos. 5 (A house in which flesh and bones grow), 6 (A house without doors and windows in which flesh and bones grow), 7 (In one room flesh and bones grow). Finnish: Lönnrot, 1390 = Henssen, 149. Gypsy: Wlislocki, 5. Arabic: Giacobetti, 200. African, Hausa: Tremearne, p. 59 (The house of the youths is full of meat). Fijian: Fison, p. 409, No. 27 (A house filled with food, and as straitly shut up, that no man can find the door. Then comes to pass a wonderful thing. The food becomes a man. Only one man, but he fills the whole house. By and by, he opens the house, leaps outside, and runs away, leaving the house burst and destroyed).

1135d. As often occurs in oral transmission, the riddler has substituted the specific detail "store" for the characteristic general conception of "house."

1136. Flemish: Joos, 484 (A little barn full of grain, and there is neither door nor window). Icelandic: Árnason, 282 (I found a house full of provisions, without mite or louse). If you should wish to use this store, you'll find no door), 284 (A house full of food, but no door is to be found). Cheremiss: Porkka, 36 (The interior of my little hut is tasty). For the comparison of a nut to a pot of food, see the headnote to No. 1187 of the present collection.

1137a through 1137e. For the comparison of an egg to gold and silver see the note to No. 1139 and the brief comment in the headnote to No. 1139.

1138a, 1138b. (Comparison to flowers, fruits, parts of plants.) Flemish: Joos, 367 (A red, white flower with a yellow heart). German: Butsch, 141; Wossidlo, 31 (yellow flower); Hanika-Otto, 65a through 65f. Renk, *Tyrol*, 191 (A white lake and yellow lilies in it). Swiss: Rochholz, 381 (A beautiful flower, red and white, round and small, in a white castle). Spanish: Demófilo, 536, 537, 546; Rodríguez Marín, 376. Argentinian: Lehmann-Nitsche, 468 (yellow [var.: red] flower). Chilean: Flores, 344 (yellow flower). Cuban: Massip, 102 (Between two walls there comes out a yellow flower). Arabic: Ruoff, p. 49, No. 14 (An apricot in a crystal glass). The Lamba "A little hole full of grass litter" (Doke, 6) may describe the yolk as similar to drying or yellowing grass. It is possible, however, that this may be related to the Turkish riddle in which an egg is said to contain two kinds of fodder (see, in the present collection, the headnote to No. 1140, n. 5).

1138b. The query in this confused and defective riddle has been inserted by the collector.

1139. (Comparisons to silver and gold.) Spanish, Argentinian: Lehmann-Nitsche, 633 (Shell of silver, heart of gold). Lithuanian: Jurgelionis, 799 = Schleicher, p. 196 (I break the ice and find silver, I break the silver and find gold). Lettish: Bielenstein, 422, 423, 424 (I strike the wall, I strike silver; I strike silver, I hit upon gold), 425. Russian: Sadovnikov, 551 (I found a ball and broke it, I beheld silver and gold). Arabic: Giacobetti, 199, 203. Turkish: Kúnos, 56 (I saw a wonderful thing. If I hit it with my fingers, it bursts open. Half of it is silver, half is gold, part of it becomes glassy); Kowalski, *Asia Minor*, 30; Kowalski, *Zagadki*, 32 (In a white bag there is some yellow gold); Moshkov in Radlov, X, 267, No. 27 (In the yard were noise and shouting. I went into the yard and found a silver ball). Armenian: Seidlitz, p. 71, No. 36 (A silver wall, within a golden liquid. When it falls in, it can't be built up again). The second theme is that of Humpty Dumpty; see Nos. 738 through 747b of the present collection. Blechsteiner (p. 1, No. 21) cites the riddle from Zelinski, *Sbornik . . . Kavkaza*, II, No. 38, but I have not been able to verify the reference. Georgian: Blechsteiner, p. 15, No. 21 (Gold within, silver without). Indonesian, Sangir: Adriani, p. 418, No. 200 (Porcelain envelops silver, silver envelops gold). Serawaj: Helfrich, *Serawaj*, p. 44, No. 2 (Gold within, silver without). Karo-Batak: Joustra, p. 96. Soenda: Holle, *Soenda*, p. 372, No. 16. Engganee: Helfrich, *Engganee*, p. 518, No. 71 (A fruit without a stalk, containing gold and silver). Javanese: Kreemer, *Java*, p. 136; Ranneft, *Proza*, p. 13, No. 63 (A white box full of gold and silver).

A few riddles mention a specific golden object; see German: Wossidlo, 32 (golden watch). Indian, Bengali: Mitra, *Chittagong*, p. 973, No. 22 (golden amulet); Mitra, *Sylhet*, p. 114, No. 17 (golden cup).

1141. Scotch Gaelic: Campbell, p. 397, No. 12 (A little clear house, and its two doors shut). Irish: Christiansen, 41 (White house, yellow house, you can't get in without breaking the white house). This has some similarity to Nos. 1159a, 1159b of the present collection. Flemish: Joos, 365 (I am a house, but no one can build me. If he who dwells in me wants to get out, he must cut the house to bits). German: Butsch, 139; Wossidlo, 82. Swiss: Zahler, *Münchenbuchsee*, 63. Latin, Reusner, ed. 1599, p. 106 = *ibid.*, ed. 1602, p. 280 = Friedreich, p. 207, No. 13; Huldreich Therander (Johann Sommer), 405. French:

Rolland, 65. Spanish, Cuban: Giménez Cabrera, 9 (A little white house which everyone knows how to open but no one knows how to shut). Porto Rican: Mason, 288. Lettish: Bielenstein, 417.

For comparisons of an egg to a box that cannot be closed after it has been opened, see the headnote to No. 1187, n. 1, of the present collection.

1142a, 1142b. Persian: Kuka, 18 (I saw a sphere containing a sphere within itself. It has three windows, of which one is open and the other two are closed). Hawaiian: Judd, 6 (A fishpond with three outlets). The riddle for a coconut usually refers to a head with three eyes; see, in the present collection, Nos. 523 through 524b and the headnote to Nos. 523–524.

The Kamba call the openings between the stones supporting a pot over the fire the doors of a house: "Tell me the rich man who has three doors to his house" (Lindblom, 1).

1143a, 1143b. French: Parsons, *Antilles*, III, 407, Guadaloupe, 119. Rumanian: Gorovei, 228. Polish: Gustawicz, 255; Saloni, *Rzeshów*, 114 (Two pigsties with a single post between them), 115 (There stand two pigsties and between them a single post); Siarkowski, 36 (Two tiny pigsties with one post). Modern Greek: Polites, *Neohellenika Analekta*, I, 250, No. 325 (There are two little windows from which hang two little girls); Stathes, p. 339, No. 40 (I have two little openings and they are always damp). Turkish: Kowalski, *Zagadki*, 69 (I have two houses, they have only one column). See also the similar riddles collected in the note to No. 1101 in the present collection. Armenian: Seidlitz, p. 71, No. 13 (Two rooms have a single prop). Georgian: Kapanadze, p. 144, No. 6 (My little pigpen is swept and swept, yet it is never swept out). Mongolian: Mostaert, 28 (Two houses with one pillar). African, Lamba: Doke, 88 (A house one doesn't close), 90 (A lean-to on an anthill). Kamba: Lindblom, 60 (Why do you allow yourself to get wet by the rain, when you have a cave to take shelter in?). Kiniramba: F. Johnson, p. 356, No. 17 (It rains and the cave is here). Ila: Smith and Dale, II, 328, No. 23 (Into the house of the red man you can push only one fire-stick). Wanamwezi: Dahl, 45 (In mother's house there are two eyes [peepholes]). SeSuto: Norton and Velaphe, 59 (Bushmen's houses are not opened, because [they are] doorless). Indian, Kashmiri: Knowles, 138 (One mosque, two doors. Come, sir, bang on it). The injunction refers to blowing one's nose; the "mosque" is the head. Baiga: Elwin, p. 475, No. 112 (One pillar and two doors), which resembles the previously cited Polish riddles. Indonesian, Engganee: Helfrich, *Engganee*, p. 517, No. 1. Samoan: Heider, 132 (Tell me a house with one main post, but two doors); Brown, p. 343 (There stands a long house with one post but with two doorways). Hawaiian: Judd, 177 (My house with two rooms and two foreigners), which resembles a Modern Greek version quoted above, 187 (My house, it has one rafter and two doors), 188, 189.

1144. A Hungarian riddle for the eyes, "A little house has two lighted windows; they are opened every morning and closed every night" (Kriza, 32), is of this pattern, but develops the theme with unusual skill.

Other comparisons of the eyes to windows may be found in the present collection, in the headnote to Nos. 1100–1108, nn. 25, 27, in the headnote to No. 1100, n. 2, and in the note to No. 1100 (Lettish: Bielenstein, 825).

The eyes are also compared to mirrors (see the headnote to No. 1100, n. 1, and Kúnos, 17, quoted in the note to No. 1100), and in at least one instance, to a sunglass, or "burning glass" (Wingate, 19, quoted in the note to No. 1100).

Comparisons of the eyes to water are collected in the notes to Nos. 1044 and 1176, and comparisons to lights are mentioned in the headnote to Nos. 1189–1191, n. 3. Riddles comparing the eyes to inanimate objects other than windows, mirrors, sunglasses, lights, and bodies of water are cited in the headnote to Nos. 1003–1004, § 3. Living creatures to which the eyes are compared are: infants (see the headnote to No. 1044, n. 5); birds (see the headnote to Nos. 1003–1004, §1, and the headnote to Nos. 1100–1108, n. 20); and quadrupeds (see the headnote to Nos. 1003–1004, § 2, and a Russian riddle, Sadovnikov, 1729, quoted in the note to No. 1100).

1145. The riddler has probably reversed the colors.

1146. (No actor is mentioned.) Flemish: Joos, 549 (A red house, white chairs, a red carpet). French: De la Suie, *Savoie*, p. 473 (Who is in a palace surrounded by little tabourets?).

1147. (In the following parallels there is an actor, who is a dancer.) German: Haffner, 111; Hanika-Otto, 223 (*Timmerl-tammerl*, it dances in the room, it cannot go far out the door; there is a bone lattice in front of it), which includes the notion of a fence discussed in the headnote to No. 1149 of the present collection; Renk, *Tyrol*, 8. Swiss: Zahler, *Münchenbuchsee*, 426. French: Dardy, *L'Albret*, p. 333 (In a little room there are four little chairs; a little lady dances in the middle; she goes out neither by night nor by day). Spanish, Argentinian: Lehmann-Nitsche, 337 (dancer in a red dress). Italian: Tschiedel, 28, 29 (white divans, red dancer); Coronedi-Berti, *Archivio*, II (1883), 576, No. 16; Salvioni, *ibid.*, IV (1885), 540, No. 9; Cimegotto, *ibid.*, XIII (1894), 436, No. 28. Turkish: Kowalski, *Zagadki*, 49 (In a gloomy glen a young lady in vermilion dances). Indian, Parsee: Munshi, p. 409 (Sunabai dances in a box).

1148. (In the following parallels, the actor is not a dancer.) Breton: Duine, *Saint-Malo*, p. 516 (A beautiful lady in her palace surrounded by her thirty-two white chickens); Sébillot, *Devinettes*, 55c. German: Haffner, 114. Danish: Kristensen, p. 93, § 233, No. 360, and p. 138, § 399, No. 638 (white chairs, red room, girl in a red dress). Walloon: Colson, *Wallonia*, IV, 108, No. 116a = *Revue des traditions populaires*, VII (1892), 10 (A king dressed in red, a palace of flesh and bone, two rows of soldiers), and p. 109, No. 121 (Thirty-two white ladies in thirty-two red armchairs). For other comparisons of teeth to soldiers see, in the present collection, the headnote to No. 841, § 1. French: Baissac, *Mauritius*, p. 421 (My salon is tapestried in red; within, many little white chairs; the man-servant wipes them with a red cloth). Spanish, Argentinian: Lehmann-Nitsche, 250 (a dark chatterer), 415 (a woman imprisoned for talking too much). Chilean: Flores, 399. Italian: Tammi, 4 (a master in red). Lithuanian: Jurgelionis, 176 (A very pretty little room full of threshers; among the threshers lies a red dog). For this comparison to threshers see, in the present collection, the headnote to No. 841, § 4; and for this comparison of the tongue to a red dog see the headnote to No. 1151, nn. 2–8. Polish: Gustawicz, 129 (A gentleman in a red mansion; sometimes he talks, sometimes he is silent). Russian: Sadovnikov, 1749 (A babbler lives in a birch grove). Indian, Bhil: Hedberg, p. 880, No. 96 (In a little chamber not bigger than a water jar a prattling woman talks).

1149. German: Wossidlo, 42d. Walloon: Colson, *Wallonia*, IV, 108, No. 113 (What is a red garden with red hedges?), and p. 109, No. 120 (A red calf that is leaping behind a white hedge). Serbian: Novaković, p. 66, No. 7 (A watermill fenced with thorns). Modern Greek: Abbott, p. 311, No. 19 (A fence of stakes all around the pen, and in the midst a squealing hen); Polites, *Neohellenika Analekta*, I, 215, No. 126 (An ivory garden and a singing nightingale). Armenian: Wingate, 15 (I have a granary the Lord hath wrought with marble pillars ranged round about). Georgian: Blechsteiner, p. xlvi; No. 2 (My little vegetable garden is bordered with stones). African, SeSuto: Norton and Velaphe, 36 (The little reed-fence of the mother Knock-knock). Kundu: Ittmann, *Kundu*, 124 (Fences that are closely surrounded with fence-posts). Nandi: Hollis, *Nandi*, 71 (What is the wall inside a man's house which was made by the spirits?).

1150a, 1150b. (Wet object.) Spaniards compare the tongue and the mouth to a well and a rope; see Demófilo, 135 and 138 through 140; Rodríguez Marín, 310 through 313. Chilean: Flores, 100 through 102. See further, German: Frischbier, *Menschenwelt*, p. 242, No. 5. French: Constantin, *Savoie*, p. 20. Italian: Schneller, *Wälschtirol*, p. 255, No. 16 (I know a little board under a roof, it is always wet). Modern Greek: Polites, *Neohellenika Analekta*, I, 219, No. 149 (An old wooden plank soaking in the water); Stathes, p. 339, No. 47 (I have a little board that is always damp). Arabic: Ruoff, p. 17, No. 10 (A well full of water. It is never dry all its life). Turkish: Katanov in Radlov, IX, 286, No. 211 (Warming a little patch in the sun, I could not dry it). African, Hausa: Tremearne, p. 59, No. 10 (I washed my calabash, I went east with it, I went west with it, but it did not dry.—Dog's tongue).

For comparisons of the tongue to a wet plank that does not rot, or to a rag, see, in the present collection, the headnote to No. 1150.

1153. Compare No. 1517.

1154. Polish: Kopernicki, 94 (It is always pottering around the poor man's hut.— Poverty). African, Slave Coast: Trautmann, p. 102 (A little switch that chases mother and daughter from their field.—Hunger). For other versions of this very obscure riddle see, in the present collection, Nos. 969 and 1050 and the note to No. 1050.

1156a through 1156g. Parallels seem to be lacking, and no collector offers an explanation of this curious sequence. Little or no light is thrown on the English riddle by the remote similarity of the curious Turkish heart riddle (Zavarin, *Brusa*, 3): "I went to the bazar. I bought a pitcher, thinking it was empty. The man gave it, saying, 'It is full.' I came home [and] mixed one *oka* [a measure] of sour milk, thinking it was very thick, with forty *okas* of water. Then, I went to Top Kanē [artillery arsenal] and seized a cannon ball in my hand, thinking it was a trumpet, and they seized me, saying, 'He's a madman!'"

1157a, 1157b. A connection with the Cup of Death discussed by Carleton Brown ("Poculum Mortis in Old English," *Speculum*, XV [1940], 389–399) seems obvious. Possibly the Turkish heart riddle, "On an unmade wall sits an unborn child" (Kúnos, 145), is related to these themes.

1158a, 1158b. The answer "ear-wax" seems to be a casual substitution without importance.

1159a through 1159d. Irish: Christiansen, 37. German: Wossidlo, 31. Swedish: Ström, p. 196, "Ägget," 4 (A yellow house in a white house; to enter the yellow house you must break apart the white house). Spanish: Demófilo, p. 395, No. 62. Russian: Sadovnikov, 545 (Strong-city, White-city, in the White-city there lives a brother to wax). Indonesian, Malay: Klinkert, p. 47, No. 7 (Chest in a chest, white and yellow in the chest).

1159d. "Posmet" or "posmat" is an obsolete word signifying "cup" or "pot."

1161. Compare Portuguese: Parsons, *Cape Verde*, 1a (My house of grass, inside my house of grass a house of tiles, inside my house of tiles a tank of water.—Coconut).

1162a through 1163. The element "on the hill" is also used in Nos. 910*h*, 916*f*.

1164. The meaning of the riddle is obscure. Probably we should supply "house" after "white."

1165a through 1165c. The Modern Greek spoon riddle, "A hollow ship with freight of slops, / Inside a cave her anchor drops" (Abbott, p. 311, No. 20), also makes a comparison to a ship. See further, in the present collection, the headnote to Nos. 412–413, n. 14; see also Polish: Gustawicz, 92 (Many guests rode over a linden bridge.—Beans). White Russian: Jurkevich, p. 293 (Little birds were running along a linden bridge, slap into a bog.—Peas).

1166. Compare No. 1070, in which the rose growing outside the garden (single man) is to be selected rather than the rose within. Both these texts bear some resemblance to the "tricky question" type of riddle quoted and discussed in the headnote to Nos. 1101 (see especially nn. 12–13).

1167. Filipino: Starr, *Philippines*, 97 (I saw two boats; only one person was aboard). Hawaiian: Judd, 191 (My double canoe, it sails by day, it sails by night, with two bowsprits and two sterns.—The feet).

1170. The riddler's intentions are not entirely clear, and the manner of description does not agree with that usually employed for the sun. In Nos. 1189, 1190, the headnote to Nos. 1189–1191, and the note to Nos. 1189, 1190, the sun or moon is called a lamp or light. Some riddles for the sun call it an article of food; see the headnote to Nos. 1230–1234.

Compare such parallels as the Irish "A golden saddle on a muddy road.—The reflection of the sun or moon in a water hole" (Delargy, 55); the Swedish "Gold lies in the courtyard; is there no one to salvage it?" (Ström, p. 207, "Solen," 13), which has a slight resemblance to the Hickamore Hackamore riddle (see the headnote to Nos. 748–749 of the present collection); the Estonian "A golden apple on a golden platter" (Dido, 30, parallels to which are cited in the present collection, in the headnotes to No. 1094, nn. 5–6, and to No. 1095, nn. 2–3); the Turkish "A handful of *mojane* [a yellow substance used to color foods] in order that the world may tint itself" (Kowalski, *Zagadki*, 134); and the Yakut "It is said that a golden ball has gone wandering of its own accord" (Popov, p. 283).

1171. The usual conception is that of a barrel without a hole. For parallels see Irish: O Dalaigh, 57 (A barrel on the shore and both ends closed), 58 (A little white bag with both ends sewn up); Delargy, 28 (A barrel on the strand with both ends closed); De Bhaldraithe, 33 (A barrel on the lake, without a stave, without measure). Flemish: Joos, 261 through 263; *Ons Volksleven*, II (1890), 104, No. 16. Luxemburg: De la Fontaine, 1. German: Wossidlo, 25. Danish; see the headnote to No. 1140, n. 2, in the present collection (a barrel without a bunghole and yet containing two kinds of wine). French: Rolland, 64 (barrel without a hoop); Mensignac, *Gironde*, 48, 49; Parsons, *Antilles*, III, 380, Martinique, 7, p. 391, Dominica, 18, p. 399, Guadaloupe, 12, p. 410, Les Saintes, 16, and p. 448, Hayti, 12. Basque: Cerquand, 43. Italian: Pitrè, 872; Ferraro, *Archivio*, XXI (1902), 541, No. 18 (barrel without a hole). Lithuanian: Jurgelionis, 803 (barrel without hoops). Polish: Gustawicz, 114 through 118, 122, 123, 124 (A tiny barrel without a stopper); Siarkowski, 7; Kopernicki, 24 (A tiny barrel of wine; there is no opening to it); Saloni, *Rzeshów*, 51 (A keg of wine, and there's no hole in it), 52 (A little keg of wine, and there's no hole in it), 53 (A little barrel of wine, and there's no hoop on it), 54. White Russian: Wasilewski, 18 (There's a keg without a nail, without a hole), 77 (A little keg full of wine, nowhere any hole). Russian: Sadovnikov, 539 (The barrel is full of wine; it has neither staves nor bottom), 540, 541. Surinam: Herskovits, p. 439, No. 29 (My mother has a barrel. It has no opening, but it holds water), 29a (My mother has a barrel. It has no hoops, but it holds water). Indian, Bhil: Hedberg, p. 881, No. 103 (One jar has no mouth).

Basque and Spanish riddlers show a particular liking for the concept of a barrel without a plug; see Basque: Demófilo, p. 378, No. 6. Spanish: Rodríguez Marín, 372. Argentinian: Lehmann-Nitsche, 489 (A little barrel without a bung), 534. Dominican Rep.: Andrade, 174. Porto Rican: Mason, 286.

For the comparison of an egg to a barrel holding two kinds of wine see the headnote to No. 1140, n. 1, of the present collection. An egg is also compared to a house that can be entered or left only with difficulty (No. 1141), to a house made by God (see the headnote to No. 1187, § 2, and to a garment without a seam (see the note to No. 1213) or a dish without a crack (No. 1213).

1172a through 1173j. Scotch Gaelic: Nicolson, p. 49. Irish: De Bhaldraithe, 57. Danish: Feilberg, *Ordbog*, III, 61, s.v. "ring." Norwegian: Christie, 66; Bugge, *Telemarken*, 108; Brox, *Ytre Senja*, 109. Swedish: Dybeck, *Runa*, 1850, p. 37, No. 35; Ericsson, *Södermanland*, II (1881), 98, No. 103; Ström, p. 166, "Ring," 1, 2; Russwurm, *Eibo*, p. 134, §316, No. 38 (A tun of flesh with an iron ring). French: Rolland, 198 (What is round and has no bottom?); Fleury, *Basse-Normandie*, p. 370; Baissac, *Mauritius*, p. 413; Parsons, *Antilles*, III, 378, St. Lucia, 24, p. 389, Martinique, 2, p. 399, Guadaloupe, 13, and p. 448, Hayti, 11. Spanish, Argentinian: Lehmann-Nitsche, 488, 646. Dominican Rep.: Andrade, 31 through 33. Italian: Pitrè, 22; Salvioni, *Archivio*, IV (1885), 542, No. 24; Balladoro, *ibid.*, XVI (1897), 230, No. 31; Tschiedel, 2 (Roundish round, basin without a bottom, it is not a basin. Whoever guesses is a great hero). Rumanian: Gorovei, 958. Lithuanian: Jurgelionis, 247 (A bottomless well), 248 (A barrel of meat, a hoop of iron), 524 (A pot full of meat, both ends open). Lettish: Bielenstein, 215 (A well without bottom), 216 (A little, little barrel full of fresh meat), 450 (A little meat barrel with brass hoop), 897 (A little tub of meat, a band of gold). Lappish: Qvigstad, 56. Finnish: Aarne and Krohn, 171 = Henssen, 140; Lönnrot, 1864 = Henssen, 70. Estonian: Wiedemann, pp. 275 (A barrel of flesh, a silver [var.: copper, iron] ring), 285. Zyrian: Wichmann, *Zyrian*, 166. Mordvin: Ahlqvist, p. 39, No. 5 = Paasonen, 261 (A hole of silver, the plug of flesh). Cheremiss: Wichmann, *Cheremiss*, 123. Gypsy: Wlislocki, 9 (It has no bottom, it has no lid, and yet it is filled with flesh).

1173c. (References to the use of the ring.) Breton: Charlec, *Dol-de-Bretagne*, 1903, p. 288 (The wisest young girl made the best use of it). Walloon: Colson, *Devinettes*, No. 37 (A very round hole which has no bottom and is good for marriage).

1173j. The riddler has carelessly substituted a reference to water for the original reference to flesh and blood. He has taken this from such riddles as Welsh: Hull and Taylor, 259 (What is exceedingly full of holes [and] still holds water?—A chain holding a pot); also No. 1461 in the present collection and the three German riddles cited in the note to Nos. 1461, 1462.

1174. Indonesian, Tabaru: Fortgens, 19 (A bamboo vat of water has been turned upside down and it does not pour out.—Sugar cane). Compare, in the present collection, Nos. 1105c through 1105e, the note to Nos. 1105a through 1105e, and many riddles quoted in the note to Nos. 1199a through 1199d.

1175. African, Kamba: Lindblom, 33 (It is a little water in the taro leaves).

1176. French: Baissac, *Mauritius*, pp. 418–419 (I have two pretty bowls, each one has a billow in the middle and plants at the edge; when they overflow, you see water pouring from each one; but you cannot see the channel leading the water to these bowls). For a comparison of the eye to a lake, a pool, or a tank with vegetation at its edge see, in the present collection, No. 1044 and the corresponding note and headnote. Portuguese: Parsons, *Cape Verde*, 211 (My little chest of *calafache* [a meaningless word], before it closes it spills over), 257b (My little gourd jar, before it fills up it spills). Spanish: Demófilo, p. 429, No. 5. Argentinian: Lehmann-Nitsche, 514. Chilean: Flores, 516 (two crystal fountains). Serbian: Novaković, p. 226, No. 1 (The rabbit jumped into the sea; the sea got tired of it but the rabbit did not.—Splinter in the eye). Mordvin: Paasonen, 243 (An oak fell in the lake, the oak began to weep). Astrakhan Calmuck: Kotvich, 12 (A camel fell into the sea; the camel feels no discomfort but the sea does), 13 (A two-year-old colt fell into the sea . . .). African, Kamba: Lindblom, 51 (Tell me the white ditch where the water never dries up). Songaï: Hamouda, 26 (I have planted my bit of straw, it made all the sea boil). Togo: Schönhärl, 72 (There are two streams. Both become murky, if an ant [the translator is uncertain of the word] falls into either one). Pangwe: Tessman, 130 (A honeysucker sits on the branch of a *Copaifera Tessmannii*, the *Copaifera* will break). The honeysucker is tiny; the *Copaifera* is the largest tree in the forest. Indian, Baiga: Elwin, p. 472, No. 82 (Touch the place and a spring gushes forth). Indonesian, Tabaru: Fortens, 7 (A sea, people are hanging round about).

The comparison of the eyes to pools, as in the Yakut "Between two lakes there is found a small knoll, so they say" (Piekarski, 174) or in the Indonesian "It is a mountain ridge, but it has two harbors" (Malay: Tauern, *Patasiwa*, p. 70), resembles some riddles in the headnote to Nos. 1100–1108 of the present collection (e.g., the riddles for a cat, cited in nn. 29–30). The comparison of pools and eyes is at least as old as the Song of Songs: "Thine eyes are like the fishpools of Heshbon, by the gate of Bethrabbin" (7:4). In a Serbian riddle (Novaković, p. 99, No. 3) and in an Albanian riddle (Hahn, p. 159, No. 1), quoted in the note to No. 1100 of the present collection, the eyes are likened to springs.

The Duala "What tool does not get dirty?" (Ebding, 39) employs an entirely different theme from any discussed here, but involves a reference to the water flowing from the eye.

1177. Compare with this riddle Nos. 1165a and the riddles for a spring cited in the headnote to No. 1193, § 3.

1180. Close parallels seem to be lacking. At least the conclusion—and perhaps more—of this English riddle is adapted from such nursery rhymes for dandling or tossing a child as "Here we go up, up, up, /And here we go down, down, down" or "Here goes my lord / A trot, trot, trot." Compare also the Argentinian Spanish "Thirty-two women seated in chairs" (Lehmann-Nitsche, 460) and similar riddles in the notes to Nos. 1146, 1147, and 1148 of the present collection. In some riddles the mouth and teeth are called a room and its furnishings (see, for example, the headnote to Nos. 1145–1148). See also No. 118, which describes a tree as continually rocking.

1181. Compare No. 398, which describes thunder as the groaning of a cow.

1182. African, Kamba: Lindblom, 14 (A wife sitting on three stools). See also, in the present collection, No. 1110 and the headnote to No. 68, n. 4.

1183. Compare No. 1070, which represents a man already married as a flower that cannot be plucked; see also the headnote to No. 1070.

1185. Compare the Evhe scorpion riddle, "My father gives me a chair. I cannot sit in it until I die" (F. Müller, p. 156, No. 1).

1187a, 1187b. Welsh: Hull and Taylor, 156, 157. Welsh Gypsy: Sampson, 17. French: Parsons, *Antilles*, III, 448, Hayti, 15. Basque: Cerquand, 43 = Demófilo, p. 372, No. 1 (A locked box without a key). Spanish: Demófilo, p. 344, No. 19. Chilean: Laval, 38. Modern Greek: Dieterich, *Rätseldichtung*, p. 93, citing Polites, *Neohellenika Analekta*, I, 209, No. 93 (On a tree there hangs a locked box). Turkish: Kowalski, *Asia Minor*, 21; Zavarin, *Brusa*, 14 (On the tree is a chest with a lock). Indian, Ho: Sarkar, p. 251, No. 26 (You cannot open a lock locked by grandmother.—Fruit of the āsan tree). Khāriā: Roy and Roy, II, 453, No. 39 (Will you be able to open the box of the princess?—Fruit of the āsan tree). Kolarian: Wagner, 16 (The king's and the queen's basket you cannot open.—The fruit of the haṭna tree).

1188. French: Parsons, *Antilles*, III, 392, Dominica, 28, p. 403, Guadaloupe, 66, and p. 413, Marie Galante, 2. Turkish: Kúnos, 60 (I have a box, there are two slices of bread in it).

1189, 1190. Irish: Christiansen, 15; Hyde, p. 170 (A great, great house it is, a golden candlestick it is. Guess it rightly, let it not go by thee); Delargy, *Inis Cé*, 25 (A house, a big house, a gold candlestick. Begin it right and don't let it go by). Portuguese: Parsons, *Cape Verde*, 266 (I have a great mirror which lights all the world.—Sun). Modern Greek: Polites, *Neohellenika Analekta*, I, 217, No. 139 (A small pot of oil lights the whole world). African, Kamba: Lindblom, 69 (The lamp ours.—Moon). Swahili: Velten,

80 (A light burns all night long without oil or wick). Togo: Schönhärl, 120 (A lighted torch of [an oily wood] looks into every city.—Moon). Kundu: Ittmann, *Kundu*, 145 (I have two lamps, they have no oil, yet they shine).

See also, in the present collection, No. 1170 and the corresponding note, and Schultz, *Bemerkungen*, p. 369.

1191. The import of the riddle is not clear.

1192. French: J. Roux, *Limousin*, 32; Haurigot, *French Guiana*, p. 120; Parsons, *Antilles*, III, 367, Trinidad, 50, p. 379, St. Lucia, 32, p. 397, Dominica, 114, p. 417, Marie Galante, 81, and p. 450, Hayti, 47. Basque: Vinson, 65; Cerquand, 23. Spanish: Demófilo, 773, 778, p. 344, No. 20, and p. 396, No. 64 (letter); Rodríguez Marín, 788, 789. Argentinian: Lehmann-Nitsche, 637. Chilean: Flores, 546, 547. Dominican Rep.: Andrade, 237. Porto Rican: Mason, 429. Italian: Pitrè, 155; Corsi, *Archivio*, X (1891), 398, No. 10; Tschiedel, 11. Rumanian: Gorovei, 938. Russian: Sadovnikov, 2139 (One will not break it against a corner, but one will break it on water). Serbian: Novaković, p. 231, Nos. 2 (Hit it against a tree and it does not break; throw it into water and it breaks), 3 (I hit it against a rock and it does not break; I hit it against water and it breaks). Bulgarian: Chacharov, 134 (Place it in water and it will suffer dissolution, place it on the ground and it will not suffer dissolution). Modern Greek: Polites, *Neohellenika Analekta*, I, 235, No. 259 (A ring like a pillar, proud and tall, fell from the tower and did not crack.—Roll of paper). Surinam: Herskovits, p. 439, No. 33 (My mother stands on the ceiling; she flings a large basket of plates on the ground, but no one is broken.—Paper), 33a (My father has a pot. Coming from the river, it fell, but did not break.—Letter). Arabic: Giacobetti, 420, 421. Turkish: Zavarin, *Brusa*, 43 (You can throw it from the minaret, and it won't die. Throw it into water, and it will die); Kúnos, 90 (I dropped it from a hill, it did not perish. I dropped it from a rock, it did not die, but it died in a spoonful of water), 199 (Falling from the minaret, it does not break; falling into water, it breaks). Crimean Tatar: Filonenko, 85 (Wherever I throw it, it doesn't break. If it falls into water, it doesn't break). The negative in the second sentence seems to be an error. Armenian: Seidlitz, p. 70, No. 6; Wingate, 10 (I rolled it down a mountain, it was not broken. I dragged it through the valley, it was borne by breezes. I placed a stone upon it, it was not broken. I dropped it into water, it fell into pieces); Zelinski, p. 58, No. 26 (I hit it against the earth, it did not tear. I hit it against a stone, it did not tear. I threw it into water, [then] it tore). Cherekessian: Tambiev, p. 61, No. 89 (If it falls from the sky, it does not break open; if it falls into the water, it breaks apart). African, Lamba: Doke, 67 (That which does not break.—A leaf when it falls from afar). Louyi: Jacottet, 3 (My father's gourd, when it falls, it does not break.—A leaf). Indian, Kashmiri: Knowles, 19 (It went to court, it went to court, and on seeing the water it died).

1193. The ants crawling in great numbers out of a hole and scattering in all directions resemble a plate. If they are disturbed, the plate is broken, but only temporarily.

1194. Modern Greek: Polites, *Neohellenika Analekta*, I, 243, No. 280 (I shine, I shine like glass. I fall and do not break). Georgian: Blechsteiner, 33 (I struck it with a saber and made no impression). Svanian: J. Nizheradze, pp. 68–69, No. 29 (One perceives no blow on it). African, Bakongo: Denis, 32 (That which is not cut). Basuto: Rolland, p. 169, No. 1 (There is a thing that falls from the top of the mountains without breaking, do you know it?). Taveta: Hollis, *Taveta*, p. 208, No. 43 (I have cut [it], yet I see no mark). Malagasy: Sibree, p. 39, No. 12 (Cut, yet no wound is seen).

1197. The arrangement of the answers seems to be confused. For discussion of the theme see the headnote to No. 1070.

1198. The import of the riddle is obscure, but see a similar description of a glass lamp chimney quoted in the headnote to Nos. 1172–1173, §4.

1199a through 1199d. Irish: Christiansen, 28; Delargy, 43 (Four smooth, soft rods walking on the mountain with their mouths beneath them); De Bhaldraithe, 25 (Four big soft rods, outside of the middle of the lake, but not oozing a drop). Scotch Gaelic: Nicolson, p. 39 (A fresh new coque my father brought from Ross, though it be turned mouth downwards not a drop will leave it). French: Parsons, *Antilles*, III, 408, Guadaloupe, 13. Portuguese: Parsons, *Cape Verde*, 81. Serbian: Novaković, p. 19, No. 5 (A little vixen trots along the hill, in a little sack it carries water, it turns abruptly to the hill, yet it does not spill anything). Albanian: Pedersen, 8 (Two pots of honey: day and night they stand with their mouths downward and the honey does not flow out). Arabic: Ruoff, p. 45, No. 22 (Four bottles of rose water, they are neither in heaven nor on earth); Stumme, *Tázerwalt*, 10. Abyssinian: Littmann, *Tigriña*, 10 (Four long-necked clay pots whose openings are turned downward). African, Wamajame: Ovir, 41 (They put it down and yet do not let it flow out). Nandi: Hollis, *Nandi*, p. 134, No. 4 (What produces liquid and yet cannot let liquid flow when it wishes?). Dschagga: Raum, p. 304, No. 3 (It is overturned without spilling). Kanuri: Lukas, p. 170, No. 19 (Even if it is upset, it is not spilled). Aandonga: Pettinen, 17 (The thing is overturned, yet the contents do not flow out). Suk: Beech, p. 45, No. 12 (I-carried-I a-jar-of-water. I-did-not-spill-it-I.—Udder). See other uses of the same conception collected in the note to No. 1174 in the present collection.

Riddlers often call the teats something good to eat; see the Turcoman "Under the park are four loaves of bread" (Samojlvich, 108, with many parallels) and the Turkish "Under a log lie four loaves of bread" (Katanov in Radlov, IX, 241, No. 82).

For references to the fact that rain does not wet the teats, see the headnote to Nos. 961–963, §5, in the present collection.

1199a. The explanation added by the riddler is evidence that he has misunderstood "throw away"; this was used in the sense of "leak" or "spill," as is clear from Nos. 1199*b* and 1199*c*.

1200a, 1200b. Breton: Sauvé, 90*a*, 90*b*; Sébillot, *Haute-Bretagne*, 48*b*. Swedish: Geijer and Campbell, 15. Italian: Salvioni, *Archivio*, IV (1885), 543, No. 30 (Five push, ten pull); Tammi, 3. Lithuanian: Jurgelionis, 261 (Ten men pulled flax across the floor.—Trousers). Polish: Gustawicz, 295, 296; Kopernicki, 38. Estonian: Wiedemann, p. 267. Turkish: Katanov in Radlov, IX, 160, No. 1324 (Mount Altay is lifted by ten men.—Hat put on by two hands), p. 241, No. 78 (Five men are putting old man Oranday on a horse.—Putting on hat), and p. 286, No. 219.

1201. Perhaps a degenerate version of the better personification is No. 1005.

1202. The import of the riddle is not clear.

1203a through 1203c. (Comparison to an animal and a rope.) Portuguese: Parsons, *Cape Verde*, 35 (My white cow tied to a hillside). Bulgarian: Chacharov, 130 (The rope gave birth to a calf). Modern Greek: Abbott, p. 311, No. 25. Arabic: Stumme, *Tázerwalt*, 9 (A green cow which is tied with a green cord.—Gourd). Turkish: Hamizade, 297 (Horses from the court, on the other side eggs.—Pumpkin), 298 (I pull like a rope, it comes like a jar), 299 (Beneath the roof a he-goat is tied, his little tail is [variant: horns are] tied to the sky); Kowalski, *North Bulgaria*, 58 (They stretch themselves long; they bear calves in the grass). Armenian: Grigorov, p. 123, No. 1 (A rope drank its fill of water, but it was a calf that became bloated.—Watermelon and vine). Tatar: Kalashev and Ioakimov, p. 49, No. 16 (The rope will take a drink, the calf will swell up.—Pumpkin). Indian, Bhil: Hedberg, p. 869, No. 20 (The rope is walking and the ox is lying down.—Cucumber). Uraon: Archer, p. 181, No. 23 (The goat sits while the string grows.—Marrow [i.e., bean]). Bengali: Mitra, *Chittagong*, p. 315, No. 25. Baiga: Elwin, p. 465, No. 8 (The ox is tied in the stall, but the yoke walks away). Kolarian: Wagner, 3 (The lamb is lying down, the string is ascending.—Cucumber). Malayalam: Schmolck, p. 242, No. 4 (A young steer lies tied in comfort in the grass to a rope that is long and strong. Yet, it creeps away. What strange thing is this? The steer lies quiet, the rope creeps.—Gourd).

1205. (Comparison to a thing without mention of an animal.) French: Parsons, *Antilles*, III, 416, Marie Galante, 63. Spanish: Demófilo, 899; Rodríguez Marín, 539. Argentinian: Lehmann-Nitsche, 534. Cuban: Massip, 38 (I sowed a plank, a rope sprang up and on the end a billiard ball). Dominican Rep.: Andrade, 41. Porto Rican: Mason, 122, 123.

1206. The import of the riddle is obscure, and the references and meanings of "spetch" (parings or scraps of hides) and of "spooin" are uncertain.

1207. The pun "years: ears" is characteristic of recent riddling. The riddle does not involve a clearly conceived comparison of a hat to another object and must consequently be rated a rather poor invention.

1209. The rather ingenious comparison to a coat is an unusual variation of the well-known coffin riddle (see Nos. 1728 through 1735, the parallels in the corresponding note and in the headnote to Nos. 1728–1737, and the discussion in that headnote). In the coffin riddle a rather vaguely conceived object, which in many instances could be an article of dress, is alluded to in terms of those who order it made, those who make it, and those who use it. A Flemish riddler thinks of a specific garment in "A vest without sleeves. He who has it must keep it; he who sees it doesn't want it; and he who has it doesn't know it" (Joos, 111). The garment is the correct answer—instead of the wrong answer implied or suggested, as it usually is—in a Javanese riddle based on the idea of something made by one who does not use it and used by one who does not make it (Ranneft, *Proza*, p. 43, No. 196). See also No. 656 in the present collection for the conception of a coffin as a black dress trimmed with silver buttons.

1210. This text based on the coffin riddle (for which see Nos. 1728 through 1735 and the headnote to Nos. 1728–1737) has absorbed elements belonging to one of the riddles for a bed (Nos. 1596a through 1596c). The effectiveness of the present riddle, and also of the bed riddle just mentioned, depends largely on punning, since the puzzle is based in part on the double meanings of both the words "made" and "keep."

1211. An unusual version of the riddle for a hole, a well, or a pit. See Nos. 1111a through 1112, which compare a hole or grave to a stick, a piece of twine, or a door, and Nos. 1691a through 1695, which compare a ditch or a hole to an unnamed something that is made larger by taking from it.

1212a, 1212b. Lithuanian: Jurgelionis, 850 (In a dark room there sits one who sews without thread or needle), 852 (There sits a maiden in a dark chamber; she weaves without a loom and heddles). Russian: Sadovnikov, 1427 (In a dark cell handsome maidens knit without thread or needle), and 1428 through 1435.

1213. Breton: Sébillot, *Haute-Bretagne*, 21a (What has neither flesh nor bone and has a little white shirt that has neither seam nor cuffs?); Kerbeuzec, *Ille-et-Vilaine*, 20 (A little pocket without a seam); Sébillot, *Devinettes*, 17a. German: Frischbier, *Thierwelt*, p. 353, No. 57, and the Masurian (a dialect related to Polish) "A bundle without a seam" (Frischbier, *ibid.*, p. 355, No. 78). Walloon: Colson, *Wallonia*, IV, 61, No. 54b. French: Rolland, 66 = Ledieu, *Démuin*, p. 132 (Who has a little white cloak without seam or cuffs?); Lacuve, *Poitou*, p. 355, No. 53 (Who has a sack of a mixture without a corner or seam?). Spanish: Demófilo, 547 (shirt without a seam). Russian: Sadovnikov, 548 (The little white sheepskin coat is sewn without seams). Malagasy: Sibree, p. 39, No. 15 (A little bag whose stitching is invisible).

1215. (Three or more comparisons.) Breton: Kerbeuzec, *Ille-et-Vilaine*, 63 (cloth, money, apple). Dutch: Sinninghe, p. 5, No. 1 (My mother knows a sheet that she can't fold. My father knows an apple that he can't peel. My sister knows stars [the riddler anticipates the answer] that she can't count); Boekenoogen, p. 40 (sheet, apple, pearls). Flemish: Joos, 536 (sheet, apple, money); *Ons Volksleven*, I (1889), 78, No. 33 (sheet, apple, money). Swedish: Dybeck, *Runa*, 1849, p. 48, No. 16 = Russwurm, 82 (Our mother [the earth] has a cover that no one can fold; our father [God] has more coins than anyone can count; our brother [Christ] has an apple that no one can bite), which includes explanatory references offered by either the riddler or the collector. It seems obvious that our mother is Our Lady. This seems to be supported by Dybeck's parallel from Södermanland: "Mother [Mary] has a bull that no one can carve, father has money that no one can count," in which the explanation of "mother" may have been made by the riddler. See further, Ericsson, *Södermanland*, II (1881), 97, No. 95 (My father has money that no one can count; he has a sheet that no one can sew; he has a wagon that no one can push; he has an apple that no one can bite), in which the wagon is Charles's Wain, or the Great Bear; Sandén, *Norra Vadsbo*, 116 ([money; sheet]; sister has a firkin that no one can open; brother a bull that no one can carve); Geijer and Campbell, 76 (sheet, money, bull, apple); Ström, p. 203, "Himmelen," 2 (money, sheet, barrel, bun). Walloon: Colson, *Wallonia*, IV, 43, Nos. 10a (A large shroud that one cannot fold, gold pieces that one cannot collect, an apple that one cannot peel), 10b through 10d. French: Rolland, 9a (My father has a cover that he cannot fold, my mother has a ball that she cannot roll, my sister has so many crowns [coins] that she cannot carry them), 9b (My father has so many crowns that he cannot count them, my mother has so large a veil that she cannot fold it, my sister has so large an apple that she cannot eat it); Rolland, *Rimes*, pp. 195–197, Nos. 2a through 2d; Orain, *Ille-et-Vilaine*, p. 153 (apple, cloth, money); Carnoy, *Picardy*, p. 53 (My father has an apple that he cannot eat; my sister has a mirror in which she cannot see herself; my mother has a cloth that she cannot fold; and my father has crowns that he cannot count); Parsons, *Antilles*, III, 393, Dominica, 52 (cheese, money, cloth), and p. 418, Marie Galante, 96 (money, cheese, cloth). Spanish, Argentinian: Lehmann-Nitsche, 555a through 555i (sheet, money, mirror); Cuban: Giménez Cabrera, 10 (sheet, money, apple). Porto Rican: Mason, 165 (sheet, marble, money). Italian: Tschiedel, 23 (cloth, money, apple).

For the comparisons of the moon (sun) to an apple see the headnote to No. 1095, nn. 1–3; of the sky to a blanket, Nos. 1217, 1219, 1221; and of the sky with stars to a blanket with objects on it, No. 1226. In a Kundu riddle quoted in the headnote to No. 1094, n. 6, the moon is called a large palm nut among small, worthless nuts.

1216. The mention of four elements is unusual; a few examples will be found in the note to No. 1215. The description of "water" shows some similarity to the riddle calling snow a blanket, quoted in the headnote to Nos. 1219–1220, nn. 2–7.

1217. Irish: Christiansen, 2b. French: Parsons, *Antilles*, III, 377, St. Lucia, 4, p. 383, Martinique, 44, and p. 411, Les Saintes, 37. Serbian: Novaković, p. 142, No. 4 (One bolt of cloth covers the whole world), which is allied to the snow riddles discussed in the headnote to Nos. 1219–1220 of the present collection). The sky and the earth are referred to as two blankets; see the note to Nos. 1252a, 1252b.

1218. This may be a confused version of Nos. 1218a, 1218b.

1219. Walloon: Colson, *Wallonia*, IV, 42, No. 4 (A great sheet that is on our roof is more beautiful than fire). Russian: Sadovnikov, 1806 (A little blue fur coat has covered the entire world).

1220. African, Kxatla: Schapera, 9 (Tell me: mat spread yourself and then remove yourself).

1221 through 1223. This special Antillean variety is an excellent illustration of the development of a local type. It is used to make riddles having different answers.

1224 through 1225b. (Sheet, money.) Afrikaans: Groenewald, p. 85, citing *De Brand*-

wag, VII, 32 (My father has more sheep than he can count; my mother has a sheet so large that she can never fold it up). The comparison to countless sheep seems to be intrusive; see Nos. 484a through 484d of the present collection. Spanish, Cuban: Massip, 58 (money, sheet). Dominican Rep.: Andrade, 116 (sheet, money). New Mexican: Espinosa, 29 (sheet, money); Campa, 63 (Jesus Christ has money which he cannot count; Mary the Most Holy, a sheet that she cannot fold). Italian: Coronedi-Berti, *Archivio*, II (1883), 576, No. 1 (sheet, money). Tatar: Kalashev and Ioakimov, p. 60, No. 2 (Grandfather has a robe, it is impossible to fold it. Its middle is full of gold pieces; one cannot count them). Indian, Kashmiri: Knowles, 5 (First rose the guru's wife with four *lakhs* [a very large number]. Then arose Shark, the Mulla, and took and lifted up his axe at her.—Moon, stars, sun). Knowles supplies "of bodies" after "*lakhs*," but the parallels suggest that "of coins" would be more suitable. The name Shark suggests an Arabic word-root used to refer to the rising of the sun.

1224. The riddler has obviously forgotten to mention the coins, but has retained the act associated with them.

1226. (A sheet, rug, or blanket filled with crumbs, stones, or lice.) Danish: Kristensen, p. 44, §111, Nos. 156a, 156b. French: Baissac, *Mauritius*, p. 410. Portuguese: Parsons, *Cape Verde*, 271 (A black shawl loaded to the mouth with chicken lice). Italian: Tschiedel, 22. Lithuanian: Jurgelionis, 85 (A cloth full of crumbs and flakes of bread), 87 (A table full of crumbs), 346. Lappish: Qvigstad, 78 (What is it, if a skin [pelt] is spread over a rooftree and it is full of lice?—Sky and spots free of clouds). Turcoman: Samojlvich, 21 (I cannot shake a heavy blanket, I cannot pour out small stones). This suggests the nomad sleeping on a rug on sand.

Other objects are occasionally mentioned in a similar context. See the Lithuanian "A yard full of wooden pokers" (Jurgelionis, 88), which may imply that the ends of the pokers are glowing, and the analogous "A cloth full of embers" (his No. 86); the Bulgarian "I have a skin covered with golden nails" (Bozhov, 81); and the Arabic "I have a cloak full of buttons; it cannot be folded or carried" (Ruoff, p. 13, No. 16 = Littmann, p. 47). The Nyika "Spread out the mat and let us eat some fruit" (Hollis, *Nyika*, p. 137, No. 5) resembles also the comparison of stars to fruit or nuts in a dish or sieve (see the headnote to Nos. 1093–1095 of the present collection).

The Votyak use this comparison to describe malt: "On the stone a blanket of lice" (Wichmann, *Votyak*, 76).

1227a through 1227c. French: Parsons, *Antilles*, III, 384, Martinique, 66; p. 402, Guadaloupe, 48. Note a special West Indian variety in "The king's table is full of quatresous" (Parsons, *Antilles*, III, 402, Guadaloupe, 59, and p. 411, Les Saintes, 51). I do not understand the Kxatla "Tell me: paper money, God knows how to write.—It is the stars" (Schapera, 5).

1229a, 1229b. For comparisons of the sun or moon to bread or biscuits see the headnote to Nos. 1230–1234.

1229b. In riddles I find no other allusion to the sky as something that does not fall, and it seems reasonable to conjecture that "fall" is a mishearing of "fol'," i.e., "fold." Several proverbs and children's songs refer to the falling of the sky; see Archer Taylor, *An Index to the "Proverb,"* FF Communications, CXIII (Helsinki, 1934), p. 58, and "Formelmärchen," *Handwörterbuch des deutschen Märchens*, II (Berlin, 1934–1940), 185, n. 126.

1230a through 1234. German: Hanika-Otto, 228b, 228c (steak). Lithuanian: Jurgelionis, 80 (A cheese in the well), 81 (Behind an old woman's cottage there hangs a mouthful of bread. Dogs bark, but cannot reach it), 83 (Behind the house a slice of bread), 84 (A loaf of bread sits amidst the peas); Schleicher, p. 204 (In the village there lies a pancake). Polish: Saloni, *Rzeshów*, 90 and 91 (like Lithuanian: Jurgelionis, 84). Serbian: Novaković, p. 129, No. 9 (There is one piece of bacon on the mountain). The usual Serbian form is "one piece of wax suffices for the whole world.—Moon or sun" (Novaković, p. 129, No. 8 = p. 218, No. 4) with the variants "one glass of butter" (p. 218, No. 3), "one cup of honey" (p. 218, No. 6), and "one loaf of bread without lard" (p. 218, No. 7). See further, Zyrian: Wichmann, *Zyrian*, 293 (A buttery boat, a tallowy boat.—Sun, moon). Hungarian: *Magyar Nyelvör*, IX (1880), 89 (A bit of wax that is enough for the whole world). Modern Greek: Dieterich, *Rätseldichtung*, p. 90, citing *Syll. Konst.*, XVIII, 120 (Two fish in a frying pan, one cold, one warm). Turkish: Kowalski, *Asia Minor*, 18 (like the Modern Greek version). Mongolian, Buryat: Gombojew, 1 (A silver dish on the ice). African, Togo: Schönhärl, 116 (My father gave us two yams, yet I do not know which is larger and which is smaller). Indian, Kashmiri: Knowles, 3 (Half a bread and a bowl of machámah [rice pudding].—Half-moon and stars). Bengali: Mitra, *Chittagong*, p. 660, No. 4 (What is like the circular wooden plate [kneading board]? It is a round earthen pot which fulfils the need of all countries alike.— Sun or moon). Kolarian: Wagner, 42 (There are two cow-dung flat cakes in the world). Indonesian, Batak: Ophuijsen, p. 467, No. 81 (A plate of warm rice and a plate cold rice.—Sun, moon). Karo-Batak: Joustra, p. 100 (One comes with hot water, one comes with cold water. Tabaru: Fortgens, 20 (A plate of pap, of which half is warm and half is cold).

1231. The import of the riddle is not entirely clear.

1234. "Duff" is similar to pie, but is boiled, not baked.

1235. This very defective riddle is intelligible only in the light of the parallels. For "bellee" read "belly to belly." Irish: See O Dalaigh, 6. Breton: Sauvé, 27; Charlec, *Dol-de-Bretagne*, 1903, p. 288. Swiss: Rochholz, 449 (Hole against hole, a plug at the hole, and a hand at the hole). Walloon: Colson, *Wallonia*, V, 132, No. 284. French: Rolland, 290; Pineau, *Poitou*, 15; Mensignac, *Gironde*, p. 299, No. 9; Westphalen, *Metz*, col. 201; Ledieu, *Démuin*, p. 136; Baissac, *Mauritius*, p. 422 (Belly on belly, the little end in the crack); Parsons, *Antilles*, III, 414, Marie Galante, 28. Italian: Pitrè, 16. Lithuanian: Schleicher, p. 204. Czech: Feifalik, p. 381, No. 82 (Four knees, two navels, a bit of flesh in the mouth). Polish: Gustawicz, 76 through 78; Siarkowski, 69 (Eye to eye, it looks sincerely; it keeps a piece of meat in a hole; water flows as over a rope). Russian: Sadovnikov, 1714 (Heart to heart, belly to belly, hands under the rump, raw flesh in the mouth).

1236. Irish: Christiansen, 41. Polish: Gustawicz, 127 = Kopernicki, 63 (Boiled in nothing but salt, yet it is never salty); Siarkowski, 96 (What is it that a man buys for three pence, boils in a quart of salt, and then salts some more after it is boiled?—Egg, which is sometimes bought for three pence, placed in a quart jar filled with salt; after it is cooked, it is salted again). Serbian: Novaković, p. 76, No. 2 (I cooked porridge in a thousand pounds of salt, and yet it is not salty). Bulgarian: Gubov, 427 (It remained seven years in salt. When they took it out, it was not salty). Arabic: Ruoff, p. 48, No. 11 (Something, you cook it until it boils, you salt it and you do not salt it). Turkish: Kúnos, 31 (I put water on the fire, I put in the thing in question with its *ōka* [a measure] of salt, and it is still saltless, still saltless). Cherekessian: Tambiev, p. 64, No. 134 (Our little old man eats a lot of salt). Yakut: Piekarski, 152 (What is it that man eats after boiling it in a pound of water to which salt has been added?), 153 (Boiled in salt that weighs a *pud* [measure of weight], man adds more salt to it when he eats it), 154 (They say you boil it a long time in bitter, salty water; just before eating it, you salt it again).

1237a through 1237j. Welsh: Hull and Taylor, 284. Irish: Delargy, *Inis Cé*, 14. German: Wossidlo, 429 (It is not alive, it is not dead; one can, however, make it live, walk, and stand, eat and drink, jump and leap, and die again). Russian: Sadovnikov, 927 (Born with neither legs nor head; when grown, legs as well as head come); Sichler, p. 119.

For the use of the conventional phrase "neither fish, flesh, nor bone" and its variants, see, in the present collection, Nos. 24d, 264a, 265, 392a, 392b, 665, the headnote to Nos. 264–265, the note to Nos. 23 through 24d, the note to No. 24d, and the note to No. 665.

1239a through 1241b. French: Parsons, *Antilles*, III, 447, Hayti, 6 (Something to eat, something to drink, something to throw away). This shows some resemblance to the description of a fruit discussed in the headnote to Nos. 806–815 of the present collection. Spanish, Dominican Rep.: Andrade, 123. Porto Rican: Mason, 178. Surinam: Herskovits, p. 437, No. 14 (My mother goes to market. She buys wood, and food, and water). Indian, Kashmiri: Knowles, 105 (Something to eat, to drink, to gnaw; food for the cow; and something to sow in the garden.—Watermelon). Knowles cites a tale to similar effect and a parallel in the *Madanakámarájankadai* (*The Dravidian Nights*), p. 63. Marco Polo, who mentions the varieties of uses to which a coconut is put, may have heard our riddle; see J. H. Herriott, *California Folklore Quarterly*, II (1943), 11. See further the Catalan fig riddle: "What is that: a thing that yields everything, honey, millet, and cordovan [leather]?" (Milá y Fontanals, 1876, p. 23, No. 5), which refers to the juice, seeds, and skin.

1240. The riddle is not completely intelligible. For a discussion of the allusion to St. John, see the note to Nos. 814a, 814b.

1244a through 1245. African, Kxatla: Schapera, 98 (Tell me: the little pot which cooks up above). Tschuana: Kuhn, *Tschuana*, 34 (A pot from which one partakes while it boils). For other riddles on a pipe or hookah see the headnote to Nos. 1440–1441 and the note to 1440 of the present collection.

1248a through 1248c. For a parallel to the idea that one cannot touch a wasp, see No. 1656.

1249. Arabic: Stumme, *Tázerwalt*, 4 (A fairy whom one may approach and who is [also] forbidden; each of us enjoys its marrow). For the explanation of the first sentence see Leviticus 15:19; the "marrow" is mother's milk. For other riddles on this and related themes see, in the present collection, Nos. 1045, 1070, 1166, and 1197, the notes to Nos. 1045 and 1070, and the headnote to No. 1070.

1252a, 1252b. A few anomalous riddles show some slight resemblances. See Turcoman: Samojlvich, 17 (Just like two frames of a cart), which the collector finds difficult to interpret. He suggests the alternative translation, "Just like two hides," which has an exact parallel in Kirghese (Vasiliev, I, No. 11) and is supported by many texts cited in his note. Compare also the African "Do you know two magnitudes that correspond to each other?—Earth and sky [and twelve other pairs of objects]" (Duala: Ebding, 14).

For comparisons describing heaven and earth as two like objects see Astrakhan Calmuck: Kotvich, 171 (You cannot step over father's sheepskin, you cannot roll up mother's sheepskin.—Earth and sky), 172 (A rug with wool and a rug without wool.—Earth and sky), in which the wool represents fog or clouds. African, Kamba: Lindblom, 25 (Our father's gourd shells are of equal size). Kxatla: Schapera, 1. Masai: Hollis, *Masai*, p. 254, No. 5 (I have two skins, one to lie on and one to cover myself with). Togo: Schönhärl, 116. Tschuana: Kuhn, *Tschuana*, 25 (Two coverlets of equal size). Nuer: Huffman, p. 105, No. 14 (Guess what are two big rugs). Nandi: Hollis, *Nandi*, p. 141, No. 36 (I slaughtered two oxen, one red and the other white, and their hides were alike). Kiniramba: F. Johnson, p. 355, No. 7 (The leaves of the palm are alike). Sesuto: Norton and Velaphe, 1 (The spread-out hides are equal). Kundu: Ittmann, *Kundu*, 33 (Two large leaves), 302 (My father has four large leaves.—Earth and firmament; moon and sun). Nyika: Hollis, *Nyika*, p. 137, No. 5 (I spread out my hyphaene-palm leaf and in the morning it is invisible), which contains a second theme. For this second theme see the headnote to No. 1094 of the present collection. Taveta: Hollis, *Taveta*, p. 205, No. 27 (Father's skin-garments are alike [in size]). Pangwe: Tessmann, 13 (Two large leaf-surfaces). Slave Coast: Trautmann, p. 102 (Immensity and immensity).

The African riddles on this general theme are obviously divisible into several distinct varieties: the comparisons to gourds or calabashes (Kamba), to skins (Masai, Nandi, Taveta), to leaves (Kiniramba, Kundu, Nyika, Pangwe), and to abstractions (Duala, Slave Coast).

1254. Surinam: Herskovits, 95 (My father sent a letter to call his child. Just as the letter arrived, then that self-same moment the child arrived at his father's.—Fisherman, fishhook, and fish).

1256a, 1256b. In both riddles the speaker includes too definite an allusion to the answer. The first of these shows additional corruption.

1275b. The meaning of "message" is obscure.

1258c. Indian, Malayalam: Schmolck, p. 242, No. 35 (The baggage arrives before the traveler).

1259. A comparison to driving a wagon. *Whimiky whamiky* is onomatopoetic. "Lamiky" is probably a rhyming corruption of "lam" (to beat, strike). The riddle draws a picture of a man standing up and lashing a horse. Compare Surinam: Herskovits, 90 (Eight foot falls, *wiriwiri, tikita*.—Two span of horses, the wheels, and the whip).

CHAPTER VIII
ENUMERATIONS OF COMPARISONS
Nos. 1260–1408

1260. Variations of the last clause also occur in riddles for sunlight (Nos. 748a, 748b), for smoke (Nos. 1268a, 1268b), and for a well (Nos. 1286a through 1288, 1315a, 1315b, 1317 through 1318c, 1323, 1325a, 1325b, 1327a, 1328, 1330 through 1332, 1334).

1261a, 1261b. The Scotch Gaelic "Not bigger than a grain of barley, and it covers the table of the king" (Nicolson, p. 37) has only a vague resemblance to this riddle. It belongs rather to the usual manner of describing sight or the eyes, for which see the headnote to No. 1471 in the present collection.

1262. For the theme "comes to the king's table" see the headnote to No. 737. Compare the Russian riddle for pepper, "She is black, she is small, she ran around the entire field and had dinner at the tsar's" (Sadovnikov, 497).

1263a, 1263b. The riddle is most popular in Germanic countries, whence riddlers in the adjoining regions to the east may have borrowed it. See Frisian: Dykstra, *Snypsnaren*, p. 106. Flemish: Joos, 179 (Larger than a louse, smaller than a mouse, in it there are more windows than in a king's house); M[one], *Anzeiger*, VII (1838), col. 371; *Ons Volksleven*, I (1889), 78, No. 40. Afrikaans: Groenewald, p. 80. German: Wossidlo, 224; Frischbier, *Menschenwelt*, p. 249, No. 81; Hanika-Otto, 118. Swiss: Rochholz, 489; Zahler, *Münchenbuchsee*, 90. Faeroic: see the headnote to Nos. 1263–1265 in the present collection. Icelandic: Árnason, 407 (What is bigger than a louse, smaller than a mouse, [it is] staring with all its eyes up to the king's house?). Danish: Kristensen, p. 59, §132, Nos. 191, 191b (Little as a house, brown as a mouse, and it can clothe all the king's house), which includes a final clause usually found in the needle riddle (see the headnote to Nos. 531–534, §2, in the present collection). Swedish: Geijer and Campbell, 71; Ström, pp. 399–400, "Fingerborgen," 1; Sandén, *Norra Vadsbo*, 88 (Larger than a louse, smaller than a mouse, with more windows than the king's house); Russwurm, 25 (A little house, but many windows round about). Walloon: Colson, *Wallonia*, V, 53, Nos. 193, 194 (What is not larger than the head of a mouse and has as many windows as the chateau of Paris?). Lettish: Bielenstein, 441 (A little, little house with countless windows), 442 (A little, little house, two [var.: three, a hundred] windows), 443 (A little, little dwelling, windows round about), 444 (A little house, windows round about, but one can't look through them). Czech: Hanika-Otto, p. 261, No. 58. Serbian: Novaković, p. 141, No. 7 (It is as little as a mouse, yet it has more windows than a king's palace). Finnish: Aarne and Krohn, 280 = Henssen, 63.

1264. Flemish: Joos, 180 (There is a thing, it is smaller than a finch, it has many eyes, and yet it does not see). For the paradox of having eyes and not seeing compare the note to No. 330 in the present collection. Arabic: Ruoff, p. 24, No. 23 (It is as large as a hazelnut and has a thousand protruding eyes).

1265. For the comparison of meshes to windows see the riddle for a fishnet, No. 906 and the corresponding headnote.

1266a, 1266b. French: Rolland, *Rimes*, p. 206, No. 47 (Who throws away his entrails on leaving?). Lithuanian: Jurgelionis, 637 (Žaidė raidė flew through pine forests, left its intestines, and ran home itself). Lappish: Qvigstad, 17. Compare the headnote to Nos. 205–207 in the present collection for the idea of leaving intestines behind, and see the survey of riddles for a gun in the headnote to No. 801.

For the introductory comparison compare also No. 1466.

1267. "Widdicote" is a Devonshire word for "sky"; see Joseph Wright, *English Dialect Dictionary*, VI (London, 1905), 486, s.v.; W. G. Smith and Janet Heseltine, *Oxford Dictionary of English Proverbs* (Oxford, 1935), p. 590.

1268, 1268b. The last clause occurs in various connections; see the English shadow riddle numbered 1260 in this collection, and the English sunlight and well riddles listed in the note to No. 1260.

1268a. According to Halliwell-Phillipps, the collector of the riddle, "wastle" signifies "twig, withy," but the *New English Dictionary*, s.v., gives the more appropriate meaning "dough of the first quality." H. D. Traill (*Social England* [London, 1894], II, 436) defines it as "bread of the second quality." The basket of "wastell cakes" in the coat of arms of Bethlehem ("Bedlam")—the old London hospital for the insane—may refer to the diet of the inmates; see D. H. Tuke, *Chapters in the History of the Insane* (London, 1882), pp. 52–53 note.

1268b. "Wasp" is a corruption of "wastle." Although it is possible that the Bermudan text is derived from Halliwell-Phillipps, the persistence of this rare word is very curious.

1269a through 1272. Most of the parallels here cited include the contrast "high: low" and one or both members of the contrast "bitter: sweet," and all have the answer "nut," though the species of nut varies. The first Rumanian riddle cited is exceptional, in that it has the contrast "bitter: sweet" only. Riddles mentioning colors are cited in the note to Nos. 1273, 1274; those mentioning something prickly or rough in the note to No. 1276.

See German: Wossidlo, 219*a* (small, high; bitter), 219*b* (high, broad; bitter, sweet); Haffner, 31 (high, little; bitter). Swiss: Rochholz, 392 (high, low; hard, small; bitter, sweet); Zahler, *Münchenbuchsee*, 281 (high, small; bitter, sweet). Latin: Reusner, ed. 1602, pp. 282–283 (high, small; sweet, bitter). Walloon: Colson, *Wallonia*, IV, 92, No. 91 (As big as a giant, as little as a mouse, as bitter as soot). French: V. S., *Mélusine*, I (1878), col. 255, No. 17 (low, high; bitter, sweet), col. 264, No. 82 (high, low; bitter, sweet). Catalan: Pelay y Briz, p. 207, No. 55 (high, round; sweet, bitter). Spanish: Demófilo, p. 385, No. 17 (high, round; sweet, bitter). Chilean: Flores, 556 (high, low; bitter, sweet). Italian: Salvioni, *Archivio*, IV (1885), 541, No. 17 (high, low; bitter, sweet); Balladoro, *ibid.*, XVI (1897), 232, No. 46 (high, little; good, bitter). Rumanian: Gorovei, 1218 (bitter, sweet), 1219 (low, high; sweet, bitter). Russian: Sadovnikov, 1371 (It is small and round and white in the middle and bitter and sweet). Serbian: Novaković, p. 155, Nos. 6 (It is bigger than a city, smaller than an egg, sweeter than honey), 7 (As big as a house, as small as a mouse; its fruit is bitter, but even the richest person eats it). Hungarian: Kálmány, I, 159, No. 11 (It is larger than a house, it is smaller than a mouse; it is sweeter than honey, and it is more bitter than poison). Albanian: Hahn, p. 161, No. 30 (Bitter, bitter as poison; sweet, sweet as honey). Crimean Tatar: Filonenko, 1 (Taller than a horse, lower than a camel; more bitter than poison, yet sweeter than sugar).

1272. The speaker has adapted the walnut riddle to the pecan.

1273, 1274. (Colors mentioned.) Breton: Sébillot, *Haute-Bretagne*, 29 (High as a house but isn't a house, green as chives but aren't chives, hard as a boulder but isn't a boulder, white as milk but isn't milk); Le Pennec, 20 (What is as white as snow, green as a meadow, sweet as milk, bitter as soot, hard as wood, and soft as an apple?). German: Butsch, 153 (High above the house, big as a mouse, white as snow, brown as clover), which is disordered in some of its details; Wossidlo, 219*c*, 219*d*; Frischbier, *Pflanzenwelt*, p. 69, No. 24 (high, small, green, white, bitter). Danish: Kristensen, p. 140, § 414, Nos. 155*a*, 155*b*. Latin: Reusner, ed. 1599, pp. 108–109 = ed. 1602, pp. 282–283 (high, small; white, sweet). French: Rolland, 107 (Green as grass, white as snow, bitter as gall, sweet as honey); Carmeau, p. 34 (Green as the meadow, bitter as gall, sweet as honey); Lacuve,

Poitou, p. 354, No. 37 (high, short, green, bitter); Dottin, *Bas-Maine*, 8 (green, sweet, bitter); J. Roux, *Limousin*, 46 (green, long, sweet), 47 (green, hard, white). Spanish, New Mexican: Campa, 105 (high, little; white, black). Italian: Corrazzini, p. 313, as cited by Gianandrea, in *Archivio*, I (1882), 566, No. 35 (high, red, sweet, bitter.—Sorb apple); Coronedi-Berti, *Archivio*, II (1883), 577, No. 27. Portuguese: Pires, *ibid.*, III (1884), 118, No. 40 (green, sweet, bitter); Braga, 34 (green, bitter, sweet); Pires de Lima, 180 (high, green, bitter), 206 (high, green, bitter, sweet). Rumanian: Gorovei, 1217 (high, green, sweet, bitter).

Some parallels contain elements borrowed from the blackberry riddle (see, in the present collection, Nos. 1561a through 1561c), in which the colors are said to occur in a chronological sequence. See, for example, the Flemish cherry riddles, collected by Joos, containing the adjectives "high, small, red, black" (481), "high, small, green, black" (482), and "high, small, green, white" (494). See also the walnut riddle in which the elements are arranged in a different order (No. 1392 in the present collection).

1274. The comparison "as sweet as milk" is unusual in English riddling. Compare the French nut riddle, "Without, as bitter as camomile; within, as sweet as milk" (A. Ferrand, *Dauphiné*, p. 226). Milk ordinarily suggests whiteness, but this allusion, too,. is no longer current in English use (see, however, Nos. 1358a through 1359c in the present collection).

1276. German: Wossidlo, 220 (high, small, prickly, shiny); Haase, *Ruppin*, 43 (high, small, prickly, shiny). French: Rolland, 111 (White within, hairy in the middle, spiny without), which represents an adjustment to the pattern of Nos. 1416, 1418 of the present collection. Modern Greek: Abbott, p. 305, No. 1 (Without, as smooth as glass; within, a woolly mass; but hid amid the wool there lurks a nice mouthful); Dieterich, *Sporades*, 15 (Soft and shiny, and hairy within, further within it is like a sack and is covered up to its face, and in its innermost parts, it conceals a good heart).

1279a, 1279b. Frisian: Dykstra, *Snypsnaren*, p. 103. Flemish: Joos, 12. Danish: Kristensen, p. 127, § 353, Nos. 563a through 563j; Feilberg, *Ordbog*, III, 577, s.v. "stjærne." Norwegian: Landstad, p. 809, No. 23 (Higher than a house, smaller than a mouse, and cannot go through a church door). Swedish: Hyltén-Cavallius, *Värend*, 35 (Higher than a house, smaller than a mouse, burns like a wax candle); Dybeck, *Runa*, 1865–1873, p. 48, No. 43 (Higher than a house, burns like a light); Wigström, p. 292, No. 66 (Higher than a house, and burns like a wax candle); Ericsson, *Södermanland*, V (1884) 67, No. 220; Ström, p. 211, "Stjärnorna," 2, and p. 276, "Gåtsagor," 1.

1279b. "Hide" is a mishearing or miswriting of "higher."

1281. Flemish: Joos, 12. German: Wossidlo, 223; Gilhoff, 713; Carstens, *Schleswig-Holstein*, p. 422. Norwegian: Stafset, 82.

1282. The riddler varies from the usual enigmatic technique in making no contrast of the qualities: "high" is not the opposite of "fine." Compare the Lappish fog riddle, "Higher than all mountains and lower than heather" (Qvigstad, 5).

1283. A confused version of the nut riddle, Nos. 1269a through 1275.

1286a through 1286c. Danish: Feilberg, *Ordbog*, II, 119, s.v. "kilde." Swedish: Ericsson, *Södermanland*, V (1884), 68, No. 223 = Geijer and Campbell, 58 (Round and narrow, a step long, the king's horses can't pull it); Ström, p. 177, "Brunnan" = Wigström, p. 290, No. 31. French: Rolland, 221a (Round as a thimble, horses can't carry it); Constantin, *Savoie*, p. 25 (Round as a cask, a hundred thousand men cannot lift it). References to the various uses of the element "horses can't pull it" are collected in the note to No. 1260 in the present collection.

This English riddle is perhaps disordered, for the comparison "round as a house" has no evident meaning. Perhaps the Cheremiss "I can't overturn the emperor's big kettle" (Porkka, 82) is a related invention.

1286a. The riddler has carelessly omitted "horses."

1287. The comparisons to colors, which are not particularly appropriate here, may have been taken from the chimney riddle (No. 1530a). The adjective "red" may refer to the painted housing of the pump.

1291. "Scrooked" may be a corruption of "as crooked," but the comparison does not seem either apposite or correct. A comparison to a bee is characteristic of riddles for a watch; see Nos. 1309a through 1310b, 1312a through 1313. This riddle is a composite of elements belonging to other riddles.

1295a, 1295b. See also Nos. 1353a, 1353b. A rainbow is like the curve of the briar as it bends to the ground.

1301a, 1301b. Spanish, Cuban: Massip, 120 (round as a cup); Sánchez, 6 (round as a plate). See also No. 1344 (sun), in the present collection.

1302 through 1308. (Versions which mention first the roundness of the frying pan.) Welsh: Hull and Taylor, 194, 195, 199. Spanish, Argentinian: Lehmann-Nitsche, 589 (cheese, neck of a stick), 617 (barrel, coal). Serbian: Novaković, p. 221, No. 3 (It is round and it has a tail, outside it is black, and out of it sweet things come).

For comparisons of a frying pan to the sun or moon see, in the present collection, Nos. 1305a through 1306, and to a round biscuit and a slick mole, see Nos. 1349a through 1349c. For versions which mention first the blackness of the pan and for anomalous versions see Nos. 1336, 1361a through 1361c.

1305a through 1306. (Comparisons to the sun or moon). Danish: Kristensen, p. 101, § 263, Nos. 414a through 414c, and p. 126, § 350, Nos. 558a, 558b. Norwegian: Brox, *Ytre Senja*, 38. Swedish: Hyltén-Cavallius, *Värend*, 17 = Wigström, p. 288, No. 6 (Round as the sun, black as the earth, it drags a long tail after it); Ericsson, *Södermanland*, II (1881), 98, No. 101; Sandén, *Norra Vadsbo*, 15; Ström, p. 145, "Grytan," 1, and p. 146, "Stekpannen."

The comparison "black as ink" is proverbial; see also the blackberry riddle, particularly Nos. 1385, 1386 varr., and 1391 var., in the present collection.

1311a, 1311b, 1312b. For the use of onomatopoetic sounds in riddles see the headnote to Nos. 445–458.

1315a, 1315b. The comparison "round as an apple," which does not seem appropriate here, has perhaps been borrowed thoughtlessly from No. 1309a.

Variants of the last element, "all the king's horses can't pull it up," occur frequently in riddles for a well; see the English examples collected in the note to No. 1260. See also Flemish: Joos, 63 (You can cover it with a tub and cannot drag it away with a thousand horses). Walloon: Colson, *Devinettes*, p. 152, No. 31 (What is no larger than a flail [?] and all the horses in Brabant cannot move [it]?); and in Colson, *Wallonia*, V, 57, No. 224 (three variants). The collector queries the word translated as "flail."

1316. Compare No. 1326 and the headnote to No. 1326.

1326. See also No. 1316.

1333a, 1333b. Lappish: Qvigstad, 65 (What is it that has more holes than the farmer has sheep?—Sieve or basket). African, Kxatla: Schapera, 105 (Tell me: the wing of the lightning bird is full of holes). Indian: Lakshīnātha Upasānī, X, 10 (It is round, but not a wheel, has many eyes but is not Indra. It does not go without a vehicle. What is it?— Sieve).

1335. Disordered and unintelligible.

1336. A poor version of the pattern exemplified in Nos. 1302 and 1304 through 1308 and discussed in the headnote to Nos. 1302–1308.

1340. See Nos. 1348a, 1348b for a description of a chestnut bur as something round and sharp.

1342. Breton: Lavenot, *Basse-Bretagne*, p. 670. Flemish: Joos, 263. German: Wossidlo, 338. Swiss: Rochholz, 488; Zahler, *Münchenbuchsee*, 349. Danish: Kristensen, p. 122, §338, No. 536. Swedish: Dybeck, *Runa*, 1865–1873, p. 81, No. 95; Ericsson, *Södermanland*, IV (1883), 73, No. 200; Ström, p. 161, "Skjortan och särken," 4, and p. 162, "Kangsnöret." Walloon: Colson, *Devinettes*, p. 149, No. 18 (Ladder by day, worm by night). French: Rolland, 140; Lacuve, *Poitou*, 22; Patry, *Normandie*, p. 643; Roque-Ferrier, *Languedoc*, p. 338. Catalan: Pelay y Briz, 40. Basque: Vinson, 1; Demófilo, p. 373, No. 7. Italian: Pitrè, 359. Lithuanian: Jurgelionis, 249 (During the day like a hoop; during the night like a snake. He will be my husband who guesses this well.—Belt, girdle). Lettish: Bielenstein, 252 (By day it is a barrel hoop; by night it is a snake). Polish: Gustawicz, 297 (Like a ring during the day, like a snake at night. He who guesses will be my mate); Saloni, *Rzeshów*, 130 (By day like a hoop, by night like a snake.—Belt). Russian: Sadovnikov, 632 (By day like a hoop, by night like a snake. Whoever guesses shall be my husband).

1344. See the moon riddle, Nos. 1301b.

1345. This somewhat disordered text may be a version of No. 1425. Part of the confusion arises from the association of pears and apples. An apple seems to be properly part of the riddle, and some association or other has caused the introduction of the reference to a pear. The fundamental idea may be related, although probably not, to the comparison of the eye to a pool of water, for which see No. 1044. Since the speaker often obscures the import of the comparison (perhaps intentionally), the parallels are widely divergent. See Welsh: Hull and Taylor, 244. German: Frischbier, *Menschenwelt*, p. 241, No. 3 (Rough round about it, and water in the middle). Indian, Panjabi: Emeneau and Taylor, p. 19, No. 21 (Red, red, red. Above, hair as long as four fingers' breadth. It is split from inside.—Wheat-ear).

1346. Russian: Sadovnikov, 1366 (There stands a shaggy tree, the shaggy one is smooth inside, the smooth one is sweet.—Nut), which may be compared with No. 1161 (walnut) and the coconut, riddle in the corresponding note. See also the Hungarian onion riddle (Meltzl, 32).

1347a. The riddler has introduced "shaller" by mistake; compare No. 1319 and the headnote to Nos. 1315–1336.

1348a, 1348b. The conception of something round and sharp ("keen") is also used, together with a third attribute, one-eyed, in an unusual English riddle for a needle, No. 1340.

1349a through 1349c. "Slick as a mole" probably refers to the greasiness of the pan. For a survey of related frying-pan riddles see the note to Nos. 1302 through 1308.

1350. See other well riddles in the note to Nos. 1315a, 1315b.

1361. A confused mixture of No. 1349a and No. 1319.

1353a, 1353b. See Nos. 1295a, 1295b, and the headnote to Nos. 1295–1296.

1355. (The kind of fruit named in the following parallels varies widely, being characteristically a fig, pomegranate, pepper, or other fruit filled with seeds. A poppy is often the answer.) See Spanish, Argentinian: Lehmann-Nitsche, 493 (A sack full of oats.—Fig). Chilean: Flores, 29 (Pepito went on a little road and found a little purse full of half-centavos.—Pepper), 31 (In a red bag there are a hundred trifles.—Pepper), 35 (A little red box full of trifles.—Pepper). Rumanian: Papahagi, 7 (A box, a little box, full of red pearls.—Pomegranate). Kashub: Patock, *Strellin*, 4 (In the midst of the sea there stands a tower, of which I can assure you that it contains thousands.—Poppy). Polish: Gustawicz, 202 (In a little garden there stands a cane and on this there is a little branch. In this little branch there are thousands, I can swear to it.—Poppy), 203 through 210; Kopernicki, 46 (There stands a little cane, on its top is a tiny globe.

You can swear there are thousands in there.—Poppy), 46a; Saloni, *Rzeshów*, 97 (Little and black, you could swear there's a thousand in it.—Poppy). Albanian: Pedersen, 10 (A box full of red buttons.—Pomegranate), 10 var. (A stall full of red horses); Hahn, p. 161, No. 29 (A food-bag with millet.—Fig), 46 (Round, with many butterflies in its stomach.—Cucumber and seeds). Modern Greek: Polites, *Neohellenika Analekta*, I, 208, No. 84 (I have a box of rubies, they are of the best. I shall call him clever who finds the answer.—Pomegranate), in which the translation of *soprarina* (of the best) is uncertain. Armenian: Zelinski, p. 55, No. 7 (Pilgrims are traveling to Mecca; they try to travel at night; from within a single egg they take from forty to fifty chicks.—Pomegranate). Maltese: Stumme, *Malta*, p. 102, No. 9 (A box within which mountains of pearls, beautiful and fine, are to be found.—Pomegranate). Arabic: Giacobetti, 69 (His cup is as large as the palm of one's hand. It contains nevertheless a thousand and one things.—Pomegranate); Bauer, p. 222, Nos. 6, 9. Turkish: Hamizade, 270 (The outside is locked, the inside is lousy.—Fig), 515 (A little, little box, its inside is full of coral.—Pomegranate), 518 (An apple is hung on the shelf, coral is pressed inside.—Pomegranate), 519 (From over there I got one, I came home and there were a thousand.—Pomegranate), 522 (In my hand there is one, inside it there are a thousand.—Pomegranate), 524 (The pilgrims go on a pilgrimage. They labor and go by night. Inside an egg thousands of dwarfs go.—Pomegranate), 525 (The stationers don't know it; within, the paper is full of coral.—Pomegranate), 530 (I have a vessel, a full box; the box-makers don't know it.—Pomegranate); Kowalski, *Asia Minor*, 5 (At the top of the branch a millet-bin.—Fig), 9 (A barrel, a little barrel, full of tiny pickled cucumbers.—Lemon); Zavarin, *Brusa*, 16 (I bought one thing at the market. I brought home a thousand pieces. —Pomegranate); Kúnos, 239. African, Bakongo: Denis, 72 (A sack full of cowries.— A fruit). Evhe: F. Müller, p. 156, No. 4 (Pearls fill a little calabash.—A plant related to the tomato). Indian: Lakshīnātha Upasānī, XIII, 1 (On a stick is placed a granary having many rooms and all are filled with grains of corn. Have you seen it?—Poppyhead). Kolarian: Wagner, 21 (Dirty, filthy, but a hundred rupees have room in it.— The jack fruit, the flesh around the seeds). Parsee: Munshi, p. 416 (A small ball containing fifty to one hundred grains.—Pomegranate). Indonesian, Tabaru: Fortgens, 90 (A chest containing only teeth.—Watermelon). Korean: Bernheisel, p. 62 (What is a red silk purse that contains hundreds of gold coins?—Red pepper).

For comparisons describing a fruit as a house or as a house and its occupants see the headnote to Nos. 1132-1138, §§ 2-3, and the headnote to No. 1134, in the present collection.

1356. I do not see the connection of the first two comparisons with a snare.

1357. Portuguese riddles for an orange, "Round as a ball, bitter as gall, and sweet as molasses" (Parsons, *Cape Verde*, 16), and for a lime, "Green as grass, white as paper, sweet as molasses, bitter as gall" (*ibid.*, 17), show some similarity to this text and are related, at the same time, to the walnut riddle discussed in the headnote to Nos. 1269-1275 in the present collection. See also No. 1365.

1361a through 1361c. (Versions mentioning first the blackness of the frying pan, and also versions containing only the element "an eye in its tail." The latter are perhaps defective versions of the comparison of a frying pan to a magpie, discussed in the headnote to Nos. 1302-1308.) Welsh: Hull and Taylor, 196 through 198. Breton: Sébillot, *Haute-Bretagne*, 59 = Kerbeuzec, *Ille-et-Vilaine*, 38 and 97 (Who has an eye in the end of its tail?). Flemish: Joos, 174 (Black within and without, and it has an eye on its tail). German: Gilhoff, 500 (Black within, black without, three legs and a long tail). French: Rolland, 159 (Who has an eye in its tail?); Bladé, *Armagnac*, 34 (Five eyes, its throat in the middle, and an eye at the end of its tail.—Warming pan); V. S., *Mélusine*, I (1878), col. 258, No. 49 (A thing that has an eye at the end of its tail); Carmeau, p. 33; Marchessou, *Velay et Auvergne*, p. 170, No. 27; Lacuve, *Poitou*, p. 355, No. 43. Italian: Tammi, 57. See also, in the present collection, Nos. 1302, 1304, 1305a, 1307, 1308.

1364, 1365. Spanish, Cuban: Massip, 63. Compare the Irish apple riddle, "As white as a swan, as sweet as honey, as round as an egg, as red as blood" (Christiansen, 55), which is very similar to the texts cited in the note to No. 1357 of the present collection.

1367. Breton: Sébillot, *Haute-Bretagne*, 35 (Green as chives but are not chives, white as snow but is not snow, red as blood but is not blood, black as ink but is not ink). For similar series of antitheses, see Nos. 1368a, 1368b, 1371, 1372, 1373b, and 1374 in the present collection. See also Dutch: Sinninghe, p. 13, No. 3. Afrikaans: Groenewald, p. 82. German: Wossidlo, 217. Swiss: Rochholz, 385 (White as snow, green as clover, red as blood, coal-black as a felt hat). Walloon: Colson, *Devinettes*, p. 148, No. 8 (Green as grass, bitter as soot, red as blood, sweet as honey).

Riddles having the answer "cherry" exhibit the varieties noted in the discussion of the bramble riddle; see the headnote to Nos. 1384–1393 of the present collection. For example, the Breton riddle above names the colors and adds a contradiction to each one; the Swedish "First as white as blood, then as green as a lake, last [it is] red and tastes sweet" (Ström, p. 126, "Körsbärsträdet," 2), which is closely paralleled by a blackthorn riddle (*ibid.*, p. 128, "Slån," 1), contains the characteristic series of comparisons and mentions the colors as occurring in a sequence (see the headnote to Nos. 1559–1561 in the present collection); the Walloon "High as a tower, green as grass, white as snow, bitter as soot, sweet as honey" (Colson, *Wallonia*, IV, 92, No. 89) contains elements characteristic of the walnut riddle, Nos. 1269a through 1271b and 1273 through 1275 in the present collection. The French "Who has a green tail, who is as round as a ball, and who is red?" (Rolland, 106a) and "Who has a red skin, a green tail, and is as bitter as rosewort?" (*ibid.*, 106b) are confused and disordered products.

1369. Spanish: Demófilo, 897 (I am as round as the earth, green as mash, red like cochineal, and black as pitch). Arabic: Giacobetti, 92 (Green as a prairie, black as coffee, red as blood, sweet as honey), 93, 94.

1370. Spanish, Cuban: Headwaiter, 5 (It is green and is not parsley; it is straw-colored and is not saffron; it has a crown and is not a king; it has a fishbone and is not of the sea). Arabic: Giacobetti, 66 (Red as coral, white as linen, yellow as a lemon).

The Portuguese riddle for a lime, "Green as grass, white as paper, sweet as molasses, bitter as gall" (Parsons, *Cape Verde*, 17), is of the same type.

1374. See Nos. 1572a through 1572c.

1376. A modification of the bramble riddle; see, for example, No. 1391. Compare Spanish: Rodríguez Marín, 534 (green, white, black). Argentinian: Lehmann-Nitsche, 625.

1378. Armenian: Glushakov, p. 29, No. 50 (Black as a blackbird, sweet as honey in the mouth, it bites like a dog).

1379. Welsh: Hull and Taylor, 204, 205. Welsh Gypsy: Sampson, 13. Danish: Kristensen, pp. 113–114, § 310, Nos. 493a through 493d. Norwegian: Bergh, *Valdres*, 50; Brox, *Ytre Senja*, 7, 90. Swedish: Ericsson, *Södermanland*, II (1881), 96, No. 91 (White as chalk, black as pitch, it dances like a lady, it gnaws like a horse); Hyltén-Cavallius, *Värend*, 11 (White as a swan, black as a raven, it hops like a hare, it walks like a man); Sandén, *Norra Vadsbo*, 64; Noreen, *Fryksdal*, 15; Geijer and Campbell, 69, 70; Ström, pp. 110–111, "Skatan," 2 through 4. Walloon: Colson, *Wallonia*, IV, 62, No. 63 (White as snow, black as soot on a pot, a back like a miner's pick, a tail like a horse). French: Rolland, 70 (Who is black and white, who skips across the field, who is like the curate when he is singing?); Guillon, *La Bresse*, p. 20. Lettish: Bielenstein, 711 (What sort of bird is it:

it is as white as chalk, black as coal, it neighs like a stallion, dances like a maiden?). Czech: Hanika-Otto, note to No. 39 (Black as coal, white as snow, green as grass, it calls in the guests), which is not completely intelligible. Hungarian: *Magyar Nyelvör*, XV (1886), 330 (It is white like a horse, black like a raven, straight like a board, curved like a *salló*, it speaks like a Jew). The meaning of *salló* is obscure.

1380. (The following parallels are contaminated versions. Few riddles have admitted foreign matter as readily as the magpie riddle.) In some versions riddlers have introduced the contrast of high and low discussed in the headnotes to Nos. 1269–1275 (walnut) and 1281 (star or road). See German: Frischbier, *Thierwelt*, p. 357, No. 91. French: Beauvillard, *Mélusine*, I (1878), col. 557, No. 9 (High as the chestnut, lower than the earth, black as a mole, white as snow). Lithuanian: Jurgelionis, 837 (Blacker than the soil, whiter than the snow, lower than the doorstep, higher than the roof). Lettish: Bielenstein, 712 (Higher than a church, lower than a sled, white as snow, black as coal). Finnish: Henssen, 113 (Blacker than a coal, whiter than snow, higher than a house, lower than a hut). Estonian: Wiedemann, pp. 270–271 (Higher than a church, lower than a sled, blacker than a coal, whiter than snow) and 281 (Blacker than a coal, whiter than snow, higher than the church). Turkish: Katanov in Radlov, IX, 143, No. 1160 (Whiter than snow and blacker than soot; lower than a dog and higher than a camel). The second pair of contrasts belongs to riddles cited in the headnote to No. 575, nn. 43–44, and the headnote to No. 1281, n. 7, of the present collection.

The Estonian "At the end like an awl, in the middle like a ball, blacker than a coal, dances like a lady" (Wiedemann, p. 283) begins with elements taken from an altogether different magpie riddle (see the headnote to No. 1435, §4, of the present collection).

1381a, 1381b. (The following parallels employ antitheses. They seem to have arisen independently, for they have no other striking resemblance in common.) See "White as a goose and is no goose, green as grass, it has a tail like a cow and is not a cow"(Kashub: Gulgowski, 7); "Speckled and yet it is not a dog, green and yet not an onion, it gads about like the very devil, holding its direction toward the forest" (Russian: Sadovnikov, 1580); "Green, yet it is not a poppy; red, yet it is not fustian stuff, it gads about . . ." (*ibid.*, 1580a).

1382. This version exemplifies a very curious contamination. The frying-pan riddle (see Nos. 1302, 1304 through 1305b, and 1308) is a comparison of a frying pan to a magpie. The riddler has kept that fact in mind and here gives the magpie as the answer to his riddle. He has also remembered the comparisons to colors and the mention of a hole in the blackberry riddle (No. 1373a) and has adapted them to his purpose.

The notion of a stick in the wrong place—a theme which properly belongs to the cherry riddle; see the headnote to Nos. 632–644, §§16–23—occurs in a Low German magpie riddle: "Something flies over the house; it has a broom in its body" (Wossidlo, 322a). With slight changes this is adapted to describe a bee (*ibid.*, 322b) and a leaf (*ibid.*, 322c).

Note also the comparison of a magpie to an object in the Cheremiss "The handle of my pantry box is long" (Genetz, 76) and the Votyak parallel, "On the hut [there is] a dipper with a long handle" (Buch, 23).

1383. Welsh: Hull and Taylor, 105. Breton: Sébillot, *Haute-Bretagne*, 38b; Orain, *Ille-et-Vilaine*, p. 147; Le Chef, *Ille-et-Vilaine*, p. 667. Flemish: Joos, 468 (Winter and summer, [it is] equally green; and it has a beard like a turkey), 472 (White, yellow, and green, a tail like a turkey, a beard like an old man. If you don't believe it, go smell it.—Leek). German: Haffner, 37, 38. Swiss: Rochholz, 415. Walloon: Colson, *Wallonia*, IV, 94, Nos. 104a (Green as a meadow, white as snow, bearded like a man), 104b (Green as a leek, a beard like a goat's, and as straight as an *i*). French: Rolland, 115. Basque: Vinson, 69. Spanish, Argentinian: Lehmann-Nitsche, 168. Italian: Pitrè, 647. Modern Greek: Abbott, p. 307, No. 7 (Hoary beard and hoary hair, 'neath the earth he has his lair.—Leek). Indian, Parsee: Munshi, p. 414 (White beard, green moustaches. If you cannot solve [the riddle], go ask your father.—Radish).

1384. The riddler has adapted the usual comparison "as black as ink" to fit the answer "huckleberries." The comparison to cotton is unusual, but see the Iraqi riddle for a caper bush: "Green, green as jasmine, but it is not jasmine; white, white as cotton, but it is not cotton. Does he know it or does he not?" (Arabic: Meissner, *Iraq*, 72).

1385. The comparison to fire is found only occasionally; see the French mulberry riddle: "Red as fire and it is not fire, black as a pot and it is not a pot" (Rolland, 100). This French text gains a special unity by limiting the means of comparison to such closely related objects as a fire and a pot.

1386. As the number of variants indicates, this is the usual form of the English riddle. The answer is ordinarily "blackberry," but the parallels below name other fruits, especially the cherry. See Irish: Delargy, 67 (As white as milk, as high as a cliff, as red as blood, as sweet as honey, as black as a beetle.—Blackberries); Hyde, p. 172 (flour, grass, blood, ink.—Blackberry). Flemish: Joos, 479 (wax, grass, blood.—Cherry), 480 (snow, grass, blood.—Cherry). Luxemburg: De la Fontaine, 58 (snow, clover, blood.—Cherry). German: Wossidlo, 217a (grass, blood, tar.—Cherry), 217b (grass, snow, blood, tar.—Cherry), 217c (Higher than a house, smaller than a mouse, greener than grass, black as the raven. He who can guess that shall have three thousand ducats and kiss my sweetheart.—Cherry); Haffner, 24 (snow, clover, blood.—Cherry); Hanika-Otto, 641, vv. 6-12 (snow, coal.—Elderberry). Norwegian: Brox, *Ytre Senja*, 20 (snow, grass, red as a coal.—Cherry). Swedish: Ericsson, *Södermanland*, III (1882), 103, No. 161 (At first as white as snow, it later becomes green, and finally as red as blood, then for the first time it is really good.—Cherry). Walloon: Colson, *Wallonia*, IV, 92, No. 90 (White as snow, green as cress, red as fire, black as charcoal, it is not charcoal.—Cherry). Spanish, Argentinian: Lehmann-Nitsche, 628 (snow, grass, blood, black as black, it is good.—Cherry). Lettish: Bielenstein, 299 (grass, snow, blood.—Cherry). Czech: Hanika-Otto, note to No. 41 (many parallels). Serbian: Novaković, p. 35, No. 6 (At first it is like the snow, then it is green and unripe, later it is sweet and red.—Grapes).

This manner of description is also applied to a woodpecker; see Hanika-Otto, 642, vv. 86-92.

1387. Swedish: Ström, p. 134, "Rovan" (green as a meadow, red as a rose, white as a cheese).

1388. Riddlers have adapted this pattern to describe a letter by adding such descriptive elements as "talks without a tongue" or "goes without feet." For examples see Danish: Kristensen, p. 18, §28, No. 33a. Basque: Vinson, 55. Spanish: Demófilo, 251 through 253. Chilean: Flores, 166. Cuban: Massip, 48, 49.

The Lithuanian "A little blind dove flutters through the whole world" (Schleicher, p. 194) equates a letter to a creature.

1392. In Nos. 1273, 1274 the riddler arranges similar elements in a different order.

1394a through 1394c. The import of the riddle is obscure, but its dissemination indicates its age and implies popular acceptance. This version, which is expressed in comparisons, is related to No. 1726, which is expressed in assertions. For parallels to this version see Danish: *Skattegraveren*, IX, 467, as cited by Kristensen, pp. 163-164, § 2, No. 2a (What is better than God, and less than shame, one eats it when one is dead, but if one eats it when one is alive, one dies). Kristensen comments that the use of *Skam* (shame, sin) in the meaning *Fanden* (Devil) is curious. See further *Skattegraveren*, IX, 298, as cited by Kristensen, p. 164, § 2, No. 2b (What is that which is better than Our Lord, worse than the Devil, the dead eat it, and when the living eat it, they die?); Feilberg, *Ordbog*, II, 27; and IV, 244, s.v. "ingen." Swedish: Dybeck, *Runa*, 1848, p. 43, No. 32 (Better than God, worse than shame; a dead man eats it, if a living man should eat it he would die); Ericsson, *Södermanland*, III (1882), 96, No. 124 = Geijer and Campbell, 92. Italian: Corsi, *Archivio*, X (1891), 400, No. 29 = Tschiedel, 52 (More than God, worse than the Devil).

The conception differs somewhat in the Icelandic "What may be called older than time, and what can be seen fairer than the sun? What can blow stronger than the winds or hotter than the bright fire?" (Árnason, 466).

1394c. (Higher than God.) Compare the Flemish "Solomon has wisdom, but what stands above wisdom?—Hair" (Joos, 801).

1400. Some elements belong to riddles for a cow; see especially Nos. 1476a through 1476e, 1477c, 1477g, 1477j through 1478a, 1479a, 1479e.

1401c. "Bando" is "ba'n do"' (barn door), but it is not clear that the collector so understood it.

1403. (Description in terms of form.) Breton: Sauvé, 131. French: Rolland, 383; Bladé, *Armagnac*, 7 (ass, cow); Millien, *Nivernais*, p. 578; Roque-Ferrier, *Languedoc*, p. 333. Spanish: Demófilo, 292 (stork), 472; Rodríguez Marín, 359. Argentinian: Lehmann-Nitsche, 969. Porto Rican: Mason, 635. Russian: Sadovnikov, 919. Hungarian: Kálmány, III, 181, No. 32 (It has the exact form of a horse, but is not a horse). Korean: Bernheisel, p. 84 (What is it that is like a cow, but without horns?—Calf).

1404a, 1494b. (Description in terms of acts.) Flemish: Joos, 423, 908. German: Wossidlo, 370a, 370b, 371; Frischbier, *Thierwelt*, p. 347, No. 28; Carstens, *Schleswig-Holstein*, p. 415; Hanika-Otto, 613. Swedish: Ericsson, *Södermanland*, V (1884), 64, No. 205. Catalan: Pelay y Briz, 239 (cow). Portuguese: Pires, *Archivio*, III (1884), 114, No. 10. Lithuanian: Schleicher, p. 201. Lettish: Bielenstein, 319 (It looks like a dog, it barks like a dog, but it isn't a dog.—Bitch). Serbian: Novaković, p. 37, Nos. 6 (It is as big as a goose, yet it is not a goose; it swims in the water like a duck, yet it is not a duck; it is as white as a swan, yet it is not a swan; and when on ice, it stands on one leg.—Gander), 7 (It cackles like a goose, yet it is not a goose; it has feathers and a bill like a goose, yet is not a goose.—Gander), p. 126, No. 4 (It looks like a cat, it mews like a cat, yet it is not a cat.—Tomcat), and p. 109, No. 10 (My father is a dog, my mother is a dog, I bark like a dog, and yet I am no dog.—Bitch). Hungarian: *Magyar Nyelvör*, XIX (1890), 185 (It lows in the stable but isn't a cow. What is it?—Ox). Gypsy: Wlislocki, 50.

1407. Snuffers are only rarely the theme of riddles. A Finnish description, "Two eyes, three legs, its takes its food from the fire" (Henssen, 167) is akin to the riddles discussed in the headnote to Nos. 46–87 of the present collection. Another variety is noted in the headnote to Nos. 1476–1494, §27. See another manner of description in No. 1697.

CHAPTER IX
ENUMERATIONS OF COMPARISONS
Nos. 1409–1495

1409. A modern Greek riddler compares a steelyard to a cock with claws and hooked feet; see Abbott, p. 305, No. 3.

1410. German: Wossidlo, 260 (Without, as black as oven-soot; within, as shining as the sun's glow).

1411. The meaning of the riddle is not entirely clear. Compare the Flemish ring riddle, "What has neither beginning nor end?" (Joos, 377) and a Jamaican wheel riddle in the present collection (see No. 1708 and the corresponding note).

1413. Welsh: Hull and Taylor, 254 through 257. Welsh Gypsy: Sampson, 34 (Full of bones, full of flesh, one large hole and many small holes), a riddle combining elements from certain shoe riddles (see, in the present collection, the headnote to No. 453, §2) with other elements from riddles for a glove (see the headnote to No. 908, n. 24). Danish: Kristensen, p. 24, §62, No. 75d (Proud and neat, little and compact, and many holes in it, yet none through it). French: Rolland, 183 (Who has a hundred holes and a plug of flesh?—The thimble and the finger). Lithuanian: Jurgelionis, 549 (Though new [it is] full of holes).

1414. The import of the riddle is completely obscure.

1415. Compare the Argentinian "It goes from the hall and enters the kitchen, managing its tail like a hen" (Lehmann-Nitsche, 131a).

1416. Welsh: Hull and Taylor, 245. Breton: Sébillot, *Haute-Bretagne*, 46c; Orain, *Ille-et-Vilaine*, p. 154. German: R. Köhler, *Kleinere Schriften*, III, 515, No. 17; Wossidlo, 244, 245; Frischbier, *Menschenwelt*, p. 245, No. 35. Walloon: Colson, *Wallonia*, IV, 110, No. 129; Colson, *Devinettes*, p. 149, No. 15. French: Rolland, 135; Bladé, *Armagnac*, 22; Lacuve, *Poitou*, p. 702, No. 5; Lespy, *Béarn*, 13; Roque-Ferrier, *Languedoc*, pp. 337–338. Catalan: Pelay y Briz, 16. Spanish: Demófilo, pp. 343–344, No. 18, p. 363, No. 17, and p. 396, No. 66; Rodríguez Marín, 623. Cuban: Massip, 126. Dominican Rep.: Andrade, 80. New Mexican: Espinosa, 71; Campa, 59. Porto Rican: Mason, 361. Portuguese: Braga, 4; Pires, *Archivio*, III (1884), 120, No. 52; Parsons, *Cape Verde*, 197. Italian: Gianandrea, *Canti popolari marchigiani*, p. 299, No. 15; Ive, *Canti popolari istriani*, p. 298, No. 8; Salvioni, *Archivio*, IV (1885), 546, No. 58; Balladoro, *ibid.*, XVI (1897), 231, No. 41; Ive, *ibid.*, XXII (1903), 118, No. 16; Tschiedel, 56, 59; Tammi, 49. Serbian: Novaković, p. 143, Nos. 7 (The naked stands in the woolly thing.—Feet in socks), 8 (I stuck the naked one into the woolly thing). Modern Greek: Carnoy and Nicolaides, 20 (The hairy one is open, the naked one entered). Turkish: Kowalski, *Zagadki*, 104 (The hairy one opened his mouth, the naked one flew in); Kúnos, 105, 184.

1417. This seems to be defective, for the parallels usually begin with a formula "Black outside, red inside," for boots (see Nos. 1538a through 1538f). See also the riddles for trousers cited in the headnote to Nos. 1416–1419, § 3, and the Turkish "I held it at its mouth and kicked it, reaching to its bottom" (Kúnos, 4); "I held it by its handle and stuffed it to the bottom" (*ibid.*, 216); and "Bifurcated hips, it stumbles to its bottom" (*ibid.*, 242); "I held it with two hands; I pushed to the bottom" (Moshkov in Radlov, X, 272, No. 94); and Kúnos, 141. See also the shirt and trouser riddles in the note to No. 1108 in the present collection.

1418. Welsh: Hull and Taylor, 277. Compare the Porto Rican riddle for cotton, "Hairy without, hairy within" (Mason, 41).

1419a, 1419b. Flemish: Joos, 590 (Hair seeks hair, and hair finds hair, and hair had a ring through which it went).

1421. Compare Nos. 1572a through 1572c and similar riddles listed in the headnote to No. 1572.

1422. Compare a somewhat similar conception in No. 1450b below.

1423a through 1423c. Scotch Gaelic: Nicolson, p. 53. Irish: Christiansen, 70 (It is not in and it is not out and one sees it every day). The last of these assertions occurs also in riddles for the fingers (see, in the present collection, No. 1629a and the parallels, especially Rolland, 374, quoted in the note to Nos. 1629a, 1629b) and in riddles about one's equal (Nos. 1715a through 1717a, 1718, 1720b). Frisian: Dykstra, *Snypsnaren*, p. 102. German: Wossidlo, 836; Böckel, *Hesse*, 6; Hanika-Otto, 134. Swiss: Rochholz, 560. Icelandic: Árnason, 415. Norwegian: Aasen, 10; Berge, 34; Stafset, 12; Brox, *Ytre Senja*, 191. Swedish: Dybeck, *Runa*, 1848, p. 45, No. 43; Ericsson, *Södermanland*, I (1879), 86, No. 30; Christofferson, p. 36, No. 23 = *Folkminnen och folktankar*, II (1915), 89, No. 23; Geijer and Campbell, 51 through 53; Ström, p. 180, "Fönstret," 1. Cheremiss: Wichmann, *Cheremiss*, 32, 33, 130. Hungarian: Arany and Gyulai, III, 294, No. 9 (It is outside and also inside); Kriza, 20 (It stands inside as well as outside), 20 var. (Outside, it is peeping; inside, it is peeping); *Magyar Nyelvör*, III (1874), 38 (Its inside and outside are alike; there is a cross in the middle.—Window-frame), which is a different theme; V (1876), 127 (It is outside, but inside, too); VI (1877), 423 (It is to be found outside as well as inside; yet it is always in the right place).

1423a. For the assertion "the house can't do without it," compare Nos. 1676 through 1679.

1424. A Russian samovar riddle cited in the headnote to Nos. 1440–1441, n. 30, also contains a reference to water in terms of its position, but with respect to vertical order (above, below), not to the order from the middle outward, as here; also, as in No. 1424, the water maintains its position seemingly in defiance of the laws of nature. For a sponge riddle involving such an apparent impossibility but not emphasizing the order of the relative positions, see No. 1459.

1425 through 1426c. German: Frischbier: *Menschenwelt*, p. 241, No. 3 (Rough round about it, and water in the middle), and p. 242, No. 4 (Hair round about it, something bad gets in). Swiss: Rochholz, 444 (Hair round about it, God forbid that anything bad gets in).

1425. Compare Nos. 1345, 1443, 1444, the headnotes to Nos. 1355 and 1443–1444, and the notes to Nos. 1443 and 1444.

1428. Polish: Gustawicz, 440 (A maiden's handicraft surrounded by an overgrowth, a hole in the center, a tiny little opening.—Wreath); Kopernicki, 43.

1429a through 1429c. See Nos. 69a through 69d.

1432a through 1432c. (Contrast of living and dead.) Welsh: Hull and Taylor, 216 through 219. Welsh Gypsy: Sampson, 26. Frisian: Dykstra, *Snypsnaren*, p. 97. Flemish: Joos, 580. German: Wossidlo, 241; Frischbier, *Menschenwelt*, p. 255, No. 152; J. Meier, *Ostfriesland*, 12; Carstens, *Schleswig-Holstein*, p. 414; Böckel, *Hesse*, 16; Renk, *Tyrol*, 179; Hanika-Otto, 96 through 100. Swiss: Rochholz, 502; Zahler, *Münchenbuchsee*, 20. Norwegian: Bugge, *Telemarken*, 65. French: V. S., *Mélusine*, I (1878), col. 265, No. 97; Marchessou, *Velay et Auvergne*, p. 166, No. 5; J. Roux, *Limousin*, 42; Fouju, *Beauce*, p. 631; Sébillot, *Auvergne*, 10. Czech: Hanika-Otto, note to Nos. 97–101. Votyak: Wichmann, *Votyak*, 67.

1433a, 1433b. (Contrast of flesh with wood and iron.) German: Wossidlo, 241 (Flesh in front and behind, and wood and iron in the middle). Hanika-Otto, 97 (Flesh in front, flesh behind, wood in the middle). Walloon: Colson, *Wallonia*, IV, 57, No. 27 (Flesh in front and behind, wood and iron in the middle). French: Rolland, *Rimes*, p. 207, No. 54.

For mention of three members—alive, dead, and baptized—see, in the present collection, the headnote to No. 1435, n. 13.

1434a, 1434b. African, Galla: Cerulli, 3 (That which is over is dead, that which is under is dead, that which is between is alive). This shows some similarity to the turtle riddle cited in the note to Nos. 594a, 594b of the present collection. For similar descriptions in a horizontal order, see the headnote to Nos. 1416–1447.

1435. This riddle contains only the last element of a description of the front, middle, and back of a cock. Examples of this description are cited here. The Welsh versions (Hull and Taylor, 201, 202) contain elements borrowed from Nos. 540a through 540h in the present collection. See further, German: Wossidlo, 240, 323; Frischbier, *Thierwelt*, p. 349, No. 37; Hanika-Otto, 36 (In front it has a comb, in the middle it is like a lamb, at the back it has a sickle). Swiss: Zahler, *Münchenbuchsee*, 132. Danish: Kristensen, p. 37, § 95, No. 124; Feilberg, *Ordbog*, II, 250, s.v. "kok." Swedish: Sandén, *Norra Vadsbo*, 31. Rumanian: Papahagi, 39, var. 1. Bulgarian: Gubov, 295 (A living feathered thing, on its head there is a red crest, on its end a sickle). This seems to be a contaminated version, containing only the last element of this riddle. Finnish: Lönnrot, 1485 = Henssen, 120 (Head like a spike, tail like a sickle, middle like a sack of meal). Estonian: Lönnrot, p. 190; Wiedemann, p. 265 (In front like a spear [or: an awl], in the middle like a bag of yarn, behind like a shovel). Cheremiss: Genetz, 28 (The back is a sickle, the head is a comb); Wichmann, *Cheremiss*, 134. Gypsy: Wlislocki, 33 (In front it is like a comb, in the middle like a barrel, behind like a sickle). Indonesian, Sangir: Adriani, p. 387, No. 1 (One end is a fishing hook, the other is a fish spear).

1436b. "Heart" should be "hat."

1437a through 1437f. (The parallels often have the answers "oven" or "stove," and refer to the bricks or tiles of which ovens and stoves are made in continental Europe.) German: Hanika-Otto, 102a through 102e; Frischbier, *Menschenwelt*, p. 247, No. 55 (In the room there stands a man; he wears a thousand patches). Swedish: Ström, p. 181, "Kakelugnen," 1, 2. Basque: Vinson, 52. Russian: Sadovnikov, 125 (A little hat called Bormontai [grumbler].—Dutch oven covered with tiles), 1051 (The little hat, the little Tatar, all patchy.—Dutch oven covered with tiles), 1052 (Patch on patch, done with no needle.—*Kamenka*, the upper part of a Russian bath). Cheremiss: Porkka, 6. Mordvin: Paasonen, 117. Zyrian: Wichmann, *Zyrian*, 18, 27, 119. Hungarian: Kriza, 18 (The skirt of my mother, many, many patches on it, but there is not a single stitch on it. —Oven); *Magyar Nyelvör*, XII (1883), 426; XXXI (1902), 334, No. 60.

1438a. In this defective version, the strong association of "cabbage" and "patch," in the common term for a plot of ground, has blocked the riddler's understanding of the intended comparison and has caused him to give an incorrect answer.

1438b. (Cabbage.) Irish: Christiansen, 63 (See my grandfather in the field with two hundred coats). German: Wossidlo, 198 (Behind the house there stands a man; he wears ninety-nine fur coats). Danish: Kristensen, p. 46, § 120, Nos. 167a through 167g, and p. 78, § 195, No. 300b; Feilberg, *Ordbog*, II, 354, s.v. "kål." Norwegian: Brox, *Ytre Senja*, 128; Bergh, *Valdres*, 61; Stafset, 217. Swedish: Russwurm, 43; Ericsson, *Södermanland*, IV (1883), 71, No. 187; Hyltén-Cavallius, *Värend*, 19; Wigström, p. 228, No. 11; Sandén, *Norra Vadsbo*, 27; Christofferson, p. 86; Ström, 131, "Kålen," 1. French: Parsons, *Antilles*, III, 404, Guadaloupe, 83, 85. Spanish, Argentinian: Lehmann-Nitsche, 547a through 547f. Italian: Pitrè, 164, 376 (lettuce). Rumanian: Papahagi, 98 (An old gray-haired man dressed in forty shirts). Lithuanian: Schleicher, p. 202; Jurgelionis, 1032 (A short, stout little gentleman clothed in a hundred suits), 1033 (A little one-legged woman wears a hundred dresses), 1034 (A hundred leaves, a hundred underleaves, and he himself stands on one foot), 1036 (Patch on patch; a needle never pierced it), 1039 (A small woman, a hundred caps), 1040, 1041, 1043. Lettish: Bielenstein, 272 (Little mother sits in the garden, a hundred coverlets laid about her back), 273 (A little, little woman, a hundred cloths about her neck), 274 (A little, little woman, three hundred caps on her head), 276 (A little, little maiden, a hundred caps on her head), 277 (A little mademoiselle; she wears a hundred skirts), 278 (Patch on patch, nowhere a stitch), 908 (A short, fat maiden, a hundred caps on her head). Polish: Siarkowski, 19 (An ugly old wretch waddled about, dressed in forty jackets); Gustawicz, 131 (It stands in the gateway, dressed in thirty jackets). Russian: Sadovnikov, 746 (Here stands Filat; he wears a hundred patches), 747 (A woman sits in the rows, all in patches), 748 (A patch on a patch, yet no needle worked here), 749 (Neither sewn nor cut, yet all in seams, clothes without count, yet all without clasps). Bulgarian: Chacharov, 53 (It wears a hundred coats, yet it freezes in winter). Finnish: Aarne and Krohn, 71 = Henssen, 125a. Estonian: Wiedemann, pp. 275 (Patch on patch, rag on rag, without piercing it with a needle), 291 (A beggar; a hundred coats without a needle having pierced through). Mordvin: Ahlqvist, p. 39, No. 6 (He wears rags, he has a long foot under him), and p. 40, No. 7 (He wears forty shirts that reach to his knee); Paasonen, 17 (A little priestling, he wears forty shirts), 196, 197. Zyrian: Wichmann, *Zyrian*, 83 (A little, little priest, but he wears a hundred garments for mass). Hungarian: *Magyar Nyelvör*, IX (1880), 37, No. 1. Modern Greek: Abbott, p. 313, No. 28 (My uncle Theodore the Short wrapped up in forty blankets); Stathes, p. 351, No. 116 (A crazy old woman in the middle of the garden; she wears a thousand cloths and her bottom always shows), which is akin to the hen riddle discussed in the headnote to No. 1437, § 10, in the present collection. Arabic: Ruoff, p. 51, No. 25 (It is short and round and wears many clothes). Maltese: Stumme, *Malta*, 14 (Mat on mat, and yet not a mat). Turkish: Kúnos, 143 (Fold on fold, a needle never penetrated it); Hamizade, 457 (It has layers and layers, this is the wisdom of God), 458 (Tiered, tiered, a little folded thing, after these folds it is a white, pure, little thing), 459 (Your grandfather has a jacket, there are patches in a thousand places), 460 (A tiered, tiered bed; whoever doesn't know this is a donkey; either you'll know or you'll die), 461 (I have a girl who is like canvas; her rump is like a sacking needle; inside forty layers of clothes the interior is like ice).

1439. (Onion.) Breton: Lavenot, *Basse-Bretagne*, p. 663. German: Wossidlo, 194; Hanika-Otto, 105. Swiss: Zahler, *Münchenbuchsee*, 444 (A woman with a hundred kerchiefs). French: Rolland, 113; Bladé, *Armagnac*, 82; Lacuve, *Poitou*, p. 352, No. 6; Pineau, *Poitou*, 23; Queyrat, *La Creuse*, I, 365; A. Ferrand, *Dauphiné*, p. 225; Lallemant, *Argonne*, p. 235 (without a seam). Portuguese: Braga, 68; A. Thomáz Pires, *Archivio*, IV (1885), 117, No. 33. Spanish: Demófilo, 257, 260, 263, 264, 266, p. 349, No. 43, p. 376, No. 1, and p. 386, No. 23; Rodríguez Marín, 510 through 514. Argentinian: Lehmann-Nitsche, 512, 547g through 547i. Chilean: Flores, 179 through 181, 186 = Rodríguez Marín, 510. Dominican Rep.: Andrade, 109. New Mexican: Espinosa, 24, 25 (Hat upon hat, hat of my own cloth. He will not guess me, not in the whole year); Campa, 67. Porto Rican: Mason, 156a through 156f, 157. Italian: Pitrè, 191. Hungarian: Meltzl, 32. Lithuanian: Jurgelionis, 1036, 1044. Russian: Sadovnikov, 737a through 737q, 739 through 744; Preobrazhenskii, p. 171 (A small little woman, all in patches, anyone who will look will weep). Bulgarian: Gubov, 215 (Ozukhin, Kozukhin with thirty fur coats), 216 (An old woman with nine fur coats); Ikonomov, 2 (Dried and dried, three to nine fur-lined coats). Cheremiss: Genetz, 65 (The Russian woman put on a hundred dresses). Albanian: Hahn, p. 162, No. 53. Turkish: Szapszal, p. 67, No. 3 (It is of such small stature, but it has forty or thirty suits of clothes); Hamizade, 596 (Tier on tier it opens up; one runs from its smell.—Garlic). Gypsy: Wlislocki, 36 (I wear many skirts and bite whomever I can bite). Ossete: Schiefner, 7. African, Kxatla: Schapera, 22, 59. Indian: Lakshīnātha Upasānī, VI, 2. Parsee: Munshi, p. 412 (A stunted little *gokuldas* [gentleman] putting on fifty, one hundred clothes), and a variant on the same page (Coat over coat do I put on, and hot and confused am I; to some do I appear white, to others red). Hindi: Mitra, *Bihar*, 28 (She is the daughter of a king and the granddaughter of Humel. She wears a thousand pieces of clothing tied round her with knots). Hummel is Humayun, but the pertinence of the name is not apparent. Bengali: Mitra, *Sylhet*, p. 110, No. 8 (The girl lives below ground and wears rags very tightly. Although the barber does not touch her and the washerman does not wash her clothes, still the girl lives clean and spruce). Bhil: Hedberg, p. 870, No. 24 (One brother has put on coat upon coat). Filipino: Starr, *Philippines*, 261 (Mary is going to church having seven or eight shirts).

1440. (Riddles with the answer "pipe" are included among the following parallels.) French: Rolland, 165 (Who is it who has neither bones nor a skeleton, who carries fire on his head?). Serbian: Novaković, p. 122, Nos. 11 (Fire burns on its head and men kiss it on its tail), 12 (Fire burns on the snake's head, and the pasha kisses it on its tail), and p. 123, No. 6 (A striped snake. On its head fire burns, but men kiss it under the tail). The "snake" is the tube of the hookah. Armenian: Grigorov, p. 124, No. 206 (Body is of clay, nose is of fire). Cherekessian: Tambiev, p. 58, No. 60 (The nose of gold, the tail of wood.—Firebrand). Buryat: Gombojew, 49 (Smoke went out of our courtyard, fire clung to the head of the cobold.—Pipe). Arabic: Ruoff, p. 39, No. 98 (A bird flies over the oceans, its heart [is] of water, its head of fire). Persian: Kuka, 16 (I saw a very wonderful thing, which has water underneath and fire on the head). Indian, Kolarian: Wagner, 38 (Below they cook water, the fire they put above). Uraon: Archer, p. 189, No. 160 (Fire above, water below). Khāṛiā: Roy and Roy, II, 455, No. 49 (The jar below, the fire above). Bhil: Hedberg, p. 874, No. 55 (The hot water is beneath and above it is the fire).

1441. (The answer to the following riddles is "samovar.") Votyak: Wichmann, *Votyak*, 321 (Fire in the middle, water round about), 329, 440 (Fire burns in the middle of water). Cheremiss: Wichmann, *Cheremiss*, 83, 151. Armenian: Seidlitz, p. 71, Nos. 27 (A sea on all sides, fire in the middle), 31 (A window at the top, a hole below, fire and water within). Persian: Phillott, 1 (A strange thing I saw in this world: water bubbling round fire). Compare the samovar riddles cited in the headnote to Nos. 1440–1441, n. 30, in the present collection.

1442. French: Parsons, *Antilles*, III, 373, Grenada, 77. See also the headnote to Nos. 1443–1444, n. 3, of the present collection. Webster defines "Mackintosh" as a waterproof outer garment.

1443. Breton: Kerbeuzec, *Ille-et-Vilaine*, p. 502, No. 8, and p. 509, No. 9. German: Wossidlo, 244, 245; Hanika-Otto, 215, 216; Jungwirth, *Zeitschrift des Vereins für Volkskunde*, XX (1910), 84, No. 14. Walloon: Colson, *Wallonia*, IV, 109, No. 123; Colson, *Devinettes*, p. 149, No. 12 (Hairy above, hairy below, the most dangerous in the middle). French: Roland, 300; Parsons, *Antilles*, III, 367, Trinidad, 55, p. 389, Martinique, 128, p. 390, Dominica, 10, p. 402, Guadaloupe, 54, and p. 410, Les Saintes, 33. Catalan: Pelay y Briz, 79, 166, 220. Spanish, Chilean: Flores, 490, 516, 557. Dominican Rep.: Andrade, 255. New Mexican: Espinosa, 83; Campa, 211. Porto Rican: Mason, 403, and compare his No. 517. Italian: Gianandrea, *Archivio*, I (1882), 397, No. 1; Rondini, *ibid.*, VIII (1889), 187, No. 77b; Cimegotto, *ibid.*, XIII (1894), 436, No. 24; Balladoro, *ibid.*, XVI (1897), 230, No. 29; Pitrè, 514; Pitrè, *Canti*, II, 66, No. 843; and Pitrè, *Saggio di critica litteraria* (Bologna, 1870), p. 28; Ive, *Canti popolari istriani*, p. 302, No. 20; Tschiedel, 56, 59. Portuguese: Parsons, *Cape Verde*, 212. Rumanian: Gorovei, 1238. Lettish: Bielenstein, 71 (Hair above, hair below, "God protect it!" between). Polish: Saloni, *Rzeshów*, 32, 33; Siarkowski, 99 (Let us go to sleep and put hair upon hair.—Close the eyes); Gustawicz, 267, 337, 338. Russian: Sadovnikov, 1783 (Shaggy meets shaggy and they embrace). Bulgarian: Stoilov, p. 59, §14 (I cannot lie down and go to sleep before I touch wool to wool). Hungarian: Arany and Gyulai, II, 360, No. 57 (Put the two hairy ones together, leave the ball between); *Magyar Nyelvör,* II (1873), 90; V (1876), 268; VI (1877), 270; IX (1880), 37, No. 5; XVIII (1889), 376; and XXV (1896), 239. Modern Greek: Dieterich, *Sporades,* 18; Abbott, p. 317, No. 45 (Hair meets hair and they protect the hole); Polites, *Neohellenika Analekta,* I, 225, No. 179 (Wool covers wool and heals the opening); Stathes, p. 354, No. 134 (Wool meets wool and closes the opening); Carnoy and Nicolaides, 33. Gypsy: Wlislocki, 48. Turkish: Kúnos, 166. Yakut: Popov, p. 285 (Hair meets hair and wishes for night); Piekarski, 161 (Wool joins with wool and longs for something of last night), 162 = Priklonskii, 5 (At night, two pieces of wool, one from above, one from below, meet and join; at daybreak, they separate), 163 (Wool adheres to wool and pleads for that which comes with night); Priklonskii, 93. Indian, Bhil: Hedberg, p. 881, No. 99 (A bird sitting in the corner is flapping its wings). Indonesian, Menangkerbau Malay: Harmsen, p. 279, No. 49 (Hairs meet hairs, almost dead with pleasure.—Sleep). Lampong: Helfrich, *Lampong,* p. 614, No. 21 (Hair above, hair below; when they meet, the world is forgotten.—Sleep). American Indian, Ten'a: Jetté, 63 (Riddle me: we are placed above each other.—Eyelashes and the eyebrows). For related ideas see the tabulation in the note to No. 1425 in the present collection.

1444. French: Mensignac, *Gironde,* p. 298, No. 4 (Hairy against hairy, to hide the little bare one.—Eye). Spanish, New Mexican: Campa, 33 (Large and hairy and at the point a knot.—Halter, bell ox). Italian: Gianandrea, *Archivio,* I (1882), 398, No. 2; Ferraro, *Canti popolari in dialetto logodurese,* p. 305, No. 21.

1445a through 1446b. Swedish: Geijer and Campbell, 9; Ström, p. 147, "Smörkärnen," 1 (A bottom above, a bottom below, a stake in the middle, the work goes forward). This conception is akin to the riddle for a pair of horses with a pole between; see the headnote to Nos. 1416–1419, §7, in the present collection.

1448a through 1449. Tupper did not print the full text of an English version (*Holme Riddles,* 83). For parallels see French: Mensignac, *Gironde,* p. 305, No. 51 (flax). Portuguese: Parsons, *Cape Verde,* 219 (Put it in straight, take it out flopping). Italian: Tammi, 13 (apple). Lithuanian: Jurgelionis, 599 (They put them in straight, they pull them out limp.—Preparing flax), 600 through 603. Polish: Saloni, *Rzeshów,* 119 (It grows strong, it hangs weakly), 120 (It stands hard, it hangs weakly, it is overgrown, its head is bald); Siarkowski, 95 (Sharp as a horn, it comes out soft and flabby, at the end it goes, "Drip, drip!"—Taking flax from water); Gustawicz, 346 (It goes in like a horn, it comes out wilted, with the end dripping, "Drip, drip."—Crescent roll). The last refers to dipping a roll in a cup of coffee. Russian: Sadovnikov, 2066 (flax). Hungarian: *Magyar Nyelvör,* XII (1883), 332 (They put it in stiff, they take it out dripping.—Straw). Indonesian, Javanese: Luinenburg, p. 383, No. 15 (It is put into water, then it becomes thick; if it is taken out, then it becomes thin.—Duckweed, an aquatic plant).

The Zyrian straw riddle, "In wet, out dry" (Wichmann, *Zyrian,* 210) is a reversal of the usual pattern.

1450a, 1450b. Compare the fish riddle, No. 406.

1453. Flemish: Joos, 176 (I throw it over the house, and it is a cross). German: Wossidlo, 333; H. Meier, *Ostfriesland,* 1. Swiss: Zahler, *Münchenbuchsee,* 327 (I shot One-Leg on the roof and it comes down as Two-Legs). Walloon: Colson, *Wallonia,* V, 55, No. 203 (What does one throw in the air straight and it comes down crosswise?); Colson, *Devinettes,* p. 152, No. 34.

The underlying concept is closely related to that of a riddle for a ball of thread; see No. 1341 of the present collection.

1454. Icelandic: Árnason, 430 (What grows in stature when it loses its head?). Swedish: Ström, p. 163, "Huvudkudden." Latin: Daly and Suchier, p. 142, No. 101 (What rises higher, if you take off the head?); W. Wilmanns, "Disputatio regalis et nobilissimi iuvenis Pippini cum Albino scholastico," *Zeitschrift für deutsches Altertum,*

XIV (1869), 543, No. 96. The solution was later explained to him by Elias Steinmeyer; see *ibid.*, XV (1872), 166 note. An ingenious solution, *castrum, astrum*, which F. Schwarz proposed, is wrong; see *ibid.*, XLIII (1926), 269. Catalan: Pelay y Briz, 307. Spanish: Demófilo, 532 (What is bigger when you leave it?).

1455a, 1455b. Breton: Sébillot, *Haute-Bretagne*, 47; Kerbeuzec, *Ille-et-Vilaine*, 70; Duine, *Saint-Malo*, p. 517; Le Pennec, 30. Flemish: Joos, 257, 258. German: Hanika-Otto, 117. Danish: Kristensen, p. 136, § 393, Nos. 627a through 627f. Norwegian: Christie, 66 (hat); Bugge, *Telemarken*, 106; Stafset, 2 (hat); Brox, *Ytre Senja*, 47, citing Riksheim, 72. Swedish: Dybeck, *Runa*, 1848, p. 47, No. 66 = Russwurm; 83. Walloon: Colson, *Wallonia*, IV, 111, No. 135; Colson, *Devinettes*, p. 149, No. 17. French: Rolland, 136, 171; V. S., *Mélusine*, I (1878), col. 262, No. 40; Marchessou, *Velay et Auvergne*, p. 169, No. 23; Lacuve, *Poitou*, 3; A. Ferrand, *Dauphiné*, p. 228; Dardy, *L'Albret*, p. 329; Bladé, *Armagnac*, 111; Westphalen, *Metz*, col. 202; Roque-Ferrier, *Languedoc*, p. 337; Baissac, *Mauritius*, p. 403. Spanish: Demófilo, 1058, and p. 367, No. 6. Argentinian: Lehmann-Nitsche, 10, 32. Italian: Pitrè, 726a; Tschiedel, 50 (stocking); Gianandrea, *Archivio*, I (1882), 403, No. 11; Rua, *ibid.*, VII (1888), 453, No. 27. Rumanian: Gorovei, 1282. Lithuanian: Schleicher, p. 208. Polish: Gustawicz, 13 (What stands empty at night but is filled with meat during the day?). Russian: Sadovnikov, 642 (A linden bush is planted. It is unlocked at night, it is locked by day.—Boot, shoe). Finnish: Aarne and Krohn, 177 = Henssen, 213; Lönnrot, 38. Lappish: Qvigstad, 24; Poestion, p. 289. Estonian: Wiedemann, p. 283 (By day a sausage, by night a gut), and, on the same page (By a day full of flesh, by night its mouth is open), and a second variant (By day full of raw flesh, at night full of wind); Lönnrot, p. 191. Modern Greek: Polites, *Neohellenika Analekta*, I, 205, No. 68 (All day long with his mouth full, and at night gaping), and p. 211, No. 104 (All day long they are full, and at night they are empty). Ossete: Schiefner, 41. Indian, Parsee: Munshi, p. 416 (There is a substance which would only walk when its stomach is full, but never when it is empty.—Slippers). See also Nos. 453a through 453f and 991a through 991c in the present collection.

1456. Breton: Sébillot, *Haute-Bretagne*, 62; Duine, *Saint-Malo*, p. 517. Walloon: Colson, *Wallonia*, IV, 151, No. 183. Spanish, Argentinian: Lehmann-Nitsche, 33, 34. Serbian: Novaković, p. 104, Nos. 3 (At night it is ready to calve; by day it is not pregnant), 4 (By day it is empty; at night it is full). The first of these resembles the Bulgarian text discussed in the headnote to Nos. 1455–1457, § 3, in the present collection. Mordvin: Paasonen, 311 (Put together by day, stretched out at night). This resembles certain riddles cited in the present collection, particularly those for a belt (see the headnote to No. 1342, nn. 5–6). Samoan: Heider, 77 (Something thick by day and thin at night.— Mattress unrolled at night and rolled up by day), 76 (the preceding reversed to describe a mosquito net). See also the headnote to Nos. 1341–1342, § 4, in the present collection.

1459. Catalan: Milá y Fontanals, 1877, pp. 6–7 (not closely parallel). Lithuanian: Jurgelionis, 1068 (What has holes but holds water?). Modern Greek: Abbott, p. 305, No. 2 (A pitcher with a thousand chinks, yet ne'er lets out the water it drinks); Polites, *Neohellenika Analekta*, I, 196, Nos. 14 (A thousand-holed pail carries water to town), 15 (A thousand-holed ship takes water to town), 16 (A thousand-holed pail that does not spill a drop of water); Stathes, p. 349, 110 (A thousand-holed pail that does not spill a drop). The last two of these resemble a riddle in the present collection describing a cow's teats as bottles that do not spill a drop (see Nos. 1199a through 1199d and the corresponding note). See also No. 1424 for a sponge riddle. A similar idea is used in the description of a ring as a bottomless cylinder which will hold liquid, flesh, and bones (see, in the present collection, Nos. 1173d, 1173e, 1173g, 1173i, and 1173j).

1461, 1462. (The answer is usually a chain.) Welsh: Hull and Taylor, 259 (quoted in the note to No. 1173j in the present collection). German: Wossidlo, 353; Gilhoff, 35; Hanika-Otto, 111 (Hole adjoining hole, and yet it holds). The Swedish "Hole to hole, but as strong as steel" (Ström, p. 170, "Kättingen") turns the concept in a different direction.

1465. The import of "two heads and nary nose" is obscure.

1466. The import of "dark as homemade thunder" is obscure.

Inasmuch as riddles having the answer "snake" are not very numerous, it is curious that the Scotch Gaelic "A little rod in Alexander's wood, neither pine is it, nor oak is it, it is no wood on earth, and you will not guess it until nightfall" (Nicolson, p. 17) should have parallels in eastern Europe. See French: Parsons, *Antilles*, III, 381, Martinique, 15. Rumanian: Papahagi, 84. Serbian: Novaković, p. 62, Nos. 3 (I went along a road and I found a stick, uncut and untouched. God said, "Leave that alone. I need it"), 4 (I went alone, unsent, and found a stick uncut. God said, "Leave that alone, that is my support"), and p. 63, No. 2 (I threw the stick into the bush and could not find its end). Hungarian: *Magyar Nyelvör*, V (1876), 127 (They are throwing iron sticks all over the roads); and VI (1887), 423 (In the forest pretty sticks are going around). Indian, Bihari: Mitra, *Bihar*, 9 (A long stick thrown away in the forest). Baiga: Elwin, p. 465, No. 10 (A king's stick that no one will lift). Uraon: Archer, p. 184, No. 78 (A fallen plough-stick that cannot be picked up). Bhil: Hedberg, p. 871, No. 30 (A fresh stick, I can't bend it and you can't bend it). Indonesian, Batak: Ophuijsen, p. 214, No. 44 (It is like a piece of wood, but one cannot step over it).

A special variety of the comparison of a snake to a stick is seen in the following: Cuman: Németh, *Codex Cumanicus*, pp. 594–595, Nos. 27, 28 (many parallels). Turkish: Kowalski, *Asia Minor*, 82 (Under the earth a fat stick); Kowalski, *North Bulgaria*, 50 (Under the earth there lies a fat thong); Kúnos, 156 (Under the ground a slimy belt); Hamizade, 735 (Underneath the earth is a greasy strap); Katanov in Radlov, IX, 242, No. 109, p. 255, No. 136, and p. 293, No. 262. Turcoman: Samojlvich, 47 (Under the earth a flat rod). This is also used for a bear in the Altai Turkish "Under the earth a fat club" (Menges, p. 77, No. 44) and for a mouse in the Turcoman "Under the ground a greasy ball" (Samojlvich, 43).

A snake is sometimes compared to a lady. See Spanish: Demófilo, 352; Rodríguez Marín, 390 through 394. Argentinian: Lehmann-Nitsche, 331. Chilean: Flores, 218 through 221.

1467. Note the echo of the wolf's reply to Little Red Riding Hood.

1469. Abyssinian: Littmann, *Tigriña*, 74 (Something that moves itself back and forth in a hole).

1471. French: J. Roux, *Limousin*, 33 (It measures the height of the sky in a single motion); Roque-Ferrier, *Languedoc*, p. 327 (What is the height of the sky?—Flash of the eye). Persian: Phillott, 18 (It travels to the sky ahead of the eye but no one has ever seen it.—Sight).

1472. For references to the value or services of an object compare the headnote to Nos. 1674–1680.

1473. (The small object is usually identified as a flaxseed, almond, grain of wheat or rice, or a chemical.) Breton: Sébillot, *Haute-Bretagne*, 60a; Orain, *Ille-et-Vilaine*, p. 152; Duine, *Saint-Malo*, p. 516. Flemish: Joos, 166. German: Wossidlo, 346. Swiss: Rochholz, 476; Zahler, *Münchenbuchsee*, 228. Walloon: Colson, *Wallonia*, IV, 150, No. 175; Colson, *Devinettes*, p. 150, No. 23 (almond). French: Rolland, 167; V. S., *Mélusine*, I (1878), col. 262, No. 65; J. Roux, *Limousin*, 8; A. Ferrand, *Dauphiné*, p. 227; Dottin, *Bas-Maine*, p. 137, No. 6; Westphalen, *Metz*, col. 196; Constantin, *Savoie*, p. 20; Carmeau, p. 34; De la Suie, *Savoie*, p. 472; Parsons, *Antilles*, III, 381, Martinique, 18, p. 413, Les Saintes, 12, and p. 437, Saint Martin, 40. Catalan: Pelay y Briz, 65, 248; Demófilo, p.

360, No. 7. Spanish: Demófilo, 621, p. 369, No. 18, and p. 394, No. 56; Rodríguez Marín, p. 317, No. 16. Argentinian: Lehmann-Nitsche, 315 through 317, 590. Dominican Rep.: Andrade, 192. Porto Rican: Mason, 335. Portuguese: Parsons, *Cape Verde*, 129a through 129c. Italian: Pitrè, 417; Gianandrea, *Canti popolari marchigiani*, p. 303, No. 34. Rumanian: Gorovei, 1046; and Gorovei, *Devinettes*, p. 506 (Of all things I am the largest. I am so large that I fill the room. During the day I am shy, and during the night I see very well). Hungarian: *Magyar Nyelvör*, III (1874), 328 (Its price is two kreuzer, but it does not fit in the house); and VII (1878), 476. The meaning is that light radiates so widely that it cannot be confined in a house. Arabic: Ruoff, p. 38, No. 90; Bauer, p. 222, No. 11; Littmann, 58; Stumme, *Tázerwalt*, 18; Giacobetti, 403, 404; Löhr, p. 107, No. 13; Socin and Stumme, 3 (A lively grain of wheat that shines in our room). Turkish: Kúnos, 48 (A chemical costing five paras will fill four corners of the house); Kowalski, *Zagadki*, 12 (Sal ammoniac to the worth of a liard [a small coin] furnishes the whole room); Moshkov in Radlov, X, 269, No. 65 (Five kopeks' worth of sal ammoniac illuminates the whole world). Mongolian: Mostaert, 128 (One jujube cannot find room in a whole house), 130 (One jujube reddens the whole felt tent). African, Kxatla: Schapera, 100 (Tell me: the little calf which fills the house of the white people), 102 (Tell me: a small pot which by itself fills a hut). Surinam: Herskovits, 78. Indian, Kolarian: Wagner, 61 (A very small bird brings light to the whole country), 62 (By one rice ear the whole house is filled). Khāṛiā: Roy and Roy, II, 451, No. 22 (The house is filled with one sheaf of paddy). Bihari: Mitra, *Bihar*, 46 (An exceedingly small buffalo, it occupies the whole room); Mitra, *Bihari Life*, p. 43, No. 24 (One pod fill the whole room with husks). Bengali: Mitra, *Chittagong*, p. 343, No. 4 (A piece of flax suffices to fill a large room). Bhil: Hedberg, p. 885, No. 126 (From a single ear the whole house is filled with chaff). This, like one of the Bihari riddles, carries out the metaphor with admirable fullness. Indonesian: Sangir: Adriani, p. 393, No. 37 (A piece of pig filled a house). Tabaru: Fortgens, 48. Atjeh: Kreemer, *Atjeh*, 71 (A head of rice as full as a house), which seems to involve a slight inaccuracy in translation. Filipino: Starr, *Philippines*, 85 (A grain of rice fills the whole house). Tagalog: Rizal, p. 45. Chinese: oral (Not big, not big, it cannot be packed in one [var.: a whole] room); Rudolph, p. 75, No. 24 (It is a thing which is not large, yet it fills the whole room except below itself).

1476a through 1489. Scotch Gaelic: Nicolson, p. 39. Irish: Christiansen, 27a through 27c; O Dalaigh, 19; Delargy, 42 (Four running, four shaking, two giving directions and Mac Oi Ghioblacháin running after them); and Delargy, *Inis Cé*, 15 (Four shaking, four running, and the son of the beggar king running after them all); De Bhaldraithe, 24. Breton: Sébillot, *Haute-Bretagne*, 16; Orain, *Ille-et-Vilaine*, p. 146; Kerbeuzec, *Ille-et-Vilaine*, 1; Charlec, *Dol-de-Bretagne*, 1904, p. 168, No. 32. Frisian: Dykstra, *Snypsnaren*, p. 104; Carstensen, p. 326, No. 17. Dutch: Sinninghe, p. 12, No. 14. The introduction is perhaps intended to suggest a hedge, and the answer should be "cow," and not "steer." Flemish: Joos, 582, 641. Afrikaans: Groenewald, pp. 62, 76. German: Wossidlo, 165, and compare his No. 120; Frischbier, *Thierwelt*, p. 344, Nos. 1, 2; Gilhoff, 24 through 31; Haase, *Ruppin*, p. 73, No. 25; Haffner, 60 through 63; A. Pichler, "Tirolische Volksdichtung," *Zeitschrift des Vereins für Volkskunde*, IV (1894), 200; Hanika-Otto, 8a through 8h. Faeroic: Hammershaimb, *Færøsk anthologi*, I, 324, No. 35 = Hammershaimb, *Antiquarisk tidsskrift*, III (1849–1851), 320, No. 54 = Karl Müllenhoff, *Zeitschrift für deutsche Mythologie*, III (1855), 129. Icelandic: Heusler, *Zeitschrift des Vereins für Volkskunde*, XI (1901), 129; Árnason, 254 (Four walk, five dangle, one swings behind and never gets in front), 255 (Four walk on the ground, five dangle near by, one lags behind and never gets any closer to the front). Norwegian: Landstad, p. 807, No. 11; Aasen, 5; Christie, 1; Berge, 9; Bugge, *Telemarken*, 16; Stafset, 64; Brox, *Ytre Senja*, 17. Danish: Kristensen, pp. 72–75, § 174, Nos. 276a through 289d, p. 75, § 176, No. 281d (which is contaminated with the theme discussed in the headnote to Nos. 976–979 of the present collection), and pp. 144–145, § 429, Nos. 679a through 679s; Feilberg, *Ordbog*, II, 240–241, s.v. "ko," and p. 538, s.v. "malke." Swedish: Russwurm, 44 = Dybeck, *Runa*, 1847, pp. 40–41, No. 8 (Four hang, four walk, two point up in the air, a little one dangles behind). See also Dybeck, *Runa*, 1847, p. 42, No. 22 (Two lights, two spits, four goers, four hangers, one dragger-after); 1848, p. 45, No. 45; 1849, p. 47, No. 8; and 1865–1873, p. 8; Ericsson, *Södermanland*, I (1879), 81, No. 6; and II (1881), 94, Nos. 81 through 83; Hyltén-Cavallius, *Värend*, 3; Noreen, *Fryksdal*, 11; Sandén, *Norra Vadsbo*, 125, 127; Waltman, *Lidmål*, 196; Geijer and Campbell, 63, and compare their Nos. 4 through 7 and 68; Ström, pp. 93–95, "Oxen, kon, kalven," 1 through 8. Walloon: Colson, *Wallonia*, IV, 58, No. 43. French: Rolland, 44, 400, and compare his No. 31; Rolland, *Rimes*, p. 198, No. 11; Bladé, *Armagnac*, 1; Ledieu, *Démuin*, p. 327 (Four strike the dew, four look at the sky, four carry breakfast); E. Rolland, *Faune populaire*, V (Paris, 1882), 113; L. Desaivre, *Mélusine*, I (1878), col. 245, No. 2; V. S., *ibid.*, col. 264, Nos. 88, 89; Fleury, *Basse-Normandie*, p. 372; Sébillot, *Auvergne*, 7; Marchessou, *Velay et Auvergne*, p. 179, No. 11; Bon, *Auvergne*, p. 204; Patry, *Normandie*, p. 643; Fesquet, p. 175; Desaivre, *Poitou*, p. 450, No. 2; Pineau, *Poitou*, 4; Queyrat, *La Creuse*, I, 363; Parsons, *Antilles*, III, 384, Martinique, 63. Basque: Vinson, 19. Catalan: Pelay y Briz, 14, 127, 147, 169, 311, 320; Milá y Fontanals, 1876, p. 26, No. 22. Spanish: Demófilo, 168 through 170, 985, 1012, and p. 347, No. 35, p. 363, No. 17, p. 382, No. 7, and p. 389, No. 8; Rodríguez Marín, 335 through 338 and pp. 323–324, n. 34; *El folklore español*, V (1884), 98–99. Argentinian: Lehmann-Nitsche, 549a through 549j. Chilean: Flores, 117, 761 through 766; Laval, 32, 33. Cuban: Massip, 196 (Two pointers, four flowers, one fly-shover); Giménez Cabrera, 46 (Four run-woods, four run-fountains, two *tus, tus*, one hit-him). The words *tus, tus* are used to call a dog. Mexican: M. Redfield, p. 50, No. 13. New Mexican: Campa, 112, 153, 171. Porto Rican: Mason, 538, 539. Portuguese: Coelho, *Zeitschrift für romanische Philologie*, III (1879), 198, No. 6; Pires, *Archivio*, III (1884), 114, No. 9; Braga, 5; Pires de Lima, 135 through 138; Parsons, *Cape Verde*, 53a through 53c. Italian: Straparola, IV, 5; A. Gianandrea, *Archivio*, I (1882), 404–405, No. 13; Coronedi-Berti, *ibid.*, II (1883), 580, No. 45; Salvioni, *ibid.*, IV (1885), 539, No. 2; Rua, *ibid.*, VII (1888), 452, No. 15; Rondini, *ibid.*, VIII (1889), 190, No. 96; G. Ferraro, *ibid.*, p. 332, No. 3; Corsi, *ibid.*, X (1891), 397, No. 3; Cimegotto, *ibid.*, XIII (1894), 435, No. 23; Menghini, *ibid.*, XIV (1895), 278, No. 7; Balladoro, *ibid.*, XVI (1897), 557, No. 51; Ferraro, *ibid.*, XXI (1902), 538–539, No. 14; Panareo, *ibid.*, XXIII (1906–1907), 236, No. 2; Bernoni, *Venice*, 25; Pitrè, 87; and Pitrè, *Canti*, II, 67, No. 846; Tschiedel, 5, 7; Ive, *Canti popolari istriani*, p. 300, No. 14; Ferraro, *Canti popolari in dialetto logodurese*, p. 304, No. 19, and p. 310, No. 37; Gianandrea, *Canti popolari marchigiani*, p. 296, No. 3; Schneller, *Wälschtirol*, p. 253, No. 3. Rumanian: Gorovei, 1920. Lithuanian: Jurgelionis, 731 (Four jump, two listen, two look, two smell), 732 (Two run, two chase, two whistle), 733 (Four clatter, the fifth sweeps the road), 734 (Four workers work, one sweeps); Schleicher, p. 205 (Two extend themselves, two stretch themselves, and the fifth fights in battle). Lettish: Bielenstein, 209 (Two wind instruments, two broad bits of cloth, four that run on the ground, a fifth that wages war), 210 (Two wind instruments, two pancakes, four that crouch on the earth, a ninth that awaits attack), 211 (Two conical bags, two leaves, four that run on the earth [var.: stamp the earth], a ninth is the military captain), 212 (Two leaves, two supports [the translator is uncertain of the meaning], four that root up the earth, a fifth that continually beats flesh), 213, 214. Czech: Feifalik, p. 369, No. 10. Polish: Gustawicz, 172 through 176p; Kopernicki, 41 (Four poles, two sticks, and the seventh is a brush), 41 var. (Four walkers, four pullers, one grinder, and two pushers); Kolberg, *Krakowskie*, IV, No. 57, as cited by Kopernicki; Saloni, *Rzeszów*, 83 (Four goers, four pullers, one *majder* [the meaning is obscure], two prickers), 84 (Four poles, two stakes, the fifth [the riddler has lost count], a wagger), 85 (Five poles, two little stakes, the fifth wags), 86; Siarkowski, 9 (Four teats, two little sticks, the seventh is a pendulum), 9 var., 35 (four walkers, four pullers, two pushers, and the eleventh is a thrower-outer). Russian: Sadovnikov, 855, 856 (Four dangle, four stamp, one shakes), 857 (Four are boots, four are noisy, two are ear-y, one is wave-y), 858, 859 (One shakes, four walk, two frighten children, four are sweet to all), 860 through 866, 873 through 876; Preobrazhenskii, p. 171 (Two gore-ish, two walk-ish, one wavers, two ear-ies). I have endeavored to suggest the strange Russian compounds by equally strange English compounds. Serbian: Novaković, p. 6, No. 7 (Three ——, four walkers, the fifth and sixth gorers, the seventh and eighth you cover, and the ninth you twist), p. 22, No. 3 (There are two binding feathers with two horns and four stalks), and p. 23, No. 1 (One, two walk; the fifth, the sixth make noise; the eighth gores, and the ninth switches its tail), which is badly disorganized. Bulgarian: Gubov, 93 (The four walked, the fifth and sixth looked at each other, the seventh and eighth listened, the ninth lagged behind). Finnish: Aarne, as cited in the headnote to Nos. 1476–1494 in the present collection. Estonian: Wiedemann, p. 281 (Four give, four bear, two keep off the dog, one beats on the milk pail) and two more versions. Lappish: Qvigstad, 94. Cheremiss: Genetz, 99 (Four dance, one clasps). Hungarian: Kálmány, II, 176, No. 21 (Two look skyward, two look downward, four bite the dew, four carry the cream container, and you'll find the broom at the back); *Magyar Nyelvör*, VI (1877), 270 (Two stand straight, four reach the dew, four prepare dinner); VII (1878), 89 (It looks at the sky with two things, it looks at the ground with two things, it carries supper in four things, it touches the dew with four things, too); XI (1882), 527 (There is a fork in front, a broom in the rear, four things on the ground, and four things pay the customs duty), which contains traits belonging to the cow riddle discussed in the headnote to No. 1435, § 3, of the present collection. See further, *Magyar Nyelvör*, XL (1911), 285 (It has four *tipi topa* [onomatopoetic words signifying "feet"], it has two shiny buttons, it carries a fork in front and a broom in the rear) has also a similar borrowing. Szendrey (*Ethnographia*, XXXII [1921], 74) cites the following additional versions, among which I have been unable to find his citations from Kálmány: *Magyar Nyelvészet*, II, 321 (Four hang down, two stand up, two stand apart, four are drawn upon); Lázár, 519 (Four are holders, two look up to Heaven, two shine like the lake, but there is no lake); Kálmány, III, 188 (Two look at the heavens, two look on the earth, four fling down the dew, four carry breakfast, the broom is in the rear); Szendrey's manuscript collection from Szalonta (With two it gazes at the heavens, with two it measures the road, it carries breakfast in four, with one it chases flies). I have discarded some versions which properly belong in the headnote to No. 1435, § 3, of the present collection. Turkish: Hamizade, 274 (Four hanging ones, four stepping ones, two piercing ones, one stepping [properly: dragging] one). Arabic: Ruoff, p. 42, No. 8 (Four make the sound *Trak, trak*, two [go] up and down, and one drives off flies). Tatar: Kalashev and Ioakimov, p. 49, No. 17 (Four are on the ground, four are in the sky), which resembles the riddle for a bed (Nos. 69a through 70 of the present collection). Yakut: Piekarski, 148 (There are eight who resemble one another, four identical ones, two peaceful ones, and two hostile ones, they say.—Hoofs, teats, horns, ears), which seems a little confused unless it refers to cloven hoofs and the last two elements of the answer are interchanged, and 149 (They say that there are four who resemble one another and eight paired ones.—Four shins and eight hoofs of horned cattle). Indian, Bhil: Hedberg, p. 873, No. 52 (Two are standing, two flapping, four are walking, and two are flashing). Kashmiri: Knowles, 136 (She treads the ground with four, four are dishes of sweets, two are lamps, two are archers, and one fans her). Uraon: Archer, p. 194, No. 223 (Four brothers who stagger while a fifth waves a switch). Filipino: Starr, *Philippines*, 3 (Four posts, one whip, two fans, and two bolos.—Carabao),

4 (Four earth posts, two air posts, and [a] whip.—Carabao), 5 (One pointing, two moving, four changing [position].—Carabao).

1476e. A "horny cow" is a cow with horns.

1477h. The use of the word "switchbox" shows that the riddler does not understand what he is saying. It is probably a city child's corruption of the word "switchabout."

1486. The riddler has introduced some elements belonging to the comparison of a man to a house; see the headnote to Nos. 1100–1108, nn. 17, 24–25, 27–28.

1488. The collector explains the word "t'under" as "thunder," but it is probably a corruption of "timber"; compare No. 1486. "Bellie bander" is probably a corruption of "dillydander"; see No. 1478a and the headnote to No. 1478.

1490. (In the parallels cited here, the answer is usually "horse" and only rarely "donkey.") German: Wossidlo, 119. French: Rolland, *Rimes*, p. 198, No. 10; Baissac, *Mauritius*, p. 401. Italian: Rondini, *Archivio*, VIII (1889), 190, No. 95. Serbian: Novaković, p. 96, Nos. 3 (One dines, two hold the light, four serve, and a thousand dance.— Horse eating oats, looking with its eyes, standing on its legs, shaking its tail so that the hairs fly about), 4 (Two bump, two thump, two look, two listen, and the ninth is Shaking Pasha). The first of these Serbian riddles is an interesting adaptation intended to suggest a banquet. Hungarian: Arany and Gyulai, II, 357, No. 45 (Four prancers, two flaps, one switch), and p. 358, No. 48 (It walks, it has two big flaps, the third is the switch); and III, 297, No. 27 (Four big prancers, two little flaps, one is the switch); *Magyar Nyelvör*, II (1873), 467, No. 58; Pap, 153 (Four prancers, two little flaps, one switch), as cited by Szendrey in *Ethnographia*, XXXII (1921), 76. Mordvin: Paasonen, 201 (Four push, four grind, Akkulima winnows). This is perhaps an adaptation of the riddles cited in the headnote to No. 841, nn. 26–32, in the present collection. Zyrian: Wichmann, *Zyrian*, 159 (It stands on four feet, two lights are burning, two dolls are playing). This is a curious adaptation to a domestic scene. Modern Greek: Georgeakis, p. 292; Polites, *Neohellenika Analekta*, I, 209, No. 90 (Four make this sound, *Tack, tick;* two this, *Tick, tick;* and one is used to drive away flies.—Mule). Arabic: Giacobetti, 153 (Four things make a noise and two are moving in the air, there is a club to chase away flies before his shop.—Donkey). Turkish: Hamizade, 20 (Four *taktak*'s [onomatopoetic], one looking, two hearing, one little one), 177 (Four hangers, two lookers, two hearers, one smeller.—Donkey).

For discussion see Aarne, *Rätselforschungen*, II, 135–145; Szendrey, *Ethnographia*, XXXII (1921), 76.

1491. A contaminated version containing elements found in Nos. 69a through 69d and 1429a through 1429c.

1492. Breton: Sauvé, 107 (Two who rest, two who work, two who bend and two who run, and two who work all the time.—Windmill). Hungarian: Kriza, 17 (*Denden* plank, *pereszlen* cube, six horses pull it, the seventh causes snow to fall.—Mill). The meanings of the italicized words are obscure.

1495. For a comparison of a pot on a man's head, in terms of the living and the dead, see Nos. 67a through 67e.

Chapter X
ENUMERATIONS IN TERMS OF COLOR
Nos. 1496–1572

1496. The magpie riddle usually lists comparisons to other things in terms of their blackness and whiteness; see Nos. 1379 through 1382. Since this text lacks such comparisons, we might infer that it is defective. A few parallels, however, mention the colors of a magpie without giving comparisons to them; see Breton: Sébillot, *Haute-Bretagne*, 22; Kerbeuzec, *Ille-et-Vilaine*, 100. Flemish: Joos, 375. Basque: Vinson, 68.

1498a through 1499. "Red" is occasionally spelled "read." This riddle does not clearly suggest an object different from the answer.

1498c. This riddle employs the technique of Nos. 1559a through 1561d. Inasmuch as the second stage is inaccurately described—a newspaper is only partially black when it is printed, the riddle is more confusing that it should properly be.

1499. The riddler seeks to accommodate the question to the technique of the true riddle by suggesting, in this instance rather imperfectly, a creature that moves about.

1504. (The following parallels contain references to two colors.) German: Haffner, 171 (It is yellow within and white without). French: Rolland, 62; Baissac, *Mauritius*, p. 400. Modern Greek: Polites, *Neohellenika Analekta*, I, 229, No. 202 (I have something that is white outside and yellow inside).

An acquaintance with this riddle is implied in a jest ascribed to Nasreddin; see René Basset, *Mille et un Contes*, I (Paris, 1924), 433, No. 137; Albert Wesselski, *Der Hodscha Nasreddin* (Weimar, 1911), I, 11, No. 15 (see also his note, p. 209).

1505a through 1505c. (The following parallel contains a reference to three colors.) Welsh Gypsy: Sampson, 12 (What is white and yellow, and yet white all over?).

1505b. The collector has probably misunderstood "foul" as "fowl"; see No. 1505c.

1506a, 1506b. (The following parallels contain references to three positions of colors.) Danish: Kristensen, § 149, § 439, No. 698 (What is white without and white within with a yellow dot in the middle?). Mingrelian: Blechsteiner, p. 157, No. 6 (White without and half red, half white within). Svanian: J. Nizheradze, pp. 68–69, No. 27 (First it is white, then it is white, then it is golden). See also No. 1553 of the present collection.

1509. The answer should be "cantaloupe"; see No. 1514.

1517. Compare No. 1153.

1531. Votyak: Buch, 20 (White without, black within). See the pot riddles cited in the note to No. 1537 of the present collection.

1536. Compare No. 1562.

1537. Low German: Frischbier, *Menschenwelt*, p. 252, No. 121 (White without, black within.—Pot), and p. 253, No. 122 (frying pan). For ideas related to the theme of "guts wallopin'" see, in the present collection, the references listed in the headnote to No. 1032, n. 1.

1538a through 1538f. Irish: Delargy, 23 (It is black outside, it is red inside, there you have it! Now, thrust into it!). For more vivid scenes of the same category, see the Lithuanian "Blackie! I thrust one who is not black into you" (Schleicher, p. 199) and "Blacken or don't blacken yourself. I shall put something into you" (Jurgelionis, 259), or the Serbian "A red hole, a white wedge, lift your leg and drive in the wedge" (Novaković, p. 238, No. 1). See also No. 1417 in the present collection, and compare No. 1416 (stocking). The theme is obscured in the French "Who is black outside and red inside?" (Mensignac, *Gironde*, 24 *bis*).

1538f. Riddlers do not often mention an act before describing the form.

1540. Compare the Rumanian "A Moor above, a Moor below, the bride in the middle" (Papahagi, 26).

1542, 1543. Mordvin: Paasonen, 303.

(The usual answer in the following parallels is "iron while it is being forged.") See Flemish: Joos, 51 (I throw it red into the water and it comes up black), 52 (I put it black into the pot and it comes out red. Guess from now until St. Gertrude's Day!). German: Wossidlo, 330a, 330b (It falls into the water a beautiful red and comes out as black as death), 331 (What goes into the fire black and comes out again red?); Hanika-Otto, 94 (Into the water white and out of it black.—Glowing iron); Haffner, 241. Swiss: Zahler, *Münchenbuchsee*, 199. Swedish: Ström, p. 379, "Sysselsättningar," 38. Spanish: Demófilo, 233 (I was a crude mountaineer who was buried without any reason, I suffered pains in a terrible fire, I emerged black and without a face; I keep it carefully.—Coal). New Mexican: Campa, 56 (They put it in hard, they take it out white, colored, and flashing.—Iron in forge). Lettish: Bielenstein, 785 (It goes into the bath black and comes out red), 786 through 788. Gypsy: Wlislocki, 47 (Red while alive, black when dead.—Coal). Turkish: Kúnos, 240 (I bought it in the market. It was jet black, it came home blazing red); Zavarin, *Brusa*, 46 (I bought it in the bazar, it was black as black. I brought it home, it was red as red); Hamizade, 416 (Over there it is very black, in the house it is red), 417 (In the winter it is a jewel, blow on it and it gets black; it is itself a very black smoke's poison.—Charcoal). African, Songaï: Hamouda, 23 (A red Targui has fallen into the water; he has turned into a black Bella [slave of the Touareg]). Indian, Baiga: Elwin, p. 474, No. 106. Indonesian, Malay: Klinkert, p. 49, No. 32 (It is brought in black, it is dragged out red, and beaten while a man sits on his haunches.—Iron). This alludes to the habit of Malay smiths, who sit on their heels while working at the forge. The scene is probably intended to suggest that of slaughtering an animal.

1544. I am not quite sure what meaning the riddler attaches to the words "in" and "out."

1547a, 1547b. Spanish, Argentinian: Lehmann-Nitsche, 688, 689 (in the house red, in the field green). Hungarian: *Magyar Nyelvör*, VIII (1879), 185 (When thrown up, it is green; when it has fallen down, it is red).

1548. The riddler has understood "green" to mean "unripe" and has therefore replaced "red" by "ripe."

1549. A confused riddle containing elements of Nos. 1547a and 1547b, and of the descriptions of objects by a series of comparisons (for which see Nos. 1384 through 1393b). See also the description of plants in a biographical sequence of colors, as discussed in the headnote to Nos. 668–669.

1550a through 1550c. (The following parallels contain no details of the situation and no comparisons for the colors.) Welsh: Hull and Taylor, 139, 140. Welsh Gypsy: Sampson, 11. Scotch Gaelic: Nicolson, p. 33. Breton: Sébillot, *Haute-Bretagne*, 21c (Who comes in white and leaves yellow?). German: Frischbier, *Thierwelt*, p. 355, No. 75; Hanika-Otto, Nos. 387a, 387b. Danish: Kristensen, p. 150, § 439, Nos. 702a, 702e. French: Rolland, 61; Pineau, *Poitou*, 31; Mensignac, *Gironde*, No. 46 (I throw a ball white. It falls yellow); Baissac, *Mauritius*, p. 403. Rumanian: Gorovei, 1311. Polish: Gustawicz, 126. Hungarian: Arany and Gyulai, II, 350, No. 10; *Magyar Nyelvör*, VIII (1879), 185; *Magazin für die Litteratur des Auslands*, 1856, p. 364.

1551a, 1551b. Flemish: Joos, 364 (I throw something over the house, and it comes down red.) The reference is probably to the half-formed chick in the shell. Compare Nos. 1505a through 1505c in the present collection.

1552. (In the following parallels the riddler elaborates "up" and "down" by references to specific places. In many of these versions the allusion to "in the air" probably means merely "up.") Welsh: Hull and Taylor, 141 (What goes white to the brink and comes yellow to the ground?). Luxemburg: De la Fontaine, 4 (on the roof). German: Wossidlo, 328; Gilhoff, 119; Frischbier, *Thierwelt*, p. 355, No. 76; H. Meier, *Ostfriesland*, 1 (on the roof); Haffner, 170 (on the table); Hanika-Otto, 387c (on the roof). Swiss: Zahler, *Münchenbuchsee*, 62 (on the roof). Danish: Kristensen, p. 150, § 439, Nos. 702b, 702d, 702e; Feilberg, *Ordbog*, III, 1144, s.v. "æg." Swedish: Ström, p. 197, "Ägget," 6. Walloon: Colson, *Wallonia*, IV, 62, No. 59 (in the air); Colson, *Devinettes*, No. 6 (in the air). French: Ledieu, *Démuin*, p. 132 (in the air); Parsons, *Antilles*, III, 391, Dominica, 19, p. 404, Guadaloupe, 72 (in the air), and p. 410, Les Saintes, 30 (on a balcony). Spanish, Argentinian: Lehmann-Nitsche, 693 (on the roof). Lettish: Bielenstein, 421 (One lays it on the table: it is white. It falls and becomes yellow). Polish: Saloni, *Rzeshów*, 56 (It will fly up white to the roof and come down gold from the roof).

1553. (In the following parallels the riddler names three elements.) Welsh Gypsy: Sampson, 12 (What is white and yellow, yet white all over?). Breton: La Calvez, *Tréguier*, p. 342 (Throw up one and three are found.—Hen, white, and yellow of egg); Lavenot, *Basse-Bretagne*, p. 667 (like La Calvez's riddle). French: Lacuve, *Poitou*, 18 (like La Calvez's riddle).

1554. (In the following parallels the riddler makes allusions to colors and elaborates them by comparisons.) Scotch Gaelic: Nicolson, p. 33 (It will be lifted up as white as the snow, but brought down golden yellow on the flagstone). Irish: Hyde, p. 170 (I threw it up as white as snow, like gold on a flag it fell below); Christiansen, 35a (I threw it up as white as snow and it fell down as yellow as gold), 35b (I threw it up as white as my skirt, and it fell as red as gold), 36 (It is Gogarde o Gog, who is as white as chalk, and if he falls out of the nest in the tree, he becomes as red as blood); De Bhaldraithe, 32 (I threw her up, white as a swan, and she fell down, yellow as gold); Delargy, *Inis Cé*, 13.

1559a. Swiss: Zahler, *Münchenbuchsee*, 76 (First as white as snow, then as green as clover, then as red as blood; it tastes as good to all children). Walloon: Colson, *Wallonia*, IV, 91, No. 86.

1559b. Tupper did not print the parallel text in *Holme Riddles*, 138. The theme is contained in several English riddles in the present collection; see Nos. 1374, 1421, and 1572a through 1572c. See also Scotch Gaelic: Nicolson, p. 41. French: Rolland, 103. Hungarian: Meltzl, 39.

1561a through 1561d. (In the following parallels, the fruits given as answers vary somewhat.) See Frisian: Dykstra, *Snypsnaren*, p. 107. Arabic: Giacobetti, 107 (Its web is white, its fabric red, and it is black when you take it from its frame.—Wild mulberry), which involves a comparison to weaving. Svanian: J. Nizheradze, pp. 68–69, No. 21 (At first it is red, then it is white, then it is reddish, and then it is black.—Blackberry).

1562. See the Lampong parallels, "A chapel on two posts, it can fly, toward morning it makes a sound" and "A chapel on two posts, a roof of split bamboo" (Helfrich, *Lampong*, pp. 612–613, Nos. 1, 14). The second of these has an Engganee parallel, "A dwelling with only two posts and with a motley thatch that can move itself about" (Helfrich, *Engganee*, p. 518, No. 11). See also, in the present collection, No. 1536, the headnote to No. 1437, n. 10, and riddles cited in the headnote to Nos. 1100–1108, nn. 32, 40.

1563. Probably a defective and unimaginative version of the pattern exemplified by Nos. 871 through 877, which contain an adequate personification.

1565c. The phrases "put 'to a bag, tied with a string," which can (if necessary) refer to coal sold in a sack, are found in Nos. 1096a through 1096d, 1096f, 1096h, and 1097 through 1099.

1568. The second half of the riddle has a parallel in a riddle for catching a louse (see Nos. 971d through 971f).

1570. Riddles for a rainbow vary greatly among themselves, and few, if any, resemble this English text. Compare as an example the Estonian "Who goes through the world bent and striped like a ribbon, and whom no one can catch?" (Dido, 25).

1571. Spanish, Argentinian: Lehmann-Nitsche, 532 (A green gourd full of sweet water). Filipino: Starr, *Philippines*, 405 (Green skin, red meat, *espectorante* they call it), which I do not fully understand.

Other riddles referring to a watermelon as something that is both green and red are Nos. 910*a*, 910*b*, 910*e* through 910*i*, 916*a* through 916*d*, 916*f*, 916*g*, 1083, 1162*a*, 1162*b*, 1369, 1376, 1508, 1518, 1528, 1547*a*, 1547*b*, and 1549 in the present collection.

1572a through 1572c. Tupper did not print the parallel in the *Holme Riddles*, 85. Compare the Welsh riddle for a leek, "In a bed I sleep, my end has been buried; the fatter I am, the better for the housewife" (Hull and Taylor, 117). See also a somewhat similar Swedish description of a nut (Ström, p. 126, "Hasel," 2).

Chapter XI
ENUMERATIONS IN TERMS OF ACTS
Nos. 1573–1748

1573. Welsh: Hull and Taylor, 209. Irish: Delargy, 41 (There is something on me and it is not heavy on me, but in any case it is on me). Breton: Sauvé, 139a. Danish: Kristensen, p. 96, § 249, No. 382. Norwegian: Bergh, *Valdres*, 46 (What is it that clings to everything?). French: Bladé, *Armagnac*, 5; Baissac, *Mauritius*, p. 409. Catalan: Pelay y Briz, 21; Milá y Fontanals, 1876, p. 27, No. 25 (What is that: a thing that every man has and the stars, too). Portuguese: Pires, *Archivio*, III (1884), 246, No. 90. Spanish: Demófilo, 726, and p. 357, No. 5. Argentinian: Lehmann-Nitsche, 992a through 992d (also with the answers "God, divinity, thought"), 1002a through 1002d. Chilean: Flores, 297, 298. Dominican Rep.: Andrade, 221 (What is it that everyone in the world has?). Porto Rican: Mason, 398, 649. Rumanian: Papahagi, 66, var. 1 (It enters into everything and is immortal), var. 2 (I am inseparable from the dead and the living). Lithuanian: Schleicher, p. 204 (What fits everything?). Russian: Sadovnikov, 2061 (Both you and I have it; both the parson and the cat have it; both the pike in the sea and the oak in the forest have it). Bulgarian: Stoilov, pp. 67–68, § 43, Nos. 1 (You have it and I have it), 4 (There is a thing that everyone in the world shares). Estonian: Wiedemann, p. 279 (What is attached to everyone?). Modern Greek: Carnoy and Nicolaides, 8 (I am necessary for everything, without me nothing could be done in this world), which resembles the Turcoman riddle quoted below and contains a theme found in No. 1680 of the present collection; Polites, *Neohellenika Analekta*, I, 197, No. 20 (I have it, you have it, but if I do not tell you mine, you cannot find it out), and p. 228, Nos. 199 (What is that thing that goes with all things?), 200 (A thing, a thing, a little thing, it can go wherever you may wish to put it); Stathes, p. 345, No. 80 (What is that thing that goes with all things?). Turkish: Kúnos, 201 = Kúnos, *Nyelvkönyv*, 29 (It is neither on the earth nor in the sky, yet every day it is near by); Kúnos, 226 (You have it, I have it, he has it); Kowalski, *Zagadki*, 83 (You have it, I have it, the stick has it). Hamizade, 283 (What is in the ground, what is in the sky, it is inside everything), 284 (It's in you, it's in me, it's also in a useless twig), 285 (It's in me, it's in you, it's in him, it's in the world, it's in everybody). Turcoman: Samojlvich, 64 (One thing is needed for all things).

A few versions from countries immediately east of Germany are couched in a negative form. See Lithuanian: Schleicher, p. 205 (What is lacking to nothing?). Polish: Gustawicz, 553 (What is it that no man is without?), 556 (What is it that nothing can be without?). Hungarian: *Magyar Nyelvör*, XXX (1901), 398, No. 3 (What is it that nothing can be without?).

1575. The riddle appears to be an adaptation of the proverb "Everything has an end, and so does the pudding" (G. L. Apperson, *English Proverbs* [London, 1929], p. 8; W. G. Smith and Janet Heseltine, *Oxford Dictionary of English Proverbs* [Oxford, 1935], p. 99).

1576. This resembles the popular saying, "I want what I want when I want it." Riddles for sleep are rather rare and usually employ altogether different patterns. See, for example, the Arabic "It comes from behind and knocks you down" (Giacobetti, 309), which is paralleled by the Argentinian Spanish "A thing that comes to you and falls upon you without touching" (Lehmann-Nitsche, 110).

1577. The pun on "without" belongs to the technique of the literary rather than to that of the popular riddle.

1578a through 1578c. In his *Quaestiones naturales* of the early twelfth century Adelard of Bath discussed the visibility and motion of the human breath; see M. Müller, *Die Quaestiones naturales des Adelardus von Bath* (Beiträge zur Geschichte der Philosophie, XXXI, ii [Münster i. W., 1934]), pp. 31–32, Nos. 24, 25. Such speculations may have given rise to the riddle. See also the headnote to No. 226, § 2, of the present collection, and Italian: Tammi, 60 (What is the thing that is seen afar and is not seen near at hand? —Fog). Compare the Lettish riddle cited in the headnote to Nos. 1586–1588 in the present collection.

1581. Spanish, Argentinian: Lehmann-Nitsche, 191 (What thing does man possess that no one can see; it flies without wings to the sky and is the cause of knowledge?). For parallels to the idea of flying without wings see the headnote to Nos. 365–366, especially §§ 7–8, in the present collection.

1582a through 1585. Breton: Duine, *Saint-Malo*, p. 518. Flemish: Joos, 98 (It is yours and remains yours, it is given [to you], but someone else uses it more than you). German: Wossidlo, 400; Hanika-Otto, 432. Danish: Kristensen, p. 96, § 249, Nos. 385a, 385b; Feilberg, *Ordbog*, II, 676, s.v. "navn." Norwegian: Christie, 91; Bugge, *Telemarken*, 110; Berge, 88; Stafset, 17, 119; Brox, *Ytre Senja*, 160 (You have it, I use it; I have it, you use it). Swedish: Sandén, *Norra Vadsbo*, 39; Waltman, *Lidmål*, 210; Ström, p. 341, "Namngåtor," 1. French: Alexandre Sylvain (A. van den Bussche), *Cinquante Ænigmes françoises* (1582), 21; Rolland, 249. Spanish, Cuban: Sánchez, 4 (It is mine and you use it more than I do). Italian: Rolland, p. 162, No. 64; Pitrè, 510; Tschiedel, 54. Lithuanian: Jurgelionis, 1111, 1112. Lappish: Qvigstad, 60. See also such other riddles for a name as Nos. 1573, 1574, and 1588 in the present collection.

1586. Welsh: Hull and Taylor, 382, 383. Irish: Christiansen, 16 (What sort of thing is that which you can keep when you give it away?).

The same comparison is applied, less successfully, to the giving of one's name: see No. 1588 in the present collection.

1587. Compare the description of money as something that goes from hand to hand (No. 1605).

1589a. The narrative style of the answer suggests that the riddle has degenerated in form. Compare the Polish "He gives wives to all men but has none himself.—Priest" (Gustawicz, 183). See also No. 1721 in the present collection, and French: Mensignac, *Gironde*, p. 298, No. 6.

A slightly different but related theme in riddles about a woman one cannot marry emphasizes the contrast, "has and yet cannot have"; see, in the present collection, Nos. 1045, 1183, and 1249, and the headnote to No. 1070; and compare the riddles listed in the note to No. 1249.

1589b, 1589c. The answer of riddles built upon the contrast of "having and yet not being permitted to have [in marriage]" is ordinarily "a woman" or "a girl" in one's immediate family. Except in the Surinam riddle quoted in the headnote to No. 1070 (n. 7), the idea that a man is not obtainable in marriage is usually applied to one already married (see Nos. 1070, 1166, and 1197) rather than to an unmarried relative. See the discussion in the headnote to No. 1070.

1591, 1592. Most versions imply a scene of hunting game; see No. 460a, the headnote to No. 460, and the note to No. 460a. For parallels limited to the paradox, see Breton: Charlec, *Dol-de-Bretagne*, 1905, p. 40, No. 54 (If you have it, you seek it; if you do not have it, you do not seek it and you do not wish to find it). Spanish: Fernán Caballero, *La estrella de Vandalia*, p. 87, as cited by R. Köhler, *Kleinere Schriften*, I, 67; H. Knust (ed.), Walter Burley, *Liber de vita et moribus philosophorum*, Bibliothek des literarischen Vereins in Stuttgart, CLXXVII (Tübingen, 1886), pp. 59–60, 198.

1593a through 1593i. Welsh: Hull and Taylor, 236. Irish: O Dalaigh, 201. Dutch:

Sinninghe, p. 8, No. 8. Flemish: Joos, 76 (I haven't it, and I don't want it, but if I had it, I wouldn't give it up for the world). Danish: Kristensen, p. 114, § 311, Nos. 495a through 495e. Norwegian: Stafset, 227. Swedish: Dybeck, *Runa*, 1849, p. 47, No. 11; Sandén, *Norra Vadsbo*, 14; Geijer and Campbell, 139; Ström, p. 81, "Huvudet," p. 393, No. 35, and p. 406, No. 35. Latin: M[one], *Anzeiger*, VIII (1839), col. 316, No. 83 (Est aliquid vere, quod nemo cupit habere; si quis haberet, pro toto mundo non daret). Spanish: Demófilo, 362.

1569a through 1596e. This literary riddle has broken down in oral tradition. Note the pun on "keep," meaning "to retain" or "to stay in bed," in No. 1596a and No. 1596c. In another bed riddle, No. 1210, which contains added elements from a coffin riddle, the same puns on "made" and "kept" are used, but the pun on "made" is confused by the introduction of the idea of not wearing a garment one has made.

1602. The answer belongs to a very widely known neck-riddle about a bird that built its nest in the skull of a dead horse. See Welsh: Hull and Taylor, 292. Scotch Gaelic: Nicolson, p. 23, German: Wossidlo, 967; Hanika-Otto, 646. Spanish, Argentinian: Lehmann-Nitsche, 694, and the note, pp. 636–639.

1604a through 1604f. Swiss: Rochholz, 497 (It can stand where an egg [stands] and cannot lie where a cow lies.—Pole for a fruit tree). Danish: Kristensen, p. 106, § 290, Nos. 453 (What is it that cannot, when upright, go in a door and yet it can go into a mousehole?—Rake handle); Feilberg, *Ordbog*, III, 71, s.v. "rivestage." Faeroic: Hammershaimb, *Antiquarisk tidsskrift*, III (1849–1851), 321, No. 67 (It can stand in a mousehole, but cannot lie in an oxstall.—Fire-tongs). Swedish: Sandén, *Norra Vadsbo*, 62. Indian, Uraon: Archer, p. 189, No. 159 (Held in the hand, but not in the house.—Umbrella). The paradox would perhaps be clearer if we read "contained" instead of "held."

Another umbrella riddle, No. 1681 in the present collection, describes an object the shape of which can be completely altered. The idea of the relative difficulty or impossibility of fitting an object into an opening or box under varied circumstances is also used in riddles for a spear and other long, slender objects (see No. 258 and the note to No. 258) and is closely allied to the theme of riddles for a fan and for a feather (see Nos. 257a, 257b and the headnote to No. 257.

1605. Swedish: Ström, p. 182, "Pengar," 1 (There is hewing in Stockholm, and another person gets the chips here). Italian: Pitrè, 480a (I have a good quality; everybody takes me, now here and now there; I always change my owner); Ferraro, *Canti popolari in dialetto logodurese*, p. 325, No. 76. Cheremiss: Wichmann, *Cheremiss*, 82 (Quite small, round; it goes from hand to hand), 216. Mordvin: Paasonen, 334 (It goes from prison to prison, it stops nowhere, it traverses all the world, it is of no service, everyone needs it). Turkish: Kowalski, *Zagadki*, 141 (A tiny thing that runs through the whole world).

1608. Spanish, Argentinian: Lehmann-Nitsche, 881. Polish: Gustawicz, 509 (Why does the crow fly to the woods?—Because the woods will not fly to her).

1610. This riddle is really a proverb; for parallels see Archer Taylor, *The Proverb* (Cambridge, 1931), p. 121, and *An Index to the "Proverb,"* FF Communications, CXVI (Helsinki, 1934), pp. 65–66; Rochholz, p. 222, No. 364. These parallels show that "spur" in this English riddle is an error for "spare."

1613. An adaptation of the carriage-wheel riddle, in which the motif of vain pursuit or a race is used, but the actors are persons (see the headnote to Nos. 952–957).

1614a through 1614d. (In the following parallels, the object making the noise varies.) Welsh: Hull and Taylor, 14 through 16. Welsh Gypsy: Sampson, 38. Irish: De Bhaldraithe, 87 (What is in the car and is not needed and doesn't help it?); O Dalaigh, 192. Spanish: Demófilo, 886. Argentinian: Lehmann-Nitsche, 675c, 675d. Dominican Rep.: Andrade, 275 (automobile).

For riddles in which the object is a mill or windmill, see French: Orain, *Ille-et-Vilaine*,

p. 158. Spanish, Argentinian: Lehmann-Nitsche, 675a, 675b. Chilean: Flores, 665. New Mexican: Campa, 246. Porto Rican: Mason, 492.

1616a through 1616f. African, Sierra Leone: Cronise and Ward, p. 193 (Ladder wey [which] pusson no duh klim.—Smoke). I should prefer "whe' " (where) to the collector's interpretation of "wey." Compare the German "Someone goes up the steps, and one doesn't hear it.—Smoke" (Haffner, 255), which is an obscure recollection of a riddle, better known in Slavic regions, to the effect that smoke, fog, or night comes silently. See also No. 1626 in the present collection.

1616f. The introduction is borrowed from nursery tales.

1619a through 1619c. Filipino: Starr, *Philippines*, 197 (My *compadre* is tiny, yet he knows how to climb a coconut tree).

1629a, 1629b. See Scotch Gaelic: Nicolson, p. 39 (What is, was, and will be?—The middle finger's excess of length over the others), and, on the same page, an example like the following parallels. Irish: Christiansen, 23 (What has never been and shall never be: stretch out your hand and get to see it?); De Bhaldraithe, 79 ("When I look carefully, I see a thing that wasn't, isn't, and won't be," says a man, separating his fingers equally, but so that you can't see what he is thinking about). Norwegian: Landstad, p. 813, No. 48; Berge, 101 (It has never happened and will never happen, but go out and you will see it); Stafset, 224. French: Rolland, 374 (What thing never was and never will be and you see it every day?). The Mordvin "I have house. Its corners are not square" (Paasonen, 183) contains a paradox that I do not understand.

The inequality in the lengths of the fingers is also the subject of a proverb; see S. W. Fallou, *A Dictionary of Hindu Proverbs* (London, 1886), p. 177; S. G. Champion, *Racial Proverbs* (New York, 1938), p. 479, No. 105 (Five fingers are not equal), a Turkish proverb.

1630. The introductory phrase "goes across the bridge" occurs frequently as a conventional introduction in German riddles. Here it serves to confuse the hearer and has only the general meaning that the object named by the riddler in the answer is out of doors. A few riddlers have described a hoe as a bird that eats grass; see No. 361a. I have noted no close parallels to this riddle, but compare Welsh: Hull and Taylor, 49 (What [thing] that is never seen goes through the bush?—A shot from a gun), cited also in the headnote to No. 801, n. 1, in the present collection. Lithuanian: Jurgelionis, 636 (Stands in the corner where it is placed, flies unseen through the fields). See also various riddles in the headnote to Nos. 379–380.

1631. Breton: Sébillot, *Haute-Bretagne*, 69; Le Pennec, 31 (I have seen you where you have never been, where you will never be, and where you cannot be. Tell me, where?). Walloon: Colson, *Wallonia*, V, 95, Nos. 242a (Could you say where [où] one is when [où, signifying also, "where"] one is not [there]?), 242b (I have seen you where you have never been and where you cannot go). French: Rolland, 190. Cherekessian: Tambiev, p. 57, No. 41 (When you look at it, it looks like you. Whatever you tell it, it repeats. You do not know what to say to it).

The Hungarian "You see him with your eyes, you recognize him; yet it is not he. You know very well that he is a good man, although he is not worth anything" (Kriza, p. 340, No. 12) contains only a few elements resembling the English riddle.

1632 through 1639. Scotch Gaelic: Nicolson, p. 85. Welsh: Hull and Taylor, 267 through 270. Welsh Gypsy: Sampson, 43. Irish: Hyde, p. 170; Delargy, 68 (I ran and I got it, I sat down and I searched for it. If I found it, I would see it, and when I did not find it, I took it home with me); De Bhaldraithe, 11. Flemish: Joos, 523, 526 (I went to Hall, I looked for it, I didn't find it and brought it home with me). Swiss: J. Müller, *Innerschweiz*, 6. Spanish: Demófilo, 433; Rodríguez Marín, 584, 585. Argentinian: Lehmann-Nitsche, 656a, 656b. Dominican Rep.: Andrade, 141 (Without seeking, I found it, and when I found it, I set myself to seeking). Indonesian, Serawaj: Helfrich, *Serawaj*, p. 69, No. 97. Atjeh: Kreemer, *Atjeh*, 38. Tabaru: Fortgens, 3. Malay: W. W. Skeat, *Malay Magic* (London, 1900), p. 484, n. 1 (What is it which you leave behind when you remember it and take it with you when you forget it?—Leech). Filipino: Starr, *Philippines*, 270 (If you do not remember, you get; but if you do remember, you do not get.—Grassburs), 282 (I sought a thing I wished to get, and as I could not find it, I kept it until my death).

1643a through 1643v. Flemish: Joos, 1st ed., 32, and 2d ed., 46 (A houseful, a barnful, and when you seize it, not a handful). German: Karl Müllenhoff, *Zeitschrift für deutsche Mythologie*, III (1855), 14, No. 17; H. Meier, *Ostfriesland*, 20; Haffner, 256. Norwegian: Christie, 34; Landstad, p. 808, No. 16. Swedish: Ericsson, *Södermanland*, II (1881) 99, No. 106; Ström, p. 385, No. 2. French: Parsons, *Antilles*, III, 374, Cariacou, 13. African, Wamajame: Ovir, 22 (The magic object of the father and mother fills a fist).

The Lappish "You can easily see it, but you can't take hold of it" (Qvigstad, 97; Donner, 21) is very similar to Eusebius' "Unus contigi patitur nec fore videtur" ("De vento et igne," 8).

A few riddles for smoke refer to its effect on the eyes. See the headnote to Nos. 1616–1627, n. 1; the Lappish "What is it that fills the house and is felt in the eyes and is lighter than a leaf?" (Qvigstad, 73); and the Indian "A swift bird flies in every direction and hurts only in the eyes" (Lakshīnātha Upasānī, VIII, 7).

1644a. The riddler must have erred in inserting the word "but."

1644b. The part in brackets is supplied from the version with which this text is associated, to replace the collector's "etc." Perhaps the riddler rhymed "hole" and "bowl." The riddler uses the formula "over the hills" unintelligently. For a parallel, see Swedish: Sandén, *Norra Vadsbo*, 89.

1646a, 1646b. Icelandic: Árnason, 850 (With long spangles it lies in the passage. It is fairer than gold, but no one can catch it). Turkish: Hamizade, 291 (It doesn't fill the palm [of the hand]; it doesn't enter the house). Yakut: Piekarski, 41 (They say there is something which never allows itself to be caught.—Reflection of the sun's rays on the snow). African, Kundu: Ittmann, *Kundu*, 132 (I see it, but can't catch it). Galla: Cerulli, 6 (By running one does not reach it. Here, take it.—Sun). The Bulgarian spark riddle, "Here I am, there I am, and yet they cannot catch me" (Chacharov, 39), may be an adaptation of this theme.

1647. The import of the riddle is obscure.

1648 through 1650. Welsh Gypsy: Sampson, 6 (A roadful, a barnful, and thou canst not catch a pipeful). Turcoman: Samojlvich, 15 (crepitus ventris). African, Lamba: Doke, 73 (That which one cannot catch.—The breeze). Chinyanja: Rattray, p. 155 (Something that cannot be bound.—Winds).

Compare the Argentinian Spanish riddle for the breath, "A thing that can neither be seized nor seen, but no one can be without it" (Lehmann-Nitsche, 645) and the Bengali "I have rolled a circular object belonging to the Râjâ. If anyone would be able to catch it, I would give him a thousand rupees.—Wind" (Mitra, *Chittagong*, p. 668, No. 6-A).

1648. For the introductory formula see No. 1644a and the riddles listed in the headnote to Nos. 1643–1654, n. 5.

1651a through 1651c. (The following parallels, which also include riddles with the answers "air" or "smoke," refer to the weight of the supposed object, or its ability to be lifted or to support something.) Swedish: Ström, p. 229, "Luften" (Wherever you go and wherever you stand, it is around you. You draw it in, you do not hold it, you expel it again. You take it up carefully anew.—Air). French: Lacuve, *Poitou*, p. 353, No. 12 (What is that which is bigger than a bull and weighs less than an egg?—Smoke). Spanish: Demófilo, 549 (Much higher than a pine and doesn't support a caraway seed); Rodríguez

Marín, 293, 294. Argentinian: Lehmann-Nitsche, 584, 585. Chilean: Flores, 367, 372. The Spanish versions, which differ very little among themselves, have some similarity to an English riddle for water, which trembles but can bear heavy burdens (see No. 728 and the corresponding headnote and note in the present collection).

1652a through 1652c. Welsh: Hull and Taylor, 273. German: Wossidlo, 343b; Hanika-Otto, 278. Swiss: Rochholz, 433 (There is a whole meadow full and yet no basketful.—Dew). Swedish: Ericsson, *Södermanland*, II (1881), 99, No. 106. Serbian: Novaković, p. 125, No. 4 (The field is full of it, yet you cannot fill a basket). Estonian: Dido, 36 (The field is full, the valley is full, and one cannot get a fistful.—Fog).

1655. This confused text is perhaps a corruption of Nos. 1643a through 1644b.

1657. Swedish: Ström, p. 205, "Solen," 6 (She touches you and you cannot touch her). Italian: Pitrè, 664. Compare the death riddle, No. 223 in the present collection.

1659a through 1659c. Russian: Sadovnikov, 1824 (Sweet milk is poured on the floor. One cannot scrape it off with either knife or teeth), 1826 (I sweep, I sweep, I cannot sweep it out. When the time comes, it will go away of its own accord). Turkish: Hamizade, 205 (Beside the door there is a spot. I rubbed and rubbed but it didn't come out), 223 (Beside the door some curdled milk is poured out. I wipe it, but it doesn't go away), 224 (In front of the door some oil is poured out. I wiped and wiped but it didn't go away).

For the comparison of sunlight to a person who cannot be driven away, see Nos. 748a through 748g of the present collection.

1660a, 1660b. Welsh: Hull and Taylor, 368 (What is that which you cannot hold for five minutes, although it is as little as a feather?).

1663a through 1663c. Swiss: Rochholz, 487. French: Rolland, 186 (What is no longer than an egg and four horses can't pull it up?—Spool of thread).

1665, 1666. Welsh: Hull and Taylor, 272. Icelandic: Árnason, 353 (If you stab it, no wound is seen when the sword is pulled out). Danish: Kristensen, p. 275, § 415, No. 10 (When one cuts through it, it straightway becomes whole again). Spanish, Dominican Rep.: Andrade, 56. Lithuanian: Jurgelionis, 103 (I chop with an ax, no mark is left). Russian: Sadovnikov, 1485 (I ride and ride and yet leave no trace, I cut and cut and yet there is no blood, I chop and chop and yet there are no splinters). African, Kundu: Ittmann, *Kundu*, 148 (I endeavored to cut it, it did not allow itself to be separated), 280 (Where I have fallen no one later sees traces). Togo: Schönhärl, 18 (What can everyone cut and he does not see where he has divided it?). Tonga-Shangaan: Junod and Jaques, p. 229, No. 7 (The thing which you can beat without leaving a scar). Malagasy: Sibree, p. 38, No. 12 (Cut and yet no wound is seen). Indian, Bhil: Hedberg, p. 881, No. 101 (If chewed, it will not get masticated. If cut, it will not get cut). Indonesian, Sangir: Adriani, pp. 397–398, No. 63 (When it is cut, it gets no scar). Filipino: Starr, *Philippines*, 230 (The king's cake, you cannot divide it), 231 (If you chop it, it heals at once). See also No. 1194 in the present collection.

Somewhat more definitely conceived is the Filipino "What is that creature which, if we strike it, at once cures itself without leaving a scar?" (De los Reyes y Florentino, p. 236). For riddles referring to rowing a boat as not leaving a track that can be seen, see the note and the headnote to No. 227 of the present collection.

1667. The import of the riddle is not clear.

1668. French: Rolland, 247. Catalan: Pelay y Briz, 260. Spanish: Demófilo, 921. Argentinian: Lehmann-Nitsche, 677. Chilean: Flores, 688, 689. Mexican: Noguera, 80. Italian: Tschiedel, 68 (Who names me breaks me).

1670. Scotch Gaelic: Nicolson, p. 25 (I shall go over my bridge of glass, I shall return over my bridge of glass, and if my bridge of glass breaks, there is not in Scotland or Ireland [one] who will repair my bridge of glass). Irish: Christiansen, 7a (A road or bridge over the sea, without stone, without clay, without wood), 7b (A bridge over the sea, without stick, without stone), 8 (like the Scotch Gaelic riddle). Swedish: Ström, p. 221, "Isen," 6. Symphosius conceives the idea in very different terms: "Water was I once, which quick methinks I'll be. Now by unbending heaven's harsh chains bound, when trod upon I cannot last nor when bare be held" (Ohl, 10).

1671. The riddle appears to be defective; it should have the same concluding phrase as that of No. 1670.

1678. "Hitch it . . . , hitch it" echoes the formula characteristic of the riddles for a wasp or a stinging plant; see Nos. 338a through 338d, 341 through 342c. In an endeavor to make sense of the formula and to fit it to the description of a broom, the riddler is only moderately successful.

1680. Welsh: Hull and Taylor, 399, 400 (What is swifter than thought?). The first of these is clearly derived from the same source as the English riddle. German: Wossidlo, 106. Danish: Kristensen, p. 133, § 384, No. 608 (What is the most certain of all things?), and compare p. 132, § 380, Nos. 601a (What is the quickest of all things?), 601b. Swedish: Ström, p. 225, "Tiden, årstiderna, dygnet," 1, and p. 304, "Gåtvisor," 3. Japanese: Starr, *Japan*, p. 25 (Why is time like a bullet?—It is faster than an arrow). For riddles that are similar but have the answer "mind," or "thought," see, in the present collection, Nos. 363a, 363b, and the headnote to Nos. 362-364.

1681. Basque: Vinson, 66 (Closed, a stick; and extended, a roof). Russian: Sadovnikov, 686 (It looks like a ladle, but when you open it, it is a pancake); Bardin, p. 244, No. 17 (When you close it, it is a spike; when you open it, it is a pancake). Filipino: Starr, *Philippines*, 365 (When pulled, it is a cane; when pushed, it is a tent). Korean: Bernheisel, p. 60 (What is it that is a handful in warm weather, but an armful in cold weather?—A cane. When warm, the cane is carried in the hand, but when cold, it is carried in the folded arms; the Korean thus folding his arms in order to keep his hands warm by inserting each in the opposite long sleeve). See also, in the present collection, Nos. 1604a through 1604f and the note to Nos. 1604a through 1604f.

1682. Russian: Sadovnikov, 1658 (Not the sun, not the fire, yet it shines).

1683. A long Breton riddle (Charlec, *Dol-de-Bretagne*, 1903, p. 395), which seems literary rather than popular, refers to a match as leaving something after it dies. See also Hungarian: Arany and Gyulai, III, 297, No. 26 (As soon as it comes into existence, it scratches; as soon as it is scratched, it dies.—Spark).

1684. Compare No. 1458, which describes putting up wallpaper.

1687. Welsh: Hull and Taylor, 381 (What is that which binds two together, but only touches one?).

1688. Compare the phrase "never can win" in the gambler riddle, No. 134.

1689. Although the fundamental conception is well suited to describe a pen, examples are rare. I have note only the Filipino "When held, it goes; when let loose, it lies down" (Starr, *Philippines*, 192).

1690. (In the following parallels, the answer is "well," or "spring.") German: Wossidlo, 398. Spanish, Cuban: Massip, 172 (The more they take away, the deeper it is.—Well). Lettish: Bielenstein, 879. Finnish: Henssen, 163. Estonian: Wiedemann, p. 271.

1691a through 1692d. (In this note, riddles having the answer "ditch" have not been separated from those with the answer "hole.") Welsh: Hull and Taylor, 237, 240, 241. Welsh Gypsy: Sampson, 29. Breton: Sauvé, 112; Milin, *Batz*, p. 56; Lavenot, *Basse-Bretagne*, p. 669. Flemish: Joos, 28, 64, 676, 677. German: Butsch, 170; Wossidlo, 397; Frischbier, *Menschenwelt*, p. 264, No. 222; Haffner, 10; Hanika-Otto, 566. Swiss: Rochholz, 511; Zahler, *Münchenbuchsee*, 230. Icelandic: Árnason, 1154. Danish: Kristensen, pp. 44–45, § 114, Nos. 160a through 160f, and p. 79, § 201, Nos. 307a, 307b. Norwegian: Berge, 89; Stafset, 1; Bugge, *Telemarken*, 79; Christie, 95. Swedish: Ericsson, *Södermanland*, III (1882), 96, No. 125; Geijer and Campbell, 93; Ström, p. 335, "Förminsknings-

och förstoringsgåtor," 1. Latin: Huldreich Therander (Johann Sommer), 290; Johannes Lorichius in Reusner, ed. 1599, p. 112 = *ibid.*, ed. 1602, p. 287 = Friedreich, p. 202, No. 15. French: Rolland, 26; Bladé, *Armagnac*, 73; Roque-Ferrier, *Languedoc*, p. 336; Parsons, *Antilles*, III, 411, Les Saintes, 44. Catalan: Pelay y Briz, 52. Spanish: Demófilo, 532; Rodríguez Marín, 916, and p. 387, n. 207. Argentinian: Lehmann-Nitsche, 870a through 870e. Dominican Rep.: Andrade, 12. New Mexican: Campa, 243. Porto Rican: Mason, 694. Portuguese: Pires, Archivio, III (1884), 246, Nos. 91, 92. Italian: Pitrè, 85. Rumanian: Gorovei, 930, 1253; and Gorovei, *Devinettes*, p. 506. Lithuanian: Jurgelionis, 1108. Lettish: Bielenstein, 89, 879. Serbian: Novaković, p. 76, No. 11 (When you add to it, it grows smaller. When you take away from it, it grows bigger), and p. 196, Nos. 3 (The more you take out of it, the bigger it grows), 4 (The more you take away, the more remains; the less you take away, the less remains). Estonian: Wiedemann, p. 271. Hungarian: Arany and Gyulai, II, 370, No. 109 (When there are more in it, it is lighter; when there are fewer, it weighs heavier. What is it?—Cheese with worms); Kriza, 65; *Magyar Nyelvőr*, II (1873), 42, No. 2 (When I eat of it, it will become larger; when I add to it, it will become smaller), and p. 515, No. 90; XII (1883), 234, No. 15 (hole in a fence); XIII (1884), 285, No. 16; and XVIII (1889), 428. Armenian: Wingate, 4. Tatar: Kalashev and Ioakimov, pp. 50–51, No. 29 (The more one scrapes it, the faster it grows; the more one cuts it short, the longer it grows.—Pit). Indonesian, Sangir: Adriani, p. 406, No. 112. Javanese: Ranneft, *Proza*, p. 15, No. 70; Ranneft, *Poëzie*, p. 65, No. 2.

1693a, 1693b. Welsh: Hull and Taylor, 238 (What grows greater by cutting its two ends?—A channel [gutter]), 239.

1695. German: Huss, *Siebenbürgen*, 52. Hungarian: *Magyar Nyelvőr*, VII (1878), 89 (When it is large, it is all right. When it is small, something has to be added to it).

1700. Turkish: Kowalski, *Zagadki*, 4 (A riddle: a little thing that I let slip from my hand).

1703a, 1703b. French: *Les Adeuineaux amoureux*, pp. lxxix–lxxx = Rolland, 27. For references to something that is small and nevertheless powerful see the headnote to No. 801, § 1, in the present collection.

1705. For discussion of this mythological theme see Axel Olrik, *Ragnarök* (Berlin, 1922). The Hungarian "They blow the horn made from bone, golden boards break, and the worms of the earth move around" (Arany and Gyulai, III, 296, No. 20; *Magyar Nyelvőr*, IX [1880], 37, and XI [1882], 527) describes a cock crowing, dawn breaking, and men stirring about. This elaborate comparison probably has no relation to the English riddle.

1706. This typical example of the literary riddle fails, as is often the case, to maintain a single, consistent idea. The riddler conceives wood as a person upholding a roof, having a fair form, and going into the grave with the hearer. Inconsistent with the idea of a person are, however, the references to closing the hearer in on every side, which is an allusion to a coffin, and to paving his dwelling. A folk riddler would, furthermore, have preferred the answer "tree" to the vaguer and more abstract "wood."

1708. The import of the riddle is not entirely clear. The notion of an endless object is applicable to water (see the Yakut "They say there is something of which there is no end" [Piekarski, 24]) and smoke (see the Yakut "There is, so they say, something to which there is no end, no matter how one pulls on it" [Piekarski, 49]). The underlying concept in this wheel riddle has some similarity to the description of a ring as "This corner, no corner at all" (No. 1411 in the present collection).

1709. For the idea of a tree that cannot be climbed or can be climbed only by one creature, see Nos. 1408, 1049, 1617g, and the Togo riddle cited in the headnote to No. 1070, n. 5.

1711. Compare the medieval Syriac "What is that which is seen and measures itself and is not a body?" (Furlani, *Azraq*, 3), which is identical with Furlani, *Enigmes philosophiques*, p. 129, No. 19. See also a longer version in his p. 135, No. 74.

1712a, 1712b. A literary riddle.

1713. Compare texts cited in the headnote to Nos. 1573–1575, nn. 7–15. The Polish "What is it that the Lord God did not and cannot create on this earth?—Sin" (Kopernicki, p. 128, No. 19) is good theology of another sort.

1714. Breton: Kerbeuzec, *Ille-et-Vilaine*, 88. Norwegian: Stafset, 28. Spanish: Demófilo, 119, 120; Rodríguez Marín, 893, 894. Argentinian: Lehmann-Nitsche, 656. Chilean: Flores, 82 through 86. Filipino: Starr, *Philippines*, 314 (The king asked from his soldier what he had not, and the soldier gave him what was not in the world).

1715a, 1715b. (In the following parallels three persons are named in a descending order. Unless otherwise indicated, the sequence is "God, king, farmer.") Breton: Kerbeuzec, *Ille-et-Vilaine*, 21 (impossible for God, difficult for a king, easy for you and me); Le Pennec, 15. Dutch: Sinninghe, p. 8, No. 3 (God, emperor, farmer). Flemish: M[one], *Anzeiger*, VII (1838), col. 264, No. 225 (God, emperor, farmer), and col. 267, No. 269; Joos, 94, var. 1; *Ons Volksleven*, I (1889), 36, No. 21. German: Butsch, 23 (God, Pope, common man); Wossidlo, 394 (God, emperor, farmer); Gilhoff, 661 (God, emperor, farmer). Danish: Kristensen, p. 79, §203, Nos. 309d (God, emperor, farmer), 309e (God, king, you and I). Swedish: Ericsson, *Södermanland*, IV (1883), 73, No. 94 (God, Pope, common man); Sandén, *Norra Vadsbo*, 65. Walloon: Colson, *Wallonia*, V, 128, No. 257 (God, king, laborer). French: Rolland, 258; Bladé, *Armagnac*, 62; Dottin, *Bas-Maine*, 9; Westphalen, *Metz*, col. 200; Roque-Ferrier, *Languedoc*, p. 322, n. 2. Italian: Bernoni, *Venice*, p. 30. Czech: Feifalik, p. 376, No. 51 (God, emperor, we). Serbian: Novaković, p. 189, No. 3 (God, tsar or king, farmer). Hungarian: *Magyar Nyelvör*, XXXIII (1904), 529, No. 5 (God never has a chance to see it; the king might see it once in a while; the peasant is always seeing it.—God can't see God, because there is only one God; a king might meet another king; the peasant always meets his like). Armenian: Glushakov, p. 38, No. 95 (God, tsar, man); Surinam: Herskovits, 102.

1716. (In the following parallels three persons are named in a confused order.) Flemish: P. Poirters, *Het Masker*, p. 119 (God farmer, king), as cited by Joos, 8; Joos, 94 (God, we, king). Swiss: Zahler, *Münchenbuchsee*, 358 (God, farmer, emperor). Russian: Arkhangel'skii, p. 79 (tsar, peasant, God). Hungarian: Arany and Gyulai, II, 355, No. 37 (Emperors and kings seldom see one of them, the men working in the fields see them every day, His Majesty the Lord never sees any).

1717a, 1717b. (In the following parallels three, or rarely four, persons are named in an ascending order. Texts having the series "farmer, king, God" are not specially indicated; other versions are given in abbreviated form.) Scotch Gaelic: Nicolson, p. 63 (we, king, God). Breton: Sauvé, 139b; A. Orain, *Mélusine*, IV (1881), col. 379. Flemish: Joos, 94, var. 2 (I, you, everyone, God). Afrikaans: Groenewald, p. 91 (one, king, God). Luxemburg: De la Fontaine, 25. German: Hanika-Otto, 209b (farmer, emperor, God); Haffner, 122 (we, emperor, God); Frischbier, *Menschenwelt*, p. 243, No. 18. Icelandic: Árnason, 403. Danish: Kristensen, p. 79, §203, Nos. 309c (anyone, king, God), 309f, 309g (we, king, God). Norwegian (all texts have "I, you, king, God"): Landstad, p. 812, No. 46; Bergh, *Valdres*, 64; Stafset, 29; Brox, *Ytre Senja*, 52; Berge, 86. Swedish: Dybeck, *Runa*, 1848, p. 44, No. 37 = Russwurm, 30 (we, king, God). Walloon: Colson, *Devinettes*, p. 153, No. 39. French: V. S., *Mélusine*, I (1878), col. 256, No. 30 = Marchessou, *Velay et Auvergne*, p. 173, No. 10 (people, king, God); Lacuve, *Poitou*, p. 355, No. 46; Desaivre, *Poitou*, p. 452, No. 18; J. Roux, *Limousin*, 11 (we, king, God). Spanish, Argentinian: Lehmann-Nitsche, 721f (man, king, Pope, God). Italian: Coronedi-Berti, *Archivio*, II (1883), 575, No. 10 (we, king, Pope, God); Ferraro, *Canti popolari in dialetto logodurese*, p. 323, No. 68

(we, king, Pope, God). Lithuanian: Jurgelionis, 149 (we, king, God). Serbian: Novaković, p. 189, Nos. 1 (we, tsar, God), 2 (farmer, tsar, God). Estonian: R. Köhler, *Kleinere Schriften*, III, 503 (we, king, God); Wiedemann, p. 276 (we, king, God).

1719. (In the following parallels two persons are named.) Irish: Delargy, 73 (I sought and found not, and it was easier for me to find the thing that God never found and never will find). Danish: Kristensen, p. 79, § 203, Nos. 309a (every man, king), 309b (we, God). French: Lallemant, *Argonne*, p. 235 (God, peasant). Portuguese: Pires, *Archivio*, III (1884), 246, No. 94 (king, God). Hungarian: Kriza, 111 (Kings and emperors seldom see one of that kind, farmers see many of them.—Farmer). For discussion see R. Köhler, *Kleinere Schriften*, III, 504.

1720a, 1720b. (In the following parallels one person is named and the verb varies much more widely than in the parallels to Nos. 1715a through 1719.) Welsh: Hull and Taylor, 2, 3. Welsh Gypsy: Sampson, 1 (What is it God does not see?—Another like Himself). Breton: Sauvé, 139a (What can't God find?). Flemish: Joos, 772. Spanish, Porto Rican: Mason, 414. Rumanian: Gorovei, *Devinettes*, p. 505 (There is a being that cannot endure one like it). Lithuanian: Jurgelionis, 2 through 4, 10 (master). Polish: Kopernicki, p. 128, No. 20 (What is it that the Lord Christ has not?—A brother). Hungarian: Arany and Gyulai, III, 297, No. 30 (What can't God ever see?—God); *Magyar Nyelvör*, V (1876), 329, No. 59 (What hasn't God created?—Something bigger than Himself); XXIX (1900), 592, No. 6 (What has God never seen?—Someone like Himself); and XXXIII (1904), 529, No. 14 (What does not God have?—He has no god).

1723. The meaning of "nitticoat, natticoat" is obscure. These and similar words also occur in some versions of the candle riddle; see in particular a variant to No. 608a.

1724a through 1724d. Irish: De Bhaldraithe, 20 (also with variant answer, "spittle"). Breton: Charlec, *Dol-de-Bretagne*, 1903, p. 395 (That which the poor throw away and the rich collect). Flemish: Joos, 71; *Ons Volksleven*, I (1889), 37, No. 22 (The beggar throws it away, and the gentleman puts it in his pocket). Afrikaans: Groenewald, p. 92. German: Wossidlo, 392; Frischbier, *Menschenwelt*, p. 243, No. 13; Haase, *Ruppin*, p. 402, No. 214; O. Schell, "Volksrätsel aus dem Bergischen," *Zeitschrift des Vereins für Volkskunde*, III (1893), 297, No. 52; E. Meier, *Kinderreime*, p. 85, No. 350; I. V. Zingerle, *Sitten, Bräuche und Meinungen des Tiroler Volkes* (2d ed.; Innsbruck, 1871), p. 278, Nos. 89, 90; Feifalik, p. 375, No. 45; Haffner, 119; Hanika-Otto, 438. Icelandic: Árnason, 426 (What does the poor man throw away that the rich man puts in his pocket?). Danish: Kristensen, p. 119, § 330, Nos. 525, 525b; Feilberg, *Ordbog*, III, 439, s.v. "snot." Norwegian: Stafset, 35. Swedish: Russwurm, 75 (The German puts it in his pocket, the peasant throws it down); Ericsson, *Södermanland*, V (1884), 72, No. 252. Walloon: Colson, *Wallonia*, IV, 109, No. 122. French: Bladé, *Armagnac*, 66, 212. Catalan: Pelay y Briz, 51; Milá y Fontanals, 1876, p. 25, No. 18; Demófilo, p. 356, No. 18. Spanish: Demófilo, p. 345, No. 24, p. 367, No. 8, and p. 390, No. 39. Argentinian: Lehmann-Nitsche, 636. Chilean: Flores, 451. Italian: Pitrè, 475; Gianandrea, *Archivio*, I (1882), 400, No. 5; Coronedi-Berti, *ibid.*, II (1883), 575, No. 6; Rondini, *ibid.*, VIII (1889), 187, No. 79; Pasquarelli, *ibid.*, XV (1896), 77, No. 17; Bernoni, *Venice*, 30. Rumanian: Gorovei, 1182. Lettish: Bielenstein, 475 (The farmer throws it on the floor, the German thrusts it in his pocket), 476 (What does the farmer throw on the ground and the landlord put in his pocket?), 477. Czech: Feifalik, p. 375, No. 45. Polish: Gustawicz, 400. Russian: Sadovnikov, 1760. Serbian: Novaković, p. 210, Nos. 6, 7 (The rich man puts me in his pocket, the rabble throw me in the road). Lappish: Qvigstad, 41. Estonian: Weidemann, pp. 276, 286. Mordvin: Paasonen, 25. Zyrian: Wichmann, *Zyrian*, 67. Hungarian: Kálmány, I, 169, No. 16 (The poor throw it away, the rich fold it in a handkerchief); *Magyar Nyelvör*, III (1874), 329, No. 59 (The peasant throws it away, the king hides it. What is it?); and XII (1883), 331, No. 50 (The beggar throws it away, the gentleman keeps it in his pocket). Modern

Greek: Polites, *Neohellenika Analekta*, I, 213, Nos. 114 = Stathes, p. 343, No. 70 (The rich gather it up, the poor throw it away. Yakut: Popov, p. 286 (The Russian puts it in his pocket, the Yakut throws it on the floor). Arabic: Ruoff, p. 18, No. 17 (The rich man puts it in his pack, the poor man throws it away). Turkish: Hamizade, 638 (The rich man collects it, the poor man throws it away). Indian, Baiga: Elwin, p. 476, No. 124 (The poor man throws it away, the rich man puts it in his pocket). Bhil: Hedberg, p. 880, No. 93 (Having kept it as silver, he goes far away and throws it away).

For discussion and parallels see Feilberg, *Ordbog*, III, 439, s.v. "snot"; G. Pitrè's note to Gianandrea, "Indovinelli marchigiani," *Archivio*, I (1882), 400, No. 5; Tupper, note to *Holme Riddles*, 45.

1726. Swedish: Ericsson, *Södermanland*, IV (1883), 70, No. 178 (He who eats me is never satisfied; he who has me is never rich; he who sees me, he is blind; he who hears me, he is deaf; and he who thinks of me, thinks nothing.—Nothing).

The following appear to be fragments of the riddle from which Nos. 1394a through 1394c, 1726, and 1727 of the present collection are derived: "What do the deaf hear and the blind see?" (Flemish: Joos, 734); "The dead eat it, and when the living eat it, they die" (Danish: Kristensen, p. 61, § 140, No. 200); "What is it that the dead eat, which if the living should eat it, they would die?" (Spanish, Argentinian: Lehmann-Nitsche, 897. Porto Rican: Mason, 389).

1727. Italian: Tschiedel, 53 (He is unfortunate who holds me, a poor man possesses me, an avaricious man gladly gives me away, a deaf man can hear me, a beast can understand me).

1728 through 1735. Welsh: Hull and Taylor, 289. Welsh Gypsy: Sampson, 28. Irish: O Dalaigh, 135 (The person who made it never used it, and the one who uses it will never see it). Breton: Sébillot, *Devinettes*, 59. Flemish: Joos, 110; Boekenoogen, p. 48. Afrikaans: Groenewald, p. 81. German: Butsch, 228; Wackernagel, 42; Wossidlo, 403; Haffner, 206; Haase, *Ruppin*, 130; Arthur Bonus, *Rätsel*, I (Munich, 1907), 79; Simrock, *Das deutsche Rätselbuch* (Leipzig, n.d.), 39; Frischbier, *Menschenwelt*, p. 243, No. 20; Gilhoff, 659, 660; Renk, *Tyrol*, 148; Hanika-Otto, 74. Swiss: Zahler, *Münchenbuchsee*, 315. Danish: Kristensen, p. 80, § 311, Nos. 311a through 311d; Feilberg, *Ordbog*, II, 422, s.v. "ligkiste." Norwegian: Brox, *Ytre Senja*, 95. Swedish: Ericsson, *Södermanland*, III (1882), 97, No. 128; Christofferson, p. 36, Nos. 19a, 19b = *Folkminnen och folktankar*, II (1915), Nos. 19a, 19b; Ström, p. 186, "Likkistan." Latin: Johannes Lorichius in Reusner, ed. 1602, pp. 290–291 = Friedreich, p. 208, No. 17; Buchler, *Gnomologia*, 3d ed. (1614), p. 454. Walloon: Colson, *Wallonia*, V, 131, No. 280. French: Rolland, 279; V. S., *Mélusine*, I (1878), col. 257, No. 32 = Marchessou, *Velay et Auvergne*, p. 174, No. 11; Guillon, *La Bresse*, p. 20; Dardy, *L'Albret*, p. 331; Mensignac, *Gironde*, p. 299, No. 10; Parsons, *Antilles*, III, 389, Martinique, 126. Catalan: Pelay y Briz, 54. Spanish: Demófilo, 188, 919, and pp. 395–396, No. 63; Rodríguez Marín, 808, 810, and p. 376, n. 179; Caballero, *Cuentos*, 26. Argentinian: Lehmann-Nitsche, 687a through 687i. Chilean: Flores, 70, 71, 882, 883. Dominican Rep.: Andrade, 39, 40. New Mexican: Espinosa, 4; Campa, 184 (burial), 248. Porto Rican: Mason, 65, 119. Portuguese: Pires, *Archivio*, III (1884), 245, Nos. 82, 83; Parsons, *Cape Verde*, 249 (grave). Italian: Rolland, p. 161, No. 33; Pitrè, 158; Gianandrea, *Canti popolari marchigiani*, p. 301, No. 26; Gianandrea, *Archivio*, I (1882), 404, No. 12; Coronedi-Berti, *ibid.*, II (1883), 578, No. 30; G. Pitrè, "Bibliografia delle tradizioni popolari in Italia," *ibid.*, p. 11; Salvioni, *ibid.*, IV (1885), 549, No. 80; Rua, *ibid.*, VII (1888), 453, No. 27; Rondini, *ibid.*, VIII (1889), 188, No. 83; Corsi, *ibid.*, X (1891), 398, No. 12; Pasquarelli, *ibid.*, XV (1896), 77, No. 15; Balladoro, *ibid.*, XVI (1897), 233, No. 56; Tschiedel, 12; Bernoni, *Venice*, 52; Ive, *Canti popolari istriani*, p. 297, No. 7; Schneller, *Wälschtirol*, p. 255, No. 23. Rumanian: Gorovei, 531; and Gorovei, *Devinettes*, p. 505; Papahagi, 71. Lettish: Bielenstein, 659. Czech: Hanika-Otto, note to her No. 74. Polish:

Kopernicki, 57 (You build it, not know for whom, and he who buys it has no use for it); Gustawicz, 432 (He who builds it does not need it; he who buys it does not want it; he who needs it knows nothing), with two parallels. Russian: Sadovnikov, 2111, 2119. Serbian: Novaković, p. 139, Nos. 8, 9. Bulgarian: Stoilov, p. 68, § 49, Nos. 1 through 3. Finnish: Lönnrot, 1749 = Henssen, 133. Estonian: Lönnrot, p. 192. Modern Greek: Dieterich, *Rätseldichtung*, p. 100; Polites, *Neohellenika Analekta*, I, 242, No. 275. Turkish: Kúnos, 144 = Kúnos, *Am Urquell*, IV (1893), 22, No. 31. Indonesian, Javanese: Ranneft, *Proza*, p. 11, No. 54 (He who makes it does not use it, he who uses it is not aware of it; he who is aware of it does not want it), and p. 16, No. 74; Ranneft, *Poëzie*, p. 26, No. 14; Mayer, 48. Filipino: Starr, *Philippines*, 90 (The one who orders it is crying; the one who has it, it is not his to give; the one who owns it does not care anything about it).

1736. Turkish: Hamizade, 488 (The maker sells it, the buyer doesn't use it, the user doesn't see it.—Gravestone).

1738. Swedish: Ericsson, *Södermanland*, I (1879), 88, No. 38; III (1882), 96, No. 124; and IV (1883), 70, No. 178; Sandén, *Norra Vadsbo*, 7; Geijer and Campbell, 89. Estonian: Wiedemann, p. 291. Latin: Reusner, ed. 1602, p. 291. Hungarian: *Magyar Nyelvör*, XVI (1887), 523, No. 44 (When inside of one, it is tight; when inside of two, it is wide [loose]; inside of three, there is no place for it).

Compare also Georg Hager's versification in a Meisterlied written on March 7, 1592. My colleague Clair Hayden Bell kindly gives me the reference to Vienna, National Library, No. 13512, fol. 567 recto. The Sanskrit saying, "That which belongs to six ears is betrayed," may refer to this idea; see M. Bloomfield, *Proceedings of the American Philosophical Society*, LVI (1917), 13.

1739 through 1740c. Somewhat similar are Lettish: Bielenstein, 859. Polish: Gustawicz, 54 through 57; Saloni, *Rzeshów*, 50; Kopernicki, 65, 78. White Russian: Wasilewski, 109. Hungarian: Arany and Gyulai, II, 369, Nos. 97, 98; *Magyar Nyelvör*, II (1873), 42, No. 4; XVIII (1889), 377; and XL (1911), 334, No. 41.

1743. Danish: Kristensen, p. 69, § 168, No. 259.

1744a through 1744c. Norwegian: Bergh, *Valdres*, 70. Swedish: Ström, p. 270, "Gåtberättelser," 16. Hungarian: Arany and Gyulai, II, 352, No. 20.

For a similar invention having the answer "well," see Hungarian: *Magyar Nyelvör*, II (1873), 90; V (1876), 329, No. 54, and p. 422, No. 63; VII (1878), 476, No. 47; and XII (1883), 474, No. 69; Arany and Gyulai, II, 352, No. 21. See also the Polish shirt riddle (Siarkowski, 70).

1746a, 1746b. (The answer in the following parallels is "baking" or "kneading bread.") Breton: Sauvé, 65; Sébillot, *Haute-Bretagne*, 84; Kerbeuzec, *Ille-et-Vilaine*, 101.

Collections of Riddles Cited

Collections of Riddles Cited

Aarne, Antti. *Vergleichende Rätselforschungen*, I–III. FF Communications, XXVI (Helsinki, 1918), XXVII (1919), XXVIII (Hamina, 1920). Cited as Aarne, *Rätselforschungen*.

———, and Kaarle Krohn. *Suomen kansan arvoituksia*. Suomalaisen kirjallisuuden seura, CLXCIII. Helsinki, 1921.

Aasen, Ivar. *Prøver af landsmaalet i Norge*. Christiania, 1853.

Abbott, G. F. *Macedonian Folklore*. Cambridge, 1903.

Les Adeuineaux amoureux. Bruges, Colard Mansion, ca. 1478. Reprinted in the series Les Joyeusetés facéties, [VI] (Paris: Techener, 1831).

Adriani, N. "Sangireesche teksten," *Bijdragen tot taal-, land- en volkenkunde van Nederlandsch-Indië*, 5th ser., X (1894), 386–449.

Ahlqvist, August. "Einige Proben mordvinischer Volksdichtung," *Journal de la société finno-ougrienne*, VIII (1890), 39–42. Cited as Ahlqvist.

———. *Forschungen auf dem Gebiete der ural-altaischen Sprachen*, I, *Versuch einer mokscha-mordwinischen Grammatik*. St. Petersburg, 1861.

———. "Wogulische Sprachtexte," *Mémoires de la société finno-ougrienne*, VII (1894), 126–129. Cited as Ahlqvist, *Vogul*.

Alcázar, Ignacio del. *Colección de cantos populares*. Madrid, 1910.

Aldhelm. *See* Pitman.

Andrade, M. J. *Folklore from the Dominican Republic*. Memoirs of the American Folklore Society, XXIII. New York, 1930.

Arany, Lászlo, and Pál Gyulai. *Magyar Népköltési Gyüjtemény*. 3 vols, Budapest, 1872–1882.

Archer, W. C. *The Blue Grove, the Poetry of the Uraons*. London, 1940.

Archivio per lo studio delle tradizioni popolari, I–XXIV, No. 2 (1882–1909). Cited as *Archivio*.

Arkhangel'skiĭ, A. "Selo Davshino, Iaroslavskoĭ gubernii, Poshekhonskago uezda," *Etnograficheskii sbornik*, II (St. Petersburg, 1854), 75–80.

Árnason, Jón. *Íslenzkar gátur*. Íslenzkar gátur, thulur og skemtanir, I. Copenhagen, 1887.

Augustiny, Julius. "Sukuma Texte," *Zeitschrift für Eingeborenen-Sprachen*, XIV (1923–1924), 42–43, 153–155.

Bacon, A. M., and E. C. Parsons. "Folklore from Elizabeth City County," *Journal of American Folklore*, XXXV (1922), 312–327. Cited as Bacon and Parsons, *Virginia*.

Baissac, Charles. *Le Folklore de l'Ile Maurice*. Les Littératures populaires de toutes les nations, XXVII. Paris, 1888. Cited as Baissac, *Mauritius*.

Balladoro, Arrigo. "Demande facete ed indovinelli veronesi," *Archivio*, XXI (1902), 41–47.

———. "Indovinelli veronesi," *ibid.*, XVI (1897), 228–233.

———. "Dubbi ed indovinelli veronesi," *ibid.*, pp. 552–558.

Bang, Willy. "Ueber die Rätsel des Codex Cumanicus," *Sitzungsberichte der k. preussischen Akademie der Wissenschaften, philosophisch-historische Classe*, 1912, i,[1] pp. 334–353.

Bardin, A. V. *Folklor*. N.p. [Moscow], 1940.

---

[1] Unless otherwise indicated, the small roman numeral in the Collections of Riddles Cited, and also in the notes and text of the present collection, represents the number of the "Part," or an equivalent subdivision of a volume.

Baring-Gould, Sabine. "Yorkshire Household Riddles," *Notes and Queries*, 3d ser., VIII (1865), 325.
Basset, René. *Contes populaires berbères*. Collection de contes et chansons populaires, XII. Paris, 1887.
———. *Nouveaux Contes berbères*. Ibid., XXIII. Paris, 1897.
Bauer, Leonhard. *Das palästinische Arabisch*. 4th ed.; Leipzig, 1926.
Bayon, Raoul. "Devinettes de la Haute-Bretagne," *Revue des traditions populaires*, V (1890), 295–298. Cited as Bayon, *Haute-Bretagne*.
Bazarov, Sh.-Lkh. B. *Dvesti zagadok aginskikh Buriat*. Trudy troitsko-savtskokiakhtinskago otdeleniia priamurskago otdeleniia imperatorskago russkago geograficheskago obshchestva, V. St. Petersburg, 1902.
———. *See also* Rudnyev.
Beauregard, G. M. Ollivier. "Devinettes malayses," *Revue des traditions populaires*, III (1888), 662–663. Cited as Beauregard.
———. "Proverbes et dictons malays," *ibid.*, V (1890), 722–724. Cited as Beauregard, *Proverbes et dictons*.
Beauvillard, Louis. "Devinettes (de Loiret)," *Mélusine*, I (1878), cols. 485, 556–557.
Beckwith, Martha W. "Hawaiian Riddling," *American Anthropologist*, XXIV (1922), 311–331. Cited as Beckwith.
———. *Jamaica Anansi Stories*. Memoirs of the American Folklore Society, XVII. New York, 1924. Cited as Beckwith, *Jamaica*.
Beech, W. H. *The Suk, Their Language and Folklore*. Oxford, 1911.
Bender, C. J. *Die Volksdichtung der Wakweli; Sprichwörter, Rätsel und Lieder*. Beiheft IV zur *Zeitschrift für Eingeborenen-Sprachen*. Berlin, 1922.
Berge, Rikard. *Norsk visefugg*. Christiania, 1904.
Bergh, Hallvar. "Folkminne ifraa Valdres og Hallingdal," *Norsk folkekultur*, X (1924), 108–114. Cited as Bergh, *Valdres*.
Bernheisel, C. F. "Korean Conundrums," *Korean Review*, V (1905), 81–87; VI (1906), 59–62.
Bernoni, Domenico-Guiseppe. *Indovinelli popolari veneziani*. Venice, 1874. Cited as Bernoni, *Venice*.
Bielenstein, August. *Tausend lettische Rätsel*. Mitau, 1881.
Bingham, C. W. "Yorkshire Household Riddles," *Notes and Queries*, 3d ser., VIII (1865), 425.
Bladé, J. F. *Proverbes et devinettes populaires, recueillis dans l'Armagnac et l'Agenais*. Paris, 1879. Cited as Bladé, *Armagnac*.
Bleakney, F. S. "Folklore from Ottawa and Vicinity," *Journal of American Folklore*, XXXI (1918), 169. Cited as Bleakney, *Canada*.
Blechsteiner, Robert. *Kaukasische Forschungen*, I. Vienna, 1919.
Boas, Franz. "Two Eskimo Riddles from Labrador," *Journal of American Folklore*, XXXIX (1926), 486. Cited as Boas, *Labrador*.
———. "Notes on Mexican Folklore," *ibid.*, XXV (1912), 227–231. Cited as Boas.
Böckel, Otto. "Volksrätsel aus dem Vogelsberg," *Hessische Blätter für Volkskunde*, II (1903), 224–229. Cited as Böckel, *Hesse*.
Boekenoogen, G. J. "Raadsels en raadselsprookjes," *Handelingen en mededeelingen van de Maatschappij der nederlandsche letterkunde te Leiden over het jaar 1900–1901*, pp. 36–81.
Boggs, R. S. "North Carolina White Folktales and Riddles," *Journal of American Folklore*, XLVII (1934), 320–325. Cited as Boggs, *North Carolina*.
Bolte, Johannes. "Eine Rätselsammlung aus dem Jahre 1644," *Zeitschrift des Vereins für Volkskunde*, XX (1910), 81–83.

Collections of Riddles Cited 873

———. "Volksrätsel aus der Mark Brandenburg," *ibid.*, XLIV (1934), 250–260.

Bon, Antoinette. "Devinettes d'Auvergne," *Revue des traditions populaires*, V (1890), 204. Cited as Bon, *Auvergne*.

The Book of Meery Riddles. London, 1629. Reprinted in Brandl, pp. 7–22. Cited as *Meery Riddles* (1629).

A Booke of Merrie Riddles. London, 1631. Reprinted in Brandl, pp. 53–63. Cited, as in Brandl's study, according to the heading of the text, as *Prettie Riddles* (1631).

Bozhov, S. D. "Gatanki ot Demir-Khisarsko," *Sbornik za narodni umotvoreniia*, V, ii (1891), 206.

Braga, Theophilo. *O povo portuguez.* Lisbon, 1886.

Brandl, Alois. "Shakespeares 'Book of Merry Riddles' und die anderen Rätselbücher seiner Zeit," *Jahrbuch der deutschen Shakespeare-Gesellschaft*, XLII (1906), 1–64.

Brewster, Paul G. "Riddles from Southern Indiana," *Southern Folklore Quarterly*, III (1939), 93–105. Cited as Brewster, *Indiana*.

Brown, George. *Melanesians and Polynesians.* London, 1910.

Brox, Arthur. "Gaater fraa Ytre Senja," *Norsk folkekultur*, XIII (1927), 15–29. Cited as Brox, *Ytre Senja*.

Brunk, August. *Osnabrücker Rätselbüchlein.* Osnabrück, 1910.

Buch Max. "Die Wotjäken, eine ethnologische Studie," *Acta Societatis Scientiarum Fennicarum*, XII (1892), 98–102.

Buchler, Johann. *Gnomologia seu sententiarium memorabilium, cum primis Germanicæ, Gallicæque linguæ, brevis & aperta Latino carmine, . . . facta descriptio; præter ænigmata.* 3d ed.; Mainz, 1614.

Büttner, C. G. *Lieder und Geschichten der Suaheli.* Berlin, 1894.

Bufe. "Die Poesie der Duala-Neger in Kamerun: Tierfabel, . . . Rätsel," *Archiv für Anthropologie*, XLI (1915), 54–60.

Bugge, Sophus. *Gaader samlede i Telemarken.* Risør, 1925. Cited as Bugge, *Telemarken*.

Bullock, C. C. See Whitney.

Burne, Charlotte S. *Shropshire Folk-Lore.* London, 1883. Cited as Burne, *Shropshire*.

Bussche, Alexander van den (pseud.: Alexandre Sylvain). *Cinquante Ænigmes françoises.* Paris, 1582.

———. *Quarenta aenigmas en lengua española.* Paris, 1581.

Busse, J. "Kaguru-Texte," *Zeitschrift für Eingeborenen-Sprachen*, XXVII (1936), 61–62.

Butsch, A. F. *Strassburger Rätselbüchlein; die erste zu Strassburg ums Jahr 1505 gedruckte deutsche Rätselsammlung.* Strassburg, 1876.

Caballero, Fernán. *Cuentos, oraciones, adivinas y refranes populares é infantiles.* Colección de autores españoles, XL. Leipzig, 1878.

Callaway, Henry. *Nursery Tales, Traditions, and Histories of the Zulus.* London, 1868.

Campa, A. L. *Sayings and Riddles in New Mexico.* University of New Mexico Bulletin, Language Ser., V, ii, No. 313. Albuquerque, N.M., 1937.

Campbell, Åke. See Geijer.

Campbell, J. F. *Popular Tales of the West Highlands.* Edinburgh, 1860.

Carmeau, Henri. *Terroirs mauges.* Paris, 1912.

Carnoy, E. H. "Devinettes picardes," *Revue des traditions populaires*, I (1886), 53–55. Cited as Carnoy, *Picardy*.

———, and Jean Nicolaides. *Traditions populaires de l'Asie Mineure.* Les Littératures populaires de toutes les nations, XXVIII. Paris, 1889.

Carstens, Heinrich. "Volksrätsel, besonders aus Schleswig-Holstein," *Zeitschrift des Vereins für Volkskunde*, VI (1896), 412–423. Cited as Carstens, *Schleswig-Holstein*.

Carstensen, A. "Nordfriesische Rätsel," *Am Urquell*, III (1892), 325–328.

Carter, Isabel G. "Mountain White Riddles," *Journal of American Folklore*, XLVII (1934), 76–80. Cited as Carter, *Mountain White*.

Casalis, Eugène. *Les Bassutos*. Paris, 1859.

———. *Etude sur la langue séchuana*. Paris, 1841. Cited as Casalis, *Séchuana*.

Cashen, William. *Manx Folk-Lore*. Douglas, 1912.

Cerquand, J. P. "Légendes et récits populaires du pays basque," *Bulletin de la société des sciences de Pau*, 2d ser., V (1876), 238–242.

Cerulli, Enrico. "The Folk-Literature of the Galla of Southern Abyssinia," *Harvard African Studies*, III (1922), 198–199.

Chabot, J. B. "Eclaircissements sur quelques points de la littérature syriaque," *Journal asiatique*, 10th ser., VIII (1906), 277–283.

Chacharov, P. A. "Gatanki ot Shchip," *Sbornik za narodni umotvoreniia*, IX, ii (1893), 207–211.

Chambers, Robert. *Popular Rhymes of Scotland*. London, 1870. Cited as Chambers, *Scotland*.

Chappell, J. W. "Riddle Me, Riddle Me, Ree," *Folk-Say*, II (1930), 227–238.

Charlec. "Quelques Devinettes populaires du pays de Dol-de-Bretagne," *Revue des traditions populaires*, XVIII (1903), 288, 395–396; XIX (1904), 168–169, 378–379; XX (1905), 40–41. Cited as Charlec, *Dol-de-Bretagne*.

Christiansen, R. T. "Iriska gåtor," *Folkminnen och folktankar*, IV (1917), 120–148.

Christie, W. F. K. *Norske gaator*. Bergen, 1868.

Christofferson, Olof. *Gåtor från Skytts härad*. Folkminnen från Skytts härad, III. Lund, 1915.

Cimegotto, Cesare. "Indovinelli molisani," *Archivio*, XIII (1894), 433–436.

Claret. V. Flajšhans, ed. *Klaret a jeho družina*. Sbírka pramenů, skupina I, řada I. Corpus I, 1 and 2 (Prague: Česka akademie, 1926, 1928). Cited as Claret.

Coelho, F. A. "Romances populares e rimas infantís portuguezes," *Zeitschrift für romanische Philologie*, III (1879), 197–198.

Colson, O. "Devinettes populaires aux pays wallon," *Revue des traditions populaires*, VII (1892), 147–153. Cited as Colson, *Devinettes*.

———. "Enigmes populaires," *Wallonia*, IV (1896), 42–46, 57–64, 90–95, 107–112, 146–152; V (1897), 53–58, 93–96, 128–132, 135–136.

Constantin, Aimé. *Littérature orale de la Savoie*. Annecy, 1882. Cited as Constantin, *Savoie*.

Cords, Rose. "'Wit's Academy; or, Six Peny-Worth for a Peny,' London, 1656," *Jahrbuch der deutschen Shakespeare-Gesellschaft*, LVII (1917), 49–68.

Cornelissen, J., and others. "Raadsels," *Ons Volksleven*, I (1889), 6–8, 36–38, 78–80; II (1890), 104–105; IV (1892), 228; V (1893), 108–110; VI (1894), 149–151; VIII (1896), 190; X (1898), 76, 166–167; XII (1900), 42–43. Cited as *Ons Volksleven*.

Coronedi-Berti, Carolina. "Indovinelli bolognesi," *Archivio*, II (1883), 575–580.

Corsi, G. B. "Indovinelli senesi," *Archivio*, X (1891), 397–404.

Courtney, M. A. *Cornish Feasts and Folk-Lore*. Penzance, 1890.

Cronise, F. M., and H. W. Ward. *Cunnie Rabbit, Mr. Spider, and the Other Beef*. London, 1903.

Dahl, E. "Hundert Rätsel der Wanamwezi," *Zeitschrift für Kolonialsprachen*, III (1913), 257–271.

Dale, A. M. *See* Edwin W. Smith.

Daleau, F. "Notices pour servir à l'étude des traditions, croyances et superstitions de la Gironde," *Bulletin de la société d'anthropologie de Bordeaux*, IV (1887), 105–106. Cited as Daleau, *Gironde*.

Daly, L. W., and Walther Suchier. *Altercatio Hadriani Augusti et Epicteti philosophi.* Illinois Studies in Language and Literature, XXIV, Nos. 1-2. Urbana, 1939.

Dames, M. Longworth. *Popular Poetry of the Baloches.* Publications of the Folk-Lore Society, LIX. London, 1907.

Damsté, H. T. "Simaloereesche teksten," *Bijdragen tot de taal-, land- en volkenkunde van Nederlandsch-Indië,* LXXI (1916), 636-637.

Dansk Folkemindesamling. Manuscript collections in the Royal Library, Copenhagen. Cited as DFS, according to year and collector's name. Many small collections of later dates are, however, included under 1906.

Dardy, Léopold. *Anthologie populaire de l'Albret, sud-ouest de l'Agenais ou Gascogne landaise.* Agen, 1891. Cited as Dardy, *L'Albret.*

De Bhaldraithe, Tomás. "Tomhaiseannaí as Cois Fhairrge," *Béaloideas,* XII (1942), 55-67.

Decary, R. "Notes ethnographiques sur les populations du district de Maromedia (Sakalava et Tsimihety)," *Revue d'ethnographie et des traditions populaires,* V (1924), 358-359.

De C[lercq], F. S. A. "Vijf-en-veertig Tounseasche raadsels," *Tijdschrift voor Nederlandsch-Indië,* 3d ser., IV, ii (1870), 237-255. Cited as De C.

De Filippis, Michele. "The Literary Riddle in Italy to the End of the Sixteenth Century," *University of California Publications in Modern Philology,* XXXIV (1948), 1-174.

Delargy, J. H. "Tomhaiseanna gaelge," *Béaloideas,* I (1927), 31-37. Cited as Delargy.

———. "Tomhaiseannaí ó inis Cé i n-iorrus," *ibid.,* XI (1941), 78-82. Cited as Delargy, *Inis Cé.*

Demaundes Joyous. London: Wynken de Worde, 1511. Reprinted (with annotations) in John M. Kemble, *The Dialogue of Salomon and Saturnus* (London, 1848), pp. 285-301.

Demófilo. *See* Machado y Alvarez.

Dempster, Miss. "Folklore of Sutherlandshire," *Folk-Lore Journal,* VI (1888), 236. Cited as Dempster, *Sutherlandshire.*

Denis, Léopold, S.J., "Devinettes de Bakongo," *Congo,* XVII, i (Brussels, 1936), 187-205.

Desaivre, Léo. "Formulettes et enfantines du Poitou," *Bulletin de la société de statistique, sciences, lettres ... des Deux-Sèvres,* IV (Niort, 1879-1881), 450-454. Cited as Desaivre, *Poitou.*

Destunis, G. S. "Ocherki grecheskoi zagadki s drevnikh vremen do novykh," *Zhurnal ministerstva narodnago prosviescheniia,* CCLXX (1890), 66-98, 262-290.

Dido, A. "Devinettes estoniennes," *Revue des traditions populaires,* IX (1894), 32-36.

Dieterich, Karl. "Neugriechische Rätseldichtung," *Zeitschrift des Vereins für Volkskunde,* XIV (1904), 87-104. Cited as Dieterich, *Rätseldichtung.*

———. *Sprache und Volksüberlieferung der südlichen Sporaden.* Vienna, 1908. Cited as Dieterich, *Sporades.*

Di Martino, Mattia. "Indovinelli inediti raccolti in Noto," *Archivio,* XIII (1894), 199-202.

Doke, C. M. *Lamba Folklore.* Memoirs of the American Folklore Society, XX. New York, 1927.

Donner, Otto. *Lieder der Lappen.* Helsingfors, 1876.

Dorsey, James Owen. "Omaha Sociology," *Report of the Bureau of American Ethnology,* III (1884), 334.

Dottin, Georges. *Glossaire des parlers du Bas-Maine.* Paris, 1898. Cited as Dottin, *Bas-Maine.*

Duine, François. "Devinettes du pays de Saint-Malo," *Revue des traditions populaires*, XVI (1901), 515–518. Cited as Duine, *Saint-Malo*.

Dumoutier, Gustave. *Les Chants et les traditions populaires des Annamites*. Collection de contes et chansons populaires, XV. Paris, 1890.

Dybeck, Rikard. *Runa*, 1847, pp. 40–42; 1848, pp. 43–48; 1849, pp. 46–50; 1850, pp. 34–37; 1865–1873, pp. 8, 29–31, 48–50, 64–65, 81, 98–99; 1874, p. 21.

Dykstra, Waling. *Uit Friesland's volksleven van vroeger en later*. 2 vols. Leeuwarden, 1894–1896. Cited as Dykstra.

———, and T. C. van der Meulen. *In doaze fol alde snypsnaren*. Frjentsjer, 1882. Cited as Dykstra, *Snypsnaren*.

Dyrenkova, N. P. *Shorski folklor*. Moscow, 1940.

Ebding, F. "Dualarätsel aus Kamerun gesammelt und übersetzt," *Mitteilungen des Seminars für orientalische Sprachen*, XIV, 3. Abteilung, Afrikanische Sprachen (1911), pp. 160–181.

Ebert, Adolf. "Ueber die Räthsel-poesie der Angelsachsen, insbesondere die Aenigmata des Tatwine und Eusebius," *Berichte über die Verhandlungen der k. sächsischen Gesellschaft der Wissenschaften, philosophisch-historische Classe*, XXIX (1877), 20–56.

Eckart, Rudolf. *Allgemeine Sammlung niederdeutscher Rätsel nebst einigen anderen mundartlichen Rätselaufgaben und Auflösungen*. Leipzig, 1894.

Edwards, G. D. "Items of Armenian Folklore Collected in Boston," *Journal of American Folklore*, XII (1899), 101–102.

Ehlers, J. *Schleswig-holsteensch Räthselbook*. Kiel, 1865.

Elwin, Verrier. *The Baiga*. London, 1939.

———, and Shamrao Hivale. *Folksongs of the Maikal Hills*. Oxford University Press (printed at Madras), 1944.

Emeneau, M. B., and Archer Taylor. "Annamese, Arabic, and Panjabi Riddles," *Journal of American Folklore*, LVIII (1945), 12–20.

Endemann, C. "Rätsel der Sotho," *Zeitschrift für Eingeborenen-Sprachen*, XVIII (1927), 55–74.

Endevinalles populars; recull d'equivochs negatius. Barcelona, 1909.

L'Enfant sage (Das Gespräch des Kaisers Hadrian mit dem klugen Kinde Epitus), edited by Walther Suchier. Gesellschaft für romanische Literatur, XXIV. Dresden 1910.

Erhart-Siebold, Erika von. *Die lateinischen Rätsel der Angelsachsen*. Anglistische Forschungen, LXI. Heidelberg, 1925.

Ericsson, Gustav. "Gåtor från Åkers och Öster-Rekarne härad," *Bidrag till Södermanlands äldre kulturhistoria*, I (1879), 79–94; II (1881), 92–101; III (1882), 96–104; IV (1883), 69–73; V (1884), 63–72. Cited as Ericsson, *Södermanland*.

Ernault, Emile. "Devinettes de la Basse-Bretagne," *Mélusine*, I (1878), cols. 292, 511; II (1884), col. 497; III (1886–1887), col. 235.

Espinosa, A. M. "New Mexican Spanish Folklore, IX, Riddles," *Journal of American Folklore*, XXVIII (1915), 319–352.

Eusebius. *See* Ebert.

Farr, T. J. "Riddles and Superstitions of Middle Tennessee," *Journal of American Folklore*, XLVIII (1935), 318–326. Cited as Farr, *Tennessee*.

Fauset, A. H. *Folklore from Nova Scotia*. Memoirs of the American Folklore Society, XXIV. New York, 1931. Cited as Fauset, *Nova Scotia*.

———. "Negro Folk-Tales from the South," *Journal of American Folklore*, XL (1927), 276–292. Cited as Fauset, *Southern Negro*.

———. "Tales and Riddles Collected in Philadelphia," *ibid.*, XLI (1928), 552–557. Cited as Fauset, *Philadelphia*.

Feifalik, Julius. "Ein Hundert Volks- und Kinderräthsel aus Mähren," *Zeitschrift für deutsche Mythologie*, IV (1859), 367–384, 392–393.

Feilberg, H. F. *Bidrag til en ordbog over jyske almuesmål*. 4 vols. Copenhagen, 1886–1914. Cited as Feilberg, *Ordbog*.

———. "Gaader," *Aarbog for dansk kulturhistorie*, 1898, pp. 10–76. Cited as Feilberg, *Gåder*.

Feit, Paul. "Das deutsche Volksrätsel," *Mitteilungen der schlesischen Gesellschaft für Volkskunde*, XIV (1905), 1–33; XVI (1906), 37–40.

Fellman, Jacob. *Anteckningar under min vistelse i Lappmarken*. 3 vols. Helsingfors, 1906.

Ferrand, Auguste. "Devinettes du Dauphiné," *Revue des traditions populaires*, X (1895), 225–228. Cited as A. Ferrand, *Dauphiné*.

Ferrand, Gabriel. *Contes populaires malgaches*. Collection de contes et chansons populaires, XIX. Paris, 1893.

Ferraro, Giuseppe. *Canti popolari in dialetto logodurese*. Turin, 1891.

———. "Indovinelli sardi," *Archivio*, XXI (1902), 529–542.

———. "Spigolature di canti popolari parmigiani e mon ferrini," *ibid.*, VIII (1889), 322–333, 497–504, esp. pp. 332–333.

Fertiault, F. "Devinettes de Bourgogne," *Revue des traditions populaires*, V (1890), 168. Cited as Fertiault, *Bourgogne*.

Fesquet, P. "Enigmes populaires recueilles à Colognac," *Revue des langues romanes*, XVI (3d ser., II; 1879), 175–177.

Filonenko, V. I. *Zagadki krimskikh tatar*. Simferopol, 1926.

Findlay, William. "Riddles," *Miscellanies of the Rymour Club*, I (Edinburgh, 1906–1911), 58–60. Cited as Findlay, *Edinburgh*.

Finlay, H. H. "Folklore from Eleuthera, Bahamas," *Journal of American Folklore*, XXXVIII (1925), 295–296. Cited as Finlay, *Bahamas*.

Fison, Lorimer. "On Fijian Riddles," *Journal of the Anthropological Institute of Great Britain and Ireland*, XI (1882), 406–410.

Fitzgerald, David. "Of Riddles," *Gentleman's Magazine*, CCLI (1881), 177–192.

Flajšhans, Václav. "Naše hádanky," *Národopisný věstník českoslovanský*, XVIII (1925), 1–32. Cited as Flajšhans.

———. "Nejstarši hádanka česka z r. 1366," *Český lid*, XXIV (1924), 50–51.

———. *See also* Claret.

Fletcher, R. S. *Hausa Sayings and Folk-Lore*. New York, 1912.

Fleury, Jean. *Littérature orale de la Basse-Normandie*. Les Littératures populaires de toutes les nations, XI. Paris, 1883. Cited as Fleury, *Basse-Normandie*.

Flores, Eliodor. "Adivinanzas corrientes en Chile," *Revista de folklore chileno*, II (1911), Parts iv and vii, 137–334 (paginated continuously).

Fontaine, Eduard de la. *Die Luxemburger Kinderreime*. Luxemburg, 1877.

Fortgens, J. "Grammatikale aanteekningen van het Tabaroesch. Tabaroesche volksverhalen en raadsels," *Bijdragen tot taal-, land- en volkenkunde van Nederlandsch-Indië*, LXXXIV (1928), 300–344, 527–542.

Fouju, G. "Devinettes beauceronnes," *Revue des traditions populaires*, IV (1889), 631. Cited as Fouju, *Beauce*.

Fourès, Auguste. "Enigmes populaires du Lauragais," *Revue des langues romanes*, XXII (3d ser., VIII; 1882), 253–255.

Franz, G. H. "The Literature of Lesotho," *Bantu Studies*, IV (1930), 155–156.

Friedreich, J. B. *Geschichte des Räthsels*. Dresden, 1860.

Friis, J. A. *Lappiske Sprogprøver*. Christiania, 1856.

Frischbier, Hermann. "Die Menschenwelt in Volksrätseln aus den Provinzen Ost- und Westpreussen," *Zeitschrift für deutsche Philologie*, XXIII (1892), 240–264. Cited as Frischbier, *Menschenwelt*.

———. "Die Pflanzenwelt in Volksrätseln aus der Provinz Preussen," *ibid.*, IX (1878), 68–77. Cited as Frischbier, *Pflanzenwelt*.

———. "Die Thierwelt in Volksrätseln aus der Provinz Preussen," *ibid.*, XI (1880), 344–359. Cited as Frischbier, *Thierwelt*.

Frison, Joseph. "Devinettes bretonnes," *Revue des traditions populaires*, XXVI (1911), 148.

———. "Devinettes di Morbihan," *ibid.*, XXVII (1912), 13.

Frohnmeyer, L. J. *A Progressive Grammar of the Malayalam Language*. 2d ed.; Mangalore, 1913.

Furlani, Giuseppe. "Di una raccolta di indovinelli in lingua siriaca," *Rendiconti della R. Accademia nazionale dei Lincei. Classe di scienze morali*, 5th ser., XXXIII (1925), 77–80.

———. "Gli indovinelli di Giovanni Azraq," *ibid.*, XXXII (1923), 37–50. Cited as Furlani, *Azraq*.

———. "Un Recueil d'énigmes philosophiques en langue syriaque," *Revue de l'orient chrétien*, 3d ser., I (1918–1919), 113–136. Cited as Furlani, *Enigmes philosophiques*.

Gardner, E. E. *Folklore from the Schoharie Hills*. Ann Arbor, 1937. Cited as Gardner, *Schoharie Hills, N.Y.*

Geijer, Herman, and Åke Campbell. *Gåtor*. Svenska landsmål ock svenskt folkliv, CXCI. Uppsala, 1930.

Genetz, Arvid. "Ost-tscheremissische Sprachstudien, I," *Journal de la société finnoougrienne*, VII (1889), 135–141.

Georgeakis, G., and Léon Pineau. *Le Folklore de Lesbos*. Les Littératures populaires de toutes les nations, XXXI. Paris, 1894. Cited as Georgeakis.

Giacobetti, A. *Recueil d'énigmes arabes*. Algiers, 1916.

Gianandrea, Antonio. *Canti popolari marchigiani*. Turin, 1875.

———. "Indovinelli marchigiani," *Archivio*, I (1882), 397–407, 554–566; II (1883), 82–88, 425–434.

Gilhoff, Johannes. *Das mecklenburgische Volksrätsel*. Parchim, 1892.

Gill, W. W. *Jottings from the Pacific*. London, 1885.

Giménez Cabrera, L. "Adivinanzas oídas en la Habana," *Archivos del folklore cubano*, II (1926), 329–336.

Giorgi, Paolo. "Indovinelli siciliani raccolti in Castro Reale," *Archivio*, XV (1896), 71–74.

Giovanetti, Julio. "Devinettes des Philippines," *Revue des traditions populaires*, XXVI (1911), 38.

Glushakov, M. W. "Pamyatniki narodnago tvorchestva Kutaisskoi gubernii, imeretinskiya zagadki," *Sbornik . . . Kavkaza*, XXXII, iii (1903), 22–39.

Gombojew, Galsang. "Sechzig burjätische Rätsel," *Bulletin de la classe historico-philologique de l'académie impériale des sciences de Pétersbourg*, XIV (1857), 169–174.

Gorovei, Artur. *Cimiliture românilor*. Bucharest, 1898. Cited as Gorovei.

———. "Devinettes populaires romaines," *Revue des traditions populaires*, VII (1892), 505–506; XII (1897), 22–34; XIII (1898), 113–119. Cited as Gorovei, *Devinettes*.

Green, Edward. "Riddles from South Antrim," *Béaloideas*, XI (1941), 178–182. Cited as Green, *South Antrim*.

Greenleaf, Elisabeth B. "Riddles of Newfoundland," *The Marshall Review*, I, No. 3 (Huntington, W.Va.), 5–20. Cited as Greenleaf, *Newfoundland*.

Collections of Riddles Cited

Gregor, Walter. *Notes on the Folk-Lore of the North-East of Scotland.* Publications of the Folk-Lore Society, VII. London, 1881. Cited as Gregor, *Northeast Scotland.*

Grigorov, N. "Selo Tatev," *Sbornik . . . Kavkaza*, XIII, i (1892), 123–124.

Grigson, W. V. *The Maria Gonds of Bastar.* Oxford, 1938.

Groenewald, C. F. *Rijmpies en raaisels.* Diss., Univ. of Groningen; Groningen, 1919.

Gruntvig, N. F. S. *Gamle danske Minder.* 3 vols. Copenhagen, 1854–1861.

Gubov, P. K. "Gatanki," *Sbornik za narodni umotvoreniia*, XXII–XXIII, Part i (1906–1907), 1–146.

Guillon, Charles. "Devinettes de la Bresse," *Revue des traditions populaires*, I (1886), 20. Cited as Guillon, *La Bresse.*

Gulgowski, L., and F. Lorentz. "Rätsel aus Sanddorf, Kr. Berent," *Mitteilungen des Vereins für kaschubische Volkskunde*, I (1910), 73–74. Cited as Gulgowski.

Guliia, D. I. *Sbornik abkhazskikh poslovits, zagadok.* Akademiia Nauk SSSR. Gruzinskiĭ filial, Otdeleniye iazika i literaturi, IX. Abgiz, 1939.

Gustawicz, Bronislaw. "Zagadki i łamigłowki ludowe," *Zbiór wiadomosci do antropologii krajowéj*, XVII (1893), 201–260.

Gutch, Eliza. *Examples of Printed Folk-Lore Concerning the East Riding of Yorkshire.* Publications of the Folk-Lore Society, LXIX. London, 1912. Cited as Gutch, *East Riding, Yorkshire.*

———, and Mabel Peacock. *Examples of Printed Folk-Lore Concerning Lincolnshire.* Publications of the Folk-Lore Society, LXVIII. London, 1908. Cited as Gutch and Peacock, *Lincolnshire.*

Gutmann, Bruno. "Zur Psychologie des Dschaggarätsels," *Zeitschrift für Ethnologie*, XLIII (1911), 522–540.

Gutsleff, E. G. *Answeisung zur ehstnischen Sprache.* Halle, 1732.

Gyulai, Pál. *See* Arany.

Haase, K. E. "Volksrätsel aus der Grafschaft Ruppin und Umgegend," *Zeitschrift des Vereins für Volkskunde*, III (1893), 71–79; V (1895), 396–407. Cited as Haase, *Ruppin.*

———. "Volksrätsel aus Thüringen," *ibid.*, V (1895), 180–183. Cited as Haase, *Thüringen.*

Haffner, Oskar. "Rätsel" in Anon., *Volkskunde in Breisgau* (Freiburg i. Br., 1906), pp. 51–106.

Hagen, Hermann. *Antike und mittelalterliche Rätselpoesie.* Biel, 1869. 2d ed.; Berne, 1877. References are to the first edition, unless otherwise designated.

Hahn, J. G. von. *Albanesische Studien.* Jena, 1854.

Haldar, Sukumar. "Ho Riddles," *Journal of the Bihar and Orissa Research Society*, III (1917), 276–278.

Halliwell-Phillipps, J. O. *Nursery Rhymes of England.* London, 1886.

———. *Popular Rhymes and Nursery Tales.* London, 1849.

Halpert, Herbert. "A Few Riddles," *Hoosier Folklore Bulletin*, III (1944), 38. Cited as Halpert, *Riddles.*

———. "Negro Riddles Collected in New Jersey," *Journal of American Folklore*, LVI (1943), 200–202. Cited as Halpert, *New Jersey.*

Hamizade, Ihsan. *Bilmeceler.* Türk halk bilgisine ait maddeler, III. Istanbul, 1930.

Hammershaimb, V. U. "Færøiske gåder," *Antiquarisk tidsskrift*, III (1849–1851), 315–322.

———. *Færøsk anthologi.* 2 vols. Copenhagen, 1891.

Hamouda, Ben. "Devinettes songaï," *Bulletin du comité d'études historiques et scientifiques de l'Afrique occidentale française*, II (1919), 278–280.

Hanika-Otto, Liesl. *Sudetendeutsche Volksrätsel.* Beiträge zur sudetendeutschen Volkskunde, XIX. Reichenberg, 1930.

Al-Harîrî. *The Assemblies.* Translated by Thomas Chenery and F. Steingass. Oriental Translation Fund, n.s., III. London, 1867–1898.

Harland, John, and T. T. Wilkinson. *Lancashire Legends, Traditions, Pageants, Sports, &c.* London, 1873.

Harmsen, L. K. "Menangkerbausch-maleische raadsels," *Tijdschrift voor indische taal-, land- en volkenkunde*, XXIII (1875), 258–281.

Harris, H. G. *Hausa Stories and Riddles.* Weston-super-Mare, 1908.

Haug, [Martin]. "Vedische Räthselfragen und Räthselsprüche," *Sitzungsberichte der philosophisch-philologischen und historischen Classe der k. bayerischen Akademie der Wissenschaften*, Bd. II for 1875 (Munich).

Haurigot, Georges. "Littérature orale de la Guyane française, Devinettes," *Revue des traditions populaires*, VIII (1893), 119–120. Cited as Haurigot, *French Guiana*.

Headwaiter, E. "Más adivinanzas cubanas," *Archivos del folklore cubano*, II (1926), 236–239.

Hedberg, Enok. "Proverbs and Riddles Current Among the Bhils of Kandesh," *Journal of the Anthropological Society of Bombay*, XIII (1928), 854–892.

Heider, E. "Samoanische Rätsel (O Tupua faa-Samoa)," *Archiv für Anthropologie*, XLII (1915), 119–137.

Helfrich, O. L. "Bengkoeleesche raadsels (Těkoq-těki)," *Tijdschrift voor indische taal-, land- en volkenkunde*, XXXVII (1893), 98–104. Cited as Helfrich, *Bengkoela*.

———. "Lampongsche raadsels, spreekwoorden en spreekwijzen," *Bijdragen tot de taal-, land- en volkenkunde van Nederlandsch-Indië*, 5th ser., VI (1891), 612–619. Cited as Helfrich, *Lampong*.

———. "Nadere bijdrage tot de kennis van het Engganeesch," *ibid.*, LXXI (1916), 517–519. Cited as Helfrich, *Engganee*.

———. "Serawajsche en besemahsche spreekwoorden, spreekwijzen en raadsels," *ibid.*, 6th ser., I (1895), 1–78, 384–386. Cited as Helfrich, *Serawaj*.

Henssen, Gottfried. "Finnische Volksrätsel," *Zeitschrift des Vereins für Volkskunde*, XLIII (1933), 47–81.

Hepding, Hugo. "Hessische Hausinschriften und byzantinische Rätsel," *Hessische Blätter für Volkskunde*, XII (1913), 161–182.

———. "Duo Pergamena ainigmata byzantines epoches," in G. K. Chronoronikos and A. Thebaiopoulos, eds., *Pergamos* (Mytilene, 1929), pp. 235–237.

Herskovitz, M. G. and F. S. *Suriname Folklore.* Columbia University Contributions to Anthropology, XXVII. New York, 1936. Cited as Herskovits.

Hertz, Wilhelm. "Die Rätsel der Königin von Saba," *Zeitschrift für deutsches Alterium*, XXVII (1883), 1–33, reprinted in his *Gesammelte Abhandlungen* (Stuttgart, 1905), pp. 412–455.

Heusler, Andreas. "Die Altnordischen Rätsel," *Zeitschrift des Vereins für Volkskunde*, XI (1901), 117–149.

Hivale, Shamrao. See Elwin.

Holle, K. F. "Soendasche raadsels," *Tijdschrift voor indische taal-, land- en volkenkunde van Nederlandsch-Indië*, XVII (5th ser., III; 1869), 369–376. Cited as Holle, *Soenda*.

Hollis, A. C. *The Masai; Their Language and Folklore.* Oxford, 1905. Cited as Hollis, *Masai*.

———. *The Nandi; Their Language and Folklore.* Oxford, 1909. Cited as Hollis, *Nandi*.

———. "Nyika Proverbs," *Journal of the African Society*, XVI (1916–1917), 137–142. Cited as Hollis, *Nyika*.

———. "Taveta Enigmas," *ibid.*, X (1910–1911), 200–212. Cited as Hollis, *Taveta*.

Hudson, A. P. "Some Folk Riddles from the South," *South Atlantic Quarterly*, XLII (1943), 78–93.

Huffman, Ray. *Nuer Customs and Folklore*. London, 1931.

Hugues, Albert, and Albert Roux. "Folklore du parage d'Uzès et du Margoirès," *Bulletin de la société d'études des sciences naturelles de Nîmes*, 1914–1917, p. 202.

Hull, Vernam E., and Archer Taylor. "A Collection of Welsh Riddles," *University of California Publications in Modern Philology*, XXVI (1942), 225–326.

Hurel, E. "Manuel de la langue kinyarwanda," *Mitteilungen des Seminars für orientalische Sprachen*, XIV, 3. Abteilung, Afrikanische Sprachen (1911), pp. 1–159.

Huss, R. "Nordsiebenbürgische Rätsel," *Jahrbuch der luxemburgischen Sprachgesellschaft*, 1928, pp. 39–63. Cited as Huss, *Siebenbürgen*.

Hyatt, H. M. *Folklore from Adams County, Illinois*. Memoirs of the Anna Egan Hyatt Foundation, [I]. New York, 1935. Cited as Hyatt, *Adams Co., Ill.*

Hyde, Douglas. *Beside the Fire*. London, 1890.

Hyltén-Cavallius, G. O. "Gåtor ock spörsmål från Värend upptecknade på 1830-talet," *Nyare bidrag till kännedom om de svenska landsmålen*, II, No. 8 (1882). Cited as Hyltén-Cavallius, *Värend*.

Ikonomov, V. "Gatanki ot Debrsko," *Sbornik za narodni umotvoreniia*, I, ii (1889), 146–148.

Indovinelli. Treviso, 1628. Reprinted in Rolland.

Ioakimov, A. *See* Kalashev.

Ittmann, J. "Aus dem Rätselschatz der Kosi," *Zeitschrift für Eingeborenen-Sprachen*, XXI (1930–1931), 25–54. Cited as Ittmann, *Kosi*.

———. "Einiges aus der Bankon-Literatur," *ibid.*, XVII (1926), 106–108. Cited as Ittmann, *Bankon*.

———. "Kundu Rätsel," *Mitteilungen des Seminars für orientalische Sprachen*, XXXVII, 3. Abteilung, Afrikanische Sprachen (1934), pp. 162–185. Cited as Ittmann, *Kundu*.

Ive, Antonio. *Canti popolari istriani*. Turin, 1877.

———. "Indovinelli in veglioto odierono," *Archivio*, XXII (1903), 116–119.

Jacobsen, M. E. "Simaloereesche sprookjes, overleveringen, raadsels en spelen," *Tijdschrift voor indische taal-, land- en volkenkunde*, LVIII (1919), 1–14.

Jacottet, E. *Etudes sur les langues du Haut-Zambèze*. 3ᵉ partie: Textes louyi. Paris, 1901.

Jaeger, M. "Assyrische Räthsel und Sprichwörter," *Beiträge zur Assyriologie*, II (1894), 274–305.

Jaques, A. A. *See* H. P. Junod.

Jetté, Julius. "Riddles of the Ten'a Indians," *Anthropos*, VIII (1913), 181–201, 630–651.

Johnson, F. "Kiniramba Folk-Tales," *Bantu Studies*, V (1931), 355–356.

Johnson, Guy B. *Folk-Culture on St. Helena Island*. Chapel Hill, N.C., 1930. Cited as Johnson, *St. Helena Island, S.C.*

Johnson, John H. "Folklore from Antigua, British West Indies," *Journal of American Folklore*, XXXIV (1921), 83–88. Cited as Johnson, *Antigua*.

Joos, Amaat. *Raadsels van het vlaamsche volk*. Ghent, 1888. [2d ed.]; Brussels, n.d. [1926]. References are to the second edition unless otherwise designated.

Joustra, M. "Een en ander uit de litteratuur der Karo-Bataks," *Mededeelingen van wege het nederlandsch zendelinggenootschap*, XLV (1901), 91–101.

Judd, H. P. *Hawaiian Proverbs and Riddles*. Bulletin of the Bernice P. Bishop Museum, LXXVII. Honolulu, 1930.

Jungbauer, Gustav. "Sartische und deutsche Volksrätsel," in *Festschrift für M. Winternitz* (Leipzig, 1933), pp. 347–357.

Jungwirth, Ernst. "Volksrätsel aus Ostermiething im oberen Innviertel," *Zeitschrift des Vereins für Volkskunde*, XX (1910), 83–85.

Junod, Henri. "Les Ba Ronga," *Bulletin de la société neuchâteloise de géographie*, X (1898), 252–263.

———. *Life of a South African Tribe*. London, 1927. Cited as Junod.

Junod, Henri Philippe, and A. A. Jaques. *Vutlhari bya Vatonga (Matšhangana). The Wisdom of the Tonga-Shangaan People*. Cleveland, Transvaal, n.d. Cited as Junod and Jaques.

Jurgelionis, Kleofas. *Misliu Knyga*. Chicago, 1913.

Jurkevich, I. "Prikhod Ostrinskiĭ, Vilenskoĭ gubernii, Lidskago uezda," *Etnograficheskii sbornik*, I (St. Petersburg, 1853), 293.

Kaindl, R. F. "Lieder, . . . und Allerlei aus der Kinderwelt in der Bukowina und in Galizien," *Zeitschrift des Vereins für Volksunde*, VIII (1898), 319–320.

Kalashev, A., and A. Ioakimov. "Tatarskie teksty," *Sbornik . . . Kavkaza*, XVIII, ii (1894), 48–51, 60–61, 66–67.

Kálmány, Lajos. *Szeged Népe*. 3 vols. Arad, 1881–1891.

Kamp, Jens. *Danske folkeminder, æventyr, gaader*. Odense, 1877.

Kapanadze, Y. "Selo Sachilavo, Kutaisskoĭ gubernii, Seanskogo uezda," *Sbornik . . . Kavkaza*, XXVII, ii (1900), 144–145.

Karutz, R. *Unter Kirgisen und Turkmenen*. Leipzig, 1911.

Katanov, N. Th. *Mundarten der Uŕianchaier (Sojenen), Abakan-Tataren und Karagassen* (Vol. IX of W. Radlov, *Proben der Volksliteratur der türkischen Stämme Süd-Sibiriens* [St. Petersburg, 1866–1907]). St. Petersburg, 1907. Cited as Katanov in Radlov. The text and the Russian translation are separately paged. The pagination used here refers to the Russian translation.

Kats, J., and M. Koesrin. *Spraakkunst en taaleigen van het Javaansch*, I. Weltevreden, 1921.

Kavanagh, Tobias. "Four Kilkenny Riddles," *Béaloideas*, IV (1933–1934), 342.

———. "Some Kilkenny Riddles," *ibid.*, II (1929–1930), 295.

Kavyopadhyaya, Hira Lal. *A Grammar of the Chhattisgarhi Dialect of Eastern Hindi*. Calcutta, 1921.

Kemble, John M. *The Dialogue of Salomon and Saturnus*. London, 1848.

Kerbeuzec, Henry de. "Devinettes du pays de Guipel, Ille-et-Vilaine," *Revue des traditions populaires*, XX (1905), 502–511. Cited as Kerbeuzec, *Ille-et-Vilaine*.

Khudiakov, E. A. *Velikorusskiia zagadki*. Moscow, 1861.

Klaret. *See* Claret.

Klinkert, H. C. "Vervolg op de maleische spreekwoorden, benevens eenige maleische raadsels en kinderspelen," *Bijdragen tot taal-, land- en volkenkunde van Nederlandsch-Indië*, 3d ser., IV (1869), 24–66.

Klukine, Innokentii A. *Kyluch k izucheniiu zhivol mongol'skoi rechi i pis'mennosti*. Trudy gosudarstvennago dal'nevostochnago universiteta, 6th ser., IV. Vladivostok, 1926.

Knortz, Karl. *Streifzüge auf dem Gebiete amerikanischer Volkskunde*. Leipzig, 1902.

Knowles, J. H. "Kashmiri Riddles," *Journal of the Royal Asiatic Society of Bengal*, LVI (1887), 126–154.

Köhler, Reinhold. *Kleinere Schriften*, I (Weimar, 1898), II–III (Berlin, 1900). *See* especially "Zwei und vierzig Rätsel und Fragen," III, 499–538.

Koesrin, M. *See* Kats.

Kopernicki, J. "Zagadki i łamigłowki górali Bieskidowych spisane w okolocach Rabki," *Zbiór wiadomości do antropologii krajowéj*, I (1877), 113–129.

Kotvich, V. *Kalmykskiia zagadki i poslovitsy*. Izdaniia fakul'teta vostochnykh iazykov imperatorskago St. Petersburgskago universiteta, XVI. St. Petersburg, 1905.

Kowalski, Tadeusz. "Türkische Volksrätsel aus Kleinasien," *Archiv orientální*, IV (1932), 295–324. Cited as Kowalski, *Asia Minor*.

———. "Türkische Volksrätsel aus Nordbulgarien," in T. Menzel, ed., *Festschrift Georg Jacob* (Leipzig, 1932), pp. 128–145. Cited as Kowalski, *North Bulgaria*.

———. *Zagadki ludowe tureckie*. Prace komisji orjentalistycznej, I. Akademji umiejetności. Cracow, 1919. Cited as Kowalski, *Zagadki*.

Kreemer, J. "Atjèhsche raadsels," *Mededeelingen van het koloniaal instituut te Amsterdam*, IX (1928), 1–67. Cited as Kreemer, *Atjeh*.

———. "Javaansche raadsels," *Mededeelingen van wege het nederlandsch zendelinggenootschap*, XXVII (1883), 134–136, 320–331; XXX (1886), 1–8. Cited as Kreemer, *Java*.

Kristensen, E. T. *Danske folkegaader efter trykte og utrykte kilder*. Struer, 1913.

Kriza, János. *Vadrószák. Székly Népköltési Gyüjtemény*, I. Koloszvár, 1863.

Kuhn, G. "Pedi Texte," *Zeitschrift für Eingeborenen-Sprachen*, XXVII (1936–1937), 165–166. Cited as Kuhn, *Pedi*.

———. "Tschuana Texte. Lieder, Rätsel und Märchen," *ibid.*, XXVI (1935–1936), 308–311. Cited as Kuhn, *Tschuana*.

Kuka, M. N. *The Wit and Humour of the Persians*. Bombay, 1894.

Kúnos, Ignaz. *Oszmán-török Népköltési Gyüjtemény*. 2 vols. Budapest, 1887–1889. Cited as Kúnos.

———. *Oszmán-török Nyelvkönyv*. Budapest, 1905. Cited as Kúnos, *Nyelvkönyv*.

———. "Türkische Volksrätsel," *Am Urquell*, IV (1893), 21–23. Cited as Kúnos, *Am Urquell*.

Kuun, Géza. *Codex Cumanicus*. Budapest, 1880.

La Calvez, G. "Devinettes; pays de Tréguier," *Revue des traditions populaires*, VII (1892), 342. Cited as La Calvez, *Tréguier*.

Lacuve, R. M. "Devinettes du Poitou," *Revue des traditions populaires*, X (1895), 352–356; XIV (1899), 702–703. Cited as Lacuve, *Poitou*.

Lallemant, Louis. *Folklore et vieux souvenirs d'Argonne, arrondissement de Sainte-Menehould*. Châlons-sur-Marne, 1921. Cited as Lallemant, *Argonne*.

Landstad, M. B. *Norske folkeviser*. Christiania, 1853.

Larivey, Pierre de. *Les Facétieuses Nuits de Straparole*. Paris, 1857.

Lauterbach, Johannes. *Ænigmata ... additis simul Nicolai Reusneri ... Ænigmatis*. [Frankfurt a. M.], 1601.

Laval, R. A. *Contribución al folklore de Carahue (Chile)*. Madrid, 1916.

Lavenot, P. M. "Devinettes de la Basse-Bretagne," *Revue des traditions populaires*, VI (1891), 666–672. Cited as Lavenot, *Basse-Bretagne*.

Leather, Ella M. *The Folk-Lore of Herefordshire*. London, 1912. Cited as Leather, *Hereford*.

Le Blanc, Paul. "Devinettes de l'Auvergne," *Revue des traditions populaires*, V (1890), 204.

Le Chef, Rodolphe. "Contes, devinettes, ... recueillis à Bréal-sous-Montfort, Ille-et-Vilaine," *Revue des traditions populaires*, X (1895), 667–668. Cited as Le Chef, *Ille-et-Vilaine*.

Ledieu, Alcus. *Traditions populaires de Démuin*. Monographie d'un bourg picard, III. Paris, 1892. Cited as Ledieu, *Démuin*.

Le Héricher, Edmond. "Littérature populaire de la Normandie," *Mémoires de la société d'archéologie, littérature ... d'Avranches et de Mortain*, VII (1885), 34–35.

Lehmann-Nitsche, Robert. *Adivinanzas rioplatenses*. Buenos Aires, 1911.

Leitner, G. W. "Dardu Legends, Proverbs and Fables," *Indian Antiquary*, I (1872), 91.

———. *Dardistan in 1866, 1886, and 1893*. Woking, 1893. Cited as Leitner.

Le Pennec, Yves. "Devinettes populaires de Basse-Bretagne: Michel Pipi Pe ar Farcer Breton," *Revue de Bretagne et de Vendée*, XXXII (n.s., III; 1888), 307–314.

Lespy, Jean Désiré, called Vastin. *Proverbes du pays de Béarn, énigmes et contes populaires.* Publications spéciales de la société pour l'étude des langues romanes, II. Paris, 1876. Cited as Lespy, *Béarn.*

Lindblom, Gerhard. "Kamba Riddles, Proverbs and Songs," *Archives d'études orientales*, XX, iii (Uppsala, 1934).

Littmann, Enno. *Morgenländische Spruchweisheit, arabische Sprichwörter und Rätsel, aus mündlicher Ueberlieferung gesammelt und übertragen.* Morgenland, XXIX. Leipzig, 1937. Cited as Littmann.

———. "Tigriña-Rätsel," *Zeitschrift der deutschen morgenländischen Gesellschaft*, XCII (1938), 611–632. Cited as Littmann, *Tigriña.*

Löhr, Max. *Der vulgärarabische Dialekt von Jerusalem.* Giessen, 1905.

Loewenthal, Fritz. *Studien zum germanischen Rätsel.* Germanistische Arbeiten, I. Heidelberg, 1914.

Lönnrot, Elias. *Arvoituksia.* Suomalaisen kirjallisuuden seura, V. 2d ed.; Helsinki, 1851.

Lorentz, F. *See* Gulgowski.

Lüpkes, Wiard. *Ostfriesische Volkskunde.* 2d ed.; Emden, 1925.

Luinenburg, S. "Javaansche raadsels," *Mededeelingen van wege het nederlandsch zendelinggenootschap*, L (1906), 381–386; LI (1907), 27–33.

Lukas, J. "Sprichwörter, Aussprüche und Rätsel der Kanuri," *Zeitschrift für Eingeborenen-Sprachen*, XXVIII (1938), 161–174.

Lyster, M. Eileen. "Two Gypsy Riddles," *Journal of the Gypsy-Lore Society*, n.s., I (1907–1908), 92.

Lytkin, G. S. "Syrjänische Sprachproben," *Journal de la société finno-ougrienne*, X (1892), 29–82.

MacGréine, Padraig, O.S. "A Longford Miscellany," *Béaloideas*, III (1931–1932), 413–418.

Machado y Alvarez, Antonio (pseud.: Demófilo). *Colección de enigmas y adivinanzas en forma de diccionario.* Seville, 1880. Cited as Demófilo.

Mackenzie, D. A. *The Spirit-Ridden Konde.* London, 1925.

Maclagen, R. C. *Games and Diversions of Argyleshire.* Publications of the Folk-Lore Society, XLVII. London, 1901.

Maenchen, O. J. (O. J. Maenchen-Helfen). *Reise ins asiatische Tuwa.* Berlin, 1931.

Magyar Nyelv. Budapest, 1905 ff.

Magyar Nyelvészet. Pest, 1856–1861.

Magyar Nyelvör. Budapest, 1872–1917.

Malein, A. *Rukopisnie predanie zagadok Aldhelma.* Zapiski istoriko-filologicheskago fakul'teta, LXXVI. St. Petersburg, 1905.

Mann, Oskar. *Persisch-kurdische Forschungen*, I (Berlin, 1909), II (1910).

Marchessou, Régis. *Velay et Auvergne.* Le-Puy-en-Velay, 1903.

Marquer, François. "Devinettes de la Haute-Bretagne," *Revue des traditions populaires*, IV (1889), 225.

Marsden, F. H. "Some Notes on the Folk-Lore of Upper Calderdale," *Folk-Lore*, XLIII (1932), 262. Cited as Marsden, *Upper Calderdale.*

Mason, J. A. "Porto Rican Folklore, Riddles," *Journal of American Folklore*, XXIX (1916), 423–504.

Massip, Salvador. "Adivinanzas corrientes en Cuba," *Archivos del folklore cubano*, I (1925), 305–339.

Materyały antropologiczno-archeologiczne i etnograficzne, I–XIV (Cracow, 1890–1919). Cited as *Materyały*.

Mayer, L. T. *Een Blik in het Javaansch volksleven.* Leiden, 1897.

Meery Riddles. See *The Booke of Meery Riddles* (1629).

Mehta, S. S. "Some Riddles Prevalent Among the Women of Gujerat, Including Cutch and Kathiawar," *Journal of the Anthropological Society of Bombay*, XV (1933), 111–123, 129–138.

Meier, Ernst. *Deutsche Kinder-Reime und Kinder-Spiele aus Schwaben.* Tübingen, 1851. Cited as E. Meier, *Kinderreime.*

Meier, Hermann. *Ostfriesland in Bildern und Skizzen.* Leer, 1868.

Meissner, Bruno. "Neuarabische Sprichwörter und Räthsel aus dem Iraq," *Mitteilungen des Seminars für orientalische Sprachen*, IV, 2. Abteilung, Westasiatische Studien (1901), pp. 167–174. Cited as Meissner, *Iraq*.

Meltzl, Hugo van. "Székler Volksrätsel und Vexierfragen," *Acta comparationis litterarum universarum*, III (Koloszvar, 1888), 9–20.

Menges, Karl Heinrich. See Potapov.

Menghini, Mario. "Indovinelli popolari romani," *Archivio*, XIV (1895), 277–280.

Mensignac, Camille de. "Notice sur plusieurs coûtumes, ... devinettes, ... du département de la Gironde," *Bulletin de la société d'anthropologie de Bordeaux et du Sud-Ouest*, IV (1887), 297–307. Cited as Mensignac, *Gironde*.

Meulen, T. G. van der. See Dykstra.

Milá y Fontanals, M. "Anciennes Enigmes catalanes," *Revue des langues romanes*, XI (2d ser., III; 1877), 5–8. Cited as Milá y Fontanals, 1877.

———. "Enigmes populaires catalanes," *ibid.*, X (2d ser., II; 1876), 22–27. Cited as Milá y Fontanals, 1876.

Milin, G. "Notes sur l'Ile de Batz, § 3, Devinettes," *Revue des traditions populaires*, X (1895), 54–56. Cited as Milin, *Batz*.

Millien, Achille. "Devinettes du Nivernais," *Revue des traditions populaires*, IV (1889), 512, 578. Cited as Millien, *Nivernais*.

Mitra, Sarat Chandra. See Mitra, "Tibetan Folklore from Kalimpong ..."

———. *Bihar.* See Mitra, "Riddles Current in Bihar," ...

———. "Bihari Life in Bihari Riddles," *Journal of the Anthropological Society of Bombay*, VII (1904–1907), 21–50. Cited as Mitra, *Bihari Life*.

———. *Chittagong.* See Mitra, "Riddles Current in the District of Chittagong ..."

———. "A Few Riddles Current in the District of Pābnā in Eastern Bengal," *Journal ... Bombay*, XI (1917–1920), 327–336. Cited as Mitra, *Pābnā*.

———. *Murshidābād.* See Mitra, "Riddles Current in the District of Murshidābād ..."

———. "Notes on Ho Riddles," *Journal ... Bombay*, XI (1917–1920), 100–119; XII (1921–1924), 246–259. Cited as Mitra, *Notes on Ho Riddles*.

———. *Pābnā.* See Mitra, "A Few Riddles Current in the District of Pābnā ..."

———. "Riddles Current in Bihar," *Journal of the Royal Asiatic Society of Bengal*, LXX, iii (1901), 33–58. Cited as Mitra, *Bihar*.

———. "Riddles Current in the District of Chittagong in Eastern Bengal," *Journal ... Bombay*, XI (1917–1920), 296–327, 960–979; XII (1921–1924), 339–368; XIII (1924–1928), 657–672. Cited as Mitra, *Chittagong*.

———. "Riddles Current in the District of Murshidābād, in Northwestern Bengal," *ibid.*, XI (1917–1920), 913–939. Cited as Mitra, *Murshidābād*.

———. "Riddles Current in the District of Sylhet, Eastern Bengal," *Journal ... Bengal*, n.s., XIII (1917), 105–125. Cited as Mitra, *Sylhet*.

———. "Tibetan Folklore from Kalimpong in the District of Darjeeling in the Eastern Himalayas," *Journal ... Bombay*, XIV (1927–1931), 465–466. Cited as Mitra.

Mittwoch, Eugen. "Proben amharischen Volkskunde," *Mitteilungen des Seminars für orientalische Sprachen*, X, 2. Abteilung, Westasiatische Studien (1907), pp. 186–187, 209–212.

Mocci, Antonio. "Indovinelli sardi logoduresi," *Archivio*, XIII (1894), 437–438.

M[one], F. J. "Räthselsammlung," *Anzeiger für Kunde der teutschen Vorzeit*, VII (1838), cols. 32–50, 258–268, 371–384. Contains: "1. Lateinische Räthsel [cols. 32–50]. 2. Teutsche Räthsel [cols. 258–268, 371–382; Flemish riddles are included]. 3. Französische Räthsel [cols. 382–383]. 4. Italienische Räthsel [cols. 383–384]. 5. Spanische Räthsel [col. 384]." Cited as M[one], *Anzeiger*, by volume and column.

———. "Zweite Räthselsammlung," *ibid.*, VIII (1839), cols. 217–229, 315–326. Contains: "A. Lateinische Räthsel [cols. 217–229, 315–317]. B. Teutsche Räthsel [cols. 317–323]. C. Italienische Räthsel [cols. 323–326]." Cited as M[one], *Anzeiger*, by volume and column.

Mont, Pol de. "Raadsels," *Volkskunde*, I (1888), 18–19, 205–209.

Monteil, Charles Victor. *Contes soudanais*. Collection de contes et chansons populaires, XXVIII. Paris, 1905.

Moshkov, V. *Mundarten der bessarabischen Gagausen* (Vol. X of W. Radlov, *Proben der Volksliteratur der türkischen Stämme Süd-Siberiens* [St. Petersburg, 1866–1907]). St. Petersburg, 1904. Cited as Moshkov in Radlov. The text and the Russian translation are separately paged. The pagination used here refers to the translation.

Mostaert, Antoine. *Textes oraux ordos*. Monumenta Serica, I; Monograph Ser., No. 1. Peiping, 1937.

Mudge-Paris, David Benji. "Tales and Riddles from Freetown, Sierra Leone," *Journal of American Folklore*, XLIII (1930), 317–321.

Müllenhoff, Karl. "Nordische, englische und deutsche Räthsel, *Zeitschrift für deutsche Mythologie*, III (1855), 1–20.

Müller, F. "Aus der Volksliteratur der Evheer," *Zeitschrift für afrikanische, ozeanische und ostasiatische Sprachen*, VI (1902), 156–157.

Müller, Josef. "Rätsel, Scherzfragen und Wortspiele aus Uri," *Schweizerisches Archiv für Volkskunde*, XIX (1929), 9–12. Cited as J. Müller, *Uri*.

———. "Scherz- und Rätselfragen aus der Innerschweiz," *Schweizer Volkskunde*, VII (1917), 1–8. Cited as J. Müller, *Innerschweiz*.

Munshi, R. N. "A Few Parsee Riddles," *Journal of the Anthropological Society of Bombay*, X (1915), 94–100, 409–425.

Neal, Janice. "Wa'n't That Remarkable!" *New York Folklore Quarterly*, I (1945), 209–220, esp. pp. 216–217.

Németh, Julius. "Die Rätsel des Codex Cumanicus," *Zeitschrift der deutschen morgenischen Gesellschaft*, LXVII (1913), 577–608. Cited as Németh, *Codex Cumanicus*.

Nergaard, Sigurd. *Eventyr. Barnevers, spurningar og ordspraak*. Folkeminne fraa Østerdalen, III (subseries); Norsk Folkeminnelag, VII. Oslo, 1923.

———. *Segner fraa Elvrom*. Oslo, 1907. Cited as Nergaard.

Nerucci, Gherardo. "Storie e cantari ninne-nanne e indovinelli del montale nel circondario di Pistoja," *Archivio*, III (1884), 39–56.

A New Collection of Enigmas. London, 1810.

The New Help to Discourse. See W. W., Gent.

A New Riddle Book; Or, A Whetstone for Dull Wits. Lichfield, n.d. [18th cent.].

Newell, W. W. "Topics for the Collection of Folklore, II," *Journal of American Folklore*, IV (1891), 155–158.

Nicolaides, Jean. See Carnoy.

Nicolson, Alexander. *Gaelic Riddles and Enigmas*. Glasgow, 1938.

Niemann, G. K. "Alfoersche vertelsels en raadsels," *Mededeelingen van wege het nederlandsch zendelinggenootschap*, XXX (1886), 13–16.

Nippgen, J. "Devinettes mordvines," *Revue des traditions populaires*, XXVI (1911), 257.

Nizheradze, J. "Svanetskie teksty," *Sbornik . . . Kavkaza*, XXXI, iv (1902), 66–69.

Nizheradze, W. S. "Svanetskiia poslovitsy, zagadki i pesni," *Sbornik . . . Kavkaza*, X, ii (1890), 1–8.

Noguera, Eduardo G. "Adivinanzas recogidas en México," *Journal of American Folklore*, XXXI (1918), 537–540.

Noreen, Adolf. "Rägglor från öfre Fryksdalen," *Nyare bidrag till kännedom om de svenska landsmålen*, II (1881), pp. v–ix. Cited as Noreen, *Fryksdal*.

Norton, W. A., and H. Velaphe. "Some SeSuto Riddles with Their Translations," *South African Journal of Science*, XXI (1924), 569–572.

Notes and Queries. London, 1849 ff.

Novaković, Stojan. *Srpske narodne zagonetke*. Panchevo, 1877.

O Dalaigh, Sean. "Tomhaiseanna o Dhúnchaoin," *Béaloideas*, XIII (1943), 80–101.

Ohl, R. T. *The Riddles of Symphosius*. Diss., Univ. of Pennsylvania; Philadelphia, 1928. Cited as Ohl, *Symphosius*.

Ohlert, Konrad. *Rätsel und Rätselspiele der alten Griechen*. Berlin, 1886. 2d ed.; Berlin, 1912. Cited as Ohlert.

———. "Zur antiken Rätselpoesie," *Philologus*, LIII (n.s., VII; 1894), 745–754; LVII (n.s., XII; 1898), 596–602. Cited as Ohlert, *Philologus*.

Olsson, Helmer. "Gåtor från Västergötland," *Folkminnen och folktankar*, XXII (1935), 124–137, 187–194. (Riddles in the second part are numbered separately). Cited as Olsson, *Västergötland*.

———. "Den halländska gåtan," *Vår bygd*, utg. av Hallands hembygsförbund, XXI (1937), 39–46.

———. "Några bohuslänska gåttyper," *Folkminnen och folktankar*, XXIII (1936), 170–175.

Ons Volksleven. See Cornelissen.

Ophuijsen, C. A. van. "Eenige Bataksche raadsels," *Tijdschrift voor indische taal-, landen volkenkunde*, XXVIII (1883), 201–215; XXX (1885), 459–472.

Orain, Adolphe. *Folklore de l'Ille-et-Vilaine*. Les Littératures populaires de toutes les nations, XXXIV. Paris, 1898. Cited as Orain, *Ille-et-Vilaine*.

Ovir, E. "Märchen und Rätsel der Wamadschame," *Zeitschrift für afrikanische und ozeanische Sprachen*, III (1897), 65–84.

Paasonen, H. "Proben der mordwinischen Literatur," *Journal de la société finno-ougrienne*, XI (1894), 24–73.

Palashev, O. "Iz zhivota i obichaitě na Banatskitě Bulgari," *Sbornik za narodni umotvoreniia*, XXII–XXIII, Part i (1906–1907), 13 (articles in Part i are separately paginated).

Panareo, Salvatore. "Indovinelli salentini," *Archivio*, XXIII (1906–1907), 236–244.

Panjab Notes and Queries, I–III (1884–1886).

Pantin, W. A. "A Medieval Collection of Latin and English Proverbs and Riddles, from the Rylands Latin MS. 394," *Bulletin of the John Rylands Library*, XIV (1930), 81–114.

Papahagi, Perikle. "Sammlung aromunischer Sprichwörter und Rätsel," *Jahresbericht des Instituts für rumänische Sprache*, II (1895), 181–192.

Papakristodoulos, P. "Ainigmata Thrakika," *Laographia*, II (1910), 193–194.

Paris, Gaston. "Préface" to Eugène Rolland, *Devinettes et énigmes populaires de la France* (Paris, 1877), pp. i–xvi.

Parker, A. "Oxfordshire Village Folk-Lore, II," *Folk-Lore*, XXXIV (1923), 330–331. Cited as Parker, *Oxfordshire*.

Parsons, Elsie Clews. *Aiken, S.C.* See Parsons, "Folklore from Aiken, South Carolina" . . .

———. *Andros Island, Bahamas.* See Parsons, "Riddles from Andros Island, Bahamas" . . .

———. *Antilles.* See Parsons, *Folklore of the Antilles* . . .

———. *Bahamas.* See Parsons, "Spirituals and Other Folklore from the Bahamas" . . .

———. "Barbados Folklore," *Journal of American Folklore*, XXXVIII (1925), 276–292. Cited as Parsons, *Barbados*.

———. "Bermuda Folklore," *ibid.*, pp. 244–265. Cited as Parsons, *Bermuda*.

———. *Cape Verde.* See Parsons, *Folklore from the Cape Verde Islands* . . .

———. *Eleuthera and Watling's Islands, Bahamas.* See Parsons, "Riddles and Proverbs from the Bahama Islands (Eleuthera and Watling's Islands)" . . .

———. "Folklore from Aiken, South Carolina," *Journal of American Folklore*, XXXIV (1921), 24–37. Cited as Parsons, *Aiken, S.C.*

———. "Folklore from St. Helena, South Carolina," *ibid.*, XXXVIII (1925), 227–228. Cited as Parsons, *St. Helena Island, S.C.*

———. *Folklore from the Cape Verde Islands*, II. Memoirs of the American Folklore Society, XV, ii. Cambridge, Mass., 1923. Cited as Parsons, *Cape Verde*.

———. *Folklore of the Antilles, French and English*, III. Ibid., XXVI, iii. New York, 1943. Cited as Parsons, *Antilles*, III.

———. "Folklore of the Cherokee of Robeson County, North Carolina," *Journal of American Folklore*, XXXII (1919), 388–390. Cited as Parsons, *Robeson Co., N.C.*

———. *Folklore of the Sea Islands, South Carolina*. Memoirs of the American Folklore Society, XVI. New York, 1923. Cited as Parsons, *Sea Islands, S.C.*

———. *Guilford Co., N.C.* See next entry.

———. "Notes on the Folklore of Guilford County, North Carolina," *Journal of American Folklore*, XXX (1917), 201–207. Cited as Parsons, *Guilford Co., N.C.*

———. "Riddles and Proverbs from the Bahama Islands (Eleuthera and Watling's Islands)," *ibid.*, XXXII (1919), 439–441. Cited as Parsons, *Eleuthera and Watling's Islands, Bahamas*.

———. "Riddles from Andros Island, Bahamas," *ibid.*, XXX (1917), 275–277. Cited as Parsons, *Andros Island, Bahamas*.

———. *Robeson Co., N.C.* See Parsons, "Folklore of the Cherokee of Robeson County, North Carolina" . . .

———. *St. Helena Island, S.C.* See Parsons, "Folklore from St. Helena, South Carolina" . . .

———. *Sea Islands, S.C.* See Parsons, *Folklore of the Sea Islands, South Carolina* . . .

———. "Spirituals and Other Folklore from the Bahamas," *Journal of American Folklore*, XLI (1928), 471–485. Cited as Parsons, *Bahamas*.

———. *See also* Bacon.

Pasquarelli, Michele. "Indovinelli di Basilicata raccolti a Missanello," *Archivio*, XV (1896), 75–78.

Patock, J. "Rätsel aus Schwarzau, Kr. Putzig," *Mitteilungen des Vereins für kaschubische Volkskunde*, II (1910), 51. Cited as Patock, *Schwarzau*.

———. "Rätsel aus Strellin, Kr. Putzig," *ibid.*, I (1910), 220. Cited as Patock, *Strellin*.

Patry, Albert. "Devinettes normandes," *Revue des traditions populaires*, IX (1894), 186, 643. Cited as Patry, *Normandie*.

Pauer, P. S. "Adivinanzas recogidas en México," *Journal of American Folklore*, XXXI (1918), 541.

———. *See also* Sahagún.

Peacock, Mabel. *See* Gutch.

Pedersen, Holger. *Zur albanesischen Volkskunde*. Copenhagen, 1898. A translation of the texts printed in *Abhandlungen der k. sächsischen Gesellschaft der Wissenschaften, philosophisch-historische Classe*, XV (1895), No. 3.

Pelay y Briz, F. *Endevinallas populars catalanas accompanyadas de variants y confrontaments ab endevinallas francesas, lituanas, vascas, gallegas, italianas, etc. seguidas de un aplech de endevinallas modernas*. Barcelona, 1882.

Penzer, N. M. *The Ocean of Story*. 10 vols. London, 1924–1928.

Perera, A. A. *Sinhalese Folklore Notes*. Bombay, 1917.

Perkins, A. E. "Riddles from Negro Schoolchildren in New Orleans," *Journal of American Folklore*, XXXV (1922), 105–115. Cited as Perkins, *New Orleans*.

Petrov, I. Ya. "Mingrel'skie teksty," *Sbornik . . . Kavkaza*, X, ii (1890), 257.

Petsch, Robert. *Das deutsche Volksrätsel*. Grundriss der deutschen Volkskunde, I. Strassburg, 1917.

———. *Neue Beiträge zur Kenntnis des Volksrätsels*. Palaestra, IV. Berlin, 1899.

———. "Rätselstudien. I. Zu den Reichenauer Rätseln," *Beiträge zur Geschichte der deutschen Sprache*, XLI (1916), 332–346. Cited as Petsch, *Rätselstudien*.

Pettinen, A. "Lieder und Rätsel der Aandonga," *Zeitschrift für Eingeborenen-Sprachen*, XVII (1926–1927), 202–230.

Pettingill, R. W. "Zu den Rätseln im Apollonius des Heinrich von Neustadt," *Journal of English and Germanic Philology*, XII (1913), 248–251.

Peuckert, W.-E. *Deutsches Volkstum in Märchen und Sage, Schwank und Rätsel*. Berlin, 1938.

Phillott, D. C. "Some Riddles Collected from Dervishes in the South of Persia," *Journal of the Royal Asiatic Society of Bengal*, n.s., II (1906), 86–93.

Piekarski, Edward. "Zagadki jakuckie (z przednowa S. E. Malowa)," *Rocznik orjentalistyczny*, IV (1928), 1–59.

Pincier, Johannes. *Ænigmatum libri tres*. The Hague, 1655.

Pineau, Léon. *Le Folklore de Poitou*. Collection de contes et chansons populaires, XVIII. Paris, 1892. Cited as Pineau, *Poitou*.

———. *See also* Georgeakis.

Pires, Antonio Thomáz. "Adivinhas portuguezas ... na provincia do Alemtejo," *Archivio*, III (1884), 113–120, 241–250.

———. "Adivinhas portuguezas ... na provincia do Douro," *ibid.*, VII (1888), 246–248; VIII (1889), 93–96.

———. Adivinhas portuguezas recolhidas na provincia do Douro," *Revista lusitana*, I (1887–1889), 262–266.

Pires de Lima, A. C. *O livro das adivinhas*. Porto, 1921.

Pitman, J. H., ed. *The Riddles of Aldhelm*. Yale Studies in English, LXVII. New Haven, 1925.

Pitrè, Giuseppe. *Canti popolari siciliani*. 2 vols. Palermo, 1871. Cited as Pitrè, *Canti*.

———. *Indovinelli, dubbi, scioglilingua del popolo siciliano*. Biblioteca delle tradizioni popolari siciliani, XX. Turin, 1897. Cited as Pitrè.

———. "Indovinelli toscani," *Archivio*, X (1891), 382–384. Cited as Pitrè, *Archivio*.

Poestion, J. C. *Lappländische Märchen, Volkssagen, Räthsel und Sprichwörter*. Vienna, 1886.

Polites, N. G. "Demode Ainigmata," *Neohellenika Analekta*, I (Athens, 1870), 193–256.

———. "Paratereseis tes Tourkikes paroimias kai ainigmata," *Laographia*, III (1911), 240–242.

Pommerel. "Devinettes de l'Auvergne," *Revue des traditions populaires*, XXIII (1908), 42. Cited as Pommerel, *Auvergne*.

Popov, A. A. *Iakutskii fol'klor*. [Leningrad?]: Sovietskii pisatel', 1936.

Poppe, N. N. *Materialy dlia issledovaniia tungusskogo iazika, nareche bargusinskikh tungusov*. Materialy po iaficheskomu iazikoznaniiu, XIII. Leningrad: Akademiia Nauk, 1927.

Porkka, Volmari. "Tscheremissische Texte mit Uebersetzung," *Journal de la société finno-ougrienne*, XIII (1895), 88–95.

Potapov, L. P., and Karl Heinrich Menges. "Materialien zur Volkskunde der Türkvölker des Altaj," *Mitteilungen des Seminars für orientalische Sprachen*, XXXVII, 1. Abteilung, Ostasiatische Studien (1934), pp. 76–78, 81, 86–87. Cited as Menges.

Pracki, W. "Zagadki ludowe ze wsi Turowa pow. radzyńskiego gub. siedleckiej," *Materyały*, IV (1900), 211–216.

Praeger, S. Rosamond. "Riddles from Co. Down," *Béaloideas*, IV (1933–1934), 144–146.

———. "Rimes and Riddles from County Down," *ibid.*, VIII (1938), 167–171.

Pratt, George. *Grammar and Dictionary of the Samoan Language*. 2d ed.; Malina, Samoa, 1911.

Preobrazhenskii, A. "Prikhod Stanilovskoĭ na Siti," *Etnograficheskii sbornik*, I (St. Petersburg, 1853), 170–173.

Prettie Riddles. See *A Booke of Merrie Riddles* (1631).

Priklonskii, V. "Iakutskiia zagadki," *Zhivaia starina*, I (1890), supplement.

Pröhle, W. "Balkarische Studien," *Keleti szemle*, XVI (1915–1916), 120.

Puckett, N. N. *Folk Beliefs of the Southern Negro*. Chapel Hill, N.C., 1926. Cited as Puckett, *Southern Negro*.

Queyrat, Louis. *Contributions à l'étude du parler de la Creuse, commune de Chavant*. 3 vols. Gueret, 1927–1930. See esp. I, 363–367. Cited as Queyrat, *La Creuse*.

Quijada Jara, Sergio. *Estampas huancavelicas*. Lima, 1944.

Qvigstad, Just. *Lappische Sprichwörter und Rätsel*. Kristiania Etnografiska Museums Skrifter, I, No. 3. Oslo, 1922.

Radlov, W. *Proben der Volksliteratur der türkischen Stämme Süd-Sibiriens*. 10 vols. St. Petersburg, 1866–1907.

———. *See also* Katanov, Moshkov.

Ramstedt, G. J. "Bergtscheremissische Sprachstudien," *Mémoires de la société finno-ougrienne*, XVII (1902), 213–214.

Randolph, Vance, and Isabel Spradley. "Ozark Mountain Riddles," *Journal of American Folklore*, XLVII (1934), 81–89. Cited as Randolph and Spradley, *Ozark*.

Randolph, Vance, and Archer Taylor. "Riddles in the Ozarks," *Southern Folklore Quarterly*, VII (1944), 1–10. Cited as Randolph and Taylor, *Ozarks*.

Ranneft, W. M. "Verklaring van de meest bekende javaansche raadsels in poëzie," *Verhandelingen van het bataviaasch genootschap van kunsten*, XLIX, No. 2 (1896). Cited as Ranneft, *Poëzie*.

———. "Verklaring van de meest bekende javaansche raadsels in proza," *ibid.*, XLVII, No. 2 (1893). Cited as Ranneft, *Proza*.

Rattray, R. S. *Some Folk-Lore Stories and Songs in Chinyanja*. London, 1907.

Raum, J. *Versuch einer Grammatik der Dschaggasprache*. Archiv für das Studium deutscher Kolonialsprachen, XI. Berlin, 1909.

Recinos, Adrián. "Adivinanzas recogidas en Guatemala," *Journal of American Folklore*, XXXI (1918), 544–549.

Redfield, Margaret Park. *The Folk-Literature of a Yucatecan Town.* Contributions to American Ethnology, III, No. 13. Washington, 1937.

Redfield, Robert, and Alfonso Villa R. *Cham Kon: A Maya Village.* Washington, 1934.

Redfield, W. A. "A Collection of Middle Tennessee Riddles," *Southern Folklore Quarterly,* I, No. 3 (1937), 35–50. Cited as Redfield, *Tennessee.*

Renk, Anton. "Volksrätsel aus Tirol," *Zeitschrift des Vereins für Volkskunde,* V (1895), 147–160. Cited as Renk, *Tyrol.*

Reusner, Nicolaus. *Ænigmata.* Frankfurt a. M., 1601.

———. *Ænigmatographia.* Frankfurt a. M., 1599. 2d ed.; Frankfurt a. M., 1602. Cited as Reusner.

Reyes y Florentino, J. de los. *El folk-lore filipino.* Manila, 1889.

The Riddles of Heraclitus and Democritus. London, 1598. Reprinted in Brandl.

Rivers, W. H. R. *The Todas.* London, 1906.

Rizal, José. "Specimens of Tagal Folklore," *Trübner's Record; a Journal Devoted to the Literature of the East,* 3d ser., I, Part i, No. 243 (1889), pp. 45–46.

Rochholz, E. L. *Alemannisches Kinderlied und Kinderspiel.* Leipzig, 1857.

Rodríguez Marín, F. *Cantos populares españoles.* Seville, 1882.

Roethe, Gustav, ed. *Die Gedichte Reinmars von Zweter.* Leipzig, 1887.

Rolland, Eugène. *Devinettes ou énigmes populaires de la France suivies de la réimpression d'un recueil de 77 indovinelli publié à Trévise en 1628. Avec une préface de Gaston Paris.* Paris, 1877. Cited as Rolland. See on pp. 167–169, "Enigmes des Wolofs," and on pp. 169–170, "Enigmes des Bassutos" (reprinted from Casalis, *Etude sur la langue séchuana*).

———. *Rimes et jeux de l'enfance.* Les Littératures populaires de toutes les nations, XIV. Paris, 1883. Cited as Rolland, *Rimes.*

Rondini, Druso. "Canti popolari marchigiani inediti," *Archivio,* VII (1888), 531–546; VIII (1889), 185–192.

Roque-Ferrier, Alphonse. "Enigmes populaires en Languedoc," *Revue des langues romanes,* VII (1875), 313–340. Cited as Roque-Ferrier, *Languedoc.*

Roux, Albert. See Hugues.

Roux, Joseph. "Enigmes populaires du Limousin," *Revue des langues romanes,* XII (2d ser., IV; 1877), 172–186. Cited as J. Roux, *Limousin.*

Roy, Sarat Chandra. *The Birhors.* Ranchi, 1925.

———. *The Mundas and Their Country.* Calcutta, 1912.

———, and R. C. Roy. *The Khaṛiās.* 2 vols. Ranchi, 1937.

Rua, Giuseppe. "Di alcune stampe d'indovinelli," *Archivio,* VII (1888), 427–465.

———. See also Straparola.

Rudnyev, A. D., ed. "Obraztsy mongol'skago narodnago tvorchestva (Mongol'ski tekst i russki perevod zagadok, sobrannykh Sh.-Lkh. Baz. Bazarovym ...)," *Zapiski vostochnago otdeleniia imperatorskago russkago arkheologicheskago obshchestva,* XIV (1902), 092–0106.

Rudolph, R. C. "The Riddle in China," *California Folklore Quarterly,* I (1942), 65–82.

Ruoff, Eric. *Arabische Rätsel gesammelt, übersetzt und erläutert; ein Beitrag zur Volkskunde Palästinas.* Diss., Univ. of Tübingen; Tübingen, 1933.

Russwurm, C. F. W. *Eibofolke oder, die Schweden an den Küsten Ehstlands und auf Runö.* Reval, 1855. Cited as Russwurm, *Eibo.*

———. "Schwedische Räthsel," *Zeitschrift für deutsche Mythologie,* III (1855), 345–356. Cited as Russwurm.

S., V. [Victor Smith]. "Quelques Devinailles du Velay et du Forez," *Mélusine,* I (1878), cols. 253–266.

Sadovnikov, D. *Zagadki russkago naroda.* 2d ed.; St. Petersburg, 1901.

Sahagún, Fray Bernardino. *Historia general de las cosas de la Nueva España.* The riddles are reprinted in P. S. Pauer, "Adivinanzas tomadas del libro Historia General de las cosas de la Nueva España escrita por el R. P. Fray Bernardino Sahagún Tomo II del Vigésimo Tercero de la Biblioteca Mexicana en la página número 369, Cápitulo XLII," *Journal of American Folklore,* XXXI (1918), 542–543.

Sakellarios, A. A. *Ta Kypriaka.* 2d ed.; Athens, 1891.

Salmon, L. "Folk-Lore in the Kennet Valley," *Folk-Lore,* XIII (1902), 421. Cited as Salmon, *Kennet Valley.*

Saloni, Aleksander. "Lud łańcucki," *Materyały,* VI, ii (1903), 260–262. Cited as Saloni, *Łańcut.*

———. "Lud rzeszowski," *ibid.,* X, ii (1908), 315–330. Cited as Saloni, *Rzeshów.*

Salvioni, Carlo. "Centurie d'indovinelli popolari lombardi," *Archivio,* IV (1885), 537–552.

Samojlvich, A. N. "Zagadki zakaspiiskikh turkmenov," *Zhivaia starina,* XVIII (1909), 52–83.

Sampson, John. "Fifty Welsh Gypsy Folk-Riddles," *Journal of the Gypsy-Lore Society,* n.s., V (1911–1912), 241–254.

Sánchez de Fuentes, Eugenio. "Más adivinanzas cubanas," *Archivos del folklore cubano,* II (1926), 124–130.

Sandén, P. A. "Gåtor från Fredsbärgs ock Hifva församlingar i Norra Vadsbo härad," *Nyare bidrag till kännedom om de svenska landsmålen,* VII, No. 4 (1887). Cited as Sandén, *Norra Vadsbo.*

Sanders, D. H. *Das Volksleben der Neugriechen.* Mannheim, 1844.

Sarkar, Girindra Nath. "Ho Riddles," *Journal of the Bihar and Orissa Research Society,* II (1916), 350–355; V (1919), 250–258.

Sauvé, L. F. "Devinettes bretonnes," *Revue celtique,* IV (1879–1880), 60–103.

Sayce, R. U. "A Survey of Montgomeryshire Folklore," *Collections Historical and Archaeological Relating to Montgomeryshire and Its Borders,* XLVII (1941), 16–18. Cited as Sayce, *Montgomeryshire.*

Sbornik materialov dlia opisaniia mestnostei i plemen Kavkaza, I–XXIX (Tiflis, 1881–1901). Cited as *Sbornik . . . Kavkaza.*

Schapera, Isaac. "Kxatla Riddles and Their Significance," *Bantu Studies,* VI (1932), 215–231.

Scheibler, P. "Bassa-Märchen und Rätsel," *Zeitschrift für Kolonialsprachen,* VII (1917), 164–166.

Schevill, Rudolph. "Some Forms of the Riddle Question and the Exercise of the Wits in Popular Fiction and Formal Literature," *University of California Publications in Modern Philology,* II (1910–1912), 183–237.

Schiefner, Anton. "Ossetische Texte," *Bulletin de l'académie de St. Pétersbourg,* VI (1863), cols. 449–453.

Schleicher, August. *Litauische Märchen, Sprichworte, Rätsel und Lieder.* Weimar, 1857.

Schmidt, Arno. *Hundert alte und neue Volksrätsel aus Westpreussen.* Heimatblätter des deutschen Heimatbundes, I. Danzig, 1924. Cited as Schmidt, *Danzig.*

———. "Die Reichenauer Rätsel," *Zeitschrift für deutsches Altertum,* LXXII (1936), 197–200.

———. "Zu dem Rätsel: ein Toter wird begraben," *Zeitschrift für Volkskunde,* XLV (1935), 164–165.

Schmolck, W. "Volksstudien von der Küste Malabar," *Das Ausland,* LXVI (1893), 242–243, 261.

Schneller, Christian. *Märchen und Sagen aus Wälschtirol.* Innsbruck, 1867. Cited as Schneller, *Wälschtirol.*

Schönhärl, Josef. *Volkskundliches aus Togo: Märchen und Fabeln, Sprichwörter und Rätsel.* Dresden, 1909.

Schrijnen, Josef. *Nederlandsche volkskunde.* 2 vols. 2d ed.; Zutphen, 1930–1933.

Schultz, Wolfgang. "Rätsel" in Pauly, Wissowa, and Kroll (eds.), *Realencyclopädie der classischen Altertumswissenschaft,* Zweite Reihe, I (Stuttgart, 1913), cols. 62–125. Cited as Schultz, *Rätsel.*

———. *Rätsel aus dem hellenischen Kulturkreise,* I–II. Mythologische Bibliothek, III, i (Leipzig, 1909); V, i (1912).

———. "Vergleichende Bemerkungen zur byzantischen Rätselüberlieferung," *Laographia,* IV (1913), 353–376. Cited as Schultz, *Bemerkungen.*

Sébillot, Paul. "Devinettes recueillies dans les Côtes-du-Nord et l'Ille-et-Vilaine," *Bulletins et mémoires de la société d'émulation des Côtes-du-Nord* (Saint-Brieuc), XXIII (1885), 93–98. Cited as Sébillot, *Devinettes.*

———. *Littérature orale de la Haute-Bretagne.* Les Littératures populaires de toutes les nations, I. Paris, 1881. Cited as Sébillot, *Haute-Bretagne.*

———. *Littérature orale de l'Auvergne.* Ibid., XXXV. Paris, 1898. Cited as Sébillot, *Auvergne.*

Seetzen, U. J. In *Fundgruben des Orients,* I (Vienna, 1809), 75–77. Cited from the reprint in J. B. Friedreich, *Geschichtedes Räthsels* (Dresden, 1860), pp. 178–179, § 61.

Seidel, August. *Geschichten und Lieder der Afrikaner.* Berlin, [1899?].

Seidlitz, R. vo ̇. "Armenische und grusinische Sprichwörter," *Das Ausland,* LVII (1884), 70–71; partially reprinted in *ibid.,* LXII (1889), 809.

Shein, P. V. "Materialy dlia izucheniia byta i iazika russkago naseleniia severo-zapadno kraia," *Sbornik otdeleniia iazika i slovesnosti, imperatorskoĭ akademiia nauk* (St. Petersburg), XLI, No. 3 (1887) = "Materialy," I, Pt. i; LI, No. 3 (1890) = "Materialy," I, Pt. ii; LVII (1893) = "Materialy," II. See especially "Materialy," II, 485–499.

Siarkowski, K. W. "Zagadki ludowe z róznych miejscowości gubernii kieleckéj," *Zbiór wiadomości do antropologii krajowéj,* VI, 3–29.

Sibree, James. "Folk-Tales of the Malagasy, II, Riddles and Conundrums," *Folk-Lore Journal,* I (1883), 38–40.

Sichler, Léon. "Devinettes russes," *Revue des traditions populaires,* I (1886), 118–120; VII (1892), 755–756; VIII (1893), 218–219.

Silva, W. A. de. "A Contribution to Sinhalese Plant Lore," *Journal of the Ceylon Branch of the Royal Asiatic Society,* XII (1891–1892), 113–143, esp. pp. 139–143.

Simpkins, J. E. *Examples of Printed Folk-Lore Concerning Fife.* Publications of the Folk-Lore Society, LXXI. London, 1914. Cited as Simpkins, *Fife.*

Simrock, Karl. *Das deutsche Rätselbuch.* Leipzig, n.d.

Singels, N. J. "Raadsels uit den ouden tijd," *Nederland,* 1898, Part ii, pp. 409–449.

Sinninghe, J. R. W. *Oudhollandsche raadsels.* Baarn, 1937.

Smiley, Portia. "Folklore from Virginia, South Carolina, Georgia, Alabama, and Florida," *Journal of American Folklore,* XXXII (1919), 375. Cited as Smiley, *Virginia, etc.*

Smith, Edwin W., and A. M. Dale. *The Ila-Speaking Peoples of Northern Rhodesia.* 2 vols. London, 1920.

Smith, Victor. See V. S.

Socin, Albert, and Hans Stumme. "Der arabische Dialekt der Houwara des Wad Sus in Marokko," *Abhandlungen der k. sächsischen Gesellschaft der Wissenschaften, philosophisch-historische Klasse,* XV (1895), No. 1, pp. 79–81, 136–137.

Sommer, Johann (pseud.: Huldreich Therander). *Ænigmatographia rhythmica.* Madgeburg, 1606.

Souché, B. "Proverbes, traditions, diverses conjurations," *Bulletin de la société de statistique, sciences, lettres ... des Deux-Sèvres*, IV (Niort, 1879–1881), 483–540.

Spenney, Susan Dix. "Riddles and Ring-Games from Raleigh, North Carolina," *Journal of American Folklore*, XXXIV (1921), 110–111. Cited as Spenney, *Raleigh, N.C.*

Spiegel, H. van den. "Eenige madoereesche versjes, raadsels en spreekwoorden," *Tijdschrift voor indische taal-, land- en volkenkunde*, XXXVII (1893), 285–309.

Spieth, Jakob. *Die Ewe-Stämme.* Berlin, 1906.

Spradley, Isabel. *See* Randolph.

Stafset, K. D. *280 gamle norske gaator.* Velden, 1908.

Stamatiadis, E. I. *Ikariaka.* Samos, 1903.

Starr, Frederick. *Aino nazo shu.* The Ainu Library. Tokio, 1911. Cited as Starr, *Ainu.* *See also* Archer Taylor.

——. "Japanese Riddles," *Transactions of the Asiatic Society of Japan*, XXXVIII (1910), 1–49. Cited as Starr, *Japan.*

——. *A Little Book of Filipino Riddles.* Yonkers, 1909. Cited as Starr, *Philippines.*

Stathes, S. E. "Kytheriaka Ainigmata," *Laographia*, II (1910), 330–370.

Stayt, H. A. *The Bavenda.* London, 1931.

Steere, Edward. *Swahili Tales.* London, 1889.

Stoilov, Ch. P. "Gatanki," *Sbornik za narodni umotvoreniia*, XXX (1914), 1–146.

Stokes, Whitley. "Irish Riddles," *Celtic Review*, I (1904), 132–135.

Straparola, M. Giovanfrancesco (Giuseppe Rua, ed.). *Le piacevoli notti.* Bologna, 1899–1908. *See also* Larivey.

Ström, Fredrik. *Svenska folkgåtor.* Stockholm, 1937.

Stumme, Hans. "Elf Stücke im Sílha-Dialekt von Tázerwalt, XI, Rätsel," *Zeitschrift der deutschen morgenländischen Gesellschaft*, XLVIII (1894), 391–392, 406. Cited as Stumme, *Zeitschrift . . .*

——. *Märchen der Schluh von Tázerwalt.* Leipzig, 1895. Cited as Stumme, *Tázerwalt.*

——. *Maltesische Märchen, Gedichte und Rätsel.* Leipziger semitische Studien, I, Nos. 4 [text] and 5 [translation]. Leipzig, 1904. Cited as Stumme, *Malta.*

——. *Tunisische Märchen und Gedichte.* Leipzig, 1893. Cited as Stumme, *Tunis.*

——. *See also* Socin.

Suchier, Walther. *See* Daly, and *L'Enfant sage.*

Suie, Jean de la. "Devinettes savoyards," *Revue des traditions populaires*, XI (1896), 472–473. Cited as De la Suie, *Savoie.*

Sylvain, Alexandre. *See* Bussche.

Symphosius. *See* Ohl.

Szapszal, H. S. *Próby literatury ludowej turków z Azerbajdzanu Perskiego.* Prace komisji orjentalistycznej, XVIII. Akademji umiejetności. Cracow, 1935.

Szendrey, Sigismund. "Találósmeséink és külföldi megfeleléseik," *Ethnographia*, XXXII (1921), 69–81.

Tafel, Albert. *Meine Tibetreise.* Stuttgart, 1914.

Talpa, M. Y., and Y. M. Sokolov. *Kabardinsk folklor.* Moscow, 1936.

Tambiev, Pago. "Adygskie zagadki," *Sbornik . . . Kavkaza*, XXVI, iii (1899), 53–65.

Tammi, Ernesto. "Indovinelli piacentini," *Il folklore italiano*, V (1930), 179–185.

Tardy, L. "Contributions à l'étude du folklore Bantou. Les Fables, devinettes et proverbes fang," *Anthropos*, XXVIII (1935), 277–303.

Tatwine. *See* Ebert.

Tauern, O. D. *Patasiwa und Patalima.* Leipzig, 1919.

Tauxier, Louis. *Nègres gouro et gagou, centre de la Côte d'Ivoire*. Paris, 1924. Cited as Tauxier, *Côte d'Ivoire*.

———. *Les Noirs du Yatenga*. Paris, 1917. Cited as Tauxier.

Taylor, Archer. "Ainu Riddles," *Western Folklore*, VI (1947), 163–173. Cited as Taylor.

———. *A Bibliography of Riddles*. FF Communications, CXXXIX. Helsinki, 1939.

———. "Twenty-three Riddles from Nellore," *Journal of American Folklore*, LIV (1941), 72–75. Cited as Taylor, *Nellore*.

———. *See also* Emeneau, Hull, and Randolph.

Tessmann, Günter. *Die Baja. Ein Negerstamm im mittleren Sudan*. Stuttgart, 1934.

———. "Rätsel der Pangwe, West Zentralafrika," *Anthropos*, X–XI (1915–1916), 695–725. Cited as Tessmann.

Therander, Huldreich. *See* Sommer.

Thorburn, S. S. *Bannú; or Our Afghan Frontier*. London, 1876.

Thurston, Helen S. "Riddles from Massachusetts," *Journal of American Folklore*, XVIII (1905), 182. Cited as Thurston, *Massachusetts*.

Torczyner, Harry. "The Riddles in the Bible," *Hebrew Union College Annual*, I (1924), 125–149.

Trautmann, René. *La Littérature populaire de la Côte des Esclaves*. Paris, 1927.

Tremearne, A. J. N. *Hausa Superstitions and Customs*. London, 1913.

Tschiedel, J. "Italienische Volksrätsel," *Zeitschrift des Vereins für Volkskunde*, VI (1896), 276–283.

Tupper, Frederic, Jr. "The Comparative Study of Riddles," *Modern Language Notes*, XVIII (1903), cols. 1–8.

———. "The 'Flores' of Pseudo-Bede," *Modern Philology*, II (1904–1905), 561–572.

———. "The Holme Riddles (MS. Harl. 1960)," *Publications of the Modern Language Association*, XVIII (1903), 210–272. Cited as Tupper, *Holme Riddles*.

———. *The Riddles of the Exeter Book*. Boston, 1910.

Turi, Johan and Per. *Lappish Texts* (ed. Emilie Demant-Hatt). Det kongelige danske videnskabernes selskabs skrifter, historisk og filosofisk afdelning, 7th række, IV, No. 2. Copenhagen, 1920. Cited as Turi.

Turner, George. *Nineteen Years in Polynesia*. London, 1861. Cited as Turner.

———. *Samoa. A Hundred Years Ago and Long Before*. London, 1884.

Udal, J. S. *Dorsetshire Folk-Lore*. Hertford, 1922. Cited as Udal, *Dorset*.

Ulanowska, Stefanie. "Łotysze polskich a w szczególności z gminy Wielońskiej powiatu Rzézyckiego," *Zbiór wiadomości do antropologii krajowéj*, XVI (1892), 203–216.

Upasānī, Lakshīnātha. *A Collection of Riddles*. Patna (Bankipur: Behar-Bandhu Press), 1888.

Velaphe, H. *See* Norton.

Velten, Carl. "Hundert Suaheli-Rätsel," *Mitteilungen des Seminars für orientalische Sprachen*, VII, 3. Abteilung, Afrikanische Sprachen (1904), pp. 1–11.

Villa R, Alfonso. *See* Robert Redfield.

Vinson, Julien. *Le Folklore du pays basque*. Les Littératures populaires de toutes les nations, XV. Paris, 1883.

Vloten, J. van. *Nederlandsche Baker- en Kinderrijmen*. 4th ed.; Leiden, n.d. [1894].

Volkskunde in Breisgau. *See* Haffner.

W., W., Gent. *The New Help to Discourse*. 9th ed.; London, 1733.

Wackernagel, Wilhelm. "Sechzig Räthsel und Fragen," *Zeitschrift für deutsches Altertum*, III (1843), 25–34.

Wagner, Paul. "Some Kolarian Riddles," *Journal of the Royal Asiatic Society of Bengal*, extra volume for 1904, pp. 62–79.

Wallner, Anton. "Sechs Rätselsprüche," *Beiträge zur Geschichte der deutschen Sprache*, XLIV (1916), 110–117.

Waltman, K. H. "Lidmål," *Bidrag till kännedom om de svenska landsmålen*, XIII, i (1894), 32–39. Cited as Waltman, *Lidmål*.

Ward, H. W. *See* Cronise.

Wasilewski, Leon. "Zagadki białoruskie," *Materyały*, II, ii (1897), 5–13.

Waugh, F. W. "Canadian Folklore from Ontario," *Journal of American Folklore*, XXXI (1918), 63–72. Cited as Waugh, *Canada*.

Weigand, Gustav. *Die Aromunen*. Leipzig, 1894.

Werner, Alice. *The Natives of British Central Africa*. London, 1906.

Westermann, Diedrich. *The Shilluk People: Their Language and Folklore*. Berlin, 1912.

Westphalen, R. *Petit Dictionnaire des traditions messines*. Metz, 1934. Cited as Westphalen, *Metz*.

Whitney, A. W., and C. C. Bullock. *Folklore of Maryland*. Memoirs of the American Folklore Society, XVIII. New York, 1925. Cited as Whitney and Bullock, *Maryland*.

Whymant, A. N. J. *A Mongolian Grammar*. London, 1926.

Wichmann, Yrjö. "Syrjänische Volksdichtung," *Mémoires de la société finno-ougrienne*, XXXVIII (1917), 146–175. Cited as Wichmann, *Zyrian*.

———. "Volksdichtung und Volksbräuche der Tscheremissen," *ibid.*, LIX (1931), 132–155. Cited as Wichmann, *Cheremiss*.

———. "Wotjakische Sprachproben, II, Sprichwörter, Rätsel, Märchen, Sagen," *Journal de la société finno-ougrienne*, XIX (1901), 10–51. Cited as Wichmann, *Votyak*.

Wiedemann, F. J. *Aus dem inneren und äusseren Leben der Ehsten*. St. Petersburg, 1876.

Wigström, Eva. *Folkdiktning, visor, sägner, sagor, gåtor samlad och upptecknad i Skåne*. Copenhagen, 1880.

Wilken, N. P. "Alfoersche vertelsels en raadsels," *Mededeelingen van wege het nederlandsch zendelinggenootschap*, XXX (1886), 291–306.

Wilkinson, T. T. *See* Harland.

Wilson, H. B. "Notes of Syrian Folklore Collected in Boston," *Journal of American Folklore*, XVI (1903), 135–156.

Wingate, J. S. "Armenian Riddles," *Folk-Lore*, XXIII (1912), 471–472.

Winstedt, Eric Otto. "Coppersmith Gypsy Notes," *Journal of the Gypsy-Lore Society*, n.s., VIII (1914–1916), 246–266.

Wintemberg, W. J. "Folklore Collected in the Counties of Oxford and Waterloo, Ontario," *Journal of American Folklore*, XXXI (1918), 150. Cited as Wintemberg, *Ontario*.

———. "Folklore Collected in Toronto and Vicinity," *ibid.*, p. 133. Cited as Wintemberg, *Toronto*.

———, and Katherine H. "Folklore from Grey County, Ontario," *Journal of American Folklore*, XXXI (1918), 123–124. Cited as Wintemberg and Wintemberg, *Canada*.

Wit and Humor of the Age. Chicago, n.d. [1901].

Wlislocki, Heinrich von. *Volksdichtungen der siebenbürgischen und südungarischen Zigeuner*. Vienna, 1890.

Woeste, F. "Volksräthsel, meist aus der Grafschaft Mark," *Zeitschrift für deutsche Mythologie*, III (1855), 179–196.

Wossidlo, Richard. *Rätsel*. Wismar, 1897.

Wright, Elizabeth M. *Rustic Speech and Folk-Lore*. London, 1913.

Zahler, H. "Rätsel aus Münchenbuchsee," *Schweizerisches Archiv für Volkskunde*, IX (1905), 81–111, 187–210. Cited as Zahler, *Münchenbuchsee*.

Zavarin, V. "Osmanskii zagadki sobranniia v Brusie," *Drevnosti vostochniia*, IV (1913), 115–129. Cited as Zavarin, *Brusa*.

Zelinski, S. P. "Etnograficheskie ocherki iz byta Armyan-pereselentsev iz Persii," *Sbornik . . . Kavkaza*, I, ii (1881), 55–59.

Zhamtsaranov, Tsyben Zh. "Materialy k izucheniyu ustnoi literatury mongol'skikh plemion," *Zapiski vostochnago otdeleniia imperatorskago russkago arkheologicheskago obshchestva*, XVII (St. Petersburg, 1907), 08–0126, esp. pp. 0120–0125.

Zingerle, I. V. *Das deutsche Kinderlied im Mittelalter*. 2d ed.; Innsbruck, 1872.

Collections Arranged According to Languages

Note: Following the collector's usage, I have occasionally adopted a geographical rather than a linguistic designation. Authors of several books and articles are cited only once in each group. The full titles will be found in the Collections of Riddles Cited.

General and Comparative. Aarne, Boekenoogen, Destunis, Feilberg, Feit, Fitzgerald, Flajšhans, Friedreich, Geijer and Campbell, Hagen, Hertz, Jungbauer, Kemble, Loewenthal, Müllenhoff, Paris, Petsch, Pettingill, Peuckert, Reusner, Schevill, Schultz, Singels, Szendrey, Taylor, Tupper, Wallner
Aandonga. Pettinen
Abchaz. Guliia
Abyssinian. Littmann, Mittwoch
Afghan. Thorburn
African. Cronise and Ward, Decary, Rolland, Seidel, Werner. *See also* Aandonga, Abyssinian, Afrikaans, Baja, Bakongo, Bankon, Bantu, Baronga, Basa, Basuto, Bavenda, Chinyanja, Dschagga, Duala, Evhe, Ewe, Gagou, Galla, Gouro, Hausa, Ila, Kaguru, Kamba, Kanuri, Kiniramba, Kinyarwanda, Konde, Kosi, Kundu, Kxatla, Lamba, Lesotho, Louyi, Mandingo, Masai, Nandi, Nuer, Nyika, Pangwe, Pedi, Sechuana, SeSuto, Shilluk, Sierra Leone, Slave Coast, Songaï, Sotho, Suk, Sukuma, Swahili, Taveta, Togo, Tonga-Shangaan, Tschuana, Wakweli, Wamajame, Wanamwezi, Wolof, Yatenga, Zulu
Afrikaans. Groenewald
Ainu. Starr, Taylor
Albanian. Hahn, Pedersen
Alfoer. Niemann, Wilken
Annamese. Dumoutier, Emeneau and Taylor
Arabic. Bauer, Emeneau and Taylor, Giacobetti, Al-Ḥarîrî, Littmann, Löhr, Meissner, Ruoff, Seetzen, Socin and Stumme, Stumme
Armenian. Edwards, Glushakov, Grigorov, Seidlitz, Wingate, Zelinski
Assyrian. Jaeger
Atjeh. Kreemer
Aztec. Sahagún (ed. by Pauer)
Baiga. Elwin
Baja. Tessmann
Bakongo. Denis
Balkar. Pröhle
Baluchi. Dames
Bankon. Ittmann
Bantu. Tardy
Baronga. H. Junod
Basa. Scheibler
Basque. Cerquand, Machado y Alvarez (Demófilo), Vinson
Basuto. Casalis, Rolland
Batak. Joustra, Ophuijsen
Bavenda. Stayt
Bengali. Mitra
Bengkoela. Helfrich
Berber. Basset
Bhil. Hedberg
Bihari. Mitra
Birhor. S. C. Roy
Breton. Bayon, Charlec, Duine, Ernault, Frison, Kerbeuzec, La Calvez, Lavenot, Le Chef, Le Pennec, Milin, Orain, Sauvé, Sébillot
Bulgarian. Bozhov, Chacharov, Gubov, Ikonomov, Palashev, Stoilov
Buryat. Gombojew. *See also* Mongolian
Calmuck. Kotvich. *See also* Mongolian
Catalan. *Endevinalles*, Machado y Alvarez (Demófilo), Milá y Fontanals, Pelay y Briz
Celtic. *See* Breton, Irish, Manx, Scotch Gaelic, Welsh
Cherekessian. Tambiev
Cheremiss. Genetz, Porkka, Ramstedt, Wichmann
Chinese. Rudolph
Chinyanja. Rattray
Coorg. Emeneau manuscript
Cuman. Bang, Kuun, Németh. *See also* Turkish
Czech. Feifalik, Flajšhans, Hanika-Otto
Danish. Feilberg, Dansk Folkemindesamling (DFS), Grundtvig, Kamp, Kristensen
Dard. Leitner
Dene. *See* Ten'a
Dschagga. Gutmann, Raum
Duala. Bufe, Ebding

Dutch. Schrijnen, Sinninghe, Vloten. *See also* Flemish
Engganee. Helfrich
English. Bacon and Parsons, Baring-Gould, Beckwith, Bingham, Bleakney, Boggs, *The Book of Meery Riddles* (cited as *Meery Riddles* [1629]), *A Booke of Merrie Riddles* (cited as *Prettie Riddles* [1631]), Brandl, Brewster, Burne, J. F. Campbell, Carter, Chambers, Chappell, Cords, Courtney, *Demaundes Joyous*, Dempster, Farr, Fauset, Findlay, Finlay, Fitzgerald, Gardner, Green, Greenleaf, Gregor, Gutch, Gutch and Peacock, Halliwell-Phillipps, Halpert, Harland and Wilkinson, Hudson, Hyatt, G. B. Johnson, J. H. Johnson, Kavanagh, Kemble, Knortz, Leather, MacGréine, Maclagen, Marsden, *Meery Riddles* (1629), Neal, *A New Collection of Enigmas*, *A New Riddle Book; Or, A Whetstone for Dull Wits*, Newell, *Notes and Queries*, Pantin, Parker, Parsons, Perkins, Praeger, *Prettie Riddles* (1631), Puckett, Randolph and Spradley, Randolph and Taylor, W. Redfield, *The Riddles of Heraclitus and Democritus*, Salmon, Sayce, Simpkins, Smiley, Spenney, Thurston, Tupper, Udal, W. W. Waugh, Whitney and Bullock, W. J. Wintemberg, W. J. and Katherine H. Wintemberg, *Wit and Humor of the Age*, Wright
Eskimo. Boas
Estonian. Dido, Gutsleff, Lönnrot, Wiedemann
Evhe. F. Müller
Ewe. Spieth
Faeroic. Hammershaimb
Fijian. Fison
Filipino. Giovanetti, Reyes y Florentino, Rizal, Starr
Finnish. Aarne and Krohn, Henssen, Lönnrot
Flemish. Cornelissen, Joos, M[one], Mont, *Ons Volksleven*
French. *Les Adevineaux amoureux*, Baissac, Beauvillard, Bladé, Bon, Bussche (Sylvain), Carmeau, Carnoy, Constantin, Daleau, Dardy, Desaivre, Dottin, A. Ferrand, Fertiault, Fesquet, Fleury, Fouju, Fourès, Guillon, Haurigot, Hugues and Roux, Larivey, Lacuve, Lallemant, Le Blanc, Ledieu, Le Héricher, Lespy, Marchessou, Mensignac, Millien, M[one], Parsons, Pineau, Pommerel, Queyrat, Rolland, Roque-Ferrier, J. Roux, Victor Smith (V. S.), Sébillot, Suie, Sylvain (pseud.) Westphalen. *See also* Walloon
Frisian. Carstensen, Dykstra
Gagou. Tauxier
Galla. Cerulli
Georgian. Blechsteiner, Y. Kapanadze
German. Böckel, Bolte, Brunk, Butsch, Carstens, Eckart, Ehlers, Feifalik, Frischbier, Gilhoff, Haase, Haffner, Hanika-Otto, Huss, Jungbauer, Jungwirth, Köhler, Loewenthal, Lüpkes, E. Meier, H. Meier, M[one], Müllenhoff, Pettingill, Renk, Roethe, Schmidt, Wackernagel, Woeste, Wossidlo, Zingerle. *See also* Luxemburg, Swiss
Gouro. Tauxier
Greek, Classical. Ohlert, Schultz
Greek, Modern. Abbott, Carnoy and Nicolaides, Destunis, Dieterich, Georgeakis and Pineau, Hepding, Papakristodoulos, Polites, Sakellarios, Sanders, Schultz, Stamatiadis, Stathes
Gujerati. Mehta
Gypsy. Lyster, Winstedt, Wlislocki. *See also* Welsh Gypsy
Hausa. Fletcher, Harris, Tremearne
Hawaiian. Beckwith, Judd
Hebrew. Hertz, Torczyner
Hindi. Kavyopàdhyaya
Hindustani. Elwin and Hivale
Ho. Haldar, Sarkar
Hungarian. Arany and Gyulai, Kálmány, Kriza, *Magyar Nyelv*, *Magyar Nyelvészet*, *Magyar Nyelvör*, Meltzl
Icelandic. Árnason, Heusler
Ila. Smith and Dale
Indian. Lakshīnātha Upasānī. *See also* Baiga, Bengali, Bhil, Bihari, Birhor, Gujerati, Hindi, Hindustani, Ho, Kashmiri, Khāṛiā, Kolarian, Malayalam, Maria Gond, Munda, Panjabi, Parsee, Sanskrit, Telugu, Toda, Uraon
Indian, American. *See* Aztec, Mayan, Omaha, Quechua, Ten'a
Indonesian. Tauern. *See also* Alfoer, Atjeh, Batak, Bengkoela, Engganee, Javanese, Lampong, Madoer, Malay, Sangir, Serawaj, Simaloer, Soenda, Tabaru, Tounsea
Irish. Christiansen, De Bhaldraithe, Delargy, Hyde, O Dalaigh, Stokes
Italian. *Archivio*, Balladoro, Bernoni, Cimegotto, Coronedi-Berti, Corsi, De Filippis, Di Martino, Ferraro, Gianandrea,

Giorgi, *Indovinelli*, Ive, Larivey (trans. of Straparola), Mocci, M[one], Panareo, Pasquarelli, Pitrè, Rondini, Rua, Salvioni, Schneller, Straparola, Tammi, Tschiedel
Japanese. Starr
Javanese. Kats and Koesrin, Kreemer, Luinenburg, Mayer, Ranneft
Kabardin. Talpa and Sokolov
Kaguru. Busse
Kamba. Lindblom
Kanuri. Lukas
Kashmiri. Knowles
Kashub. Gulgowski and Lorentz, Patock
Khāriā. S. C. and R. C. Roy
Kiniramba. F. Johnson
Kinyarwanda. Hurel
Kolarian. Wagner
Konde. Mackenzie
Korean. Bernheisel
Kosi. Ittmann
Kundu. Ittmann
Kxatla. Schapera
Lamba. Doke
Lampong. Helfrich
Lappish. Donner, Fellman, Friis, Poestion, Qvigstad, Johan and Per Turi
Latin. Aldhelm (ed. by Pitman), Buchler, Claret (ed. by Flajšhans), Daly and Suchier, Ebert, Malein, M[one], Pantin, Pincier, Reusner, Schmidt, Sommer (Therander), Symphosius (ed. by Ohl), Tupper
Lesotho. Franz
Lettish. Bielenstein, Ulanowska
Lithuanian. Jurgelionis, Schleicher
Louyi. Jacottet
Luxemburg. De la Fontaine
Madoer. Spiegel
Malagasy. G. Ferrand, Sibree
Malay. Beauregard, Harmsen, Klinkert, Tauern
Malayalam. Frohnmeyer, Schmolck
Maltese. Stumme
Mandingo. Monteil
Manx. Cashen
Maria Gond. Grigson
Masai. Hollis
Mayan. R. Redfield and Villa R
Mingrelian. Blechsteiner, Petrov
Mongolian. Bazarov, Klukine, Kotvich, Mostaert, Rudnyev, Whymant, Zhamtsaranov. *See also* Buryat, Calmuck
Mordvin. Ahlqvist, Nippgen, Paasonen
Munda. S. C. Roy
Nandi. Hollis

Norwegian. Aasen, Berge, Bergh, Brox, Bugge, Christie, Landstad, Stafset
Nuer. Huffman
Nyika. Hollis
Omaha. Dorsey
Ossete. Schiefner
Pangwe. Tessmann
Panjabi. Emeneau and Taylor, *Panjab Notes and Queries*
Parsee. Munshi
Pedi. Kuhn
Persian. Kuka, Mann, Phillott
Portuguese. Braga, Coelho, Parsons, A. T. Pires, Pires de Lima
Polish. Gustawicz, Kopernicki, Pracki, Saloni, Siarkowski
Pushto. *See* Afghan
Quechua. Quijada Jara
Rumanian. Gorovei, Papahagi, Weigand
Russian. Arkhangel'skii, Bardin, Destunis, Khudiakov, Preobrazhenskii, Sadovnikov, Sichler
Ruthenian. Kaindl
Samoan. Brown, Gill, Heider, Pratt, Turner
Sanskrit. Haug, Penzer
Sart. Jungbauer
Sangir. Adriani
Scotch Gaelic. Nicolson
Sechuana. Casalis, Rolland
Serawaj. Helfrich
Serbian. Novaković
SeSuto. Norton and Velaphe
Shilluk. Westermann
Shor. Dyrenkova
Sierra Leone. Cronise and Ward, Mudge-Paris
Simaloer. Damsté, Jacobsen
Sinhalese. Perera, Silva
Slave Coast. Trautmann
Soenda. Holle
Songaï. Hamouda
Sotho. Endemann
Spanish. Andrade, Boas, Bussche (Sylvain), Caballero, Campa, Demófilo (pseud.), Espinosa, Flores, Giménez Cabrera, Headwaiter, Laval, Lehmann-Nitsche, Machado y Alvarez (Demófilo), Mason, Massip, M[one], Noguera, Pauer, Recinos, M. Redfield, R. Redfield and Villa R, Rodríguez Marín, Sánchez, Sylvain (pseud.). *See also* Catalan
Suk. Beech
Sukuma. Augustiny
Surinam. M. G. and F. S. Herskovits
Svanian. J. Nizheradze, W. Nizheradze

Swahili. Büttner, Steere, Velten
Swedish. Christofferson, Dybeck, Ericsson, Hyltén-Cavallius, Noreen, Olsson, Russwurm, Sandén, Ström, Waltmann, Wigström
Swiss. J. Müller, Rochholz, Zahler
Syriac. Chabot, Furlani
Syrian. Wilson
Tabaru. Fortgens
Tagalog. See Filipino
Tatar. Filonenko, Kalashev and Ioakimov
Taveta. Hollis
Telugu. Taylor
Ten'a. Jetté
Tibetan. Mitra, Tafel
Toda. Rivers
Togo. Schönhärl
Tonga-Shangaan. Junod and Jaques
Tounsea. De C[lercq]
Tungus. Poppe
Turcoman. Karutz, Samojlvich

Turkish. Hamizade, Katanov, Kowalski, Kúnos, Maenchen, Moshkov, Polites, Potapov and Menges, Radlov, Szapszal, Zavarin. *See also* Cuman
Tschuana. Kuhn
Uraon. Archer
Vogul. Ahlqvist
Votyak. Buch, Wichmann
Wakweli. Bender
Walloon. Colson
Wamajame. Ovir
Wanamwezi. Dahl
Welsh. Hull and Taylor
Welsh Gypsy. Sampson
White Russian. Jurkevich, Shein, Wasilewski
Wolof. Rolland, Seidel
Yakut. Piekarski, Popov, Priklonskii
Yatenga. Tauxier
Zulu. Callaway
Zyrian. Lytkin, Wichmann

Index of Solutions

Index of Solutions

Note: Numbers separated by a short dash refer to the headnotes indicated by those numbers. Italicized solutions refer to English riddles; solutions given in roman type refer to riddles in languages other than English cited in the headnotes, or in footnotes to the headnotes. Numbered notes indicate footnotes to the headnotes. Most subdivisions of numbers, i.e., 1281d, are ignored in the Index; when such a subdivision is mentioned, as under "apple," it usually indicates an answer different from others in the group.

A (letter of the alphabet)
   airy creature set in glass, 469
acacia
   chair cannot be rocked in, 1185
ackee
   pick laughing woman for wife, 691
   black man sits on white man's head, 880
   children with black heads, 923
   shipload of children with black heads, 936
   white and black within, red without, 1511
acorn
   supplies spoon, cup, beam, 1239–1241
   two troughs, a spit, a cap, 1476–1494 § 18
adze
   eats at back, voids at front, 240 § 3
   See also ax
age
   haven't it, don't want it, wouldn't give it up, 1593–1595 § 6
air
   can't get spoonful (thimbleful), 1649
   See also wind
almond
   wood above and below, man between, 1436–1447 n. 9
alphabet
   brothers rule the world, 984 n. 16
amor (a plant)
   white, black, sweet, bitter, 1384–1393 n. 17
anchor
   come up, let us go, 938
Androgius, a eunuch
   a man and not a man, 823
anger
   too small for one, right for two, too much for three, 1738 n. 5
anka bird
   more crooked than sickle, whiter than snow, 1379–1382 n. 14
annata
   children with red hats, 920
[answer lacking], 215, 378, 410, 411, 567, 587a, 632d, 653, 702, 747b, 963, 981, 1084c, 1140, 1206, 1222b, 1427, 1650
ant(s)
   six legs, 46–87
   four feet, runs day and night, 83
   leaves no tracks, 181–185 § 12

   little titchie above ground, 337
   neither men, women, nor children, 838
   can't tell men from women, 839
   people nicky, nacky, color of tobacco, 888
   people going up heeple steeple, colored like gingersnaps, 889
   (people), nick, nack, gingersnap, 890
   people the color of old straw kelly, 891
   brown, red, black men, 892
   people going across London Bridge, nicker, nacker, color of tobacco, 901
   can't climb chip cherry, 1619
anthill, ant nest
   plate broken and repaired, 1193
   pot boils at edge of field, 1193 § 1
anvil
   dwarf beaten, 818
anxiety
   flies without wings, 365–366 § 7
apple
   man with foot in backside, 632–644 § 19
   red house, colored people, 913
   high, red, white, sweet, 1269–1275 § 1
   high, wide, yellow, 1281 n. 16
   red outside, white inside, 1512
   old man shook it, 1739
   See also bell apple; custard apple; maiden apple; mammy apple; sorb apple; sugar apple
apple tree
   brings forth young without tongues, 1021
   old lady took it, 1740
arch of bridge
   brothers in vain pursuit, 996–1001 § 2
arrow
   leaves no track, 181–185 § 10
   bird flies without life, 379–380
   flying maiden with iron beak, 379–380
   bull, goose, smith made it, 403
   camel opens mouth, flash of light follows, 436
   See also bow and arrows
ashes
   works all day, lies in dung, 785
   dead buries living, 835
   when living becomes dead, 836
   man doesn't go to heaven, 941
   See also fire; fire and ashes; spark, smoke, and ashes

905

ashter. *See* oyster
ass
   four make a noise, two shake, 1476–1494 n. 3
atsuete (Filipino fruit)
   round, hairy, red, 1345
ax
   girl lies with face to wall, 191
   goes to wood, looks homewards, 191
   eats and spits out, 240 § 3
   has one eye, 280
   barking dog, 438–444 § 7
   makes house, sleeps outside, 791
axle
   goes, does not move, 119–132 § 2

baby
   cradled and threshed like wheatfield, 671
   lay a year in a dark house, 674–680
   nine run, one comes, two run, 939
   haven't it, wouldn't sell it, if I had it, 1595
baby in cradle
   two downstumps, four upstanders, 1476–1494 § 13
bag
   eats and voids with mouth, 240 § 12
   stands when belly is full, 771
bagpipes
   shepherdess complains, 521
bait
   dead catches living, 828–836 § 4
baking. *See* bread, loaves of bread
baking pan, fire, cassava
   black, red, white, 1541
ball
   goes to water, doesn't quench its thirst, 246–253 § 7
   goes without feet, 260–265 § 14
   egg thrown without breaking, 1196
   round, cannot rest, 1468
ball of thread
   high, but will pass under cup, 1281 n. 17
   round, long, 1341 n. 1
   throw it and yet hold it, 1341 n. 6
   up round, down long, 1341 n. 7
   cannot throw it over roof, 1341 n. 8
   horses cannot take it over mountain, 1341 n. 11
   See also bottome (ball) of thread
bamboo
   man without guts, 555
   clothed when young, naked when old, 587
bamboo briar
   round as rainbow, 1353a
bammie (pancake), fire (griddle)
   white man on black man's head, 881

Redman boxes Blackman, Whiteman laughs, 886
white on top, black in middle, red on bottom, 1540
banana
   baby with three heads, 515
   sick, it looks to heaven, 692
   undress and eat Negro, 806–815 n. 5
   grows on tree, throw away skin, eat flesh, 1092
banana bush, banana leaf
   man with torn coat, 593
   woman with many garments, 1438–1439 n. 10
banana shoot
   shoots earth, not God, 800
bank. *See* riverbanks
baptism
   servant had it not, but gave it to master, 1589–1590 § 1
   God could do it, but didn't, 1714
bar of door
   man got up and put it in, 1744
barbs of rose
   five brothers, 990a
bark
   goes about wood, can't get in, 198
barley
   born in March, makes man fall, 670
barrel
   two heads, one body, 30
   two heads, no neck, no ears, 74
   drinks with its side, 240 § 9
   man with two heads, 516
   man with two ears, one body, 516c
   man with two heads stands on one, 516e
   bones on its skin, 588 § 1
   girt with many girdles, 678 § 1
   wears nine garments, 1437 § 7
   two ears, four feet, 1476–1494 § 24
   See also cask; staves in barrel; tub
bars of grate
   family in bed do not touch one another, 1027
baseball team
   has eighteen legs, catches flies, 271
basket
   thousand eyes, 10–16 § 6
   See also clothesbasket, man carrying basket, little
   like basket, 1403–1404 n. 5
bat
   bird and not a bird, 823
bathtub
   round and deep, 1470

Index of Solutions

bay. *See* sun and bay
beach
   can't climb chip cherry, 1623
beam(s)
   goats' horns project, 412–413 § 5
   man in room, beard outside, 544 § 6
   Long Anthony, 575 § 1
   family lies in one bed, 1027–1028 § 3
   See also girder(s); post(s); rafters
bean(s)
   trees, branches, cradles, children, 1161–1164
   See also castor bean(s)
bean, white
   grows on a tree, 1081
beard
   bush 'grows with root upwards, 1055–1057 § 3
beau
   bunch of flowers, 1068
beauty
   wounds heart, pleases eye, 799
bed
   four legs up, soft in middle, 69
   two legs up, four legs down, soft in middle, 69d
   four legs up, one broad top, 70
   four legs, one foot, 75
   head, foot, feathers, 76
   four legs can't walk, 307
   four legs can't walk, feathers can't fly, 318
   four legs can't walk, head can't talk, 334
   harnessed all night, rests in the day, 445–458
   maker doesn't wear it, 1210
   soft in middle, hard around, 1429
   live in middle, dead at ends, 1434
   pregnant at night, but not by day, 1455–1457 § 3
   mountain in morning, meadow in evening, 1455–1457 n. 15
   empty by day, full at night, 1456
   four groundholders, 1491
   formed long ago, made today, 1596
   never comes to you, 1608
   old man jumped at it, 1741, 1742
   See also mattress
bed, door, window
   easy for it during day, during night, at no time, 138–140
bedbug
   bites, never stings, 343
   Tatar boy sells needles, 576
   wears red jacket, 632–644 § 12
bedposts
   men lying in one bed, 1027–1028 § 8

bee(s)
   yellow, black, green bird, 353
   steed does not wet its feet, 431–432 § 4
   guinea pigs (swine), nik, nak, color of tobacco, 479
   not maiden, widow, or wife; rears children, 586
   girl sings strange song, 649
   lives in air, 685
   smith without a hand, 793
   naked white and yellow-packed binny ewes, 894
   going up heeple steeple, nicky, nacky people, 899
   going across London Bridge, wix, wax, color of tobacco, 900
   going across London Bridge, nicker, nacker, color of tobacco, 901, 902
   workmen with yellow toes and clothes, 947
   one brother spoke, one went on, 1006
   bears young, young kill it, 1007 § 8
   meat forbidden, milk permitted, 1070 n. 13
   See also bumblebee
bee, beehive, honey
   high, small, valuable, 1269–1275 § 3
beehive
   lift tail of gray mare, 407
   house with many people, 909 § 2
   mistress in barn in clearing, 1100–1108 n. 34
   house with many doors (rooms), 1128–1131 § 4
   locked box on tree, 1187 n. 13
   checkety cloth, 1212
beer
   born of barley, it knocks a man down, 670
   merry son, 1017 § 7
beer bottle
   suck man's blood, leave his body, 805*i*
beet
   man's hair projects, 544 § 4
   man with red hair, 632–644 § 11
   maiden with forty skins, 1438–1439 n. 1
beetle
   through a rock, through a reel, 707
   carries house on back, 727 § 4
bell
   the more you pull it, the more it cries, 3–4 n. 7
   iron horse, flaxen hair, 3–4 n. 10
   head, no hair, 4
   goes to water, does not drink, 247
   jingles to water, doesn't drink, 252
   speaks without tongue, cries without lungs, 259–265

bell—*Continued*
  tongue, no head, yet speaks, 268
  cow lows (horse neighs), 398 § 2
  cuckoo raises voice, leaves fall, 398 § 2
  animal with flaxen tail, 437
  bird with single wing, long tail, 472
  bellows between mountains, 665–667 n. 3
  lives high in air, 685 § 3
  keeps out of sight, 708
  hollers vainly for water, 764
  dead speaks, 830–834 n. 12
  perched high, makes women run, 1039 n. 4
  yolk summons people, 1039
  round as apple, deep as pail, 1316
  round, deep, cries when caught by tail, 1326
  cock (bull, donkey) with long tail, 1326
  old woman with one tooth, 1326
  egg in nest, thread in egg, egg cries out, 1326 n. 4
  See also cowbell
bell, sound of
  chips fly about, 1605 § 4
bell apple
  brown outside, seeds inside, 1527a
  yellow outside, juice inside, 1527b
bellows
  cow calved it, it grew in wood, 402
  wooden belly, leather sides, 553
  breathes without soul, lies in ashes, 785–786
  makes wind, wind feeds it, 1007 § 6
belly
  accompanies one everywhere, 113
  full during day, empty at night, 1455 § 5
  See also stomach
belt
  dead holds back the living, 828–836 § 7
  snake heads come out of two holes, 1108
  round by day, long at night, 1342
  See also girdle
berry
  red, small, makes man dismount, 632–644 n. 17
  See also blackberry; bra'berry; cranberry; eglantine berry; gooseberry; huckleberry; mulberry; raspberry; squashberry; strawberry
besom
  goes round the house, lies in corner at night, 695f
  See also broom
betel
  mother tall, children mad, son round, 1017 §7
  in green, out red, 1544 n. 4

Bible
  man obeys Lord's commands, 827
  deaf, dumb, blind old lady, 940
bicycle
  sitting man walks, 717
billhook
  walks without bones, 264–265 § 12
birch
  man with fur coat, 587 n. 10
birch sap
  strip calf, throw away hide, 806–815 § 3
bird
  makes noise in house with one door, 229
  lady (man) can't pick up handkerchief, 730
  man can't pick up hat, 731
  lower than weeds, higher than tree, 1281 n. 13
  load of hay, 1606
  See also anka bird; blackbird; buzzard; chicken(s); cock; crow; duck; eagle; goose; grassquit; hen; herneshaw and frog; hopingay; magpie; nightingale; owl; parrot; partridges; peacock; quail; robin; rooster; sea gull; swallow; turkey; woodpecker
bird and dragonfly
  Two-Wings chases Four-Wings, 465
bit in horse's mouth
  in dry, out wet, 1448–1452 § 7
blackberry
  person is white, green, then red, 668–669 § 3
  suck man's blood, leave body, 806
  black as ink, red inside, 1364
  green as grass, black as coal, 1373
  red as blood, black as ink, 1378
  black, sweet, bites, 1384–1393 n. 6
  white, green, red, sweet, 1385
  white as paper, green as grass, 1387
  white as snow, green as grass, 1389
  white as snow, and snow it isn't, 1391
  all black, white bottom, 1497
  first green, then white, then red, 1561
blackbird
  boy in black suit, 659
  woman can't pick up handkerchief, 730
blacking and brush
  put hairy-hairy in blackey-blackey, 863
blast of horn
  goes through a wood without touching, 154
blood
  house, shelf, cup, 1156a
  mill (house), chest, cup, 1156e
  everyone has it, 1573–1575 § 2
boat
  two heads, no foot, 30

Index of Solutions

goes on its back, 372
dead carries the living, 828
See also ship; vessel
bolt of door
  outside during day, inside at night, 1423 § 3
  See also door and bolt
bone
  Two-Legs throws One-leg, 461
book
  goes on its back, 372
  has leaves, is not a tree, 760
  not a man, yet speaks, 760
  covered with spots, makes all talk, 760
  white as snow, black as crow, 1388
  See also hymnbook; prayerbook
bookworm
  fed by learning, 770
boot(s)
  tongue can't talk, 296b
  walks all day, sits under bed at night, 445b
  sits under table, gapes for bones, 453a
  Blackey covers ten, 864
  two brothers full all day, 991
  one coco full pot, 1243
  hoist your foot, shove it in, 1417
  full by day, empty at night, 1455b
  swells and collapses, 1448–1452 § 8
  red inside, black outside, 1538
  See also feet; leg(s); shoe(s); stocking(s)
boots, stockings, legs
  yurt, little yurt, stag's cheeks, 1156–1160 n. 13
  house, small house, boy, 1156–1160 n. 14
bottle
  neck, no head, 6
  big belly, broad foot, short neck, 270
  pulled off rabbit's head, drank blood, 388
  pull out horse's tongue, 416
  takes off hat when we are sick, 514
  black man, red head, 583–584
  half a 'tumpy, 736
  man falls, no one can put him together, 738–747 § 2
  Humpy Dumpy dead and never runs, 746
  pull off head, drink blood, 805
  Little Johnny never drowns, 822
  dead serves the living, 828–836 § 6
  Guinea people with heads turned down, 929
  two brothers can't help each other, 994
  sisters can't wash each other, 1013
  children can't bathe each other, 1031
  long, round, black, has hole, 1362
  up white, down black, 1555
  See also Greybeard

bottome (ball) of thread
  round as ball, longer than Paul's steeple, 1341
bough
  has eyes, can't see, 278
bow and arrows
  children (men) run from woman, 801 § 4
  humpbacked mother, straight children, 1017 § 5
bowling match
  hounds chase hares, 476
boy
  kills butterfly, 824
  Whitey drives Whitey, 842d, 844c, 844d, 849
  Blackey goes into Whitey, 865
boy and cherry
  stick in tail, stone in throat, 637
boy and pot
  three feet up, two feet down, 67e
bra'berry
  white, green, black, 1561b
braids
  people can't be seen, 918
  trees standing on heads, 1055–1057 § 3
brains
  food in a dish, 1187 n. 11
brakes on wagon
  born in woods, 1058–1062 § 8
bramble blossom
  white as milk, 1386
brandis (tripod)
  without bottom, holds water, 1462
brazier
  one going, one coming embrace bride, 712
bread, loaves of bread
  white horses turn black or brown, 493
  white boys turn brown, 919
  punning names, 970–975 n. 11
  father is being born, son walks about, 985 § 3
  first soft, then hard, 1448–1452 § 4
  in damp, out dry, 1448–1452 § 4
  in white, out red, 1542–1546 § 2
  See also loaves and oven fork
bread and coffee
  in dry, out wet, 1448–1452 § 3
bread and shovel
  two round, one long, 958–960
breadfruit
  outside green, inside white, 1089
breast, cow's. See teats
breath
  goes, never comes back, 136
  comes, goes, isn't seen, 226 § 2
  black lamb with blue fleece, 389
  have it here, see it yonder, 1578

breath—*Continued*
  cannot hold it, 1660
  cannot hang it up, 1661–1662
briar, brier, brier-bush
  many noses, 41
  crooked as a rainbow, teeth like cat, 1295
  crooked as a ram's horn, 1299
  round as a rainbow, 1353
  See also bamboo briar
brick
  maiden in red coat, 632–644 § 14
  red within, red without, 1535
bridge
  short girdle on long man, 678 § 9
  the greater the less feared, 1703
bridge, crossing a
  above water, below water, never touch water, 165
  water below, water above, 173
bridge of ice
  no man can make it, 1212 n. 2
  See also ice
bridle
  goes to water, never drinks, 248
  goes to water "gink, gink," doesn't drink, 251a
  dead holds back the living, 828–836 § 7
brier. *See* briar, brier, brier-bush
broom
  makes a thousand tracks, 179
  goes through a hundred rooms, 221
  feet can't walk, 305–310
  hundred legs, hides behind door, 559
  people girt with belt, 678 § 3
  goes around house and into corner, 695
  drill (jig) hall, lean behind door, 696
  sits in corner at night, goes over house by day, 697
  long pole, bushy tail, 1415
  in green, out red, 1544 n. 1
  cannot do without it, 1678
  long hairy something, 1747
  See also brush
broom handle
  goes around house, never enters, 202
  works all day, stands in corner at night, 698
broth pot
  mouthed like mill door, 1397
brother
  God has none, 1715–1720 § 2
brush
  goes around house, lies in corner, 695e
  grows in woods, whinnies in moor, 1058
  See also blacking and brush; broom

bubble
  thousand men can't lift it, 1661
bucket
  rump touches water first, 144
  ears cannot hear, 285
  down laughing, up crying, 768
  in dry, out wet, 1448–1452 § 6
  barren going, pregnant coming, 1455–1457 § 1
  See also pail; woman carrying bucket
buckwheat
  green dress, red for mourning, then black, 668–669 § 6
  Whitey in Whitey, 850
  three-cornered house without doors, 1132–1138 § 3
  tree, branch, nest, egg, 1161–1164 n. 7
buggy
  runs, never walks; tongues never talk, 313
buggy wheel(s)
  four men talking, 964
  big and little sister, 1014
  can't tell where it will end, 1708
  See also wheel(s)
bugs
  men working in green coats, 948
bullet
  runs without flesh or blood, 260–265 § 16
  bird flies, 379–380
  animal runs, 436
  born without skin, 667 n. 7
  man speaks, 755
  man spits, 781
  man spits fire, 781
  man small but powerful, 801 § 1
  mad children, 801 § 2
  messenger, 801 § 5
  messenger doesn't return, 801 § 6
  well with water that kills, 801 § 10
  kills a man, 801
  recipient is sad, 1591–1592 n. 3
  cuts hay, can't be seen, 1630
bullet and gun
  cow lows, calf runs, 436
  iron father, tiny children, 1017 § 5
bull's-eye thistle
  nine heads, nine tails, 60
  See also thistle
bumblebee
  Bum! Bum! everywhere it goes, 232
bundle of wood (grain)
  entrails outside, flesh inside, 588 § 8
  man with girdle, 678 § 2
buoy
  can't move in water, 1609
bur. *See* chestnut; chestnut bur

bush. *See* gorse bush
butter
  beat silver, gold appears, 1138 n. 8
  water washes it, sun can't dry it, 1214
butterfly
  round, small, lives in cell, 672
  bird that is not a bird, 824
button
  head and eye only, 35
  eyes can't see, 284
  each man has a room, 908 § 2
  round as apple, flat as chip, 1337
buttonholes and fingers
  men get hold of each other, 966–968 n. 3
buzzard
  cleans up the earth, 219

cabbage
  heart in head, 32a
  heart in head, stands on one leg, 32b
  head can't think, 273
  cut off head, leave body, 806–815 § 6
  stands on one leg, 1121–1126 § 4
  patch on patch, 1438
  man with many coats, 1438
  first stiff, then limber, 1448
  first stiff, then flops, 1449
cabbage (cabbage palm)
  man drops coat, can't pick it up, 729
  body of dragon, tail of phoenix, 1405–1408 n. 18
cabbage patch
  swans resting, 946–950 n. 17
  patch on patch, 1438a
cabbage patch, dog (cow) in
  Whitey in Whitey, 849
cable
  ten men can't set it on end, 1663a
  ten men can't tear it, 1664b
cake
  thin and plain, rich and sweet, 1474
calabash
  grows on tree, 1080
  See also gobee
calf in cow's belly
  goes through bush without touching, 160
calf of leg
  back in front, stomach behind, 191 § 8
camel
  composed of members of various animals, 1405–1408 n. 12
  two pancakes, two glass pieces, 1476–1494 § 6
  five Russians sow, two stand watch, 1476–1494 § 6

camomile
  becomes young lady, 650–652
can. *See* skelion
canary, horse, man
  eight legs, three heads, wings, 51
candle(s)
  outside fat (naked), inside wool (flesh, hair), 588 § 7
  grows shorter as it stands, 607 through 630
  tall white man with red cap, 631
  man grows down, not up, 681
  woman dissolves in tears, 689
  Miss Nancy always dropping, 689a
  girl dirties dress, 689b
  sits in corner, does chores in house, 695–699 § 3
  lillilow set up on end, 703
  eats own flesh, drinks own blood, 774a
  three lie close, take heat, die, 974
  tree grows smaller, 1047
  created on mountain, dies on altar, 1058–1062 n. 3
  many shining lights, 1191
  small, but fills house, 1473
  twenty in tankard, one fills house, 1473
  sequence of colors, 1559–1561 § 11
candle snuffers
  box gets fuller when one takes more pinches, 1697
  See also snuffers
candlestick
  grows shorter as it stands, 619
candy
  more it leaks, more it goes, 1607
cane
  leaves track at side of road, 174–185
  grandmother walks about all day, sits in small space, 699
  See also staff; walking stick
cane (sugar cane)
  wears a white cap every year, 650–652
  man bows when addressed, 756
  drink John's blood, throw away his flesh, 808
  water stands up, 1105
  long, juicy, sweet stick, 1109
  well without bottom holds water, 1174
  tall and sweet, 1285
  See also sugar cane
cane mill
  chews, doesn't swallow, 241
  two ground holders, two cross-standers, 1492
cane tree
  tree that is not a tree, 824

cantaloupe
  pink house in cream house in yellow house, 1163
  yellow inside, white outside, 1514
  See also muskmelon
cap, fur cap
  hairy without, hairy within, 1416–1419 § 4
  full by day, empty at night, 1455 § 2
  lies flat, when empty; sits up, when full, 1689 n. 1
  See also fez; hat
card (for wool or cotton)
  ten thousand teeth, no mouth, 20
  brothers eat off each other, 966–968 n. 7
  scratches all day, sits in corner at night, 966
  fight all day, embrace at night, 968
  See also hand card
cardamon
  goes into water red, remains red, 1542–1543 § 3
carob
  born white, becomes black, 668–669 § 7
carriage wheel. See wheel(s)
carrot
  girl's hair sticks out, 544 § 4
  first white, then red, 1572b
cart
  dead follows living, 1432–1434
  See also pole of cart; wagon
cart wheel. See wheel(s)
casha (cashot, cushia) seed
  Nanny (Kitty) with bent nose, 537
cask
  man bound and beaten, 678 n. 2
  girt with belts, 678 § 1
  See also barrel; tub
casket (coffin)
  maker didn't want it, 1730
  user didn't know of it, 1734
cassava
  grows from father's bone, 661
  high, bitter, 1283
cassava, pan, and fire
  red beneath, black in middle, white above, 1541
castor bean(s)
  cock crows, 377
  guinea pigs with one-quality head, 477
  children with white heads, 922
  Negroes with white heads, 935
  wives dance, 946–950 n. 6
  See also bean(s)
castor-bean pod
  three brothers in one house, 1005
  bag holds three, 1201

cat
  around floor all day, sleeps under stove at night, 446
  neither maiden, man, nor wife; wears one kind of robe, 586
  woman with stick in her rump, 632–644 § 23
  in front like ball (button), behind like awl (stick), 1435 § 1
  two look, two hear, 1476–1494 § 9
  See also kitten; she-cat
cat and mouse
  up with four, down with eight legs, 61
  Four-Feet on Four-Feet waits for Four-Feet, 463
  hairy in hairy's mouth, 1419
cat and pot
  no head, seven legs, one tail, 62
cat, herring, and grill
  Four-Legs, No-Leg, Four-Legs, 466–468 n. 7
caterpillar
  black at ends, red in middle, 1529
cattle, milking. See cow, milking a; fingers milking
cedar
  branch, nest, eggs, 1161–1164 n. 9
  red as blood, green as grass, 1377
  white man, 1627
ceiling and floor
  look at each other, 1003–1004
  never meet, 1027–1028 § 4
cemetery
  insatiable, 236–239
  See also churchyard; graveyard
cennep
  green inside, white outside, black seeds, 1520
centipede
  twenty feet on one side, 84
chaffcutter
  eats and voids, 240 § 5
  four hangers, ten reachers, 1476–1494 n. 1
chain
  jingles to water, doesn't drink, 253
  See also brandis (tripod); reeken hook (brandis, trivet)
chair
  legs without body, 26
  four feet, one back, 87
  legs can't walk, 306
  horse can't walk, 434
chair and cat
  Four-Feet on Four-Feet, 463

Index of Solutions

chair and man
  went out on two legs, came back on four, 464
  See also stool
chamber pot. See utensil
charcoal
  black, tires horses, 1565b
cheese
  child begets (kills) parent, 1007 § 11
cheese, half of
  like other half, 1403–1404
cherry (fruit)
  red flesh, white (wooden) heart, 579
  black hat, a taste like wine, 632–644 n. 7
  fire burns on branch, 632–644 n. 42
  Dick Redcap (Pat, Uncle Jack), 632 through 644
  man with stick in hand, 635
  hurble purple with red girdle, 638
  Uncle Jack with stone in throat, 639
  man in red coat holds staff, 640
  Little May Margery, 643
  petticoat lined with scarlet, 644
  white, green, then red, 668–669 § 2
  sweet, but bitter as gall in middle, 1269–1275 § 1
  sequence of colors, 1556–1561 § 2
cherry (tree)
  girl with bent-down nose, 538
cherry and boy
  stick in his hand, stone in his throat, 637
cherry and girl
  girl in red petticoat, 642
cherry myres
  green as grass, white as milk, 1367
chest
  body of wood, guts of rags, 553–554 § 5
chestnut
  coat with thousand lancets, 576 n. 11
  kernel surrounded by people, 908–916 n. 13
  high, rough, sharp, 1276
  high, round, sharp, 1277
  thousand outside, satin within, 1355 n. 12
  skin above and below, morsel between, 1436–1447 § 6
chestnut bur
  round as ball, sharp as awl, 1348
chicken(s)
  Whitey drives out Whitey, 843b
  nuts together at night, scattered by day, 1094 n. 3
  narrow face Virginia, 1414
  See also cock; hen; rooster
chicken, hatching
  dead gives birth to living, 828–836 § 1
  becomes skin and bone in two weeks, 1238

chicken and eggs
  cattle of various colors, 493 § 4
  dead gives birth to living, 828–836 § 1
  daughter begets mother, 1007 § 10
chicken in egg
  over water, under water, doesn't touch water, 169d
chigger (jigger)
  dig stump out of wood, 1114
child
  Christian person, 837
  given what one has not, 1589
  easily begotten, 1590
  cedar, chipcherry, beer, 1627
  See also baby; child, suckling a
child, christened
  goes on its back, 372
  receives a gift, 1253
child, illegitimate
  apple fallen to the ground, 836 n. 2
child, suckling a
  hand round back, meat fills crack, 1235
child, unborn
  anklebone with concave or convex side up, 373
  sex of unhatched chick is unknown, 373
  goes to town, doesn't know town, 711
  See also baby; woman, pregnant
child and mother
  eight feet, four eyes, four ears, 57
  flesh in crack, 1235
children
  limbs of tree, 1046
chile
  colors in biographical sequence, 668–669 n. 6
chimney
  eats with rump, voids with mouth, 240 § 11
  has four legs, but can't walk; smokes a pipe, 319
  four brothers wear one cap, 993 § 3
  grows with root up, top below, 1055–1057 § 5
  stands on one leg, smokes, 1121–1126 § 9
  patch on patch, hole in middle, 1437
  black within, red without, 1530
  black within, white without, 1531
  horse can't climb chipcherry, 1618
china plate
  in green, out red, 1542–1546 § 3
chink in wall
  born in house, without parents, 667
  patched without needle or thread, 793–794
  See also holes in wall

chinkapin
    white child, black nurse, red mother, 1019*b*
    in green, out mahogany color, 1544
chinkapin tree
    tall daddy, sticky mammy, 1019*a*
Christmas tree
    bride stands on one leg, 1121–1126 § 5
church
    oak, nest, egg, yolk, 1039
churchyard
    four hurdles (fences), two stiles, 1476–1494 § 29
    See also cemetery; graveyard
churn
    tigers roars in well, 387
    wagon being driven, 1259
    big at bottom, little at top, 1445
    narrow at bottom, wide at top, 1446
    biff it to the bottom, goes flippety-flop in middle, 1447
churn-dash
    grown in the wood, 1058–1062 § 6
churning
    frog jumps in well, 349
cider
    child and mother, 1007 § 12
cinder sifter
    thousand eyes, can't see, 331
    See also coal sifter; sieve; sift, sifter
cistern floor, cistron plain
    can't spread sheet, 1223
clam cherry
    grows on tree, yellow inside and outside, 1088
cloak
    broader than God, 1394
clock
    face, no mouth, 9
    hands, no fingers, 22
    runs day and night, 117
    moves while standing still, 125
    works without salary, 125–127
    runs, but never runs away, 126
    runs without legs, 262
    has face, can't see, 283
    hands can't wash face, 301
    has two hands, doesn't wash, 302
    has hands, can't work, 303
    has hands, can't feel, 304
    runs, can't walk, 321
    has eyes, can't see, 322
    has hands, can't touch, 323
    has legs (feet), doesn't walk, 324
    long waist, brazen face, 565*a*
    hands move, runs all day, 565*b*
    two legs, face, two hands, 566
    cries constantly, 751–754 n. 6
    never eats, 780*a*
    chops (saws) without chips, 789
    can't do without it, 1679
clock, hands of
    brothers pursue each other, 996–1001 § 7
clothes
    Whitey drives Whitey (duck) away from Whitey, 851
    Whitey drives Whitey (cow) away from Whitey, 852
    Whitey drives Whitey (horse) away from Whitey, 853
clothesbasket, man carrying
    over and under water, doesn't touch water, 167
clothes chest
    body of wood, belly of rags, 553–554 § 5
clotheshorse
    horse without head, 409
clothesline
    tied at both ends, raised in middle, 1430
cloud(s)
    moves without legs, 260–265 § 5
    flies without wings, 365–366 § 3
    flock of sheep, 485
    gray horse drinks up water, 489–490 § 2
    Hickamore, Hackamore sits over king's door, 749
    can't fold table cloth, 1218
    sheet covers world, 1220
    sheet can't be spread, 1222
    can't fold (stretch) cloth, 1224
    patch on patch without seam, 1437 § 9
    See also stars and clouds
cloud and earth
    two packey of equal size, 1252*b*
coach
    eight feet, two heads, 48–55
coal
    black, much admired, 1565
    black, tires horses, 1566
coal(s) of fire
    red horses, 493 § 2
    stone is fire, black is red, 1475
    in red, out black, 1543
    See also fire
coal(s) and ashes
    dead buries living, 835
coalpit (charcoal pit)
    blood remains where cow was killed, 396
coal-pot
    two ears, one foot, can't use them, 326

Index of Solutions

coal sifter
  hundred eyes, no nose, 10
  See also cinder sifter; sieve; sift, sifter
coat
  neck, no head, 6 § 2
  maker does not use it, 1728–1737 n. 13
cobweb
  one who cares has none, 1728–1737 § 4
cock
  barking dog, 441
  sings, but not the mass, 539–543 § 3
  man with spurs, 539
  beard of flesh, mouth of horn, 540
  head of fire, 541
  feet of griffon, 543
  prophet or Turk with many wives, 585
  wears red jacket, 632–644 § 13
  clothes not spun or woven, 793–794
  sack of feathers on two rakes, 1100–1108 n. 40
  patch on patch, 1437 § 10
  See also chicken(s); hen; rooster
cockerel
  tail a sickle, 1435
coco leaf
  catches dew, not rain, 1175
coconut
  has two eyes, cries out of one, 279
  man with three eyes cries out of one, 523
  man with three eyes sees out of one, 524
  Miss Nancy can't reach bread, 709
  suck blood, eat flesh, throw away bones, 812
  pick Zion fruit, 814
  speaks when grown, 830–834 n. 1
  three sons, one blind, two can't see, 987
  black mother, rough nurse, white baby, 1020
  grows on tree, contains water, 1072
  grows on tree, outside green, 1085
  sky above, sky below, water between, 1105–1106 n. 1
  water in a pond never stirs, 1106
  house on one post, glass windows, green children, 1124a
  house on one post, no windows or door, 1124b
  house without opening, 1132–1138 § 3
  house with three doors, only one opens, 1142
  hide within skin, bone within hide, 1156–1164 n. 10
  jungle, rock, something white, water, 1156–1160 n. 15
  furnishes wood, milk, meat, 1239
  eat and drink out of St. John, 1240

  see a drink and a chaw, 1241a
  a chaw in a cup, 1241b
  hard as rock, but not rock, 1358
  white, but not as white as snow, 1393
  outside green, inside white, 1500
  up brown, down white, 1557
coconut, picking a
  he rides and arrives before me, 951a
  doctor arrives before me, 951b
  corn arrives before buyer, 1255
  fruit leaves before picker, 1256
  message arrives before sender, 1257
  bread (ship, trunk) arrives before servant (traveler), 1258
coconut palm, climbing a
  face town when going to town, 724
  no one can climb chip cherry like me, 1620
coconut, shoot in
  drinks up water, 489–490 § 5
cocoon(s)
  barber in house without doors, 1134 n. 2
  bulls tied in forest, 1203–1205 n. 13
coffee
  born in white, dies in red, buried in black, 668
  punning names, 970–975 n. 12
  See also bread and coffee; milk in coffee
coffee berry, coffee blossom
  white, green, red, 1390
coffeepot(s)
  man with arms akimbo, 551
  shipload of men with arms akimbo, 932
coffee pulper
  cries for crop, 234
coffin
  Mary Mack dressed in black, 656
  born in ground, bears man, 1058–1062 § 3
  maker of coat doesn't want it, 1209
  maker doesn't use it, 1728 through 1735
coffin and bearers
  four men in rain are wet, one man is dry, 962
cold
  invisible, 226 § 5
comb
  teeth can't bite, 299
  teeth along its back, 299 n. 1
  woman separates entangled men, 966–968 § 11
  animal grazes, 1042–1044
  tickles where it is tender, 1465
  See also flax comb; honeycomb
comb and lice
  dead drives out the living, 495–460
  drives pigs from thicket, 459–460
  has many teeth, drives deer, 459

916   *English Riddles*

combing hair
    snowshoe slides over roof, 1143-1148
conscience
    not subject to fear, 1710
cook
    greasy miller, 1169
cookstove
    eyes can't see, 317
cooking pot
    crow sits on three trees, 371
    Negro with three feet, 930
    See also pot.
cord
    can't be tasted, 1667
cork
    horse's tongue pulled out, 416
    man never drowns, 821
    goes in white, comes out red, 1542-1546 § 4
corn (maize or wheat)
    ear can't hear, 285
    brown bull dashes head on stone, 397
    man in room, beard in hall, 544
    sequence of colors, 668-669 n. 7
    house, 1127
    person with many garments, 1438-1439
corn and crows (pigeons)
    if he comes, I no come, 944
corn and rat
    if it comes, it doesn't come, 945
corners of graveyard. *See* graveyard
cornfield
    Whitey runs Whitey out, 845
corn grain
    supports all Jamaica, 1053
corn mill
    boy never perspires, 784
corn silk
    dry one's self on unspun silk, 1104c
corner of hut, beam at
    long Anthony, 575 § 1
corners of pillow
    four brothers lie in one bed, 1027-1028 § 7
corpse
    goes on its back, 372 n. 13
    goes through rain, is not wet, 962
    less of it but weighs more, 1690-1697 n. 7
    man who orders something without knowing, 1728-1737 n. 6
corpse and bearers
    five heads, four souls, 56-57
    four carry him, one guards him, 56-57
    See also coffin and bearers

corset
    opens like barn door, ears like cat, 1399a
    opens like barn door, shuts like trap, 1399c
corsetlace
    ladder by day, ring at night, 1342
cotton
    bush dresses all the world, 531-534 § 2
cotton cards
    teeth, no mouth, 20
cotton field
    Whitey drives Whitey (cow) out of Whitey, 842
    Whitey (dog) drives Whitey (animal) out of Whitey, 843
    Whitey (man) sends Whitey (person) to drive out Whitey, 844
    Blacky goes into Whitey, 865
cotton jenny
    eats and voids, 240 § 6
cough
    bellows between mountains, 665-667 n. 1
cow
    goes about, drops piece, 418
    two posts on top of a mountain, 1100-1108 n. 33
    opens like a barn door, 1400
    seamless coat, white chessmen, 1405-1408 n. 13
    in front a fork, in middle a basket, at back a broom, 1435 § 3
    patch on patch, 1437 § 11
    four turned up, four turned down, 1476-1494 n. 6
    two hookers, two lookers, 1476
    four standers, four hangers, 1477
    four dillydanders, 1478
    two lookers, a wigwag, 1479
    four downstanders, four (two) upstanders, 1480
    four little landers, 1481
    four streetwalkers, 1482
    four yellow sandals, 1483
    four groundholders, 1484
    four groundholders, goes "Moo!," 1485
    two top timbers, 1486
    four standing posts, 1487
    two top thunder, 1488
    four feet shaking, 1489
    out black, in white, 1545
cow, dappled
    patch on patch, 1437 § 11
cow, white
    Whitey drives Whitey out of Whitey (cotton field), 842
    Whitey drives Whitey out of Whitey (cornfield), 845

Index of Solutions

Whitey drives Whitey out of Whitey (cabbage patch), 849b
Whitey drives Whitey out of Whitey (buckwheat), 850
Whitey drives Whitey out of Whitey (white clothes), 852
Whitey drives Whitey out of Whitey (house), 854
cow, milking a
   Two-Legs sits on Three-Legs, 462
   down she squat, 734
   See also cow, calf, woman milking; fingers milking
cow and bell
   goes to water, doesn't drink, 247b
cow, calf, woman milking
   ten feet, two hands, four legs, three livers, 55
cowbell
   goes about, doesn't drink (eat), 247
   mouth can't swallow, 291
   tongue can't speak, 294
   hollers for water, can't get it, 764
   found it in field, 1642
   See also bell; sound
cow-tie
   all hair except head, 34
crab
   two arms, eight legs, 48–55 § 7
   lives in river, crawls on four feet, 99
   bones outside, flesh inside, 588 § 2
   tells me to carry, 725
   carries house on back, 727 § 3
   eight stand, two crack, 982
   in black, out red, 1542–1543 § 2
cradle
   six legs, two eyes, 48–55 § 6
   dead bears the living, 828–829 § 2
   born in wood, carries soul, 1058–1062 § 10
   wood on both sides, flesh in middle, 1416–1447 n. 7
cranberry
   looks sweet, tastes sour, 1246
crane (in fireplace)
   pinchbacked pappy, 1017
   can't catch bowlful, 1647
crayfish
   priest becomes cardinal after death, 1542–1543
creek
   crooked as arrow, 1291
crepitus ventris
   born between two mountains, 665–667
   makes noise when born, 665
   born without skin, 667

cannot pick it up, 729–731 § 5
See also wind
cresset
   Andy stands on one leg, 1121–1126 § 8
crook
   sleeps with finger in its eye, 687
crow
   Blackman drops handkerchief, 730e
   never builds house until it rains, 792
crown
   higher than God, 1394
crows and corn
   if they come, they don't come, 944
crucifix
   two heads, four arms, three feet, 48–55 § 4
cucumber
   people in house without doors or windows, 909
   house filled with people, 910–915 § 1
   bosom full of gold pieces, 1355 n. 8
cup
   one coming, one going kiss girl, 712
curtain
   grows downward with roots above, 1055–1057 § 6
cushia seed. See casha seed
custard
   pots boil without fire, 1178a
custard apple
   green fruit grows on tree, 1075

dandelion
   first in yellow, then in white, 651
   yellow petticoat, green gown, 652
darkness
   enters without sound, 164 § 3
   can't catch it, 1643–1654 § 6
   the greater it is, the less you see, 1690–1697 § 1
dash churn
   narrow at bottom, wide at top, 1446b
daughter(s)
   fruit on trees can't be eaten, 1045
   best furniture, 1179
   chair not to be sat in, 1183
   bananas can't be eaten, 1249
day and night
   persons pursuing one another, 1001
   black and white people, 1001
   brothers born one after another, 1001
   black hen hatches white hen, 1007 § 5
days of week
   six sons, 983
   seven birds in nest, 1037
   See also week; year

death
looks at you, you can't look at it, 223
little boy slays all, 803
in a pond, boat, and cup a sup that all must taste, 1157
less than God, greater than emperor, 1394 n. 7
can't do without it, 1573–1575 n. 3
he who has it can't give it, 1589–1590 § 3
See also debt; hunger; war
debt
kills whole world, 802
grows as you contract it, 1698
deer
cut throat, drink blood, 815
Devil
father of sin, 1009
dew
sun finds lost brooch, 367–369
broadest water, 1103
has neither rained nor run, 1104
caught by coconut leaf, 1175
can't get hands full, 1654
dew and sun
water to wash in, towel to dry hands, 1104
dice
blind eyes, 275
deaf man is cursed, 782
men fight, 966–968 § 12
dime
round as apple, thin as knife, 1352
dipper
in dry, out wet, 1448–1452 § 6
dirtdauber (wasp)
big at both ends, little in middle, 1431
dishcloth, dishclout, dishrag
in, it's easy; out, it slips about, 1451
most used, least thought of, 1674
cannot live without me, 1675
distaff
leaves no trace, 181–185 § 9
guts of rags, 553–554 § 6
five wet men under roof, 961–963 § 8
crooked father, ragged mother, 1017 § 2
grown in wood, 1058–1062 § 7
in front like button, 1435 § 6
See also spindle
ditch
the more taken from it, the more it grows, 1692
cut ends to make it longer, 1693
short, cut it to make it longer, 1695
dog
leaves out tongue, hot or cold, 103

wagon with tongue toward village, 191 n. 2
runs from yard to yard, 222
has legs, but can't be ridden, 310
boy can't walk, 766
two shine, four spread, 1476–1494 § 10
dog and deer
I cut man's throat, drink blood, 815
dog and pot
seven legs, tail, tongue, 62 n. 3
mouth to mouth, seven legs, 63
half living, half dead, tail wagging, 1495
dog chasing cow
Whitey drives Whitey, 842, 845, 846, 850, 852
dog, mutton (ham), and man
Two-Legs sits on Three-Legs and holds One-Leg, 461
dog flea
boy sleeps with man, runs when called, 686
See also flea(s)
dogwood
dog can't bark, 444
doll
mouth can't eat, 287
donkey
boy bawls every hour of the day, 752
four groundstanders, 1490
door
comes, goes, never leaves, 127
goes in but never out, 133–135
comes to house but does not enter, 198–202 § 6
bird flies but does not leave, 356 n. 4
goes out in morning, returns in evening, 445–458
stork comes, goes, stands on one foot, 1121–1126 n. 1
both inside and outside, 1423 § 2
two stand, two lie, 1476–1494 § 26
See also key(s); latch
door and bolt
sisters girt with belt, 678 § 8
embrace each other, 968 nn. 2–4
door-bar (door-peg)
get up and put it in, 1744
doorjambs
never meet, 1003–1004
doorknob
animal's horns project, 412–413 § 7
door-peg. *See* door-bar
dot of *i*
higher than God (*dieu*), 1394 n. 5
dough
climbs without feet, 260–265 § 11

Index of Solutions 919

dragonfly and bird
  Two-Wings chases Four-Wings, 465
draw well
  Hoddy Toddy, all legs, no body, 560
dream
  enters locked house, 112 n. 5
  goes a thousand leagues in an hour, 1680 § 1
dreamer
  walks, does not go, 715
dress
  full during day, empty at night, 1455 § 1
  See also belt; boot(s); boots, stockings, legs; button; buttonholes and fingers; cap, fur cap; cloak; clothes; coat; corset; fez; girdle; glove(s); hat; knapsack; mittens; muff; pants; parasol; purse; shirt; shoe(s); skirt; sleeve; slippers; trousers; umbrella; vest; waistcoat; watch pocket
drinking
  mouth to mouth, palm on back, 1235 n. 1
drum
  growls when touched, 387 n. 9
  barking dog, 438–444 § 6
  Two-Legs beats Four-Legs, 461–462 n. 32
  wooden ribs, leather belly, 553–554 § 3
  kiss me asleep, kiss me awake, 758
  put down silent, picked up noisy, 768–769 § 3
  grown in wood, 1058–1062 § 2
drum, song of
  goes through wood, doesn't touch leaf, 155
drying hands
  is done if you don't do it, 1104 n. 5
duck
  mouth in tail, 42
  flies up, dives, 359
  flies, wears shoes without feet, 366
  green head (cap), yellow toes, 606
  Whitey drives Whitey out of Whitey, 851
  in front like a broomstick, 1435 § 5
duck egg. *See* egg, duck's
dumplings
  sheep (balls) jump in water, 489–490 § 4
dung
  born without skin, 667 n. 6
dust
  flies without wings (feet), 365
  house full, yard full, can't catch bowl full, 1645

E (letter of the alphabet)
  found in "yet," 469
eagle
  casts bill, 354

ear(s)
  two flop, 960
  two hear fruit fall, 980
  Jack can't see Tom, 1004
  children stand beside ash-heaps, 1102–1106
  two ponds, 1102
ear of corn
  can't hear, 285
  man in room, beard in hall, 544
  man makes house, 1127
earwax
  something in box on shelf in house, 1158
earth
  bears, does not weary, 138–140
  insatiable, 236–239
  beaten, repays with good, 674–680 n. 10
  travels far, does not sweat, 784 n. 3
earth and sky
  calabash can't be opened, 1141–1142 § 5
  two planks (leaves, rugs), 1252
  two packey of equal size, 1252a
  See also wind, sky, and earth
earthquake
  men and beasts tremble, 1705
earthworm
  creature without bones, 264–265 § 3
  See also worm(s)
eating
  threshing, grinding, 841, § 4
  mill grinds, 841 § 5
  kneading bread, 841 § 6
  girl pushes green stone, 841 § 7
  See also fingers eating
eating a bird
  series of tortures, 674–680 n. 37
eating a fish
  caught not an animal, stripped it of not feathers, 367–369
eaves
  roots up, branches grow down, 1055–1057 § 5
echo
  goes through woods without touching, 149, 150
  goes through branches without touching, 153
  is not seen, 226 § 3
  speaks without tongue, 259–265
  I am here, I am found there, 1578 n. 9
egg
  [described according to form]
  stone wall, golden lady, 580
  bones outside, flesh within, 588 § 4
  fruit and flower, 1138 n. 3
  silver and gold, 1138

egg—Continued
  marble stone, golden ball, 1139
  two liquids in barrel, 1140
  two liquids do not mingle, 1140 nn. 12–16
  cup of honey under ice, 1140 n. 9
  barrel without staves, 1171
  barrel without hoops, 1171 n. 1
  without seams, 1213
  See also lining of egg
  [described as house or stronghold]
  house without door or window, 1132
  white house without doors or windows, 1133
  house without door has occupant, 1134
  house full of meat without windows or doors, 1135
  house, fountain, gold, 1137
  crystal fountain within marble walls, 1138
  castle on seaside, 1140
  house cannot be reëntered, 1141
  food in cup in house, 1159
  house made by God, 1187 § 2
  [described in terms of colors]
  motley cattle, 493 § 4
  lady with yellow petticoat, 647
  green as grass, ripe as apple, 1366
  white outside, yellow inside, 1504
  white outside, red inside, 1505
  white outside, white and yellow inside, 1506
  white outside, additional details, 1507
  up white, down yellow, 1550
  up white, down red, 1551
  up in the air white, down on the ground yellow, 1552
  up white, down yellow and white, 1553
  up white as snow, down yellow as gold, 1554
  [described in terms of function]
  born without skin, 667 n. 5
  lies in own dung, 785
  neither living nor dead, 828–836 n. 24
  living above, dead below, 828–836 § 11
  begets parent, 1007 § 10
  food in ivory, 1187 n. 11
  boiling it in salt leaves no taste, 1236
  can't be picked up, 1661–1662
  can't hang it on a nail, 1661–1662
egg, broken
  Biddy Widdy (Miss Mary, Tommy Tucker) tears gown, 589, 590, 592
  Humpty Dumpty tears gown, 591
  cup (barrel) can't be repaired, 738–747
  Humpty Dumpty falls, can't be put together, 738

Humpty Dumpty falls, can't be put back, 739
Humpty Dumpty falls, can't stand, 740
Humpty Dumpty falls, can't be cured, 742
Humpty Dumpty falls, can't be mended, 743, 744
Humpty Dumpty falls, can't be picked up, 745
Humpty Dumpty falls (defective versions), 747
egg, hatched
  daughter begets mother, 1007 § 10
  neither fish, flesh, nor bone, I kept it till it ran alone, 1237
  neither skin nor bone, 1238
  See also chicken hatching; chicken and eggs
egg, laid
  born without skin, 667 n. 5
  Whitey went upstairs, Whitey came downstairs, 860
  Whitey went upstairs, Whitey came downstairs, left Whitey, 861
  Mrs. Black went in black, left white, 866
  Blackey went in Blackey, left Whitey, 867
  Blackie upstairs, Whitie downstairs, 868
  Blackey went uphill, put down Whitey, 869
egg, duck's
  over water, under water, doesn't touch water, 169
  doesn't get wet, 170
  leaves no track, 171
egg, partridge. See partridge egg
egg, silkworm's
  round, small, lives in cell, 672
eggplant
  man with green cap (turban), 632–644 § 6
  black jug contains paddy, 910–916 n. 9
eggs and chicken(s). See chicken and eggs
eglantine berry
  rough within, red without, 1421
end
  everything has it, 1575
engine
  brass toes, brass nose, 267
entrails
  throw away meal, eat bag, 805–818 n. 4
equal (like)
  God never sees it, king seldom, we every day, 1715
  king seldom, God never, we everyday, 1716
  we see it every day, king seldom, God never, 1717
  God never sees it, George Washington scarcely ever, we every day, 1718

Index of Solutions 921

President has seen it, the Lord has not, 1719
man found it, God did not, 1720
eunuch
  man, yet not a man, 823
euphorbia tree
  stands on one leg, 1121–1126 § 5
eye(s)
  runs, doesn't move, 125–130
  goes through river, is not wet, 165–173 § 8
  insatiable, 236–239
  man leaves hair outside, 544 § 12
  two see fruit, 980a
  two brothers ahead of four, 996
  two brothers can't see each other, 1003
  two birds can't see each other, 1003–1004 § 1
  two animals can't see each other, 1003–1004 § 2
  two separated objects, 1003–1004 § 3
  two girls never kiss, 1016
  two sisters can't see each other, 1016
  well overhung by tree, 1044
  two colored liquids, 1140
  candles, 1144
  windows, 1144
  tank filled by a little dirt, 1176
  no bigger than plum but leads king, 1261
  round as an apple, 1345
  breakers on both sides, dark water between, 1425–1428
  round, split, hair around it, 1425
  long, hair around (on) it, 1426
  hair above and below, dance in middle, 1443
  hair above and below, round thing in middle, 1444
  stones thrown far, 1471 n. 2
  pole reaches the sky, 1471 nn. 15–16
  small but holds the world, 1471 n. 19
  rolled up and unrolled, 1471 n. 23
  sow a field, 1471 nn. 28–29
  birds fly far, 1471 nn. 30–35
  horses go far, 1471 nn. 36–37
  persons go far and return, 1471 nn. 39–50
  reaches the sky, 1471
  here it comes, there it goes, 1578 n. 13
  wouldn't want to lose it, 1593 § 1
eye of a needle. See needle(s)
eyebrows
  sables (men, snakes) lying end to end, 1042–1044
  two little gardens, 1100 n. 3
eyelashes
  man inside, hair outside, 544 § 12

men fighting, 1003–1004
geese on shores of lake, 1044 n. 3
men striking with poles, 1044 n. 8
hair above and below, 1443
eyelids, eyewinker
  chop and leave no chips, 788–789 § 2
  embrace each other at night, 968 n. 7
  chop and leave no mark, 1665–1666 § 3
eyes and feet
  two brothers arrive before four, 996

face
  brothers sit on chair but do not touch, 1003–1004 n. 22
  landscape, 1100–1108
  house, windows, door, 1144 n. 4
  See also head (and its several parts—ears, eyes, etc.)
fan
  lies in box, not in a field, 257b
fan, winnowing
  two kites kick each other, 397 n. 13
fat, bubbles of
  hundred eyes, 10–16
fatwood
  fat but does not eat, 245
faucet
  grown in wood, 1058–1062 § 6
feather
  falls in water, doesn't splash, 164 § 2
  lies in box, not in a field, 257a
  girl drops kerchief, 730
  man drops hat, 731
  cannot throw it over roof, 1341 n. 9
  picked and left behind, 1632–1642 n. 4
  See also quill, quill pen
February
  youngest of twelve sons, 984
feet
  Whitey up, Whitey down, 858
  men never catch each other, 996–1001 § 8
  four brothers preceded by two, 996
feet of pot
  sisters cannot touch one another, 1012
  children never touch one another, 1027–1028 § 10
fence
  goes round house, never comes in, 201
  men girt with belt, 678 § 4
  warriors stand motionless, 992–993
  shirt without stitches, 1437 § 6
  See also rail, rail fence, railing
fetlocks
  men with beards on backward, 191 § 6
fez
  Red rides Black, 871–877 n. 34

fez—*Continued*
  turned down, full; turned up, empty, 1455 § 2
fiddle
  ten teeth without tongue, 21
  two holes, bridge betwixt, 106
  humpbacked father, hollow mother, seven children, 1017 *bis* § 3
  once green, now singing, 1059
  grows in wood, bellows in town, 1060
  grows in wood, earns for master, 1061
  cries in wood, 1062
  See also violin
field of cotton. *See* cotton field
field of flax
  maidens dancing, 946
fig
  sack of oats, 1355 n. 1
  box full of nits, 1355 n. 2
file
  eats with belly, voids at sides, 240 § 3
  pimply man (child), 576–577
finger(s)
  men entering house, 908 § 1
  tree with green and dry wood, 989 nn. 10–12
  men born on same day but of unequal size, 1040–1041
  five geese on rack, 1040–1041
  five boughs on tree, 1040
  ten trees, 1041
  can't eat bunch of plantains, 1247
  never of equal length, 1629
fingers catching louse
  take boy to court, 970
  five take one to jail, 971
  five after one, 972
  kill boy on two tables, 973
fingers eating
  five brothers enter a hollow, 908 § 1
  five pick fruit, 980
fingers knitting
  ten upon four, 979
fingers milking
  buttocks up, buttocks down, ten draw four, 976–979
  stub stands, mill goes, ten draw four, 976–979 n. 11
  four hang, ten draw, 976–979 § 6
  ten draw four, 976
  ten against four, 977
  ten upon (above) four, 978
  See also cow, milking a; cow, calf, woman milking
fingers picking nose. *See* nose, picking the
fingers sewing. *See* sewing

fingers spinning
  five dry, five wet men, 961–963 § 8
fingers writing. *See* writing
fingernail(s)
  apron on back, 588
  goats on fence, 989 n. 8
  caps on backs of ten sons, 989
fire
  gets out when locked in, 112
  dies when fed water, 235
  moves without legs, 260–265 § 7
  walks without bones, 264–265 § 11
  bird flies without wings, eats without mouth, 367–369
  rooster stays in only one coop, 374
  red eggs in nest, 375b
  traces cannot be erased, 396
  red heifer (cow) dies on drinking water, 399
  man with queue and sores, 576–577 n. 5
  dressed in evening, undressed in morning, 587 n. 7
  dancing girl, 721
  man goes out, when locked in, 721
  Kitty Brannie eats stone, drinks no water, 776
  buried, turns into bars of gold, 785–786
  dead gives birth to the living, 828–836 § 2
  chief in the middle, slaves round about, 841 § 1
  black child born of red mother, 871–877 n. 5
  man goes halfway to heaven, 941
  men fighting, 966–968 § 5
  bigger than louse, smaller than mouse, 1263–1265 n. 4
  small, large, sweet, bitter, 1269–1275 § 4
  dregs above and below, beer between, 1436–1447 n. 6
  red, makes hot, 1563
  goes up chimbly chip chirrup, 1625
  See also coal(s) of fire
fire and ashes
  shines all day, is raked up in its dirt, 786
  dead buries the living, 835
  when the dead covers the living, 836
  See also spark, smoke, and ashes
fire and pot
  dead sits on the living, 828–829 § 6
  women warming livers, 871–877 n. 14
  red animal licks black animal, 871–877
  red man makes black man sing, 871
  red man tickles black man, 872
  red man makes black man's belly boil, 873
  red man makes black man gallop, 874
  black man rides red horse, 875–877 n. 8

Index of Solutions

black man sits on red man's head, 875
black man sits on chair, 876
Ber Reddy sticks Ber Blacky, 885
three catch, ten reach over, 976–982 n. 2
fire and smoke
  mule in stable, tail outside, 413
  man in house, beard outside, 544 § 9
  son on roof, father not born, 985
  daughter begets mother, 1007 § 7
  See also fire, smoke, and pot (stove); stove, fire, and smoke; wood, fire, and smoke
fire and weeds
  husband and wife fight, 966–968 § 5
fire, pan, and cassava
  red beneath, black in middle, white above, 1541
fire, pan, and pancake
  Redman boxes Blackman, Whiteman laughs, 886
fire, pot, and stones
  thing on three incombustible sticks, 1110
fire, smoke, and pot (stove)
  father, mother, son, 1017 *bis*
fire, spark, and smoke
  red mother, stout daughter, son goes to sky, 941–942
  one goose flies away, one disappears, one eats insatiably, 941–942
  three men start for heaven, 941–942
firebrand
  twenty-four ladies dance, 949
firefly
  lights the fields, 1682
fireplace
  patched up, hole in middle, 1437c
  black within, red without, four corners round about, 1532
fire stick
  in red, out black, 1542
firestones and pot
  children go to school, 1033
  See also fire, pot, and stones
fish
  lives in river, 98
  horse slippery, 406
  boy lives far from home, 684
  seamless coat, 1213 § 3
  flops about when out, 1450
  old man had something good, 1748
  See also eating a fish
fish, bird, man, and dog
  Footless, Two-Foot, Three-Foot, Four-Foot, 466–468 n. 6
fish and bait (weir)
  dead catches the living, 828–836 § 4

fish in net
  men in house, house leaps out, 906
fish in pan (pot)
  child cries when fed, 778b
  Ber Reddy sticks Ber Blacky, Ber Whitey laughs, 885
fish, stool, and dog
  No-Legs and Four-Legs, 466–468 n. 5
fishhook
  dead kills the living, 828–836 § 4
fishing
  ride not on road, hit not with stick, 823–824 n. 9
  men fighting, 970–975 § 2
  sent a letter, 1254
fish net
  house with countless windows, 1130a
fishpot
  many windows, one (two) door(s), 1130
fishtrap
  can enter but not leave it, 1141–1142 § 2
flag
  heart of wood, head of steel, 553–554 § 7
  patch on patch, 1437 § 3
flail
  grown in wood, barks at home, 1058–1062 § 7
flame
  consumes mother, 774c
  See also candle; fire; lamp
flatiron
  three-fourths square, black as a bear, 1360
  See also iron; self-heater
flax
  man in room, beard outside, 544 § 2
  green, then white, 668–669 § 4
  they beat me, they drowned me, 679
  threw away meat, kept bones, 806–815 § 1
  pillars with green caps, 946–950 n. 18
  dancing in green gowns, blue hats, 946
  white, stands in bed, 1572 n. 4
flax-break (flail)
  two heads, can't talk, 335
  born in wood, barks at home, 1058–1062 § 7
flax comb (heckle)
  feet, no mouth, 19
flaxseed
  dresses all the world, 531–534 § 2
flea(s)
  leaves no track, 185
  has legs, rarely walks, 309
  bird without feathers, 344
  a sharp knife, 344
  makes king (beam) move, 344
  hip, hop, jump wide, 344

flea(s)—*Continued*
  little boy sleeps with man, 686
  black, it leaps, can't be fettered, 1379–1382 n. 15
  don't want it, but seek it, 1593–1595 §7
  See also dog flea; lice; vermin
flood
  red bull tears down field, 399–400
floor and ceiling. *See* ceiling and floor
flour
  dogs drink much water, 489–490 n. 1
  goes up brown, comes down white, 1550–1554
flour sifter
  thousand eyes, no nose, 10
  See also sieve; sift, sifter; strainer
flowers
  bloom in morning, wilt in evening, 1066
flute
  born in wood, 1058–1062 §2
fly (flies)
  bird with six legs, 46–87
  buffalo walks sea without wetting feet, 431–432 §2
  Miss Nancy gives everyone a kiss, 735
  comes to king's table, 737 §1
  three prisoners in glass, 975
foam
  goes crying as river flows, 750–767
food in pan
  moon in tank, 1230–1234 n. 46
fool, mind of
  flies without wings, 365–366 §8
foot. *See* feet
foot, cut
  did it in wood, brought it home, 1640
footsteps
  headless fox ate goose without shadow, 367–369 n. 60
  can't do without them, 1580
forge
  bull bulled it, 401
fork
  cut in woods, thrives in meadow, 1058–1062 §8
fowl
  Whitey drives out Whitey, 848
fowl egg. *See* egg
fox and goose
  Jack with pack on his back, 726
frog
  long legs, short thighs, bullet eyes, 82
  dances in swamp, 347
  green cap, yellow shoes, 605
frog in bird's mouth
  six legs, one tail, 352

frost
  leaves white glove in window, 213
  priest loses key, sun hides it, 367–369
  ox drinks pool, 489–490 §1
  Hicky-picky locks gate without iron, 794
  builds bridge without tools, 794
  through a rock, through a wheel, 1600
fruit. *See* ackee; apple; atsuete; banana; berry; breadfruit; cantaloupe; cardamon; carob; cassava; cennep; cherry; chile; clam cherry; coconut; eggplant; fig; grape(s); grenade; guava; hip; lemon; lime; mango; melon; muckle lime; muskmelon; olive; orange(s); papaw; papaya; peach; pear; pineapple; plum; pomegranate; popo fruit; poppy; prickle (prickly) pear; raisin; skinnip; sloe; soursop; vine and fruits; watermelon
frying pan
  servant bawls when fed, 778a
  bird with tail, 1302–1308
  round as apple, black as coal, 1302
  round as hoop, 1304
  round as moon, black as coon, 1305
  round as moon, black as ink, 1306
  round as ring, 1308
  round as well, deep as bowl, 1336
  round as biscuit, slick as mole, 1349
  little round hole, black as coal, 1361
  hell atop, hell abottom, 1441
  See also skillet; spider
funeral procession. *See* coffin and bearers; corpse and bearers
fungee (corn flour)
  black sits on red man's head, 877
furrow
  heads at both ends, 30

gallows
  stands outdoors, kills many thieves, 804
gambler
  in and out, never wins, 134
garden
  Whitey drives Whitey out of Whitey, 847
girder(s)
  lie in one bed (pillow), 1027–1028 §3
  long beam with twelve nests, 1037–1038 n. 38
  See also beam(s); rafters
girdle
  round as hoop, long as snake, 1342
  See also belt
girl. *See* cherry and girl; woman carrying bucket

Index of Solutions 925

girl, milking
   down, out, up, home, 734
   See also fingers milking
girl, unmarried
   partially filled glass on table, 1197
gizzard
   flesh outside, skin inside, 588 § 9
glass
   imprisons flies, 975
   will not hold drop, 1198
glove(s)
   fingers, no toes, 23
   fingers, no flesh, 24
   sisters (brothers) have own rooms, 908 n. 8
   five rooms, one door, 908 n. 20
   five holes in one, 908 n. 24
   cartful of fingers and thumbs, 1250
   hairy one opens, naked one enters, 1416–1419 § 5
gnimabraein (mythical animal)
   drowns when out of sea, 346
goat
   horns point to village, 191 § 4
   Four-Foot jumps on No-Foot, 466
   Whitey drives Whitey out of Whitey, 849a
   four stand, two candles, 1476–1494 § 8
gobee (calabash)
   grows green, has seeds, 1080
   green as grass, 1371
goose
   supported by shovels, it eats grass, 360–361
   bin on two poles, 1100–1108 n. 32
   boat, paddle, trumpet, 1405–1408 nn. 7–8
   in front like broomstick, 1435 § 5
   patch on patch, 1437 § 10
gooseberry
   red cap, stick in hand, 636
gopher
   black hair, red beard, 547
gorse bush
   deer with five thousand teeth, 390
   yellow, green, can't ride it, 1569
gourd
   hen lays eggs, 381–382
   sow gives birth, 382
   house full of children, 908–916
   man raises flag (drags shield), 1017–1035
   father tethers child and departs, 1017–1035 n. 3
   tree, branch, nest, egg, 1161–1164 n. 6
   See also calabash; gobee
grain
   throw away flesh, keep bones, 806–815 § 2
   supports all Jamaica, 1053

   See also barley; buckwheat; corn (maize or wheat); maize; millet; rice; wheat
grape(s)
   hair extends beyond fortress, 544 § 3
   stalk in rump, 632–644 § 16
   bird eaten, 806–815 n. 1
   kill man, drink his blood, 806–815 n. 10
   house without door, full of juice, 1135–1136
   round as marble, green as grass, 1339
grape, vine, shoot, wine, brandy (some or all of these)
   son visits church on holy days, father annually, grandson never, 1017–1035
   woman bears handsome son, mad grandson, 1017–1035
   wooden mother, straight father, humpbacked son, 1017 § 6
   sequence of colors, 1559–1561 § 6
grass
   makes thousand tracks, 178
   only Johnny rides, 433
   company of dancers, 946–950 § 2
   children born in hedge, 1021–1024 n. 3
   only Johnny can climb tree, 1048
grasshopper
   big head, no a——, 8
   fears rooster, not dogs, 561
   members resemble those of various animals, 1405–1408
grassquit (a tropical finch)
   only Johnny rides, 433
grate
   family in bed can't touch one another, 1027
grater
   rat eats cassava, 1054
grave
   insatiable, 236–239
   kills none, swallows a hundred, 236–239
   stick grows longer when cut, 1111a
   twine grows longer when cut, 1111c
   door grows longer when cut, 1111d
   house without doors, 1132–1138 § 4
   house without doors, occupant can't speak, 1134 n. 11
   locked box, 1187
   green coat grows longer when cut, 1211
   grows longer when cut, 1694
   cut it to make it longer, 1695
graveyard
   eats meat, not bread, 483
   has no parents or children, 667
   See also cemetery
graveyard, corners of
   four insatiable boars, 483

grenade (fruit)
   not a king, but wears a crown, 595
Greybeard (stone bottle)
   man without teeth or tongue, 549
greyhound
   head like snake, neck like drake, 1406
grief
   flies without wings, 365–366 § 7
grinder. *See* sausage grinder
grinding
   men fighting, 966–968 § 3
   See also mill
grindstone
   growls when tail is caught, 387 n. 8
gristmill
   hog squeals, 387
ground
   white, with black seed, 1063c
groundnut (peanut)
   can open but not close trunk, 1187
   trunk holds two kinds of clothes, 1188
grubs
   each has own room, 908 § 3
grudge
   old when born, 664
grugru (pecan) tree
   can't beat drum, 1709
guava
   grows on trees, 1078
   carpenter in house without door, 1134 n. 8
guitar
   hen with six chicks, 475
gums. *See* mouth; teeth
gun
   looks homeward, 191 § 3
   eats and voids, 240 § 14
   cock crows fire, 379
   cock crows, lightning follows, 380
   tiger roars, 387
   lion bellows, 398 § 3
   donkey brays fire, 436
   dog barks here, bites yonder, 438
   dog barks fire, 439
   Jamaica bully-dog barks, 440
   twins girt with three belts, 678 § 6
   dances about, stands in corner, 695–699 § 2
   long black fellow bellows, 755
   man spits fire, spews lead, 781
   blue dog never sweats, 784 n. 1
   kills you, you can't kill it, 819
   dead kills the living, 828–836 § 4
   iron father, wooden mother, tiny children, 1017 § 5
   long, slinky, sings when guts come out, 1266
   round, deep, death of many things, 1329
   body of python, voice of lion, two feet, 1405–1408 n. 15
   maiden wears nine shirts, 1437 § 5
   See also bullet; bullet and gun; rifle; shotgun
gungo peas
   pen of guinea pigs, holler when touched, 480
gutter
   comes to house, doesn't enter, 198–202 § 5

hail
   many feet, 86
hair
   snow on ridge of Khangay, 46 n. 12
   meadow and animals, 459–460
   cannot be split, 1043
   grove of trees, 1043
   wands that only God can count, 1116
   cannot be counted, 1116
   tree without branches, 1116 n. 22
   over the head, under the hat, 1436
   grows and becomes less, 1690–1697 n. 2
   See also combing hair; queue; shaving; tail, cow's; tail, horse's; tears and hair
hair rope
   hair without, hair within, 1418
halibut head
   wobbly gut, 1251
halter
   cries â, 246–253
ham
   half a——, no hole, 25
   Four-Legs carries off One-Leg, 461
hand
   five pick fruit, 980
   tree with five branches, 1040
   See also drying hands; finger(s)
hand card
   thousand teeth, can't chew, 297
   See also card (for wool or cotton)
hands of clock
   brothers pursue each other, 996–1001 § 7
hanger
   many noses, 40
hare
   cow with leather horns, 393
   protect me from a dog, 561–562 n. 2
   See also rabbit
harrow
   born in wood, scratches dirt, 1058–1062 § 8

Index of Solutions

harrow, teeth of
  sister pursues sister, 1014–1015 § 6
harrowing
  Twenty-five Legs pursues Four-Legs, 461–462 n. 29
hat
  wear it over two years, 1207
  lies flat if empty, sits up if full, 1689 n. 1
  See also cap, fur cap; fez
hatchet
  looks homeward, 191a
hawk
  comes low, catches chickens, 360
  child learns to be thief, 797
hawk, horse, and man
  eight legs, two hands, wings, 50
hawthorn
  sequence of colors, 1559–1561 § 3
hayricks, prop for
  dressed in summer, undressed in winter, 587
  child born before father, 985 § 6
haystack
  sequence of colors, 1559–1561 § 7
head
  mountain with snow, 46
  dough on post, 208–209
  hillside where sheep graze, 488
  house and people, 918
  meadow and trees, 1043
  mountain, grass, two glasses, 1100
  block with seven holes, 1101
  house, door, side doors, windows, 1143–1151 n. 4
  theater, windows, people, red stage, 1147
  See also face (and the several members—ears, eyes, mouth, etc.)
head, bald
  haven't it, but wouldn't take the world for it, 1593
head, broken
  owner will not forget it, 1594
heads, two
  wouldn't want to lose them, 1593–1595 § 4
hearnshaw. *See* herneshaw and frog
hearse
  black as the De'il, runs on four wheels, 1363
  black, tires horses, 1567
heart
  goes, does not go away, 119–132 § 14
  tree without branches, bird without wings, 823–824 n. 11
  house, table, plate, saucer, 1156a

without it, yet I have it, 1577
never saw it, never will, 1579
hearth
  four sisters have one hat, 993 § 1
  See also fire, pot, and stones; firestones and pot
heat
  invisible, 226 § 5
  son appears before father's birth, 985 § 2
heaven and earth
  two packey of equal size, 1252a
  See also earth and sky
heckle
  grown in wood, barks in yard, 1058–1062 § 7
hedgehog
  makes many tracks, 180
  donkey loaded with needles, 576
  ball stuck with pins, 576
  Mr. Rusticap (Uncle Ned) with pins and needles on his back, 576
heel
  back is in front, 191 § 9
hemp
  one wears the hide, throws away flesh, 805–818 n. 3
  ladies dance, 946a
  See also flax
hen
  patch on patch, 1437 § 10
  house with two posts and roof of a hundred pieces, 1437 § 10
  two pink pillars, 1562
  See also chicken(s); cock; rooster
hen and chickens
  drags guts after itself, 206
  drags harrow after itself, 214
  woman with many children, 1023
hen and egg
  Mrs. Black goes in black, leaves white, 866
  Black man sits on white man's head, 879
  See also egg, laid
henhouse
  house with many windows, 1128–1131 § 5
henna
  in green, out red, 1544 n. 3
herneshaw and frog
  six legs, one tail, 352
highway
  rough, smooth, low, high, 578
  See also road
hip (fruit)
  Pat in red petticoat and black hat, 634
hip, right
  like left hip, 1403–1404

hobbyhorse. *See* stick-horse
hoe
  flies high and low, eats grass, 361
hog
  great lips, hairy beard, 546
  two things flap, 960
  hairy thing, 1746
holdfast (vise)
  the more it holds, the weaker it is, 1702
hole
  gig grows larger when pared, 1112
  brought stab, left hole, 1113
  the more it grows, the less it weighs, 1690–1697 n. 6
  the more you take from it, the larger it becomes, 1691
holes in horseshoe
  six and four wait for twenty-four, 937
holes in wall
  eyes, 10–16
  See also chink in wall
holly
  has horns, but is not beast, 601
  large, pointed, 1276–1277 § 1
honey
  sop bread under gray mare's tail, 407
  yellow men working at vat, 947
  dish full of flowers, 1069
honeycomb
  many eyes, 10–16 § 7
  sheet neither spun nor woven, 1212
  bridge on bridge, 1437 § 4
hoof(s) of horse
  four pursue one another, 952–957 § 9
  does not soften in water, 1448–1451 n. 1
hook and eye
  couple part at night, meet in morning, 968 n. 5
hook and line
  hunchback with long intestines, 205-207 § 4
  See also fish and bait
hookah
  sea above, fire below, 1440–1441 n. 5
  woman with fire on her head, 1440–1441 n. 6
  snake charmer and snake, 1440–1441 n. 13
hoops. *See* barrel; cask
hopingay
  green like a mead, talks like man, 1405
hops
  moves without legs, 260–265 § 18
  straight father, twisted mother, son, 1017 § 7
  cannot throw it over roof, 1342 n. 10

horn
  looks backward, 191 § 1
horn, blast of
  goes through wood without touching, 154
hornets
  hickey, hackey, old tobacky, 893
horns of goat
  point to village, 191 § 4
horse
  four legs, no arms, 46–87
  turns apron (fetlocks) homeward, 191 § 6
  wild and woolly, 408
  boy can't talk, 767
  in front like tub, back like broom, 1435 § 2
  uphill gallop me not, 1610
  See also donkey; mule
horse, pregnant
  only four feet are wet in water, 432
horse, rump of
  watered with blood, it brings forth herbs, 1042
horse and cart
  hair against hair, peg in middle, 1416–1419 § 7
horse and man
  boat and outriggers, 48–55
  three heads, two souls, 48–55
  six legs, two heads, two hands, 49
  Whitey drives Whitey out of garden, 847
  Whitey drives Whitey out of clothes, 853
  Whitey locks up Whitey, 855
  Whitey sends Whitey to chase Whitey out of stable, 856
  See also horse and woman; horse, man, and bird; horse, man, and woman
horse and reins
  drags guts, 205–207 § 7
horse and saddle
  lock of blood, bed of wood, steps of iron, 1436–1447 n. 8
horse and shafts
  wood on each side, hairy one between, 1416–1447 n. 13
horse and wagon
  two push, six eyes, 1476–1494 § 3
horse and woman
  four legs on one side, two on the other, 53
horse, man, and bird
  eight legs, two hands, three lives, 50
  eight legs, two arms, wings, 51
horse, man, and plow. *See* man plowing
horse, man, and pot
  black on black, three legs up, six legs down, 64
  patch on patch, two legs up, four legs down, 65

Index of Solutions

three legs up, cold as a stone, six legs down, 67
horse, man, and saddle. *See* man, saddle, and horse
horse, man, and woman
  five legs on one side, three on the other, two breasts, 52
  three bodies, eight legs, three mouths, 54a
  five legs on one side, two eyes in forehead, four eyes on back, 54b
horse collar
  high and low, 1281 n. 11
horseshoe
  looks backward, 191 § 12
  burned, tortured, nails driven in, 674–680 n. 17
  shoes made without an awl, 796a
  shoes made without leather, 796c
  six and four wait for twenty-four, 937
horseshoe (horseshoe nail)
  goes to water with head down, 246
horseshoe in churn
  big to bottom, little to top, goes whipperty-whop, 1445f
horseshoe nail. *See* nail
horsetail (*Equisetum*)
  barrel on barrel, 1105–1106
horsewhip
  tickles where it is tender, 1464
hours
  twenty-four brothers rule world, 984 n. 15
hours of sleep
  Nature requires five, 1722
house
  legs can't walk, 308
  sits on four blocks, 733
  living within, dead without, 828–836 § 12
  catches fish at night, loses them by day, 906 n. 8
  worms go in and out of cow, 906 n. 12
  man rich at night, poor by day, 906 n. 15
  man with head of grass, sides of wood, 1100–1108 n. 41
house, oven, oven-mouth, fire
  storehouse, trunk, kerchief, gold, 1156–1160 n. 3
house roof
  ride horse with broken back, 435
huckleberry
  white as cotton, green as grass, 1384
humpback
  haven't it, wouldn't want to lose it, 1593–1595 § 5

hunger
  branch flicks all, 969 n. 2
  dog does not cry when beaten, 969 n. 3
  fights without speaking, 969 n. 4
  thousand men kill thousand bullocks, 969
  painted out, painted in, 1154
  have it, don't want it, 1728–1737 § 2
hunting
  two chase, two wait, 976–982 n. 4
husband
  man can give it to a lady, 1589
  See also man, married
husband, wife, lover
  have it, don't give it, 1589–1590 nn. 1–4
hut, corner of. *See* corner of hut, beam at
hymnbook
  old lady deaf, dumb, and blind, 940

I (letter of the alphabet)
  seen in tin, 469
i, dot over. *See* dot
ice
  neither burns nor drowns, 165–173 § 9
  can't repair it, 738–747 § 4
  bridge made without tools, 794
  longest bridge, 1103
  bridge can't be mended, 1670
  bridge breaks when crossed, 1671
  See also bridge of ice
ice and water
  son rides, father not yet born, 985 § 4
  mother begets child, child begets mother, 1007
icicle
  can't be put together again, 738–747 § 4
  grows with root up, 1055a
  grows with head down, 1055b
  lives in winter, dies in summer, 1057
ignis fatuus
  Jackatawad runs over moor, 704
ingratitude
  I owe most, pay naught, 574
ink
  black man dances (sits) on white man's table (sheet, head), 883
  black seen on white field, a good scholar can guess, 1063b
inkstand
  narrow at top, wide at bottom, 1445–1447
insanity
  flies without wings, 365–366 § 8
instrument, musical
  dumb when alive, 830–834 n. 15
iron (flatiron)
  humpback, smooth belly, 45b

930 English Riddles

iron (flatiron)—*Continued*
  runs without feet, 260
  See also flatiron; self-heater

jack (turnspit)
  mill with two wings, 1169
jack-spaniard, jack spaniel
  bites, 341
  mother can't touch children, 1028
Jackatawad (*ignis fatuus*)
  runs over the moor, 704
jackdaw
  peasant goes to wood, wagon tongue peeps out of the wood, 191
jack plane
  eats through belly, voids through back, 240
  horse (cattle) eat, 415
jar
  leaves entrails at home, 205–207 § 6
jigger. *See* chigger
jug
  lives on water, doesn't drink, 779
  cut her head, suck her blood, 805f
June bug
  a Chinese when small, a Papuan when big, 587 n. 12

kasava root. *See* cassava
kesair nut
  earth above and below, pebble between, 1105–1106
kettle
  black on black, three legs up, 64
  red man makes black man sing, 871
  See also pot; teakettle
key(s)
  goes, never moves, 119–132 § 12
  goes through keyhole, 197
  leaves mouth at home, 205–207 § 5
  horns (tail) project, 412–413 § 6
  maiden in corn crib, braids outside, 544 § 7
  lord ties woman with cords, 678 n. 1
  does what force cannot do, 705
  all hands play on it, 712c
  one went in, two hung by, 958
  often used, rarely named, 1674–1680 § 3
kissing
  too few for one, right for two, 1738 n. 4
kite
  yellow house within a green house, 1164
kitten
  head like a cat, isn't a cat, 1403
  acts like a cat, isn't a cat, 1404
knapsack
  looks homeward, 191 § 2

kneecap
  box cannot be opened, 1187 n. 5
knife
  animal in barn, horns (tail) outside, 412–413 § 4
  components taken from animals and earth, 553–554 n. 6
knitting. *See* fingers knitting
knitting needles
  brothers captured and released, 996–1001 § 4
  four women go on a journey, 1014–1015 § 5
knob. *See* doorknob
knot
  bull in stall, horns in wall, 412–413 § 7
kulak
  once held in esteem, 1674–1680 n. 5

ladder
  man carries his way 190
  man sleeps outdoors, 790
  long father, many children, 1027–1028 § 2
ladle
  horse (bird) and tail, 412–413 § 3
lady
  Whitey drives Whitey out, 844a, 848, 852b
lady carrying pail
  over and under water and never touches water, 165
lady riding horse
  two heads, two feet on one side, four feet on other side, 53
  See also horse, man, and woman
lamb
  Whitey chases Whitey, 844a
  See also sheep
lamp
  eats out of stomach, voids at its sides, 240 § 13
  sleeps all day, awake at night, 254–255
  bird drinks with tail, 413
  lady's locks flutter, 607–631 n. 9
  man with running nose, 689
  drinks own blood, eats own flesh, 774b
  icy father, dirty mother, woolly child, 1017 § 4
  bottom water, top fire, 1440
  fire burns in sea, 1440–1441 n. 3
  small but fills a room, 1473
lamp chimney
  round, bottomless, 1172–1173 § 4
lampwick
  petticoat becomes shorter when worn, 617

Index of Solutions 931

lane
  small, straight messenger, 706
  See also path
lantern
  iron roof, glass walls, 1155
latch
  ram in stall, horns in wall, 412–413 § 7
  everybody plays on Tom Tittymouse, 712
laws
  sin begets, 1009
lawsuit
  wouldn't want to lose it, 1593–1595 § 8
  have it, seek to get rid of it, 1632–1642 n. 5
leaf (leaves)
  up and down, in and out, 135
  Nancy comes downstairs, 720
  cannot drown, 821–822
  walk on dead, dead hollers, 834a
  runs when dead, 1021–1024
  See also banana bush, banana leaf; coco leaf
leaves and tree
  mother stands still, children dance, 946–950
  mother bears many children, 1022
  mother lives, children die, 1022c
leech
  walks without bones, 264–265 § 4
leek
  bearded grandfather, 544 § 4
  green, white, goat's beard, 1273–1274
leg(s)
  Jack cannot help Jill, 943
  fat boy in small house, 1156–1160 n. 14
  See also calf of leg; feet
leg, wooden
  haven't it, wouldn't want to lose it, 1593 § 3
lemon
  comes to king's table, 737 § 3
  many spears cannot protect wife, 1017–1035 n. 7
  house without door, 1132–1138 § 2
Lent and Easter
  lettuce with fifty leaves, red rose, 983 n. 16
  bridge of seven versts, flower at end, 983 n. 17
lesswana bulb
  mistress with thousand dresses, 1438–1439
letter
  goes through water without being wet, 165–173 § 11
  goes without legs, 260–265 § 17

  travels without flesh or blood, 264–265 § 13
  mute messenger talks without mouth, 760
  bird without wings, 760 n. 13
  dead speaks to living, 830–834 n. 3
  white face, speckled thoughts, 1063 n. 23
  chips fly about, 1605 § 3
letters of the alphabet. *See A; E; I; O; U*
lettuce
  heart in its head, 31
lice (rarely: louse)
  six feet, 46–87
  walks without bones, 264–265 § 2
  pigs (animals) in forest, 459–460
  hunter leaves those he has killed, brings back those he has not killed, 460
  hunt with eagles (beagles?), 474
  animals grazing (roaming) on hillside, 488 n. 1
  haven't it but look for it, 1593–1595 § 7
lice, killing
  man captured and executed, 970–975
  animal slaughtered as sacrifice, 970–975 n. 15
  sentence passed on fingernail, 970
  five take one to jail, 971
  five after one, 972
  kill boy on two tables, 973
  lose what I take, keep what I take not, 1591
lice and comb. *See* comb and lice
licks (blows)
  up laughing, down bawling, 769d
life
  longer it gets, the shorter it is, 1690–1697 § 3
light
  goes through water, is not wet, 165–173 § 1
  man inside, head outside, 544 § 11
  small, fills room, 1473
  See also candle(s); lamp; moonshine; sun; sunbeam; sunlight, sunshine
lightning
  unbridled horse, 398
  through a rock, through a reel, 1601
  See also thunder and lightning
like
  shepherd sees it, God does not, 1715–1720 n. 15
  See also equal
lily
  sequence of colors, 1559–1561 § 5
lime (fruit)
  grows on tree, is green, black, yellow, 1079

lining of egg
  shirt neither washed nor sewn, 1104
lintel
  neither in nor out, 1423 § 2
lips
  come and do not come, 944–945
  persons quarrel, 966–968 n. 11
  sisters kiss, 1016 n. 4
liquor
  one is enough, two too many, 1738 n. 10
liquor, bottle of
  pull off his head, drink his blood, 805d
loaves and oven fork
  two round, one long go into hole, 958–960
  smooth children, long father, 1017 § 3
lobster
  something wears red coat, 646
  in black, out red, 1542–1543 § 2
lock
  goes, never moves, 119–132 § 12
  all hands play on it, 712c
  See also key(s)
locomotive
  two biscuits, one cup of coffee, 1242
  See also engine
log
  runs around house, 192–197
  Mrs. Black went in black, 863
  in black, out white, 1542–1546 § 6
  See also sawyers and log
log and hen
  Mrs. Black went in black, 866
looking glass
  turn my back, I am nobody, 825a
  scratch my back, I am nobody, 826
  See also mirror
loom
  hundred teeth, two ribs, 18–21
  tiger roars, 387
  garden, tree, cradle, child, 1161–1164 n. 8
  boards on both sides, hole in middle, 1416–1447 n. 17
lotus
  stick in its eye, 632–644 § 17
louse. *See* lice
love
  tree without branches, bird without wings, 823–824 n. 11
  string breaks, 1202
lunatic, mind of
  flies without wings, 365–366 § 8

macaroni
  man mounts horse, dangles feet, 412–413 § 3
  See also vermicelli

machine in corn mill
  chews, doesn't swallow, 241
machine (sewing machine)
  saddled on back, ridden at tail, 425
machine (unidentified)
  chick chick up, chick chick down, 1624
  See also engine; locomotive; threshing machine
madman, mind of
  flies without wings, 365–366 § 8
maggots
  through the rock, through the reel, 1598
magpie
  tail looks backward, 191 § 7
  wears yellow boots, walks by jumps, 1379–1382 n. 9
  white as milk, black as coal, 1379
  white as milk, hops like foal, 1380
  black as ink, but not ink; white as milk, but not milk, 1381
  white as milk, has long tail, 1382
  in front like book (pickax), 1435 § 4
  white and black, 1496
maid on stool
  Two-Legs sat on Three-Legs, 462
maiden apple
  red outside, red seeds inside, 1526
maize
  storks gather on high ground, 489–490 n. 2
  everyone takes off my clothes, 587 n. 6
  hair in belly, 588 § 8
  girt with pearls, 650–652 n. 1
  white beard becomes black, 668–680 n. 6
  child gives birth to mother, 1007 § 12
  poor at foot and head, rich in middle, 1436–1447 n. 5
  wears many garments, 1438–1439 n. 12
  See also corn
maltsack
  belly bigger than all the rest, 269
mammy apple
  has a big seed, 1073
man
    [described in terms of form]
  two hands, twenty fingers (i.e., digits), 46–87
  first four, then two feet, 46
  in the morning four feet, at noon two feet, 47
  two poles, mill, etc., 1100–1108
  log with nine holes, 1101 n. 7
    [described in terms of function]
  Christian person, 837
  two walk, two dangle, 1476–1494 § 5

[qualified by descriptive adjective]
man, black
  can't do without white man, 1677
man, married
  rose in garden, 1070
  flower of Virginia, 1099
  rigged ship, 1166
man, old
  three legs, four eyes, 46–87
  mountain is covered with snow, 46
  three legs, two arms, 48
man, unmarried
  rose outside of garden, 1070
  unrigged ship, 1166
  glass not full, 1197
man, white
  Whitey runs out (locks up) Whitey, 842
    through 844, 847, 850, 852, 854, 855, 856
  cedar, chipcherry, 1627
  can't do without black man, 1677

[man in action]
man beating drum
  kiss me asleep, kiss me awake, 758
man carrying basket
  over water, under water, doesn't touch water, 167
man carrying hatchet. See hatchet
man carrying pig
  living at both ends, dead between, 1432–1434 § 2
man carrying pot. See man and pot
man cutting foot
  done in the woods, brought it home, 1640
man dreaming
  walks but does not go, 715
man eating. See eating; fingers eating
man milking. See cow, milking a; fingers milking
man playing bagpipe
  shepherdess complains, 521
man plowing
  ten feet, six eyes, 48–55 § 1
  Three-Legs chases Four-Legs, 461–462 n. 30
  hair against hair, 1416–1419 § 7
  two heads, middle contrasting, 1430–1431 § 3
  dead in middle, alive at each end, 1432
  flesh in front and behind, wood and iron in middle, 1433
  soul behind, noisemaker in middle, blower at head, 1435 n. 2
  alive in front, dead in middle, eats bread at back, 1435 n. 7
  alive in front, dead in middle, baptized at back, 1435 n. 13

  two poke, two pull, 1476–1494 § 4
man pulling on pants
  ten men haul bag up hill, 1200a
m n reading book
  has bound servant, 690
man riding bicycle
  rides, yet sits, 717
man riding horse. See horse and man; horse, man, and bird; horse, man, and pot; horse, man, and woman
man scratching head
  hunt with eagles, 474
man selling nuts, 1749
man threshing
  two stand, two strike, two look at each other, two bow, 1476–1494 § 16
man walking on ice
  Two-Legs walks on No-Foot, 466–468 n. 4

[man and various persons or objects]
man and chair
  goes out on two legs, comes back on four, 464
man and children
  can't get spoonful, 1653
man and daughters
  cannot eat fruit, 1045
man and fish
  Two-Legs walks on No-Leg, 466–468 n. 4
man and hammock
  runs but does not go away, 119–132 § 11
man and pot
  three feet dead, two feet alive, 67
man and shadow
  two men racing, 952–957 § 8
man and sods on his head
  goes away above ground, returns underground, 168
man and umbrella
  goes through rain, is not wet, 961–963 § 3
man and woman
  flower of Virginia, 1099
man, dog, and boot
  Two-Legs, Four-Legs, One-Leg, 461–462 n. 4
man, dog, and ham (leg of mutton)
  Two-Legs, Four-Legs, One-Leg, 461
man, dog, and pot
  Four-Legs broke Three-Legs, Two-Legs beat Four-Legs, 461–462 n. 12
man, goat, and cabbage
  Two-Legs drives Four-Legs from One-Leg, 461–462 n. 16
man, saddle, and horse
  alive above and below, dead between, 1436–1447 § 1
man, woman, and child
  Christian people, 837

mangle
  two stand in front, two lie below, 1476–1494 § 23
mango
  skin on hair, hair on bone, 588 § 8
  child gives birth to parent, 1007 § 12
  bears green fruit, 1086
  throw away skin, eat flesh, 1091
  yellow outside and inside, white door inside, 1153
  yellow outside, yellow inside, 1517
mango tree
  flock of goats, 491
manioc
  coarse cloth outside, white robe inside, 588 § 8
manioc, pulling
  men fighting, 966–968 § 4
mare. *See* horse
marker on scale
  comes, goes, doesn't leave, 125–130 § 4
marriage, giving in
  man given what he hasn't, 1589
  too little for one, right for two, 1738 n. 3
marriage of brother and sister
  never will be, 1628
marrow
  take out gold, discard box, 805–818 n. 5
marsh hen
  nests in marsh, 355
martagon (lily)
  dressed in ninefold coat, 1438–1439
mason
  carries way on neck, 190
master
  God has none, 1715–1720 § 3
mat
  four ears, hundred eyes, 10–16 § 5
  man has teeth on his back, 299
  knock and stand up, 1672
  See also mattress
match (matches)
  head can't think, 272
  horse and spur, 429
  man with red hair, 583
  man with red face, black (blue) hair, 584
  can't be put together again, 738–747 § 3
  men in flat-top house, 907
  redhead children in flat-top house, 924
  little thing swallows mother, 1008 n. 4
  piece of wood flares up, 1683
match at bowls
  hounds chase hares, 476
matter (mucus, pus)
  egg does not break when thrown, 1195

mattress
  rolled up, spread out, 1341–1342 § 4
meal. *See* flour; fungee (corn flour); wheat
mealie
  bone within, marrow without, 588 § 8
  woman with thousand petticoats, 1438–1439
medicine bottle
  man removes hat when we are sick, 514
melon
  red house, green furniture, 1145
  red, white, black inside, green outside, 1518
  green outside, red and white inside, brown eyes, 1528
  See also calabash; cantaloupe; gobee; gourd; muskmelon; watermelon
men threshing
  two stand, two strike, 1476–1494 § 16
men, women, and children
  Christian people, 837
mileposts
  ladies can't catch one another, 953
milk
  turns without moving, 132
  goes over field, sits by fire, 447
  goes over pasture, sits in cupboard, 449
  goes over hillsides, sits on shelf, 450
  goes in fields, sits on table, 451
  goes over fields, sits in water, 452
milk in coffee
  white cow, 493 § 3
milk bottle
  up white, down black, 1555
milking
  down she squat, 734
  See also fingers milking
Milky Way
  long person, 575 § 5
mill
  goes, yet stands still, 125–130 § 5
  eats with eye, voids at side, 240 § 4
  doesn't drink, 246–253 § 6
  insatiable hen, 376
  squealing hog, 387
  animals fight, drop foam, 397
  narrow fold, many sheep, butting ram, 397
  five swine cry loudly, 481
  stands all night in dew, 688
  woman sings when full, 768–769 § 5
  feeds world but does not eat, 776–777
  more a man eats, more he wants, 777
  boy works all day, never perspires, 784
  grows in the wood, rattles on the water, 1058–1062 § 12

house with one post, 1125
two groundholders, two cross-standers, 1492
See also cane mill; corn mill; grinding; gristmill; sawmill; sugar mill; windmill
mill-point
four men can't catch one another, 952
mill roller
boars eating and refusing, 482
horses can't catch one another, 494
mill saw
rolling trout, 345
millet
man with red hair, 632–644 § 10
millipede
Two-Legs eats Twenty-Legs, 461–462 n. 33
millstone
swine cry more when fed, 481a
mimosa
green cow, white calves, 1036–1099
mind
often changes, 363
flies without wings, 365–366 § 8
me here, me there, 1578 n. 2
See also thought
mink
black hair, red beard, 547
mirror
draws without hands, 259
back, nobody; face, somebody, 825b
see you where you will never be, 1631
two who cannot touch each other, 1631
See also looking glass
Mississippi River
four eyes, can't see, 328a
four eyes, goes to sea, can't see, 328b
runs, has eyes, can't see, 328c
mist
touches every twig, 146
leaves no track, 181–185 § 6
cannot gather handful, 1651
cannot catch bowlful, 1652
See also cloud(s)
mittens
house occupied by five brothers, 908 n. 6
show two, hide ten, 976–982 n. 9
naked one enters hairy one, 1416–1419 § 5
See also glove(s)
mole
four legs, two ears, no eyes, 72
kettle boils, 1193 § 2
money
makes no track, 181–185 § 8

moves without legs, 260–265 § 15
have it, can't keep it, 1587
goes from hand to hand, 1605
See also penny; sovereign
money, counterfeit
if you see it, you don't take it, 823–824 n. 6
taker doesn't know it, 1728–1737 § 1
mongoose
four legs, eats chickens, 73
monkey
wide mouth, long beard, 545
months
birds without wings, 367–369 n. 58
twelve sons, second is the youngest, 984
twelve branches, 1037–1038
twelve apples, 1095
See also year
moon
grows young again, 89
four weeks old when Adam died, 90
four days old when Adam was four days old, 91
four weeks old when Cain was born, 92
here since the creation of the world, 93
here since creation, not yet a month old, 94
goes up and down, 120
goes, but makes no sound, 164 § 1
falls in water, doesn't splash, 164 § 2
doesn't get wet in water, 165–173 § 2
goes through, makes no hole, 181–185 § 3
sleeps all day, awake at night, 254–255 n. 1
deer walks alone, 392a
gray horse, 405
ram in stall, horns on wall, 412–413 § 9
mare never wets feet, 431
uncastrated ram, 484–486 n. 7
beauty spots on face, 513
Peep-peep has one eye, 527
long (tall) person, 575 § 4
lady with yellow petticoat, 648
baby is born and vanishes, 663
woman four weeks old, 682
see my face in town, 723
single king in land, 798
princess or girl, 1001 n. 13
pumpkin in meadow, 1071 n. 14
calabash vanishes in morning, 1094 n. 2
lamp shines over world, 1189
falls, doesn't break, 1192–1196 § 6
loaf (loaf among beans), 1230–1234
sour milk (cheese) in cup, 1230–1234
cup, bucket, 1230–1234
pancake travels, 1230–1234 n. 6
cheese cannot be cut, 1230

moon—*Continued*
  pancake (shingle), 1231
  white yam, 1232
  dumpling, 1233b
  higher than tree, 1278
  round as apple, 1301
  more crooked than sickle, whiter than snow, 1379–1382 n. 14
moon, half of
  like other half, 1230–1234 n. 2
moon and stars. *See* stars and moon
moon and sun. *See* sun and moon
moon, stars, and sky
  apple, money, blanket, 1215
moon, stars, sun, and water
  apple, money, diamond, sheet, 1216
moon, sun, and river. *See* sun, moon, and river (wind)
moon, sun, and stars. *See* sun, moon, and stars
moonshine
  sheet that none can weave, 1219–1220 n. 13
mortar. *See* matter (mucus, pus)
mortar (for grinding)
  born in forest, shouts in house, 1058–1062 § 9
moth
  through a rock, through a reel, 1603
mother, wife, and daughter
  milk and flesh allowed or prohibited, 1070 n. 11
mould
  has hair, no bones, 264–265 § 6
mountain
  born when mother was born, 1007 § 4
mouse
  around house, in cupboard, 448
mouse and cat. *See* cat and mouse
mouse nest in cat's ear
  never was, never will be, 1628
mousetrap
  full by day, empty at night, 1455 § 4
mouth
  cherry-red mill, 1101
  red house, white galleries, 1148
  well never dries, 1150 n. 5
  field without drafts, 1150 n. 41
  red garden, white fence, 1151
  you have it, I have it, 1573–1575 n. 2
  See also face; head; teeth; teeth and tongue; tongue
mowing machine
  insatiable red bull, 400c
muckle lime
  grows on tree, inside black, 1079

mucus
  five men catch girl, 970–975 § 4
  falls, doesn't break, 1192–1196 § 5
  See also matter; snot
mud men (dig mud, make bricks)
  twenty-four carpenters, some with blue bonnets, some with straw hats, 950
mud turtle
  Mother Hubbard with blanket on her back, 594a
muff
  covered with hair, 1428
mulberry
  wears two gowns a year, 650
mule
  people willing, something else is not, 1743
mule, Negro, and pot
  three legs up, six legs down, 64
mushroom
  walks without bones, 264–265 § 7
  man with red cap, 632–644 n. 29
  house (animal, man, tree) on one leg, 1121–1126 § 3
  umbrella in field, 1121–1126 § 3
  folded, no needle passed through, 1438–1439 n. 7
muskmelon
  green, full of yellow Negroes, 912
  See also cantaloupe
music
  goes through bush, never touches, 159
  See also drum, song of; echo; horn, blast of; noise; sound
mussel
  bones outside, flesh within, 588 § 3
mustard tree
  a tree and not a tree, 823
mutton, leg of
  One-Leg is carried off by Four-Legs, 461

N (letter of the alphabet)
  I (ben) have it, man (adam) does not, 1573–1575 n. 6
nail (horseshoe nail; nail in house, ship, or shoe)
  in water, out of water, 172
  goes about, sleeps on head, 187
  walks with head down, 188
  says "clink, clink" under water, doesn't drink, 251b
  man walks on head, 719
  chicken with fuzzy head, 787
  man has head out of doors, 787
  men with heads out of doors, 917
  See also fingernail(s); horseshoe (horseshoe nail); shoe nail, shoe tack

Index of Solutions

name
  follows with everything, 113
  does not drown or burn, 165–173 § 10
  clings to everyone, 1573–1575 nn. 8–13
  falls from heaven, 1573–1575 n. 14
  everyone has it at the same time, 1573
  teakettle has it, 1574
  you have it, others use it, 1582
  you have it, I use it more than you, 1583
  you rarely use it, 1584
  everyone has it but rarely uses it, 1585
  everybody takes it, I still have it, 1588
narcissus
  emerald, gold, silver, 668–669 n. 16
needle(s)
  eye, no head, 5
  one leg, one eye, 36
  one foot, one eye, 37
  leaves a track, 176
  leaves tail behind, 203
  snake, 203
  drops piece, 204
  goes through water (trees, hedge), leaves guts, 205
  has one eye, never closes it, 281
  has one eye, cannot see, 282
  bird with long tail, 351
  pig leaves trail, 386
  bull drags halter, 394–404
  cow breaks and builds wall, 394
  horse cannot gallop without tail, 419–435
  horse goes over bridge, 420
  horse jumps, reins get shorter, 421
  horse jumps, loses piece of tail, 422
  horse jumps, loses gut, 423
  horse jumps, stops a gap, 424
  saddle at head, ride at tail, 426
  animal with flaxen tail, 437
  dog with iron tail, 437
  sheep with one eye, 486
  horse and mare go to mountain, 495
  man with one eye, 528
  named person with one eye, 529
  unnamed person with one eye, 530
  man plowing, 531–534 n. 6
  person goes over whole world, 531–534 § 1
  person dresses whole world, 531–534 § 2
  man with one eye and tail, 531
  woman with one eye and tail, 532
  named woman with one eye and tail that is gradually lost, 533
  named woman with one eye and a tail, 534
  person with one hair, 535–536
  man loses half his tail, 535
  named person with tail, 536
  Miss Nancy with long frock, 597
  long dress grows shorter, 598
  series of tortures, 674–680 n. 31
  shiney jumps, whitey holds back, 710
  Miss Witty Wit wits out last wit, 820
  soldiers with one eye, 931
  round, keen, one eye, 1340
  in wet, out dry, 1448–1452 § 9
  put it here, find it there, 1578 n. 10
  thousand men can't bring it down, 1662
Negro and pot
  Black on Black, 64
nest, ants'
  mashed plate is repaired, 1193
nest, hen's
  black man on white man's head, 879
nest, mouse's
  never in cat's ear, 1628
nest, sparrow's
  neither in nor out, 1423 § 1
nest, wasp's
  bananas can't be touched, 1248
net
  many eyes, 10–16 § 4
  children hang round mother, 1026
  house with countless windows, 1130a
net and fish
  house leaps out of window, occupants are caught, 906
nettle
  Hitty Titty bites, 342
  man in red cap, 342 note
  soldier, 342 note
newspaper
  dog barks, 443
  opens like barn door, spotted like cat, 1398
  black, white, red all over, 1498
  first white, then black, then red, 1498c
  black, white, red all over, goes to Dover, 1499
night. *See* day and night
nightingale
  small, but pleases hearer, 336
  frying pan above, cotton below, 1436–1447 § 4
noise
  wagon (train) can't go without it, 1614
  never seen after it is made, 1628
  See also echo; horn, blast of; music; sound
noose
  dead catches living, 828–836 § 4
  See also snare
north wind
  Father Boris (Boreas) makes din, 762b

nose
  bridge between two lakes, 1044
  grows with root upward, 1055–1057 § 4
  house with two doors (rooms), 1143
  See also nostrils
nose, dog's
  never dries, 1150 n. 3
nose, hog's
  goes in and out, 960
nose, picking the
  two walk, five wait, 970–975 § 4
  five men seize girl, 970–975 § 4
nostrils
  brothers are not alive but have power of life, 1003–1004 n. 21
  holes in a hill, 1101
  brothers with mouths turned down, 1143–1151 n. 10
  See also nose
nothing
  better (greater, higher) than God, 1394
  rich don't want it, 1726
  rich want it, 1727
nut
  seize it, open it, don't carry it off, 125–130
  beaten, flayed, swallowed, 674–680 n. 14
  hard mother, bearded father, fat son, 1017 § 6 n. 14
  grown in wood, 1058–1062 § 14
  four live in house without door, 1134 n. 4
  house full of meat, 1136
  can't close house when opened, 1141–1142 § 4
  box made only by God, 1187 § 1
  pot of tasty food, 1187 n. 9
  doesn't get salty when lying in salt, 1236
  See also almond; betel; chestnut; chinkapin; coconut; groundnut; kesair nut; peanut; pecan; walnut
nut, wormy
  pick it up, if you don't see it, 823–824
  house has occupant, 1134
  See also worm(s)

O (letter of the alphabet)
  found in box, 469
oak (acorn, tree, ship)
  alive, it feeds the living; dead, it bears the living, 828
ocean. See sea
ocean and river
  father (mother) devours children, 1007 § 3
  See also sea

okra boiling in pot
  hog jumps in pen, 385
old age. See age
olive
  stick in backside, 632–644 § 20
  people in house, 910–915 § 11
  large, round, sweet, bitter, 1269–1275 § 1
  sequence of colors, 1559–1561 § 4
onion
  old man with beard in ground, 544 § 4
  head down, feet up, 544 § 5
  sold by father, tail cut off, causes weeping, 668–680 n. 21
  eat meat, throw away bones, 806–815 § 5
  green as grass, not grass, 1374
  white as milk, has beard, 1383
  woman with many garments, 1439 n. 2
  horse with many blankets, 1439 n. 7
  weep on undressing woman, 1439
  patches on patches, 1439
orange(s)
  yellow-backed guinea pigs, 478
  ate flesh, sucked blood, threw away skin, 809
  ladies dressed in yellow in a house, 910–915 § 12
  grows green, yellow when ripe, 1082
  yellow inside and outside, white windows, 1152
  round, bitter, sweet, 1269–1275 § 1
  round as moon, yellow as ochre, 1357
oven
  always yawning, 104
  belly full of meat, mouth of dirt, 233
  insatiable animal, 387
  steep hill with hole, 1101 n. 14
  house without post, 1126
  black within and without, 1534
oven and coals, custards, loaves
  father and children, 1017 § 3
owl
  sleeps all day, walks at night, 254
  bald old man squawls, 542
  mouth like barn door, ears like cat, 1396
ox (oxen)
  Four-Legs breaks up fight, 465
  two boys walking together, 1002
  See also man plowing
ox (oxen) and plow
  beast with forty feet, 59
  two poke, two pull, 1476–1494 § 4
ox and wagon
  two pierce, two push, 1476–1494 § 3

Index of Solutions 939

oxen and pole
  flesh on both sides, pole between, 1416–1447 n. 16
oyster
  rough outside, smooth inside, 1420

pail
  arse touches water first, 144
  over and under water, doesn't touch water, 165
  out between two woods, in between two waters, 166c
  hangs on tree like candle, 1704
  See also bucket; woman carrying bucket
palm
  white, black, then red, 1559–1561 § 9
  See also cabbage (cabbage palm); coconut, picking a; coconut, climbing a; salak
palm, sacred
  born in field, becomes daughter of God, 1058–1062 § 14
pan. See baking pan; cassava, pan, and fire; food in pan; frying pan; skillet; warming pan
pancake. See bammie
pane. See windowpane(s)
pants
  legs can't walk, 333
  ten men haul bag up flat hill, 1200a
pap
  round as moon, white as snow, 1354
  run after it, 1612
papaw
  yellow house, black people, 914
  grows on tree, red outside, 1077
  green outside, yellow inside, 1502
  black inside, yellow outside, 1515
papaya
  box full of hail, 1355 n. 10
paper
  falls, does not break, 1192–1196 § 1
  plate breaks only in water, 1192
  See also newspaper
paper and ink
  black man dances (sits) on white man's table (head, sheet, chair), 883
  white land, black seed, he who guesses is clever, 1063
paper and pen
  one cannot do without the other, 1676
parasol
  many rafters, one post, 1123
parchment
  calf, bee (wax), goose (quill) rule world, 511

parents
  you have them, I have them, 1573–1575 § 3
park (path?)
  small, straight messenger, 706
parrot
  Itum Paraditum (handsome protector) wears green coat, 602
  wears green coat, talks of many things, 604
  green as grass and speaks in prison, 1372
partridges
  nick, nack people, colored across the back, 895
  nickle, nackle, brown tobacco people going up heeple steeple, 896
  nicker, nacker, brown tobacco people going across London Bridge, 901
  through a rock, through a reel, 1602
partridge egg
  neither fish, flesh, nor bone, walks alone, 1237b
patch (Patch)
  man named Patch on motley horse, 65
  man has it, God does not, 1721 n. 1
path
  comes to house, makes no track, 182
  comes to door, never comes in, 199
  goes to house, never comes in, 200
  goes to spring, doesn't drink, 250
  comes to river, breaks its neck, 458
  sleeps out at night, 688
  See also highway; lane; park; road
pea. See pease
peach
  heart in its head, 33
peacock
  eyes in tail, 39
peanut
  goes out naked, returns in fur coat, 587 n. 5
  wears large overcoat, 657
  plant one, many get up, 1052
  can open but not close trunk, 1187a
  See also groundnut
pea pod
  house full of children, 910–915 § 10
pear
  man with stick in backside, 632–644 § 19
  high, hard, yellow, 1269–1275 § 1
  green inside, one seed, 1519
pease
  touch one guinea pig, others cry out, 480
  sheep dry a river, 490
  one boy speaks, other cannot, 830
  children cry out, 831
  old can, young can't talk, 832

pease—*Continued*
  dead speak, living are silent, 833
  touch one child, others cry out, 926
  children cry out when wind blows, 927
  children (boys) turn drummer, 928
  older daughter speaks, younger can't, 1011
  crooked father, hollow mother, children, 1017 *bis* § 2
  girl doesn't want to see brothers, 1035
  tree, branch, nest, eggs, 1161–1164 n. 5
  See also gungo peas; pigeon peas
pease tree (vine)
  children cry out when touched, 831
pecan (nut)
  large, small, bitter, sweet, 1272
pecan tree
  can't climb soldier tree, 1049
  See also grugru tree
peg (for blankets)
  full by day, empty at night, 1455 § 3
peg (for door)
  old man put it in, 1744
pen
  goose, calf (vellum), bee (wax) rule world, 511
  born as flesh and blood, given drink, head cut off, 674–677
  makes enmity between kings, 674
  makes peace between kings, 675
  does naught without guide, 675
  flesh and blood do not remain in it, 676
  makes lovers glad, 677
  dead speaks to living, 830–834 n. 4
  white man dances on black lady's floor, 883c
  in dry, out wet, 1448–1452 § 10
  when held, it goes; when released, it lies down, 1689
pen and paper. *See* paper and pen
pencil
  shut up in wooden case, 101
pencil and slate
  black man walks on black road, 884
penny
  goes through wood without touching, 148
  hill, house, closet, dress, pocket, Indian head, 1160
  round as apple, flat as pond, 1338a
  round as apple, half of a woman, whole of a man, 1338b
pepper, pepper seed
  teeth, no mouth, 18–21
  lady in red petticoat, 645
  green skirt becomes red, 668–669 § 5
  Miss Nancy dances rough, 694
  at king's table, 737 § 2
  house full of people, 910–915 § 5
  white, green, then red, 1559–1561 § 10
periwinkle
  I can open but not close house, 1141–1142 § 3
person
  something lives under the hill, 88
person in bed
  live in middle, dead at both ends, 1434
pies
  pots boil without fire, 1178b
pig
  flesh, not milk, eaten, 1070 n. 12
  cow's hoofs, gazelle's ears, wolf's eyes, 1405–1408 n. 17
  two shine, four spread, 1476–1494 § 11
pig, young
  like pig, 1403–1404
pigeon(s)
  horse crosses river without wetting feet, 431–432 § 1
  if they come, they don't come, 944b
pigeon peas
  old can talk, young cannot, 832a
  grow on tree, shake with wind, 1090
pigs and sow
  ten heads, ten tails, 56
pillow
  lower with than without a head, 1454
  See also corners of pillow
pillow beare (pillowbere), pillowcase
  goes to water, leaves guts at home, 207
pimiento
  church full of people, 910–915 § 5
pimpler
  threw it away, 1637
pin
  head, no body, 1
  head, no hair, 3
  head, no eyes, 5
pineapple
  bone inside, marrow outside, 588 § 8
  stick in backside, 632–644 § 18
  chief surrounded by slaves, 841 § 1
  window on window, 1438–1439 n. 14
pingwing (pinguin?)
  buttons from head to foot, 1208
pipe
  stick hog's head, tail bleeds, 383
  ride horse on tail, 427
  pot of hominy cooked at top and raw at bottom, 1244
  pot of food boils at top, 1245
  headed like thimble, tailed like rat, 1402
  two straights, one crook, 1494
  See also hookah

Index of Solutions

pirogue (meat pie)
  bast above and below, butter between, 1436–1447 n. 7
pitcher
  neck, no head, 6 § 1
  eats and voids, 240 § 9
  goes aslant, returns erect, 1448–1458 nn. 7–8
pitchfork
  looks homeward, 191 § 1
plane
  son eats and vomits, 772
  See also jack plane
plantation
  work de finny, 783
Pleiades
  animals, 988 note
  seven sons can't converse, 988
  seven sisters lie in one bed, 1027–1028 § 9
plow
  goes to woods and looks homeward, 191 § 1
  insatiable, 236–239
  born in woods, digs in ground, 1058–1062 § 8
  See also man plowing
plow and oxen. See ox (oxen) and plow
plow handles
  chopped in wood, squeals in field, 1058–1062 § 8
plum
  girl bears only twins, 662
  eat pot, throw away contents, 805–818 n. 8
  sucked Davy's blood, left body, 813
  smaller than mouse, higher than castle, 1263–1265 n. 5
  white, black, small, high, 1269–1275 § 1
pocket. See trousers; watch pocket
pod
  people sit in chairs, 1145–1148 n. 5
  See also pea pod
pod of castor bean
  three brothers in one house, 1005
  one bag holds three, 1201
pole
  upright in day, flat at night, 1455 n. 6
pole of cart
  looks backward, 191 § 1
  See also wagon tongue
policeman
  brass button, blue coat, 660
pomegranate
  stick in hand, stones in throat, 633
  eat bag, throw away wheat, 805–818 n. 7
  people in house without door, 909
  mother and thousand children, 1021–1024
  red outside, seeds inside, 1084
  goblet filled with pearls, 1355 n. 5
  green as grass, yellow as gold, 1370
pond
  grows larger as you take from it, 1690
poplar
  man in fur coat, 587 n. 10
popo fruit
  man with spear in heart, 632–644 § 22
poppy
  man with red cap, 632–644 § 8
  maiden, bride, crone, then crawls out of eyes, 668–680 n. 16
  barracks (house) full of soldiers, 910–915 § 9
  woman with many children, 1023–1024 n. 6
  tenants in manor on post, 1100–1108 n. 35
  stands on one leg, 1121–1126 § 5
  container with thousands in it, 1355 n. 3
porridge
  black outside, guts walloping, 1537
Portington, Robert
  heard thing cry, 564
post(s)
  girt with belt, 678 § 4
  brothers quarrel, 966–968 § 13
  brothers stand together, 993
  men surround king, 993 n. 6
  See also beam(s); bedposts; fence; mileposts; pole; rafters
pot
  person with hundred eyes, 10–16
  body without intestines, feet without nails, 68
  three feet, mouth, two ears, 68
  three feet, 85
  eats and voids, 240 § 9
  mouth can't speak, 325
  John Crow on three trees, 371
  black hen on red nest (eggs), 375
  bull feeds on three ridges, 395
  black man (woman) with arms akimbo, 550
  stands with arms akimbo, lies with arms akimbo, 551
  three legs, wooden (iron) cap, 558
  man suffers tortures, 674–680
  can't be repaired, 738–747 § 2
  Negroes with three feet, 930
  men with arms akimbo, 932
  hollowhearted mammy, 1017
  daughter sits on three chairs, 1182
  full, yet holds more, 1457
  two lookers, three standers, 1493
  black without, black within, 1537

pot—Continued
  living buy it, dead do not need it, 1726–1727 n. 3
  See also broth pot; chamber pot; coalpot; coffeepot(s); cooking pot; teakettle; teapot; utensil. Compare boy and pot; cat and pot; dog and pot; fire and pot; Negro and pot; horse, man, and pot; man and pot; or man, dog, and pot
pot and spoon
  ship and propeller, 1165
pot and stove
  four brothers go to school, 1033e
pot-foot. See feet of pot
pothook
  bent legs knotted in middle, 563
  See also reeken hook (brandis, trivet)
potrack
  hangs, bears, never blooms, 1067
potato
  many eyes, no nose, 11
  many eyes, no mouth, 16
  buried alive, the young live, the old die, 95
  many eyes, never cries, 276
  eyes can't see, 277
potato vine
  horse in stable, mane outside, 412
pounds
  rich man wants more, 1725
power gun
  gun that is not a gun, 824
prayer
  five apples fall from heaven, 983 n. 19
  God cannot do it, 1714
prayerbook
  man obeys the Lord, 827
  old lady, 940
prickle, prickle (prickly) hedge
  chair cannot be sat in, 1184b, 1184c
prickle (prickly) pear
  chair can't be sat in, 1184a
  bed can't be lain in, 1886
  green outside, red inside, 1510
prickly-otchin (sea urchin)
  Uncle Ned carries needles, 576b
promise. See word
pudding (black pudding, plum pudding)
  flour of England, fruit of Spain, met in rain, 1096
  flour of England, fruit of Spain, wet an old lady, 1097
  bound with napkin, tied with string, 1098
pulling manioc
  men fighting, 966–968 § 4

pump
  voids, 240 § 10
  has one leg, hand, and eye; shake his hand, 568
  shake his hand, leave him standing, 816
  shake his hand, he bleeds, 817
  strike him, he bleeds, 818
pumpian, pumpkin
  all head, no body, 520
  people in house without doors, 909
  forty soldiers in green chapel, 909
  red children in green and white house, 911
  mother bears son, son bears mother, 1007 § 12
  red or yellow when ripe, 1087
  round, yellow, many things in it, 1355
  yellow inside, green outside, 1503
  green outside, small seeds inside, 1525
  first green, then yellow, 1560
  See also calabash; gobee; gourd
pumpkin vine
  bears pigs all about, 381
  horse goes anywhere, 419
  man ties mat, 795
  rope runs, horse (cow) stands, 1203
  runs off, covers whole ground, 1204
  every bump of rope a sheet of paper, 1205
  See also vine
purse
  gully with two notches, 1107
quail
  nickey, nackey people, colors of their back, 897
  nicky, nacky people, color of brown tobacco, 898
queue
  something dangles behind house, 1145–1148 n. 5
quill, quill pen
  lies in box, not in field, 257 n. 1
  goose, calf (parchment), bee (wax) rule world, 511
  goose, calf (parchment), bee (wax) rule England, 512
  series of tortures, 674 through 677
rabbit
  runs, jumps, stops, humps, 220
  Whitey in Whitey, 843a
  ears like mule, tail like cotton boll, 1408
  four flic-flac and tail, 1476–1494 § 12
  See also hare
rabbit, unborn
  eat what was not born, 823–824

radish
  hair sticks out, 544 § 4
  white, red, stands up, 1572a
rafters
  men surround king, 993 n. 6
  lie in one bed, 1027-1028 § 3
  See also beam(s); girder(s)
rag
  holds water, water doesn't hold it, 1463
rail, rail fence, railing
  uphill, downhill, never moves, 121
  goes in and out, never moves, 133
  goes up, never down, 142
railroad
  goes to Yarmouth without moving, 128
railroad track
  two backbones, thousand ribs, 43
  runs without moving, 129
railroad train, railway train. *See* train
rain
  leaves black glove in window, 211
  girl loses keys (pearls), sun finds them, 367-369
  says "Blirp-blarp!," 445-458
  long person, 575 § 3
  novices stand in a file, 992-993 n. 6
  fruit for which one looks up, 1055-1057 § 5
  cannot be caught, 1643-1654 § 7
rainbow
  little blue man in green boat, 654
  Sandy in red, 655
  man who is not a man carries water on way that is no way, 823-824 n. 8
  high as world, red as blood, 1284
  purple, yellow, red, green, king can't reach it, 1570
raisin
  wrinkled woman carries stick, 632-644 § 16
rake
  teeth can't eat, 300
ram. *See* sheep
raspberry
  red mortar, white pestle, 632-644 n. 41
  white head puts on beautiful cap, 650-652
rat
  Titty titty bites, 340
  brother becomes ferocious, 573
rat and cat
  Four-Feet waits for Four-Feet, 463
rat and corn
  when it comes, it doesn't come, 945
rattlesnake
  old man with walking stick, 757

razor
  animal (person) grazes (roams), 1042-1044
  ax, stick, plow, 1042-1044
  mad one enters hairy one, 1416-1419 § 6
reed(s)
  people dance, 946-950 § 2
  barrel on barrel, 1105-1106 n. 11
  See also grass; rushes
reed, weaver's
  walks, remains in same place, 119-132 § 3
reeken hook (brandis, trivet)
  full of holes, holds water, 1461
reel
  white man sits on black man's head, 878
  horses (horsemen, children) pursue one another, 952-957 § 2
  brothers pursue one another, 996-1001 § 3
  sisters pursue one another, 1014-1015 § 4
  hold thread, but not bread, 1686
  See also distaff; spindle
reins. *See* horse and reins
rhubarb
  green, slender, ten bring it, 1568
rice
  flowers bloom in water, 489-490 n. 6
  sheep dry up a river, 489
  Browney goes in, Whitey comes out, 870
  white man sits on black man's chair, 882
  men bowing, 946-950 n. 8
  children (men) bathe and dry up water, 1032
rice in pot
  man leans against wall, 1032
riddle (enigma)
  seems mysterious at first, 100
ridgepole
  rides, doesn't move, 125-130 § 6
rifle
  wooden belly, iron back, 554
  Negro bellows between mountains, 665-667 n. 2
  See also bullet; bullet and gun; gun; shotgun
ring
  man with no legs or body, 571
  slave with heart on back, 933
  bottomless tub, 1172
  bottomless tub holds flesh, 1173
  no corner, 1411
  See also wedding ring
river
  horse runs, 114-118
  runs without stopping, 114
  goes, never moves, 119-132 § 10

river—*Continued*
  caravan does not return, 136
  never runs up, 143
  moves without legs, 260-265 § 4
  mouth can't talk, 288
  has bed, but never sleeps; is always moving, 289
  has bed, never sleeps; has mouth, never eats, 290
  devoured by parent, 1007 § 3
  chop tree, leave no scars, 1194-1196
  crooked, horses cannot pull it straight, 1292
  crooked, smooth as slate, 1294
  See also Mississippi River; ocean and river; Sissiboo River; stream; sun, moon, and river (wind); water
river, stones reeds
  one goes, one stands, one plays, 138-140
riverbanks
  bulls ready to fight, 966-968 n. 2
  never meet, 1003-1004 n. 42
road
  accompanies one constantly, 113
  up hill and down hill, yet stands still, 122
  up hill and down hill, never stands still, 123
  up hill and down hill, stands still, goes to mill, 124
  turns around and never moves, 131
  up hill and down hill, never tires, 137
  goes to mill, makes no tracks, 181
  goes to house, never enters, 200
  is not seen, 226 § 4
  bull in yard, horns on river, 412-413 § 8
  long animal, 575 n. 2
  long plant, 575 n. 5
  rope, turban, thong, stick, 575 n. 13
  has no end, 575 n. 19
  cannot roll it up, 575 n. 22
  if upright, would touch sky; if with ears, would hear all; if with tongue, would tell all, 575 n. 45
  long Aunty Long-long, 575
  higher than tree, lower than grass, 1281
  follow it, can't catch it, 1643-1654 § 8
  See also highway; lane; path
road, block, tree trunk
  "I go"; "I lie"; "I stand," 138-140
robin
  little, red, called by man's name, 658
rock and goat
  Four-Foot jumps on No-Foot, 466
rock and sea. *See* sea and rock
rolling pin
  two heads, one body, 519

roof
  brothers bear a plate, 993 n. 2
  patch on patch, 1437 § 1
  See also house roof; ridgepole; straw roof
room
  four robbers in one nightcap, 993 § 3
rooster
  Kingston bully-dog barks, 441
  maker never uses it, 1737
  See also cock
rope
  ten men can't set it on end, 1663
  ten men can't tear it, 1664
  See also hair rope
rose
  five brothers, 990
rudder
  bears no fruit, 1064
rum, bottle of
  No-Foot (One-Foot) man brings down Two-Foot, 467
  No-Sense on table won't trouble you, 468
  chop off man's head, drink his blood, 805b
runners. *See* sled runners
rushes
  man beard waves, 544 § 2
  people dance, 946-950 § 2
  See also grass
rust
  eats, never swallows, 243
rye in sacrificial vessel
  rams in iron sheepfold, 489-490 n. 4

sack. *See* bag; maltsack
saddle(s)
  back of skin, belly of rags, 553-554 § 4
  peasant with three belts, 678 § 5
  two men talking, 965
  born in woods, 1058-1062 § 8
  lower than dog, higher than horse, 1281 n. 7
  steps of iron, bed of wood, 1436-1447 n. 18
  tires horse, worries man, 1564
saddlebags
  men pulling each other's beards, 966-968 § 7
  sisters (brothers) do not see each other, 1016
sail(s)
  over water, under water, 172c
  leaves on tree, 1036
sails of windmill
  sister pursues sister, 1015b

Index of Solutions 945

salak (palm)
  person with red hair, 632–644 § 9
salt
  comes to king's table, 737 § 2
  water kills it, 1008
  kings eat it, dogs don't, 1262 n. 2
  fruit good to eat, 1262 nn. 3, 5
  grows without blossoms (root), 1262 nn. 6–7, 9
  little bit serves king, 1262
salt and water
  lives in water, water kills it, 1008
saltcellar
  round head, small body, 96
samovar
  fire burns in water, 1440–1441 n. 4
sand
  small but bears church, 728 n. 5
sandals and feet
  four feet, two heads, 48–55 n. 18
sausage grinder
  eats and never gets full, 237
saw
  hundred teeth, no mouth, 18
  chews fine, never wearies, 239
  eats and voids, 240 § 1
  teeth cannot eat, 298
  insatiable, 776–777
  long, bares its teeth, 1295–1296 nn. 1–2
  crooked as rainbow, teeth like cat, 1296
sawdust
  neither straight nor crooked wood, 1117
sawing
  men fighting, 966–968 § 2
sawmill
  hums all day, 231
  See also mill saw
sawyers and log
  alive above and below, dead between, 1436–1447 § 2
scale, marker on. *See* marker on scale
scales
  six legs, two heads (soles), 48–55 § 5
  See also steelyard
scissors
  long legs, crooked thighs, 81
  creature with eyes in back, 228
  blind it to use it, 228
  eyes can't see, legs can't walk, 305–310
  horse with two ears bites at tail, 417
  brother (birds, animals) fight, 966–968 § 1
  brothers kiss, 968 n. 6
  five guide, two watch, 970–975 § 6
  opens like barn door, shuts like trap, 1395

up straight, down cross, 1453
two rings, two ends, 1476–1494 § 28
scorpion
  saddle can't be mounted, 1183–1186
scythe
  teeth, no mouth, 18–21
  looks homeward, 191 § 1
  rises high, is driven into ground, 361
  goes over field, rests at home, 445–458
sea
  reaches both poles, 105
  goes day and night, never stops, 116
  man's mouth foams, 750
  talks constantly, 751
  tree with good fruit, 1262 n. 3
  grumbling crone carries good fruit, 1262 n. 5
  See also ocean and river; surf; swell; tide; wave(s)
sea and rock
  goes day and night, cannot fill belly, 238
  cannot converse, 765
sea-egg (sea urchin)
  monk loaded with pegs, 576 n. 3
  house covered with pins, 1119
sea gull
  great big tee, 700
seasons
  four men pursue one another, 952–957 § 7
  four persons of different natures, 984
  See also months; winter; year
secret
  too much for one, enough for two, 1738
self-heater (flatiron)
  back as round as belly, 44
  humpback, smooth belly, 45a
servant
  Whitey sends Whitey, 847, 852, 853
sewing
  five carry the judge, 979 n. 2
sewing machine. *See* machine
shadow
  cannot be seen in the dark, 113
  catch it when one sits down, 113
  cannot walk across it, 113
  follows wherever you go, 113
  goes over and under water without touching, 147
  does not rustle, 164 § 3
  does not get wet, 165–173 § 3
  goes to water, doesn't drink, 246–253 § 9
  neither flesh nor bone, yet goes about, 265
  falls, is not broken, 1192–1196 § 3
  big, light, sixty horses can't pull it, 1260
  everyone has it, 1573–1575 § 1
  seek it, do not take it, 1591–1592

946   English Riddles

shadow—*Continued*
  cannot go without it, 1614–1615
  no one can touch it, 1643–1654 § 6
  can't be cut, 1665–1666 § 2
  the larger it is, the less you see, 1690–1697 § 2
  nothing but has a name, 1712
  God hasn't it, 1721 n. 5
shadow and man. *See* man and shadow
shaving
  cutting grass (trees), 1116
sheaf (sheaves)
  defend me from hens, 561–562 n. 1
  man beaten, shaved, stabbed, 674–680
  girt with belts, 678 § 2
  brothers wear one hat, 993 § 2
shears. *See* scissors
she-cat
  like cat, 1403–1404
sheep
  leaves rags on bushes, 209
  meadow and fountain, 1100–1108 n. 23
  four run, two look, 1476–1494 § 7
shepherd
  sees his like, 1715–1720 n. 15
ship
  fish with two heads, 30
  beast with ten tails, one foot, 58
  leaves no track, 227
  bird flies high, robs, kills, 358
  goes on its belly, 372
  goose walks without legs, 372
  horse never eats, 414a
  horse carries many things in belly, 414b
  village goes over the sea, 828 n. 12
  dead carries the living, 828
  woman dresses and undresses, 1036
  tree with root and leaves, 1036
  born in wood, 1058–1062 § 1
  floor up, roof down, 1120
  can't go without weight, 1615
  See also boat; vessel
shirt
  arms, no legs, 6 § 2
  neck, no head, 6 § 2
  dances all day, rests all night, 695–699 § 6
shoe(s)
  many eyes, no nose, 14
  tongue, no mouth, 17
  cries without tears, 274
  tongue can't talk, 296
  tongue can't talk, eyes can't see, 311
  soul can't be saved, tongue can't talk, eyes can't see, 312
  five eyes can't see, 329

  goes "trip-trap" all day, 445–458
  runs about all day, rests under bed at night, 445
  eats meat all day, gapes at night, 453 § 1
  full of flesh all day, empty at night, 453 § 2
  runs about all day, gapes for bones at night, 453
  runs about, sits with tongue out, 454
  runs about, sits in corner, 456
  goes to river, stops, 458
  dead bears the living, 828–829 § 1
  two blacks leap, 862
  five rooms, one door, 908
  house with five people, 908
  brothers full all day, empty at night, 991
  house inhabited by five unequal brothers, 1040–1041 n. 6
  two boats, one man aboard, 1167
  full all day, empty at night, 1455a
  tied, it goes; loosened, it stops, 1689
  See also boot(s); slippers
shoe, wooden
  grown in forest, 1058–1062 § 13
shoelace
  ladder by day, ring at night, 1342
shoe nail, shoe tack
  goes on its head, 188
  goes on its head, sits in house at night, 189
shoemaker and bench
  six feet, two heads, one mind, 48–55 § 3
shoot. *See* banana shoot; coconut, shoot in
shot. *See* bullet
shotgun
  bites, never swallows, 242
  long, black fellow bellows, 755b
  See also gun; rifle
shovel
  man with beard, 544 § 8
shrub
  throw it away, 1637
shuttle
  Polly Pickett runs with one leg tied, 557
sieve
  room with thousand windows, 10–16
  forty (hundred, thousand) eyes, no nose, 12
  thousand eyes, no mouth, 15
  voids through eyes, 240 § 7
  woman with boil can't sit, 576 n. 10
  woman bleeds from nose, 817
  cut down in wood, lay with horses, 1058–1062 § 5
  deep as well, sea can't fill it, 1289
  round, deep, Mississippi can't fill it, 1319
  round as saucer, shallow as cup, 1347

Index of Solutions   947

the more holes, the less it weighs, 1690–1697 n. 5
See also sift, sifter; strainer
sift, sifter
  hundred (thousand) eyes, no nose, 10
  thousand eyes, no mouth, 15
  one door, thousand windows, 1131
  round, deep, river can't fill it, 1321
  round as saucer, thousand holes, 1333a
  round as biscuit, thick as mole, 1351
  pit de patte', three times a day, 1707
  See also cinder sifter; sieve
sight
  reaches sky, 1471
  this came, that went, 1578 n. 11
  moves swiftly, 1680 § 3
  See also eye(s)
silence
  talking breaks it, 1668
  have it all the time, talking breaks it, 1669
silkworm
  round, then slender, then a hermit, 672
  buried before it is dead, 673
silver
  series of tortures, 674–680 n. 36
sin
  raven without wings on oak without branches, 367–369 n. 57
  you come out, I go in, 959
  Devil's daughter, 1009
  can't take it off, 1713
  all but God have it, 1721 n. 3
sinkhole
  round, deep, can't lift it, 1327b
Sissiboo River
  crooked as a ram's horn, 1298
sister
  cannot marry her, 1070
skelion (can)
  baby without belly, 556
skillet
  round as moon, black as coal, 1305c
  round as pail, black as coal, 1307
  round as biscuit, slick as mole, 1349
  black as mole, long tail, 1361
  See also frying pan
skinnip
  grows on tree, 1076
  See also cennep
skirt
  bottomless tub, 1172–1173 § 3 . .
sky
  face clean by day, scabby by night, 576–577 n. 11
  horse runs without sweating, 784 n. 2
  silk without seams, 1213 § 4

sheet (blanket) can't be folded, 1217
blanket covers world, 1219
blanket can't be spread, 1221
tablecloth can't fall, 1229b
nothing so broad or so long, 1267
higher than house, 1280
patch on patch, 1437 § 9
no rider mounts chip cherry, 1622
See also earth and sky; moon, stars, and sky; stars and sky; wind, sky, and earth
slander
  too heavy for one, enough for two, 1738 n. 7
slate
  black man walks on black road, 884
sled
  runners can't walk, tongue can't talk, 315
  Eight-Legs chases Four-Legs, 461–462 n. 31
  dead pursues living, 1432–1434 n. 1
sled runners
  dogs race, 952–957 § 10
  brothers pursue on another, 996–1001 § 5
  sisters pursue one another, 1014–1015 § 3
sleep
  dead buries the living, 835 n. 3
  have it without knowing, 1576
  maker doesn't need it, 1728–1737 § 3
sleep, hours of
  Nature requires five, 1722
sleeve
  first stiff, then slack, 1448–1452 § 8
slippers
  lie at bedside, gape for bones, 453f
  See also shoe(s)
sliver. *See* thorn (splinter)
sloe
  stick in backside, 632–644 § 21
smith (horseshoer)
  makes shoes without awl, 796a
  makes shoes without leather, 796c
smoke
  goes up, never down, 141
  touches water, is not wet, 165–173 § 6
  makes no track, 183
  goes out through keyhole, 196
  seen, not felt, 226
  smokes, can't chew, 244
  moves without legs, 260–265 § 6
  moves without bones, 264–265 § 11
  can't catch Hitty-titty, 339
  flies without feathers, 365–366 § 2
  climbs without legs, 365–366 § 2
  black lamb, blue feet, 389b
  mule in stable, tail outside, 413

smoke—Continued
  man in room, beard outside, 544 § 9
  long man reaches sky, 575 § 2
  can't bear a leaf, 728
  horses can't pull it out, 748–749 § 3
  man who sees it doesn't want it, 823–824 n. 7
  Whitey can't climb Whitey, 859
  man goes to sky, 941
  weeps, goes to heaven, dies, is begot by another, 942
  son on roof, father not yet born, 985
  mother begets child, 1007 § 7
  high as castle, horses can't pull it, 1268
  higher than palace, as fine as silk, 1282
  can't climb chip cherry, 1616, 1617
  can't climb cloud, 1626
  can't catch handful, 1643
  goes about house, can't catch bowlful, 1644
  doesn't touch people in house, 1655
  can't hit or knock it, 1673
  See also fire and smoke
snail
  moves without legs, 261
  bloodless, boneless, yet goes about, 264
  casts skin, 350
  horse drops silver, 418
  flesh within, bones outside, 588 § 3
  neither fish nor flesh, but has horns, 603
  carries house on back, 727
  small, but fills house, 1473 n. 4
snake
  big (bald) head, no a——, 7
  makes but one track, 175
  walks without feet, 263
  thief without feet, 367–369 n. 62
  eyeless, armless, crawls on belly, 561–562 n. 6
  wears seamless dress, 1213 § 2
  crooked as rainbow, slim as ja', 1293
  crooked as rainbow, thieving as cat, 1297
  stick on ground, 1466 note
  lady, 1466 note
  long, slim, slender, 1466
snare
  dead catches the living, 828–836 § 4
  round, two strings, 1356
  See also noose
snot
  lords (rich) keep it, beggars throw it away, 1724
  See also mucus
snow
  touches every twig in wood, 145
  makes no track, 181–185 § 7
  leaves white cap on stump, 208

  leaves glove (sheet) in window, 210
  flies without wings, 365–366 § 6
  hen lays eggs, 367–369 n. 66
  white bird featherless, 367, 368
  dove flies down, king eats it, 369
  gull lights on every tree, 370
  maiden with white kerchief, 607–631 n. 11
  falls, doesn't break, 1192–1196 § 4
  blanket covers everything but water, 1219–1220 n. 2
  blanket covers world, 1219–1220 n. 5
  patch on patch, 1437 § 9
  falls from heaven, sticks to earth, 1573–1575 n. 18
  chips fall, 1605 § 1
snuff
  Miss Mary going upstairs, 596
  can't pick it up, 1658
  young throw it away, old treasure it, 1724
snuff taking
  two take me to two caves, 970–975 § 3
snuffers
  ears like barn door, belly like box, 1407
  two little rings, two poles, 1476–1494 § 27
  See also candle snuffers
soap
  black goat turns white, 1542–1546 § 1
  grows thinner the more it works, 1700
song of a drum
  goes through woods without touching, 155
soot
  grows with root above, 1055–1057 § 5
  goes up black, comes down and covers all, 1558
sorb apple
  large, bitter, sweet, 1269–1275 § 1
soul
  can't be seen, 1715–1720 n. 16
sound
  goes through bush without touching, 157
  goes through rick without touching, 161
  touches water, is not wet, 165–173 § 4
  goes without a shadow, 186 n. 1
  is not seen, 226 § 3
soursop
  child wears prickles (bumps), 577
  green house, black children, 915
  green, white, has seeds, 1074
  house with nails outside, 1118
  green as grass, white as milk, 1368
  green outside, white inside, 1501
  black inside, white inside, green outside, 1516

Index of Solutions 949

green outside, white inside, black seeds,
  1521
sovereign (coin)
  small, worth a lot, 1472
sow
  stands on this side of wood, looks over, 224
sow and pigs
  ten heads, ten tails, forty feet (nails), 56
spark
  flies without wings, 365–366 § 2
  geese fly to heaven, 941–942
  man goes halfway to heaven, 941
  twenty-four dancing (riding) ladies, 949
  here it is, now it's not, 1578 n. 6
  See also fire, spark, and smoke; spark, smoke, and ashes
spark, smoke, and ashes
  three men start for heaven, 941
spear
  cannot lie in chest, 258
  travels about, takes no space at home, 695–699 § 4
spear grass
  two stand, two fly, 1476–1494 § 17
spectacles
  I see when eyes are covered, 228
  ridden without bridle, 428
  man carries eyes in case, 522
  stick your nose in, 1723
Sphinx, Riddle of
  creature walks on four, two, and three legs, 46
  on four legs in morning, two at noon, three at night, 47
spider
  sleeps all day, walks all night, 255
  moves without wings between silken strings, 356
  frog jumps without touching water, 348
  lives on high, 685 § 2
  through a rock, through a reel, 1599
spider (frying pan)
  round as a biscuit, black as ink, 1303
spider and web
  lesser than mouse, more windows than house, 1265
spindle
  woman (animal) becomes pregnant (fat), 1455–1457 § 2
  See also distaff
spinning
  five under roof are wet, 961–963 § 8
  five drive, five wait, 979 n. 5
spinning wheel
  beast snarls, 387
  sings, can't talk; runs, can't walk, 714

spinning wheel, treadle of
  headless fox ate white goose, 367–369 n. 59
spit (turnspit)
  long father, potbellied mammy, 1017c
  the slower the work, the sooner done, 1701
spittle
  can't pick it up, 729–731 § 3
splinter
  can't be put together again, 738–747 § 3
  brought it home, 1633
  the more I looked for it, the more I hated it, 1636
  ran and found it, looked for it, ran away with it, 1638
spoke(s)
  twenty-four men pursue another, 957
  brother pursues brother, 997
  brothers in one pair of drawers, 1005 n. 6
  lie in one bed, never meet, 1027–1028 § 5
sponge
  holes around it, holds water, 1424
  full of holes, holds water, 1459
spool
  noody, nawdy, two heads, one body, 517
spoon
  horse (bird, cow) with tail, 412–413 § 3
  loaded ship goes to cave, 412–413 § 3
  born in woods, stabs men's throats, 1058–1062 § 6
  ship and propeller, 1165
  in dry, out wet, 1448–1452 § 6
spring (of water)
  kettle boils, 1193 § 3
  full of holes, holds water, 1460
spring. *See* seasons
squash
  green, long, white, has seeds, 1522
  See also calabash; gobee; gourd
squashberry
  chop off man's head, drink his blood, 807
squeak
  accompanies wagon, 1614b
  See also noise
staff
  runs about, sits on small spot, 695–699 § 5
  See also cane; walking stick
stake
  high, low, 1281 n. 12
standpipe
  man always bleeding, 817b
star(s)
  lost without being stolen, 470
  countless sheep, 484

star(s)—Continued
  rollers plunge into water, 489–490 § 3
  Peep-peep has one eye, 525
  Little hittie wrapped in a whittle, 599
  seven sons can't converse, 988
  people seen by night, not by day, 1023–1024
  can't count children, 1024
  children glitter, 1025
  flowers in field (garden), 1071
  roses on bush, 1071
  dish of nuts (peas, rice), 1093–1095
  vegetables, 1093–1095
  nuts (sand) scattered about, 1093–1095
  peppers ripe at night, 1093
  fruits vanish in daylight, 1094
  countless apples (fruits), 1095
  candles (lights), 1189–1191
  can't be found in morning, 1217–1218
  blanket full of lice, 1226 note
  bones, 1227 § 1
  household objects, 1227 § 3
  pustules, 1227 § 4
  pearls, jewels, stones, 1227 § 5
  buttons, 1227 § 6
  eggs, 1227 § 7
  countless coins, 1227
  can't count things, 1227c
  plates washed in evening vanish during night, 1228
  articles of food, 1230–1234
  higher than house, higher than tree, 1279
  higher than house, smaller than mouse, 1281
  scattered chips, 1605 § 2
  See also Pleiades; sun, earth, stars, and road
stars and clouds
  money cannot be counted, sheet cannot be folded, 1225a
  biscuits cannot be counted, cloth cannot be folded, 1229a
stars and moon
  mare and foal, 496b
  minaret, flowers, tulip, 1071
  king's son, flowers, 1071
  See also moon, stars, and sky; moon, stars, sun, and water; sun, moon, and stars
stars and sky
  sheet full of small change, 1226
statue
  maiden in red jacket, 632–644 § 15
staves in barrel
  men lie in one bed, 1027–1028 § 6
  two trees project from forest, 1040–1041

stays (corset)
  twelve legs, 569
steam
  touches water, is not wet, 165–173 § 6
  cries "Oh!" and runs out, 445–458
  son appears before father's birth, 985 § 2
steam engine
  brass toes, brass nose, 267
  See also engine; locomotive
steelyard
  horse bucks when ridden, 430
  crooked, notched, straight, 1409
  See also scales
stick. *See* cane; Sphinx, Riddle of; staff; walking stick
stick for beating clothes
  born in woods, cries out in village, 1058–1062 § 7
stick-horse
  man rides and yet walks, 718
stocking(s)
  only feet and legs, 27
  two thick worms with open mouths, 453
  sausage by day, gut at night, 453
  small house in large house, 1156–1160 n. 14
  ten drag woolly bag, 1200b
  naked one slips into furry one, 1416–1419 n. 2
  hairy without, hairy within, 1416
  wider the hole, the better to get in, 1467
stomach
  flesh outside skin, 588 § 9
  chest cannot be opened, 1187 n. 7
stool
  Two-Legs (man) sat on Three-Legs, 461
  Two-Legs (maid) sat on Three-Legs, 462
storm
  Arthur O'Bower roars, 762a
stove
  four eyes, four legs, 77
  insatiable, 236
  sits on four legs, smokes pipe, 320
  eyes can't see, 327
  legs can't walk, eyes can't see, 332
  man with beard outside, 544 § 9
  lady in winter, servant in summer, 695–699 n. 29
  black father, black brothers, red sisters, 1018
  too much for one, enough for two, 1738 n. 9
  See also cookstove; pot and stove
stove, fire, and smoke
  fat mother, pretty daughter, skipping son, 1017 § 3

Index of Solutions

strainer
  round, deep, river can't fill it, 1321
  round as saucer, Mississippi can't fill it, 1333b
  thousand holes, 1412
  See also sieve; sift, sifter; tea strainer
strap
  up laughing, down crying, 769
strawberry
  red cow, 632–644 n. 35
  woman with red cap, 632–644 § 2
  red spot where lady squat, 732
  pulled off red soldier's head, ate flesh, 806–815 § 4
  first white (green), then red, 1559
straw roof
  holes hold water, 1459–1463 § 2
stream
  runs, never gets tired, 138
  flat as plate, crooked as snake, 1300
  See also creek; river; water
stump and hen
  Blackey goes in Blackey, leaves Whitey, 867
suckling a child
  meat fills the crack, 1235
sugar apple
  child with bumpy skin, 577b
  black as soot, 1365
  white, green, has seeds, 1523
sugar cane
  child's head gives birth to mother, 1007 § 12
  well, without top or bottom, holds water, 1174
  goes in wet, comes out dry, 1448–1458 n. 1
  in green, out yellow, 1546
  See also cane
sugar mill
  six milching cows, 392
Śukrācarya
  three legs, six eyes, 48–55
sun
  comes from beyond ocean, 102
  enters locked house, 112
  never wearies, 140
  never touches house (wood), 164
  makes no sound, 164 § 1
  falls in water, doesn't splash, 164 § 2
  goes through water, isn't wet, 165–173 § 1
  goes through, makes no hole, 181–185 § 3
  looks in window, 192
  goes through keyhole, 194
  goes to door, doesn't knock, 216
  goes to water, doesn't drink, 246–253 § 10
  moves without legs, 260–265 § 8
  sits on oak, no one can catch it, 367–369 n. 51
  hare runs on ice, 388
  ox falls in ravine, 390–392
  bull bears calves and eats them, 390–392
  deer cannot be shot, 391
  deer runs alone, 392b
  horse in stable, tail projects, 412–413 § 9
  old lady has one eye, 526
  branches of tree extend into room, 544
  man outside, beard in room, 544 § 10
  chariot rolls from behind mountain, 716
  man makes no track, 716
  Hickamore, Hackamore can't be pulled away, 748
  eats nurse, 775
  son rules world, 798
  two hundred eagles, three hundred wings, 1037–1038 n. 27
  oak with thousand branches, 1037–1038 n. 37
  flower, 1071 n. 18
  apple among nuts, 1095
  unwoven towel dries hands, 1104
  barrel of gold, 1170
  house can't be opened, 1187 n. 6
  golden pot (pan), 1189–1191 n. 13
  golden stick, 1189–1191 n. 23
  golden candlestick in tall house, 1190
  falls, doesn't break, 1192–1196 § 6
  dish of butter, 1230–1234
  johnny cake serves world, 1233
  round, plump, mounts meetinghouse, 1344
  red as apple, 1375
  many climb chipcherry, 1621
  can't catch bowlful, 1646
  can't touch it, 1657
  can't take it off, 1659
  moves fastest, 1680 § 2
  See also sunbeam; sunlight, sunshine
sun and bay
  boy doesn't want to leave mother, 701
sun and cloud
  gray horse drinks up water, 489–490 § 2
sun and moon
  two cows (falcons), 496
  mare and colt, 496a
  man with two eyes, 525–534 n. 4
  twin children of different natures, 967
  men fighting, 967
  boats cannot overtake each other, 1001 n. 14
  brothers race, 1001
  two duff serve world, 1234
  two stumps, 1252
  two walk, two stand, 1476–1494 § 14

English Riddles

sun and moon—*Continued*
  goes away red, comes back white, 1542–1546 § 5
sun and snow. *See* snow
sun and stars
  ram and many sheep, 484 note
sun, earth, stars, and road
  stallion, coffers, belt, cloth, 1215–1216 n. 5
sun, moon, and river (wind)
  one works by day, another by night, a third all the time, 138–140
sun, moon, and stars
  two geese, one hundred and twenty sparrows, 484–486 n. 4
  camels, 484–486 n. 8
sunbeam
  enters lady's chamber, 192b
  goes in window (keyhole), 192c
  flies without wings, 365–366 § 4
  Hickamore, Hackamore on a kitchen door, 748d
sunlight, sunshine
  white gloves lie in window, 212
  comes to king's table, 737 § 4
  Humpty Dumpty falls, can't stand, 741
  Hickamore, Hackamore can't be driven away, 748
  house full, can't catch bowl full, 1646
  milk spilled at door, 1659 n. 3
  men can't take it off, 1659c
  See also light; moonshine; sun; sunbeam
surf
  beats day and night, 751–754
  See also sea; swell; wave(s)
swallow
  in front like a fork, 1436–1447 § 3
swallow (meaning obscure)
  sits when you sit, 737
swan
  ship with sails whiter than snow, 1168
sweat
  can't get handful, 1654
swell (wave)
  brothers can't catch one another, 1000
sword
  born in smithy, 401–404 § 4
  horse (goat) in stable, tail projects (horns project), 412–413 § 4
  boards above and below, man between, 1436–1447 n. 7
table
  hoof, no head or tail, 28
  one top, two ends, four legs, 78
  man with silken kerchief, 208–209

  legs can't walk, 305
  four brothers under one hat, 993
table, platter, peas, bacon
  clay on oak, peas on clay, pig on peas, 1156–1160 n. 9
tache (boiler in sugar refinery)
  milking cow, 492
tack. *See* shoe nail, shoe tack
tadpole
  all head, no body, 2
tail, cow's
  moves, doesn't leave spot, 125–130 § 8
  grows downward, 1056
tail, horse's
  herbs watered and tilled, 1042
  one goes in, thousands come out, 1448–1458
tail, peacock's
  more eyes than forty men, 39
talking machine
  talks without life, 761
tap (faucet)
  grows in woods, 1058–1062 § 6
taro
  foot like pot, body like stick, head like umbrella, 1436–1447 n. 14
tea
  black rams in courtyard, 489–490 n. 3
teakettle
  red lips, black beard, 548
  sings all day, 754
  round, black, 1410
  See also teapot
team, baseball
  eighteen legs, catches flies, 271
teapot
  nose can't smell, 286
tea strainer
  round, deep, river can't fill it, 1322
tears and hair
  wash in water not rained, wrap in cloak not woven, 1104 n. 3
teats
  four trees not wet by rain, 961–963 § 5
  upside down, bottles do not leak, 1199
  See also fingers milking
teeth (very rarely: tooth)
  dogs (wolves), 497–510 § 4
  sharks, 497–510 § 6
  chickens, geese or other white birds, 497–510 § 7
  insects, 497–510 § 8
  sheep, 497
  cows, 501
  horses in a meadow, 502
  white horses on red hill, 503

Index of Solutions 953

horses on blue hill, 504
horses in rows, 505
horses gallop in unison, 506
horses on bridge, 507
man (girl) on red horse, 581
white man binds hand, 582
white children play in red, 841
soldiers, 841 § 1
monks (nuns) in white, 841 § 2
company of people, 841 § 3
persons threshing, 841 § 4
mill, 841 § 5
kneading bread, 841 § 6
Whitie all around town, 857
people in chapel, 908–916 § 3
men fighting, 966–968 § 6
tree with crown down, root up, 1055–1057 § 4
red house, white seats, 1146
house with white galleries, 1148
red house, white fence, 1149
axes, knives, 1150 § 1
bones, 1150 § 2
stones, 1150 § 3
pearls, shells, 1150 § 4
chips, 1150 § 5
fence always wet, 1150
box of worms, 1355 n. 11
See also face; head; mouth; teeth and tongue
teeth and tongue
snake guarded by soldiers (stones), 497–510 § 5
fish in water, 497–510 § 6
white and red sheep, 498
white cows licked by red bull, 499
white and red cattle, 500
cows and whip, 501
white horses and one red horse, 508
white horses licked in by red horse, 509
red man whips horses, 510
armies with ambassador between, 966–968 n. 6
men fighting, 966–968 § 6
red dog behind fence, 1151
flower in a garden, 1151 n. 1
devil above and below, McKintosh between, 1442
marble above and below, bride plays between, 1443–1444
See also face; head; mouth; tongue
teeth of harrow. See harrow, teeth of
telephone
two frogs in double pond, 471
know voice, can't see face, 1685

tennis ball
round, can't rest, 1468
tent
legs cannot walk, wings cannot fly, 305–310
thimble
forty (thousand) eyes, no nose, 13
thousand eyes can't see, 330
man covered with pockmarks, 576–577
many windows, wouldn't hold mouse, 1128
many windows, one door, 1129
barrel filled with flesh, 1172–1173 § 2
small with many windows, 1263
small with many eyes, 1264
round, deep, as many windows as a hotel, 1320
small with many holes, 1333 n. 2
many holes, none goes through, 1413
thistle
nine heads, nine tails, 60
man with red cap, 632–644 § 7
stands on one leg, 1121–1126 § 5
See also nettle
thorn (splinter)
went to wood and got it, 1632, 1634, 1635, 1639, 1641
thornbush
Cicily sage in cage, children die, 1022d
thought
flies high, doesn't leave place, 364
never seen, 1581
quickest in the world, 1680 § 1
See also anxiety; mind
threshing machine
insatiable bull (cow), 400
thread. See needle; reel
thread, ball of
horses can't pull it, 748–749 § 4
See also bottom of thread
threshold
grew in woods, 1058–1062 § 11
neither in nor out, 1423 § 2
thunder
is not seen, 226 § 3
rattling wagon, 398
cow groans, is heard over world, 398
dog barks, 442
not fish, flesh, or voice; makes noise when born, 665
no carpenter can make Holderdebolder, 738–747 n. 5
grumbles over world, 763
noise of chair pulled about, 1181
thunder and lightning
sword strikes here, tip flashes there, 398

954   *English Riddles*

thunder and lightning—*Continued*
  horse here, reins there, 398
  through the rack, through the reel, 1601d
tick of watch
  goes through bush without touching, 156
tide
  goes night and day, 115
tie. *See* cow-tie
tiler
  carries way on his neck, 190b
tiles
  thousand legs up, thousand legs down, 64–70
time
  only one, neither past nor future exists, 97
  runs without legs, 262 n. 1
  tree with leaves black on one side, white on other side, 1037–1038 n. 31
  longest, shortest, swiftest, 1680
tobacco
  done on top, raw on bottom, 1244
  See also hookah; pipe
today
  named yesterday, 97
toe(s)
  Blackey covers ten, 864
  five people in house, 908
  ten prisoners, 970–975 § 7
tomato
  red outside, seeds inside, 1524
tombstone
  maker doesn't need it, 1736
tomorrow
  always will be, 97
tongs
  long legs, short (crooked) thighs, little head, 79
  long legs, short thighs, bald head, 80
  dead digs up the living, 835 n. 5
tongue
  moves, doesn't leave the place, 125–130 § 7
  goes without bones, 264–265 § 8
  red dog barks, 438–444 § 5
  snake, 497–510 § 5
  fish (crocodile), 497–510 § 6
  rooster, 497–510 § 7
  red (brown) sheep, 498
  red bull (cow), 499
  wet red calf, 499–501 n. 2
  whip, 501
  red horse, 508, 509
  red man, 510
  rag always wet, 1150 n. 8
  wet lady, 1150 n. 16

  wet plank doesn't rot, 1150 n. 21
  rocker on a red hill, 1180
  out, it wriggles about; ill, it's still, 1422
  round, it rolls all day, stops at night, 1469
  See also teeth and tongue
tongue of wagon. *See* wagon tongue
toothpick
  two bring it, five use it, 970–975 § 8
tow, distaff, spindle
  mother, father, son, 1017 § 2
towel
  you here, I there, 1578 n. 14
  See also drying hands
town clock
  head without hair, 4a
  See also bell; clock
track
  needle leaves it everywhere, 176
  the first drop in a field, 1051
  See also railroad track
train
  can run, can't walk, 217
  can holler, can't talk, 230
  moves without legs, 260–265 § 12
  man going to town faces town, 722
  dead bears the living, 829
  can't overtake it, 1611
trap
  dead catches the living, 828–836 § 4
trash
  silent in morning, man speaks in evening, 759
  dead cry out when stepped on, 834b
tree(s)
  one leg, many hands, 71
  rocks, never stands still, 118
  pig dies when tail is cut, 384
  gladdens me in spring, cools me in summer, 587
  pretty in spring, naked in winter, 587
  brings forth tongueless young, 1021
  children die, but mother lives, 1022
  never of equal height, 1040–1041 n. 2
  gets shorter when it is cut, 1696
  See also apple tree; birch; bough; cabbage (cabbage palm); cedar; cherry; chestnut; chinkapin tree; Christmas tree; coconut, picking a; coconut palm, climbing a; dogwood; euphorbia tree; fatwood; grugru (pecan) tree; leaves and tree; mango tree; mimosa; mulberry; mustard tree; oak (acorn, tree, ship); palm; palm, sacred; pecan tree; pomegranate; prickle (prickly) pear; salak (palm). Fruits and nuts are separately listed. In the

Index of Solutions

West Indies, "tree" is often used as a generic term for "plant," as in the term "cane tree" (sugar cane)
tree, climbing a
　man faces town, 724
　See also coconut, picking a; coconut palm, climbing a
tree, felling a
　kill ox, burn flesh, 806–815 n. 4
tree and leaves. See leaves and tree
trees in a colonnade
　stand at a distance from one another, yet they meet, 1003–1004 n. 47
tripod
　three lads girt with belt, 678 § 7
trousers
　five push, ten pull, 976–982 n. 3
　man sees and takes two roads, 1108
　hairy within, hairy without, 1416–1419 § 3
　hold it at both sides, thrust in middle, 1416–1419 § 3
　See also pants
tub
　over water, under water, never touches water, 165d, 165e
　round as mill wheel, luggit like cat, 1343
　See also barrel; cask; staves in barrel
tumblers (glasses)
　three daughters, 1010
turf
　black within, black without, 1533
turfstack
　patch on patch, 1437 § 8
turkey
　feathers outside, pink inside, 1535
turmeric
　earth above and below, girl between, 1105–1106 n. 4
turn-stick
　Miss Nance wheels thrice, 693
　rain doesn't cover it, 1115
turnstile
　four arms stop no one, 266
turtle
　eat insides, throw away skin, 805–818 n. 10
　carries house on back, 727 § 2
　brass sky, straight earth, cat's paws, 1405–1408 n. 6
　plate above and below, flesh between, 1436–1447 § 5
　many patches on clothing, 1437 § 12
　See also mud turtle

U (letter of alphabet)
　if pursued, does not fly from you, 469
udder. See teats
umbrella
　child without leg, arm, back, or belly, 570
　bones outside, flesh inside, 588 § 6
　animal (person) with several ribs, one leg, 1121–1126 § 1
　house with one prop (post, rafter, leg), 1121
　many rafters on one post, 1122
　opens like barn door, shuts like trap, 1401
　black outside and inside, 1513
　won't go up chimney (drain), 1604
　pulled, it is a cane; pushed, it is a tent, 1681
utensil (chamber pot)
　Miss Nancy with arm akimbo, 552

vanes of windmill
　sisters pursue one another, 1015a
　See also windmill
vat. See barrel; cask; tub
vellum
　calf, goose (pen), bee (wax) rule world (England), 511, 512
vermicelli
　goes in wooden door, out iron door, takes hot and cold baths, 680 n. 9
　See also macaroni
vermin
　taken and lost, not taken and kept, 1592
vessel
　goes, cannot see, 227
　dead carries the living, 828d
　can't see where it divides water, 1666
vest
　opens like barn door, 1399b
vine
　walks without feet, 264–265 § 7
vine and fruits
　snake lays eggs, 381–382
　lady in house, sleeves in yard, 412–413 § 2
　See also gourd; grape, vine, shoot, wine, brandy; potato vine; pumpkin vine
violin
　linden sings, horse flicks tail over ram, 1058–1062 n. 27
　once green and growing, now dead and roaring, 1059a
　grew in woods, winters in town, 1061a
　See also fiddle
viper
　child kills mother, 1007 § 9
virgin
　unplanted pomegranate, 1070 n. 4

vise. *See* holdfast
voice
  does not touch anything, 151
  goes through woods, does not touch limb, 152
  goes through branches, does not touch limb, 153
  goes through bush without touch, 153
  goes through house, does not touch anything, 162
  goes through air, does not touch earth, 163
  goes without shadow, 186 n. 1
vulture on dead horse
  dead bears the living, 828–829 § 5

wagon
  makes two tracks, 177
  looks backward, 191 § 10
  never drinks, 249
  moves without legs, 260–265 § 11
  four legs, goes to water, doesn't drink, 293
  over water, under water, doesn't drink, 295a
  has tongue, goes to water, doesn't drink, 295b
  tongue can't eat, 295c
  tongue can't talk, 314
  can run, not walk, tongue can't talk, 316
  runs all day, stands with tongue out at night, 455
  See also buggy; cart
wagon rope
  ten men can't rear it, 1663b
wagon tongue
  never rests, goes to creek, never drinks, 256
  never drinks, 292
  See also pole of cart
waistcoat
  opens like barn door, 1399
walking stick
  white to the end, black to the middle, 1539
  See also cane; staff
wallpaper
  up ready, down unready, 1458
  when dirty, not worth dime, 1684
walls
  look at each other, 1003–1004 n. 23
  See also ceiling and floor
walnut
  merchant descends leaving cloak, 951
  green house in brown house, 1161
  locked chest on tree, 1187 n. 12
  high, bitter, soft, white, 1269
  high, low, bitter as gall, 1270
  high, low, sweet, 1271
  high, low, green, bitter, 1273
  sweet, green, bitter, high, little, 1274
  tall, low, has many rooms, 1275
  round as apple, rough as bear, 1346
  soft, white, bitter, green coat, 1359
  white as snow, green as herbs, 1392
war
  tree fights, 1050
warming pan
  up red, down black, 1556
washboard
  in dry, out wet, 1452
wasp(s)
  Hitty Titty will bite, 338
  blue coat, yellow breeches, 649
  nicky, nacky people brown as tobacco, 887
  pernicky people, 899
  nicker, nacker people going across London Bridge, 901
  soldiers in red and yellow jackets, 903
  black, blue people color of shoe, 904
  bananas can't be picked, 1248a
  big at both ends, 1431d
  no one could touch it, 1656
  See also dirtdauber; hornets; yellow jackets
wasp nest
  bridge on bridge, 1437 § 4
watch
  stopped at North Pole, 130
  goes through bush, never touches bush, 156
  looks backward, 191 § 13
  little informer in armor, 600
  Pippety-poppety eats neither corn nor hay, 780b
  round as apple, busy as bee, 1309
  round as biscuit, busy as bee, 1310
  round as biscuit, goes "Tick!," 1311
  round as dollar, busy as bee, 1312a
  round as dollar, goes "Tick!," 1312b
  round as ring, busy as bee, 1313
  round as moon, clear as crystal, 1314
  cannot win, 1688
watch, tick of
  goes through bush without touching, 156
watch pocket
  round, deep, 1335
water
  runs smooth, cannot climb, 218
  moves without feet, 260–265 § 4
  trembles at breath, bears burdens, 728
  pots boil without fire, 1177
  never gets smashed, 1194
  can't fold sheet, 1216
  can't hold it, 1643–1655 § 7
  can't hang it up, 1661–1662 n. 12

Index of Solutions

chop it and leave no chips, 1665–1666 n. 2
field without paths, 1665–1666 n. 4
can't see where it is cut, 1665
See also ice and water; salt and water
water, hot
   girl doesn't want to see brothers, 1035
   never freezes, 1711
waterfall
   roars without mouth, 751–754
waterfall and cliff
   men fighting, 966–968 § 6
watermelon
   water below, water above, 173
   child lives in bush, 683
   white pearls, emerald green, ruby red, 668–669 § 8
   comes to king's table, 737 § 3
   eat man, drink blood, 810
   eat woman, drink blood, 811
   little white children play in red, 840
   children stay in bush, 905
   house with iron key, 908–916
   pupils in church without door, 909 n. 7
   black cow eating red hay in green stable, 910–915 n. 2
   green, white, red house, black children, 910
   little niggers in a red house within a green house, 916
   mother lies in child, 1007 § 12
   grows on tree, green outside, red inside, 1083
   wash hands in water neither rain nor run, 1104d
   vault without door, 1132–1138 § 2
   green house on hill, in green house a white house, 1162
   God makes it, a knife opens it, 1187 § 3
   basin with black fish, 1355 n. 6
   green as grass, white as milk, 1369
   red as blood, but is not blood, 1376
   green outside, red inside, 1508
   green outside, yellow inside, 1509
   up green, down red, 1547
   up green, down ripe, 1548
   up green as grass, down red, 1549
   green rind, red meat, full of syrup, 1571
   See also melon
wave(s)
   eagles fight and leave foam, 397 n. 12
   girl opens kerchief, 713
   neighbors never greet, 966–968 § 9
   See also surf; swell
wax
   bee, calf (parchment), goose (pen) rule world (England), 511, 512

throw meat away, keep broth, 805–818 n. 11
   See also earwax; honeycomb
weapon
   horse in stable, 412–413 § 4
weaver's reed. *See* reed, weaver's
weaving
   horse goes through forest (brook), 459–460 n. 35
   series of tortures, 674–680 n. 38
   dead men pulling each other's hair, 967 n. 7
web, spider's
   small with many windows, 1265
wedding ring
   without bottom or top, yet holds flesh, 1173d
   fastens two, touches one, 1687
   no right woman without it, 1745
week
   seven passengers (horsemen), 983
   fir in six pieces, stork on top, 983 n. 13
   six leaves in book, seventh golden, 983 n. 20
   seven planks, 983 n. 28
   six sons, six shirts, 983
   birds (eggs) in nest, 1037
   See also days of week; year
weight
   ship can't go without it, 1615
weir
   eats and voids, 240 § 8
   dead catches the living, 828–836 § 4
well
   man voids, 240 § 10
   iron head, stone belly, 1100–1108 n. 43
   pot without bottom, 1170–1178 n. 4
   deep as cup, round as house, 1286
   black within, red without, deep, 1287
   deep as sea, horses can't pull it up, 1288
   round as an apple, deep as a cup, 1315
   round as ball, deep as cup, 1317
   round as biscuit, deep as cup (sea, well), 1318
   round as cup, oxen cannot draw it up, 1323
   round as hoop (hook), deep as cup, 1325
   round as a marble, deep as cup, 1327a
   round as an orange, deep as cup, 1328
   round as a riddle (sieve), deep as cup, 1330
   round as ring, deep as cup, 1331
   round as ring, deep as spring, 1332
   round as saucer, deep as cup, 1334
   round and long, 1341–1342 § 1
   round as apple, sweet as nothing, 1350
   grows bigger when more is taken away, 1690–1697

well sweep
  born in wood, lifts up tail at house, 1058–1062 § 6
wheat
  laid in grave, begets children, 95
  sequence of colors, 668–669 n. 8
  cradled and threshed, 671
  cut and beaten, 680
  men with clubs, 946–950 n. 9
  head in man, middle in ox, end in ground, 1436–1447 n. 8
  up with its name, down without it, 1547–1558 n. 1
  up brown, down white, 1550–1554
  See also sheaf (sheaves)
wheel(s)
  horses pursue one another, 954–957 § 1
  cattle pursue one another, 954–957 § 2
  wolves pursue one another, 954–957 § 3
  dogs pursue one another, 954–957 § 4
  swine pursue one another, 954–957 § 5
  devils, madmen pursue one another, 954–957 § 6
  four walking can't catch one another, 954
  big man pursues little man, 955
  something run after something, 956
  big brother pursues little brother, 998
  big sister pursues little sister, 1014
  children run after one another, 1029
  children can't go without one another, 1030
  See also buggy wheel(s)
wheelbarrow
  makes one track, 174
  walks on head to save its feet, 187–189
  in every window seen around, 225
  two heads, one body, 518
  feet don't touch ground, 572
  thing never catches up, 1613
whetstone
  goes, never moves, 119–132 § 13
  gives edge that it has not, 1589–1590 § 4
  more one lays it on, the faster it wastes, 1699
whey and cheese
  child kills parent, 1007 § 11
whip
  tickles where it's tender, 1464
whitewash
  small amount illuminates house, 1473 n. 5
wife
  hen and chickens, 373
  a good that one cannot have, 1070 n. 9
  chipcherry, beer, cedar, 1627
  Christ had it not, Napoleon had it, 1721

wife, name of
  man gives what he has not, 1589–1590 § 2
wig
  with and without head and tail, 29
will-o'-the-wisp
  runs over the moor, 704
wind
  goes, yet never moves, 119–132 § 9
  goes day and night, never wearies, 139
  goes through water, is not wet; through fire, is not burned, 165–173 § 5
  leaves no track, 184
  passes sun without shadow, 186
  peeps in crack, 193
  peeps in keyhole, 195
  fills house, you can't see it, 226
  moves without legs, 260–265 § 9
  walks without bones, 264–265 § 10
  flies, never rests, 357
  flies as high as sky, 362
  flies without wings, 365–366 § 1
  takes without hands, 365–366 § 1
  boy talks but you can't see him, 753
  Arthur O'Bower roars, 762
  feeds bellows, 1007 § 6
  can't catch colts, 1643–1654 n. 6
  can't catch spoonful, 1648
  See also north wind
wind (crepitus ventris)
  born without sin, 666
wind, sky, and earth
  son-in-law, father, mother, 1017 § 8
windmill
  moves without legs, 260–265 § 10
  man loses cap, can't pick it up, 729–730 § 6
  sons sent to school, 986
  brothers pursue one another, 999
  grown in the wood, 1058–1062 § 12
  See also mill-point; sails of windmill; vanes of windmill
window
  weeps and laughs, 768–769 § 2
  perspires daily, 784
  bears no fruit, 1065
  neither in nor out, 1423
  patch on patch, 1437 § 2
  cloud at night, open in day, 1455 n. 15
windowpane(s)
  eight eyes all in white, 38
  live side by side, never see each other, 1003–1004
winds (wings) of windmill
  man in west pursues woman in east, 996–1001 § 1
  four sisters pursue one another, 1015

wine. *See* bottle; grape(s)
wings of cart
  can't fly, 356
winter
  no teeth, yet bites, 297-300
  See also seasons
woman
  Two-Legs sat on Three-Legs, 461a
  Christian person, 837
  See also horse and woman; horse, man, and woman
woman, married
  bird flying, 473
  met in shower of rain, 1099
  filled glass, 1197
woman, pregnant
  four legs, forty nails, 57
  eight hands, eight feet, 57
  I eat in town, I don't know town, 711
  two go through rain: one is wet, one is not, 961
  See also child, unborn
woman, single
  bird sitting, 473
woman, white
  chases white lamb (horse), 844
  sends white dog after cow, 846
  sends white dog after fowl, 848
  sends servant, 852, 853
woman carrying bucket of water on bridge
  over water, under water, 165
  water above, below, and on each side, 165i
woman kneading bread
  two look, two poke, 1476-1494 § 15
woman milking cow
  four legs on ground, two legs on ground, 1476-1494 § 4
  See also fingers milking
woman nursing child
  flesh fills crack, 1235
woman riding horse. *See* horse and woman; horse, man, and woman
woman sewing
  brass whip drives steel horse over bone bridge, 420c
woman and children
  tree and limbs, 1046

wood
  goes with you into the grave, 1706
wood, fire, and smoke
  mother stabs, father burns, daughter pinches, 1017-1035 n. 10
woodpecker
  cuts wood, never gets bundle, 788
  children with red caps, 921
  shipload of people with red cap, 934
word
  goes through rain, is not wet, 961-963 § 4
  given and kept, 1586
worm(s)
  long man legless fears hens, not dogs, 562
  I am fed by learning, 770
  eat's mother in grandam's belly, 773
  rich men assemble in club, 1134 n. 12
  through a rock, through a reel, 1597
writing
  five hold, two watch, 970-975 § 6
  black animals, white field, 1058-1062
  white land, black seed, 1063

yam
  living man buried with corpse, 835
yarn. *See* ball of yarn
year
  twelve months old, 88-95
  father, twelve sons, 984
  tree, part green, part dry, 1037-1038
  animals (other than birds), 1037-1038 § 2
  birds, 1037-1038 § 3
  wagon, 1037-1038 § 4
  wheel, 1037-1038 § 5
  building, 1037-1038 § 6
  cask, 1037-1038 § 7
  household objects, 1037-1038 § 9
  tree, twelve boughs, fifty-two nests, 1037
  tree, twelve limbs, 1038
  See also day and night; months; seasons; week
yellow jackets
  pernicky, pernacky, people the color of brown tobacco, 899
yoke
  stood in woods, carpenter made it, 404
  two wooden, two crooked, 1476-1494 § 25